To Shirin

from Gary

Family Law

Jurisdictional comparisons **Second edition 2013**

General Editor:
James Stewart
Manches LLP

General Editor
James Stewart
Manches LLP

Commercial Director
Katie Burrington

Commissioning Editor
Emily Kyriacou

Senior Editor
Caroline Pearce

Design and Production
Dawn McGovern

Editorial Assistant
Magdalena Wika

Published in July 2013 by Sweet & Maxwell,
100 Avenue Road, London NW3 3PF
part of Thomson Reuters (Professional) UK Limited
(Registered in England & Wales, Company No 1679046.
Registered Office and address for service:
Aldgate House, 33 Aldgate High Street, London EC3N 1DL)

A CIP catalogue record for this book is available from the British Library.

ISBN: 978-0-414028-70-8

Contents

Foreword

James Stewart Partner, Manches LLP; Governor at Large, International Academy of Matrimonial Lawyers

During the past decade there has been a steady rise in the number of transnational marriages and relationships. The growth in the number of cases with an international dimension has made it vital for family law practitioners to understand the complexities involved in dealing with modern day cross-jurisdictional matters. The outstanding success of the first edition of *Family Law Jurisdictional Comparisons* is indicative of the fact that family lawyers throughout the world must, by necessity, have a thorough understanding of international family law.

Cases involving conflict of laws and questions as to the application of foreign law or the role of foreign courts are becoming increasingly common. Likewise, public international family law issues arising from a myriad of international treaties, regulations and conventions have given rise to a new body of international jurisprudence which all family law practitioners are now forced to grapple with. Against this background, I felt it was vital to provide family law professionals with a second edition of *Family Law Jurisdictional Comparisons*, which not only updates 30 of the original chapters, but which includes 16 new jurisdictions as diverse as Canada, Chile, Monaco, Spain and the United Arab Emirates. The book has also been expanded to include nine core US jurisdictions ranging from California and the state of Washington on the west coast, to New York and Maryland on the east coast.

I hope that this second comparative edition, with its ease of access and template style, will help simplify and raise awareness of the multifaceted issues surrounding family law in the jurisdictions which it covers.

The primary aim of this second comparative overview is to provide an accessible resource to family lawyers around the globe who are acting in cases with an international dimension. Each chapter has the same basic structure covering core areas of law as it is applied in each jurisdiction, conflict of laws, pre-nuptial and post-nuptial agreements, divorce (including financial claims after overseas divorce), children (including international child abduction, parental responsibility, adoption and surrogacy), cohabitation and same-sex relationships and the different forms of family dispute resolution. The chapters also address European and international conventions and the impact that such conventions have on domestic family law.

There are many common threads in family law across different jurisdictions. However, there are also very significant differences. For example, the way in which property is distributed on divorce varies widely. Certain jurisdictions have a system based on the notion of community of property, while others give a wide discretion to the court and consider distribution based on need and resources. Similarly, there is a broad spectrum of approaches in relation to the award of post-marital maintenance. In certain jurisdictions an award is very rare, in some, maintenance may be limited to a fixed 'rehabilitative' period of time, while in others an open-ended award is favoured. The treatment of marital or pre-/post-nuptial agreements also varies markedly from jurisdiction to jurisdiction, with civil law jurisdictions traditionally giving contractual force to such agreements, in contrast with many common law jurisdictions where judicial discretion prevails.

There are also major differences in the recognition of rights for cohabitants and those in same-sex relationships, and while a number of jurisdictions have written constitutions in which fundamental family law rights are protected, in others there are no such constitutional rights.

A consequence of the disparities between family law regimes across jurisdictions is that parties may be able to select a jurisdiction that will better facilitate the resolution of their particular case. This may be a choice based on national procedure, or law. For example, the parties may choose a jurisdiction which favours forms of mediation or alternative dispute resolution (ADR), or one where there are likely to be fewer procedural delays.

My heartfelt gratitude goes to the leading family law and divorce practitioners in many countries who have worked so diligently to compile the chapters in the second edition. Most of these contributors are Fellows of the International Academy of Matrimonial Lawyers (IAML). I would also like to thank my colleagues at Manches' family department who have assisted me with this project, in particular my brilliant PA, Chryssie Louca, my partner Rebecca Carlyon and my trainees, Charlotte Doherty and Charlotte Eccles. Thanks too must go to my friend and colleague, Louise Spitz, for all her hard work on the English chapter of this edition. Louise is rightly recognised in Chambers' Guide to the Legal Profession as the 'senior statesman' of English family law.

Thanks too must go to Katie Burrington, Emily Kyriacou, Magda Wika and the entire reference book team at the European Lawyer without whose efforts this book would not have been produced.

Finally, I would like to personally thank Cheryl Hepfer (President of the IAML), William Longrigg (President-Elect), Sylvia Goldschmidt (President, USA Chapter), Alfred Kriegler (President, European Chapter), and the rest of my friends and colleagues in the IAML who have been so supportive of this project.

James Stewart
London, July 2013

Preface

Cheryl Lynn Hepfer Principal, Offit Kurman; President, International Academy of Matrimonial Lawyers

Many of our clients now work and reside around the world. They reside and own assets in more than one country. There has been an increase in truly international cities, such as New York, London, Hong Kong and Tokyo. As a result, family has become much more international. International treaties and conventions, which include Council Regulation EC No 2201/2003 (Brussels IIR), as well as legislation within the United States, such as the Uniform Child Custody Jurisdiction and Enforcement Act (UCCJEA), have proliferated. Perhaps the most crucial of them all is the Convention on the Civil Aspects of International Child Abduction (The Hague Convention). Those family law practitioners who deal with international clients must remain informed of the latest legal developments so that they can provide advice to their clients.

As President of the International Academy of Matrimonial Lawyers (IAML), I know the importance of having resources available that can lead practitioners through the intricacies of the laws that affect their clients. I am delighted, therefore, to endorse and contribute to *Family Law Jurisdictional Comparisons*, a unique publication which summarises family law regimes in 46 jurisdictions around the world. In such a complex area, there can be no substitute for the advice of specialists. I am very pleased, therefore, that so many of the contributors to this publication are Fellows of the IAML.

The IAML is a worldwide association of practising lawyers, who are recognised by their peers as the most experienced and expert family law specialists in their respective countries. The IAML has more than 600 Fellows in jurisdictions across the globe. The Academy's primary objective is to improve the practise of international family law throughout the world. One of the ways to best accomplish this objective is through its creation of a network of expertise in international family law which is available to other lawyers and to the wider public, whether they are considering an international marital agreement, choice of jurisdiction for divorce or if they find themselves involved in international child abduction proceedings.

This publication will be a tremendous resource for all family lawyers who are addressing international issues in their practices, which are bound to have more intricate components. The ability to compare the laws and procedures of so many jurisdictions in one book make this publication very worthwhile and applicable to our practices. The fact that the information is provided by so many Fellows of the IAML, who have the knowledge and expertise to identify and favourably resolve international issues, contributes significantly to its value.

I congratulate and commend James Stewart, the General Editor of this fine publication, and thank him for the opportunity to provide the Preface to this invaluable resource for those who practice international family law.

Cheryl Lynn Hepfer
Bethesda, MD, July 2013

Argentina

Perez Maraviglia & Horton Abogados Diego Horton

A. JURISDICTION AND CONFLICT OF LAW

1. SOURCES OF LAW

1.1 What is the primary source of law in relation to the breakdown of marriage and the welfare of children within the jurisdiction?

Argentina is organised as a Federal Republic, ruled by the National Constitution of 1853 and its amendments, the latest passed in 1994. The constitution has been inspired by the Constitution of the United States of America and the liberal doctrine of the time. Under this model, the country's states, known as provinces, are each ruled by their Provincial Constitutions and local provincial laws. Thus, both the Federal Government and the Provinces hold their own legal and judicial system. There are then national laws in force throughout the country, and provincial laws ruling only in a specific province. The Civil Code, which derives from the Roman law tradition, in force nationwide, is the main legal instrument under which family law is ruled. The primary sources of law are the legislative statutes passed in Congress as a mandatory source. Statutory rules are arranged in hierarchical order, the National Constitution ranking first, followed by the international treaties embodied in domestic laws after being approved by Congress, national federal laws, provincial laws and municipal laws. There are also formal or mandatory sources of law in jurisprudence and case law conformed by the different Courts of Appeal's plenary rulings and Supreme Court judgments, as well as custom *secundum legem* or custom referred to by the law.

Specifically in the field of Argentine family law, case law has grown to be a very powerful instrument and in many cases the primary source of posterior laws passed in Congress. Many family law modifications were first accepted by the courts and later adopted by the laws that amended family law institutions along the lines set by judicial precedents. Case law has the virtue of being more dynamic than the law and can uphold the obligation to impart justice in each particular case. It has played and keeps playing the role of law construction, adopting modern changes in legislation in order to adapt the law to the new social, economic and political realities of the country.

For family law, the Civil Code is still the main source of law, complemented by both national and provincial legislation that have been either inserted in the Civil Code as amendments, or complement the Code's principles as independent complementary laws. There are also some provinces that have procedural laws which have served as main laws in order to solve overall conflicts; for example, the law against domestic violence (a procedural law only valid in some provinces), establishing a quick drastic procedure to stop the initial violent acts, ie, to obtain a restraining order, and a subsequent procedure to work on the causes of violence together with therapeutic solutions to the problems arising from the violent situation.

1.2 Which are the main statutes governing matrimonial law in the jurisdiction?

Matrimonial law in Argentina has been always ruled by the Civil Code, together with subsequent amendments and incorporations to the Code. The first matrimonial regulation was enacted as Law 2393 in year 1888, followed by those laws approving the Montevideo Treaties of 1889 and 1940, which complemented the primary legislation with different matrimonial rules to be applied between citizens of different nationalities. With the return of democracy in 1983, Law 23264, enacted in 1985, introduced major changes in matters of filiation and minority.

Moreover, Law 23515, enacted in 1987, established major changes in marriage legislation, incorporating divorce for the first time in Civil Code history, as a cause of marriage dissolution allowing divorced spouses to re-marry under the same legislation.

There are other complementary laws governing different related matters such as adoption (through a substantial amendment to the Argentine Civil Code made by Law 24779, in 1997), child and adolescents rights protection, passed in Congress as Law 26061, and domestic violence laws, enacted as Laws 26485 and 26486, protecting life, physical integrity, personal safety and dignity, of all family members.

There are also criminal laws 13944 and 24270 each protecting alimony payment compliment, which protects beneficiaries from non-compliment with an alimony payment obligation, as well as visitation for non-custodial parents, punishing parents who breach child support agreements and judgments, and parents who impede the non-custodial parent from visiting the child.

In July 2010, by enacting law 26618, Argentina became the first country in Latin America to allow and regulate same-sex marriage.

2. JURISDICTION

2.1 What are the main jurisdictional requirements for the institution of proceedings in relation to divorce, property and children?

Different sections in the Civil Code determine the law of the last marital domicile as the applicable law and court jurisdiction in cases of personal separation, divorce and marriage nullity. In a federal country like Argentina, this principle applies within the provinces: while the applicable law is always the Civil Code as a national law, court jurisdiction will definitely be the provincial court where the last marriage residence was settled.

Personal separation and marriage dissolution cases shall be governed by the law of the spouses' last marital residence. However, if the last marital residence happens to be located in a foreign country, the parties may file for divorce in that country, and then register the foreign court sentence before the Argentine Civil Registry with the intervention of the Argentine judge, who will have received all foreign certified divorce sentence documents.

Also in relation to international jurisdiction of courts in private law, the Argentine Civil Code establishes that filings for divorce, personal separation and marriage invalidity, as well as those relating to the effects of marriage, may be brought before the court of the last actual marital residence or before the court of the respondent spouse's residence, opening a potential concurrent jurisdiction.

In relation to marital property, it is proper to maintain the rules of international jurisdiction applicable to separation and divorce. As to applicable law, it is established that marriage covenants and the relationships between spouses relating to marital property shall be governed by the law of first marital residence concerning everything that, in matters of a strictly real nature, is not prohibited by the law of marital property location.

With respect to alimony and child support, Argentine law provides that 'the right to receive alimony/child support, as well as the eligibility, opportunity and scope of the alimony/child support agreement, if any, shall be governed by the law of marital residence. Alimony/child support payments shall be regulated by the law of the respondent's domicile. The option clearly benefits the claimant for alimony and child support by allowing a wide range of alternative courts for the beneficiary to resort to.

Parental rights are governed by the law of the place where said rights are exercised. The legal principle of court effectiveness establishes, for example, that visitation rights have to be filed before the court of the child's habitual residence to ensure a more expedite and effective jurisdictional protection.

3. DOMICILE AND HABITUAL RESIDENCE

3.1 Explain the concepts of domicile and habitual residence as they apply to the jurisdiction in relation to divorce, the finances and children

In Argentine family law the concept of domicile, as a formal notion (or even a contractual stipulation), is only used in settlements that are formerly submitted to the judge for approval. In the rest of the cases, we always refer to habitual residence as the legal denomination applied to jurisdiction and applicable law. Domicile is home. Domicile is family settlement. Domicile is the child´s habitual residence or the parent's habitual residence. It is the nature of family law to ensure court proximity and effectiveness to the family as a way of ensuring the correct application of the law and protect the rights of all family members. Therefore, the concept of habitual residence always prevails as the real family law concept versus a domicile that may be formally established, but not necessarily the place where family interactions occur.

4. CONFLICT OF LAW/APPLICABLE LAW TO BE APPLIED

4.1 What happens when one party applies to stay proceedings in favour of a foreign jurisdiction? What factors will the local court take into account when determining forum issues?

The National Commerce Court of Appeal has decided: *'Issues relating to international jurisdiction are resolved by specific rules of a conventional or domestic source, by standards deriving from jurisdiction based on domestic venue, or by case law issued by Argentina's Supreme Court of Justice for the resolution of jurisdictional issues.'*

In order to examine jurisdictional matters, the court shall determine firstly if there are legally binding treaties between the two or more potential jurisdictions that define and address the issue. Secondly, if there is no binding treaty dealing with jurisdictional matters, the court shall examine international private law provisions on jurisdictional matters and determine the connection points of the particular case with each potential jurisdiction to decide upon declining or accepting jurisdiction.

In cases of concurrent jurisdiction it is advised that the judge should only have jurisdiction if the action was filed first, or where the applicable law coincides with the jurisdiction; if the applicable law governing the case is foreign law, intervention by the foreign court may prove to be more convenient.

B. PRE- AND POST-NUPTIAL AGREEMENTS

5. VALIDITY OF PRE- AND POST-NUPTIAL AGREEMENTS

5.1 To what extent are pre- and post-nups binding within the jurisdiction? Could you provide a brief discussion of the most significant recent case law on the issue?

Under Argentine Civil law, there are no pre- or post-nups allowed, in the way these are understood in international civil law. Hence, there is no option for spouses (before or after marriage) to reach agreements by which the property and income legal matrimonial rules can be modified.

As far as pre-nups are concerned, the only allowance in the Civil Code is established as follows: *'before the celebration of marriage, the spouses may execute marriage covenants solely based on the following purposes: (i) to designate property that each spouse contributes to the marriage; and (ii) to designate donations and gifts made by husband to wife'*.

After marriage, no prior agreement made by spouses can be modified, altered or revoked in any way, under penalty of nullity. Even once the divorce process is underway, any agreement between spouses needs to be made after the divorce sentence, or simultaneously with the joint petition of divorce sentence.

Under Argentine international private laws, the marital property system is to be ruled by the law of the first marital residence, even if the property is purchased or arranged upon after changing their place of residence. So, in a case in which an Argentine court must intervene in a dispute between spouses who, for example, are now residing in Argentina, but had their first marital residence in another country, the court must enforce the law of the foreign country in order to determine the validity of eventual pre-nuptial agreements.

However, during 2012 a very important Proposed Civil Code Amendment project was delivered to Congress for consideration. One of the key amendments included in this project is the allowance of pre- and post-nuptial agreements in a really flexible way. If the law is finally passed, it will amend more than 120 years of unmodified marital property rules.

C. DIVORCE, NULLITY AND JUDICIAL SEPARATION

6. RECOGNITION OF FOREIGN MARRIAGES/DIVORCES

6.1 Summarise the position in your jurisdiction

Argentina's legal system recognises marriages celebrated in a foreign country under foreign rules, provided the legal requirements established by Argentine law for a marriage celebrated in Argentina, have been complied with in that said foreign country and no legal impediments have occurred.

With regard to personal separation and marriage dissolution cases, we have seen already that these are to be governed by the law of the spouses' last marital residence. Therefore, if the last marital residence happens to be located in a foreign country, spouses obtaining divorce judgment in a foreign country will then register that foreign court sentence before the Argentine Civil Registry with the intervention of the Argentine judge who will have received all foreign certified divorce sentence documents.

7. DIVORCE

7.1 Explain the grounds for divorce within the jurisdiction (please also deal with nullity and judicial separation if appropriate)

Since the introduction of the ability to dissolve the marriage tie through divorce in 1987, there have been three different forms of marital disruption: divorce, personal separation and marital nullity.

Divorce

Divorce (dissolving marriage tie and releasing the parties to allow further remarriage) has mainly two forms of process:

(1) Fault-based divorce. Either party may file a petition of divorce against the other spouse, based on five causes limitedly established in the Civil Code:
   - (i) adultery, strictly defined as sexual unfaithful misconduct;
   - (ii) murder attempt against the denouncing spouse and/or their children;
   - (iii) instigation to commit a crime performed by one spouse to the other;
   - (iv) serious defamation or offences (physical and/or psychological), taking under consideration, for its evaluation, the social and educational position of the spouses;
   - (v) marital residence abandonment.

(2) No-fault divorce. There are two alternatives for this process:
   - (i) after three years of non co-habitation, either party may file a no-fault petition of divorce;
   - (ii) after three years of marriage, both parties can jointly file a petition for divorce and also obtain a no-fault divorce decree.

Personal separation

Personal separation (does not allow further remarriage, but releases the parties from their marital obligations), has a very similar process to the divorce case. The fault-based personal separation process requires the same grounds as those shown in the fault-based divorce. In the case of a no-fault personal separation, the three-year requirement is reduced to two years in both cases shown in paragraph 2 hereinabove.

Marital nullity

Marital nullity may be pleaded when one or more of the impediments to a valid marriage take place. These are specific requirements contained in the Civil Code, that allow the declaration of absolute nullity (nullity encumbering public order), which are listed as follows:

(1) marriage between direct line blood relatives;
(2) marriage between brother and sister or half-brother and sister;
(3) marriage between direct line adopted relatives;
(4) validity of a previous marriage of one or both spouses at the moment of marriage;
(5) one spouse being the author, accomplice or instigator of attempted homicide against the other.

There are also some other causes of relative marital nullity (those not encumbering public order that only could be filed by one of the spouses), such as:

(1) marriage performed by a minor;
(2) marriage performed by a temporary or permanent mentally disabled person;
(3) sexual impotence absolutely impeding sexual intercourse, in one or both spouses;
(4) when marital consent is obtained through lie, fraud, error or with violence from one spouse to the other.

8. FINANCES/CAPITAL, PROPERTY

8.1 What powers does the court have to allocate financial resources and property on the breakdown of marriage?

The Argentine legal system establishes two different kinds of marital estate, known as the property earned or purchased by husband or wife during marriage. This marital property can then by classified in marital estate administered by the husband during marriage, and marital estate administered by the wife during marriage, regardless of who holds title for the specific good. This means that any spouse can hold title of a property and that property will still be considered marital estate, only that it will be administered by the spouse holding its title.

Marital estate is to be allocated to both spouses in halves, after the divorce sentence is passed. These allocations and the proportions of such allocations (that may include compensations due to values being different in each property) will have to be agreed upon, as they can never be imposed or decided by the judge. If the parties do not reach an agreement, the judge, upon petition, may order the public selling of the goods, and the 50:50 distribution of the funds obtained through that form of liquidation.

8.2 Explain and illustrate with reference to recent cases the court's thinking on division of assets

As stated above, the judge is unable to divide non-liquidated assets between the parties.

However, different conflicts may arise concerning the nature of the assets: whether they are marital property or they belong to either spouse as separate or private unencumbered property (known as those goods received through donation or inheritance during marriage or goods acquired by a spouse before marriage).

Today, the mainstream of Argentine legal scholars and judges construe and interpret that if a married person disposes of a portion of separate property, and fails to prove that he has purchased another good with the product of the selling of the first property, it is legally assumed that the monies derived from the sale of separate property were consumed by the selling party with no right to reward against the marital estate. On the other hand, if the party is able to prove that the monies obtained by the selling of a separate property have been assigned to the purchase of a portion of marital property, this amount shall constitute a credit in favour of the owner of the separate property previously sold. This credit is to be claimed at the time of legal separation or divorce sentence. The spouse who claims the right to seek reward for the proceeds from the sale of separate property shall only be required to give proof of the nature and sale of such property, and of the fact that he has received the corresponding funds. However, the spouse who challenges the right to the reward, denying that the monies have really been used for the benefit of the marital estate (by way of reinvestment, gift or concealment) shall be required to go beyond their mere denial and give positive evidence of any such circumstances.

The courts have also interpreted that *'it is proper to admit the right to grant reward to one of the spouses for the sale of separate property after the celebration of marriage because it is assumed that the proceeds there from were used for the benefit of the marital estate and require that the other spouse challenging such a right gives proof that the monies received were reinvested or spent in personal obligations or designed for acts that are alien to the marital estate, such as gifts or bequests'*.

9. FINANCES/MAINTENANCE

9.1 Explain the operation of maintenance for spouses on an ongoing basis after the breakdown of marriage

9.2 Is it common for maintenance to be awarded?

9.3 Explain and illustrate with reference to recent cases the court's thinking on maintenance

The Argentine Civil Code establishes the concept of 'innocent' spouse in a divorce or legal separation process, as the party not giving cause for the marital dissolution. It is in this case where the innocent party is entitled to claim alimony further to the divorce decree. The judge must set alimony in order to preserve the economic standard of living that the spouses used to have when they were living together, taking into account the resources of both parties. For purposes of setting alimony or spousal support the following are to be considered:

(i) the age and health of the spouses;
(ii) the involvement in child care and education by the parent being granted residential custody of the children;
(iii) job training and job accessibility by the beneficiary of spousal support;
(iv) the potential loss of pension rights; and
(v) the existence of both personal assets and personal needs of the party after settlement of marital property.

There is also a right to alimony in the case of personal separation caused by mental illness, alcoholism or drug addiction.

In every case, however, the amounts established for alimony will necessarily vary according to the real needs of the obligee and the ability to pay and income of the obligor, factors that are always examined thoroughly by the judge. Maintenance rights, as we can see, are always dynamic and are never ruled as definitive, because of the principles taken into consideration when judged: real necessities, affordability of payment by the obligor, increasing needs in case of overcoming illness of the obligee, decreasing affordability because of job loss of the obligor, re-marriage or cohabitation of the obligee, and many other factors that may cause a petition in court for modification of the alimony.

10. CHILD MAINTENANCE

10.1 On what basis is child maintenance calculated within the jurisdiction?

The obligation to support minor children is mandatory for both parents. It is ruled that the parent holding custody is not liable to pay a defined monthly quota, as it is implicit in his custodial status. The other parent is always liable to pay a fixed monthly amount until the child turns 21 years of age.

Child alimony is always based on the conjunction of the real needs of the children and the income/possibilities of payment of the parent.

There are two main principles ruling the issue: (i) alimony can always be modified according to new upcoming needs of the children and the increasing or decreasing income of the parent; and (ii) it is intended that the children maintain similar living standards to those they had when their parents were living together.

It is generally ruled by the courts, that the non-custodial parent should directly pay for the health insurance and education of the child, plus a monthly amount in cash to cover unspecific daily needs.

The parent holding custody receives and administrates alimony, legally representing the children, until they reach 18. From the age of 18 to the age of 21, when the alimony right terminates, the obligor may pay directly to the child as he is no longer a minor. Moreover, if during an alimony legal filing a child turns 18, he is no longer represented by his mother, and is therefore expected to stand in court and to continue proceedings against his father for the alimony part he is entitled to.

Inflation rates in Argentina, which are usually high, have caused, unfortunately, a great number of filings in court to adjust the alimony sum. Some ways of establishing on going adjustments have been both ordered by court and agreed upon by the parties, for example, establishing alimony as a percentage of the obligor's salary, or pre-establishing an automatic increase in alimony matched with increases seen in education or healthcare costs. But, again, these mechanisms are not always fair and generate a great deal of conflicts.

A parent failing to comply with alimony obligations may lose parental rights and duties, and may also face a criminal law offence for non-compliment of family financial assistance.

11. RECIPROCAL ENFORCEMENT OF FINANCIAL ORDERS

11.1 Summarise the position in your jurisdiction

There are different measures that the judge may order during or after fault-based divorce or alimony collection court cases. When a divorce case is filed, the plaintiff usually files for preliminary injunction for seizure of 50 per cent of the defendant's income during trial (income and salaries are defined by Argentine law as marital estate), and over marital property in general. These measures could include real estate, vehicles, vessels, bank accounts and equity. Another common order during divorce is the filing of the inventory of goods (usually works of art, jewellery and furniture), as, again, they are preliminary and presumably considered marital property, unless the defendant proves ultimately that they are separate property. It is also frequent, in some cases, to order the intervention of an auditor in defendant's businesses, including collection powers to withdraw 50 per cent of the defendant's income in those businesses. These usually take place in corporations where the defendant is shareholder and/or a member of the board of directors.

When executing alimony sentences or judicially approved alimony agreements, there are also similar preliminary injunctions which can be ordered by the judge, to secure the goods over which the execution will target. These orders may include also separate goods, as the objective is to collect alimony regardless of the nature of the defendant's property.

In these cases, there is no legal requirement for the complainant to show irreparable injury nor the urgency nor the legal grounds he has for the petition. The orders are taken, also, without prior hearing or notification of the defendant.

In the case of a foreign force, or a force passed in another Argentine province, if it is final and is duly certified in its original jurisdiction, it can be enforced before the jurisdiction of the defendant's domicile, or where the defendant's property is located.

12. FINANCIAL RELIEF AFTER FOREIGN DIVORCE PROCEEDINGS

12.1 What powers are available to make orders following a foreign divorce?

As discussed under question 11, Argentina will admit a foreign judgment to be executed in its jurisdiction. There are particular bilateral international treaties that establish proceedings for foreign divorce to be enforced in the country. In the case of a foreign judgment passed in a country with which there is no particular treaty, every Procedural Code in any Argentine state will admit the petition of orders from other jurisdictions, by the process of what is known as *exequatur*, that is, the execution of a foreign judgment as if it was passed in Argentina, provided it complies with certain requirements, such as the judgment being final, duly notified to the defendant, that it does not breach public order and that it does not oppose another judgment passed in Argentina.

D. CHILDREN

13. CUSTODY/PARENTAL RESPONSiBILITY

13.1 Briefly explain the legal position in relation to custody/parental responsibility following the breakdown of a relationship or marriage

13.2. Briefly explain the legal position in relation to access/contact/visitation following the breakdown of a relationship or marriage

The Argentine Civil Code defines parental rights and duties (PR&D) to be exercised by both parents jointly. In case of separation or divorce, the legal use of PR&D is reserved to the custodial parent, without prejudice of the rights of the non-custodial parent to supervise the education of the child, and to have frequent and adequate visitation. Also, the non-custodial parent's authorisation is always required when the child travels abroad or for medical treatments and surgery, for example.

Custody is always assigned to the mother in the cases of children under five years of age, except where this does not best serve the interests of the child. After that age, if the parties do not agree on custody, the judge will decide who will use custody right, taking under consideration some priorities: to try to maintain the original home organisation of the child, not to separate brothers and sisters and always hearing the child, with the intervention of a minority officer, who will represent the child through the judicial process.

Visitation by the non-custodial parent is to be wide, open, frequent and organised, not to interfere in the child's habits and usual schedules. As stated previously, it is a criminal offence in Argentina to in any way impede or obstruct normal visitation and parental contact.

The visitation schedule is nearly always agreed upon by the parties. In the case of non-agreement, it is established and ruled upon by the judge, although there are many opportunities given by the court for the parties to agree upon visitation, in order to avoid visitation judgment. Needless to say, judicial imposition of a visitation schedule is always a negative issue for both parents and children.

14. INTERNATIONAL ABDUCTION

14.1 Summarise the position in your jurisdiction

By law 23.857, which was passed by Congress in 1990, Argentina ratified its participation and adhesion to the international abduction treaty signed in 1980 in The Hague XVIII Conference. The country has firmly supported the principles set forth in that Conference and the judicial system has always acted accordingly. The principle of peaceful and rapid restitution of the child that has been taken out of the country without consent of the other parent has been present in our legislation ever since. Argentina's system requires both parents' consent for a child to leave the country either by himself or in the company of one of his parents. Argentina's immigration office requires written proof granted before notary public by the non-travelling parent to be exhibited at every border. Even when both parents are travelling with a minor son or daughter, they must prove at the border their parental condition towards the child with the necessary documents.

Despite the fact that, as far as civil law is concerned, it is a priority to restitute the child and find quick solutions other than just punishing the offender, Argentina's Criminal Code severely punishes both child cross-border abduction and contact impediment performed by the custodial parent towards the non-custodial parent.

15. LEAVE TO REMOVE/APPLICATIONS TO TAKE A CHILD OUT OF THE JURISDICTION

15.1 Summarise the position in your jurisdiction

15.2 Under what circumstances may a parent apply to remove their child from the jurisdiction against the wishes of the other parent?

Removing a child from its habitual residence is a very complex issue with mixed and concurrent rights of all the parties involved. When these cases arise, parents usually have serious reasons for petitioning that the residence should be fixed in another jurisdiction.

In Argentina, legal use of parental rights on duties is jointly exercised by both spouses. However, our legislation provides the right of the child who is separated from one or both parents to maintain personal relationships and keep direct contact with both parents regularly, except that such circumstance is contrary to the best interests of the child. Where one of the parents opposes the child leaving the country to temporarily or permanently reside abroad, the court shall determine if such an objection is admitted.

In principle, the right to oppose is granted by the mere legal use of parental rights. However, this is not an absolute right. The Supreme Court of Argentina has ruled that *'for purposes of preserving the stability of children who have suffered the impact of family disintegration, there should be very serious causes associated with child safety and/or child moral and material health that may warrant the temporary removal of a child from his/her habitual residence, thereby changing the status in life that the child enjoyed at the time of filing the separation or divorce suit'*.(Supreme Court of the Argentine Nation. Date: 04/29/2008 Parties: M. D. H. c. M. B. M. F.)

For its part, the competent Court of Appeal to adjudge an issue like the foregoing, held that *'jurisdictional intervention, as an alternative to such conflicts, is never geared to placing the parties at a crossroads where they shall be forced to choose; but it is directed both at understanding whether the father's objection to the minor child residing abroad is warranted or not, and at making the most advisable decision for the party involved'*.(National Court of Civil Appeals, Chamber K. Date: 05/29/2006 Parties: P., M. E. c. S., J. C).

For the purpose of evaluating whether the father's objection is warranted and in order to determine the best interest of the child, the courts will generally evaluate the factors as a whole, such as the habitual residence of the child and the type of relationship between the non-resident parent and the child, ie, whether they see each other regularly or sporadically and whether the resident parent is actively involved in the upbringing of the child or is an absent parent. The courts shall also consider if the child has his needs provided for within the country, and, of course, his opinion will be heard, according to his age and maturity, as well as the centre of living of the child; a notion defined by law as 'the place where the child has lived the greatest part of his existence'. This relates to how the child's identity is closely linked to the child's residence.

E. SURROGACY & ADOPTION

16. VALIDITY OF SURROGACY AGREEMENTS

16.1 Briefly summarise the position in your jurisdiction

Argentina's legal system does not recognise surrogacy agreements, as a biological mother will always be able to claim, lawfully, the filiation with the child to be born or already born. This biological link will always prevail against an agreement made unlawfully as the object of that said contract will always be illegal.

The Proposed Civil Amendment of 2012 includes provisions on the subject, yet to be discussed. Under such provisions, surrogacy agreements may see the light of day, only if they do not include an economic price, and they are only performed for free.

17. ADOPTION

17.1 Briefly summarise the position in relation to adoption in your jurisdiction. Is adoption available to individuals, cohabiting couples (both heterosexual and same-sex)?

Adoption is Argentina is judicially granted. Adoption, either simple (revocable) or permanent (extinguishes biological parental link), can only be granted and decided by a family law judge, after verifying the parent's age requirements (over 30 years of age, or married couples over three years of marriage), parents' residence in the country for more than five years, biological parents' consent, adopted person's consent (if he or she were over 18) and other requirements.

Law 26.618, passed in 2010, allows individuals and cohabiting couples (both heterosexual and same-sex) to file for adoption of a child.

F. COHABITATION

18. COHABITATION

18.1 What legislation (if any) governs division of property for unmarried couples on the breakdown of the relationship?

There is currently no legislation governing division of property in cohabitation in Argentina. The National Constitution allows and protects the rights of individuals deciding not to get married. This principle has continued to be in force in the Civil Code. Unmarried couples, therefore, are subject to the rules of joint ownership set forth in the Civil Code. The proposed Civil Code Amendment of July 2012, still to receive treatment in Congress, includes some rights for unmarried couples, which may be similar to those applied in matrimony. The extension and characteristics of these are yet to be seen.

G. FAMILY DISPUTE RESOLUTION

19. MEDIATION, COLLABORATIVE LAW AND ARBITRATION

19.1 Briefly summarise the non-court-based processes available in your jurisdiction and the current status of agreements reached under the auspices of mediation, collaborative law and arbitration

19.2 What is the statutory basis (if any), for mediation, collaborative law and arbitration in your jurisdiction? In particular, are the parties required to attempt a family dispute resolution in advance of the institution of proceedings?

As a Federal Republic, every state or province in Argentina has its own procedural laws. The Federal Capital (City of Buenos Aires) has a compulsory mediation statutory law that has been valid for more than 15 years. Every patrimonial family law matter (ie, alimony, division of marital assets), has to be filed before a registered mediator, prior to filing in court. This process is confidential and each party has to have legal advice during however many hearings are necessary. Mediation ends with an agreement act, with the mediator intervention, who submits the agreement in court for approval. If no agreement is reached, the mediator issues a non-agreement act that allows the requiring party to file in court.

Mediation has proved to be effective and satisfactory in most cases. A key factor of success in mediation is the absence of a sentence passed by a judge, deciding 'in favour' of one party and 'against' the other party. In family law, these issues are extremely important as they prevent later conflicts caused by non-satisfaction of the losing party. The mediator is a relevant figure who collaborates with the parties in order to help them reach an agreement. There might also be participation from other professionals, such as psychologists and counselors, helping the parties to reach a solution in the particular case.

After the City of Buenos Aires' experience with mediation, most provinces have passed similar laws imposing these proceedings in their jurisdictions. The province of Buenos Aires, Argentina's most important state, began this in 2012.

Mediation has been such an effective solution that some judges, at a relevant point during litigation, have acted as mediators, using mediation skills in one or more subsequent hearings, in order to persuade the parties to reach an agreement

H. OTHER

20. CIVIL PARTNERSHIP/SAME-SEX MARRIAGE

20.1 What is the status of civil partnership/same-sex marriage within the jurisdiction?

20.2 What legislation governs civil partnership/same-sex marriage?

Same-sex marriage was introduced by Law 26618 enacted in July 2010. The law provides that married same-sex couples shall have the same rights and duties as those provided for by heterosexual marriages. It modifies the terms of the matrimonial act by changing the word husband and wife, and father and mother, for the terms 'spouses' and 'parents' respectively, which include both genders.

Act 26.618 also changed the institution of adoption, which is now allowed for same-sex couples under the same terms as those required for heterosexual couples.

21. CONTROVERSIAL AREAS/RAPIDLY DEVELOPING AREAS OF LAW

21.1 Is there a particular area of the law within the jurisdiction that is currently undergoing major change?

21.2 Which areas of law are most out-of-step? Which areas would you most like to see reformed/changed?

I believe the Proposed Amendment of the Civil Code, submitted to Congress in July 2012 will have a great impact in family law, regardless of the extension and characteristics of what will finally became the enacted law. It comprises nearly every aspect in matrimony and divorce, admitting both pre-nups and post-nups, and allows divorce proceedings to be much simpler, not depending on both spouses wills, hence allowing one of the spouses to request a non-fault divorce. The actual legislation allows unilateral petitions only after three years of separation. In many cases, a situation in which a couple persists in living together simply because one of them refuses to separate, has caused and continues to cause family suffering, at the least, and domestic violence, at the worst.

Issues of the importance of artificial conception and birth, egg donation regulation or surrogacy are also part of the Proposed Project, the outcome of which is still to be seen in the final enacted law.

Again, legislation on domestic violence has been another achievement in Argentina during the past 10 years, establishing new and modern ways of preventing violence and creating multidisciplinary teams to work with the problem and to find solutions, and establishing drastic preliminary injunction orders, such as home exclusion of the violent subject, and psychological treatment for every member in the family.

Finally, I strongly believe there is a pendant issue in our jurisdiction with regards to parental alienation. I would like see both legislators and judges more concerned about the damage caused in a child's mind when one parent continuously delivers negative and aggressive messages to a child regarding the other parent. This tends to be silent in family law, is very difficult to prove, is very difficult to avoid, and has very little to do with how a parent really is, and very much to do with how one parent sees the other parent during or after divorce. It is a complex and painful matter that requires the whole of the legal profession to start working devotedly and much harder on the subject.

The author would like to thank Karina Carrano and Agustina Canullo for their assistance in compiling this chapter

Australia

Meyer Partners Family Lawyers Max Meyer

A. JURISDICTION AND CONFLICT OF LAW

1. SOURCES OF LAW

1.1 What is the primary source of law in relation to the breakdown of marriage and the welfare of children within the jurisdiction?

Australia is a federation of states. The Constitution of the Commonwealth of Australia defines the powers allocated to the Commonwealth Government. The rest is left to the states. The states may also, by agreement, delegate powers to the Commonwealth.

Since the passage of the Family Law Act (1975) (FLA), that law of the Commonwealth of Australia has become and remains the primary source of law in relation to the breakdown of marriage.

It is also the primary source of law in relation to children within the jurisdiction. However, there are still laws of each state that operate in relation specifically to child welfare but not to parenting matters.

Western Australia uniquely opted to enter into an agreement with the Commonwealth to set up its own state Family Court. (For the somewhat Alice in Wonderland result, see *Eckett & Eckett* [2010] FamCAFC39.) That court still applies the FLA as the principal, if not the only, source of its law.

Australian courts also rely upon the authority of decided cases.

Finally, the Family Court of Australia has inherited the *parens patriae* jurisdiction previously found in the English Court of Chancery, which is the court's inherent jurisdiction to make orders for the benefit of, in this case, children. (See *Secretary, Department of Health & Community Services & JWB & SMB* (1992) 175 CLR 218 (Marion's case) and *ZP v PS* (1994) FLC 92-480.)

1.2 Which are the main statutes governing matrimonial law in the jurisdiction?

The Marriage Act 1961 of the Commonwealth of Australia sets out the requirements for a valid marriage.

The Domicile Act 1982 of the Commonwealth of Australia and the state Domicile Acts largely codify the common law relating to domicile.

By far the principal statute governing matrimonial law in Australia is the FLA. The Act and regulations incorporate international treaty obligations to which Australia is a state party, such as the Convention of the Recovery Abroad of Maintenance and the Hague Convention of 25 October 1980 on the Civil Aspects of International Child Abduction.

2. JURISDICTION

2.1 What are the main jurisdictional requirements for the institution of proceedings in relation to divorce, property and children?

Divorce

Section 39(3) of the FLA provides that proceedings for a divorce order may be instituted if, at the date on which the application is filed, either party to the marriage is an Australian citizen, is domiciled in Australia or is ordinarily resident in Australia and has been resident for one year immediately preceding that date.

Australia recognises a domicile of origin, domicile of choice and domicile of dependence. Essentially a domicile of dependence applies now only to minors.

The Family Court in *Woodhead v Woodhead* (1998) FLC92-813 said: ' 'ordinary residence' is not a term of art, it refers to a person's voluntary place of abode and the question where a person is ordinarily resident is one of fact'.

Section 4(1) of the FLA defines 'ordinarily resident' to include 'habitually resident'.

Property and spouse maintenance

Proceedings in relation to property or spouse maintenance may be started in Australia if either party to the marriage is an Australian citizen, is ordinarily resident in Australia, or is present in Australia at the date the Application was filed (see section 39(4)(a)) FLA.

Citizenship and ordinary residence have been discussed in the preceding paragraphs. 'Present in Australia' requires no explanation, even among lawyers.

Children

Proceedings may be instituted in Australia in relation to a child only if:

- the child is present in Australia;
- the child is an Australian citizen or is ordinarily resident in Australia;
- the parent of a child is an Australian citizen, is ordinarily resident in Australia or is present in Australia;
- a party to the proceedings is an Australian citizen, is ordinarily resident in Australia or is present in Australia;
- it would be in accordance with a treaty or arrangement enforced between Australia and an overseas jurisdiction, or the common law rules of private international law, for the court to exercise jurisdiction in the proceedings (see section 69E FLA).

The terms 'citizen', 'ordinarily resident' and 'present' have been discussed above. Each criterion relates to the date on which the application began.

3. DOMICILE AND HABITUAL RESIDENCE

3.1 Explain the concepts of domicile and habitual residence as they apply to the jurisdiction in relation to divorce, the finances and children

To some extent domicile has been discussed above under 'divorce'. The Domicile Acts recognise three kinds of domicile, which are domicile of origin, domicile of choice and domicile of dependence. There are two fundamental assumptions:

- that each person must have a domicile at all times;
- that a person cannot simultaneously have more than one domicile for the same purpose (see *Radich v Bank of New Zealand* (1993) 45FCR101).

At common law domicile of origin was never entirely displaced. If the subject acquired a domicile of choice, and abandoned it without acquiring a new one, then the subject would revert to domicile of origin. That rule has now been abolished by the Domicile Act (section 7) and the existing domicile continues until a new domicile is acquired.

A person acquires a domicile of choice by being lawfully present in the country with the intention of remaining in that country indefinitely. Physical presence does not mean residence (*Ferrier-Watson v McElrath* (2000) 26FamLR169). The two elements of physical presence and intention must occur simultaneously.

The subject's presence in the country must be lawful (*Ah Yin v Christie* (1907) 4CLR1428).

Australian courts must in all cases apply the law of the forum (*lex fori*) to determine the concept of domicile (Re *Annesley* (1926) Ch692).

Habitual residence

The concept of habitual residence applies only in so far as it is included within the concept of 'ordinary residence', which is a foundation for jurisdiction under the FLA. The concept of habitual residence is also relevant to cases involving the Hague Convention on International Child Abduction. In Australian domestic law this is enacted in the *Family Law (Child Abduction Convention) Regulations 1986*. In *LK v Director-General, Department of Community Services* (2009) 237CLR582 the High Court of Australia recently said that in considering a child's place of habitual residence, the enquiry is not necessarily whether there is a settled and unequivocal intention on the part of the party who is looking to establish no change, as is the case with acquiescence, but rather there are a whole range of relevant matters to be considered of which the intentions of the parties are but one. The High Court also said that the term 'habitual residence' though used long ago, has not been defined but 'if the term 'habitual residence' is to be given meaning, some criteria must be engaged at some point in the enquiry and they are to be found in the ordinary meaning of the composite expression'. Accordingly the High Court directs attention to a wide variety of circumstances relating to where a person is said to reside and whether it is to be described as habitual, and second, intentions are relevant to the circumstances of residence as well.

4. CONFLICT OF LAW/APPLICABLE LAW TO BE APPLIED

4.1 What happens when one party applies to stay proceedings in favour of a foreign jurisdiction? What factors will the local court take into account when determining forum issues?

Section 42 FLA provides that Australia applies its own law to determine a forum case.

Conflict of law

The High Court of Australia broke with English law in *Voth v Manildra Flour Mills Pty Limited* (1990) 171CLR358. The court held that a stay of Australian proceedings should be granted if the local court is a clearly inappropriate forum, which will be the case if continuation of the proceedings in that court would be oppressive in the sense of being 'seriously and unfairly burdensome, prejudicial or damaging', or vexatious, in the sense of being 'productive of serious and unjustified trouble and harassment'.

In determining whether the local court is a clearly inappropriate forum, legitimate personal or juridical advantage is a factor.

The principle in *Voth* was subsequently considered by the High Court in *Henry v Henry* (1996) FLC92-685. The Court first affirmed that its prior decision in *Voth* applied equally to matrimonial proceedings. Next, it applied *Voth*, emphasising that the notion of any *prima facie* right in the party moving the local forum was overstated. It should be read more appropriately as indicating that the onus lies on the party seeking a stay to establish that the chosen forum is clearly inappropriate.

The court said that 'it is *prima facie* vexatious and oppressive, in the strict sense of those terms, to commence a second or subsequent action in the courts of this country if an action is already pending with respect to the matter in issue'.

The High Court held that all of the disputes arising out of the marital relationship were concerned with the same controversy. 'The marital relationship lies at the heart of all proceedings between husband and wife.'

The following principles can be derived from the case:

- no question arises unless the courts of the respective countries have jurisdiction;
- if there is a question as to the jurisdiction of the foreign court, it may be necessary to adjourn the local proceedings for that question to be determined;
- if both have jurisdiction it will be relevant to consider whether each will recognise the other's orders; if the foreign court will not have its order recognised in Australia that will ordinarily dispose of any suggestion that the local proceedings should not continue;
- if the orders of the foreign court will be recognised in Australia, it will be relevant to consider whether any orders may need to be enforced in other countries and, if so, the relative ease with which that can be done;
- which forum can provide more effectively for complete resolution of the matter involved in the parties' controversy;
- the order in which the proceedings were instituted, the stage they have reached and the costs incurred will be relevant, as will be the connection of the parties and their marriage with each of the jurisdictions and the issues on which relief might depend in those jurisdictions;
- it will be relevant to consider whether, having regard to their resources and their understanding of language, the parties are able to participate in the respective proceedings on an equal footing.

In *ZP & PS* (1994) FLC92-480 the High Court determined that:

- the Family Court had *parens patriae* jurisdiction;
- that jurisdiction was guided by the welfare of the child as the paramount consideration;
- even the question of forum, therefore, must be determined by reference only to that principle and not to forum conveniens principles.

The Full Court of the Family Court of Australia recently had occasion to reconsider an apparent conflict between *ZP & PS* (1994) and *B & B (re jurisdiction)* (2003) FLC 93-136. In *Pascarl & Oxley* [2013] FamCAFC 47, the Full Court determined wherever the relevant application involved the best interests of the child test, then it is that test, not *forum conveniens* principles, that will apply.

B. PRE- AND POST-NUPTIAL AGREEMENTS

5. VALIDITY OF PRE- and POST-NUPTIAL AGREEMENTS

5.1 To what extent are pre- and post-nuptial agreements binding within the jurisdiction? Could you provide a brief discussion of the most significant recent case law on the issue

In Australia, these agreements are called financial agreements. Since 2001, people have been able to enter into binding financial agreements made before marriage, during marriage or after a divorce order is made. Those agreements may deal with property interests, spouse maintenance and superannuation or pensions.

If all statutory requirements are complied with, these agreements are binding upon the parties and exclude the jurisdiction of the Family Court to the extent that the agreements deal with all of the matters referred to. The relevant statutory provisions are sections 90B, 90C and 90D of the FLA, which set out the basic requirements for an agreement to become binding.

Sections 90DA, DB, E, F and G set out further requirements. Section 90K of the FLA sets out the circumstances in which the court may set aside a financial agreement. Section 90KA sets out the criteria for the validity, enforceability and effect of financial agreements. Section 90G of the FLA sets out what is required as follows:

- that the agreement be in writing;
- that is be signed by all parties;
- that, before signing the agreement, each spouse party was provided with independent legal advice about the effect of the agreement on the rights of that party and about the advantages and disadvantages of that party of making the agreement;
- that each legal practitioner provide a signed statement of advice;
- that each spouse party receive a copy of the statement (but not the advice) given to the other.

A court can set aside a financial agreement if:

- it was obtained by fraud;
- a party entered into it to defraud a creditor or creditors, or with reckless disregard to the interests of a creditor;
- the agreement is, for some reason, void or unenforceable or voidable;
- in circumstances arising since the agreement was made, it is

impracticable for the agreement to be carried out;

- if there has been a material change in circumstances since the making of the agreement, where that change relates to the care, welfare and development of a child of the marriage and, as a result of that change, the child or the carer for the child being a party to the agreement will suffer hardship if the agreement is not set aside; or
- if a party behaved unconscionably in the making of the agreement.

When the Australian government passed these provisions, it did so to allow people to regulate their own financial affairs freely.

That spirit did not survive long. The court, in *Black & Black* [2008] 38 FamLR 503, made it clear that 'strict compliance with the statutory requirements is necessary to oust the court's jurisdiction to make adjustive orders under section 79 of the FLA'. In that case, purely because of a technical defect, the court set aside the agreement and considered itself free to reorder the financial affairs of the parties.

In January 2010, the Commonwealth government changed section 90G FLA broadly by inserting what some commentators have called a 'get out of jail free card'. To summarise, the new provision (section 90G(1A)) is to the effect that, if the agreement was signed and some of the mandatory criteria had not been met, but nonetheless the court was satisfied that it would be unjust and inequitable if the agreement were not binding, then the court can make an order declaring the agreement to be binding. There are major potential ambiguities in this provision.

The prediction in the first edition of this work has come to pass. There is a flood of litigation. Some of that litigation is against the lawyers drawing the agreements, when they were overturned by the courts. Many agreements have been set aside by the courts for technical failures. However, the most worrying development appears to be attacks on the nature and quality of the legal advice given to the parties or one of them and the consequent setting aside of the agreements. Examples are *Cording & Oster* [2010] FamCA 511, *Pascot & Pascot* [2011] FamCA 945, *Hoult & Hoult* [2011] FamCA 1023. However, some cases have descended to absurdity in addressing technical failures. For example, *Suffolk v Suffolk* (2) [2009 FamCA 917] where an agreement was set aside because, contrary to the specifics of the legislation, one party did not get the original and the other a copy.

In short, the courts have been assiduous in finding ways to set aside agreements that appeared to give effect to the wishes of the parties. They have done so by a combination of focusing narrowly on technical compliance with the legislation and a proper regard to any circumstance of unconscionability between the parties at the time of signing the agreement.

C. DIVORCE, NULLITY AND JUDICIAL SEPARATION

6. RECOGNITION OF FOREIGN MARRIAGES/DIVORCES

6.1 Summarise the position within your jurisdiction

Part VA of the Marriage Act 1961 came into effect in April 1986 and governs the recognition of foreign marriages. This ratified the Hague Convention on Celebration and Recognition of the Validity of Marriages of 1978.

A marriage is recognised as valid in form and substance if, at the time of the marriage, it was valid under the *Lex Loci Celebrationis*.

The exceptions set out in section 88D(2) and (3) are:

- if either of the parties was at the time of the marriage validly married under Australian law to another person;
- if either of the parties was at the time not of marriageable age (if domiciled in Australia, 18 years; if domiciled elsewhere, 16 years);
- if the parties were within prohibited relationships as defined under Australian law (see above);
- if the marriage under Australian law would be void for lack of consent or mental incapacity.

Section 88E(1) of the Marriage Act provides that Australia will recognise as valid a marriage in a foreign country that would not otherwise be recognised under the previous provisions of the Marriage Act if that marriage is valid under the common law rules of private international law.

Recognition of foreign divorces

Section 104 FLA, based on the Hague Convention on Recognition of Divorces and Legal Separations 1 June 1970, provides recognition of any dissolution, annulment or legal separation 'effected in accordance with the law of an overseas jurisdiction' provided either party had a specified connection with that foreign jurisdiction at the date the proceedings began that resulted in that decree.

The connection may be ordinary residence, domicile or nationality. Each of those concepts has been discussed earlier in this chapter.

As in the case of foreign marriages, section 104(5) of the Family Law Act provides that any dissolution, annulment or legal separation recognised as valid under the common law rules of private international law, but not otherwise entitled to recognition for the foregoing reasons, shall still be recognised as valid in Australia. Again, as the rules of private international law are common.

7. DIVORCE

7.1 Explain the grounds for divorce within the jurisdiction (please also deal with nullity and judicial separation if appropriate)

Firstly, divorce or principal relief is, in Australia, dealt with independently of other forms of matrimonial relief. Section 48(1) FLA provides that 'an application under this Act for a divorce order in relation to a marriage shall be based on the ground that the marriage has broken down irretrievably'.

Irretrievable breakdown of marriage is the only one ground of divorce, proved by living apart for 12 months. There is no concept of matrimonial fault.

While the parties need to have lived separately for 12 months before filing a divorce application, there is no waiting time before the parties may apply for any other kind of matrimonial relief in relation to children, property or maintenance.

Nullity

An application for a decree of nullity must be based on the ground that the marriage is void. A marriage is void if:

- it is bigamous;
- the parties are too closely related;
- the marriage was not a proper marriage ceremony in accordance with the Marriage Act;
- the consent of either party was not a real consent by reason of fraud, mistake as the identity of the other party or the nature of the ceremony, or mental incapacity or either party was too young to marry.

Most of these propositions are self-evident and later in this chapter the question of the recognition in Australia of an overseas marriage ceremony will be discussed. However, lack of consent for any of the reasons set out above will cause Australia not to recognise a marriage contracted overseas, even if otherwise valid in accordance with the laws of the country in which it was contracted (see section 88D(2)(d) Marriage Act 1961).

By section 11 of the Marriage Act the marriageable age for both sexes is 18.

Judicial separation

Though section 8(2) of the Family Law Act abolished an application for judicial separation, a modern form of similar relief is found under section 114(2) FLA, where the court may issue an injunction relieving a party from any obligation to perform marital services or render conjugal rights.

8. FINANCES/CAPITAL, PROPERTY

8.1 What powers does the court have to allocate financial resources and property on the breakdown of marriage?

There are three possible ways in which a discussion of the court's powers may be understood.

What are the court's powers, in the sense of what orders may it make?

The types of property orders the Family Court can make are set out in section 80 of the FLA. Those powers are comprehensive. Moreover, the courts have the power to make orders on an interim basis, including, importantly, the power to order a party to make interim property settlement before a final hearing and the power to make an order that a party provide a lump sum for the other party's legal costs and expert witness fees. Since the decision in *Strahan & Strahan* (Interim Property Orders) (2009) FamCAFC166, it may be that orders that are specifically for interim costs become less usual. In *Strahan* the Full Court determined that it was necessary only to assess whether the applicant was likely to receive a property settlement in excess of what she was to receive in the interim and that the respondent had the capacity to pay and the applicant did not. The powers of the Family Court extend to orders and injunctions. Section 114 FLA entitles the court to make orders for the personal protection of a party to the marriage, restraining a party to the marriage from entering or remaining in the matrimonial home, in relation to the property of a party to the marriage and injunctions whether interim or final where it appears to the court to be just or convenient.

As the Family Court is a statutory court, it is a court of limited jurisdiction. However, even courts of limited statutory jurisdiction have been held to have implied powers (see *DJL v The Central Authority* [2000] FLC 93-015). These implied powers are for the court to make such orders as are necessary for them to exercise their statutory jurisdiction with justice and efficiency.

Against whom may such orders be made?

Orders may, of course, be made against the parties to a marriage. If one of the parties dies after proceedings have been started then the other party may continue those proceedings, and obtain an order against the deceased party's estate.

In December 2004 the FLA was amended to give the court wide powers to make orders against third parties. Before that date the court was very cautious about interfering with the rights of third parties as a result of *Ascot Investments Pty Limited v Harper* (1981) FLC 91-000. In that case the High Court said that an order may not be made if its effect will be to deprive a third party of an existing right or to impose on that third party a duty which the party would not otherwise be liable to perform. There was an exception made in the case of the rights of that third party being only a sham, a device to allow a party to evade his or her obligations under the FLA. Such sham transactions may always be disregarded.

Similarly, if a company were completely controlled by one party to a marriage, so that in reality an order against the company is an order against the party, the fact that in form the order appears to affect the rights of the company may not necessarily invalidate it.

The new sections 90AE to section 90AJ inclusive (comprised in Part VIIIAA), expand the reach of the Family Court's powers considerably but those powers may be exercised only in limited circumstances.

Section 90AE(2) states that the court may make any order that directs a third party to do a thing in relation to the property of a party to the marriage or alters the rights, liabilities or property interests of a third party in relation to the marriage.

The strength and breadth of this law comes from section 90AC. If this law is inconsistent with any other Commonwealth or state law, or any Trust Deed or other instrument, Part VIIIAA overrides any such provision.

There are some safeguards. Section 90AK prohibits the court from making an order if it would result in the acquisition of property from a person other than on just terms. The order must be reasonably necessary. Procedural fairness must be observed.

There is still considerable uncertainty about the reach of these provisions and there are some contradictions embodied within it, as discussed in *Hughes-Kempe & Kempe & Ors* (2005) FLC 93-237. A more recent case has tested the limits of the third party provisions. In *AC & Ors and VC & Anor* [2013] FamCAFC 60, the Full Court of the Family Court, while overruling the trial judge in the particular circumstances, found no difficulty in principle with an order compelling the trustees of a trust to bring forward a vesting date of a trust where the court found that the beneficiaries had an irrevocable entitlement to share in the trust fund.

What property may be the subject of orders?

Section 4(1) FLA provides a definition of the word 'property', which is already wide but has been expanded by recent cases. In that definition 'property' means 'in relation to the parties to a marriage or either of them – means property to which those parties are, or that party is, as the case may be, entitled, whether in possession or reversion...'.

In keeping with the decision in *Ascot Investments & Harper*, the Family Court has always been able to deal with the property of a sham structure, such as a company or trust, as though the property of that structure were the property of the parties or either of them.

Similarly, the court has also dealt with the property of a structure, be it a company or a trust, where that structure is no more than the alter ego of a party to the marriage.

Specifically in the case of trusts, the Family Court has treated the property of a trust as the property of a party to the marriage if that party is the *de facto* or *de jure* controller of the trust, by reason of circumstance or by reason of a position as appointor, protector or controller.

In *Kennon v Spry; Spry v Kennon* 238 CLR 366, the High Court found within the definition of 'property' in the FLA, the right of the wife as a beneficiary to require the due administration of a trust. If that right were removed from the wife, the Family Court could use its power to set aside such a transaction as the husband had a fiduciary duty as the trustee of the trust to consider whether and in what way the power should be exercised.

To go even further, at least one Judge of the High Court considered that the nature of the assets of the trust, having been acquired through the efforts of one party or both during the marriage, contributed to their being treated as the property of the parties to the marriage. Three Judges of the High Court gave the widest interpretation possible to the Family Court's definition of property.

Then there are orders that deal with property that does not exist. This may take a number of forms. Firstly, the court may take into account assets that have been 'wasted' (see *Kowaliw & Kowaliw* (1981) FLC91-092).

Secondly, there is what are known as 'add backs'. Generally, the legal costs spent by both parties have been added back into a notional pool of property. Moreover, as in *Konitza & Konitza* (2009) FamCACF171, the Full Court deals with a premature distribution by one party of marital property to a relative.

The extent to which the court will add back notional property has recently been discussed and may be curtailed: *Sebastian & Sebastian (No 5)* [2013] FamCA 191. This now appears to be more of a discretionary matter and not something to be dealt with by entering into a balance sheet necessarily.

8.2 Explain and illustrate with reference to recent cases the court's thinking on division of assets

There are two main sections of the FLA that deal with division of assets and much case law. The two key sections are section 79 and section 75(2).

Section 79 has two key sub-sections. Section 79(2) states that 'the court shall not make an order under this section unless it is satisfied that, in all the circumstances, it is just and equitable to make the order'.

Section 79(4) requires the court to take into account:

- direct and indirect financial contributions by or on behalf of a party to the marriage to the acquisition, conservation or improvement of any of the property of the parties to the marriage;
- non-financial contributions, whether direct or indirect, by or on behalf of a party to the marriage towards the acquisition, conservation or improvement of the property of the parties to the marriage;
- contribution made by a party to the marriage to the welfare of the family constituted by the parties to the marriage and any children of the marriage, including any contribution made in the capacity of homemaker or parent;
- the effect of any proposed order on the earning capacity of either party;
- matters referred to in section 75(2) FLA.

There are other sub-sections of minor relevance.

The matters referred to in section 75(2) are compendious. To some degree, where section 79(4) refers to past contributions, section 75(2) refers to present or prospective factors, such as the future earning capacity of each party, their financial commitments, standard of living that is and was reasonable for them, the duration of the marriage and the extent to which it affected the earning capacity of a party, the need to protect a parenting role of a party, the financial circumstances of any subsequent cohabitation of a party and other similar matters.

The High Court of Australia in the recent decision of *Stanford v Stanford* (2012) FLC 93-518 has potentially introduced a significant change to the way in which assets are divided upon the breakdown of relationships. To some degree the changes may be less real than apparent. Before the High Court's decision in *Stanford* there were four steps involved:

- identify and value the asset pool;
- assess the contributions;
- take into account the matters referred to in section 75(2) of the FLA; and
- determine whether the orders are just and equitable: *Coghlan & Coghlan* (2005) FLC 93-220, *Hickey & Hickey & Attorney-General for the Commonwealth of Australia (Intervenor)* (2003) FLC 93-143.

The High Court emphasised that the requirement to make a just and equitable order was a separate, preliminary and distinct requirement. It did not otherwise confirm the four-step approach and many lawyers question whether there is now one step, are three steps or five steps. If this sounds like a dance routine…

One thing is clear from the High Court's judgment and that is that the first task is to identify, according to common law and equitable principles, the existing rights of the parties in whatever property in the broadest sense exists, and then and only then to determine whether it is just and equitable to make any order, not just the particular order. It is too early to see exactly what effect this decision will have, but it now seems possible that the court will consider not making any property settlement order if:

- the parties kept their financial affairs separate;
- the relationship was very short;
- where there was a pre-nuptial agreement that is not necessarily valid under Australian law and the parties adhered to it;
- where the parties ordered their property relationship in a way that is consistent with their current legal and equitable ownerships.

Otherwise, it is clear that the requirements of section 79(4) of the FLA will continue to come into play.

There is no principle that equality of outcome is either a starting point or a finishing point in the evaluation of contributions, even where assets are built up by the joint efforts of the parties to a marriage over a significant period of time (see the High Court of Australia decision in *Mallet v Mallet* (1984) FLC 91-507). However, the same decision is authority for the proposition that a non-income earning spouse must have just and equitable treatment by the recognition of her or his contribution in a real and substantial way, not in a token way.

An approach in keeping with the principle enunciated by the High Court is that which refers to special or extraordinary contributions by the exercise by one of the parties of an entrepreneurial skill or an extraordinary or special skill.

In *Ferraro & Ferraro* (1993) FLC 92-335, by the exercise of the husband's business acumen and entrepreneurial skill, there were produced assets worth approximately A$12 million. The court found that this was an extra contribution and, where the exercise of special skills had produced assets only in the 'normal range', the contributions would normally be equal. However, in this case the husband's contributions were valued at 62.5 per cent.

In the (still) leading case of *JEL & DDF* (2001) FLC 93-075, the asset pool of A$44 million was divided by the Full Court as 72.5 per cent to the husband and 27.5 per cent to the wife on the basis of the same general principles, enunciated as follows:

- there is no presumption of equality of contribution or 'partnership';
- there is a requirement to undertake an evaluation of the respective contributions of each party;
- although in many cases the direct financial contribution of one party will equal the indirect contribution of the other as homemaker and parent, that is not necessarily so in every case;
- in qualitatively evaluating the roles performed by marriage partners, there may arise special factors attaching to the performance of the particular role of one of them;
- the court will recognise any such special factors as taking the contribution outside the 'normal range';
- the determination of whether a contribution is special or extra is not

necessarily dependent upon the size of the asset pool or the 'financial product'.

While this decision has been repeatedly and strongly criticised, for example, by a differently constituted Full Court in *Figgins & Figgins* (2002) FLC 93-122, it still remains the authoritative statement of the law. Despite predictions, it has been resilient.

The factors identified in section 75(2) comprise the third phase. Although the Full Court has criticised this approach, in general, adjustments for these factors tend to be in a much narrower range than those for the factors identified under section 79(4) as contributions (see *Clauson & Clauson* (1995) FLC 92-595).

While previous cases referred to contributions that were 'special' or 'extraordinary', in the case of *Smith & Fields* [2012] FamCA 510 a judge put new clothes on more or less the same body. He rejected the notion of such special contributions, while at the same time rejecting the notion of a marital partnership with its implication of equality of outcome, in this big money case. He referred to and found a superior contribution by the husband because of the nature of the husband's contributions, being of the nature not of special skills, but of ingenuity and stewardship.

9. FINANCES/MAINTENANCE

9.1 Explain the operation of maintenance for spouses on an ongoing basis after the breakdown of marriage

Section 72 FLA provides that a party to a marriage is liable to maintain the other party if, and only if, the other party is unable to support herself or himself adequately, and then only if the first party is reasonably able to do so. The court can make orders for periodic payments or for a lump sum. 'Adequately' refers to the standard of living that the couple enjoyed when they were together. It does not mean mere subsistence. The court takes into account all of the matters set out in section 75(2) FLA, previously addressed in the context of property settlement.

Spouse maintenance may be ordered on an interim basis or on a final basis.

9.2 Is it common for maintenance to be awarded?

It is a sad fact that, in most Australian states, there is often between one year and two years for cases to come to trial. It is also often the case that one party controls the purse strings. In those circumstances, it is very common for the court to order interim maintenance, ie, an order for maintenance up until the time of final hearing.

However, it is less common for maintenance orders to be made on a final basis as part of an application for final property settlement. There is a disjunction between what the cases have said and what the courts and the parties to litigation are actually doing. As early as 1986, the Australian Institute of Family Studies reported that long-term maintenance was being ordered, or agreed upon in only six per cent of the couples it surveyed. Later studies have found similar results. In part this is because the philosophy of a clean break is embodied in section 81 FLA. The court is required to make such orders as will finally determine the financial relationship between the parties to the marriage and avoid further proceedings between them, so far as practicable.

Another factor may be the court's reluctance to order different financial provisions, but building upon the same factors. In ordering property settlement, the court takes into account prospective matters under the heading of section 75(2) FLA and it is that same section that provides many of the indicia for maintenance orders.

9.3 Explain and illustrate with reference to recent cases the court's thinking on maintenance

In the early to middle 1990s a spate of maintenance orders was made at a final hearing and for a relatively long period. The court was influenced by a landmark Canadian decision and social research on the feminisation of poverty. The Full Court found in *Mitchell & Mitchell* (1995) FLC92-601 a new purpose for spouse maintenance to compensate for economic disadvantage. It may be noted that this does not appear in the Australian legislation, but in fact little has changed as an expression of the law since *Bevan & Bevan* (1995) FLC92-600 laid down the following principles:

- there must be a threshold finding that the applicant has a need and the measure of that need is a variable factor;
- the order must be reasonable and based on the various criteria in section 75(2);
- there is no principle that a party should automatically support the other at a pre-separation standard of living when an order for post separation spouse maintenance is made simply because that party has the means to do so;
- there is an exercise of discretion based on what is reasonable and adequate.

Even in those cases where the facts create an anticipation of spouse maintenance, with a small asset pool and one party having large income, the orders are still rare. An example is *Best & Best* (1993) FLC92-418. It will be seen that these are not new cases.

New cases tend to emerge from unusual situations. In *Brown v Brown* (2007) FLC93-916, a husband had transferred out of his name all of his Australian assets, refused to come to Australia, had assets of about (by that time) A$150 million and an income of at least A$1 million *per annum*. In that context the trial judge made an order for lump sum spouse maintenance of A$3.75 million, reduced on appeal to A$2.25 million.

It is difficult to avoid the view that this case represents an aberration, and, while there is no inconsistency of principle, it seems more born of circumstance than any change to the way in which maintenance is addressed. However, it may herald a trend. Pre and post-nuptial agreements may deal both with property settlement and spouse maintenance. There are technical requirements in order to exclude any spouse maintenance application that are even more stringent than in relation to property settlement.

In *Adamidis v Adamidis* (2009) FMCA Fam1104, the wife applied to set aside a financial agreement, excluding both property and maintenance rights. She failed as to property settlement, but succeeded as to spouse maintenance. The husband then applied for lump sum spouse maintenance and one could anticipate a kind of retributive adjustment where the court's jurisdiction has been excluded in one aspect but made available in another. This decision may represent not a principled approach to the issue of spouse maintenance but an opportunistic one dictated by the circumstances of the individual case.

10. CHILD MAINTENANCE

10.1 On what basis is child maintenance calculated within the jurisdiction?

In most instances provision of financial support for children is determined by a Child Support Assessment instead of an order of a court for child maintenance.

The Child Support Agency (CSA) was formed to assist separated parents to take responsibility for the financial support of their children. The CSA administers the Child Support Scheme.

The Child Support (Assessment) Act 1989 introduced a formula for the administrative assessment of child support. The scheme involves the assessment of child support in accordance with a formula, as well as the collection and enforcement of court orders, child support agreements and child support assessments.

From 1 July 2008, a new formula is applied for the purposes of child support assessments.

Features of the new formula include:

- it uses an 'income shares' approach to calculate and share the costs of children. This concept uses a parent's share of the income available to support a child as an indication of their ability to meet the costs of the child. The costs of the child are divided between the parents according to their share of the combined child support income;
- both parents have the same self support amount. The self support amount is the amount deducted from the parent's adjusted taxable income for their own support. The amount is the same for both parents as indexed each year;
- the cost of the children is divided between the parents in proportions equal to their share of the combined income;
- it recognises the costs of contact as a contribution to the costs of the children;
- it treats the children of first and second families as equally as possible by using the actual costs of the children from the second family in determining the child support payable (rather than a flat increase).

In the majority of cases the rate of child support will be assessed using the first formula. The CSA has an online estimator on its website to assist parties to calculate the support payable.

Parents can object to particular decisions made under the Child Support

(Assessment) Act. There are avenues of review, both administrative and judicial.

11. RECIPROCAL ENFORCEMENT OF FINANCIAL ORDERS

11.1 Summarise the position within your jurisdiction

Common law

- The foreign court must have had jurisdiction over the defendant, either by the presence of the defendant in that jurisdiction or by voluntary submission to it.
- The foreign judgment must be final.
- The plaintiff and defendant in the foreign judgment must be identical with the parties to any proceeding in Australia.
- The judgment may be enforced only if it is for a fixed sum of money.

A number of defences exist, among them, if the original judgment was obtained by fraud or a judgment is contrary to the public policy of Australia.

However, suing for recognition and enforcement at common law requires a proceeding that pleads the foreign judgment and the foreign judgment cannot simply be registered.

However, for family law matters, the long-held view is that an order for property settlement must be ancillary to a divorce decree and the recognition of the property settlement order depends upon the recognition of the decree for divorce (as to which see the earlier discussion of that topic).

Statute

The Foreign Judgments Act 1991 permits registration of judgments in Australia by reciprocal arrangements with certain nominated courts only in some 30 countries and provinces. While at common law foreign decrees for property settlement were held to be judgments *in personam,* under the Foreign Judgments Act by statutory definition judgments in family law matters are not judgments *in personam* but fall into a third category.

Such a judgment is entitled to recognition in Australia if the foreign court exercised a jurisdiction which would have been entitled to recognition under the law of Australia.

If the proceedings in the foreign court were contrary to a choice of forum agreement between the parties, the judgment will not be registered.

If the proceedings giving rise to the judgment were ancillary to divorce proceedings then they will probably be recognised and registrable in Australia.

The judgment must be final and conclusive and for a fixed sum.

Australia is not party to any international agreement or convention governing the recognition and enforcement of orders in relation to property settlement between spouses.

Spouse maintenance

Australian law provides for the registration and enforcement in Australia of maintenance orders made in certain overseas countries. The Child Support Regulations permit the enforcement of both spouse and child maintenance obligations that arise overseas.

An Australian court may vary an overseas spouse maintenance order in two ways. If the overseas order comes from certain countries, and is registered in Australia, the court here may vary the order or discharge it. In respect of certain other countries, the Australian court may only provisionally vary the overseas order and the variation must be confirmed by the country in which the order was originally made. Unless the overseas order is registered in Australia, no Australian court may vary or discharge the overseas order.

Australia is party to an agreement with New Zealand on spouse maintenance, to the Hague Convention on the Recognition and Enforcement of Decisions Relating to Maintenance Obligations, and to an agreement with the USA for the Agreement for the Enforcement of Maintenance (support) Obligations, as well as to the United Nations Convention on the Recovery Abroad of Maintenance (UNCRAM).

12. FINANCIAL RELIEF AFTER FOREIGN DIVORCE PROCEEDINGS

12.1 What powers are available to make orders following a foreign divorce?

Australia will still have jurisdiction to entertain an application for financial relief after the making of a foreign divorce if one of the jurisdictional facts referred to in part 2 is established.

If the foreign divorce proceedings are current, in the sense that any aspect of those proceedings, be it principal or ancillary relief or even parenting proceedings, remains undetermined, then there will no doubt be argument as to whether Australia is a clearly inappropriate forum for the determination of the Australian application. This is discussed in part 4.

If there are no foreign proceedings still current, and the court determines that Australia is not a clearly inappropriate forum to determine the issues before the Australian court, then an Australian court may, in certain circumstances, still deal with some aspects of financial relief.

In *Pagliotti & Hartner* (2009) FLC 93-393, the Full Family Court dealt with an application by the wife to deal with property in Australia, despite the fact that the husband and the wife had litigated already after the breakdown of their marriage in the Roman Tribunal. The Full Court determined that Australia could grant an order altering the interests of the parties in the Australian property.

The Roman proceedings did not have the power to make orders in relation to property outside Italy. Nonetheless, it was submitted by the respondent that, apart from forum issues, the application was *res judicata* or there was an estoppel.

The Full Court accepted that there was no identity of proceedings between Australia and Italy because the ownership of the Australian property was not determined in those proceedings, that the Australian proceedings were different in kind and raised different issues from the Italian proceedings and that the Italian proceedings were primarily concerned with spouse maintenance and not property settlement. The Full Court, therefore, determined that there was neither *res judicata* nor estoppel.

Pagliotti & Hartner was followed by *Chen & Tan* [2012] FamCA 225 to the effect that once Australian jurisdiction is enlivened, Australia applies its own law and may adjust the rights of parties in property located overseas regardless of the rights of those parties under foreign law.

Therefore, it seems that in limited circumstances parties who can establish jurisdiction in Australia may maintain proceedings for financial relief, notwithstanding that orders for a divorce and even orders for financial relief have been made in a foreign court. In most cases, the forum conveniens or oppression arguments will be the most daunting obstacle.

D. CHILDREN

13. CUSTODY/PARENTAL RESPONSIBILITY

13.1 Briefly explain the legal position in relation to custody/parental responsibility following the breakdown of a relationship or marriage

Until any court orders to the contrary, both parents have joint parental responsibility for their children. The paramount consideration in any decision concerning children is their welfare or their best interests.
The main object of the FLA is to ensure the children receive help to achieve their full potential and to ensure parents fulfil their duties and meet their responsibilities concerning the care, welfare and development of the children.

Parental responsibility may be altered by the court. It may be altered both wholly, so that one party has the sole responsibility to make long term decisions for the children, or partially so that some aspects of parental responsibility are shared and other aspects, for example education, might be given to one parent and not the other. There is a presumption that it is in the best interests of the children for parents to have equal shared parental responsibility. This does not apply if there is abuse or family violence or it is not in the best interests of the child.

If there is shared parental responsibility or that question is in dispute, the court must consider whether the children spending equal time with each parent is in their best interest and reasonably practicable. If it is not, the court must then consider whether a child spending substantial and significant time with each parent is in the child's best interests and reasonably practicable. 'Substantial and significant time' is referred to in the FLA to include weekends, holidays, weekdays, time that allows each parent to be involved in the child's daily routine as well as occasions and events of particular significance both to the children and to the parents.

As to what is practicable, the court will look at the distance between the parents' homes, the parents' actual and future capacity to do what they say they want, their communications, the impact of the proposed arrangement on the children and other matters.

In all of this there are primary considerations:

- the benefit to the children of having a meaningful relationship with both parents;
- the need to protect them from harm;

- greater emphasis is now placed on need to protect from harm and family violence. It is an issue of increased significance and expanded meaning.

There are additional considerations including:

- the wishes of the children;
- their relationship with each parent and others;
- the attitudes of parents to the children and their parental responsibilities;
- family violence;
- the need to make an order least likely to lead to further litigation.

It is worth noting, that unless in exceptional circumstances, the parties cannot take parenting proceedings without first attempting to resolve their parenting disagreement with a counsellor called a family dispute resolution practitioner.

14. INTERNATIONAL ABDUCTION

14.1 Summarise the position within your jurisdiction

Australia is a party to the Hague Convention on the Civil Aspects of International Child Abduction (the Hague Convention).

Article 5(a) refers to the term 'rights of custody'. Australia has abandoned the words 'custody' and 'access' in family law matters but section IIIB(4) of the Family Law Act was enacted to resolve doubts about the implications of those changes for Convention purposes. In short:

- each parent is regarded as having a right of custody unless that parent has no parental responsibility for the child because of any court order;
- subject to any court order, a person with whom a child is to live or who has parental responsibility for a child under any parenting order has a right of custody;
- a person who is responsible for the day-to day-care, welfare and development of a child has a right of custody, subject to any court order;
- a person with whom a child is to spend time or with whom a child is to communicate under any court order is regarded as having a right of access.

The applicant under a Hague Convention case must establish that the child was habitually resident in one Hague contracting state and then wrongfully removed to, or retained in, a different contracting state. Determination of habitual residence is therefore central. The High Court of Australia in *LK v Director General, Department of Community Services* (2009) HCA 9 held that 'the relevant criterion is a shared intention that the children live in a particular place with a sufficient degree of continuity to be properly described as settled'. This differs from mere physical presence and intention and is focused on what each parent intends for the child. The court declined to identify a set of criteria that bear upon a child's habitual residence or to settle a hierarchy of importance. This decision has been criticised as giving too much weight to parental intentions that may, in some respects, be uncertain or difficult to interpret.

In relation to the acquiescence defence, *Department of Community Services & Frampton* (2007) FamCA 450 determined that a finding of acquiescence to a change of habitual residence requires 'clear and unequivocal evidence of acquiescence and/or evidence of circumstances which were wholly inconsistent with a request for summary return'.

In relation to the grave risk of physical or psychological harm defence (or 'intolerable situation defence'), the Full Court in *Murray & Director-General of Family Services* (1993) FLC 92-416 ordered the return of children to New Zealand, despite the high risk that they may be exposed to domestic violence at the hand of the left behind parent because the returning parent and children could be protected by the New Zealand courts and authorities. Thus, as in *Gsponer v Director General Department of Community Services (VIC)* (1989) FLC 92-001, the return of the child to a harmful or intolerable situation is determined in the context of the place, not the parent left behind. In *DP & Commonwealth Central Authority; JLM v Director General NSW Department of Community Services* (2001) 206CLR 401, the High Court of Australia said that the grave risk defence requires clear and compelling evidence.

In *Gernish-Grant v Director General Department of Community Services* (2002) FLC 93-111, two judges of the Full Court referred to *Friedrich v Friedrich* 78F2d1060 (6th Circuit 1996), a decision of the US Court of Appeal. This effectively confirmed the focus on risk from the country to which the child is to return, but raised the second category of a grave risk of harm in cases of serious abuse or neglect or extraordinary emotional dependence, coupled with the incapacity or unwillingness of the court in the country of habitual residence to give the child adequate protection. In *Director General Department of Community Services v Harris* (2010) 43FamLR 170 where the grave risk of harm test was applied.

In relation to the 'mature child objects to return' defence:

- 'objects' must refer to an objection to being returned to the country from which it was removed, not the parent;
- the objection must show a strength of feeling beyond mere expression of a preference;
- there is no strict rule requiring the child to be a certain age, although 12 is a rule of thumb;
- where there are siblings, an older sibling's objection may carry the objection of a younger.

The public policy defence requires evidence that the fundamental principles of the requested state did not permit the return, rather than mere incompatibility with those principles should the child be returned (see *McCall & McCall; State's Central Authority; Attorney General of the Commonwealth* (1995) FLC 92-551).

The best interests of the child have no place in the application of the Hague Convention in Australia (see *De L v Director General, NSW Department of Community Services* (1996) 187CLR 640).

However, in relation to return of a child to a non Hague Convention country, and subject to earlier comments in relation to jurisdiction and to *forum conveniens* in parenting matters, the best interests of the child determine the outcomes.

15. LEAVE TO REMOVE/APPLICATIONS TO TAKE CHILD OUT OF A JURISDICTION

15.1 Under what circumstances may a parent apply to remove their child from the jurisdiction against the wishes of the other parent?

It is necessary to deal with what the FLA states as some core values:

- that children receive help to fulfil their full potential and to ensure parents fulfil their duties and responsibilities;
- that unless, the court otherwise orders both parents have joint shared parental responsibilities, they have equal obligations and responsibilities towards the children and the right to be equally involved in decisions about their long term welfare;
- there is a presumption that it is in the best interests of the children for the parents to have equal shared parental responsibility;
- where there is shared parental responsibility, or it is in dispute, the court must consider whether the children spending equal time with each parent would be in their best interests and reasonably practicable;
- if, having considered the issue, the court believes it is not in a child's best interests to spend equal time with each parent, the court must then consider whether a child spending 'substantial and significant time' with each parent is in the best interests of the child and reasonably practicable.

In determining whether it is reasonably practicable for the child to spend equal time or substantial and significant time with each parent the court will consider:

- how far the parents live from each other;
- the ability of the parents now and in the future to implement an arrangement for the children spending equal time, or substantial and significant time with each parent;
- communication issues between the parents;
- the children's best interests are paramount;
- the impact of such an arrangement on the child.

There is a range of subsidiary factors, but these may be stated as the core objectives.

Very clearly, there is no presumption in favour either of a mother or of a parent with whom a child has lived predominantly. Given the core value of at least substantial and significant time, it is to be wondered that there are any successful relocation applications, especially where the distances are substantial (as, even within Australia, they often are). Yet there has been a plethora of such cases, as the mobility of Australia's population continues to grow nationally and internationally, and it is unlikely that this will change.

The leading case is now *MRR v GR**. That case has now been followed many times, for example in *Saver v Radcliff & Anor* [2012] 48 FamLR 298.

The court said the legislation 'obliges the court to consider both the question of whether it is in the best interests of the child to spend equal time with each of the parents and the question of whether it is reasonably practicable that the child spend equal time with each of them'.

While this decision charts a logical path for judicial officers, it does not seem to necessitate any new approach. The court will look at the proposals advanced by the parties but is not bound by them. There is no onus on either party to show compelling reasons. The court will look at the existence of family networks in the place of relocation or the lack of them in the place from which relocation is sought, the history of the residence of the parents and the child, the ability of the relocating parent to obtain employment, financial considerations, the child's wishes and whether or not the relocating parent's reasons for leaving are held in good faith or constitute an attempt to undermine the relationship between the child and the other parent.

E. SURROGACY AND ADOPTION

16. VALIDITY OF SURROGACY AGREEMENTS

16.1 Briefly summarise the position in your jurisdiction

The law relating to surrogacy is not federal but state based. However, to all practical effect, the law in Australia is uniform in relation to surrogacy agreements. When a surrogate mother undergoes donor insemination and utilises her own ovum to conceive the child, this is known as traditional surrogacy; gestational surrogacy is the harvesting of the ovum from a third person or one of the intended parents depending on the circumstances, and fertilised using the sperm donated from the intended parent or a third person.

Altruistic surrogacy arrangements are privately organised. These are legal in all Australian states. There is a restriction in one of the Australian territories that those wishing to enter into altruistic surrogacy arrangements must be a couple and the surrogate must also be a couple. In South Australia altruistic surrogacy is legally available to heterosexual relationships and in Western Australia altruistic surrogacy is available only to married, cohabiting couples, or single women but not to same-sex couples.

Commercial surrogacy is outlawed in all states of Australia except for the Northern Territory. Three states impose extra-territorial criminal sanctions for those who engage in commercial surrogacy overseas and return with the child.

17. ADOPTION

17.1 Briefly explain the legal position in relation to adoption in your jurisdiction. Is it an option available to individuals, cohabiting couples (both heterosexual and same-sex)?

The law in relation to adoption in Australia, if inter country children are involved, is controlled by each state and territory and also by federal law. The federal law is the Migration Act 1958, the Family Law Act 1975 and the Australian Citizenship Act 2007. Australia is also a party to the Hague Convention of Intercountry Adoption, and has enacted domestic legislation accordingly. The controls are strict.

While adoptions within Australian states depend in part upon federal law, each state and territory has its own law and the laws differ. With the exception of one state, however, an adoption legal in an Australian jurisdiction will be recognised in each other Australian jurisdiction.

Criteria are the age of prospective adopters, the longevity of their relationship, the health of the prospective adopters including emotional and physical health, life experience, stability and security of their emotional and physical environment, financial circumstances, capacity to maintain the child's cultural identity and religious faith, if any, appreciation of the need to facilitate or retain contact with birth parents and family of the child, and parenting history.

In most Australian jurisdictions it is possible for one person to adopt a child but the circumstances have to be exceptional and the rules are very restrictive.

In five of the seven Australian jurisdictions, heterosexual cohabiting couples may adopt on the same basis as heterosexual married couples. In four Australian jurisdictions same-sex cohabiting couples are able to adopt but in three not able to do so.

F. COHABITATION

18. COHABITATION

18.1 What legislation (if any) governs division of property for unmarried couples on the breakdown of the relationship?

Until December 2008, each Australian state and territory had its own legislation dealing with cohabitants. However, all but two Australian states referred their powers over this area to the Commonwealth, which passed the Family Law Amendment (De Facto Financial Matters and Other Measures) Act. That Act came into effect on 1 March 2009. The effect is that, for the referring states, the rights of cohabitants equal those of parties to a marriage except for a few jurisdictional niceties.

The FLA now defines the relationship of cohabitation, referred to here as a *de facto* relationship, as follows:

'A person is in a de facto relationship with another person if:

(a) the persons are not legally married to each other; and

(b) the persons are not related by family; and

(c) having regard to all the circumstances of their relationship, they have a relationship as a couple living together on a genuine domestic basis'.

The Act applies equally to relationships of opposite sexes and the same sex.

The Act (section 44(5)) provides that a financial application may be brought only if made within two years from the end of the *de facto* relationship. The Act applies to those relationships that broke down after 1 March 2009. So far as the referring states are concerned, therefore, there is limited use in discussing the pre-amendment position of cohabitant couples.

The South Australian legislation is the Domestic Partners Property Act 1996. It also applies to same-sex and heterosexual relationships. That of Western Australia is the Family Court Act 1997. Likewise, the Western Australian legislation is applicable to same-sex or heterosexual relationships.

There are differences in detail between the legislation of these two states and also between these two states and the legislation that, before the Commonwealth assumed powers, prevailed in the other states.

The significant differences between the rights of cohabitants under the former legislation and the legislation in the two non-referring states, and the rights of those that may now be dealt with under the FLA, reside chiefly in the subsidiary criteria for property adjustment and the rules governing maintenance of one of the parties to such a relationship.

In both the FLA and the *de facto* legislation for cohabitants, the overriding criterion is justice and equity. However, where the FLA refers to the prospective factors set out in section 75(2) and discussed above, there is no such reference whatsoever to those factors in the *de facto* laws that did apply and still apply.

This worked very much to the disadvantage of that partner to such a relationship who was at an economic disadvantage, having most likely made lesser financial contributions during the relationship and having no compensation from the court for ongoing economic disadvantage after the relationship ended, whether because of a commitment to the relationship or not.

Moreover, orders for 'spouse' maintenance are greatly attenuated, being usually rehabilitative and always for a brief period.

The West Australian statute contains no such limitation and its provisions mirror those of the FLA.

G. FAMILY DISPUTE RESOLUTION

19. MEDIATION, COLLABORATIVE LAW AND ARBITRATION

19.1 Briefly summarise the non-court-based processes available in your jurisdiction and the current status of agreements reached under the auspices of mediation, collaborative law and arbitration

Each of mediation, collaborative law and arbitration is available in Australia. The popularity and frequency of the use of each vary from state to state and from place to place. Both mediation and collaborative law are gaining in popularity. Arbitration, curiously, is little used. In addition, particularly in relation to parenting matters, family dispute resolution is available and frequently used. However, agreements reached by those means, with one exception, have no legal status unless subsequently made into, or registered as, court orders. For example, an award of an arbitrator, if registered in court, has effect as if it were a court order.

One exception is in relation to parenting matters, where parties may conclude a parenting plan. It must be in writing, signed by the parents and dated. Lawyers are required to inform clients that they could consider a parenting plan and advise where they can get help to develop one. However, parenting plans do no bind a court: at best a court will have regard to its terms. Neither is the parenting plan of itself enforceable.

19.2 What is the statutory basis (if any), for mediation, collaborative law and arbitration in your jurisdiction? In particular, are the parties required to attempt family dispute resolution in advance of the institution of proceedings?

Arbitration has a statutory basis in the FLA (section 13E). A court in relation to financial proceedings may order referral to arbitration with the consent of the parties but not otherwise. In a general sense, neither mediation nor collaboration, except as set out below, has a statutory basis. The court refers all cases to court sponsored mediation during the course of any proceedings.

However, in parenting matters, with some exceptions, it is mandatory that parties attempt family dispute resolution with a registered family dispute resolution practitioner before being entitled to start court proceedings. Only if the practitioner provides a certificate that the parties have done so and failed, will the court accept a parenting application subject to the exceptions previously referred to. This is set out in section 60I of the FLA.

H. OTHER

20. CIVIL PARTNERSHIPS/SAME-SEX MARRIAGE

20.1 What is the status of civil partnership/same-sex marriage within the jurisdiction?

The institution of marriage is still reserved for heterosexuals. Section 5 of the Marriage Act of the Commonwealth states that 'marriage means the union of a man and a woman to the exclusion of all others, voluntarily entered into for life'. It is likely that, if that was what defined a marriage, this publication would be superfluous.

Nonetheless, while same-sex couples may not marry within Australia, several Australian states now afford some recognition to same-sex relationships.

20.2 What legislation governs civil partnership/same-sex marriage?

There is no legislation permitting same-sex marriage. Tasmania, by means of the Relationships Act 2003, instituted a registry system intending partners sign a certificate witnessed by a state official. That is then sent to the Registrar of Births, Deaths & Marriages and is known as a Deed of Relationship. It includes same-sex partners living as a 'significant relationship'. The significant benefit of registering the relationship is that it is evidence of the relationship, without having the need to prove its existence elsewhere and for other purposes.

In the Australian Capital Territory, the Civil Partnership Act 2008 came into effect on 19 May 2008. This Act permits the registration by couples, of whatever gender, of their civil partnership. It imports legal recognition. It confers automatic recognition as being in a domestic partnership for the law of the Australian Capital Territory. They must, however, live in that place.

In Victoria, the Relationships Act 2008 also had as its main purpose the overcoming of the need to prove the existence of the relationship. Registration is permitted of 'registrable relationships' and, again, there are no limitations of gender.

In order for a couple to bring themselves within the ambit of the FLA as *de facto* partners, they must prove the existence of the *de facto* relationship. Registration of a relationship is not determinative of the existence of the relationship, but a very significant factor.

21. CONTROVERSIAL AREAS/RAPIDLY DEVELOPING AREAS OF LAW

21.1 Is there a particular area of the law within the jurisdiction that is currently undergoing major change?

In the first edition of this work I referred to nuptial agreements. That is still an area of rapid change. The law is still evolving and it is to be hoped that the number of such agreements that are coming before the courts will decline as it becomes more and more apparent to the legal and lay communities that these agreements must be done with proper professional skill and considerable care. Unfortunately lawyers are more and more featuring in the nuptial agreement litigation themselves, as defendants both in separate suits and joined as parties to the proceedings.

In the area of cohabitants, no jurisprudence has developed to distinguish their legal rights and obligations from those of parties to a marriage, but the ambit of cohabitation as a notion is being widened rather than narrowed by court decisions.

21.2 Which areas of law are most out of step? Which areas would you most like to see reformed/changed?

The Family Court lags behind the courts of some other signatories to the Hague Convention on International Child Abduction in the relative slowness of its dealing with applications for return, and its tolerance for argument and protracted appeals process.

No doubt, a shift in judicial attitude would be assisted by better government funding and more judges.

It is still the case that the attitude of the court to pre- and post-nuptial agreements is contrary to the spirit of the legislation that established them, and there is community pressure to use these agreements, but intense concern about their efficacy and survival rates.

There is still no recognition of same-sex marriage despite changing community attitudes with which the law appears to be out of step.

The conflict of values that big money cases throw up, between the assessment of contributions, and the partnership model, remains unresolved; and the recent High Court decision in *Stanford* referred to above may yet have a role to play; otherwise, it must await appellate intervention because it is most unlikely that there will be any from the legislature.

Austria

Rechtsantwaltskanzlei Dr Alfred Kriegler
Dr Alfred Kriegler

A. JURISDICTION AND CONFLICT OF LAW

1. SOURCES OF LAW

1.1 What is the primary source of law in relation to the breakdown of marriage and the welfare of children within the jurisdiction? Which are the main statutes governing matrimonial law in the jurisdiction?

The Austrian Civil Code (*Allgemeines Bürgerliches Gesetzbuch, ABGB*) governs legal relationships between spouses, relationships between parents and children, and also issues of succession and property rights. The Austrian Marriage Act (*Ehegesetz, EheG*) contains provisions concerning engagements, the requirements for entry into a marriage and for the dissolution of a marriage by divorce, annulment or nullity, as well as maintenance obligations after divorce, the distribution of assets and articles for daily use in conjugal community and matrimonial savings. The Resolution Act relating to non-litigious proceedings (*Außerstreitgesetz, AußStrG*) applies to special procedural matters in parent and child law, divorces by mutual consent and the distribution of matrimonial property. Provisions on litigious proceedings in general and the jurisdiction of Austrian courts can be found in the Code of Civil Procedures (Zivilprozessordnung, ZPO) and the Act governing the Jurisdiction of Austrian courts (*Jurisdiktionsnorm, JN*).

There are no separate family courts in Austria. District Courts (*Bezirksgerichte*) have first-instance jurisdiction in family matters and specialist family law departments are in situ. Unlike many other European states, individual rulings are not used as general precedents for other similar cases in Austria but such decisions are important when it comes to the interpretation of laws. One exception to this rule is the calculation model which was developed through the established practice of the courts and is applied throughout the country in decisions relating to maintenance.

2. JURISDICTION

2.1 What are the main jurisdictional requirements for the institution of proceedings in relation to divorce, property and children?

The Act governing the jurisdiction of Austrian courts (JN) sets out the international jurisdiction of the Austrian courts.

Austrian courts have jurisdiction in cases of divorce, annulment or nullity of marriage and declaratory judgments relating to the validity of a marriage if one of the following conditions is met:

- one of the parties is an Austrian national;

- the respondent, or at least one respondent, where a petition for nullity is brought by both spouses or both registered partners has their habitual residence in Austria;
- the petitioner has their habitual residence in Austria and the last common address and the habitual residence of either spouses or registered partners was located in Austria, or where the petitioner is stateless or was an Austrian national at the time the marriage or registered partnership was entered into.

Domestic courts have jurisdiction in proceedings concerning the distribution of assets and articles for daily use in conjugal community and matrimonial savings if one of the parties is an Austrian national or has their habitual residence in Austria.

In parent and child law cases, the jurisdiction of the Austrian courts is contingent on the following:

- the minor child is an Austrian national;
- their habitual residence or, in urgent matters, their temporary place of abode is in Austria;
- the minor holds assets in Austria, if the dispute concerns such assets.

At the same time, the jurisdiction of the Austrian courts is governed by the relevant EU regulations when cases involving EU member states are considered. Under the regulation concerning jurisdiction and the recognition and enforcement of judgments in matrimonial matters and matters of parental responsibility (Brussels IIA Regulation), the jurisdiction of the courts of a member state in matters of divorce, legal separation or annulment of a marriage, depends on whether the member state is:

- where both spouses have their habitual residence;
- where both spouses had their last habitual residence, provided that one of them still resides there;
- where the respondent has their habitual residence;
- in case of a joint petition, where one of the spouses has their habitual residence;
- where the petitioner has their habitual residence, provided that they have lived there for at least one year immediately prior to filing the petition;
- where the petitioner has their habitual residence, provided that they stayed there for at least six months immediately prior to filing the petition and provided that they are either a national of that member state or has their domicile there (in case of the United Kingdom and Ireland);
- where both spouses are nationals of that member state or, in case of the United Kingdom and Ireland, their common domicile is located there.

Under the above regulation, the courts having jurisdiction in matters of parental responsibility are the courts of the member state where the child had their habitual residence at the time when the petition was filed.

3. DOMICILE AND HABITUAL RESIDENCE

3.1 Explain the concepts of domicile and habitual residence as they apply to the jurisdiction.

Persons are considered to have their domicile in Austria if they have taken up their abode with the intention of residing in Austria permanently. When determining habitual residence, the duration of stay, as well as the personal circumstances and job situation indicating a long-term connection between the person and their stay, will be taken into consideration. According to precedent, a period of about six months has been determined to be indicative of such a long-term connection.

4. CONFLICT OF LAW/APPLICABLE LAW TO BE APPLIED

4.1 What happens when one party applies to stay proceedings in favour of a foreign jurisdiction? What factors will the local court take into account when determining forum issues?

Provisions governing the law applicable in cases which have effect beyond the Austrian borders are set out in the Act on Private International Law (*Internationales Privatrecht-Gesetz, IPRG*).

The legal effect of a marriage and the legal effects of divorce are determined as follows:

- the common, or in the absence thereof, the last common domicile of the spouses, provided that one spouse retained it;
- according to the law of the state where both spouses have their common habitual residence, or in the absence thereof, according to the law of the state where both spouses had their last common habitual residence, provided that one spouse retained such residence.

If the marriage did not come into effect under the law applicable in the jurisdiction described in the first paragraph above, but is valid in Austria, the legal effects of the marriage are adjudicated under Austrian law. If the spouses are more strongly connected to a third country, and the marriage is also effective there, the law of the third country will be applied instead of Austrian law.

If none of these situations applies, the divorce will be adjudicated according to the domicile of the petitioning spouse at the time of the divorce.

The matrimonial property regime will be adjudicated under the law which was expressly chosen by the parties, and in the absence of such choice of law, it will be subject to the relevant law at the time of the marriage.

B. PRE- AND POST-NUPTIAL AGREEMENTS

5. VALIDITY OF PRE AND POST NUPTIAL AGREEMENTS

5.1 To what extent are pre- and post-nups binding within the jurisdiction? Could you provide a brief discussion of the most significant recent case law on this issue

The situation in Austria differs from that in other countries as future spouses rarely enter into pre-nuptial agreements here. Related legislation was reformed with effect from 1 January 2010 to facilitate entry into pre-nuptial agreements.

Pre- and post-nuptial agreements can be used for arrangements relating to the legal consequences of marriage, maintenance and contributions to earnings of the spouse's death, the distribution of marital property and other arrangements in the event of separation or divorce.

Pre- and post-nuptial agreements may be only be entered into by spouses or fiancées and are contingent upon marriage.

Under the Austrian Act on Private International Law, formal requirements for pre- and post-nuptial agreements are subject to the laws of the country where the agreement was entered into. If a valid pre- or post-nuptial agreement was entered into abroad, it is recognised in Austria. For the law applicable in relation to the distribution of matrimonial property, please refer to chapter A4.

The scope of maintenance to be agreed between spouses will be discussed in chapter C9. It is permissible to exclude a spouse's right to maintenance *vis-à-vis* the other in the event of dissolution of a marriage. However, it is not possible to predict what future rulings the Austrian courts will decide in cases of spousal maintenance. For this reason, it is advisable to agree to the waiver of any maintenance providing more than modest subsistence in case a total exclusion of maintenance is found to be invalid.

Decisions on child custody in separation or divorce proceedings are taken by the Austrian custody courts. These will consider the best interests of any children of the marriage at the time of divorce. Any pre-existing agreement relating to children will be accepted only as an expression of the spouses' wishes, but the court will respect such wishes if they are also in the best interests of the children. The same principles apply to arrangements concerning visitation rights for the non-care-giving parent.

To protect the assets of one spouse, it is also customary in pre or post-nuptial agreements to include a waiver of all the statutory rights of the surviving spouse to (part of) the estate of the other spouse. Dispositions on death for the benefit of a surviving spouse are possible irrespective of such a waiver.

Where a marriage is dissolved, Austrian law differentiates between matrimonial savings, the matrimonial home and the other matrimonial assets and articles for daily use in the distribution of matrimonial property.

Before the Austrian Family Law Amendment Act 2009 *(Familienrechtsänderungsgesetz)* came into effect, pre- or post-nuptial agreements concerning matrimonial savings needed to be in the form of a notarial deed in order to be valid. Any arrangements relating to matrimonial assets, articles for daily use and the matrimonial home were unenforceable. The courts were, however, allowed to take such arrangements into consideration, in so far as it was equitable, in distribution proceedings.

Since 1 January 2010, it has been possible to include a matrimonial home, which would not normally be subject to distribution, in the distributable assets to benefit the financially disadvantaged spouse (opting in). Conversely, it is also possible to exclude the transfer of ownership or rights *in rem* from one spouse to the other in respect of any matrimonial homes which one spouse owned, inherited or received as a gift prior to the marriage (opting out). Nevertheless, the judge may order mandatory rights of use in the distribution proceedings.

Apart from agreeing on opting in or opting out, spouses may also enter into other arrangements concerning the matrimonial home, such as arrangements concerning the use or financial compensation to be paid to the spouse who would not retain the home. Pre- or post-nuptial agreements concerning the matrimonial home have to be executed in the form of a notarised deed.

The court may decide to overrule an agreement on the use of the matrimonial home by one spouse if the other spouse, or a child of the marriage, is unable to afford basic necessities or would have to accept living in clearly worse circumstances, for example, if relocation resulted in job loss or school change.

Written agreements concerning the remaining matrimonial assets and articles for daily use may be entered into without requiring the formalities of a notarised deed. Such agreements are subject to the same legal provisions which relate to matrimonial savings.

Agreements on matrimonial savings have to be executed in the form of notarised deeds. Courts may overrule these agreements if they would lead to an unfair and unreasonable disadvantage for one spouse at the outset, for example, if one spouse was effectively left destitute. In distribution proceedings, the judge may also decide to deviate from a previously equitable and reasonable agreement if adherence to such an agreement has become unreasonable for one spouse, ie, it puts them at an unfair disadvantage under the circumstances prevailing at the time of the distribution. These decisions are taken on a case-by-case basis, for example, if one spouse loses their entire property during the marriage. Issues of fault will also be considered in this context.

If the court overrules a pre- or post-nuptial agreement, the matrimonial circumstances, the duration of the marriage, the question as to whether the agreement was made with the benefit of legal advice and the actual form of the agreement will be considered in making the decision.

Pre- or post-nuptial agreements concerning proceedings for divorce, annulment or nullity of marriage do not have to meet any formal requirements.

If no proceedings for the distribution of assets are commenced within the foreseen period, ie, one year from the date on which the dissolution of the marriage became final and unappealable, pre- or post-nuptial agreements may be rescinded for nullity on grounds of a violation of law or bad faith within 30 years from the date of the agreement.

C. DIVORCE, NULLITY AND JUDICIAL SEPARATION

6. RECOGNITION OF FOREIGN MARRIAGES/DIVORCES

6.1 Summarise the position in your jurisdiction

The provisions governing the recognition of marriages entered into abroad or divorces pronounced abroad are set out in the Austrian Act on Private International Law *(Internationales Privatrecht-Gesetz, IPRG)*.

A marriage entered into abroad is valid in Austria if either the requirements of each spouse's personal statute were met, or the formal requirements applicable in the place where the marriage was solemnised were fulfilled.

A foreign decree for judicial separation without divorce, a divorce decree or the annulment of a marriage as well as a declaratory judgment as to whether a marriage does or does not validly exist will be recognised in Austria if it is final and unappealable and there is no other reason for the refusal of recognition. Recognition may be adjudicated separately as a preliminary question without requiring special proceedings.

Recognition has to be refused if:

- the decision or decree clearly contradicts the fundamental values of the Austrian legal system (*ordre public*);
- one of the spouses was not granted due process of law unless they evidently agree to the decision or decree;
- the decision is incompatible with an Austrian precedent or an earlier decision (in relation to the particular case) was made which satisfied the requirements of recognition in Austria whereby the spouses were separated or divorced or the marriage was annulled or its valid existence or non-existence was declared;
- the issuing authority would not have had international jurisdiction if Austrian law were applied.

Recognition does not fall within the remit of the Austrian Federal Ministry of Justice, as was the case in former times; each authority has to clarify the preliminary question whether there exists an impediment to the marriage of the (future) spouses or not.

As Austria is a member state of the European Union, Austria has to apply the relevant EU regulations concerning jurisdiction and the recognition and enforcement of judgments in matrimonial matters and matters of parental responsibility (Brussels II A Regulation) in cases involving other member states. Judgments pronounced in one member state will be recognised in the other member states without requiring special proceedings. Reasons for refusing recognition are similar to those stated in Austrian national law. Recognition has to be refused in the following cases:

- if recognition clearly contradicts *ordre public* in the member state where it is applied for;
- if the respondent who did not enter an appearance was not served with the writ instituting the proceedings or an equivalent writ in a timely manner and in such a way so as to enable them to defend themselves unless it is found that they clearly agreed to the judgment;
- if the judgment is incompatible with a judgment pronounced in proceedings involving the same parties in the member state in which recognition is applied for;
- if the judgment is incompatible with an earlier judgment pronounced in proceedings involving the same parties in another member state or a third country, provided that the earlier judgment fulfils the requirements for recognition in the member state where recognition was applied for.

7. DIVORCE

7.1 Explain the grounds for divorce within the jurisdiction (please also deal with nullity and judicial separation if appropriate)

Austrian law draws a distinction between divorce arising from fault, divorce for other reasons and divorce by mutual consent.

In a fault divorce, one spouse has to have committed serious wrongdoing such as adultery, physical violence or mental cruelty or dishonest or immoral conduct causing the marriage to break down irretrievably. The spouse committing such wrongdoing cannot petition for divorce as this would be morally unjustified. A petition for divorce is not admissible on these grounds if the wrongdoing was forgiven or not perceived as destructive to the marriage. Divorce must be petitioned for within six months from the time when the reason for divorce came to the notice of the other spouse and is no longer admissible if 10 years have passed since the reason for divorce became known.

Divorce may also be petitioned for if the marriage has irretrievably broken down due to one spouse's behaviour resulting from a mental disorder, or if one spouse suffers from a mental illness or an infectious disease or medical condition which cannot be expected to be cured within the foreseeable future. A petition for divorce will not be morally justified in case of undue hardship for the spouse concerned. After six years of judicial separation, a divorce decree has to be granted if requested.

Divorce may be applied for if conjugal community has been terminated for three years and the marriage has irretrievably broken down. Hardship grounds may again be applied, ie, that divorce would cause more hardship to the respondent than a dismissal of the divorce petition to the petitioner. Again, the divorce has to be granted if conjugal community is not resumed within six years. In this type of divorce, the respondent may apply for a finding in the divorce decree that the petitioner was at fault in the breakdown of the marriage. This is important for older spouses because after the ex-spouse's death, an ex-spouse who is not at fault will be entitled to a full widower's pension regardless of the amount of maintenance previously paid.

Divorce by mutual consent requires conjugal community to have ended for at least six months. Further requirements are that the marriage has irretrievably broken down, a joint petition for divorce is to be submitted and the spouses draw up a written agreement on matters of custody and visitation rights for children from the marriage, child support and maintenance of the ex-spouse, as well as for the distribution of matrimonial property.

A marriage can be declared a nullity if the marriage was not entered into in the required form, if one spouse did not have legal capacity or the ability to make informed decisions at the time of the marriage, if the marriage was exclusively entered into to assume the other spouse's name or citizenship, if one spouse is already married or if the spouses are relatives by blood. The consequences of a divorce are the same as after a divorce.

8. FINANCES/CAPITAL, PROPERTY

8.1 What powers does the court have to allocate financial resources and property on the breakdown of marriage? Explain and illustrate with reference to recent cases the court's thinking on division of assets.

After a divorce, annulment or declaration of nullity of the marriage, the distribution of matrimonial savings and matrimonial assets and articles for daily use may be made by the spouses by consent or can be ordered by the court at the request of one spouse. The request for distribution has to be submitted within one year from the date on which the dissolution of the marriage became final and unappealable. The fundamental idea behind the distribution of matrimonial property is the equitable division of the assets acquired during the marriage between the spouses. Fault is not a decisive criterion for the distribution of assets. However, the spouse who is not at fault is to be given a right of first refusal when choosing objects to be distributed.

Matrimonial savings and matrimonial assets and articles for daily use have to be divided up. Related debts, if any, have to be set off against assets. Matrimonial assets and articles for daily use are defined as movable and immovable property used by both spouses during the marriage, eg, the household effects or the matrimonial home. Matrimonial savings include investments usually held for utilisation and acquired during the marriage, in particular cash, savings deposits, securities or art objects.

The date of the marriage (only assets acquired during the marriage will be distributed) and the date when conjugal community was terminated are the two dates that are relevant in deciding whether an asset will be subject to distribution or not. The cut-off date for valuation of the distributable objects is the date of the first-instance judgment.

Assets which one spouse brought to the marriage, inherited or received as a gift, as well as assets for the sole utilisation by one spouse or in the exercise of an occupation will not be subject to distribution. One special feature of Austrian law is that assets belonging to a company or shares in a company are not subject to distribution unless they are held for investment purposes. If one spouse brought the matrimonial home to the marriage, inherited it or received it as a gift, it will be subject to distribution if the other spouse depends on it because they have no other adequate housing and need the home to satisfy their current housing needs, or if a child from the marriage depends on the continued use of the home. The same applies to household effects, ie, furniture and household articles for daily use, if the other spouse depends on being able to use them. According to recent decisions, gifts from relatives which have not been expressly earmarked will be allocated to the spouse related to the giver. Gifts one spouse made to the other will be included in the distributable assets. If assets brought to the marriage, inherited or received as gifts are sold and other assets are bought from the proceeds, or if the proceeds are subsequently deposited in a savings account, their equivalent will remain excluded from distribution, if it is clearly defined.

Distribution has to be equitable and the contributions of each spouse to the acquisition of matrimonial assets, the best interests of the children and existing debts have to be taken into account. Household work, as well as care-giving and the upbringing of children, will be equivalent to the financial contributions of the breadwinning spouse. The ratio applied in most decisions is 1:1.

If, during the two years prior to the termination of conjugal community or to the divorce petition, annulment or declaration of nullity of the marriage, one spouse has reduced the matrimonial assets without the other spouse's consent in a manner inconsistent with conjugal life during the marriage, the value of the missing assets will be included in the distribution. The same applies if matrimonial assets were invested in a company. This provisions helps avoid disadvantages for one spouse by the other's tampering with matrimonial assets.

In the course of the distribution of matrimonial assets, the court may also order the transfer of ownership and other rights in property from one spouse to the other. If the property in question is owned by a third party, transfer is contingent on the latter's consent. Matrimonial savings may also be transferred. The consent of any third party who may be involved is not required if the property in question is the matrimonial home. If there is no other way for a distribution to be made, the court may order one spouse to pay compensation to the other.

9. FINANCES/MAINTENANCE

9.1 Explain the operation of maintenance for spouses on an ongoing basis after the breakdown of marriage. Is it common for maintenance to be awarded? Explain and illustrate with reference to recent cases the court's thinking on maintenance.

The question as to whether a spouse is entitled to maintenance after divorce, and the amount thereof, will depend on the type of divorce and any finding of fault.

Divorce by mutual consent requires the spouses to agree on spousal maintenance beforehand. A waiver of maintenance is also a possible option in this context.

In the event of a fault divorce, the spouse who the court found to be solely or primarily at fault in the breakdown of the marriage has to pay maintenance to the other spouse if the latter does not have sufficient income of their own or cannot be expected to earn a sufficient income or does not have sufficient assets to live on. The spouse entitled to maintenance is obliged to take up work if this is reasonable with due regard being given to their age, state of health, training and previous work experience. Continuation of work to the same extent as during the marriage is considered reasonable. If maintenance payments jeopardise the subsistence of the person obliged to pay, the amount of maintenance will be reduced to an equitable level. However, the existing assets of a person obliged to pay maintenance (not only income yielded from such assets) will be taken into account here.

Spouses with no income of their own are entitled to 33 per cent of the net income of the other spouse. Spouses who earn their own money are entitled to 40 per cent of the common income, less their own income. Additional obligations to maintain children or another ex-spouse will reduce maintenance by three to four per cent.

In case of a divorce where both spouses are equally at fault, spouses are not entitled to mutual maintenance. If a spouse is unable to maintain themselves, they are entitled to equitable maintenance of about 10-15 per cent of the other's net income.

Regardless of fault, entitlement to maintenance exists for the spouse for whom it is unreasonable to maintain themselves because of care-giving obligations for children, or who took care of the household, the upbringing of children or had care-giving obligations for a relative and was, therefore, unable to take up gainful work.

In the event of a divorce for other reasons, the maintenance provisions for fault divorces apply if there is a finding of fault in the judgment. The same amount of maintenance as that given during the marriage is due after a divorce decree granted after conjugal community has been terminated for at least three years and when the court decides one spouse to be solely or primarily at fault. As a matter of principle, maintenance obligations towards a new spouse will not be taken into account. If the judgment does not state any fault, the spouse petitioning for divorce has to pay equitable maintenance to the other. In this instance, the needs, financial situation, income and maintenance entitlements from relatives of the other spouse will be taken into account.

Maintenance obligations end when the ex-spouse entitled to maintenance re-marries and, according to the established practice of the courts, they are suspended during such time as the ex-spouse lives in non-marital cohabitation. Ex-spouses entitled to maintenance lose their entitlement in case of serious wrongdoing against the person obliged to pay maintenance after the divorce or if they lead an immoral or dishonest life against the maintenance payer's wishes.

10. CHILD MAINTENANCE

10.1 On what basis is child maintenance calculated within the jurisdiction?

Both parents are obliged to contribute to meeting the needs of any children. Taking care of the household and giving care to children is considered to be the contribution made by the care-giving parent. If parents and children live in the same household, maintenance is provided in kind as a matter of principle. After a separation, maintenance has to be paid in cash.

The amount of maintenance will depend on the personal circumstances of the parents as well as the abilities, talents and development opportunities of the children. Over a period of time the courts have developed precedents setting out the percentages of the average net income of the parent which should be paid as maintenance for the children, although consideration is also given to the other maintenance obligations of such parent. The average maintenance needs of various age groups are published every year. As a matter of principle, monthly maintenance should not amount to more than two-and-a-half times the average need. Internationally, this maintenance limit is not very high if the parent obliged to pay maintenance has a large income. Apart from entitlement to normal maintenance, children may also have special requirements. These are additional financial needs exceeding the general average of what children of the same age need in Austria. Such special requirements have to be extraordinary and urgent in nature. They include expenses for orthodontic treatment, costs of medical treatment or special education to foster the talents of the children. The higher the normal maintenance payments, the lower the additional payments for special requirements will be.

The obligation to pay maintenance ends once the child is able to maintain themselves. If parents are unable to fulfil their maintenance obligations, the grandparents have to take care of maintenance.

11. RECIPROCAL ENFORCEMENT OF FINANCIAL ORDERS

11.1 Summarise the position in your jurisdiction

Acts and deeds executed abroad have to be declared enforceable in Austria if they are enforceable under the law of the state where they were executed and reciprocity is ensured by state treaty or regulation.

Reciprocity has to be reviewed on a case-by-case basis. Maintenance matters are governed by the Brussels I regulation (Regulation 44/2001 of 22 December 2000). However, it has to be borne in mind that a new EU regulation will be effective as from June 2011. A multilateral treaty applicable in this respect is the New York Convention on the Recovery Abroad of Maintenance. The Austrian Foreign Maintenance Act (*Auslandsunterhaltsgesetz*) applies in matters involving the United States of America.

12. FINANCIAL RELIEF AFTER FOREIGN DIVORCE PROCEEDINGS

12.1 What powers are available to make orders following a foreign divorce?

A typical feature of Austrian law is that the sale or encumbrance of real property can be prohibited by an entry to that effect in the Land Register.

Acts and deeds executed abroad have to be declared enforceable in Austria if they are enforceable under the law of the state where they were executed and reciprocity is ensured by state treaty or regulation.

D. CHILDREN

13. CUSTODY/PARENTAL RESPONSIBILITY

13.1 Briefly explain the legal position in relation to custody/parental responsibility following the breakdown of a relationship or marriage.

In case of a divorce or in case of a separation of the parents, both parents keep joint custody. However, the parents can agree sole custody for the one caring parent or to restrict the rights of the other parent. The parents with shared custody have to agree at court in which home the children will be mainly looked after.

If such agreement is not possible after a period of at least six months ('stage of parental temporary responsibility') the court has to decide either sole custody for one parent or joint custody and in which home the children will be mainly looked after.

13.2 Briefly explain the legal position in relation to access/contact/visitation following the breakdown of a relationship or marriage

The child and both parents are entitled to have regular contact according to the needs of the child. This contact should be agreed by consensus. If this is not possible, a parent can ask the court to determine the parents' contact with the child and their duties in relation to the child's welfare. The decision shall consider and guarantee the close relationship between parents and children and shall embrace times of leisure and times of caring. The decision will depend on the age, the needs and the wishes of the child as well as on the closeness of the relationship in the past. The contact can be reduced or forbidden, in as much it is especially necessary because of violence against the child or an important attachment figure.

The parent not living with the child shall not be forced into the position of an occasional visitor. This parent shall be involved in the everyday life of the child.

14. INTERNATIONAL ABDUCTION

14.1 Summarise the position in your jurisdiction

Austria is a signatory party to the Hague Convention of 25 October 1980 on the Civil Aspects of International Child Abduction. Likewise, EU Council Regulation number 2201/2003 of 27 November 2003 and its provisions governing child abduction are applicable in Austria.

15. LEAVE TO REMOVE/APPLICATIONS TO TAKE A CHILD OUT OF THE JURISDICTION

15.1 Summarise the position in your jurisdiction. Under what circumstances may a parent apply to remove their child from the jurisdiction against the wishes of the other parent?

Every parent is allowed to leave the territory of Austria with a minor if they (also) have sole custody. The other parent may prevent this from happening if the well-being of the child is jeopardised, for example, if the planned trip is to a war zone.

E. SURROGACY & ADOPTION

16. VALIDITY OF SURROGACY AGREEMENT

16.1 Briefly summarise the position in your jurisdiction.

Surrogacy is forbidden in Austria. However the Austrian Constitutional Court found that decisions of other countries, ie, concerning cases outside of Austria, have to be respected.

17. ADOPTION

17.1 Briefly explain the legal position in relation to adoption in your jurisdiction. Is adoption available to individuals, cohabiting couples (both heterosexual and same sex)?

Austria has kept the tradition that the adopter and the adoptee must enter into a contract that requires approval by a court. Adults can also be adopted as there is no upper age limit. The adoption of a child by more than one person is only permissible if those persons are married. There are no special rules with regard to same sex couples, they cannot adopt jointly.

F. COHABITATION

18. COHABITATION

18.1 What legislation (if any) governs division of property for unmarried couples on the breakdown of the relationship?

Although more and more couples deliberately decide against marriage, the rights and obligations of cohabiting partners are not enshrined in legislation in Austria, with the exception of a few provisions in secondary laws where non-marital cohabitation is equivalent to marriage. Legal provisions governing the dissolution of marriage are not applicable to non-marital cohabitation. Each partner remains the owner of their assets when cohabiting. In case of separation, the general provisions on assets, gains, damages, etc, apply. Cohabiting partners are not obliged to pay maintenance to each other.

There is no legal choice between marriage and cohabitation for heterosexual couples in Austria. The registered partnership introduced in Austria on 1 January 2010 only applies to same-sex couples.

G. FAMILY DISPUTE RESOLUTION

19. MEDIATION, COLLABORATIVE LAW AND ARBITRATION

19.1 Briefly summarise the non-Court-based processes available in your jurisdiction and the current status of agreements reached under the auspices of mediation collaborative law and arbitration

In practice only mediation is accepted by parties to divorces in Austria, as Collaborative Law is not known and practised. Mediation is regulated in a law (*Zivilrechtsmediationsgesetz*), Collaborative Law is not regulated and arbitration in family matters not foreseen.

Agreements for a divorce by consent prepared in a mediation have to be signed at Court.

Mediation stops prescription.

19.2 What is the statutory basis (if any), for mediation, collaborative law and arbitration in your jurisdiction? In particular, are the parties required to attempt a family dispute resolution in advance of the institution of proceedings?

N/A.

H. OTHER

20. CIVIL PARTNERSHIP/SAME-SEX MARRIAGE

20.1 What is the status of civil partnership/same-sex marriage within the jurisdiction? What legislation governs civil partnership/same-sex marriage?

Until recently, there was no legal basis for same-sex partnerships in Austria. This situation changed with the coming into effect of the Act on Registered Partnerships (*Eingetragene Partnerschaft-Gesetz 2009, EPG*). Since 1 January 2010 there is a legal basis for the cohabitation of homosexual couples which does, however, strongly differ from the legal basis of marriage in some respects.

Clearly, one main difference between marriage and registered partnership is the nature of the participants since registered partnerships may only be entered into by same-sex couples. The other main difference is in the way in which each is entered into. Registered partnerships are entered into without the presence of witnesses and without ceremony by simultaneous and personal declaration of intent made by the partners before a representative of the local administrative authority or municipality. There is no engagement and the partnership may only be entered into by persons who are of age (past the age of 18 years). Marriages may be entered into by declaration before a court from the age of 16, provided that the legal representatives of the parties and the persons having custody of the minor give their consent.

The effects of a registered partnership also differ significantly from those of a marriage. Registered partners keep their surnames; a common surname requires an additional procedural stage, ie, an application for a name change. The Act on Registered Partnership does not oblige the partners to mutual faithfulness. Adoption by registered partners is expressly ruled out and the same holds true for medically assisted reproduction. The dissolution of a registered partnership is easier than obtaining a divorce. Dishonest or immoral conduct is not defined as serious wrongdoing entitling a partner to demand the dissolution of the partnership on grounds of fault. If a registered partnership has broken down and cohabitation has ceased for three years, either partner may apply for dissolution and the application must be granted. In divorce law, there is a hardship clause, stating that a divorce petition has to be rejected if the divorce would cause more hardship to the respondent than a dismissal of the divorce petition to the petitioner; in such cases the marriage will continue for another three years.

The Austrian Constitutional Court ruled that there is no violation of the equal treatment principle in excluding same-sex couples from marriage. However, recent rulings of the European Court for Human Rights have stated that allowing privileges for the institution of marriage does not automatically mean that it is also acceptable to treat same-sex couples differently, at random, without objective justification. For this reason, it remains to be seen what reasons can be given for the differences between marriages and same-sex partnerships under the Act on Registered Partnerships and to what extent a need will arise to reform Austrian marriage law.

21. CONTROVERSIAL AREAS/RAPIDLY DEVELOPING AREAS OF LAW

21.1 Is there a particular area of the law within the jurisdiction that is currently undergoing major change? Which areas of law are most out-of-step? Which areas would you most like to see reformed/ changed?

Discussions about the abolition of fault in divorces have been going on for several years but have not led to any changes since there has been no satisfactory solution to the issue of how to calculate maintenance after marriage.

Joint custody will become the standard, the 'stage of parental temporary responsibility' will be abolished and the rights of the non-caring parent will be strengthened.

The possibilities for pre- and post-nuptial agreements will be broadened. However, there is a need to wait and see how the practice of the courts develops after the most recent reform.

The current law on registered partnerships is a half-hearted solution. However, now that legislators have established the ability to enter into a registered partnership, sooner or later they will have to make such partnerships fully equivalent to marriage.

Surrogacy and 'ARTS' in general might be legalised in the future.

Wouters Sosson & Associés Dr Jehanne Sosson,
Silvia Pfeiff & Sohelia Goossens

A. JURISDICTION AND CONFLICT OF LAW
1. SOURCES OF LAW
1.1 What is the primary source of law in relation to the breakdown of marriage and the welfare of children within the jurisdiction?

Breakdown of marriage

Since 21 June 2012, the rules of conflict of laws are governed by the Rome III Regulation (Regulation [EU] N° 1259/2010 of 20 December 2010 implementing enhanced cooperation in the area of the law applicable to divorce and legal separation). There is a possibility for the spouses to choose the law to be applied (Article 5 to 7). In case there is no choice of law, Article 8 of this regulation governs the conflict of laws.

For requests for divorce or separation made before 21 June 2012, Article 55 of the Code of Private International Law (CPIL) is applicable to resolve the conflict of law.

Since the reform of divorce regulation in Belgium, ie, by the law of 27 April 2007, there are two kinds of divorce (see section 7).

Regarding the welfare of children

The conflict of laws rules concerning parental responsibility are contained in Article 35 CPIL. There also are some international conventions that bind Belgium, for example, the Hague Convention regarding the guardianship of minors dd. 12 June 1902.

The law dd. 8 April 1965 regarding the welfare/protection of the youth is applied by the Juvenile Courts (civil and criminal sections).

Parental responsibility is governed by Article 371ff. of the Belgian Civil Code (BCC). The physical custody of the child is governed by Article 374 BCC. The principle of guardianship if the child has no parent able to exercise parental responsibility is mentioned in Article 375 BCC.

1.2 Which are the main statutes governing matrimonial law in the jurisdiction?

The rules relating to matrimonial property are contained in Articles 1387 to 1479 BCC. It includes general provisions for married couples, marriage contracts, particular rules where no contract has been concluded and also rules concerning registered partnership.

2. JURISDICTION

2.1 What are the main jurisdictional requirements for the institution of proceedings in relation to divorce, property and children?

Divorce

International jurisdiction rules

Belgian Courts have jurisdiction if the case meets the requirements of Articles 3 to 7 of the Regulation Brussels II revised. If none of the criteria mentioned in that Regulation leads to the jurisdiction of the Belgian Courts, and if none of the EU member states, except Denmark, has jurisdiction, and if the defendant is not habitually resident nor a national of a member state, jurisdiction can be based on Article 5 CPIL (domicile or habitual residence of the defendant), 6 (widening of international jurisdiction by agreement between the parties), 9 (related actions) and 11 (*forum necesitatis*) CPIL.

Belgian jurisdiction rules

For divorce proceedings the court having jurisdiction is the Court of First Instance (*Tribunal de Première Instance*) of the spouses' last common residence or where the defendant's residence is situated. However for divorces by mutual consent the spouses can choose any Court of First Instance.

Property

International jurisdiction rules

Division of matrimonial assets: The provisions on jurisdiction concerning all matrimonial matters can be found in Article 42 CPIL. The criteria mentioned in this article are similar (but not identical) to those of Article 3 of the Regulation Brussels II revised. The only difference exists in Article 42, 2 which states that Belgian courts also have jurisdiction if the last joint habitual residence of the spouses was in Belgium not more than 12 months before the application was introduced. Articles 5, 6, 9 and 11 of CPIL can also be applied.

Belgian jurisdiction rules

Division of matrimonial assets: The procedure is dealt with by the Court of First Instance dealing with the divorce or the defendant's place of residence (Articles 569 and 624 BJC).

Children

International jurisdiction rules

The general rule is contained in Article 8 of the Regulation Brussels II revised. The main criteria is the habitual residence of the child. Articles 9, 12, 13, and 20 of the Regulation may also apply. If no EU member state (except Denmark) has jurisdiction according to this Regulation, Articles 5, 9, 11, 32 and 33 of CPIL can be applied. For example, this allows Belgian courts to have jurisdiction if the child has Belgian nationality and lives in a non-EU country.

Belgian jurisdiction rules
The local Family Court having jurisdiction is the one where the residence of the child is situated.

3. DOMICILE AND HABITUAL RESIDENCE

3.1 Explain the concepts of domicile and habitual residence as they apply to the jurisdiction in relation to divorce, the finances and children

In Belgian law, the domicile is a legal concept and is defined in Article 102 BCC as follows: '*The domicile of a Belgian person, regarding the exercise of his/her civil rights, is at the place where he/she has his/her main establishment*'. This article refers only to Belgian nationals, but also applies to foreigners. Articles 103 and 108 provide that: 't*he change of the domicile will be proceeded by the fact of an effective habitation in another place, together with the intention of fixing there his/her principal establishment*'; '*The unemancipated minor's domicile is the common residence of their father and mother or, if they don't live together, at the residence of one of them. The person upon guardianship has his/her domicile with his/her tutor*'.

The habitual residence is a factual concept, which has been defined on several occasions by the European Court of Justice and for example, the habitual residence is the place where the party involved has '*fixed, with the wish to vest it with a stable character, the permanent or habitual centre of his/her interests*' (ECJ, 22 December 2010, *Mercredi*, C-497/10 PPU, section 51, *Rec*. 2010 I-14309). Belgian courts are bound by this definition whenever they apply EU law.

Article 4 of CPIL provides the following definition: '*the place where a person has established his main residence, even in the absence of registration and independent of a residence or establishment permit; in order to determine this place, the circumstances of personal or professional nature that show durable connections with that place or indicate the will to create such connections are taken into account*'.

4. CONFLICT OF LAW/APPLICABLE LAW TO BE APPLIED

4.1 What happens when one party applies to stay proceedings in favour of a foreign jurisdiction? What factors will the local court take into account when determining forum issues?

When a person wants to stay a proceeding before a Belgian jurisdiction in case a similar procedure has been introduced abroad, this person has to argue for it before any other defence on the merits.

The general rule of *lis pendens* in international cases is contained in Article 14 of the Belgian CPIL. This article provides that: '*When an action is pending before a foreign jurisdiction and it is anticipated that the foreign decision shall be amenable to recognition or enforcement in Belgium, the Belgian court that is later seized of a request between the same parties with the same object and cause of action, can stay its proceeding until the foreign decision has been rendered. The court takes into account the requirements of due process. The court declines jurisdiction when the foreign decision can be recognized in virtue of the present law*'.

Between the EU countries concerned, one has to apply Article 19 of the Regulation Brussels II revised in matters relating to divorce, legal separation, marriage annulment, and questions of parental responsibility, and Article 12 of the Regulation (EC) N° 4/2009 of 18 December 2008 on jurisdiction, applicable law, recognition and enforcement of decisions and cooperation in matters (called later on maintenance Regulation) that concern alimonies issues. In those regulations, Article 16 and Article 9 define respectively when a court is deemed to be seised.

The main difference between Article 14 CPIL and the *lis pendens* rules contained in the two above-mentioned regulations is that the Belgian judge *can* stay the proceeding if he applies Article 14 CPIL, but he *has to* stay the proceeding in application of the two above-mentioned European regulations.

B. PRE- AND POST-NUPTIAL AGREEMENTS

5. VALIDITY OF PRE- AND POST-NUPTIAL AGREEMENTS

5.1 To what extent are pre- and post-nups binding within the jurisdiction? Could you provide a brief discussion of the most significant recent case law on this issue?

In Belgium, pre-nuptial agreements are called *marriage contracts*. In a marriage contract the spouses can determine the property of their assets, and also the law that applies to their divorce and to maintenance. But it is contrary to Belgian public policy to foresee an amount of spouse's alimony after divorce (*pension alimentaire après divorce* – see section 9) before the end of the divorce. As a consequence, it is forbidden to allow for an amount of pension after divorce within the marriage contract.

Post-nups do not exist as such in Belgium. But the parties can settle an agreement at any stage of a divorce proceeding as long as what they decide is not contrary to Belgian public policy (for example, one parent cannot be excused paying for the child's education).

The provisions of a foreign post-nuptial agreement would be recognised and enforced in Belgium under certain conditions only (Article 22 and 25 CPIL). However, when on the basis of the Hague protocol of 2007 (The Hague Protocol of 23 November 2007 on the Law Applicable to Maintenance Obligations), the parties decide validly to apply a foreign law to their post-nuptial agreement, Belgian public policy can be invoked only in extreme cases.

C. DIVORCE, NULLITY AND JUDICIAL SEPARATION

6. RECOGNITION OF FOREIGN MARRIAGES/DIVORCES

6.1 Summarise the position in your jurisdiction

Recognition of marriages

The Belgian International Private Law Code provides that a foreign act of marriage is recognised in Belgium without any judicial procedure and gives the power of acknowledging the validity of this act of marriage to any authority.

The authorities have to check if this act of marriage was established in accordance with the CPIL and that this act fulfils all the necessary conditions of authenticity in virtue of the right of the state where it was established (Article 27 CPIL). It means that the foreign act of marriage has to respect Belgian public order and doesn't constitute a *fraus legis*.

In principle, a marriage certificate has to be legalised.

Recognition of divorces

Divorces pronounced by a European member state

In accordance with Article 21 of the Regulation Brussels II revised, divorces pronounced in any other member state are recognised in Belgium without any new judicial procedure.

However, a decision of divorce is not recognised in certain cases listed in Article 22 of the above-mentioned regulation (points a to d).

Divorces pronounced by non-member states

There are two possibilities:

In the case of a judiciary divorce that respects the principle of equality between parties, the decision is recognised (Article 22 CPIL) if it respects the conditions mentioned in Article 25 CPIL.

A foreign deed establishing the intent of the husband to dissolve the marriage without the wife having the same right cannot be recognised in Belgium. However, such a breakdown of marriage could be recognised in Belgium if it fulfils some cumulative conditions (in fact, five conditions, including the respect of Article 25 CPIL, that contains at least nine other conditions).

7. DIVORCE

7.1 Explain the grounds for divorce within the jurisdiction (please also deal with nullity and judicial separation if appropriate)

There are two kinds of divorce proceedings:

(1) Divorce for irreparable breakdown

On basis of Article 229 BCC, the divorce has to be pronounced if it is proven that there is an irreparable breakdown of the marriage, which can be proven as follows.

(a) Article 229, section 3 BCC

A person solely requesting to divorce has to prove that the parties have lived in separate residences for at least one year at the moment he/she appears for the first time before the court. In this case (and if all relevant documents are given to the judge), the divorce will be pronounced automatically.

If the parties have been living in separate residences for less than one year, the judge postpones the case and lists a second hearing one year either after the first appearance or just after the time at which the duration of the separation reached one year. At this second hearing, if the applicant repeats that he/she wants to divorce, it will be pronounced automatically.

When the conditions are fulfilled, the respondent cannot oppose the divorce.

(b) Article 229, section 1 BCC
Irreparable breakdown can also be proven by one of the parties in the sense that living (back) together is impossible. This requires significant facts or thoughts (for example, adultery) which need to be proven by legal means.

(c) Article 229, section 2 BCC
When both parties introduce the divorce (they only agree on the principle of divorce) or when the defendant accepts the divorce at the first hearing (requests based on Article 229, section 3 BCC), proof of disunion is considered to be established by the fact that the parties have been living in separate residences for six months.

If the parties have lived apart for less than six months, both parties have to repeat their will to divorce at the second hearing, which is fixed at least three months after the first hearing.

The separate residences fact is generally proven as follows: at least one of the parties has to bring an extract of the Population Register to the judge.

(2) Divorce by mutual consent
The spouses who both want to divorce may choose to divorce by mutual consent (Article 1287 to 1304 BJC). In this case, all questions have to be discussed between parties before the introduction of a divorce application. Indeed, the parties settle and sign conventions, in which the questions regarding children, alimonies, pension after divorce, division of matrimonial assets etc. are decided. After it isi signed, a divorce application can be registered at court. The parties have to appear personally before the judge and ask for the divorce. They may do it only once if they have been separated for at least six months. The conventions could be refused if the judge considers that some points are contrary to public policy or children's interests. Once the judgment of divorce is pronounced, the conventions have a judiciary value.

Nullity of marriage
The rules governing the question of nullity of marriage are contained in Article 180ff. BCC. These rules are distinct from those concerning divorce. They suppose that an impeachment to marriage existed at the moment it was celebrated.

Judicial separation
Judicial separation (*séparation de corps*) still legally exists in Belgium (Article 308 to 311bis BCC) but is very rarely used.

8. FINANCES/CAPITAL, PROPERTY

8.1 What powers does the court have to allocate financial resources and property on the breakdown of marriage?

Under Belgian law the question of division of assets is submitted to the matrimonial regime of the parties. The parties can choose certain rules of the matrimonial property regime by establishing a marriage contract (eg, a regime of division of assets). If there is no such contract, the legal regime of community of assets acquired during the marriage applies.

The division of assets on the one hand, and the pension after divorce that could be allowed on the other hand, are based on various rules and criteria. As a consequence, there is no automatic link between the pension after divorce – if any – and the division of assets. But a judge allowing a pension after divorce to one of the ex-spouses can take into account how the assets are shared between parties in order to valuate each of the ex-spouses' resources.

The liquidation of the matrimonial regime and the division of assets are realised by a public officer called notary, appointed by the judge of divorce. In that process of liquidation of the matrimonial regime, there would be a legal proceeding only in case there is an unresolved issue. Both the notary and the judge have to apply the legal rules regarding the division of assets.

In the framework of a divorce by mutual consent, the parties can choose how they share their assets. In litigated divorce, the parties are submitted to the rules governing their matrimonial regime, but they still can try to negotiate during the process of liquidation with the notary.

8.2 Explain and illustrate with reference to recent cases the court's thinking on division of assets

The courts have to apply the law. The courts' decision in the matter of division of assets concern very specific and technical questions.

9. FINANCES/MAINTENANCE

9.1 Explain the operation of maintenance for spouses on an ongoing basis after the breakdown of marriage

There are two kinds of maintenance: those between spouses and those between ex-spouses. The first one is an effect of the marriage and constitutes one of the obligations between spouses (Article 213 BCC). In case of separation of the spouses, one party may be required to pay maintenance to the other (if there is no agreement between parties) until the dissolution of the marriage. This spousal maintenance (*secours alimentaire*) is based on the standard of living that the couple enjoyed before the separation.

After the divorce of the parties, they can decide on a pension after divorce for one of them (Article 301, section 1 BCC). In case there is no agreement, the judge can allow to the ex-spouse having the *need* of a maintenance a pension after divorce paid by the other ex-spouse (Article 301, section 2 BCC). In order to evaluate this need, several criteria are taken into account: the age of the applicant, her/his ability to have a full- or part-time job, the applicant's health, the duration of the marriage, etc. The judge may refuse to order such a pension if the defendant can prove that the applicant committed a serious fault which made the continuation of common life impossible. In any case, there is no pension after divorce if the applicant committed or tried to commit certain crimes (violence) against his/her ex-spouse.

9.2 Is it common for maintenance to be awarded?

Practically, even if the criteria to allow spousal maintenance are more favourable for the creditor than those concerning the pension after divorce, the period between a request for maintenance and the dissolution of the marriage has in many cases become very short since the introduction of the new law of divorce.

Regarding the pension after divorce, the Belgian courts and the legal criteria are strict compared with other European countries. The applicant has to prove a *need*, which is not the same concept as the standard of living. The court determines the amount of pension that has to cover at least the beneficiary's needs. It takes into account the incomes and possibilities of the ex-spouses, as well as the significant deterioration of the beneficiary's economic situation (Article 301, section 3 BCC). In order to evaluate this deterioration, several criteria are taken into account: the duration of the marriage, the age of the parties, behaviour regarding the management of their needs during the marriage, charge of children during the common life or after it. The court can decide for a decreasing pension and to what extent it decreases (Article 301, section 3 BCC).

In particular, for short marriages or for women or men who are quite young when they divorce, a pension after divorce is very difficult to obtain, but this has to be examined case by case.

Lastly, Belgian law foresees a maximum of one-third of the debtor's income in case the judge allows a pension after divorce (Article 301, section 3 BCC). Also the period allowed for such a pension cannot exceed the duration of the marriage (Article 301, section 4 BCC), except in extraordinary circumstances.

9.3 Explain and illustrate with reference to recent cases the court's thinking on maintenance

The courts apply legal criteria in order to allow maintenance between (ex)/spouses. They do an analysis on a case-by-case basis. The concepts of standard of living (maintenance between spouses) and need (pension after divorce) have been illustrated in the courts' precedents.

A decision of the Belgian Supreme Court (*Cour de Cassation*) dd. 12 October 2009 can be summarised as follows: the minimum amount of pension after divorce consists in the needs of the beneficiary and the maximum in the standard of living during marriage. In order to fix that amount the courts take into account the deterioration of the beneficiary's economic situation that results from the choices of the spouses during their common life, but also the significant deterioration of the beneficiary's economic situation as a result of the divorce.

A published decision of the Brussels' Court of Appeal dd. 16 December 2010, for example, states that the applicant for maintenance has to show that his/her standard of living decreased because of the divorce proceedings.

10. CHILD MAINTENANCE

10.1 On what basis is child maintenance calculated within the jurisdiction?

The rules regarding child maintenance were changed by the Legislator in 2010: they became more precise, with the aim of making them more objective.

The parents have an obligation to assume, proportionally to their financial capacity, the maintenance, supervision, education and the training of their children (Article 203, section 1 BCC).

Financial capacity includes all professional, investment, moveable and property incomes, and also all advantages that assure them of their standard of living and that of their children (Article 203, section 2 BCC). The judge must now consider all those criteria in order to determine the amount of child maintenance.

The necessary elements for calculating child maintenance are:

- the budget of the child (or a general budget which takes into account the age of the child and standard of living);
- all relevant documents needed to establish both parents' incomes (and at least the two last tax documents called *'avertissements-extraits de rôle'* of each parent); and
- any specific criteria of the case.

In order to calculate the amount of child maintenance, the family allowance is usually deducted from the budget of the child. The balance of that budget is to be shared between parents according to their 'contributory abilities' on the one hand, and the dispatching of physical custody between parents on the other hand.

For example, if the physical custody of the child is shared equally between parents, their total incomes (with a deduction of the expenses relative to the principal residence at which each lives) are similar, and the family allowance is also shared between parents, then no child maintenance is due. On the other hand, if the child stays for longer periods at one of his/her parents, and/or the income of this parent is lower than the income of the other parent, then this parent can claim alimonies for the child.

Moreover, it is important to emphasise the fact that, in Belgian law, a list of extraordinary costs has to be settled or decided by the judge, costs which will be shared between the two parents accordingly to their faculties. These costs are supposed to be exceptional or unpredictable, and not included in the ordinary costs – which are covered by the child maintenance (Article 203bis, section 3 BCC).

Finally, child maintenance is due until the end of child's school education (this generally includes college, graduate school and/or university).

11. RECIPROCAL ENFORCEMENT OF FINANCIAL ORDERS

11.1 Summarise the position in your jurisdiction

The rules concerning the enforcement of foreign financial orders in Belgium depend on the country in which the order was pronounced.

For EU countries, the maintenance Regulation, and the Hague protocol of 2007 apply.

Concerning the procedures engaged after 18 June 2011 (date of its application) but for orders pronounced before that date, there will be a short judicial procedure of *exequatur*.

Concerning the procedures engaged after the 18 June 2011 for orders pronounced after that date, the EU order regarding alimonies is automatically and directly enforceable in Belgium.

However, the Hague protocol of 2007 does not apply with regard to the UK and Denmark. As a consequence, for those states, the procedure of *exequatur* has to apply anyway (decisions pronounced before or after the 18 June 2011) and on the basis of the above-mentioned Regulation (Article 23ff) for procedures engaged after that date.

For orders pronounced by a non-EU country, each case must be considered. Several conventions may apply, for example: the Lugano Convention or the Convention of 15 April 1958 concerning the recognition and enforcement of decisions relating to maintenance obligations towards children. When no specific convention applies, a procedure of *exequatur* is necessary in application of Article 22 CPIL. In the framework of this procedure, the foreign order on alimonies is enforceable in Belgium if the requirements of Article 25 CPIL are respected.

The second stage is to enforce the order (a Belgian order or foreign order recognised and declared enforceable in application of the above-mentioned rules). The creditor needs the assistance of a public officer called a bailiff. In order to recover some amounts of alimonies due in virtue of an order, the creditor can ask the assistance of a bailiff in order to do a seizure. There are four main kinds of seizure: on salary, on a real-estate property, on a bank account and on moveable assets. There are very specific rules for a seizure and the debtor may be able to defend himself/herself in seizing the judge in case the amounts due are contested.

Usually, the bailiff costs have to be prepaid by the creditor, and if *in fine* the debtor pays or the judge (seized by the debtor) considers that the creditor was 100 per cent right in doing the seizure, then those bailiff costs are charged to the debtor.

Finally, a creditor of alimonies may be able to obtain the right (settled in the order) to receive the debtor's income directly.

In any of the above-mentioned possibilities, as far as the order regarding alimonies is recognised in Belgium, the creditor can take some conservatory measures on the debtor's properties in Belgium.

12. FINANCIAL RELIEF AFTER FOREIGN DIVORCE PROCEEDINGS

12.1 What powers are available to make orders following a foreign divorce?

This question leads to the one about whether the Belgian courts allow a pension after divorce to someone who did not obtain any (or a very little one) in a foreign country.

Concerning the European Union decisions over divorce, as stated in section 11.1, the orders pronounced and enforced after 18 June 2011 are automatically and directly recognised and enforceable in Belgium. The possibility to review a foreign order in this case is mainly contained in Article 19ff of the Regulation on maintenance in case the right of defence had not been respected. This leads to a procedure before the foreign judge, ie, the one who pronounced that decision.

For divorces pronounced in the UK and Denmark, Article 23 of above-mentioned regulation has to apply: there is an *exequatur* of the foreign order. This is also the case for the decisions pronounced by non-European countries. For those orders, and in case there is no bilateral convention, there is an *exequatur* to make them enforceable in Belgium, on basis of Articles 22-25 CPIL.

In application of Article 23 of the above-mentioned regulation and Article 25 CPIL, the Belgian courts can, for example, refuse to enforce a foreign order on divorce and pension after divorce if it is contrary to public policy. Under no circumstances will the foreign order be reviewed on its merits.

In case the foreign judge was not even seized of any application regarding pension after divorce, such a request can be made before a Belgian court if the criteria of international jurisdiction and application of the Belgian law are fulfilled. As a consequence, Article 301 BCC which contains a certain number of conditions will be applied (cf. sections 9.1 and 9.2).

D. CHILDREN

13. CUSTODY/PARENTAL RESPONSIBILITY

13.1 Briefly explain the legal position in relation to custody/parental responsibility following the breakdown of a relationship or marriage

Following the breakdown of a relationship or marriage, both parents retain parental responsibility over the child and continue to exercise it jointly. If it is in the child's interest, the court can decide that one of the parents will exercise sole parental authority, subject to the ultimate supervision of the other, who retains the right to be informed of all important decisions taken for the child (Article 374 of the BCC).

Concerning physical custody (*hébergement*), the judge homologates the agreement of the parents, unless it is clearly against the child's interest. In case there is no agreement, the law of 18 July 2006 foresees that the court has to analyse first and foremost the possibility of fixing an equal shared physical custody between parents. But if the court considers that this custody is not the most appropriate for the child, it can decide on another system. In this case, the court designates which parent has the main residence of the child and which one has subsidiary residence. A parent cannot be deprived of any contact with his/her child, except for very serious reasons.

The parties can agree on all matters related to the child, but such agreements are not enforceable until endorsed by the court.

13.2 Briefly explain the legal position in relation to access/contact/visitation following the breakdown of a relationship or marriage

As mentioned, the principle is that physical custody is equally shared between parents. When the parents or the court decide otherwise, it is common to fix a principal residence and a subsidiary residence, but still with overnight contacts for both parents.

It is only under certain exceptional circumstances that one of the parents would have contact for only a little time and without overnight stays.

Finally, in case a parent is facing criminal charges for example, there still can be some contact in a specific meeting centre/area.

14. INTERNATIONAL ABDUCTION

14.1 Briefly summarise the position in your jurisdiction

The cases of removal of a child to/from Belgium can be governed by one or several of the following legal texts:

- the Hague Convention of 25 October 1980 on the Civil Aspects of International Child Abduction ;
- the Regulation Brussels II revised; or
- a bilateral convention (eg, the bilateral protocol between Belgium and Tunisia dd. 27 April 1989).

In child abduction cases, the Belgian Central Authority will help the parent whose child has been abducted by several means, including:

- the localisation of the child;
- making contact and seeing the abducting parent in order to try to encourage he/she to return the child to his/her habitual residence;
- receiving the application forms filled in and signed by the parent requesting a return of the child on basis of the Hague Convention of 1980;
- acting as intermediary between the parent requesting the return of the child, the courts, and the Central Authority of the state in which the child is abducted (in cases where a child was removed from Belgium);
- appointing either the Public Prosecutor or an attorney in order to introduce the procedure requesting the return of the child (in cases where the child was removed from a foreign country to Belgium).

The Belgian Central Authority is an organ of the Ministry of Justice. Its address is: boulevard de Waterloo 115, 1000 Brussels (tel: 02 542 67 19; fax: 02 542 70 06).

There are also rules of procedure specific to abduction cases in the Judiciary Code (Article 1322bis to quaterdecies).

The procedures requesting the return of the child from Belgium to a foreign country in application of the Hague Convention – and also, for what concerns European member states, the Regulation Brussels II revised – can be summarised as follows.

The Public Prosecutor or an attorney introduces an application before the President of the Court of First Instance linked to the Court of Appeal of the place where the child lives at the moment the request is registered or sent to court. This is an urgent procedure called *'comme en référé'*. There are briefs, evidence and pleadings. The Belgian courts try to deal with these procedures as quickly as possible. Some orders are pronounced several weeks after the introduction of the procedure, but there are cases that take longer. An appeal of these orders is possible (except if it is a decision of non-return based on Article 11.6 of Regulation Brussels II revised).

The enforcement of those orders is possible with the help of a bailiff, often with a member of the police, and sometimes a psychologist. Moreover, a civil and daily penalty is often ordered in order to force the parent who committed the abduction to bring the child back to his/her place of habitual residence.

Finally, a parent who abducted a child can also be pursued on a criminal level (Article 432 of the Belgian Criminal Code).

15. LEAVE TO REMOVE/APPLICATIONS TO TAKE A CHILD OUT OF THE JURISDICTION

15.1 Summarise the position in your jurisdiction

Each parent has to legally respect the rights of the other parent and those of the child. Since, as a principle, the exercise of parental responsibility is joint between parents, a person who wants to leave the country with the child has to obtain an authorisation from the other parent before moving. Even in cases where only one parent has parental responsibility, that parent still has to respect the access rights of the other parent.

As a consequence, without an express agreement of the other parent to remove a child from Belgium, a specific order is necessary.

The application to take a child out of the jurisdiction is to be introduced before the Juvenile Court, civil section. In order to examine such a request, the judge will take into account all the circumstances of the case in order to find the best solution as regards the child's best interests, which are linked to the child being able to keep close contact with both of his/her parents.

Finally, the judge has to offer every child who has reached at least 12 years' old the right to be heard by him. The child's statement is not binding.

15.2 Under what circumstances may a parent apply to remove their child from the jurisdiction against the wishes of the other parent?

The following points are taken into account by the court:

- It is important to show the judge that there will be, if possible, a certain continuation of the child's education and standard of living.
- The ties of the applicant (the parent who is asking to relocate with the child abroad) with Belgium and with the country of destination.
- The applicant should provide the judge with various evidence, such as proof of job proposal(s), possibilities of a place to live, contacts taken with schools at which the child could be registered, and any other evidence that can show that the plan of living is realistic, reasonable and in the child's interests.
- The applicant should propose large periods of school breaks with the other parent.
- The applicant must also propose regular phone calls/Skype (webcam).

More generally, it is essential for the applicant to show his/her ability to respect the place of the other parent: to keep her/him informed of all important information concerning the child (health, school, etc.) and to keep sending pictures of the child.

Often, the travel costs (created by this removal) required in order for the child to see the other parent are to be met by the applicant.

E. SURROGACY AND ADOPTION

16. VALIDITY OF SURROGACY AGREEMENTS

16.1 Briefly summarise the position in your jurisdiction

Surrogacy is not legally regulated in Belgium yet. In practice, however, cases of surrogacy do exist (this is possible in some hospitals, upon certain conditions and serious supervision). A surrogacy contract is considered void, so a surrogate mother (being or not the genetic mother of the child) cannot be forced to give up the child after the birth. But if all parties enforce their contract, and if the surrogate gives up the child, the parentage with the intended parents has to be established by adoption as the name of the surrogate is written on the birth certificate and the surrogate is considered the legal mother. Belgian courts generally agree to pronounce adoptions in such cases if it is in the best child's interest and if it was not a commercial surrogacy. When the surrogate is not married, the intended father can acknowledge the child if the surrogate agrees. Only the intended mother has to adopt the child in this case.

17. ADOPTION

17.1 Briefly explain the legal position in relation to adoption in your jurisdiction. Is adoption available to individuals, cohabiting couples (both heterosexual and same-sex)?

Adoption was legally reviewed with the law of 24 April 2003 (but came into force on 1 September 2005).

There are different kinds of adoption in Belgium, submitted to different principles or proceedings:

- Simple adoption (*adoption simple*): in this case, the adopted person maintains a tie with his/her family of origin. This adoption is revocable.
- Plenary adoption (*adoption plénière*): this adoption is only possible for minor children. In this case, the adopted child ceases entirely to be part of his/her family of origin. It is irrevocable.
- International adoption: this adoption implies the international removal of a child (Article 360-1 ff BCC and 1231-26 ff of the Judicial Code).
- Internal adoption: it implies no international removal of a child (1231-2 ff of the Judicial Code).

Regarding the *adoption simple* and *adoption plénière*, there are several legal requirements contained in Article 344.1 to 348.11 BCC. A proceeding is in any case needed as the adoption has to be pronounced by a judge.

Adoption is available to the following persons:

- a single person: that person could be married or cohabitant, but in those cases, she/he must obtain the consent of her/his partner;
- a married couple: heterosexual or homosexual (law of 18 May 2006): there is no condition of length of the marriage;
- cohabiting couples (heterosexual or homosexual – law of 18 May 2006) in the sense of '*two persons having signed a declaration of legal cohabitation*

or two persons living together permanently and emotionally for at least three years at the moment of introduction of the adoption procedure, if they are not linked by a parental link involving a marriage obstacle from which they cannot be excused by the King' (Article 343, section 1b BCC).

F. COHABITATION

18. COHABITATION

18.1 What legislation (if any) governs division of property for unmarried couples on the breakdown of the relationship?

In Belgium, civil partnerships called 'legal cohabitation' have existed since 1998 (Articles 1475 to 1479 BCC). Regarding their assets, each cohabitant keeps sole property on his/her incomes, but property for which neither cohabitant is able to prove ownership are presumed to belong to both of them. As a consequence, in the event of a breakdown of the relationship, in principle the properties of each legal cohabitant will be shared unless one of them can prove his/her sole ownership.

Alongside legal cohabitation and marriage remains the simple *de facto* cohabitation. There are no legal statutes organising *de facto* cohabitation. As a consequence, there are no legal rules governing disunion. Regarding division of property, there are no particular rules, and the general rules of civil law have to apply. Each partner keeps the property of the assets he/she owned before the *de facto* cohabitation, as well as the property of assets acquired during this cohabitation. However, the acquisition of properties in joint names remains possible, but there is no presumption of joint possession for the properties acquired during the common life. The civil common rules for property and proof of the right of property are the following:

- for real-estate, the notary deed will be used;
- to prove ownership of a moveable asset, a written document is needed (invoice, purchase order...) or, if there is no written document, testimonies and corroborative presumptions.

G. FAMILY DISPUTE RESOLUTION

19. MEDIATION, COLLABORATIVE LAW AND ARBITRATION

19.1 Briefly summarise the non-court-based processes available in your jurisdiction and the current status of agreements reached under the auspices of mediation, collaborative law and arbitration

In Belgium, the non-court-based ways of dispute resolution available are negotiation, mediation, collaborative law and arbitration.

A negotiation can be made with the attorneys and the parties or only between attorneys. An agreement reached at the end of a negotiation process can be homologated by a court. Therefore, it is necessary to seise the court if there is no procedure pending.

Family mediation can be defined as a cooperation process in view of the resolution of a family conflict in which a neutral third party, professional and qualified (either an attorney or other people with relevant training and accreditation), is solicited by the protagonists in order to help them find a lasting agreement that is mutually acceptable and fairly felt by each of them. If the mediation process succeeds, the agreement of the parties can be homologated by the relevant court.

The collaborative family law is a voluntary and confidential process of resolution of conflicts by negotiation. In this framework, there are at least four people: the parties involved in a family dispute, who are the main negotiators, and their respective attorneys, who assist them and give them advice. The attorneys are only involved in the collaborative law process; if it fails, they have to stop their intervention. If this process succeeds, a convention is settled by the attorneys and signed by the parties. This convention is official and should be homologated by the relevant court.

For those three possibilities, the court verifies that the agreement respects the child's best interest and public order.

These three processes are confidential. The attorneys and mediators are bound by client legal privilege for all discussions and for the documents used.

Finally, arbitration is used very infrequently in family law cases as it is authorised only if the parties can compromise, which is not allowed in many family issues.

19.2 What is the statutory basis (if any), for mediation, collaborative law and arbitration in your jurisdiction? In particular, are the parties required to attempt a family dispute resolution in advance of the institution of proceedings?

Mediation is governed by Articles 1724 to 1737 BJC. A mediation is 'judiciary' when it is ordered by a judge. However, the parties are not required to necessarily attempt a family mediation in advance of the institution of proceedings. But the court appreciates that the parties are trying to resolve their dispute by mediation. In any case the mediation is voluntary and both parties have to agree to mediate and on who should be mediator. Each of the parties can stop the mediation whenever he/she wishes. The mediation can be global or partial.

The rules regarding collaborative family law are contained in a specific charter settled and approved by the attorney's Bars.

Finally, the rules regarding arbitration are contained in Articles 1676 to 1723 BJC.

H. OTHER

20. CIVIL PARTNERSHIP/SAME-SEX MARRIAGE

20.1 What is the status of civil partnership/same-sex marriage within the jurisdiction?

The marriage of same-sex couples is subject to the same conditions of access as a heterosexual marriage, namely the absence of any obstacles associated with kinship (Articles 161 to 164 BCC), the absence of bigamy (Article 147 BCC), the fulfilment of age conditions (18 years unless allowed by the Juvenile Court – Articles 144 and 145 BCC), legal capacity and a valid consent (Article 180 BCC).

Same-sex marriage produces the same effects as heterosexual marriage: there are the same reciprocal rights and duties between spouses, the same rules apply to property, the same rules apply to its dissolution by divorce or death, and therefore the same rights of inheritance exist for the surviving spouse. There is, however, a major exception for this principle regarding children who may be born (necessarily by medically or 'amicably' assisted reproduction) within the context of that marriage: the legal rule called 'presumption of paternity' (Article 315 BCC) is not applicable if the marriage was contracted between people of the same sex (Article 143 BCC). Adoption is, however, allowed (cf. section 17.1 *supra*).

20.2 What legislation governs civil partnership/same-sex marriage?

The law of 13 February 2003 made marriage accessible under Belgian law to people of the same sex. This is contained in Article 143 BCC. Belgian law also organises a registered partnership for same-sex and heterosexual couples.

21. CONTROVERSIAL AREAS/RAPIDLY DEVELOPING AREAS OF LAW

21.1 Is there a particular area of the law within the jurisdiction that is currently undergoing major change?

There are for the moment in Belgium many discussions and work (mostly confidential until today) that are ongoing in order to change several rules regarding property, in particular inheritance and matrimonial property regime matters.

Regarding the inheritance area, there were very recently the following changes in the law: grandchildren can inherit directly from their grandparents if their parents renounce their succession.

The cases in which a person is considered undignified to inheritance are more important than previously. Any person recognised as having committed (or tried to commit) criminal offences against the testator is now considered undignified to inherit.

21.2 Which areas of law are most out-of-step? Which areas would you most like to see reformed/changed?

Not applicable.

Bermuda

Marshall Diel & Myers Ltd
Rachael Barritt & Adam Richards

A. JURISDICTION AND CONFLICT OF LAW

1. SOURCES OF LAW

1.1 What is the primary source of law in relation to the breakdown of marriage and the welfare of children within the jurisdiction?

1.2 Which are the main statutes governing matrimonial law and jurisdiction?

In the Supreme Court, the core legislation relating to divorce, financial proceedings and to children born to married couples or those children determined to be children of the family is the Matrimonial Causes Act 1974 (MCA 1974).

Unmarried parents may choose to address issues relating to the welfare of children by bringing an application in either the Supreme Court or the Magistrate's Court. Applications in the Supreme Court will be determined by reference to the provisions of the Minors Act 1950 (MA 1950).

In the Magistrate's Court, applications in relation to children and their welfare whether born within marriage or outside of marriage including issues of maintenance, are determined in accordance with the Children Act 1998(CA 1998) as amended by the Children's Amendment Act 2000.

Other Acts which are relevant include the following:

- Matrimonial Proceedings (Magistrate's Court) Act 1974 (financial relief for a married woman or a married man prior to the issue of a divorce petition).
- Adoption of Children Act 2006.
- Domestic Violence (Protection Order) Act 1997.
- Law Reform (Husband and Wife) Act 1977 (includes provisions for the determination of the title or possession of property between a husband and wife).

The Constitution of Bermuda 1968 has a number of sections applicable to family law.

2. JURISDICTION

2.1 What are the main jurisdictional requirements for the institution of proceedings in relation to divorce, property and children?

Divorce

Section 2 of MCA 1974 provides that the court has jurisdiction to entertain proceedings for divorce, judicial separation or nullity of marriage where either of the parties is domiciled in Bermuda on the date when the proceedings are begun, or, either of the parties are ordinarily resident in Bermuda throughout the period of one year prior to the proceedings being initiated.

Property

Sections 27 and 28 of MCA 1974 empower the court to determine applications for financial relief on the granting of a decree of divorce, a decree of nullity of marriage or a decree of judicial separation, or at any time thereafter.

Children

Where proceedings for divorce, nullity or a decree of judicial separation are continuing in Bermuda, or at any time thereafter, the Supreme Court has jurisdiction to make orders in relation to children of the family pursuant to Section 46 of MCA 1974.

The MA 1950 is silent as to the jurisdiction of the court. The court has held that it can accept jurisdiction over a child present in Bermuda applying its 'paternal jurisdiction'. In considering the most convenient forum the court must apply a discretionary exercise having regard to the welfare of the child being the first and paramount consideration.[1]

Under Section 36L of the CA 1998 the court in Bermuda has jurisdiction where:

(i) the child is habitually resident in Bermuda at the commencement of the application, or

(ii) the child is physically present in Bermuda and;

- substantial evidence is available;
- no application for custody of, or access to, the child is pending before an overseas tribunal;
- no overseas order in respect of custody or access to the child has been recognised by a court in Bermuda;
- the child has a real and substantial connection with Bermuda;
- on the balance of convenience it is appropriate for jurisdiction to be exercised in Bermuda.

3. DOMICILE AND HABITUAL RESIDENCE

3.1 Explain the concepts of domicile and habitual residence as they apply to the jurisdiction in relation to divorce, the finances and children

As Bermuda is a common law jurisdiction based primarily on the law of the UK, the determination of domicile has been determined in accordance with the common law of England and Wales. Domicile of origin will be acquired at birth: a child born to married parents will receive the domicile of his father; a child born to unmarried parents or born after the death of the child's father will receive the domicile of the mother.

Any person may acquire a new domicile by residing in another country with the intention of continuing to reside there and not to return to reside permanently in the country in which they had previously been domiciled. The burden of establishing a change of domicile is on the person asserting it. In *Burrows v Burrows,* Divorce Jurisdiction 1999 No. 37, the court held,

[1] *J (A Minor)* Civil Jurisdiction 1996 No. 44

citing the UK authority of *Boldrini v Boldrini* 1932 Probate Division, that residing in Bermuda subject to a work permit did not preclude one from choosing Bermuda as a domicile of choice. The term habitual residence is interchangeable with the term ordinary residence. The courts have construed the term according to its ordinary and natural meaning and have adopted the definition that a person is ordinarily resident in a place if he habitually and normally resides lawfully in such place from choice and for a settled purpose, apart from temporary or occasional absences.

CA 1998 specifically defines when a child is habitually resident for the purposes of applications pursuant to that Act (see Question 2, *supra*)

4. CONFLICT OF LAW/APPLICABLE LAW TO BE APPLIED

4.1 What happens when one party applies to stay proceedings in favor of a foreign jurisdiction? What factors will the local court take into account when determining foreign issues?

Schedule 1 of MCA 1974 provides for divorce proceedings to be stayed where proceedings have been commenced in a foreign jurisdiction. The power is discretionary and will be applied on the balance of fairness and convenience. The court is directed to have regard to all relevant factors including the convenience of witnesses and any delay or expense which may result from the proceedings being stayed. The court will have regard to the principle of *forum non conveniens* and will consider which is the more natural or appropriate forum to try the case.

The factors which the court will consider include: the place of residence of the parties and the location of their assets; the convenience of witnesses; any delay or expense which may result in a decision to stay; the extent to which one set of proceedings can deal comprehensively with all the issues between the parties, including issues as to financial provision.

The Bermuda court does have jurisdiction, which it will exercise sparingly and with great caution, to enjoin a party from carrying on proceedings including matrimonial proceedings in a foreign court. The jurisdiction has been confirmed by the Bermuda Supreme Court[2] citing the Privy Council decision of *Soc. Nat. Ind. Aerospatiale v Lee Kui Jak* [1987] AC 871 (PC) as binding on Bermuda.

In relation to matters pursuant to CA 1998 in the Magistrate's Court, the issue of jurisdiction is determined by Section 36L (see Question 2, *supra*). Section 36N permits the court to decline jurisdiction where it is more appropriate for jurisdiction to be exercised outside Bermuda.

B. PRE- AND POST-NUPTIAL AGREEMENTS

5. VALIDITY OF PRE- AND POST-NUPTIAL AGREEMENTS

5.1 To what extent are pre- and post-nuptial agreements binding within the jurisdiction? Could you provide a brief discussion of the most significant recent case law on this issue?

The courts of Bermuda have significant regard to decisions of the English

[2] *Scandia International Insurance Company and others v Al amana Insurance and Reinsurance Company Limited* Civil Jurisdiction 1993 No. 381

Court of Appeal. In the case of *Remington v Remington* [Civil Appeal No 1 of 1977] the Court of Appeal held that the Bermuda courts:

'...pay great respect to the English Court of Appeal's construction of a statute and seek to benefit from the guidance thus provided. In the absence of cogent reasons to the contrary the tendency would, I think, almost certainly be to follow the English decision, particularly in matters where English law or practice is applicable'.

This pronouncement applies to decisions of the Supreme Court (formerly House of Lords) which are highly persuasive.

Additionally the Court of Appeal in the case of *Grayken v Grayken* Civil Appeal No 14 of 2010 confirmed that: 'Privy Council decisions are binding in Bermuda whether or not the appeal is from Bermuda'.

In the case of *McLeod v McLeod* [2008] UKPC 64, the Privy Council considered the legal position regarding the enforceability of a post-nuptial agreement and held that such agreements were 'maintenance agreements' according to the statute. The Privy Council held that post-nuptial agreements are binding and enforceable, and will be varied only if circumstances have changed or where inadequate provision was made for any child of the marriage. As the Privy Council is Bermuda's highest appellate court and given the similar provisions in the Matrimonial Causes Act 1973 of the UK (UK MCA 1973) and MCA 1974, the decision in *McLeod* is binding on the courts of Bermuda. In *McLeod* the Board made comments in relation to pre-nuptial agreements which strictly were obiter.

Historically, pre-nuptial agreements were unenforceable as against public policy, but were viewed as a circumstance of the case that the court could take into account. The UK Supreme Court judgment in the case of *Radmacher v Granatino* [2010] UKSC42 altered this position considerably and deviating from what was said by the Board in *McLeod* concerning pre-nuptial agreements, provided that the court should give effect to both pre-nuptial and post-nuptial agreements that are freely entered into by each party with a full appreciation of its implications, unless in the circumstances it would be unfair to hold the parties to their agreement. Therefore, the UK Supreme Court established a rebuttable presumption that the court should give effect to pre- and post-nuptial agreements.

As a decision of the Supreme Court of the UK, the decision in *Radmacher* is highly persuasive to the Bermuda courts in relation to both pre- and post-nuptial agreements. Potential difficulty, however, may arise in light of the earlier Privy Council decision of *McLeod*. It remains to be seen whether the guidance in *Radmacher* will be followed in relation to pre-nuptial agreements and whether the comments of the Board on pre-nuptial agreements in *McLeod* will be considered obiter. The Bermuda courts will need to reconcile the differing approaches to pre-nuptial agreements.

C. DIVORCE, NULLITY AND JUDICIAL SEPARATION

6. RECOGNITION OF FOREIGN MARRIAGES/DIVORCES

6.1 Summarise the position in your jurisdiction

Marriages

Section 18 of MCA 1974 is in similar terms to section 14 of the UK MCA

1973 and provides that the validity of a foreign marriage shall be determined in accordance with the rules of private international law. Whether a foreign marriage is to be recognised in Bermuda will be determined by reference to the legal position in the UK.

By the rules of private international law, the form of marriage will be governed by the local law of the place of celebration. For the marriage to be valid, it must comply with the local formalities of the place where the marriage was celebrated.

The capacity of the parties to marry will be determined, however, not by reference to the law of the place where the marriage took place, but having regard to the law of each party's ante-nuptial domicile. Where the ante-nuptial domiciles of the parties marrying differs, the courts in Bermuda have held that the location of the intended matrimonial home will govern the applicable law as to capacity[3].

Divorce/annulment

The Recognition of Divorces and Legal Separations Act 1977 sets out the criteria in which a divorce obtained in a country other than Bermuda shall be recognised. The divorce must have been obtained by means of judicial or other proceedings in a country outside of Bermuda and be effective under the law of that country. The validity of an overseas divorce will only be recognised in certain circumstances, namely:

- where either spouse was habitually resident in that country; or
- where both spouses were nationals of the country; or
- if the petitioner was a national of the country and was habitually resident there; or
- the petitioner was a national of the country and was present in the country on the date in which he instituted the proceedings provided that he and the respondent last resided in a country which did not allow for divorce to be obtained.[4]

Where a country uses the concept of domicile as a ground of jurisdiction, the Act provides that habitual residence is interchangeable with any reference to domicile.

7. DIVORCE

7.1 Explain the grounds for divorce within the jurisdiction (please also deal with nullity and judicial separation if appropriate)

Section 7 of MCA 1974 precludes the filing of a petition for divorce before a period of three years from the date of marriage. An application can be made to present a petition within the three-year period on the ground that the petitioner has suffered exceptional hardship or the actions of the respondent show exceptional depravity.

Section 5 of MCA 1974 provides that the only ground for filing for divorce is where the marriage has broken down irretrievably. In order to satisfy the court that the marriage has broken down irretrievably the petitioner must

[3] *Burrows v Burrows* 1999 Divorce jurisdiction No. 37
[4] Section 3 Recognition of Divorces and Legal Separations Act 1977

prove one of the following facts:
(i) that the respondent has committed adultery and as a result of that adultery the petitioner finds it intolerable to live with him/her;
(ii) the respondent has behaved unreasonably and the petitioner cannot be expected to live with the respondent;
(iii) that the parties to the marriage have lived apart for a continuous period of two years prior to issuing the divorce petition and that they both consent to a divorce being granted;
(iv) that the respondent has deserted the petitioner for a continuous period of two years prior to issuing a divorce petition; or
(v) that the parties to the marriage have lived separate and apart for five years. The consent of the respondent is not required.

Judicial separation
Section 21 of MCA 1974 allows a party to petition for judicial separation in the event that any of the five facts required to prove that a marriage has broken down irretrievably exist. The court is required to enquire into the facts as is necessary but does not need to find that the marriage has broken down irretrievably.

Nullity
Section 15 of MCA 1974 states that in respect of any marriage celebrated after 31 December 1974, the marriage will be deemed void if:
(i) the marriage was not valid pursuant to the Marriage Act 1944. The Marriage Act sets out the formalities for a valid marriage, including, who may perform a marriage, the requirement for giving notice of a marriage and the recording of the said marriage;
(ii) that at the time of the marriage either party was already lawfully married; or
(iii) that the parties are not respectively male and female.

In such circumstances the marriage will be void. A decree of nullity will not be required as the marriage will be considered not to have existed.

In contrast, Section 16 of MCA 1974 sets out circumstances in which a marriage will be considered voidable. A voidable marriage will be treated as valid and subsisting until a decree absolute is obtained. A marriage will be voidable where the marriage has not been consummated due to incapacity or wilful refusal; where either party to the marriage did not validly consent; where either party was suffering from a mental disorder; where the respondent was suffering from a venereal disease; or where the respondent was pregnant by a person other than the petitioner at the time of the marriage.

Proceedings for the granting of a decree of nullity must be commenced within three years from the date of marriage. The relief will not be granted where the petitioner was aware that the marriage could be avoided but conducted himself in such a manner that the respondent would believe he did not intend to seek a decree of nullity.

8. FINANCES/CAPITAL/PROPERTY

8.1 What powers does the court have to allocate financial resources and property on the breakdown of marriage?

The powers of the courts in Bermuda are based on the largely analogous provisions of the UK MCA 1973. The court therefore has a similarly wide range of powers to make orders for financial provision which largely mirror the powers available in the UK. There are, however, some limited, albeit significant, differences between the two Acts. The powers of the court at a final hearing are provided for in Sections 27 and 28 of MCA 1974 and permit the court to make any one, or more than one, of the following orders:

- periodical payments such a period of time as the court determines;
- lump sum or sums provision;
- lump sum provision for the benefit of a child;
- transfer of property to the other party, to a child of the family, or to a third person for the benefit of a child of the family;
- settlement of specific property for the benefit of the other party and/or children of the family;
- variation of any nuptial settlement or trust which was established for the benefit of a party to the marriage.

The MCA 1973 does not empower the court to order the sale of property. Furthermore, there are no provisions in relation to the sharing or splitting of pension funds nor provisions for the making of a 'clean break' order.

Section 29 MCA 1974 largely mirrors Section 25 of the UK MCA 1973. The court is therefore required to have regard to:

- the financial resources of the parties, including their income and assets;
- the relative needs of the parties, including their respective needs in the foreseeable future;
- the standard of living enjoyed during the marriage;
- the ages of the parties and the length of marriage;
- any disability which the parties may be suffering;
- the relative contributions made to the welfare of the family; and
- the value of any benefit either party may lose by reason of the divorce. (This subsection specifically refers to pensions as an example of such a benefit. In the absence of specific legislation regarding the splitting or sharing of pensions, it is this section to which the court will have regard in addressing pension provisions. The options available regarding pensions are therefore quite limited and in most circumstances, the determined value of the pension will simply be off-set against a lump sum provision.)

There are three important distinctions between MCA 1974 and the UK MCA 1973:

(i) Subsection 1 of MCA 1974 does not include a provision requiring the court to have regard to the welfare of any children under the age of 18 years. Nonetheless, the practice of the court will be to have regard to the welfare of any child under the broad requirement for the court to consider all the circumstances of the case.

(ii) Section 29 continues to include the commonly entitled 'tailpiece' which requires the court to seek to place the parties in the financial position they would have been had the marriage not broken down. This section was repealed in the UK leading to debate in Bermuda as to how that distinction should be applied when considering precedent from the UK. The courts have now made it clear that, in applying this section, the objective of the court must be to achieve a fair outcome and in that regard have fallen into line with the stated objective in the UK, despite the 'tailpiece' remaining.

(iii) MCA 1974 does not require the court to seek to achieve a 'clean break' between the parties so that neither will have any further financial claim upon the other in the future. Where possible, the court will seek to bring finality to proceedings and accept the desirability of a clean break. The present position remains, however, that the court in Bermuda does not have power to dismiss a claim for periodical payments without the consent of the party against whom the order is being made. As such, where a claim for periodical payments has not been dismissed by consent, a party may return to the court and ask for those payments to be reviewed.

8.2 Explain and illustrate with reference to recent cases the court's thinking on the division of assets

The starting point and seminal case for consideration of Ancillary Relief claims in Bermuda remains the UK authority of *Miller v Miller; McFarlane v McFarlane* [2006] UKHL 24. The House of Lords approved in that case the main principles set out in *White v White* [2000] 2 FLR 981 namely that the objective in ancillary relief cases was to achieve fairness. Furthermore, the Lords approved the non-discriminatory approach such that there should be no distinction between the roles of bread-winner and home-maker in assessing the contributions each makes to the welfare of the family.

Miller elaborated on the guidance provided and confirmed that in distributing the assets fairly the court must have regard to the considerations of needs (generously assessed), compensation (for any financial disadvantage caused by the marriage) and sharing. With respect to sharing the House of Lords held that 'when the partnership ends each is entitled to an equal share of the assets of the partnership, unless there is good reason to the contrary'.

The primary reasons why the court in Bermuda might depart from equality relate to the source of the assets – for example, where the assets were gifted or inherited, or where the wealth was acquired prior to the marriage or post-separation. Significant debate and case law has been generated in relation to this issue.[5] The significance of pre-acquired property will be fact specific and discretionary. Factors which may impact upon whether there should be a departure from equality in such circumstances will include the length of the marriage, the liquidity of the parties and their respective needs. Where the needs of the parties require an equal division of

[5] See for example *Humprey v Humprey* Divorce Jurisdiction 2006: No 220, *T v T*, Divorce Jurisdiction 2007: No 216, *De Smith v Smith*, Divorce Jurisdiction 2007: No 80, *Wainwright v Wainwright* Divorce Jurisdiction 2011: No 1, *Woolridge v Woolridge* Divorce Jurisdiction 2007 No. 204 and *Butterfield v Butterfield* Divorce Jurisdiction 2008 No. 17 and *Dill v Dill*, Divorce Jurisdiction 2010, No. 23

the assets, the source of the assets is likely to have insignificant weight.

Trust assets

As an offshore jurisdiction, matrimonial attorneys in Bermuda will deal with assets held in trust more frequently than some other jurisdictions. There will typically be two approaches by a spouse seeking to unlock those trust assets of which the other party is a beneficiary:

Where the trust is deemed a nuptial settlement, the court has wide-ranging powers to vary the terms for the benefit of the other spouse or child of the family.[6]

Where it can be shown that the assets in a trust are a financial resource to a spouse who is a beneficiary of the trust, the court will take the benefit received from the trust assets into account when determining to what extent the trust assets are a financial resource and what, if any, judicial encouragement should be placed on the trustees to make funds available to the respondent. In the recent case of *Simmons,*[7] the wife was one of five beneficiaries of a trust set up by her husband during the marriage. The other beneficiaries were the husband and his three adult children. The Court of Appeal for Bermuda allocated a notional 20 per cent of the value of the assets in the trust to the wife.

9. FINANCES/MAINTENANCE

9.1 Explain the operation of maintenance for spouses on an ongoing basis after the breakdown of marriage

Section 26 of MCA 1974 allows the court to make an order for 'maintenance pending suit' defined as an order for either party to pay periodical payments to the other for his/her maintenance. The court can back date the payments to the date of the petition but maintenance pending suit will cease upon the grant of decree absolute or the dismissal of the petition.

Section 27 of MCA 1974 provides similar powers to order periodical payments after the decree of divorce or judicial separation. In addition, the court can require the paying party to provide security for the periodical payments. The court has no jurisdiction to dismiss a party's application for maintenance of its own volition so as to effect a clean break.

The length and duration of an order for periodical payments is provided for in section 32 of MCA 1974. An order for periodical payments shall begin not earlier than the date of the application and shall extend for such term as the court considers appropriate but will come to an end on the death or remarriage of the party in whose favour the order is made.

9.2 Is it common for maintenance to be awarded?

While the court strives to effect a clean break between parties, where there is no consent to periodical payments being dismissed or while there is a demonstrated need on the part of the applicant, it is not unusual for maintenance to be awarded, particularly pending the outcome of the

[6] Section 28 (1) (c)

[7] *Simmons v Simmons*, Civil Appeal No 2 of 2010, (Judgment dated 9 May 2011)

substantial ancillary relief application, often for substantial monthly sums. In addition, orders providing a sum of maintenance specifically for the provision of legal fees are permissible and have become increasing common in recent years. In the case of *F v F* Divorce Jurisdiction 2010: No. 22 the court held that there was a flexible discretionary power to order a sum of maintenance specifically for the provision of legal fees. In *F v F,* the court awarded $20,000 per month for legal costs from the date of the application until the interim award and continuing thereafter at $10,000 per month until final determination of the applications.

9.3 Explain and illustrate with reference to recent cases the court's thinking on maintenance

In relation to applications for maintenance pending suit, *F v F, supra,* confirmed the proposition that the court has a wide and unfettered discretion to make such orders for periodical payments until the hearing as the court thinks reasonable, having regard to the means and needs of the parties. In *F v F,* the court awarded maintenance, in addition to the award for the provision of legal fees, at the rate of $22,000 per month, having regard not only to disclosure provided but also based on inferences derived from the husband's standard of living.

In exercising the discretion to make an order for periodical payments, the court shall have regard to the factors set out in section 29 of the MCA 1974 which are discussed in detail above. The court will approach each case on a fact specific basis having regard to the needs of the parties compared against their earning potential, both in the present and foreseeable future. In balancing these competing interests, the courts will have regard to the approach and guidance formulated in the leading UK authorities subject to the differences in the MCA 1974 referred to in section 8.1 above. The court will seek to bring finality to proceedings notwithstanding that there is no express power to dismiss a claim for periodical payments. The court strives to obtain the consent of the party against whom the order is being made.

10. CHILD MAINTENANCE

10.1 On what basis is child maintenance calculated within the jurisdiction?

There are three Acts which set out the court's jurisdiction to make maintenance orders for the benefit of children. They are the MCA 1974, the CA 1998 and the MA 1950.

MCA 1974 – Sections 25-29

The orders that can be made for children of the family in connection with divorce proceedings include periodical payments, secured periodical payments and lump sum provision.[8] The obligation to pay maintenance for a child of the family continue to the child's eighteenth birthday unless the court specifies a later date or if the child will be or is receiving instruction at

[8] Lump sum payments for the benefit of a child of the family is possible for the purpose of enabling a party to meet any liabilities or expenses reasonably incurred before making an application for periodical payments. Sections 27(3) of the MCA 1974

an educational establishment or undergoing training for a trade, profession or vocation.[9]

The court must have regard to all of the circumstances of the case including:

(a) the financial needs of the child;
(b) the income, earning capacity (if any), property and other financial resources of the child;
(c) any physical or mental disability of the child;
(d) the standard of living enjoyed by the family before the breakdown of the marriage; and
(e) the manner in which the child was being and in which the parties to the marriage expected the child to be educated or trained.

The court must, so far as it is practicable, place the child in the financial position in which the child would have been if the marriage had not broken down and each of those parties had properly discharged his or her financial obligations and responsibilities towards him. [10]

CA 1998- Part IVB (Support Obligations)

This Act governs unmarried parents' maintenance obligations.[11] Every parent has an obligation, to the extent the parent is capable of doing so, to provide support, in accordance with need, for his or her child. This obligation applies to an unmarried child who is under the age of 18 years or, if over 18 years of age, is enrolled in a full-time education or is unable, by reason of illness, disability or other cause, to withdraw from the charge of his or her parents or to obtain the necessaries of life.[12] The obligation does not extend to a child who is 16 years of age or older and has withdrawn from parental control.[13]

[14] The factors that the court must consider include:

(a) parents' joint financial responsibility to maintain the child;
(b) the relevant abilities of the parents to contribute;
(c) the current assets and means;
(d) the assets and means that each parent is likely to have in the future;
(e) each parent's capacity to provide support for the child;
(f) the age and physical and mental health of each parent;
(g) the needs of the child;
(h) the measures available for the parents to become able to provide for the support of the child and the length of time and cost involved to enable the mother or father to take those measures;
(i) any legal obligation of each parent to provide support for another person;
(j) the desirability of the mother or father remaining at home to care for the child. [15]

[9] Section 33 (1) and Section 33 (3) of MCA 1974.
[10] Sections 29(2) of the MCA 1974.
[11] In January 2004, the Children Act was amended by the Children Amendment Act 2002. The amendments removed any distinction in law between children born inside or outside marriage, and revised the law relating to the obligation of parents to support their children.
[12] Section 36.1B(1) of the Children Act 1998
[13] Section 36.1B(2) of the Children Act 1998
[14] Section 36.1C(2) and section 82 of the Children Act 1998
[15] Section 36.1C(3) and section 36.1C(4) of the Children Act 1998

MA 1950 – Section 12

The MA 1950 empowers the Supreme Court to make orders related to the 'maintenance' of a minor[16] when an application is made by the parents of a minor, the guardians of a minor or the person who has care and control of a minor. [17] The welfare of the minor is the first and paramount consideration under the MA 1950 and the court can make 'such orders as it sees fit' having regard to 'the welfare of the child and to the conduct and to the wishes or representations of either party or any guardian or of any person having the actual charge of the minor'.[18]

Recent decisions in the Supreme Court have held a judge determining an application under the MA 1950 could apply the relevant provisions of the CA 1998 as these statutes are of concurrent jurisdiction.

Calculation of child maintenance

There is no prescribed formula for the quantum of maintenance awarded and each case will be decided on its own circumstances. The courts have wide discretionary powers but will seek to balance between the needs of the child and the means of the parties involved while attempting to ensure that the child's best interests are met. The Court of Appeal provided some guidance in relation to child support in its decision in *M v W* (Civil Appeal No 14 of 2009) as decided under section 36.1 of the CA 1998. The Court of Appeal held that 'neither adherence to a rigid principle of proportionality nor a contribution by each parent on the basis of equality should be strictly followed.'[19]

11. RECIPROCAL ENFORCEMENT OF FINANCIAL ORDERS

11.1 Summarise the position in your jurisdiction

There is a limited statutory framework for the registration and enforcement of maintenance orders and for the registration and enforcement of judgments.

The Maintenance Orders (Reciprocal Enforcement) Act 1974 makes provision for maintenance orders made in other signatory countries to be registered and enforced in Bermuda, and vice versa. The list of reciprocating countries is limited to those set out in the Maintenance Orders (Reciprocal Enforcement) (Designation) Order 1975 (the 1975 Order). [20]

The Judgments (Reciprocal Enforcement) Act 1958 makes the registration of an English judgment possible so long as the court in the UK had jurisdiction to make the orders sought to be registered and the courts in the UK will be held to have had jurisdiction in relation to judgments where the jurisdiction of the court giving the judgment is recognised by the law of Bermuda. In cases involving the enforcement of judgments against a Bermuda trust, regard must be had to Section 11 of the Trusts

[16] A minor is defined as a person who has not yet reached the age of 18.
[17] Minors Act 1950, section 12
[18] Minors Act 1950, section 12
[19] *M v W* (Civil Appeal No 14 of 2009) at paragraph 18.
[20] Barbados, Guernsey, Hong Kong, Jamaica, Jersey, New South Wales, Saint Vincent, The Isle of Man, The Leeward Islands, California, Connecticut, Florida, Hawaii, Maryland, Missouri, New Jersey, Ohio and the United Kingdom of Great Britain and Northern Ireland.

(Special Provisions) Act 1989 as amended by the Trusts (Special Provisions) Amendment Act 2004 ('the amended 1989 Act').

Non-UK judgments and maintenance orders from countries that are not listed in the 1975 Order are enforced in accordance with the Common Law by bringing an action on the foreign judgment and applying for summary judgments under the relevant Rules of the Supreme Court on the ground that the defendant has no defence to the claim.[21]

12. FINANCIAL RELIEF AFTER FOREIGN DIVORCE PROCEEDINGS

12.1 What powers are available to make orders following a foreign divorce?

The Recognition of Divorces and Legal Separations Act 1977 (1977 Act) provides the legislative framework whereby an individual can apply to the Supreme Court of Bermuda for relief under Part IV of the Matrimonial Causes Act 1974.

The 1977 Act sets out the narrow jurisdiction of the Supreme Court of Bermuda which extends only to *in relation to any land or any interest in land* in Bermuda when the following two circumstances exist:

- the divorce or legal separation was obtained in proceedings in a country outside of Bermuda; and
- the validity of the divorce or legal separation is recognised by the law of Bermuda. [22]

Section 6 of the 1977 Act confirms that no overseas divorce or legal separation shall be recognised as valid in Bermuda except as provided for in the Act, and sections 2 through 8 of the 1977 Act provides the framework for having an overseas divorce or legal separation recognised in Bermuda. (see question 6, *supra*)

D. CHILDREN

13. CUSTODY/PARENTAL RESPONSIBILITY

13.1 Briefly explain the legal position in relation to custody/parental responsibility following the breakdown of a relationship or marriage

13.2 Briefly explain the legal position in relation to access/contact/visitation following the breakdown of a relationship or marriage

MCA 1974 – Section 46

The Supreme Court has jurisdiction to make such orders as it sees fit for the custody and education of a child of the family who is under the age of 18 years in cases of divorce. Custody is defined by the Act as including access to the child.

MCA 1950 – Section 12

The Supreme Court also has jurisdiction to make orders related to the custody and right of access to a child when an application is made by the parents of a

[21] *Ellefsen v Ellefsen*, Civil Jurisdiction No 202 of 1993
[22] Section 9 of The Recognition of Divorces and Legal Separations Act

minor, the guardians of a minor or the person who has care and control of a minor under section 12 of the MA 1950. The court can make 'such orders as it sees fit' having regard to 'the welfare of the child and to the conduct and to the wishes or representations of either party or any guardian or of any person having the actual charge of the minor'. Neither parent has a more superior claim in an application before the court than that of the other parent.

CA 1998 – Part IVA (Custody Jurisdiction and Access)
Section 6 and section 36B of the CA 1998 sets out the welfare principle and provides that in the administration and interpretation of the Act, the welfare of the child shall be the paramount consideration when determining custody and incidents of custody and access to children.

The starting point is that a father and mother have parental responsibility for a child, are joint guardians of the child and are equally entitled to custody of the child.[23] A person entitled to custody has the rights and responsibilities of a parent including the right to care and control of the child and the right to direct the education and religious training of the child.[24] The entitlement to access under the CA 1998 includes the right to make reasonable inquiries and to be given information as to the health, education and welfare of the child. Where parents live separate and apart and the child lives with one of them with the consent of the other, the right of the other to custody and the incidents of custody (but not the entitlement to access) is suspended.[25]

Based on the decision in *M v W* outlined above, when exercising its discretion under section 12 of the MA 1950, the court may take into consideration the framework set out in the CA 1998 in relation to custody and access.

Relevant jurisprudence
The guiding principle in custody and care and control applications is that the welfare of the minor is paramount, and that neither parent has a more superior claim in an application before the court than that of the other parent. While some guidance can be obtained from the relevant jurisprudence, each decision will turn upon the facts of the particular case. Early cases stand for the proposition that, as a general rule, a single home is most likely to be consistent with the best interests of children, but that those interests must always be determined on a case-by-case basis.[26] In more recent cases, the courts have found that in certain circumstances joint care and control is in the best interest of the child and despite having no statutory framework to do so have used guidance provided by *A v A* [2004]1 FLR to help manage the shared care and control order and to forestall future miscommunications.[27]

[23] Section 36C(1) of the CA 1998
[24] Section 36C(2) of the CA 1998
[25] Section 36C(4) of the CA 1998
[26] *Coles v Coles* Divorce Jurisdiction 2001 No 13, *Re J & H* (Minors) (Care and Control) 2004, *Re D (a child)* (Care and Control) Divorce Jurisdiction 2004: No 62, *J v J*, Divorce Jurisdiction 2005: No 182
[27] *Re T, S v T* [2010] Bda LR 8, *S v S*, Divorce Jurisdiction 2004: No 187 (The initial decision of Justice Greaves [2009] Bda LR 49 was appealed and the Court of Appeal upheld the appeal and remitted the case back to the Supreme Court for rehearing).

It is worth noting that in its Throne Speech in 2013, the newly-formed government in Bermuda confirmed that it would introduce amendments to the CA 1998 to include a provision for shared parenting orders. These amendments, if enacted, could potentially change the court's view and approach in relation to joint care and control and access applications both in the Magistrates' Court and the Supreme Court.

14. INTERNATIONAL ABDUCTION

14.1 Briefly summarise the position in your jurisdiction

Domestic laws and regulations implementing the Hague Convention

The United Kingdom extended the Hague Convention on the Civil Aspects of International Child Abduction (the 'Convention') to Bermuda through a Note that was filed with the Ministry of Foreign Affairs in the Netherlands in December 1998.[28] The extension of the Convention to Bermuda was recognised by the United States in March 1999.

The Convention was implemented in Bermuda by way of the International Child Abduction Act 1998 (1998 Act) and the subsequent International Child Abduction (Parties to Convention) Order 1999 (1999 Order). The Central Authority in Bermuda is the Attorney General.

Applications under the Convention are made by way of originating summons to the Supreme Court and the Order 118 of Rules of the Supreme Court sets out the procedure when making such an application. [29]

Domestic laws regarding child abduction

The CA 1998 provides the court with the power to enforce custody and access orders and preventative measures to stop the removal of children from Bermuda. [30]

The MA 1950 specifically sets out the procedure for emergency non-removal applications, which may be made on an *ex-parte* basis. [31]

To prevent the abduction of children during divorce proceedings, a parent can make an *ex-parte* application to the Supreme Court for an order prohibiting the removal of a child of the family without the leave of the court. [32]

15. LEAVE TO REMOVE/APPLICATIONS TO TAKE A CHILD OUT OF THE JURISDICTION

15.1 Summarise the position in your jurisdiction

15.2 Under what circumstances may a parent apply to remove their child from the jurisdiction against the wishes of the other parent?

Upon the grant of *decree nisi*, travel restrictions are automatically put in place in respect of any child of the family ensuring that neither parent can remove the child from the jurisdiction without the express written consent

[28] Article 39 of the Convention.
[29] Order 118 of the Rules of the Supreme Court
[30] Section 36O and Sections 36S to 36Y of the CA 1998
[31] Section 22 of the MA 1950 along with Minors Act (Applications under section 22) Rules 1964
[32] Section 94 of the MCR 1974.

of the other parent or permission from the court. The order includes a prohibition on the issue of any further travel documents by the Department of Immigration for the said child.

Parties can agree to waive these restrictions at the divorce hearing or any time thereafter. Barring agreement, the parent wishing to travel with the child or to relocate with the child must either obtain the written consent of the other parent or make an application to the court for permission to do so.

Applications to remove a child are primarily governed by the welfare principle and the determination of the child's best interests.[33] The Supreme Court typically deals with three main types of removal applications. The first where the parent is seeking to return to his or her permanent overseas home; the second is where a Bermudian parent seeks to relocate abroad either on a permanent or temporary basis; and the third when a party wishes to travel for holiday purposes with the child.

In the permanent removal cases, the Bermuda courts have endorsed the approach and principles outlined in the UK decision of *Payne v Payne* [2001] 1 FLR1052 and the UK decisions that have followed. [34] The Bermuda courts have also relied on the principle outlined in the decision of *M v M* [2007] Bda LR 66 that:

'The right of freedom of movement is protected by section 11 of the Bermuda Constitution and matrimonial courts should surely be reluctant...to make orders which...punish primary carers, be they Bermudians or foreign nationals, for seeking to exercise constitutional mobility rights.'[35]

E. SURROGACY AND ADOPTION

16. VALIDITY OF SURROGACY AGREEMENTS

16.1 Summarise the position in your jurisdiction

There is currently no specific legislative framework in place in relation to surrogacy, and the issue has not been dealt with in any reported Bermudian jurisprudence.

Recourse could be had to section 12 of the MA 1950, which allows any person having 'actual charge of a minor' to apply to the court seeking orders related to guardianship, custody, maintenance or access or to section 36D of the CA 1998 which allows 'any other person' to apply to the court for an order respecting custody of or access to a child or to determine any aspect of the incidents of custody of or access to the child. Further, the provisions of the Adoption of Children Act 1963 may offer some assistance.

17. ADOPTION

17.1 Briefly explain the legal position in relation to adoption in your jurisdiction. Is adoption available to individuals, cohabiting couples (both heterosexual and same-sex)?

The Magistrates' Court, upon application made in the prescribed manner

[33] Section 94 of the MCR 1974, section 12 and 22 of the MA 1950 along with Minors Act (Applications under section 22) Rules 1964, section 36U of the Children Act 1998.

[34] *Fisher v Fisher and Stirling* 1997 Divorce Jur. No. 88 [2001] Bda LR 71, *Robinson v Robinson* 2001 Divorce Jur. No. 149 (2004), *M v M* [2007] Bda LR 66, *C v C* (Re T) Divorce Jurisdiction 2008 No 42

[35] *M v M* [2007] Bda LR 66, paragraph 13

by a person domiciled in Bermuda[36], may make an order authorising an applicant to adopt an infant.[37] An adoption order may only be made in respect of an infant who:

- was born in Bermuda;[38] or
- is the child of a person possessing Bermudian status under the Bermuda Immigration and Protection Act 1936;[39] or
- is resident in Bermuda with the specific permission of the Minister responsible for immigration.[40]

An applicant must be:

- the mother or father of the infant[41]; or
- a relative of the infant, and has attained the age of 18 years; [42] or
- a person who has attained the age of 25 years[43] .

An adoption order may be made on the application of two spouses authorising them jointly to adopt an infant; but shall not in any other case be made authorising more than one person to adopt an infant. As such, common law partners and same-sex couples are precluded from adopting together. The Act prohibits adoption of a female infant in favour of a sole male applicant, unless the court is satisfied that there are special circumstances which justify the making of an adoption order.[44]

The infant must also have been in the care and possession of the applicant for at least three consecutive months immediately preceding the date of the order, not counting any time before the date which appears to the court to be the date on which the infant attained the age of six weeks. This requirement will not apply where at least one of the parents of the infant is the applicant for the adoption order. [45]

Consent to an adoption order must be given by every person who is a parent or a guardian of the infant. Consent can only be given after the infant reaches the age of six weeks.[46] Such consent must be in writing and signed by the person giving the consent, unless it is given orally before the court hearing the application. The court can dispense with any consent required if it is satisfied that the person whose consent is to be dispensed with has either abandoned, neglected, or persistently ill-treated the infant; cannot be found; is incapable of giving his consent; or is withholding his consent unreasonably. However, there are circumstances where the court can dispense with consent.[47]

There is a restriction on sending children abroad for adoption unless the person is granted the authority of a licence by the court as provided for in section 16 of the Act.

---

[36] Where an applicant to adopt an infant is not domiciled in Bermuda and it is shown to the satisfaction of the court that the infant, if adopted, would be permitted to enter the country of the domicile of the applicant, then the court may make an order authorising the applicant to adopt the infant, section 10 of the Adoption of Children Act 1963.

[37] 'Infant' is defined as a person under the age of 18 but does not include a person who is or has been married.

[38] Section 4 (i) of the Adoption of Children Act 1963.

[39] Section 4 (ii) of the Adoption of Children Act 1963.

[40] Section 4 (iii) of the Adoption of Children Act 1963.

[41] Section 3 (1) (i) of the Adoption of Children Act 1963.

[42] Section 3 (1) (ii) of the Adoption of Children Act 1963. Relative is defined by the Act as meaning a grandparent, brother, sister, uncle or aunt, whether full blood or half blood or by affinity.

[43] Section 3 (1) (iii) of the Adoption of Children Act 1963.

[44] Section 3 (3) of the Adoption of Children Act 1963.

[45] Section 5 of the Adoption of Children Act 1963.

[46] Section 6 of the Adoption of Children Act 1963.

[47] Section 7 of the Adoption of Children Act 1963.

F. COHABITATION
18. COHABITATION
18.1 What legislation (if any) governs the distribution of property for unmarried couples on the breakdown of the relationship?

Bermuda does not recognise 'common-law marriages'. Save for claims brought pursuant to the CA 1998 in relation to financial support for any children[48], and common law claims relating to real property, there is no legislation governing the financial rights as between unmarried couples.

Cohabitees that hold property in their joint names (as 'joint tenants') or in unequal shares (a 'tenant in common') can look to the Partition Act 1855 and Partition Act 1914 for relief. Generally, properties held in joint tenancy will be shared equally and property held in tenancy in common will be shared in accordance with each party's relative share. However, in *Hassell v Furbert and Furbert,* Civil Jurisdiction 2004 No 248, the court determined that it could treat joint tenants as tenants in common in cases where the parties had contributed in unequal shares to the property's purchase. In that case, the court calculated each party's contribution to the property and determined the percentage that each party would receive based on their percentage contribution.

In the case of *Stevens v Astwood,* Civil Jurisdiction 2010 No 365, the court considered its jurisdiction to make a *Mesher* order postponing the sale of a property jointly owned by unmarried cohabitees who had children together. It held that the matrimonial statutory regime explicitly placed marital assets into a separate legal box and subjected them to distinct legal rules. The court concluded that there would need to be express legislation for the court to interfere with the property rights of non-married couples under the general law. To do otherwise would potentially represent a compulsory acquisition of property in violation of section 13 of the Bermuda Constitution. Justice Kawaley did expressly state that this case did serve to identify a need for law reform.

To establish an interest in a property which is not in joint names, a cohabitant would have to rely on the doctrine of constructive and resulting trust.

G. FAMILY DISPUTE RESOLUTION
19. MEDIATION, COLLABORATIVE LAW & ARBITRATION
19.1 Briefly summarise the non-court-based processes available in your jurisdiction and the current status of agreements reached under the auspices of mediation, collaborative law and arbitration

There is a movement towards utilising alternative dispute resolution processes in Bermuda in an effort to reduce costs and acrimony in proceedings. There are a number of experienced practitioners who are trained as mediators and arbitrators.[49] A Collaborative Law Alliance has been established in Bermuda and there are a number of trained collaborative law specialists as well. It is also common for parties and their attorneys to engage

[48] Section 31.6 of the CA 1998

[49] Arbitration is not commonly used in matrimonial or family proceedings as parties find that its procedure and the associated costs as too similar to those in court proceedings to gain any advantage.

in without prejudice roundtable discussions to reach resolution of claims without proceeding through the courts. Parties are able to take advantage of these processes on a voluntary basis.

The agreements reached under the auspices of mediation, arbitration and collaborative law often contain their own provisions for the enforcement or review of the agreement.[50] However in divorce proceedings, these agreements are typically reduced to a consent order and produced to the court for approval. These processes may also result in separation agreements, the terms of which are eventually entered as orders of the court upon pronouncement of *decree nisi*.

19.2 What is the statutory basis (if any) for mediation, collaborative law and arbitration in your jurisdiction? In particular, are the parties required to attempt a family dispute resolution in advance of the institution of proceedings?

The Rules of Supreme Court 1985 (as amended) which apply in matrimonial proceedings[51] include as part of the overriding objective the court's duty to 'encourage parties to use an alternative dispute resolution procedure if the court considers that appropriate, and to facilitate the use of such procedure'.[52]

The CA 1998 (as amended) gives the court limited jurisdiction to order parties to engage in mediation in circumstances where it is satisfied that a parent has failed to comply with an existing order for access. [53]

H. OTHER

20. CIVIL PARTNERSHIP/SAME-SEX MARRIAGE

20.1 What is the status of civil partnership/same-sex marriage within the jurisdiction?

There is no legislative framework in place for the establishment or recognition of civil partnerships.

There is no recognition of same-sex marriages in Bermuda. While the Human Rights Amendment Act 2013 added sexual orientation to the list of prohibited grounds of discrimination, during the debates in the House of Assembly, many of the members of parliament were careful to clarify that the government considered marriage to be between a man and a woman only.

20.2 What legislation governs civil partnership/same-sex marriage?

There is no legislation governing civil partnerships or same-sex marriages in Bermuda.

[50] With collaborative law, if there is a breakdown in the agreement, the parties have the option of reactivating the collaborative law process to resolve any breakdown as a starting point with the option of seeking the assistance of the court if the agreement has been entered as an order.
[51] Rule 3(1) of the Rules of Supreme Court 1985
[52] Rules 1A, 1A4 of the Rules of Supreme Court 1985
[53] Section 36F(1) of the Children Act 1998 as amended by the Children Amended Act 2002

21. CONTROVERSIAL AREAS/RAPIDLY DEVELOPING AREAS OF LAW

21.1 Is there a particular area of the law within the jurisdiction that is currently undergoing a major change?

21.2 Which areas of law are most out of step? Which areas would you most like to see reformed/changed?

Matrimonial and family law legislation in Bermuda is, for the most part, outdated and out of step with modern legislation in other common law jurisdictions. There have been many calls for immediate and urgent reform. The Family Law Reform Sub-Committee was created in 2008 under the championship of Justice Norma Wade Miller. In 2009, the Sub-Committee produced a report entitled 'Justice for Families: a Review of Family Law in Bermuda'. The Sub-Committee's conclusions were made after review of submissions from organisations, professionals and from the general public and upon review of the current legislation and the present infrastructure.

As part of its recommendations, the report recommended a major overhaul of the current legislation related to families with the aim of modernising the legislation in order to keep pace with the changes in the UK legislation which have occurred over the past 30 years. The Committee also recommended improving the family court system in Bermuda by establishing a Unified Family Court (UFC) bringing together the Magistrates' and Supreme Court's jurisdiction under one roof, providing a central administrative base and incorporating mediation as a cornerstone in the process. While the report did not deal with the rights of 'common law' spouses and the rights of same-sex partners, it recognised that these topics required a more detailed assessment and possible eventual incorporation into the proposed Unified Family Court.

It is hoped that the newly-formed government will carefully consider the recommendations of the report and implement the three key reforms: the overhaul of the legislation, the inclusion of mediation as a vital step in the process, and the establishment of the Unified Family Court. In June 2013, the Chief Justice along with the Honorable Justice Wade-Miller of the Supreme Court commenced a review Bermuda's family law regime in order to assess the necessity for legislative reform and it is hoped that this will result in major changes to the current legislation.

Canada – Ontario

Lenkinski Family Law & Mediation
Esther Lenkinski & Lisa Eisen

A. JURISDICTION AND CONFLICT OF LAW

1. SOURCES OF LAW

1.1 What is the primary source of law in relation to the breakdown of marriage and the welfare of children within the jurisdiction?

Canada is broken down into 10 provinces and three territories[1]. Both the federal and provincial governments have jurisdiction over family law[2]. The federal government presides over matters of marriage and divorce while the provincial government has jurisdiction over the solemnisation of marriage and property and civil rights.

Custody, child support and spousal support generally fall within the ambit of provincial legislation. However, where those issues arise in connection with a divorce, there is jurisdiction for them to be considered under federal legislation.

1.2 Which are the main statutes governing matrimonial law in the jurisdiction?

The Divorce Act[3] (DA) is federal legislation which governs divorce and corollary relief including custody, child support and spousal support for all of Canada's provinces and territories.

In Ontario, the Family Law Act[4] (FLA), specifically Part I, sets out the method by which property is to be divided following the breakdown of marriage. Child and spousal support obligations are included in Part III of the FLA while child custody is prescribed by the Children's Law Reform Act[5] (CLRA).

2. JURISDICTION

2.1 What are the main jurisdictional requirements for the institution of proceedings in relation to divorce, property and children?

Divorce

A court in a province has jurisdiction over divorce proceedings if either spouse has been ordinarily resident in the province for at least one year

[1] Provinces: Alberta, British Columbia, Manitoba, New Brunswick, Newfoundland and Labrador, Nova Scotia, Ontario, Prince Edward Island, Quebec, Saskatchewan. Territories: Northwest Territories, Nunavut, Yukon

[2] Constitution Act, 1867 R.S.C. 1985, App II., No. 5, ss. 91 & 92

[3] Divorce Act, R.S.C. 1985, c. 3 (2nd Supp.)

[4] Family Law Act, R.S.O. 1990, c. F.3, as am.

[5] Children's Law Reform Act R.S.O. 1990, c. C.12, as am.

immediately preceding the commencement of the proceedings.[6]

Property
Because the FLA does not address the issue of jurisdiction *simplicter*[7], the common law 'real and substantial connection' test is used to determine whether the Ontario courts have jurisdiction[8].

Ontario's FLA provides that property rights of spouses are governed by the internal law of the place where both spouses had their last common habitual residence or by the laws of Ontario if there was no common habitual residence[9].

Children
Where custody support is requested separately from divorce, those claims can be heard by a court in a province where either former spouse is ordinarily resident at the commencement of the proceedings or in a province where both former spouses accept the jurisdiction of the court.[10]

Where custody proceedings are instituted outside of divorce, the court in Ontario can only exercise jurisdiction in two circumstances: where the child is habitually resident in Ontario at the commencement of the application; or where the child is not habitually resident in Ontario but the court is satisfied that:

(i) the child is physically present in Ontario at the commencement of the application;
(ii) the substantial evidence concerning the best interests of the child is available in Ontario;
(iii) no application for custody or access is pending in a place where the child is habitually resident;
(iv) no extra-provincial order in respect of custody or access has been recognised by a court in Ontario;
(v) the child has a real and substantial connection with Ontario; and
(vi) on the balance of convenience, it is appropriate for jurisdiction to be exercised in Ontario[11].

Support for a child may be made outside of divorce proceedings by a parent if the child is under 18 and in school[12].

3. DOMICILE AND HABITUAL RESIDENCE

3.1 Explain the concepts of domicile and habitual residence as they apply to the jurisdiction in relation to divorce, the finances and children

Divorce
The language of the DA provides that a spouse has to have been 'ordinarily resident' in a province for at least one year immediately preceding the commencement of the proceedings.

[6] Divorce Act, R.S.C. 1985, c. 3 (2nd Supp.), s.3(1)
[7] *Wang v Lin* 2013 CarswellOnt 530 (Ont . C.A.)
[8] *Wang v Lin* 2013 CarswellOnt 530 (Ont . C.A.)
[9] Family Law Act, s .15
[10] Divorce Act, R.S.C. 1985, c. 3 (2nd Supp.), s.4(1)
[11] Children's Law Reform Act R.S.O. 1990, c. C.12, as am. s. 22(1)
[12] Family Law Act, R.S.O. 1990, c. F.3, as am., s.31

Finances

Under the DA, a court has jurisdiction as long as either of the former spouses are ordinarily resident in the province at the commencement of the proceedings or both accept the jurisdiction of a particular province's court. As 'ordinarily resident' is not defined within the DA, it is a question of fact determined on the specific circumstances.

Under the FLA, an Ontario court has jurisdiction to deal with property if the parties have no 'last common habitual residence'. The term 'last common habitual residence' refers to the place where the spouses most recently lived together and participated together in family life[13].

Children

Habitual residence of a child is defined as the place where the child resided:

(a) with both parents;

(b) where the parents live separately, with one parent under a separation agreement or with the consent, implied consent or acquiescence of the other under a court order; or

(c) with a person other than a parent on a permanent basis for a significant period of time;

whichever last occurred[14]

A parent cannot change the habitual residence of the child by removing or withholding the child without the consent of the parent having custody of the child.[15]

4. CONFLICT OF LAW/APPLICABLE LAW TO BE APPLIED

4.1 What happens when one party applies to stay proceedings in favour of a foreign jurisdiction? What factors will the local court take into account when determining forum issues?

Divorce and corollary relief

A party seeking a stay of domestic proceedings must be able to establish that the foreign court is a clearly or distinctly more appropriate forum[16]. Where the corollary relief will need to be dealt with by the foreign court, severing the divorce from the corollary relief is not appropriate.[17]

Where no divorce or after divorce

Where a stay of proceedings in favour of a foreign court is sought under provincial legislation in respect of custody, an Ontario court will, unless there are exceptional circumstances, refrain from exercising jurisdiction in cases where it is more appropriate for the matter to be determined by a tribunal in the place where the child has a closer connection.[18]

---

[13] *Adam v Adam* [1994] O.J. No. 1930 (Ont. Gen. Div.); affd [1996] O.J. No. 3266 (Ont. C.A.)

[14] Children's Law Reform Act R.S.O. 1990, c. C.12, as am. s. 22(2)

[15] Children's Law Reform Act R.S.O. 1990, c. C.12, as am. s. 22(3)

[16] *Kornberg v Kornberg* [1990] M.J. No. 659, 30 R.F.L. (3d) 238 (Man. C.A.)

[17] *Struck v Struck*, [2008] O.J. No. 2808, 56 R.F.L. (6th) 224 (Ont. S.C.J.)

[18] Children's Law Reform Act R.S.O. 1990, c. C.12, as am. s. 19(b)

B. PRE- AND POST-NUPTIAL AGREEMENTS

5. VALIDITY OF PRE- AND POST-NUPTIAL AGREEMENTS

5.1 To what extent are pre- and post-nups binding within the jurisdiction? Could you provide a brief discussion of the most significant recent case law on this issue?

In Ontario, these agreements are referred to as marriage contracts. To be valid, a marriage contract must be in writing, signed by the parties and witnessed.[19] Married couples, or those intending to marry, can make agreements dealing with any matter, however, terms purporting to deal with custody of or access to a child or limiting a spouse's right to possession of the matrimonial home are unenforceable.[20] Marriage contracts, along with other domestic contracts such as separation agreements, are binding on the parties.

A court may set aside an agreement or a provision in it if one party failed to disclose to the other significant assets or debts existing at the time the contract was made, if a party did not understand the nature or consequences of the contract, or otherwise in accordance with the law of contract.[21] Setting aside a contract or a provision thereof is essentially a two-step process. First, the party seeking to set aside the contract must be able to show that he or she fits within one of the criteria listed above. Second, the court makes a discretionary decision based on the facts.[22]

In *LeVan v Levan*[23] the OCA agreed with the trial judge and set aside a marriage contract on the basis that the husband had deliberately breached his statutory obligation to provide financial disclosure and that neither the wife nor her lawyer understood the nature and consequences of the marriage contract. The husband's leave to appeal to the SCC was denied.

The findings in *LeVan* and other cases make it abundantly clear that in order for a marriage contract to survive judicial oversight, there must be sufficient financial disclosure such that the other party knows exactly not only the rights he or she is releasing but the potential amounts at stake. The onus is on both the spouse with the assets/income to disclose, as well as on the other spouse to seek to compel further disclosure if he or she is not satisfied with what has been provided. Marriage contracts must be negotiated and signed well in advance of the wedding date to avoid a claim of duress. The parties must also consider the need for independent legal advice.

C. DIVORCE, NULLITY AND JUDICIAL SEPARATION

6. RECOGNITION OF FOREIGN MARRIAGES/DIVORCES

6.1 Summarise the position in your jurisdiction

Foreign marriages

The formalities of a marriage are determined by the law of the place where the marriage is celebrated. An Ontario court can inform itself of the law in a

[19] Family Law Act, R.S.O. 1990, c. F.3, as am., s.55

[20] Family Law Act, R.S.O. 1990, c. F.3, as am., s.52

[21] Family Law Act, R.S.O. 1990, c. F.3, as am., s.56(4)

[22] *Quinn v Keiper*, [2007] O.J. No. 4169 (Ont. S.C.J.), affirmed [2008] O.J. No. 3788 (Ont. C.A.)

[23] *LeVan v LeVan*, [2008] O.J. No. 1905 (Ont. C.A.), leave to appeal refused [2008] S.C.C.A. No. 331 (S.C.C.)

foreign jurisdiction to determine whether to annul a foreign marriage.[24]

Foreign divorces

Foreign divorces are recognised in Canada pursuant to three possible bases under the DA.[25] First, a foreign divorce will be recognised where either spouse was 'ordinarily resident' in that country for at least one year immediately preceding the commencement of proceedings for the divorce. Second, foreign divorces obtained after 1 July, 1968 are recognised based on the wife's domicile in a country other than Canada as if she were an unmarried adult. Third, foreign divorces granted under common law are recognised. As long as the divorce was properly obtained in accordance with the laws of the other country, it is rare for the foreign divorce not to be recognised.[26]

7. DIVORCE

7.1 Explain the grounds for divorce within the jurisdiction (please also deal with nullity and judicial separation if appropriate)

Canada is a 'no fault' jurisdiction which means that the reason the marriage is at an end is irrelevant to determinations of custody, access and support. Where there has been a breakdown of the marriage, a court may grant a divorce. Breakdown of a marriage is established on two possible bases: one, if the spouses have lived separate and apart for at least one year immediately preceding the determination of the divorce proceeding and were living separate and apart at the commencement of the proceedings; or two, the spouse against whom the divorce proceeding is brought has committed adultery or treated the other spouse with physical or mental cruelty such that continued cohabitation is intolerable.[27]

Living separate and apart

To be living 'separate and apart' requires only the intention of one spouse. While it does require a physical separation, spouses can live separate and apart under the same roof.

Adultery

Although adultery is still included in the DA, it is rarely invoked today. Firstly it is expensive, onerous, and time consuming to make a successful claim. Secondly, the courts are critical of spouses who claim marriage breakdown-based adultery; they are seen as unnecessarily trying to embarrass their former spouse and the person with whom the alleged adultery was committed. Finally, although a divorce cannot be *granted* until the spouses have been living separate and apart for one year, a claim may be *commenced* as soon as the spouses are separated, making that ground far more practical.

---

[24] Annulment of Marriages Act (Ontario) R.S.C. 1970, c. A-14, s. 3; *Torfenejad v Salimi*, [2006] O.J. No. 4633 (Ont. S.C.J.), affd [2008] O. J. No. 3165 (Ont. C.A.)
[25] Divorce Act, R.S.C. 1985, c. 3 (2nd Supp.), s.22
[26] *Martinez v Basail*, [2010] O/J/ No. 1432 (Ont. S.C.J.)
[27] Divorce Act, R.S.C. 1985, c. 3 (2nd Supp.), s.8

Cruelty

To establish cruelty, the conduct must be of a 'grave and weighty' nature. The conduct cannot be simply a manifestation of incompatible temperaments between the spouses.[28]

Actions in nullity

As a divorce can be obtained based on one year of separation, actions in nullity are not particularly common.[29] Where the parties both reside in a province, a court in that province can deal with a claim for annulment[30]. Grounds for an annulment may be based on lack of formalities or lack of capacity to marry[31].

8. FINANCES/CAPITAL, PROPERTY

8.1 What powers does the court have to allocate financial resources and property on the breakdown of marriage?

Support

Pursuant to the DA, a court in Ontario can require one spouse to pay child support in accordance with the applicable guidelines (see section 10 below for more on how child support is calculated). In the order, the court can impose terms, conditions, or restrictions as it thinks fit and just.[32]

The DA also provides a court in Ontario with the power to order a spouse to pay spousal support.[33]

Property

In Ontario, only married spouses are entitled to division of property as provided for in the FLA.[34] Common law spouses may still make claims for property, but can only do so by way of common law trust principles, which are also available to married spouses[35].

Courts in Ontario do not have jurisdiction to divide property *in specie*; rather, all property acquired by the spouses during the marriage should be equalised at separation by the transfer of money from the spouse who during the marriage accumulated more and at separation owns property with a greater value to the other spouse. This equalisation model applies to property owned by the spouses on valuation date[36]. First, the courts determine each spouse's net family property, which is defined as the value

[28] *Knoll v Knoll*, [1970] O.J. No. 1443

[29] *Chirayath v Chirayath*, [1980] O.J. No. 262 (Ont. C.A.)

[30] *Torfenejad v Salimi*, [2006] O.J. No. 4633 (Ont. S.C.J.), affd [2008] O. J. No. 3165 (Ont. C.A.)

[31] *Halsbury's Laws Of Canada, First Edition*, LexisNexis Inc., 2010 pages 144-145; Marriage (Prohibited Degrees) Act S.C. 1990, c. 46

[32] Divorce Act, R.S.C. 1985, c. 3 (2nd Supp.), s.15.1

[33] Divorce Act, R.S.C. 1985, c. 3 (2nd Supp.), s.15.2; See Question 9.3 for more on how spousal support is calculated

[34] Family Law Act, R.S.O. 1990, c. F.3, as am., ss.1 & 5

[35] *Rawluk v Rawluk* 1990 CarswellOnt 217 (S.C.C.); For changing trust law principles in family law context, see discussion under Question 22.1

[36] 'Valuation date' is defined as 'the date of separation, the date of divorce or a declaration of nullity, the day before the date of the death of a spouse or the date of commencement of an application for improvident depletion' at section 4 of the Family Law Act.

of all the property a spouse owns at separation after deducting the spouse's debts and liabilities and the value of property, other than a matrimonial home, that the spouse owned on the date of marriage[37]. A spouse's net family property cannot be less than zero. The spouse whose net family property is the lesser of the two is entitled to one-half the difference between them. Essentially, the spouse with the larger 'ownership pile' pays money to the spouse with the smaller 'ownership pile' to ensure that they leave the marriage with assets, whether property or money, of equal value[38]. The courts also retain some limited discretion to order an unequal division where it would otherwise be unconscionable.[39] Unconscionable means more than unfair or inequitable; it is something that would 'shock the conscience of the court'[40].

8.2 Explain and illustrate with reference to recent cases the court's thinking on division of assets

In 1990 the SCC considered the division of property in *Rawluk v Rawluk*[41] and explained that it is a two-step test which distinguishes between ownership and equalisation. At the first step, ownership[42] is determined. At the second step, the spouses' assets are equalised. Each spouse's assets are equalised based on the value of each asset at the date of valuation[43], not the date of trial. Therefore, if a non-titled spouse has made contributions to a property which has increased in value after the date of valuation, that spouse would not be entitled to share in the increase. In *Rawluk* however, the SCC made it clear that 'ownership' includes beneficial ownership which allows the non-titled spouse to make a claim for a constructive trust interest in the property.

In *Serra* v *Serra*[44] the OCA considered the situation where after separation the husband suffered a substantial decline in the value of his business, the major asset, as a result of market factors. Equalisation was determined on the value of each spouse's property *on valuation date*, but by the time the amount of the payment was calculated, it was actually more than (possibly even double) the husband's net worth. The court found that equalisation would be unconscionable and instead ordered an unequal division.

The definition of a spouse's 'net family property' refers to the value of property after deducting debts and liabilities. Effective 14 May, 2009, the FLA was revised to expressly include contingent tax liabilities in respect of property[45].

---

[37] There is also provision for the exclusion of the value of certain property from a spouse's net family property calculation
[38] *Rawluk v Rawluk* 1990 CarswellOnt 217 (S.C.C.)
[39] Family Law Act, R.S.O. 1990, c. F.3, as am., ss.4 & 5
[40] *Ward v Ward* 2012 CarswellOnt 8658 (Ont. C.A.)
[41] *Rawluk v Rawluk* 1990 CarswellOnt 217 (S.C.C.)
[42] Ownership is far more than a share in the property; it includes additional legal rights, control and responsibility as well as psychological benefits: Annotation to *Rawluk* by James McLeod
[43] See footnote 42 for the definition of "valuation date"
[44] *Serra v Serra*, [2009] O.J. No. 432 (Ont. C.A.)
[45] Family Law Act, R.S.O. 1990, c. F.3, as am., s. 4(1.1)

9. FINANCES/MAINTENANCE

9.1 Explain the operation of maintenance for spouses on an ongoing basis after the breakdown of marriage

Where maintenance, or spousal support as it is known in Canada, is requested as part of a divorce, a court must consider the condition, means, needs and other circumstances of each spouse including the length of time the spouses cohabited (not just the length of the marriage), the functions performed by each spouse during cohabitation, and any order, agreement or arrangement related to the support of either spouse. The objectives of a spousal support order under the DA is to:

(a) recognise the economic advantages or disadvantages to the spouses arising from the marriage or its breakdown;
(b) apportion between the spouses any financial consequences arising from the care of any child of the marriage over and above any obligation for the support of any child of the marriage;
(c) relieve economic hardship of the spouses arising from the breakdown of the marriage; and
(d) in so far as practicable, promote the economic self-sufficiency of each spouse within a reasonable period of time.[46]

Under Ontario legislation, spousal support is available to married and common law couples[47] or the parents of a child who are in a relationship of some permanence.[48] The purposes under the FLA are similar to those set out under the DA.

9.2 Is it common for maintenance to be awarded?

Generally, the longer the spouses have cohabited, the larger the discrepancy between their incomes, and/or the closer their relationship resembles the 'traditional' relationship where one spouse worked outside the home while the other was responsible for the home and the children, the more likely it is that spousal support will be awarded.

9.3 Explain and illustrate with reference to recent cases the court's thinking on maintenance

Before a court will order spousal support, an applicant must establish entitlement to support. In *Bracklow v Bracklow*[49], the SCC set out the three possible bases for entitlement. Where the basis is compensatory in nature, a spouse will have established his or her inability to support him or herself as a result of foregoing education or career opportunities during the marriage in favour of the other spouse's education and/or career goals. Additionally, where a spouse has taken on the more traditional roles of child-rearing and household management, a compensatory basis may be found. A contractual basis is established where the spouses have an express or implied agreement about entitlement to and the provision of support or conversely an express

[46] Divorce Act, R.S.C. 1985, c. 3 (2nd Supp.), s.15.2
[47] Having lived together continuously for at least three years
[48] Family Law Act, R.S.O. 1990, c. F.3, as am., s. 29
[49] *Bracklow v Bracklow*, [1999] S.C.J. No. 14

or implied agreement about the lack of entitlement to or the provision of spousal support. Where there are no grounds for compensatory support, but a spouse is unable as a result of the marriage or its breakdown to be self-sufficient, non-compensatory spousal support may be established.

Miglin v Miglin[50] was a seminal case as the SCC established a two-stage process for setting aside a waiver of spousal support in an agreement. In the first stage, which has two separate steps, the court must examine the circumstances at the time of the formation of the agreement. At the first step of the first stage, the court determines whether there were any circumstances of pressure and examines the conditions under which the negotiations were held including whether there was professional assistance. At the second step of the first stage the court looks to the substance of the agreement and determines the extent to which the agreement takes into account the factors and objectives listed in the DA. The court only intervenes if there has been a significant departure from the DA. At the second stage, the court considers the current circumstances to determine whether the agreement continues to be an accurate reflection of the parties' intentions.

The OCA's decision in *Fisher v Fisher*[51] came as a surprise to many in the family law bar. After a 19-year marriage where the parties had no children, the court restricted the wife's support to a maximum of seven years. The decision marked a departure from the court's previous practice of ordering indefinite support on the breakdown of long-term marriages. The OCA found that the wife's claim was essentially non-compensatory in nature and ordered time-limited, transitional support to allow her to adjust to the lifestyle her income allowed. The decision was also significant for the court's acknowledgement that the Spousal Support Advisory Guidelines (SSAGs), although only advisory in nature and not binding, are useful. The SSAGs use an income-sharing model of support, rather than one based on budgets, in an effort to bring consistency and predictability to the amount of spousal support to be ordered.

In the 2011 decision of *Davis v Crawford*[52] the OCA reviewed the trial judge's decision to award lump sum spousal support. While the court disagreed that lump sum support is to be used only in 'very unusual circumstances', they did note that for practical reasons most spousal support would be ordered to be made periodically. Ultimately, lump sum spousal support was ordered as there was a real concern the husband would not pay periodic support.

10. CHILD MAINTENANCE

10.1 On what basis is child maintenance calculated within the jurisdiction?

Since 1 May, 1997, child support in Ontario has been calculated in accordance with the Child Support Guidelines. The amount of support is based on the income of the payor and the number of children living with the recipient parent. The Guidelines are grids that provide a specific amount

[50] *Miglin v Miglin*, [2003] S.C.J. No. 21
[51] *Fisher v Fisher*, 2008 ONCA 11 (Ont. C.A.)
[52] *Davis v Crawford*, 2011 ONCA 294 (Ont. C.A.)

of support to be paid for every income level, above a minimum threshold income of $9,000, depending on the number of children for whom support is paid, (the 'Table' amount). Table child support accounts for the payor's contribution to the costs incurred by the recipient parent for the childrens' food, clothing, rent, utilities and transportation.

In addition to the Table amount many payors are obligated to contribute to the children's special or extraordinary expenses such as childcare, summer camp, education, extracurricular, and health related expenses. Both parents are required to contribute to these special expenses in proportion to their respective incomes.

11. RECIPROCAL ENFORCEMENT OF FINANCIAL ORDERS

11.1 Summarise the position in your jurisdiction

The Interjurisdictional Support Orders Act, 2002[53] (the ISOA) governs the enforcement of support orders both where the recipient lives in Ontario but the payor lives elsewhere as well as where the payor lives in Ontario but the recipient lives in a different jurisdiction.

Under Part III of the ISOA a claimant is able to register a support order made in a reciprocating jurisdiction for enforcement in Ontario. The process begins with a copy of the order, along with information about the payor living in Ontario, being sent to the designated authority in Ontario. The court clerk in the court closest to where the payor lives registers the order which has the same effect as though it had been made by an Ontario court. The payor receives notice and then has 30 days to bring a motion to an Ontario court to have the registration set aside which will only be granted if the payor did not have notice or an opportunity to participate in the proceedings in which the order was made, the order is contrary to public policy in Ontario, or the court that made the order did not have jurisdiction to make it.[54]

The order is then filed with the Director of the Family Responsibility Office (the FRO). The FRO can garnish funds directly from the payor's employment wages to satisfy the order. Where a payor is in arrears of support, the FRO has a number of additional enforcement mechanisms available including garnishing federal money owed to the payor such as income tax refunds, suspending a payor's driver's licence or revoking his passport. In extreme cases, the payor may be incarcerated[55].

12. FINANCIAL RELIEF AFTER FOREIGN DIVORCE PROCEEDINGS

12.1 What powers are available to make orders following a foreign divorce?

Under the Federal Divorce Act

Where the parties obtain a divorce in a foreign jurisdiction, the Ontario

[53] Interjurisdictional Support Order Act, 2002, S.O. 2002, c. 13
[54] Interjurisdictional Support Order Act, 2002, S.O. 2002, c. 13, Part III
[55] Family Responsibility and Support Arrears Enforcement Act, 1996, S.O. 1996, c. 31, as am.

courts have no power to vary its terms or to make an order for support and custody under the federal DA[56].

Custody under provincial legislation

An order for custody of a child can be brought by a former spouse and determined by an Ontario court under the CLRA so long as the court has jurisdiction under s.22.

Support under provincial legislation

Under the FLA, parents are obligated to support each unmarried child who is a minor (under 18) and is enrolled in a full-time programme of education[57].

An Ontario court has no power to order spousal support following a foreign divorce.[58]

Equalisation under provincial legislation

A court in Ontario does have jurisdiction to make an order for equalisation.[59]

D. CHILDREN

13. CUSTODY/PARENTAL RESPONSIBILITY

13.1 Briefly explain the legal position in relation to custody/parental responsibility following the breakdown of a relationship or marriage

Custody is accepted as referring to decision-making authority with respect to the child, specifically education, religion and non-emergency medical decisions.

Under the Divorce Act

Either or both spouses can apply for custody of a child following the breakdown of a marriage and the court is required to consider only the best interests of the child. The willingness of the person making an application for custody to facilitate the child's contact with the other parent is a factor to be taken into consideration by the court.[60]

Under the Children's Law Reform Act

While never actually defining the term 'custody', the provincial legislation in Ontario explicitly provides that both parents are equally entitled to custody of the child, but where the parties separate and the child lives with one of them with the consent or acquiescence of the other, the entitlement of the parent with whom the child does not live is suspended until a separation agreement or court order provides for custody. The parent with custody, or both parents where custody is jointly held, must exercise their rights and responsibilities in

---

[56] *Okmyansky v Okmyansky*, [2007] O.J. No. 2298 (Ont. C.A.); *Rothgeisser v Rothgeisser*, [2000] O. J. No. 33 (Ont. C.A.)

[57] Family Law Act, R.S.O. 1990, c. F.3, as am., s. 31

[58] *Okmyansky v Okmyansky*, [2007] O.J. No. 2298 (Ont. C.A.); *Rothgeisser v Rothgeisser*, [2000] O. J. No. 33 (Ont. C.A.)

[59] *Okmyansky v Okmyansky*, [2007] O.J. No. 2298 (Ont. C.A.)

[60] Divorce Act, R.S.C. 1985, c. 3 (2nd Supp.), s.16

respect of the chid in accordance with the child's best interests.[61]

13.2 Briefly explain the legal position in relation to access/contact/ visitation following the breakdown of a relationship of marriage

Under the Divorce Act

A parent who is granted access has the right to information about the health, education and welfare of the child. Courts are required to give effect to the principle of maximum contact which provides that a child should have as much contact with each spouse as possible, so long as such contact is in the child's best interest.[62]

Under the Children's Law Reform Act

Where a child lives with one parent after separation, the other parent continues to have entitlement to access to the child, including the right to visit with the child and to ask and be provided with information about the health, education and welfare of the child.[63]

14. INTERNATIONAL ABDUCTION

14.1 Briefly summarise the position in your jurisdiction

Canada is a signatory to the Hague Convention[64].

Part III of the CLRA, which provides for custody, access and guardianship of children, was drafted specifically to deter forum shopping and child abduction. One of the stated purposes of the CLRA is to discourage child abduction[65] and at s.46, the Hague Convention has been codified. The CLRA also clearly and unequivocally confirms that a child's habitual residence, for the purpose of establishing a court's jurisdiction, cannot be changed by the removal or withholding of a child without the consent of the person having custody.[66] Ontario courts do have discretion to accept jurisdiction in respect of custody of or access to a child where the child is physically present in Ontario and the court believes that the child would suffer serious harm if the child remains in the custody of the person legally entitled to custody, is returned to the custody of the person legally entitled to custody, or the child is removed from the province.[67]

15. LEAVE TO REMOVE/APPLICATIONS TO TAKE A CHILD OUT OF THE JURISDICTION

15.1 Summarise the position in your jurisdiction

In Ontario, removal of a child from a jurisdiction is generally referred to as 'mobility rights' and was considered by the SCC in *Gordon v Goertz*[68]. While the best interest of the child is the paramount consideration, a court

[61] Children's Law Reform Act R.S.O. 1990, c. C.12, as am. s. 20
[62] Divorce Act, R.S.C. 1985, c. 3 (2nd Supp.), s.16
[63] Children's Law Reform Act R.S.O. 1990, c. C.12, as am. s. 20
[64] Convention on the Civil Aspects of International Child Abduction
[65] Children's Law Reform Act R.S.O. 1990, c. C.12, as am. s. 19(c)
[66] Children's Law Reform Act R.S.O. 1990, c. C.12, as am. s. 22(3)
[67] Children's Law Reform Act R.S.O. 1990, c. C.12, as am. s. 23
[68] *Gordon v Goertz*, 19 R.F L. (4th) 177 (S.C.C.)

hearing a mobility application will consider the existing custody and access arrangements, as well as the child's relationship with each parent, the goal of maximising the child's contact with both parents, the views of the child, the custodial parent's reason for moving, and the disruption to the child[69]. As mobility cases are so fact driven, it is extremely difficult for family law lawyers to predict whether a court will grant the request for a move in any specific situation.

15.2 Under what circumstances may a parent apply to remove their child from the jurisdiction against the wishes of the other parent?

A parent can apply under any circumstances but will only be successful if he or she can persuade the court that there has been a material change of circumstances necessitating the move and that the best interest of the child will be met by permitting the move.[70]

E. SURROGACY AND ADOPTION

16. VALIDITY OF SURROGACY AGREEMENTS

16.1 Briefly summarise the position in your jurisdiction

Surrogacy, along with other assisted reproductive technologies, is in a state of flux in Canada. The Assisted Human Reproduction Act [71] (AHRA), a federal piece of legislation, came into force on 22 April, 2004. However, by 2010 a number of its provisions had been repealed, having been deemed unconstitutional by the SCC[72]. While the AHRA acknowledges surrogacy, it prohibits payment to a surrogate and payment for arranging for the services of a surrogate. The AHRA permits surrogates to be reimbursed for expenses 'in accordance with the regulations' but those regulations have yet to be drafted. There are, as yet, no reported Canadian cases dealing with the enforceability of surrogacy agreements. However, in February 2013, the Royal Canadian Mounted Police, Canada's national police service, laid 27 criminal charges against an Ontario surrogacy agent and her firm.

17. ADOPTION

17.1 Briefly explain the legal position in relation to adoption in your jurisdiction. Is adoption available to individuals, cohabiting couples (both heterosexual and same-sex)?

In Ontario all individuals, including married and unmarried heterosexual and same-sex couples are potential adoptive parents. Adoption has been codified in the Child and Family Services Act[73] (CFSA)where the primary objective is the best interest of the child. The individuals must undergo a home study which is comprised of a series of interviews in which

---

[69] *Gordon v Goertz*, 19 R.F L. (4th) 177 (S.C.C.)

[70] Section 17 the Divorce Act does not specifically refer to the change being 'material' but it has been read into the section by the common law in *Willick v Willick*, [1994] S.C.J. No. 94, (S.C.C.). Section 29 of the Children's Law Reform Act includes the phrase 'material change in circumstances'.

[71] S.C. 2004, c. 2

[72] Reference re Assisted Human Reproduction Act, 2010 SCC 61

[73] R.S.O. 1990, c. C.11, as am. at Part VII

the practitioner will assess the adoptive parents' skills and ability to parent and will prepare a report for approval. The CFSA also provides for openness agreements whereby birth parents, and other specified persons, can negotiate the terms of the agreement prior to the finalisation of the adoption[74].

F. COHABITATION

18. COHABITATION

18.1 What legislation (if any) governs division of property for unmarried couples on the breakdown of the relationship?

There is no legislation in Ontario governing the division of property for unmarried couples on the breakdown of the relationship. Prior to the SCC's 2011 decision in *Kerr v Baranow*[75] common law couples, in making a claim to property held by the other spouse, invoked various trust principles, including the resulting trust and constructive trust. In *Kerr* the SCC made it clear that the resulting trust, and its concomitant 'common intention' of the parties no longer has any role to play. Where an unjust enrichment claim is made, the SCC determined the manner in which a monetary remedy is to be quantified in a domestic situation and expressly rejected the fee-for-service calculation. The SCC held that 'where the unjust enrichment is best characterised as an unjust retention of a disproportionate share of assets accumulated during the course of ... a 'joint family venture' to which both partners have contributed, the monetary remedy should reflect that'[76]. Factors which point to the existence of a 'joint family venture' include mutual effort, economic integration, actual intent and priority of the family.

G. FAMILY DISPUTE RESOLUTION

19. MEDIATION, COLLABORATIVE LAW AND ARBITRATION

19.1 Briefly summarise the non-court-based processes available in your jurisdiction and the current status of agreements reached under the auspices of mediation, collaborative law and arbitration

Alternative dispute resolution processes, including mediation, arbitration and collaborative law, are available in Ontario for parties who choose to opt out of the court system. A hybrid of mediation and arbitration, known as Med/Arb, has been voluntarily used by litigants over the past number of years. In a Med/Arb process, the parties choose one person, generally a well-respected senior family law lawyer, to act first as mediator, and failing resolution, as arbitrator.

Where agreement is reached through mediation or the collaborative law process and the agreement is reduced to writing, signed by the parties and witnessed, that agreement becomes a domestic contract as defined in Part IV of the FLA.

[74] Child and Family Services Act, R.S.O. 1990, c. C.11, as am. s.153.6
[75] *Kerr v Baranow* 2011 CarswellBC 240 (S.C.C.)
[76] *Kerr*, para. 80

19.2 What is the statutory basis (if any) for mediation, collaborative law and arbitration in your jurisdiction? In particular, are the parties required to attempt a family dispute resolution in advance of the institution of proceedings?

Under the CLRA[77] and the FLA[78] parties can request that the court, by order, appoint a person the parties have chosen, and who has agreed to act, to mediate.

Family arbitrations, agreements and awards are all governed by both the FLA and the Arbitration Act, 1991[79], but where there is a conflict between the two pieces of legislation, the FLA prevails[80]. The provisions in respect of family arbitrations, agreements and awards were added to the Family Law Act by the Family Statute Law Amendment Act, 2006, S.O. 2006, c. 1 which came into force in Ontario on 30 April, 2007. The legislation provides that arbitrations are to be guided by the laws of Ontario or another jurisdiction within Canada. Parties must have independent legal advice prior to entering into an arbitration agreement.

Where a separation agreement, court order, or arbitration award requires parties to engage in a particular process prior to the institution of proceedings, the court will generally enforce those provisions.

There is currently no requirement that parties attempt family dispute resolution in advance of the institution of proceedings, although parties are free to do so. In Ontario, there is a Family Law Information Centre located at most courthouses. There are court connected family mediation services at 17 separate court house locations across the province[81]. Once proceedings have been instituted, all family law litigants are required to attend a Family Law Information Session and as a first step in the proceedings, participate in a case conference, which is an early opportunity to sit with a judge in an informal setting to get a judge's view of the merits of the case.

H. OTHER

20. CIVIL PARTNERSHIP/SAME-SEX MARRIAGE

20.1 What is the status of civil partnership/same-sex marriage within the jurisdiction?

Same-sex marriage is legal in all Canadian provinces and territories.

20.2 What legislation governs civil partnerships/same-sex marriage?

Pursuant to the 2005 Civil Marriage Act[82] same-sex couples across Canada are entitled to equal access to marriage. The preamble to the Act makes it clear that only marriage, as opposed to some other civil union, would offer same-sex couples equal access and ensure their human dignity.

---

[77] Children's Law Reform Act, s.31
[78] Family Law Act, s.3
[79] S.O. 2006, c. 1, s.5
[80] Family Law Act, s. 59.1
[81] Ministry of the Attorney General (Ontario) *www.attorneygeneral.jus.gov.on.ca/english/family/family_justice_services*
[82] S.C. 2005, c.33

21. CONTROVERSIAL AREAS/RAPIDLY DEVELOPING AREAS OF LAW

21.1 Is there a particular area of law within the jurisdiction that is currently undergoing major change?

Pension law in Ontario underwent a major change effective 1 January, 2012[83]. The value of a pension is an asset to be included in the calculation of a spouse's net family property. For a spouse who has worked for many years and contributed to a pension, that pension can be of significant value. The recent pension reform is meant to address two significant challenges faced by separating spouses.

First, prior to January 2012, pensions were valued by actuaries, only some of whom specialised in valuation of pensions in the family law context, in circumstances where there was no specific formula required to be followed. Effective 1 January, 2012, pension plans registered in Ontario are valued by the plan administrators in accordance with a prescribed formula. For other plans, the calculation will still be made by independent valuators but they must value the pension in accordance with the same prescribed formula.

The second challenge the legislation was designed to deal with was the difficulty faced by many pension-holding spouses who owed a significant equalisation payment to the other spouse (as a result of the large value of the pension) but who were unable to satisfy the equalisation amount without access to the funds held in the pension (until retirement when the pension was in pay) or who had to transfer assets to the non-pension holding spouse to satisfy the equalisation obligation, leaving the pension-owning spouse with little but the future income stream from the pension at retirement. Effective January 2012, the pension-holding spouse can transfer up to 50 per cent of the pension value to a registered investment vehicle in the non-pension-holding spouse's name to satisfy an equalisation payment.

Although the pension reform has streamlined the process and has provided some relief, it has also created a host of additional challenges for separating spouses, family law lawyers and the courts.

As a result of the SCC's decision in *Kerr* and the introduction of the concept of a joint family venture, the constructive trust claim has now possibly been expanded. It remains to be seen whether married spouses will now be able to make more successful claims to a constructive trust interest in property which has increased in value since separation. Additionally, although constructive trust principles are not applicable to property gifted to the other spouse, the SCC's decision may have opened that door.

21.2 Which areas of law are most out-of-step? Which areas would you most like to see reformed/changed?

The laws surrounding assisted reproductive technologies are most out-of-step with the reality of the way in which families are formed. It has been reported that the Ontario surrogacy agent facing criminal charges under the AHRA will challenge the constitutionality of some of its remaining provisions[84].

[83] Family Statute Law Amendment Act, 2009 S.O. 2009, c. 11

[84] Article by Tom Blackwell in *The National Post* – online – 17 March, 2013

Regardless of whether a challenge of constitutionality of the AHRA is successful, further change in the law of assisted reproductive technologies is required.

A second area where change would be welcome is with respect to the equity in a home brought into marriage. In calculating a spouse's net family property under the FLA, there is a deduction given for all property a spouse has brought into the marriage, with the exception of the equity in a home that the parties use as a matrimonial home (or where the proceeds of a home owned at date of marriage are used to purchase a matrimonial home). The FLA provides a matrimonial home with special protection. At the time the FLA was drafted, there was a great deal of debate about this specific issue as many felt it was simply unfair for the spouse who brought a home, as opposed to any other asset, into the marriage, to lose the deduction for it on separation. Currently, the only way for a spouse who owns a home at marriage to protect the equity of that home (or one into which the equity is transferred), is to enter into an agreement with their spouse in which it is agreed that in the event of marriage breakdown, the equity in the home the on the date of marriage will be deducted from the home-owning spouse's net family property. Given the rate of divorce, the fact that people are now marrying later in life, and that many have already purchased a home by the time they enter marriage, legislative reform is advisable.

Chile

Horvitz and Horvitz Abogados Daniela Horvitz Lennon

A. JURISDICTION AND CONFLICT OF LAW

1. SOURCES OF LAW

1.1 What is the primary source of law in relation to the breakdown of marriage and the welfare of children within the jurisdiction?

In Chile, the applicable rules in relation to matrimonial rupture and protection of children have their starting point in the Political Constitution of the Republic, which states that the family is the fundamental basis of society and that the life of the child that is expected to be born is protected. However, and most importantly, international agreements ratified by Chile have a Constitutional status, hence granting the International Convention on the Rights of the Child, as well as other agreements relating to infancy, access to said status.

Regarding legal status, the Civil Code basically applies, which regulates marriage, the property regimes, family assets, obligations between parents and their children, and between spouses, child support set forth by law, as well as custody and guardianships. Such dispositions complement or further each other by the following laws: Child Support Law (14.908), Minors' Law (16.618), Law of Civil Marriage (19.947) and Law of Family Courts (law 19.968), notwithstanding other laws of specific character. Finally, there are regulations which serve to implement the legal rules.

One of the criticisms that UNICEF has of our legislation is the absence of one sole organic body which regulates, in a joint manner, all matters concerning the family, especially childhood and adolescence.

1.2 Which are the main statutes governing matrimonial law in the jurisdiction?

The requisites and characteristics of marriage are regulated in the Civil Code, beginning in Article 102 and following. In 2004, the Law of Civil Marriage (19.947) was promulgated, which *'regulates the requisites to marry, the form of entering such contract, the separation of the spouses, the declaration of matrimonial nullity, the dissolution of the bond and the means to remedy or relieve the ruptures between the spouses and its effects'*. (Article 1°).

2. JURISDICTION

2.1 What are the main jurisdictional requirements for the institution of proceedings in relation to divorce, property and children?

Article 15 of the Civil Code states, as an exception to the general rule of the territoriality of the law, that: *'Chileans will remain subject to the native laws that rule the obligations and civil rights, notwithstanding the residence or domicile in a foreign country. 1° In everything relative to the condition of the persons and to their aptitude to execute certain acts, which are to have effect in Chile; 2° In the obligations and rights that arise from family relations; but only with regards to their spouses and Chilean relatives.'*

This is regardless of their place of residence, when dealing with the matters set out above with respect to Chileans, our judicary will be competent to adjudge. If dealing with foreigners who want to regulate their family relations in Chile, national regulations will apply with regard to marriage, separation, divorce, filiation, support and compensatory renderings, since it is a question of public order rules.

3. DOMICILE AND HABITUAL RESIDENCE

3.1 Explain the concepts of domicile and habitual residence as they apply to the jurisdiction in relation to divorce, the finances and children

Article 62 of the Civil Code sets out that: 'The place where an individual is settled, or where he or she habitually exercises his or her profession or trade, will determine his or her civil domicile or legal residence.' The concept of 'habitual residence' has been academically and jurisprudentially developed because a legal definition does not exist. Unlike other countries, it is not a concept that is very much used, since the rules of competence are determined by a person's domicile. For example, the competent court to have jurisdiction over the action of alimony is the court of the domicile of the alimony payer or of the alimony plaintiff, to the election of the latter.

4. CONFLICT OF LAW/APPLICABLE LAW TO BE APPLIED

4.1 What happens when one party applies to stay proceedings in favour of a foreign jurisdiction? What factors will the local court take into account when determining forum issues?

Family matters are considered to be matters of public order, so they do not admit either jurisdictional extensions, or application of foreign law. In Chile only substantive rules and Chilean procedures are going to apply. Within domestic and cultural circumstances which must guide a ruling, for example in matters of support and economic compensation, foreign rules can be considered to be a parameter, but never in an imperative manner. On the other hand, if it is a question of executing foreign rulings in Chile, this must be carried out of by means of an *exequatur* procedure, and the courts will only make such orders that do not adversely affect the public order. The best example to illustrate this point is that, before 2004 foreign divorces were not even recognised in Chile because in Chile marriage was indissoluble.

B. PRE- AND POST-NUPTIAL AGREEMENTS

5. VALIDITY OF PRE- AND POST-NUPTIAL AGREEMENTS

5.1. To what extent are pre- and post-nups binding within the jurisdiction? Could you provide a brief discussion of the most significant recent case law on this issue?

In Chile, the term 'pre-nuptial agreement' is known only through doctrine, without having legal structure of its own. The only agreements that can be entered into earlier, or in parallel, with the marriage, are the conventions of patrimonial character, which are called 'marriage capitulations', established in Article 1715 of the Civil Code. Although pre-nuptial agreements are not prohibited, their recognition and validity are again restricted to the concept of public order rules. Hence, the fulfilment of a pre-nuptial agreement in which a woman resigns — anticipatedly – to the economic compensation that arises from the termination of the marriage would not be enforceable, since it is understood that public interest is involved, therefore making the above mentioned resignation illegitimate. In practice very few pre-nuptial agreements are entered into, and those that are practised basically have a more declarative character than any other thing, serving as proof of certain circumstances (for example: that at the moment of marriage the woman was not working, that the parties consider the exchanges of letters of a personal nature to be evidence of infidelity, etc.).

Those pre-nuptial agreements that are recognised and have validity are those which relate to the establishment of the patrimonial regime of marriage: total separation of assets, partial separation of assets and participation in joint assets.

On the other hand 'post-nuptial' agreements are widely recognised and constitute a condition precedent for a certain category of divorce. Article 21 of the Civil Marriage Law states: '*If the spouses separated* de facto, *they will be able, by mutual agreement, to regulate their mutual relations, especially the support that is outstanding and all matters related to the property regime of marriage*'.

In order for a court to be able to declare the divorce, after one year has passed, a post nuptial agreement is required in addition to the mutual assent of the parties. In Chile this is called a Regulative Agreement of Family Relations, in which matters set forth in the above-mentioned Article 21 have to be considered. It is an obligation of the court to revise the mentioned agreement, verifying that the inalienable rights awarded by law are respected, and finally to declare that it complies with the requirements of completion and sufficiency required by law.

C. DIVORCE, NULLITY AND JUDICIAL SEPARATION

6. RECOGNITION OF FOREIGN MARRIAGES/DIVORCES

6.1 Summarise the position in your jurisdiction

Chile expressly recognises marriages entered into abroad in Article 80 of Law 19.947, with the sole limitation that they must be '*the union between a man and a woman*'. Nor will Chile recognise those marriages entered into without the free and spontaneous assent of the contracting spouses, which is grounds for nullifying the matrimonial contract.

Marriages entered into abroad that are registered in Chile will be understood to be entered into under the regime of total separation of goods.

Concerning divorce and nullity of marriage ruled abroad, they will be admitted in Chile in accordance with the general rules as established by the Code of Civil Procedure.

In order for the recognition of a foreign divorce or nullity to take place, it must be:

(a) product of a judicial resolution (administrative divorces are not equivalent);
(b) not to have been ruled in opposition to Chilean Public Order;
(c) not to have been granted with fraud to the law.

The latter circumstance refers to those divorces that should have been requested in Chile and were obtained in a foreign jurisdiction.

7. DIVORCE

7.1 Explain the grounds for divorce within the jurisdiction (please also deal with nullity and judicial separation if appropriate)

In Chile, legislation exists in relation to matrimonial nullity, *de facto* separation, judicial separation and divorce.

Nullity of marriage

Until 2004 it was the only manner of dissolving a marriage, since divorce did not exist.

At present, nullity is specifically regulated in the Civil Marriage Law N° 19.947. in its Chapter V. The grounds for the declaration of nullity – in generic terms – are based upon any of the spouses having any legal incapacity whatsoever or the assent not being free or spontaneous.

It is relevant to indicate that a marriage which is declared null produces the same civil effects as a valid marriage regarding the spouse who acted in good faith or just cause of error.

On the other hand, the filiation of the children that has already been determined will not be altered by the nullity.

Separation

Legislation regulates *de facto* separation and judicial separation.

With respect to *de facto* separation, the law basically grants the parties the faculty to regulate their family relations by mutual agreement, and the guide to grant a true date to the cessation of the cohabitation.

Judicial separation, on the other hand, implies a judicial procedure, in which one of the spouses sues the other, or both enter it by mutual agreement. This lawsuit can be based upon fault, in which the defendant is charged with a serious violation of the obligations imposed by marriage; or it can be based upon the objective fact of the cessation of cohabitation (articles 26 and 27 of Law 19.947).

Necessarily, after the separation is ruled upon, either by joint or unilateral request, family relations must remain sufficiently regulated. In this respect, both Articles 21 and 27 of this regulation set out for the judge the matters and the criteria of completion and sufficiency. As for the matters, spousal support must be regulated, and also those matters linked to the regime of marital property, child support, personal care and communication regime. And '*it will be understood as sufficient if it protects the superior interest of the children, assuring to reduce the economic impairment that could be caused by the rupture and establishing the equitable relations, towards the future, between the spouses whose separation is being requested'*. (Article 27, paragraph 2°, Law 19.947.)

A judicial separation leaves all the rights and personal obligations that exist between the spouses unaffected, except those whose exercise is incompatible with the separation (duty of cohabitation and duty of faithfulness), which will be suspended.

It is of the essence of the concept of judicial separation that it can be temporary, hence, revocable. With the renewal of life together between the spouses, carried out with the intention of permanence, the marital status of 'separated' terminates, and for the purposes of evidentiary value, a rescission must be requested – if it has been a guilty separation – or there must be registration of the proof of the renewal, for both spouses, before the competent authority.

Divorce

It is regulated in spite of the fact that the definition of the contract of marriage contained in Article 102 of the Civil Code still contemplates that it is an 'indissoluble' contract.

It terminates the marriage but it does not affect filiation. A divorce must always be obtained by means of a judicial process, in which the divorce is declared by legal sentence.

There are basically three reasons for which one can request a divorce:

- Request by mutual agreement of the spouses, once one full year or more has passed from the cessation of cohabitation, given that their mutual relations are regulated in a complete and sufficient manner.
- Unilateral request by one of the spouses, once three years or more have passed from the cessation of cohabitation, without any marital conciliation between the parties having occurred.
- Request by one party attributing a fault imputed to the other spouse, *'whenever it constitutes a serious violation of the duties and obligations that the marriage imposes on them, or of the duties and obligations towards the children, which makes life together intolerable'* (Article 54 of Law 19.947). This means that this is a subjective ground, because the sole infraction is not enough, one has to also take into consideration the personal consequences that this infraction has on the other spouse.

A peculiarity of the divorce trial is that the judge, in the first hearing, has to 'urge to the parties to reach an agreement' that will allow the parties to overcome their conflicts 'and to verify the intention of the parties to allow the conservation of the matrimonial bond as possible' (Article 67 Law 19.947). This rule that may seem curious is aimed at satisfying those legislators who strongly opposed the approval of the law of divorce, who insisted that divorce weakened the family and thus deemed this institution as unconstitutional. As a consequence it is seen as a duty of the state, represented by the judge, to urge the parties to maintain the marriage, as foundation of the family.

8. FINANCES/CAPITAL, PROPERTY

8.1 What powers does the court have to allocate financial resources and property on the breakdown of marriage?

One must distinguish between the economic or patrimonial aspects that can be discussed when the family rupture occurs. On one hand alimony rights exist, be they major (between adults) or minor (towards the minors of age), the term of the patrimonial regime of the marriage, and finally, the possibility of gaining access to an economic compensation.

With regard to alimony, we will refer in detail to this in the following section 9 and 10 below, hence we will refer in this section to the patrimonial regimes and economic compensation.

In Chile three marital property regimes exist related to marriage: separation of assets (entire or partial), marital partnership (supplementary regime) and participation in joint property.

In marital partnership, in a very general way, all the goods that are generated during the marriage enter into a community, which, at the end of the regime (that can be before, or independent of the divorce) will be divided into equal parts. The husband administers all the goods while the marital partnership stays in force, with a series of limitations that have been introduced to the legislation in order to reduce the discrimination that this regime meant towards women. Within the frame of this regime, the figure of the reserved patrimony of the married woman was created, consisting of those goods that are acquired by the married woman under the marital partnership regime with her professional savings (product of her remunerated work), which she can administer separately from the husband. When the marital partnership ends, she can choose to be awarded her own goods and to resign from the joint property of the marital partnership, or to contribute her goods to the marital partnership and gain access to 50 per cent of the joint property.

At present a series of modifications to this regime are being discussed in the Congress, basically to grant both husband and wife an equal right to the administration of their joint property.

In the joint property regime, the goods acquired during the marriage are administered as if they were the separate property of every spouse, and when this regime ends, the joint property is distributed in equal parts. For the purposes of this calculation the goods that the spouses had at the moment of the marriage must be considered, for which an inventory can be prepared jointly with the matrimonial capitulation.

Although theoretically this regime seemed to be the most suitable one, the legislative technique used in its implementation has caused this regime to be of very little use, due to the practical difficulties involved in its liquidation.

On the other hand, and independent from the existing marital property regime during the marriage, along with the establishment of the divorce in 2004, in Chile the legal institution of economic compensation was created.

The legal nature of the institution has been widely debated, being assigned with proper elements of support, others of compensation and others of unjust enrichment. Finally, the majority of the doctrine has preferred to understand that it is a unique and special legal institution, with elements of its own.

Article 61 of Law 19.947 establishes: *'If, as consequence of having devoted herself to the care of the children or to the labors proper of the common hearth, one of the spouses could not develop a gainful or lucrative occupation during the marriage, or it did it in a minor measure of what he or she could have and wanted, she or he will have the right to be compensated, when the divorce takes place or the nullity of the marriage is declared, for the impairment suffered by this cause'*. For this right to be born, the following requisites must be met copulatively:

(i) not having worked outside of the hearth or to have done it in a minor measure of what was wanted and desired;
(ii) that the aforementioned was a consequence of having devoted him or herself to the care of the children or housework; and
(iii) economic damage is produced as a consequence of the two previous factors.

It is relevant to point out that in Spanish the word 'damage' refers to a loss or reduction, which is to say that a person who had an expectation of generating economic resources which turned out to be frustrated by the family option has suffered economic damage.

During the parliamentary discussion, the difference that existed between this institution and a possible quest for patrimonial or economical equality between the parties at the end of the marriage was debated. The latter alternative was discarded.

The same law establishes – in Article 62 of the Civil Marriage Law – the elements that must be considered for the determination of the existence of the damage and the quantity of the compensation. For example; the patrimonial situation of both parties, good or bad faith, the state of health of the beneficiary spouse, etc.

Compensation can be established by mutual agreement by the spouses, or by judicial sentence.

If settled by judicial sentence, the amount and forms of payment must be established. And for the latter, the law sets forth that it can establish the following modalities: *'1. Delivery of a sum of money, actions or other assets. Concerning money, it can be paid in one or several readjustable installments, which to its regards the judge will settle guarantees for their payment. 2. Constitution of rights of usufruct, use and room, regarding assets that are of property of the debtor spouse. The constitution of these rights will not harm the creditors that the proprietary spouse had to the date of the constitution, nor will it affect any of the creditors that the beneficiary spouse could have in any time'*.

For the purposes of protecting timely fulfilment, when the payments are settled in installments, every quota will be considered as alimony. This means that there is personal coercion for compelling the debtor.

Although the establishment of economic compensation is an advance in the protection of the members of the family concerning the matrimonial rupture, the practice has shown that it has left out a series of family situations that deserve coverage and which are not framed within the hypotheses proposed at present by the law.

I cannot leave out the institution of family assets. It is concerned with the right that the non-proprietary spouse has to request that the building that serves as principal residence of the family, as well as the furniture within it, be covered by a special protection, which will prevent the proprietor of the building from being able to sell it or mortgage it without the assent of the other spouse. This institution is regulated in Articles 141 and following of the Civil Code.

This institution is also foreseen for the rights or actions that the spouses have in proprietary societies of a building that serves as principal residence.

8.2 Explain and illustrate with reference to recent cases the court's thinking on division of assets

In Chile, jurisprudence is only referential and does not generate any precedent.

In light of the above, instead of making punctual reference to certain judgments, it is better to allude to a jurisprudential tendency, which is that the amount of economic compensation has been increasing, and the criterion to qualify the grounds of origin have become more lax, especially privileging the principle of family law, which is the superior interest of the child and the protection of the most vulnerable spouse.

9. FINANCES/MAINTENANCE

9.1 Explain the operation of maintenance for spouses on an ongoing basis after the breakdown of marriage

The Civil Code establishes who holds the right to receive alimony. Between these holders, first of all, is the spouse (Article 321 of the Civil Code). But in order for the right to proceed, the support receiver must lack proper means of subsistence which would allow him or her to survive in a manner corresponding to his or her social position (Article 330 of the Civil Code), this is to say that he or she is in a condition of need.

This is the essential element at the time of regulating alimony between adults, this is to say between spouses, because the condition of need – in case of the adults – is not presumed, therefore it must be demonstrated.

Chilean society is, and has been, chauvinist, so in general, when dealing with a question of major alimony, it is the woman who sues the husband.

The granting of this alimony has become more restricted, probably because of the greater access of women to education and to the labour market, and also because of the concept of gender equality. In a very simplified way, we might point out that alimony is granted today in Chile, only and exclusively when the woman does not have the skills or the economic means to sustain herself, in accordance with her social level. The latter point is important, because in Chile the criterion is related more to a modest subsistence than to the maintenance of a certain social status. Certainly, the economic level of the husband is not necessarily a reference point when granting this major alimony.

9.2 Is it common for maintenance to be awarded?

The possibility of obtaining a sentence that settles alimony in favour of a spouse is going to be directly related to the training of the woman, number of children, age and patrimony.

Nevertheless, even in cases in which major alimony is settled, when doing a comparative analysis with countries like Canada or England, alimony amounts are usually low.

9.3 Explain and illustrate with reference to recent cases the court's thinking on maintenance

On the subject of conjugal support, Chilean courts have not limited themselves to the existence of current economic capacity as grounds to deny, or to limit major alimony, even considering the training or qualification that the support receiver has to obtain her own sustenance. On this matter a ruling of the Illustrious Court of Appeals of Santiago, dated 11 August, 2006, states (where pertinent): '*It has been duly proved in the species that the actor is not developing at present a profitable activity. Consequently, given that resources are being generated, the lady is holder of the alimony right ... it is still a pacific fact that the claimant is a forty four-year-old person of age to the date of this ruling, healthy, of profession publicist and who is enabled to exercise any profited activity, which leads us to sustain that the alimony that the defendant must pay her and in accordance with that set forth in article 330 of the Civil Code, is only owed in the measure that the means of subsistence of the support receiver does not allow her to survive in a manner corresponding to her social position. Therefore, considering that she has the certain possibility to carry out a stipendiary work, the alimony that will be regulated in her favor will only increase the alimony that was settled in cash in the first grade.*' (the emphasis is ours).

10. CHILD MAINTENANCE

10.1 On what basis is child maintenance calculated within the jurisdiction?

The alimony that is owed to the children has the greatest and best juridical protection within our legislation. This is because there are several securities that only exist regarding these alimony receivers. Namely:

(i) the obligation of the judge to settle provisional alimony with the only merit of the lawsuit presentation;
(ii) the capacity of the alimony payer to pay is presumed;
(iii) in case of insufficiency of the alimony payer, the grandparents must assume the obligation; and
(iv) the law settles a minimum that every alimony payer must pay in favour of an alimony sum. (Article 3 of Law 14.908)

For the purposes of determining the amount that the alimony payer must pay, it is necessary to refer to the parameters set forth in Article 323 of the Civil Code, which states: 'The support must enable the alimony receiver to modestly survive in a manner which corresponds to his or her social position'. The word 'modest' has been interpreted on many occasions as giving the alimony a welfare character. Nevertheless, when the rule considers the 'social position', the possibility has been opened to settle alimony in accordance with the lifestyle that the alimony receivers used to maintain.

On the other hand, the Law on Family Abandonment and Payment of Alimonies, number 14.908, establishes the greatest restriction that applies in Chile regarding alimony support. In its Article 7° it indicates that the court will not be able to settle as an alimony amount a sum or percentage that exceeds 50 per cent of the revenues of the alimony payer. This ceiling does not distinguish within the number of support receivers, so it is understood that between all of the alimony that a person owes, he or she will never be asked to pay a sum that exceeds 50 per cent of his or her revenues.

As for the manner of distributing to the alimony load, Chilean legislation establishes that if the parents are married under the regime of marital partnership, the maintenance of the children corresponds to the Marital Partnership. If the parents are married under separation of goods, each parent will have to contribute in a proportional manner to his or her economic capacity, and when establishing the amount of the support, the capacities and the domestic conditions of the parts shall be considered.

11. RECIPROCAL ENFORCEMENT OF FINANCIAL ORDERS

11.1 Summarise the position in your jurisdiction

The resolutions that settle alimonies, or those which approve transactions between the parties regarding this matter, have executory merit, with a special enforcement procedure regulated by Law 14.908.

There is also the possibility that the judge arranges that the payment of the support is guaranteed, on the part of the debtor, with a mortgage or pledge.

Finally, there is an obligation for the judge, when facing non-compliance with an alimony order, of imposing on the debtor, as a means of enforcement, arrest for up to 15 days. Upon this non-compliance continuance, a judge can impose a national restriction order and extend the arrest for up to 30 full days.

Other measures to obtain compliance with the support obligation, are the suspension of the driver's licence and ordering the retention of a possible tax return of the alimony payer once every year (Article 16 Law 14.908).

Finally, as sanction for the contumacious defaulter, the law establishes the possibility of decreeing the separation of goods of the spouses, authorising the woman married in marital partnership with exceptional faculties and authorising the departure from the country of minor children without the need for the assent of the alimony payer.

Regarding the payments that proceed because of economic compensation, they lack a special regime, unless the court has settled these payments in installments. In this case the installments will be considered to be alimony for the purposes of the securing of its payment.

In the international arena, Chile has signed the Convention on the Recovery Abroad of Maintenance of 20 June, 1956 and the Inter-American Convention on maintenance obligations of 15 July, 1989.

12. FINANCIAL RELIEF AFTER FOREIGN DIVORCE PROCEEDINGS

12.1 What powers are available to make orders following a foreign divorce?

As has been already indicated, foreign sentences of divorce are recognised in Chile only to the extent they do not infringe public order. If they fulfill the homologation requirements, they are fully enforceable in Chile.

The most specific rules that are applied in case of foreign resolutions that contain maintenance obligations or renderings between spouses, are contained in the Inter-American Convention on Maintenance Obligations, which in Chile has constitutional status. In its Article 11 it establishes the requirements that must be complied with by foreign orders in order for them to have extraterritorial efficacy. The great benefit of the application of the Convention is that the examination of the fulfillment of the requirements is done directly by the judge who must take the execution forward, thus avoiding the process of *exequatur* before the Supreme Court which governs the homologation of foreign judgments in general.

D. CHILDREN

13. CUSTODY/PARENTAL RESPONSIBILITY

13.1 Briefly explain the legal position in relation to custody/parental responsibility following the breakdown of a relationship or marriage

Until June 2013 (when this chapter was written), in Chile the personal care of the upbringing and education of the children has until now been a joint obligation of the parents, as established by Article 224 of the Civil Code. Nevertheless, 'if the parents live separately, the mother has the personal care of the children' as stated by Article 225 of the Civil Code.

The personal care of the children could be held by the father only in the event that the mother granted it to him voluntarily by means of a public deed or when established by a Family Court, 'when the interest of the son makes it indispensable, being it for maltreatment, oversight or another qualified cause'.

Chilean legislation did not allow shared custody; hence it could not be agreed upon voluntarily nor be established judicially.

Notwithstanding the above, the legislation guaranteed that the parent who did not live with the children had the right to maintain direct and regular contact with them, with the frequency and freedom that was most suitable for the children.

However, all of the above has become obsolete since June 2013, when Articles 225 and following of the Civil Code were modified. The following general changes were implemented:

- parents can agree to shared custody, and the court is able to settle for shared custody to be implemented;
- both parents are equally able to hold the personal care of the children in case of separation;
- the rule of supplementary attribution of personal care does not automatically correspond to the mother any more, but to the parent

who is coexisting *de facto* with the children.
(The legislative procedure can be verified at *www.bcn.cl*)

13.2 Briefly explain the legal position in relation to access/contact/ visitation following the breakdown of a relationship or marriage

The right of the non-resident parent to have contact with his or her children is not only legally, but also constitutionally protected, as Chile has ratified the International Convention of the Rights of the Children, and thus, must respect its contents (Article 9 number 3°).

Article 229 of the Civil Code refers to the right-duty to maintain a direct and regular relation between a non-resident parent and his or her children.

With this regulation, this relationship that used to be called a 'right of visitations' is now called 'communicational regime'. The change in the wording of the rule and denomination was intended for this relationship to be understood not as something exceptional, but instead as a way of incorporating the concept of co-parenthood.

Although it has been a gradual process, Chilean jurisprudence today recognises in a better way and to a greater extent the importance of promoting an ongoing bond between children and a non-resident parent.

14 INTERNATIONAL ABDUCTION

14.1 Briefly summarise the position in your jurisdiction

This topic appears less frequently in Chile than in many other countries due in large part to the existence of Article 49 of the Law 16.618. which states that a minor's departure from Chile to move abroad must be expressly authorised by both parents in a private deed executed by a notary public.

Therefore, the circumstances under which an international abduction might take place are that once the departure abroad has been authorised and certain conditions put in place, the parent who has gone abroad in the company of the minor does not comply with returning the child in the agreed manner.

In the latter case one must distinguish between the parent who has care of the child (ie, residence) and the one who only has contact with that child. When the parent who keeps the child abroad is the mother (who in Chile is generally the parent with care in whose favour a residence order has been made), this is not treated as an abduction but instead as a serious non-compliance with the contact regime. If, on the contrary, the parent who is keeping the child abroad does not hold the personal care of the child, that is the commission of a criminal offence.

15. LEAVE TO REMOVE/APPLICATIONS TO TAKE A CHILD OUT OF THE JURISDICTION

15.1 Summarise the position in your jurisdiction

15.2 Under what circumstances may a parent apply to remove their child from the jurisdiction against the wishes of the other parent?

As has been already indicated, in Chile both parents must authorise the departure of children from the country, by express disposition of the law.

The same applies when a parent who must authorise that departure is not able to do so, or when, without justification, he or she refuses to do so. In this case, authorisation to travel can be granted by the family judge who has the authority to determine where the minor should reside.

For the purposes of granting or denying the authorisation, the judge will take into consideration the benefit that the trip will have for the minor, and will indicate the period of time for which the authorisation is granted.

A major issue is that the law indicates that when the minor does not return to the country within the established time frame and without a legitimate reason 'the judge will be able to decree the suspension of the alimonies that have been decreed', without taking into consideration the most serious issue which is the minor's relationship with the parent who has been 'left behind' in Chile.

When dealing with a definitive change of place of residence, the law does not indicate different criteria, thus the general rules and principles of family procedure become applicable, as set forth in Articles 9° and following of Law 19.968 International Conventions. This lack of objective criteria implies that in practice the likelihood of obtaining permission to remove a minor from Chile will depend on the requirements imposed by the judge who hears the case.

E. SURROGACY AND ADOPTION

16. VALIDITY OF SURROGACY AGREEMENTS

16.1 Briefly summarise the position in your jurisdiction

In Chile there is no legal regulation of surrogacy, and hence there is no definition of surrogacy in Chilean law.

Using the concept of a surrogacy agreement set out by the Supreme Court of New York, ie, 'agreements in which a surrogate mother promises to be implanted by the fertilized ovum of another woman or inseminated artificially, and she promises to give her assent to the adoption of the child born as a result of the implantation or the insemination', the situation in Chile might be summarised in the following manner:

Specific regulatory framework

In Chile, surrogacy is not governed by any regulatory body.

Rules of filiation

The Chilean Civil Code, in its Article 183, states that, it is the fact of childbirth that determines maternity, without distinguishing between who contributed a child's genetic material and who gave birth to that child. The mother of a child is the woman who gives birth to that child.

Validity and enforceability of the contract

As for the legitimacy of contracts for leasing a womb, although they are not prohibited by Chilean legislation, they are not regulated by any disposition, either in the Civil Code, the Sanitary Code, or in law 19.451 on organ transplants.

The national doctrine refers to the topic, for example in the Agreement of

Civil Rights: Preliminary and General Parts, of professors Arturo Alessandri R., Antonio Vodanovic H, y Manuel Somarriva U., as a way to illustrate the situation of unnamed contracts. Concerning the substance of the matter, the opinion of the majority is that a contract of this nature adversely affects the National Public Order and thus suffers from illicit object.

Article 182 of the Civil Chilean Code, addresses the legal status of children conceived by means of the use of Assisted Reproduction (AR) techniques, but clarifies: '*the father and the mother of the child conceived by means of the application of human assisted reproduction techniques are the man and the woman that were submitted to them*' excluding the participation of a third party.

Therefore, in accordance with prevailing regulations, those who enter into surrogacy agreements, are absolutely unprotected and have no ability in law to assert parental rights with regard to any children conceived with a surrogate.

17. ADOPTION

17.1 Briefly explain the legal position in relation to adoption in your jurisdiction. Is adoption available to individuals, cohabiting couples (both heterosexual and same-sex)?

Adoption is fully recognised in Chilean legislation and protected by the Civil Code and special rules, such as Law 19.620. Chile has also ratified the Inter-American Convention on Conflicts of Laws on the subject of minors' adoption and the Convention on Protection of the Child and cooperation on the subject of international adoption.

Articles 20 and following of law 19.620 state who is authorised to adopt. An absolute priority exists for married couples, be they Chilean or foreign. Only in the event that 'there are no interested spouses to adopt a minor', 'a single, divorced person or widow' will be able to become an adoptive parent.

In Chile there is no regulation whatsoever of either co-habiting nor *de facto* unions of homosexuals, so the situation in which a homosexual couple would want to adopt is not contemplated in the law.

F. COHABITATION

18. COHABITATION

18.1 What legislation (if any) governs division of property for unmarried couples on the breakdown of the relationship?

De facto unions are not regulated in our legislation within the framework of family law. Some references to cohabitation exist in special rules, such as the Law of Intrafamiliar Violence, the Regulation on Residential Subsidies, etc. But organic regulation does not exist in relation to this matter.

At present a project of law exists called 'Agreement of Life in Couple' which seeks to regulate the patrimonial relationship of those are *de facto* cohabitants, be they heterosexual or homosexual; nevertheless it has not yet been approved.

Faced with the factual situation of cohabitation or concubinage, in which a community of assets exists, the courts have resolved the matter by applying civil rules of the *de facto* society or community.

G. FAMILY DISPUTE RESOLUTION

19. MEDIATION, COLLABORATIVE LAW AND ARBITRATION

19.1 Briefly summarise the non-court-based processes available in your jurisdiction and the current status of agreements reached under the auspices of mediation, collaborative law and arbitration

19.2 What is the statutory basis (if any), for mediation, collaborative law and arbitration in your jurisdiction? In particular, are the parties required to attempt a family dispute resolution in advance of the institution of proceedings?

Since the creation of the Family Courts in 2004, family mediation has also become institutionalised. Shortly after the law establishing the Family Courts came into effect, it was imposed as an obligatory step prior to the majority of actions being heard by the Family Courts.

At present, Articles 103 and following of Law 19.968 refer to family mediation.

For the purposes of bringing a legal action in relation to personal care, maintenance and/or a contact regime, the parties must previously submit to a process of mediation. Attendance at mediation can be directly requested by the parties, or ordered by the Family Courts. Only once this process has failed can the parties resort to the Courts of Justice and ask them to intervene.

The agreements that are adopted in the process of mediation have the same value as a court order as long as the Family Court that has jurisdiction is made aware of the existence of the agreement.

Even when the conflict has become a matter for the courts, the principle of collaboration is legally consecrated, as demonstrated by Article 14 of the Law 19.968: '*Collaboration. During the procedure and in the resolution of the conflict, alternatives will be sought in order to mitigate the confrontation between the parties, privileging the solutions agreed by them.*'

It is worth mentioning the existence of technical advisers to the courts, who are generally psychologists and/or social workers who collaborate with the judge in the course of any family proceedings. Although their legal role is focused on advising the judge in respect of matters within their knowledge, in practice, they often operate as mediators or conciliators, trying to obtain agreements between the parties before they come before a judge.

As for arbitration, Chile does not designate arbitrators for the resolution of disputes in relation to family matters. The only matter linked to family law that requires arbitration is the liquidation of the community property that remains at the end of the marital partnership.

H. OTHER

20. CIVIL PARTNERSHIP/SAME-SEX MARRIAGE

20.1 What is the status of civil partnership/same-sex marriage within the jurisdiction?

20.2 What legislation governs civil partnership/same sex marriage?

In Chile there is no legal regulation of *de facto* cohabitation for either heterosexuals or homosexuals.

Cohabitation or concubinage are mentioned in family law in different circumstances, which means that they are recognised in some form, but no rights are established for cohabitants as a result.

Homosexual marriage does not exist in Chile, and homosexual marriages entered into abroad are not recognised in Chile, because the definition of the matrimonial contract is that it is between a man and a woman, hence, same-sex marriages do not fulfil the legal requirements to be recognised in Chile.

At present a project of law exists in the Congress to give legal recognition to *de facto* unions or cohabitations, named AVP. Its advances can be checked on *www.bcn.cl.*

21. CONTROVERSIAL AREAS/RAPIDLY DEVELOPING AREAS OF LAW

21.1 Is there a particular area of the law within the jurisdiction that is currently undergoing major change?

At present in Chile there is a great deal of discussion and controversy in relation to many matters inherent in family law. We are in an historical moment in which family institutions that have been deeply rooted in our society for many years are being revised.

Modifications to the Civil Code with reference to the care of the children have just been approved (June 2013). This currently means a radical change to the last 100 years of law, in which the mother was automatically entitled to have care of the children following the breakdown of the marriage. It also recognises for the first time in Chile the possibility of shared custody, and gives priority to it.

On the other hand, there is also discussion regarding legislation concerning the recognition and regulation of *de facto* cohabitation, including between people of the same sex, consecrating the so-called 'agreement of life in couple', and introducing legislation in relation to homosexual relationships for the first time.

Another regulation that is being discussed and that will result in great changes, is the modification to the patrimonial regime of the marital partnership.

Finally, and at the request of UNICEF and aiming to fulfill international standards, the creation of an organic body that concentrates all regulation concerning infancy and adolescence is being discussed.

21.2 Which areas of law are most out-of-step? Which areas would you most like to see reformed/changed

Although the rules on care and custody of minor children are being reformed in order to make them more egalitarian between both parents and to favour co-parenting/shared care, there is a well founded fear that the wording of the rules, or the legislative technique to be used could result in the increased involvement of the courts within family conflicts.

As for matters which it is necessary to reform and to improve, clearly the rules on the subject of compliance with maintenance obligations must be mentioned, given that at present they are time consuming with a high percentage of evaders.

Finally, there is an ongoing debate as to the rights that children and adolescents have to be heard during court proceedings. Although they have the right to be heard during trial, there is no specialist legal support for them in the court process and it is highly advisable that a minors' public defender office be established.

Denmark

Nyborg & Rørdam Maryla Rytter Wróblewski

A. JURISDICTION AND CONFLICT OF LAW

1. SOURCES OF LAW

1.1 What is the primary source of law in relation to the breakdown of marriage and the welfare of children within the jurisdiction?

1.2 What are the main statutes governing matrimonial law in the jurisdiction?

The primary sources of law in relation to the breakdown of marriage are:

- The Formation and Dissolution of Marriage Act *(Ægteskabsloven),*
- The Legal Effects of Marriage Act (*Retsvirkningsloven*),
- Act on Division of Matrimonial Property (*Ægtefælleskifteloven*)
- Act on Registered Partnership (*Lov om registrerede parforhold*) (allow same-sex couples to form a registered civil partnership).

EC council regulation no. 4/2009 is applicable in Denmark. The rest of the EC regulations dealing with family law are not applicable.

Denmark has ratified a number of international conventions dealing with the international aspects of family law and the 1970 Hague Convention on Divorce, the 1958 Hague Convention on Maintenance for Children and the 1973 Hague Convention on Maintenance Obligations.

In the area of the welfare of children the Act on Parental Responsibility (*Forældreansvarsloven*) is the primary source of law. As a large part of cases dealing with children is not dealt with in court but by administrative authorities, there are also administrative guidelines about the subject.

Denmark has ratified the existing international instruments about child abduction, namely the 1980 Hague Convention and the 1980 European Council Convention.

Denmark has also ratified the 1996 Hague Convention on Protection of Children.

2. JURISDICTION

2.1 What are the main jurisdictional requirements for the institution of proceedings in relation to divorce, property and children?

In Denmark issues of property division and issues of children are not dealt with within the divorce case – but in separate processes. There is also a separate process for determining the size of a spousal maintenance.

The divorce and the length of a possible spousal maintenance obligation are dealt with in the courts if the spouses cannot agree. The courts have jurisdiction in relation to divorce under article 448C and The Danish Administration of Justice Act (*Retsplejeloven*) on the following grounds:

(i) the respondent has his/her domicile in Denmark;
(ii) the petitioner has his/her domicile in Denmark and has had this Danish domicile for the past two years or for a longer period before;
(iii) the petitioner is a Danish subject and it is proven that because of this citizenship he/she cannot file for divorce where he/she resides;
(iv) the petitioner and the respondent are both Danish subjects and the respondent does not oppose that the divorce is handled in Denmark;
(v) the petitioner and respondent have obtained a legal separation from Danish authorities within the past five years.

These are the rules that apply to international jurisdiction in general. When it comes to Nordic subjects there is a Nordic convention that applies and which sets up jurisdictional grounds that are identical with the grounds found in EU regulation no. 2201/2003.

Division of property is dealt with in the Probate Court (*Skifteretten*). The court's international jurisdiction to hear claims about property division is regulated in Sections 4 and 5 of the Act on Division of Matrimonial Property (*Ægtefælleskifteloven*) on the following grounds:

- if the petitioner or the respondent has his/her residence in Denmark;
- if either the petitioner or the respondent has a connection with Denmark the parties can agree on Danish jurisdiction when the dispute arises.

Finally, there is jurisdiction to handle assets situated in Denmark if they are not included in a property division handled outside Denmark.

Children's jurisdiction is governed by the 1996 Hague Convention in relation to countries that are parties to the 1996 Hague Convention. According to Articles 5-14 of the 1996 Hague Convention, jurisdiction can be based on grounds mostly relating to the habitual residence of the child.

There is a possibility within the Convention for a court in one state to invite a court in another state to take jurisdiction if they find that this other state is in a better position to consider the child's best interest, ref. articles 8 and 9.

The 1996 Hague Convention entered into force in Denmark on 1 November 2011 and applies to cases started after that date.

In relation to other countries Section 448 f of the Administration of Justice Act (*Retsplejeloven*) governs jurisdiction for cases relating to children in a way that is very similar to the 1996 Hague Convention – as the following jurisdictional grounds are accepted:

(i) the child has his/her habitual residence in Denmark;
(ii) the child is wrongfully removed or retained in another country and the child had his/her habitual residence in Denmark just before the wrongful removal or retention;
(iii) the child is exiled from his/her home country due to disturbances and the child is present in Denmark;
(iv) the child is present in Denmark and the child's habitual residence is not known;
(v) the child is present in Denmark and the case is so urgent that it is not possible to wait for a decision from the country of the child's habitual residence.

Number (ii) does not apply if more than one year has passed since the parent with parental rights was aware of where the child is, and that parent has not asked for the child's return within that one year and the child is now adjusted to that new country.

Numbers (i) and (iv) do not apply if the habitual residence is based on a wrongful removal or retention, unless the habitual residence has been in place for more than one year and the parent left behind has not asked for the child's return within that one year, or unless the parent left behind has asked for a return but the application has been rejected.

3. DOMICILE AND HABITUAL RESIDENCE

3.1 Explain the concepts of domicile and habitual residence as they apply to the jurisdiction in relation to divorce, the finances and children

In Danish law texts there is no distinction when reference is made to simple residence, habitual residence or domicile. Regardless of which concept is to be used the law only refers to the 'residence'. Hence one needs to consult preparatory documents or case law to find out whether the specific use of the term 'residence' in a particular law refers to the concept of simple residence, habitual residence or domicile.

Having said that, so far case law indicates that there is only one concept of simple residence, one concept of habitual residence, and one concept of domicile. In other words the concept does not change its meaning/content depending on whether it relates to divorce, the finances and children.

In Denmark all people register at a central register where they live. This applies regardless of the nationality of the person. When a person moves he/she has to change the registration to the new address within a limited period of time. If this is not done in time the person can be fined. This obligation to register means that the registration is often taken as important evidence when proof is needed about where a person had his/ her residence, habitual residence or domicile.

However, the mere fact that a person has registered at an address in Denmark is not enough to prove habitual residence or domicile. This being said it can often be concluded that a person has his/her simple residence in Denmark if he/she is registered here. This is because the concept of the simple residence is the place a person lives. In most situations it is solely a factual concept (there are exceptions for diplomats working temporarily abroad that keep their Danish residence). A person can have more than one residence in different countries at the same time.

Habitual residence is mostly used in Danish family law in relation to children. The leading judgment about the concept is a Supreme Court judgment from 2007 (ref. U.2007.1205H) regarding an application for return under the 1980 Hague Convention. In that case the parents had entered into a written agreement in February 2004 that their four-year-old daughter should reside in Denmark with her mother until 1 May 2005 when they would return to Australia. When the agreement expired the mother refused to return the daughter to Australia. The Supreme Court ruled that the girl should be returned as the habitual residence had not changed from Australia to Denmark during the stay here. The conclusion based on this judgment is that Denmark has chosen an approach to the concept of habitual residence where it includes subjective elements or a reference to the parent's intentions.

Under Danish law a person has his/her domicile where that person resides with the intention of staying there. If a person changes his/her residence but only with the intention of staying there for a limited period of time then the domicile is not changed. A person can only have one domicile. There is case law to support the interpretation that a person cannot be without a domicile. The concept seems to put a lot of emphasis on subjective factors, however, objective elements need to support the intention described. Hence if a stay abroad (and away from the original domicile) is very long the domicile will change regardless of the person's intentions. There is no time limit but a guideline would be that a stay abroad for more than two years indicates a change of domicile. However, if the stay abroad includes moves between different countries there might not be such an indication.

4. CONFLICT OF LAW/APPLICABLE LAW

4.1 What happens when one party applies to stay proceedings in favour of a foreign jurisdiction? What factors will the local court take into account when determining forum issues?

Danish courts generally apply the principle of *lis pendens*, meaning that the jurisdiction in which the proceedings were commenced first has priority to deal with the proceedings and those started second are halted. The principle is applied as a general principle, but in some areas, for instance in cases about maintenance, the EC regulation 4/2009 forms the basis. In cases of separation or divorce there will often also be a reference to Article 12 of 1970 Hague Convention on divorce about the application of the principle of *lis pendens*.

Danish courts do not apply principles of forum convenience.

B. PRE- AND POST-NUPTIAL AGREEMENTS

5. VALIDITY OF PRE- AND POST-NUPTIAL AGREEMENTS

5.1 To what extent are pre- and post-nuptial agreements binding within the jurisdiction? Could you provide a brief discussion of the most significant recent case law on this issue?

Pre-nuptial as well as post-nuptial agreements are legally binding in Denmark if they meet the requirements stipulated by law. The agreements have to be in writing and signed by both spouses. The agreement also needs to be submitted to the court for registration in order to be valid.

In Denmark it is possible for spouses to contract in pre- or post-nuptial agreements for different property regimes, ie, separate property in different forms. It is also possible for the spouses to make agreements that provide that pension rights are divided upon divorce (which they are not as a general rule under the default regime).

It is not possible for spouses to make binding agreements about spousal maintenance obligations or lump sum compensations. This principle applies regardless of whether the agreement on spousal maintenance or compensation would provide better for the weaker spouse than the law. However, agreements based on regulation no. 4/2009 can be included in a pre- or post-nuptial agreement and can be registered.

Under Danish law pre- and post-nuptial agreement cannot specify a particular foreign law to be applied to the division of property However, an exception probably applies when the property regime of a couple is governed by foreign law according to Danish private international law rules on choice of law. In that situation if a choice of foreign law is valid under the foreign law that governs the regime, then the choice made is probably accepted by Danish courts although Danish substantial law would not allow that choice.

The Danish choice of law rule is that the property regime is determined by the law of the state where the husband had his domicile when the marriage was entered into. However if the husband changes his domicile in connection with the marriage then the law of the state of the first communal domicile of the spouses will be applied.

There is case law where the validity of pre- and post-nuptials is challenged based on principles of contract law. So far the courts have been very reluctant to declare nuptials to be not binding – and they have for instance not required in general that the parties have obtained independent legal advice or for full disclosure to have been made. However, if the agreement is made as a post-nuptial agreement at a time where one or both spouses is aware that there is a real risk that the marriage is breaking down, the courts tend to demand more proof that the consequences of such nuptial are understood by the spouse that is giving up property rights under the agreement.

C. DIVORCE, NULLITY AND JUDICIAL SEPARATION

6. RECOGNITION OF FOREIGN MARRIAGES/DIVORCES

6.1 Summarise the position in your jurisdiction

Danish law recognises a marriage entered into abroad if it complies with the formalities of the country in which it was entered into.

If a marriage is properly conducted then it will usually be recognised in Denmark. This includes religious marriages, even if the equivalent Danish religious authority does not have the right to conduct marriages.

When a person resides in Denmark that person can register his/her foreign marriage with Danish authorities. If there are doubts about the validity of the foreign marriage the Division of Family Affairs at the National Social Appeals Board can be asked for advice/its opinion.

Denmark does not permit polygamous marriages. Marrying a second person without dissolving a previous marriage constitutes bigamy which is a criminal offence.

Denmark is a party to the 1973 Hague Convention but also recognises divorce ordered abroad in most circumstances. However Danish law will not necessarily accept the financial terms, if there was Danish jurisdiction for divorce when the application was handed in.

7. DIVORCE

7.1 Explain the grounds for divorce within the jurisdiction (please also deal with nullity and judicial separation if appropriate)

Both parties are entitled to legal separation regardless of the position of the other party. A legal separation is a suspension of the marriage. The separation suspends all rights of inheritance and any obligation to maintain the other spouse. If the parties start to cohabit after a legal separation (but before a divorce) the separation terminates and the parties continue their marriage.

After half a year of legal separation the spouses can obtain a divorce if they are in agreement. If one spouse opposes, the other spouse is entitled to a divorce after one year of legal separation.

Direct divorce is available only in the following situations:

- adultery;
- severe violence against the spouse or his/her children;
- bigamy;
- child abduction out of Denmark; or
- the spouses have been living apart for two years due to disagreements.

When it comes to adultery, violence, bigamy and child abduction it is only the party who is the 'victim' who can apply. With regard to adultery and child abduction the application has to be handed in within certain time limits.

8. FINANCES/CAPITAL, PROPERTY

8.1 What powers does the court have to allocate financial resources and property on the breakdown of marriage?

The court dealing with the separation/divorce can only make orders about the length of spousal maintenance and only when applied for. Orders about the size of the obligation are made by the State Administration also upon application. The standard rule for calculating the size of the spousal maintenance is one-fifth of the difference of the income of the payor and the payee. However, there is a ceiling for the income of the payee of 270,000-310,000 DDK per year. If the income of the payee including the maintenance calculated as explained above exceeds this ceiling the maintenance obligation is reduced.

According to case law Danish authorities always apply Danish law when dealing with maintenance issues.

The power to allocate property on the breakdown of marriage lies with the probate court. The probate court is competent both to divide marital property and to decide that compensation (a lump sum payment) shall be paid if the spouses have separate property.

The choice of law rule regarding property is described above. The choice of law regarding compensation is probably Danish law.

8.2 Explain and illustrate with reference to recent cases the court's thinking on division of assets

On divorce the value of the marital property is divided equally between the spouses. Any property that is separate property is not included when the division is made.

The starting point in Danish law is that all property is marital property, regardless of whether the asset was acquired before or after the marriage. However, pension rights are treated according to special rules and are as a general rule not divided. Also spouses can have separate property that applies in whole or in part to the assets of the parties jointly. Separate property can be created according to:

- a pre- or postnuptial agreement;
- a deed of gift, where the donor has specified that the gift should be the separate property of the beneficiary;
- a last will, where the testator has specified that the inheritance shall be the separate property of the heir.

There is very little case law on asset division as until 2012 this was mainly dealt with privately. This was due to the fact that until 2012 the fees for the courts for handling an asset division case were very high and the process was very inefficient.

Since March 2012 the court has had the power to appoint (upon application) an independent property division executor to carry out the asset division. The executors are all lawyers. The task of the executor is to make an inventory of the assets (based on his/her legal judgment) and assist the spouses with practical issues.

The new system is much more efficient and less expensive. However, this has not greatly increased court rulings in relation to the division of assets as the executor is also in a position to suggest compromise solutions to the spouses.

Most existing case law concerns situations where separate property or money has been invested in an asset that are included in the the community of property. It is difficult to say anything general about the results in these cases.

9. FINANCES/MAINTENANCE

9.1 Explain the operation of maintenance for spouses on an on-going basis after the breakdown of marriage

Whether there shall be a right to spousal maintenance after the breakdown of a marriage and for how long that obligation shall continue needs to be agreed/decided upon. If the parties reach an agreement no authority checks will be needed if the agreement is in accordance with case law. In the absence of an agreement a decision is made by the court. The parties cannot obtain a legal separation or divorce if there is no agreement or decision on the length of a possible spousal maintenance right/obligation.

An obligation that is limited in time has a maximum duration of 10 years. In this regard case law is often divided into two categories: One category of short obligations of up to five years (in practise mostly one, two or three years) and one category of long obligations of eight or 10 years.

The court can also set up an obligation that maintenance is for the joint lives of the parties). However, such obligations are only set up if the marriage has lasted more than 20 years (although in practice today the criterion is more like 25 years of marriage).

9.2 Is it common for maintenance to be awarded?

Short obligations are not uncommon – but long obligations are very rare. This is because maintenance obligations are only set up if the weaker spouse has a no ability to create an income of her/his own and cannot be expected to obtain such an ability in the period where the maintenance is to be paid.

9.3 Explain and illustrate with reference to recent cases the court's thinking on maintenance

The criteria considered when deciding maintenance is:

- ability to pay by the payor;
- lack of ability to create income of his/her own by the payee;
- the length of the marriage.

Within the last few years a further criterion has been developed, namely that the lack of ability to work needs to be due to the marriage. The criterion is sometimes referred to as 'co-habitation damage'. This means that maintenance is mainly awarded if one party due to family life has given up working. This can be as a result of childcare commitments or because they had followed their spouse abroad for work. If one party is working part-time and can provide for his/herself than it is unlikely that they will be able to successfully claim maintenance. The mere fact that the weaker party cannot support herself/himself at the same standard that the parties had enjoyed during the marriage does not give grounds for maintenance.

10. CHILD MAINTENANCE

10.1 On what basis is child maintenance calculated within the jurisdiction?

If the child spends a maximum of five days out of 14 days with the non-resident parent child maintenance is calculated solely based on the income of the non-resident parent and the number of minor children that the resident parent is supporting. Decisions are taken by the State Administration who calculate the support based on standard rates.

Danish authorities always use Danish law regarding child support. The minimum child support is 1,104 DDK per month – or 13,248 DDK per year. If there is only one child the non-resident parent pays four times the minimum if he/she earns more than 1,200,000 DDK. It is possible to make orders for five times the minimum. There are no examples of orders above five times the minimum regardless of the income of the non-resident parent.

11. RECIPROCAL ENFORCEMENT OF FINANCIAL ORDERS

11.1 Summarise the position in your jurisdiction

Denmark only enforces financial orders when obliged by either EU regulation or international convention.

EU regulation 4/2009 applies in Denmark. Therefore all orders about maintenance (in the EU sense of the word) are enforced based on this regulation.

Denmark has ratified the 1958 Hague Convention on Child support and the 1973 Hague Convention on maintenance obligations. Hence maintenance orders from states party to these conventions are also enforced.

Denmark has no international system of enforcement of financial orders from states that with no convention base. This also applies to orders on division of assets.

12. FINANCIAL RELIEF AFTER FOREIGN DIVORCE PROCEEDINGS

12.1 What powers are available to make orders following a foreign divorce?

There are no general powers for Danish courts to make financial orders following a foreign divorce.

However, if a foreign divorce has been obtained but there has been no order for the division of assets, and there is Danish jurisdiction to deal with the matter, the Danish probate court can divide the assets. This is, however, not a specific power to deal with overseas matters – it is simply a consequence of the fact that the processes are not interlinked in Denmark.

It might be possible based on regulation 4/2009 to commence a standalone application in relation to spousal maintenance if the question has not been dealt with in the separation/divorce case. The question is currently being considered by the Appeal Court.

Jurisdiction for child support is regulated by regulation 4/2009 and is always a standalone process under Danish law.

D. CHILDREN

13. CUSTODY/PARENTAL RESPONSIBILITY

13.1 Briefly explain the legal position in relation to custody/parental responsibility following the breakdown of a relationship or marriage

Upon divorce in Denmark, parents will have joint custody of a child/ children. Decisions regarding custody or residence is always dealt with in separate proceedings and only if specifically requested by one or both parents.

The court can decide that the parents shall remain having joint custody – and make a decision about the residence of the child accordingly. Sole custody is only awarded if that is considered to be in the best interest of the child.

All cases about custody and residence start as an application to the State Administration. The matter can only proceed to court upon application if the parents cannot agree about residence or custody.

The State Administration can make temporary orders for custody and residence if necessary but not final orders. Final orders can only be made by the courts.

13.2 Briefly explain the legal position in relation to access/contact/ visitation following the breakdown of a relationship or marriage

The jurisdiction to set up contact orders lies with the State Administration. A normal visitation schedule for a child above three years is a so called 9/5 arrangement – meaning nine days out of 14 with the resident parent (and five days with the contact parent). The State Administration can also set up less contact or more contact. The latter up to a so-called 7/7 arrangement.

Holidays are usually split 50-50. It is difficult to obtain a different split even if the contact parent lives abroad and therefore has less everyday/ weekend contact.

14. INTERNATIONAL ABDUCTION

14.1 Briefly summarise the position in your jurisdiction

Denmark has ratified both the 1980 Hague Convention on the Civil Aspects on Child Abductions and the 1980 European Council Convention on Recognition and Enforcement of Decisions Concerning Custody of Children. With regard to the latter, Denmark has reserved the right, in cases covered by Articles 8 and 9, to refuse recognition and enforcement of decisions relating to custody on the grounds provided under Article 10. Both conventions are implemented in Danish law in the Act on Child Abduction (*Børnebortførelsesloven*)

The Ministry of Social Affairs and Integration is the Central Authority for both conventions.

In the Danish courts cases regarding abduction are dealt with in the enforcement court in the local area where the child is being retained. The Danish central authority will, when they receive an application from foreign central authority, send the application to the local court. However, it is the parent left behind – not the Central Authority – who will act as the applicant at the return hearing in court.

The parent left behind is entitled to legal aid without having to fulfil the normal financial criteria. If the left behind parent has not chosen a lawyer himself/herself the court will appoint a lawyer. There is a list created by the Ministry of Justice of 19 lawyers practicing in different areas of Denmark who have been appointed as experienced in abductions cases.

The time frame for an abduction case in the first instance is about two to six months depending on the circumstances of the case. In the first instance there will normally be a hearing where both parents are expected to give evidence.

The time frame for an appeal is about two to three months. A hearing on appeal is only granted upon application if the appeal court finds it necessary. This is very seldom.

The issues discussed in court today in abduction cases are:

(i) the 'habitual residence' of the child and
(ii) the 'grave risk defence'.

With regard to the first issue the Supreme Court found in 2007 that habitual residence of a child had not changed to Denmark despite a residence of one year and three months in Denmark with the Danish mother, because the parents had agreed in writing before the mother and the child left Australia that the child would return after that period, ref. U.2007.1205H. This judgment has since been used to show that the Danish approach to habitual residence is not merely objective but includes the intentions of the parents as well.

With regard to the grave risk defence, this is often raised but seldom leads to non-return orders being made. However, with small children abducted by the primary caretaker it is difficult to predict what the court will decide.

If a child has been abducted from a non-convention country there is no legal basis for ordering a return. Therefore, the legal steps are firstly to 'create' jurisdiction for a custody/leave to remove case and then to pursue a return based on an evaluation of the 'child's best interest' in that case. Unfortunately this can be a rather long process.

15. LEAVE TO REMOVE/APPLICATIONS TO TAKE A CHILD OUT OF THE JURISDICTION

15.1 Summarise the position in your jurisdiction

Since 2007 the law in Denmark has provided for shared parental responsibility regardless of whether one party argues against it. Since that time it is possible for the courts to make decisions on 'leave to remove' in cases where the parents share parental responsibility. Before that time an application to remove the child from Denmark would necessarily involve claims for sole custody.

15.2 Under what circumstances may a parent apply to remove their child from the jurisdiction against the wishes of the other parent?

A parent can always apply for an order to remove the child. An order is only granted if it is considered to be in the child's best interest. In that test it is an important factor if a continued residence in Denmark provides the possibility for 'normal' contact with the other parent. In such cases it can be difficult to move children aged between three and eight, provided there is normal contact with the parent that intends to stay in Denmark. This applies even if the grounds for the move are acceptable, ie, a foreign parent wanting to move back home due to difficult integration or lack of network in Denmark.

With older children their own opinions are important for the result of the proceedings.

E. SURROGACY AND ADOPTION

16. VALIDITY OF SURROGACY AGREEMENTS

16.1 Briefly summarise the position in your jurisdiction

Agreements about surrogacy are not valid and cannot be enforced under Danish law. However, it is possible after the birth of a child for the biological mother (that gives birth to the child) to transfer custodial rights to the receiving couple by agreement that is binding, provided the child has also been handed over. Also if the biological mother gives agrees to an adoption that agreement is binding provided there is basis for adoption.

17. ADOPTION

17.1 Briefly explain the legal position in relation to adoption in your jurisdiction. Is adoption available to individuals, cohabiting couples (both heterosexual and same-sex)?

Adoption of a child that you do not know beforehand is only available for married couples or individuals. Neither cohabiting persons nor registered partners can adopt together. Adoption is only possible if the parents have been approved as adoptive parents by the Danish Authorities.

The general requirements for approval are:

- the age difference between child and applicant must not exceed 40 years;
- the adoptive parents should as a minimum have lived together for two-and-a-half years and they must be married at the time of approval;
- the adoptive parents' physical and mental health must not be such that it could have a negative influence on the child's situation;
- the adoptive parents must have adequate housing;
- the adoptive parents' financial situation must be adequate;
- the adoptive parents must not be convicted of any offences that may raise doubts as to whether they are suitable adopters.

There are special rules for adoption of relatives, for example adopting the child of your spouse. In those situations no official approval is necessary.

Registered partners can adopt children of their partner if the child is conceived based on artificial insemination and that happened while the partners were living together.

F. COHABITATION

18. COHABITATION

18.1 What legislation (if any) governs division of property for unmarried couples on the breakdown of the relationship?

There is no legislation governing division of property for unmarried couples on the breakdown of the relationship. There are court procedures that can result in compensation being granted, but it is difficult to obtain such compensation.

G. FAMILY DISPUTE RESOLUTION

19. MEDIATION, COLLABORATIVE LAW AND ARBITRATION

19.1 Briefly summarise the non-court-based processes available in your jurisdiction and the current status of agreements reached under the auspices of mediation, collaborative law and arbitration

So far there are not many non-court-based processes available.

Under Danish law parties can in any kind of agreement include a clause of enforceability – with reference to the Danish Civil Procedure Act. Such a clause has the effect that the agreement (to the extent it is precise enough) can be enforced in the enforcement court without obtaining a judgment. If this clause is included in an agreement reached by mediation, collaborative law or arbitration it is enforceable.

19.2 What is the statutory basis (if any), for mediation, collaborative law and arbitration in your jurisdiction? In particular, are the parties required to attempt a family dispute resolution in advance of the institution of proceedings?

Parties are not required to try family dispute resolution – but all cases regarding divorce and children start in the State Administration and start with an information meeting. Depending on the parties and the caseworker at the meeting, the meeting can have a format that looks a bit like mediation – but it is not always so.

H. OTHER

20. CIVIL PARTNERSHIP/SAME-SEX MARRIAGE

20.1 What is the status of civil partnership/same-sex marriage within the jurisdiction?

Civil partnership is available to homosexual couples only. Their status is the same as married couples in relation to the access to legal separation and divorce and all financial conditions. Inheritance rights are also the same as for married couples.

20.2 What legislation governs civil partnership/same-sex marriage?

The Act on Registered Partnership.

21. CONTROVERSIAL AREAS/RAPIDLY DEVELOPING AREAS OF LAW

21.1 Is there a particular area of the law within the jurisdiction that is currently undergoing major change?

Currently a law preparation committee is considering how to modernise the system of property regimes. This work includes considering whether the default regime in Denmark needs changes. It only includes considering how the regime of pre- and post-nuptial agreements can be made more flexible when it comes to content (but maybe less flexible when it comes to conditions for validity).

21.2 Which areas of law are most out-of-step? Which areas would you most like to see reformed/changed?

There has not been any joint initiative to look at international family law cases. This means that the criteria for jurisdiction are very different when it comes to different process that most people would regard as one case – namely their divorce and all that follows about finance and children. Also the rules regarding choice of law have never been reformed.

Dominican Republic

Aaron Suero & Pedersini
Dr. Juan Manuel Suero & Elisabetta Pedersini, J.D.

A JURISDICTION AND CONFLICT OF LAW

1. SOURCES OF LAW

1.1 What is the primary source of law in relation to the breakdown of marriage and the welfare of children within the jurisdiction?

The Dominican Republic Constitution, Civil Code, Divorce Law and Code for the Protection of Minors' Fundamental Rights are the primary source of law in relation to the breakdown of marriage and the welfare of children. Const. R.D., Articles. 55(3), 56, 109, 111, 151, G.O. 10561 (2010); Cod. Civ. R.D., Ley 1529 (1876); Ley 1306-Bis, G.O. 5034 (1937); Ley 136-03, G.O. 10234 (2003).

1.2 Which are the main statutes governing matrimonial law in the jurisdiction?

The main Dominican Republic statutes governing matrimonial law are according to the following legal hierarchy:

- The Dominican Republic Constitution. Const. R.D., G.O. 10561 (2010);
- The Dominican Civil Code and its amendments. Cod. Civ. R.D., Ley 1529 (1876);
- The Dominican Civil Procedure Code and its amendments. Cod. Proc. Civ. R.D., Dec. 1668 (1878);
- The Dominican Commerce Code and its amendments. Cod. Com. R.D. (1884).
- Civil Status Acts Law 659 and its amendments. Ley 659, G.O. 6114 (1944);
- Divorce Law 1306-Bis and its amendments. Ley 1306-Bis, G.O. 5034 (1937);
- Code for the Protection of Minors' Fundamentals Rights and its amendments. Ley 136-03, G.O. 10234 (2003).

2. JURISDICTION

2.1 What are the main jurisdictional requirements for the institution of proceedings in relation to divorce, property and children?

Jurisdiction of proceedings in relation to divorce is determined by considering where the marriage contract was celebrated or executed, based on the legal principle of *lex loci contractus*, Cod. Civ. R.D., Article 1156 (1876), the landmark case of *Cristóbal Montero vs Maria Ortega*, SCJ, B.J. 534, Pág. 80

(1955), the last known domicile of the defendant or the domicile agreed by the parties in the stipulation agreement for the dissolution of the marriage.

Meanwhile, the marital property division is determined by the legal nature of property, ie, whether or not the property is real property ('immoveable property') or personal property ('moveable property'), Cod. Civ. R.D., Article 2123, 2128 (1876), the last known domicile of the defendant or the domicile agreed by the parties in the stipulation agreement for the dissolution of the marriage.

The competent court is the Civil Chamber of First Instance Tribunal located in the Judicial District of the defendant's domicile or in the jurisdiction agreed by the spouses in the stipulation agreement. Const. R.D., Articles 8, 9, 12, 26, 55, 109, 111, 112, 151, 154 (4), 160, G.O. 10561 (2010); Cod. Proc. Civ. R.D., Article 59 (1878); Ley 821, Articles 42, 45, 49, G.O. 3921 (1927); Ley 1306-Bis, Articles 3, 4, 26, 28, G.O. 5034 (1937); SCJ Res. 439-2004 (2004); SCJ Res. 1371-2004 (2004); Jaquez v Echavarria, SCJ B.J. 1108, Sent. 27 (2003); *In re: Santa Isabel Morillo,* SCJ B.J. 1186, Sent. 2, (2009); *Martinez et al v Cubilette*, SCJ B.J. 1182, Sent. 32 (2009).

With regard to children, jurisdiction is determined by the last known domicile of the child. The competent court is the Civil Chamber of the Tribunal for Minors located in the Judicial District of the minor's domicile. Const. R.D., Articles 8, 9, 12, 26, 56, 109, 111, 112, 151, 154 (4), 160, G.O. 10561 (2010); Ley 136-03, Articles 65, 209, 211, 213, G.O. 10234 (2003); SCJ Res. 1471-2005 (2005); SCJ Res. 1841-2005 (2005); SCJ Res. 480-2008 (2008); *In re: Morillo*, SCJ B.J. 1186, Sent. 2, (2009).

3. DOMICILE AND HABITUAL RESIDENCE

3.1 Explain the concepts of domicile and habitual residence as they apply to the jurisdiction

The Dominican Republic Civil Code defines domicile as 'the place of principal establishment for a Dominican citizen'. Cod. Civ. R.D., Article 102 (1876). A citizen is any person of 18 years old or emancipated. Const. R.D., Article 21 (2010). But, when it comes to a married woman, the Civil Code indicates that 'the domicile of a married woman is her husband's domicile'. Cod. Civ. R.D., Article 108 (1876).

And in cases of non-emancipated minors, the Civil Code provides that 'the domicile of a non-emancipated minor is his parents' or tutor's domicile.' Idem; Ley 136-03, Articles 65, 209, 211, 213, G.O. 10234 (2003); SCJ Res. 1471-2005 (2005); SCJ Res. 1841-2005 (2005); SCJ Res. 480-2008 (2008).

In 2003, the Dominican Republic Supreme Court of Justice (SCJ) construed domicile as '...an element of individualization of personal character, which marks an individual all the time and in all the places, which allows distinguishing him from the others in connection to territorial demarcation, judicial existence, statute of limitation and a specific place' *Rayer v Tapi Muebles Plaza*, SCJ B.J. 1111, Sent. 18 (2003).

In 2009, the SCJ determined 'if the domicile is the result of a contract, the stipulation made upon reciprocal consideration by the parties, it abolishes the standard effects of domicile, to a point that trial judges cannot decide the validity of a legal notice made to another address' *Banco de Desarrollo Financiero del Caribe v Sanchez et al*, SCJ B.J. 1186, Sent. 3 (2009).

Even though the concept of 'habitual residence' is mentioned in the Code for the Protection of Minors' Fundamental Rights (Ley 136-03, Articles 64, 110, G.O. 10234 (2003)), and in several multilateral treatises ratified by the Dominican Republic government, such as The Hague Convention of 25 October 1980 on the Civil Aspects of International Child Abduction, this concept has not been defined yet by the Dominican Legislative Branch nor by the Dominican Judicial Branch.

In 2007, the SCJ used the concept of habitual residence for the first time, but the highest court of the country did not define this concept nor construed the basic elements or requirements for determining the habitual residence of a minor. *Santelises v Zayas*, SCJ B.J. 1156, Sent. 6 (2007).

4. CONFLICT OF LAW/APPLICABLE LAW TO BE APPLIED

4.1 What happens when one party applies to stay proceedings in favour of a foreign jurisdiction? What factors will the local court take into account when determining forum issues?

If a party applies to stay proceedings in favour of a foreign jurisdiction, the Dominican Republic court must take into account one or all of the three following factors when determining forum issues:

(a) whether or not the request to stay proceedings in favour of a foreign jurisdiction violates the Dominican Republic Constitution or public policy statutes. Const. R.D., Articles 8, 9, 12, 26, 55, 56, 109, 111, 112, 151, 154 (4), 160, G.O. 10561 (2010);

(b) whether or not the foreign court had personal and subject matter jurisdiction prior to the Dominican Republic court (*Litispendencia or Lis pendens*). Ley 834, Articles 28, 29, G.O. 9478 (1978);

(c) whether or not the Dominican Republic court has personal and subject matter jurisdiction on the defendant, considering the defendant's last known domicile or the minor's domicile or habitual residence (*Exepcion de Incompetencia*). Ley 834, Articles 1, 2, 3, 20, G.O. 9478 (1978); Ley 1306-*Bis,* Articles 3, 4, 28, G.O. 5034 (1937); Ley 136-03, Articles 65, 209, 211, 213, G.O. 10234 (2003); *In re: Morillo*, SCJ B.J. 1186, Sent. 2, (2009); *Martinez et al v Cubilette*,SCJ B.J. 1182, Sent. 32 (2009).

The burden of proof is on the party filing the motion to stay proceedings. The Dominican Republic court, upon evaluation of the facts and documents submitted to the court, will accept or deny the motion to stay proceedings. The decision of the court can be appealed before the Court of Appeals. Ley 834, Articles 8, 9, 10, G.O. 9478 (1978).

B. PRE- AND POST-NUPTIAL AGREEMENTS

5. VALIDITY OF PRE- AND POST-NUPTIAL AGREEMENTS

5.1 To what extent are pre- and post-nups binding within the jurisdiction? Could you provide a brief discussion of the most significant recent case law on this issue?

The validity of pre- and post-nuptial agreements is subject to the constitutional legal principles of territoriality and public policy. Const. R.D., Articles 8, 9, 26, 109, 111, G.O. 10561 (2010); *de la Cruz vs. Alvino*, SCJ B.J. 1060, Sent. 28 (1999). In view of the above, there are two classifications:

(a) domestic pre- and post-nuptial agreements; and
(b) foreign pre- and post-nuptial agreements.

Domestic pre- and post-nuptial agreements

Domestic pre-nuptial agreements are those executed pursuant to Dominican Republic statutes for a marriage contract to be performed in the Dominican Republic territory. Const. R.D., Articles 9, 55, 109, 111, G.O. 10561 (2010); Cod. Civ. R.D., Articles 1395-1398 (1878); Cod. Com. R.D., Articles 67-70 (1884); Ley 2125, G.O. 7001 (1949).

Although a marriage is considered a civil contract executed by and between a man and a woman, Ley 659, Article 55 (1), G.O. 6114 (1944), in the Dominican Republic, there is no case precedent allowing or denying the validity of post-nuptial agreements. However, it is our understanding, that due to the civil nature of the marriage contract, and the implied amendments that the spouses perform during the existence of the marriage, it shall not be considered as an irrevocable contract, therefore post-nuptial agreements shall be allowed *if* their stipulations are not contrary to Dominican Republic public policies. Const. R.D., Articles 9, 55, 109, 111, G.O. 10561 (2010); *Reyes v Reyes*, SCJ B.J. 1146, Sent. 9 (2006).

Foreign pre- or post-nuptial agreement

A foreign pre- or post-nuptial agreement shall be considered valid by the Dominican Republic authorities if it was executed in compliance of the formalities established in its country of origin (*lex loci contractus*) Const. R.D., Articles 26, 111, G.O. 10561 (2010); Ley 659, Article 58 (14), G.O. 6114 (1944); Ley 834, Article 122, G.O. 9478 (1978); *Chu Yin v Chu-Ching*, SCJ B.J. 1141, Sent. 5 (2005); *Reyes v Reyes*, SCJ B.J. 1146, Sent. 9 (2006); *Gallardo v Gallardo et al*, SCJ B.J. 1039, Sent. 3 (1997); de la Cruz v Alvino, SCJ B.J. 1060, Sent. 28 (1999); *Geo Reisen GMBH v Connex Caribe*, SCJ B.J. 1192, Sent. 27 (2010); *Biwater Intl., Ltd. v Abreu*, SCJ B.J. 1195 (2010); but in the Dominican Republic, there is no case precedent allowing or denying the homologation or validity of foreign pre- or post-nuptial agreements.

To conclude, the validity of domestic post-nuptial agreements and foreign pre- or post-nuptial agreements is a grey area in the Dominican Republic legal and judicial systems, due to an outdated Dominican Civil Code, the lack of legislation and no case precedent.

C. DIVORCE, NULLITY AND JUDICIAL SEPARATION

6. RECOGNITION OF FOREIGN MARRIAGES/DIVORCES

6.1 Summarise the position in your jurisdiction

When it comes to the recognition of foreign marriages or divorces, the rule of thumb in the Dominican Republic is that 'Judgments rendered by foreign courts and documents received from foreign officers are enforceable in the territory of the Republic in the manner and in the cases provided by the law.' Cod. Proc. Civ. R.D., Article 546, Dec. 1668 (1878); Ley 834, Article 122, G.O. 9478 (1978); Ley 659, Article 59 1(c), G.O. 6114 (1944); but the Dominican Civil Procedure Code creates a loophole because it does not provide further instructions on the minimum requirements, proceedings and venue for the recognition of foreign marriages or divorces.

In view of the above, the Dominican Republic courts must take into account whether or not the foreign marriage or divorce is from a signatory country of the Convention on Private International Law (Bustamante Code), Res. 1055, G.O. 4042 (1928) or the Hague Convention of 19 October 1996 on Jurisdiction, Applicable Law, Recognition, Enforcement and Co-operation in Respect of Parental Responsibility and Measures for the Protection of Children, Res. 261-09, G.O. 10534 (2009). If the marriage or divorce is from a signatory country of the Bustamante Code, the provisions of Articles 36-56,423-433, shall be applicable; if the marriage or divorce is from a non-signatory country of the Bustamante Code or the above mentioned Hague Convention, the rules established in *Chu Yin v Chu-Ching*, SCJ B.J. 1141, Sent. 5 (2005), shall be applicable.

In *Lopez v Alcantara*, SCJ B.J. 1103, Sent. 21 (2002), the Dominican Republic Supreme Court of Justice held that 'only foreign *constitutif* or *déclaratif* judgments, such as those relating to the status and capacity of the people, do not need the homologation or *exequatur*'; but, if the foreign divorce judgment is a condemnation which condemns a person to a positive or negative obligation, (to be bound to do, to give, to pay or to forbear), it must be homologated by a Dominican Republic court, in order to be enforceable in the Dominican Republic territory. In 2007, the SCJ ratified its *Lopez v Alcantara* jurisprudence in *Banco Gubernamental de Fomento para Puerto Rico v Vicioso et al,* SCJ B.J. 1157, Sent. 6 (2007).

In Chu Yin v Chu-Ching, SCJ B.J. 1141, Sent. 5 (2005), the SCJ established the minimum requirements that a petitioner for the recognition of a foreign judgment must provide to the Dominican Republic courts:

(1) the foreign judgment must have *res judicata* in its jurisdiction of origin;
(2) the foreign judgment must have been rendered by a competent foreign court;
(3) the foreign judgment must not be subject to further appeals;
(4) the foreign judgment must be enforceable within its statute of limitations;
(5) the foreign judgment must have been obtained with due process; and
(6) the foreign judgment must not be contrary to Dominican Republic public policies.

In view of the above, foreign marriages and foreign *constitutif* or *déclaratif* divorce judgments that do not have a condemnation, are recognised by Dominican authorities based on the common law principle of comity, without a need of homologation proceeding.

7. DIVORCE

7.1 Explain the grounds for divorce within the jurisdiction (please also deal with nullity and judicial separation if appropriate).

Pursuant to Dominican Republic Divorce Law 1306-Bis, Article 2, G.O. 5034 (1937), the grounds for divorce are:

(a) the mutual consent of the spouses;
(b) irreconcilable differences justified by facts whose magnitude is the cause of unhappiness of the spouses and social disruption, sufficient to justify a divorce;
(c) the absence ordered by a court in accordance with the requirements contained in Chapter II, Title IV, Book I of the Civil Code;
(d) the adultery of either spouse;
(e) the condemnation of one spouse to a criminal penalty. (Divorce shall not be granted for this cause if the condemnation is the punishment of political crimes.);
(f) the abuse or serious injuries committed by one spouse against the other;
(g) the voluntary home abandonment by one spouse, provided that the spouse does not return within two years;
(h) habitual drunkenness of one of the spouses, or the habitual or immoderate use of narcotic drugs.

The Dominican Republic also allows foreign citizens to obtain a bilateral or mutual consent divorce. Ley 1306-Bis, Article 28 (V), G.O. 5034 (1937); Ley 142, G.O. 9229 (1971).

Pursuant to Dominican Republic Law 659, Article 61, G.O. 6114 (1944), the grounds to request the nullity of a marriage are:

(a) if the marriage contract was made under duress or without the consent of one or both spouses;
(b) when there was misrepresentation by one or both spouses.

Finally, in connection with judicial separation, the Dominican Republic legislative and judicial branches have not defined nor established the grounds for a judicial separation, even though the term 'judicial separation' appears in the Dominican Constitution, Article 55 (3), G.O. 10561 (2010); Dominican Republic Tax Code, Cod. Trib. R.D., Ley 11-92, Article 295, G.O. 9835 (1992); in the Code for the Protection of Minors' Fundamentals Rights, Ley 136-03, Article 82, G.O. 10234 (2003); and in *Dominguez v Ortiz*, SCJ B.J. 1182, Sent. 64 (2009).

8. FINANCES/CAPITAL, PROPERTY

8.1 What powers does the court have to allocate financial resources and property on the breakdown of marriage?

Dominican Republic courts, *per se*, do not have powers to allocate financial resources or property on the breakdown of the marriage, because Dominican Republic courts are bound and limited to rule according to the pleadings made by the litigating parties. Const. R.D., Article 151, G.O. 10561 (2010); Cod. Proc. Civ. R.D., Articles 78, 141, Dec. 1668 (1878); *First Intl. Timber Sales Inc. v Idoprema*, SCJ B.J. 1193, Sent. 32 (2010).

The right to request allocation of financial resources and property during the breakdown of marriage belongs to the spouses or former spouses. The SCJ held that 'a court makes an *extra* and *ultra petita ruling* when it grants a right that has not been requested or claimed or when it decides in addition to the pleadings made by the litigating parties' *Guzman v Lara*, SCJ B.J. 1137, Sent. 12 (2005); *Polanco et al v Rosado et al*, SCJ B.J. 1144, Sent. 2 (2006); *Burgos v Diaz*, SCJ B.J. 1196, Sent. 92 (2010).

For the duration of the divorce proceeding, the wife is entitled to a provisional allocation of financial resources (alimony *ad litem*) and property with an inventory, until the end of the divorce proceeding. Ley 1306-Bis, Articles 22, 24, G.O. 5034 (1937).

Once the divorce is published, the spouses have a period of two years to complete the division of financial resources and community property; after the expiration of the two year period, each former spouse retains the financial resources and property under his/her possession if it was not claimed by the other former spouse within that period, except for real estate property ownership rights, because these rights are not subject to the statute of limitation. Cod. Civ. R.D., Ley 1529, Article 815 (1876); *Mariñez v Lorenzo*, SCJ B.J. 1189, Sent. 15 (2009).

8.2 Explain and illustrate with reference to recent cases the court's thinking on division of assets

When it comes to division of marital assets or cohabitation assets, the Dominican Republic is a community property jurisdiction, meaning that each spouse or concubine is entitled to an equal percentage or 50 per cent of the community created during the marriage or concubinage. Cod. Civ. R.D., Ley 1529, Articles 815, 1393, 1399, 1400, 1401, 1402, 1404 (1876); *Lajara v Herrera*, SCJ B.J. 1135, Sent. 16 (2005); *Morel v Diaz*, SCJ, B.J. 1140, Sent. 6 (2005).

The community of property begins with the celebration of the marriage and ends with the publication of the divorce decree. Cod. Civ. R.D., Ley 1529, Articles 815, 1393, 1399, 1400, (1876). The community of property consists in:

(i) all the movable and personal assets under the spouses' possession at the celebration of the marriage;
(ii) all the financial benefits, income, rent and interest earned during the marriage;
(iii) all the real estate properties acquired during the marriage.

In connection to concubines, the community of property begins when the concubines have a public and notorious relationship as a more *uxorio* cohabitation, *Quiterio et al*, SCJ, B.J. 1091, Sent. 44 (2001); but there is no clear judicial guideline to determine the end of the concubinage. The principles and rules for division or partition of the community of property created during the concubinage are the same for the division of martial community property. Cod. Civ. R.D., Ley 1529, Article 815, (1876); *Lajara v Herrera*, SCJ B.J. 1135, Sent. 16 (2005).

9. FINANCES/MAINTENANCE

9.1 Explain the operation of maintenance for spouses on an on-going basis after the breakdown of marriage

The maintenance for spouses after the breakdown of the marriage is regulated pursuant to Ley 1306-Bis, Articles 22, 24, 25, G.O. 5034 (1937). The duty to pay and secure maintenance for spouses is mandatory until the expiration of the two-year period for the division of the all assets of the community property. Cod. Civ. R.D., Ley 1529, Article 815, (1876); *Mariñez v Lorenzo*, SCJ B.J. 1189, Sent. 15 (2009).

9.2 Is it common for maintenance to be awarded?

Maintenance for spouses is awarded in most cases, if it is requested by one of the spouses to the court and if the court considers the pleading for maintenance to be reasonable and fair according to the community of property and the income of the other spouse. Furthermore, the maintenance for spouses is a matter of public policy and social interest. Const. R.D., Article 111, G.O. 10561 (2010); Ley 1306-Bis, Articles 22, 24, 25, G.O. 5034 (1937). In *re Risk Gonzalez*, SCJ B.J. 1093, Sent. 42 (2001); *Abreu v Santana*, SCJ B.J. 1188, Sent. 32 (2009).

In 2000, the SCJ held that 'a judgment ordering maintenance for spouses and child support cannot be considered as an interlocutory judgment, because these are provisional measures for public policy, and do not finally determine or complete the suit'. *Matos v Peña*, SCJ B.J. 1077, Sent. 13 (2000).

9.3 Explain and illustrate with reference to recent cases the court's thinking on maintenance

In the past two decades, the SCJ has made several decisions in connection with maintenance for spouses, providing the guidelines regarding the grounds, nature and scope to determine maintenance. Herein are the landmark cases:

In 1994, the SCJ held 'considering that the evaluation of the husband's financial condition to establish the amount of the maintenance for the spouse that he shall provide to the wife, during the divorce proceeding, pursuant Article 22 of the Divorce Law 1306-Bis (1937), is a matter of trier of fact under the sovereign appreciation of the lower court, that escapes of the censorship of the Supreme Court of Justice, as Court of Cassation.' *Carbonell v Crestar*, SCJ, B.J. 1008, Sent. 16 (1994).

In 2000, the SCJ held that 'a judgment ordering maintenance for spouses and child support cannot be considered as an interlocutory judgment, because these are provisional measures for public policy, and do not finally determine or complete the suit.' *Matos v Peña*, SCJ B.J. Sent. 13 (2000).

Later, in 2001, the SCJ held that 'if it is reasonable, fair and compatible with the income of the spouse' and 'considering the financial capacity of the father' the lower court decision shall not be the object of criticisms by the SCJ. *In re Risk Gonzalez*, SCJ, B.J. 1093, Sent.42 (2001).

10. CHILD MAINTENANCE

10.1 On what basis is child maintenance calculated within the jurisdiction?

The basis for calculating child maintenance is as follows:

- Child maintenance consists of all the care, services and products towards the fulfilment of the basic and indispensable needs of the child, for his support and development; such as but not limited to: food, shelter, clothing, assistance, medical assistance, medicine, recreation, integrity and academic education; because, these duties are public policy. Ley 136-03, Article 170, G.O. 10234 (2003).
- Parents' obligation to maintain their child is irrevocable, joint and several. Const. R.D., Article 55(10), 56, G.O. 10561 (2010); Ley 136-03, Article 171, G.O. 10234 (2003).
- To determine child maintenance, the defendant must provide: (a) an affidavit of income; and (b) the last income tax return; or (c) an affidavit of income issued by the employer. Ley 136-03, Article 178, G.O. 10234 (2003); *Batista v Mena*, SCJ B.J. 1154, Sent. 24 (2007).
- If the defendant is an employee, the employer cannot make a monthly deduction that exceeds 50 per cent of the net monthly salary of the employee. Ley 136-03, Article 187, G.O. 10234 (2003).

11. RECIPROCAL ENFORCEMENT OF FINANCIAL ORDERS

11.1 Summarise the position in your jurisdiction

In connection with the enforcement of financial orders regarding child support, the Dominican Republic is a signatory of the following treaties:

- The Convention on Private International Law (Bustamante Code); Res. 1055, G.O. 4042 (1928);
- The United Nations Convention on the Rights of the Child (1989); Res. 8-91, G.O. 9805 (1991);
- The Hague Convention of 19 October 1996 on Jurisdiction, Applicable Law, Recognition, Enforcement and Co-operation in Respect of Parental Responsibility and Measures for the Protection of Children; Res. 261-09, G.O. 10534 (2009).

The Dominican Republic is not a signatory member of the following multilateral treaties:

- The Inter-American Convention on Support Obligations (1989);
- The Hague Convention of 2 October 1973 on the Recognition and Enforcement of Decisions Relating to Maintenance Obligations; and
- The Hague Convention of 23 November 2007 on the International Recovery of Child Support and Other Forms of Family Maintenance.

If the judgment for child maintenance is from a country that does not have a bilateral or multilateral treaty for the recognition and enforcement of foreign judgments with the Dominican Republic, the proceeding to enforce a financial order will be pursuant to Const. R.D., Article 55(10), 56, 109, 111, 112, G.O. 10561 (2010); Ley 136-03, Article 105, 211(j), G.O. 10234 (2003); SCJ Res. 1841-2005 (2005).

If the judgment for child maintenance is from a country that is a signatory of the Convention on Private International Law (Bustamante Code) or the The Hague Convention of 19 October 1996 on Jurisdiction, Applicable Law, Recognition, Enforcement and Co-operation in Respect of Parental Responsibility and Measures for the Protection of Children; Res. 261-09, G.O. 10534 (2009), the proceeding to enforce a financial order will be pursuant to the Constitution Const. R.D., Article 26, 55(10), 56, 109, 111, 112, 151 G.O. 10561 (2010); Bustamante Code, Articles 59, 67, 68, 423-433, Res. 1055, G.O. 4042 (1928); Ley 136-03, Article 105, 211(j), G.O. 10234 (2003); SCJ Res. 1841-2005 (2005); *Gallardo v Gallardo et al*, SCJ B.J. 1039, Sent. 3 (1997); *Chu Yin v Chu-Ching*, SCJ B.J. 1141, Sent. 5 (2005).

The Dominican Republic Supreme Court of Justice has not yet created jurisprudence in connection with recognition and enforcement of a foreign judgment on child maintenance.

12. FINANCIAL RELIEF AFTER FOREIGN DIVORCE PROCEEDINGS

12.1 What powers are available to make orders following a foreign divorce?

When the foreign divorce judgment has a condemnation (an obligation to do, to give or to pay), the first issue that a Dominican Republic court must take into account is whether or not the foreign divorce is from a signatory country of the Convention on Private International Law (Bustamante Code), Res. 1055, G.O. 4042 (1928) or the Hague Convention of 19 October 1996 on Jurisdiction, Applicable Law, Recognition, Enforcement and Co-operation in Respect of Parental Responsibility and Measures for the Protection of Children; Res. 261-09, G.O. 10534 (2009). If the divorce is from a signatory country of the Bustamante Code or the above Hague Convention, the provisions of Const. R.D., Articles 26, 55 (10), 56, 109, 111, 112, G.O. 10561 (2010); Articles 52-56, 423-433 of the Bustamante Code; and *Gallardo v Gallardo* et al, SCJ B.J. 1039, Sent. 3 (1997); *Chu Yin v Chu-Ching*, SCJ B.J. 1141, Sent. 5 (2005) shall be applicable. If the divorce is from a non-signatory country of the Bustamante Code or the aforementioned Hague Convention, the rules established in *Lopez v Alcantara*, SCJ B.J. 1103, Sent. 21 (2002) and *Chu Yin v Chu-Ching*, SCJ B.J. 1141, Sent. 5 (2005), shall be applicable.

The condemnatory foreign divorce judgment must obtain the *exequatur* or be homologated by a Dominican Republic court, in order to be enforceable in the Dominican Republic territory. Const. R.D., Article 55(10), G.O. 10561 (2010); Cod. Civ. R.D., Article 2123, Ley 1529 (1876); Cod. Proc. Civ. R.D., Article 546, Dec. 1668 (1878); Ley 834, Article 122, G.O. 9478 (1978); *Lopez v Alcantara*, SCJ B.J. 1103, Sent. 21 (2002); *Chu Yin v Chu-Ching*, SCJ B.J. 1141, Sent. 5 (2005); *Banco Gubernamental de Fomento para Puerto Rico v Vicioso* et al, SCJ B.J. 1157, Sent. 6 (2007).

In *Lopez v Alcantara*, SCJ B.J. 1103, Sent. 21 (2002), the SCJ held that 'although according to the law, the judgments rendered by foreign courts must have, for its enforcement in the national territory, an *exequatur* by a national court, nonetheless the non-compliance of this formality does not dispose to the substantive right of the interested party to exercise a legal proceeding, but merely causes, once initiated the legal action, a stay of proceedings, until the satisfaction of the *exequatur* legal requirement'.

Later in *Chu Yin v Chu-Ching*, SCJ B.J. 1141, Sent. 5 (2005) the SCJ held that 'judges in an *exequatur* proceeding can take any action concerning to the enforcement of foreign judgments, such as for example: to order a provisional remedy, agree on a grace period pursuant Article 1244 of the Civil Code, and to order the conversion to Dominican currency of a condemnation issued in foreign currency'.

In view of the above, foreign condemnatory divorce judgments must have an *exequatur* or homologation by a Dominican Republic court, in order to be enforced in the Dominican Republic territory.

D. CHILDREN

13. CUSTODY/ PARENTAL RESPONSIBILITY

13.1. Briefly explain the legal position in relation to custody/parental responsibility following the breakdown of a relationship or marriage

Custody and parental responsibility are legal institutions. It is public policy that both parents have a duty to guarantee, within their possibilities and economic means, the protection of a minor's integrity, child support and a family environment. In the event of the death of one parent, the custody and parental responsibility will pass to the living or surviving parent; and in the event of the death of both parents, the Dominican Republic Government will appoint custody. The District Attorney must provide an opinion to approve or revoke the custody; and according to the minor's maturity level, the minor shall provide an opinion about his custody. Ley 136-03, Articles 70, 82, 83, G.O. 10234 (2003). All court decisions shall be subject to the best interest of the child. *Pedro Diaz v. Jose Moreno*, SCJ, B.J. 1109, Sent. 15 (2003).

13.2. Briefly explain the legal position in relation to access/contact/ visitation following the breakdown of a relationship or marriage

Access/contact/visitation is subject to the best interest of the child; the terms and conditions established in a socio-familial report enacted by CONANI (national council for childhood and adolescence); any previous agreement by and between the parents; the divorce judgment (if any); any violation of a previous agreement or the divorce judgment; and the judge's opinion over the evidence provided to the court, considering the habitual residence of the minor, parents' transportation possibilities, the frequency of visits and vacations, etc. Ley 136-03, Articles 102 and 103, G.O. 10234 (2003). *Claudia Lopez v. Adrian Karter,* SCJ, B.J. 1112, Sent. 42 (2003); *Claudia Lopez v. Adrian Karter*, SCJ, (en banc) B.J. 1163, Sent. 1 (2007).

14. INTERNATIONAL ABDUCTION

14.1 Summarise the position in your jurisdiction

The Dominican Republic is signatory of The Hague Convention of 25 October 1980 on the Civil Aspects of International Child Abduction Res. 177-04, G.O. 10278 (2004); but the country is not a signatory member of The Inter-American Convention on the International Return of Children (1989) and The Inter-American Convention of International Traffic in Minors (1994).

The Civil Chamber of the Tribunal for Minors has jurisdiction in International Child Abduction cases. Ley 136-03, Article 211(j), G.O. 10234 (2003); SCJ Res. 480-2008, Article 2 (2008).

The court must take into account whether or not the petition for the return of the child is from a signatory country of the Hague Convention on the Civil Aspects of International Child Abduction (1980). If the petition is from a signatory country of the Hague Convention, then the provisions of the Hague Convention, the SCJ Res. 480-2008, *Gallardo v Gallardo et al*, SCJ B.J. 1039, Sent. 3 (1997); *Chu Yin v Chu-Ching*, SCJ B.J. 1141, Sent. 5 (2005) shall be applicable. See also *In re CONANI*, SCJ 1175, Sent. 3 (2008). If the petition is from a non-signatory country of the Hague Convention, the rules established in Const. R.D., Articles 26, 55 (10), 56, 109, 111, 112, G.O. 10561 (2010); Ley 136-03, Articles 104, 110, 211(j), 405-406, G.O. 10234 (2003); and *Morales et al v Montes de Oca*, SCJ B.J. 1189, Sent. 17 (2009), shall be applicable.

15. LEAVE TO REMOVE/APPLICATIONS TO TAKE A CHILD OUT OF THE JURISDICTION

15.1 Summarise the position in your jurisdiction

No child shall be allowed to leave the Dominican Republic jurisdiction without both parents; in the event that the child is traveling with one of the parents or an adult (relative or non-relative) the non-traveling parent must provide a written and notarised travel authorisation to the parent or adult traveling with the child. If the parents do not provide the authorisation to travel, the Civil Chamber of the Court of Minors could issue an order to authorise the child to travel. Ley 136-03, Articles 110, 204, 211(p), 213, G.O. 10234 (2003).

If the child is illegally taken out of the Dominican Republic jurisdiction, the parent or adult in violation of the Code of Minors could be subject to the sanctions established in Ley 136-03, Articles 13, 110, 391, 405-406, G.O. 10234 (2003); *Morales et al v Montes de Oca*, SCJ B.J. 1189, Sent. 17 (2009).

15.2 Under what circumstances may a parent apply to remove their child from the jurisdiction against the wishes of the other parent?

The doctrine and principle of the 'best interest of the child' prevails to determine the circumstances that could allow a parent to apply to remove a child from the Dominican Republic jurisdiction against the wishes of the other parent. Ley 136-03, Principio V, Articles 8, 59, 72-74, 78, 84, 95, 102, 108, 288, 345 and 461, G.O. 10234 (2003); *Diaz v Moreno* et al, SCJ B.J. 1109, Sent. 15 (2003); *Lopez v Karter*, SCJ B.J. 1112, Sent. 42 (2003); *Lopez v Karter*, (en banc) SCJ B.J. 1163, Sent. 1 (2007).

The circumstances to apply for removal of a child could be:

- suspension of parental authority;
- fault, negligence or unjustifiable non-compliance of parental duties;
- threat by one or both parents;
- risk to child's security and welfare;
- abandonment;

- civil or judicial interdiction;
- a negative socio-familial report made by CONANI;
- violation of previous custody agreements executed by the parents;
- violation of custody rights;
- a divorce judgment; and
- any other circumstance determined by a judge.

E. SURROGACY & ADOPTION

16. VALIDITY OF SURROGACY AGREEMENTS

16.1 Briefly summarise the position in your jurisdiction

In the Dominican Republic there is no specific legislation or case law that addresses the legal issue of surrogacy agreements. However, surrogacy agreements are executed and performed under the legal principles of freedom of contract, *lex contractus* and privity of contract. Cod. Civ. R.D., Articles 1134, 1156, 1165, 1351, Ley 1529 (1876). Surrogacy agreements can be construed in a foreign language, governed according to foreign laws and interpreted by a foreign court, under the legal principle of *locus regit actum,* if the terms and conditions of the contract are not contrary to Dominican Constitution and public policies. Const. R.D., Articles 6, 47, 50, 111, G.O. 10561 (2010); *de la Cruz v. Asetesa*, SCJ, B.J. 1133, Sent. 16 (1005).

In the event of a dispute, if the surrogacy contract is contrary to the provisions of the Dominican Constitution or public policies, local laws shall prevail over any foreign law and the surrogacy contract will be governed and interpreted pursuant to Dominican Republic laws and Courts. Const. R.D., Articles 6, 111, 149, G.O. 10561 (2010); *de la Cruz v. Alvino,* SCJ, B.J. 1060, Sent. 28 (1999).

17. ADOPTION

17.1 Briefly explain the legal position in relation to adoption in your jurisdiction. Is adoption available to individuals, cohabiting couples (both heterosexual and same-sex)?

Adoption is regulated by Law 136-03, G.O. 10234 (2003). The adoption is an irrevocable privilege, a judicial and social institution protected by public policies granted by a Dominican Court for children issues. It creates a legal bond similar to the biological bond of the father and son; it has a social and human character to integrate and protect families for adopted children, considering their best interest and under the utmost supervision by the Dominican state. Ley 136-03, Articles 111, 112, 116, G.O. 10234 (2003).

Adoption is available to individuals and heterosexual couples who meet the following criteria:

- adopting parents must be between the ages of 30-60 years old;
- a minimum of five years of marriage or continuous cohabitation; and
- with moral character and qualifications for an optimal development of the adopted children.

Ley 136-03, Articles 117, 118, 119, G.O. 10234 (2003). There is no case precedent of approval of adoption granted to homosexual or same-sex couples.

F. COHABITATION

18. COHABITATION

18.1 What legislation (if any) governs division of property for unmarried couples on the breakdown of the relationship?

The division of property for unmarried couples on the breakdown of the relationship is considered as a division of cohabitation assets or as a division of a *de facto* partnership. As mentioned, the Dominican Republic is a community property jurisdiction; therefore, each partner is entitled to an equal percentage or 50 per cent of the community created during the relationship. Const. R.D., Article 55, 151, G.O. 10561 (2010); Cod. Civ. R.D., Ley 1529, Articles 815, 1393, 1399, 1400, 1401, 1402, 1404 (1876); *Quiterio et al*, SCJ, B.J. 1091, Sent. 44 (2001); *Lajara v Herrera*, SCJ B.J. 1135, Sent. 16 (2005); *Morel v Diaz*, SCJ, B.J. 1140, Sent. 6 (2005).

G. FAMILY DISPUTE RESOLUTION

19. MEDIATION, COLLABORATIVE LAW & ARBITRATION

19.1 Briefly summarise the non-court-based processes available in your jurisdiction and the current status of agreements reached under the auspices of mediation, collaborative law and arbitration

In the Dominican Republic there is no specific legislation for non-court-based processes under the auspices of collaborative law or arbitration. However, in 2006, the Dominican Supreme Court created a Centre for Family Mediation. SCJ, Res. 886-2006 (2006). Mediation is the only authorised non-court-based process available for family conflict. SCJ, Res. 886-2006 (2006).

19.2 What is the statutory basis (if any), for mediation, collaborative law and arbitration in your jurisdiction? In particular, are the parties required to attempt a family dispute resolution in advance of the institution of proceedings?

The statutory basis for mediation is SCJ, Res. 886-2006 (2006). Mediation is voluntary and the parties are not required to attempt it prior to the institution of divorce proceedings or any other type of family law issues or litigation. SCJ, Res. 886-2006, Articles 1, 3 (2006).

H. OTHER

20. CIVIL PARTNERSHIP/SAME-SEX MARRIAGE

20.1 What is the status of civil partnership/same-sex marriage within the jurisdiction?

Although the Dominican Republic Constitution protects and respects human dignity and equal rights and promotes the right of intimacy, it also defines that a marriage consists of 'the natural or legal bond, by the free decision of a man and a woman to be bound by a marriage or by their voluntary responsibility to be bound accordingly.' Const. R.D., Articles 4, 7-8, 38-39, 44, 55(3), G.O. 10561 (2010).

Even though the new Dominican Republic Constitution provides sufficient fundamental civil and political constitutional rights to justify the recognition of civil partnership/same-sex marriage, Const. R.D. 38, 39, 40 (13), 42-45, 47, 48, G.O. 10561 (2010), the Dominican Republic judicial branch has not defined nor established the grounds for the recognition of a domestic or foreign civil partnership/same-sex marriage. Indeed, the terms civil partnership and same-sex marriage have not been used by the judicial branch.

In 2008, the President of the SCJ made the following statements in connection to civil partnership/same-sex marriage: 'The family bond, which previously consisted in a social support and in certain occasions as an economic support, today has collapsed considerably. We must take into account the rise of unconventional families. Single women with children, sentimental partners of the same sex that are living together under the same roof. In reality, our patterns of conduct have changed.' Dr. Jorge Subero Isa, La Ética del Funcionario Judicial, Conferencia Pontificia Universidad Catolica Madre y Maestra – RSTA, May 28, 2008.

20.2 What legislation governs civil partnership/same-sex marriage?

The Dominican Republic does not have legislation that specifically governs civil partnership/same-sex marriage, because it is against the principles of a marriage pursuant to the Dominican Republic Constitution. Const. R.D., Articles 55(3), 109, 111 G.O. 10561 (2010); Ley 659, Article 55(1) G.O. 6114 (1944). The new Dominican Republic Constitution provides several fundamental civil and political constitutional rights that could allow the judicial recognition of civil partnership/same-sex marriage if this legal issue reaches the Dominican Republic Supreme Court of Justice. Const. R.D. 38, 39, 40 (13), 42-45, 47, 48, G.O. 10561 (2010).

If litigation involves a civil partnership/same-sex marriage, it is most likely that the Dominican Republic judicial authorities will handle this issue as a *de facto* partnership, subject to division of assets pursuant to Article 823 of the Dominican Republic Civil Code. *Morel v Diaz*, SCJ, B.J. 1140, Sent. 6 (2005).

21. CONTROVERSIAL AREAS/RAPIDLY DEVELOPING AREAS OF LAW.

21.1 Is there a particular area of the law within the jurisdiction that is currently undergoing major change?

The Dominican Republic Civil Code is undergoing a major reform, and the Dominican Republic legislative and judicial branches are drafting a Family Code, which should include a compilation of all the marriage and family sections of the Napoleonic Civil Code with current legislation on marriage, cohabitation, divorce, division of assets, wills, children issues and international treaties ratified by the Dominican Republic Congress.

21.2 Which areas of law are most out of step? Which areas would you most like to see reformed/changed.

Most of the areas of the marriage, divorce, division of assets and wills are out of step because the vast majority of the laws, rules and regulations are based on the legal principles of the original Napoleonic Civil Code. Cod. Civ.

R.D., Ley 1529 (1876), issued more than 50 years ago, when the concepts of marriage and nuclear family were based upon the marriage of a man and a woman, and not according to the social reality of this millennium that a marriage or a family could be the result of a consensual non-marital union of two adults.

However, vast reforms or broad changes are not expected because the Dominican Republic legislative and judicial branches are ultra conservative.

England & Wales

Manches LLP James Stewart & Louise Spitz

A. JURISDICTION AND CONFLICT OF LAW

1. SOURCES OF LAW

1.1 What is the primary source of law in relation to the breakdown of marriage and the welfare of children within the jurisdiction? Which are the main statutes governing matrimonial law in the jurisdiction?

Common law constitutes the basis of the legal system of England and Wales. No codified system of law exists and family law is to be found instead in Acts of Parliament (legislation or statute law), as applied and interpreted by the Higher Courts (precedent).

The Matrimonial Causes Act 1973 (MCA 1973) is the core legislation relating to divorce and financial proceedings. The Children Act 1989 (CA 1989) is the primary source of law in relation to children, their upbringing and welfare. Other important statutes are:

- The Married Women's Property Act 1882 (declaration of existing property rights).
- The Domicile and Matrimonial Proceedings Act 1973 (DMPA 1973) (jurisdiction disputes within the jurisdictions of England, Scotland, Northern Ireland, Jersey, Guernsey and the Isle of Man).
- The Matrimonial and Family Proceedings Act 1984 (MFPA 1984), Part III (financial relief in England and Wales after an overseas divorce).
- The Family Law Act 1986 (FLA 1986).
- The Child Support Act 1991 (CSA 1991).
- The Family Law Act 1996, (Part IV, family homes and domestic violence).
- The Human Rights Act 1998 (incorporating the European Convention on Human Rights into English law).
- The Civil Partnership Act 2004 (CPA 2004) (allows same sex couples to form registered civil partnerships).

A number of EC Regulations are applicable in England and Wales, notably Council Regulation (EC) No 2201/2003 (Brussels IIR). The UK has also ratified a number of international conventions dealing with the international aspects of family law including The Convention on the Civil Aspects of International Parental Child Abduction 1980 (The Hague Convention).

2. JURISDICTION

2.1 What are the main jurisdictional requirements for the institution of proceedings in relation to divorce, property and children?

Divorce

The court has jurisdiction in relation to divorce and ancillary relief under

Article 3(1) of the Brussels II Regulation on the following grounds:-

- the petitioner and the respondent are both habitually resident in England and Wales;
- the petitioner and the respondent were last habitually resident in England and Wales and one of them continues to reside there;
- the respondent is habitually resident in England and Wales;
- the petitioner is habitually resident in England and Wales and has resided there for at least one year prior to presentation of the petition;
- the petitioner is domiciled in England and Wales and has been habitually resident in England and Wales throughout the period of at least six months prior to presentation of the petition;
- the petitioner and the respondent are both domiciled in England and Wales; or
- no court of a contracting state has jurisdiction and either party is domiciled in England and Wales when proceedings are begun.

Property

Under section 24 of the MCA 1973 the court's ability to hear a financial claim depends on whether or not it has jurisdiction to hear a petition for divorce, nullity or judicial separation.

Children

Jurisdiction in children cases is governed by Brussels IIR and the FLA 1986. The court may also stay proceedings in relation to children under its general case management jurisdiction, applying the principle of *forum non conveniens*, ie, if it considers that there is a jurisdiction which is more appropriate and where proceedings have already been started.

For international cases where Brussels IIR does not apply, the courts will turn to the *forum non conveniens* principles. The relevant considerations will be: the child's habitual residence; the parents' connections with the competing jurisdictions; the child's welfare; the ease with which the parties could participate in the process and the range of orders available in the competing jurisdictions.

Brussels IIR provides that jurisdiction as between member states in matters of parental responsibility is based on a child's habitual residence (Article 8). If a child's habitual residence cannot be established, jurisdiction will be based on the child's physical presence in England and Wales (Article 13).

The FLA 1986 applies principally to jurisdictional conflicts between jurisdictions within the UK and covers any application under section 8 Children Act 1989 (including applications for residence orders, similar to custody orders, or contact orders, similar to access or visitation orders).

3. DOMICILE AND HABITUAL RESIDENCE

3.1 Explain the concepts of domicile and habitual residence as they apply to the jurisdiction, in relation to divorce, the finances and children

The meaning of domicile in civil jurisdictions, where the term often equates to the place where a person habitually resides, is not the same as in common law jurisdictions such as England and Wales. Domicile may be 'of origin', 'of dependence' or 'of choice'. Domicile of origin is acquired at birth and, where a person is born to married parents, is determined by the domicile of the father. Where the mother is unmarried or widowed, an individual will acquire the domicile of origin of the mother. Until the age of 16, a person's domicile is dependent on that of their parents.

A domicile of origin may be displaced by a domicile of choice, when a person has an intention to reside permanently in a jurisdiction where he is physically present. The burden of establishing a change of domicile is on the applicant. A special legal status is associated with domicile and indeed Brussels IIR provides that the court can have jurisdiction for divorce under Article 3(1) if the petitioner and the respondent are both domiciled in England and Wales, even if they have not lived there during the marriage.

Habitual residence

In common law the term habitual residence is taken to mean the country of ordinary residence. This is essentially the country where a person is living for purposes such as work or family life, except for the occasional absence. It is a question of fact and it must be shown that the person was present in the country voluntarily, with a settled intention and for an appreciable period of time. It should be noted that a person is capable of having more than one habitual residence.

Habitual residence for the determination of jurisdiction under Brussels IIR has a different meaning compared with that under English domestic law. In *Marinos* [2007] 2FLR 1088 the High Court described the phrase 'habitually resident' as 'the place where the person has established, on a fixed basis, his permanent or habitual centre of interest'. The interpretation of habitual residence under Brussels IIR does not permit a person to be habitually resident in two countries at the same time.

In cases relating to international child abduction under The Hague Convention, habitual residence refers to the country regarded as the home of the child in question.

4. CONFLICT OF LAW/APPLICABLE LAW TO BE APPLIED

4.1 What happens when one party applies to stay proceedings in favour of a foreign jurisdiction? What factors will the local court take into account when determining forum issues?

Within the EU

Within the EU (except Denmark) Brussels IIR rules on jurisdiction apply. Where proceedings for divorce, nullity or judicial separation are begun in two EU states, where both have jurisdiction, the proceedings commenced first in time must be allowed to continue and those started second must be halted. Proceedings will be considered to have 'commenced' once the required documents are lodged with the court, provided the necessary steps to effect service on the respondent are taken.

Within 'related jurisdictions'

In related jurisdictions (Scotland, Northern Ireland, Jersey, Guernsey, Alderney, Sark and the Isle of Man) paragraph 8 of Schedule 1 to the DMPA 1973 provides that the English court must stay divorce proceedings if, before the beginning of trial or first trial, one party to the marriage applies for a stay and:

- there are already divorce proceedings in existence in a related jurisdiction; and
- the parties to the marriage have resided there together; and
- the place where they resided together when the proceedings in the court were begun, or if they did not then reside together, where they last resided together before those proceedings were begun, is in that jurisdiction; and
- one of the parties was habitually resident in that jurisdiction throughout the year ending with the date on which they last resided together before the date on which the proceedings were begun.

Non-EU countries

When one party suggests that the English court is not the appropriate forum, and that another, non-EU country, is more appropriate, paragraph 9 to Schedule 1 DMPA 1973 confers a discretionary power on the court to order a stay if there are concurrent proceedings in any other jurisdiction, other than proceedings governed by Brussels IIR. The court will apply the principle of *forum non conveniens* and will consider if the balance of fairness (including convenience) as between the parties means that it is appropriate for the proceedings in the other jurisdiction to be disposed of before further steps are taken in the English proceedings.

The respondent will have to satisfy the court that there is some other available non-EU forum, which is clearly a more appropriate forum, to try the case. Important criteria which the court will consider include:

- which forum was involved in the case first and is most likely to reach a final decision first;
- the location of family assets (whether they are wholly or mainly in England); and
- whether foreign proceedings would result in a decision which is incompatible with English concepts of justice.

The English court has little influence over the continuation of the proceedings in the other non-EU country. If the English court refuses to stay the English proceedings, there may be two sets of proceedings concerning identical subject matter, between the same parties, in two places concurrently. In the divorce context this usually results in a race to see which legal system will produce a final result first.

B. PRE- AND POST-NUPTIAL AGREEMENTS

5. VALIDITY OF PRE- AND POST-NUPTIAL AGREEMENTS

5.1 To what extent are pre- and post-nuptials binding within the jurisdiction? Could you provide a brief discussion of the most significant recent case law on this issue?

Historically, pre- and post-nuptial agreements have not been legally binding.

The Supreme Court's judgment in the case of *Radmacher v Granatino* [2010] UKSC 42 marked a shift in the attitude of the courts towards upholding such agreements. While it did not make pre-nuptial agreements binding in England and Wales upon divorce, it took a purposeful step towards that eventuality. The judgment comprises four key principles:

- there is now a rebuttable presumption that courts should give effect to pre-nuptial agreements;
- nuptial agreements cannot oust the jurisdiction of the court;
- the substance of nuptial agreements must be fair. They cannot be allowed to prejudice the reasonable requirements of any children of the family and a failure to meet a party's needs or to compensate them for relationship-generated loss could render it unfair to hold that party to the terms of the agreement; and
- the circumstances surrounding the making of nuptial agreements will affect the weight given to the agreement upon divorce. If there is evidence of duress, fraud or misrepresentation, the agreement may be ignored. The weight attached to the agreement may be reduced if the parties do not take legal advice or have the benefit of disclosure prior to its execution. Best practice suggests that each party should have independent legal advice and that there should be disclosure prior to entering into the agreement.

Following *Radmacher*, great weight will now be given to both pre- and post-nuptial agreements unless the terms are manifestly unfair. The status of nuptial agreements in England is being considered by the Law Commission.

C. DIVORCE, NULLITY AND JUDICIAL SEPARATION

6. RECOGNITION OF FOREIGN MARRIAGES/DIVORCES

6.1 Summarise the position in your jurisdiction

Marriages

Two independent factors must be present for a marriage celebrated in a foreign jurisdiction to be recognised as valid in England. First, the marriage must be 'formally' valid and secondly each of the parties to the marriage must have 'capacity'.

English law follows the principle of *lex loci celebrationis* (the law of the place of celebration). A foreign marriage will be recognised if it complies with the formalities of the country in which it was celebrated.

Any procedural error which means that the marriage is not properly conducted in the country where it is celebrated will almost certainly mean that it is not recognised in the UK.

If an overseas marriage is properly conducted, it will usually be recognised in England, Scotland, Wales and Northern Ireland. It will not be possible to remarry in the UK without the overseas marriage being dissolved.

Capacity to marry is governed by the law of each party's pre-marital domicile. If there is any doubt as to the validity of the marriage, it is possible to ask a court for a declaration of status under section 55(1) FLA 1986.

Traditional religious marriages will be recognised in the UK if they are valid in the country in which they took place.

Divorce/annulment

The recognition of foreign divorces within Europe is governed by the provisions of Brussels IIR which provides a straightforward set of rules for recognition, which in most cases will be automatic.

The FLA 1986, section 44(1) provides that divorces, annulments and judicial separations granted in one UK jurisdiction will automatically be recognised throughout the UK if they were granted by a court of civil jurisdiction.

Under section 46(1) of the FLA 1986 a divorce obtained by means of judicial or other proceedings in a country which is not a signatory to Brussels IIR will be recognised if the divorce is effective under the law of the country in which it was obtained and if, at the date of the commencement of the proceedings either party to the marriage was habitually resident, domiciled in or was a national of that country. FLA 1986, section 46(2) deals with divorces obtained other than by means of proceedings. Such a divorce will only be recognised if it is effective under the law of the country in which it was obtained and at the date on which it was obtained each party to the marriage was domiciled in that country or either party to the marriage was domiciled in that country and the other party was domiciled in a country under whose law the divorce is recognised as valid.

Recognition of civil partnerships

Schedule 20 of the CPA 2004, as amended, sets out the specified overseas relationships which will be specifically recognised as civil partnerships in the UK. The civil partnership will be treated as having been formed when the overseas relationship was registered in the relevant country, but it is important to note that no civil partnership can be deemed to have been formed before 5 December, 2005. In certain circumstances, partners may apply to the English court for a declaration as to the validity of their overseas relationship.

7. DIVORCE

7.1 Explain the grounds for divorce within the jurisdiction (please also deal with nullity and judicial separation if appropriate)

Divorce

The provisions of Part II FLA 1996, which would have introduced no fault divorce, have not been implemented. Accordingly, England and Wales remains a fault based jurisdiction.

A divorce petition cannot be presented to the court before a period of one year has elapsed from the date of the marriage. It can be issued either at the Principal Registry of the Family Division, in London, or at any divorce county court in England and Wales. The sole ground for divorce is that the marriage has broken down irretrievably. This can be established if one of the following five facts is proved:

- adultery by the respondent which means the petitioner finds it intolerable to live with the respondent;
- behaviour by the respondent which means that the petitioner cannot

reasonably be expected to live with the respondent;
- desertion by the respondent for a period of two years;
- separation for two years and the parties agree to divorce; or
- separation for five years.

Judicial separation

Section 17(2) MCA 1973 provides that an application for a decree of judicial separation can be made if one of the five facts listed above exists but the petitioner does not need to demonstrate that the marriage has broken down irretrievably.

Nullity

A decree of nullity may declare that a marriage is either void from the outset or voidable. Proceedings must be instituted within three years of the marriage. If it is declared to be voidable, the marriage will be treated as valid and subsisting until the decree is obtained.

Section 11 of the MCA 1973 sets out that a marriage will be deemed void if:

- the parties are too closely related;
- either party is under the age of 16;
- the formalities required for a valid marriage were not adhered to;
- the marriage is bigamous;
- the parties are not respectively male and female; or
- in the case of a polygamous marriage celebrated abroad, one of the parties was domiciled in England and Wales.

If it is decided that the marriage is indeed void, a decree of nullity is not necessary as the marriage is considered never to have existed.

Section 12 MCA 1973 sets out the circumstances in which a marriage will be voidable:

- because of lack of consent;
- failure to consummate through the incapacity of either party or the wilful refusal of the respondent;
- the mental incapacity of either party; or
- venereal disease or pregnancy by another at the time of the marriage.

8. FINANCES/CAPITAL, PROPERTY

8.1 What powers does the court have to allocate financial resources and property on the breakdown of marriage?

The courts have a wide discretion when it comes to the division of assets on divorce or judicial separation. Its powers are set out in sections 22-24A of the MCA 1973; and include orders to:

- make, or arrange, periodical payments to the other party for as long as the court decides is necessary – sometimes known as maintenance;
- pay a lump sum or sums to the other party;
- make, or arrange, periodical payments for the benefit of any children – known as child maintenance (subject to certain restrictions set out in the Child Support legislation;
- pay a lump sum for the benefit of any children;

- transfer specified property to the other party;
- make a settlement of specified property, that is set up in trust, for the benefit of the other party and/or a child of the family;
- vary any nuptial settlement or trust made for the benefit of one of the parties;
- sell specified property and distribute the proceeds; and/or
- share a pension fund.

8.2 What factors are relevant to the exercise of the court's powers?

The court must give first consideration to the welfare of any children under the age of 18. All the factors the court must take into consideration when deciding what orders to make are set out in section 25 MCA 1973.

They are:

- the financial resources which each party has, or is likely to have in the foreseeable future;
- the financial needs of each party now and in the foreseeable future;
- the standard of living enjoyed by the family before the breakdown of the marriage;
- the age of the parties and the duration of the marriage;
- any physical or mental disability of either party;
- the contributions made by each party to the welfare of the family, including any contribution by looking after the home or caring for the family, and any contributions which either is likely to make in the foreseeable future; and
- the conduct of each of the parties, if that conduct is such that it would be unjust to disregard it (it is very rare for the court to take conduct into consideration unless it has been serious financial misconduct).

The Court has a duty, both at the time of making the original periodical payments order and on any subsequent application to vary it, to consider imposing a 'clean break' by terminating the maintenance order immediately or on payment of a capital sum. It is possible to challenge a final order relating to capital only in highly exceptional circumstances, specifically if, shortly after the order was made, a totally unforeseen event takes place which completely invalidates a fundamental assumption made by the judge when making the order, for example the death of one of the parties.

The starting point in respect of costs is that each party should bear their own costs, unless there has been litigation misconduct by one of the parties, in which case the other party may be able to recover the costs directly referable to that misconduct.

8.3 Explain and illustrate with reference to recent cases the court's thinking on division of assets

In *White* [2000] 2 FLR 981 the House of Lords reviewed the operation of section 25 MCA 1973 and considered the way in which the lower courts had been applying the law. The court's objective must be to achieve a fair outcome and, in considering how fairness is best achieved, the House of Lords established two key principles:

- There should be no bias in favour of the money-earner against the home-maker. Whatever the division of roles between the husband and wife, their contribution to the marriage, and to the family assets, should be seen as having equal value.
- A judge exercising his discretion pursuant to section 25 MCA 1973 should check his tentative views against the yardstick of equality of division and should depart from it only if, and to the extent that fairness requires it. Judges who give a spouse less than half of the matrimonial assets should be able to explain why they have 'departed from equality'.

In the subsequent cases of *Miller/McFarlane* [2006] UKHL 24, the House of Lords confirmed the two main principles set out in *White*, but went much further in exploring the issues facing the courts when making financial orders on divorce. The Lords agreed on three key principles justifying the redistribution of property on divorce, disagreeing to some extent on the detailed application of those principles. When dividing assets on divorce, judges should consider:

(i) the needs (generously interpreted) generated by the relationship between the parties;
(ii) compensation for any financial disadvantage generated by the relationship; and
(iii) the sharing of the fruits of the matrimonial partnership.

The court should consider all three, being careful to avoid double counting.

The ultimate objective of the court is to give each party an equal start on the road to independent living. In *Charman* [2007] EWCA Civ 1791, the Court of Appeal reviewed the three principles identified in *Miller/McFarlane*, and discussed how to apply the principles in practice. The court made the general point that in the event of irreconcilable conflict between the principles, the overriding criterion is fairness.

Reasons to depart from equality of division

- Shortness of marriage – *Miller v Miller* [2006].
- Inheritance – only in cases where there is a surplus of assets required to meet the parties' reasonable needs.
- Illiquidity – difficulties in borrowing and the nature of assets may justify a departure from equality.
- Special contribution – to be taken into account, such a contribution must be wholly exceptional.
- Wealth generated prior to the marriage and after separation – assets brought into the marriage or acquired or created by one party after separation may qualify as non-matrimonial property. This factor will only carry weight in cases where the assets available for distribution exceed the parties' reasonable needs and where the non-matrimonial property can be clearly identified.
- Needs exceed resources – equality may be departed from in cases where the parties' needs exceed the assets available for distribution, ie, where

most of the capital is required to house the wife and children. In such cases, equality may be deferred by giving the party who receives less an interest realisable at a later date, for example a share in the family home secured by a charge on the property realisable when the youngest child completes full-time education.

9. FINANCES/MAINTENANCE

9.1 Explain the operation of maintenance for spouses on an ongoing basis after the breakdown of marriage

As an interim measure, either party can apply at any time until the final hearing for maintenance pending suit (interim financial assistance) by virtue of section 22 MCA 1973. This can include provision for legal costs as part of a monthly maintenance award.

Section 23(1) MCA 1973 enables the court to order either party to the marriage to pay periodical payments to the other and to provide that such payments should be secured. An order, which can be backdated to the date of the application, will terminate by operation of law on the remarriage of the recipient, the death of either party, or the making of a further court order.

Section 28(1) MCA 1973 affords the court a discretion to fix a term for the making of periodical payments, and in certain circumstances, to bar the recipient from applying to extend the term.

9.2 Is it common for maintenance to be awarded?

The courts recognise that both parties require an income and therefore it is common for periodical payments to be awarded, particularly to the person who is the children's primary carer and whose earning capacity is temporarily or permanently reduced by childcare obligations.

9.3 Explain and illustrate with reference to recent cases the court's thinking in relation to maintenance

The general principle is that the quantum of any order will be assessed with reference to the section 25 MCA 1973 criteria, after first consideration has been given to the welfare of any minor children of the family. There is no prescribed formula and each case will be decided on its own facts and circumstances. In fixing the amount, the court has a wide discretionary power but will generally try to achieve a balance between the budgetary needs of the parties and the income resources available to them. *McFarlane* illustrated that, in cases where there is surplus income, the courts can order maintenance to enable one party to build up capital for the future.

10. CHILD MAINTENANCE

10.1 On what basis is child maintenance calculated within the jurisdiction?

The legal requirement for parents to support their children financially continues after divorce or a separation. Non-resident parents are required to provide payment to the parent with care in respect of children who are under the age of 16 or under the age of 20 and in full-time secondary education. For parents who cannot agree maintenance arrangements and who are both resident in England and Wales, there is a complex set of laws and regulations commencing with the Child Support Act 1991 and a series of amending statutes and regulations. These have effectively resulted in three child support regimes, the most recent of which is the 2008 regime which has not yet been fully implemented. The great majority of existing and new cases, save where the payer has four or more relevant children, are currently administered by the Child Support Agency (CSA) or Child Maintenance Service.

The CSA calculates the payments on the basis of a fixed statutory formula which provides for the 'non-resident' parent to pay 15 per cent of income, net of tax, national insurance and pension contributions, for one child; 20 per cent for two and 25 per cent for three or more children. Net income for these purposes is capped at £2,000 per week. If the non-resident parent's weekly net weekly income exceeds £2,000, the parent with care may make an application to the court for increased maintenance (a 'top up' order). The court can also make orders for the payment of school fees, maintenance for step-children and where the child is over the child support age but has a disability which requires extra financial support.

The figure can be adjusted to take into account the number of nights in excess of 52 a year a child stays with the non-resident parent. Additionally, if the non-resident parent has other children living with them, a percentage of their net income will be disregarded.

The Child Maintenance Service will ultimately take over from the CSA and will work on the basis of the paying parent's yearly gross income using information supplied by HM Revenue & Customs or information about benefits received by unemployed parents. The percentages of gross income will be 12 per cent, 16 per cent and 19 per cent of weekly gross income up to £800 and 9 per cent, 12 per cent and 15 per cent to any excess over £800 gross per week.

The court can also order lump sum payments or the settlement of property for the benefit of a child under Schedule 1 of the CA 1989.

11. RECIPROCAL ENFORCEMENT OF FINANCIAL ORDERS

11.1 Summarise the position in your jurisdiction

Part II of The Maintenance Orders (Reciprocal Enforcement) Act 1972 makes provision for maintenance orders made in signatory countries to be registered and enforced in the UK, against a UK resident. Once an application made by the relevant foreign authority is received by the Reciprocal Enforcement of Maintenance Orders (REMO) section at the Department for Constitutional Affairs, it can be registered with the appropriate court and enforced accordingly. The list of reciprocating countries is extensive and is contained in the Recovery Abroad of Maintenance (Convention Countries) Order 1975 (SI 1975/423), as amended. The United States (excluding Alabama, Mississippi, South Carolina and the District of Columbia) are signatories, albeit with some modifications as to the procedure to be followed, by virtue of the Reciprocal Enforcement of Maintenance Orders (United States of America) Order 1995, SI 1995/2709.

Similarly, a UK resident can make use of reciprocal arrangements and enforce maintenance orders made by a UK court in other signatory countries.

The Civil Jurisdiction and Judgment Act 1982, as amended, gives effect to the EC Regulation on the Enforcement of Judgments in civil and commercial matters and further allows for the recognition and enforcement of maintenance orders as well as the enforcement of judgments, other than maintenance orders, made in a Brussels IIR or Lugano Convention country.

12. FINANCIAL RELIEF AFTER FOREIGN DIVORCE PROCEEDINGS

12.1 What powers are available to make orders following a foreign divorce?

Part III MFPA 1984 provides the framework within which an individual can, in certain circumstances, apply through the English courts for financial relief following an overseas divorce.

Permission needs to be obtained from the court before applying for financial relief. Section 15 MFPA 1984 sets out the circumstances in which the court will have jurisdiction to hear such an application:

- either party is domiciled in England and Wales either on the date of the application for permission (leave) or on the date on which the divorce, annulment or legal separation obtained in the overseas country took effect in that country;
- either party was habitually resident in England and Wales throughout the period of one year ending either with the date of the application for leave or with the date on which the divorce, annulment or legal separation obtained in the overseas country took effect; or
- either or both had, at the date of the application for leave, a beneficial interest in possession in a dwelling-house situated in England or Wales, which was at some time during the marriage a matrimonial home.

Under section 13(1) MFPA 1984, permission to bring Part III proceedings will be granted if there is 'substantial ground for the making of an application for such an order'. The relevant facts to which the court will have regard are contained in section 16(2) and include the parties' connection to England and Wales, the jurisdiction in which the marriage was dissolved, the ability of the applicant to apply for financial orders in that jurisdiction and the availability of any property in the jurisdiction of England and Wales.

The Supreme Court case of *Agbaje* [2010] UKSC 13 has confirmed that it is not necessary that the applicant should prove that any financial award made by a foreign court has resulted in a real hardship or serious injustice. At the same time, the court will not intervene merely because one party wants their financial award 'topped-up' to the equivalent award that would have been granted under English law.

D. CHILDREN

13. CUSTODY/PARENTAL RESPONSIBILITY

13.1 Briefly explain the legal position in relation to custody/parental responsibility following the breakdown of a relationship or marriage.

Following the breakdown of a marriage or relationship, the parents may decide between themselves who any children are to live with and what contact they will have with each parent. If the parents do not agree about the arrangements, either may apply to the court under section 8 CA 1989 to determine the position. The court may specify the child is to live with one parent, or may make a shared residence order providing that the child lives with both parents. This does not necessarily mean the child spends an equal amount of time with each parent, but it is seen as giving parity of parental status. At the time of going to press, the Government is seeking to introduce a statutory presumption in favour of shared parenting through the Children and Families Bill.

The fact that both parents retain parental responsibility gives them, in theory, an equal say in major decisions in the child's life such as schooling, religious upbringing and medical treatment. Day-to-day decisions will inevitably be made by the parent with whom the child resides for the majority of the time.

When making any order under section 8, the child's welfare must be the court's primary consideration. When determining whether an order is in the child's best interests, the court must consider the welfare checklist set out in section 1(3) CA 1989. The factors to be considered include the child's physical, emotional and educational needs, and how capable each of their parents is of meeting their needs. The wishes of the child may be taken into consideration if they are of sufficient age and understanding. The court must give consideration to the 'delay' and 'no order' principles under sections 1(2) and 1(5) CA 1989 respectively. These state that any delay in proceedings is likely to be prejudicial to the welfare of the child and that the court should only make an order if it is better for the child than if no order were made.

13.2 Briefly explain the legal position in relation to access/contact/visitation following the breakdown of a relationship or marriage

The position with regard to contact is similar to that of residence. Parents are free to determine contact between themselves, with the court able to make an order under section 8 CA 1989 if they are unable to reach agreement. In all cases which come before the court, safeguarding checks are undertaken by CAFCASS (Child & Family Court Advisory & Support Service). Where there are allegations of or proven domestic violence, contact may be limited to indirect means such as cards and letters or may be supervised.

Conditions may be attached to contact, eg, where the parent with care fears abduction, the non-resident parent may have to surrender their passport for the duration of contact.

Where a parent is in breach of a contact order, the other parent may apply for an enforcement order for breach of which there are penalties including a requirement to undertake unpaid work.

As with residence orders, the court must consider the welfare checklist and the 'no order' principle. Contact is seen as a right of the child and not the parents.

14. INTERNATIONAL ABDUCTION

14.1 Summarise the position in your jurisdiction

England is a party to The Hague Convention which sets out strict rules on the wrongful removal of a child from its place 'of habitual residence', or the wrongful 'retention' of a child away from its place of habitual residence, in breach of the other parent's 'custody rights'. The Convention provides that the courts of signatory states will generally return an abducted child to the country it came from, although there is a limited discretion in certain circumstances to allow the child to stay in the new country.

Where the child's country of habitual residence is not a Convention signatory, the English courts will be guided by whether or not the return would be in the child's best interests taking into account such factors as nationality, language, race and how familiar the child is with England. An English parent trying to secure the return of a child from a country which is not a Convention signatory could face substantial difficulties.

The Convention sets out strict rules about what constitutes abduction. It occurs where a parent takes a child out of the home country without the permission of the other parent or where the child has been taken out of the home country with the other parent's permission, but is not returned as agreed. The 'habitual residence' of the child is usually straightforward as it is the country where the child lives on a day-to-day basis. If the child was in the process of moving home abroad, this can be more difficult. Abduction will not result in a change in the habitual residence of the child.

Abduction requires the violation of 'custody rights' and this term is not well defined. It seems to involve having the right to help make decisions about the care of the child, particularly in relation to determining where the child is to live. As custody arrangements operate differently from country to country, the circumstances of each individual case must be carefully considered. In England and Wales, the question of whether a parent has 'parental responsibility' under the CA 1989 will be relevant.

Defences which may prevent the return of a child to a home country include clear evidence of consent or acquiescence to the removal of the child, or where there is a real and substantial risk that the return of the child would expose them to physical or psychological harm or otherwise place the child in an intolerable situation. If a parent seeking a child's return under the Convention applies less than one year after the abduction, the court in the new country must order the return of the child unless one of these defences has been established. If the application was made over a year after the abduction, the new country must return the child unless one of the defences has been established or it is demonstrated that the child is now settled in the new country. The court may refuse to order the return of the child who objects to being returned and has attained an age and degree of maturity at which it is appropriate to take account of their views.

Brussels IIR places emphasis on the views of the children but this defence is not often upheld due to the possibility that the child's views have been influenced by the adult with whom they are living. In England and Wales it has traditionally been very difficult to establish this defence.

15. LEAVE TO REMOVE/APPLICATIONS TO TAKE A CHILD OUT OF THE JURISDICTION

15.1 Summarise the position in your jurisdiction. Under what circumstances may a parent apply to remove their child from the jurisdiction against the wishes of the other parent?

A parent who shares parental responsibility with another parent cannot remove a child from the jurisdiction without written consent of that person or permission of the court.

In contrast to the approach adopted in much of the US, the English approach is generally said to favour the mother who wishes to relocate to a foreign jurisdiction, particularly if she is the sole carer.

Applications for leave to remove are governed by the welfare principle as set out in section 1 CA 1989. Most applications for leave to remove are made by mothers (and primary carers of children). The courts have until recently endorsed the approach taken in *Payne* [2001] 1FLR1052 where, as well as considering the welfare of the child and whether the application was genuine, the court looked at the impact of refusing the application on the mother.

This approach has been seen as increasingly out of touch with modern shared parenting arrangements. The decision in *MK v CK* [2011] EWCA Civ 793 recognised that where shared parenting exists, the role of each parent in the child's life may be 'equally important'.

E. SURROGACY & ADOPTION

16. VALIDITY OF SURROGACY AGREEMENTS

16.1 Briefly summarise the position in your jurisdiction

The key legislation is the Surrogacy Arrangements Act 1985 (SSA 1985) and the Human Fertilisation and Embryology Act 2008 (HFEA 2008). Under section 1A SSA 1985 surrogacy agreements are currently unenforceable under English law. Further, section 3 SSA 1985 creates a number of criminal offences in relation to surrogacy, including advertising for a surrogate mother.

Despite this, people still enter into surrogacy agreements. The legal consequences in terms of the parent/child relationship are governed by sections 33 to 42 of HFEA 2008. The surrogate is the legal mother of the child and any husband of hers the legal father. If she is in a civil partnership, her partner will be a legal parent. If the woman is unmarried at the time of the surrogacy, the intended father can be named as the legal father.

Once the child is born, legal parenthood can be transferred from the surrogate (and her husband or partner) to the intended parents. At present, only couples (heterosexual or same-ex, married or long-term cohabiting) can apply to become the legal parents of a surrogate child. The intended parents have six months from the birth of the child to apply for a parental order. The court must be satisfied that the surrogate mother and any other deemed legal parent give their full and informed consent, that no money or benefits other than 'reasonable expenses' have been transferred to anyone involved in the surrogacy arrangement.

With international surrogacy arrangements, the courts have confirmed that English law takes precedence over foreign surrogacy laws – foreign court orders and birth certificates will not be recognised. In *Re X (Children) (Parental Order: Foreign Surrogacy)* [2008] EWHC 3030 (Fam) the court granted a parental order despite the parents' payment to a surrogate. This was primarily because the welfare of the child demanded it and the parents had not exploited the surrogate.

17. ADOPTION

17.1 Briefly explain the legal position in relation to adoption in your jurisdiction. Is adoption available to individuals, cohabiting couples (both heterosexual and same-sex)?

Married people, civil partners, cohabiting couples and individuals can all adopt under English law. The key legislation governing adoption is the Adoption Act 1976 and the Adoption and Children Act 2002 (ACA 2002).

Section 19 ACA 2002 stipulates that parental consent is required for an adoption but this can be, and often is, dispensed with via section 52 ACA 2002 by the court making a placement order.

Once a placement order is granted or consent to adoption is given, a period of prospective adoption is required before an application for a final adoption order can be made.

Following an application, the court has to consider a number of factors in determining whether to grant an adoption order.

The primary consideration is the child's welfare throughout his life. The factors outlined in section 1(4) ACA 2002 include the child's needs, any harm they are at risk of suffering and any relationship they have with the birth family. The court must also consider the delay principle – section 1(3) ACA 2002. In addition, section 1(5) ACA 2002 requires the court to give due consideration to the child's religious, racial, cultural and linguistic background. At the time of going to press, the Government has proposed the removal of this requirement in its Children and Families Bill.

Generally, the effect of an adoption order is to treat the child as if they were born to the adopter(s) – section 67 ACA 2002. Contact with the birth parents may be granted through a contact order, but there is no automatic right to it. The adopted child may choose to make contact with their birth parents once they are 18.

F. COHABITATION

18. COHABITATION

18.1 What legislation (if any) governs division of property for unmarried couples on the breakdown of the relationship?

Unlike marriage, no legal or financial responsibility between couples will arise from the simple fact of cohabitation. Despite a common misconception, England and Wales does not recognise so-called 'common-law marriage' (whereby a couple who live as man and wife without getting married acquire legal rights in relation to each other), regardless of the length of their cohabitation. Cohabitants have little legal protection and any claims that arise from the relationship fall into two categories: claims brought on behalf of children and claims for an interest in property. To establish an interest in a property which is not in joint names, a cohabitant must rely on property law and the principles of 'constructive trusts' and 'proprietary estoppel'.

Properties held in joint names (a 'joint tenancy') will generally be shared equally upon relationship breakdown. If the property is held in unequal shares based on initial contribution to the purchase price (a 'tenancy in common'), each cohabitant will take back their relative share upon sale.

To establish a constructive trust, the claimant must show that there was an agreement, arrangement or understanding to own a property jointly. The agreement can be express or inferred from conduct. The claimant must then have acted to his or her detriment, for example by making financial contributions, on the understanding that he or she would thereby acquire an interest in the property. Alternatively, the claimant can rely on proprietary estoppel, which has traditionally been applied where the claimant was led to believe that the property would be owned jointly, and acted to their detriment upon that assurance.

While there is growing pressure for change, there are no immediate plans for reform.

G. FAMILY DISPUTE RESOLUTION

19. MEDIATION, COLLABORATIVE LAW & ARBITRATION

19.1 Briefly summarise the non-court-based processes available in your jurisdiction and the current status of agreements reached under the auspices of mediation, collaborative law and arbitration

Mediation is a form of negotiation using a neutral third party to assist in identifying and narrowing the issues between the parties. Mediators do not provide advice and usually the parties involved rely on their own lawyers for advice.

Collaborative law is a process whereby the parties and their lawyers negotiate face to face through a series of meetings. The collaborative process requires all the lawyers involved to sign an agreement stating they will not continue to represent the parties if the collaborative approach fails.

Arbitration was introduced in February 2012. It is governed by the provisions of the Arbitration Act 1996 in conjunction with the rules of the Institute of Family Law Arbitrators (IFLA). The process is similar to a final hearing in a court with the arbitrator presiding and making a final award. The IFLA Scheme covers most financial disputes, but not disputes about children.

Alternatively, the parties may opt for a private financial dispute resolution (FDR) hearing. These are 'judge' mediated meetings at which the 'judge' will make a recommendation as to the likely range of outcomes should the parties progress their financial dispute to a final hearing. It is hoped this will focus the minds of the parties and encourage them towards settlement.

Mediation, collaborative law and private FDR hearings do not, by themselves, produce binding decisions. Agreements will need to be finalised by a court order to be legally binding and enforceable.

Although English law does not allow parties to make final agreements as to finances following divorce or separation without the possibility of court review and any arbitration decision must be approved by the court, indications are that the awards will be upheld.

19.2 What is the statutory basis (if any) for mediation, collaborative law and arbitration in your jurisdiction? In particular, are the parties required to attempt a family dispute resolution in advance of the institution of proceedings.

Mediation, collaborative law and private hearings do not have any statutory basis under English law.

Parties are not under any compulsion to attempt alternative dispute resolution before issuing proceedings. However, they are strongly encouraged to do so and the Family Procedure Rules 2010 (FPR), contain a number of provisions promoting alternative resolution.

The FPR contain an 'overriding objective' at Part 1 which requires the court to deal with the matter justly and the parties to assist the court in achieving this aim. Dealing with the matter justly includes saving expense and dealing with the case expeditiously. This clearly requires the parties to attempt to settle where possible. Costs could be awarded against a party who takes a wholly unreasonable stance in refusing to negotiate or attempting to settle.

Practice Direction 3A FPR 2010 requires parties to attend a Mediation Information and Assessment Meeting prior to issuing financial and Children Act proceedings. This requires the parties to consider mediation but it does not commit them to the procedure.

Moreover, Part 3 FDR requires the court to consider, at every stage of the case, whether alternative dispute resolution is appropriate. A case may be adjourned so that the parties can attempt to settle out of court.

H. OTHER

20. CIVIL PARTNERSHIP/SAME-SEX MARRIAGE

20.1 What is the status of civil partnership/same-sex marriage within the jurisdiction? What legislation governs civil partnership/same-sex marriage?

Governed by the CPA 2004, civil partnerships are often said to be civil marriage in all but name, but there remains an important legal distinction between the two institutions. *Rayden on Divorce* summarises the position: 'marriage requires the participation of two persons one a man the other a woman'.

The Marriage (Same-Sex Couples) Bill, which aims to introduce same-sex marriage in England, received its third reading on 21 May 2013, passing by a large majority in the House of Commons of 366 to 161.

21. CONTROVERSIAL AREAS/RAPIDLY DEVELOPING AREAS OF LAW

21.1 Is there a particular area of the law within the jurisdiction that is currently undergoing major change? Which areas of law are most out-of-step? Which areas would you most like to see reformed/changed.

One of the mostly controversial issues is the removal of almost all legal aid in family matters with effect from 1 April 2013. Legal aid will still be available for care proceedings and cases involving domestic violence. Parties will have to find alternative ways of funding any other proceedings involving children and any financial disputes. Concerns have been raised that this will deny people access to justice and that an increased number of people will act as 'litigants in person', resulting in a slowing down of the court system.

In autumn 2013, the Law Commission is due to publish its report into the division of matrimonial property on divorce or separation and marital property agreements. In an interim announcement, the Commission stated its belief that court decisions on the division of assets on divorce are currently far too unpredictable. It hinted that it may recommend legislation to provide further guidance to judges on the division of assets. It is hoped this may lead to greater certainty.

Finland

Asianajotoimisto Juhani Salmenkylä Ky, Attorneys at law Hilkka Salmenkylä

A. JURISDICTION AND CONFLICT OF LAW

1. SOURCES OF LAW

1.1 What is the primary source of law in relation to the breakdown of marriage and the welfare of children within the jurisdiction?

The Finnish legal system is based on statutes enacted by the Parliament. The most important of the sources of law is legislation. The interpretation of the law may draw on the legislative materials, legal practice, general legal principles and jurisprudence. It seems that the content of family legislation has, intentionally even, been left unclear in order to force us to use these other measures.

1.2 Which are the main statutes governing matrimonial law in the jurisdiction?

There are several provisions, Acts and decrees concerning family law in Finland. The main ones are:

- Marriage Act
- Code of Inheritance
- Child Custody and Rights of Access Act
- Act on the Enforcement of a Decision on Child Custody and the Right of Access
- Child Maintenance Act
- Paternity Act
- Act on Registered Partnerships

Brussels II (Council Regulation (EC) No 2201/2003), Maintenance Regulation (Council Regulation (EC) No4/2009) and the Convention on the Rights of a Child and the European Convention on Human Rights are also in force as nationally binding law.

2. JURISDICTION

2.1 What are the main jurisdictional requirements for the institution of proceedings in relation to divorce, property and children?

Brussels II and Maintenance Regulation apply, and the following applies only in so far as otherwise not provided for in them.

Under the Marriage Act, the Finnish court has jurisdiction if either spouse is domiciled in Finland, or the petitioner has been domiciled in Finland or has a close link to Finland and is unable to obtain a divorce in the foreign state where either spouse is domiciled, or if this would cause unreasonable inconvenience to the petitioner, and the admissibility of the matter in Finland is justified in view of the circumstances.

The Finnish court has jurisdiction on a matter pertaining to the personal legal consequences of marriage if the respondent is domiciled or habitually resident in Finland, and on a matter pertaining to maintenance, and also if the person entitled to maintenance is domiciled or habitually resident in Finland.

The Finnish court has jurisdiction on a matter pertaining to matrimonial property if the respondent is domiciled or habitually resident in Finland, if the petitioner is domiciled or habitually resident in Finland and the law of Finland is to apply on the matter pertaining to matrimonial property, if the last common domicile or place of habitual residence of the spouses was in Finland and one of the spouses is still domiciled or habitually resident there, if the property is located in Finland, or if the respondent accepts that the matter be admissible in Finland.

A Finnish court competent in a matter pertaining to divorce may, at the same time, hear an ancillary matter pertaining to the maintenance payable to a spouse or another matter pertaining to the personal legal consequences of marriage, if the resolution of the latter is necessary owing to the divorce.

Under The Child Custody and Rights of Access Act, a Finnish court may consider a case if the child is habitually resident in Finland. A child, who has lived in Finland continuously for at least one year immediately prior to the case being brought before the court, is considered to be habitually resident in Finland. Even if the child is not habitually resident in Finland, a Finnish court may consider a case relating to child custody or rights of access if the child lives in Finland or if there is good reason for it or if the child has, with regard to all the relevant circumstances, another close connection with Finland.

3. DOMICILE AND HABITUAL RESIDENCE

3.1 Explain the concepts of domicile and habitual residence as they apply to the jurisdiction, in relation to divorce, the finances and children

The concepts of 'habitual residence' and 'domicile' are very similar in Finland. Habitual residence should mean where you actually live and work and where your children go to school, so where the centre of your life is, and domicile in which population register you are registered in. The use of these terms has not been systematic in Finnish legislation or jurisprudence, especially in translations of Conventions.

4. CONFLICT OF LAW/APPLICABLE LAW TO BE APPLIED

4.1 What happens when one party applies to stay proceedings in favour of a foreign jurisdiction? What factors will the local court take into account when determining forum issues?

In relation to the personal legal consequences of marriage, the law of the state where both spouses are domiciled will apply. If they are not domiciled in the same state, the law of the state where both spouses were last domiciled during the marriage will apply. In other situations the law of the state to which they have the closest link will apply.

In relation to matrimonial property matters, unless otherwise agreed, the law of the country which, upon marriage, became the domicile of both spouses, will apply. If the spouses subsequently changed domicile, the law of the new domicile would apply, provided the spouses had resided there for at least five years. The law of the new domicile would apply immediately if the spouses had been domiciled there earlier in the marriage or if both of them were citizens of the new domicile. If no country has become the domicile of both spouses, the law of the country to which, taking all circumstances into account, the spouses have the closest link will apply.

If questioned, the court needs to determine whether the case is brought up in the correct forum. If not, the case should be dismissed.

If one party were to demand a foreign law be applied, that party would, if applicable, have to clarify the content of that law, otherwise the court will apply the Finnish law. Content of law means the Acts, legislative materials, legal praxis and legal literature.

The law allows the spouses to decide in advance or during the marriage which law will govern their matrimonial property matters, provided that at least one of the spouses has a connection based on nationality or domicile to the state whose law they want to apply.

They can choose the law of the country in which one or both of them are domiciled or were last domiciled or they can choose the law of the country of which one of the spouses is a citizen at the time of the agreement. The agreement must be in writing in order to be valid, but does not have to be witnessed or registered anywhere.

B. PRE- AND POST-NUPTIAL AGREEMENTS

5. VALIDITY OF PRE- AND POST-NUPTIAL AGREEMENTS

5.1 To what extent are pre- and post-nups binding within the jurisdiction? Could you provide a brief discussion of the most significant recent case law on this issue?

The spouses can, either before the conclusion of the marriage or during the marriage, execute a marriage settlement. In a marriage settlement, the engaged persons or spouses may exclude from the marital right any property owned or later acquired by a spouse. In a marriage settlement, the spouses can agree that, when the marriage is dissolved, the property of the spouses is not divided equally, but that each spouse keeps their property. The marriage settlement can also stipulate that a spouse has no matrimonial right to certain property belonging to the other spouse, such as real estate or property obtained as inheritance.

The spouses may also agree to restore the marital right of a spouse to property previously excluded from the said right by way of a prior marriage settlement.

The marriage settlement is concluded in writing. It is dated and signed. In addition, two non-disqualified persons – persons without any close connection, like a relationship to the spouses – must attest it. The marriage settlement enters into force when it has been registered by the local register office.

A marriage settlement affects the distribution of matrimonial assets. A marriage settlement relates to the distribution when the marriage is dissolved through the death of a spouse and when the distribution is carried out on the basis of a divorce.

However, a marriage settlement is not necessarily binding. Its stipulations may be derogated from, or it may be set aside altogether, in the adjustment of the distribution of matrimonial property in case compliance with the marriage settlement would result in an unreasonable result.

Since 2000, it has been possible, according to the Supreme Court decision KKO:2000:100, to exclude marital right only in case of divorce. This decision has, however, been criticised to be false and against the clear wording of the law.

C. DIVORCE, NULLITY AND JUDICIAL SEPARATION

6. RECOGNITION OF FOREIGN MARRIAGES/DIVORCES

6.1 Summarise the position in your jurisdiction

A marriage solemnised according to laws of another country is legally recognised in Finland after the marriage has been registered in Finland.

A marriage between a woman and a man in a foreign state is valid in Finland if it is valid in the state where it was concluded or in a state where either spouse was a citizen or where either spouse was habitually resident at the time of the marriage.

A marriage that has been entered into in a foreign state after the death of one engaged person or without one engaged person being present in person at the time of the marriage, or that has been entered into merely by practice and without a ceremony or other formality, shall be valid in Finland only if it is valid in a state referred to above and there is a special reason why the marriage should be deemed valid in Finland.

Special attention shall be given to the links of the engaged persons to the state where the marriage was entered into and to the duration of the cohabitation of the spouses.

A matter pertaining to the validity of a marriage may be ruled admissible in Finland if a matter pertaining to the divorce of the spouses would be admissible in Finland. If the resolution of a matter depends on the validity of a marriage, a Finnish authority may determine the validity in connection with the resolution of this matter, even if the matter of validity would otherwise be inadmissible.

A foreign judgment about divorce shall be deemed valid in Finland without any specific validation if, at the time of the judgment, both spouses were citizens of the state whose authority issued the judgment or if the judgment pertains to spouses where neither of them was a Finnish citizen at the time of the judgment, and the judgment is deemed valid in both spouses' home countries. If at least one of spouses was a Finnish citizen at the time of the judgment, it shall be valid in Finland only if specifically validated.

A judgment may be validated here, if either spouse, in view of their citizenship or domicile, has such a link to the foreign state in question that the authorities of that state can be deemed to have had adequate grounds of being seised of the matter, and if the judgment is not in essential conflict with Finnish public policy (*ordre public*).

7. DIVORCE

7.1 Explain the grounds for divorce within the jurisdiction (please also deal with nullity and judicial separation if appropriate)

A marriage is dissolved by a court order (divorce). A divorce is granted after a reconsideration period of six months or after the spouses have lived separately for two years without interruption.

A divorce case becomes pending in the District Court by a written application, which can be made by the spouses together or by one spouse alone. The application can also be sent by mail, telefax or email.

When handling a case of divorce, the court does not examine the grounds for divorce nor the personal relationship between the spouses. It is enough to write simply 'I want a divorce'. A spouse is always entitled to obtain a divorce. A spouse cannot prevent the other spouse from obtaining a divorce by objecting to it.

After a reconsideration period of at least six months, the spouses or just one of them can apply for divorce, also now only stating 'I want a divorce'. The original applicant cannot withdraw the original application. The request has to be made within one year of the beginning of the reconsideration period; otherwise the divorce case shall lapse. No oral hearing is organised.

In connection with proceedings relating to divorce, the following matters can also be decided:

- maintenance to a child or the spouse;
- the custody and visiting rights of a child;
- ordering one of the spouses to continue to live in the common home and the other spouse to vacate the common home (until division of property only); or
- appointing an estate distributor.

Alternatively, the spouses can agree on these matters or even leave them unresolved and have separate judicial proceedings at a later date if needed.

Previously and until 1988, the divorce system in Finland was based on guilt on the part of the spouse. Grounds for guilt were those such as adultery, assault or habitual abuse of alcohol or drugs.

The Marriage Act no longer has regulations on 'cancellation of marriage' or 'nullification of marriage'. Today, according to the Supreme Administrative Court, there is only one way of dissolving a marriage (besides death) and that is divorce. Even if one of the spouses was mentally ill and could not understand the ceremony or the marriage, the marriage could not be cancelled (KHO: 2003:69).

8. FINANCES/CAPITAL, PROPERTY

8.1 What powers does the court have to allocate financial resources and property on the breakdown of marriage?

The property that a spouse has when entering into the marriage remains theirs. The spouse also owns what they have acquired during the marriage. Each spouse has a marital right to the property of the other spouse. According to this right, each spouse acquires half of the net property of the spouses at the distribution of matrimonial property.

A spouse does not have a marital right to property excluded from the scope of the marital right by a marriage settlement, a gift deed or a will, nor to property acquired in *lieu* of such property.

When proceedings relating to divorce are pending, a distribution of matrimonial property will be carried out if a spouse so demands. It is not obligatory, they can also leave it undistributed. If either spouse has a marital right to the property of the other spouse, a separation of the property of the spouses will be carried out instead of the distribution.

The distribution of the matrimonial assets can be carried out by the parties themselves in accordance with a mutual agreement (distribution by agreement – more than 90 per cent of all distributions) or the distribution can be carried out by an estate distributor appointed by the court (official distribution). Division of assets is not carried out by the court.

When the distribution is carried out by agreement, the distribution shall be reduced to a document, which must be dated and signed and attested by two non-disqualified persons. If an estate distributor carries out the distribution, they draft it in the form of a document, which they must sign. A distribution of matrimonial property is carried out according to the provisions on the distribution of a decedent's estate, according to the Code of Inheritance and to the further provisions in the Marriage Act.

If a spouse so demands, the distribution shall be carried out by an estate distributor. On petition, the court appoints a suitable person as the estate distributor. In practice, a suitable person is a member of the bar, which means a private practising advocate. If the spouses have different candidates, the court most often chooses the one first suggested.

A spouse who wishes to contest a distribution carried out by an estate distributor shall bring an action against the other spouse within six months of the date of the distribution in a district court.

The right to have a distributor appointed does not become statute barred. There has been a case where an estate distributor was appointed 30 years after the divorce as the other spouse could not prove that the division of property had been carried out!

A marriage settlement affects the distribution of matrimonial assets. A marriage settlement relates to the distribution when the marriage is dissolved through the death of a spouse and when the distribution is carried out on the basis of a divorce.

The distribution of matrimonial assets can be adjusted. Adjustment is always an exception to the main rule of dividing all the assets in half.

The adjustment of the distribution means that, in an individual case on the basis of consideration, the rules otherwise applicable to the distribution of matrimonial property may be derogated from. A spouse can demand adjustment during the proceedings from the very start, any time during the proceedings, and also in court contesting the estate distributor's decision.

The distribution can be adjusted if the distribution would lead to an unreasonable end result or to the other spouse receiving unjust financial benefit. When considering the adjustment of the distribution, special attention shall be paid to the duration of the marriage, the activities of the spouses for the benefit of their common household or for the accumulation and preservation of the property, and to other comparable facts regarding the finances of the spouses.

Therefore, the adjustment of the distribution of matrimonial assets takes place paying attention to perspectives of reasonableness and justice separately in each individual case. No general rules can be set in advance as to when the adjustment of the distribution of matrimonial assets is possible, how the adjustment shall be carried out or how often the adjustment shall be applied.

8.2 Explain and illustrate with reference to recent cases the court's thinking on division of assets

There are about 13,000 divorces per year in Finland. About 750 estate distributors are appointed. Only about 75 cases to contest the distribution are handled in court. Most of them stay at district court level.

Sometimes the divorce lapses after distribution has been carried out. Then you have no marital right to the other spouse's property. Supreme Court, KKO:2010:92: A and B had signed an agreement on distribution of property on 15 May 1991 after divorce was pending. They continued their marriage and the divorce lapsed. A asked the court to appoint an estate distributor to carry out a distribution of their assets or a separation of their property. An estate distributor was appointed to carry out a separation of property.

A practical question was answered by the Supreme Court in an augmented division. Supreme Court KKO:2011:31: The lawyer proposed as distributor was disqualified for this task as the application was drawn up by a lawyer from the same law office.

9. FINANCES/MAINTENANCE

9.1 Explain the operation of maintenance for spouses on an ongoing basis after the breakdown of marriage

When married, both spouses should contribute to the household finances and maintenance, according to their financial capacities. The spouses have a mutual maintenance obligation towards one another. The provisions on spouses are also applied to the parties of a registered partnership. In other types of relationships, the parties have no duty to maintain one another.

A spouse may ask for maintenance during the marriage or in connection with divorce.

9.2 Is it common for maintenance to be awarded?

Involuntary maintenance after divorce, although possible according to the

Marriage Act, is practically non-existent. In Finnish legal practice, it is very rare for a spouse to be obliged to pay maintenance to the other spouse. As a rule, after the divorce, the spouses shall support themselves, earn their own living, or if they cannot, the social security system is supposed to take care of them.

When the spouses are granted a divorce by a court and a spouse is deemed to be in need of maintenance, the court may, upon request, order the other spouse to pay the requesting spouse maintenance deemed reasonable with a view to the paying spouse's capability to pay maintenance and other circumstances.

The maintenance may be confirmed payable in periodic installments or as a lump sum. Maintenance may be ordered to be paid until further notice or until the period determined in the order. The obligation to pay maintenance in periodic instalments shall lapse if the spouse to whom it is granted remarries.

The amount of maintenance and its method of payment can also be confirmed by agreement.

9.3 Explain and illustrate with reference to recent cases the court's thinking on maintenance

The Supreme Court, KKO:2010:3, upheld its praxis. The question was whether the wife had right to maintenance after divorce. She was of foreign origin, she did not speak good Finnish, she was without professional training and the marriage had lasted for about 10 years. At the time of divorce, the wife was about 50, the husband 65. The parties had three young children who stayed living with the father. The mother was practically evicted.

According to the court's reasoning, the judgment will be based on the fact that the spouse is in need of maintenance. If there is no need, there is no obligation to pay. Secondly, the other spouse must be capable of paying and, thirdly, the circumstances must be so that the obligation to pay can be deemed reasonable.

As it was stated earlier in KKO:2004:104, the principal rule is that the financial bond created by the marriage ceases in divorce and the liability to provide maintenance ends. The obligation to pay maintenance might be an issue only when the other spouse has been left totally without the ability to support himself/herself because of the marriage. Divorce as such, does not give cause to claim maintenance.

The Supreme Court thus ordered, voting 4-1, that the husband pay a small sum of money monthly for three years starting from the date of the divorce. The lower courts had refused the application. The one minority member of the court would have refused the claim.

In KKO:2011:97 the Supreme Court applied the Swiss law and ordered, voting 3-2, that the husband must pay the ex-wife, living in Switzerland, maintenance until further notice. The minority refused the claim. The marriage had lasted for more than 20 years.

10. CHILD MAINTENANCE

10.1 On what basis is child maintenance calculated within the jurisdiction?

Child maintenance is regulated by the Child Maintenance Act. A child is entitled to maintenance from its parents. If a parent neglects to maintain a child, or if the child does not live permanently with a parent, the parent can be ordered to pay maintenance to the child.

A claim for child maintenance can be handled separately. It may also be presented in connection with paternity, divorce or custody and rights of access proceedings.

A child is entitled to maintenance from the parents until the age of 18. The parents are responsible for the costs incurred by education, even after the child has turned 18, if deemed reasonable. The term 'education' refers primarily to upper secondary education.

As a rule, maintenance is payable in cash on a monthly basis and in advance, unless otherwise agreed or stipulated.

There is a fixed formula for calculating maintenance, an instruction given by the Ministry of Justice. It is not legally binding but most courts use it. Regardless of this instruction, the final consideration of the amount of maintenance is made on an individual basis. This was confirmed by two Supreme Court decisions KKO:2010:37 and KKO:2010:38.

A child has the right to adequate maintenance. That consists of the satisfactory fulfillment of the child's needs, necessary care and education and payment of the resulting costs. The parents are responsible for the maintenance of the child based on their financial capacity. Consideration shall be given to the parents' age, ability to work and opportunity to take part in gainful employment and the amount of assets available to them.

When assessing the extent of the parents' maintenance duty, the child's ability and possibility to maintain himself/herself are also taken into account, as are any circumstances in which child maintenance does not incur any costs to the parents, or the costs are minimal.

The amount and payment method of maintenance can be adjusted by agreement or judgment, if the circumstances that are considered when validating maintenance have changed remarkably. These adjustments must be considered reasonable and must take into account both the child and the liable parent's circumstances. A maintenance agreement can be amended if it is considered to be unreasonable.

11. RECIPROCAL ENFORCEMENT OF FINANCIAL ORDERS

11.1 Summarise the position in your jurisdiction

The core rule is that judgments cannot be enforced without an international agreement or a national provision forming the basis of the enforcement action.

The enforcement of civil judgments may be based on the Lugano Convention and a Council Regulation (EC) No 44/2001 on jurisdiction and the recognition and enforcement of judgments in civil and commercial matters, the Brussels I-regulation.

International family matters are regulated by the Council Regulation (EC) No 2201/2003 concerning jurisdiction and the recognition and enforcement of judgments in matrimonial matters and the matters of parental responsibility, the Brussels II-regulation.

Maintenance is regulated by the Council Regulation (EU) No 4/2009 on jurisdiction, applicable law, recognition and enforcement of decisions and cooperation in matters relating to maintenance obligations.

Additionally, there are conventions making it possible to enforce judgments within specific fields, such as, for example, the Hague Convention concerning the Recognition and Enforcement of Decisions Relating to Maintenance Obligations towards Children, the New York Convention on the Recovery Abroad of Maintenance and the Nordic Convention on Maintenance Obligations.

There are also some reciprocal arrangements with Ontario, Canada and the United States. Finland also recognises and enforces decisions on maintenance without an international instrument.

In Finland, the Ministry of Justice sees to matters related to international maintenance obligations, as the central authority.

Between the Nordic Countries, the Convention on the Recognition and Enforcement of Civil Judgments also has to be taken into account.

12. FINANCIAL RELIEF AFTER FOREIGN DIVORCE PROCEEDINGS

12.1 What powers are available to make orders following a foreign divorce?

Divorce, child custody, maintenance and division of assets are all separate issues. If these other matters have not been decided on the foreign divorce proceedings, the party can make an application about these in Finland in case Finland has jurisdiction. If there is a decision from abroad, and the decision is recognised in Finland, it is possible to apply for a change, if the reasons meet the normal requirements for change in an order.

D. CHILDREN

13. CUSTODY/PARENTAL RESPONSIBILITY

13.1 Briefly explain the legal position in relation to custody/parental responsibility following the breakdown of a relationship or marriage

Brussels II applies. The Finnish law does not have an exact definition of parental responsibility.

The provisions on custody of children are to be found in the Child Custody and Right of Access Act. If the parents of the child are married to one another at the time of the birth of the child, they shall both have custody of the child. If the mother of the child is not married, she gets sole custody. Also after the establishment of paternity, the mother will remain the sole custodian unless otherwise agreed. Custody can be decided in a court order or an agreement between the parents.

The law states very little about how to decide a case about custody. The main argument should be the best interest of the child.

The objectives of custody are to ensure the well-being and the balanced development of a child according to his/her individual needs and wishes, and to ensure close and affectionate relationships in particular with his/her parents.

After the breakdown of a relationship or marriage, joint custody is the main rule. In general it is then also agreed with whom the child will reside and how the other parent is to maintain contact and visit the child. If the parents cannot reach an agreement on the question of custody, the matter will be settled in court. The court should obtain a report from the municipal social welfare board. The court will then decide not only on the custody, but also on with which of the parents the child is going to reside.

When the parents have joint custody, the consent of both custodians is, as a rule, necessary when significant matters relating to the child are decided, for instance residence, education, or surname of the child and passport for the child. The parent with whom the child resides, decides on all day-to-day practical things.

If the parents have joint custody, neither parent has the right to take the child abroad without the consent of the other parent.

13.2 Briefly explain the legal position in relation to access/contact/ visitation following the breakdown of a relationship or marriage

The purpose of visitation right is to safeguard the rights of the child to meet the parent with whom the child doesn't live. The parents can agree on the visitation right and they do not have to take any legal measures. They can also go to court to have an order. The decision must be made in accordance with the child's best interests. The court should obtain a report from the municipal social welfare board.

The most normal schedule for access is every other weekend, perhaps from Thursday from school until Monday morning to school, and one night on the other week. Nowadays young couples tend to divide the time equally. Even if the time is divided, the child resides with one parent and has access to the other parent.

14. INTERNATIONAL ABDUCTION

14.1 Summarise the position in your jurisdiction

The Hague Convention on Child Abduction applies. Finland has been a member since August 1994. The Ministry of Justice is the central authority.

Pursuant to the Child Custody and Right of Access Act, the state and municipal welfare authorities shall, upon request, provide the Ministry of Justice with executive assistance for ascertaining the whereabouts and the circumstances of a child, for securing return of a child and for preventing the wrongful removal of a child.

The Ministry of Justice provides active advice and help relating to the interpretation of the Child Abduction Convention and to the practical measures in applying for return.

When the ministry receives a request for the return of a child, it assigns the case to a lawyer, whose first duty, generally, is to attempt to achieve a voluntary return of the child. Failing this, the lawyer will bring action for the return of the child in the Helsinki Court of Appeal, where all cases of child abduction are concentrated in Finland. The petitioner parent is granted free legal representation with costs. Appeals against decisions made by the Court of Appeal can be lodged with the Supreme Court. Normally, no oral hearings are held.

If a decision on the return of a child is not voluntarily complied with, it can be enforced through coercive measures. The Court of Appeal decision can be enforced in spite of appeal. This happens in a couple of days.

If a child has been wrongfully removed to a state that is not a party to the Child Abduction Convention, the parent shall contact the Ministry for Foreign Affairs.

Child abduction is also regarded as an offence, subject to punishment according to the Penal Code. According to this provision, whoever takes a child arbitrarily into custody and removes the child from its country of residence to a foreign country, or fails to return the child to its state of residence, renders themselves guilty of child abduction. In addition, the abductor may be guilty of a more serious offence against personal liberty, for instance, of deprivation of liberty, aggravated deprivation of liberty or hostage taking.

Supreme Court, KKO:2009:85 refers to a 14-year-old child who, trusted to foster parents' custody in Estonia, had arrived to her mother in Finland. The issue was whether the child, who had turned 15 during the proceedings, should be returned to Estonia, despite her objection. The Helsinki Court of Appeal ordered the girl to be returned. The Supreme Court found that the child objected to being returned and had attained an age and degree of maturity where it was appropriate to take her opinion into account, and overturned the decision.

Supreme Court, KKO:2008:98 refers to spouses who had lived in Finland since 2000 and who had travelled to Scotland with their children in October 2007. The children were born in 2005 and 2007. The mother had travelled with the children to Finland on 28 April 2008, without the approval of the father. The issue was whether the children were habitually resident in Scotland at that time and whether the children should be returned to Scotland (3-2).

The Helsinki Court of Appeal held that, at the time of the removal of the children, their place of habitual residence had already been established in Scotland. The children were to be returned to Scotland. The Supreme Court held that habitual residence was in Finland. The children could not be ordered to be returned to Scotland. The minority agreed with the Court of Appeal.

Supreme Court, KKO:2004:76 refers to a mother who, without permission, had not returned the children (nearly 13 and nine years' old) back to their father in the United States, where the children habitually resided. The issue was whether the children resisted the returning and whether the opinion of the children should be taken into account. The children were ordered to be returned.

Supreme Court, KKO:2004:129 concerns the issue of whether to enforce the order to return children (the boys in KKO:2004:76). The mother and the boys had been hiding. The enforcement process went through the district court, the Court of Appeal and then the Supreme Court. When the children were found they were hospitalised (now aged 13 and 10), strongly opposing the return. The court ordered the decision to be enforced.

15. LEAVE TO REMOVE/APPLICATIONS TO TAKE A CHILD OUT OF THE JURISDICTION.

15.1 Summarise the position in your jurisdiction

Joint custody is retained in 75 per cent of divorce cases. The father, when the parents are not married, is not automatically granted joint custody, but most cohabiting couples agree about it.

If the parents cannot agree about relocation, the 'near-parent' can go to court for a new court order, asking to get sole custody or an order about residing abroad. The other parent, the 'far-parent', can also ask for sole custody or an order that the child shall reside with them, or a change in the right of access schedule.

While a case relating to child custody or right of access is pending in court, the court may issue an interim order on the person with whom the child is to reside, on the right of access and on the conditions of visiting rights. The court may also order someone to act as the custodian for the child until the final decision is made. The interim order is enforceable and guarantees that the child cannot be relocated during the process.

If the custodian has sole custody, there are no legal means to prevent the custodian moving abroad and taking the child with them. If the other parent gets this information early enough, they can take the case to court, asking for change of custody, or at least try to ensure a right of access under the new circumstances in order to maintain contact with the child.

An interim order can be issued and it can be more effective in this situation as the non-custodian has no other legal means to prevent the relocation.

15.2 Under what circumstances may a parent apply to remove their child from the jurisdiction against the wishes of the other parent?

There are not any published cases from the Supreme Court on relocation. The legal literature about the interpretation of the law is also limited. Legal practise of the lower courts is of particular importance in guiding the interpretation of the family law.

The child's best interest should always be the most important factor.

The first matter to consider is whether the plan to move abroad is genuine, or if it is motivated by the attempt to exclude the other parent from the child's life. Several other following factors have to be considered:

- the age of the child and whether the child is mature enough to make a decision
- has the child expressed their will independently without any pressure or manipulation by either parent;
- relations and history between the child and both parents, whether the

far-parent has exercised their right of access and to what extent;
- the reason for moving and, if the near-parent has a new family, compared with a situation where there is just a new partner, met abroad, without any history of living together;
- whether there is a new job, why it is necessary to change jobs, possible career opportunity; and
- the effects to the right of access, how far abroad is the near-parent moving and whether it is possible to maintain relations between the child and the far-parent so that the child is able to remain in contact with that parent.

There might also be a practical question of money. Together with a new schedule for the right of access, the court can order the near-parent to pay part or most of the travelling costs needed to keep up the contact. In that case, the maintenance order at least must be amended.

E. SURROGACY AND ADOPTION

16. VALIDITY OF SURROGACY AGREEMENTS

16.1 Briefly summarise the position in your jurisdiction

Surrogacy has been prohibited in Finland in all circumstances since 2007 when the Fertility Treatment Act came into force. However, in 2011 the National Social and Health Care Ethics Advisory Committee stated that surrogacy should be accepted in certain situations, for example if the woman doesn't have a womb.

The Ministry of Justice has given out a memorandum and asked several institutions for opinions. The opinions differed. The Ministry has not decided yet if it is pursuing new legislation or not.

A case has now started in a district court about adopting the husband's biological child given birth by a Russian woman in Russia, who had been paid for surrogacy. Adoption should be denied as surrogacy is forbidden in Finland, but the child's best interest seems to say differently. A similar case involving India is upcoming.

17. ADOPTION

17.1 Briefly explain the legal position in relation to adoption in your jurisdiction. Is adoption available to individuals, cohabiting couples (both heterosexual and same-sex)?

The new law pn adoption, the Adoption Act, entered into force on 1 July 2012. The purpose of adoption is to promote the welfare of a child by creating a child-parent relationship between the adoptee and the prospective adopter. In all decisions and other measures concerning the adoption of a minor child, the best interests of the child shall be the paramount consideration.

The adoption of a minor child may be granted if it is deemed to be in the best interests of the child and if it has been established that the child will be well taken care of and brought up. In decisions on the matter, the child's wishes and views shall be taken into consideration having regard to his or her age and degree of maturity. The adoption of an adult may also be granted in certain circumstances.

Remuneration is prohibited. An adoption may not be granted if any remuneration for the adoption has been given or promised.

The Act provides minimum and maximum age for the adopter. The minimum age is 25 (in special circumstances lower) and the maximum age is 50 (when the adoptee is a minor). The age difference between the adoptee and the adopter shall be at least 18 years and no more than 45 years.

An adoption is available for individuals. Married spouses may only adopt a child jointly. A spouse may, however, alone adopt a child of the other spouse or their own child who has previously been adopted by someone else. This goes for registered partnerships too. Persons other than married couples may not adopt a child jointly. Registered partners or cohabiting couples may thus not adopt jointly.

An adoption shall be granted by judicial decision. Permission from the Adoption Board is needed in most cases, both for domestic adoption and for adoption from foreign state. Permission may be granted if the conditions for adoption are fulfilled and the prospective adopter has been granted adoption counselling. Permission for adoption from a foreign state without using a service provider as an intermediary may be granted only if a child is a close relative of the prospective adopter or their spouse or if a child has been taken care of by the prospective adopter other than with a view to adoption.

Once an adoption has been granted, the adoptee shall be deemed the child of the adoptive parents and not of the former parents, unless otherwise expressly provided by law or unless otherwise follows from the nature of adoption.

The court can decide that a minor adoptee shall have the right to meet his or her former parent or maintain contact with him or her in another manner. The granting of a right of contact shall be subject to the condition that the former parent and the adoptive parents have agreed upon the maintenance of contact and there is no reason to assume that the maintenance of contact would be contrary to the child's best interests.

F. COHABITATION

18. COHABITATION

18.1 What legislation (if any) governs division of property for unmarried couples on the breakdown of the relationship?

The Act on the Dissolution of the Household of Cohabiting Partners entered into force on 1 April 2011. The Act applies to the dissolution of the household of cohabiting partners when the partnership ends. Cohabiting partner refers to partners who live in a relationship in a shared household and who have lived in a shared household for at least five years or who have, or have had, a joint child or joint parental responsibility for a child. However, a person who is married shall not be deemed a cohabiting partner. The Act is short, having only 12 sections.

If a cohabiting partner so demands, a separation of the cohabiting partners' property shall be carried out when the cohabiting partnership ends.

Separation of property can be agreed on by making a separation deed of the property as provided by the Code of Inheritance. The cohabiting partner can also apply to the district court to appoint an estate distributor to separate the property in accordance with the provisions governing the distribution of inheritance.

A cohabiting partner is entitled to compensation if, through contributions for the benefit of the shared household, they have assisted the other cohabiting partner in accumulating or retaining their property so that dissolution of the household, solely on the basis of ownership, would result in unjust enrichment at the expense of the other.

In the field of public law, however, there have also earlier been several statutes that recognise cohabitation as a significant legal relationship.

G. FAMILY DISPUTE RESOLUTION

19. MEDIATION, COLLABORATIVE LAW AND ARBITRATION

19.1 Briefly summarise the no-court-based processes available in your jurisdiction and the current status of agreements reached under the auspices of mediation, collaborative law and arbitration

According to the Marriage Act, family conflicts and legal issues should be resolved by negotiation or by an agreement. The family can get mediation help from the Social Welfare Board. Mediation includes personal conversation with a social worker or a psychologist and it is possible to have a family negotiation.

19.2 What is the statutory basis (if any), for mediation, collaborative law and arbitration in your jurisdiction? In particular, are the parties required to attempt a family dispute resolution in advance of the institution of proceedings?

The Act on mediation in civil matters and confirmation of settlements in general courts applies to child issues too. The precondition for court mediation is that the matter is amenable to mediation, and a settlement is appropriate in view of the claims of the parties.

Besides, since the beginning of 2011 there has been the so-called Follo-mediation, mediation with the help of a specialist, normally a psychologist, as an experiment in four district courts which probably will widen out nationally in a couple of years. The parties can choose to go into this mediation directly or after starting a court case. The Ministry of Justice is planning to make legislation about this mediation.

H. OTHER

20. CIVIL PARTNERSHIP/SAME-SEX MARRIAGE

20.1 What is the status of civil partnership/same-sex marriage within the jurisdiction?

20.2 What legislation governs civil partnership/same-sex marriage?

The Act on Registered Partnerships came into force in 2002 and, for the most part, contains the same legal provisions as those that govern marriage. Instead of marriage, it creates a separate institution. Registered partnerships, which are available only to same-sex couples, are registered and dissolved using a procedure similar to that for marriage. The legislation also permits joint custody of children and grants immigration rights to a foreign partner. Same-sex couples cannot have a religious marriage ceremony, adopt a child together or take a common surname. However, since 1 September 2009, a partner in a civil partnership has been able to adopt the other partner's biological child.

The legal affairs committee in Parliament has discussed same-sex marriage, which was one issue in the previous elections. It was a close vote not to continue to the legislation.

Now a Citizens' Initiative has been collecting names, which at the time of writing (May 2013) numbered more than 151,000. Once a petition receives more than 50,000 names, the initiative has to be considered in Parliament. As the law about citizens' initiative is new, it has not been decided yet what is the correct procedure.

21. CONTROVERSIAL AREAS/RAPIDLY DEVELOPING AREAS OF LAW

21.1 Is there a particular area of the law within the jurisdiction that is currently undergoing major change?

21.2 Which areas of law are most out-of-step and which areas would you most like to see reformed/changed.

N/A.

France

Cabinet CBBC Véronique Chauveau,
Charlotte Butruille-Cardew & Alexandre Boiché

A. JURISDICTION AND CONFLICT OF LAW

1. SOURCES OF LAW

1.1 What is the primary source of law in relation to the breakdown of marriage and the welfare of children within the jurisdiction?

In French family law, the primary source of law for the breakdown of the marriage is Article 230-309 of the French Civil Code (FCC).

Rules concerning the welfare of children and parental responsibility can be found in Articles 372 to 381.

There are no specific rules relating to conflict of laws in the FCC. Rules of conflict of laws about the welfare of children or parental responsibility are contained in the Hague Convention, dated 19 October 1996, in force in France since 1 February 2011.

There is no code of private international law in France. There are some general rules in the FCC, such as Article 3, marriage (Article 202-1 and 202-2), parentage (Articles 311-14 to 311-18), adoption (370-3 to 370-5), PACS (Article 515-7-1).

The other rules of conflict of law are from international conventions or case law.

1.2 Which are the main statutes governing matrimonial law in the jurisdiction?

In France, matrimonial law is predominantly governed by the First Book of the FCC, (Articles 7 to 515-8). These articles cover a wide range of matters relating to the family, such as right of the persons, identification, name, surname, domicile, marriage, rights and duties arising out of marriage, divorce, parentage, adoption, parental responsibility, adults protected by the law, PACS and cohabitation.

The rules relating to matrimonial property and marriage contracts are contained in Articles 1387 to 1581.

The rules relating to succession are contained in Articles 720 to 1100.

2. JURISDICTION

2.1 What are the main jurisdictional requirements for the institution of proceedings in relation to divorce, property and children?

In matters relating to divorce, legal separation or marriage annulment, the rules of Articles 3 to 7 of the Regulation 1347/2003 Brussels II revised shall be applied first by the French court. If the French court has no jurisdiction under Brussels II revised, and no court of another member state has jurisdiction based on the Regulation, and if the defendant is not a national of a member state or domiciled in the United Kingdom or Ireland, the French court could have jurisdiction based on the French rules of jurisdiction. These rules are based on an extension of the French internal rules of jurisdiction at the international level. For divorce or separation, these rules can be found in Article 1070 of the French Code of Civil Procedure. In application of this Article, the French court will have jurisdiction if the family was living in France and one of the spouses is still living there, if the spouse living with the children is habitually resident in France and if the defendant is still a resident in France.

If the French court has no jurisdiction based on Article 1070 of the French Code of Civil Procedure, Article 14 and 15 of the FCC could be used. These rules are based on the petitioner's or defendant's French citizenship. The rules are subsidiary and they can be used only when the Brussels II revised and the regular rules of jurisdiction do not give jurisdiction to the French court.

In relation to property, in general, when the French judge decrees the divorce, he or she orders in the same decision the division of the properties and designate a notary to divide the properties.

If the divorce has taken place abroad and no division of the properties has been made or ordered, or if the defendant is habitually resident in France or one of the spouses is a French national, a petition to share the matrimonial properties can be filed before the French court.

In relation to parental responsibility, the Brussels II revised regulation will be applied if the child is habitually resident in a member state. If the 1996 Hague Convention does not apply, the internal rules may apply.

For maintenance obligations, the European regulation n°4/2009 of 18 December 2008 is applicable.

3. DOMICILE AND HABITUAL RESIDENCE

3.1 Explain the concepts of domicile and habitual residence as they apply to the jurisdiction

In French law, the domicile is a legal concept and is defined by Article 102 of the FCC as 'the domicile of a French person, as to the exercise of his civil rights, is at the place where he has his main establishment'. The text refers only to a French person, but it also applies to foreigners.

There is no definition of habitual residence, because this is a notion of fact, whereas a domicile is a legal concept. However, in the application of the divorce rules set forth in the European Regulation Brussels II, the *Cour de Cassation* ruled on 14 December 2005 that 'habitual residence, an autonomous notion of community law, is defined as the place where the party involved has fixed, with the wish to vest it with a stable character, the permanent or habitual centre of his or her interests'.

This definition shall be applied to determine French jurisdiction in case of divorce, separation or annulment of marriage.

Concerning the habitual residence of the child, in application of the same regulation, the French court will have to follow the definition given by the ECJ in its case law dated 2 April 2009.

4. CONFLICT OF LAW/APPLICABLE LAW TO BE APPLIED

4.1 What happens when one party applies to stay proceedings in favour of a foreign jurisdiction? What factors will the local court take into account when determining forum issues?

If a party wants to challenge the French jurisdiction or to stay a proceeding when a similar proceeding has been previously filed abroad, they should argue this point before any defence on the merits.

To stay a proceeding in favour of a European jurisdiction, the French court will apply the rules of the Brussels II Regulation.

A French court could also decide to stay proceedings in favour of a foreign court already seised in a case with the same object between the same parties. To this classical requirement in *lis pendens* case, the French law adds another condition that the foreign order should be able to be enforced in France.

A French court is considered seised of a divorce petition when the request for divorce, which is the first document filed, is lodged at the court.

In a case where the French court and the English court had been seised on the same day, the *Cour de Cassation* refers to the hour of seisure.

When the stay is asked for a proceeding in a non-European country, the party should establish that the foreign order would be able to be recognised after in France.

To be recognised in France, a foreign order should comply with the following three conditions:

- jurisdiction of the foreign court – this condition will be satisfied when a strong link between the case and the court is established;
- conformity to public policy – through this condition the French judge will control the content of the foreign order and will also control the foreign proceeding; and
- absence of fraud – the jurisdiction of the foreign court should not be the result of fraud from the party.

If these three conditions are met, the foreign order would be recognised in France.

B. PRE- AND POST-NUPTIAL AGREEMENTS

5. VALIDITY OF PRE- AND POST-NUPTIAL AGREEMENTS

5.1 To what extent are pre- and post-nups binding within the jurisdiction? Could you provide a brief discussion of the most significant recent case law on this issue

There is no similar concept in French law such as the Anglo-Saxon pre-nuptial or post-nuptial agreement, whereby the parties may contractually, and in advance, organise all the financial consequences of their divorce, as well as the assets administration and allocation both during marriage and in case of divorce. However, French law has a long established tradition of recognising the validity and enforceability of post- and pre-nuptial agreements, the goal of which is to organise the matrimonial regime of the parties. French law recognises, in that respect, the freedom of the spouses to organise a *contrat de mariage,* with the sole condition that it conforms to public policy. This right is often referred to as the principle of the 'freedom of matrimonial agreements'. The parties could, therefore, insert special clauses in relation to the administration or the winding up of the matrimonial estate during their lifetime in the event of a divorce or upon death.

The provisions of a pre- or post-nuptial agreement, whose goal would be to organise the matrimonial regime of the parties, would be, under certain conditions, recognised and enforced in France.

Pursuant to the Hague Convention dated 14 March 1978, the future spouses may choose the applicable law to their matrimonial regime, provided one spouse has sufficient connecting factors with the chosen applicable law (nationality, habitual residence or the first state in which they will reside after marriage (Article 3).

The separation of property regime (Articles 1536 and following the FCC) is often recommended in the case of international pre-nuptial agreements, as it is very close the English regime and often known in other countries. Furthermore, it is the regime which affords the maximum protection to the parties with respect to their personal assets and often advised for couples where one of the parties is wealthy and wants to protect their own assets from the other spouse in case of breakdown of the marriage.

C. DIVORCE, NULLITY AND JUDICIAL SEPARATION

6. RECOGNITION OF FOREIGN MARRIAGES/DIVORCES

6.1 Summarise the position in your jurisdiction

A marriage contracted abroad is valid in France if the essential conditions have been fulfilled under the national law of each spouse, if the conditions conform to French public policy and if it was celebrated pursuant to the *lege fori*.

For immigration purposes, the French law is very strict about the conditions of a marriage between a French citizen and a foreigner celebrated abroad. Some conditions will need to be fulfilled so that the local French consulate registers the marriage in France, if the couple wishes to live in France.

For a long period of time (see *Bukley, Cour de Cassation,* 28 February 1860) the French court directly recognised a divorce pronounced abroad in France. As a consequence, a divorce pronounced abroad is presumed valid until it has been challenged and shown not to comply with the conditions of recognition of a foreign order in France (see section 11). Besides, if a divorce is pronounced in an EU member state, EU Regulation 2201/2003 Bruxelles II revised applies. Its Article 21.1 provides that a judgment given in a member state shall be recognised in the other member states without any special procedure being required. Article 22 provides for the grounds of non-recognition for judgments relating to divorce, legal separation or marriage annulment.

French courts frequently have had to deal with repudiation pronounced in Morocco and Algeria. Since 2004, the *Cour de Cassation* decided that this kind of divorce should not be recognised in France when one of the spouses is French or habitually resident in France because it is contrary to equality between men and women and contrary to the rules of the European Convention on Human Rights.

7. DIVORCE

7.1 Explain the grounds for divorce within the jurisdiction (please also deal with nullity and judicial separation if appropriate)

Grounds for divorce

The 2004 Divorce Act establishes the grounds for divorce, which are mutual consent, the acceptance of the principle of marital breakdown, fault and breakdown of communal life. Clearly, it must be discussed separately from the nullity of marriage, which is regulated by Articles 180-184 of the FCC.

Divorce by mutual consent is agreed by the parties and is always an option for spouses during the course of any divorce proceedings on different grounds (Article 230, FCC). Practitioners will often prefer to use the standard request to initiate a divorce proceeding, conferring all options on their client, if an agreement is not rapidly reached.

In a divorce, on acceptance of the principle of marital breakdown, the spouses agree on the principle of a marital breakdown, but not on issues relating to children and ancillary relief, which are consequently dealt with by the court. The spouses need to agree that there has been a marital breakdown (Article 233, FCC). The acceptance of this principle can be made at any stage of the proceedings.

A divorce based on fault is granted when the actions of a spouse render the continuation of married life intolerable (Article 242, FCC). Reconciliation of the spouses can constitute a discretionary bar to divorce and faults on either side could lead to a decree being made against both spouses. Alternatively, the judge may refuse a decree if satisfied that neither spouse has established that the marriage has irretrievably broken down.

In the case of irretrievable breakdown of communal life, divorce can be granted on the basis of a two-year separation period with no financial consequences attached (Article 237, FCC). No consent is necessary and the defendant cannot oppose the decree of divorce. The two-year separation needs to be evidenced at the date of lodging the petition for divorce.

The non-conciliation order sets interim measures organising the life of the spouses and the children, up to 30 months as from the date of the order.

Nullity

The annulment can be pronounced when the essential conditions for the formation of marriage are not met. Thus, a marriage might be annulled if the consent of one of the spouses was defective, notably in the case of an error on the person (error on the identity) or on the substantial characteristics of the person (in that case, error must meet a subjective criterion – the error must have been a determining factor of the party's consent – and an objective criterion – the error must be 'sociologically determining'), or in the case of duress (Article 180 FCC). A marriage might also be annulled for lack of authorisation of the legal representative (for a minor for instance) (Article 182 FCC). An annulment on the basis of one of these two grounds can only be sought by one of the spouses, the Public Prosecutor, or by the ones whose authorisation was required.

Besides, nullity might be pronounced on several grounds that address public policy such as the non-respect of the minimum age to marry, bigamy, incest, absence of one of the spouses, etc. Nullity might be pronounced also for default of matrimonial intention (Article 146 FCC), this is used generally to cancel marriage concluded only for immigration purposes

Nullity can then be sought by the spouses themselves, the Public Prosecutor or any person who has an interest in such action (Article 184 FCC).

The consequences of the annulment (retroactive disappearance of the marriage) do not apply to the children of the former spouses who are treated as divorcees' children. Parents keep on exercising joint parental responsibility. If one spouse entered into the marriage in good faith he or she could benefit from the putative marriage rules that will maintain the effect of the marriage to his or her benefit. On this basis, he or she for example will be able to obtain a compensatory lump sum as in a divorce proceeding.

8. FINANCES/CAPITAL, PROPERTY

8.1 What powers does the court have to allocate financial resources and property on the breakdown of marriage?

Article 270 of the FCC provides that the compensatory benefit (*prestation compensatoire*) aims to compensate, as much as possible, the disparity in the breakdown of the marriage created in the respective spouses' lives. It must be distinguished from interim measures and measures taken during the winding up of the matrimonial regime.

In order to determine the compensatory benefit, the judge will not only take into consideration the parties' current resources, but he or she will also make predictions based on the parties' situation at the time of the divorce as to what will happen in the near future.

Article 271 lists the key elements a judge should take into account to determine the compensatory benefit:

- the duration of marriage or the level of education;
- the time spent or to be spent for the education of children;
- the ability to find a job;
- the retirement plan; and
- the amount of wealth received in the process of winding up matrimonial assets.

The compensatory benefit should take the form of capital given to the creditor. It is only if this is not possible that compensatory benefit should be paid by instalments.

Capital can take the form of a lump sum, goods, or even the attribution of a right of use. The notion is extensive and judges have considerable power assessing both the form and the content of the compensatory benefit.

When compensatory benefit is paid in instalments, and if revision is necessary, it can only be decreased. It cannot be paid for more than eight years.

The compensatory benefit can also take the form of a lifetime rent. For example, a lifetime rent will be granted to a senior citizen with a meagre pension and very little chances of finding employment. The rent is fixed or variable.

8.2 Explain and illustrate with reference to recent cases the court's thinking on division of assets

The division of assets depends on the marital regime adopted by the spouses.

The spouses may enter into a pre-nuptial agreement and adopt the separation of assets regime, where the assets of each spouse remain clearly separated, whether they have been acquired before or during the marriage.

When the spouses do not enter into a pre-nuptial agreement, the marital regime that will automatically apply is the community of property regime. From the date of the marriage, a distinction is made between the common assets or acquired property (*les acquêts*) and the assets that belong exclusively to one of the spouses or own property (*les biens propres*). The *biens propres* are mainly the assets that were already the property of one of the spouses before the marriage or have been acquired by inheritance or legacy during the marriage. The *acquêts* are all the assets acquired by the spouses or by one of them during the marriage, or that result through work or as income from own property. The principle set out by Article 1402 of the FCC is that all assets are presumed to be *acquêts* unless it is proven that they belong exclusively to one of the spouses. Articles 1404 to 1408 of the FCC define the different categories of *biens propres*.

When the marriage is dissolved, each of the spouses takes his or her *biens propres* back. Indeed, own property is not subject to division. Division only concerns the community, which is actively made up of the *acquêts* and passively made up of the debts contracted during the marriage. The difference between those two sums represents the net amount of the assets subject to division. Each of the spouses is entitled to half of this sum, which represents their share in the community. Then, the assets are divided between the spouses, up to their share in the community. Since it is rather difficult to divide the spouses' assets so that each of them gets exactly the equivalent of the sum he or she is entitled to, the spouse who recovers more pays a balancing payment to the other (*soulte*).

As an example: Mr. and Mrs Dupond are married under the French community of property regime. A divorce proceeding is instituted and the assets of the couple need to be divided. The community is actively made up of two main assets: a house in Paris (€500,000) and a house in Nice (€350,000). The total amount of the debts amounts to €40,000. The net amount of the assets subject to division is then €500,000 + €350,000 – €40,000 = €810,000. The share of each spouse in the community is €810,000/2 = €405,000. Each spouse is then entitled to recover assets up to €405,000. The parties decide to award the house in Paris to Mr. Dupond and the house in Nice to Mrs Dupond. Mr Dupond recovers the equivalent of €500,000, which is more than his share in the community. Mrs Dupond recovers the equivalent of €350,000, which is less than her share in the community. Mr Dupond will then pay to Mrs Dupond a *soulte* of €55.000 (€405,000 – €350,000).

9. FINANCES/ MAINTENANCE

9.1 Explain the maintenance support for spouses on an ongoing basis following the breakdown of the marriage

Article 212 of the FCC binds each spouse to provide support and assistance for the other. During marriage, where one of the spouses does not fulfil their obligations, they may be compelled by the other to do so it. In such case, and based on a request filed in Family Court, the family judge will award maintenance support for living costs during marriage.

Upon separation or pending a divorce, maintenance is awarded to the economically weaker spouse and may be decreased or increased proportionately to each party's income and needs if circumstances change. In the presence of children, the judge will award a separate amount to the custodial parent.

Pursuant to Article 255 of the FCC, periodical payments and allowance for costs may be ordered to be paid by one spouse to the other. French law does not provide a scale or a limited list of criteria, but there is a sole duty to provide to the economically weaker spouse a monetary amount to maintain the standard of living to which they have become accustomed. However, the Family Court recognises that two households cost more that a common one and that this justifies payment of a smaller amount as the debtor will also have needs.

The spouses' income (from work and assets) and fixed expenses, such as, income tax, property tax, car and home insurance, loans, rent or mortgage, etc, will be taken into consideration. This is awarded at the preliminary hearing, in case of separation or divorce and will last until divorce is definitive.

Upon dissolution of marriage, Article 271 of the FCC provides that the economically weaker spouse should receive compensatory benefit, which is generally paid in capital and in one lump sum. It may also be paid by the attribution of an asset or life interest in an asset or if the debtor spouse cannot afford capital payment. See section 8, above.

9.2 Is it common for maintenance to be awarded?

A compensatory payment is ordered after divorce in only 17 per cent of cases. This is due to two main reasons. Firstly, it is now common that both spouses work and have similar incomes. Secondly, because of the low income of many couples, where the debtor has no means to pay their spouse maintenance, a social benefit may be awarded.

A lifetime maintenance is very seldom awarded after divorce, due to the extreme criteria required by the leading cases. It should be noted that, in the latest orders, this mainly happens for elderly wives, who have not been able to work due to their spouse's situation and who are obviously unable to obtain a qualification.

Pursuant to Article 276-4 of the FCC, this lifetime maintenance may be substituted by a capital payment if it is justified by a change of circumstances. It cannot be raised if circumstances change.

9.3 Explain and illustrate with reference to recent cases the court's thinking on maintenance

On 14 May 2010, the 1st chamber, 3rd section of the Appellate court of Caen awarded a lifetime maintenance of €2,500 per month to the wife. The husband was 67 years old and his income was €7,500 per month, but he was only expected to receive €3,280 per month from his retirement fund. The husband paid a monthly mortgage of €2,000 per month. The wife was 66 years old and received €290 per month from her retirement fund and paid €610 per month on rent. Lifetime maintenance was awarded, even though the marriage lasted 39 years and the wife had not only sold an asset and donated €96,000 to her children, but she had also not disclosed what she still had. The husband was also a partner in a real estate company, of which he had 50 per cent of shares. The court ruled that instead of disposition *inter vivos*, the wife should have bought herself a flat. This may help to explain the low amount of maintenance awarded.

On 12 June 2010, the 1st Chamber of the Appellate Court of Nancy overturned the appeal of a husband who, in first instance, had been required to pay €762 per month lifetime maintenance to the wife. Although the husband's income was reduced by retirement (€4,486 per month) he had other income from real estate (€14,121 per month) and assets totalling almost €5 million. Based on Article 276-4 of the FCC, the court ruled that the husband's assets showed that the loans he contracted were not necessary. The marriage had lasted for 23 years and the wife had gone through cancer in 2004.

Therefore, clearly lifetime maintenance does not allow the economically weaker spouse to keep up with their previous standard of living on this sole basis. Nevertheless, French courts keep a strict position on condition. The debtor may ask to change the lifetime maintenance into capital payment.

10. CHILD MAINTENANCE

10.1 On what basis is child maintenance calculated within the jurisdiction?

The FCC provides that each parent, married or not, has a duty to participate in the needs of common children proportionately to their resources. As France has a family benefit system based on the number of children from the age two upwards, and not related to the income of the parents, the court will take into account this amount, as well as other criteria such as home state allowance and any income of the parents. This child support does not include any right for the mother, for example, to have a 'roof over her head'. In broad terms, the judge will determine the 'available' income of each parent after deducting compulsory expenses. This support is based on living costs.

This support may vary if the resident parent relocates far away from the other parent, with the judge having the power to decide which parent will have to pay travel costs.

In France, child support is taxable by the Internal Revenue Service for the creditor and deductible for the debtor.

11. RECIPROCAL ENFORCEMENT OF FINANCIAL ORDERS

11.1 Summarise the position in your jurisdiction

A distinction must be made between the enforcement of French and foreign financial orders. There are some specific rules about the enforcement of financial orders in family matters. For example, if the debtor does not pay the maintenance, the creditor could directly seize their salary. This proceeding is called 'direct payment'. The assistance of a *huissier de justice* (process server) is necessary to do all the enforcement in French law. If the creditor does not receive payment of the maintenance, they could ask for help from the tax administration or obtain an allowance from the social security services, which will then file against the debtor. The regular rules of enforcement are also available for the creditor and they could seize the bank account of the debtor.

The non-payment of maintenance is also a criminal offence (Article 227-3 of the French Criminal Code) in French law. The non-paid creditor could decide to file a criminal complaint to the public prosecutor or to seize directly the criminal court against the reluctant debtor.

The rules related to the enforcement of foreign financial orders in France depend on the country where the order has been made. If the order has been made in an EU country, the rules of the Regulation CE 44/2009 will be applicable. If the order has been made in a country member of the Lugano Convention, the rules of this convention will be applicable. In these two cases the enforcement of the foreign order will be very easy. The order could be made in a country member of the Hague Convention of 2/10/1973 or the Hague Convention of 1958, which is still applicable in Surinam. There are also many bilateral conventions with specific rules on enforcement with some African states (for example, Morocco, Algeria, Ivory Coast, Tunisia, Senegal), some South American states (for example, Argentina, Uruguay, Brazil) and some Asian states (for example, Laos, China).

If there is no convention between the foreign states, the foreign order could be enforced through the regular *exequatur* proceedings and the claimant will have to establish that the foreign order fulfilled the following three conditions:

- jurisdiction of the foreign court;
- conformity to French international public policy; and
- absence of fraud.

Before the enforcement of the foreign order, the creditor could take some conservatory measures on the debtor properties in France.

A criminal claim for non-payment of maintenance could be made only when the foreign order had been enforced by the French court.

12. FINANCIAL RELIEF AFTER FOREIGN DIVORCE PROCEEDINGS

12.1 What powers are available to make orders following a foreign divorce?

If the French court has jurisdiction, it could be according to Regulation EC 44/2009 or to the Lugano Convention. For example, a French court will have jurisdiction to make orders to vary or to order maintenance following a foreign divorce. If the case is related to spousal maintenance after divorce, the applicable law will be determined by application of Article 5 of the Hague Protocol dated 23 November 2007 on the applicable law to maintenance obligations. If it concerns child maintenance, the applicable law will be the one of the child's habitual residence by application of Article 3 of the same Protocol.

D. CHILDREN

13. CUSTODY/PARENTAL RESPONSABILITY

13.1 Briefly explain the legal position in relation to custody/parental responsibility following the breakdown of a relationship or marriage

Article 373-2 of the FCC provides that the breakdown of a marriage or a relationship has no impact over the rules governing the exercise of parental responsibility. Thus, separated parents keep on exercising joint parental responsibility over their children, which is the general principle provided for by Article 372 of the FCC. However, the judge might entrust only one of the parents with parental responsibility when the best interest of the child requires so. Serious reasons must be evidenced in order for the judge to grant unilateral parental responsibility. In determining the methods of parental responsibility, the judge will take several elements into consideration, such as the agreements previously entered into by the parents, the feelings expressed by the child, the ability of each parent to assume their duties and to respect the rights of the other and the results of the social and psychological investigations (Article 373-2-11 FCC).

Following the breakdown of a relationship or marriage, the judge will also determine custody of the child. Two options are available: the judge will either decide to award custody to one of the parents or to allow alternate residence (one week at the mother's place, one week at the father's place for instance), although this last option will only be chosen if several conditions are met (age of the child, availability of the parents, material conditions of accommodation, proximity of the parents' places, etc).

13.2 Briefly explain the legal position in relation to access/contact/visitation following the breakdown of a relationship or marriage

When child custody is awarded to one of the parents, the non-custodial parent will benefit from a visitation right (for example, the first, third and fifth weekend of each month and half of the school vacation).

Visitation rights can be denied to the non-custodial parent but only if it is justified by serious reasons. Or the judge might decide that the non-custodial parent's visitation right will be exercised in a special meeting space, when the best interest of the child requires so. The same can be decided concerning the presentation of the child, that might take place in a special meeting space or with the assistance of a trustworthy third party, when the best interest of the child requires so or when direct presentation of the child to the other parent presents a risk for one of them (Article 373-2-9 FCC).

Finally, the parents can agree on parental responsibility, child custody and visitation rights and submit to the judge their plans for the same. The judge will ratify the agreement, unless it does not sufficiently protect the best interest of the child or the parents' consent has not been given freely (Article 373-2-7 FCC).

14. INTERNATIONAL ABDUCTION

14.1 Summarise the position in your jurisdiction

France and other member states of the Hague 1980

France ratified the Hague Convention dated 25 October 1980 and it came into effect in 1983.

The French central authority is part of the French Ministry of Justice and is called *Bureau de coopération internationale civile et commerciale*. When receiving a request from another central authority, this office will immediately advise the general prosecutor of the jurisdiction of the Appellate Court where the abducting parent has taken residence. An inquiry will be made and the police or the *Gendarmerie* will ask the abducting parent if they agree to bring back the child. If they do not agree, the general prosecutor will request that the prosecutor of the local court files an emergency petition for return.

Normally, the 'left behind' parent has no obligation to retain a lawyer, whereas this is strongly recommended if the abducting parent raises exceptions for defence. The hearing will take place relatively quickly (delays differ from one court to another) and the abducting parent will appear, generally assisted by a lawyer. France does not have an automatic system of assistance by specialised solicitors or barristers, but it is relatively easy to obtain legal aid based on low income, although the lawyer will generally not have any training in such matters. While French jurisprudence is, in broad terms, in accordance with the guide of good practice of The Hague, difficulties sometimes arise when the enforcement of the order is refused by the abducting parent. France has specialised jurisdiction to judge this kind of case.

France and European member states

While the entering into effect of EU regulation 2201/2003 dated 27 November 2003 should have sped up the process, it is obvious that in most cases the delay of six weeks is illusory.

However, Article 11 of this regulation, which grants the court of habitual residence jurisdiction to order return, even if court of refuge has overturned return on Article 13b, is generally respected by French judges who have benefited from extensive training in European Law.

Bilateral conventions

France is linked with many foreign states by bilateral conventions on judicial cooperation. Some work and some do not. The 1981 Franco-Moroccan Convention has good results for children abducted to France and the system is not so different from the Hague. On the other hand, it appears to be more difficult to retrieve children illegally removed to Morocco, although this largely depends on the court with jurisdiction in this country.

The Franco-Egyptian convention requests that an order is already standing, but Egypt rarely sends back any child.

Some conventions or agreements exist 'on paper', such as the agreement signed with Algeria, Tunisia or Lebanon. No child has ever been sent back on this basis, although in the past some parents have benefited from some limited access.

France and other states not linked by any convention

As France has an efficient body of rules to domesticate foreign orders, it is possible to obtain an order to the effect that children brought to France in violation of a residence order are returned to their habitual place of residency in an expeditious manner. The judge will check that this fulfils the child's best interests.

The criminal path

When the 'left behind' parent has no idea where the abducted children are, or if the country of refuge is not a member of any convention, it is possible, under French criminal law, to obtain an international warrant for arrest. In such circumstances, if the abducting parent tries to move from their place of refuge, they may be arrested and this sometimes leads to the return of the children (Articles 227-5, 227-7 and 227-9 of the FCC).

15. LEAVE TO REMOVE/APPLICATION TO TAKE A CHILD OUT OF THE JURISDICTION

15.1 Summarise the position in your jurisdiction.

The FCC (Article 373-2) rules as follows:

'Separation of the parents has no influence on the rules of devolution of the exercise of parental authority. Each of the father and mother shall maintain personal relations with the child and respect the bonds of the latter with the other parent. Any change of residence of one of the parents, where it modifies the terms of exercise of parental authority, shall be the subject of a notice to the other parent, previously and in due time. In case of disagreement between them, the most diligent parent shall refer the matter to the family causes judge who shall rule according to what the welfare of the child requires. The judge shall apportion removal expenses and adapt accordingly the amount of the contribution to the support and education of the child.'

In France both parents have to agree on relocation, otherwise the family judge will decide. They are very keen to protect the child's best interest, which is clearly linked to the child's ability to keep close contact with both parents. There are no special rules about relocation abroad. If the resident parent is relocating for professional reasons, the judge will be more lenient. If contact has to be changed (as alternating weekends are not a viable option), the non-resident parent may obtain a larger part of school breaks. When making an order, the judge will see that the non-resident parent is still able to see their children and will adapt the child support if they have to pay travel costs.

15.2 Under what circumstances may a parent apply to remove their children from the jurisdiction against the wishes of the other parent?

If the residential parent wishes to relocate abroad, the judge will make sure that the continuation of education is coherent, such as whether the children are to be registered in French or international school, the dates of school breaks and the feasibility of the trips back and forth. The court will also see if the new jurisdiction will enforce and/or domesticate the French order without varying it. When applying for leave to relocate against the wishes of the other parent, it is useful to provide the judge with a file of pictures of the house, school, affidavits from family and/or neighbours and a study by a local lawyer explaining, if the jurisdiction is not in the EU, how easy domestication would be.

E. SURROGACY AND ADOPTION

16. VALIDITY OF SURROGACY AGREEMENTS

16.1 Briefly summarise the position in your jurisdiction

Since a 1991 decision of the *Cour de Cassation*, surrogacy agreements are strictly prohibited in France as being contrary to the principle of the inalienability of the human body. This prohibition has been confirmed by the 1994 bioethics law and is now outlined in Article 16-7 of the FCC, which provides that surrogacy agreements are null and void. They are also liable to penal sanctions. There are no exceptions to this rule.

In spite of that legal prohibition, many couples who are confronted by the infertility of the woman decide to go abroad, in a country where surrogacy agreements are legal or tolerated. The question that was asked then was to determine whether those overseas surrogacy agreements, which are legal under the national law of the country in which they are concluded, were to be recognised in France, ie, whether the commissioning parents can obtain registration in France of the child's foreign birth certificate mentioning them as his or her legal parents.

The answer to that question was given by the *Cour de Cassation* in 2011. In three decisions the Court reiterated that a surrogacy agreement was contrary to the principle of the inalienability of the human body and, hence, could not produce any effect in France as regard to filiation, even though it was entered into in a country in which such practice is legal. As a consequence, the Court ruled that a foreign judgment giving effect to a surrogacy agreement by recognising the commissioning parents as being the legal parents of the child was contrary to essential principles of French law and thus to the French conception of international public order, so that the registration in France of the foreign birth certificate could be refused or annulled. The direct result of such a decision is that filiation between the commissioning parents and the child can never be recognised.

Recently, the French Ministry of Justice has required the public prosecutor to register the foreign birth certificate when the father was the biological father of the child.

17. ADOPTION

17.1 Briefly explain the legal position in relation to adoption in your jurisdiction. Is adoption available to individuals, cohabiting couples (both heterosexual and same sex)?

The French rules of conflict of laws are contained in Article 370-3 of the FCC, which provides that the conditions of adoption are subject to the national law of the adopting parent, or, in the case of an adoption by a married couple, to the law governing the effects of their union (which is the national law if they have the same nationality, or the law of their domicile if not) However, adoption can never be pronounced if the national law of both spouses prohibits it. Besides, the adoption of a foreign minor cannot be pronounced if his or her national law prohibits this institution, unless the minor is born and habitually resident in France. Finally, whatever the applicable law to adoption is, it requires the consent of the child's legal representative.

Under French law, adoption is available to individuals. Any person aged above 28 can adopt, whether he or she is married or not, living alone or cohabiting. Adoption is also available to spouses who have been married for more than two years or both aged above 28. However, this last condition is not applicable if the adoption concerns the child of the other spouse.

Cohabiting couples (whether heterosexual or same sex) cannot adopt a child together; the child can only be adopted by one of the cohabitants. Partners who have entered a PACS are in the same situation. Thus, two persons have to be married if they want to adopt a child together.

The principle is that the adopting parent shall be 15 years older than the adopted child, unless the adopted child is the child of the spouse (the age difference is then lowered to 10 years).

Adoption in France, whether the candidate is a national or a foreigner, is conditioned by obtaining an approval given by the President of the Conseil General unless the adopted child is the child of the spouse.

There are two types of adoption. *Adoption plénière* and *adoption simple*. *Adoption plénière* or plenary adoption's effects are very strong; the child is considered to be the child of the adopting parent and a new birth certificate is established with their name as genitors. The adoption is final and cannot be revoked. *Adoption simple* or simple adotption, which is also possible for adults, is where the child is considered to be a member of the adopting family but maintains their inheritance rights within their original family (as well as taking inheritance rights from the adopting family). This adoption can be revoked.

The effects of an adoption pronounced in France are the ones provided by French law. An adoption that has been regularly pronounced abroad will have the effect of a plenary adoption in France if it breaks the pre-existing link of filiation in a complete and irrevocable way. Failing that, it will have the effect of a simple adoption.

F. COHABITATION

18. COHABITATION

18.1 What legislation governs division of property for unmarried couples on the breakdown of the relationship?

Article 515-8 of the FFC defines 'concubinage' as a 'union in fact, characterised by a life in common, offering a character of stability and continuity, between two persons, of different sexes or of the same sex, who live as a couple'. The assets acquired, given or inherited during the cohabitation remain in the name of the cohabitant who acquired, benefited from or inherited them. Each cohabitant retains full ownership of their separate property. If a house is bought in the sole name of one of the cohabitants, that cohabitant will have the complete administration and benefit from it, regardless of the financial contribution made by the other.

Unmarried cohabitants' occupation rights in the family home in France are determined by reference to ordinary property law and the non-owning partner will have limited, if any, property rights. When the joint ownership is being wound-up, the other cohabitant will have no right or share in the asset acquired solely by their partner. For both to benefit, the asset must be in joint names.

In general, financial claims between cohabitants have little chance of success. Neither maintenance support nor compensatory benefit is due in cohabitation without marriage.

When the cohabitation has been very long and one of the cohabitants can prove that their cohabitant has become richer with their help (promotion of the other's career, for example), they could possibly obtain some compensation.

G. FAMILY DISPUTE RESOLUTION

19. MEDIATION, COLLABORATIVE LAW AND ARBITRATION

19.1 Briefly summarise the non-court-based processes available in your jurisdiction and the current status of agreements reached under the auspices of mediation, collaborative law and arbitration

Conciliation

Conciliation is a compulsory step in the dissolution of marriage action (except in the mutual consent). When a dissolution of marriage action is introduced, both parties are summoned to a conciliation hearing before the judge who will try and conciliate them on both the principle and the consequences of the divorce. If the judge succeeds in conciliating the parties, which is very rare in practice, conciliation is recorded and the legal proceedings end. In practice the judges never try to conciliate the spouses.

Mediation

Mediation can either be contractual – the parties decide to try and settle the dispute out of court with the support of a neutral third person, a mediator – or judicial – the mediator is designated by the judge, with the consent of the parties.

Both contractual and judicial mediation are governed by the same fundamental principles: the free choice of the parties to turn to it, confidentiality, expertise of the mediator who has to comply with professional ethics and the good faith of all of the participants.

Mediation can lead the parties to enter into an agreement. Mediation agreements are not, in themselves, legally binding. They need to be ratified by the judge in order to become enforceable. The non-ratification of the agreement does not make it void, but only deprives it of its immediate enforceability. If the parties fail to reach an agreement, the judge records the failure of the mediation measure and settles the dispute.

Collaborative law

Collaborative law relies on a contractual commitment of the parties and their lawyers to forbid themselves from introducing legal proceedings to resolve their dispute. The purpose is to allow the parties, helped by their counsels or other collaborative law practitioners if necessary, such as psychiatrists, therapists, notaries, or mediators, to formulate their own solutions that will be considered as being acceptable by both parties. These solutions are then subject to ratification by the judge.

Arbitration

Arbitration is prohibited in family law by Article 2060 of the FCC, but it could be used in partition of matrimonial property or inheritance cases.

19.2 What is the statutory basis (if any) for mediation, collaborative law and arbitration in your jurisdiction? In particular, are the parties required to attempt a family dispute resolution in advance of the institution of proceedings?

Conciliation

Applicable dispositions can be found in Articles 252 to 252-4 of the FCC and in Articles 1108 to 1113 of the French Civil Procedure Code.

Mediation

As part of a dissolution of marriage action, Article 255 of the FCC provides that the judge can suggest a family mediation to the spouses and, with their consent, designate a family mediator. The judge can also order the spouses to meet with a family mediator who will give them information on the purpose and the proceedings of the mediation measure. The same powers are granted to the judge by Article 373-2-10 of the FCC in order to favour the common exercise of parental responsibility. The decision ordering the spouses to meet with a mediator is not appealable (Article 1071 al. 3 of the French Civil Procedure Code). However, the parties have no obligation to go through a mediation measure.

Collaborative law

There is no statutory basis for collaborative law. It can only be implemented on a voluntary basis.

H. OTHER

20. CIVIL PARTNERSHIP/SAME-SEX MARRIAGE

20.1 What is the status of civil partnership/same-sex marriage within the jurisdiction? What legislation governs civil partnership/same-sex marriage?

Article 515-1 of the FCC provides a different definition of the PACS, defining it as: 'a civil covenant of solidarity is a contract entered into by two natural persons of age, of different sexes or of a same sex, to organise their common life'. If the parties conclude a PACS after 1 January 2007 (amendment of the PACS's provisions by the law 23 June 2006) they will be treated as spouses married under a separation of assets regime, and when valuing their respective shares in the property consideration will be given to the difference between the price of the purchase of the property and the price of its sale. Hence it may differ in its regime from the winding up of cohabitants.

If they have opted for a limited community regime, which is close to the French legal regime for spouses, the matrimonial home will be considered as a joint asset. Consequently, the price will be divided equally between the partners who have entered the PACS.

As far as the PACS is concerned, things are a little different, as a mutual and material assistance exists between the partners. This duty is considered to be more formal than practical and many authors consider that it could be difficult to obtain an order requiring a partner to pay support to the other.

21. CONTROVERSIAL AREAS/RAPIDLY DEVELOPING AREAS OF LAW

21.1 Is there a particular area of the law within the jurisdiction that is currently undergoing major change?

21.2 Which areas of law are most out of step? Which areas would you most like to see reformed/changed?

On 23 April 2013, the French Parliament adopted a legislative bill on same-sex marriage. It aims to extend the institution of marriage to homosexual couples and allow the adoption of a child by a homosexual married couple (which would directly result from their status of spouses).

A recourse against this law has been filed by the opposition before the *Conseil Constitutionnel* and it is currently pending. The recourse has been rejected and the law published on 17 May 2013.

Therefore now in France same-sex marriage is allowed and a same-sex married couple could adopt a child.

The new law also introduces a rule of conflict of law Article 202-1 FCC which designated the national law applicable to the matrimonial capacity of the spouses. But if the national law of one spouse prohibits same-sex marriage and if the law of the nationality of the other, or the domicile or the residence of one spouse admits same-sex marriage then the French authorities will be able to celebrate the marriage.

Germany

Kanzlei, Dr. Kreidler-Pleus & Kollegen
Dr. Daniela Kreidler-Pleus

A. JURISDICTION AND CONFLICT OF LAW

1. SOURCES OF LAW

1.1 What is the primary source of law in relation to the breakdown of marriage and the welfare of children within the jurisdiction?

The primary sources of law are as follows:

- Statutes;
- Decisions/case law of the Regional Courts of Appeal (*Oberlandesgerichte*/OLG);
- Decisions of the Federal Supreme Court of Justice (*Bundesgerichtshof*/BGH);
- Decisions of the Federal Constitutional Court (*Bundesverfassungsgericht*/BVerfG);
- Directing lines/guidelines of the Regional Court of Appeal;
- Düsseldorf Scale.

1.2 Which are the main statutes governing matrimonial law in the jurisdiction?

The main statutes are as follows:

- *Bürgerliches Gesetzbuch (BGB)*/German Civil Code §§ 1297 to 1921;
- *Versorgungsausgleichsgesetz*/Law on the Balance of Pension Entitlements;
- *Gesetz über das Verfahren in Familiensachen und in Angelegenheiten der freiwilligen Gerichtsbarkeit* (FamFG) sections 111 to 270/ Law Concerning the Proceedings in Family Law Cases and Cases of Noncontentious Matters.

2. JURISDICTION

2.1 What are the main jurisdictional requirements for the institution of proceedings in relation to divorce, property and children?

To start proceedings an application has to be initiated at the local competent family court. With the application court fees have to be advanced.

Divorce

The applicant has an obligation to be represented by a lawyer when initiating divorce proceedings (section 114 FamFG). The written application has to include the following points:

- name and address of the parties;
- name and address of the competent court;

- application of divorce;
- grounds for divorce;
- name and date of birth of the common minor children and their habitual residence;
- declaration of the parents that they agree upon the care, visitation rights and alimony for the minor children, if such agreement exists;
- declaration that the parties agree upon the spousal maintenance, marital home and household effects, if such agreement exists;
- information on whether other applications are pending concerning the family, where both spouses are involved;
- signature of the lawyer;
- the number of required transcripts;
- marriage certificate and birth certificates of the common minor children.

Property

In proceedings concerning the balance of accrued gains and maintenance, an application has to be initiated at the local competent family court. As long as divorce proceedings are pending, the local competent court is exclusively the court where the divorce proceedings were initiated.

As a rule the parties have to be represented by a lawyer, according to section 115 FamFG.

Children

Legal proceedings concerning the care of children or visitation rights normally start with an application at the local competent Family Court. As long as divorce proceedings are pending, the local competent court is exclusively the court where the divorce proceedings were initiated.

In proceedings concerning care and visitation rights, the parties do not have to be represented by a lawyer. The court has to appoint a guardian, if this is necessary, for the child to exercise their rights (section 158 FamFG).

The parents and the youth welfare office have to be heard. The court has to hear the child from their 14th birthday upwards. If the child is under 14 years, they have to be heard if the biases, relationships or the will of the child is important for the decision, or if there are other reasons to hear the child. As a rule, even very young children are heard by the court, starting at about the age of four or five years old.

In proceedings concerning care and visitation rights, the court has the obligation to reach an amicable arrangement.

3. DOMICILE AND HABITUAL RESIDENCE

3.1 Explain the concepts of domicile and habitual residence as they apply to the jurisdiction.

German law follows the concept of habitual residence, not domicile. Habitual residence is understood as described in the Hague Convention of 5 October 1961 concerning the Powers of Authorities and the law applicable in Respect of the Protection of Minors and the Hague Convention on Child Protection.

A person is a habitual resident of a country or state where they have the most social and economic relations, the person's centre of life (BGH FamRZ 2002, 1182 f.). The stay must be of certain duration and more than a simple stay. In addition, further family and professional relationships, which support the argument that this is the person's centre of life, are necessary (see *OLG München,* 30.06.2005, No. 5, IPRspr. 2005, No. 198, 543-545).

If there is more than one residence, the habitual residence is where the person mostly stays overnight. Habitual residence means factual integration in the social environment for a certain period of time. The intention for such an integration is not necessary (see BGH FamRZ 81, 135 f.; 93, 798, 800).

Registration at the registration office is only an indication (see BGH FamRZ 95, 1135; 96, 171 f.).

The intention to establish a residence is necessary; ie, a person who moves to a new place with the intention to stay there immediately has a new habitual residence at the this place. A temporary stay of less than three weeks is not sufficient to establish a residence (see BGH FamRZ 95, 728 f). This intention is especially important if the person is absent for a more lengthy time; ie, for professional reasons. If the person intends to come back, they must keep the habitual residence (see BGH FamRZ 93, 798 f.). Unintended or involuntary moves do not establish a new habitual residence (see Köln FamRZ 2003, 1124). They only can establish a new habitual residence if the move back is unforeseeable or the stay is a very long one (see Köln FamRZ 2003, 1124).

The habitual residence of children is where their lives are centred (see Hamm FamRZ 91, 1466). This can differ from the residence of the parent who has care of the children (see BGH FamRZ 97, 1070). As long as the child is young, the habitual residence will be the same as that of the person who has child care. When the child is older, the social relations to family, friends and school, etc, become more and more important. If the stay is only a temporary stay, it depends on the duration and the view of the child. Some courts assume that the residence becomes habitual after six months (see BGHZ 78, 293, 301; Köln FamRZ 91, 363 f.; Hamm FamRZ 91, 1346; Bamberg FamRZ 96, 1224 f.).

In the case of child abduction, the habitual residence of the child can change, even if the change of residence was against the law, if the child's centre of life has changed (see BGH, NJW 1981, 520 ff.; EuGH, FamRBint 3, 2009, 53).

4. CONFLICT OF LAW/APPLICABLE LAW TO BE APPLIED

4.1 What happens when one party applies to stay proceedings in favour of a foreign jurisdiction? What factors will the local court take into account when determining forum issues?

German law follows, as a rule, the principle of priority. Germany has signed most of the International Conventions and in particular the Brussels I Regulation offers rules for priority.

With regard to other International Conventions, for example, the European Convention on Jurisdiction and Enforcement of Judgments in Civil and

Commercial Matters of 27 September 1968 in the form of 29 November 1996 (EUGVÜ), the European Court refers to the *lex fori* concerning the question of pending actions.

If there is no provision in the International Conventions, pending actions according to German law will only be given if an action is filed. It is only filed if the service of the action to the other party has taken place. It is not sufficient that the action is presented to the court. This very often leads to a disadvantage for the German jurisdiction because many other countries do not demand for the service of the action, only the presentation to the court.

If it is not clear which court was first in time, the consequences depend on whether the Brussels Regulations are applicable, or other international conventions that do not offer rules for priority, or no conventions are applicable.

According to Brussels II bis, the later seised court will temporarily suspend the proceedings until the jurisdiction is clear. If the first seised court declares that it has jurisdiction, the German court will declare that it has no jurisdiction. If the first seised court declares that it has no jurisdiction, the second seised court in Germany will continue. If there is no decision from the first seised court, or the German court does not have notice of such a decision, the German court will temporarily suspend the proceedings.

The question whether the German court could continue will depend on the question of the recognition of the decision of the first seised court. In all other cases, the second seised court will temporarily suspend the decision according to section 148 ZPO.

If the principle of priority is not respected by the foreign court, the consequences will depend on whether an international convention or regulation is applicable. According to Article 21 of Brussels II bis, for example, the decision of a foreign court will be recognised and enforced, even if the foreign court makes a decision without respecting the principle of priority.

If there is no international regulation/convention, and the foreign court takes a decision without respecting German priority, the judgment will not be recognised (section 109 I No. 3 FamFG).

The prior decision of a foreign court will not be respected in Germany if this leads to unreasonable prejudice for the applicant in Germany, for example, if the foreign court needs a disproportionately long time to decide without pertinent reasons (BGH NJW 83, 1269, AG Leverkusen, FamRZ 2003, 41).

If the German court makes a decision without respecting the foreign priority, the judgment will, nevertheless, be valid.

B. PRE- AND POST-NUPTIAL AGREEMENTS

5. VALIDITY OF PRE- AND POST-NUPTIAL AGREEMENTS

5.1 To what extent are pre- and post-nups binding within the jurisdiction? Could you provide a brief discussion of the most significant recent case law on this issue

The freedom to enter into marriage contracts (pre- and post-nuptial agreements) complies with the German tradition of law and can be traced back to the Middle Ages.

An agreement has to be concluded in a notary public's office with both parties present. The parties to an agreement do not have to be represented by legal counsel before or during the signing of the agreement. Full disclosure of the assets of the parties before signing is not required.

The notary does not represent either of the parties, but is an independent, impartial consultant for the parties involved. The notary is obliged to explore the parties' intent, clarify the facts in the case and instruct the parties on the legal consequences of the transaction and reflect their statements clearly and unambiguously in the transcript. The entire transcript must be read to the parties.

The marriage contract in a closer sense is defined in section 1408 I BGB as a contract in which the married couple settle their relationship on their status of property. Status of property is to be understood in a sense that the legal status of property can be changed or varied.

There are three different categories of legal status in which property can be held:

- community of accrued gains (*Zugewinngemeinschaft*);
- separation of property;
- community of property.

The community of accrued gains is the default statutory regime of matrimonial property, ie, if the spouses do not agree to choose another one.

According to sections 1408 II BGB, 6 I 2 VersAusglG, the married couple can exclude the balance of the pension entitlements in a marriage contract.

All arrangements concerning the marriage of a couple for the regulation of general matrimonial questions, the matrimonial property rights and the consequences of a divorce, can be made in a marriage contract. The German courts do have jurisdiction to set aside those agreements (or aspects of them) in certain circumstances.

Case law/Jurisprudence has fundamentally changed since the Federal Constitutional Court (*Bundesverfassungsgericht*) and the High Court of Justice (*Bundesgerichtshof*) changed their jurisdiction in 2001 and 2004 (BVerfG 06.02.2001, BGH 29.03.2001).

These two decisions are diametrically opposed to the previous rulings where it was held that a court cannot interfere with the freedom of a husband and wife to contract according to their wishes. They gave new criteria according to which marriage contracts are valid or not. The main principle is that a marriage contract may not undermine the proper application of the law. If the marriage contract starts with unequal negotiating positions (eg, pregnancy) or leads to an obvious unilateral and unjustified burden for one party, that may be seen as undermining the proper application of the law.

When considering the marriage contract we have to keep two dates in mind; the date of the marriage contract and the date of the divorce. If the contract had undermined the proper application of law at the date the parties concluded it because it was against morals (*contra bonus mores*), the whole marriage contract would be invalid according to section 138 BGB.

If the facts had changed within the time between the marriage and the divorce, and at the time of the divorce the marriage contract or specific provisions within the contract undermine the proper application of the law, then only these specific provisions have to be adapted to the new situation. According to section 242 BGB, the rest remains valid.

These are the most important recent decisions of the High Court of Justice (*Bundesgerichtshof*) are detailed below:

BGH 17.10.2007 – XII ZR 96/05

The waiver of the balance of accrued gains is not invalid because one spouse had been self-employed during the marriage – which both parties had expected when concluding the agreement – and, therefore, had not gained pension entitlements, so that no balance of pension entitlements took place.

BGH 09.07.2008 – XII ZR 6/07
BGH 18.03.2009 – XII ZB 94/06

The exclusion of the balance of pension entitlements is invalid if both parties declare that the wife would retire from professional life to take care for the children and could, therefore, not gain her own pension entitlements.

If the agreement was concluded when the wife was pregnant in the ninth month and first saw the draft at the notary's office, the agreement could be invalid as a whole.

C. DIVORCE, NULLITY AND JUDICIAL SEPARATION

6. RECOGNITION OF FOREIGN MARRIAGES/DIVORCES

6.1 Summarise the position in your jurisdiction

There are no special proceedings for the recognition of foreign marriages. However, the question of the validity of a marriage can be a preliminary question for other decisions, for example, taxes, family registration, naming, etc. This preliminary question has to be answered by the competent administration or authority.

As a rule Germany acknowledges the validity of foreign marriages if the laws (rules) of the foreign country (home country or country of marriage) concerning marriage were obeyed. Furthermore, the fiancés have to fulfill the requirements of their home country or the place where they were married for a marriage, for example, unmarried, minimum age, no relation by blood (Article 11 I, 13 II EGBGB).This means that German law accepts only religious marriages, Nevada marriages, common-law marriages according to North American law, registered Soviet Union marriages, Imam marriages according to Turkish law, etc, if the marriages followed the law of the fiancés' home country or the country where the marriage took place.

Foreign divorces have to be recognised. There must be an application for recognition. Foreign divorce is effective only after recognition. The rules are to be found in section 107 ff. FamFG.

However, there are foreign divorces which are recognised '*ipso jure*'.

This happens, as a rule, if the Brussels II bis Regulation is applicable. Those covered are divorces which took place after 1 March 1 2001 within the European Union, with the exception of Denmark. Formal recognition is necessary only if there are exceptions according to Articles 22 and 23. There are other divorces which do not need formal recognition. These are cases where both parties are members of the state whose court or authority granted the divorce (section 107 I 2 FamFG).

In all other cases, the *Landesjustizverwaltung* or a regional Court of Appeal has to declare the preconditions for the recognition as given.

The preconditions can be found in bilateral agreements (Switzerland and Tunisia). In all other cases the recognition takes place. If the preconditions of section 109 FamFG are given, this is not possible if:

- the divorce is not final;
- the foreign courts had no jurisdiction according to German law (section 109 I 1 FamFG);
- it was given default of appearance if the respondent was not served with the document which instituted the proceedings, or with an equivalent document, in sufficient time and in such a way as to enable the respondent to arrange for their defence, unless it is determined that the respondent has accepted the judgment unequivocally (section 109 I 2 FamFG);
- the decision is irreconcilable with a German judgment or a previous foreign judgment, which has to be recognised in Germany, or if the proceeding is incompatible with previous pending German proceedings (section 109 I 3 FamFG);
- the recognition of the divorce would lead to a result that is incompatible with the leading principals of German law (*ordre public*) (section 109 I 4 FamFG).

7. DIVORCE

7.1 Explain the grounds for divorce within the jurisdiction (please also deal with nullity and judicial separation if appropriate)

According to section 1565 I BGB, a marriage may be dissolved by divorce if it has broken down. This is given if the conjugal community no longer exists and the spouses cannot be expected to restore it;

The breakdown is presumed according to section 1566 BGB if the spouses have lived apart for a year and both of them want the divorce or if the spouses have lived apart for three years and one spouse wants the divorce.

Living apart means separation of board and lodging, no common meals, no services for the other spouse and no other similarities. If conditions are respected, a separation can take place within the same house or apartment.

A divorce can take place, even if the spouses have not separated for one year, if the continuation of the marriage could lead to an unbearable hardship for the applicant. The reasons must lie in the person of the respondent. These reasons can be severe verbal abuse and rude violations of the other, such as frequent mistreatment of the spouse, alcoholism and frequent alcohol abuse or an unawareness of any previous convictions.

However, a divorce cannot take place if its continuation until the end of the first year of separation is in the interest of the common minor children. Furthermore, a divorce cannot take place if the divorce leads the respondent, because of extraordinary circumstances, to significant hardship, so that maintaining the marriage would be expected of the applicant. This could be the case if the respondent was, for example, in the final stages of muscular sclerosis and there was a danger of deterioration.

Annulment according to section 1313 ff BGB

A marriage can be annulled by a judgment if there is a reason for the dissolution. The law provides the following reasons:

- when concluding the marriage, one partner was not able to be married;
- when concluding the marriage, one partner was incapable of acting in law;
- when concluding the marriage, one partner had already been married to a third party;
- if the partners are related by lineal descent or full or half brothers and sisters;
- if the parties did not give their statement to conclude the marriage personally and if both parties were not present;
- if one spouse had concluded the marriage in a state of unconsciousness or disturbance of the mind;
- if one spouse had not known that a marriage was taking place;
- if one party had concluded the marriage because of fraud. However, if the fraud concerned property or was concluded by a third party, this would not lead to a suspension;
- if one party had been led into the marriage by an unlawful threat;
- if both parties had agreed before they married that they did not want to be bound in wedlock.

8. FINANCES/CAPITAL, PROPERTY

8.1 What powers does the court have to allocate financial resources and property on the breakdown of marriage? Explain and illustrate with reference to recent cases the court's thinking on division of assets

German law differs between maintenance, the balance of pension entitlements, the balance of accrued gains, the division of the household effects and the division of joint property. The courts do not have the right to put all these aspects together and make one judgment considering the whole case. Every aspect is ruled in separate proceedings, but by the same judge. The pension entitlements have to be balanced together with the divorce and the other aspects are dealt with only if applied for.

Community of accrued gains is the statutory regime of matrimonial assets. The principle of community of accrued gains is based on the separation of assets. Even after marriage, each spouse remains the sole proprietor of his or her assets, also of assets that he or she has acquired during the marriage. The balance of accrued gains means that only the increase in the assets' value will be balanced. The increase in the assets' value is defined as the surplus, resulting from the difference between the initial assets of a spouse and the assets at the end of the marriage.

The marriage date and the service date of the divorce petition to the other party are the two deadlines required for the calculation of the balance of the increase in assets' value. The initial and final assets at the above-mentioned deadlines will be listed and it will then be calculated which assets each spouse owned at the respective deadlines.

The initial assets will be calculated with the cost of living index in settlement of the loss of purchasing power. Furthermore, these amounts are added to the initial assets that one spouse will acquire as a result of death, with regard to a future inheritance, by gift or as furnishings. The cost of living index at the date of the gift or inheritance will be applied for the added assets.

Should the increase in the assets' value (*Zugewinn*) of one spouse exceed the share of the other spouse, the latter will be entitled to half of the surplus in money. There will not be any possibility of acquiring half of the assets.

The equalisation of the accrued gains only applies to assets acquired during the marriage. There is no balancing of the assets acquired when the parties lived together before the marriage took place.

Maintenance and balance of accrued gains are only to be paid in money. The court does not have the right to allocate real estate or other assets. The separation of common assets goes by an execution sale. The balance of pension entitlements takes place by transferring entitlements from one pension account to the other.

Only proceedings to divide up the matrimonial household effects lead to an allocation of specific objects. For the specific objects of the household, this means that the spouse becomes the final owner of the former common object.

Proceedings concerning the marital home are comparable. One spouse can apply to stay in the marital home if the move would lead to unbearable hardship for the spouse. However, this would only mean that the parties conclude a rental agreement. The remaining spouse does not become the owner of the real estate.

9. FINANCES/MAINTENANCE

9.1 Explain the operation of maintenance for spouses on an ongoing basis after the breakdown of marriage. Is it common for maintenance to be awarded? Explain and illustrate with reference to recent cases the court's thinking on maintenance.

German law offers the possibility for the financially weaker party of the divorce to gain maintenance. Fundamentally, German law takes the autonomy of the spouse after the divorce as its starting point. This idea of autonomy was strengthened by a new law which came into force on 1 January 2008.

A spouse only has the right to post-matrimonial maintenance under the following circumstances:

- if the spouse has taken care of the children;
- if the spouse is no longer able to earn their own living because of age;
- if the spouse is unable to earn their own living because of illness or weakness;
- if the spouse is unable to find adequate employment after the divorce;
- if the spouse is unable to earn as much as the other spouse;
- if the spouse loses a secure job;
- if the spouse needs maintenance to obtain further education;
- maintenance of equity.

The maintenance can be limited in relation to time as well as with regard to the level of maintenance. The court must decide on a limitation in the initial proceeding. No limitation will be possible after that. It must be ascertained whether the limitation on the maintenance is adequate in every single case. The criteria are as follows:

- to what extent was the spouse disadvantaged throughout the marriage to earn their own maintenance;
- how long did the spouse take care of the common children;
- who took care of the household and who was responsible for earning the income;
- how long did the marriage last.

The judge also has to take into consideration how much time the spouse will need to become autonomous.

The court can deny, reduce or limit the level of the right to maintenance if the payment of the maintenance would be a gross inequity for the other spouse. The judge will have to take the interests of the children into consideration, if, for example, the children are being looked after by the other spouse, when deciding on this.

As a rule, maintenance must be paid monthly in advance. A spouse may only ask for a lump sum in special cases. There must be an important reason to ask for such a sum, for example, if the spouse has the intention to leave the country. On the other hand, the spouse who owes the maintenance must be living in very good financial conditions in this case, so that paying a lump sum would not be a problem for them. If there is no important reason, the judge will be unable to decide on a lump sum. Consequently, the payment of a lump sum is then only possible by means of an agreement between the parties.

Germany had a reform of the right to maintenance which came into force on 1 January 2008. Since then maintenance claims have been more often limited to a certain period of time and also lowered after a certain time.

Before the law came into force, the weaker party to the marriage could claim for life-long maintenance according to the marital circumstances of living if the marriage had lasted more than 20 years. Now the maintenance claim can be limited and reduced even in those cases. The important point is whether the one who has taken care of the children or took charge of the household had a break in their career. If so, the other party has to pay maintenance.

The jurisdiction differs from state (*Bundesland*) to state. There is a frontier in the middle of Germany; south of this frontier the judges are still very generous, north of this they are very strict in limiting and reducing the maintenance.

In the south of Germany the courts do not normally cut off maintenance directly after the divorce. Even if there is no break in the career, maintenance has to be paid for a third or quarter of the time of marriage, as a rule, because of the marriage. If there was a break in the career, maintenance can be payable for a lifetime. However, the amount of the maintenance will be limited after a certain time to the amount which the person would have earned if they had not married (BGH 14.10.12009, XII ZR 146/08).

The second big change is the fact that, according to the new law, the one who takes care of the child has to start working when the child is three years old. For this period of time, meaning the first three years, the one who takes care of the child has the right to maintenance. After that time they have to prove that, because of the child, there is no possibility to work. Therefore, the person who takes care of the child has to prove that there is no kindergarten place available and no possibility to find another person to take care of the child. This seems to be a very tough rule. In fact, the judges only expect the one who takes care of the children to have a €400.00 net income when the child is three years old. When the child is older than eight to 10 years, they expect part-time work and full-time work only after the child's twelfth birthday (BGH 18.03.2009, XII ZR 74/08).

10. CHILD MAINTENANCE

10.1 On what basis is child maintenance calculated within the jurisdiction?

The parent who does not look after the child is obliged to pay child maintenance. The amount of the child maintenance depends on the income of the parent who does not look after the child. All forms of income by the parent who is obliged to pay maintenance are relevant. If the parent is self-employed the average income of the last three years is used.

If the parent is employed, the salary of the last 12 months is relevant.

If there is income from rent and lease an average is also built out of the last three years.

Income from capital is the income of the last year.

If the parent who has to pay maintenance lives in a house or apartment of their own, the saved rent is put into consideration. Income taxes, social insurance contributions and age care contributions are deducted from the whole sum. Loans are considered in an appropriate amount. Furthermore, professional expenses are considered.

Once this is done, the so-called *Düsseldorfer Tabelle*/Düsseldorf scale is used.

The Düsseldorf scale has four classes for the ages from nought to five, six to 11, 12 to 17 and starting from 18 years. Furthermore, there are 10 income groups. The lowest starts from up to €1,500.00. In this group a child at the age of nought to five years receives a minimum maintenance of €317.00 per month. This amount is pro-rated with the state child allowance, so the amount that has to be paid is €225.00 per month.

The highest income group is between €4,701.00 and €5,100.00. In this group the child between nought to five years receives child maintenance in the amount of €508.00 per month. After pro-rating the state allowance, the amount that has to be paid is €416.00 per month.

A student who does not live in the house of the parents will normally receive a fixed child maintenance amount of €670.00 per month.

If the income of the parent who owes the child maintenance is over €5,100.00 per month, the child maintenance has to be fixed according to the individual needs of the child. The monthly needs of the child have to be listed.

11. RECIPROCAL ENFORCEMENT OF FINANCIAL ORDERS

11.1 Summarise the position in your jurisdiction

Foreign financial orders can be enforced according to international conventions.

Within the EU the EUGVVO (Council Regulation (EC) No 44/2001 on Jurisdiction and the Recognition and Enforcement of Judgements in Civil and Commercial Matters) and the EUGVÜ (European Convention on Jurisdiction and Enforcement of Judgements in Civil and Commercial Matters) are relevant.

The new EU Maintenance Regulation, Council Regulation (EC) No I/2009 of 18 December 2008 and the Protocol of 23 November 2007 on the Law Applicable to Maintenance Obligations came into force on 18 June 2011. They replaced and amended (in relation to maintenance claims) the jurisdiction and enforcement provisions of the Brussels IRegulation(Article 68) in family cases. The regulation applies to Germany and some other European countries.

Furthermore, the Lugano Convention sets the rules in relation to Iceland, Norway, Switzerland and in relation to former Polish judgments.

Normally the most favourable international convention is applicable according to the so-called *'Günstigkeitsprinzip'*. If no international convention applies, the enforcement follows section 107 ff. FamFG.

Enforcement is only possible if the foreign decision can be recognised in Germany. The recognition will take place *ipso jure*. Only if the following preconditions according to section 109 FamFG are given, the recognition of financial orders cannot take place, if:

- they are not final;
- the foreign courts had no jurisdiction according to German law (section 109 I 1 FamFG);
- they were made in default of the appearance of the party, if the respondent was not served with the document which instituted the proceedings or with an equivalent document in sufficient time and in such a way as to enable to respondent to arrange for their defence, unless it is determined that the respondent has accepted the judgment unequivocally (section 109 I 2 FamFG);
- the order is irreconcilable with a German judgment or a former foreign judgment which has to be recognised in Germany or if the proceedings are incompatible with former pending German proceedings (section 109 I 3 FamFG);
- the recognition of the divorce would lead to a result that is incompatible with the leading principles of German law (*ordre public*) (section 109 I 4 FamFG).

There must be reciprocity. This means that German courts only acknowledge decisions of foreign countries in which comparable decisions of German courts are acknowledged (section 109 IV FamFG).Then the decision has to be declared enforceable according to section 110 FamFG in formal proceedings.

12. FINANCIAL RELIEF AFTER FOREIGN DIVORCE PROCEEDINGS

12.1 What powers are available to make orders following a foreign divorce?

A German court can make orders following a foreign divorce if the foreign court has not yet decided on ancillary consequential matters. This is very often the case if the foreign law does not recognise a balance of pension entitlements. According to section 102 FamFG, German courts have jurisdiction if the applicant or respondent are habitual residents in Germany, if the court has to decide on German pension entitlements or a German court has already decided on the divorce.

If a foreign decision cannot be recognised, the German court can make a new order in the same area. If a foreign decision on an ancillary consequential matter has to be recognised, a variation can be possible.

If there is a maintenance claim, a variation can take place according to sections 238-240 FamFG, saying a variation is only possible if the facts on which the decision was based have changed essentially after the decision.

If there is a decision on child care or visitation rights, a variation is possible if the best interest of the child requires a variation of the foreign decision.

D. CHILDREN

13. CUSTODY/PARENTAL RESPONSIBILITY

13.1 Briefly explain the legal position in relation to custody/parental responsibility following the breakdown of a relationship or marriage

German law strictly differs between parental custody and the right of visitation.

Parental custody in section 1626 I of the BGB is described as the duty and the right of the parents to care for the minor child. Parental custody includes the care for the person and the property of the person.

In the care and upbringing of the child, the parents take account of the growing ability and the growing need of the child for independent responsible action (section 1626 II BGB).

If the parents are or were married, as a rule the parents retain, even after separation and divorce, joint parental custody of their children.

Joint custody, according to German law, means that the parents have to consult each other and take joint decisions in relation to long-term issues which relate to the child, as for example, religion, education and medical care. In relation to long-term issues there is no right of one parent to decide without consulting the other parent. Only if the parents cannot reach a consent and the court decides, then one parent is allowed to decide on a concrete issue on his/her own.

Only in very exceptional cases will the courts give one parent sole parental custody.

The parent with whom the child lives or who has a visitation right can decide on day-to-day issues without the consent of the other parent.

If necessary, one parent can ask the court to decide where the child should live.

The rules concerning parents who are not married are described in section 1626 a I BGB. If the parents, at the date of the birth of the child, are not married to each other, they have joint parental custody if they:

- declare that they wish to take over joint parental custody (declarations of parental custody); or
- marry each other.

Otherwise the mother has sole parental custody (section 1626 a II BGB).

The European Court of Human Rights decided in December 2009 that section 1626a I BGB violated the rights of a legal father and that the German parliament therefore must amend the law. After the decision of the ECoHR and before the new law was adopted, German courts changed their jurisdiction to section 1626a BGB.

If the father wished to change the sole custody of the mother into joint custody he could initiate a court proceeding in order to prove that the mother alone or at all could not care enough for the child.

The legal father could already initiate a court proceeding and obtained parental custody together with the mother if there were no significant reasons which justified a refusal; for example if the father initiated the court proceeding by not giving his consent just to disallow the mother from making important decisions.

On 19 April 2013 the new Law to reform the Parental Care of Non Married Parents of 16 April 2013 was promulgated in the Bundesgesetzblatt (law gazette) and came into force on 19 May 2013.

It gives the father the possibility to apply for joint parental custody. The family court shall now decide in principle in favour of the father, if the welfare of the child is not harmed. If the legal mother does not react or does not present relevant facts which justify refusal of the joint parental custody to the applicant, there is a legal presumption that the parental custody of the father does not harm the welfare of the child.

On 25 April 2013 the German Bundestag adopted the Law on the Strengthening of the Rights of the Physical, not Legal Father. If the physical father shows sustainable interest in the child he will gain visitation rights and the right to information concerning the child. Only if this is against the best interest of the child will those rights not be granted.

The law still has to pass the Bundesrat which is assumed as sure and then has to be proclaimed.

13.2 Briefly explain the legal position in relation to access/contact/visitation following the breakdown of a relationship or marriage

In principle every legal parent has the right to contact with their own child, section 1626 III, 1684 BGB. The rights of contact of a genetic father who is not the legal father are very limited.

In such cases the father only has the same right of contact as a non-related person, according to section 1685 II BGB, even if he does have a close socially-familiar bond to the child and did or does have actual responsibility for the child. If these requirements are not fulfilled, even if not due to the fault of the genetic father, he does not have the right of contact.

According to the change in law which passed the legislation on 31 January 2013, these rights will be improved if the genetic father has shown constant interest in the child. He shall also be allowed to request personal information on his child. If it is uncertain that he is the genetic father, there is the right to ask the mother and the child to contribute genetic information to a procedure in order to ascertain who the father is (section 1598 a BGB).

The right of visitation can be limited if it endangers the welfare of the child. But the limitation shall always be by the mildest means.

For example the '*Kinderschutzbund*' (child protection organisation) can be asked to accompany the visits (*begleiteter Umgang*) of a parent in order to observe if the danger to the welfare of the child disappears in time or if the child begins to become familiar with a parent whom they had previously not seen for a long time. This sort of contact normally starts with a brief contact time, aiming to increase to unaccompanied contact with the parent. Sometimes the accompanied contact is a means to ease the concerns of the one parent that the other is not able to care for the child. But courts tend to respect those concerns only if there are facts that justify them. In the case of separation of the parents, regardless of whether they are married or not, where the parents cannot agree on the contact, each parent can ask the Family Court to decide on the extent and content of the right of contact.

There is a gradual change in the right of contact according to the age of the child. While children are young, courts normally offer contact more often, but for a shorter period of time and without a stay overnight. When children become older the courts usually decide in favour of contact every second weekend, half of the school holidays and with a stayover for one or two nights.

If the parent who does not live with the child lives far away from the child, there might be changes to the principles mentioned above.

14. INTERNATIONAL ABDUCTION

14.1 Summarise the position in your jurisdiction

Germany is a contracting state of the Hague Child Abduction Convention, the Brussels II a Regulation and the European Custody Convention.

The Central Authority is located at the Federal Office of Justice (*Bundesamt für Justiz*). Their website under *www.bundesjustizamt.de* (English translation available) is very helpful.

The jurisdiction for child abduction proceedings has been centralised. Only 22 out of 600 Family Courts in Germany have jurisdiction for abduction cases.

There is a decrease in the number of abduction cases going to court. On average the length of the proceedings exceeds six weeks.

The exceptions under Article 13 of the Hague Convention not to return the children are now handled very consistently within the intentions of the Convention.

Enforcement of Return Orders is controlled by the court but is, nevertheless, very time consuming and hard-going. Voluntary return settlements with undertakings, safe harbour decisions, etc, are in the meantime established.

Communication between judges of the countries involved in the matter is no longer the exception.

15. LEAVE TO REMOVE/APPLICATIONS TO TAKE A CHILD OUT OF THE JURISDICTION

15.1 Summarise the position in your jurisdiction

Parents have joint care of their children born during the marriage. Therefore, it is a joint decision of the parents where the children should live. If one parent, after the separation, wants to move, this is only possible with the consent of the other parent.

If a child was born out of wedlock, the mother still has the sole care. Joint care is only possible if the mother agrees to this. However, this will change in the near future according to a decision of the EUGH. If the mother has the care, it is only up to her to decide where the child should live. If the mother wants to move, she does not need the consent of the father.

Under what circumstances may a parent apply to remove their child from the jurisdiction against the wishes of the other parent?

If one parent wants to move with a child to another place, especially to a foreign country, this parent has to apply for the sole care or the right to decide where the child will have their habitual residence.

Joint care is the rule, so the sole care for one parent is only possible if the other parent does not care enough for the child, or if the child should move to a foreign country.

The parent will only get sole care or the right to decide where the child should live if this is in the best interests of the child. For the best interests of the child, the following criteria have to be taken into consideration:

- the principle of continuity;
- the principle of promotion/support;
- relationship to the parents and brothers and sisters;
- will of the child.

Principle of continuity refers to the question of which parent brought up the child most of the time. Principle of continuity is based on the experience that the continuation of familiar and social relations is very important for a stable and healthy development of a child.

Principle of promotion/support means the court has to decide which parents will be better able to promote/support the child.

It is the constitutional right of a child that their will be considered as far as this complies with the interests of the child. The older the child becomes, the more important the will of the child becomes (BVerfG FamRZ 2007, 105; BVerfG FamRZ 2007, 1078).

The court has to check in every single case whether the wishes of the child are stable and objectively comply with its interests. If the court comes to the decision that the wishes are stable and the child has good reasons for them, the court will then consider the wishes of the child.

Before the court takes a decision, the local youth welfare office is asked for an opinion. As a rule the court will also put a guardian to stand by the child. In addition, there is a possibility to call on psychological expertise.

E. SURROGACY AND ADOPTION

16. VALIDITY OF SURROGACY AGREEMENTS

16.1 Briefly summarise the position in your jurisdiction

Since 1991 the *Embryonenschutzgesetz* (ESchG) has prohibited a doctor from supporting the execution of surrogacy agreements. Furthermore section 13 c AdVermiG (Law Concerning the Agencies for Adoption) prohibits an agency from arranging the conclusion of surrogacy contracts. The doctor might be sentenced according to criminal law with imprisonment of up to three years or a fine, section 1 I ESchG for supporting surrogacy agreements. The agency might be sentenced in the same way according to section 14b AdVermiG.

There is no prosecution of the host mother or the contracting parents.

If there is a legally prohibited surrogacy agreement, the mother of a child is the woman who gave birth to it, ie, the host mother, not the contracting, ordering or genetic mother (section 1581 BGB).

It is not possible to change the legal situation by using foreign (legal) documents or concluding a foreign contract.

The contracting male might only be the legal father if:

- he is the genetic father and initiates a court proceeding in order to receive recognition of fatherhood; or
- he, (no matter whether he is the genetic father or not), obtains the consent of the host mother who acknowledges that he is the father, section 1595 I BGB.

Surrogacy agreements are prohibited if the host mother is a woman who carries a baby who is genetically the baby of two other people or if she is a woman willing to give away her own child to other people permanently.

If there is an agreement between a host mother and the contractors to give away an own child of the host mother by adoption, the contract is void and the promise to pay the host mother is not valid either.

17. ADOPTION

17.1 Briefly explain the legal position in relation to adoption in your jurisdiction. Is adoption available to individuals, cohabiting couples (both heterosexual and same-sex)?

According to section 1741 I BGB an adoption is admissible if it serves the best interests of the child and it is to be expected that a parent-child relationship will arise between the adoptive parent and the child.

The adoption may not be pronounced if the overriding interests of the children of the adoptive parent or of the child to be adopted prevent it or if it is to be feared that interests of the child to be adopted are endangered by children of the adoptive parent (section 1745 BGB).

There should be an appropriate time allowed for the child and the adoptive parent in order to see if they are suited to one another.

In principle:

- a married couple only are allowed to adopt a child together;
- an unmarried person is only allowed to adopt a child alone;
- a married person can adopt the child of the husband/wife alone if the husband/wife did adopt the child before they got married or it is the

genetic legal child of the spouse; and

- a married person at the age of 25 or more can adopt the child of the husband/wife alone if the partner is not yet 21 years' old or is not legally competent.

It takes the consent of the legal representative of the child or/and the legal parents in order to adopt a child. If the child is 14 years' old or older it requires the consent of the child, too. If the child and the adoptive parents are of different nationalities, the Family Court has to agree.

The consent of one parent or both parents for the adoption by another person/couple can be substituted by the Family Court, if they have persistently grossly violated their duty to the child.

The consent has to be certified by a notary and presented to the Family Court.

By adoption the child becomes the legal child of the adoptive parents/ person/couple who receive/s parental custody by law. The legal relationship to the previous parents, to former siblings, grandparents, great-grandparents or cousins ends. The child receives the family name of the adoptive family.

A homosexual partner is allowed to adopt the legal genetic child of the other homosexual partner if they are registered according to section 9 *Lebenspartnerschaftsgesetz* (LPartG) (Law of Homosexual Couples). If a homosexual person wants to adopt a child alone, it would be against article 14 EMRK (European Convention on Human Rights), if he/she were refused, simply because of his/her sexual orientation. But if there are other reasons to protect the welfare of a child then an exception could be made. BVerfG FamRZ 03, 149. On 19 February 2013 the Federal Constitutional Court decided that a homosexual partner in a registered homosexual relationship may adopt the child of the other partner if he/she adopted the child before they were registered. The Federal Constitutional Court has not yet decided whether a joint adoption of a child by a registered homosexual couple is possible. But the jurisdiction may develop in that direction.

An adult can be adopted if there is an ethical justification for it.

F. COHABITATION

18. COHABITATION

18.1 What legislation (if any) governs division of property for unmarried couples on the breakdown of the relationship?

Rules for a married couple are usually not applicable to unmarried couples. According to German law 'the family' is specially protected by Article 6 of the Constitution of the Federal Republic of Germany (*Grundgesetz*).

In principle in the case of separation there is no compensation:

- for one partner's larger share to payment for living costs in times of cohabitation;
- for lower pension claims as a result of the disadvantage of cohabitation, eg, if one partner raised the common children, this parent would be unable to have pension claims as high as the other parent who was not prevented from working;
- for less income when the common child was raised by one partner who

was disadvantaged in his/her career; or
- for less capital or property one partner could save/earn because of the disadvantages of cohabitation, (eg, if children were raised by one partner or one partner gave up work in order to care for the household).

There are some cases in which compensation could be given: these are, however, not provided by law, but set up by jurisdiction:
- If there is a partnership between a couple which goes beyond living private everyday-life together, eg, if the couple built up a business together which was considered to be a joint business with joint investment of work and/or money, even if only one partner were the single owner of the business, the other partner could ask the owner of the business to pay off his/her share.
- If one partner worked ambitiously in the business of the other partner and did not get paid for his/her work and if the business of the other increased in value or the other partner were able to save money this way, the partner leaving could ask for compensation for the time of cohabitation and work, but only to the limit of saved expenses/raised value of the business and only if the contribution of one partner were more than one could expect in a regular partnership.
- If a couple built up a house, but only one partner was the legal owner of it, the other partner could ask for compensation for the work he/she invested if the house increased in value or the owner of the house could avoid other expenses because of the work/investment of the other partner. Additionally it must contravene the principle of good faith to refuse compensation.
- If, on the contribution of both partners, there was an agreement by both to achieve a special aim, and even if they had not spoken expressly of this common aim, but the receiving partner had understood and not contradicted the contributor's wish to promote this aim, then there might be compensation for the contributor if the aim was not achieved. The aim might be the expectation of a long-term participation in the benefit of a house built with the help of the partner claiming compensation.

There is no reason for compensation if the cohabitation ended due to the death of the contributing partner. Compensation claims are not inheritable.

In tax law there are some financial advantages for married people which do not apply to cohabiting couples.

G. FAMILY DISPUTE RESOLUTION

19. MEDIATION, COLLABORATIVE LAW AND ARBITRATION

19.1 Briefly summarise the non-court-based processes available in your jurisdiction and the current status of agreements reached under the auspices of mediation, collaborative law and arbitration

19.2 What is the statutory basis (if any), for mediation, collaborative law and arbitration in your jurisdiction? In particular, are the parties required to attempt a family dispute resolution in advance of the institution of proceedings?

On 26 July 2012 the law concerning the promotion of mediation and other methods of settling conflicts out of Court of 21 July 2012 (Law on Mediation) came into force.

Mediation

Mediation is defined in section 1 Law on Mediation (*MediationsG*) as a confidential and structured proceeding where the parties try to find voluntarily and autonomously a consensual solution to their conflict with the help of a mediator. The mediator is usually a specially qualified person, independent and neutral, who will guide the parties through the process of mediation. The mediator has no power to impose a binding decision on the parties. Mediation is a private civil contract between the parties and between the parties and the mediator.

Mediation is not restricted to cross-border cases but is also comprehensive. It covers family law-related conflicts as well as other civil law-related ones. It can take place before or without starting court proceedings. There is also the option to stop a court proceeding and ask a judge who specialises in mediation or is a mediator for help. If the mediation fails the court proceedings can continue.

The mediator is bound by secrecy and has the right to refuse to give evidence in court, section 4 Law on Mediation (*MediationsG*), section 383 I Nr. 6 Code of Civil Procedure (*Zivilprozessordnung*). An exception is only possible if there are reasons of public interest, for example if there is danger to the welfare of a child.

The mediator has to point out that the parties should seek the advice of external advisors, for example lawyers.

When starting court proceedings it should be mentioned if a mediation has taken place or if there were any reasons that prevented the parties from pursuing mediation. The court may order that the parties have to attend a meeting to discuss the possibility of mediation and present a confirmation of attendance.

Mediation is not convenient in all family law proceedings, for example in adoption or descent proceedings.

Proceedings where children are concerned shall be continued within three months if there was a break in the court proceedings in favour of a mediation and if the mediation did not lead to an agreement within that time. If the case is related to violent matters, the Family Court has to consider the interests of the victim in any suggestion for mediation.

It will be some time before German people become familiar with mediation.

Collaborative law

In Germany there is no legal basis for collaborative law and it is poorly known. But, of course, parties can agree to proceed as such on a private contract basis.

Arbitration

In contrast with mediation, arbitration transfers the power of decision to third persons without having a classic court proceeding.

It is only possible concerning the maintenance of spouses, the division of property and equalisation of accrued gains. Divorce, equalisation of pension entitlements and children's matters are not open to arbitration. The legal basis of arbitration can be found in section 1030 I Code of Civil Procedure (ZPO).

The parties agree on one or more private persons as arbitrators and agree that this person/these persons have the power to decide on their legal issues if an agreement between the parties is not possible.

Arbitration in family law matters is not yet common in Germany.

In Munich three retired family judges established Family Arbitration. In Stuttgart two judges did the same.

A family law arbitration is only possible if both parties are represented by lawyers. The result of the arbitration can be the following:

(a) agreement on the discussed matters;
(b) decision of the arbitrator; or
(c) decision of both parties not to finish the family arbitration.

The parties are bound by the arbitrator's decision.

H. OTHER

20. CIVIL PARTNERSHIP/SAME-SEX MARRIAGE

20.1 What is the status of civil partnership/same-sex marriage within the jurisdiction? What legislation governs civil partnership/gay marriage?

German law provides special status for same-sex partnerships, the *Lebenspartnerschaftsgesetz.*

Two people of the same sex can apply the so-called *Lebenspartnerschaft.* This is possible if they declare before the Registrar General that they want to set up a partnership for life. This is also only possible if both parties are older than 18 years and not yet married or part of another partnership, according to the *Lebenspartnerschaftgesetz.* They cannot be relatives of direct descent or brothers or sisters. Furthermore, they must take the declaration seriously. The partners can take the name of the other partner as their common name, as well as a double name, or each partner may keep their own name. If the partners do not choose another status of property they live according to the status of community of accrued gains. As married couples the partners can conclude a contract. The partners owe each other maintenance and the rule follows the rules of married couples. The dissolution of the partnership follows the same rules of the divorce of married couples. The pension entitlements are balanced as if the partners were married.

There are also special rules for the children of one of the partners. A child of a partner can choose the name the partners have chosen as their partnership name. If one of the partners, as parent of the child, has the sole care, the other partner could have the right to decide together with their partner on decisions regarding the day-to-day life of the child. This is called little custody and cannot happen if the parents have common custody. A partner is allowed to adopt the children of the other partner if both parents of the children agree to this. It may be that the children have parents of the same sex. In this case the partners have common care of the children. If the child was adopted by the other partner, this partner could be obliged to pay the support for the child.

German inheritance law is the same for spouses and same-sex partners. The only difference is the taxation. Married couples have privileged tax rates while partners do not have that privilege.

21. CONTROVERSIAL AREAS/RAPIDLY DEVELOPING AREAS OF LAW

21.1 Is there a particular area of the law within the jurisdiction that is currently undergoing major change?

21.2 Which areas of law are most out-of-step and which areas would you most like to see reformed/changed?

Concerning maintenance for spouses a change of law in relation to long lasting marriages came into force on 1 March 2013. Section 1578 b GCC was changed so that the length of the marriage has become more important.

It is difficult to foresee how the courts will deal with that change in the future.

Rules concerning parents who are not married were changed by the new law which was discussed in section 13 above on custody/parental responsibility.

Gibraltar

Triay & Triay Charles Simpson

A. JURISDICTION AND CONFLICT OF LAW

1. SOURCES OF LAW

1.1 What is the primary source of law in relation to the breakdown of marriage and the welfare of children within the jurisdiction?

The primary source of law in relation to the breakdown of marriage and the welfare of children within the jurisdiction is statutory and is contained in the Matrimonial Causes Act and the Children Act. The court also has inherent jurisdiction to deal with matters including those in relation to children, eg, wardship.

1.2 Which are the main statutes governing matrimonial law in the jurisdiction?

The main statutes governing matrimonial law in the jurisdiction are:

- the Matrimonial Causes Act;
- the Married Women's Property Act;
- the Children Act;
- the Maintenance Act.

2. JURISDICTION

2.1 What are the main jurisdictional requirements for the institution of proceedings in relation to divorce, the finances and children?

The main jurisdictional requirements for the institution of proceedings are detailed below.

In relation to divorce and judicial separation, the jurisdiction requirements are set out in section 4 of the Matrimonial Causes Act and the court has jurisdiction to entertain proceedings for divorce or judicial separation if:

- the court has jurisdiction under Council Regulation (EC) No 2201/2003 (Brussels II (revised));
- no court of a member state has jurisdiction under Brussels II (revised) and either of the parties to the marriage is domiciled in Gibraltar on the date when the proceedings are begun.

Under Article 3(1) of Brussels II (revised), in matters relating to divorce, judicial separation or nullity of marriage, jurisdiction lies with the courts of the member state. Under Article 3(1) (a) in whose territory there is the following:

- the spouses are habitually resident;
- the spouses were last habitually resident, in so far as one of them still resides there;

- the respondent is habitually resident;
- in the event of a joint application, either of the spouses is habitually resident;
- the applicant, if they have resided there for at least one year immediately before the application was made;
- the applicant is habitually resident if they have resided there for at least six months immediately before the application was made and is a national of the member state in question or, in the case of United Kingdom and Ireland, has their domicile there.

Under Article 3(1) (b) jurisdiction shall lie with the courts of the member state of the nationality of both spouses or, in the case of the United Kingdom and Ireland, of the domicile of both spouses.

In relation to finances, jurisdiction is generally founded under the relevant provisions of the Matrimonial Causes Act, which give the court wide discretionary powers, or under the Married Women's Property Act, normally when divorce, judicial separation or nullity proceedings are not taking place. In relation to the latter jurisdiction, the applicable principles are derived from the law of real property, equity and trusts.

In relation to children, the jurisdiction requirements are set out in section 3 of the Children Act 2009, which provides that subject to Council Regulation (EC) No 2201/2003 as implemented in Gibraltar by the Civil jurisdiction and Judgments (Amendment Act) 2005, a court shall have jurisdiction under this Act if the applicant or the respondent or any of the respondents, or a child to whom the application relates, resides in Gibraltar.

Council Regulation (EC) No 2201/2003 applies to civil matters relating to the 'attribution, exercise, delegation, restriction, or termination of parental responsibility'. The scope of the regulation includes those set out in Article 1(2).

The Supreme Court of Gibraltar also has inherent jurisdiction with respect to children.

Gibraltar has also recently incorporated into domestic law the Hague Convention dated 19 October 1996 on Jurisdiction, Applicable Law, Recognition, Enforcement and Co-operation in respect of Parental Responsibility and Measures for the Protection of Children.

3. DOMICILE AND HABITUAL RESIDENCE

3.1 Explain the concepts of domicile and habitual residence as they apply to the jurisdiction in relation to divorce, the finances and children

Council Regulation (EC) 44/2001 (Brussels II) applies to Gibraltar and makes provision for determining domicile for the purpose of the application of this Regulation. In addition, the Civil Jurisdiction and Judgments Act (CJJA) make specific provision for determining domicile for the purpose of the CJJA.

Section 24 (2) of the CJJA provides that an individual is domiciled in Gibraltar if and only if:

- he or she is resident in Gibraltar;

- the nature and circumstances of his or her residence indicate that he or she has a substantial connection with Gibraltar.

The concepts are, therefore, derived from local statute, common law and European decisions given and subject to the application of Brussels II. In relation to matrimonial causes, the domicile of an individual is determined according to those legal principles which are recognised in Gibraltar and/or which have been enacted in Gibraltar. Those principles are derived from English or European law.

Domicile is the legal relationship between a person and a particular territorial area and, generally speaking, arises either from that person's residence there, coupled with the intention of making it a permanent home, or from it being or having been the domicile of a person on whom they are, for this purpose, legally dependent; eg, the domicile of origin is acquired at birth and is the domicile of the person upon whom the child is dependent. In that regard, a legitimate child born in the lifetime of their father receives the domicile of the father, whereas an illegitimate child receives the domicile of the mother. The concept of domicile in Gibraltar is the same as that in England.

A person cannot have more than one domicile at any time and can acquire a domicile of choice by residing in another country with the intention of continuing to reside there for an indefinite period of time, coupled with the genuine intention of residing there permanently and not returning to reside permanently in the country in which they were previously domiciled or which represents their domicile of origin.

In non-Brussels II cases, Gibraltar also follows English law in relation to the concept of 'habitual residence'. As a matter of domestic law, a person is habitually resident in the jurisdiction where a person lives voluntarily and has settled for the regular order of that person's life. A person will not, therefore, be considered to be habitually resident in Gibraltar unless they have taken up residence and lived in Gibraltar for an appreciable period of time, although there is no concrete definition of the latter.

With regard to the application of Brussels II, 'habitual residence' has an autonomous meaning as a matter of European law and the author is of the view that, in the absence of further authority, the Supreme Court should follow the approach adopted by Mr Justice Munby in the English case of *Marinos v Marinos* [2007 EWHC 2047]. In the context of that case, reference was made to the explanatory report on Brussels II of Dr Borras (Official Journal of the European Communities, C221/27, 16 July 1998) and the definition of habitual residence is as follows: '*the place where the person had established, on a fixed basis, his permanent or habitual centre of interests, with all the relevant facts being taken into account for the purpose of determining such residence.*'

Mr Justice Munby added in his analysis of the meaning that, in deciding where the habitual centre of someone's interests has been established, one has to have regard to the context and have examined various European case authorities. Given the application of Article 3 to family matters, he concluded that the place where the matrimonial home is to be found, the place where the family lives *qua* family, is equally obviously an important factor in ascertaining the location of the habitual centre of a spouse's interests. The author is of the view that the Supreme Court of Gibraltar would follow this approach in appropriate circumstances where jurisdiction is claimed under Brussels II and, given the definition of the domicile of individuals in section 24 of the CJJA. Furthermore, as a matter of community law, it does not appear to be the case following *Marinos v Marinos* that an applicant can be habitually resident in two different countries at the same time; whereas, as a matter of domestic law, there can be more than one place of residence (see English case of *Ikimi v Ikimi*).

It should be noted that in the local case of *W v W D & M No 24* of 2008, the court struck out a local petition on the basis that it did not consider the court had jurisdiction under the former section 4 of the Matrimonial Causes Act, which then provided as follows: '*The court shall have jurisdiction to entertain proceedings for divorce or judicial separation if (and only if) either of the parties to the marriage:*

a) is domiciled in Gibraltar on the date when the proceedings are begun; or

b) was habitually resident in Gibraltar throughout the period of one year ending with that date.'

Both spouses had moved to Gibraltar and acquired category II tax statuses and become resident in Gibraltar and, as a requirement for that status, they had purchased approved accommodation in Gibraltar. However, the couple also subsequently purchased property in Spain and, based on the relevant facts before it, the court did not consider it had jurisdiction under the previous section 4 on the basis that neither party was resident or domiciled in Gibraltar based on the interpretation of those facts. The case of *Marinos v Marinos* was not considered in the judgment and the court appear to have followed domestic/English law to determine the matters before it in relation to the question of habitual residence/domicile. The question of jurisdiction under Brussels II was not considered in the judgment and it does not appear that the court was addressed on this, despite the apparent application of the Regulation. It should be noted, however, that the case predated the local amendment of section 4 of the Matrimonial Causes Act, albeit the Regulation was in application.

The local case of *Fisher v Small* 2005-06 Gib LR 1 provides local authority (although it is not a family case) to the effect that a category II individual is not to be considered as domiciled in Gibraltar within the meaning of section 24 of the CJJA, or considered resident in Gibraltar in the absence of evidence of actual residence in Gibraltar.

In the case of *T v T* (divorce jurisdiction: nationality and domicile), the court found that the court had jurisdiction under the Regulation in the case of two Gibraltarians given that both were domiciled in Gibraltar and Gibraltar was considered part of the United Kingdom for the purpose of the ruling. This decision was not appealed.

4. CONFLICT OF LAW/APPLICABLE LAW TO BE APPLIED

4.1 What happens when one party applies to stay proceedings in favour of a foreign jurisdiction? What factors will the local court take into account when determining forum issues?

What happens and what principles apply depends on whether jurisdiction is claimed either in Gibraltar or in the foreign court under Brussels II (revised), or whether no contracting state has jurisdiction under Brussels II (revised).

Assuming that Brussels II applies, the court will need to consider whether an automatic stay should be granted pursuant to Article 17. The latter requires an examination as to jurisdiction by the court of a member state which is seised of a case over which it has no jurisdiction under the regulation and over which a court of another regulation state has jurisdiction by virtue of the regulation. In those circumstances, if the local court is satisfied that the court of another regulation state has jurisdiction by virtue of the regulation, then it must declare of its own motion that it has no jurisdiction.

Where proceedings relating to divorce, legal separation or marriage annulment between the same parties are brought before courts of different member states, the court second seised shall of its own motion stay its proceedings until such time as the jurisdiction of the court first seised is established. Pursuant to Article 19(3), where the jurisdiction of the court first seised is established, the court second seised shall decline jurisdiction in favour of that court. If the court first seised does not have jurisdiction then the court second seised will have jurisdiction subject to jurisdiction having been established there.

In addition, section 8 of the Matrimonial Causes Act provides:

'The schedule to this Act shall have effect as to the cases for which matrimonial proceedings in Gibraltar may be stayed by the court where there are concurrent proceedings elsewhere in respect of the same marriage, but nothing in this schedule prejudices the power to stay proceedings which is exercisable by the court apart from the schedule.'

The schedule to the Act places a duty under paragraph 2 on the petitioner to furnish particulars in respect of any matrimonial proceedings they know to be continuing in another country outside Gibraltar. Pursuant to paragraph 3, where before the trial or first trial in any matrimonial proceedings which are continuing in the court in Gibraltar, it appears that:

- any proceedings in respect of the marriage in question or capable of affecting its validity or subsistence, are continuing in another jurisdiction;
- the balance of fairness (including convenience) as between the parties to the marriage is such that it is appropriate for the proceedings in that jurisdiction to be disposed of before further steps are taken in the proceedings, so far as they consist of a particular kind of matrimonial proceedings.

The court may then in its discretion order that the proceedings in the court be stayed or that those proceedings be stayed so far as they consist of matrimonial proceedings.

Pursuant to paragraph 1(2) of the schedule, the court, in considering the balance of convenience and fairness shall have regard to all factors appearing to be relevant including the convenience of witnesses and any delay or expense which may result from the decision whether to stay proceedings or not.

The court also has jurisdiction to stay proceedings under its inherent jurisdiction. The inherent power is exercised by applying the principle of *forum non conveniens*. In simple terms, the court will consider whether there is another available forum which is clearly more appropriate for the trial of the action and determine whether a stay should be granted, unless there are circumstances where justice, nevertheless, requires that a stay be granted.

B. PRE- AND POST-NUPTIAL AGREEMENTS

5. VALIDITY OF PRE- AND POST-NUPTIAL AGREEMENTS

5.1 To what extent are pre- and post-nuptial agreements binding within the jurisdiction? Could you provide a brief discussion of the most significant recent case law on this issue

Following the application of the amended Matrimonial Causes Act, which came into effect in January 2010, pre- and post-nuptial agreements are binding as financial agreements provided they come within the definition of financial agreement in section 31B, section 31C or section 31D of the MCA and subject to the provisions of section 31A to 31M. Prior to this Gibraltar law largely followed English law on this issue, although there is no local reported decision in relation to pre-nuptial agreements. There is, however, the Privy Council decision in *Macleod v Macleod* 2008 UKPC 64, which it submitted prior to the implementation of the amended Matrimonial Causes Act and part VIA was a binding authority.

The relevant sections provide as detailed below.

Section 31B(1) provides that if people who are contemplating entering into a marriage with each other make a written agreement with respect to any of the matters mentioned in section 31B(2), at the time of making the agreement, the people are not the spouse parties to any other binding agreement with respect to any of those matters and the agreement is expressed to be made under section 31B(1) that agreement constitutes a financial agreement.

Section 31B(2), in turn, permits a financial agreement before marriage in relation to the following matters:

- in the event of the breakdown of the marriage, all or any of the property or financial resources of either or both of the spouse parties, at the time when the agreement is to be made, or at a later time and before divorce, is to be dealt with;
- the maintenance of either of the spouse parties during the marriage, after divorce or both during the marriage and after the divorce.

Under section 31B(3), a financial agreement made under section 31B(1) may also contain matters incidental or ancillary to those mentioned in subsection 2 and other matters (although the latter is undefined).

Under section 31B(4), a financial agreement made as mentioned in subsection (1) may terminate a previous financial agreement, however made, if all of the parties to the previous agreement are parties to the new agreement.

Under section 31C, financial agreements can also be made during marriage by the parties to a marriage subject to the provisions of that section and the subsections thereunder. The subsections generally follow those outlined under section 31B and the financial agreement can cover the same matters. However, the agreement must be expressed to be made under section 31C and it should be noted that under section 31C (3) a financial agreement under section 31C may be made before or after the marriage has broken down.

Under section 31D, financial agreements can also be made after a decree of divorce is granted in relation to a marriage (whether it has taken effect or not) provided the agreement is expressed to be made under section 31D and the parties are not parties to any other binding financial agreement under sections 31B, 31C or 31D of the Matrimonial Causes Act. It should be noted that a financial agreement under section 31D may also terminate a previous financial agreement, however made, if all of the parties to the previous agreement are parties to the new agreement.

Pursuant to section 31E (1), a financial agreement that is binding on the parties to the agreement to the extent to which it deals with how, in the event of the breakdown of the marriage, all or any or the property or financial resources of either or both of the spouse parties at the time when the agreement is made or at a later time and before the termination of the marriage by divorce are to be dealt with, is of no force or effect until a declaration of separation is made.

Under section 31E (5), the declaration of separation must be signed by both parties to the agreement and it must state that the spouse parties have separated and are living separately and apart at the time of the declaration. Separated is defined in section 31E (7) as meaning that the parties separated and thereafter lived separately and apart for a continuous period of two years immediately preceding the date of the filing of the application for a decree of divorce.

Under section 31G, it should be noted that a provision of a financial agreement which relates to maintenance of a child or children of the family is void unless it has been referred to the court and the court has expressed its opinion that the provision is reasonable and gives appropriate directions. It would, however, appear that such a clause could be expressed to be made as a maintenance agreement, provided it is compliant with the relevant provisions of part V of the maintenance agreement. The latter is reviewable by the court in any event.

In considering the above, it should be noted that a financial agreement under section 31 can be set aside under section 31L if the court is satisfied that:

- the agreement was obtained by fraud (section 31L (1) (a));
- a party to the agreement entered into the agreement for the purpose of defrauding or defeating a creditor or creditors of that party, or with

reckless disregard of the interests of a creditor or creditors of the party (section 31L (1) (b));
- the agreement is void, voidable or unenforceable (section 31L (1) (c));
- in the circumstances that have arisen since the agreement was made, it is impracticable for the agreement or a part of the agreement to be carried out (section 31L (1) (d));
- since making the agreement, a material change of circumstances has occurred (such as circumstances relating to the care welfare and development of a child of the family) and as a result the child, or if the applicant is the primary carer, a party to the agreement will suffer hardship if the court does not set the agreement aside;
- in respect of the making of the financial agreement, a party to the agreement engaged in conduct that was in all circumstances unconscionable.

There has not been any significant case law on pre-nuptial or post-nuptial agreements given the recent application of the amended Matrimonial Causes Act.

C. DIVORCE, NULLITY AND JUDICIAL SEPARATION

6. RECOGNITION OF FOREIGN MARRIAGES/DIVORCES

6.1 Summarise the position in your jurisdiction

Part IX of the Matrimonial Causes Act deals with the recognition in Gibraltar of divorces and legal separations obtained elsewhere. Under section 54 of the Matrimonial Causes Act, the validity of a divorce or legal separation obtained in a country outside Gibraltar shall be recognised if at the date of the institution of the proceedings in the country in which it was obtained:
- either spouse was habitually resident or domiciled in that country;
- either spouse was a national of that country.

Council Regulation (EC) No 2201/2003 / Brussels II (revised) also provides for the recognition and enforcement of judgments in matrimonial matters and, as stated above, applies in Gibraltar. The latter is applied by virtue of section 38A of the CJJA and under schedule 11 to the CJJA the minister responsible for justice is the central authority in Gibraltar for the purpose of Article 53 of Regulation 2201/2003. The Supreme Court may in turn make orders recognising or enforcing regulation state judgments in Gibraltar.

It should also be noted that under part V of the CJJA, Gibraltar and the UK are to be treated as if each were a separate regulation state for all purposes connected to the operation of Regulation 2201/2003 in relation to the respective jurisdictions.

7. DIVORCE

7.1 Explain the grounds for divorce within the jurisdiction (please also deal with nullity and judicial separation if appropriate)

Under section 16 of the Matrimonial Causes Act, and subject to the provisions of section 18 of the MCA, a petition may be presented to the Supreme Court by either party to a marriage on the ground that the marriage has broken down irretrievably.

Section 18 of the MCA imposes a restriction on petitions for divorce within three years from the date of the marriage (the specified period) in that no petitions can be presented within the specified period in the absence of the court granting permission to allow the presentation of such a petition.

Under section 18 (2) the court can grant such permission on either of the following grounds:

- section 18 (2) (a) – that the case is one of exceptional hardship suffered by the petitioner or exceptional depravity on the part of the respondent (subject to the interests of any child of the family and having regard to whether there is a reasonable probability of a reconciliation of the parties during the three-year period);
- section 18 (2) (b) – in any case where the petitioner is under the age of 16 years at the date of the marriage.

On a petition for divorce and pursuant to the provisions of section 16 (2), the Supreme Court shall not hold the marriage to have broken down irretrievably in the absence of the petitioner satisfying the court of one or more of the following facts:

- that the respondent has committed adultery, rape, sodomy or bestiality or is homosexual, and in any such case, that the petitioner finds it intolerable to live with the respondent;
- that the respondent has behaved in such a way that the petitioner cannot reasonably be expected to live with the respondent;
- that the respondent has deserted the petitioner for a continuous period of at least two years immediately preceding the presentation of the petition;
- that the parties have lived apart for a continuous period of at least two years and the respondent consents to a decree being granted on the basis of two years' separation;
- that the parties to the marriage have lived apart for a continuous period of at least three years immediately preceding the presentation of the petition.

The court cannot hold for the purpose of section 16 (2) b) that the respondent has behaved in such a way that the petitioner cannot reasonably be expected to live with the respondent unless the petitioner satisfies the court that the behaviour is one or more of the following:

- conduct by the respondent that involves actual and reasonably substantial physical or mental injury to the petitioner or to any child of the marriage or either party, or the reasonable apprehension by the petitioner or any such child of such injury;
- constructive desertion by the respondent of the petitioner;
- unsoundness of mind or other mental disorder on the part of the respondent, where the condition is likely to be incurable and the condition has existed for at least three years or, in exceptional circumstances, the condition has lasted for less than three years and the effects of the behaviour of the respondent are directed towards the petitioner or towards any child of the marriage or of either party.

A petition for judicial separation may be presented to the Supreme Court under section 30 of the MCA by either party to a marriage on the ground that any such fact that is mentioned in section 16 (2) exists. There is no minimum requirement that the parties have lived together for a period of three years prior to a petition for judicial separation being presented.

A petition for nullity may be presented to the Supreme Court by a husband or a wife asking that their marriage may be declared null and void under section 24 of the MCA.

A marriage is void on any of the grounds set out in section 25 (1) as listed below:

- that it is not a valid marriage under the provisions of the Marriage Act;
- that, at the time of the marriage, either party was already lawfully married;
- that the parties are not respectively male and female;
- that, in the case of a polygamous marriage entered into outside Gibraltar, either party was at the time of the marriage domiciled in Gibraltar.

The grounds on which a marriage is voidable are set out in section 25A and are as follows:

- the marriage has not been consummated owing to the incapacity of either party to consummate it;
- the marriage has not been consummated owing to the wilful refusal of the respondent to consummate it;
- either party to the marriage did not validly consent to it, whether in consequence of duress, mistake, unsoundness of mind or otherwise;
- at the time of the marriage either party, though capable of giving a valid consent, was suffering, whether continuously or intermittently, from a mental disorder within the meaning of section 3 of the Mental Health Act of such a kind or to such an extent as to be unfit for marriage;
- at the time of the marriage the respondent was suffering from venereal disease in a communicable form;
- at the time of the marriage the respondent was pregnant by some other person other than the petitioner.

The bars to relief where the marriage is voidable are contained in section 25B of the MCA and the court shall not grant a decree of nullity on the ground that a marriage is voidable if the respondent satisfies the court that:

- the petitioner, with knowledge that it was open to have the marriage avoided, so conducted themself in relation to the respondent so as to lead the respondent to reasonably believe that they would not seek to do so;
- it would be unjust to the respondent to grant the decree.

Under section 25B (2), the court shall not grant a decree of nullity by virtue of section 25A on the grounds mentioned in paragraph 25A(c) (either party to the marriage did not validly consent to it whether in consequence of duress, mistake, unsoundness of mind or otherwise), (d) (mental disorder of either party at time of marriage within section 3 of Mental Health Act), (e) (respondent suffering from venereal disease in communicable form at time of marriage) or (f) (pregnancy by someone else at time of marriage) unless it is satisfied that proceedings were issued within the period of three years from the date of the marriage or leave for the institution of such proceedings has been granted after the expiration of that period. Under section 25A(3), the court also cannot grant a decree of nullity by virtue of section 25A on the grounds mentioned in paragraphs (e) or (f) unless it is satisfied the petitioner was ignorant of the relevant fact alleged.

Under section 25A(4), the court cannot grant permission to institute proceedings for nullity after three years of marriage unless it is satisfied the petitioner has at some time during that three-year period suffered from a mental disorder within the meaning in section 3 of the Mental Health Act and considers that, in all the circumstances of the case, it would be just to grant leave to institute nullity proceedings after the expiry of the three-year period.

8. FINANCES/CAPITAL, PROPERTY

8.1 What powers does the court have to allocate financial resources and property on the breakdown of marriage?

The Supreme Court of Gibraltar has wide discretionary powers to allocate financial resources and property in divorce, judicial separation or nullity proceedings. These powers are derived from the MCA and include the following powers under part VII of the MCA:

- power to make an order for periodical payments in favour of a party to a marriage under section 34(1)(b) or 40(6)(b), or in favour of a child of the family under section 34(1)(f), (2) or (4) or 40(6)(f);
- power to make an order for secured periodical payments in favour of a party to a marriage or in favour of a child of the family;
- power to make an order for a lump sum provision in favour of a party to a marriage under section 34(1)(c) or 40(6)(c), or in favour of a child of the family under section 3491)9f), (2) or (4) or section 40(6)(f);
- power to make a property adjustment order which includes an order for the transfer and/or settlement of property;
- power to order maintenance pending suit;
- power to vary nuptial settlements, although it should be noted under the current provisions of the amended Matrimonial Causes Act, the power to vary is limited under section 35(1)(c) to varying for the benefit of children of the family. It is understood this is likely to be the subject of further amendment to permit variation for the benefit of a spouse to the marriage.

The court also has power to make pension sharing orders under part VIIA of the MCA.

Under section 37(1), it is the duty of the court in deciding whether to exercise its powers under section 34 to 36 of the Matrimonial Causes Act and, if so, in what manner to give first consideration to the welfare of any child of the family who has not attained the age of 18, and to have regard in the application of financial provision to a party to a marriage, the court shall have regard to the following matters:

- the income, earning capacity, property and other financial resources which each of the parties to the marriage has or is likely to have in

the foreseeable future, including, in the case of earning capacity, any increase in that capacity which it would in the opinion of the court be reasonable to expect a party to the marriage to take steps to acquire;
- the financial needs, obligations and responsibilities which each of the parties to the marriage has or is likely to have in the foreseeable future;
- the standard of living enjoyed by the family before the breakdown of the marriage;
- the age of each party to the marriage and the duration of the marriage;
- any physical or mental disability of either of the parties to the marriage;
- the contributions which each of the parties has made, or is likely to make in the foreseeable future, to the welfare of the family, including any contribution by looking after the home or caring for the family;
- the conduct of each of the parties, whatever the nature of the conduct, and whether it occurred during the marriage or after the separation of the parties or dissolution or annulment of the marriage, if that conduct is such that it would in the opinion of the court be inequitable to disregard it;
- the value to each of the parties to a marriage of any benefit which, by reason of the dissolution or annulment of the marriage, that party will lose the chance of acquiring.

8.2 Explain and illustrate with reference to recent cases the court's thinking on division of assets

The courts in Gibraltar have tended to follow English case law. This is best illustrated by the reported case of *Caruana v Caruana DM 49 of 2000*, which followed and approved the approach adopted by the House of Lords in the English case of *White v White 3 WLR 1571* as the starting point on division of assets. The first instance decision and approach adopted by the then chief justice in the case was subsequently approved by the local Court of Appeal. The object of applying the criteria (as now enshrined in section 37) is to achieve the overarching objective of fairness and the starting point by which this is to be measured is against the yardstick of equality, although the courts have not gone as far as to say that the starting point should be equal division.

9. FINANCES/MAINTENANCE

9.1 Explain the operation of maintenance for spouses on an ongoing basis after the breakdown of marriage

Generally speaking, this will depend on a number of factors, including the age of the marriage, the age of the parties, the employment prospects of the wife and the respective financial circumstances and needs of the parties.

9.2 Is it common for maintenance to be awarded?

It is relatively common, subject to the particular circumstances of the case, although it should be noted that under section 38(1) it is the duty of the court to consider the practicality of a clean break between the parties and, naturally, that militates against the granting of maintenance in appropriate circumstances. However, the latter is clearly dependent on the facts of each case and relevant considerations being applied in determining the issue.

9.3 Explain and illustrate with reference to recent cases the court's thinking on maintenance

An example of the court's approach to maintenance is illustrated by the local case of *Gonzalez v Gonzalez D & M 15 of 2004*, which was the subject of an appeal to the Court of Appeal. The judgment in respect of the latter is reported in 2005-2006 Gib LR 216. The Court of Appeal approved the approach adopted by the Supreme Court considering that it has given appropriate weight to the factors set out in the then section 32(1) of the MCA (now section 37(1)). Those factors included the parties' respective incomes, earning capacity, property and other financial resources, their financial needs and the ages and the duration of the marriage. The case illustrates that the court's general obligation was to apply the principle of equality of division and only depart from it if, and to the extent that there was, a good reason for doing so.

10. CHILD MAINTENANCE

10.1 On what basis is child maintenance calculated within the jurisdiction?

There is no prescribed formula. Under section 37(3) of the Matrimonial Causes Act, the court is to have regard to the following matters (non exhaustive):

- the financial needs of the child
- the income, earning capacity (if any) property and other financial resources of the child;
- any physical or mental disability of the child;
- the manner in which the child was being and in which the parties expected the child to be educated or trained;
- the considerations mentioned in relation to the parties as set out in paragraphs (a), (b), (c) and (e) of section 37(2) (see sub-paragraphs 8.3.1, 8.3.2, 8.3.3 and 8.3.5 above).

The Magistrates Court also has power to award maintenance under the provisions of the Maintenance Act.

11. RECIPROCAL ENFORCEMENT OF FINANCIAL ORDERS

11.1 Summarise the position in your jurisdiction

As stated above, Brussels I and Brussels/Lugano Conventions apply to Gibraltar by virtue of the CJJA. An application for the registration of a maintenance order in appropriate circumstances is made to the Magistrates Court.

In addition to the provisions of Brussels I, the Maintenance Orders (Reciprocal Enforcement) Act applies to Gibraltar and this is the statutory mechanism for the enforcement of maintenance orders emanating from designated countries and territories designated as reciprocating countries regarding maintenance orders generally, namely British Columbia, Malta, Nova Scotia, Ontario and UK and, in respect of maintenance orders of specified classes, Australia.

The Judgments (Reciprocal Enforcement) Act also applies to Gibraltar. This provides for the enforcement of foreign judgments in Gibraltar and is equivalent to the English Judgments (Reciprocal Enforcement) Act 1933. Lump sum and costs orders made by a recognised foreign court may be capable of enforcement, provided the judgments are final and conclusive between the judgment creditor and judgment debtor and a sum of money is payable thereunder. However, foreign maintenance orders fall outside the scope of this Act on the basis that they are capable of variation. It should be noted that the judgment cannot be registered unless pronounced within six years prior to application for registration.

In the absence of reciprocal enforcement provisions, a judgment or order of a competent foreign court will be enforceable in Gibraltar at common law by an action *in personam* on the judgment debt if, firstly, the foreign judgment is for a definite sum of money and, secondly, it is final and conclusive. A foreign judgment for a lump sum or for costs may, therefore, be enforced at common law.

12. FINANCIAL RELIEF AFTER FOREIGN DIVORCE PROCEEDINGS

12.1 What powers are available to make orders following a foreign divorce?

There are currently no statutory powers available to make orders following a foreign divorce.

D. CHILDREN

13. CUSTODY/PARENTAL RESPONSIBILITY

13.1 Briefly explain the legal position in relation to custody/parental responsibility following the breakdown of a relationship or marriage

The position depends on whether the parents in question have parental responsibility for the child in question. Under section 11(1) of the Children Act, where a child's father and mother were married to each other at the time of the birth, they each have the right and duty of parental responsibility for that child. In the case of an unmarried couple who subsequently marry after the birth of the child then parental responsibility vests in the mother and in the father as well if he is named on the birth certificate of the child, or by virtue of a parental responsibility agreement between the parents or alternatively, by order of the court or if the child becomes legitimate under section 3 of the Legitimacy Act (which provides for the legitimacy of a child in the event of the subsequent marriage of that child's parents after his or her birth).

Under section 10 of the Children Act, parental rights are equal and subject to any court order or agreement. Statutory parental rights can be summarised as follows:

- the right to have the child living with him or her or to regulate that child's residence;
- the right to control, direct or guide in a manner appropriate to the stage of the development of the child, the child's upbringing;

- if the child is not living with the parent concerned, the right to maintain personal relations with the child and to have direct contact with the child on a regular basis;
- the right to act as the child's legal representative.

The legal position after breakdown of the marriage is therefore usually determined by agreement between the parents or by court order. If the latter then the first and paramount consideration for the court in determining any issue as to the upbringing of the child in question or in relation to the administration of that child's property or any income arising therefrom is the child's welfare. In determining whether to make an order under the Act, the no order principle is enshrined under section 4(5) which means that the court should not make any order unless it considers that the making of the order in question would be better for the child in question than making no order at all.

The types of order that can be made under section 25 of the Children Act are:

- residence order;
- contact order;
- prohibited steps order;
- a specific issue order.

13.2 Briefly explain the legal position in relation to access/contact / visitation following the breakdown of a relationship or marriage

The non-residential parent has the right under section 10 of the Act to maintain personal relations with the child and to have contact with him or her unless such right is curtailed by court order or agreement. If necessary, then an application can be made to court under section 25 for a contact order.

14. INTERNATIONAL ABDUCTION

14.1 Summarise the position in your jurisdiction

Until 18 March 2010, the International Child Abduction Act was passed by the local parliament. This Act extends the application of the Convention on the Civil Aspects of International Child Abduction, signed at the Hague on 25 October 1980, to Gibraltar. However, no commencement date has yet been given. The Act is therefore not yet in operation pending a commencement date being issued by the Government by notice in the local *Gazette*. It is however an offence under section 184(1) of the Crimes Act 2011 for a person, including a parent, to take a child under the age of 18 out of Gibraltar without appropriate consent and the requisite consent includes the other parent provided that parent has parental responsibility. Furthermore, the Children Act contains provisions giving effect to the 1996 Convention on Jurisdiction, Applicable law, Recognition, Enforcement and Co-operation in Respect of Parental Responsibility and Measures for the Protection of Children, signed at the Hague on 19 October, 1996 as referred to above.

In the event of abduction to a non-Convention/non-EU state, then the appropriate course would be to obtain declaratory relief to the effect that the removal was unlawful and to then seek the summary return of the child from the relevant jurisdiction. This is likely to be in the context of local wardship proceedings which may be commenced.

15. LEAVE TO REMOVE/APPLICATIONS TO TAKE A CHILD OUT OF THE JURISDICTION

15.1 Summarise the position in your jurisdiction

The application is normally made under the Children Act.

15.2 Under what circumstances may a parent apply to remove their child from the jurisdiction against the wishes of the other parent?

A person in whose favour a residence order has been made may take the child out of the jurisdiction for up to one month at a time, with no limit on the number of occasions, without the need for the consent of the other holders of parental responsibility, subject to the provisions of section 30. This provides that, where a residence order is in force, no person may remove the child from Gibraltar without the written consent of every person who has parental responsibility of the child, with the exception that, where a person in whose favour a residence order is made wishes to remove a child from Gibraltar for a period of less than one month, they can do so in the absence of a contrary order being made by the Supreme Court.

It should be noted that section 30(4) also permits a child to be removed from Gibraltar by a person in whose favour a contact order has been made during the period stipulated in that order, unless the child is a ward of court or subject to a care order, supervision order or emergency protection order, in which case leave must be sought before removing the child from the jurisdiction.

Therefore, subject to the above, permission is required to remove a child from the jurisdiction permanently or temporarily on holiday if it is against the wishes of the other parent or anyone else with parental responsibility for the child. That application is normally made for an appropriate order under the Children Act.

The first and paramount consideration for the court to consider under the Children Act is the child's welfare and, under section 4(2) of the Children Act, the child's welfare is considered to be best promoted by a continuing relationship with both parents as long as it is safe to do so. In approaching the question of whether leave should be granted for permanent removal, the court will also consider whether the application is genuine and not motivated by a selfish desire to exclude the other parent from the child's life and whether the proposed plans are realistic, well researched and investigated and in the best interest and welfare of the child. If the court is satisfied that the plans are *bona fide* and well researched, it will then consider the position of the other parent to see if they are motivated by a genuine concern for the child's welfare or a rather more selfish motive. The wishes of the child can also, in appropriate circumstances, be taken into account. Reference to the checklist contained in section 4(3) of the Children Act is not mandatory but those factors can be a useful point of reference for the court and include the wishes of the child, their physical, emotional or educational needs, the likely effect on the child of a change of circumstances, their age, sex, background and any characteristics of the child which the court considers relevant.

In considering the issue of temporary visits, the court usually carries out a balancing exercise to weigh the benefit of the child of the proposed visit against the risk that the child might not be returned and, depending on the relevant facts, appropriate safeguards may need to be built into any order granting temporary removal.

E. SURROGACY AND ADOPTION

16. VALIDITY OF SURROGACY AGREEMENTS

16.1 Briefly summarise the position in your jurisdiction

Gibraltar law follows English law on this issue and surrogacy agreements are not enforceable locally.

17. ADOPTION

17.1 Briefly explain the legal position in relation to adoption in your jurisdiction. Is adoption available to individuals, cohabiting couples (both heterosexual and same-sex)?

The position is governed by the Adoption Act 1951. Jurisdiction to make adoption orders is vested in the Magistrates Court and the Supreme Court of Gibraltar. An application for an adoption order can be made under section 5 of the Adoption Act by an individual resident or domiciled in Gibraltar who is the mother or the father of the minor, a relative of the minor (grandfather, brother, sister, uncle or aunt) who has attained the age of 21 years or by an individual applicant who is over 25 years old. Under section 5(2) an application can be made on the joint application of two spouses provided one of the applicants is the mother or father of the minor and the other one is over 21 and section 5(3) specifically prohibits an adoption order being made authorising more than one person to adopt a minor unless the application is made by two joint spouses under section 5(2). This aspect of the legislation was successfully challenged in the case of *P v HM Attorney General for Gibraltar* (judgment of Dudley C.J. dated 10 April 2013) (unreported) where the Supreme Court held that the provisions of the Adoption Act which excluded a same-sex couple from jointly applying for adoption violated section 7 (the right to family life) and section 14 (discrimination) of the Gibraltar Constitution.

The Adoption Act sets out the requirements for the making of an adoption order. In short, the applicant(s) must be eligible to make an application for adoption under the Adoption Act under section 5, the child must have been in the care and custody of the applicant for the probationary period namely at least three consecutive months immediately preceding the date of the order, the welfare officer must have been put on notice of the intention to adopt in accordance with section 7 and the court must be satisfied under section 8 that requisite consents have been given under section 6 by every parent or guardian of the child unless the requisite consent is dispensed with by the court on recognised statutory grounds. The court must also be satisfied under section 8(1)(b) that the order, if made, will be for the welfare of the minor and that the applicant has not received or agreed to receive any payment as a reward or in consideration of the adoption (except as the court may sanction) under section 8(1)(c).

F. COHABITATION

18. COHABITATION

18.1 What legislation (if any) governs division of property for unmarried couples on the breakdown of the relationship?

There is no legislation in place. The division of property for unmarried couples is governed by trust and equitable principles.

G. FAMILY DISPUTE RESOLUTION

19. MEDIATION, COLLABORATIVE LAW AND ARBITRATION

19.1 Briefly summarise the non-court-based processes available in your jurisdiction and the current status of agreements reached under the auspices of mediation, collaborative law and arbitration

The most popular non-court based alternative dispute process is family mediation. The latter is a voluntary process and the parties concerned enter into a mediation agreement with the mediator concerned in order to try to resolve the matters in dispute. Family mediation is encouraged in appropriate situations.

Arbitration can also take place subject to the agreement of the parties to arbitrate and the fact that an arbitration award cannot seek to oust the jurisdiction of the court.

Collaborative law is not seen in family practice in Gibraltar at present and the author is not aware of any locally trained collaborative lawyers.

19.2 What is the statutory basis (if any), for mediation, collaborative law and arbitration in your jurisdiction? In particular, are the parties required to attempt a family dispute resolution in advance of proceedings?

Arbitration is governed locally by the Arbitration Act. Mediation is encouraged, where appropriate, in the context of the furtherance of the overriding objective by active case management as enshrined in rule 4(6)(b) of the Family Proceedings (Matrimonial Causes) Rules 2010. There is no requirement for the parties to attempt a family dispute resolution prior to the institution of legal proceedings.

H. OTHER

20. CIVIL PARTNERSHIP/SAME-SEX MARRIAGE

20.1 What is the status of civil partnership/same-sex marriage within the jurisdiction?

There is currently no statutory recognition of such status in Gibraltar although it should be noted that the Gibraltar Constitution Order 2006 affords protection against discrimination (whether direct or indirect) as well as recognising the right to family life. Indeed the latter is amply illustrated by the recent case of *R v HM Attorney General for Gibraltar* (2013) where the Supreme Court held that the provisions of the Adoption Act which excluded same-sex couples from jointly applying for adoption violated section 7 (the right to family life) and section 14 (discrimination) of the Gibraltar Constitution.

20.2 What legislation governs civil partnership/same-sex marriage?

There is currently no equivalent provision to the English Civil Partnership Act 2004 in force in Gibraltar, although it is understood that the current Government has stated that it intends to promote and implement legislation governing civil partnership. At the date of writing, no bill has been published. It is understood that the proposals do not intend to include same-sex marriage.

21. CONTROVERSIAL AREAS/RAPIDLY DEVELOPING AREAS OF LAW

21.1 Is there a particular area of the law within the jurisdiction that is currently undergoing major change?

There has been a substantial and extensive review of the Matrimonial Causes Act which has led to various amendments to the MCA. In addition, the Minors Act was repealed and replaced by the Children Act. Civil Partnership legislation is pending.

21.2 Which areas of law are most out of step? Which areas would you most like to see reformed/changed?

Prior to the first edition of this text, there had been a substantial overhaul of family law in Gibraltar. Since then family rules were introduced to compliment the MCA and the Children Act. However, there are some discrepancies in those rules which need to be reviewed and updated.
The author would also like to see an amendment to the MCA to enable applications for ancillary relief in respect of foreign divorce proceedings, as indeed is the case in England.

Guernsey

F Haskins and Co Advocate Felicity Haskins

A. JURISDICTION AND CONFLICT OF LAW

1. SOURCES OF LAW

1.1 What is the primary source of law in relation to the breakdown of marriage and the welfare of children within the jurisdiction? Which are the main statutes governing matrimonial law in the jurisdiction?

The primary source of law in relation to the breakdown of marriage and the welfare of children within the jurisdiction of the Bailiwick of Guernsey is statute law.

1.2 Which are the main statutes governing matrimonial law in the jurisdiction?

The main statutes are The Matrimonial Causes (Guernsey) Law 1939, as amended (dealing with decrees of divorce, judicial separation, nullity of marriage and ancillary relief); The Children (Guernsey and Alderney) Law 2008 (dealing with children) and The Domestic Proceedings and Magistrates Court (Guernsey) Law 2008 (dealing with, inter alia, spousal and child maintenance).

2. JURISDICTION

2.1 What are the main jurisdictional requirements for the institution of proceedings in relation to divorce, property and children?

The jurisdictional requirements for the institution of proceedings in relation to divorce is that either party is either domiciled in the jurisdiction of the Bailiwick of Guernsey on the date the proceedings are begun or has been resident in the Bailiwick of Guernsey for 12 consecutive months immediately preceding the presentation of the Petition.

In respect of finances, the court is seized when a decree of divorce, judicial separation or nullity of marriage has been granted.

In respect of children, the court has jurisdiction after the making of a decree of divorce, judicial separation or nullity of marriage in the Island of Guernsey.

3. DOMICILE AND HABITUAL RESIDENCE

3.1 Explain the concepts of domicile and habitual residence as they apply to the jurisdiction in relation to divorce, the finances and children

A person's domicile is either their domicile of origin or their domicile of choice (defined as the country or place in which, in the opinion of the

Matrimonial Causes Division of the Royal Court ('the court'), he has last resided with the intention of there having his settled home). Unless the contrary is proved, the court presumes the continuance of a proved domicile of origin or choice, as the case may be.

The domicile of a child under the age of 16 years or married under that age is generally taken as that of his mother if he then has his home with her and no home with his father, or he has any time had her domicile with her and has not since had a home with his father.

4. CONFLICT OF LAW/APPLICABLE LAW TO BE APPLIED

4.1 What happens when one party applies to stay proceedings in favour of a foreign jurisdiction? What factors will the local court take into account when determining forum issues?

If proceedings in respect of the marriage or capable of affecting its validity or subsistence are pending in another jurisdiction, and the trial in those proceedings has not begun, details must be provided to the court of those proceedings which are known to be continuing in that other jurisdiction. On an application by either party the court must stay the proceedings if the proceedings in that other jurisdiction are:

(a) in respect of the same marriage; and
(b) the parties to the marriage have lived together after its celebration; and
(c) the place they resided together when the proceedings in the court were begun, or, if they did not then reside together, where they last resided together before those proceedings were begun is in that jurisdiction; and
(d) that either of the parties was habitually resident in that jurisdiction throughout the year ending with the date on which they last resided together before the date on which the proceedings in the court were begun.

The court has the discretion to stay the trial in matrimonial proceedings if it appears that any proceedings are continuing in another jurisdiction. In exercising its discretion the court considers the balance of fairness and convenience as between the parties to the marriage and has regard to all factors appearing to be relevant, including the convenience of witnesses and any delay or expenses which may result from the proceedings being stayed, or not being stayed.

B. PRE- AND POST-NUPTIAL AGREEMENTS

5. VALIDITY OF PRE- AND POST-NUPTIAL AGREEMENTS

5.1 To what extent are pre- and post-nups binding within the jurisdiction? Could you provide a brief discussion of the most significant recent case law on this issue?

The court has the power to cancel, vary, modify or terminate a pre- or post-nuptial settlement (made in any jurisdiction) as it thinks just, having regard to the means of the parties, the conduct of the parties or the interests of the children of such marriage.

Parties cannot oust the jurisdiction of the court, but the court gives increasing weight to agreements made between two consenting adults, providing such agreements make fair and reasonable provision. The mere fact the result is not what the court would have done is not enough to set such agreements aside. Much depends on the circumstances that existed at the time the agreement was signed; whether the agreement was signed under duress or undue influence, whether there had been disclosure of assets and/or an opportunity for both parties to seek independent legal advice.

So while such agreements are not strictly legally binding in Guernsey, as the overriding duty of the court is to make a fair order taking into account the provisions of the law, the execution of a contract is one of the factors to be considered, and an increasingly persuasive factor.

In Guernsey, while English case law is not binding, it is of considerable persuasion and guidance is sought therefrom. Mature adults are generally bound by agreements freely entered into which do not offend against Thorpe LJ's list in *Radmacher v. Granatino* (2010) UKSE 42.

A body of local case law is slowly building up. In *E v. E* (2003-2004) GLR Note 22, the parties had entered into a 'non-negotiable' pre-nuptial agreement in which they agreed that upon divorce neither would be entitled to the other's assets. The agreement was drawn up by the husband's advocate; the wife was advised to seek independent legal advice but failed to do so due to lack of funds. It was held that the court had an overriding duty to arrive at a solution which was fair in all the circumstances, and therefore made provision for the wife despite the terms of the agreement. Carey, Bailiff found that while the courts would generally hold parties to properly negotiated agreements, in these circumstances 'properly negotiated' included both parties obtaining competent legal advice. As the wife was not separately advised, and in light of the parties' respective financial circumstances (the husband having a substantial estate and the wife having a negligible estate), the Bailiff did not give the agreement the weight it might otherwise have had.

C. DIVORCE, NULLITY AND JUDICIAL SEPARATION

6. RECOGNITION OF FOREIGN MARRIAGES/DIVORCES

6.1 Summarise the position in your jurisdiction

The Recognition of Divorces and Legal Separations (Bailiwick of Guernsey) Law 1972 as amended provides that divorces or judicial separations granted by means of judicial or other proceedings in any country: (a) in any part of the British Islands shall be recognised in the Bailiwick; and (b) outside the British Islands and that are effective under the law of that country will be recognised as valid if, at the date of the institution of the said proceedings either spouse was habitually resident or domiciled (defined in accordance with the law of that country) in, or a national resident of, that country.

There are some exceptions to this rule, for instance if there was no valid marriage subsisting at the time between the parties, or if at the time the divorce or judicial separation was obtained no sufficient steps were taken to give notice of the proceedings to the other spouse or the other spouse was unreasonably not given an opportunity to take part therein, or if its recognition would be manifestly contrary to public policy.

In respect of the validity of marriages, foreign marriages are invariably recognised in Guernsey. The formalities of the marriage abroad must have been carried out according to the law of the country where the marriage took place and each party must have the capacity to marry according to the law of their home country before they were married.

7. DIVORCE

7.1 Explain the grounds for divorce within the jurisdiction (please also deal with nullity and judicial separation if appropriate)

The sole ground for a petition for divorce is that the marriage has broken down irretrievably. The petitioner must also prove one or more of the following facts:

(a) the respondent has committed adultery and the petitioner finds it intolerable to live with him/her;
(b) that the respondent has behaved in such a way that the petitioner cannot reasonably be expected to live with the respondent;
(c) that the respondent has deserted the petitioner for a continuous period of at least two years immediately preceding the presentation of the petition;
(d) that the parties to the marriage have lived apart for a continuous period of at least two years immediately preceding the presentation of the petition and the respondent consents to a decree being granted; or
(e) that the parties to the marriage have lived apart for a continuous period of at least five years immediately preceding the presentation of the petition.

In respect of a petition for judicial separation, the applicant need prove one of the above facts only.

It is also possible to proceed by way of a judicial separation by consent, without the requirement to prove any fact, but both parties must agree the terms.

A decree of nullity can be obtained if the marriage is by law void or voidable, or if one of the following grounds is proved:

(a) the continuing impotency of one party or both since the celebration of the marriage;
(b) the marriage was celebrated through fraud, threats or duress by the respondent upon or to the petitioner;
(c) the marriage has not been consummated owing to the wilful refusal of the respondent to do so;
(d) the respondent was at the time of the marriage pregnant by some other person other than the petitioner, unless the pregnancy resulted from intercourse which occurred between the respondent and a former husband during the subsistence of that marriage;
(e) that the respondent was at the time of the marriage suffering from venereal disease in a communicable form;
(f) that either party was at the time of the marriage of unsound mind or a mental defective within the meaning of the *Loi ayant rapport aux Faibles d'Esprit* 1926;

(g) either party to the marriage was at the time of the marriage subject to recurrent fits of insanity or epilepsy;
(h) the marriage was bigamous on the part of the respondent;
(i) the marriage has been annulled by another court of competent jurisdiction in which the respondent in the proceedings for nullity in this jurisdiction was domiciled at the time proceedings for such annulment were instituted (subject to certain requirements).

8. FINANCES/CAPITAL, PROPERTY

8.1 What powers does the court have to allocate financial resources and property on the breakdown of marriage?

The court has a wide discretion in the allocation of financial resources and property on the breakdown of marriage. This can include a power to cancel, vary or modify, or terminate the trusts of any marriage contract, marriage settlement, post-nuptial settlement or terms of separation between the parties, having regard to the conduct of the parties or interests of the children as the court deems just. The court has power to re-vest property in one or other of the parties on terms or otherwise. There is no power at present to order a sale of property. That said, the result can be achieved by making capital/lump sum orders or by re-vesting property in undivided shares so that a forced sale can ensue in appropriate circumstances. There are no provisions for pension sharing/splitting at present and thus the benefit of these assets has to be dealt with in other ways, such as a compensatory payment or ongoing spousal maintenance, deferred lump sum etc.

The overall aim is to achieve fairness and justice. All factors are borne in mind. In reaching its decision the court takes into account the provisions of s.25 of the English Matrimonial Causes Act 1973. That said, care is taken not to apply English legislation 'lock, stock and barrel' – for instance conduct under Article 47(1) of the Matrimonial Causes (Guernsey) Law 1939, as amended, contains no qualification in respect of the consideration of conduct as is found in s.25(2) of the Matrimonial Causes Act 1973. However, English case law is of considerable guidance.

8.2 Explain and illustrate with reference to recent cases the court's thinking on division of assets

In *I v I (Royal Court)* 2003-04 GLR N (36) it was held that the reasonable capital and income needs of parties must be considered (housing being the most important consideration); if there are dependent children, the housing of the parent with care is the first priority even if the other parent is not then housed as he wishes. It was further held that the court should be wary of making *Mesher*-style orders[1] as they may cause unfairness in the future and that consideration should be given to alternatives.

In *D v D (C.A.)* 2007-08 GLR 334 it was held that if a husband's share of capital is secured by a charge on the home, payable on the occurrence

[1] *Mesher* orders allow the parent with care to remain in the matrimonial home with the children. Once the children are no longer dependent the home will be sold and the capital divided between the former husband and wife in accordance with the court order.

of specified events, it is legitimate to specify a definite termination date and that the court may increase the charge and enhance the husband's final share to compensate for deferral and greater borrowing/repayment difficulties encountered in old age. It was further held that giving the wife sole ownership and indefinite occupation would only be appropriate if the husband was not in need of accommodation or a stake in the housing market.

In *E v E (C.A.)* 2007-08 GLR 133 it was held that if the husband's share of capital is secured on the home and payable on children's majority or earlier specified events, it was wrong to discount for early payment, but that the court should try to preserve the real value of the capital share by suitable orders. That case further provided that if appropriate, co-ownership may be the best recognition of the principle of equality between spouses, with capital shares to be realised as soon as the needs of the children permit (eg, on attaining majority, ceasing to live in home, or the death of the mother with care and control); but that it was inappropriate to order sale merely because of the mother's remarriage or cohabitation, because her responsibilities to the children then continue.

In *C v C (C.A.)* 2005-06 GLR 199 it was held that allocation of a spouse's liabilities (eg, debts to third parties) was not possible under the provisions of the law, which only permit allocation or division of 'interests in property'; however, such situations can be dealt with by way of contributions for support. That said, mortgage liabilities on the matrimonial home can be part of a fair allocation of parties' assets so as to give maximum flexibility in reaching equitable division of parties' property *(E v E (C.A.)* 2007-08 374).

9. FINANCES/MAINTENANCE

9.1 Explain the operation of maintenance for spouses on an ongoing basis after the breakdown of marriage

The court has a wide discretionary power to make awards for ongoing spousal maintenance (including interim provision), having regard to all the circumstances of the case, including the financial position and conduct of the parties. As a matter of practice, the court takes into account the provisions of s.25 of the English Matrimonial Causes Act 1973 (see supra). There is power to order such payments to be paid as a lump sum or to be secured. Consideration is given to the appropriateness of a clean break.

9.2 Is it common for maintenance to be awarded?

Maintenance is awarded in appropriate cases, such as where:

(a) there are young children such that the wife's earning capacity is hampered;

(b) if there are inadequate assets for both parties to achieve self-sufficiency or the assets that exist are tied up in a family business which is not to be sold;

(c) if parties are older and unlikely to have an earning capacity in their own right; or

(d) in order to compensate for pension income.

There is, however, a marked emphasis on encouraging spouses to adapt and thus term maintenance orders often granted, rather than for life. At the date hereof maintenance does not automatically cease on remarriage.

9.3 Explain and illustrate with reference to recent cases the court's thinking on maintenance

In *I v. I* (supra) it was held that the court should consider a clean break, but only if it is obvious the parties will achieve self-sufficiency.

Secured periodical payments are rarely ordered; in *C v C (Royal Court)* 2003-2004 GLR N (20) it was held such orders may be appropriate if the paying party intends to leave the Island for a jurisdiction not covered by Maintenance Orders (Facilities) (Enforcement) (Reciprocating Countries) (Guernsey) Ordinance 1959 and there is no employment in view. In *J v J* (Royal Court) 2009-10 GLR N (14) it was emphasised that they are rarely ordered, as lump sum and property adjustment orders are available instead. In exercising its powers the court balances all the circumstances, including the extent to which freezing assets hinders the ability to earn income, the likelihood of moving out of the jurisdiction to avoid payments, the likelihood or otherwise of failure to honour maintenance commitments and the whole financial structure of the parties' assets.

10. CHILD MAINTENANCE

10.1 On what basis is child maintenance calculated within the jurisdiction?

The court has a wide discretion on the level of child maintenance to be ordered. Such payments are usually made until each child attains the age of 18 years or ceases full time education or training, and there is a recent tendency to include provision for children to take a gap year. An annual increase in accordance with the Guernsey Official Index of Retail Prices is also standard. Variations are only granted if there has been a material change in circumstances.

In determining the level of maintenance, the court takes into account all of the circumstances of the case, first consideration being given to the welfare of minors of the family. This includes a consideration of the following factors:

(a) the income, earning capacity, property and other financial resources which each party to the marriage has or is likely to have in the foreseeable future (including any increase in earning capacity either party could reasonably achieve in the opinion of the court);

(b) the financial needs, obligations and responsibilities each party has or is likely to have in the foreseeable future;

(c) the standard of living enjoyed by the family;

(d) the financial needs of the child;

(e) the income, earning capacity, property or other financial resources of the child;

(f) any physical or mental disability of the child; and

(g) the manner in which the child was being and in which the parties to the marriage expected him to be educated or trained.

As a matter of practice, the court compares the result of the above analysis with the outcome under the English CSA guidelines, which are being given increasing weight in this jurisdiction.

11. RECIPROCAL ENFORCEMENT OF FINANCIAL ORDERS

11.1 Summarise the position in your jurisdiction

Under the Judgment (Reciprocal Enforcement) (Guernsey) Law 1957, it is possible to register a foreign judgment of a recognised superior court (ie, the High Court or above in the UK) provided the judgment is:

- final and conclusive between the parties; and
- for a specified sum of money (other than taxes, penalties and fines).

If proceedings are not covered as above, the common law applies, in respect of which foreign financial orders made in matrimonial proceedings (excluding maintenance) can only be enforced by suing on the foreign judgment itself. The order of the foreign judgment will only be enforced if the foreign court:

(a) was a competent jurisdiction (determined on English rules of conflict);
(b) there was no fraud on the party in whose favour the judgment was given;
(c) there was no fraud on the part of the foreign court;
(d) the enforcement would not be contrary to public policy; or
(e) the proceedings in which the judgment was obtained were not contrary to natural justice.

It is unlikely the local court would consider the foreign court had jurisdiction to order a transfer of property situated in this jurisdiction.

The Maintenance Orders (Reciprocal Enforcement) (Bailiwick of Guernsey) Law 1984 provides, *inter alia*, that maintenance orders made in Guernsey or in a reciprocating country, can be transmitted for enforcement either in Guernsey (if the payer resides in Guernsey) or the reciprocating country; such orders are transmitted via the Lieutenant Governor and the payer is notified of such application and given an opportunity to establish a defence, before the order is registered/confirmed. A registered order can be enforced in the Bailiwick as if it had been made in this jurisdiction.

There is also power to make provisional maintenance orders against people residing in reciprocating countries in certain circumstances.

12. FINANCIAL RELIEF AFTER FOREIGN DIVORCE PROCEEDINGS

12.1 What powers are available to make orders following a foreign divorce?

The court has power to deal with financial relief as regards real and personal property of either party to the marriage following a recognised decree of divorce or nullity of marriage or judicial separation, in the same manner as if the decree of divorce or nullity of marriage or judicial separation had been granted in this jurisdiction.

D. CHILDREN

13. CUSTODY/PARENTAL RESPONSIBILITY

13.1 Briefly explain the legal position in relation to custody/parental responsibility following the breakdown of a relationship or marriage

Both parties to a marriage who were married at the time of the child's birth have joint parental responsibility for that child.

In principle, if the parties were not married after the commencement of s.7 of the Children (Guernsey and Alderney) Law 2008 and the father did not have parental responsibility or its equivalent under the law of any part of the British Isles (other than Guernsey or Alderney), the mother has parental responsibility of that child but the father can acquire parental responsibility in certain circumstances, such as if he was registered as the child's father in the registration of births occurring within Guernsey or Alderney, or by written agreement with the child's mother, or by application to the court. He will then share parental responsibility with the child's mother.

13.2 Briefly explain the legal position in relation to access/contact/visitation following the breakdown of a relationship or marriage

Orders for residence, contact or other specific issues (including prohibited steps orders), can be made by the court. This may be either on application by the parties or of the court's own volition if a question in respect of the welfare of a child arises during proceedings.

In determining what orders to make the welfare of the child is paramount; the court has a duty to consider 'the child welfare principles' and 'the child welfare checklist' which are set out at sections 3 and 4 of the Children (Guernsey and Alderney) Law 2008.

There is a Safeguarder Service in Guernsey which is often appointed by the court to provide reports to the court in cases of dispute (akin to CAFCASS in the UK).

14. INTERNATIONAL ABDUCTION

14.1 Summarise the position in your jurisdiction

Section 74 of the Children (Guernsey and Alderney) Law 2008 deals with the offence of child abduction out of the jurisdiction. The offence is committed if a person takes or sends a child under the age of 16 years out of the jurisdiction of Guernsey or Alderney (save for periods not exceeding 28 days or certain other exceptions) without the consent of every person with parental responsibility of the child (or the consent of the States Health and Social Services Department if the child is subject to a care requirement) or without leave of a relevant court.

It is a defence if the person can show on a balance of probabilities that he reasonably believed any other person required had consented or would have consented had they been aware of all of the relevant circumstances or he had taken reasonable steps to communicate to such person but was unable to do so.

The court has certain powers of enforcement including a power of arrest.

As yet, Guernsey is still not a signatory to the Hague Convention on the Civil Aspects of Child Abduction; nor is it bound by Brussells II. The court currently deals with such matters applying the welfare principle and the welfare checklist.

15. LEAVE TO REMOVE/APPLICATIONS TO TAKE A CHILD OUT OF THE JURISDICTION

15.1 Summarise the position in your jurisdiction

A contested application for leave to take a child out of the jurisdiction is determined in accordance with the overriding statutory principle that the child's welfare is paramount. The court considers all of the circumstances of the case and takes guidance from English case law (such as *Payne v Payne* (2001) 1 FLR 1052), which, while not binding, is of considerable persuasive value.

15.2 Under what circumstances may a parent apply to remove their child from the jurisdiction against the wishes of the other parent?

A parent may apply to remove their child from the jurisdiction against the wishes of the other parent; however he must satisfy the court such a removal is in the child's best interests. The court will consider all of the circumstances of the proposed move.

E. SURROGACY & ADOPTION

16. VALIDITY OF SURROGACY ARRANGEMENTS

16.1 Briefly summarise the position in your jurisdiction

At present there is no law governing surrogacy agreements in Guernsey.

However, section 54 of the Human Embryology and Fertilisation Act 2008 in England allows parental orders to be made in favour of people domiciled in the Channel Islands; the application would currently need to be made in family proceedings in England.

Consideration could also be given to adoption in such circumstances.

17. ADOPTION

17.1 Briefly explain the legal position in relation to adoption in your jurisdiction. Is adoption available to individuals, cohabiting couples (both heterosexual and same sex)?

An adoption order can be made on the application of two spouses to adopt a child; or one person only in any other case. Cohabiting couples cannot both adopt, however the partner of the single parent who adopts can apply for parental responsibility if the parties are not married.

The proposed applicant must be either the mother or father of the child, a relative of the child who is over 20 years of age, or be over 25 years of age.

An adoption order will not be made for a female child in favour of a single male applicant, unless there are special circumstances which justify the making of such an order as an exceptional measure.

The consent of both the parents or guardian is generally required; albeit in some circumstances there is power to dispense with consent.

F. COHABITATION

18. COHABITATION

18.1 What legislation (if any) governs division of property for unmarried couples on the breakdown of the relationship?

There is no specific legislation governing the division of property for unmarried couples on the breakdown on their relationship in Guernsey and the matter is dealt with in accordance with general property law. If one cohabitee provides all or most of the funds to purchase the property in which both cohabit, the court may nevertheless, upon licitation (forced sale), order an equal division of the proceeds of sale if both intend the property to be held jointly. Intention of joint ownership may be evidenced by transfer into joint ownership and registration of title in both names. Equitable presumptions of English law (eg, advancement or resulting trust) are not incorporated into Guernsey land law. Norman law principles are applied, whereby joint owners *prima facie* are entitled to property or proceeds of sale in equal shares.

G. FAMILY DISPUTE RESOLUTION

19. MEDIATION, COLLABORATIVE LAW AND ARBITRATION

19.1 Briefly summarise the non-court-based processes available in your jurisdiction and the current status of agreements reached under the auspices of mediation, collaborative law and arbitration.

Parties can agree to submit to mediation, a process which remains voluntary. An agreement reached through mediation is generally binding in the same way as any other written contract.

Collaborative law and arbitration in family proceedings do not yet take place in Guernsey; however, it is likely that any agreements reached under collaborative law or arbitration would be binding in the same way as a mediated settlement.

19.2 What is the statutory basis (if any), for mediation, collaborative law and arbitration in your jurisdiction? In particular, are the parties required to attempt a family dispute resolution in advance of the institution of proceedings?

As yet there is no statutory basis for mediation, collaborative law or arbitration.

The parties are required to attempt a judge-led family dispute resolution hearing in advance of the actual ancillary relief hearing.

H. OTHER

20. CIVIL PARTNERSHIP/SAME-SEX MARRIAGE

20.1 What is the status of civil partnership/same-sex marriage within the jurisdiction?

Civil partnership and same-sex marriage have no status in Guernsey; that said, any agreement reached between such parties are likely to be enforced in the same way as any other written contract.

20.2 What legislation governs civil partnership/same-sex marriage?

None.

21. CONTROVERSIAL AREAS/RAPIDLY DEVELOPING AREAS OF LAW

21.1 Is there a particular area of the law within the jurisdiction that is currently undergoing major change?

Changes have been recommended by the Policy Council to the States to extend the powers of the divorce court to ensure justice is done between parties in matrimonial proceedings. In particular:

(a) to transfer real or personal property to a wider range of people, to include children of the family or another person for those children's benefit;
(b) to create trusts or settlements or vary trusts of settlement of real or personal property of the spouses; and to vest real or personal property in trust generally including for the children of the family and other persons for those children's benefit;
(c) to direct payments or periodic payments out of the sale of real or personal property;
(d) to direct that real or personal property, or any interest therein, should be held on trust for sale with power to postpone sale either indefinitely or to a fixed time or until further order of the divorce court;
(e) to suspend the ability of co-owners to require a licitation (supra) for a period of time;
(f) to create a right of usufruct or habitation, or possession (eg, lease/licence for either party);
(g) to secure a fixed charge on the interest of either or both owners of real property.

Consideration is also to be given to amending the legislation to make provision for pension sharing orders and/or payments of lump sums. In addition, there are plans to detail specific matters to be taken into account in Guernsey when making financial orders, rather than relying on section 25 of the English Matrimonial Causes Act 1973.

The amended law on these issues has been drafted.

21.2 Which areas of law are most out-of-step? Which areas would you most like to see reformed/changed?

The areas most out of step are those set out in 21.1 above, the fact re-marriage does not automatically terminate maintenance and the fact Guernsey is still not a signatory to the Hague Convention on the Civil Aspects of Child Abduction.

Hong Kong

Stevenson, Wong & Co Catherine Por

A. JURISDICTION AND CONFLICT OF LAW

1. SOURCES OF LAW

1.1 What is the primary source of law in relation to the breakdown of marriage and the welfare of children within the jurisdiction?

The primary sources of law are the common law and statutory law.

1.2 Which are the main statutes governing matrimonial law in the jurisdiction?

The Matrimonial Causes Ordinance (chapter 179) (MCO), the Matrimonial Proceedings and Property Ordinance (chapter 192) (MPPO), the Marriage Ordinance (chapter 181) and the Guardianship of Minors Ordinance (chapter 13) (GMO) are the main ordinances in Hong Kong governing divorce, children issues and financial relief on the breakdown of a marriage.

2. JURISDICTION

2.1 What are the main jurisdictional requirements for the institution of proceedings in relation to divorce, property and children?

Hong Kong courts will have jurisdiction in proceedings for divorce if:

- either of the parties to the marriage is domiciled in Hong Kong at the date of the petition or application;
- either of the parties to the marriage is habitually resident in Hong Kong throughout the three years immediately preceding the date of the petition or application;
- either of the parties to the marriage has a substantial connection with Hong Kong at the date of the petition or application.

Under Part IIA of the MPPO, an application for an order for financial relief, including orders in relation to property, can be made in Hong Kong by a party whose marriage has been dissolved or annulled or the parties to the marriage have been legally separated, by means of judicial or other proceedings, in a place outside Hong Kong. Certain jurisdictional requirements, analogous to the court's jurisdiction in divorce proceedings in Hong Kong, need to be met for the court to entertain such an application. Leave of the court to make such an application must first be obtained.

Child custody and maintenance can be dealt with within divorce proceedings under the MPPO or without, under the GMO.

3. DOMICILE AND HABITUAL RESIDENCE

3.1 Explain the concepts of domicile and habitual residence as they apply to the jurisdiction in relation to divorce, the finances and children

Where the divorce jurisdiction is concerned, a person is considered domiciled in Hong Kong if Hong Kong is their permanent principal home to which they return or intend to return to. As far as habitual residence is concerned, and in the context of divorce jurisdiction, a period of residence in a place one considers the 'home' to which one routinely returned denotes habitual residence.

For financial orders under Part IIA of the MPPO, jurisdictional requirements are analogous to the Court's jurisdiction in divorce proceedings.

A child's domicile is that of the country or territory with which he/she is for the time being most closely connected. Where the child's parents are domiciled in the same country or territory and the child has his/her home with either or both of them, it shall be presumed, unless the contrary is proved, that the child is most closely connected with that country or territory. Where the child's parents are not domiciled in the same country or territory and the child has his/her home with one of them, but not with the other, it shall be presumed, unless the contrary is proved, that the child is most closely connected with the country or territory in which the parent with whom he has his/her home is domiciled.

The habitual residence of a child living with both parents is that of the parents. The habitual residence of such parents refers to their abode in a particular place or country which they have adopted voluntarily and for settled purposes as part of the regular order of their life for the time being, whether of short or long duration.

4. CONFLICT OF LAW/APPLICABLE LAW TO BE APPLIED

4.1 What happens when one party applies to stay proceedings in favour of a foreign jurisdiction? What factors will the local court take into account when determining forum issues?

Hong Kong has adopted the principles set out by the House of Lords in *Spilada Maritime Corp v Cansulex Ltd, The Spiliada* [1987] AC 460, in *Louvet v Louvet* [1990] 1 HKLR 670, and more recently confirmed by the Court of Appeal in *DGC v SLC nee C* [2008] HKLFR 160, governing stay of a Hong Kong proceeding by reason of *forum non conveniens* or *forum conveniens* (they mean the same). The principles are:

- The single question to be decided is whether there is some other available forum having competent jurisdiction, which is the appropriate forum for the trial of an action, ie, in which the action may be tried more suitably for the interests of all the parties and the ends of justice.
- In order to answer this, the applicant for the stay has to establish that, firstly, Hong Kong is not the natural or appropriate forum ('appropriate' in this context means the forum that has the most real and substantial connection with the action) and, secondly, that there is another forum

available which is clearly or distinctly more appropriate than Hong Kong. Failure by the applicant to establish these two matters at this stage is fatal.

- If the applicant is able to establish both of these two matters, the plaintiff in the Hong Kong proceeding has to show that they will be deprived of a legitimate personal or juridical advantage if the action is tried in a forum other than Hong Kong.
- If the applicant is able to establish this, the court will have to balance the advantages of the alternative forum with the disadvantages that the plaintiff may suffer. Deprivation of one or more personal advantages will not necessarily be fatal to the applicant for the stay if they are able to establish to the court's satisfaction that substantial justice will be done in the available appropriate forum.

B. PRE- AND POST-NUPTIAL AGREEMENTS

5. VALIDITY OF PRE- AND POST-NUPTIAL AGREEMENTS

5.1 To what extent are pre- and post-nuptial agreements binding within the jurisdiction? Could you provide a brief discussion of the most significant recent case law on this issue.

Pre- and post-nuptial agreements are not binding in Hong Kong. They are considered a 'circumstance' or 'conduct' of the parties which a court has a statutory obligation to take into account when deciding what financial provision to make. It is for the court, in the exercise of its discretion, to decide what weight should be given to such agreements.

The Hong Kong Court of Final Appeal has yet to consider whether the Supreme Court decision of *Radmacher v Granatino* [2010] UKSC 42 will be adopted here.

It is also unknown if Hong Kong will follow the Privy Council decision of *MacLeod v MacLeod* [2010] AC 298.

C. DIVORCE, NULLITY AND JUDICIAL SEPARATION

6. RECOGNITION OF FOREIGN MARRIAGE/DIVORCES

6.1 Summarise the position in your jurisdiction

Hong Kong courts can recognise an overseas divorce in Hong Kong provided that, if at the date of the institution of the proceedings in the country in which it was obtained: (a) either spouse was habitually resident in that country; or (b) either spouse was a national of that country.

7. DIVORCE

7.1 Explain the grounds for divorce within the jurisdiction (please also deal with nullity and judicial separation if appropriate)

The sole ground for presenting or making a petition or application for divorce shall be that the marriage has broken down irretrievably. The court hearing a petition for divorce shall not hold the marriage to have broken down irretrievably unless the petitioner satisfies the court of one or more of the following facts:

- the respondent has committed adultery and the petitioner finds it intolerable to live with the respondent;

- the respondent has behaved in such a way that the petitioner cannot reasonably be expected to live with the respondent;
- the parties to the marriage have lived apart for a continuous period of at least one year immediately preceding the presentation of the petition and the respondent consents to a decree being granted;
- the parties to the marriage have lived apart for a continuous period of at least two years immediately preceding the presentation of the petition;
- the respondent has deserted the petitioner for a continuous period of at least one year immediately preceding the presentation of the petition.

There is a restriction on applying for divorce within the first year of marriage, although the court may allow a petition to proceed within the first year of marriage on the grounds of exceptional hardship.

There is also provision in the MCO for a joint application for divorce based on the parties' separation of at least one year.

Judicial separation

A petition for judicial separation may be presented to the court by either party to a marriage on one or more of the five facts above. However, with a judicial separation, as distinct from divorce, the court is not concerned with irretrievable breakdown and shall grant a decree of judicial separation if it is satisfied on the evidence of any of the five facts. A petition can also be presented within the first year of marriage.

Nullity

A petition for a decree of nullity may be presented to the court by either party to a marriage on the grounds provided in section 20 of the MCO, which provides for void and voidable marriages.

8. FINANCES/CAPITAL, PROPERTY

8.1 What powers does the court have to allocate financial resources and property on the breakdown of marriage?

The court has powers under sections 4, 5, 6 and 6A of the MPPO to make orders for periodical payments, secured periodical payments and lump sum order for the other party to the marriage, periodical payments, secured periodical payments and lump sum order for the child of the family, transfer and settlement of property, variation of settlements and sale of property.

It is only upon the grant of a decree absolute that the court can make orders in respect of sections 4, 6 and 6A of the MPPO. The court has jurisdiction on parties' assets wherever situated.

8.2 Explain and illustrate with reference to recent cases the court's thinking on division of assets

LKW v DD [FACV 16 of 2008], the Hong Kong Court of Final Appeal considered the proper approach to making financial provision orders on and after the dissolution of a marriage. The Court identified 4 principles from *White v White* [2001] 1 AC 1996 and various landmark English cases which followed thereafter. The principles are the objective of fairness, rejection of any gender or role discrimination, yardstick of equal division which should be departed from only for good articulated reasons and rejection of minute retrospective investigation. With a view to achieving a fair financial outcome, the court further provided a framework as guidance for a systematic consideration of issues relevant to the court's exercise of its discretion under section 7 of the MPPO (see 9.3 below). The first step is to ascertain the final resources of each of the parties as at the date of the hearing; the second step is to assess the parties' financial needs; the third step is, if there are surplus assets after the parties' needs have been catered for, to apply the sharing principle to the parties' total assets, leaving the 'needs' question previously considered to be dealt with under that principle; the fourth step involves whether good reasons exist for departing from the principle of equal division, leading to the fifth step, which is deciding on the award, taking into account the overall impact of all relevant factors.

9. FINANCES/MAINTENANCE

9.1 Explain the operation of maintenance for spouses on an ongoing basis after the breakdown of marriage

As far as maintenance pending suit is concerned, the court has stated that the principles for the court to consider at this stage are, firstly, the reasonable needs of the spouse and the children of the family who ask for maintenance, and the other spouse's ability to pay, and, secondly, this being an interim provision, the court will not make a detailed investigation of the financial positions of the parties but will adopt a broad brush approach (see *Wong Wai Susanna v Lim Min Sup Mark* (CACV 263/98)).

9.2 Is it common for maintenance to be awarded?

Spousal maintenance in Hong Kong is common. Where assets are sufficient to achieve a clean break, this is usually the preferred course.

9.3 Explain and illustrate with reference to recent cases the court's thinking on maintenance

The court is obliged to consider all the factors in section 7.(1) of MPPO:

- the income, earning capacity, property and other financial resources
- which each of the parties to the marriage has or is likely to have in the foreseeable future;
- the financial needs, obligations and responsibilities which each of the parties to the marriage has or is likely to have in the foreseeable future;
- the standard of living enjoyed by the family before the breakdown of the marriage;
- the age of each party to the marriage and the duration of the marriage;
- any physical or mental disability of either of the parties to the marriage;
- the contributions made by each of the parties to the welfare of the family, including any contribution made by looking after the home or caring for the family;
- in the case of proceedings for divorce or nullity of marriage, the value to either of the parties to the marriage of any benefit (for example,

a pension) which, by reason of the dissolution or annulment of the marriage, that party will lose the chance of acquiring.

10. CHILD MAINTENANCE

10.1 On what basis is child maintenance calculated within the jurisdiction?

There is no formulaic assessment for children's maintenance.

The relevant statutory factors to be considered are set out in section 7(2) of the MPPO, which are:

- the financial needs of the chid;
- the income, earning capacity (if any), property and other financial resources of the child;
- any physical or mental disability of the child;
- the standard of living enjoyed by the family before the breakdown of the marriage;
- the manner in which the child was being, and in which the parties to the marriage expected the child, to be educated.

11. RECIPROCAL ENFORCEMENT OF FINANCIAL ORDERS

11.1 Summarise the position in your jurisdiction

Hong Kong has reciprocal arrangements, under the Maintenance Orders (Reciprocal Enforcement) Ordinance (Chapter 188), for facilitating the recovery of maintenance by or from persons in Hong Kong from or by other persons in reciprocating countries.

Reciprocating countries for maintenance orders generally are the United Kingdom, Bermuda, the Province of Manitoba, the Province of Saskatchewan, the Province of Ontario and Isle of Man.

Reciprocating countries for maintenance orders other than affiliation orders (orders adjudging, finding or declaring a person to be the father of a child, whether or not it also provides for the maintenance of the child) are the Commonwealth of Australia and its territories, the State of British Columbia, the State of Brunei, Malaysia, New Zealand, the Republic of Singapore, the Solomon Islands, the Republic of South Africa and the Republic of Sri Lanka.

12. FINANCIAL RELIEF AFTER FOREIGN DIVORCE PROCEEDINGS

12.1 What powers are available to make orders following a foreign divorce?

Under Part IIA of the MPPO, an application for an order for financial relief, including orders in relation to property, can be made in Hong Kong by a party whose marriage has been dissolved or annulled or the parties to the marriage have been legally separated, by means of judicial or other proceedings, in a place outside Hong Kong. Certain jurisdictional requirements, analogous to the court's jurisdiction in divorce proceedings in Hong Kong, need to be met for the court to entertain such an application. Leave of the court to make such an application must first be obtained. If leave is granted, the court also has power to make interim maintenance orders, to avoid transactions intended to defeat applications for financial relief and to prevent transactions intended to defeat prospective applications for financial relief.

D. CHILDREN

13. CUSTODY/PARENTAL RESPONSIBILITY

13.1 Briefly explain the legal position in relation to custody/parental responsibility following the breakdown of a relationship or marriage

Under section 19 of the MPPO, the court may make such orders as it thinks fit for the 'custody and education' of any child of the family under the age of 18. In section 10 of the GMO, the court may make orders regarding the custody of the minor and the right of access to the minor of either of his or her parents.

The first and paramount consideration in an application under either of the above ordinances is the best interests of the child.

The term 'custody' is not defined in the legislation. Courts have interpreted it to mean making the decisions of a child's life, decisions of real consequence in safeguarding and promoting the child's health, development and general welfare. Custody can be held jointly by the parents, or solely by one parent.

Hong Kong does not have the concept of 'parental responsibility' as yet.

13.2 Briefly explain the legal position in relation to access/contact/visitation following the breakdown of a relationship or marriage

Following the breakdown of a marriage, the court will make orders providing for the custody, care and control of and access to the child/children. The concept of 'care and control' is also not defined in the legislation. It is generally said to mean the day-to-day looking after of the child/children. Orders for care and control are usually to one parent solely. Joint care and control orders can be made, usually only by consent, as they normally require a high level of cooperation between the parents.

Access is the right of the child/children to see the non-custodial parent, or in the case of joint custody, the right of the child to see the parents without care and control. The normal order is for reasonable access, with details to be worked out between the parents. Alternatively, access can be defined. Access can also be supervised.

In the case of a child/children of parents who are not married, the mother has custody of the child/children. The father will only have rights as may be ordered by a court.

14. INTERNATIONAL ABDUCTION

14.1 Summarise the position in your jurisdiction

The People's Republic of China is not a signatory to the Hague Convention, but Hong Kong is a signatory. The Convention is given recognition under the Child Abduction and Custody Ordinance (chapter 512).

15. LEAVE TO REMOVE/APPLICATIONS TO TAKE A CHILD OUT OF THE JURISDICTION

15.1 Summarise the position in your jurisdiction

When a court in Hong Kong makes a custody order, it also directs that the child/children may not be removed from Hong Kong without leave of the court. There is therefore a positive requirement to make an application to the court for leave to permanently remove a child/children from the jurisdiction of Hong Kong.

In *SMM v TWM* [CACV 209/2009], the Court of Appeal concluded that the principles in *Payne v Payne* [2001] Fam 473 should be applied and adopted in Hong Kong. The two propositions applied by the Hong Kong court are firstly, that the welfare of the child is the paramount consideration and secondly, that refusing the primary carer's reasonable proposals for relocation is likely to impact detrimentally on the welfare of the child.

15.2 Under what circumstances may a parent apply to remove their child from the jurisdiction against the wishes of the other parent?

It is usually the primary carer parent who makes the application and generally the motivation arises out of the parent's remarriage or an urge to return home. The other parent's opposition is usually a reduction in contact, influence and being a part of the child/children's life/lives.

The removing parent's application must be genuine and not motivated by some selfish desire to exclude the other parent from the child/children's life/lives. The application must also be realistic, well thought out and investigated. Assuming so, the remaining parent's opposition would be given careful consideration including the extent of the detriment to him and his future relationship with the child/children in the event of removal. The impact on the removing parent of a refusal of his/her application would also be considered. The child's welfare would, ultimately, be the paramount consideration.

E. SURROGACY AND ADOPTION

16. VALIDITY OF SURROGACY AGREEMENTS

16.1 Briefly summarise the position in your jurisdiction

The law on Surrogacy in Hong Kong is governed by the Human Reproductive Technology Ordinance (HRTO) (Cap 561, Laws of Hong Kong).

Only the gametes of a married couple can be used in a surrogacy arrangement (section 14 of the HRTO). The Code of Practice on Reproductive Technology and Embryo Research prepared and maintained by the Council on Human Reproductive Technology, a statutory body established under section 4 of HRTO, further provides, *inter alia*, that a reproductive technology procedure may only be provided to the wife who is unable to carry a pregnancy to term and no other treatment option is practicable for her.

The surrogate mother is the legal mother of the child at birth by virtue of her giving birth to the child. In order to obtain parental rights to the child, the commissioning couple must apply to the court for a parental order in their favour in place of the surrogate mother. Under section 12 of the Parent and Child Ordinance (PCO)(Cap 429, Laws of Hong Kong), the court may make an order providing for a child to be treated in law as the child of the parties to a marriage in circumstances where the child has been carried by a woman other than the wife, as a result of the placing in her of an embryo or sperm and eggs or her artificial insemination following the use of gametes of one or both of the spouses. Therefore, only those who can apply to the court for the parental order can use a surrogacy arrangement to become the legal parents of the child.

The commissioning couple must apply for the order under section 12 of the PCO within six months of the birth of the child. The child's home must be with the husband and the wife or either of them and the husband or wife or both of them must be domiciled in Hong Kong, have been habitually resident in Hong Kong throughout the immediately preceding period of one year, or have a substantial connection with Hong Kong.

In considering an application for an order under section 12 of the PCO, the court must be satisfied, among other things, that both the commissioning couple and the surrogate mother have a full understanding of the matter and have unconditionally agreed to the making of such an order. As a matter of good practice, the surrogacy agreement should clearly state that the implications of the necessary arrangements and procedures have been fully and clearly explained to each of the parties by their respective legal and medical representatives and that the parties have had the opportunity to raise any issues which they may have had before the start of the surrogacy arrangement.

Pursuant to section 17 of the HRTO, no person shall, whether in Hong Kong or elsewhere, make or receive any payment for a surrogacy arrangement. Reasonable expenses incurred by the surrogate mother in the course of the pregnancy may, however, be paid to her.

Under section 18 of the HRTO, no surrogacy arrangement is enforceable by or against any of the persons making it.

Where a parental order is made under section 12 of the PCO, the Registrar of the Court shall notify the Registrar of Births and Deaths, enabling the registration of the commissioning couple as the child's legal parents.

17. ADOPTION

17.1 Briefly summarise the position in relation to adoption in your jurisdiction. Is adoption available to individuals, cohabiting couples (both heterosexual and same-sex)?

Adoption is governed by the Adoption Ordinance (Chapter 290). Adoption by Chinese customary law was abolished in 1973.

Under the Adoption Ordinance, a sole applicant, being either the mother or father of the child, a relative of the child and who has attained the age of 21 years, a person who is married to a parent of the child or a person who has attained the age of 25 years, can adopt a child. There is one restriction on the eligibility of the applicant in that a sole male applicant cannot adopt a female child unless the court is satisfied that there are special circumstances justifying it.

A joint application can be made by two spouses provided one of the applicants is the mother or father of the child, is a relative of the child and the other applicant has attained 21 years or has attained the age of 25 years and the other applicant has attained 21 years.

The consent of the every person who is a parent or guardian of the child or who is liable by virtue of any of any order or agreement to contribute to the maintenance of the child is required. In the case of an application by one of two spouses, the consent of the other spouse is required.

The applicant and the child must reside in Hong Kong.

F. COHABITATION

18. COHABITATION

18.1 What legislation (if any) governs division of property for unmarried couples on the breakdown of the relationship?

There is no legislation in Hong Kong governing the division of property for unmarried couples upon the breakdown of their relationship.

G. FAMILY DISPUTE RESOLUTION

19. MEDIATION, COLLABORATIVE LAW AND ARBITRATION

19.1 Briefly summarise the non-court-based processes available in your jurisdiction and the current status of agreements reached under the auspices of mediation, collaborative law and arbitration

Family mediation was introduced in Hong Kong in 2000. It was then and remains a voluntary process, pro-actively encouraged by the Government, the courts and the profession. An application to the court, by way of a consent summons, is required to make a mediated agreement an order of the court and thereby enforceable.

Collaborative practice, being a contractual agreement between trained professionals and the parties to act collaboratively to resolve their family disputes, is a relatively new process in Hong Kong. Not only lawyers but also health professionals and financial specialists have been trained in the collaborative process. Any agreement reached would need to be made into an order of the court.

Family arbitration has yet to be introduced to Hong Kong. This process is, however, being explored at this time.

19.2 What is the statutory basis (if any), for mediation, collaborative law and arbitration in your jurisdiction? In particular, are the parties required to attempt a family dispute resolution in advance of the institution of proceedings?

While mediation has been introduced in family and civil disputes in Hong Kong, it is not mandatory, whether in advance of or during the course of proceedings. There may, however, be costs consequences to a party who unreasonably refuses to mediate. Collaborative practice is also a voluntary process.

H. OTHER

20. CIVIL PARTNERSHIP/SAME-SEX MARRIAGE

20.1 What is the status of civil partnership/same-sex marriage within the jurisdiction?

Same sex marriages are not recognised in Hong Kong. The Marriage Ordinance recognises 'the voluntary union for life of one man and one woman to the exclusion of all others'.

In *W v Registrar of Marriages* [FACV 4 of 2012], W, a post-operative male-to-female transsexual was not permitted to marry her male partner. The Registrar of Marriages decided that W did not qualify as a 'woman' under the Marriage Ordinance and the Matrimonial Causes Ordinance. W challenged that decision, contending that she should in law be counted as a woman for the purposes of marriage. W was unsuccessful in her challenge at first instance and on appeal. The Court of Final Appeal, in May 2013, allowed W's appeal by a majority (one judge dissenting). W was granted a declaration that the Marriage Ordinance and the Matrimonial Causes Ordinance must be read and be given effect so as to include within the meaning of the words 'woman' and 'female' a post-operative male-to-female transsexual person whose gender has been certified by an appropriate medical authority to have changed as a result of sex reassignment surgery and a further declaration that W is in law entitled to be included as 'a woman' within the meaning of the Marriage Ordinance and the Matrimonial Causes Ordinance and therefore eligible to marry a man. The court, however, recognised that there could be difficult issues arising in various areas and called upon the Government and the legislature to consider enacting legislation to deal with such areas. The court was also of the view that there is a strong case for a comprehensive review of the legislation concerning problems facing transsexuals.

20.2 What legislation governs civil partnership/same-sex marriage?

None. Nothing in *W v Registrar of Marriages* is intended to address the question of same-sex marriages.

21. CONTROVERSIAL AREAS/RAPIDLY DEVELOPING AREAS OF LAW

21.1 Is there a particular area of the law within the jurisdiction that is currently undergoing major change?

None.

21.2 Which areas of law are most out of step? Which areas would you most like to see reformed/changed.

The law relating to child custody and access remains the most out of step. Although a Consultation Paper was published in 1998 and a Law Reform Commission Report was published in March 2005 to, among other things, adopt the concept of 'parental responsibility' in place of the concepts of 'custody' and 'care and control', there has yet to be legislative change. This is long overdue and out of line with other common law jurisdictions.

India

Chambers of Ms Pinky Anand Ms Pinky Anand, senior advocate, Supreme Court of India

A. JURISDICTION AND CONFLICT OF LAW

1. SOURCES OF LAW

1.1 What is the primary source of law in relation to the breakdown of marriage and the welfare of children within the jurisdiction?

Breakdown of marriage

India is a secular country and a wide number of religions are freely practised here. The major religions practised in India include Hinduism, Islam and Christianity. People solemnize marriages in accordance with religious rituals and ceremonies which are mostly codified by statutory personal laws. Thus, the matrimonial laws in India, including laws on marriage, divorce and other connected issues, are essentially governed by the personal laws of the parties depending upon their religion.

There has also been promulgation of a secular legislation, which applies to all persons of all religion, called the Special Marriage Act 1954. This Act is a civil legislation and parties from all religions, caste, and/or community can elect to get married under this Act. The breakdown of marriage would then be governed by this Act.

All these laws are central Acts and apply throughout the State of India, except the State of Jammu and Kashmir and Goa.

Welfare of children

Every personal law governing the marriage between two parties lays down provisions for ensuring the welfare of the children born from the wedlock. There is a general law called the Guardian and Wards Act 1890, which is applicable to all communities.

The Guardian and Wards Act 1890 is a complete code defining the rights and liabilities of guardians and wards. It applies to minor children of any caste and creed, although, while approving and declaring a person as the guardian of the minor, the court will take into consideration the personal law of the minor. The Act has been promulgated with a view to protect the person and property of the minor.

1.2 Which are the main statutes governing matrimonial law in the jurisdiction?

All persons Special Marriage Act 1954

Hindu – the Hindu Marriage Act 1955

Muslim – a Muslim marriage is a contract under Muslim law. Every Muslim who has attained puberty and who is of sound mind may enter into a contract of marriage. A Muslim marriage can be dissolved by way of divorce by the parties without recourse to court or, on certain grounds, by recourse to court. There are three ways to dissolve a Muslim marriage:

- by the husband – a Muslim husband of a sound mind can divorce his wife at his will by way of *talak*. He may divorce his wife whenever he desires without assigning any cause;
- by mutual consent – divorce may take place by mutual consent of the husband and the wife. It is then called *khula* (or *khul*) or *mubara*;
- divorce by delegation – under Muslim law, it is only the husband who can pronounce *talak* on his wife, not vice versa. However, the husband may delegate this power to the wife or any third person by an agreement. This is known as divorce by delegation or *talak-e-tafweez*.

A Muslim woman can obtain a decree for dissolution of the marriage under the Dissolution of Muslim Marriages Act 1939, which lays down the grounds for divorce.

Christian – the Indian Christian Marriage Act 1872 and the Divorce Act 1869.

Parsi – the Parsi Marriage and Divorce Act 1936.

2. JURISDICTION

2.1 What are the main jurisdictional requirements for the institution of proceedings in relation to divorce, property and children?

All of the Indian matrimonial statutes lay down jurisdictional rules.

For jurisdiction, two matters require attention:

- the place at which the petition or suit in a matrimonial cause is filed; and
- the court in which the petition or suit in a matrimonial cause should be filed.

In a matrimonial case, the jurisdiction of the court depends on the domicile of the parties, the place of solemnisation of marriage, the marital residence and the residence of the respondent, or, in cases where the respondent resides outside India, where the petitioner resides. Where a number of courts have jurisdiction, a party can choose one of them.

The normal considerations applicable in cases where the existence of jurisdiction in a court is in question are generally those which help to resolve the doubt in favour of the existence of jurisdiction, rather than its absence. The same is because of the principle that it is the duty of the courts to grant relief sought and not lightly abdicate the jurisdiction vested by the law.

Under the Hindu Marriage Act 1955 and the Special Marriage Act 1954, jurisdictional requirements are the same. A divorce petition may be presented to the district court within the local limits of whose original civil jurisdiction:

- the marriage was solemnised;
- the respondent, at the time of the presentation of the petition, resides;
- the parties to the marriage last resided together;
- in case the wife is the petitioner, where she is residing on the date of presentation of the petition;

- the petitioner is residing at the time of the presentation of the petition, in a case where the respondent is, at that time, residing outside the territories to which this Act extends, or has not been heard of as being alive for a period of seven years or more by those persons who would naturally have heard of him/her if he/she were alive.

The applicability of the Special Marriage Act is not merely restricted to Indians. The parties need not be domiciled in India to solemnise their marriage under the Special Marriage Act.

Under the Indian Divorce Act 1869, a petition in a matrimonial cause may be presented in the court of the district judge within the local limits of whose ordinary jurisdiction:

- the husband and wife reside; or
- where the husband and wife last resided together.

3. DOMICILE AND HABITUAL RESIDENCE

3.1 Explain the concepts of domicile and habitual residence as they apply to the jurisdiction in relation to divorce, the finances and children

Domicile denotes the place in which a man has voluntarily fixed the habitation of himself and his family, not for a special or temporary purpose, but with the intention of making a permanent home until some unexpected event shall occur to induce him to adopt some other permanent home. Domicile, as recognised in India, is of two types:

- domicile by origin;
- domicile acquired by choice.

Every person is assumed to have a domicile. An individual is considered to have acquired the domicile of the country they are born in by virtue of their birth. Such domicile is called domicile of birth.

A person receives a domicile of origin at birth, which remains their domicile until and unless they acquire a new domicile. Domicile of choice is that which the individual has elected and chosen for him- or herself to displace the domicile previously obtained.

The Indian courts follow the concept of domicile as laid down in common law. Some of the general rules in respect of domicile are:

- no person can be without a domicile;
- a person cannot choose to be without a domicile, even though they can choose to change their domicile. Every independent person must have a domicile, either of origin or of choice. Every dependent person must also have a domicile, either that of the person on whom they are dependent or that otherwise attributed by law; and
- no person can, at the same time and for the same purpose, have more than one domicile.

In *Central Bank of India Ltd v Ram Narain* AIR 1955 SC 36, the Apex Court acknowledged the concept of domicile as established under English law and held that the two constituent elements that are necessary by English law for the existence of domicile are a residence of a particular kind and an intention of a particular kind.

It has been held that there must be the *factum* and there must be the *animus*. The residence need not be continuous but it must be indefinite and not purely fleeting. The intention must be a present intention to reside forever in the country where the residence has been taken up.

As held in *Kedar Pandey v Narain Bikram Sah* [1965] 3 SCR 793, the only intention required for proof of a change of domicile is an intention of permanent residence. In other words, what is required to be established is that the person who is alleged to have changed their domicile of origin has voluntarily fixed the habitation of him- or herself and their family in the new country, not for a mere special or temporary purpose, but with a present intention of making it their permanent home.

The test for establishing change of domicile as held in *Louis De Raedt v UOI and Ors.* (1991) 3 SCC 554, is that a person acquires a new domicile when they settle in a new country with the intention of making their permanent home in the country of residence and of continuing to reside there permanently.

Section 1(2) Hindu Marriage Act 1955 provides that 'the Act extends to the whole of India, except the State of Jammu and Kashmir, and applies also to Hindus domiciled in the territories to which this Act extends who are outside the said territories'. The Hindu Marriage Act is applicable to persons who are not residing in India but continue to be domiciled in India.

The Bombay High Court in its recent judgment, *Ms. Kashmira Kale v Mr. Kishore Kumar Mohan Kale* Writ Petition No.1242 of 2010, held that domicile in India is a necessary requirement for the application of matrimonial statutes in India. Where the parties are domiciled in a country other than India, the Hindu Marriage Act 1955 cannot apply to them.

In India the concept of habitual residence is not defined but it is recognised by Indian courts. However, statutes require residence as a ground of jurisdiction.

In *Smt. Satya v Teja Singh* [1975] 2 SCR 1971, the Supreme Court held that residence, for the purposes of application of Indian matrimonial statutes, does not mean a temporary residence but a habitual residence or a residence which is also intended to be permanent for the future.

The concept of residence is of importance in India as the courts to which a petition under the matrimonial statutes can be presented include:

- the place where the parties to the petition last resided; or
- the place where the respondent, or the petitioner if she is the wife, resides.

Divorce

The law relating to the concepts of domicile and habitual residence as they apply to the jurisdiction in relation to divorce has been unsettled until now, although in the landmark judgment of *Y. Narasimha Rao and Ors. v Y. Venkata Lakshmi and Ors.* (1991) 3 SCC 451, it was held that marriages which take place in India can only be dissolved under either the customary or the statutory law in force in this country. Hence, the only law that can be applicable to the matrimonial disputes is the one under which the parties are married, and no other law.

The confusion occurs where the parties are permanently settled abroad and come to India for the sole purpose of solemnisation of marriage. When such parties enter into matrimonial disputes, the question which arises is whether the divorce petition would be maintainable in India if the parties are not domiciled in India. The Supreme Court of India has not adjudicated on the issue as yet, but the cogent proposition which emerges from the views of the different high courts is one held by the Bombay High Court as in *Ms. Kashmira Kale v Mr. Kishore Kumar Mohan Kale* Writ Petition No.1242 of 2010, where it was held that domicile in India is a necessary requirement for the application of matrimonial statutes in India. Where the parties are domiciled in a country other than India, the Hindu Marriage Act 1955 cannot apply to them. The same is not confirmed by the Supreme Court of India and is not binding on the other High Courts. For the purposes of jurisdiction, the Indian domicile of one of the parties is sufficient to confer jurisdiction on the Indian Court.

Children

In matters of child custody, the best interest and welfare of the child is of primary importance. The issues regarding child custody are adjudicated by the courts in whose jurisdiction the child resides and who has the closest contact with the child. The Indian courts can decide on the issue of the custody of a child who is a foreign citizen only if the child is within the territorial jurisdiction of Indian courts.

The Supreme Court of India in *Ruchi Majoo vs Sanjeev Majoo* (AIR 2011 SC 1952) has held that simply because a foreign court has taken a particular view on any aspect concerning the welfare of the minor, it is not enough for the courts in this country to shut out an independent consideration of the matter. Objectivity, and not abject surrender, is the mantra in such cases.

The Supreme Court held since the interest and welfare of the child was of primary concern, a competent court in India was fully entitled and, indeed, duty-bound to examine the matter independently, taking the foreign judgment, if any, only as an input for its final adjudication. The Apex Court allowed the trial court to hear the mother's application for custody of the child.

4. CONFLICT OF LAW/APPLICABLE LAW TO BE APPLIED

4.1 What happens when one party applies to stay proceedings in favour of a foreign jurisdiction? What factors will the local court take into account when determining forum issues?

A party can apply to stay proceedings in a foreign jurisdiction by way of seeking an injunction against the other party from proceeding in any other jurisdiction. The same can be applied under Order 39 (3) of the Code for Civil Procedure.

In *Harmeeta Singh v Rajat Taneja* 102 (2003) DLT 822, the parties were married in New Delhi in accordance with Hindu religious ceremonies. The parties departed for the USA soon after their marriage. Subsequently, the wife was compelled to leave the matrimonial home and the husband filed for divorce in the courts in the USA. The Delhi High Court observed that matrimonial disputes between estranged spouses are the most bitterly fought litigation and raise a myriad of awkward questions. Often, the jurisdiction of more than one court can be invoked where the husband and wife have started residing in different territories, either nationally or internationally. It must then be decided which court should be best suited and, therefore, competent to exercise jurisdiction. The endeavour of judges in every corner of the world should be to look only towards alleviating the human suffering that is endemic in every matrimonial dispute, since persons who may otherwise be willing to forgo their rights and go a long way to arrive at a compromise in other litigation, would fight to the very end. The Delhi High Court in this case, restrained the defendant (husband) from continuing with the proceedings in the United States of America.

In *Nimitt Rai Tiwari v Nishma Ramesh Karia,* CS (OS) 304/2010, the marriage between the parties was solemnised in India and the parties resided within the territory of India after the solemnisation of their marriage. Thereafter disharmony brewed between the parties and the wife left India to reside in Kenya with her parents. Subsequently the defendant wife filed a case for divorce in Kenya. The Honourable High Court of Delhi restrained the wife from continuing with the divorce case in the foreign country on the ground that the cause of action had arisen within the territory of India and if the husband was to pursue the case in Kenya, grave prejudice would be caused to him.

In *Magotteaux Industries Pvt. Ltd. and Ors v AIA Engineering Ltd.* 155 (2008) DLT 73, the Delhi High Court held that the powers vested in the court for granting anti-suit injunction should be used sparingly. The principle behind granting an anti-suit injunction sparingly is that the same is not merely inconvenient to the parties to the proceedings but also amounts to interference with the process of administration of justice of the foreign court.

The Honourable Supreme Court of India laid down the principles governing anti-suit injunctions in *Modi Entertainment Network and Anr. v W.S.G. Cricket PTE. Ltd* (2003) 1SCR 480.

In exercising discretion to grant an anti-suit injunction, the court must be satisfied of the following aspects:

- the defendant, against whom injunction is sought, is amenable to the personal jurisdiction of the court;
- if the injunction is declined, the ends of justice will be defeated and injustice will be perpetuated;
- the principle of comity (respect for the court in which the commencement or continuance of an action/proceeding is sought to be restrained) must be borne in mind;
- in cases of multiple forums, the court will consider the appropriate forum to be *forum conveniens,* having regard to the convenience of the parties, and may grant an anti-suit injunction in regard to proceedings which are oppressive or vexations or in a *forum non conveniens.*

B. PRE- AND POST-NUPTIAL AGREEMENTS

5. VALIDITY OF PRE- AND POST-NUPTIAL AGREEMENTS

5.1 To what extent are pre- and post-nups binding within the jurisdiction? Could you provide a brief discussion of the most significant recent case law on this issue?

The proposition of law concerning pre- and post-nuptial agreement is still controversial and not fully evolved. In India, marriages are not considered a civil contract but a sacred alliance that cannot be broken or dissolved, except with regard to the strict provisions of the personal laws and civil law.

The concept of a post-nuptial agreement has not been defined in any of the personal laws, such as the Hindu Marriage Act 1955, the Parsi Marriage Act 1936, the Christian Marriage Act 1872 or the Special Marriage Act 1954.

In India, a pre- and post-nuptial agreement is considered to fall into the category of a contract. Therefore, a legally binding pre-nuptial or post-nuptial agreement would have to satisfy the conditions of a valid contract under the Indian Contract Act 1872. One of the conditions that a valid contract is required to fulfil is that it should not be against public policy. Where an agreement envisages the breakdown of a marriage, it may not be considered a valid contract, being against public policy.

However, where the marriage has broken down and the parties enter into an agreement in order to amicably settle family issues, such agreements are upheld by the courts which will consider such agreements.

C. DIVORCE, NULLITY AND JUDICIAL SEPARATION

6. RECOGNITION OF FOREIGN MARRIAGES/DIVORCES

6.1 Summarise the position in your jurisdiction

Foreign marriages and divorces are given recognition in India as long as they satisfy the provisions of section 13 of the Civil Procedure Code.

Section 13 provides that a foreign judgment shall be conclusive as to any matter thereby directly adjudicated upon between the same parties or between parties under whom they or any of them claim litigating under the same title except:

- where it has not been pronounced by a court of competent jurisdiction;
- where it has not been given on the merits of the case;
- where it appears on the face of the proceedings to be founded on an incorrect view of international law or a refusal to recognise the law of India in cases in which such law is applicable;
- where the proceedings in which the judgment was obtained are opposed to natural justice;
- where it has been obtained by fraud; or
- where it sustains a claim founded on a breach of any law in force in India.

The Supreme Court in *Y.Narasimha Rao and Ors. v Y. Venkata Lakshmi and Ors.* (1991) 3 SCC 451 held that Indian courts would not recognise a decree of divorce passed by courts of foreign countries if the petition of divorce is not based on the substantive and jurisdictional grounds provided for divorce under the Hindu Marriage Act, 1955 and one of the nine grounds of divorce which are required to be satisfied.

The Supreme Court held that, where a party only technically satisfied the requirement of residence in a foreign country with only the purpose of obtaining the divorce and the party is neither domiciled in that state nor has an intention to make it their home, and that there is no substantial connection with the forum, then the decree of divorce passed by the court of such a foreign country will not be recognised by the Indian courts.

In *Smt. Satya v Teja Singh* [1975] 2 SCR 1971, the Supreme Court derecognised the decree of divorce of the foreign country on the ground that one party obtained the divorce decree by fraud on the foreign court by representing incorrect jurisdictional facts. The Apex Court held that 'residence' does not mean a temporary residence for the purpose of obtaining a divorce, but habitual residence or residence which is intended to be permanent for future as well.

In *Y. Narasimha Rao and Ors. v Y. Venkata Lakshmi and Ors.* (1991) 3 SCC 451, it is held that the relevant provisions of section 13 of the CPC are capable of being interpreted to secure the required certainty in the sphere of this branch of law in conforming with public policy, justice, equity and good conscience, and the rules so evolved will protect the sanctity of the institution of marriage and the unity of family, which are the cornerstones of our society.

It is held that the marriages which take place in India can only be dissolved under either the customary or the statutory law in force in this country. Hence, the only law that can be applicable to the matrimonial disputes is the one under which the parties are married, and no other law. When, therefore, a foreign judgment is founded on a jurisdiction or on ground not recognised by such law, it is a judgment which is in defiance of the law. Hence, it is not conclusive of the matters adjudicated therein and therefore, unenforceable in this country. For the same reason, such a judgment will also be unenforceable under clause (f) of Section 13, since such a judgment would obviously be in breach of the matrimonial law in force in this country.

It has been held by the Supreme Court that *'the jurisdiction assumed by the foreign court as well as the grounds on which the relief is granted, must be in accordance with the matrimonial law under which the parties are married. The exceptions to this rule may be:*

- *where the matrimonial action is filed in the forum where the respondent is domiciled or habitually and permanently resides, and the relief is granted on a ground available in the matrimonial law under which the parties are married;*
- *where the respondent voluntarily and effectively submits to the jurisdiction of the forum as discussed above and contests the claim, which is based on a ground available under the matrimonial law under which the parties are married;*
- *where the respondent consents to the granting of relief, although the jurisdiction of the forum is not in accordance with the provisions of the matrimonial law of the parties'.*

7. DIVORCE

7.1 Explain the grounds for divorce within the jurisdiction (please also deal with nullity and judicial separation if appropriate)

Judicial separation

With the exception of Muslim law, all other matrimonial statutes contain a provision for judicial separation, although provision is not identical in all statutes. Under Muslim law there is nothing like a decree of judicial separation.

Under the Hindu Marriage Act 1955, a wife or husband can file for judicial separation under section 10 on any one of the fault grounds for divorce stated in section 13 (1), and the wife can sue for judicial separation on any one of the additional fault grounds laid down in section 13 (2).

Under the Special Marriage Act 1954, the husband and wife may file for judicial separation under section 23 on any of the grounds specified in section 27 (other than the grounds specified in clause (I) and (j) thereof on which a petition for divorce might have been presented or on the ground of failure to comply with a decree for restitution of conjugal rights.

Under the Divorce Act 1869, grounds on which judicial separation decree may be obtained are adultery, cruelty and two years' desertion.

Nullity

Section 5 of the Hindu Marriage Act 1955, provides that a marriage may be solemnised between any two Hindus if the following conditions are fulfilled:

- neither party has a spouse living at the time of the marriage;
- neither party is mentally impaired or insane at the time of the marriage;
- the bridegroom is 18 years or over and the bride 15 years or over at the time of the marriage;
- the parties are not within the degrees of prohibited relationship, unless the custom or usage governing each of them permits of a marriage between the two;
- the parties are not *sapindas* ie, lineal ascendants of each other or have a common lineal ascendant as far as third generation (inclusive) in the line of ascent through the mother, and the fifth (inclusive) in the line of ascent through the father, unless the custom or use governing each of them permits a marriage between the two; and
- where the bride is under the age of 18 years, the consent of her guardian in marriage, if any, has been obtained for the marriage.

It is only the violation of prohibition of bigamy and marriage within a prohibited relationship that render the marriage void. Being under age does not render the marriage void or voidable. Insanity renders a marriage voidable.

Under the Special Marriage Act 1954 and the Hindu Marriage Act 1955, distinction between a void and voidable marriage is made and separate grounds of both are laid down. However, under the Indian Divorce Act 1869, only the grounds of void marriages are laid down. No grounds of voidable marriage are provided. The same is true of the Parsi Marriage and Divorce Act 1936, however, some of the traditional grounds of voidable marriages have been made grounds of divorce.

Muslim law recognises only void marriages known as *'batil'* marriages. There is no concept of voidable marriage. Muslim law has a unique concept of irregular marriage called *'fasid'* marriage.

A void marriage means no marriage. It is a marriage which does not exist from its beginning. In respect of void marriage, no decree of court is necessary. Even when the court passes a decree, it merely declares it null and void. It is not the decree of the court which renders such a marriage void, it is an existing fact that the marriage is void and the court merely makes a judicial declaration on that fact.

A voidable marriage is a perfectly valid marriage so long as it is not avoided. A voidable marriage can be avoided only on the petition of one of the parties to the marriage. If one of the parties does not petition for annulment of marriage, the marriage will remain valid. So long as a voidable marriage is not avoided, all legal consequences of a valid marriage flow from it.

Divorce

Dissolution of marriage under all Indian personal laws is based on guilt or fault theory of divorce. Under the Hindu Marriage Act 1955, the Special Marriage Act 1954 and the Parsi Marriage and Divorce Act 1936, there is a provision for divorce by mutual consent. However, under the Dissolution of Muslim Marriage Act 1939, where the wife can alone sue for divorce, the grounds are all fault grounds. Muslim law also recognises divorce by mutual consent.

Fault theory

Hindu law – section 13 of the Hindu Marriage Act 1955 recognises nine fault grounds of divorce, which are available to both the parties, and four additional fault grounds are available to the wife alone under section 13 (2).

Section 13 of the Hindu Marriage Act, 1955 states that any marriage solemnised, whether before or after the commencement of this Act, may, on a petition presented by either the husband or the wife, be dissolved by a decree of divorce on the ground that the other party:

- is living in adultery;
- has ceased to be a Hindu by conversion to another religion;
- has been incurably of unsound mind for a continuous period of not less than three years immediately preceding the presentation of the petition;
- has, for a period of not less than three years immediately preceding the presentation of the petition, been suffering from a virulent and incurable form of leprosy;
- had, for a period of not less than three years immediately preceding the presentation of the petition, been suffering from venereal disease in a communicable form;
- has renounced the world by entering any religious order;
- has not been heard of as being alive for a period of seven years or more by those persons who would naturally have heard of them, had that party been alive;
- has not resumed cohabitation for a period of two years or more after the

passing of a decree for judicial separation against that party;
- has failed to comply with a decree for restitution of conjugal rights for a period of two years or more after the passing of the decree.

Section 27 (1) of the Special Marriage Act 1954 contains 10 fault grounds of divorce on which either spouse can seek divorce. Section 27 (1A) contains two fault grounds on which the wife alone can seek dissolution of marriage.

Section 2 of the Dissolution of Muslim Marriages Act 1939 contains nine fault grounds on which the wife alone can sue.

For Christians, subsection 10 of the Indian Divorce Act 1869 contains grounds of divorce.

The Parsi Marriage and Divorce Act 1936 contains 10 fault grounds of divorce on which either spouse may seek divorce.

Under the Indian personal laws, divorce by mutual consent is recognised under the Hindu Marriage Act 1955, the Special Marriage Act 1954, the Parsi Marriage and Divorce Act 1939, the Dissolution of Muslim Marriage Act 1939, and now also under Divorce Act 1869.

The only requirement for divorce by mutual consent is that the parties should have been living separately for a period of one year or more. In order to provide a cooling-off period so that the parties can reconsider their decision to separate, the following procedure has been stipulated:

- the parties must have been separated for a period of one year;
- the first motion is filed and presented;
- after six months and before 18 months, the parties will have to present the second motion;
- statements of the parties will be recorded by the court and only then will the decree of divorce will be granted.

The Supreme Court of India held in *Anil Kumar Jain v Maya Jain* (2009)10SCC415 that the language of section 13 B of the Hindu Marriage Act 1955 is very specific in which it intends that, on a motion presented by both of the parties made no earlier than six months after the date of presentation of the petition and not later than 18 months after the said date, and if the petition is not withdrawn in the meantime, the court shall, on being satisfied after hearing the parties and after making such inquiry as it thinks fit, pass a decree of divorce declaring the marriage to be dissolved with effect from the date of the decree. It is held that only the Supreme Court can waive the mandatory period of six months which the parties need to observe before decree of divorce by mutual consent can be granted to the divorcing parties. The said period of six months is given to the parties so that they can reconcile and get back together if possible.

8. FINANCES/CAPITAL, PROPERTY

8.1 What powers does the court have to allocate financial resources and property on the breakdown of marriage?

Matrimonial laws are singularly lacking in provisions relating to the settlement of properties of the spouses and the matrimonial home. Section 27 of the Hindu Marriage Act 1955 provides only for the settlement of property presented jointly to the husband and wife at or about the time of marriage. It does not talk about the settlement of the property of the spouse owned by them, jointly or separately. This is because there is no concept of matrimonial property in India, thus, there is no division of assets.

However, maintenance is available to the wife as a statutory right upon the breakdown of marriage. The courts have very widely interpreted the term 'maintenance' in order to allocate financial resources and property to wife on the breakdown of the marriage. The courts have powers under the respective personal laws, as well as under section 125 of the Criminal Procedure Code and section 20 of the Protection of Women from Domestic Violence Act 2005.

8.2 Explain and illustrate with reference to recent cases the court's thinking on division of assets.

Since there is no concept of matrimonial property, there is, therefore, no concept of division of assets. However, the concept of 'maintenance' has been widely interpreted by the Indian courts. The husband is required to provide/maintain the wife in accordance with the same status that the wife enjoyed during the subsistence of marriage.

9. FINANCES/MAINTENANCE

9.1 Explain the operation of maintenance for spouses on an ongoing basis after the breakdown of marriage

Maintenance is available as a statutory right by way of independent relief, both under civil and criminal laws, and also as an ancillary relief.

Maintenance to Hindus is provided for under the Hindu Marriage Act 1955, section 24 (maintenance pending suit) and section 25 (permanent alimony and maintenance) and the Hindu Adoptions and Maintenance Act 1956, section 18.

With regard to Muslims, the wife is entitled to maintenance from her husband as provided under section 3 of the Muslim Women (Protection of Rights on Divorce) Act 1989, after the breakdown of the marriage. Section 3 provides that a divorced woman shall be entitled to:

- a reasonable and fair provision and maintenance to be made and paid to her within the period of *iddat* by her former husband;
- where she maintains the children born to her before or after her divorce, a reasonable provision and maintenance to be made and paid by her former husband for a period of two years from the respective dates of birth of such children;
- an amount equal to the sum of *mahr* or dower agreed to be paid to her at the time of her marriage or at any time thereafter according to Muslim law;
- all the properties given to her before or at the time of marriage or after the marriage by her relatives, friends, husband and any relatives of the husband or his friends.

With regard to Christians, section 36 of the Indian Christian Marriage Act 1872 regarding maintenance pending suit, provides that alimony pending the suit of divorce shall in no case exceed one-fifth of the husband's average net income for the three years preceding the date of the order, and shall continue, until the decree for dissolution of marriage or of nullity of marriage, is made absolute or is confirmed.

Section 37, regarding permanent maintenance, states that the court shall order the husband to secure to the wife such gross sum of money, or such annual sum of money, for any term not exceeding her own life, to the satisfaction of the court, after holding in consideration:

- the wife's fortune (if any);
- the ability of the husband to pay; and
- the conduct of the parties.

There is a provision for interim and permanent maintenance. The right to claim maintenance extends till remarriage.

A controversy arose some time back when there was dispute as to the time period for which a Muslim husband is obligated to pay maintenance to his divorced wife. The Muslim Women (Protection of Rights on Divorce) Act 1989 was enacted to codify and regulate the obligations of the Muslim husband to pay maintenance to the divorced wife. However a controversy arose as to the time period for which a muslim husband is obligated to pay maintenance to the divorced wife. The Supreme Court in the judgment of *Danial Laitifi v Union of India* AIR 2001 SC 3958, held that:

- a Muslim husband is liable to make reasonable and fair provision for the future of the divorced wife which obviously includes her maintenance as well. Such a reasonable and fair provision extending beyond the *iddat* period must be made by the husband within the *iddat* period in terms of section 3(1) (a) of the Muslim Women (Protection of Rights on Divorce) Act 1989;
- the liability of a Muslim husband to his divorced wife arising under section 3(1) (a) of the Act to pay maintenance is not confined to the *iddat* period;
- a divorced Muslim woman who has not remarried and who is not able to maintain herself after the *iddat* period can proceed as provided under section 4 of the Muslim Women (Protection of Rights on Divorce) Act 1989 against her relatives, who are liable to maintain her in proportion to the properties which they inherit on her death, according to Muslim law, including her children and parents. If any of the relatives are unable to pay maintenance, the magistrate may direct the State Wakf Board, established under the Act, to pay such maintenance.

9.2 Is it common for maintenance to be awarded?

Maintenance is commonly awarded in favour of the wife.

9.3 Explain and illustrate with reference to recent cases the court's thinking on maintenance

The concept of maintenance has evolved in leaps and bounds over the years. Prior to this, low maintenance was being awarded by the Indian courts and the concept was more of survival rather than right to live in the same lifestyle as the husband. However, with changing times, the Indian courts have been awarding maintenance in accordance with the status and lifestyle of the parties.

In *Vimalben Ajitbhai Patel v Vatslabeen Ashokbhai Patel and Ors.* (2008) 4 SCC 649, the Supreme Court of India held that it is the right of the wife to be maintained by the husband.

Although no set formula has been laid down in the statute for determining the quantum of maintenance, the Supreme Court of India in *Jasbir Kaur Sehgal v District Judge, Dehradun & Ors.* (1997) 7 SCC 7, held that maintenance should be in accordance with the lifestyle of the parties.

The right to residence has also been recognised under the Protection of Women from Domestic Violence Act 2005 and by the Supreme Court in *S.R. Batra v Taruna Batra* (2007) 3 SCC169.

The factors which are considered for deciding maintenance include, but are not limited to, the following:

- status of the parties;
- reasonable wants of the applicant;
- the independent income and property of the applicant;
- the number of persons the non-applicant has to maintain;
- the amount required to provide the applicant with a lifestyle similar to that enjoyed during the marriage;
- non-applicant's liabilities, if any;
- provision for food, clothing, shelter, education, medical attendance and treatment of the applicant;
- payment capacity of the non-applicant.

Some discretion cannot be ruled out when estimating the income of the non-applicant if all sources or correct sources are not disclosed.

10. CHILD MAINTENANCE

10.1 On what basis is child maintenance calculated within the jurisdiction?

Section 125 Cr.P.C provides that where any person having sufficient means neglects or refuses to maintain his legitimate or illegitimate minor child, whether married or not, or neglects or refuses to maintain his legitimate or illegitimate child (not being a married daughter) who has attained majority, where such child is, by reason of any physical or mental abnormality or injury unable to maintain itself, may be ordered to make a monthly allowance for the maintenance of his child by a magistrate.

Under the Hindu Adoptions and Maintenance Act 1956, a Hindu father or a Hindu mother is under a statutory obligation to provide maintenance to their children. The obligation to maintain the children is to be shared equally by the mother and father. However, with the social set up in India, the father is called upon to primarily maintain the children as he is still considered to be the primary breadwinner for the family. In a situation where the father has no means or insufficient means, the mother is under the obligation to provide for maintenance.

In *State of Haryana & Ors. v Smt. Santra* (2000) 5 SCC182, the Supreme Court held that maintenance would obviously include provision for food, clothing, residence, education of the children and medical attendance or treatment. The obligation to maintain the children, besides being statutory in nature, is also personal in the sense that it arises from the very existence of the relationship between parent and the child. The obligation is absolute in terms and does not depend on the means of the father or the mother.

It is has been held that, in determining the amount of maintenance to be awarded to children, regard shall be had to the position and status of the parties and the reasonable wants of the child.

Ordinarily, an order of maintenance would end when the child attains the age of majority, but if the welfare of the child requires it, it may be continued beyond it, particularly when the child is engaged in higher education.

In *Jagdish Jugtawat v Manjulata and Ors.* (2002) 5SCC422 it was held that a female child has a right to be maintained by her parents even after she attains majority.

Under the Mohammedan law, a father is bound to maintain his sons until they have attained the age of puberty. He is also bound to maintain his daughters until they are married.

11. RECIPROCAL ENFORCEMENT OF FINANCIAL ORDERS

11.1 Summarise the position in your jurisdiction

Foreign orders/decrees/judgments cannot be directly executed in India unless they are the judgments of courts in what are called 'reciprocating territories'. In all other cases, the only mode of giving effect to a foreign judgment is to file a suit on the judgment in an appropriate Indian court, which has to be tested by section 13 of the CPC.

Section 44 A of the CPC provides for the execution of decrees passed by courts in a reciprocating territory, when the following conditions are satisfied:

- where a certified copy of decree of any of the superior courts of any reciprocating territory has been filed in a district court, the decree may be executed in India as if it had been passed by the district court;
- together with the certified copy of the decree, a certificate shall be filed from such superior court stating the extent, if any, to which the decree has been satisfied or adjusted and such certificate shall, for the purposes of proceedings under this section, be conclusive proof of the extent of such satisfaction or adjustment; and
- the provisions of section 47 shall, as from the filing of the certified copy of the decree, apply to the proceedings of a district court executing a decree under this section, and the district court shall refuse execution of any such decree, if it is shown to the satisfaction of the court that the decree falls within any of the exceptions specified in clauses (a) to (f) of section 13.

Explanation 1 – 'reciprocating territory' means any country or territory outside India which the central government may, by notification in the official *Gazette*, declare to be a reciprocating territory for the purposes of this section; and 'superior courts', with reference to any such territory, means such courts as may be specified in the said notification.

Explanation 2 – 'Decree', with reference to a superior court, means any decree or judgment of such court under which a sum of money is payable, (not being a sum payable in respect of taxes or other charges of a like nature or in respect to a fine or other penalty) but shall in no case include an arbitration award, even if such an award is enforceable as a decree or judgment.

12. FINANCIAL RELIEF AFTER FOREIGN DIVORCE PROCEEDINGS

12.1 What powers are available to make orders following a foreign divorce?

There do not appear to be any decisions on the subject of the right of an Indian court to make orders following a foreign order of divorce or annulment of marriage. However, in our opinion, where a particular relief is available to a party under the matrimonial statute, and the same has been agitated before the foreign court, the party would not have a right to re-agitate the issue before the Indian court. However if the issue of financial orders has not been decided by a foreign court, it may be agitated in appropriate proceedings in India.

D. CHILDREN

13. CUSTODY/PARENTAL RESPONSIBILITY

13.1 Briefly explain the legal position in relation to custody/parental responsibility following the breakdown of a relationship or marriage

There is no standard formula which is applied in relation to custody/ parental responsibility following the breakdown of a relationship or marriage. The most important principle which governs the decisions of the courts in relation to children is the best interest and welfare of the child.

Generally speaking, the mother has a preferential right to custody of infants, children below the age of five years and female children. However, where the court upon substantial evidence reaches the conclusion that the mother cannot secure the best interest and welfare of the child, the primary custody of infants can be entrusted to fathers.

13.2 Briefly explain the legal position in relation to access/contact/ visitation following the breakdown of a relationship or marriage

The courts in India are very favourable to permitting access/contact/ visitation following the breakdown of a relationship or marriage to the parent who does not have custody of the child. It is settled law that a child should not miss out on the love and affection of both the parents as a result of breakdown of marriage. Depending on the facts and circumstances of the case, the courts may permit, weekly, fortnightly or overnight visitation. The court may also permit sharing of the holidays between the parents.

14. INTERNATIONAL ABDUCTION

14.1 Summarise the position in your jurisdiction

In recent times, India has witnessed an alarming number of cases involving trans-border child abduction.

India, not being a signatory to the Hague Convention on the Civil Aspects of International Child Abduction (1980), is not under an obligation to return the child to the country from which the child had been wrongfully removed. However, recently the Supreme Court of India has held that, where children have been wrongfully removed from the jurisdiction of foreign countries to which they belong, the principle of comity of nations would apply and the parties should be sent back to the jurisdiction of the court who had the most intimate contact and the courts in that country should conclusively adjudicate the issue of custody.

The law laid down by the Apex Court of India has changed over the course of time and the same can be witnessed from the judgments pronounced by it. One of the earliest ones includes *Surinder Kaur Sandhu v Harbax Singh Sandhu* (AIR 1984 SC 1224), in which the Supreme Court held that the modern theory of conflict of laws recognises and, in any event, prefers the jurisdiction of the state which has the most intimate contact with the issues arising in the case. The Supreme Court held that jurisdiction is not attracted by the operation or creation of fortuitous circumstances such as the circumstance as to where the child, whose custody is in issue, is brought or for the time being lodged. To allow the assumption of jurisdiction by another state in such circumstances will only result in encouraging forum-shopping. Ordinarily jurisdiction must follow on functional lines. For example, that in matters relating to matrimony and custody, the law of that place must govern which has the closest concern with the well-being of the spouses and the welfare of the offspring of the marriage.

In *Elizabeth Dinshaw v Arvand M. Dinshaw & Anr.* (1987) 1 SCC 42, the Supreme Court of India held that, whenever a question arises before a court pertaining to the custody of a minor child, the matter is to be decided not on considerations of the legal rights of the parties but on the sole and predominant criterion of what would serve best the interest and welfare of the minor.

Dr. V. Ravi Chandran v Union of India & Ors. [2009(14) SCALE 27] is a groundbreaking case fought by the author, where mother and father lived in USA and litigated in the US court leading to a consent order regarding their child. Subsequently the mother came to India with the child in violation of US court order and was untraceable. In this case, the Supreme Court had directed the Central Bureau of Investigation (CBI) to find the child as the mother had been fleeing from the course of justice.

The Supreme Court of India held that the US court was the only competent court to adjudicate any disputes relating to the child and, if the mother had any grievance, she could seek modification of the consent order in the US court.

Despite the explicit orders by the Supreme Court that if the parties did not return to the jurisdiction of the US courts within stipulated time to settle their disputes regarding child custody, the child will be handed over to the petitioner father, the saga continued. The mother sought extension of time to return to the jurisdiction of US courts for obtaining her visa but thereafter was untraceable. The Honourable Supreme Court again directed the CBI to trace the child. This time after the child was traced, the Supreme Court directed the CBI to hand over the child to the father. The child was recovered by CBI in Chennai and handed over to the father and they returned to the jurisdiction of US courts.

In *Shilpa Aggarwal v Aviral Mittal* 2009(14) SCALE 511, both the parties, who were permanent residents of the UK, came to India for a visit with their three-year-old daughter. The wife refused to return to her matrimonial home in the UK with the daughter. The husband filed for the custody of his daughter. The Supreme Court of India held that matters of child custody should be adjudicated by the courts which had the most intimate contact with the issue in question. The Supreme Court placed reliance on the principle of comity of courts and the best interest of the child and directed that the final decision with regard to the custody of the child would be taken by the English courts where both the parents permanently resided.

While dealing with a case of custody of a child removed by a parent from one country to another in contravention of the orders of the court where the parties had set up their matrimonial home, it has been held that the court in the country to which child has been removed must first consider the question of whether the court could conduct an elaborate enquiry on the question of custody or, by dealing with the matter, summarily order a parent to return custody of the child to the country from which the child was removed and that all aspects relating to child's welfare be investigated in a court in their own country.

Recently in *Ruchi Majoo vs. Sanjeev Majoo* (2011) 6SCC 479, the Supreme Court has clarified that the duty of a court exercising its *Parens Patraie* jurisdiction in cases involving custody of minor children is all the more onerous. Welfare of the minor in such cases being the paramount consideration, the Supreme Court has held that simply because a foreign court has taken a particular view on any aspect concerning the welfare of the minor that is not enough for the courts in India to shut out an independent consideration of the matter. Objectivity and not abject surrender is the mantra in such cases. That does not, however, mean that the order passed by a foreign court is not even a factor to be kept in view. But it is one thing to consider the foreign judgment to be conclusive and another to treat it as a factor or consideration that would go into the making of a final decision.

15. LEAVE TO REMOVE/APPLICATIONS TO TAKE A CHILD OUT OF THE JURISDICTION

15.1 Summarise the position in your jurisdiction

In India both of the parents are assumed to be the natural custodians of their child. Therefore, there is no bar against a parent removing the child from the jurisdiction against the wishes of the other parent. Only in the case where the court has passed an order granting one parent the exclusive custody of the child, or there is a restraining order of the court, or the matter adjudicating child custody is pending in the court of law, would it be necessary for a parent to seek permission of the court to remove the child from the jurisdiction.

It is important to mention that in India, matters relating to family and custody are considered to be of a civil nature. Therefore, even in a case of child abduction by one parent, the matter is considered to be of a civil nature and, unlike in Western countries, arrest warrants are not issued.

In cases of child abduction, the other parent has remedy in the form of filing a writ of *habeas corpus* or by seeking relief of restoration under the Guardians and Wards Act 1890.

15.2 Under what circumstances may a parent apply to remove their child from the jurisdiction against the wishes of the other parent?

Ordinarily, a parent does not require permission of the court to remove a child to a place they like, unless:

- such action is objected to by the other parent;
- there is a restraining order of the court; or
- the child is a ward of the court.

E. SURROGACY AND ADOPTION

16. VALIDITY OF SURROGACY AGREEMENTS

16.1Briefly summarise the position in your jurisdiction

In India, three types of surrogacy are permitted as per law.

- Voluntary and gratuitous surrogacy,
- Paid surrogacy like any commercial transaction according to the agreement between the commissioning couple and the woman who agrees to bear the child,
- altruistic surrogacy, where the surrogate receives no financial reward for bearing or relinquishing the child.

Surrogacy in India is not governed by statutory law. Although the Indian Council of Medical Research (ICMR) has set 'national guidelines' to regulate surrogacy, these are simply guidelines. The said Guidelines were made in 2005 regulating Assisted Reproductive Technology procedures. These guidelines are limited in their scope and although they provide that surrogate mothers must sign a 'contract' with the childless couple, there are no stipulations for an event where the 'contract' is violated and what the rights of a child born from such arrangement would be.

In August 2009 with the objective of further formalising the law on surrogacy, the Law Commission of India submitted the 228th Report on Assisted Reproductive Technology procedures discussing the importance and need for surrogacy, and also the steps taken to control surrogacy arrangements.

With India fast emerging as a hotspot for the rent-a-womb phenomenon, the Union Health Ministry has finalised the Assisted Reproductive Technologies (ART) Regulation Bill 2010, which has been sent to the Law Ministry for its approval. The Union Cabinet will shortly examine the draft

Assisted Reproductive Technology (Regulation) Bill, 2010, and then table it in Parliament.

Floated earlier in 2008, the Bill envisages a national framework for the regulation and supervision of Assisted Reproductive Technology (ART). The new law will protect the rights of children born through surrogacy and preserve the social order where infertility can lead to breakdowns of marriages.

Salient Features and highlights of the ART Bill 2010:

- It legalises commercial surrogacy for single persons, married or unmarried couples.
- When it becomes law, the surrogate mother will have to enter into a legally enforceable surrogacy agreement.
- The Bill details procedures for accreditation and supervision of infertility clinics (and related organisations such as semen banks) handling spermatozoa or oocytes outside of the body, or dealing with gamete donors and surrogacy, ensuring that the legitimate rights of all concerned are protected, with maximum benefit to the infertile couples/ individuals within a recognised framework of ethics and good medical practice.
- The Bill allows only 21 to 35-year-olds to be surrogate mothers and says no woman would act as a surrogate for more than five successful live births in her life, including those of her own children.
- The draft law prohibits In Vitro Fertilization (IVF) clinics from advertising for surrogates on behalf of infertile couples and seeks to create ART Banks to do the advertising for commissioning parents.
- These banks will screen surrogate mothers and donated sperm and oocytes for infections while ART clinics will simply offer ART services.
- The Bill guarantees legal protection to parents, surrogate mothers and children and mandates legally enforceable agreements between the stakeholders. Any violation would be a cognisable offence punishable with imprisonment and fine.
- Foreigners from countries that don't recognise commercial surrogacy will be barred from hiring surrogate mothers in India. 'Foreigners and NRIs can hire surrogacy service only if they give an undertaking that their country permits surrogacy and the child born will get citizenship of the foreign country'.
- It mandates foreigners to hire local guardians to support the surrogate mother in their absence.
- Once the Bill gets the asssent, it will become binding on a surrogate mother to relinquish all her filial rights over the baby. And, the birth certificate of the baby born through surrogacy will bear the name of the individual or individuals who commissioned the surrogacy as parents. The commissioning parents could be a single man or woman, a married couple or an unmarried couple, who are in a live-in relationship.
- No woman can be treated with gametes or embryos derived from the gametes of more than one man or woman during any one treatment cycle. An ART clinic cannot mix semen from two individuals before use.

- Renting of a womb is legal in India but there is no law at present to regulate surrogacy. If Parliament passes the ART Bill, renting a womb by Indian and foreign couples looking for surrogate mothers is expected to become hassle-free.
- The Draft Bill gives homosexual people and single people the legal right to have surrogate babies. It defines a 'couple' as two persons living together and having a sexual relationship.
- A woman in the age-group of 21-35 can become a surrogate mother. She will be allowed five live births, including her own children. She will not be allowed to donate oocytes more than six times in her life.
- In case of a single man or woman, the baby will be his/her legitimate child.
- A child born to an unmarried couple using a surrogate mother and with the consent of both parties shall be the legitimate child of both of them.
- During the gestation period, the couple will bear the surrogate's expenses and give monetary help to her. The couple may enter into an agreement with the surrogate.
- Foreign couples must submit two certificates — one on their country's surrogacy policy and the other stating that the child born to the surrogate mother will get their country's citizenship.
- Foreign couples have to nominate a local guardian who will take care of the surrogate during gestation.
- ART banks, accredited by the government, will maintain a database of prospective surrogates as well as storing semen and eggs and details of the donor.
- State boards will give accreditation to ART banks – private and government. The board will have a registration authority which, in turn, will maintain a list of all In-Vitro Fertilisation (IVF) centres and monitor their functioning.

The Law Commission of India (2009) described ART industry as a 'Rs 25,000-crore pot of gold'. It recommended only altruistic surrogacy arrangements and not commercial ones. But the Draft Bill legalises commercial surrogacy as well. The basis of commercial surrogacy is a surrogacy agreement which demarcates the liabilities and intentions of the parties concerned. The surrogacy agreement is based on free consent and a meeting of the minds of the parties concerned towards a particular outcome, has been held to be valid in India and is interpreted in light of the provisions of the Indian Contract Act, 1872.

The law relating to surrogacy is different in each country, hence the legal consequence of breaching the surrogacy agreement depends on the statutory law and case law prevailing in each individual country.

In the landmark case of *Baby Manji Yamada v Union of India* (2008) 13 SCC 518, the view of Supreme Court was not only pro-surrogacy it was also extremely pro-contract. Baby Manji, a surrogate child of a Japanese couple who were having legal difficulties getting a visa for the child born in Gujarat. The Supreme Court of India came to the rescue by giving custody of the child to the surrogate grandmother. The Supreme Court of India held that commercial surrogacy is permitted in India, and therefore there is manifold increase in the international confidence in going for surrogacy in India.

In another matter of *Jan Balaz v Anand Municipality* AIR 2010 GUJ 21, a German couple entered into a contract with a surrogate mother. Twin children were born. The question which arose was whether a child born in India to a surrogate mother, an Indian national, whose biological father is a foreign national, would get citizenship in India, by virtue of birth. This was a momentous question which had no precedent in this country.

The High Court of Gujarat keeping in view the findings of the Supreme Court in Baby Manji's case held that this case is primarily concerned with the relationship of the child with the gestational surrogate mother, and with the donor of the ova. In the absence of any legislation to the contrary, the High Court is more inclined to recognise the gestational surrogate who has given birth to the child.

The facts of this case are peculiar because, the petitioner was a German national and was the biological father of two babies given birth to by a surrogate mother who was an Indian citizen. The petitioner's wife was a German national. The petitioner & his wife were both working in the UK at the time and were desirous of staying there. The petitioner and his wife had entered into a surrogacy agreement with the surrogate mother. Further the surrogate mother had also agreed that she would not take any responsibility about the well being of the child and the biological parents would have a legal obligation to accept the child that the surrogate mother would deliver and the child would have all inheritance facts of a child of biological parents as per the prevailing law. The surrogate mother gave birth to two baby boys. On birth an application for passports was made in India; the petitioner's name was shown as the father and the surrogate mother's name was shown as the mother. The Regional Passport Office asked for the passports back and issued a certificate of identification. The father submitted that Germany would never recognise the babies as their citizens, so he filed a writ petition stating that the denial of passports to the children was violative of Article 21 (right to life) of the Indian Constitution.

The High Court held that this case was primarily concerned with the relationship of the child with the gestational surrogate mother, and with the donor of the ova. In the absence of any legislation to the contrary, we are more inclined to recognise the gestational surrogate who has given birth to the child as the natural mother. She has a right to privacy that forms part of right to life and liberty guaranteed under Article 21 of the Constitution of India. Nobody can compel her to disclose her identity. Babies born are not in a position to know who is the egg donor and they only know their surrogate mother who is real. The wife of the biological father, who has neither donated the ova, nor conceived or delivered the babies, cannot in the absence of legislation be treated as a legal mother and she can never be a natural mother. The Gujarat High Court held that, by providing ova, a woman will not become a natural mother. Life takes place not in her womb, nor does she receive the sperm for fertilisation. In the present legal framework, the High Court held that the courts have no other option but to hold that the babies born in India to the gestational surrogate are citizens of this country and therefore, are entitled to receive passports. It directed the Passport Authorities to release the passports forthwith.

It is clear that in the case of *Jan Balaz* the contract proved to be insufficient in demarcating the rights of the parties and it also brought out residual issues such as citizenship and identity that are matters of vital importance to the children but do not have a place in the surrogacy agreement.

In both the above case laws, the Indian courts have taken a very pro-contract stand, possibly as a way of encouraging commercial surrogacy, which contributes millions of dollars to India's economy. However it seems from the above that the Indian Contract Act in its current form is not able to quite comprehend the complex questions and requirements that surround surrogacy and surrogacy agreements. Unlike most contracts that deal with the inanimate, which indirectly has an an impact on the lives of human beings, the main entity being given for consideration here is a human child. What actually defines breach of a surrogacy agreement is not given anywhere in the Indian Contract Act making it easier for certain parties to evade liability and accountability which will leave the innocent child unprotected and vulnerable. In light of the above mentioned arguments it becomes clear that more than an issue of contract, commercial surrogacy is an issue of rights, mainly, the rights of the intending parents, the rights of the donors, the rights of the surrogate mother and last but definitely not least, the rights of the child. It is also an issue of human rights because of the cramped and heavily controlled living conditions of the surrogate mother.

Issues such as whether the parent country of the commissioning couple recognises and accepts the citizenship of the surrogate child are of great importance since The Citizenship Act of India does not accord citizenship to a child born out of surrogacy and such matters can leave the child in a no-man's land where citizenship is denied from both countries. For example both Japan and Germany do not recognise surrogacy and therefore will not grant citizenship to surrogate children born in India. This was evidenced in the *Baby Manji Yamada* case and the *Jan Balaz* case mentioned above. This is an important issue for consideration since it directly harms the child who is not at fault and this factor should be a pre-requisite for surrogacy agreements. The Contract Act does not mention any such requirement, which is an important issue of international citizenship and identity of the surrogate child.

The absence of a legislation to elaborate on certain issues that are peculiar to only the issue of surrogacy results in the courts of India handling these delicate and life-changing matters. One of the most distinguishing features of a surrogacy agreement from other agreements is that it directly deals with the exchange of a human child for consideration. In the event of a problem the matter is taken to court, which will take a long time to give a decisive verdict, and this will hamper and traumatise the child during its formative years because of the uncertainty and insecurity in its life.

The ART Regulation Bill 2010 guarantees legal protection to parents, surrogate mothers and children and mandates legally enforceable agreements between the stakeholders. Any violation would be a cognisable offence punishable with imprisonment and fine.

17. ADOPTION

17.1 Briefly explain the legal position in relation to adoption in your jurisdiction. Is adoption available to individuals, cohabiting couples (both heterosexual and same-sex)?

An adopted child post satisfying all the legal formalities, acquires the same rights as a biological child. The law governing adoption is also governed by the personal law of the parties. Guardian and Wards Act, 1890 is a statute which protects the rights and interests of children but this does not provide for adoption. This legislation provides that a person can become a 'Guardian' of a child, which for all purposes is akin to adoption but not a parent.

Traditional Hindu law specifically provided for adoption by religion as well as culture as the last rites of the father are to be performed by the son. This was codified under the Hindu Adoptions and Maintenance Act, 1956.

Since a large number of Indian children are available for adoption being helpless, destitute, delinquents or orphaned, a number of foreign countries started looking at India for adoption. The only secular Act available was the Guardian and Wards Act but it did not provide for a formal procedure of adoption and only defined guardianship as a concept.

Today adoption of orphan, abandoned and surrendered children in India is governed by a set of guidelines notified by the Government of India. Central Adoption Resource Authority (CARA) is an autonomous body under the Ministry of Women & Child Development, Government of India. It functions as the nodal body for the adoption of Indian children and is mandated to monitor and regulate in-country and inter-country adoptions. CARA is designated as the Central Authority to deal with inter-country adoptions in accordance with the provisions of the Hague Convention on Inter-country Adoption, 1993, ratified by the Government of India in 2003. It primarily deals with the adoption of orphan, abandoned and surrendered children through its associated/recognised adoption agencies.

By means of a progressive judgment by the Supreme Court, judicial guidelines were laid down in *Lakshmi Kant Pandey vs Union of India* (UOI) 1985 Supp SCC 701 under which foreigners could become guardians of Indian children and adopt them in accordance with the laws of their home country.

Lakshmi Kant Pandey's judgment provided that a Central Adoption Resource Agency (CARA), be set up by the Government of India with regional branches at a few centres which are active in inter-country adoptions. Every social or child welfare agency, taking children under its care could be required to send to the CARA the names and particulars of children under its care available for adoption and the names and particulars of such children could be entered in a register to be maintained by the CARA for adoption.

In *Lakshmi Kant Pandey v UOI* (2012) 12 SCC 735, a writ petition was filed putting forth the difficulties faced by adoptive parents coming from abroad and it was highlighted that many Indian courts were not accepting documents executed and authenticated abroad, with the result that the adoption of children by foreign parents was being delayed. The Supreme Court allowed the application and stated that:

(a) direct the courts of competent jurisdiction dealing with adoption/ guardianship cases to accept documents authenticated by officers competent to issue certification by 'Apostille' in the country of their execution as provided and covenanted in the Hague Apostille Convention;

(b) direct the court of competent jurisdiction to hear and dispose of cases in accordance with the time frame fixed in *Lakshmi Kant Pandey v. Union of India* 1985 Supp SCC 701.

S. Banu v Raghupathy H.C.P. No. 1139/2006, the Madras High Court held that in cases of complaints, the District Social Welfare Officer shall hold public hearing into complaints and conduct enquiry; and in cases of questionable documents relating to adoption, direct the parties to approach the police, if needed, to seek assistance from Legal Services Authority of the concerned District. The Madras High Court also observed that when a *prima facie* case is made out raising doubts as to genuineness of adoption and documents, the District Social Welfare Officer himself shall refer the matter to the police for investigation.

In *Stephanie Joan Becker v. State & Ors.* 2013 (2) SCALE 312, the Supreme Court restated the principles established in *Lakshmi Kant Pandey v Union of India* and also said that guidelines for adoption from India 2006 and 2011 must be adhered to. The Apex Court also observed that if the adoption is in best interest of the child it should be allowed without any hindrance.

In *Craig Allen Coates v State and Anr.* 2010 (8) SCC 794 it was held that for inter-country adoptions the procedure followed heretofore could include a reference to an Expert Committee on the lines constituted in the present case to ensure that inter-country adoptions are allowed only after full and proper satisfaction is recorded by all the agencies including a committee of experts wherever reference to such a committee is considered necessary.

Until very recently, there was a prohibition under the personal laws to adopt two children of the same sex. Moreover the Guardian and Wards Act was badly lacking particularly with delinquent and juvenile children.

While the Juvenile Justice Act, 1986 dealt with the care and protection of juveniles, it did not enter the domain of adoption. This lacuna was filled by the enactment of Juvenile Justice (Care and Protection of Children) Act, 2000 which contains specific provisions for adoption as one of the ways for rehabilitation and social reintegration of juveniles in conflict with law. The J.J. Act being secular in nature, supersedes HAMA and does not impose restrictions upon the number of adopted children from the same gender.

The Bombay High Court in *In Re: Adoption of Payal @ Sharinee Vinay Pathak and his wife Sonika Sahay @ Pathak* 2010(1) Bom CR 434 held that when the child to be adopted is orphaned, abandoned or surrendered or a child in need of care and protection as defined in Juvenile Justice Act, the bar imposed by Section 11 (i) and (ii) of the Hindu Adoption and Maintenance Act does not bar adopting the child of same gender after having a biological child of the same gender.

F. COHABITATION

18. COHABITATION

18.1 What legislation (if any) governs division of property for unmarried couples on the breakdown of the relationship?

There is no legislation which governs the division of property for unmarried couples if the relationship breaks down. However, the Protection of Women from Domestic Violence Act 2005 bestows all benefits on a woman living in such a type of arrangement as available to a married woman, by reason of being covered within the term 'domestic relationship' under section 2(f).

The Supreme Court of India has held in *Savitaben Somabhai Bhatiya v State of Gujarat and Ors.* (2005) 3 SCC 636 that a relationship 'in the nature of marriage' is akin to a common law marriage. However, the couple must hold themselves out to society as being akin to spouses in addition to fulfilling all other requisite conditions for a valid marriage.

In *D. Velusamy vs D. Patchaiammal* (2010)10SCC469, the Supreme Court observed that a 'relationship in the nature of marriage' is akin to a common law marriage. Common law marriages require that although not being formally married:

(a) the couple must hold themselves out to society as being akin to spouses;
(b) they must be of legal age to marry;
(c) they must be otherwise qualified to enter into a legal marriage, including being unmarried; and
(d) they must have voluntarily cohabited and held themselves out to the world as being akin to spouses for a significant period of time.

Further, the Supreme Court has held that a 'relationship in the nature of marriage' under the 2005 Act must also fulfill the above requirements, and in addition the parties must have lived together in a 'shared household' as defined in section 2(s) of the Act. Merely spending weekends together or a one night stand would not make it a 'domestic relationship'.

Hence, not all live in relationships will amount to a relationship in the nature of marriage to get the benefit of the 2005 Act. The conditions mentioned by above must be satisfied, and this has to be proved by evidence.

In *Chanmuniya vs Chanmuniya Virendra Kumar Singh Kushwaha and Anr.* (2011)1SCC141 the Supreme Court held that in those cases where a man has lived with a woman for a long time and even though they may not have undergone the legal necessities of a valid marriage, he should be made liable to pay the woman maintenance if he deserts her. The man should not be allowed to benefit from the legal loopholes by enjoying the advantages of a *de facto* marriage without undertaking the duties and obligations.

Through the judgment in *Chanmuniya*, the Supreme Court has extended relief for maintenance under S.125 Cr.P.C to women in live-in relationships. It has been held that monetary relief and compensation can be awarded in cases of live-in relationships under the Act of 2005, they should also be allowed in a proceeding under section 125 of Cr.P.C.

Sections 18-23 of the Protection of Women from Domestic Violence Act 2005 provide a large number of reliefs as legal redress. An aggrieved woman can claim reliefs through the courts in the form of protection orders, residence orders, monetary relief, custody orders for children, compensation orders and interim/*ex parte* orders.

The benefits available to a woman under the Protection of Women from Domestic Violence Act 2005 include a woman's right to reside in the shared household with her husband or a partner.

If a husband/partner of the complainant violates protection orders, it will be deemed a punishable offence. Punishment for violation of the rights enumerated above could extend to one year's imprisonment and/or a maximum fine of Rs. 20,000.

Section 17 of the Act gives all married women or female partners in a domestic relationship, the right to reside in a home that is known in legal terms, as the 'shared household'. The same provision applies even if the woman does not have any right, title or beneficial interest in the same.

The law provides that if an abused woman requires it, she has to be provided with alternate accommodation. The accommodation and her maintenance has to be paid by her husband or partner.

The law, significantly, recognises the need of the abused woman for emergency reliefs to be provided by the husband. She has the right to the services and assistance of the protection officer and service providers, shelter homes and medical establishments stipulated under the provisions of the law.

A woman who is the victim of domestic violence will have the right to the services of the police. She also has the right to simultaneously file a criminal complaint under section 498A of the Indian Penal Code. Charges under section 498A can be framed by the magistrate. The offences are cognisable and non-bailable.

G. FAMILY DISPUTE RESOLUTION

19. MEDIATION, COLLABORATIVE LAW AND ARBITRATION

19.1 Briefly summarise the non-court-based processes available in your jurisdiction and the current status of agreements reached under the auspices of mediation, collaborative law and arbitration

There have been proactive attempts by the Indian judiciary in the past few years to have a formal framework which provides mediation and arbitration services to help litigants resolve their disputes in an amicable fashion. There have been numerous mediation and conciliation centres which have been opened which run under the aegis of the High Courts of various states. The Supreme Court of India also has its own mediation and conciliation centre.

In family disputes, the medium for amicable settlement adopted is mediation. There is no legal recognition for 'Collaborative Law' in India, however, lawyers do participate in facilitating settlements.

In India family matters are not the subject matter of arbitrations.

The mediation and conciliation centre are governed by the rules formulated by the High Courts of various states from time to time.

The agreements reached under the auspices of mediation and collaborative law have the sanctity of law. Parties who do not abide by the term and conditions are liable to be sued for breach of contract and may even be liable for contempt of court.

19.2 What is the statutory basis (if any), for mediation, collaborative law and arbitration in your jurisdiction? In particular, are the parties required to attempt a family dispute resolution in advance of the institution of proceedings?

An attempt at reconciliation is mandatory under the Hindu Marriage Act, 1955 and the Special Marriage Act, 1954. Other Indian matrimonial statutes do not provide for it and there is therefore no statutory mandate to attempt settlement in other cases.

Reconciliation is provided for under section 23(2) and section 23(3) of the Hindu Marriage Act (HMA).

Section 23 (2) HMA states that before proceeding to grant any relief under it, there shall be a duty of the court in the first instance, in every case to make every endeavour to bring about reconciliation between parties where a divorce is sought on most of the fault grounds for divorce specified in section 13 HMA. Section 23 (3) HMA makes a provision empowering the court on the request of parties, or if the court thinks it just and proper, to adjourn the proceedings for a reasonable period not exceeding 15 days to bring about reconciliation. It must be borne in mind that a Hindu marriage is a sacrament and not a contract. Even if divorce is sought by mutual consent, it is the duty of the court to attempt reconciliation in the first instance. Accordingly, Hindu law advocates rapprochement and reconciliation before dissolving a Hindu marriage.

The provisions of sections 34 (2) and 34 (3) of the Special Marriage Act are pari materia to the provisions contained in sections 23 (2) and 23 (3) of the HMA. Even though the marriage contracted under the SMA does not have the same sacramental sanctity as marriage solemnised under the HMA, the Indian Parliament retained the provisions for reconciliation of marriages in the same terms as they exist in the HMA.

It may be noticed that the provisions under both the statutes are almost identical and accordingly every endeavour to bring about reconciliation is mandatory.

The mediation and conciliation centres are established under the Rules of the High Courts within whose jurisdiction they are established.

H. OTHER

20. CIVIL PARTNERSHIP/SAME-SEX MARRIAGE

20.1 What is the status of civil partnership/same-sex marriage within the jurisdiction?

Civil partnership/ gay marriages are not recognised within the territory of India. Homosexuality is considered to be a crime in India punishable under section 377 of the Penal Code.

However, in *Naz Foundation v Govt. of NCT and Ors.* 160 (2009) DLT277, the Delhi High Courttook the first step towards dismantling the legal discrimination provided by section 377 of the Penal Code in its present form by interpreting the Constitution of India as requiring a 'reading down' of the offence of 'carnal intercourse against the order of nature'. The Delhi High Court ruled that section 377 IPC insofar as it criminalises consensual sexual acts of adults in private, violates the fundamental rights of the citizens of India under the Constitution. It was held that if not amended, section 377 IPC violates Article 14 of the Indian Constitution, which states that every citizen has equal opportunity of life and is equal before law. The High Court clarified that the provisions of section 377 IPC will continue to govern non-consensual penile non-vaginal sex and penile non-vaginal sex involving minors. However, consensual intercourse between adults of any gender cannot be a criminal offence.

Currently the judgment of the Delhi High Court has been challenged in the Supreme Court and the matter is pending adjudication.

20.1 What legislation governs civil partnership/same-sex marriage?

Civil partnership/same-sex marriages are not legally recognised in India. There is no bar on persons of the same sex consensually living together.

21. CONTROVERSIAL AREAS/RAPIDLY DEVELOPING AREAS OF LAW

21.1 Is there a particular area of the law within the jurisdiction that is currently undergoing major change?

Section 377 of the Indian Penal Code criminalises even consensual sexual intercourse 'against the order of nature' – 'order of nature' being sexual intercourse between adults of opposite gender. The said provision in the Penal Code has not been amended since 1860. Therefore, for a country where, even in the 21st century consensual intercourse between adults of the same gender is considered to be a heinous crime punishable with imprisonment of life, decriminalisation of homosexuality would be a welcome change.

The matter is pending a decision before the Supreme Court of India.

21.2 Which areas of law are most out-of-step? Which areas would you most like to see reformed/changed?

Today, a lot of Indians with different personal laws have migrated and are migrating to different countries, either to make foreign countries their permanent abode or their temporary residence. Concepts like domicile and habitual residence emerge as the necessary ingredients for the courts to assume jurisdiction of disputes within the domain of private international law. Domicile needs to be defined by statute. Habitual residence for a defined length of period needs to be incorporated as a condition for application of laws.

There are several cases of international abduction of children in cases of inter-country marriages. India should seriously consider being a signatory to the Hague Convention on the Civil Aspects of International Child Abduction (1980). Judicial guidelines need to be clearly set out in such cases.

The concept of division of matrimonial property needs to be incorporated in family laws.

Natasha Sahrawat, advocate, assisted Ms. Anand in the compilation of this chapter.

Israel

Law Offices of Edwin Freedman Edwin Freedman

A. JURISDICTION AND CONFLICT OF LAW

1. SOURCES OF LAW

1.1 What is the primary source of law in relation to the breakdown of marriage and the welfare of children within the jurisdiction?

The primary source of law in Israel in matters of family law is found both in common law and in statutes. Common law in Israel has its roots in English precedents. Today there is greater impact of American common law. Statutory law in Israel is bifurcated in to civil and religious law due to the fact that Israel maintains a system of concurrent jurisdiction between religious and civil courts.

Religious courts base their rulings on religious precedent and are only subject to civil statutes in cases where the statute so specifies, as in the law guaranteeing equal protection to women, or when the Supreme Court rules that they apply. Approximately 80 per cent of the Israeli population is Jewish and therefore the overwhelming majority of case law and legislation in the area of matrimonial law relates to the implementation of Jewish law.

1.2 Which are the main statutes governing matrimonial law in the jurisdiction?

Legislation enacted during the British mandate period is still in force today. The Palestine Order in Council, 1922 determines matters of personal status according to the religious affiliation of each individual. The Order includes a list of recognised religious communities in Israel. Those who belong to a designated religious community are subject to those communities' laws in all matters of personal status. Those that are not affiliated with any of the listed religious communities are subject to the civil law.

Religious law is implemented in two ways. Firstly, each recognised religious community has a system of religious courts that are authorised by the state. These religious courts have jurisdiction over married couples only when both spouses are affiliated with the same religious community. Secondly, when litigating matters in civil courts, the applicable law applied by those courts is based on the religious affiliation of the party.

There are several acts which are of significance in matrimonial matters. The Spouses (Property Relations) Law (1973) encodes many of the principles that existed under relevant case law. The principal doctrine of this law states that there is a complete separation of each spouses' property during the course of the marriage. The parties' assets with certain specified exception are considered in total at the time of divorce and divided between them.

Another significant act which determines the relationship between parents and children is the Legal Capacity and Guardianship Law (1962). This act provides that both parents have equal custodial rights *vis-a-vis* their children. These rights include matters of education, health, welfare and place of residence. An additional act of significance in matrimonial matters is the Family Amendment (Maintenance) Law, 1959 (hereinafter Maintenance Law). This act establishes the basis for the obligation to pay child support for minor children up to the age of 18 years.

In 1995 the Family Court Act was passed. This Act established a system of family courts with sweeping jurisdiction. All matters involving family members, from probate to business disputes even though unrelated to matrimonial cases are litigated in the family courts.

2. JURISDICTION

2.1 What are the main jurisdictional requirements for the institution of proceedings in relation to divorce, property and children?

Matrimonial matters are divided into several jurisdictional categories. The dissolution of marriage is within the exclusive domain of religious courts. The Rabbinical Courts Act (Marriage and Divorce) states that petitions regarding matters of marriage between Jewish spouses are in the exclusive jurisdiction of the rabbinical courts. Similar acts exist regarding exclusive jurisdiction of Muslim and Catholic courts.

Matters that are ancillary to divorce are within the concurrent jurisdiction of both civil and religious courts. Thus, matters of division of assets, child custody, spousal and child maintenance can be adjudicated by either one of the separate legal systems. Jurisdiction is determined according to who is first in time. The party that files their petition first is the one who determines jurisdiction. A recent Supreme Court case has even held that a difference of 15 minutes will determine which court has obtained jurisdiction.

The religious and civil courts exist on parallel paths including separate appellate levels. However, the Supreme Court in Israel, sitting in its capacity as the High Court of Justice, may void decisions made by supreme religious courts. This authority is granted to the Supreme Court of Israel to exercise its jurisdiction as a court of equity in matters in which the religious courts have exceeded their jurisdiction or diverged from rules of natural justice. Furthermore, where religious courts fail to comply with legislation that specifically obligates them, the Supreme Court may also intercede (*Vilogeny v High Rabbinical Court*, Bagatz 323/81, P.D. 36(2)733).

The Supreme Court has developed a set of rules that are not found in any legislative enactment in order to limit the damage to principals of equity and due process in religious courts. For example, the Supreme Court has established a good faith test for the inclusion of ancillary matters to divorce proceedings filed in a rabbinical court. Where divorce petitions include matters of child custody or support or division of assets solely for the purpose of preventing the family court from litigating these issues the rabbinical court's jurisdiction will be denied. This is due to the generally inferior status of woman in the religious courts, who naturally prefer to litigate in the civil courts.

The Supreme Court has also held that the religious courts, although generally not subject to civil law, are required to implement certain fundamental rights. For example, the Equal Protection of Women Law must be implemented when the religious courts are determining distribution of marital assets. (*Bavli v High Rabbinical Court, et. al.,* Bagatz 1000/92, P.D. (2) 221. The Supreme Court has also held that matters of child support cannot be determined by the rabbinical court, even if it has attained initial jurisdiction without the express agreement of the mother.

The Rabbinical Courts have jurisdiction over any Jewish couple as long as one is a citizen of the state, regardless of residency. It has been held that a non-resident Israeli spouse can file proceedings if they have some connection to the country. Broad jurisdiction of the Israeli Rabbinical Courts is due to the fact that a religious bill of divorce (Get) is required by observant Jews in order to remarry. Since Rabbinical Courts which exist outside of Israel do not have powers of enforcement, as they are not a state authorised court, Israeli Rabbinical Courts attempt to provide relief for those seeking a Get and are unable to do so in the state of their residence.

For matters of divorce in civil court, there are no particular jurisdictional requirements. It is sufficient for both parties to be residents of Israel. Civil divorce proceedings may only be instituted in cases where the parties are affiliated with different religious communities or are not affiliated with any of the recognised religious communities.

Property proceedings may be instituted by either spouse in the civil courts or the religious courts, where applicable. Property proceedings may be commenced prior to the filing of divorce. However, division of assets may only take place 12 months after an action for the dissolution of marriage or an action concerning marital property was initiated.

Actions regarding children are controlled by the Legal Capacity and Guardianship Law (1962). Under paragraph 76 of the Law the courts in Israel are competent to act in any manner regarding minor children wherever the need to do so arises in Israel. This paragraph gives the court broad jurisdiction to act in matters concerning minors even when there are no other pending proceedings between the parents.

3. DOMICILE AND HABITUAL RESIDENCE

3.1 Explain the concepts of domicile and habitual residence as they apply to the jurisdiction in relation to divorce, the finances and children

Domicile and habitual residence in Israel are interpreted in accordance with the meanings of these concepts as used in various Hague Conventions on private and international law. Domicile contains elements of intent regarding future residence as well as the centrality of the location in the life of the individual. Habitual residence is determined by the physical location of the individual over a continuous period of time and is not necessarily the state to which the individual has the greatest connection.

4. CONFLICT OF LAW/APPLICABLE LAW TO BE APPLIED

4.1 What happens when one party applies to stay proceedings in favour of a foreign jurisdiction? What factors will the local court take into account when determining forum issues?

Courts in Israel will respond to an application to stay proceedings in favour of a foreign jurisdiction if it can be shown that there is an action *pendent lite* in another jurisdiction, a court in a foreign jurisdiction has issued a judgment which is binding on the parties and is *res judicata* or there is a showing of *forum non conveniens*.

The factors taken in to account will depend on the argument presented for deferring to the foreign court. If the argument is made that there is a pending proceeding or a final decision in a foreign court the courts will determine the following factors:

- was the foreign court's jurisdiction properly obtained;
- were the parties properly notified of the proceeding;
- were fundamental rules of due process followed;
- does the foreign court's decision violate public policy.

If the argument of *forum non conveniens* is made, the court will consider several factors. The efficiency with which the court can conduct the proceedings is a vital factor. It will consider the accessibility to the courts by the parties, availability of witnesses including expert testimony, the applicable law and the need to interpret foreign law, and the availability of documentary evidence. The court will also consider the ability to enforce its judgment as opposed to the foreign court and finally the costs involved in conducting the proceedings in Israel as opposed to the foreign court.

The tendency of courts in Israel is to accept arguments of *forum non conveniens* only where there is a clear cut advantage to conducting the proceedings in a foreign court. It is not sufficient to argue that a court in another jurisdiction is preferable. The courts have held that advances in modern technology, including video conferencing, have diminished the weight of the *forum non conveniens* argument.

B. PRE- AND POST-NUPTIAL AGREEMENTS

5. VALIDITY OF PRE- AND POST-NUPTIAL AGREEMENTS

5.1 To what extent are pre- and post-nups binding within the jurisdiction? Could you provide a brief discussion of the most significant recent case law on this issue.

The Division of Spousal Property Law (1973) authorises parties to sign pre-nuptial agreements. There are several ways of ratifying pre-nuptial agreements before the marriage. Ratification can be done by the Family Court, a religious court, by a person authorised to perform marriage or by a notary. Both parties must be present for ratification in any of the above procedures. Pre-nuptial agreements can also be signed after the marriage but may only be ratified by the courts.

Pre-nuptial agreements that are not ratified are not valid under the Division of Spousal Property Law. However, the courts have recognised pre-nuptial agreements that were not ratified as being valid under contract law.

While ratification is still the preferred method, in all likelihood a pre-nuptial agreement that has not been ratified may still be valid.

In the matter of *YS v TTS*, Family File No. 37224-03-10, of March 19, 2012, the Jerusalem Family Court addressed the issue of a post-nuptial agreement that was not ratified by the court as required by law. The case involved the heirs of the petitioner's deceased former spouse, who challenged her claim to enforce the post-nuptial agreement against the estate. The court upheld the petitioner's claim. It ruled that although the agreement was not court ratified as required by law, courts may give practical effect to post-nuptial agreements based on legal principles of contract law and equity; including the doctrine of good faith, estoppels and acquiescence.

In a clash between the Marital Finances Law and the Inheritance Law, the Family Court held that the terms of a marital agreement ratified by the court prevails. The Inheritance Law states that an agreement regarding the disposition of assets after death can only be done by will. In the matter of *A v C*, Family File No. 37302-02-10, of May 3, 2012, the court upheld the terms of a ratified marital agreement, even though it disposed of property rights after the death of the spouse. The court gave several reasons for its decision: the Marital Finances Law is both more specific and legislated after the Inheritance Law; the Marital Finances Law addresses the division of assets when the marriage dissolves and death is also an act of dissolution; and as a matter of policy to encourage marital agreements that resolve financial issues.

C. DIVORCE, NULLITY AND JUDICIAL SEPARATION

6. RECOGNITION OF FOREIGN MARRIAGES/DIVORCES

6.1 Summarise the position in your jurisdiction

For the purpose of marital status Israel divides each person according to her or his religious affiliation. Marriages performed abroad will be recognised in Israel for purposes of registration in the Population Registry. This entitles the couple to receive any benefits extended by Israeli law to married couples, for example: attaining subsidised mortgages or for tax purposes.

However, due to the dual system of civil and religious law applicable in matrimonial matters, a couple may be recognised by the civil authorities as married but not be recognised as such by the religious authorities. Thus, a Jew and a Muslim married abroad will be recognised by the civil authorities in Israel as married. Regardless of their civil registration as a married couple, they can be married in Israel in each of their respective religious court without necessitating a divorce.

The Family Court, in a precedent setting case, granted a divorce to an Israeli same-sex couple who were married abroad. Israel does not permit same-sex marriages, although the Ministry of Interior registered the parties as married. To further complicate the issue, the exclusive jurisdiction for divorce of Jewish couples lies with the Rabbinical Court. The couple, being Jewish, attempted to file for divorce in the Rabbinical Court, but the court refused to process their petition as it does not recognise the marriage. Turning to the Family Court, which has divorce jurisdiction when the parties are of different religions, the parties argued that since they were recognised as married in Israel, the legal system cannot deny them the right to divorce. The Family Court of Tel Aviv, in Family File No. 11264-09-12, ruled on November 21, 2012 that it had the inherent authority to grant relief where no other court had jurisdiction to do so. The court therefore dissolved the marriage.

7. DIVORCE

7.1 Explain the grounds for divorce in the jurisdiction (please also deal with nullity and judicial separation if appropriate)

Grounds for divorce in the Rabbinical Courts are very narrow. Unless the divorce is by consent, the petitioner must prove that the spouse has committed adultery; is incapable of conceiving children after 10 years of marriage; commits continuous acts of spousal abuse or refuses to fulfill their spousal obligations to engage in sexual relations. If the parties agreed to divorce upon request in a pre-nuptial agreement, it is not enforceable. The Get must be granted willingly by the husband and accepted by the wife of her own free will. A Get that is granted due to an agreement is not considered to be given willfully but as the result of an obligation made within the framework of negotiations.

If the husband refuses to grant the Get and the wife cannot prove one of the grounds for divorce, she may remain married indefinitely. On the other hand, a husband who seeks a Get but is unable to prove a cause of action against the wife, may seek special dispensation to remarry. This requires the approval of 100 rabbis and is rarely granted, but its very existence creates an imbalance in divorce proceedings among Jews.

Grounds for divorce in Sharia Courts are simpler for the husband. A Muslim husband may divorce his wife by declaring three times that she is divorced. A wife must prove adultery or ongoing violence in order to receive a divorce. The Eastern Orthodox Church follows Byzantine law which permits divorce primarily on grounds of adultery.

Separation is not a legally recognised status in Israel. The courts will take note of the date of actual separation when determining the distribution of assets. However, as there are no prescribed circumstances which establish a distinct status, the issue often becomes a matter of contentious litigation.

The Rabbinical Court can nullify a marriage where deceit which goes to the fundamental relationship of the marriage is proven. Nullity of a marriage exists in Catholic Courts according to the Cannons of the Catholic Church.

8. FINANCES/CAPITAL, PROPERTY

8.1 What powers does the court have to allocate financial resources and property on the breakdown of marriage?

Assets that were acquired during the course of the marriage and until its breakdown are considered marital property to be divided equitably between the spouses. Assets acquired prior to the marriage which were not co-mingled with marital assets, remain separate property. Assets which were inherited or received as a gift during the course of the marriage are likewise considered to be separate assets assuming that they remain under the sole control of the recipient spouse.

Civil and religious courts have concurrent jurisdiction to allocate marital assets. The division of assets is implemented according to two separate property regimes. Prior to 1 January, 1974 assets acquired during the course of a marriage were joint property. The underlying supposition was that all assets acquired during the marriage were the result of a joint effort by the parties within the marital framework. Such property was to be evenly distributed. No significance was attributed to the name in which property ownership was registered. There was no requirement for the parties to divorce in order to request a distribution of assets.

On 1 January, 1974 the Spouses (Property Relations) Law went into effect. The law encoded many of the principles existing under the relevant case law but introduced a significant and very problematic change. Marital property was to be distributed under the doctrine of the balancing of assets.

The principle underlying this doctrine states that there is a complete separation of each spouse's property during the course of the marriage. The parties' assets, with certain specified exception, are considered in total at the time of divorce and divided between them. The division, however, only takes place 'with the dissolution of the marriage'.

The property relations law does not apply retroactively. Therefore, marriages that took place prior to the enactment of the law are still subject to the division of marital assets according to the law prevailing at that time.

Due to the difficulty in obtaining a Get in contested divorces, Jewish couples married after 1974 were often unable to divide their assets over the course of many years of litigation. In October of 2008, the Property Relations Law was amended, enabling the equitable distribution of assets prior to the dissolution of marriage. The amendment provides that if one year has passed after filing an action either for the dissolution of marriage and for the equitable distribution of property, the courts are authorised to distribute the marital assets even if the parties are still married.

Another alternative provided by the amendment permits dissolution of assets in the event that there are irreconcilable differences between the parties for a period of at least nine months within a consecutive 12-month period. The amendment is retroactive and therefore applies to all who were married subsequent to January 1974. Paragraph 8 of the original Property Relations Law authorised the court to distribute marital assets on an equitable rather than an equal basis.

The amendment adds a specific dimension to this formula. The court is now authorised (paragraph 8 (2) of the Law) when balancing the assets to consider, in special circumstances, the reputation and future earning capacity of each spouse. Prior to this amendment courts generally rejected the concept of future earnings as a divisible family asset.

Due to the Supreme Court ruling in the case of *Bavli (id)*, religious courts are also required to apply civil law when distributing family assets. It was held that equal rights of women in family matters are a fundamental right in Israeli jurisprudence. Religious courts were therefore forbidden from implementing precepts of religious law which discriminate against women. For example, rabbinical courts will take into account the formal title to property as an indication of how to distribute the asset, whereas under the joint property regime of Israel the formal title is not a factor. In reality, religious courts often fail to implement the ruling in the *Bavli* case, necessitating repeated petitions to the Supreme Court in its capacity as the High Court of Justice.

8.2 Explain and illustrate with reference to recent cases the court's thinking on division of assets

A leading decision in the matter of defining reputation as a marital asset was made by the Supreme Court in 2004. The court rejected the wife's claim that her husband's reputation as a lawyer is a distributable asset. The court did recognise however that it is possible in certain circumstances to consider a reputation as such an asset. It was reticent to turn such a possibility into a reality and questioned whether it could clearly define the circumstances necessary for such distribution. (Family Motion to Appeal) 5879/04 *Anonymous v Anonymous*, 59 (1) P.D. 193 (2004)).

In the short time since the amendment to paragraph 8 of the Spouses Relations Law was enacted, the courts have shown greater willingness to take into account future earnings and reputation as marital assets. A recent decision of the Tel Aviv District Family Court held that where the doctor husband's earning capacity was seven or eight times that of his attorney wife, the court would consider future earning capacity when dividing marital assets (*A v S*, Family Docket number 46385/08, Dec. 28th, 2009).

A recent court decision reflects the wariness with which the courts are applying the amendment enabling the division of future earnings capacity. The Tel Aviv Family Court upheld the claim of a housewife who managed the home while the husband developed his career to include future earning capacity in the marital assets. The court made its ruling based on three fundamental conditions: (a) one party is a homemaker while the other has a career in the work force; (b) there is a dramatic difference in the parties' future earning capacity; and (c) the couple has been married for a significant amount of time (no distinct period was defined).

9. FINANCES/MAINTENANCE

9.1 Explain the operation of maintenance for spouses on ongoing basis after the breakdown of marriage

The Family Amendment (Maintenance) Law, section 2 (a) states that a person is liable for the maintenance of their spouse in accordance with the provisions of personal law applying to him. In this context personal law refers to the law of the religious community with which the individual is affiliated as set out in article 2 of the 1922 Palestine Order in Council. Individuals who are not affiliated with any of the recognised religious communities (for example, the Protestant Churches) are considered to have no personal status law. Such individuals are subject by the above maintenance law to Israeli law. However, the law is silent regarding the extent of spousal support for those who have no personal law.

Under the law applicable for Jewish marriages there is no obligation for spousal support after the issuance of a Get. This creates situations in which the wife will take contrary positions in the Rabbinical and Family Courts regarding the breakdown of a marriage. On the one hand, the wife may petition for division of assets in Family Court. On the other hand, she may oppose the husband's petition for divorce in the Rabbinical Court in order to continue receiving spousal support for as long as possible. If the wife is gainfully employed spousal support is generally not granted. This is due to the principle under Jewish matrimonial law that the income of the wife belongs to the husband and therefore by allowing her to keep her earnings, the husband is free of his obligations to support her.

One Family Court case did rule that a Jewish husband was obligated to continue paying spousal support after the divorce, although this case is an exception and has not been adopted as a precedent. Ironically, common law spouses, who are recognised in Israel, are in a superior position to married wives under Jewish law. Due to the fact that Jewish law in silent regarding the obligation to support a common law wife after the breakdown of the relationship, courts have awarded alimony to common law wives after the termination of the relationship.

10. CHILD MAINTENANCE

10.1 On what basis is child maintenance calculated within the jurisdiction?

Child support is within the jurisdiction of civil courts and can only be adjudicated in the religious courts if the wife gives explicit consent. Under the Maintenance Law (paragraph 3) a person is obligated to support her or his minor children up to the age of 18 years. Under paragraph 4 (2) of the Maintenance Law, between the ages of 18 and 21 years a parent is responsible for one third of the monthly support paid prior to the age of 18 years. That obligation is contingent upon the child serving in compulsory military service or studying full time in an institute of higher learning.

The religious law applicable to Jews divides the obligation to pay child support into different categories. Up until the age of six years, the obligation to pay child support is the exclusive responsibility of the father, without regard to his financial ability. Between the age of six and 15 years, the father is exclusively responsible only for the child's necessities. From the age of 15 years until the age of 18 years, a father's obligation to pay child support is not absolute and is dependent upon his ability to bear the burden. Practically speaking, the courts will obligate an unemployed father with no assets to pay a minimum level of child support (currently deemed to be in the amount of NIS 1,250) for a child up to the age of 15 years. Between the ages of 15 and 18 years, the father will only be obligated to pay support if he has the financial ability to do so. Furthermore, from the age of 15 years, the mother may also be obligated to contribute to the support of the child according to her ability as the obligation is not exclusively on the father.

Israeli law does not have child support guidelines and therefore amounts vary from case to case even where incomes and needs are the same. The standard under Israeli law is that the child is supposed to be able to continue the same standard of living to which he or she was accustomed prior to the divorce (CA (Civil Appeal) 210/82 *Gelbar v Gelbar*, 35 P.D.(2)14, Supreme Court of Israel).

Divorce agreements between the parents which establish child support levels even when ratified by the court do not obligate the children. A child may file an action against the parent to increase the level of child support beyond the amount set in the divorce agreement without concern of estoppel. (C.A. 411/76 *Sher v Sher*, 32 P.D.(1) 449).

In cases where the father is not capable of providing for the child's minimal requirements, the grandparents of the child may be sued and obligated to pay support where they have the financial means to do so. A child who unjustifiably refuses all contact with the father and is old enough to do so knowingly may have their child support payments reduced by the court (C.A 1880/97 *Katan v Katan*, 39 P.D.(1) 215).

In cases where the personal status law is Islamic, the father has absolute obligation to pay child support until the age of 18 years. Under article 52 of the Palestine Order in Council, the applicable Islamic law is the 1917 Ottoman Family Law. The said law is based on the Khanafi school of thought. Interpretation of that law therefore must be based on the Khanafi Sharia Law (Crim. A 353/62 *Muhammad Alfakir v Attorney General of Israel*, 18 P.D.(2) 200, p.221). The obligation of the father to pay child support under Muslim Law differentiates between sons and daughters. The father is obligated to support his son to the age where he can support himself. It is customary that said age is attained with the completion of the child's studies. The obligation to support a daughter is until she is married without any age limitation.

Under Muslim law a wealthy father is obligated to pay support – *yasar* – (in abundance) and a poor father is only obligated to pay – *a'aser* – (minimum necessities).

11. RECIPROCAL ENFORCEMENT OF FINANCIAL ORDERS

11.1 Summarise the position in your jurisdiction

Foreign financial orders in matrimonial matters are enforced under the same procedure as any foreign financial judgment would be in Israel. The Enforcement of Foreign Judgment Law, 1983 establishes the criteria for enforcement in Israel of a judgment issued abroad. The requirements as set out in section 3 of the law are as follows:

- a judgment was rendered by a court that had authority to do so according to the laws of that state;
- the judgment is no longer appealable;
- the judgment is enforceable in the state in which it was issued;
- the judgment does not violate public policy.

Under paragraph 6a of said law a judgment will not be enforced if one of the following can be proven:

- the judgment was obtained by fraud;

- basic principles of due process were not observed;
- the court issuing the judgment did not have authority to do so under rules of international law;
- the judgment is contrary to a prior judgment still valid between the same parties in the same matter;
- at the time the foreign proceeding was initiated, a matter was pending in an Israeli court concerning the same issues and the same parties.

Where foreign judgments contain both financial orders and orders concerning the personal status of the parties' marriage, Israeli courts will distinguish between the two. The financial aspect of the judgment will be enforced while the issues of marital status will not be.

12. FINANCIAL RELIEF AFTER FOREIGN DIVORCE PROCEEDINGS

12.1 What powers are available to make orders following a foreign divorce?

In the event of relocation to Israel following a foreign divorce, Israeli courts have the authority to adjudicate petitions for child support against the foreign resident. Under section 17 (b) of the Maintenance Law, the law of the child's residence is the controlling law in the proceeding against the person responsible for child support.

In order to initiate such proceedings the court must grant a motion for service of process abroad against the respondent. Once proper service is performed on the respondent, the proceedings will be conducted in Israel.

There is controversy in Israeli law and professional literature as to the applicable law in such cases. The question is whether the personal law applicable to the respondent is that of the law of her or his state of residence or the law applicable according to the respondent's religious affiliation under the Palestine Order in Council. Logic would seem to dictate that the Palestine Order in Council only applies to those who are residents of Israel, yet some courts have given it a broad interpretation and applied it to foreign residents as well.

D CHILDREN

13. CUSTODY/PARENTAL RESPONSIBILITY

13.1 Briefly explain the legal position in relation to custody/parental responsibility following the breakdown of a relationship or marriage

13.2 Briefly explain the legal position in relation to access/contact/visitation following the breakdown of a relationship or marriage

The Legal Capacity and Guardianship Law, 5728-1962, states that both parents are equal guardians of their children. This applies whether or not the parents are married. The courts interpret this to mean that both parents have an equal right to determine significant issue regarding the health, education and welfare of their children. Where parents are unable to agree, the courts are empowered to make the determination, generally after receiving a report of the social services agency or a psychological evaluation by a court appointed expert.

The law creates a legal presumption that the custody of a child until the age of six is with the mother. In cases where both parents are considered equally suited to have custody, the presumption will work in favour of the mother. This presumption can be overcome by a showing that it is not on the child's best interest.

A government-appointed committee has spent six years developing recommendations to revise and update child custody law. The report was submitted in 2011 and has yet to be adopted. Despite the fact that the no legislative action has yet been taken, the report has already been cited by the courts while referring to some of its recommendations. The most controversial recommendation was to abandon the legal presumption of custody for children up to the age of six.

The committee recommended replacing the current legal presumption with a presumption of joint parental responsibility from birth. The guiding principle in determining custody will always be the best interests of the child, as per Article 18 of the UN Convention on the Rights of the Child. Among the considerations which the committee recommended be weighed by the court in custody matters are the following: the child's right to have direct and regular contact with both parents; the care which each parent gave the child prior to the divorce; the ability to provide for the child's development, stability and particular needs; the willingness and ability of each parent to insure the child's rights.

The committee also recommended that terms such as custody and visitation be replaced with 'parental responsibility'. Some courts have adopted the report's terminology, which is meant to create a different perception of children's interest in divorce cases.

14 INTERNATIONAL ABDUCTION

14.1 Summarise the position in your jurisdiction

Israel is a member of the Hague Conference on Private International Law. It ratified the 1980 Convention on the Civil Aspects of International Child Abduction, which came into effect in Israel on 1 December, 1991.

Legal proceedings under the Convention are within the exclusive jurisdiction of the family courts. Specific procedural regulations have been adopted which apply to Hague Convention proceedings, (Regulations of Civil Procedure-1984, Rule 295(a-z)). A time framework is established which attempts to comply with the Convention's objectives.

Proceedings in the court of first instance are to be completed within six weeks of the date of filing (Rule 295(13)). No court filing fees are imposed nor are bonds or guarantees permitted (Rule 295(15)). The petitioner is not required to testify in court. They may submit an affidavit which cannot be voided even though the petitioner did not appear for cross examination.

Judgments of the Family Court are appealable by right. Appeals must be filed within seven days of the judgment. The District Court, which has jurisdiction to hear appeals, must make its decision within 30 days of filing of the appeal (Rule 295(14)). Appeals from the District Court can only be made by leave to the Supreme Court. Requests for leave to appeal must be made within seven days of the District Court's judgment.

Family Courts have recently become more permissive in the use of testimony by video conference in Hague Convention cases. Its use is permitted where the petitioner, or a key witness, is unable to appear in Israel due to complications which are likely to occur as a result, for example, loss of legal status in the requesting state.

Actual Hague Convention proceedings are rarely completed within the time periods set by the Regulations. It is not unusual for proceedings to take more than a year before a final judgment is issued. There are no designated Hague Convention judges in Israel although most of the Family Court jurisdictions tend to concentrate the Hague Convention cases among a few unofficially designated judges.

As the Convention applies to the inhabitants of the signatory states, the question has arisen regarding the application of the Convention to abductions to the territories occupied by Israel since 1967 but not incorporated into the state. Israeli courts have implemented the Convention to instances where the abduction is an area under its administrative rule (*Bork v Stegman*, 49 P.D.(2) 431). The Supreme Court has ruled that areas under Israeli administrative control will not be used as a hiding place for abducted children, even though there is no formal provision subjecting such territory to the Convention, (*Eden v Eden*, 51 P.D.(4) 197).

Israeli courts have held that the defences under the Hague Convention are to be narrowly interpreted (*Gabai v Gabai*, 51 P.D.(2)241).

To prove the defence of consent, the evidence must be unequivocal, (*Issak v Issak*, Personal Status File 5097/92, Tel Aviv District Court, Judge H. Porat). Consent given in the heat of an argument does not meet the required standard. The case law has also adopted the position that negotiations conducted to resolve the conflict, including the option that the abducted children remain in the requested state, are not held to constitute consent (*Gabai, id)*.

Consent requires both objective proof of the intent of the left behind parent and the subjective belief of the abducting parent that permission to relocate has been granted.

Acquiescence can be proven by either active or passive behaviour. The case law holds that acquiescence, once given, cannot be retracted (*Leibowitz v Leibowitz*, 47 P.D.(3) 254). This is a comparatively harsh holding in view of the more demanding requirements to prove consent. Whereas the abductor may change their situation in reliance upon consent, an act of acquiescence, which occurs subsequent to abduction, will generally not cause a change of circumstances. This is an issue that would appear to require further deliberation.

The Israeli Civil Rules of Procedure have adopted the American standard of proof for this defence, that of clear and combing evidence. A leading case which has applied this standard is (*Roe v Roe*, 50 P.D.338). The respondent mother raised an Article 13b defence, claiming that the petitioner was a violent, abusive alcoholic who had never held a job. It was argued that a return to the habitual residence in England would be to deny the child even minimal living conditions, as the mother had no ability to support herself.

The Supreme Court held that this did not meet the standard of grave risk. The court and social service agencies in England were capable of addressing the issues raised by the mother. Abduction of the child was not the way to resolve the problems.

It has also been held that the abducting parent cannot create an Article 13b defence by claiming that his or her refusal to return with the child places him or her in grave risk of insufferable psychological harm. (*Foxman v Foxman*, Personal Status File 2898/92 Tel Aviv District Court, October 28th, 1992, C.A. 5271/92 Supreme Court, November 19th, 1992).

Israeli Courts have been inconsistent in their interpretation of the meaning of habitual residence. Some courts hold that there is a dichotomy between two approaches; that which is based solely on the perspective of the child (*Dagan v Dagan*, 53 P.D.(2) 241); and that which is based on parental intent (*Alon v Alon*, Family Appeal Request 2967/05, Supreme Court, July 12, 2005). Courts which have followed the parental intent model have created further confusion by disagreeing as to the point in time when parental intent is determined.

Other courts have taken a more comprehensive approach, recognising that habitual residence is a consequence of two elements; the physical location of the child prior to the removal and parental intent. The balance between these two elements is determined according to the fact pattern of each case. Where the relocation of a family to another country has been for an extended, undefined period, the parent's intent will carry less weight. Where relocation was for a specific purpose for a defined period, (eg a visiting professor on a year's sabbatical) the physical presence of the child have far less significance.

The issue of dividing the siblings has been raised in two cases within the framework of international abduction. In the case of *M v M*, the Israeli mother and French father lived in France, where their first son was born. While pregnant with the party's second son, the mother convinced the father that it would be best to give birth in Israel, where she had her family to assist. After giving birth in Israel to their second son, the mother immediately cut off the father from both children, even refusing to put his name on the birth certificate of the newborn.

As the newborn never had habitual residence in France, a petition under the Hague Convention was filed for the return of the older child. The petition was granted and the older child ordered returned to France, (Family Appeal 233/09, Supreme Court, April 1, 2009). In parallel, a *habeas corpus* petition was filed for the return of the newborn, as there is no requirement of habitual residence in the requesting state in a *habeas corpus* proceeding. The claim of unlawful detention was based on the proven purpose of the visit to Israel and the intent to return to France. The mother declared that she would not return to France under any circumstances. It was also argued that separating the siblings would create severe psychological harm to them both and since the infant had new ties to either country, it was fitting to send him to France along with the older brother.

The father's petition in the Family Court was rejected. His claim regarding the infants' ultimate custody was reinforced by the fact that the mother, after the ruling of the Supreme Court in The Hague Convention matter, went underground for nine months with both children. Although the mother had been brazenly in contempt of court and endangered the welfare of both children, his appeal to the District Court was unsuccessful. Not only was his appeal rejected, the District Court tried to convince the father that he should return the elder sibling to Israel, so as not to be apart from his brother and mother. The father rejected this proposal and the children remain separated, each in his respective country, *M v M*, (Family Appeal 46826-05-10, Haifa District Court).

The other case of divided siblings involved a Dutch father and an Israeli mother who lived in Holland with their two children, aged five and two. The parties were not married and under Dutch Law, an unmarried father must register his rights as a parent in order to obtain custodial rights. In this case, the father had registered as the parent of the older child but not of the younger one. While custody proceedings were being conducted in Holland, but before the father's custodial rights had been recognised, the mother abducted the children to Israel. The court held that the Hague Convention applied to the older child and therefore ordered his immediate return. Regarding the younger child, the court held that the father did not have custodial rights under Dutch Law and therefore the removal was not unlawful.

The mother appealed, claiming that the separation of the children would cause them severe psychological harm. As she would not return to Holland, her solution was to leave both children in Israel. The case reached the Supreme Court, which upheld the decision to return the older child, even though the younger one would remain in Israel. The court ruled that although the situation would produce unfortunate results, the alleged harm was not within the scope of Article 13(b). Furthermore, the court stated that there was no impediment to the mother returning with the younger child. Thus, it was not true that implicit in the return of the older child was the separation of the children, (*Doe v Roe*, Family File Request to Appeal 2270/13, Supreme Court, April 25, 2013).

15. LEAVE TO REMOVE/APPLICATIONS TO TAKE A CHILD OUT OF THE JURISDICTION

15.1 Summarise the position in your jurisdiction

15.2 Under what circumstances may a parent apply to remove their child from the jurisdiction against the wishes of the other parent?

The criteria for removal cases have evolved from an examination of the petitioning parent's motives to the best interests of the child. The case of *Goldman v Goldman* (Personal Status File 2069/92, Tel Aviv District Court, Judge H. Porat, August 27, 1993) was for many years the guiding case. Goldman held that the test for removal is a multi-faceted one, in which the factors weighed are: the impact on the relationship between the minor and the left behind parent; the petitioner's motivation to relocate and the impact on the child.

In *Anonymous v Anonymous*, (Civil Appeal Request 4574/00, January 8, 2001), the Supreme Court of Israel rejected the criteria set out in Goldman. It held that the best interests of the child are the only determinant when adjudicating matters of relocation. While overturning Goldman, the court did not completely abandon its analysis. Thus, the impact on the relationship between the child and the left behind parent is still considered, not as a separate criteria but as it impacts on the best interests of the child.

The courts have held that relocation cases are so individual that precedents are of little relevance. Two examples demonstrate how courts have responded to unique fact patterns. In the case of *LS v SM*, a divorced mother of four remarried and had primary custody of the children. She and her husband decided to relocate to Brazil for a period of up to two years. The mother and former husband concluded an agreement by which the children would relocate with the mother and the father's support arrears would be reduced. The Family Court rejected the parents' agreement, ruling that it was not in the best interests of the children.

On appeal, the District Court overturned the Family Court's ruling in a scathing decision, (Family Appeal 1066/06, Jerusalem District Court, Judge M. Drori). It held that where parents reached an agreement regarding the living arrangements of their children, the courts will not usurp the parent's prerogative to determine their children's best interests. Barring unusual situations in which their welfare is endangered, the courts will not substitute the parent's judgment for its own.

The second example also involved a divorced couple where the mother was the primary custodial parent. The father maintained regular visitation with the children. The mother remarried to a man who was offered a diplomatic position entailing relocation to Africa. The mother's petition to relocate for one year to Africa was opposed by the father.

The court accepted the mother's petition, but ordered that the relocation be subject to a number of conditions. It required the mother to submit a bank guarantee in the amount of $250,000 to the court that would be released to the father if the children were not returned to Israel at the conclusion of one year. The court also set out a detailed visitation schedule both in Africa and in Israel during the year (*TBY v ABY*, Family File No. 52122/05, Tel Aviv District Family Court).

E. SURROGACY AND ADOPTION

16. VALIDITY OF SURROGACY AGREEMENTS

16.1 Briefly summarise the position in your jurisdiction

Surrogacy in Israel is regulated by the Surrogacy Agreement Law (Ratification of Agreement and status of the Infant), 5756-1996. The law subjects all surrogacy agreements to specific, restrictive conditions. Under paragraph 2, the following conditions must be met as a prerequisite to approving a surrogacy agreement; the parents must be a man and woman; the agreement between the birth mother and the adoptive parents must be in writing and approved by the ratification committee established by the Act; the surrogate mother is not married nor is she a relative of one of the parents;

the adoptive and surrogate mothers are of the same religious affiliation; the sperm is that of the adoptive father and the egg is not that of the surrogate mother. The ratification committee has a certain flexibility to deviate from some of the requirements. It can, for instance, approve of an agreement where the surrogate mother is married or where the surrogate mother and the adoptive mother are not of the same religion.

The committee consists of seven members from various professions; two obstetricians or gynecologists, a specialist in internal medicine, a clinical psychologist, a social worker, a representative of the public who is an attorney and a religious authority according to the parties' religious affiliation. The committee is charged with reviewing all agreements to ascertain, among other facets, that the parties understand the ramifications of the agreement; that there is no exploitation of the surrogate mother or of the adoptive parents and that there is no harm to the surrogate mother or the infant.

17. ADOPTION

17.1 Briefly summarise the position in relation to adoption in your jurisdiction. Is adoption available to individuals, cohabiting couples (both heterosexual and same-sex)?

The Adoption of Children Law, 5741-1981, establishes the criteria for declaring a child adoptable where the parents have not given their consent. The Law provides for a two-stage process. The first stage is to ascertain the existence of one of the 13 grounds for adoption. Included in those grounds are the following situations; there is no reasonable possibility of identifying the parent; the child resides with the parent but there is an unreasonable refusal to permit him to remain in the house; the parent abandoned the child or has had no contact with him for six consecutive months without reasonable grounds; the child has been residing outside the house for six consecutive months, commencing before the child attained the age of six, and the parent unreasonably refuses to let him reside in the house; the parent is incapable of caring for the child to the parent's behaviour or situation and there is chance that the parent's behaviour will change in the foreseeable future, despite financial and social assistance from the welfare authorities.

The second stage is to determine whether it is in the child's best interests to be adopted or placed in an alternative framework. If it is determined that no alternative framework exists, then the child is put up for adoption. At that point, the type of adoption is determined, whether it is an open adoption or a closed one. An open adoption permits contact with the biological parent, while closed adoption does not.

According to paragraph 3 of the Law, adoption can only be granted to 'a man and his wife together'. Despite the clear intent of the legislature to restrict adoption to heterosexual couples, the courts have found a way around this limitation. In the case of *Yaros Hakak v The State Attorney*, (Civil Appeal File 10280/01), the Supreme Court approved the adoption of a child by a same-sex couple. The court relied on section 25(2) of the Law which provides that under extraordinary circumstances which shall be recorded by the court, if the adoption is found to be in the child's best interest, a single parent can adopt a child. The court held that if a single parent can adopt a child under such conditions, then certainly two parents, even if they are of the same sex, can also adopt a child.

F. COHABITATION

18. COHABITATION

18.1 What legislation (if any) governs division of property for unmarried couples on the breakdown of the relationship?

Common law marriages are recognised in Israel both by legislation and case law. Common law marriages are increasing due to several factors. Religious control of personal status has created a segment of the population which is unable to legally marry. A growing number of couples who are entitled to marry choose not to in order to avoid being subject to religious laws.

There are more than two dozen laws in which the common law spouse is explicitly mentioned. The first law to recognise common law spouse was enacted in 1949, one year after the establishment of the State of Israel. (see Handicapped Law (*Payments and Rehabilitations-1949*). Most of these statutes confer rights and benefits on the common law wife. Generally those acts confer social and economic benefits regarding pensions, retirement funds and protected tenant's rights.

The Succession Law – 1965 extends to either surviving common law spouse the same right to inherit the partner as a legally married spouse. The Single Parent Law – 1992 applies in part to both genders and in certain aspects only to women. The benefits provided by the law are extended to any single parent as such is defined by the act. Most definitions are inclusive of both genders. However, amongst the categories of single parents are women whose husbands will not provide them with a Jewish bill of divorce (Get). Husbands whose wives refuse to accept the Get are not included.

In order to qualify as a common law spouse the claimant must prove that the parties cohabitated as husband and wife and maintained a common household (*Rosenberg v Stessel*, 29(1)P.D. 505 (Supreme Court, 1973). Recently, a court has held that even though a couple maintained two separate apartments to which the woman returned every evening, she still qualified as a common law wife.

In some cases, courts will also recognise as a common spouse a married individual who is unable to obtain a divorce in the religious court.

The court will not, however, recognise two common law wives simultaneously. In *Simantov v State of Israel* (Leave to Appeal 20/05/10, March 15, 2010) the Supreme Court rejected the request of a prisoner to have conjugal visits with his common law wife. The reason for denial was that the prisoner previously had conjugal visits with a different woman whom he declared was his common law wife.

G. FAMILY DISPUTE RESOLUTION

19. MEDIATION, COLLABORATIVE LAW AND ARBITRATION

19.1 Briefly summarise the non-court-based processes available in your jurisdiction and the current status of agreements reached under the auspices of mediation, collaborative law and arbitration

Due to the concurrent jurisdiction of the civil and religious courts in Israel, there is often a race to court as jurisdiction is established in most cases by the first in time rule (see section 2 above). Since the applicable law in each court system varies in some aspects, and their interpretation of laws applicable to both systems may also vary, parties are anxious to establish jurisdiction in the court most favourable to their position. This creates a disincentive to mediate or apply collaborative law rules. For the most part, where mediation occurs it is after proceedings have been filed.

Collaborative law has no formal framework and depends entirely on the trust between opposing attorneys to not engage in litigation. It is a highly uncommon occurrence.

19.2 What is the statutory basis (if any), for mediation, collaborative law and arbitration in your jurisdiction? In particular, are the parties required to attempt a family dispute resolution in advance of the institution of proceedings?

There is no statutory basis for mediation, collaborative law or arbitration in family law proceedings. Parties are not required to attempt a dispute resolution before the institution of proceedings. Once proceedings have been instituted, the court may determine that the case should be referred to the Assistance Unit within the Family Court to help the parties resolve the dispute prior to a preliminary hearing. The Assistance Unit primarily deals with custody and maintenance disputes.

H. OTHER

20. CIVIL PARTNERSHIP/SAME-SEX MARRIAGE

20.1 What is the status of civil partnership/same-sex marriage within the jurisdiction?

Until very recently, civil partnership was not recognised in Israel. The recent enactment of legislation in this area was not adopted to provide a solution to same sex couples, but rather is intended for those who cannot marry under the archaic religious laws governing marital status.

Some courts have ratified pre-nuptial agreements of same sex couples, holding that the law does not define a couple.

Other courts have reached the opposite result, defining a couple as a man and a woman only. The Supreme Court has yet to rule on this issue and there is no legislation which addresses the subject.

20.2 What legislation governs civil partnership/same sex marriage?

The Civil Partnership Law for Religiously Unaffiliated was adopted in Israel on 22 March, 2010. The law applies only to a couple that consists of a man and a woman. The law permits a civil union only where both parties are not affiliated with a recognised religious community and cannot marry under the existing religious laws. The impact of this law is negligible as it affects a very small segment of the targeted population.

There is no law which recognises same-sex marriage.

21. CONTROVERSIAL AREAS/RAPIDLY DEVELOPING AREAS OF LAW

21.1 Is there a particular area of the law within the jurisdiction that is currently undergoing major change?

21.2 Which areas of law are most out-of-step? Which areas would you most like to see reformed/changed?

The area most out of step with the tenets of a judicial system based on equality and due process is the application of matrimonial law according to religious affiliation. While the Supreme Court and the legislator have narrowed, to some extent, the impact of religious courts, attempts to separate religion and state in family law have failed.

This system has produced several highly detrimental aspects to matrimonial proceedings:

- gender discrimination;
- race to the court house;
- lack of regularity;
- different results for those affiliated with different religions;
- subjection to religious based law by those who reject any religious identity;
- inconsistency in regard to litigants rights to due process as religious court judges are not required to be trained as lawyers;
- resistance to change.

Religious laws are more impervious to societal developments, for example, same sex marriages. While ongoing efforts are made to reduce the friction resulting from religious courts determining disputes in a democratic society, there is little chance of fundamental change.

Some attempts are being made to diminish the impact of this problematic system of jurisprudence. However, as long as the present political system remains intact there is scant hope for any fundamental changes.

An area of the law which is destined to undergo change is the establishment of child support guidelines. At present the matter is left to the discretion of the individual judge. A state appointed commission is preparing recommendations to establish uniform guidelines.

Child support in Israel is determined by the relevant personal status law of each parent, according to the Law to Amend the Law of the Family (Maintenance), 5719-1959. The personal status law is that of the religious community with which he is ethnically affiliated, regardless of whether there is an active affiliation. In the case of Jewish residents, the law obligates only the father to pay the necessary expenses of a child until the age of 15. Beyond that age, both parents can be obligated to support their minor children, according to the resources of each parent.

Despite the clear and absolute obligation under Jewish law for fathers alone to bear all necessary expenses of the child until the age of 15, the courts have began to take a more egalitarian approach to child support. They have done so by attempting to eradicate the distinction between 'essential' expenses and those categorised as 'non-essential', as the mother can also be obligated to pay for the 'non-necessities'.

Two Supreme Court cases form the legal precedent for this change. The cases of *Chinboy v Chinboy* (Family Appeal 2433/04) and *Ohana v Ohana* (Family Appeal 5750/03) both held that when determining child support the courts should require the mother to participate in essential support payments and not just in the non-essential. Courts are obligated to examine the mother's financial capabilities as well as the father's when awarding child support and the obligation should be imposed on both. The result is that there is a trend for courts to minimise what is defined as essentials in order to more evenly divide the obligation for child support.

Italy

Pirola Pennuto Zei & Associati
Andrea Russo & Benedetta Rossi

A. JURISDICTION AND CONFLICT OF LAW

1. SOURCES OF LAW

1.1 What is the primary source of law in relation to the breakdown of marriage and the welfare of children within the jurisdiction?

Under the Italian system, separation is governed by Articles 150-158 of the Italian civil code, while divorce is regulated by Law number 898 of 1/12/1970. The rules on the welfare of children are contained in the Civil Code, titles VII through XIII.

Law number. 218 of 31/5/1995, entitled Private International Law, provides the rules as to the scope of Italian jurisdiction and the criteria to determine the applicable law and enforcement of foreign judgments when foreign nationals/residents are involved. Pursuant to Articles 26-45 of this law, in certain circumstances, Italian courts can have jurisdiction and apply governing foreign law. Of course, as Italy is part of the European Union, European legislation must also be considered to be a primary source in the specific fields:

(I) Separation and Divorce
- (i) Jurisdiction: Council Regulation (EC) No 2201/2003 of 27 November 2003 (Brussels II)
- (ii) Governing law: Council Regulation (EC) No. 1259/2010 of 20 December 2010, (this Regulation is significant, particularly for foreign citizens resident in Italy. Before the regulation came into force non-Italians of the same nationality living in Italy would have had their separation/divorce governed by their common national law; now Italian law applies);

(II) Maintenance obligations:
- (i) Jurisdiction: Council Regulation (EC) No 4/2009 of 18 December 2008;
- (ii) Governing Law: the Hague Protocol of 23 November 2007.

1.2 Which are the main statutes governing matrimonial law in the jurisdiction?

Matrimonial law in Italy is governed predominantly by the First Book of the Italian Civil Code, Articles 1 to 455. These articles cover a wide range of matters relating to the family, including marriage, rights and duties arising out of marriage, dissolution and separation and marital property.

2. JURISDICTION

2.1 What are the main jurisdictional requirements for the institution of proceedings in relation to divorce, property and children?

Where both spouses are Italian citizens, Italian courts have jurisdiction over Italian citizens whether or not the spouses are resident in Italy and separation or divorce are regulated by the ordinary rules governing jurisdiction within Italy. Jurisdiction in cases of judicial separation proceedings (art. 706 Italian civil procedure code) or judicial divorce (art. 4 L. 1/12/1970 n. 898) is determined on the basis of the last common residence of the spouses or, failing that, on the basis of the residence or the domicile of the defendant spouse. Should the divorce petition be joint, it can be filed either at the tribunal in the municipality of residence or domicile of one of the spouses. Maintenance between spouses is determined during the separation or divorce proceedings and therefore, even if there are later proceedings to modify the terms of the separation or divorce, the jurisdiction will be determined applying the ordinary rules.

A second situation relates to where both parties are Italian citizens, at least one of whom is resident in a European Union state outside of Italy and to citizen spouses of other European Union states of whom one or both are Italian resident(s). In such a case, in order to determine which European state has jurisdiction over separation or divorce proceedings, reference must be made to Article 3 of Council Regulation (EC) No 2201/2003 (Brussels II). Jurisdiction lies with the state in which both spouses are habitually resident; in which they were last habitually resident, insofar as one of them still resides there; where the respondent is habitually resident; where either of the spouses is habitually resident, in the event of a joint application; where the applicant is habitually resident if he or she resided there for at least a year immediately before the application was made; or the applicant is habitually resident if he or she resided there for at least six months immediately before the application was made and is either a national of the Member State in question or, in the case of the United Kingdom and Ireland, has his or her 'domicile' there.

The third situation involves an Italian citizen married to a non-EU citizen, Italian citizens where at least one is resident in an non-EU state, and non–EU citizens of whom one or both are resident in Italy or have been married in Italy. Here reference must be made to L.118/1995, Italian Private International Law, according which (arts. 32 and 3) in cases of separation or divorce Italian jurisdiction applies if the defendant is either domiciled or resident in Italy, or has a representative who is authorised by virtue of article 77 Italian Code of Civil Procedure to be brought to trial in Italy, if one of the spouses is an Italian citizen, or if the marriage has been celebrated in Italy.

Maintenance obligations and actions relating to property are excluded from the scope of this Regulation, as these are already covered by Council Regulation (EC) No 4/2009 of 18 December 2008;

As far as parental responsibility is concerned, Brussels II defers the jurisdiction to judges where the minor has habitual residence (Article 8).

The exception to this general principle is set out in Article 12.1:

jurisdictional authorities of a member state which have jurisdiction to decide claims for separation and divorce can also have jurisdiction over the respective claims relating to the parental responsibility connected to these claims for separation and divorce.

3. DOMICILE AND HABITUAL RESIDENCE

3.1 Explain the concept of domicile and habitual residence as they apply to the jurisdiction in relation to divorce, finances and children

According to Article 43 of the Italian Civil Code, domicile and residence are two different juridical concepts reflecting the actual situation in which a person finds themselves.

'The domicile of a person is in the place where that person has established the principal centre of his/her business and interests. Residence is in the place in which the person has his/her habitual abode.'

Abode, as such, is not defined by the Civil Code, but is considered to be the place where the person is actually staying at any one time. Case law precedent has interpreted the concept of residence, as set out in Article 43 of the Civil Code, to mean the habitual and voluntary abode of a person in a determined place. This includes the objective fact of the person staying at that address and the subjective fact of their intention to continue to stay there, which can be proven by their usual lifestyle and social activities. The 'habitual' requirement is not evaluated only according to the duration of the stay or of the interest to remain in a certain place, but must be supported by the will of the 'resident'. Should the person be absent for holidays, travel, studies or work, residence status is not lost, but persists if the resident keeps their home there, returning whenever possible and maintaining the centre of their family and social relations at that location.

Residence is a matter of fact, *res facti*, which can be proven by any form of evidence, not only through the registration certificate.

It should be noted that jurisdiction in matters relating to minors, (if separation or divorce proceedings are not pending, in which case issues of custody and maintenance are to be decided by the court in which the pending separation or divorce proceedings are held) is not settled on the basis of domicile but on the habitual residence of the minor.

As far as the Hague Convention on child abduction is concerned, the habitual residence of a minor need not coincide with the 'residence agreed by the spouses', as stated in Article 144 of the Italian Civil Code, but is linked to a situation of mere fact, being 'the place where the minor, according to a long term and continuous stay, has the centre of his/her emotional ties, deriving from his/her everyday relationships'. (Supreme Court number 22507/2006.)

Therefore, a minor can be considered habitually resident in a place different from that of the residence of their parents and such determination is to be made by the judge of the proceedings.

Of note in relation to minors is the passing of Law no. 219 on 10 December 2012, which came into force on 1 January 2013, which has finally put children born out of wedlock on an equal standing with legitimate children and which has moved almost all matters related to children born out of wedlock from the jurisdiction of the Juvenile Court to the Ordinary Court, thus eliminating some lack of clarity in the identification of the appropriate court.

4. CONFLICT OF LAW/APPLICABLE LAW TO BE APPLIED

4.1 What happens when one party applies to stay proceedings in favour of a foreign jurisdiction? What factors will the local court take into account when determining forum issues?

Conflicts of law and jurisdiction issues in Italy are governed by Council Regulation (EC) No. 1259/2010 of 20 December 2010, EU Regulation Brussels II and Law 218/1995.

According to Article 19 of Brussels II, when proceedings relating to divorce, legal separation or marriage annulment between the same parties are brought before courts of different member states, the court second seised shall, of its own motion, stay its proceedings until such time as the jurisdiction of the court first seised is established.

Should the Italian case have been initiated first in time, the Italian court is obliged to continue, as it may not decline jurisdiction based on a discretionary evaluation of the best interest of the parties.

The only exception to the rule is that provided in Article 15 of Brussels II (mentioned in question 2 above).

B. PRE- AND POST-NUPTIAL AGREEMENTS

5. VALIDITY OF PRE- AND POST-NUPTIAL AGREEMENTS

5.1 To what extent are pre- and post-nups binding within the jurisdiction? Could you provide a brief discussion of the most significant recent case law on this issue?

Strictly speaking pre- and post-nuptial agreements are not envisaged within the Italian system.

When Italian law is that governing the marital property of the spouses, the only agreement permitted is the covenant by which the spouses agree to change their marital property regime from assets in common to separated or vice versa, and that choice affects only the assets purchased during the marriage, having no relevance to the spouses' right to maintenance and/or inheritance rights. This choice must take place after the marriage.

The covenant must be done by way of public deed before a notary, and noted on the marriage certificate. It should also be borne in mind that cohabiting partners are free to reach any agreement they wish.

Generally speaking, the purpose of pre-nuptial agreements is for spouses to waive their respective rights to alimony, maintenance, inheritance rights, etc. Such waivers are not permitted under Italian law, as doing so would be considered a violation of both internal and international public order principles.

The concept of these principles should be explained here.

Dispositions of Italian law that may not be avoided are those which are considered to be part of internal public order, ie, they are laws and articles whose application are, as a rule, mandatory, but which may be overridden by foreign law in certain circumstances.

Principles of international public order, on the other hand, are considered to be the core principles of the Italian juridical system and are common to the majority of Western states. These may not be overridden by foreign law in any circumstances.

If spouses of different nationalities choose, according to Article 30 of Law 218/1995, the law of nationality or the residence of one of them to be that which governs their marital property (derogating the application of the law of common nationality or the law of the place where family life is predominantly established), the application of such a law is permitted provided that it is not contrary to international public order.

The issue of whether or not a pre-nuptial agreement is valid enters into play when a foreign law, which allows the spouses to make such agreements, is the law governing the marriage.

Thus, when foreign law is applicable, it may only override an Italian law that embodies a principle of internal public order and not of international public order, which, as included in the core principles of the Italian legal system, must be upheld. Given that pre-nuptial agreements containing derogations to these core principles are considered null and void, pre-nuptial agreements are not commonly utilised in Italy by either Italian or foreign citizens.

Council Regulation (EU) No 1259/2010 of 20 December 2010 which recently entered into force, regulates spouses' choice for the law applicable to their potential divorce/separation (art. 5). This choice, which used to be considered as being against international public order, seems now to be admissible, even if made by non-EU citizens.

Issues which may be included in foreign pre-nuptial agreements, but which would be considered null and void due to the violation of the rules of international public order, are agreements as to maintenance payments, as this would imply a violation of the binding nature of the rights and obligations provided by Article 160 of the Italian Civil Code, being an illegitimate influence on the freedom of the parties to express consent as to divorce and contrary to the freedom of determination relative to personal status.

The application of the law in Italy in relation to the enforceability of pre-nuptial agreements, even between two foreign citizens who have chosen foreign law to govern their relationships, is cloudy at best. There is very little case law on the point and two of the most relevant cases treat the matter in general terms, not discussing the merits of specific types of clauses.

The Supreme Court decisions of 3/5/1984, number 2682 and 28/5/2004, number 10378, seem to confirm that pre-nuptial agreements are effective in theory, even if entered into between an Italian and non-Italian citizen, as, according to Article 30 of Law 218/1995, spouses are entitled to choose a foreign law as that governing their marital property. However, the Supreme Court pointed out that should any specific clause of a pre-nuptial agreement derogate from the obligatory rights and duties arising from marriage, according to Article 160 of the Italian Civil Code, it would be considered null and void.

However, even if certain clauses of the agreement may be considered null and void, the principle of severability permits other clauses to be considered valid and binding (eg, the choice of the law governing the spouses' marital property pursuant to Article 30 of Law 218/1995).

If the Supreme Court case law position is firm in denying the validity of pre-nuptial agreements governed by Italian law (Court of Cassation, decision 6857/1992), albeit not being as clear cut in relation to foreign pre-nuptial agreements, a large number of scholarly opinions have been published in favour of their lawfulness and, in particular, as to the validity and enforceability of foreign pre-nuptial agreements.

One very recent decision of the Supreme Court however, published on 21 December 2012, number 23713, seems to open the possibility that the strict approach may be reconsidered, and it is worth discussing here.

In this decision, in a case governed by Italian law, the Court declared an agreement between the spouses to be valid. Under the agreement one of the two was bound, in case of divorce, to transfer the ownership of certain real property to the other, who had contributed to the refurbishment of another property owned by the former.

The Court, pointing out that such an obligation is 'within the framework of so-called "pre-nuptial agreements" [...], often used abroad, particularly in Anglo-Saxon countries, where they have the very useful role of defusing situations in family disputes and divorce'. Keeping in mind its own strict view about pre-nups, the Court confirmed that agreements of this kind cannot be considered null and void *per se* but only if they do not protect the weaker spouse, being the only party entitled to claim nullity, and stated the following important principle.

Only if the obligation (in this case, the transfer of real property) could be considered to be a type of 'punishment' in the case of divorce would it violate the intangible principle of free determination to divorce, and would therefore be null and void. However, in this particular case, as the obligation to transfer the property matched the economic sacrifice already made by the spouse who had borne the costs for the restructuring the other spouse's apartment, it can therefore be considered valid.

The divorce that 'triggered' the obligation is only considered here to be a valid 'suspensive condition' as per art. 1353 et seq. Civil Code, leading the Court to state that '...it is an atypical contract, an expression of the free negotiation of the spouses, aimed to meeting interests worthy of protection, according to art. 1322, para. 2'.

In our opinion, this decision could be considered to be a watershed. It should now be possible to structure pre-nuptial agreements in accordance with these principles in order to try to have them recognised as valid in Italy, and they could, in certain cases, not be considered contrary to Italian public order. The question is still open, but an important step has been taken.

C. DIVORCE, NULLITY AND JUDICIAL SEPARATION

6. RECOGNITION OF FOREIGN MARRIAGES/DIVORCES

6.1 Summarise the position in your jurisdiction

It must first be stated that Italy permits and regulates:

(i) civil marriage;
(ii) concordat marriage (*matrimonio concordatario*), celebrated according to the Catholic rite, regulated by canon law and following the canonical form, which also has civil effects recognised by the Italian Republic by way of a specific agreement between Italy and the Holy See; and
(iii) marriage celebrated by ministers of non-Catholic faiths (art. 83 Civil Code) specifically recognised in Italy.

Marriages are recorded in the civil registry (*registro di stato civile*) of the relevant municipality.

Recognition of marriages

Resident and non-resident foreigners are entitled to marry in Italy pursuant to art. 116 Civil Code. That article provides that the marriage is valid, provided that:

(i) the limitations in the following Civil Code articles are not contravened:
    article 85 (no person of unsound mind can contract marriage);
    article 86 (no person bound by a previous marriage can contract marriage);
    article 87 (marriage cannot be contracted between: ascendants and descendants in direct line, full or half siblings and persons connected by affinity in a direct line);
    article 88 (no marriage can be contracted when one of the spouses has been convicted for the murder or attempted murder of the spouse of the other); and
    article 89 (a woman cannot contract marriage until 300 days from the dissolution, annulment or cessation of the civil effects of her previous marriage have passed);

and

(ii) that both bride and groom provide evidence that they are entitled to marry according to the law of their country of origin through a Certificate of No Impediment (*nullaosta*) issued by the relevant authority in their country. If, according to the non-Italian law, the authorisation is subject to conditions considered against the public order, for example conversion to a specific religion, that foreign law will not apply and the authorisation certificate will be considered not subordinated to such conditions.

Celebrations in Italy of non-Catholic religious marriages between foreign citizens will have civil effects if there is a specific agreement between Italy and that particular faith. If there is no such agreement the designation of the religious minister who celebrates the marriage must have been approved by way of decree by the Minister of Interior and the registrar must issue a specific written authorisation to that marriage ceremony.

Marriages celebrated abroad or before a foreign consular authority in Italy for Italian resident foreign citizens can be registered in the civil registry as per article 19 D.P.R. 396/2000 if expressly provided for in a specific convention with that foreign country. To be registered, the marriage certificate must be accompanied by a sworn translation into Italian, be legalised and apostilled.

According to a recent decision of the *Consiglio di Stato*, later agreements between the foreign spouses (for example the agreement to choose Italian law as governing the personal and marital property relations between them and to select the separation of assets regime) can be annotated in the margin of the marriage deed. However, registrations of foreign marriages only have informative value, not the probative value of certainty.

Pursuant to Italian Private International Law, a marriage is formally valid within the Italian jurisdiction if it is valid according to:

- the law of the place where the marriage was celebrated;
- the law of the country of nationality of at least one party at the moment of celebration of the marriage; or
- the law of the state where the couple were jointly resident at the time of the marriage (art. 28 Law 218/1995).

The only marriages not recognised in Italy are marriages that are contrary to public policy, such as polygamist marriages or marriages of minors without authorisation, which cannot be registered in the civil registry.

Recognition of divorces

Pursuant to Article 64 of Law 218/1995 and Article 21 of Brussels II, a foreign decision declaring a divorce is recognised in Italy without the need for any further proceedings, provided the following criteria are met:

- the judge who issued the decision was empowered to do so;
- the defendant was notified of the proceedings and their right to a defence was not violated;
- the parties appeared before the court and the trial is not defective according to the foreign local law;
- the decision is no longer appealable under the foreign local law;
- the decision is not contrary to another un-appealable Italian decision;
- there are no Italian proceedings still pending between the same parties and concerning the same matter which was initiated before the foreign proceedings;
- the decision does not go against the rules of Italian public order.

These requirements will be ascertained by the registrar when registration of the decision is requested.

According to Article 67 of Law 218/1995, the matter only needs to be brought before the Court of Appeal should the foreign decision not be recognised, the recognition is challenged or enforcement of the foreign decision is required.

7. DIVORCE

7.1 Explain the grounds for divorce within the jurisdiction (please also deal with nullity and judicial separation if appropriate).

Grounds for nullity

According to Article 117 of the Italian Civil Code, either or both of the spouses, their direct ascendants, the public prosecutor and anyone else who has a lawful and current interest, can start proceedings to have a marriage declared null and void. The grounds to file such an action are indicated by

Articles 84, 86, 87 and 88 of the Civil Code and are related to a marriage contracted:

- while a party is already married;
- by a minor not authorised by the court;
- between related spouses;
- when one of the spouses has been convicted for the murder of the spouse of the other party;
- by a woman before 300 days have passed from a previous separation, annulment or divorce;
- by an incompetent person or if one of the spouses was not of sound mind;
- after consent has been extorted by threats or by the instilling of considerable fear;
- as a consequence of a mistake made by one of the spouses as to the identity or the essential qualities of the other spouse.

The proceedings take place as an ordinary trial and the effects of the nullity are applied differently in time depending on the good or bad faith of the spouses and whether or not there are children.

Grounds for separation

Pursuant to Italian family law and in relation to parties subject to Italian law, no spouse can start divorce proceedings before having obtained a court order declaring a legal separation.

Legal separation can be requested by one or both of the spouses when, even independently of the will of the spouses, such facts occur that make the continuation of cohabitation intolerable or cause serious prejudice to the upbringing of the children.

The legal separation is mutual if the spouses agree as to the separation and to its conditions. Such proceedings will normally involve a single hearing and the approval of the court.

On the contrary, legal separation will be judicial if the spouses disagree on the separation and/or on its conditions. These proceedings involve an ordinary judicial process, with the giving of evidence and a final decision being made.

Grounds for divorce

As in the case of separation, a divorce can be either by consent between the parties or contentious.

The decisive factor in obtaining a divorce, is the demonstration that the spiritual and material communion that once existed between the spouses has disappeared and can no longer be rebuilt. The grounds for divorce are indicated in Article 3 of the Divorce Law 898/1978, which specifies that divorce can be requested if, after celebration of the marriage, the circumstances detailed in that article exist.

The most common grounds for divorce are filed pursuant to paragraph 6 of Article 3, when a judicial separation has been ordered or a separation by mutual consent has been established between the spouses before the president of the court. Prior to presenting the petition for divorce, under paragraph 6, at least three years must have passed from the date of separation, ie, from the date of the first hearing for separation. If the separation is informal and not registered, the three-year period will not start to run. Any interruption of the separation period, such as reconciliation, results in the cancellation of the time accrued up to the day of the interruption. Therefore, should the parties again decide to proceed with divorce, they must begin the three-year period again.

Other grounds are related to one of the spouses being condemned to life imprisonment or to a prison term exceeding 15 years.

Divorce can also be granted for aggravated assault or the 'taking advantage of a weaker person' to the detriment of the spouse or the children, if the marriage has not been consummated or a final declaration of sex-change has been issued.

No minimum duration of the marriage is required before a divorce can be requested, with the exception of the three-year period under paragraph 6.

8. FINANCE/CAPITAL PROPERTY

8.1 What powers does the court have to allocate financial resources and property on the breakdown of marriage?

The economic and legal status of the family is that of common ownership of property, as provided under Article 159, et seg, of the Italian Civil Code. Real and personal assets purchased either jointly or individually by the spouses during the marriage fall under common ownership, with the exception of those specified in Article 179 of Civil Code (mainly personal and inherited assets). Individual ownership may be achieved when the purchasing spouse uses money which was already their exclusive property.

This status can be changed by the spouses if they so desire (see point 5 above).

Common ownership of property ends before the divorce is pronounced. At the time the parties separate, each spouse becomes severally the owner of 50 per cent of the family assets.

However, the judge presiding over the separation or divorce proceedings only has the power to issue orders for alimony (maintenance for the spouse) and/or child support and has no power to issue orders for the transfer of assets (real or personal) or the allocation of financial resources from one spouse to the other. Therefore any such dispute must be brought in completely separate proceedings.

In cases of separation by mutual consent or joint petitions for divorce the judge can approve the parties' agreement for the transfer of real estate properties or related *in rem* rights between them. However, such an agreement, even if approved by the Court, will have only binding effects between the parties but will not directly affect the transfer of the property. A subsequent notarial deed for the transfer must take place.

Nevertheless, this does not exclude the Italian judge, while applying foreign law in cases of foreign spouses separating or divorcing in Italy and which are to be regulated by that law according to Italian international private law, from making an order as to the division of assets or the allocation of financial resources from one spouse to the other if this is permitted under the foreign law. Recently, the Ordinary Court of Milan, applying South African law (pursuant to Article 31 of Law 218/1995), issued a decision (no. 6599/2012) pronouncing the divorce pursuant to South African law and at the same time ordering the 50/50 division of the spouses' assets wherever located (including outside of Italy) which had been purchased after the wedding, some jointly, some individually, transferring ownership quotas from one spouse to the other (even though this is not permitted under Italian divorce law).

8.2 Explain and illustrate with reference to recent cases the court's thinking on division of assets

Division and the possible (forced) sale of assets does not take place during the separation/divorce proceedings, but during separate proceedings that may even take place contemporaneously with the separation trial (*Corte di Cassazione* 26/2/2010 number 4757).

Due to the fact that the court does not have the power to issue orders for the transfer of assets in separation and divorce proceedings, there are no cases on this particular issue.

9. FINANCES/MAINTENANCE

9.1 Explain the operation of maintenance for spouses on an ongoing basis after the breakdown of marriage

Maintenance payments can be awarded both after separation and after divorce. In order to determine the amount of alimony, the respective income and assets of each spouse are taken into consideration, including any property deriving from the separation of ownership. Also the reasons for the limited financial means of the spouse to be supported are considered. If one of the spouses is declared 'guilty' for the separation, he/she will not be entitled to request alimony. Even if the guilty spouse is not entitled to receive alimony, should the specific requirements detailed in art. 438 Civil Code exist (he/she is in a state of need and cannot support him/herself), he/she will be entitled to receive 'basic support'.

The Divorce Law provides, in particular, that upon the dissolution of the marriage, if the spouse entitled to alimony as above cannot provide for themselves for objective reasons (ie, an inability to work due to disability, old age, etc.), then alimony is established accordingly. If, on the other hand, the spouse is able but unwilling to support him/herself or is negligent in taking measures towards that end, it is possible that alimony will be reduced or even denied altogether.

In determining the amount of alimony, the court must consider the conditions of the couple, the reasons for the decision, the personal and financial contribution to the family given by each spouse and the assets of each party or the common property and the income of both parties. Having evaluated all these elements, even in light of the duration of the marriage, the court may order one of the spouses to periodically pay an allowance in favour of the other.

There is no set timeframe for the payments, although they tend to be made monthly. In place of alimony, and only when the divorce is pronounced, it is possible to make a one-off payment to the spouse entitled to support, provided both parties are in agreement and provided the judge approves the amount of the payment. In such a case, no further request of a financial nature can be submitted. Such a one-off payment is not tax deductible, unlike regular long term periodic payments.

In cases of separation or divorce, the parties must present income statements and any other documentation pertaining to revenue or personally and commonly-owned property. In cases of dispute, the judge may order an investigation of incomes, assets and lifestyle, and may turn the matter over to the taxation and revenue police.

The obligation to pay the allowance ceases if the spouse to whom the alimony is being paid remarries.

9.2 Is it common for maintenance to be awarded?

It is quite usual for the court to issue maintenance orders. The main problem is in getting a clear picture of the spouse's income and assets, as discussed below.

9.3 Explain and illustrate with reference to recent cases the court's thinking on maintenance

There are currently no automatic percentages to be applied regarding the calculation of alimony. Even though there is no specific principle of 'equity' a judge in Italy may use his discretion and will determine alimony on a case-by-case basis.

Case precedent has clarified that the weaker spouse is entitled to receive alimony if:

- they do not have adequate income to maintain the same lifestyle that they enjoyed during the marriage, and
- if there is and inbalance between the sum of the income and general wealth of the entire position of that spouse and the wealthier spouse (ex multis *Corte di Cassazione* 07/02/2006 number 13747).

Therefore, not only the income of the wealthier spouse must be considered, but also their total assets, inclusive of real estate, stocks, shares etc., (*Corte di Cassazione* 24/4/2007, number 9915).

According to case precedents, alimony in separation cases is based upon the inadequacy of the means of the weaker spouse, being insufficient to allow them to enjoy the same standards of living as enjoyed during the marriage (*ex multis Corte di Cassazione* 5/7/2006, number 15326).

According to article 156, paragraph 7 Civil Code and article 9, paragraph 1 of Law 898/1970, it is always possible to revise separation/divorce decisions if a change in the circumstances of the spouses or the family have occurred. This is due to the fact that financial orders issued during separation or divorce proceedings never become final.

10. CHILD MAINTENANCE

10.1 On what basis is child maintenance calculated within the jurisdiction?

According to Articles 147 and 148 of the Civil Code, parents must maintain, educate and instruct their children, taking into account their ability, natural inclination and aspirations, and must fulfil this obligation in proportion to their respective means and according to their working ability both professionally and at home.

According to Article 155 of the Civil Code, the judge who declares the separation and/or divorce is also to set the amount and the manner in which each parent is to contribute to the child's support, care, education and upbringing.

Similarly to Article 155 of the Italian Civil Code, Article 6, paragraph 3 of the Divorce Law provides that the court is to establish to what extent and in which manner the non-custodian parent must contribute to the support, care, education and upbringing of the children.

Unless the parties come to a different agreement, each parent is responsible for the support of the child proportionally to his/her income and earning capacity. The judge, where necessary, will order one party to make child-maintenance payments.

The same criteria used for determining spousal maintenance are used in determining the amount of child support.

In the case of a mutually agreed separation, the spouses can agree to the amount of child maintenance. As in cases of mutual separation, in joint petitions for divorce the court will approve the parent's agreement.

The obligation to support children lasts at least until the child is economically independent, even if of age, unless he/she can be found guilty of neglecting his/her duties (*ex multis Corte di Cassazione* 17/11/2006, number 24498). However it must be noted that this deciding factor is to be declared by Court.

A court decision of Tribunal of Florence, 3/12/2007, number 3931, used, for the very first time, a specific model with determined elements and an index to calculate the amount of the maintenance. This decision is very relevant as usually the determination of the amount of maintenance has always been left entirely to judicial discretion.

11. RECIPROCAL ENFORCEMENT OF FINANCIAL ORDERS

11.1 Summarise the position in your jurisdiction

The enforcement of Italian financial orders follows the ordinary rules established for execution. Enforcement is legally based on the judgment of separation or divorce, as well as any temporary orders issued by the judge while the separation/divorce proceedings are pending.

Italian law provides two approaches to guarantee the fulfilment of financial orders. The first is a preventive measure giving the judge the possibility of requiring a guarantee such as a personal security guarantee or a collateral security from the party who has to pay alimony. The second measure is actionable only in case of default and allows the creditor spouse to request the seizure of the assets of the defaulting spouse or to seek an order against a third party (such as the defaulter's employer, tenant or pension institution) to pay part of the amount directly to the creditor spouse. The real or personal property of the defaulter may be seized, along with their financial assets.

12. FINANCIAL RELIEF AFTER FOREIGN DIVORCE PROCEEDINGS

12.1 What powers are available to make orders following a foreign divorce?

In order to enforce foreign financial orders in Italy, both in relation to EU and non-EU orders, an *exequatur* as per EC Regulation 44/2001 and the Hague Convention of 2/10/1973 (law applicable to spousal and child maintenance obligations) is required by way of proceedings before the Court of Appeal.

D. CHILDREN

13. CUSTODY/PARENTAL RESPONSIBILITY

13.1 Briefly explain the legal position in relation to custody/parental responsibility following the breakdown of a relationship or marriage

Law 54/2006 has introduced shared custody as the preferred arrangement for the custody of children, as in this way both parents must actively participate in the care and education of their children. The custodial duties are divided and allocated by the court in the most appropriate manner.

Article 155 Civil Code, as amended by Law 54/2006, regulates this matter.

When shared custody is granted in cases of separation and/or divorce, both parents exercise parental authority, therefore any major decision regarding the child should be taken jointly, taking into consideration the best interests of the child, even if the minor is living just with one of the two parents. However in practice, especially during the first, often acrimonious, stage of separation, although parents should be attempting to cooperate in the interests of the children, it is most common for the judge to decide that they carry out their duties separately.

The new law has provided the courts with a flexible instrument, able to be modified to fit the specific facts of individual family groups. If the parents have come to an agreement as to the child's upbringing, the judge will accept the agreement and will only determine the placement, residence and visiting times of the child. Should the parents not have reached any agreement, the court will rule on the spheres of action of each parent, eliminating any form of commonality in the child's routine activities.

Only in cases in which the judge grants 'sole custody' to one of the parents (which is now very rare in Italy and requires positive proof that it is in the best interests of the minor: cf. *ex multis Cassazione*, sez. I, 17 February 2009, no. 26587 in Foro it., 2010, I, 428) even if both have parental authority, the custodian parent is to exercise that authority. Nevertheless, the non-custodian parent must still be consulted and involved in major decisions relating to the child.

Article 4 of Law no. 54/2006 extended the application of shared custody to children born out of wedlock, who are now therefore governed by identical legislation.

13.2 Briefly explain the legal position in relation to access/contact/visitation following the breakdown of a relationship or marriage

Although according to Law 54/2006, parents exercising shared custody rights do so with absolute equality, this does not mean that the child should be placed with both parents and spend the same amount of time with each of them, as it is unlikely that the child's best interests will be served by continuously alternating between the homes of the parents. Exceptions are made for special cases where the interests of the child are best met by spending an equal amount of time with each parent. In most cases therefore the minor will live mainly with one parent, spending most of the time with her/him.

Even if not expressly stated in the legislation, the Court therefore decides with which parent the child is to be based, taking into consideration that this residence must be the core of the child's interests and relationships. Consequently, in order to ensure the least disturbance to the child's habits and environment, necessary for their peaceful and balanced development, the judge is to order that the family home be awarded to the parent with whom the child is placed (Article 155 quater Civil Code).

However, despite the fact that the child's centre of interests is located with one of the parents, both parents must have absolute equality in the tasks of education and care, and the possibility of dealing with the child.

The court must also determine the manner and timing of the child's stay with the other parent. In the event that there is dialogue and collaboration between the parents, the court may limit itself to broad and generic terms such as 'when they decide,' 'prior arrangements' 'according to mutual agreement', while in cases of conflict, the judge must decide upon a specific and precise visiting timetable.

We note that in practice, in the event of conflict between the parents, the visiting regime has remained largely unchanged with respect to the situation prior to the reform, when single-parent custody was the norm.

14. INTERNATIONAL ABDUCTION

14.1 Summarise the position in your jurisdiction

This area is governed by the Hague Convention on the Civil Aspects of International Child Abduction, signed on 25/10/1980 and ratified in Italy with Law 15/1/1994, number 64 (Convention).

Article 12, Chapter III of the Convention provides that an order for the immediate return of a child can only be issued in the case of wrongful removal of a child from the person actually exercising the custody. If, instead, the custodian parent is moving abroad, the non-custodian parent can only apply to have their access rights rendered effective.

In Italy the designated central authority involved in the process of having the child returned is the Ministry of Justice, Office for Juvenile Justice.

If a foreign minor is abducted and brought to Italy, the petition of repatriation can be filed either through the foreign designated central Authority or directly at the Italian Ministry of Justice. While the authority examines the petition, the Italian police locate the child and make initial contact with the parent who removed the child to evaluate if he/she is willing to return the minor.

If this attempt fails, the central authority sends the petition, with all the documentation, to the office of the public prosecutor in the Juvenile Court where the minor is located and a hearing is scheduled. The parent filing the petition can participate in the hearing, setting out their position. The court will also meet the parent who removed the minor.

Although the parties can appeal the decision before the Supreme Court, the decision of the Juvenile Court is immediately actionable and is not suspended by the lodging of an appeal.

15. LEAVE TO REMOVE/APPLICATIONS TO TAKE A CHILD OUT OF THE JURISDICTION

15.1 Summarise the position in your jurisdiction

According to Article 316 of the Civil Code, a child is subject to the authority of its parents until majority or emancipation. The authority is exercised by both parents by mutual agreement.

In the case of separation and/or divorce, if shared custody is granted, both parents exercise parental authority, therefore, any decision regarding the minor must be made jointly, taking into consideration the best interests of the child. It is now undisputed that when parents have shared custody, the decision of moving the child's residence overseas must be agreed upon by both parents and, in default thereof, by the Court (Bologna Juvenile Court, 6 February 2007 in Famiglia e dir., 2007, 813, n. ARCERI).

Should the parents not be in agreement, the principles of the Italian law regarding the rights and duties of the parents require that the authorisation of the court for moving a minor abroad be obtained, both in the case of shared custody and sole custody.

This interpretation appears to be supported by some precedents, which state that although there is no limitation to granting custody to parents residing, or who wish to reside, abroad, a deeper evaluation of the best interests of the child is needed, making particular reference to the possible move.

15.2 Under what circumstances may a parent apply to remove their children from the jurisdiction against the wishes of the other parent?

There are no set rules as to when such an application can be made, and the judge is required to review each matter on a case-by-case basis to ascertain the best interests of the child.

E. SURROGACY AND ADOPTION

16. VALIDITY OF SURROGACY AGREEMENTS

16.1 Briefly summarise the position in your jurisdiction

Law 19 February 2004 no. 40 prohibits surrogacy agreements in Italy.

Pursuant to Article 12 of that law, anyone who produces, organises or advertises the sale of gametes or embryos or surrogacy in any form, is to be punished.

Although the law does not impose criminal responsibility on Italian intended parents who enter into surrogacy agreements outside of Italy, they may face criminal charges when they return to Italy with the child born from the surrogate mother. This stems from the fact that, according to Italian law (Article 269 paragraph 3 Civil Code) the woman who gives birth to the child is that child's mother. Therefore, in theory, the registration of the newborn in the register of births as the child of the intended mother could be construed as the offence of 'tampering with the civil registry' (Article 567 paragraph 2 Criminal Code). However, it should be noted that recent cases precedent recognises the possibility of registering a baby born under a surrogacy agreement outside Italy, in a country that admits such practices, as the child of the intended parents (Bari Court of Appeal decision 13 February 2009 and Naples 14 July 2011). In the first decision, the judges declared that surrogacy agreements are not against International Public Order and, in the interests of the child, there should be certainty as to his status, to avoid the records showing him as having different mothers in more than one country. In the Naples decision, the judges stated that the consequences of the foreign law regulating surrogacy agreements were not contrary either to Italian constitutional principles or the principles adopted by the international community to which Italy belongs and with which it shares values.

17. ADOPTION

17.1 Briefly explain the legal position in relation to adoption in your jurisdiction. Is adoption available to individuals, cohabiting couples (both heterosexual and same-sex)?

Under Italian legislation there are three types of adoption. Full and legitimating adoption ('*adozione piena e legittimante*' articles 1 et seq. Law 184/1983); adoption in 'special cases' (articles 44 et seq. Law 184/1983) and adoption of adults (Articles 291 et seq. Civil Code).

There are two procedures for full adoption depending on whether the adopted child is Italian or foreign (Law 184/1983). National and international full adoptions are only available to couples who have either been married for at least three years or have cohabitated for three years prior to the marriage. With this kind of adoption the minor severs all ties with their family of origin and acquires the status of legitimate child in the new family.

For national adoptions the Juvenile Court must ascertain that the applicant parents match all the requirements listed by law (art. 6) and that the minor is adoptable (full national adoption is available for abandoned, or orphaned minors with no relatives up to the fourth degree of kinship who can take care of them). The Court then orders a preliminary year of pre-adoption fostering, and after that time, the adoption order is issued. If during the year of pre-adoption fostering the applicant parents separate, in the interests of the minor, adoption can be granted to just one parent, as the requirements to be met by the adoptive parents need only exist at the time of the issue of the pre-adoption fostering order.

When the adoption order becomes final, the adoption is effective and it is noted in the margin of the birth registry by the registrar.

Another category is 'special cases'adoption. 'Special cases' adoption, however, does not give rise to a legitimate parent-child relationship, replacing that of the family of origin, but establishes a relationship of adoptive affiliation that joins and adds to the family of origin. In this case the adopted child retains the rights and obligations *vis-à-vis* their original family and, at the same time, acquires them in relation to their adoptive family. The child keeps his/her original surname, hyphenating it after the surname of the adopting parent, and has inheritance rights from both the natural and adoptive families. However, the adopting parents are not recognised with survivorship rights over the adoptee and the child has no legal relationship to the relatives of the adopter.

This is the only kind of adoption available to unmarried persons, but it is only allowed in the specific cases provided for in Article 44 Law 184/1983:

(i) when the minor is an orphan and the adopter is a relative within the sixth degree of kinship or, as an unrelated person, established a long-term relationship with the minor before the death of the parents;
(ii) when the minor is an orphan and is disabled (art. 3 paragraph 1, Law 104/1992); or
(iii) when the impossibility of pre-adoption fostering has been ascertained.

Article 37 bis, Law 184/1983 provides that the laws governing national adoption apply to foreign minors abandoned in Italy.

Article 36 Law no. 184/1983 states that adoption declared abroad upon application of Italian citizens who have resided in that foreign country continuously for two years is recognised in Italy if the conditions set out in the Hague convention are met.

Two recent court rulings related to the right of adoption of unmarried people are worth noting here.

The decisions of the Supreme Court no. 3572 of 14 February 2011 and the Tribunal of Caltanissetta of 18 July 2011 found that unmarried couples can obtain recognition in Italy of a foreign decision ordering an adoption, but only with the effects of the 'special cases' adoption and not those of full adoption. The judges of the Supreme Court held that full adoption is permitted only to married couples, but invited the Italian government to extend the possibility for unmarried people in particular circumstances to adopt children with full adoption effects.

As far as same-sex couples are concerned a recent Supreme Court decision declared that 'there is no scientific certainty that can prove that a minor cannot grow up in a balanced way with a same sex couple' (Court of Cassation number 601 of 11 January 2013).

F. COHABITATION

18. COHABITATION

18.1 What legislation (if any) governs division of property for unmarried couples on the breakdown of the relationship?

Pursuant to Italian legislation, marriage is considered the only personal relationship having any legal effect. Thus, there is no legislation governing cohabitation.

Although cohabitation is a fairly widespread social behaviour, there is to date no jurisprudence establishing that financial support during the life of the relationship is the responsibility of one of the cohabitants. This derives from the fact that any disbursement or expenses from one party in favour of the other is considered merely a duty dictated by moral principles.

It follows that there is no law whatsoever providing for the payment of alimony upon the cessation of the relationship, even if the end of the relationship is unjustified.

One limited effect of cohabitation is the partner's right of succession under rental contracts.

G. FAMILY DISPUTE RESOLUTION

19. Mediation, Collaborative Law and Arbitration

19.1 Briefly summarise the non-court-based processes available in your jurisdiction and the current status of agreements reached under the auspices of mediation, collaborative law and arbitration

Pursuant to D. Lgs. 4 March 2010 no. 28 there exist various types of mediation in civil and commercial matters in Italy. This law provides that mediation:

(i) is compulsory for specific matters (however the Constitutional Court declared on 6 December 2012, case no. 272, that the mandatory nature of such an instrument of settling disputes is unconstitutional, and as a consequence mediation is no longer compulsory);
(ii) can be suggested by the judge;
(iii) is optional for civil and commercial disputes relating to available rights;
(iv) can be agreed by contract in case of dispute.

However, this kind of mediation is not available in family matters.

The only types of mediation available in family matters arise within the court proceedings and are:

(i) the judge's attempt at conciliation at the first hearing in separation or divorce proceedings; and
(ii) the family mediation that the judge can suggest during the proceedings, which, if accepted by both spouses, causes a suspension of proceedings.

The transcript of an agreement reached between the parties at a family mediation can be written up as a record of separation by mutual consent (or a joint application for divorce) but the contents must be approved by the Court. For agreements that cannot be approved by the Court, it has been held that they are valid if they do not interfere with the arrangements made with the approval of the Court.

Law 54/2006, regulating family mediation, provides (Article 4) that all its provisions also apply 'to proceedings for the children of unmarried parents', while family mediation does not apply to unmarried couples without children.

Pursuant to Article 806 Code of Civil Procedure, arbitration is not available in family law matters .

19.2 What is the statutory basis (if any), for mediation, collaborative law and arbitration in your jurisdiction? In particular, are the parties required to attempt a family dispute resolution in advance of the institution of proceedings?

Article 708 Code of Civil Procedure and art. 4 paragraph 7, L. 898/1970 provide that at the first hearing at which the parties appear personally in separation and divorce proceedings, the judge must try to reconcile the spouses, hearing them first separately and then jointly. Rather than resulting in the reconciliation of the couple and renunciation of the separation request, this attempt most often leads the spouses to modify a contentious separation petition making it into a separation by mutual consent.

Although pursuant to the rules of procedure, after having heard the spouses and the respective counsel at the first hearing, the judge usually makes the temporary and urgent decisions deemed necessary to protect the interests of the minor(s) and the spouses and then the judge may decide that family mediation is advisable (Article 155 sexies Civil Code) and, if both the spouses give their consent, suspend the proceedings and decisions as to temporary and urgent orders in order to allow the spouses to reach a settlement with the support of an expert, taking into consideration the moral and material interests of any children.

However, given that both parties must give their consent, that the proceedings in such cases are extended without temporary orders being issued to regulate custody and maintenance, and that at this time there are no public entities able to perform such a service, this mechanism is rarely used in practice.

H. OTHER

20. CIVIL PARTNERSHIP/SAME-SEX MARRIAGE

20.1 What is the status of civil partnership/same-sex marriage within the jurisdiction?

Currently under the Italian system, homosexual couples do not have the right to marry or even register their marriage celebrated abroad. Civil partnerships are not envisaged either under Italian legislation, which does not recognise foreign civil partnerships.

However, recent court decisions have granted same sex couples certain specific rights.

The Reggio Emilia Tribunal, 13 February 2012, decided that since European citizens have the right to freely move their residence within the European Union together with their family, a non-EU man who legally married an Italian in Spain has the right to obtain a residence card in Italy should his husband decide to set up home there. Similar decisions have been made in relation to other specific issues, granting same-sex couples the same rights as heterosexual couples such as the right to damages for unlawful death; the right to sublet real property; the right of the same-sex partner not to witness a signature; the right of the same-sex partner to be registered with a supplementary insurance institution.

20.2 What legislation governs civil partnership/same-sex marriage?

Even if in the recent past proposals have been presented to Parliament to regulate this matter, at present no legislation governs same-sex marriages. Nevertheless recent interpretations of laws issued by the European Parliament have had effects on the attitude of the Italian Supreme Court.

In 2010, with decision no. 138, the Constitutional Court refused a petition calling for a ruling that that the Constitution guarantees the right of two persons of the same sex to marry, but also stated that:

(i) homosexual unions – understood as the stable cohabitation of two people of the same sex – can be considered as part of the 'social formations' regulated by art. 2 of the Italian Constitution, to which the fundamental right to freely live as a couple belongs;
(ii) it is up to Parliament in its discretion to determine how such unions are to be recognised and guaranteed;
(iii) the Constitutional Court has the power to intervene in specific cases of discrimination between married couples and homosexual couples.

The decision of the Supreme Court no. 4184, 15 March 2012, also stated that a stable homosexual couple cohabiting *de facto*, has the right to 'family life' and that gender difference is no longer a prerequisite for the existence of marriage. The Court also stated that such a union cannot be registered in the civil registry, not due to its 'non-existence' or its 'invalidity', but because such unions do not produce any legal effects in Italy.

21. CONTROVERSIAL AREAS/RAPIDLY DEVELOPING AREAS OF LAW

21.1 Is there a particular area of the law within the jurisdiction that is currently undergoing major change?

Pre-nuptial agreements, cohabitation and same-sex marriage are areas of law in which there are current draft bills and in relation to which Supreme Court precedents may lead to significant changes in the near future.

21.2 Which areas of law are most out of step? Which areas would you most like to see reformed/changed?

An area that requires regulation is the 'reconstituted or blended family', when two people marry or cohabitate and one or both have at least one child from a previous relationship living part-time or full-time in the household. This kind of family and the step-parenthood stemming from it are becoming more and more common, but are regulated by *ad hoc* legislation, which is causing anomalies and hardships.

In addition, legislation should be passed governing all the 'new' situations related to minors in the different types of families that have come into being, such as unmarried couples or same sex couples who have either adopted or 'had' surrogate children abroad, thus constituting a de facto family. However, notwithstanding the fact that such families effectively exist, they are not regulated by law.

Japan

Tokyo Public Law Office Mikiko Otani

A. JURISDICTION AND CONFLICT OF LAW

1. SOURCES OF LAW

1.1 What is the primary source of law in relation to the breakdown of marriage and the welfare of children within the jurisdiction?

1.2 Which are the main statutes governing matrimonial law in the jurisdiction?

The primary source of law in Japan is statutory law. The main statute governing matrimonial law in relation to the breakdown of marriage, child custody and financial issues in Japan is the Civil Code.

2. JURISDICTION

2.1 What are the main jurisdictional requirements for the institution of proceedings in relation to divorce, property and children?

At the moment, there is no statutory law providing jurisdictional requirements for the institution of proceedings in relation to divorce, property and children in international family cases. However, certain jurisdictional rules for international family cases have been established in the jurisprudence of the Supreme Court decisions, which have been followed by the lower courts.

Jurisdiction over international divorce cases

When deciding whether a Japanese court has jurisdiction over a divorce with an international element, the guiding principle is set by the leading decision of the Supreme Court Grand Bench of 25 March 1964 (*Minshu* 18-3-486). The Supreme Court Grand Bench set the principle that the jurisdictional requirement is the domicile of the defendant in Japan. It also set the exceptions when the Japanese court has jurisdiction over the international divorce cases even if the defendant does not have domicile in Japan. The requirements for the exceptions are the domicile of the plaintiff in Japan AND the existence of one of the following situations:

(i) if the plaintiff was abandoned by the defendant;
(ii) if the whereabouts of the defendant are unknown; or
(iii) other equivalent situations.

By applying this rule the Supreme Court affirmed jurisdiction over the divorce case filed by the Korean wife residing in Japan against the Korean husband who had never been to Japan and whose whereabouts were not known.

While this decision was made in the divorce case between the couples where both parties were foreigners, the rule set out by the Supreme Court Grand Bench has been followed and applied by the lower courts as the general principle for all the divorce cases with an international element, irrespective of the nationality of the parties.

The Supreme Court Second Petty Bench decision of 24 June 1996 (*Minshu* 50-7-1451) is another leading case, in which the Supreme Court set additional exceptional grounds for the Japanese courts having jurisdiction over international divorce cases. Within the general framework set by the Supreme Court Grand Bench decision of 1964 that the domicile of the defendant in Japan is required in principle, the court indicated the existence and its extent of legal or factual impediment to the plaintiff in initiating a divorce action in the country of the domicile of the defendant should be considered in determining jurisdiction if there is nexus between the divorce claim and Japan because of the residence of the plaintiff in Japan and other factors. The Supreme Court held that the Japanese court had jurisdiction in the present case despite the fact the defendant wife was domiciled in Germany. This was because the German divorce judgment was not recognised in Japan because service of the divorce proceedings was via publication (see section 6.1 below). Further divorce proceedings therefore had to be initiated in Japan.

Jurisdiction over matrimonial property issues of international divorce

It is understood that the same criteria for jurisdiction over international divorce cases applies to the matrimonial property issues of international divorce. The Tokyo High Court decision of 29 March 1993 (*Kasai Geppo 45-10-65*) dismissed the suit for financial relief asking for compensation and confirmation of the ownership of the matrimonial properties existing in Japan for the reason that the Japanese court lacks the jurisdiction in this case where the both parties have US nationality and neither party has domicile in Japan.

Jurisdiction over child custody/access issues of international family cases

There are different views on the rule for jurisdiction over the child issues of international family cases. The dominant position taken in the case laws is that if the Japanese court has the jurisdiction over the divorce case, it also has the jurisdiction over the ancillary child custody/access claims to the divorce claim, irrespective the domicile of the child. On the contrary, the dominant view among scholars is that the court of the country of domicile of the child has jurisdiction over the child custody/access issues, whether or not brought as ancillary claims to the divorce claim or independently. According to this view, there may be cases where the Japanese court has jurisdiction over the divorce case but not over the child issues as the child is not domiciled in Japan.

As regards child issues claims filed independently from the divorce claim, there is no dispute over the rule that the country of domicile of the child has jurisdiction.

Conflict of jurisdiction

Article 142 of the Code of Civil Procedure prohibits the parties of the case pending before the court from filing another petition on the same case. However, it is interpreted that this article does not apply to the international conflict of jurisdictions. In other words, the Japanese court will not automatically dismiss the petition filed by a party of the case pending before a foreign court on the same subject matter. It is generally understood that the Japanese court may exercise jurisdiction over the same matter as long as the Japanese court has jurisdiction over the said matter according to the jurisdictional rule explained as above. While which court is seised first does not matter, once the foreign court makes the decision, which becomes final and is recognised as valid in Japan, the Japanese court will dismiss the petition on the same matter for the reason that there is no longer interest of the petition (the case becomes moot).

Motion to dismiss the petition because of lack of jurisdiction

If the defendant objects to the jurisdiction of the Japanese court, the court can determine the jurisdictional issue first before proceeding further to consider the merits. It may also proceed to consider the merits while holding a decision on jurisdiction until it makes a final decision. If the court finds it lacks the jurisdiction, the petition will be dismissed. If the court finds it has jurisdiction, it generally makes such jurisdictional decision together with the decision on the merits in a final judgment. However, the court, when the jurisdictional dispute becomes ripe, may make an interlocutory judgment on the jurisdictional issue (Article 245 of the Code of Civil Procedure).

3. DOMICILE AND HABITUAL RESIDENCE

3.1 Explain the concepts of domicile and habitual residence as they apply to the jurisdiction in relation to divorce, the finances and children

Domicile

As explained above, the main factor of the jurisdictional requirements established by the jurisprudence in Japan is domicile of the parties or the child. Domicile is defined as the principle place wherein a person lives (Article 22 of the Civil Code). A Japanese national residing in Japan has an obligation to notify the municipal office of a change of domicile under the Basic Resident Registration Law. This Law was amended to apply also to a foreigner granted a residential status for more than three months as of 9 July 2012. However, it should be noted that the mere fact that domicile of a person is recorded under the Basic Resident Registration Law does not mean that the person has domicile for the purpose of jurisdictional requirement. For the jurisdictional purpose, whether a person has domicile in Japan is decided by substantive elements. However, no clear criteria to establish domicile such as the duration or purpose of residence have developed in the case law. It is observed that the courts tend to find domicile of a person simply based on the fact of the physical residence.

Registered domicile

Every Japanese national has registered domicile where that person's each incident of personal affairs such as birth, marriage, divorce, adoption and death is registered according to the Family Registry Act. As far as a person is a Japanese national, he/she has registered domicile in Japan, irrespective of in which country he/she has domicile. Therefore, the fact that a Japanese national has registered domicile in Japan does not mean that he/she has domicile in Japan for the purpose of jurisdictional requirements.

Habitual residence

As explained above, the main factor of the jurisdictional requirements established by the jurisprudence in Japan is domicile. Unlike some jurisdictions, the concept of habitual residence is not used in Japan for the jurisdictional decision. However, it is understood that the concept of domicile for the jurisdictional decision under the Japanese law is practically the same as the concept of habitual residence.

4. CONFLICT OF LAW/APPLICABLE LAW TO BE APPLIED

4.1 What happens when one party applies to stay proceedings in favour of a foreign jurisdiction? What factors will the local court take into account when determining forum issues?

Please see section 2.1 above for conflict of jurisdiction.

Statutory law on conflict of law

In Japan, the Act on General Rules for Application of Laws (GRAL) provides the rules for issues of conflict of law and provides which law governs the legal matter in issue.

Law applicable to international divorce

Articles 25 and 27 GRAL provide the rule of application of law to international divorce. If the national law of the husband and wife is the same, the same nationality law applies to their divorce. If their nationality law is not the same but the law of the habitual residence is the same, the same law of habitual residence applies. If neither is the case, the law of the place most closely connected with the husband and wife applies. However, if either husband or wife is a Japanese national who has habitual residence in Japan, Japanese law applies.

To determine if the nationality law of the husband and wife is the same in the case where either or both of them have more than one nationality, Article 38 GRAL provides the rule. Where a party has more than one nationality, the nationality law of that party shall be the law of the country of his/her nationality where he/she has habitual residence. If there is no such country of his/her nationality where the party has habitual residence, the party's nationality law shall be the law of the country with which the party is most closely connected. However, if one of those nationalities is Japanese, Japanese law shall be the party's nationality law.

The same law that governs divorce as determined above also applies to division of matrimonial properties.

Law applicable to child issues

Article 32 GRAL provides the rule on the applicable law to child issues such as custody and visitation but not to the child maintenance. The child's nationality law applies if it is the same as the nationality law of either the father or the mother (in cases where one parent died or is unknown, the nationality law of the other parent). In other cases, the law of the child's habitual residence applies.

With regard to child maintenance, the Act on Applicable Law to Maintenance provides the applicable law. Under the Article 2 of this Act, the law of the child's habitual residence applies in principle.

B. PRE- AND POST-NUPTIAL AGREEMENTS

5. VALIDITY OF PRE- AND POST-NUPTIAL AGREEMENTS

5.1 To what extent are pre- and post-nups binding within the jurisdiction? Could you provide a brief discussion of the most significant recent case law on this issue?

A pre-nuptial agreement regarding the properties is valid between a husband and wife as long as it was entered into prior to notification of marriage (Article 755 of the Civil Code). However, to assert the validity of a pre-nuptial agreement against the successor in title of the husband or wife, or a third party, it also needs to be registered prior to notification of marriage (Article 756). A post-nuptial agreement regarding the property rights of a husband and wife is not valid if it adopts a different property system other than the statutory property system as it may not be altered after the notification of marriage (Article 758 (1)).

As pre-nuptial agreements have been rarely used in Japan, there are only a few court decisions reported with regard to pre-nuptial agreements and those decisions are on the issue of taxation. When a husband and wife enter into a pre-nuptial agreement, how the Japanese court would decide on division of matrimonial properties upon divorce is not clear as no relevant court decision on this issue has been reported.

C. DIVORCE, NULLITY AND JUDICIAL SEPARATION

6. RECOGNITION OF FOREIGN MARRIAGES/DIVORCES

6.1 Summarise the position in your jurisdiction

The foreign marriage is recognised in Japan if it is valid in two aspects on formalities and the substantive requirements according to the applicable law to be determined by Article 24 of GRAL. Formalities for a marriage shall be governed by the law of the place where the marriage is celebrated (*lex loci celebrationis*). Formalities that comply with the nationality law of either party to a marriage shall be also valid. Therefore, foreign marriage celebrated in a foreign country that meets the formality requirements of the law of that country or the nationality law of either party to a marriage is valid regarding the formality aspect. With regard to the substantive requirements for the

formation of a marriage, the nationality law of each party applies.
Foreign divorce concluded by the decision of a foreign court is recognised when such a foreign court divorce judgment (decision, order or decree) is final and meets the following conditions provided by Article 118 of the Code of Civil Procedure:

(i) The jurisdiction of the foreign court is recognised under laws or regulations or conventions or treaties.
In determining if the foreign court has jurisdiction over the case, the same jurisdictional rule explained earlier applies. For example, Tokyo Family Court decision of 11 September 2007 (*Kasai Geppo* 60-1-108) refused to recognise a divorce order of the Australian court. One of the reasons for the refusal was lack of jurisdiction of the Australian court on the divorce, as both parties in this case, a Japanese wife and an Australian husband, had domicile in Japan.

(ii) The defeated defendant has received a service (excluding a service by publication or any other service similar thereto) of a summons or order necessary for the commencement of the suit, or has appeared without receiving such services.
To meet this condition, the international service from that foriegn country to the defendant in Japan needs to be conducted by a method valid through international judicial cooperation, such as through the consuls or the central authorities and with the translation attached thereto in compliance with the treaty if there is a treaty on service to which both that foreign country and Japan are parties.

(iii) The content of the judgment and the court proceedings are not contrary to public policy in Japan.
Not many precedents in which a foreign court decision was not recognised by applying this clause have been reported. The Tokyo Family Court decision of 11 September 2007 mentioned earlier refused recognition of the divorce order of the Australian court on this ground as well as the lack of jurisdiction in the circumstances where the divorce petition of the Australian husband should not have been admitted due to his act of unchastity according to the established jurisprudence of the Supreme Court of Japan (See Section 7 for details of the jurisprudence on this issue).

(iv) A mutual guarantee exists.
This condition is met as far as the Japanese court judgment may be recognised under the similar conditions in that foreign country which issued the judgment. There is no reported court decision that refused to recognise a foreign court divorce judgment applying this clause.

7. DIVORCE

7.1 Explain the grounds for divorce within the jurisdiction (please also deal with nullity and judicial separation if appropriate)

Divorce by agreement

Under Japanese law, couples may divorce by agreement (Article 763 of the Civil Code). Divorce by agreement can be concluded as far as both parties agree on divorce whether or not there is a ground for judicial divorce. Procedure for divorce by agreement is administrative in nature with no involvement of the court. Divorce shall take effect upon acceptance of notification of divorce by the municipal office. The notification of divorce is made by submission of the divorce paper with signatures of the husband and wife and two adult witnesses. If a party changes a mind after signing a divorce paper or has a fear that his/her spouse would submit a divorce paper without his/her consent by forging his/her signature may request in writing that the municipal office shall not accept a divorce paper if submitted by the other spouse (request not to accept notification). While the condition for divorce by agreement is simply the consent of the parties on divorce, by agreement couples with a minor child have to agree on which parent will have parental authority over the child as well to conclude divorce (Article 819 of the Civil Code).

Grounds for judicial divorce

Article 770 of the Civil Code provides grounds for judicial divorce. When the couples cannot agree on divorce, they may file a suit for divorce after having tried but failed to reach an agreement by the Family Court mediation. A petition for judicial divorce may be filed on one or some of the five grounds provided in Article 770 (1):

(i) if a spouse has committed an act of unchastity.
An act of unchastity (adultery) is interpreted to mean having a sexual relationship with a person of a different sex, other than the spouse;

(ii) if abandoned by a spouse in bad faith.
Abandonment in bad faith may include such acts as leaving the spouse or refusing to live with the spouse without reasonable reasons, kicking the spouse out of the house, and refusing to provide financial support to the spouse;

(iii) if it is not clear whether a spouse is dead or alive for not less than three years;

(iv) if a spouse is suffering from severe mental illness and there is no prospect of recovery; or

(v) if there is any other grave cause making it difficult to continue the marriage.

The last ground is interpreted in practice to mean practically the same as 'irrecoverable breakup of the marriage'. Factors often brought to claim this ground include violence, abuse, serious insult, alcoholism, gambling, commitment of crimes, failure to work despite the ability to work, failure to cooperate with the spouse to run the family, conflict with the spousal family, difference in personal characteristics, etc. The length of separation is often considered as one of the most important factors in establishing the irrecoverable breakup of the marriage, although separation is not an indispensable factor.

One of the most important rules established by the Supreme Court decisions is the doctrine on the admissibility of divorce petition made by the spouse who is responsible for the breakup of the marriage. The Supreme

Court decision of 19 February 1952 (*Minshu 6-2-110*) denied the petition for divorce by the husband who left his wife and lived with another woman and had a child with her on the ground of Article 770 (1) (v). The succeeding Supreme Court decisions followed this doctrine but qualified the conditions when this doctrine should apply. The Supreme Court Grand Bench decision of 2 September 1987 (*Minshu 41-6-1423*), while holding the doctrine, revised the precedent Supreme Court decisions to allow divorce even if the spouse responsible for the breakup of the marriage filed a petition provided that the three conditions are met:

(i) the duration of separation is considerably long considering the ages of the parties and compared with the duration of co-habitation;
(ii) there are no dependent children of the couple; and
(iii) there are no outstanding circumstances considerably against social justice to admit a divorce petition such as the situation where the spouse objecting to the divorce will be placed into extremely severe mental, social or economic conditions by divorce.

While these three conditions, in particular, the duration of the separation period, has been gradually loosened in the case law, the doctrine and the three conditions for exceptions to grant divorce still remain. This doctrine has generally applied only to the cases where the plaintiff has committed adultery.

Judicial separation

There is no judicial separation under Japanese law. However, it is possible for the separated couples to enter into a separation agreement in mediation at the Family Court to formally agree on such issues as child custody, visitation and maintenance during separation.

8. FINANCES/CAPITAL, PROPERTY

8.1 What powers does the court have to allocate financial resources and property on the breakdown of marriage? Explain and illustrate with reference to recent cases the court's thinking on division of assets

Financial orders in relation to divorce

One party to divorce can file a claim for distribution of properties on or following divorce within the period of two years after divorce (Article 768(1)(2) of the Civil Code). In the case of judicial divorce, one party can file a claim for distribution of properties in the divorce proceedings (Article 771). The court who issued the divorce order, shall have jurisdiction over the claim for distribution of properties in the divorce judgment (Article 32 of the Code of Personal Procedures). Article 768(3) of the Civil Code gives the court wide discretionary powers to make an order for distribution of properties providing that *'the family court shall determine whether to make a distribution, and the amount and method of that distribution, taking into account the amount of property obtained through the co-operation of both parties and all other circumstances'*.

Distribution of properties under Japanese law is generally understood to cover the following three elements:

(i) distribution of matrimonial properties that are acquired during marriage;
(ii) compensation for the mental damage caused by divorce;
(iii) post-divorce maintenance.

Distribution of matrimonial properties that are acquired during marriage

Irrespective of the holder of the properties, whether a husband or wife, the properties acquired by the contribution of the both parties after the marriage and maintained until the divorce (or separation when separation precedes) are to be considered as matrimonial properties and distributed according to the level of the contribution of each parties. Except for special cases, the levels of contribution of the parties are assumed equal.

Compensation for the mental damage caused by divorce

If one of the parties is responsible for the breakdown of the marriage, the other party can claim compensation for the mental damage caused by divorce under the Article 709 of the Civil Code (Supreme Court decision of 21 February 1956 (*Minshu* 10-2-124). The claim of compensation can be included in the claim for distribution of properties or can be filed as a separate ancillary claim in the divorce proceeding. The party who claims compensation may also file a civil lawsuit within the period of three years after the date of divorce.

Post-divorce maintenance

The case law indicates the general understanding that this element is of a supplementary nature. It means that the court considers this element in making an order of distribution of properties only when one party cannot support her/his living after divorce even with the properties that she/he would receive from the other party as the first two elements, ie, distribution of matrimonial properties and/or compensation.

In the proceeding for the distribution of properties, the court is not constrained by the claims of the parties and can make decisions exercising its discretionary power by taking into account 'all other circumstances' (Article 768 (3)).

Division of pension

If either or both of the parties are covered by Employee Pension Insurance, one party to the divorce can file an application for the decision of the ratio for the division of the record of the payment for the pension on or within two years after divorce. Unless exceptional circumstances exist, the ratio to be decided by the court upon such an application is 50:50.

This claim is based on the Employee's Pension Act and does not apply to private pension schemes. If the parties are covered by private pension schemes, such benefits may be considered as part of matrimonial properties to be distributed to the parties according to the level of contribution as explained earlier.

9. FINANCES/MAINTENANCE

9.1 Explain the operation of maintenance for spouses on an ongoing basis after the breakdown of marriage

9.2 Is it common for maintenance to be awarded?

9.3 Explain and illustrate with reference to recent cases the court's thinking on maintenance

As long as the parties are married even after its breakup and separation, they have a legal obligation to share the expenses that arise from the marriage (Article 760 of the Civil Code). According to this Article, the spouse who has the greater income has a legal obligation to pay maintenance to support the financially disadvantaged spouse. In Japan the spousal maintenance during marriage includes the child maintenance paid by the non-resident parent. The amount is calculated based on the annual incomes of the husband and the wife. In the family court practice, a simplified chart is generally used for calculation (See section 10).

After divorce there is no spousal maintenance obligation except for the cases where the element of post-divorce maintenance is considered when the court determines distribution of properties (See section 8 above).

10. CHILD MAINTENANCE

10.1 On what basis is child maintenance calculated within the jurisdiction?

The parent who does not reside with the dependent child has a legal obligation to pay child maintenance to the other parent who resides with the child. Parents have responsibilities to ensure their dependent child enjoys the same standard of living as the parents themselves enjoy. Child maintenance covers the regular expenses of the child's clothes, food, residence, education and medication of the standard level. There is no cut-off age provided by law at which the child maintenance obligation of the parents finishes. However, the standard practice in the family courts is to have a cut-off point at age 20, which is the age of majority (Article 4 of the Civil Code), unless an extension until, for example, the end of college education, is otherwise agreed by the parents.

The amount of child maintenance is calculated using a formula designed to reflect the concept that the parents are responsible for ensuring their dependent child enjoys the same standard of living as the parents. A simplified chart has been created for ease of reference. The chart and the guidance on how to use it are available at the official website of the Tokyo Family Court (only in Japanese) at *www.courts.go.jp/tokyo-f/vcms_lf/santeihyo.pdf*.

The simplified chart is created from the formula for calculation so that the standard amount of child maintenance can be found easily by using the chart based on the annual gross income (taxable income) of the parents, type of income (salary or self-employment income), number and ages of children. The chart is not legally binding and only used as a tool to find the standard amount easily and quickly.

When there are special circumstances which result in the amount calculated under the formula being considerably unfair, the court may order an amount departing from the chart taking into consideration of special expenses. Typical examples of such special circumstances include the case where the child is attending an expensive private school by the agreement of the parents and the amount of child maintenance is increased to cover the school expenses.

11. RECIPROCAL ENFORCEMENT OF FINANCIAL ORDERS

11.1 Summarise the position in your jurisdiction

There is no different treatment of financial orders of foreign courts and the same conditions for the recognition of the foreign court judgment explained in section 6 applies to the effect of financial orders of foreign courts in Japan. To enforce the financial orders of foreign courts, the creditor has to file a suit in a district court seeking an execution judgment under Article 24 of the Civil Execution Act. An execution judgment will be issued provided the foreign court order meets the conditions for recognition of the foreign court judgment under Article 118 of the Code of Civil Procedure.

12. FINANCIAL RELIEF AFTER FOREIGN DIVORCE PROCEEDINGS

12.1 What powers are available to make orders following a foreign divorce?

If the divorce is concluded by a foreign court judgment that is recognised in Japan meeting the conditions for recognition of foreign court judgments, the Japanese court may issue an order for distribution of properties as explained in section 8 as far as the Japanese court has jurisdiction over the distribution of properties in relation to divorce. It is understood that if the Japanese court has jurisdiction over the divorce case, it also has jurisdiction over the financial relief such as distribution of properties and compensation in relation to divorce. The Tokyo High Court decision of 29 March 1993 (*Kasai Geppo* 45-10-65) dismissed the suit for financial relief asking for compensation and ownership of the properties in Japan filed by the American ex-wife residing in the US against the American ex-husband residing in New Zealand following the divorce order issued in the US court for the reason that the Japanese court does not have jurisdiction as neither ex-wife or ex-husband has residence in Japan.

D. CHILDREN

13. CUSTODY/PARENTAL RESPONSIBILITY

13.1 Briefly explain the legal position in relation to custody/parental responsibility following the breakdown of a relationship or marriage

Under the Japanese law, at the time of divorce, by agreement or by order of the court, one of the parents shall be given parental authority (Article 819 of the Civil Code). In Japan parental authority includes both legal and physical custody. Parental authority has to be given to either a father or a mother upon divorce and there is no system in the Japanese law for the divorced parents to jointly hold parental authority.

When the parties cannot agree on parental authority, the court decides which parent shall have parental authority. There is no clear principle or criteria stipulated in the law for the decision on parental authority but it is understood the overall principle is the 'welfare of the child'. Although the parenting abilities and appropriateness of as a caregiver are important factors, continuity of the care arrangement is given considerable weight in practice. Views of the child are heard and considered depending the maturity and circumstances of the child. Other factors to be generally considered include non-separation of siblings. Preference of the mother is not generally used in the reasoning for the decision but when the mother is a primary caretaker, it may be considered as part of the factors of continuity of the care arrangement and parenting abilities and appropriateness.

13.2 Briefly explain the legal position in relation to access/contact/visitation following the breakdown of a relationship or marriage

The amended Article 766(1) of the Civil Code which became effective as of 1 April 2012 provides that visitation shall be determined by the agreement of the parents if they divorce by agreement. If such agreement has not been made or cannot be made, visitation shall be determined by the family court (Article 766(2)). The general principle of the 'welfare of the child' has been used by the family court when making decisions on visitation.

Before the amendment of the Article 766, when the Article did not mention 'visitation', but it was understood that the family court had the power to determine visitation as included in 'the matters regarding custody', the 'welfare of the child' had been sometimes used to deny visitation of the non-custodial parent to the child. It seems that the amendment has encouraged the divorcing parents to agreement on the issue of visitation and has encouraged a more positive approach toward visitation in the family courts. The Supreme Court First Petty Bench decision of 28 March 2013 made it clear that the visitation order or the mediated agreement on visitation can be enforced by way of indirect compulsory execution (Article 172(1) of the Civil Execution Act) which sets out monetary sanction against the party who does not perform the obligation. This decision also set the condition for the visitation order or mediated visitation agreement to be enforceable by the indirect compulsory execution order. The condition is that the visitation is sufficiently specified in terms of dates and times, frequency, duration, pick-up and return of the child.

14. INTERNATIONAL ABDUCTION

14.1 Summarise the position in your jurisdiction

As of July 2013 Japan is not a state party to the Hague Convention of 25 October 1980 on the Civil Aspects of International Child Abduction. However, after a long debate, the Japanese government decided to prepare to join the Convention in May 2011. The implementing legislation was adopted by the Diet in June 2013 and the Diet at the same time approved entering into the Convention. It is expected Japan will actually join the Convention in early 2014. The Ministry of Foreign Affairs is designated to be the Central Authority of Japan. Only two family courts, Tokyo Family Court and Osaka Family Court will hear the return cases under the Convention.

Abduction of the child from Japan to foreign countries is a crime of kidnapping for transportation out of country punishable by imprisonment with work for a definite term of not less than two years under Article 226 of the Penal Code of Japan when abduction is done by force or enticement.

15. LEAVE TO REMOVE/APPLICATIONS TO TAKE A CHILD OUT OF THE JURISDICTION

15.1 Summarise the position in your jurisdiction. Under what circumstances may a parent apply to remove their child from the jurisdiction against the wishes of the other parent?

There is no specific procedure for seeking the permission of the court to remove a child out of Japan. If a parent has sole parental authority over the child, they may remove the child out of the jurisdiction without the consent of the other parent.

E. SURROGACY AND ADOPTION

16. VALIDITY OF SURROGACY AGREEMENTS

16.1 Briefly summarise the position in your jurisdiction

Surrogacy is not prohibited or regulated by law in Japan. There has been only one relevant court decision involving the surrogacy issue, the Supreme Court Second Petty Bench decision of 23 March 2007 (*Minshu* 61-2-619). Here, the municipal office rejected the registration of the non-birth parents as parents of the children born to a surrogate mother. The children were delivered by the American surrogate mother inside whom the fertilised eggs of the Japanese wife with the sperm of her Japanese husband were implanted. While the Japanese couples obtained a judgment from the court in the United States that declared them to be the parents of the children, the Japanese Supreme Court found that such judgment cannot be recognised in Japan as it is contrary to the public policy (Article 118 (iii) of the Civil Code Procedure. see section 6.1) and upheld the rejection by the municipal office by finding that the mother who delivered the child is the mother under the Civil Code of Japan.

There has been no court decision on the validity of surrogacy agreements.

17. ADOPTION

17.1 Briefly summarise the position in relation to adoption in your jurisdiction. Is adoption available to individuals, cohabiting couples (both heterosexual and same-sex)?

A person who has obtained the age of majority may adopt another person as his/her child (Article 792 of the Civil Code). If a married person adopts a minor child, such adoption shall be made only jointly with the spouse of the adopting parent except for the case where the adopted child is the child born from the marriage of the spouse (Article 795). There is no scheme where cohabiting couples can jointly adopt a child.

F. COHABITATION

18. COHABITATION

18.1 What legislation (if any) governs division of property for unmarried couples on the breakdown of the relationship?

There is no legislation that governs division of property for unmarried cohabiting couples on the breakdown of the relationship. However, it has been established by case law that Article 768 of the Civil Code provides that division of property for married couples on divorce applies *mutatis mutandis* to unmarried cohabiting couples.

G. FAMILY DISPUTE RESOLUTION

19. MEDIATION, COLLABORATIVE LAW AND ARBITRATION

19.1 Briefly summarise the non-court-based processes available in your jurisdiction and the current status of agreements reached under the auspices of mediation, collaborative law and arbitration

As explained below, Japan has a long history of family court mediation for family dispute resolution. Private mediation provided outside court is available for family dispute resolution but has not been actively used. There is no court decision reported on the question of whether agreements reached by private mediation are binding on the courts. There is no practice of using arbitration for family dispute resolution. Collaborative law is not practised in Japan.

19.2 What is the statutory basis (if any), for mediation, collaborative law and arbitration in your jurisdiction? In particular, are the parties required to attempt a family dispute resolution in advance of proceedings?

A party who wants to divorce shall first try mediation in the family court before filing a lawsuit for divorce (Article 257(1) of the Code of Procedure for Family Affairs Disputes).

H. OTHER

20. CIVIL PARTNERSHIP/SAME-SEX MARRIAGE

20.1 What is the status of civil partnership/same-sex marriage within the jurisdiction?

20.2 What legislation governs civil partnership/same-sex marriage?

There is no legislation that governs civil partnership/same-sex marriage. Under Japanese law marriage is possible only between a man and a woman. There is no legal recognition or protection of same-sex marriage. It has been reported that same-sex couples who want to form a legally recognised relationship enter into an adoption agreement, as adoption between adults is possible under the Japanese law.

Case law has developed to give common marriage legal protection similar to that given to the legal marriage under the Civil Code in certain aspects of marriage. Special laws also treat common law marriage as providing some types of social benefits. However, there has been no court decision on the question of whether such legal protection given to common law marriage applies to same-sex partners.

21. CONTROVERSIAL AREAS/RAPIDLY DEVELOPING AREAS OF LAW

21.1 Is there a particular area of the law within the jurisdiction that is currently undergoing major change?

21.2 Which areas of law are most out-of-step? Which areas would you most like to see reformed/changed?

One of the most controversial areas of family law is child custody law. As outlined previously, currently the Civil Code does not allow divorced parents to share parental authority. It is allowed to give parental authority to one parent and physical custody to the other parent under the Civil Code, though what kind of rights are actually held and may be solely exercised by the custodial parent are not clear. While the law does not explicitly prohibit shared custody and there is a positive view on the possibility for the divorced parents to share physical custody by agreement, the legal rights of the parents sharing physical custody while one of them has sole parental authority are not clear. Parents who want to share parental authority have used these schemes as a practical alternative to shared parental authority under the current Civil Code. However, there has been an increasing number of voices calling for reform to the Civil Code to introduce joint custody. On the other hand, there is strong objection against the joint custody system and the reform of the existing custody law is a controversial debate.

Another controversial, as well as rapidly developing, area of family law is child abduction. Currently there is no statutory law which regulates one parent from taking the child without consent of the other party. It is not prohibited by law if one parent removes the child from the situation where both parents who jointly hold parental authority were residing with the child. However, if the left behind parent takes back the child from the parent who first removed the child, such action is sometimes found illegal in a civil sense or even found criminal as kidnapping of the minor (Article 224 of the Penal Code) in the case where removal of the child was conducted by use of force. These practices are criticised and confusing to the parties involved. Furthermore, the discrepancy is pointed out between the existing law and current practice for parental child abduction occurring within the country and the remedies that will soon become available for the left behind parents of the international parental child abduction under the Hague Convention when Japan joins the Convention.

Jersey

Hanson Renouf Advocate Barbara Corbett

A. JURISDICTION AND CONFLICT OF LAW

1. SOURCES OF LAW

1.1 What is the primary source of law in relation to the breakdown of marriage and the welfare of children within the jurisdiction? Which are the main statutes governing matrimonial law in the jurisdiction?

Jersey family law is predominantly derived from Jersey statute. However, some elements of English law have been incorporated into Jersey law through case law such as the English 'section 25 criteria' in financial remedy matters and the requirement for scrutiny of the care plan in public law children cases. Jersey case law, both reported and unreported, is available from *www.jerseylaw.je*. Jersey case law is supplemented by English and Guernsey case law where appropriate.

1.2 What are the main statutes governing matrimonial law in the jurisdiction?

The main statutes of interest to the family lawyer in Jersey are the Matrimonial Causes (Jersey) Law 1949 (as amended) and the Children (Jersey) Law 2002, although there are other statutes on specific issues such as adoption, child abduction and recognition of foreign divorces. The statutes are supported by the Matrimonial Causes Rules 2005 and the Children Rules 2005.

2. JURISDICTION

2.1 What are the main jurisdictional requirements for the institution of proceedings in relation to divorce, property and children?

Jersey is not part of the United Kingdom, or a member of the European Union, so Brussels II does not apply and the relevant law is Jersey law.

The family court (the Family Division of the Royal Court of Jersey) has jurisdiction in relation to divorce, nullity and judicial separation where the parties are domiciled in Jersey when proceedings are started or if either of the parties has been habitually resident in Jersey for the year immediately preceding the date proceedings are begun or, in the case of nullity or presumption of death, the year preceding the death (Matrimonial Causes (Jersey) Law 1949, Articles 3 and 6).

The jurisdictional limitations on applications in relation to children are found in the Child Custody (Jurisdiction) (Jersey) Law 2005. Within matrimonial proceedings, orders for residence, contact, specific issue orders and prohibited steps orders (pursuant to Article 10 Children (Jersey) Law

2005) can be made as long as proceedings are continuing, unless the court considers it would be more appropriate for such matters to be determined outside Jersey. For Article 10 orders not brought within matrimonial proceedings, the child must be either habitually resident in Jersey or present in Jersey but not habitually resident in Jersey or any part of the United Kingdom. An exception to this is where there are ongoing matrimonial proceedings anywhere in the United Kingdom involving the child's parents. The Royal Court can, however, make an order under its inherent jurisdiction if a child is present in Jersey and the court considers that it must exercise its powers immediately for the child's protection.

Financial remedies are generally applied for within divorce proceedings or Schedule 1 Children (Jersey) Law 2002, although there is the little used Separation and Maintenance Orders (Jersey) Law 1953 which provides for applications to be made in the Petty Debts Court for maintenance between spouses and the transfer of tenancies.

3. DOMICILE AND HABITUAL RESIDENCE

3.1 Explain the concepts of domicile and habitual residence as they apply to the jurisdiction in relation to divorce, the finances and children

The domicile of a married woman is the same as that of her husband under Jersey law (domicile of dependence). Therefore a married woman cannot be domiciled in Jersey, no matter what her connection to the island, if her husband is domiciled elsewhere. Either party to a marriage can, however, bring proceedings if either of them has been habitually resident in Jersey for the year ending with the date of issue of proceedings. A legitimate child takes the domicile of her father, an illegitimate child, the domicile of her mother.

4. CONFLICT OF LAW/APPLICABLE LAW TO BE APPLIED

4.1 What happens when one party applies to stay proceedings in favour of a foreign jurisdiction? What factors will the local court take into account when determining forum issues?

If the Jersey courts have jurisdiction to accept an application then an application can be made in Jersey regardless of any other proceedings already being extant elsewhere. Jersey is not subject to Brussels II or Brussels II *bis*, so issuing proceedings first in another jurisdiction does not necessarily oust the Jersey court. A divorce petition must include details of any other proceedings which there have been or which are continuing in Jersey or elsewhere which relate to the marriage or any children. If there is a dispute as to forum, a stay of the Jersey proceedings can be requested, this is decided on *forum conveniens* grounds. The appropriate forum has been described as: *'that in which the case may be tried most suitably in the interests of all the parties and the ends of justice... that with which the action had the most real and substantial connection'. Federal Republic of Brazil v Durant International Corporation* [2010] JLR 421 para 19. In *De Sa v Luis* [2009] JRC 027 it was held that where there were extant proceedings in Jersey, on the facts it was wrong for the respondent to bring ancillary relief proceedings in Madeira.

The correct forum was Jersey and the respondent's actions in bringing the Madeiran proceedings were unconscionable.

Decisions in respect of forum in financial remedy applications are made at the case review hearing at which both parties must be present.

Jersey law is applied in Jersey courts.

B. PRE- AND POST-NUPTIAL AGREEMENTS

5. VALIDITY OF PRE- AND POST-NUPTIAL AGREEMENTS

5.1 To what extent are pre- and post-nups binding within the jurisdiction? Could you provide a brief discussion of the most significant recent case law on this issue?

The position in respect of pre-nuptial agreements in Jersey is very similar to that in England and Wales and Guernsey. Such agreements do not bind the court, but their existence can be taken into account in the exercise of the court's discretion. The court has full power to vary any marriage settlement or post-nuptial settlement (Article 27 Matrimonial Causes (Jersey) Law 1949) or to order that a settlement of any property one party is entitled to, should be made for the benefit of the other party or any child of the family (Article 28) as long as a decree of divorce or nullity or judicial separation has been made. Agreements made prior to marriage by adults with the benefit of full disclosure and legal advice and the absence of duress or undue influence will be seriously considered by the court, but no agreement can oust the jurisdiction of the court in respect of applications pursuant to the Matrimonial Causes (Jersey) Law 1949. There is no case law in Jersey in respect of pre-nuptial agreements.

C. DIVORCE, NULLITY AND JUDICIAL SEPARATION

6. RECOGNITION OF FOREIGN MARRIAGES/DIVORCES

6.1 Summarise the position in your jurisdiction

Foreign marriages are recognised in Jersey if they were validly contracted according to the law of the jurisdiction in which they took place.

Under the Recognition of Divorces and Legal Separations (Jersey) Law 1973 a decree of divorce or judicial separation granted in any part of the British Islands is recognised in Jersey, as are any divorces and legal separations which have been obtained by judicial or other proceedings in any other country and which are effective under the law of that country.

Where a divorce is recognised under the law, neither spouse shall be precluded from re-marrying in Jersey on the ground that the divorce is not recognised as valid in another country.

There is an exception to recognition of a foreign divorce where, according to the law of Jersey (including its rules of private international law), there was no subsisting marriage between the parties.

7. DIVORCE

7.1 Explain the grounds for divorce within the jurisdiction (please also deal with nullity and judicial separation if appropriate)

Divorce is only available after three years of marriage, except in exceptional circumstances. The grounds for divorce are: adultery, desertion for two years, unreasonable behaviour, incurable mental illness or serving a prison sentence of more than 15 years (or life) on the part of the respondent. The concepts of collusion, condonation and connivance attach to the above grounds. Irretrievable breakdown is not a ground for divorce.

A divorce may also be granted on the basis of a year's separation with consent, or two years' separation, immediately preceding the presentation of the petition. For separation the parties must have 'lived apart' for either one or two years, continually. There is no provision for attempted reconciliation, if cohabitation is resumed, the period of separation has to start again.

Judicial separation is available on all the same grounds as divorce, with the addition of the respondent being 'an habitual drunkard'.

A marriage may be annulled if it is void (ie, one or both of the parties is under 16, the parties are not a man and a woman or at the time of the marriage one or both of the parties was already married) or voidable on one of the following grounds:

(a) the impotency of one or both parties to the marriage since its celebration;
(b) the marriage was celebrated through fraud, threats or duress;
(c) the marriage has not been consummated owing to the wilful refusal of the respondent;
(d) the respondent was at the time of the marriage pregnant by some person other than the petitioner (or a former husband, while married);
(e) the respondent was suffering from a venereal disease at the time of the marriage;
(f) either party to the marriage was at the time of the marriage of unsound mind or was then suffering from mental disorder of such a kind or to such an extent as to be unfitted for marriage and the procreation of children or subject to recurrent attacks of insanity or epilepsy;
(g) an interim certificate has, after the time of the marriage, been issued to either party to the marriage (pursuant to the Gender Recognition (Jersey) Law 2010);
(h) either party has taken steps for the recognition of his or her change of gender
(i) the respondent is a person whose gender at the time of the marriage had become the acquired gender.

Under (d), (e), (f) or (g), the court shall not grant a decree unless it is satisfied:

(i) that the petitioner was at the time of the marriage ignorant of the facts alleged;
(ii) that proceedings were instituted within a year from the date of the marriage; and
(iii) that marital intercourse with the consent of the petitioner has not taken place since the discovery by the petitioner of the existence of the grounds for a decree.

The procedure for nullity is the same as for divorce and judicial separation in that undefended causes can be dealt with without the parties attending a hearing, following the issue of a Greffier's Certificate confirming that the petitioner is entitled to a decree of divorce, judicial separation or nullity.

8. FINANCES/CAPITAL, PROPERTY

8.1 What powers does the court have to allocate financial resources and property on the breakdown of marriage?

The overriding objective in respect of ancillary relief is to deal with cases justly (Matrimonial Causes Rules 2005 rule 47). The court has the power to vary trusts, marriage settlements, post-nuptial settlements or separation agreements having regard to means and conduct or in the interests of children. There is a power to transfer any property to the other party, or to the children of the family or anyone else for the benefit of the children, power to order periodical payments, lump sums (more than one is permissible and any sums may be ordered to be paid in instalments) and to secure such payments, for both the other spouse and any children of the family. The court can order that property is sold and order who should receive the proceeds of sale, can insist that property is offered for sale to specific people or that there is a deferred sale. It is also possible for the court to order execution of documents by others where a person does not comply with an order for sale. There is also a power to vary, suspend or discharge orders and the court shall have regard to all the circumstances of the case including any increase or decrease in the means of the parties. There is no power to make pension sharing orders or any power to set aside prior transactions which may have been made with the intention of defeating claims. However, Pauline actions[1] and tracing claims are available if necessary.

8.2 Explain and illustrate with reference to recent cases the court's thinking on division of assets

Where needs allow, there is a starting point of an equal division of assets, but the court retains a wide discretion. 'The touchstone in all cases involving a division of matrimonial assets is fairness. The court must try to achieve fair financial arrangements between the parties, and the welfare of the children is a primary consideration... Nonetheless a ruthless application of the principle of equality will seldom lead to fairness'; *J v M* 2002 JLR 330. The 'section 25'[2] factors – from the English Matrimonial Causes Act 1973 section 25 – are frequently referred to in Jersey cases. These are absent from the Matrimonial Causes (Jersey) Law 1949, but have been brought into the equation through Jersey case law (*Howarth v McBride* (1984) JJ 1 and *In the Matter of S* [2011] JRC 119). Although there can be no pension sharing orders made in Jersey, the fact that a party has a pension can be taken into account when dividing the other assets and such pension assets be 'off-set' (*Brownbill v Southern* 1999 JLR 94 and *S v W* 1999 JLR N9).

Generally assets are divided equally unless the needs of the parties

[1] Setting aside certain transfers into trusts made with the intent of defrauding existing creditors

[2] The 'section 25' factors are from the English Matrimonial Causes Act 1973 section 25

dictate that one party should have a greater share in all the circumstances, particularly the care of young children (*O v O* 2005 JLR 535). Wherever possible, the court will endeavour to preserve the matrimonial home for one of the parties, especially where there are children (*In the Matter of P* [2009] JRC 159C). The Jersey courts do follow English case law and such a course of action has been expressly encouraged by the court. (*The Matter of L* [2010] JRC 082A where the English cases of both *Charman* and *J v J* were considered).

Where there is inadequate or misleading disclosure the court will set aside orders if appropriate, it is no defence that the other party could have discovered the true position: *P-S v C* 2006 JLR 463. Where there are trusts the court can order disclosure of information if it suspects that the husband is hiding behind the trust *M v G* 2003 JLR N28.

9. FINANCES/MAINTENANCE

9.1 Explain the operation of maintenance for spouses on an ongoing basis after the breakdown of marriage

Generally it is expected that parties will seek to maximise their income and earning capacity (*Warn v Connetta* [2009] JRC 202), although in that case the wife's ill health precluded her from doing so and maintenance was payable. A clean break is considered preferable wherever possible, but spousal maintenance can be ordered and secured under Article 29 Matrimonial Causes (Jersey) Law 1949. When making maintenance orders the court must have regard to 'all the circumstances of the case including the conduct of the parties' and 'their actual and potential financial circumstances'. Maintenance orders can be made on a joint lives basis or for a specified term. Maintenance does not cease on re-marriage, but orders can be discharged, varied or suspended (and revived) and if they are so varied the court must have regard to all the circumstances of the case, including any increase or decrease in the means of the parties.

Interim maintenance can be ordered to maintain a spouse during proceedings, including maintenance for legal fees (*S v C* 2003 JLR N24 and *In the Matter of O* 2010 JLR Note 18).

9.2 Is it common for maintenance to be awarded?

Maintenance is awarded in Jersey and in recent times, perhaps because of the current economic climate, maintenance seems to be being awarded in more cases than perhaps five years ago. Maintenance for a fixed period, to enable a party to re-train, or while children are very young is relatively common.

9.3 Explain and illustrate with reference to recent cases the court's thinking on maintenance

There are few recent cases in respect of spousal maintenance, but in the case of *Leapingwell v Sinclair* [2012] JRC 215 an application for nominal spousal maintenance made by a mother of two children, one of whom had developmental difficulties was dismissed on the basis that it prevented there being a clean break. Although the mother benefited from accommodation provided through a trust, she was reliant otherwise on state benefits. However, in other (unreported) cases spousal maintenance has been ordered where the incomes and needs of the spouses dictate. There is a general desire to facilitate a clean break, so while significant sums of interim maintenance can be ordered (including for legal fees) substantive orders for spousal maintenance are less prevalent, maintenance being capitalised wherever possible.

10. CHILD MAINTENANCE

10.1 On what basis is child maintenance calculated within the jurisdiction?

There is no Child Support Agency or C-MEC in Jersey. Child maintenance is determined by the court, if not agreed. The family court tends to set the level of child maintenance at a rate consistent with English child support levels, using the English rates as a guide.

An order for child maintenance can be made within divorce proceedings, and such maintenance can be secured, but not beyond the age of 21 (Article 25 Matrimonial Causes (Jersey) Law 1949). The court can make such provision 'as appears just'. The case of *Byrne v Hall* 2001 JLR 690 determined that maintenance can be paid in respect of children beyond the age of majority (in that case 25) if in full-time education.

Child maintenance orders usually allow for index linking and although it used to include provision in respect of higher education, the current practice is that maintenance is agreed or ordered up to the end of secondary education with provision for a review if the child goes on to higher education. Frequently at that stage the payments are made directly to the child and not the parent. In addition to child maintenance there are frequently orders for the payment of school fees and doctors' fees, school uniforms and school activities.

Orders for child maintenance, lump sum payments and transfer of property can be made under Schedule 1 of the Children (Jersey) Law 2002. These applications can be made whether or not the parents are married. People over 16 can apply for orders for financial relief under Article 2 of the Law, if in education or training. The court has to have regard to all the circumstances when making an order, including the current and future means of the parties, the financial needs, obligations and responsibilities of the parties and the child, the income, earning capacity, property and financial resources of the child, any physical or mental disability the child may have and the manner in which the child was being or was expected to be educated or trained.

11. RECIPROCAL ENFORCEMENT OF FINANCIAL ORDERS

11.1 Summarise the position in your jurisdiction

By virtue of the Maintenance Orders (Facilities for Enforcement) (Jersey) Law 2000 certain financial orders (principally maintenance) can be registered in Jersey if the payer is resident in Jersey, and once registered can be enforced as if it were an order made in Jersey. Registration is straightforward, the court where the order is made sends a certified copy of the order to the Lieutenant-Governor who in turn forwards the order to Greffier for registration. Reciprocal arrangements included in the Law allow for orders made in Jersey to be registered and enforced in foreign jurisdictions by transmission to the other jurisdiction through the Lieutenant-Governor.

12. FINANCIAL RELIEF AFTER FOREIGN DIVORCE PROCEEDINGS

12.1 What powers are available to make orders following a foreign divorce?

There are no provisions in Jersey to make orders following a foreign divorce. Applications can be made under the Children (Jersey) Law 2002, regardless of divorce.

D. CHILDREN

13. CUSTODY/PARENTAL RESPONSIBILITY

13.1 Briefly explain the legal position in relation to custody/parental responsibility following the breakdown of a relationship or marriage

Where a child's father and mother were married to each other at the time of the birth they each have parental responsibility for the child. Where the parents are unmarried, only the mother has parental responsibility (Article 3 Children (Jersey) Law 2002). The father can gain parental responsibility either by entering into a parental responsibility agreement with the mother, or by order of the court.

When parents separate or divorce there is no necessity for any custody order, each parent retains parental responsibility. It is assumed that parents will make their own arrangements for the care of their children without any intervention from the court. There is a principle of no order under the Children (Jersey) Law 2002. However, if parents cannot agree with whom the child lives, then an application can be made to the court for a residence order pursuant to Article 10. An order under this article can designate who a child lives with and with whom the child has contact or there can be a shared residence order. With a shared residence order the court can determine the time the child spends with each parent and also impose other conditions as necessary. The order relates to whom the child lives with, not to where the child lives. When making orders in respect of children pursuant to the Children (Jersey) Law 2002 the child's welfare is paramount and the court must have regard to the 'welfare checklist' ie, the ascertainable wishes of the child, her physical, emotional and educational needs, the effect of change on the child, the child's age, sex, background and other characteristics, any harm the child has suffered or is at risk of suffering, how capable the child's parents are of meeting her needs and the range of powers available to the court.

When an application is made for an Article 10 order, an officer of the Jersey Family Courts Advisory Service (JFCAS) is appointed to meet the parents to see if an agreement can be reached. They may then be required to prepare a report to assist the court.

13.2 Briefly explain the legal position in relation to access/contact/visitation following the breakdown of a relationship or marriage

Orders for contact (and prohibited steps orders and specific issue orders) are made pursuant to Article 10 Children (Jersey) Law 2002. The same provisions apply as for residence orders.

14. INTERNATIONAL ABDUCTION

14.1 Summarise the position in your jurisdiction

Jersey is a signatory to the Hague Convention on the Civil Aspects of Child Abduction. Child abduction is dealt with through the Child Abduction and Custody (Jersey) Law 2005. The central authority for child abduction purposes in Jersey is the Attorney General. The costs of applications under this Law are not at the expense of the States of Jersey unless the applicant is otherwise eligible for legal aid. The Law also deals with the recognition and enforcement of custody decisions made in other jurisdictions. There are specific provisions in respect of orders pursuant to the Children (Jersey) Law 2002 contained in Article 77 of that Law in respect of orders made in any other part of the British Islands giving effect to such orders as if they had been made in Jersey.

15. LEAVE TO REMOVE/APPLICATIONS TO TAKE A CHILD OUT OF THE JURISDICTION

15.1 Summarise the position in your jurisdiction

Where a residence order is in force no-one can remove a child from Jersey without either the written consent of everyone who has parental responsibility for the child or leave of the court. This does not, however, preclude the removal for a period of less than one month by the person in whose favour the residence order is made. A court can grant general leave to remove to any person when making a residence order. If a person wishes to prevent a child being removed from Jersey an application can be made for a prohibited steps order, or an injunction can be applied for in the Royal Court. The former course of action is to be encouraged as this is within the Children Law and the child's welfare remains paramount. If a person wishes to remove a child from Jersey, an application can be made for a specific issue order under Article 10. When such applications come before the court, the court has to be satisfied that the arrangements proposed are in the child's best interests. There is a tendency to consider that a child will be better off living in Jersey if she has lived here and is settled, but the interplay of the regime of housing qualifications can have an influence on the facts of any case.

15.2 Under what circumstances may a parent apply to remove their child from the jurisdiction against the wishes of the other parent?

If a person wishes to remove a child from Jersey, an application for a specific issue order should be made under Article 10. When such applications come before the court, the court has to be satisfied that the arrangements proposed are in the child's best interests. Where a residence order is in force the person in whose favour the residence order is made may remove a child from Jersey for up to a month without the consent of anyone else with parental responsibility for the child.

E. SURROGACY & ADOPTION

16. VALIDITY OF SURROGACY ARRANGEMENTS

16.1 Briefly summarise the position in your jurisdiction

There is no law relating to surrogacy in Jersey. If parents who are domiciled in Jersey enter into a surrogacy arrangement they may apply for a parental order in a Family Proceedings Court in England or Wales under s54 Human Embryology and Fertilisation Act 2008.

17. ADOPTION

17.1 Briefly explain the legal position in relation to adoption in your jurisdiction. Is adoption available to individuals, cohabiting couples (both heterosexual and same-sex)?

Adoption in Jersey is dealt with by the Adoption (Jersey) Law 1961. A child may be adopted in Jersey by either a single person or a married couple or civil partners domiciled in the British Islands, but not a cohabiting couple. A child may be adopted by 'strangers' who must be 25 or over, a relative, who must be 20 or over or by her mother or father. A man may not be the sole adopter of a female child except where there are special circumstances. Everyone with parental responsibility for a child has to consent to an adoption unless their consent is being withheld unreasonably or they cannot be found, or have abandoned or neglected the child or are incapable of caring for the child. There is also provision for the making of an order freeing a child for adoption. There is no concept of 'special guardianship' in Jersey.

F. COHABITATION

18. COHABITATION

18.1 What legislation (if any) governs division of property for unmarried couples on the breakdown of the relationship?

Cohabitants do not have any rights over and above their general civil and property rights. Applications for child maintenance can be made under Schedule 1 of the Children (Jersey) Law 2002. There is no power to order sale or transfer property between co-owners of property who are not married, although an older concept of *licitation* can be used to order sale by auction of jointly owned property. The law in respect of cohabitation, confirming the position, was considered in *Flynn v Reid* [2012] JRC 100 and [2012] JCA 169.

G. FAMILY DISPUTE RESOLUTION

19. MEDIATION, COLLABORATIVE LAW & ARBITRATION

19.1 Briefly summarise the non-court-based processes available in your jurisdiction and the current status of agreements reached under the auspices of mediation, collaborative law and arbitration

Mediation, collaborative law and 'private FDRs' are available in Jersey, but not arbitration. Mediation on the family model (as would be recognised in England and Wales) has hitherto only been available for children issues, although this is expected to change in the near future. Mediation is frequently used, especially in higher value cases using the civil and commercial model, usually with mediators coming from England and the mediation taking place over one or two days. Private FDRs are done in much the same way. These have developed because financial dispute hearings are not available in Jersey, largely because of the limited size of the judiciary dealing with these matters. Collaborative law occurs in a minority of cases, but is gradually gaining ground. Any agreement reached as a result of mediation, collaborative law or private FDR is usually converted into a consent order, which once made is enforceable as any other order.

19.2 What is the statutory basis (if any), for mediation, collaborative law and arbitration in your jurisdiction? In particular, are the parties required to attempt a family dispute resolution in advance of proceedings?

There is no statutory basis for mediation, collaborative law or arbitration, but equally there is nothing to prevent agreement being reached in any way in which the parties agree to work. Once an agreement becomes a consent order it has the same validity as any other. There is judicial encouragement for dispute resolution methods which avoid court proceedings, especially in relation to children. Adjournments are granted readily to encourage negotiation or mediation.

H. OTHER

20. CIVIL PARTNERSHIP/SAME-SEX MARRIAGE

20.1 What is the status of civil partnership/same-sex marriage within the jurisdiction?

In Jersey, the Civil Partnership (Jersey) Law 2012 allows same-sex couples to become civil partners and recognises same-sex unions from other jurisdictions. Civil partners have the same rights and responsibilities towards each other as married couples, the minor differences in the legislation from the Matrimonial Causes (Jersey) Law 1949 relate mainly to grounds (ie, no adultery) and consummation in the context of nullity. There are many venues now registered for civil partnerships to take place and the new legislation has been welcomed.

20.2 What legislation governs civil partnership/same-sex marriage?

Civil Partnership (Jersey) Law 2012.

21. CONTROVERSIAL AREAS/RAPIDLY DEVELOPING AREAS OF LAW

21.1 Is there a particular area of the law within the jurisdiction that is currently undergoing major change?

The main area of family law currently undergoing change is mediation. A new mediation service is being set up and mediators are being trained by the court service to ensure that mediation is more readily available to those who need it. Collaborative law is slowly gaining acceptance within the legal profession.

21.2 Which areas of law are most out of step? Which areas would you most like to see reformed/changed?

Jersey is not yet a signatory to the United Nations Convention on the Rights of the Child.

- Divorce law needs to be changed to move from the current largely fault-based grounds.
- Pension sharing orders are needed.
- Consideration should be given to developing a system of financial dispute resolution hearings, despite the challenges of a small jurisdiction.
- The law of domicile needs to be changed to enable married women to have a domicile separate from that of their husbands.
- Married men are responsible for the completion of the tax returns of their wives. All people should be responsible for their own tax returns.
- There are forced heirship arrangements of dower and légitime which need to be reconsidered to meet modern demands.
- Jersey is a beautiful, diverse and inclusive island. Our laws need to reflect that.

Malaysia

Y N Foo & Partners Foo Yet Ngo & Kiran Dhaliwal

A. JURISDICTION AND CONFLICT OF LAW

1. SOURCES OF LAW

1.1 What is the primary source of law in relation to the breakdown of marriage and the welfare of children within the jurisdiction?

In Malaysia, there are two sets of laws applicable in personal matters of intestacy, marriage, divorce, custody of children and division of assets upon the breakdown of a marriage, ie, one set governing non-Muslims and the other Muslims. They are distinct and separate jurisdictions. The law governing non-Muslims is applied in the civil courts while that governing Muslims, ie, Islamic Syariah Law is applied in the religious courts. We set out herein only the laws applicable to non-Muslims which are applied in the Civil Courts.

While we have our own Malaysian Statutes governing the breakdown of marriage and the welfare of children, Section 27 of the *Malaysian Civil Law Act 1956* which reads:

'In all cases relating to the custody and control of infants, the law to be administered shall be the same as would have been administered in like cases in England as at the date of the coming into force of this Act (ie, 7th April 1956), regard being had to the religion and customs of the parties concerned, unless other provision is or shall be made by any written law.'

allows for the application of English common law as at April 1956 to fill in any lacuna in our legislation or where there is a statute *in pari materia* with an English statute to assist in the interpretation of such statute.

1.2 What are the main statutes governing matrimonial law in the jurisdiction?

- Law Reform (Marriage & Divorce) Act 1976 (Act 164) (LRA)
- Guardianship of Infants Act 1961 (GIA)
- Child Act 2001, which deals primarily with children in need of care protection and rehabilitation and related matters.
- Married Women Act 1957
- Married Women & Children (Maintenance) Act 1950 (MWCMA)
- Married Women & Children (Enforcement of Maintenance) Act 1968

2. JURISDICTION

2.1 What are the main jurisdictional requirements for the institution of proceedings in relation to divorce, property and children?

The main jurisdictional requirements for the institution of proceedings:

In relation to divorce

Where the marriage has been registered under the LRA or where the marriage was contracted under a law providing that or in contemplation of which, marriage is monogamous; and the domicile of the parties to the marriage at the time when the petition is presented is in Malaysia.

A wife does not have a separate domicile of her own under Malaysian law, but acquires her husband's domicile upon marriage. Under an exception in the LRA, a wife, although the husband is not domiciled or resident in Malaysia may petition for divorce:

- if the wife has been deserted by the husband, or the husband has been deported from Malaysia and the husband was before the desertion or deportation domiciled in Malaysia; or
- the wife is resident in Malaysia and has been ordinarily resident in Malaysia for a period of two years immediately preceding the commencement of the proceedings.

In relation to property

The Malaysian Court has power, when granting a decree of divorce or judicial separation, to order the division between the parties to a marriage (or the sale and division of the proceeds of sale) of any assets acquired by them during the marriage by their joint efforts or by the sole effort of one party to the marriage. The Court's powers herein only arise when the Court hears and pronounces either a decree of divorce or a decree of judicial separation in Malaysian proceedings.

In relation to children

So long as a child is physically present within the jurisdiction the Malaysian Court has jurisdiction to deal with his person and property under the provisions of the following:

- The Courts of Judicature Act 1964
- The LRA
- The GIA
- an inherent jurisdiction derived from the Crown's prerogative powers as *parens patriae*.

3. DOMICILE AND HABITUAL RESIDENCE

3.1 Explain the concepts of domicile and habitual residence as they apply to the jurisdiction in relation to divorce, the finances and children

Jurisdiction to hear a divorce and make orders in relation to the parties' finances and assets and the children of the marriage only arises where the domicile of the parties to the marriage at the time when the petition is presented is in Malaysia.

Under the LRA, a citizen of Malaysia shall be deemed, until the contrary is proved, to be domiciled in Malaysia.

A wife does not have a separate domicile of her own but acquires her husband's domicile upon marriage.

Domicile in the case of *Re Bhagwan Singh Decd (1964) MLJ 360*, is that country in which a person either has or is deemed by law to have his permanent home, so that in order to acquire a domicile in a country, that person must intend to reside in it permanently or indefinitely.

'The law on this point quite clearly is that a person who has formed the intention of leaving a country does not cease to have his home in that country until he acts according to his intention. Domicile whether of origin or of choice continues until it is abandoned. It is divested only when the country of domicile has been actually abandoned with the intention of abandoning it forever.'

Case law has established the following principles:

- Clear evidence is required to establish a change of domicile. The oath of the person as to his intention to change his domicile is not conclusive.
- To displace the domicile of origin in favour of the domicile of choice, the standard of proof goes beyond a mere balance of probabilities.
- While the test that a person must have 'burnt his boats' remains, a review of all the circumstances to prove that the petitioner not only resided in Malaysia but has the intention to make that residence permanent for an indeterminate period of time appears to suffice. See: *James Sloan v Sarala Devi Sloan (2010) 4 CLJ 483.*
- A person does not have to divest his nationality to show that he has acquired a domicile of choice (supra).

4. CONFLICT OF LAW/APPLICABLE LAW TO BE APPLIED

4.1 What happens when one party applies to stay proceedings in favour of a foreign jurisdiction? What factors will the local court take into account when determining forum issues?

A Malaysian Court faced with a stay application will consider the following.

Firstly whether the Malaysian Court has jurisdiction to deal with the case. Even if the answer is yes, the Malaysian Court will nevertheless consider whether there is some other tribunal having competent jurisdiction in which the case may be tried more suitably for the interests of all the parties and for the ends of justice (doctrine of *forum non conveniens* in the English House of Lords case of *Spiliada Maritime Corp v Consulax Ltd (The Spiliada) (1987) AC 460* applied in the Malaysian case of *American Express Bank Ltd v Mohamed Tonfic Al-Ozier & Anor (1995) 1 MLJ 160.*

In this regard, the Malaysian Court will consider *inter alia* whether any particular forum is one with which the action has the most real and substantial connection and whether it would be unjust to the plaintiff to confine him to remedies elsewhere.

B. PRE- AND POST-NUPTIAL AGREEMENTS

5. VALIDITY OF PRE- AND POST-NUPTIAL AGREEMENTS

5.1 To what extent are pre- and post-nups binding within the jurisdiction? Could you provide a brief discussion of the most significant recent case law on this issue?

While we have provisions allowing for the importation of English principles in certain limited circumstances, for example, where our statute is *in pari material* with an English statute or where common law applies, Malaysian judges have cautioned against relying uncritically on cases of other jurisdictions, including England.

In the area of pre-nuptial and post-nuptial agreements, the following principles will apply over matters regarding maintenance and division of matrimonial assets.

The ultimate power resides in the court to order division of matrimonial assets and maintenance. The court is statutorily bound to consider the factors set out in the LRA itself. In relation to the division of matrimonial assets, these factors do not include a provision allowing the court a discretion to consider any agreements between the parties.

As regards maintenance, the LRA specifically provides:

- an agreement in settlement of all future claims to maintenance must be approved by the court;
- the court may at any time and from time to time vary the terms of any maintenance agreement made between spouses where there has been any material change in the circumstances and notwithstanding any provision to the contrary in any such agreement.

Up until the present we have taken the position pre-nuptial agreements are contrary to public policy, not binding and cannot oust the jurisdiction of the court. The recent development of the law in England where courts are taking cognisance of pre-nuptial agreements have hinged substantially on a provision in the English statute allowing the English Court to consider 'all the circumstances of the case' (See: Section 25(1) Matrimonial Causes Act 1973). This factor unfortunately does not exist in Sections 76 or 78 of our LRA governing the court's exercise of discretion in division of assets and ordering maintenance. In the circumstances, we are of the view there is no provision in our LRA allowing for the reception of pre-nuptial agreements.

C. DIVORCE, NULLITY AND JUDICIAL SEPARATION

6. RECOGNITION OF FOREIGN MARRIAGES/DIVORCES

6.1 Summarise the position in your jurisdiction

Foreign marriage

A marriage contracted outside Malaysia is recognised as valid if:

- it is contracted in a form required or permitted by the law of the country where it is contracted;
- each of the parties had, at the time of the marriage, capacity to marry under the law of the country of his or her domicile; and
- where either of the parties is a citizen of or is domiciled in Malaysia, both parties had capacity to marry according to the LRA.

Foreign divorce

Where there is a foreign divorce or annulment by a court of competent jurisdiction outside Malaysia of a marriage solemnised in Malaysia under the provisions of the LRA, either of the parties may apply to the Registrar-General for the registration of such foreign decree.

Where the marriage was not solemnised under the LRA, a party may nevertheless apply to court for an order recognising an order of dissolution or annulment by a court of competent jurisdiction outside Malaysia.

7. DIVORCE

7.1 Explain the grounds for divorce within the jurisdiction (please also deal with nullity and judicial separation if appropriate)

Under the LRA, one can petition for divorce as follows:

- dissolution on the ground that one party to the marriage has converted to Islam;
- dissolution by mutual consent by presenting a joint petition with proper provisions agreed in relation to custody of children, maintenance and division of matrimonial assets;
- either party petitioning for a divorce on the ground that the marriage has irretrievably broken down by reason of one or more of the following facts:
  - (a) that the respondent has committed adultery and the petitioner finds it intolerable to live with the respondent;
  - (b) that the respondent has behaved in such a way that the petitioner cannot reasonably be expected to live with the respondent;
  - (c) that the respondent has deserted the petitioner for a continuous period of at least two years immediately preceeding the presentation of the petition;
  - (d) that the parties to the marriage have lived apart for a continuous period of at least two years immediately preceding the presentation of the petition.

Grounds for judicial separation

A petition for judicial separation may be presented on one or more of the same four facts as in a petition for divorce.

Grounds for nullity

One may petition to void a marriage if:

- at the time of the marriage either party was already lawfully married and the former husband or wife of such party was living at the time of the marriage and such former marriage was then in force;
- a male person marries under 18 years of age or a female person who is above 16 years but under 18 years marries without a special licence granted by the Chief Minister;
- the parties are within the prohibited degrees of relationship unless the Chief Minister grants a special licence; or
- the parties are not respectively male and female.

A marriage is voidable if:

- the marriage has not been consummated owing to the incapacity of either party to consummate it;
- the marriage has not been consummated owing to the wilful refusal of the respondent to consummate it;

- either party did not validly consent to the marriage, whether in consequence of duress, mistake, unsoundness of mind or otherwise;
- at the time of marriage either party, though capable of giving a valid consent, was (whether continuously or intermittently) a mentally disordered person within the meaning of the Mental Disorders Ordinance, 1952 of such a kind or to such an extent as to be unfit for marriage;
- at the time of marriage the respondent was suffering from veneral disease in a communicable form;
- at the time of marriage the respondent was pregnant by some person other than the petitioner.

The court will not grant a decree of nullity on the grounds where the marriage is voidable if the petitioner with knowledge that it was open to him/her to have the marriage avoided, so conducted himself/herself as to lead the respondent reasonably to believe that he would not seek to do so and that it would be unjust to the respondent to grant the decree.

8. FINANCES/CAPITAL, PROPERTY

8.1 What powers does the court have to allocate financial resources and property on the breakdown of marriage?

Under the LRA, the court's power to order the division between the parties of any assets acquired by them during the marriage by sole or joint efforts, or to order the sale of any such assets and the division between the parties of the proceeds of sale, only arises upon the grant of a decree of divorce or judicial separation.

Where the asset has been acquired by joint efforts the court shall consider:

'(a) the extent of the contributions made by each party in money, property or work towards the acquiring of the assets;
(b) any debts owing by either party which were contracted for their joint benefit;
(c) the needs of the minor children,
and subject to those considerations, the court shall incline towards equality of division.'

Where the asset has been acquired by the sole effort of one party, the court shall consider:

'(a) the extent of the contributions made by the other party who did not acquire the assets to the welfare of the family by looking after the home or caring the family;
(b) the needs of the minor children,
and subject to those considerations, the court may divide the assets or the proceeds of sale in such proportions as the court thinks reasonable; but in any case the party by whose effort the assets were acquired shall receive a greater proportion.'
(Section 76 *LRA*)

Assets acquired during a marriage include assets owned before the marriage by one party which have been substantially improved during the marriage by the other party or by their joint efforts.

8.2 Explain and illustrate with reference to recent cases the court's thinking on division of assets

The following principles may be discerned from Malaysian cases:

- Parties' matrimonial assets are pooled together and subjected to division.
- There is no automatic percentage applicable. The court endeavours to reach a fair and just outcome in each case.

Although English case law and principles were initially imported to assist in interpreting the LRA, there are now enough local cases to assist in the interpretation of the LRA. See *Ching Seng Woah v Lim Shook Lin (1997) 1 MLJ 96.*

The court does not do an accounting of all the assets acquired or improved during the marriage and the income thereof, nor a determination of who had benefitted more or less, and then award a shortfall to the party found to have benefited less. The function of the court is to make a fair and equitable division of the matrimonial assets that exist at the time of the divorce, taking into account the factors set out in Section 76 of the *LRA*. see *Sivanes a/l Rajaratnam v Usha Rani a/p Subramaniam (2002) 3 MLJ 273.*

The LRA does not define what constitutes matrimonial assets. During the subsistence of a marriage, the matrimonial home (even if acquired solely by one party) and everything which is put into it by either spouse shall be considered a matrimonial asset. *'The purchase by the wife of kitchen cabinets, crockery, pots and pans and the payment of servant's salary and food in grocery bills' all add up as her contribution along with her keeping the house, maintaining and servicing it as a going concern and the contributions she made to the family'.* Its increase in value during the marriage constitutes an asset acquired by the parties' joint efforts. See *Ching Seng Woah v Lim Shook Lin (1997) 1 MLJ 109.*

9. FINANCES/MAINTENANCE

9.1 Explain the operation of maintenance for spouses on an ongoing basis after the breakdown of marriage

After breakdown of marriage, a wife can apply for maintenance under:

- MWCMA 1950 and/or
- Section 77 and 78 of the LRA

Under the MWCMA

If a man neglects or refuses to maintain his wife, a court, upon due proof thereof, may order him to pay a reasonable monthly maintenance to his wife, in proportion to his means.

However, if any person against whom an order as aforesaid has been applied for or made, offers to maintain his wife on condition of her living with him, and his wife refuses to do so, the court shall consider any grounds of refusal stated by the wife, and may make or enforce the order, notwithstanding such offer, if it is satisfied that such person is living in adultery or for any other reason it is just so to do. (Section 5 of the *MWCMA*)

A wife is not entitled to maintenance under the Act if she is living in adultery or if, without any sufficient reason, she refused to live with her husband.

Under the LRA

The court may order a man to pay maintenance to his wife during the course of any matrimonial proceedings; and upon or subsequent to the grant of a decree of divorce or judicial separation.

The court shall have the corresponding power to order a woman to pay maintenance to her husband or former husband where he is incapacitated, wholly or partially, from earning a livelihood by reason of mental or physical injury or ill-health, and the court is satisfied that having regard to her means it is 'reasonable so to order.'

The court considers primarily the means and needs of the parties, regardless of the proportion such maintenance bears to the income of the husband or wife but shall have regard to the degree of responsibility which the court apportions to each party for the breakdown of the marriage (Section 78 of LRA).

Unsecured maintenance expires on the death of the husband or wife, and secured maintenance expires on the death of the spouse in whose favour it was made.

Maintenance ceases on the remarriage of the spouse receiving maintenance or living in adultery with any other person.

9.2 Is it common for maintenance to be awarded?

The LRA does not have provision for the Court to make an order for a lump sum in lieu of maintenance, only monthly maintenance for a spouse.

Where the wife was a home-maker during the marriage and would have difficulty seeking employment upon divorce, the Malaysian Court will generally make an order of maintenance in favour of the wife.

However, with the increasing number of wives being gainfully employed during marriage and able to do so after divorce there is an increasing trend not to award maintenance to such wives or ex-wives.

9.3 Explain and illustrate with reference to recent cases the court's thinking on maintenance

In assessing maintenance the Malaysian Court considers primarily the means and needs of the parties and the standard of living the parties were accustomed to during the marriage. There is no rigid formula.

Although the Royal Commission in their Report leading up to the LRA recommended recognising irretrievable breakdown of the marriage as the sole ground for dissolution, the final Act still retained elements of fault in determining breakdown.

To make matters worse, Section 78 of the LRA setting out the factors the court must have regard to in ordering maintenance, requires the court to have regard to the degree of responsibility which the court apportions to each party for the breakdown of the marriage.

Fortunately however, in *SS v HJK (1991) 1 LNS 99*, the court held that only conduct which is 'both obvious and gross' so much so that to order one party to support another whose conduct falls into this category is repugnant to anyone's sense of justice should be taken into account. Short of cases falling into this category, the court should not reduce its order for financial provision merely because of what is regarded as guilt or blame.

10. CHILD MAINTENANCE

10.1 On what basis is child maintenance calculated within the jurisdiction?

Maintenance for a child can be applied for under:

- MWCMA 1950 and/or
- LRA, Sections 92 and 93

Under the MWCMA

The court may order a person who neglects or refuses to maintain his wife or a legitimate child to pay a monthly allowance in the maintenance in proportion to the means of such person, as is reasonable.

Reasonable maintenance can also be ordered for an illegitimate child.

Under the LRA

The Act provides that *'except where an agreement or order of court otherwise provides, it shall be the duty of a parent to maintain or contribute to the maintenance of his or her children, whether they are in his or her custody, either by providing them with such accommodation, clothing, food and education as may be reasonable having regard to his or her means and station in life, or by paying the cost thereof.'*

The court can make an order of maintenance at any time where the man has refused or neglected reasonably to provide for the child, he has deserted his wife and child, and during and subsequent to any matrimonial or custody proceedings.

The court has a corresponding power to order a woman to pay or contribute to the maintenance of her child where, having regard to her means, it is reasonable to do so.

The order for maintenance ceases upon a child attaining the age of 18 years or where the child has a physical or mental disability, on the ceasing of such disability, whichever is the later.

A man who has accepted a child who is not his child as a member of his family has a duty to maintain such a child if his father and mother fail to do so.

11. RECIPROCAL ENFORCEMENT OF FINANCIAL ORDERS

11.1 Summarise the position in your jurisdiction

There are two acts that allow for reciprocal enforcement of Maintenance Orders between Malaysia and a number of reciprocating countries:

- Reciprocal Enforcement of Judgments Act 1958 (REJA); and
- Maintenance Orders (Facilities For Enforcement) Act 1949 (Revised 1971) (MOFE).

The *REJA* allows for orders of reciprocating countries to be registered in Malaysia and enforceable here if the orders are:

- final and conclusive as between the parties (even if an appeal is pending);

- there is payable a sum of money; and
- a judgment of a reciprocating country.

However, orders cannot be registered if:

- six years have lapsed from the date of judgment; or
- the judgment has been wholly satisfied; or
- it cannot be enforced by execution in the reciprocating country.

The MOFE provides the mechanism for a certified copy of the maintenance order made in a reciprocating country to be registered in the appropriate Malaysian local court by the Minister charged with responsibility for the judiciary. Once registered, the maintenance order will be of the same force and effect as if it had been originally obtained in the local court, and is enforceable in Malaysia.

Similarly, upon proof to the Malaysian court that the person against whom the order was made is resident in a reciprocating country, the court shall then send a certified copy of the order to the Minister charged with responsibility for foreign affairs for transmission to the appropriate authority in the reciprocating country.

The MOFE also provides the court with the discretion to make provisional orders of maintenance against persons resident in reciprocating countries, even in the absence of that person. This provisional order will have no effect unless and until confirmed by a competent court in the reciprocating country by a summons being issued calling upon the person to show cause why that order should not be confirmed. Similarly, a local court can enforce provisional orders from reciprocating countries against persons resident in Malaysia.

12. FINANCIAL RELIEF AFTER FOREIGN DIVORCE PROCEEDINGS

12.1 What powers are available to make orders following a foreign divorce?

The provisions in the LRA enable a Malaysian court to make orders for maintenance for a spouse in the course of matrimonial proceedings and upon or subsequent to the grant of a decree of divorce or judicial separation. Division of matrimonial assets can only be ordered if the Malaysian court hears and grants a decree of divorce or judicial separation.

Under existing provisions of the LRA, a Malaysian court has no powers to make financial relief orders of its own after foreign divorce proceedings. This position is reinforced by the Federal Court decision of *Manokaram Subramaniam v Ranjid Kaur Nata Singh (2008) 6 CLJ 209* which states that 'an Order for division of matrimonial assets is limited to the time when granting a Decree of divorce or judicial separation and not at a later stage'.

Hence one should always have the ancillary issues of maintenance and division of assets determined in the same jurisdiction as the divorce.

One can only look to enforcement provisions in Malaysia for financial orders made in foreign jurisdictions.

D. CHILDREN

13. CUSTODY/PARENTAL RESPONSIBILITY

13.1 Briefly explain the legal position in relation to custody/parental responsibility following the breakdown of a relationship or marriage

Following the breakdown of a marriage, a parent or any other relative of the child, any child welfare association or any suitable person may apply for the custody of a child of the marriage.

In deciding custody:

- the paramount consideration shall be the welfare of the child;
- subject to the above welfare consideration the court shall have regard to the wishes of the parents of the child; and
- to the wishes of the child, where he or she is of an age to express an independent opinion.

There is a rebuttable presumption that it is for the good of a child below the age of seven years to be with his/her mother, but in deciding whether that presumption applies in a particular case, the court shall have regard to the undesirability of disturbing the life of a child by a change of custody. Where there are two or more children the court is not bound to place both or all in the custody of the same person but shall consider the welfare of each independently.

The person given custody shall be entitled to decide all questions relating to the child's upbringing and education.

The GIA has provisions empowering the court to appoint a guardian over the person and property of a child. The Act states that a mother and a father have equal rights and authority over a child. The court exercises its powers based primarily on the welfare of the child and shall consider the wishes of a parent/s. The GIA applies to both legitimate and illegitimate children.

13.2 Briefly explain the legal position in relation to access/contact/ visitation following the breakdown of a relationship or marriage.

The court, when making an order for custody may provide for visitation and rights of access to a parent deprived of custody or any member of the family of a parent who is dead or has been deprived of custody at such times or for such periods as the court considers reasonable.

Frequently made orders in relation to access/visitation are:

- alternate weekends;
- one half of school holidays;
- alternate public holidays;
- important festivals.

14. INTERNATIONAL ABDUCTION

14.1 Briefly summarise the position in your jurisdiction

Malaysia is not a signatory to the Hague Convention on the Civil Aspects of International Child Abduction. Hence there is no mechanism in place for the automatic return of children abducted to Malaysia.

Although a Malaysian court will take into consideration the custody order of a foreign court of competent jurisdiction, it is not bound to give effect to it if this would not be for the child's benefit. It is the welfare and interests of the child that are the paramount considerations to which all others yield, including the order of a court of competent jurisdiction.

Once a child is physically within the jurisdiction, the Malaysian court has jurisdiction over the child and is entitled to enter into the merits afresh and form an independent judgment of its own on custody, applying Malaysian law, based on what it considers is in the best interests of the welfare of the child in question and in so doing will give proper weight to any such foreign order as the circumstances of the case dictates.

The Malaysian courts have since held that if the court is satisfied no obvious real or immediate harm would befall the child if returned, children of foreign nationals who are only transient visitors to Malaysia will be returned to the country to which the child belongs, ordinarily resides or has the most real and substantial connection, without a full inquiry into the dispute. The Court of Appeal held that the duration of protection afforded should only be for as long as the children can lawfully remain in the country. See *Neduncheliyan Balasubramaniam v Kohila Shanmugam (1997) 3 MLJ 768* and *Herbert Thomas Small v Elizabeth Mary Small (2006) 6 MLJ 373.*

15. LEAVE TO REMOVE/APPLICATIONS TO TAKE A CHILD OUT OF THE JURISDICTION

15.1 Summarise the position in your jurisdiction

An order for custody may prohibit the person given custody from taking the child out of Malaysia. However, a parent who, pursuant to an agreement or order of court has sole custody may obtain the consent of the other parent or apply to court for leave to take the child out of Malaysia.

15.2 Under what circumstances may a parent apply to remove their child from the jurisdiction against the wishes of the other parent?

The Malaysian Federal Court in *Teh Eng Kim v Yew Peng Siong (1977) 1 MLJ 234* adopting English principles from the case of *Poel v Poel (1970) 1 WLR 1469*, held the following principles shall apply:

- the welfare of the child must be the paramount consideration; and
- refusing the primary carer's reasonable proposals for relocation of her family life is likely to impact detrimentally on the welfare of her dependent child.

Therefore the application to relocate will be granted unless the court concludes that it is incompatible with the welfare of the child to do so.

The Malaysian court will expect the parent wanting to relocate to make reasonable proposals for access for the parent left behind, including paying the costs of travel and access in the country to which a child has been relocated, using a webcam, telephone arrangements etc. For protection, one may consider obtaining an order in the courts to which the child will be moving, setting out the access arrangements.

E. SURROGACY AND ADOPTION

16. VALIDITY OF SURROGACY AGREEMENTS

16.1 Briefly summarise the position in your jurisdiction.

There are no reported cases on surrogacy, which involves an agreement whereby a gestational or surrogate mother agrees to bear a child for someone else, ie, the commissioning parent or parents. If the gestational mother does hand over the baby after birth to the commissioning parent and consents to the commissioning parent adopting the child, there is no prohibition in the Malaysian Adoption Act 1952 preventing the child from being legally adopted by the commissioning parent.

However, should there be a dispute, for example where the surrogate mother reneges on her agreement, any attempt to compel an adoption following surrogacy will most certainly not be upheld by a Malaysian court, it being in all probability be held to be contrary to public policy.

17. ADOPTION

17.1 Briefly explain the legal position in relation to adoption in your jurisdiction. Is adoption available to individuals, cohabiting couples (both heterosexual and same-sex)?

There are two forms of adoptions recognised under Malaysian law:

- Court authorised adoption under the Adoption Act 1952:
  - an applicant or in the case of a joint application by two spouses, the applicants/and the child must be ordinarily resident in West Malaysia;
  - the applicant or one of the applicants has attained the age of 25 and is at least 21 years older than the child (unless there are special circumstances);
  - the applicant has attained the age of 21 and is a relative of the child or is the mother or father of the child;
  - an adoption order will not be made where the sole applicant is a male and the child is a female save where there are special circumstances;
  - cohabiting couples whether heterosexual or same-sex will not be allowed to adopt a child jointly.
- Registration of *de facto* adoptions under the Registration of Adoptions Act 1952:
  - an application may be made to the Registrar of Adoptions to adopt a child who has been in the custody of and has been brought up, maintained and educated by the applicant or by two spouses in a joint application continuously for not less than two years;
  - both the applicant/s and the child must be ordinarily resident in West Malaysia at the time of the adoption;
  - unlike the court authorised adoptions under the Adoption Act 1952, which vests in the adoptive parents all the rights duties, obligations and liabilities of a natural parent and the rights of the natural parent/s is/are extinguished, an adoption through this administrative process, merely confers on the adoptive parents

custodial rights to look after, care for the child and make decisions in respect of the child.

Adoptions via registration are available to Muslims who, under their religious law, are not allowed to adopt, as the natural parents always retain, *inter alia* the right to give consent for marriage.

F. COHABITATION

18. COHABITATION

18.1 What legislation (if any) governs division of property for unmarried couples on the breakdown of the relationships?

Cohabitation is not recognised under Malaysian law.

G. FAMILY DISPUTE RESOLUTION

19. MEDIATION, COLLABORATIVE LAW AND ARBITRATION

19.1 Briefly summarise the non-court-based processes available in your jurisdiction and the current status of agreements reached under the auspices of mediation, collaborative law and arbitration

The Malaysian Mediation Centre set up by the Bar Council offers mediation as an alternative to the court process. Parties must sign an agreement to mediate. Once agreement is reached, parties sign a settlement agreement witnessed by the mediator. Parties are at liberty to pursue court action should the outcome be unsatisfactory. Mediation remains unattractive to parties as an alternative to matrimonial dispute resolution as it involves addition expense and is not final.

19.2 What is the statutory basis (if any), for mediation collaborative law and arbitration in your jurisdiction? In particular, are the parties required to attempt a family dispute resolution in advance of the institution of proceedings.

Except in a joint petition where parties have reached consensus on all terms, parties are mandatorily required to refer their matrimonial difficulty to a conciliatory tribunal. The tribunal must certify that they have failed to reconcile the parties before any divorce proceedings can be commenced by either party.

Save for the above, there is no statutory compulsion for mediation in Malaysia. However, following a Practice Direction dated 13 August 2010, after the close of pleadings in a matrimonial dispute, the court will normally fix a date for an in-court mediation, either before a registrar or a judge with solicitors present. If parties do reach agreement on terms, a consent order is recorded.

H. OTHER

20. CIVIL PARTNERSHIP/SAME-SEX MARRIAGE

20.1 What is the status of civil partnership/same-sex marriage within the jurisdiction?

20.2 What legislation governs civil partnership/same-sex marriage?

Civil partnership/same-sex marriage is not recognised under Malaysian law.

21. CONTROVERSIAL AREAS/RAPIDLY DEVELOPING AREAS OF LAW

21.1 Is there a particular area of the law within the jurisdiction that is currently undergoing major change?

The dual system of laws has given rise to much controversy especially when the line is crossed by a party to a non-Muslim marriage who converts to Islam. Under an amendment to the Malaysian Federal Constitution ie, Article 121(1A) it was intended that the civil courts exercising jurisdiction in personal law matters over non-Muslims and the Syariah courts exercising jurisdiction over Muslims shall be distinct and separate and neither shall encroach on the other where the matter is within the exclusive purview of the other.

However, an increasing number of cases have since arisen where one party to a non-Muslim marriage converts to Islam, and in some cases also converts the children without the knowledge of the other parent, and then seeks relief including custody of his/her child, in the Syariah court where the non-Muslim spouse has no right of audience. The Syariah courts had proceeded to make orders sought by the converted spouse, without regard to the rights of the non-Muslim spouse. The Federal Court to which the non-Muslim spouse appealed, refused to interfere in the decision of the Syariah court stating they were bound by Article 121(1A) of the Federal Constitution. See *Subashini Rajasingam v Saravanan Thangathoray & Other Appeals (2008) 2 CLJ 1.*

21.2 Which areas of law are most out of step? Which areas would you most like to see reformed/changes?

Under the LRA, unless a child has a disability, a parent's obligation to maintain a child ceases upon the child attaining 18 years. This provision should be amended for the obligations to continue if the child is pursuing a first degree or tertiary education until the child completes that first degree or tertiary education.

The author would like to see an amendment to the existing law so that all matrimonial disputes including custody in relation to a non-Muslim marriage (even where one spouse subsequently and while the civil marriage subsists, converts to Islam) shall be within the sole exclusive jurisdiction of the civil court.

Mexico

Müggenburg, Gorches, Peñalosa & Sepúlveda SC
Alfonso Sepúlveda García & Habib Díaz Noriega

A. JURISDICTION AND CONFLICT OF LAW

1. SOURCES OF LAW

1.1 What is the primary source of law in relation to the breakdown of marriage and the welfare of children within the jurisdiction?

State Civil Codes and State Codes of Civil Procedures are applicable to the marriage based on the marital domicile. Additionally, there are supplementary laws such as Migration Law, International Treaties, as well as mandatory judicial precedents.

1.2 Which are the main statutes governing matrimonial law in the jurisdiction?

State Civil Codes and State Codes of Civil Procedures.

2. JURISDICTION

2.1 What are the main jurisdictional requirements for the institution of proceedings in relation to divorce, property and children?

As a general rule, to file a divorce and related issues documents such as the marriage certificate, birth certificate of children, titles of property, etc must be submitted along with the divorce petition. In order for Mexican Courts to have jurisdiction over the divorce case the parties must have a marital domicile within Mexico.

If marriage takes place between a Mexican and a foreigner abroad, the marriage certificate should be registered with the Mexican Civil Registry located in the State where the spouses settle their marital domicile.

On the other hand, if foreigners get married overseas and they establish their domicile in Mexico, no additional requirement to having their marriage certificate registered with the Mexican Civil Registry is needed.

3. DOMICILE AND HABITUAL RESIDENCE

3.1 Explain the concepts of domicile and habitual residence as they apply to the jurisdiction in relation to divorce, the finances and children

The domicile of individuals is the place where they normally reside; in its absence, the location of their principal place of business; in its absence, the place where they simply live, or if there is not any, where the person is found. It is presumed that a person usually resides in a place when he has continued living there for more than six months.

The legal domicile of an individual is the place where the law establishes his residence in order to exercise his rights and fulfill his obligations, even if the person is not there.

The marital domicile is where the spouses live together, which is the place they mutually agreed as their home. Said marital domicile gives jurisdiction to courts in order to decide a divorce petition and related items.

In connection with the finance issue between spouses, the relevant statute applicable is the State Civil Code where the marital domicile is located.

As to children, the applicable statutes are the Mexican Federal Constitution (best interest of children principle), the international treaties and conventions (rights and obligations of children), federal law (protection of children) and state law (replicates the legal provisions included in the above listed statutes).

4. CONFLICT OF LAW/APPLICABLE LAW TO BE APPLIED

4.1 What happens when one party applies to stay proceedings in favour of a foreign jurisdiction? What factors will the local court take into account when determining forum issues?

Regarding the first question, the answer is that a party is not entitled to apply to stay proceedings in favour of a foreign court, since that will be considered a denial of justice according to the Mexican Federal Constitution.

In response to the second query, the local court will consider the marital domicile in order to determine forum issues, provided that such court is dealing only with a divorce proceeding and related issues (ie, spousal support obligation, child support obligation, finances, care and custody, visitations, property regime, etc.).

If the local court is solving a case that is associated with alimony only, the competent court would be the one within the jurisdiction where the creditor or debtor domicile is located, at election of the creditor. Therefore, the statutes applicable for that specific case will be those effective in the state where the petition is file by the plaintiff/creditor.

B. PRE- AND POST-NUPTIAL AGREEMENTS

5. VALIDITY OF PRE- AND POST-NUPTIAL AGREEMENTS

5.1 To what extent are pre- and post-nups binding within the jurisdiction? Could you provide a brief discussion of the most significant recent case law on this issue?

The spouses may choose between the following property regimes:

(i) marital property

(ii) separation of property; or

(iii) mixed property regime.

Under Mexican law pre-nuptial agreements are understood as contracts entered into between spouses to decide their property regime and the administration of their assets which is legally assigned to both spouses unless something different was agreed upon.

Please also bear in mind that post-nuptial agreements are allowed to be executed in Mexico.

Some formalities must be complied with for pre- and post-nuptial agreements to be valid, including executing that agreement before a Family judge or notary public.

There exist judicial precedents issued by the Mexican judicial system, which are very recent due to a new amendment to the property regime between spouses, which covers the compensation in favour of the spouse in charge of household duties and the children's care. The issue of compensation is only relevant if the spouses chose the separated property regime.

C. DIVORCE, NULLITY AND JUDICIAL SEPARATION

6. RECOGNITION OF FOREIGN MARRIAGES/DIVORCES

6.1 Summarise the position in your jurisdiction

Mexican citizens that marry abroad must attend the Civil Registry for the recording of their marriage within the first three months since establishing their residence in Mexican territory, proving their marriage with evidence or records that credit and made valid said marriage.

If the recording is made within those three months, its consequences will become effective as of the date the marriage was executed. However, if it is made after the above said three months the marriage will only take effect from the date the recording was made.

In the case that spouses marry abroad complying with the legal regulations of that country and then validate their marriage with the consul of said country in Mexico, it is not necessary to have the marriage registered in the Civil Registry of Mexico.

If spouses get divorced abroad in order to consider them divorced in the Federal District, they shall present the documents that confirm the divorce subjecting themselves to provisions established in the Civil Procedure Code for the divorce to be recorded in the Mexican Civil Registry.

The general immigration law and its regulations prevent the judicial and administrative authorities proceeding to invalidate a marriage where foreigners are involved, unless a government authorisation is given and their migratory status allows said proceeding. Authorisation will not be required when the plaintiff is Mexican.

The applicable law to nullify a marriage that took place abroad shall be the law where the marriage was held, which the Mexican judge shall review and resolve accordingly. Once the marriage is nullified the judge must follow all the necessary procedures in order to record this act in the Civil Registry.

7. DIVORCE

7.1 Explain the grounds for divorce within the jurisdiction (please also deal with nullity and judicial separation if appropriate)

Divorce in Mexico terminates the bond of marriage between both spouses, leaving them free to marry another person should they wish to do so.

The claim requesting divorce shall be filed before the court in the state where the marital domicile is located, applying the Civil Code and Civil Procedure Code of said state. The Civil Code of each state establishes different grounds for divorce.

In accordance with the Civil Code of the Federal District it is not necessary to establish a cause to justify the divorce decree, provided that a minimum of one year has elapsed since the marriage took place.

Regarding judicial separation, according to the Civil Code of the Federal District, in some cases a spouse may ask the court/Family judge to suspend his obligation to cohabit when he proves the other spouse:

(i) suffers an incurable disease which may be contagious or hereditary;
(ii) suffers a permanent sexual impotence provided that it was not originated as a result of ageing; or
(iii) suffers a mental disorder that has been judicially declared.

Even if the cohabitation obligation is suspended the other marriage obligations will subsist.

The grounds for a marriage to be nullified are:

(i) when there is an identity misunderstanding between the spouses, where one believes he is marrying certain person but in reality enters marriage with another person;
(ii) when the marriage takes place with the existence of a legal impediment such as lack of legal age, blood relation between spouses, adultery, physical or psychological violence etc.

8. FINANCES/CAPITAL, PROPERTY

8.1 What powers does the court have to allocate financial resources and property on the breakdown of marriage?

The Civil Code of the Federal District provides two types of regime of property in marriage:

(i) common property, which implies that all the assets obtained during the marriage are in equal parts property of the spouses; and
(ii) separate property, which implies that all the assets acquired during the marriage are the property of the spouse who acquired them.

The Civil Code and the Civil Procedure Code of the Federal District gives the court the power to make orders and/or rulings to allocate financial resources and property as a consequence of a divorce.

It is important for the court to take into consideration the property regime of the marriage.

The property regimes for marriage are marital partnership (common property) or separate property.

In the common property regime all assets are presumed to be part of said regime, unless is proven differently. For instance, in the common property regime each spouse will keep ownership of their assets and rights acquired before the time they got married or those acquired by sale, exchange, *usucapio*, inheritance, bequest, donation or gift of fortune during the marriage; as well as all objects for personal use and all the necessary instruments for their profession, art or occupation.

The separation of property regime can be absolute or partial. It is partial when the assets that are not included in the separation agreement are considered to be part of the common property regime. This property regime does not need to be recorded in a public document, but must contain an inventory of the assets and debts of each spouse at the time of the marriage.

In the separate property regime, the court shall award the spouse who was in charge of the home duties and, if relevant, taking care of children with compensation that cannot be higher than 50 per cent of all assets acquired during the marriage.

8.2 Explain and illustrate with reference to recent cases the court's thinking on division of assets

Nowadays, the most recent and important judicial precedents issued in the Federal District in connection with division of assets, are those dealing with compensation in favour of the spouse who was in charge of home duties and taking care of children, if any.

In recent cases, the criteria of the courts resolving division of assets has been based on equity and to protect the spouse who cannot obtain assets/properties during the marriage.

Judicial precedents of the Circuit Courts provides that such compensation is to be granted with the purpose of preventing unjust enrichment of a spouse or impoverishment of the other one, based on the fact that one of them was in charge of home duties and children, if any, and the other one was earning money.

9. FINANCES/MAINTENANCE

9.1 Explain the operation of maintenance for spouses on an on-going basis after the breakdown of marriage

After terminating a marriage, the Family judge shall decide on the spousal support issue, considering the need to receive it, that the main activities of the spouse claiming for support were home duties and care of children, and is unable to work or lacks assets. The judge shall take into account the following circumstances:

(i) the age and health of the spouses;
(ii) their professional skills and their ability to obtain a job;
(iii) length of marriage and past and future commitments to the family;
(iv) collaboration with work or activities of the other spouse;
(v) financial means of either spouse; and
(vi) other obligations the spouse obligated to provide financial support.

The right for alimony is extinguished if the creditor remarries, enters concubinage or a term equal to the duration of the marriage has elapsed.

9.2 Is it common for maintenance to be awarded?

Yes. It is a matter of public policy.

9.3 Explain and illustrate with reference to recent cases the court's thinking on maintenance

The criteria of the Circuit Courts is that alimony shall be established as a percentage of the total incomes (including bonuses) obtained by the individual obliged to provide the relevant financial support, that way the relevant payment will adjust to the current and actual earnings of the alimony provider – the most recent judicial precedent is identified with record number VI.2o.C. J/325 (9a.)-.

However, in some cases the courts determine a specific amount to be paid monthly which will be increased in line with inflation.

10. CHILD MAINTENANCE

10.1 On what basis is child maintenance calculated within the jurisdiction?

The calculation for determining alimony for children is established in each state Civil Code and is generally based on two items:
(i) lifestyle; and
(ii) the economic capacity of the alimony provider.
Therefore, the courts decide an award in proportion (percentage) to the total income of the alimony provider.

11. RECIPROCAL ENFORCEMENT OF FINANCIAL ORDERS:

11.1 Summarise the position in your jurisdiction

Some requirements must be complied with for a foreign order to be enforced in Mexico. The first requirement is for a foreign court to request international judicial cooperation through a letter rogatory and/or letter of request in order to enforce a foreign order. The second is that said foreign order meets certain conditions.

The Mexican law requirements for the relevant letter rogatory and/or letter of request to be accepted are that it:
(a) be issued a written form.
(b) be issued by an official authority (judge or court).
(c) contain a clear request addressed to the Mexican Court regarding the assistance required for the foreign order to be duly enforced.
(d) contain enough background information about the foreign proceeding in connection with the international judicial cooperation needed (ie, names of the parties involved, the subject matter of the foreign proceeding – kind of proceeding, assertions, etc – a brief summary of the case factual background, as well as the foreign judge/court's conclusions about the case – judgment summary).
(e) be apostilled/legalised.
(f) be translated into Spanish by a translator authorised to act as such by the Mexican courts.

On the other hand, the requirements for the foreign order to be enforced are that:
(a) the order cannot be the result from an action *in rem* – actions that are those brought for the specific recovery of lands or tenements.
(b) the foreign judge/court should have held jurisdiction in the foreign proceeding, in terms of the rules of international law and according to the provisions of the Federal Code of Civil Procedures.
(c) the defendant or defendants should have been personally summoned in compliance with the due process of law in the relevant foreign proceeding.

(d) the foreign order should be final – *res judicata*.
(e) no pending legal action/proceeding in Mexico should exist between the same parties on the same subject.
(f) the foreign order cannot be contrary to the Mexican public policy.
(g) the judgment should be authenticated and apostilled.
(h) the judgment should be translated into Spanish by a translator authorised to act as such by the Mexican courts.

12. FINANCIAL RELIEF AFTER FOREIGN DIVORCE PROCEEDINGS

12.1 What powers are available to make orders following a foreign divorce?

The Mexican courts are authorised to recognise foreign rulings issued in divorce proceedings by means of a specific proceeding in which the courts verify if the foreign divorce ruling is compatible with the Mexican public policy (ie, spousal support obligation, child support obligation, finances, care and custody, visitations, property regime, etc.).

Once the courts decide that the foreign divorce complies with Mexican public policy, said ruling will be enforced in the same way that the corresponding foreign judge would have done, for which the Mexican Family Court judge needs all the necessary information about the text, validity, meaning and legal scope of the relevant foreign law.

Foreign laws may apply except when they come into conflict with Mexican laws. However, it would not be considered an obstacle to apply a foreign law in Mexico, even if Mexican laws do not include any of the foreign law figures provided that similar figures may exist, that can be applied by analogy.

D. CHILDREN

13. CUSTODY/PARENTAL RESPONSIBILITY

13.1 Briefly explain the legal position in relation to custody/parental responsibility following the breakdown of a relationship or marriage

Both parents will have obligations, such as:
(i) ensuring physical, psychological and sexual security;
(ii) encouraging proper eating habits, personal hygiene and physical development;
(iii) showing affection; and
(iv) determining limits and standards of conduct to preserve best interest of minors.

These obligations will apply, regardless of whether the parent lives under the same roof as the minor or not.

The parents may agree upon the terms of an order with regard to parental responsibilities and with regard to the custody of minors, but a Family judge must then approve the agreement. If they fail to agree, the Family judge shall resolve the matter.

Agreement
Parents may agree on (i) shared-custody of the minors or (ii) that the minors will live with one of them under the same roof. The judge in the divorce decree must ensure the divorcing parents will comply with their obligations regarding child support.

Judgment
In the absence of such agreement, the Family judge must determine which parent will have care and custody rights (living under the same roof), taking into account the minors' best interest. The other parent will still need to provide child support and will have visitations with his/her child.

In this sense, the judge must take into account the minor´s opinion; however, it is not mandatory for the judge to follow the minor's opinion.

According to the Civil Code of the Federal District, children less than 12 years' old should remain in the care of the mother, except in cases of domestic violence caused by the mother or when there is a serious danger for the normal development of children. However, nowadays the Federal Supreme Court of Justice criterion seeks to grant custody to either parent based on the fact they should be treated as equals and considering the child's best interest.

13.2 Briefly explain the legal position in relation to access/contact/visitation following the breakdown of a relationship or marriage
Children are entitled to have visitations with the parent who they do not live with. The parents may determine in an agreement duly approved by the court the manner in which the contact, access or visitation shall take place. In the event that the parents do not reach any agreement the Family judge will decide on that matter.

Agreement
Parents may agree on the days when the visitations will occur and the place. Parents may also decide if visitations may allow children to stay for one or more nights in the house of the parent who they do not live with.

Judgment
If the parents do not agree, the Family judge shall resolve the manner of access or socialising rights they have with the parent who the child does not live with, taken into account the children's best interest.

The parents or the Family courts usually fix the regime of contact, access or visitation during the weekends or throughout the week, always respecting the minor's meal, rest and study times.

14. INTERNATIONAL ABDUCTION
14.1 Briefly summarise the position in your jurisdiction
Mexico is party of The Hague Convention for Child Abduction which establishes that the parent who has custody of the child cannot unilaterally change the address of the latter, as the ownership of these rights does not

imply having an exclusive and absolute power to determine the place where the child should live because in this decision the other parent shall also intervene, as he has rights to socialise and coexist with the minor.

The Central Authority which resolves cases involving international abduction in Mexico is the Ministry of Foreign Affairs (*Secretaría de Relaciones Exteriores*).

In accordance with the Convention, the states parties will be obliged to return the child and will not have the jurisdiction to judge the possible rights of custody for the child, since this is within the jurisdiction of the requesting state in which the child had his habitual residence before the abduction.

In matters of child abduction, the requested state is obliged to enact the necessary measures for the location of the child and return him to his habitual residence.

However, in Mexico there are some difficulties in complying with the Convention:

Problems of locating the child

Due to cultural and geographical configurations of Mexico, the location of the abductor and the child is sometimes almost impossible since Mexico does not have specialised police for investigating and locating abducted children.

Long proceedings for restitution of the child (evidence stage)

The Mexican Federal Constitution recognises a due process fundamental right, which can be exercised by either parent (including abductor) through the 'Amparo' proceeding which will cause the delay of the restitution.

In this sense, all types of evidence are allowed in Mexican judicial proceedings. Evidence from abroad is often obtained through a letter of request/letter rogatory process, which can take six months or so to be completed.

Opposition through the Mexican 'Amparo' proceedings

The Mexican 'Amparo' is a judicial proceeding by which private individuals and entities complain before federal courts as to any violation to human rights from any governmental activities, acts, including statutes/laws.

The plaintiff in the 'Amparo' proceeding (either parent in an abduction case) is entitled to request from the 'Amparo'/federal courts an interim remedy which is a stay order to prevent the governmental authority from continuing violating human rights while the 'Amparo' dispute is solved, which in a Hague Convention means that the the restitution of the child is stayed.

15. LEAVE TO REMOVE/APPLICATIONS TO TAKE A CHILD OUT OF THE JURISDICTION

15.1 Summarise the position in your jurisdiction

When both parents agree and express their consent that either one of them may take the minors to a foreign country they may do so giving prior notice to the other spouse.

If parents are in disagreement and one of them wishes to take a minor to a foreign country she/he will need the other spouse's consent or a judicial authorisation.

15.2 Under what circumstances may a parent apply to remove their child from the jurisdiction against the wishes of the other parent?

A parent may take a child to a foreign country without the other parent's consent if he/she obtains a judicial authorisation from a Family Court judge. In this case the parent who wishes to remove the child to another country shall demonstrate before the court that such decision was made in order to provide the minor a better life aligned with his/her best interest. The issues that a Family judge will consider include, but are not limited to:

(i) the children's right to a home;
(ii) the children's right to education;
(iii) the children's right to recreation;
(iv) the children's right to health services;
(v) the children's right to live within an environment free of domestic abuse; and
vi) the children's right to have visitations with the parent who they do not live with.

E. SURROGACY AND ADOPTION

16. VALIDITY OF SURROGACY AGREEMENTS

16.1 Briefly summarise the position in your jurisdiction

In Mexico surrogacy is still not regulated nor forbidden. Notwithstanding, in the Federal District some congressmen have filed bills with the House of Representatives to try and ensure the development of legislation in this area.

However, there exists a general principle which says 'for private individuals what is not forbidden by law then is permitted'. Therefore, we are of the opinion that surrogacy agreements are allowed in Mexico, provided that those agreements are gratuitous pursuant to articles 320 and 466 of the General Health Act.

17. ADOPTION

17.1 Briefly explain the legal position in relation to adoption in your jurisdiction. Is adoption available to individuals, cohabiting couples (both heterosexual and same-sex)?

In the Federal District, adoption is considered to be the legal act through which the Family judge constitutes in an irrevocable manner a legal relationship between the adoptee and the adopter, which shall be also considered as a blood relation between the adoptee and the family of the adopter and between him/her and the descendants of the adoptee (siblings).

Regarding adoption by homosexuals, while the Federal Supreme Court of Justice criterion states that the rights of minors subject to adoption are in a prevalent position against the interest of the adopter or adopters, it is also true that this does not mean that the sexual orientation of a person or a couple bars them from being eligible to adopt a minor under Articles 1 and 4 of the Mexican Federal Constitution. In other words, if homosexual couples are not considered capable of adopting a minor by court, purely because they are homosexual, such governmental act shall be considered as discriminatory and against the fundamental rights of that couple.

F. COHABITATION

18. COHABITATION

18.1 What legislation (if any) governs division of property for unmarried couples on the breakdown of the relationship?

The applicable law for concubinage is the Civil Code of each State.

In accordance to the Civil Code of the Federal District, upon cessation of cohabitation, concubines that lack sufficient income or assets to sustain themselves are entitled to receive alimony for an equal period of time to the duration of the concubinage. The concubine who has demonstrated ingratitude, lives in concubinage with another person or gets married cannot claim alimony. This right may only be exercised during the year following the termination of the concubinage.

Also the concubinage generates between concubines, rights of alimony and heirs rights.

In the Federal District for 'cohabitation/coexistence' there is a specific applicable law – Law of cohabitation/coexistence in the Federal District.

G. FAMILY DISPUTE RESOLUTION

19. MEDIATION, COLLABORATIVE LAW AND ARBITRATION

19.1 Briefly summarise the non-court-based processes available in your jurisdiction and the current status of agreements reached under the auspices of mediation, collaborative law and arbitration

Mediation

Mediation is a public and private service offered to the population in order to settle disputes. The Alternative Justice Law of the Superior Court of Justice of the Federal District defines mediation as a voluntary procedure by which two or more people involved in a dispute, seek and build a satisfactory solution for the dispute, with the assistance of an impartial third party called mediator.

The matters that can be resolved by a mediation procedure are: civil, commercial, family, criminal or juvenile justice.

The mediation seeks to avoid contentious proceedings or bring to an end an ongoing contentious one. The mediators are empowered to mediate regarding family disputes arising from marriage, cohabitation, domestic partnership and any other conflict in which children are involved.

Collaborative law

This is not applicable in Mexico since agreements regarding any family issue must be approved by a Family judge.

Arbitration

Not applicable in Mexico since divorce proceedings and related matters (ie, spousal support obligation, child support obligation, care and custody, visitations, etc.) need to be resolved before a Family judge due to the fact that those subjects are considered as a matter of public policy.

19.2 What is the statutory basis (if any), for mediation, collaborative law and arbitration in your jurisdiction? In particular, are the parties required to attempt a family dispute resolution in advance of the institution of proceedings?

The Alternative Justice Law of the Federal District is the statutory basis for mediation. Please bear in mind that collaborative law and arbitration are not allowed for family disputes and related issues in Mexico. However, some other states in Mexico have their own applicable local laws named 'Mediation Law' or 'Alternative Justice Law'.

Parties may initiate a mediation process at any time without having to initiate a dispute resolution in advance.

H. OTHER

20. CIVIL PARTNERSHIP/SAME-SEX MARRIAGE

20.1 What is the status of civil partnership/same-sex marriage within the jurisdiction?

The Civil Code of each Mexican state shall regulate the items regarding marriage. In the Federal District, Article 146 of the Civil Code was amended in 2009, in order to establish that marriage is *'The free union of two people that have a life in common, where both seek mutual respect, equity and reciprocal aid. That must be held before the Judge of the Civil Registry, complying with the formalities stipulated by this Code'.*

The previous amendment is supported by a non-mandatory judicial precedent (number 161268) issued by the Federal Supreme Court of Justice. This states that a person's sexual orientation is part of their personal identity and responds to a relevant element in their life project, which includes the desire to have a life in common with a person of the same or opposite sex. From the above, the court establishes that homosexual or heterosexuals persons have the right to the free development of personality, which also involves deciding to marry or not.

This kind of marriage is only permitted in the Federal District and in the State of Quintana Roo, since other Mexican states do not approve this type of marriage.

20.2 What legislation governs civil partnership/same-sex marriage?

Since civil partnership/same-sex marriage is not federally regulated or recognised, the applicable legislation for marriage is the Civil Code of each state, according to the domicile where they will get married. However, so far the only legislation available acknowledging the existence of civil partnership/same-sex marriage is the one provided by the House of Representatives in the Federal District.

21. CONTROVERSIAL AREAS/RAPIDLY DEVELOPING AREAS OF LAW

21.1 Is there a particular area of the law within the jurisdiction that is currently undergoing major change?

No.

21.2 Which areas of law are most out-of-step? Which areas would you most like to see reformed/changed?

We consider that the areas of law most out-of-step are those regarding the relocation of children, enforcement of providing alimony, international pre-nuptial agreements, surrogacy agreements and the property regime of spouses married abroad. Therefore, those areas of law need to be reformed/changed.

Monaco

PCM Avocats Christine Pasquier-Ciulla & Alison Isabella Torti

A. JURISDICTION AND CONFLICT OF LAW

1. SOURCES OF LAW

1.1 What is the primary source of law in relation to the breakdown of marriage and the welfare of children within the jurisdiction?

The primary source of law for the breakdown of marriage is Articles 197 to 206-12 of the Monegasque Civil Code (MCC). There are no rules of conflict of law concerning divorce in the MCC. They have been set out by case law.

Rules relating to the welfare of children and parental responsibility can be found at articles 298 to 410 MCC. The MCC does not contain any rules of conflict of law concerning the welfare of children.

However, Monaco ratified the New York Convention on the rights of the child (20 November 1989) and is also a party to the Hague Conference and has signed and ratified the following Hague Conventions on:

- The Civil Aspects of International Child Abduction (25 October 1980);
- The Protection of Children and Cooperation in Respect of Inter-country Adoption (29 May 1993);
- The Protection of Minors (19 October 1996).

When no Convention is applicable, Article 3 MCC (which lists cases where Monegasque law is applicable) is interpreted *a contrario* by Monegasque courts to consider that the child's national law is applicable to issues relating to the child's welfare (*TPI, 7 May 1987, E c H*). On this same basis, Monegasque courts apply a party's national law to all personal status and capacity issues.

The Monegasque Code of Civil Procedure (MCCP) contains specific procedural rules regarding matrimonial regimes at articles 816 to 829. Articles 830 to 848-1 MCCP relate to the guardianship judge (*juge tutélaire*), who has jurisdiction over family matters, minors and adults protected by the law.

There is no specific private international law code or statute in Monegasque law. Some general rules on jurisdiction issues can be found in the MCCP (Articles 1 to 5bis), and in the above-mentioned case law interpretations.

1.2 Which are the main statutes governing matrimonial law in the jurisdiction?

In Monaco, matrimonial law is predominantly governed by the First Book of the MCC (articles 116 to 410-36°). These articles cover a wide range of matters relating to family law, such as domicile, marriage, divorce, separation, parentage, adoption, parental responsibility, minors and adults protected by the law.

Rules relating to matrimonial property and marriage contracts are contained in articles 1235 to 1261 MCC.

2. JURISDICTION

2.1 What is the main jurisdictional requirement for the institution of proceedings in relation to divorce, property and children?

The general rules relating to jurisdiction can be found at Articles 1 to 5bis MCCP.

The Monegasque court of first instance (*Tribunal de Première Instance, TPI*) has jurisdiction over any dispute where the defendant's domicile is located in Monaco (Article 2 MCCP). It also has jurisdiction when the family domicile is outside Monaco if one of the spouses is a Monegasque national.

Article 3 MCCP lists the cases where the TPI has exclusive jurisdiction, whatever the defendant's domicile, which include but are not limited to proceedings:

- relating to real property situated in Monaco;
- arising from obligations created or due to be executed in Monaco, or contracted abroad and concerning a Monegasque national.

For matters relating to family law and personal status, Article 4 MCCP provides an exception to Article 2 MCCP, and allows foreign nationals to decline the Monegasque courts' jurisdiction if they can prove that both their legal and factual domicile is situated in their country of origin (see question 4.1 below)

If the defendant refuses to appear before the court, the TPI has jurisdiction if the last known family domicile is Monaco (*Court of Appeal, 10 November 1992, P c A*).

3. DOMICILE AND HABITUAL RESIDENCE

3.1 Explain the concepts of domicile and habitual residence as they apply to the jurisdiction in relation to divorce, the finances and children

'Domicile' is a legal concept and is defined by Article 78 MCC as follows: 'the domicile of a person is, regarding the exercise of its civil rights, the place where the person's main establishment is' (*TPI, 27 May 2004, N c M*). A person can only have one domicile.

In relation to spouses, Article 187 MCC states that the spouses choose, together, the family residence which constitutes their 'main establishment'. The family residence will be established *de facto* on a case by case basis (*CA, 10 November 1992, P c A*).

The 'habitual residence' of underage children in the event of a divorce is a factual concept. Since the 2003 reform of Monegasque law, this concept is attached to that of 'parental responsibility': both parents (failing that, the judge) decide on the child's habitual residence. It is defined as the place where the child effectively lives and cannot leave without authorisation from its parents or a judge (Article 304 MCC).

4. CONFLICT OF LAW/APPLICABLE LAW TO BE APPLIED

4.1 What happens when one party applies to stay proceedings in favour of a foreign jurisdiction? What factors will the local court take into account when determining forum issues?

For matters relating to civil and personal status, Article 4 MCCP sets out an exception to the general Monegasque jurisdiction rules (see question 2.1). Foreign nationals can raise a jurisdictional objection and apply to stay proceedings in favour of a foreign jurisdiction, if they can justify that both their 'legal and factual domicile' are situated in that foreign jurisdiction (*CA, 18 April 1989, DF c NS*).

This jurisdictional objection must be raised *in limine litis* (Article 262 MCCP). For this reason, when a defendant raises the jurisdictional objection before the judge ruling on interim measures, the latter rules on said measures but refers the parties to the TPI concerning the jurisdictional objection (*TPI, 4 January 1990, D c L*).

As a consequence, parties requesting interim measures are granted a certain degree of security, as they are ensured that the interests linked to measures listed in Article 202-1 MCC can be protected by a non-conciliation order until jurisdiction issues are solved (*CA, 7 April 1992, A c M; TPI 13 July 2010, A c C*).

In case of conflict between Article 3(2°) and Article 4 MCCP, Monegasque nationals benefit from a privilege of jurisdiction which trumps the jurisdictional objection of Article 4 (*CA, 18 April 1989, DF c NS*).

The exception of *litispendence* is not admitted by Monegasque courts. According to current case law, if a divorce petition is filed in Monaco after having previously been filed abroad, the Monegasque court is not required to give priority to the foreign courts to avoid potentially conflicting decisions (*CA, 18 December 1984, H c Sté Usinor; CA 18 April 1989 DF c NS; CA 26 March 1996, V c P*).

Conflict of laws

If Monegasque courts are deemed to have jurisdiction over disputes which involve an international element, the question arises as to which law is applicable to the dispute.

Article 3 MCC states that Monegasque law is always applicable in relation to real property situated in Monaco (*lex rei sitae* principle). Monegasque law is also applicable to procedural and formal requirements (*locus regit actum* principle).

An *a contrario* interpretation of Article 3 MCC has led Monegasque courts to apply the party's national law to questions relating to personal status and capacity (this includes but is not limited to marriage, divorce, parentage, adoption, minors, adults protected by the law) (*TPI, 7 May 1987, E c H*).

Therefore, concerning divorces:

- if the spouses share a foreign nationality, they can request that the law of the foreign nationality be applied to the divorce (*CA, 9 March 1993, M c M*);
- if the spouses do not share a foreign nationality, Monegasque law will be

applied (*lex fori*) (*T, 20 February 1975, B c CB*);

However, there are two exceptions to this principle:

- the foreign law must not be contrary to Monegasque mitigated public policy (*TPI 6 April 1995, B c B*);
- Monegasque judges do not automatically apply a foreign law to a dispute if they are not expressly requested to do so by the parties (*TPI 29 March 2012, S c BS*). The parties must also provide proof of the content of the foreign law.

B. PRE- AND POST-NUPTIAL AGREEMENTS

5. VALIDITY OF PRE- AND POST-NUPTIAL AGREEMENTS

5.1 To what extent are pre- and post-nuptial agreements binding within the jurisdiction? Could you provide a brief discussion of the most significant case law on this issue?

Pre-nuptial agreements

When a marriage is due to be celebrated in Monaco, Monegasque law allows the spouses to sign a marriage contract (pre-nuptial agreement).

Under Monegasque law, the validity of a marriage contract regarding its form is governed by the *lex fori*. Monegasque law imposes the following formal conditions:

- the marriage contract must be signed prior to the celebration of the wedding and takes effect on the day of the celebration of the wedding (Article 1240 MCC).
- the marriage contract must be drawn up in the form of a notarial deed (Article 1241 MCC).
- any modifications brought to the contract prior to the celebration of the wedding must also comply with these formal requirements (Article 1242 MCC).

If the above conditions are not met, the marriage contract will be deemed null and void.

The parties can choose what law is applicable to the substance of the marriage contract, in keeping with the general principle of 'freedom of matrimony agreements'. They can also refer to a foreign legal provision, or to a specific Monegasque or foreign matrimonial regime.

However, parties cannot derogate from 'public policy' rules (Article 1236 MCC), particularly rules relating to:

- rights and obligations imposed on spouses by the institution of marriage;
- parental authority; and
- inheritances and legal reserves.

Spouses therefore have the possibility to make provisions regarding:

- administration and management of property;
- property rights and disposal of real and personal property;
- modalities for each spouses' contribution to household expenses;
- gifts between spouses; and
- successional rights and obligations of the surviving spouse.

In the absence of a valid marriage contract, and unless the parties have agreed on a different Monegasque legal matrimonial regime, the separation of property regime (Articles 1244 to 1249 MCC) will be automatically applied to the marriage (Article 1235 MCC).

The matrimonial property regime can be modified at any time throughout the marriage if justified by 'the family's best interests' (Article 1243 MCC). The modification must be done by notarised deed and is subject to judicial homologation (articles 819 and 829 MCCP).

If these conditions are fulfilled, it is possible to:

- change the clauses of a marriage contract;
- select a different legal matrimonial regime;
- replace the previously selected legal matrimonial regime by a marriage contract;
- modify the law governing the matrimonial regime or marriage contract (*TPI 12 January 1990, époux M*).

Judges tend to be thorough when checking that the purported changes are indeed in 'the family's best interests', especially when a separation of property regime is changed for a community regime (*T, Ch. Cons., 3 March 1998, époux P*).

The above conditions apply to foreigners having celebrated their wedding in Monaco, or when their marriage contract or matrimonial regime is governed by Monegasque law.

Post-nuptial agreements

Prior to the 2007 reform of Monegasque divorce law which introduced mutual consent divorces into Monegasque law, 'divorce contracts' were not recognised.

There is no concept under Monegasque law similar to the Anglo-Saxon post-nuptial agreement, whereby the parties may contractually, in advance, organise the asset management and allocation of property, as well as all financial consequences, in the event of a divorce.

The new Article 202-5 MCC does however provide the possibility for the parties to sign a 'divorce convention' setting out the consequences of the divorce, at any moment during divorce proceedings. It becomes legally binding after judicial homologation (Article 202-5 MCC).

At this stage, it is unclear whether a pre-nuptial agreement on the consequences of a divorce as regards spousal compensation would be considered valid by Monegasque courts, as there is no case law available on this matter. However, such validity is not unlikely, as the 2007 divorce law reform introduced the possibility for spouses to divorce by signing a private agreement and having it judicially homologated (Article 202-5 MCC).

C. DIVORCE, NULLITY AND JUDICIAL SEPARATION

6. RECOGNITION OF FOREIGN MARRIAGES/DIVORCES

6.1 Summarise the position in your jurisdiction

Marriages

A marriage contracted abroad is valid under Monegasque law if:

- the essential conditions have been fulfilled under the national law of each spouse (*a contrario* interpretation of Article 3-3° MCC);
- the conditions conform to Monegasque mitigated public policy;
- the wedding was celebrated pursuant to *lege fori*.

If one or both spouses are Monegasque nationals, further formal conditions must be fulfilled for the marriage celebrated abroad to be valid in Monaco (Article 143 MCC):

- the marriage announcement must be formally published (Article 51 MCC);
- the Monegasque national spouse(s) must not be in violation of the various grounds for nullity (see below 7.1).

Divorces

Foreign divorce judgments are directly enforceable in Monaco, as they concern the personal status of the parties (*TPI, 8 January 1987, MM c Ministère d'Etat; TPI, 26 February 2004, F c K; CA 17 October 2012, L c S*). However, Monegasque courts can be asked to review such judgments and check:

- the compliance with formal conditions imposed by *lex fori* ;
- the absence of fraud to the law;
- the conformity of the decision with Monegasque mitigated public policy.

Ancillary measures regarding custody or maintenance are not automatically enforceable in Monaco and must be declared as such to produce legally binding effects in the Principality (see question 11.1). Depending on the country in which the judgment was pronounced, the enforcement might be governed by either:

- a bilateral convention;
- the Hague Convention on the service abroad of judicial and extrajudicial documents in civil or commercial matters (14 November 1965), or;
- the general *exequatur* procedure (Articles 470 to 486 MCCP).

7. DIVORCE

7.1 Explain the grounds of divorce within the jurisdiction (please also deal with nullity and judicial separation if appropriate)

Grounds for nullity (Articles 147 to 157 MCC)

The grounds to file an action to have a marriage declared null and void relate to a marriage contracted:

- in the absence of the spouse's consent, or after consent was extorted by threats or by instilling considerable fear;
- after consent was given as a consequence of a fundamental mistake made by one of the spouses as to the identity or essential qualities of the other spouse;
- by boys under the age of 18 and girls under the age of 15 (additional consent conditions are imposed regarding minors);
- while already married;

- between people of the same sex;
- by a woman, before a period of 300 days has passed since the death of her husband;
- between two persons who are closely related.

Depending on the cause of nullity invoked, either spouse, or both spouses, their direct ascendants, the general prosecutor or anyone whose consent was required, can start proceedings to have a marriage declared null and void.

Grounds for judicial separation (Articles 206-1 to 206-12 MCC)
Judicial separation puts an end to the obligation of cohabitation but, unlike divorce, it doesn't put an end to the duties to provide assistance and to remain faithful to one's spouse. Judicial separation can be pronounced on the same grounds as divorce. After two years, either spouse can request that the judicial separation be changed to divorce.

Grounds for divorce
The Divorce Act of 12 July 2007 greatly reformed Monegasque law, by modifying the grounds, procedures and effects of divorces. Prior to this reform, only fault-based divorces were allowed.

The new grounds for divorce are: fault, breakdown of marital life (after three years' separation), and a criminal conviction or serious illness of a spouse likely to compromise the family's balance (Article 197 MCC). The 2007 Divorce Act also introduced divorce by mutual consent (Articles 198 and 199 MCC).

A fault-based divorce can be requested when the actions of a spouse constitute a serious or repeated breach of marital obligations which renders the continuation of married life intolerable. Establishing fault on both sides leads to a decree against both spouses (*divorce aux torts partagés*).

In the case of irretrievable breakdown of communal life, a divorce can be granted after a three-year separation period on the date of lodging the divorce petition. After this mandatory separation period, the divorce is granted automatically and the other spouse's consent is irrelevant.

However, if the other spouse files for a fault-based divorce, the court will examine the fault-based request first. If no fault can be established, the court will may pronounce a divorce for irretrievable breakdown of marital life (Article 200-11 MCC).

Divorce proceedings end in the event of a reconciliation between the spouses. If a second divorce petition is then filed, facts having occurred prior to the reconciliation can only be invoked if similar facts occur after the said reconciliation (Article 200-16 MCC).

8. FINANCES/CAPITAL, PROPERTY

8.1 What powers does the court have to allocate financial resources and property on the breakdown of marriage?

In the absence of a pre-nuptial agreement, the separation of property regime, defined at Article 1244 MCC, is automatically applicable to marriages celebrated in Monaco. Spouses remain free to administer, use and dispose of their personal property, and bear the burden of their personal debts alone.

In the divorce judgment, the Court names a notary who will proceed to the liquidation of the matrimonial regime and divide any property that might be owned jointly by the spouses. If the parties fail to reach an agreement, a new procedure is triggered, as defined under Article 204-4 MCC.

At any stage during the divorce proceedings or during the subsequent liquidation of the matrimonial regime, the judge can order an expertise of the reciprocal incomes and assets (Articles 344 to 368 MCCP) or may appoint a notary to propose a draft for the liquidation of assets.

8.2 Explain and illustrate with reference to recent cases the court's thinking on division of assets

Recent constant case law shows that judges are increasingly willing and ready to order expert assessments of the spouses' respective financial situations to help them establish the allocation of property and maintenance.

Experts' missions are quite broad, and include the evaluation of the spouses' income and expenses during marital life, the interrogation of the spouses' accountants, or the lifting of banking secrecy or other professional confidentiality rules. (*CA 17 January 2012, C c K; unpublished order, 12 November 2012, V c T; unpublished order, 11 March 2013, S c V*).

In practice, however, experts are faced with various obstacles and results are often unsatisfactory (see question 21.2). In the absence of published case law at this stage, it is unclear how professionals and bankers are going to react to the lifting of confidentiality rules.

9. FINANCES/MAINTENANCE

9.1 Explain the operation of maintenance for spouses on an on-going basis after the breakdown of marriage

During divorce proceedings

Spouses have a mutual obligation to provide support and assistance (Article 181 MCC). During the marriage, the spouse that does not fulfil this obligation may be compelled to do so and upon request, the judge will award maintenance support for living costs during marriage.

Upon separation or pending divorce, alimony (*pension alimentaire*) can be awarded to either spouse in proportion to each spouse's income and needs, and may be decreased or increased if circumstances change. If there are children, the judge will award a separate amount to the custodial parent (see question 10.1).

The judge may order one spouse to pay the other spouse periodical amounts, to enable the latter to maintain the living standard to which he/she has become accustomed (Article 202-1 MCC).

In assessing the amount due, the judge *'must take into account the creditor's needs and the debtor's contributory faculties; the needs concern daily life and are appreciated, to a certain extent, in relation to the spouses' lifestyle; however, the 'needs of the wife' cannot be defined and determined as resulting necessarily and automatically from the husband's fortune and income, even if, during marital life, he used to give her considerable sums for strictly personal expenses'* (*CA 8 June 2010, VB c. FR*, where the Court granted the wife a monthly alimony of €30,000 to allow her to maintain the lifestyle she had grown accustomed to during her 20-year marriage).

This is awarded at the preliminary hearing and lasts until the divorce is final. It can be modified during the divorce proceedings if new circumstances occur.

After the divorce is final

Upon the dissolution of the marriage, the spouses no longer have a duty to support each other: payment of alimony ceases once the divorce judgment has the force of *res judicata*.

However, either spouse can receive a compensatory benefit (*prestation compensatoire*), which is usually paid in capital, in one lump sum, but can also be paid in up to five yearly instalments (or more, under exceptional circumstances), or by the attribution of an asset or life interest in an asset (Article 204-5 MCC).

Examples of the criteria taken into account in assessing the amount due are:

- the duration of the marriage;
- the age and health of the spouses;
- their qualifications and professional situation;
- the consequences of the professional choices made by one of the spouses during marital life, for the (past and future) education of the children, or to favour the other spouse's career at the expense of one's own;
- the estimated or predictable amount of wealth (both capital and income) received in the process of winding up matrimonial assets;
- the spouses' existing or predictable rights regarding social coverage and retirement plans.

Unlike French law, Monegasque law does not allow for the compensatory benefit to be fixed in the form of a lifelong annuity, as it considers that maintaining a legal obligation indefinitely after the dissolution of the marriage would not be justified.

In the case of a fault-based divorce, the 'guilty' spouse loses any advantage that the 'innocent' spouse might have granted by marriage contract or otherwise. The 'guilty' spouse also loses any right to a compensatory benefit (Articles 205-2 and 205-2 MCC).

However, exceptions can be made on the basis of equity, to compensate considerable disparities in the spouses' respective situations following the divorce (Article 205-5 MCC). For example, it was decided that, although deemed guilty in the sense of Article 197-1° MCC, a 57-year-old wife should receive compensation in a divorce pronounced after a 38-year-long marriage, during which she gave up her teaching career in order to bring up the couple's seven children (*TPI 24 November 2011, E c C*; also *TPI 17 January 2013, D c. PDS*).

Moreover, Article 205-3 MCC states that the spouse against whom the divorce was pronounced can be sentenced to pay damages to the 'innocent' spouse for the moral (*TPI, 21 November 2011, E c C*) or material (*CA, 8 February 2011, G c M*) prejudice caused by the breakdown of marriage.

9.2 Is it common for maintenance to be awarded?

As the Monegasque divorce law reform is fairly recent (Divorce Act 2007), there are no statistics providing an objective analysis and quantification of the courts' thinking on this matter. There are no official guidelines to help direct the courts regarding the allocation and calculation of maintenance.

The relatively limited case law shows that the courts consider the issue on a case-by-case basis, taking into consideration precise factual elements, as set out above.

Usually the courts grant maintenance when the divorce creates a disparity between the spouses, which is quite frequent. However, the courts seem less willing to grant maintenance in cases where the marriage was very brief and the spouses very young. In such cases, the courts think that the spouses can easily 'bounce back' from the divorce.

9.3 Explain and illustrate with reference to recent cases the court's thinking on maintenance

See questions 9.1 and 9.2.

10. CHILD MAINTENANCE

10.1 On what basis is child maintenance calculated within the jurisdiction?

Child maintenance under Monegasque law is based on the principle of parental responsibility. The child is placed under the responsibility of both his parents, who together have a duty to ensure its 'custody, supervision and education' (*autorité parentale conjointe*, Article 300 MCC).

On this basis, each parent has the obligation to 'contribute towards the child's care and education', in proportion to their respective resources and the child's needs. This obligation does not end automatically when the child reaches the age of 18.

In the event of a divorce, both parents continue to exert parental authority over the child, unless its best interests dictate otherwise (Article 204-7 MCC).

In the absence of a judicially homologated agreement between the spouses setting out the divorce modalities, the judge names the parent with whom the child will 'habitually reside' and grants the other parent a visitation right. The judge takes into consideration the child's best interests in decisions relating to the child.

The judge also orders the payment of child maintenance, known as 'contribution to the child's care and education' (*part contributive à l'entretien et à l'éducation de l'enfant*). In practice, there is no compulsory calculation mechanism. The amount due is based on the parents' respective resources and the child's needs.

Courts are insistent upon the fact that the superior interests of the child dictate that he be allowed to maintain his living standard. To this end, they take into consideration the advantages (and corollary expenses) of living in Monaco, and thus include in the child maintenance amounts the rent costs which can be quite high in Monaco (*TPI 10 January 2013, M c I*).

The amount granted is usually based on living costs and revised annually in accordance with indexes for urban families (published yearly by the system of economic statistics).

11. RECIPROCAL ENFORCEMENT OF FINANCIAL ORDERS

11.1 Summarise the position in your jurisdiction

There are specific rules on the enforcement of Monegasque financial orders in relation to family matters.

If debtors fail to pay maintenance, creditors can request an order to seize the amounts due directly from their salary as well as to obtain conservatory measures on debtors' properties in Monaco. The non-payment of maintenance for more than two months is a criminal offence (Article 296 of the Monegasque penal code) which can justify a criminal complaint.

The assistance of a bailiff (*huissier de justice*) is necessary for any enforcement.

Different provisions apply to the enforcement of foreign financial orders, depending on the state in which the order was issued.

Monaco has ratified the Hague Convention on the Service Abroad of Judicial and Extrajudicial Documents in Civil or Commercial Matters (15 November 1965), which sets up a procedure coordinated by central authorities, which ensure the follow-up on the service of judicial and extrajudicial documents in another member state. This procedure ensures that recipients have effective knowledge of the documents and facilitates proof of transmission.

Monaco has also signed several bilateral cooperation conventions, with countries such as France, which set out simplified procedures for the enforcement of foreign financial orders.

If no convention is applicable, foreign orders can be enforced through the regular '*exequatur*' procedure (Articles 470 to 486 MCCP). The claimant must establish that the foreign order complies with the following conditions (Article 473 MCCP):

- the foreign order is valid in its form;
- the foreign court had jurisdiction to issue the order;
- defence rights were respected;
- the order is enforceable in the jurisdiction where it was pronounced;
- the order is not contrary to Monegasque public policy.

12. FINANCIAL RELIEF AFTER FOREIGN DIVORCE PROCEEDINGS

12.1 What powers are available to make orders following a foreign divorce?

See above question 11.1.

With regard to the simplified procedures set out in bilateral conventions, the Monegasque judge, in ordering the enforcement of foreign orders, cannot:

- modify modalities of enforcement (*TPI, 12 March 1987, Société Fruehauf France c P*);
- modify or interpret foreign decisions (*TPI, 12 December 1985, Société Sofinco c B*);
- postpone payment (*TPI, 12 December 1985, Société Sofinco La Hénin c B*).

On the contrary, in the context of the regular '*exequatur*' procedure, in the absence of reciprocity, the courts may examine the form and the merits of a foreign decision (Article 474 MCCP) and may:

- check the decision complies with public policy (*TPI 28 June 1990, G c M*);
- check the foreign court's reasoning in reaching the decision (*TPI 24 January 2002, SA Gilsim c Trademark Management*).

In any event, even if a foreign decision on maintenance rights is not enforceable in Monaco, the courts consider that it establishes the 'essence' of a debt (*principe certain de créance*). On this basis, the courts have authority to order provisional and protective measures.

D. CHILDREN

13. CUSTODY/PARENTAL RESPONSIBILITY

13.1 Briefly explain the legal position in relation to custody/parental responsibility following the breakdown of a relationship or marriage

Parental responsibility (Articles 300 to 332 MCC) is a set of rights and obligations the parents exercise jointly to ensure the well-being of their child and its 'custody, supervision and education'.

The concept includes the parents' rights to:

- determine the child's residence;
- oversee and monitor the child's everyday life and education;
- administer the child's property.

Any decision relating to the child must be taken jointly by both parents or, failing that, by the guardianship judge.

However, if one parent is momentarily unable to exercise this right (in case of absence, geographical distance or incapacity), joint parental responsibility is momentarily attributed in its entirety to the other parent. However, the first parent remains entitled to oversee the child's welfare.

Under exceptional circumstances (such as a criminal conviction), parents can have their right to parental responsibility itself partially or totally withdrawn by the judge (Article 323 and 324 MCC).

During divorce proceedings, this principle is maintained but its modalities of enforcement must be adjusted. Bearing in mind the child's best interests, the parents or the judge must determine its principal residence, and the visitation rights of the spouse with whom it does not habitually reside (Article 202-1 §6 MCC).

The child can be heard on this matter, if it is capable of discernment and is not being manipulated (Article 12 of the New York Convention on

Children's Rights, 1989, which Monaco ratified on 21 June 1993).

13.2 Briefly explain the legal position in relation to access/contact/visitation following the breakdown of a relationship or marriage

Following a separation, the exercise of parental responsibility must inevitably be amended to suit a new factual situation. In practice, one parent is granted habitual residence and the other a more or less extensive visitation right.

Parents are encouraged to reach an agreement themselves. Failing that, the judge decides, bearing in mind the child's best interests, and taking into consideration criteria such as:

- the necessity to preserve family links and contact between the child and both parents (*TPI, 17 January 2002, M c E*);
- the capability of the parent requesting exclusive parental responsibility to provide for the child's needs and education (*CA, 2 June 2006, VB c BP*);
- the parents' geographical estrangement (*CA, 20 February 2007, NL c AM*);
- the strained relationship existing between child and parents (*CA , 2 June 2006, VB c BP*);
- the child's wishes, if it is capable of discernment and is not being manipulated (Article 202-3 MCC) (*TPI, 10 June 2010, RF c F; CA, 18 October 2010, EG c CB*).

14. INTERNATIONAL ABDUCTION

14.1 Briefly summarise the position in your jurisdiction

Monaco ratified the Hague Convention on Civil Aspects of International Child Abduction (25 October 1980).

If the other state is a party to the Convention

The Convention refers to the wrongful removal of a child from its place of habitual residence – or the wrongful retention of a child away from its place of habitual residence – in breach of a parent's custody rights.

Therefore, an order for the immediate return of a child can only be issued in the case of a wrongful removal of a child from the person actually exercising custody. In such cases, the Convention has set up a mechanism allowing the immediate return of the abducted child to the custodial parent.

If the custodial parent is moving abroad, the non-custodial parent can only apply to have its access rights rendered effective.

The Monegasque central authority dealing with international abductions is the Direction des Services Judiciaires (DSJ). In practice, the DSJ is very efficient and reacts promptly to ensure the child's safe return home.

In the event of an international abduction, the custodial parent must immediately petition the DSJ. When the child's location is known, the DSJ will alert and liaise with the relevant central authority.

If the other state is not party to the Convention

The custodial parent must enforce the Monegasque judgment granting custody or obtain an '*exequatur*' enforcement order for a foreign judgment.

In any event, there are criminal provisions for the abduction or illegal removal of children (Articles 289 to 294 MCC), but there is no published case law on the application of these provisions to custodial parents.

15. LEAVE TO REMOVE/APPLICATIONS TO TAKE A CHILD OUT OF A JURISDICTION

15.1 Summarise the position in your jurisdiction

15.2 Under what circumstances may a parent apply to remove their child from the jurisdiction against the wishes of the other parent?

In principle, parents share joint parental responsibility (see question 13.1). On this basis, both parents' consent to the child's relocation abroad is necessary.

To remove a child from the jurisdiction against the other parent's wishes, the residential parent must obtain the permission of the guardianship judge, whose main concern is the protection of the child's best interests (Article 304 MCC).

Judges recognise that the child's best interests are linked to the possibility of keeping close contact with both parents. They tend to be more lenient if the parent is relocating for professional reasons or if the move doesn't unduly disrupt the child's life.

Depending on the factual situation, visitation rights can be amended. In such cases, provisions are also made concerning the child's travel expenses, which can be included in maintenance payments or paid directly by either parent.

Procedural rules are set out in Articles 839 to 848-1 MCCP.

If the judge considers that the move is not in the child's best interests, he can issue an interim injunction to:

- order that the child's passports be submitted to police authorities for safekeeping (unpublished order 30 May 2011);
- forbid the child's move abroad (unpublished order, 21 April 2011).

E. SURROGACY AND ADOPTION

16. VALIDITY OF SURROGACY AGREEMENTS

16.1 Briefly summarise the position in your jurisdiction

There are no legal provisions or published case law relating to the validity of surrogacy agreements under Monegasque law. It must be noted that, following the Concordat signed with the Vatican in 1751, Catholicism is the official state religion in Monaco. This strong Catholic tradition suggests that surrogacy agreements are likely to be considered as contrary to public policy.

17. ADOPTION

17.1 Briefly explain the legal position in relation to adoption in your jurisdiction. Is adoption available to individuals, cohabitating couples (both heterosexual and same-sex)?

Full adoption (*adoption légitimante*, Articles 242 to 263 MCC)

Full adoption completely severs the adoptee from his or her biological family and creates a new parentage situation with the adoptive parents, giving the adoptee the same status as a biological child. It cannot be revoked.

The request can only be filed jointly by a couple who has been married for more than five years without legitimate children who have been granted an exemption from the Prince. One of the two must be over the age of 30.

The adoptee must have lived with the family for at least one year before reaching the age of six. His or her consent is also required over the age of 15. The adoptee's biological parents' consent is also necessary.

Simple adoption (*adoption simple*, Articles 264 to 287 MCC):
The adoptee maintains all its rights in its biological family but the adoptive parents exercise parental authority. A simple adoption can be judicially revoked if the adoptee's behaviour is severely troubling.

Simple adoption is open to a married couple or a single person over the age of 30, without legitimate descendants who have been granted an exemption from the Prince. The adoptive parent must be at least 15 years older than the adoptee.

The adoptee's biological parents' consent is necessary. The adoptee's consent is also required when over the age of 15.

Full and simple adoptions are not available to cohabitating heterosexual or homosexual couples.

International adoptions
Monaco ratified the Hague Convention on the Protection of Children and Cooperation in Respect of Inter-country Adoptions (29 May 1993). The *Direction des Services Judiciaires* (DJS) is the designated central authority in charge of overseeing international adoptions.

If an adoption is pronounced in due form by the competent authority of a country party to the Convention, it is automatically recognised in other party states. If the Convention is not applicable, an enforcement procedure has to be brought before Monegasque courts to have foreign adoptions recognised in Monaco and *lex fori* procedures apply. The merits of the case are governed by the national law of the adoptee (*CA, 11 November 1975, Procureur Général c V*).

F. COHABITATION
18. COHABITATION
18.1 What legislation (if any) governs division of property for unmarried couples on the breakdown of a relationship?
There are currently no legal provisions concerning cohabitation under Monegasque law.

G. FAMILY DISPUTE RESOLUTION
19. MEDIATION, COLLABORATIVE LAW AND ARBITRATION
19.1 Briefly summarise the non-court-based processes available in your jurisdiction and the current status of agreements reached under the auspices of mediation, collaborative law and arbitration
See question 19.2.

19.2 What is the statutory basis (if any) for mediation, collaborative law and arbitration in your jurisdiction? In particular, are the parties required to attempt a family dispute resolution in advance of the institution of proceedings?

There are no independent and non-court-based processes capable of producing binding results regarding family dispute resolution. However, within the court-based framework, mediation and collaboration between the parties are encouraged and private agreements become binding once they have been judicially homologated.

During divorces, to avoid lengthy and costly proceedings, spouses are entitled (and encouraged), at any time, to submit a private agreement concerning the consequences of the divorce, for judicial homologation (Article 202-5 MCC).

Mediation is built into the judicial process. When a spouse files for divorce, both spouses are summoned to a 'conciliation' hearing. The judge interviews each spouse separately, then together, and finally with their lawyers present, to attempt reconciliation. If this fails, the judge issues an '*Ordonnance de non conciliation*' and the spouses have one month from this date to file for divorce (Article 200-8 MCC).

At any time during the divorce proceedings, spouses can be advised or ordered to resort to family mediation (Article 202-4 MCC).

Concerning parental authority, the guardianship judge can advise or order parents to resort to family mediation (Article 303 MCC).

Finally, lawyers play an essential role by helping their clients reach out-of-court settlements.

H. OTHER

20. CIVIL PARTNERSHIP/SAME-SEX MARRIAGE

20.1 What is the status of civil partnership/same-sex marriage within the jurisdiction?

There are no legal provisions concerning civil partnerships under Monegasque law.

Monegasque law does not recognise same-sex marriages and considers them null and void (Article 147 MCC).

To our knowledge, the courts have not yet been faced with the issue of the recognition or the divorce/separation of a foreign, same-sex couple, legally married abroad and currently living in Monaco.

However, bearing also in mind that Monaco signed a Concordat with the Vatican making Roman Catholicism the official state religion, it is likely that such unions will be considered as contrary to public policy.

20.2 What legislation governs civil partnership / same sex marriage?

Not applicable.

21. CONTROVERSIAL AREAS/RAPIDLY DEVELOPING AREAS OF LAW

21.1 Is there a particular area of the law within the jurisdiction that is currently undergoing major change?

There is currently growing consensus around the idea that cohabitation needs to be regulated. The current absence of legal provisions is clearly out-of-step with changing social realities and the consequent increasing frequency of cohabitation of both heterosexual and homosexual couples.

21.2 Which areas of law are most out-of-step? Which areas would you most like to see reformed/changed?

The area of Monegasque family law which is most out of step is the law relating to access to evidence in divorce cases.

The person asking for financial support in divorce proceedings bears the burden of proof regarding the other spouse's financial means. It is for the spouse asking to be granted financial support following the divorce proceedings to prove the existence and extent of the other spouse's financial capabilities, to convince the judge what financial support should be ordered.

However, the elements of proof required are difficult to access, especially considering the private and sensitive nature of this kind of information.

Judges cannot order the parties to produce the relevant documentation to establish their financial situation, but are increasingly willing and likely to order expert assessments, which can be quite extensive (see question 8). Unfortunately the experts themselves are often faced with various types of obstacles: banking secrecy laws, client privilege rules (eg, accountants) and mechanisms set up to conceal assets (eg, shell companies, trust funds), and often do not investigate beyond the *prima facie* evidence they are given.

Despite the judges' efforts to broaden experts' missions, their powers unfortunately remain limited as there is no way to compel a party to reveal information. There is no equivalent to the Anglo-Saxon 'contempt of court' or the French 'solemn declaration' (*déclaration sur l'honneur*).

Please note that in this subject matter most of the Monegasque case law is not published. We therefore used unpublished decisions from our practice and also wish to thank the Direction des Services Judiciaires for kindly putting at our disposal some of the recent unpublished decisions of Monegasque courts.

The Netherlands

Smeets Gijbels B.V.
Carla L. M. Smeets & Caroliene Mellema

A. JURISDICTION AND CONFLICT OF LAW

1. SOURCES OF LAW

1.1 What is the primary source of law in relation to the breakdown of marriage and the welfare of children within the jurisdiction?

The current source of law for divorce in the Netherlands is the Dutch Civil Code (Book 1 'Persons and Family Law', Title 9 'Dissolution of marriage', Articles 1:150 to 1:166, Title 10 'decree of judicial separation and the dissolution of the marriage after judicial separation', Articles 1:169 to 1:183) and the Dutch Code of Civil Procedure (Book 3, Title 6, Articles 814 to 827). The current source of law in relation to the welfare of children is the Dutch Civil Code (Book 1, Title 14, 'Custody over minor children', Articles 1:245 to 1:377, and Title 15, 'Right to contact and information', Articles 1:377a to 1:377h). Also relevant are the European Convention on Human Rights (ECHR) and the Convention on the Rights of the Child (CRC).

Book 10 of the Dutch Civil Code (Particularly Title 3, Section 4, 'Dissolution of the marriage and legal separation', Articles 10:54 to 10:59 of the Dutch Civil Code, and Section 1, 'Solemnisation and recognition of the validity of marriages', Articles 10:27 to 10:34 of the Dutch Civil Code) governs marriage and divorce under international private law. The Convention of 5 October 1961 concerning the powers of authorities and the law applicable in respect of the protection of infants (1961 Hague Convention) governs the welfare of children in matters involving international private law. With respect to the protection of minors, the Hague Child Protection Convention of 1996 replaces the Hague Child Protection Convention of 1961 between the contracting States. The Hague Child Protection Convention of 1961 continues to apply in respect of non-contracting States. Finally, the case law handed down by the Dutch Supreme Court and the lower Dutch courts are important sources of law.

1.2 Which are the main statutes governing matrimonial law in the jurisdiction?

Titles 6 to 8 of the Dutch Civil Code (Book 1, Title 6, 'Right and duties of the spouses', Articles 1:81 to 192a, Title 7, 'The statutory community of property', Articles 1:93 to 1:113, Title 8, 'Marriage contracts', Articles 1:114 to 1:143) are relevant with respect to matrimonial property law. If there is a community of property between spouses, Articles 3:166 to 3:200 of the Dutch Civil Code are also relevant. Book 10 of the Dutch Civil Code

(Particularly Title 3, Section 2, 'Legal relationship between spouses', Articles 10:35 to 10:41 of the Dutch Civil Code, and Section 3, 'The Matrimonial Property Regime', Articles 10:42 to 10:53 of the Dutch Civil Code) is relevant with respect to international private law.

Finally, the relevant legal literature and the case law handed down by the Dutch Supreme Court and the lower Dutch courts must also be taken into consideration.

2. JURISDICTION

2.1 What are the main jurisdictional requirements for the institution of proceedings in relation to divorce, property and children?

Divorce

The answer to the question of whether the Dutch court has jurisdiction with respect to a divorce petition can be found in the Brussels II *bis* Regulation and Article 4 of the Dutch Code of Civil Procedure. The latter article specifically refers to the applicability of the Brussels II *bis* Regulation. Article 4 of the Dutch Code of Civil Procedure is a residual provision insofar as the other jurisdiction in question is not governed by a convention or regulation. Pursuant to Article 3 of the Regulation, the Dutch court has jurisdiction to take cognisance of a unilateral divorce petition in the following cases:

- if the defendant has his or her habitual residence in the Netherlands (Article 3(1)(a), third enumeration);
- if the petitioner has his or her habitual residence in the Netherlands, provided that:
    - the most recent marital address was in the Netherlands (Article 3(1)(a), second enumeration);
    - the petitioner has had his or her habitual residence in the Netherlands for at least one year immediately preceding the petition (Article 3(1)(a), fifth enumeration); and
    - the petitioner has Dutch nationality and has had his or her habitual residence in the Netherlands for at least six months prior to the petition (Article 3(1)(a), sixth enumeration); or
- if both spouses have Dutch nationality (Article 3(1)(b).

The Dutch court has jurisdiction to take cognisance of a joint divorce petition if:

- at least one of the spouses has his or her habitual residence in the Netherlands (Article 3(1)(a), fourth enumeration); and
- both spouses have Dutch nationality (Article 3(1)(b).

Property

Pursuant to Article 8 of the Dutch Code of Civil Procedure, parties to international marital property disputes may explicitly choose the court that has jurisdiction if the case in question involves issues that only affect their own interests. Thus, the parties may choose the Dutch court unless they have no reasonable interest in doing so. Such a choice of forum agreement must be laid down in writing. Article 9 of the Dutch Code of Civil Procedure provides for the possibility to tacitly choose the Dutch court as the forum; if the Dutch court does not have jurisdiction in respect of a matrimonial property dispute under the rules governing jurisdiction. Article 9 allows for jurisdiction if the defendant appears in the proceedings in the Netherlands and does not dispute the Dutch court's jurisdiction. However, the Dutch court will not accept jurisdiction if there is no reasonable interest in doing so.

In the context of divorce proceedings, the court may render decisions with respect to any ancillary relief requested, such as relief with respect to the division of matrimonial property or the settlement of a pre-nuptial or post-nuptial agreement. Article 3 and Article 4(2) of the Dutch Code of Civil Procedure are relevant in respect of matrimonial property issues such as ancillary relief. The Dutch divorce court also has jurisdiction in respect of ancillary relief related to matrimonial property issues. If the ancillary relief requested relates to a request to be permitted to continue using the marital residence (whether owned or rented), the Dutch court will have jurisdiction only if the residence is located in the Netherlands (Article 4(3)(a) of the Dutch Code of Civil Procedure).

In the event that a decision must be rendered with respect to a matrimonial property dispute that is not related to ancillary relief in connection with a divorce, in most cases such a dispute will have to be instituted by means of a petition, in which case the jurisdiction rule contained in Article 3 of the Dutch Code of Civil Procedure will apply. The Dutch court will have jurisdiction if one or more of the petitioners or interested parties have their domicile or habitual residence in the Netherlands (Article 3(a) of the Dutch Code of Civil Procedure), or if the case is otherwise sufficiently related to the Dutch legal sphere (Article 3(c) of the Dutch Code of Civil Procedure). Proceedings must, in any event, be instituted by means of a writ of summons, such as a claim for division of the marital property. In that case, the Dutch court will have jurisdiction if the defendant has his or her domicile or habitual residence in the Netherlands (Article 2 of the Dutch Code of Civil Procedure). Finally, the Dutch court will have jurisdiction on the ground of Article 9(b) and (c) of the Dutch Code of Civil Procedure if it is not possible to conduct legal proceedings outside the Netherlands or if the proceedings must be instituted by means of a writ of summons, are sufficiently related to the Dutch legal sphere, and it would be unacceptable to expect the plaintiff to subject the case to the determination of a foreign court.

Finally, Article 13 of the Dutch Code of Civil Procedure provides that the court's power to grant injunctive relief or protective measures in interlocutory proceedings cannot be disputed solely on the ground that the court in question does not have jurisdiction in respect of the proceedings on the merits of the case.

Children

The general rule contained in Article 8 of the Brussels II *bis* Regulation provides that in cases relating to parental responsibility, the court of the member state in whose jurisdiction the child has his or her habitual residence at the time at which the case is brought will be the legal authority that has jurisdiction. If the child's place of residence is legally changed to another member state, on the ground of Article 9 of the Brussels II *bis* Regulation, in principle, the court in the jurisdiction where the child had his or her prior habitual residence will retain jurisdiction to amend parental contact arrangements that have already been established up to three months after the actual removal.

Article 12 of the Brussels II *bis* Regulation will apply if an issue comes up that is related to parental responsibility in the context of pending divorce proceedings, in which case the divorce court will have jurisdiction if the following conditions have been met:

- at least one of the spouses has parental responsibility;
- the court's jurisdiction has been accepted explicitly or in some other unequivocal way by the spouses and by the persons who have parental authority at the time at which the case is brought before the court; and
- the jurisdiction is justified by the child's interests.

In addition, the Dutch court may accept jurisdiction on the ground of Article 12(3) of the Brussels II *bis* Regulation if the following three conditions have been met:

- the child has strong ties to the Netherlands, in particular because one of the persons who has parental responsibility has his or her habitual residence in the Netherlands or the child is a Dutch citizen;
- the jurisdiction has been explicitly and unequivocally accepted by all the persons who have parental responsibility at the time at which the case is brought; and
- the jurisdiction is justified by the child's interests.

Therefore, in a certain sense, the parties are given the opportunity to choose the court that has jurisdiction.

The Hague Child Protection Convention of 1996 applies as a supplement to the Brussels II *bis* Regulation in respect of jurisdiction, the law that applies, recognition, execution and collaboration with regard to parental responsibility in the EU member states, with the exception of Denmark. Authorities in an EU member state will apply the Convention if the case in question involves a child who has his habitual residence in a state that is not an EU member state but that is a contracting party to the Convention. In the event that the child has his habitual residence in an EU member state, the Regulation will be applied. The Brussels II *bis* Regulation does not provide for the law that will apply in respect of a measure that is related to parental responsibility. Therefore, the Convention designates the law that applies in respect of a measure that is taken in an EU member state, regardless of whether the measure is taken on the ground of the Regulation or the Convention. An EU member state will also determine on the basis of the Convention whether there is a custody relationship between a child and his parents by operation of law.

The intention is to concentrate jurisdiction with the authorities of the state in which the child has his habitual residence (Article 5). In the event that the child is taken away without authorisation or illicitly is not brought back, the authorities of the contracting state in which the child had his habitual residence immediately prior to his being taken away will have jurisdiction until the child has acquired a habitual residence in another State. By way of an exception, the authority of a contracting state that has jurisdiction in accordance with Articles 5 and 6 may refer the case in the event that it is of the opinion that with respect to a specific case the authority of another contracting state would be better able to assess the child's interests.

Finally, pursuant to Article 20 of the Brussels II *bis* Regulation the Dutch court will have jurisdiction to take urgent measures, even if the court of another member state has jurisdiction to take cognisance of the substance of the case pursuant to that Regulation.

3. DOMICILE AND HABITUAL RESIDENCE

3.1 Explain the concepts of domicile and habitual residence as they apply to the jurisdiction in relation to divorce, the finances and children

Divorce

The rules governing jurisdiction laid down in Article 3(1)(a) of the Brussels II *bis* Convention are all based on the concept of 'habitual residence'. That concept is not defined in the Brussels II *bis* Convention. The concept of 'habitual residence' must be understood based on autonomous interpretation of the Convention. The Court of Justice of the European Communities explained the term 'habitual residence' within the meaning of Article 8 of the Brussels II *bis* Regulation as follows (15 September 1994, case C-452/93): *'the place in which the [person] concerned has established, with the intention that it should be of a lasting character, the permanent or habitual centre of his interests. However, for the purposes of determining such residence, all the factual circumstances which constitute it must be taken into account'*. The relevant Dutch case law has also applied that autonomous interpretation of the Convention.

Financial issues related to matrimonial property law fall outside the scope of the Brussels II *bis* Regulation. They also fall outside the scope of the Regulation on Jurisdiction and the Enforcement of Judgments in Civil and Commercial Matters. Since there are no convention rules that apply, the jurisdiction of the Dutch court must be determined exclusively on the basis of the ordinary rules that govern jurisdiction. In the section that governs civil actions the concept of 'habitual residence' has been derived from the convention law as laid down in Article 5 of the Convention on Jurisdiction and the Enforcement of Judgments in Civil and Commercial Matters of 1988 and Article 1 of the 1961 Hague Convention and stands for a person's social place of residence (*residence habituelle*). The determination of where a person has his habitual residence is predominantly a question of evaluating the facts of the case at hand. A certain duration is required, albeit that duration may be limited from the outset.

Children

The Hague Child Protection Convention of 1996 does not define the meaning of the 'habitual residence' of a child. It can be inferred from the background history that underlies the Convention that the term relates to a concept based on an autonomous interpretation of the Convention, which must be determined in more detail on the basis of the facts and circumstances of the particular case in question. In the explanatory report it is noted that what is primarily relevant is the place with which the child has his most significant social connections. The duration of the residence will play an important role in the determination. However, the duration will not be determinative in all cases. That would be the case, for example, if it is to be expected that the minor will remain in this country for an extended period of time. This will once again require an evaluation of the specific facts of the case at hand.

The Court of Justice interpreted the term 'habitual residence of a child' as used in Article 8(1) as follows (Court of Justice of the European Union, 22 December 2010, no. C-497/10): *'The concept of 'habitual residence' must be interpreted as meaning that such residence corresponds to the place which reflects some degree of integration by the child in a social and family environment. The factors which must be taken into consideration include the duration, regularity, conditions and reasons for the stay in the territory of that member state and for the family to move to that state and, second, with particular reference to the child's age, the family origins and social connections which the family and child have with that member state. It is for the national court to establish the habitual residence of the child, taking account of all the circumstances of fact specific to each individual case'.*

4. CONFLICT OF LAW/APPLICABLE LAW TO BE APPLIED

4.1 What happens when one party applies to stay proceedings in favour of a foreign jurisdiction? What factors will the local court take into account when determining forum issues?

Article 12 of the Dutch Code of Civil Procedure contains a scheme that governs the situation where different proceedings are pending in the Netherlands and abroad between the same persons with respect to the same subject. If the foreign proceedings were commenced earlier than the Dutch proceedings and the decision of the foreign court can be recognised or, if appropriate, enforced in the Netherlands, the Dutch court can stay the proceedings that were commenced previously until the foreign court has rendered a decision. As soon as it appears that the foreign decision can be recognised or enforced, the Dutch court will declare that it lacks jurisdiction. Article 19 of the Brussels II *bis* Regulation goes even further and provides that the court to which the case has been submitted second must stay the proceedings *ex officio* until the jurisdiction of the court to which the case was first submitted has been established.

B. PRE- AND POST NUPTIAL AGREEMENTS

5. VALIDITY OF PRE- AND POST NUPTIAL AGREEMENTS

5.1 To what extent are pre- and post-nups binding within the jurisdiction? Could you provide a brief discussion of the most significant recent case law on this issue?

Marriage contracts may both be made by the (prospective) spouses prior to and during their marriage. In order to be valid, marriage contracts must be entered into by notarial instrument. Since 1 January 2012 district court approval is no longer required for making or altering a marriage contract during a marriage.

The parties may derogate in their marriage contracts from the provisions of the statutory community property regime, provided that the stipulations are not in conflict with provisions of mandatory law, *bonos mores* or Dutch public policy. The parties may not stipulate that a spouse is committed to a larger share of the liabilities than shared by that spouse in the community property. The parties may not derogate from the rights arising from parental authority or from the rights conferred by law to a surviving spouse.

By making a marriage contract, the general community property regime can be deviated from. To a large extent, there is freedom of contract upon drafting the marriage contract, with the exception of provisions which are intended to protect the family; these cannot be deviated from. Consequently, the consent of the other spouse is always required for, among other things, selling the house inhabited jointly, encumbering this house with a mortgage or making gifts. The duty to support each other is also an important mandatory provision.

Pre-nuptial or post-nuptial agreements can, among other things, include the following points detailed below.

- 'Cold exclusion' or marriage contract precluding any claim of one spouse on assets accruing to the other spouse during the marriage.
  In Dutch law, the term 'cold exclusion' is used when referring to a marriage contract whereby no community property regime whatsoever exists between the spouses. The word 'cold' refers to the fact that the spouses do not set off their income and increase in wealth in any way whatsoever.
- Limited community of property.
  The law offers the possibility to choose a limited community of property in the marriage contract, for instance, a community of the house or a community of household effects; a combination of 'cold exclusion' and a limited community of property. The acquisitions of each separate spouse shall remain private capital.
- Netting clauses: periodical netting clauses or final netting clauses.
  A periodical or final netting clause can be added to each marriage contract which contains an exclusion of any community of property. These clauses comprise a settlement, which needs to be paid periodically or at the end of the marriage. If netting needs to be effected periodically, this is referred to as a periodical netting clause. A choice is thus made for keeping the private assets separate and to, mandatorily or optionally, set off the income to be defined in more detail in the contract after deducting the household expenses at the end of each year. Netting is often limited to the income from labour.
  However, in practice, many people, although having committed themselves to this setoff, omit the yearly setoff. This has resulted in much case law with regard to the question as to what is right by law

in these cases. This case law has resulted in the Dutch Settlement Provisions Act (*Wet Regels Verrekenbedingen*), which came into effect on 1 September 2002. If netting does not need to be effected periodically, but at the end of the marriage (as a result of divorce or death) only, this is referred to as a final netting clause.

It is important to remember that all marriage articles are different. Although a number of provisions from the pre-nuptial or post-nuptial agreements (such as exclusion of any community of property combined with a periodical or final netting clause) will be included often, each contract will have to be assessed and explained individually. As to the manner in which pre-nuptial or post-nuptial agreements must be explained, the defining factor is the meaning which the parties could mutually attach to the provisions in all reasonability under the circumstances given and what they could reasonably expect from each other in this respect (Dutch Supreme Court, 13 March 1981, NJ 1981, 635).

In recent years, the Dutch Supreme Court has been more inclined to attach significance to the actual conduct of the spouses during the marriage. The Dutch Supreme Court delivered an interesting judgment on 18 June 2004 (*NJ* 2004, 399), in which it ruled that in a situation in which parties have acted as though they were married in accordance with a statutory community of property, the principles of reasonableness and fairness could imply that the parties are not bound by the pre-nuptial or post-nuptial agreement. The Court of Appeal of Amsterdam passed a similar judgment (19 January 2006, *LJN* AV9260). The actual conduct must be differentiated from an agreement between the spouses (not in the form of a pre-nuptial or post-nuptial agreement) through which they wish to deviate from the pre-nuptial or post-nuptial agreement system that applies between them. The Dutch Supreme Court has ruled that an agreement made during the marriage that has not been laid down in the form of a notarial deed will not lead to a different interpretation of the pre-nuptial or post-nuptial agreement (see Dutch Supreme Court, 27 June 2003, *NJ* 2003; Court of Appeal of Leeuwarden, 19 September 2007, *NJN* BB4425; Court of Appeal of Amsterdam, 11 October 2007, *LJN* BC0891).

C. DIVORCE, NULLITY AND JUDICIAL SEPARATION

6. RECOGNITION OF FOREIGN MARRIAGES/DIVORCES

6.1 Summarise the position in your jurisdiction

Recognition of foreign marriages

Two schemes govern the recognition of a foreign marriage: the Hague Convention of Celebration and Recognition of the Validity of Marriages and Book 10 of the Dutch Civil Code (Title 3, Section 1, 'Solemnisation and recognition of the validity of marriages', Articles 10:27 to 10:34 of the Dutch Civil Code). Pursuant to the Hague Convention of Celebration and Recognition of the Validity of Marriages, the rules governing recognition may be supplemented by Book 10 of the Dutch Civil Code (Title 3, Section 1, , 'Solemnisation and recognition of the validity of marriages', Articles 10:27 to 10:34 of the Dutch Civil Code). The general rule can be distilled from

Article 10:31: a marriage that is solemnised outside the Netherlands that is legally valid in accordance with the laws of the state where it was solemnised or subsequently became legally valid will be acknowledged as such.

The term 'solemnisation of the marriage' relates to both an official marriage ceremony and a formless marriage. The condition that the marriage must be 'legally valid' pertains to both the validity of the form and to the material requirements in accordance with that law. A marriage must be presumed to be legally valid on the ground of that article if declaration of marriage has been issued by a competent authority.

Recognition of divorce orders pronounced in the EU (with the exception of Denmark)

The recognition of divorce orders that are pronounced within the EU is governed by the Brussels II *bis* Regulation. Pursuant to Article 21 of that Regulation, divorces that are pronounced in a member state will be acknowledged in the other member states without any judicial process being necessary. Pursuant to Article 22 of the Brussels II *bis* Regulation, recognition may be refused on the following grounds:

- the recognition is manifestly contrary to the public order;
- if the document initiating the divorce proceedings has not been served on the defendant and the defendant has not appeared or if the defendant has not otherwise been given notice of it, unless it has been established that the defendant unequivocally accepts the decision; or
- the decision is irreconcilable with a decision that has already been rendered in the member state being requested or with a decision that has already been rendered in a third state that has been acknowledged in the member state being requested.

In principle it is not possible to recognise repudiation in the Netherlands unless a number of requirements have been met. The repudiation must have taken place outside the Kingdom, must be in accordance with the 'personal law of the man', must have legal effect in the place where the repudiation took place, and it must be apparent that the wife has explicitly or tacitly accepted the dissolution of the marriage.

Recognition of non-European divorce judgments

Article 10:57 of the Dutch Civil Code provides a scheme that governs the recognition of non-European divorces. Article 10:57 of the Dutch Civil Code requires that, in order for such a judgment to be recognised, the marriage must have been dissolved after a proper administration of justice by means of a decision rendered by a court or another competent authority. If that requirement has not been met, recognition will be possible nonetheless if it is clear that the opposing party in the proceedings has explicitly or tacitly accepted the dissolution of the marriage, unless such recognition cannot be tolerated on the ground of the Dutch public order. It is not possible to recognise repudiation in the Netherlands unless that form of dissolution is in accordance with the 'personal law of the man', the dissolution is legally effective in the place where it took place and the wife has explicitly or tacitly accepted the dissolution of the marriage.

7. DIVORCE

7.1 Explain the grounds for divorce within the jurisdiction (please also deal with nullity and judicial separation if appropriate)

Grounds

Pursuant to Dutch law there is only one ground on which to pronounce a divorce, which is irretrievable breakdown of the marriage. That ground will be deemed to apply if the continuation of the cohabitation has become unbearable and there are no prospects of a return to proper matrimonial relationship. If one of the spouses argues that the marriage has irretrievably broken down, the court will generally assume that that is the case, even if the other spouse disputes it.

Annulment of a marriage

A marriage may be annulled on the grounds detailed below:

- The requirements that govern entering into a marriage have not been met. Various requirements must be met in order to enter into a marriage. For example, in principle, the husband and the wife must both be 18 years of age and they must have 'healthy' mental faculties through which they are able to express their will. Bigamy is not permitted. In some cases permission is required from a third party (such as a parent, a judge of the Cantonal Division of the court or a trustee) in order to enter into a marriage. If one or more of those requirements have not been met, the marriage may be annulled.
- Unauthorised official or insufficient number of witnesses. If the marriage was solemnised by an unauthorised official or if it was solemnised in the presence of an insufficient number of witnesses, the marriage may be annulled at the request of the parents, the spouses and the public prosecutor.
- Threat or error. If the marriage was entered into under the influence of wrongful serious threat the spouse may request that it be annulled. An annulment can also be requested if, at the time at which the marriage was solemnised, one of the spouses made an error with respect to the identity of the other spouse or with respect to the meaning of the declaration that he or she made (for example in the event that a spouse has no command of the Dutch language).
- Marriage of convenience. If the marriage is one of convenience, ie, a marriage between a Dutch citizen and a foreigner in respect of which it can be deduced from the circumstances that the marriage was aimed solely at allowing the foreign spouse to be admitted to the Netherlands, the public prosecutor may request the court to annul the marriage. If the court annuls the marriage, the declaration of annulment will be effective retroactively to the time at which the marriage was solemnised.

Legal separation
As with divorce, irretrievable breakdown of the marriage is the only ground on which spouses can legally separate. A legal separation will not lead to the marriage being dissolved. It is traditionally an option primarily for spouses who do not wish to have the marriage dissolved because of their religious beliefs.

An important consequence of a legal separation is the dissolution of the community of property between the spouses. In addition, separate rules apply with respect to the children, living expenses and the continued use of the residence.

The legal separation can end if the spouses reconcile. The law also contains a scheme pursuant to which the marriage can be dissolved after a legal separation. The marriage can be dissolved at the request of one of the spouses three years after the legal separation. The marriage can be dissolved after one year if the spouses request the dissolution jointly.

8. FINANCES/CAPITAL, PROPERTY

8.1 What powers does the court have to allocate financial resources and property on the breakdown of marriage?

If the spouses have not entered into a pre-nuptial or post-nuptial agreement, the statutory community of property regime will apply. The community of property will be dissolved as a result of divorce, in which context each of the spouses, in principle, will be entitled to one-half of the community property. The spouses may deviate from that rule and make other agreements in a divorce agreement. Upon request, the court may order one or both spouses to determine the manner in which the community of property will be divided. The court may also determine how the community property will be divided itself. The following forms of division are possible:

- allocation of part of the property to each of the spouses;
- over-distribution of one of the spouses in exchange for payment of the excess value;
- distribution of the net proceeds of all or part of the property after it has been sold in a manner to be determined by the court.

A distribution in which all the co-owners have not participated will be null and void. However, the co-owner who did not participate must invoke the nullity within one year after he or she has become aware of the distribution. The court may nullify or change the distribution in the event that one of the co-owners has made an error in respect of the value of one or more pieces of property to be distributed and, as a result, has been disadvantaged by more than one-quarter. A co-owner who intentionally conceals goods that form part of the community of property will forfeit his or her share of those goods to the other co-owners.

8.2 Explain and illustrate with reference to recent cases the court's thinking on division of assets

Court of Appeal of Leeuwarden (16 September 2008, LJN: BF0905): The Court of Appeal ruled that the share of a partner in a general partnership forms part of the partner's private assets and thus it does not form part of the matrimonial community of property. As a result the debts that the partner incurred in connection with conducting the general partnership also formed part of his private assets.

Supreme Court (30 March 2012, LJN BV1749): in a case in which the marriage had only lasted a couple of months, the fact that the wife found out during the divorce that the husband had a large amount of debts and the fact that the husband had incurred most of these debts prior to the marriage, the Supreme Court found that there was a cause to divide the property in such a way that each of the spouses was responsible for the debts that he or she had incurred, rather than applying the general rule that the spouses share the dissolved community of property equally.

In conclusion, in general, spouses share the dissolved community of property equally. The court will only deviate from this rule when there are special circumstances and the principles of reasonableness and fairness demand this is so. This also applies for the spouses who deviate from that general rule and make other agreements in a divorce agreement (see: Court of Appeal Amsterdam, 14 August 2012, LJN BY 1478; District Court of Dordrecht, 18 July 2012, LJN BX2203; District Court of Utrecht, 1 August 2012, LJN BX4241). However, for reasons of legal certainty any deviation should be approached with caution.

9. FINANCES/MAINTENANCE

9.1 Explain the operation of maintenance for spouses on an ongoing basis after the breakdown of marriage.

9.2 Is it common for maintenance to be awarded?

9.3 Explain and illustrate with reference to recent cases the court's thinking on maintenance

Standards

Ex-spouses are also liable to maintain each other after their marriage has been dissolved. After a marriage has been dissolved, or a registered partnership has been terminated, the court may determine that maintenance payments must be made. Ex-cohabitants do not have any liability to maintain each other.

The amount of the maintenance will be determined on the basis of needs, on the one hand, and earning capacity on the other. The need must be inferred from the level of prosperity that the spouses had during the last years of the marriage. In determining the needs, the court will take into consideration both the income and the expenditures and the possibility of capital formation. The court will also take into consideration the earning capacity of the spouse who is entitled to maintenance.

The financial means/ability to pay will be determined taking into consideration the income and the reasonable expenses, such as housing expenses, health insurance, pension contributions, etc. The calculation method to be used by the court has been laid down in guidelines that have been established by a workgroup of experts, which are known as the '*Tremanormen*'. However, the guidelines do not have the status of law and, thus, the court is not bound by them.

If there is a change of circumstances after the maintenance has been set, the court may change the amount of the maintenance at the request of one of the parties.

In cases in which both partner maintenance and child maintenance are appropriate, the child maintenance will always have priority over the partner maintenance. Thus, the court will take into consideration the child maintenance in determining the financial means/ability to pay of the person paying the maintenance.

The amount of the maintenance must be indexed annually by a percentage determined by the Dutch Minister of Justice.

Duration

If a marriage has lasted less than five years and no children were born of the marriage, in principle, the duration of the maintenance obligation will not exceed the duration of the marriage. If a marriage has lasted longer than five years or if children were born out of a brief marriage, in principle, the maintenance obligation will end after 12 years. However, if the termination of the maintenance would be of such a drastic nature that, on the basis of the principles of reasonableness and fairness, the person who is entitled to receive the maintenance cannot be expected to bear its consequences, upon request the court may nonetheless set a term after 12 years. The parties may also agree on a shorter term or may request the court to set a term.

The maintenance obligation will definitively end by operation of law if the person who is entitled to receive the maintenance remarries or starts cohabitating with a new partner 'as though they were married or as though they had had their partnership registered'.

Finally, it should be noted that the Dutch court may not order a lump sum payment in lieu of maintenance, as is the case in many other countries. The spouses may make such an agreement when they divorce, which they can lay down in a divorce agreement.

10. CHILD MAINTENANCE

10.1 On what basis is child maintenance calculated within the jurisdiction?

Both parents have a duty to maintain their minor children (up to the age of 18 years) and their young children of full age (up to the age of 21 years). The following factors are used to determine how much each parent must contribute to the costs of their children's upbringing.

The child's needs

The child's need is inferred from the level of the parents' prosperity at the time of the marriage or cohabitation. On the basis of the number of children, the age of each child and the net joint disposal family income at the time of the marriage or cohabitation, it is possible to derive from the 'tables of the share in children's costs' the average amount that parents spend on their children's upbringing. Those tables are drawn up by the Dutch National Institute for Family Finance Information (*Nationaal Instituut voor Budgetvoorlichting* or 'Nibud' (see *www.nibud.nl*)). The 'child-specific budget' must be deducted from the amount derived from those tables in order to determine the child's needs.

Each parent's financial means/ability to pay

After the court has determined the children's needs, it must determine the earning capacity of each parent. Factors such as the parent's income and earning capacity, reasonable expenses, such as housing expenses, health insurance expenses and cost of living are relevant in that respect. If child maintenance is awarded, the financial means for the payment of child maintenance will also be determined on the basis of the '*Tremanormen*'.

Determination of each parent's contribution in proportion to their earning capacity and the amount of care

After the earning capacity of each parent has been determined, each parent's contribution to the costs of the children's upbringing will be calculated in proportion to each parent's ability to pay. If the earning capacity is sufficient to cover the needs of the child, the maintenance debtor can get a reduction. This reduction is based on the average number of days a week – holidays included – that the child spends with this parent. The reduction is a percentage of the need, which varies from 15 per cent (one day a week) to 35 percent (three days a week). Exceptions to the application of the reduction percentages are possible, if the parent does not fulfil his obligation to share the care.

Changes to the child maintenance

After the amount of each parent's contribution to the costs of the children's upbringing has been determined it may be changed if there is a legally relevant change in the circumstances. Such a change could be based on an increase or decrease in one of the parent's financial means. The court will critically assess such a change of circumstances.

11. RECIPROCAL ENFORCEMENT OF FINANCIAL ORDERS

11.1 Summarise the position in your jurisdiction

If the obligation to pay maintenance has been laid down in an order, but the person who must pay the maintenance fails to comply, the person who is entitled to receive the maintenance may engage the Dutch National Maintenance Collection Agency (*Landelijk Bureau Inning Onderhoudsbijdragen* or 'LBIO', see *www.lbio.nl*) to collect both the child maintenance and the partner maintenance in arrears. The LBIO is an agency that has been established by law, which has special power to collect maintenance in the event that the following conditions have been met:

- the contribution has been determined by a court;
- there have been arrears for at least one month;
- the arrears amount to at least €10;
- the arrears are not older than six months;
- the person who is obliged to pay the maintenance must know to what

bank account number the payments must be transferred.

The LBIO can also collect maintenance in other countries via collaborating convention partners of the 1956 Convention of New York.

In addition to the option of engaging the LBIO, the person who is entitled to receive the maintenance may also use other means of coercion, such as having a bailiff levy an attachment on earnings or requesting leave to commit the defaulter for failure to comply with a judicial order. However, such leave may not be requested if there is a non-attributable inability to pay. Committal for failure to comply with a judicial order may not be applied until all other means have failed, which is known as an *ultimum remedium*.

A maintenance order in arrears will be time barred after five years.

12. FINANCIAL RELIEF AFTER FOREIGN DIVORCE PROCEEDINGS

12.1 What powers are available to make orders following a foreign divorce?

Pursuant to Article 431 of the Dutch Code of Civil Procedure, a foreign judgment may not be enforced in the Netherlands unless such enforcement is based on a treaty or law. If no treaty or law applies, the party for whose benefit the judgment was pronounced abroad must commence new proceedings before the Dutch court in order to obtain an enforcement order in the Netherlands. If, during such proceedings, it appears that the foreign judgment is in compliance with the requirements that govern recognition under general law, the court may refrain from fully handling the case and proceed to order the opposing party to do what he or she was ordered to do in the foreign judgment.

If a treaty does apply, and on the ground of that treaty the foreign judgment may be enforced in the Netherlands, it is first necessary to obtain leave from the court before that judgment may be enforced. Those are known as '*exequatur*' proceedings. The procedure for acquiring such leave to enforce is governed by Articles 985 to 994 of the Dutch Code of Civil Procedure. Those articles also govern the *exequatur* proceedings insofar as the law and the treaty do not provide otherwise.

The Regulation on Jurisdiction and the Recognition and Enforcement of Judgments in Civil and Commercial Matters governs the enforcement of maintenance decisions. The enforcement of decisions with respect to divorces and parental responsibility is governed by the Brussels II *bis* Regulation. The general rule that applies under both regulations is that decisions rendered in a member state will be recognised in another member state without new proceedings being required. Decisions that are rendered and enforceable in another member state may be enforced in another member state after they have been declared enforceable by means of *exequatur* proceedings. Each regulation provides its own rules governing the *exequatur* proceedings. The Brussels II *bis* Regulation offers the courts of a member state the possibility of recognising a foreign decision by issuing a certificate as referred to in Articles 37 to 39 of the Regulation.

This is only different in respect of member states that are parties to the Maintenance Regulation of 18 December 2008, which governs the law that applies, recognition and the enforcement of decisions and collaboration in respect of maintenance obligations for these member states. In respect of these member states, the Maintenance Regulation of 18 December 2008 is applicable to maintenance decisions. The Maintenance Regulation differentiates between decisions that are rendered in member states that are bound by the Hague Protocol of 2007 and decisions rendered by member states that are not bound by that Protocol (Article 16 of the Maintenance Regulation). The Protocol provides rules of conflict that must be used to determine the law that governs the maintenance. In the event that the decision in respect of maintenance has been rendered in a member state that is bound by the Protocol, no declaration of enforceability (*exequatur*) is required. On the other hand, the declaration of enforceability is required for a decision that comes from a member state that is not bound by the Protocol, and a European Enforcement Order (EEO) can also be used.

D. CHILDREN

13. CUSTODY/PARENTAL RESPONSIBILITY

13.1 Briefly explain the legal position in relation to custody/parental responsibility following the breakdown of a relationship or marriage

Article 1:251(2) of the Dutch Civil Code provides that parents who have joint custody will continue to have joint custody after their marriage has been dissolved. The parenthood and the related rights and obligations towards the minor will continue to apply. That statutory provision is based on the tenet that in the event of a divorce, any interference in the right to respect for private and family life (Article 8 of the European Convention for the Protection of Human Rights and Fundamental Freedoms) must be limited to every extent possible.

In the event that parents exercise joint custody outside of a matrimonial relationship, that joint custody will continue after the parents have separated. If during the relationship only the mother has custody of the child, she will continue to have custody after the relationship has ended. If the father has acknowledged paternity he can request the Cantonal Division of the court to grant him custody of the child (Article 1:253c(1) of the Dutch Civil Code).

13.2 Briefly explain the legal position in relation to access/contact/visitation following the breakdown of a relationship or marriage

Pursuant to Article 1:377a(1) of the Dutch Civil Code, the child and the parent who does not have custody have a right to have contact with each other. The law does not provide that the parents and the child have a right to contact with each other in the event that the parents have joint custody; they derive the right directly from the custody relationship that they already have. In the event that parents who are not married end their relationship, pursuant to Article 1:252 of the Dutch Civil Code the custody will simply continue in the same form. The parent with whom the child does not have his principal place of residence can request parental contact arrangements in accordance with Article 1:377h of the Dutch Civil Code. In the event that only one of the parents had custody during the relationship, the parent who does not have custody may request the court to establish parental contact arrangements on the ground of Article 1:377a of the Dutch Civil Code.

14. INTERNATIONAL ABDUCTION

14.1 Summarise the position in your jurisdiction

There will be deemed to be a case of international child abduction if a child under the age of 16 years is taken abroad or kept there without the consent of a parent or guardian.

The Hague Convention of 25 October 1980 on the Civil Aspects of International Child Abduction (referred to below as the '1980 Hague Convention') applies in the Netherlands with respect to international child abduction. The Convention applies in respect of minor children under the age of 16 years and provides that, if necessary, the court can be engaged to force the child's return. The Convention will apply in respect of abduction from the Netherlands only if the child is abducted to a state that is a party to the Convention. The Brussels II *bis* Regulation also applies. The Brussels II *bis* Regulation constitutes a supplement and tightening of the 1980 Hague Convention in the relations between member states.

The Brussels II *bis* Regulation prescribes that a court in an EU member state must render a decision within six weeks with respect to a request to have a child returned and that, in principle, the child and the person requesting the child's return must be heard in respect of that request. The Brussels II *bis* Regulation also provides that, in principle, a court is obliged to order that the child be returned if it has been established that adequate measures have been taken to ensure that the child will be protected once he or she has returned. The Regulation thereby limits the application of the ground for refusal contained in the 1980 Hague Convention to the effect that the child need not be returned if there is a serious risk that, as a result of the return, the child will be exposed to bodily or psychological danger or will be put in an unbearable situation in any other way.

The Dutch court will also apply the provisions contained in the 1980 Hague Convention by analogy if the child abduction relates to a state that is not a party to the Convention. In handling an international child abduction case, the cross border mediation method forms a permanent part of the procedure. See also *www.kinderontvoering.nl*.

The Hague Child Protection Convention of 1996 was enacted as a supplement to the Hague Child Abduction Convention of 1980. The European Child Abduction Convention of 1980 is a recognition and enforcement convention, as opposed to the Hague Child Abduction Convention, which has the character of a convention governing mutual assistance. Both conventions apply only in respect of children who have not yet reached the age of 16.

15. LEAVE TO REMOVE/APPLICATIONS TO TAKE A CHILD OUT OF THE JURISDICTION

15.1 Summarise the position in your jurisdiction

A child will follow the place of residence of the person who has custody of that child. If the parents have joint custody over their minor child, which is the case in most situations, the child will follow the place of residence of the parent with whom he or she actually resides. In principle, parents who have joint custody over a child will jointly determine the place of residence of their minor child. If the parent with whom the child actually resides intends to move abroad, the other parent who has joint custody will have to give permission to do so. If the other parent refuses to grant such permission, the parent who cares for the child can request the court to grant replacement permission to move on the ground of Article 1:253a of the Dutch Civil Code (dispute with respect to the exercise of joint custody).

15.2 Under what circumstances may a parent apply to remove their child from the jurisdiction against the wishes of the other parent?

It can be inferred from the relevant case law that, after a divorce, the parents must be given an opportunity to live their own independent lives, in which context the children will generally follow the parent with whom they reside (often the mother). The interests of the mother, the father and the children will not always be the same. If there are conflicting interests the mother must be deemed to have a certain degree of discretion in this regard. In its judgment of 25 April 2008 (*LJN*: BG5054), the Dutch Supreme Court ruled that in that context the court must render the decision that it considers to be in the child's interest. However, the court is bound to consider all the circumstances of the case. This may lead to other interests weighing more heavily despite the child's best interests being that of first consideration. The following factors can play a role:

- the need to move house;
- the manner in which the move has been considered and prepared;
- the rights and the interests of the parent who is moving and his or her freedom to freely organise their new life;
- the alternatives and measures offered to the parent who is moving in order to alleviate and/or compensate the consequences of the move for the child and the other parent;
- the degree to which the parents are able to communicate and consult;
- the rights of the other parent and the child to continue having unabated contact with each other in their familiar surroundings;
- the division of the care duties and the continuity of the care;
- the frequency of the contact between the child and the other parent before and after the move;
- the child's age, his or her opinion, and the degree to which he or she is rooted in his or her environment or is used to moving; and
- the extra costs related to access after the move.

E. SURROGACY AND ADOPTION

16. VALIDITY OF SURROGACY AGREEMENTS

16.1 Briefly summarise the position in your jurisdiction

Surrogate motherhood involves a situation in which the surrogate mother and the commissioning parents make agreements prior to the birth of the child with respect to the conception of the child and the relinquishment after the child is born. Being a surrogate mother is not prohibited in the Netherlands. A differentiation must be made between surrogate motherhood for commercial purposes, in which context payment for carrying and giving birth to the child is an essential characteristic, and altruistic surrogate motherhood, in which context agreements are made with respect to compensation of the costs but the commissioning parent does not pay the surrogate mother any financial compensation for carrying and giving birth to the child.

In the Netherlands it is prohibited to offer a financial incentive for a surrogate mother to carry another person's child. Surrogate motherhood for commercial purposes is punishable under the law, as is intermediating in surrogate motherhood or publishing information showing that commissioning parents are looking for a surrogate mother. However, compensating the surrogate mother's costs is permitted. There are no established guidelines in the Netherlands with respect to the question of what amount constitutes reasonable compensation of such costs.

17. ADOPTION

17.1 Briefly explain the legal position in relation to adoption in your jurisdiction. Is adoption available to individuals, cohabiting couples (both heterosexual and same-sex)?

The ability to adopt a child under Dutch civil law is regulated by Articles 227 to 232 of Title 12, Book 1, of the Dutch Civil Code, including the related procedural rules contained in Articles 970 to 984 of Title 8, Book 3, of the Dutch Code of Civil Procedure. The condition that only a married couple may adopt a child has been revoked. Two persons of different sexes who cohabitate but are unmarried may adopt a child. A person who lives alone or who cohabitates with a parent of the child to be adopted may also adopt a child (Article 1:227 of the Dutch Civil Code).

Four sets of regulations play a role in respect of international adoptions: the Hague Convention on the Protection of Children and Cooperation in respect of Intercountry Adoption of 1993, the related implementation act, the Dutch Adoption (Conflict of Laws) Act (*Wet conflictenrecht adoptie*) (which since 1 January 2012 has been replaced by Articles 10:103 to 10:112 of Book 10, Title 6, of the Dutch Civil Code) and the Dutch Placement of Foreign Children for Adoption Act (*Wet opneming buitenlandse kinderen ter adoptie*). The Netherlands is also a party to the UN Convention on the Rights of the Child of 20 November 1989 (Treaty Series 1990, 170).

The Dutch Kingdom Act of 19 May 2011 Approving the European Convention on the Adoption of Children (revised) of 27 November 2008 (Treaty Series 2009, 141) entered into effect on 10 June 2011. That

Convention is a revision of the European Adoption Convention of 1967, which the Netherlands did not ratify. The Convention constitutes a supplement to the Hague Adoption Convention of 1993. Pursuant to the European Convention registered partners and same-sex partners are permitted to adopt children. The content of the Convention does not deviate from Dutch adoption law

F. COHABITATION

18. COHABITATION

18.1 What legislation (if any) governs division of property for unmarried couples on the breakdown of the relationship?

Dutch law does not contain any statutory scheme governing the assets of unmarried cohabitants. The parties may draw up a cohabitation agreement in which they arrange for matters related to their cohabitation. A cohabitation agreement is usually drawn up in the form of a notarial deed, but that is not obligatory. It is not possible to create a general community of property by drawing up a cohabitation agreement. However, in such an agreement the parties can arrange for which assets they will own jointly. Those assets will be governed by a simple community rather than a marital community of property. The division of such property will be governed by Title 7 of Book 3 of the Dutch Civil Code (property law). In addition to the provisions contained in Book 3, the provisions contained in Book 6 (the law of obligations) will also apply, in particular, the general provisions of contract law contained in Title 5 of Book 6 of the Dutch Civil Code.

G. FAMILY DISPUTE RESOLUTION

19. MEDIATION, COLLABORATIVE LAW AND ARBITRATION

19.1 Briefly summarise the non-court-based processes available in your jurisdiction and the current status of agreements reached under the auspices of mediation, collaborative law and arbitration

There are three alternative means to resolve disputes in the Netherlands: mediation, arbitration and collaborative divorce. Mediation is a form of voluntary intermediation in conflicts, without commencing legal proceedings. The parties resolve their conflict together, under the supervision of an independent mediator. In general one mediator is sufficient. That mediator helps the parties to clarify their interests and positions. The court must uphold the result of the mediation by including the divorce agreement that the parties have concluded in its order. As a result, the divorce agreement becomes enforceable.

Arbitration offers spouses the opportunity to resolve problems by mutual consent, without involving the court. The arbitration tribunal will handle the conflict in a manner that is similar to that used by the court. The statutory rules that govern arbitration are laid down in Articles 1020 to 1076 of the Dutch Code of Civil Procedure. Arbitration is based on an arbitration agreement (Article 1020 of the Dutch Code of Civil Procedure). A consequence of such an agreement is that the regular court must declare that it lacks jurisdiction (Article 1022 of the Dutch Code of Civil Procedure).

In the case of a collaborative divorce, the parties conclude a joint agreement in which they lay down their agreements in order to resolve the dispute without involving the court. In that context the parties work together, assisted by their own lawyers and possibly other experts, in order to separate in a respectful manner. In the event that a party withdraws, the team is dismantled and its members will no longer be entitled to assist the parties. The court must uphold the result of the collaborative divorce by including the divorce agreement that the parties have concluded in its order. As a result, the divorce agreement becomes enforceable.

It should be noted that the parties are not free to determine all the legal consequences of matters related to the law of persons and family law, including those in respect of matters such as personal status, parental custody, guardianship, contact, marriage and divorce, etc.

19.2 What is the statutory basis (if any), for mediation, collaborative law and arbitration in your jurisdiction? In particular, are the parties required to attempt a family dispute resolution in advance of proceedings?

At the present time there still is no statutory scheme with respect to mediation. On 21 May 2008 the Directive of the European Parliament and of the Council on certain aspects of mediation in civil and commercial matters (Official Journal of the European Union 2008, L136/3, also referred to as the 'Mediation Directive') entered into effect. The Mediation Directive applies only in respect of cross-border mediations. The EU is not permitted to intervene in respect of the national legislation of the member states. Nonetheless, the legislature took that Directive into consideration in order to implement relevant schemes. A legislative proposal with respect to the regulation of mediation is currently being considered by the Lower House of the Dutch Parliament.

H. OTHER

20. CIVIL PARTNERSHIP/SAME-SEX MARRIAGE

20.1 What is the status of civil partnership/same-sex marriage within the jurisdiction?

20.2 What legislation governs civil partnership/same-sex marriage?

Civil partnership

Registered partnerships are governed by Title 5A of Book 1 of the Dutch Civil Code. Since 1 January 1998 both same-sex couples and mixed-sex couples may enter into a registered partnership. At the time, the registered partnership was intended to be an equivalent alternative to marriage. A registered partnership has the same consequences as a marriage, with the exception of the relationship with children pursuant to family law. Another important difference is that a registered partnership can be terminated without judicial intervention, on the condition that no minor children are involved. If minor children are involved, the registered partnership must be terminated by the court, in which case the registered partners must draw up a parenting plan in which they lay down their agreements with respect to their minor children, as will be discussed in section 21 of this contribution. A registered partnership can be converted into a marriage.

Same-sex marriage

On 1 April 2001 the institute of marriage was opened to two people of the same sex. The fact that two people having either different sexes or the same sex may get married is arranged in Article 1:30 of the Dutch Civil Code. The conditions and rules for entering into, solemnising and terminating a marriage between same-sex couples are the same as those that apply with respect to a marriage between a man and a woman. The obligations and the rights of the spouses are also the same for same-sex couples and mixed-sex couples.

There is one difference between a marriage between a same-sex couple and a marriage between a man and a woman which is, if a child is born of the marriage of a same-sex couple, the other spouse will not automatically be the child's legal parent. In such cases the other spouse must adopt the child.

As the Netherlands is one of the few countries in which it is possible for same-sex couples to get married, the recognition of such marriages abroad may be problematic.

21. CONTROVERSIAL AREAS/RAPIDLY DEVELOPING AREAS OF LAW

21.1 Is there a particular area of the law within the jurisdiction that is currently undergoing major change?

The Dutch Continued Parenthood and Well-Planned Divorce Act (*Wet bevordering voortgezet ouderschap en zorgvuldige scheiding*) entered into effect on 1 March 2009. Pursuant to that Act, in the event of a divorce, termination of a registered partnership or legal separation involving children, the parents must draw up a parenting plan before the divorce or legal separation can be pronounced or the registered partnership can be terminated. Cohabitating parents who have joint custody over their children must also draw up such a parenting plan if they terminate their cohabitation.

The parenting plan is an agreement in which the parents make agreements regarding how they will arrange their parenthood after they break up. The parenting plan must at least contain arrangements governing:

- the division of the care and upbringing duties;
- the manner in which information will be provided and the parties will consult regarding important matters; and
- the division of the costs of care and upbringing.

The rationale behind the parenting plan is to lay down concrete details with respect to the parents' obligation to promote the development of the ties between the child and the other parent, which has been included in the law since 1 March 2009.

21.2 Which areas of law are most out-of-step? Which areas would you most like to see reformed/changed?

There is a growing group that is in favour of limiting the term and amount of partner maintenance. For example, partner maintenance could be abolished or a maximum of five years could be set. Another possibility would be to oblige the partner who is claiming maintenance to submit a development plan showing what concrete steps will be taken in the coming years to provide for his or her own livelihood as quickly as possible and to every extent possible. That will give persons who apply for maintenance an incentive to build their own future and not to remain dependent on maintenance from their ex-partner. The amount and term of the maintenance can be based on that plan. The Dutch court may not provide one party with a lump sum in lieu if maintenance, as is the case in many other countries. The spouses may make such an agreement when they divorce, which they can lay down in a divorce agreement.

There is currently a legislative proposal respect of lesbian parenthood. The issue being discussed is the differentiation that is made between the parenthood of married different-sex couples and that of same-sex couples. The legislative proposal pertains to a scheme that would govern the legal motherhood of the female partner of the birth mother, other than by means of adoption. In the event that a lesbian couple has used an unknown donor, both will be the legal mother by operation of law of the child who is born within their marriage. In all other cases the co-mother will be able to acknowledge maternity of the child, with the approval of the birth mother.

There is also a legislative proposal pending that is intended to equalise the legal position of married couples and registered partners. It has been proposed that when a child is born within a registered partnership, the father will be deemed to be the legal father by operation of law. Further, under current law a woman who is married to another woman cannot acknowledge maternity of a child unless a court has determined that certain conditions have been met (Article 204(1)(e)). However, a male registered partner can acknowledge paternity of a child of a woman other than his registered partner without any judicial intervention being required. It is now considered desirable to cease requiring that judicial assessment, in order to ensure equal treatment under the law.

New Zealand

Princes Chambers Anita Chan

A. JURISDICTION AND CONFLICT OF LAW

1. SOURCES OF LAW

1.1 What is the primary source of law in relation to the breakdown of marriage and the welfare of children within the jurisdiction?

1.2 Which are the main statutes governing matrimonial law in the jurisdiction?

Family law in New Zealand is primarily found in acts of Parliament.

The main statutes governing family law are listed below.

- The Family Courts Act 1980 establishes the Family Court and provides for its constitution, jurisdiction, powers and procedures.
- The Marriage Act 1955 and Civil Union Act 2004 provide for the legal union of couples by marriage or civil union.
- The Family Proceedings Act 1980 regulates matrimonial and Family Court proceedings and provides for paternity, partner maintenance, dissolution and voiding of marriage and civil union.
- The Property (Relationships) Act 1976 provides a code for how the property of married, civil union and *de facto* couples (including same sex couples) is to be divided when they separate, or when one of them dies.
- The Child Support Act 1991 provides for the assessment, collection and payment of child support, and the collection and payment of partner maintenance (by the Child Support Agency). There is provision for the enforcement of overseas orders in New Zealand and of New Zealand orders overseas.
- The Care of Children Act 2004 defines and regulates the custody and guardianship of children. Subpart 4 of the Act enacts into domestic law New Zealand's obligations under the Hague Convention on the Civil Aspects of International Child Abduction.
- The Children, Young Persons and their Families Act 1989 provides for state intervention in respect of children in need of care and protection, and children and youth who criminally offend.
- The Domestic Violence Act 1995 provides for protection from family violence.

2. JURISDICTION

2.1 What are the main jurisdictional requirements for the institution of proceedings in relation to divorce, property and children?

Divorce/dissolution

'Divorce' no longer exists under New Zealand law. Instead, marriages and civil unions are legally terminated by 'dissolution' under the Family Proceedings Act.

A New Zealand court has jurisdiction to make a dissolution order if at least one party is domiciled in New Zealand at the time of filing the application.

Rights in respect of property, children and financial support may be pursued upon separation, without any requirement for dissolution.

Property

The Property (Relationships) Act governs the division of property following separation. Under section 7 the court has jurisdiction to make orders in respect of the following categories of property:

- immovable property situated in New Zealand;
- movable property situated in New Zealand if one of the parties is domiciled in New Zealand at the date of application;
- movable property situated outside New Zealand if one of the parties is domiciled in New Zealand at the date of application (although if any order is sought against a person who is neither domiciled nor resident in New Zealand, the court may decline to make an order in respect of any movable property that is situated outside New Zealand);
- any property where the parties have agreed, in writing, that New Zealand law is to apply.

Classification of property as movable or immovable is decided by reference to the law of the country where the property is situated (*lex situs*).

Under section 7A, parties may agree before or at the time of entering into a marriage, civil union or *de facto* relationship that the relationship property law of a country other than New Zealand shall apply to their property. Such agreement must be in writing or otherwise valid according to the law of that country.

A party asking the court to apply foreign law must provide sufficient evidence of the law of the relevant country. If sufficient evidence is not provided, New Zealand law will be applied (*Birch v Birch* [2001] 3 NZLR 413).

Under section 7A(3), the New Zealand court may override or disregard such agreement if application of the foreign law would be contrary to justice or public policy.

Children

Under section 126(1) of the Care of Children Act, the courts have personal jurisdiction to determine a dispute about the custody or guardianship of a child when at the time proceedings are commenced:

- any party resides or is domiciled in New Zealand; or
- the child resides or is domiciled or is present in New Zealand.

However under section 126(2), a court may refuse to make an order under the Act if:

- neither the respondent nor the child are resident in New Zealand; or
- no useful purpose would be served by making the order, or the making of the order would be undesirable in the circumstances.

3. DOMICILE AND HABITUAL RESIDENCE

3.1 Explain the concepts of domicile and habitual residence as they apply to the jurisdiction

Domicile

Domicile is governed by the Domicile Act 1976, which, inconveniently, does not define the term. Case law provides limited assistance as the courts have determined domicile in a very fact-specific way. However, the general concept of domicile invokes the notion of a permanent or indefinite home in a particular country, state or territory.

Among other things, the Act provides that a child whose parents are living together has the domicile of the father. If the parents are not living together, the child has the domicile of the parent with whom they have their home.

Habitual residence

There is a close nexus between domicile and habitual residence, however, the concept of domicile has more permanent connotations. The courts have determined habitual residence with reference to concepts of 'settled purpose' and 'actual residence for an appreciable period'. A child's habitual residence will usually be that of the child's custodial parent.

4. CONFLICT OF LAW/APPLICABLE LAW TO BE APPLIED

4.1 What happens when one party applies to stay proceedings in favour of a foreign jurisdiction? What factors will the local court take into account when determining forum issues?

If an issue or dispute has already been decided in a foreign court, the doctrines of *res judicata* and judicial comity may be invoked to argue that a New Zealand court should decline to exercise jurisdiction.

A New Zealand court will grant a stay of proceedings in favour of a foreign jurisdiction if the applicant can establish that the New Zealand court is *forum non conveniens*.

In *Gilmore v Gilmore* [1993] NZFLR 561, the High Court adopted the legal principles articulated by the House of Lords in *Spiliada Maritime Corporation v Cansulex Ltd* [1987] AC 460, and set out an eight proposition test to assist in determining issues of *forum conveniens*. The *Gilmore* test was extended by the High Court in *Howson v Howson* (2/5/02, Master Faire, HC Hamilton, CP 52/01).

However, the High Court in *Wang v Yin* [2008] 3 NZLR 136 criticised the *Gilmore* test, preferring the approach taken by the House of Lords in *de Dampierre v de Dampierre* [1987] 2 All ER 1. That case promotes a two-step enquiry determining, firstly, what factors there are which connect the facts of the case with the foreign forum and, secondly, whether these factors show that the foreign forum is clearly more appropriate to hear the case. If so, a stay would normally be granted.

Children's cases

The relevant principles applying to *forum conveniens* in the specific context of child issues cases have been summarised by the Family Court in *CG v SG* (2005) 24 FRNZ 502. After reviewing the cases, the court stated at paragraphs 34 and 35:

'[34] *From those various cases I have distilled the following as being the key principles applying to forum conveniens applications in the context of child issue cases:*

- *The overriding consideration in all cases must be the objectives of the statutory provision under consideration, in this case s 23 of the Guardianship Act (now s 4 Care of Children Act). The decision of which forum is best capable of achieving a decision must be framed on the best interests of the child,*
- *The onus rests on the party seeking foreign adjudication,*
- *The burden of showing greater suitability of the other jurisdiction is not merely to show New Zealand is not the natural or appropriate forum but to establish the foreign forum is 'clearly and distinctly more appropriate',*
- *In reaching the decision the Court must not be reactive to the conduct of the parent removing or retaining the child, but on what is in the best interests of the child,*
- *The issue is not one primarily of jurisdiction but whether, in all the circumstances, and having regard to the child's welfare as the first and paramount consideration, the foreign Court or the New Zealand Court is best able to determine all custody access and related questions,*
- *Although the Hague Convention does not apply (because Malaysia is not a signatory) it is appropriate for the Court to have regard to its policy,*
- *I am of the view that the Court must also recognise the import of the United Nations Convention on the Rights of the Child (UNROC), particularly as both New Zealand and Malaysia have either accepted it or ratified it.*

[35] *In determining the application according to those principles, the Court may draw from a range of considerations including, but certainly not limited to:*

- *Trial mechanics and evidentiary considerations,*
- *Timeframe for determination,*
- *Personal circumstances,*
- *Where is the child living?*
- *Connection with each country,*
- *Qualitative comparison of competing jurisdictions,*
- *Genuine proceedings or judicial advantage?*
- *Enforcement,*
- *Existing or proposed concurrent proceedings and effect of different outcomes,*
- *Submission to jurisdiction.'*

New Zealand is currently considering signing the Hague Convention on Jurisdiction, Applicable Law, Recognition, Enforcement and Co-operation in Respect of Parental Responsibility and Measures of Child Protection.

B. PRE- AND POST-NUPTIAL AGREEMENTS

5. VALIDITY OF PRE- AND POST-NUPTIAL AGREEMENTS

5.1 To what extent are pre- and post-nups binding within the jurisdiction? Could you provide a brief discussion of the most significant recent case law on this issue?

Contracting out and settlement agreements

Section 21 of the Property (Relationships) Act allows couples either before, during or after the relationship (marriage, civil union or *de facto* relationship) to make any agreement they think fit with respect to the status, ownership, and division of their property (including future property) for the purpose of contracting out of the provisions of the Act (contracting out agreements). Contracting out agreements may be entered into either before or during a *de facto* relationship, marriage or civil union.

Section 21A allows couples to enter into any agreement they think fit with regard to the status, ownership and division of their property for the purpose of settling any differences between them (settlement agreements). Settlement agreements are entered into after a couple has separated.

How binding are agreements?

Any validly executed section 21 and section 21A agreement is enforceable unless it has been set aside by the court.

An agreement shall be validly executed if the requirements of section 21F have been complied with.

Any agreement that does not comply with these formal requirements is void, subject only to the power of the court to validate the agreement under section 21H. This power is sparingly exercised.

Particular caution should be practised if one party to the agreement is overseas at the time proposed for signing, since the witnessing lawyer is likely not to be able to provide the requisite advice to a satisfactory standard. To ensure proper compliance with the strict requirements of section 21F, it is highly advisable for either the lawyer or the signatory to travel, in order that both can be physically in attendance for the face-to-face provision of advice, witnessing and certification.

In *Thom v Davys Burton* [2009] NZLR 437; [2008] NZFLR 1030, a contracting out agreement was declared void as the wife did not receive adequate advice from the notary public in America (where she was residing and signed the agreement).

The court can set a validly executed agreement aside if it is satisfied that giving effect to the agreement would cause serious injustice (section 21J). Section 21J also preserves recourse to any enactments, rules of law or rules of equity that allow the contract to be void, voidable, or unenforceable on any other ground.

Curiously, there is no requirement for contracting out agreements to reflect the parties' respective entitlements under the Act.

A settlement agreement, on the other hand, is at risk of being set aside by the court on the ground of serious injustice if the agreed property division departs substantially from the parties' respective entitlements under the Act.

The Court of Appeal in *Harrison v Harrison* [2005] 2 NZLR 349 and other cases have made it clear that the courts will not set aside a contracting out agreement on the basis that one party signed under express or implicit threat that if they did not sign it, the relationship would be at an end. In *DR v NLS* (30/6/05, Judge Whitehead, FC Nelson FAM 2003-42-217), the agreement was signed eight days before the wedding on the husband's demand that the wedding would not go ahead unless the agreement was signed. The wife was already pregnant with their first child. These circumstances were considered to be normal pressure and not a basis for setting aside the agreement.

C. DIVORCE, NULLITY AND JUDICIAL SEPARATION

6. RECOGNITION OF FOREIGN MARRIAGES/DIVORCE

6.1 Summarise the position in your jurisdiction

Recognition of foreign marriages

Generally, marriages that have taken place in a foreign jurisdiction in accordance with the laws of that jurisdiction are recognised by New Zealand law. There is no legal obligation to register a foreign marriage in New Zealand.

Recognition of foreign divorces

Section 44(1) of the Family Proceedings Act provides a code for a New Zealand court to recognise overseas orders for divorce, dissolution or nullity of marriage (or civil union).

Essentially, the validity of such orders will be recognised in New Zealand where:

- one or both of the parties were domiciled in the overseas country where the order was made at the time it was made; or
- the overseas court or authority exercised jurisdiction on the basis of one of grounds specified in section 44(1)(b); or
- the order is recognised as valid in the courts of a country in which at least one of the parties to the marriage or civil union is domiciled.

7. DIVORCE

7.1 Explain the grounds for divorce within the jurisdiction (please also deal with nullity and judicial separation if appropriate).

Dissolution of marriage and civil union

Divorce is no longer available in New Zealand. Instead, marriages and civil unions are terminated by dissolution.

The Family Proceedings Act provides only one ground for dissolution, which is that the marriage or civil union has broken down irreconcilably. That ground can only be established if, and only if, the parties have been living apart for at least two years immediately preceding the filing of the application for dissolution.

There is no legal process for terminating a *de facto* relationship.

Nullity

The court has jurisdiction to declare a marriage or civil union to be void *ab initio*; however, such declarations are rarely sought.

Separation

In New Zealand, parties to a marriage, civil union or *de facto* relationship are legally separated as from the date that they cease to live together as a couple (sections 2A, 2AB and 2D of the Property (Relationships) Act). Parties to a marriage or civil union may apply for a separation order under Part 3 of the Family Proceedings Act 1980. However, such applications are rare because a separation order is not required in order for proceedings to be initiated in respect of property, children or dissolution.

Living apart requires both a mental and physical element. A couple may, for instance, be 'living apart' even though they continue to share a common residence. Conversely, they may be living together as a couple despite residing in separate residences.

8. FINANCES/CAPITAL/PROPERTY

8.1 What powers does the court have to allocate financial resources and property on the breakdown of marriage?

8.2 Explain and illustrate with reference to recent cases the court's thinking on division of assets

New Zealand has a codified system of deferred community of relationship property, which is codified in the Property (Relationships) Act.

Application of the Act

The Act applies to married couples and, since April 2005, couples united by civil union. It applies also to couples in a *de facto* relationship if the *de facto* relationship has lasted for more than three years (or shorter if there is a child of the relationship).

A unique feature of the Act is that it applies to govern the rights of parties in contemporaneous multi-party relationships, provided each of the component relationships qualify as a 'relationship' in terms of the Act.

Any party to a qualifying relationship may apply for orders under the Act provided the court would have jurisdiction in respect of the property under the terms of section 7 of the Act (see above section titled 'Jurisdiction').

New Zealand law allows a party to apply for division of relationship property upon separation. There is no requirement for dissolution of marriage or civil union. In many instances, proceedings are instituted long before dissolution.

Principles of division

The general scheme of the Act is that, after the end of the relationship, all relationship property shall, with very limited exceptions, be subject to equal division, provided the qualifying relationship has lasted for three years or longer. Separate property is not shared, but may be the subject of compensatory awards.

While the simplicity of the general scheme suggests a high degree of certainty of outcome, in reality numerous statutory qualifications and exceptions provide considerable scope for uncertainty and litigation.

Classification of property

The classification of property as either relationship property or separate property is of crucial importance. The Act sets out rules for classification.

Relationship property generally comprises the family home and family chattels (whenever acquired) and any other property acquired by the parties during the course of their relationship.

Relationship property includes property acquired by one of the parties immediately before the relationship began, if it was acquired in contemplation of the relationship, and was intended for the common use or common benefit of both parties (section 8).

Separate property is all property that is not relationship property. It will generally comprise property owned by a party before the commencement of the relationship, or property acquired by a party as a beneficiary under a trust, or by gift or inheritance, and property acquired out of separate property even if acquired during the relationship (section 9).

Note, however, that it is possible for separate property to acquire the status of relationship property, based on the use to which it is put.

Trust owned property

Since property owned under a trust is neither relationship property nor separate property, family trusts are commonly utilised in New Zealand as a means of placing property out of the reach of the Property (Relationships) Act.

Both that Act and the Family Proceedings Act allow the court to provide remedies to a party whose rights to relationship property have been subverted through the use of a trust, but those powers are limited and are often ineffective to provide adequate redress.

Economic disparity

A unique aspect of New Zealand relationship property law is that the courts have been given explicit statutory power to make a compensatory adjustment at the time of division of relationship property on the grounds of significant future economic disparity between the parties (sections 15 and 15A).

Economic disparity in terms of the Act is typically seen where one party, usually the female partner, has sacrificed a career in order to look after the family, thereby freeing the other partner to build a high-earning career.

Compensation for economic disparity can only be made as a lump sum payment at the time of division of relationship property, out of relationship property.

Both the restrictive statutory framework and the conservative manner in which the courts have interpreted the provision have meant it has been difficult for applicants to succeed in obtaining relief and such relief, where it has been granted, has been modest.

The courts' recent thinking

A recent case that illustrates the courts' recent thinking on the division of assets is *B v B* (23/9/09, Judge Ullrich, FAMC, Wellington, FAM-2008-086-764).

At paragraph 92, the court held that the facts of the case brought it within the sole statutory ground for departing from equal sharing, (ie, extraordinary circumstances exist that would make equal sharing of property repugnant to justice, section 13).

The extraordinary circumstances in that case included:

- the respondent provided all financial means and was the major income earner;
- the respondent provided all of the relationship property;
- the respondent performed all of the work in the building of the new family home;
- the respondent made the greatest contribution toward the performance of the household duties;
- the respondent assisted the applicant in gaining educational qualifications;
- the applicant only contributed some wages, minor household tasks and a little bit of painting.

The discretion to depart from the equal sharing principle on the grounds of extraordinary circumstances has been exercised by the courts only in exceptional cases.

9. FINANCES/MAINTENANCE

9.1 Explain the operation of maintenance for spouses on an ongoing basis after the breakdown of marriage

9.2 Is it common for maintenance to be awarded?

9.3 Explain and illustrate with reference to recent cases the court's thinking on maintenance

The operation of maintenance

Under the Family Proceedings Act, maintenance may be awarded either during marriage or civil union, or after dissolution. In the case of a *de facto* relationship, the *de facto* relationship is normally required to have lasted for three years before maintenance will be awarded, and an award can only be made after the *de facto* relationship has ended.

Liability to pay maintenance arises if the court is satisfied that the maintenance is necessary to enable the applicant to meet their reasonable financial needs, where the applicant cannot practicably do so because of certain statutory circumstances (sections 63 or 64).

Maintenance is designed to provide temporary relief and will ordinarily end after just a few years.

Liability may be continued beyond the court-ordered period on certain grounds. A maintenance order will cease when the applicant enters into a marriage, civil union or *de facto* relationship with some other person.

On separation, a party may seek an interim maintenance order under section 82 of the Act. An interim maintenance order may continue for no longer than six months.

The court may order payment of maintenance by periodical sums, a lump sum or a combination of both.

A maintenance order can be enforced by the Child Support Agency (notwithstanding that it is partner maintenance and not child maintenance).

9.2 Is it common for maintenance to be awarded?

An applicant is likely to be successful in obtaining a maintenance order if they can establish that they have an inability to be financially self-supporting which has been caused by one of specified circumstances. These include:

- the effect of the division of functions within the relationship while the parties lived together;
- disparity in the likely earning capacity of each party;
- the standard of living of the parties while they lived together;
- responsibilities for the ongoing care of children of the relationship;
- the undertaking by one party of a reasonable period of education or retraining to increase their ability to become self-supporting.

10. CHILD MAINTENANCE

10.1 On what basis is child maintenance calculated within the jurisdiction?

Liability to pay child maintenance is governed by the Child Support Act.

Liability under the Act can only exist if the child in respect of whom support is sought is ordinarily resident or domiciled in New Zealand. If the child is not, it is possible to bring an application for maintenance under the residual provisions of the Family Proceedings Act.

A person can be a 'liable parent' if they are a New Zealand citizen, ordinarily resident in New Zealand or resident of a country with which New Zealand has a reciprocal agreement for enforcement of maintenance (currently only Australia).

The Child Support Agency, which is a section of the Department of Inland Revenue, will calculate and collect child support if requested by a custodian.

The amount of child support that a liable parent has to pay is determined according to a statutory formula.

The proportion of time that a liable parent has the care of the child may operate to modify the amount of child support payable. The court's role is residual in that it deals with applications for departure from the formula assessment.

Parties may voluntarily agree to an arrangement for payment of child support other than that prescribed by the Child Support Act.

A voluntary agreement will not be enforceable if the parent having primary care is in receipt of a state-funded pension or benefit. Registration of a voluntary agreement does not prohibit either party from applying for formula assessment at any time.

11. RECIPROCAL ENFORCEMENT OF FINANCIAL ORDERS

11.1 Summarise the position in your jurisdiction

Child support and maintenance orders

Under section 215 of the Child Support Act, New Zealand can enter into a reciprocal enforcement agreement with another country for the reciprocal enforcement of child support or partner maintenance orders. So far, however, New Zealand has a reciprocal enforcement agreement only with Australia.

If there is no reciprocal enforcement agreement with the country in question, it may be possible for it to be enforced under residual provisions of the Family Proceedings Act.

Although New Zealand has not ratified the United Nations Convention on the Recovery Abroad of Maintenance, it has, nevertheless, adopted the general approach of the Convention. Part VIII of the Family Proceedings Act prescribes the procedures which apply when one party lives overseas.

Broadly speaking, maintenance proceedings are to be heard exclusively in the debtor's country, with the claimant's country acting as an agent requesting the recovery of maintenance in the foreign jurisdiction.

The Act provides a procedure for applicants from Convention countries to apply for maintenance orders when the respondent is resident in New Zealand.

If the person claiming maintenance is in a Commonwealth country and has obtained a maintenance order in that country (or another Commonwealth or designated country), a special procedure is available. If the claimant has obtained a full maintenance order, that order may be registered in New Zealand. Alternatively, if the claimant has obtained a provisional order, that order may be confirmed by a New Zealand court.

Once an order has been confirmed or registered in New Zealand, it shall take effect as though it is a maintenance order made in New Zealand. An order that has been confirmed in another Commonwealth or designated country must be registered in New Zealand before it is enforceable in New Zealand.

A debtor in New Zealand can apply to have the registration set aside, or to vary or discharge the registered order.

Following the Court of Appeal decision in *Ross v Ross* [2010] NZCA 447, [2011] NZFLR 440, it is also clear that the High Court has an inherent jurisdiction to recognise and enforce maintenance judgments of foreign courts, as part of its inherent jurisdiction to recognise an *in personam* judgment of a foreign court of competent jurisdiction.

Relationship property orders

There are three ways by which an order of a foreign court relating to relationship property can be enforced in New Zealand:

- by registration of the judgment under the Reciprocal Enforcement of Judgments Act 1934;
- by registration of a memorial of the judgment under the Judicature Act 1908;
- at common law.

The appropriate method of enforcing the foreign order will depend on which jurisdiction the order was made in and whether it was made by a superior court, ie, a court of unlimited jurisdiction.

Reciprocal Enforcement of Judgments Act 1934

The Reciprocal Enforcement of Judgments Act 1934 applies to judgments from the UK and other specified countries including France, India, Hong Kong and Australia.

Generally, the Act only applies to decisions of superior courts, however, the Governor General of New Zealand may, by order in council, specify inferior courts to which the Act is to apply. Orders have been made to include some District and Magistrates Courts of Australian states.

The Act generally applies only to judgments under which money is payable and this limits its applicability in relationship property cases.

Applications for registration of a foreign order must be made to the High Court and, if registered, a foreign order will have the same force and effect as if the judgment had originally been given in the High Court.

Judicature Act 1908

The Judicature Act provides a means of enforcement of foreign judgments under which a sum of money is payable. Under section 56, any person who has obtained such a judgment from 'any court of her Majesty's dominions' may file a memorial of that judgment with the High Court. The judgment debtor can then be summonsed to show cause as to why the judgment should not be executed. If the person does not appear, or fails to show cause, the court may make an order for execution of the judgment subject to such terms and conditions (if any) as the court sees fit. This has been held to relate only to the 'method or timing of execution' and is not an opportunity to examine the merits of the foreign decision.

The Judicature Act does not require that the judgment be that of a superior court. Foreign judgments must be enforced in their entirety or not at all.

Common law

Common law is the only method of enforcing a foreign judgment in respect of property. A judgment *in rem* will be eligible to be enforced if it is final and conclusive, and the foreign court's jurisdiction to give the judgment is recognised by New Zealand law.

Applications must be made to the High Court for registration and, if registered, the foreign judgment shall have the same force and effect as if the judgment had originally been given in the High Court.

12. FINANCIAL RELIEF AFTER FOREIGN DIVORCE PROCEEDINGS

12.1 What powers are available to make orders following a foreign divorce?

Provided the jurisdictional requirements of the Property (Relationships) Act and/or the Family Proceedings Act are met, there is no barrier to a party seeking financial relief after a foreign divorce or separation.

D. CHILDREN

13. CUSTODY/PARENTAL RESPONSIBILITY

13.1 Briefly explain the legal position in relation to custody/parental responsibility following the breakdown of a relationship or marriage

13.2 Briefly explain the legal position in relation to access/contact/visitation following the breakdown of a relationship or marriage

The terms 'custody' and 'parental responsibility' do not appear in New Zealand legislation. However, 'day to day care' is comparable with custody, and 'guardianship' closely resembles 'parental responsibility' as those terms have been used in other jurisdictions.

In most cases, a child's parents will be their guardians. Additional guardians may be appointed by the court.

Co-guardians hold rights equally until such time as a court determines otherwise.

Generally speaking, the duties, powers, rights and responsibilities of a guardian relate to important issues affecting a child's life, such as education, religion and health.

After the breakdown of the relationship or marriage, in the absence of a parenting order neither guardian has a better right than the other to have day-to-day care of the child.

In any proceedings under the Care of Children Act (except proceedings invoking the Hague Convention), the welfare and best interests of the child shall be the court's paramount consideration.

In deciding what the best interests are, the court must consider, to the extent they are relevant, the principles listed in section 5 of the Care of Children Act.

Where there is an allegation of domestic violence in relation to a party to Care of Children Act proceedings, the court may not make any order allowing that party to have any unsupervised contact with a child who is the subject of the proceedings, unless the court is satisfied on evidence that the child will be safe.

14. INTERNATIONAL ABDUCTION

14.1 Summarise the position in your jurisdiction

Child removed from a Hague Convention state to New Zealand

New Zealand's obligations under the Hague Convention have been enacted into domestic law and reside in sections 94 to 124 of the Care of Children Act. The Convention itself is appended as a schedule of the Act for reference purposes.

The New Zealand courts have adhered rigorously to a policy of immediate return.

The term 'rights of custody' has been interpreted very widely by the courts. As a result, left-behind parents have been held to have the requisite rights of custody when they had no custody order, and even when they only had rights of access to the child (*Fairfax v Ireton* [2009] NZFLR; 433 [2009] NZCA 100).

New Zealand provides free legal representation for left-behind parents in Hague Convention cases. The New Zealand Central Authority may enlist the assistance of the New Zealand police to locate the abducting parent and child. The court will appoint a lawyer to represent the Central Authority and apply to the court for return. The left-behind parent is not normally required to attend at the New Zealand court proceedings.

New Zealand courts take seriously the obligation to hear and dispose of Hague Convention applications expeditiously and most cases are resolved within two to four months.

It is worth noting that the court has jurisdiction to make an order preventing the removal of the child from New Zealand and, if necessary, a warrant to uplift the child until he or she is returned to the country of habitual residence.

Child removed from a non-Convention state to New Zealand

Where a child has been abducted from a non-Hague Convention state to New Zealand, and the child is present in New Zealand, the left-behind parent may apply to a New Zealand court for the following orders under the Care of Children Act:

- provided the left-behind parent is a guardian, an order resolving a dispute between guardians as to where (in which country) the child should live;
- a parenting order vesting the day-to-day care of or contact with the child in the applicant or imposing a condition that a child must reside in a specified country;
- a warrant enforcing the parenting order.

In determining such applications (and indeed in all proceedings under the Care of Children Act, with the sole exception of Hague Convention applications), the court must determine the case in the best interests of the child. Thus, it would order the return of the child to the original jurisdiction only if satisfied that such an order is in the child's best interests.

Child removed from New Zealand to a non-Convention state

When a child has been removed from New Zealand to a non-Convention state the remedies available to the left-behind parent are very limited.

In *Jayamohan v Jayamohan* [1996] 1; [1995] NZFLR 913, NZLR at 172; Blanchard J held that, where children have been unlawfully taken from New Zealand but the abductor is present within the jurisdiction, the High Court has power to issue a writ of *habeas corpus* directing the abductor to bring the children back to New Zealand and brought before the court.

In *H v J* [1997] NZFLR 307, the abduction occurred in India and both parents returned to New Zealand. Gendall J exercised the court's wardship jurisdiction, stating: '*... jurisdiction to appoint children wards of the Court... exists expressly when the parents are present within the jurisdiction, where the child or children are citizens of New Zealand and domiciled in New Zealand taking their domicile from that of their parents*'.

The wardship jurisdiction has since been used in several more cases. The usefulness of this remedy is limited, however, by the extent to which the justice system in the non-Convention country is prepared to enforce the

New Zealand court order and order the return of the child to New Zealand.

15. LEAVE TO REMOVE/APPLICATIONS TO TAKE A CHILD OUT OF THE JURISDICTION

15.1 Summarise the position in your jurisdiction

15.2 Under what circumstances may a parent apply to remove their child from the jurisdiction against the wishes of the other parent?

Relocation of children, whether within New Zealand or internationally, is a guardianship decision and, as such, it may not be made by one guardian unilaterally. Thus, a parent proposing to relocate a child is required to obtain the consent of the other guardian or guardians to do so. Failing that, they are expected to apply to the court under the Care of Children Act for permission to relocate. If permission is not obtained before relocation takes place, there is a good chance that on application by the non-consenting parent or guardian, the court will order the child to return to his or her original place of residence.

The overriding consideration for the court in determining relocation cases shall always be the welfare and best interests of the child. Some of the factors to be considered in determining best interests include continuity of the child's relationship with each parent and their wider family group, the child's safety and preservation of the child's cultural identity.

The court's inquiry is intensely fact specific and multifaceted. No presumptive weight is to be given to one or more factors (*Kacem v Bashir* [2010] NZSC 112, [2011] 2 NZLR 1) and it is inappropriate for the court to apply a 'one size fits all' checklist in determining relocation cases. This means that it is often impossible to predict a likely outcome in any given relocation case.

In any contested relocation case, the court must appoint a lawyer to represent the child. The child must be given an opportunity to express their views and those views must be taken into account by the court.

A parent who fears, on reasonable grounds, that the other parent or guardian is proposing to remove a child from New Zealand without consent or court permission may apply to the court for an order preventing removal of the child from the jurisdiction, and for a CAPPS listing. A CAPPS listing places a computer alert at every New Zealand international airport, and this operates to prevent the child from passing through New Zealand customs. It is thus a practical and highly effective means of preventing their removal from the jurisdiction.

E. SURROGACY AND ADOPTION

16. VALIDITY OF SURROGACY AGREEMENTS

16.1 Briefly summarise the position in your jurisdiction

The main statute relevant to surrogacy is the Human Assisted Reproductive Technology Act 2004, which defines a surrogacy arrangement as 'an arrangement under which a woman agrees to become pregnant for the purpose of surrendering custody of a child born as a result of the pregnancy'.

Section 14 of the Human Assisted Reproductive Technology Act specifically states that altruistic surrogacy agreements are not illegal. However, such arrangements are also not enforceable.

Commercial surrogacy arrangements are illegal. Allowed payments include payments to cover the costs of insemination, counselling and legal advice for the woman who is to become pregnant.

The Status of Children Act 1969 provides that a woman who gives birth to a child shall always be its mother, even if the ovum has been donated by another woman (section 17).

Commissioning parents have no formal status either as parents or as guardians. Parties are free to enter informal arrangements under which the commissioning parents shall fulfil the role of parents, but the only way for the commissioning parents to become the legal parents is by adopting the child.

Adoption applications cannot be made until after the child has been born, and at present, neither same-sex *de facto* partners, nor civil union partners can make a joint application for adoption (see section 17 on adoption below).

Before an adoption order can be made, consent must be given by both birth parents (or their consent must be dispensed with by the court) that is, not only the birth mother, but also her spouse or partner if she has one.

A child born overseas in a surrogacy arrangement will not automatically be eligible for New Zealand residency and citizenship just because there is demonstrable genetic consanguinity with a New Zealander.

17. ADOPTION

17.1 Briefly explain the legal position in relation to adoption in your jurisdiction. Is adoption available to individuals, cohabiting couples (both heterosexual and same-sex)?

Adoption is governed by the Adoption Act. An application for adoption may be made by an individual, or jointly by a couple.

Restrictions apply to both types of application. In respect of individual applications, an individual male may not adopt a female child unless the court is satisfied that he is the father of the child, or that there are special circumstances which justify the making of the order (section 4(2)).

Additionally, although a married person may make an individual application, the adoption cannot go ahead without the consent of the applicant's spouse (section 7(2)(b)).

Joint applications can only be made by 'two spouses'. Until recently, this was thought to limit applications to married couples. In *Re AMM* [2010] NZFLR 629 (HC), the High Court ruled that unmarried opposite-sex couples in a stable *de facto* relationship were 'two spouses' for the purposes of the Act.

Some former anomalies have been resolved by the 2013 amendments to the Marriage Act, which were enacted to allow same-sex marriages. As a result of consequential amendments to the Adoption Act, married couples may now jointly adopt children, regardless of whether theirs is a heterosexual or same-sex marriage. However, there remains an anomaly that civil union partners, and possibly same-sex *de facto* partners, may not jointly adopt.

F. COHABITATION

18. COHABITATION

18.1 What legislation (if any) governs division of property for unmarried couples on the breakdown of the relationship?

The Property (Relationships) Act applies to govern the property rights of couples in *de facto* relationships (except those that ended before 1 February 2002) of three years duration or longer (shorter if there is a child of the relationship), in the same way as if they were married or in a civil union.

A *de facto* relationship is one between two persons who are aged 18 years or older, who live together as a couple, and who are not married to each other or in a civil union. The Act provides a list of factors that the court may take into account when determining whether or not a *de facto* relationship exists (section 2D).

A *de facto* relationship may be between heterosexual or same-sex parties.

It is possible for parties to be in a *de facto* relationship in terms of the Act without having lived together in the same house, and without having engaged in sexual relations.

The Act will also apply to persons in multiple-party relationships. Hence, in *C v S* (28/9/06, Judge Smith, FAMC Dunedin, FAM-2005-012-157), a mistress applied unsuccessfully for orders against a husband with whom she had enjoyed a covert relationship for several years. Had she been successful in persuading the court that their relationship was a *de facto* relationship for the purposes of the Act, she would have been entitled to an equal share of any relationship property that they had.

There are numerous cases which demonstrate the difficulty that the courts have had in determining, retrospectively, whether parties were in a *de facto* relationship and, if so, when it began and when it ended. Thus, it can be very difficult to assess whether a client is or was in a qualifying relationship in terms of the Act and, if so, when it began and when it ended (ie, duration). However, if they are or were in a *de facto* relationship, then, provided the relationship has lasted for the requisite period of time, they will be subject to the sharing principles of the Property (Relationships) Act.

G. FAMILY DISPUTE RESOLUTION

19. MEDIATION, COLLABORATIVE LAW AND ARBITRATION

19.1 Briefly summarise the non-court-based processes available in your jurisdiction and the current status of agreements reached under the auspices of mediation, collaborative law and arbitration

Counselling is made available by the state both before and/or during court proceedings, to assist parties to resolve their differences by agreement.

The state also funds 'Parenting through Separation' educational courses, which separated parents may attend free of charge.

Mediation is often directed by the court in disputes involving children. In the past this has been arranged and paid for by the state and facilitated by judges and lawyers, however there are moves afoot to shift the process away from the courts, and the cost away from the state.

Judicial settlement conferences are available for proceedings involving family property, including relationship property.

Whenever agreement is reached, the agreement can be sealed by the court as a court order or recorded in a formal written agreement.

Collaborative law is practised in New Zealand, but not extensively.

Parties may privately appoint and pay for an arbitrator.

19.2 What is the statutory basis (if any), for mediation, collaborative law and arbitration in your jurisdiction? In particular, are the parties required to attempt a family dispute resolution in advance of the institution of proceedings?

The Family Court Rules provide a statutory basis for mediation for proceedings relating to parenting orders, and for judicial settlement conferences in any Family Court proceedings.

At present, parties are under no obligation to attempt a family dispute resolution in advance of the institution of proceedings. However, there is currently a Bill before Parliament to introduce such a requirement.

H. OTHER

20. CIVIL PARTNERSHIP/SAME-SEX MARRIAGE

20.1 What is the status of civil partnership/same-sex marriage within the jurisdiction?

20.2 What legislation governs civil partnership/same-sex marriage?

Same-sex marriage

Following 2013 amendments to the Marriage Act, same-sex marriage is now possible.

Civil union

Both same-sex couples and opposite-sex couples may enter into a civil union under the Civil Union Act. Couples who have entered into a civil union have the same legal rights as married couples, except that they may not jointly adopt a child.

Recognition of an overseas civil union in New Zealand

There is no provision for a civil union solemnised overseas to be registered in New Zealand. However, if the parties have entered into one of the relationships listed in the Civil Union (Recognised Overseas Relationships) Regulations 2005, their relationship is recognised as a civil union in New Zealand. The five types of registered relationships currently prescribed by the Regulations are:

- Registered partnership (Finland);
- Life partnership (Germany);
- Civil partnership (United Kingdom);
- Domestic partnership (New Jersey, USA);
- Civil union (Vermont, USA).

(See also the sections above titled 'Divorce/dissolution' and 'Recognition of foreign divorce'.)

21. CONTROVERSIAL AREAS/RAPIDLY DEVELOPING AREAS OF LAW

21.1 Is there a particular area of the law within the jurisdiction that is currently undergoing major change?

21.2 Which areas of law are most out-of-step? Which areas would you most like to see reformed/changed?

Areas of law currently undergoing or in need of reform include the following:

- the Adoption Act 1955, which despite recent amendments enacted as a result of amendments to the Marriage Act, still contains provisions that breach the Human Rights Act 1993 (see section 17 above on adoption);
- domestic violence and child protection laws, which need to be modified to provide better protection for victims of domestic violence, including children;
- legislation to provide better financial support to grandparents who raise their grandchildren.

Law changes that the author would most like to see enacted include:

- changes to the Property (Relationships) Act so that the Act would only apply to parties to a *de facto* relationship on an 'opt in' basis, because of the difficulty in being able to assess one's legal position, and thus make choices about one's property rights;
- changes to sections 15 and 15A of the Property (Relationships) Act to remove the statutory constraints on the court's ability to grant effective redress when it has been established that there will be significant economic disparity between separated couples, due to the respective roles of the parties during the relationship;
- changes to provide more effective remedies for a party whose rights under the Property (Relationships) Act have been defeated through the use of trusts.

Poland

Wiercinski Kancelaria Adwokacka
Dr Joanna Kosinska-Wiercinska & Dr Hab Jacek Wiercinski

A. JURISDICTION AND CONFLICT OF LAW

1. SOURCES OF LAW

1.1 What is the primary source of law in relation to the breakdown of marriage and the welfare of children within the jurisdiction?

The Constitution of the Republic of Poland (Act of 2 April 1997, Journal of Statutes 1997, no. 78, item 483, with subsequent amendments) (CRP) guarantees fundamental family rights by stipulating that Poland protects family, maternity and parenthood (Article 18 of the CRP), welfare of the child (Articles 71 and 72 of the CRP) and family life (Articles 47, 48 of the CRP). It also provides a freedom for parents to raise their children in accordance with their values, which also includes freedom of religious upbringing of their choice (Article 48 and 53 section 3 of the CRP). The primary source of law in relation to the breakdown of marriage and welfare of the children is the Family and Guardianship Code (FGC) of 1964 (Act of 23 April 1964, Journal of Statutes 1964, no. 16, item 93 with subsequent amendments).

1.2 What are the main statutes governing matrimonial law in the jurisdiction?

Matrimonial law is addressed in Title I of FGC. This title is further divided into five parts, covering almost every aspect of issues surrounding the creation of marital union, relations between spouses, marital property, termination of marriage and judicial separation. Other statutes may also concern issues relevant to matrimonial law. For example, procedural matters connected with matrimonial law are contained in the Polish Code of Civil Procedure (PCCP – Act of 17 November 1964, Journal of Statutes 1964, no. 43, item 269 with subsequent amendments), mainly in Articles 425-458, 561-667[5]. The issues of civil status are covered by The Law on Civil Status Registry of 1986 (Journal of Statutes 2004, no.161, item 1688, with subsequent amendments).

2. JURISDICTION

2.1 What are the main jurisdictional requirements for the institution of proceedings in relation to divorce, property and children?

The issues of jurisdiction in matrimonial proceedings are regulated in PCCP Articles 1103-1103[1] and 1106[2]. Generally in Poland, pursuant to PCCP Article 1103, the cases which are resolved by the courts in a trial belong to domestic jurisdiction, if a defendant has a domicile or habitual residence in the territory of the Republic of Poland. However Polish courts also have jurisdiction over the subject matter of matrimonial and marital property proceedings if:

- both spouses had their last domicile or their last habitual residence in Poland, if one of them still has domicile or habitual residence in Poland; or
- the plaintiff spouse had, for at least one year preceding the initiation of proceedings, domicile or residence in Poland; or
- the plaintiff spouse is a Polish citizen and had for at least six months preceding the initiation of proceedings, domicile or residence in Poland; or
- both spouses are Polish citizens.

According to Article 1103[1] § 2 of PCCP Polish jurisdiction is exclusive if both spouses are Polish citizens and have domicile and habitual residence in the Republic of Poland. Polish jurisdiction in matrimonial cases also includes parental authority disputes over common minor children (Article 1103[1] § 3 of PCCP).

Polish courts' jurisdiction over the subject matter of parents and children is based upon domicile or habitual residence of a particular child (see: Article 1103[2] PCCP)

3. DOMICILE AND HABITUAL RESIDENCE

3.1 Explain the concepts of domicile and habitual residence as they apply to the jurisdiction in relation to divorce, the finances and children

The concept of domicile involves permanent, factual location of the party within Poland. Domicile of a natural person is a place (eg, city, village, etc.) where a person stays with the intention to remain there permanently (Article 25 of the Polish Civil Code: PCC). Temporary absences will not destroy domicile. The domicile of a minor child under parental authority is the domicile of his parents or of the one of the parents who has exclusive parental authority or to whom the exercise of parental authority is entrusted. If both parents have equal parental authority and have separate domiciles, the domicile of the child is with the parent with whom a child permanently resides. If the child does not reside permanently with either of the parents, the guardianship court will decide on its domicile (Article 26 PCC).

The notion of habitual residence is based strictly on factual situation. It is not thought of in permanent terms. A residence may be a place where a person lives for any period of time. One can have several residences, but only one domicile (Article 27 PCC).

In Poland, pursuant to PCCP Article 1103, the Polish court has jurisdiction to hear cases where the defendant has domicile or factual residence in Poland. For the application of domicile and factual residence to the jurisdiction in relation to divorce, the finances and children: see question 2.1.

4. CONFLICT OF LAW/APPLICABLE LAW TO BE APPLIED

4.1 What happens when one party applies to stay proceedings in favour of a foreign jurisdiction? What factors will the local court take into account when determining forum issues?

When one of the parties applies to stay proceedings in favour of a foreign jurisdiction the court has to consider both PCCP (Article 1103 – 1103[1] PCPC) and European Regulations or any relevant international agreements related to that issues signed by Poland.

In case one of the parties in a divorce proceeding applies for a change of jurisdiction in favour of one of the other member states of the European Union, the Polish court takes into consideration Council Regulation (EU) No 2201/2003 of 27 November 2003 concerning jurisdiction and the recognition and enforcement of judgments in matrimonial matters and the matters of parental responsibility, repealing Regulation (EC) No 1347/2000.

B. PRE- AND POST-NUPTIAL AGREEMENTS

5. VALIDITY OF PRE- AND POST-NUPTIAL AGREEMENTS

5.1 To what extent are pre- and post-nups binding within the jurisdiction? Could you provide a brief discussion of the most significant recent case law on this issue?

Pursuant to Polish FGC Article 47, spouses may, through an agreement concluded in a notarial deed only, limit or expand the statutory joint property regime (community property), or establish a separation of property, or a separation of property with compensation for possession acquired. The agreement on marital property may be entered before or during marriage. It may be amended or terminated. If it is terminated during the marriage, community property is formed between the spouses unless they agree otherwise.

Whether the marital property agreement is effective in relation to the creditors' claims depends on the actual knowledge of creditors about its conclusion and nature (Article 47 FGC). The Polish Supreme Court in a decision of 2 July 2009 (V CSK 471/2008, LexPolonica nr 3854143) clarified that a separation of spousal property made in the form of an agreement signed by the spouses is not effective against the creditor if it was concluded after the creation of an obligation (the duty to pay that may arise from contract or tort), as opposed to a court's decision introducing such a separation. Moreover a spouse can plead a lack of responsibility because of the marital agreement against the creditor only if the creditor had obtained such information before the creation of an obligation. The burden of proving it stays on one of the spouses.

C. DIVORCE, NULLITY AND JUDICIAL SEPARATION

6. RECOGNITION OF FOREIGN MARRIAGES/DIVORCES

6.1 Summarise the position in your jurisdiction

Recognition of foreign marriage

Polish law does not require any form of recognition of a marriage that was concluded abroad. According to Article 1138 PCCP foreign official documents have generally probative value equal to Polish official documents. Only in case of documents which a party has claimed are not authentic is there a requirement to produce a copy certified by a Polish diplomatic or consulate post.

However there is a possibility to enter a foreign act of marriage into the Civil Status Registry but it is not a form of validation of such an act (see: Article 73 of The Law on Civil Status Registry of 1986).

Recognition of foreign divorce decrees

PCCP regulates the recognition of divorce decrees rendered by foreign countries in Articles 1145 – 1149[1]. Generally foreign decrees in all civil cases are recognised by operation of law (Article 1145 PCCP). Article 1146 PCCP enumerates the impediments to recognise a foreign court's verdict. A decree cannot be recognised, for example, if it is not binding in the country in which it was issued or a decree was issued in a case which belongs to exclusive Polish jurisdiction. Two other reasons for refusal to recognise the decree are based on the inability of one of the parties to participate in proceedings. The court shall also refuse to recognise a foreign decree when proceedings were initiated in Poland prior to proceedings in a foreign country or where recognition would be against public policy.

7. DIVORCE

7.1 Explain the grounds for divorce within the jurisdiction (please also deal with nullity and judicial separation if appropriate)

A marriage can only be terminated by death of one of the spouses, a judgment of nullity of marriage or a judgment of dissolution of marriage by a divorce. A judgment of legal separation is available, but it will not terminate a marriage.

The action for nullity of marriage presumes that the marriage was not valid. The grounds upon which a nullity can be brought are specific and are provided by FGC Articles 10-16 (see Article 17 FGC). They are:

- age at the time of marriage;
- full legal incapacitation;
- the mental illness or retardation or the bigamy of one of the spouses;
- the consanguinity, the affinity and the bonds of adoption between the spouses.

Article 10 FCG provides that a marriage can be annulled if the spouse was under the age of 18. However if there are important reasons, the Family Court may permit a woman who has reached the age of 16 to marry, where circumstances show that the marriage would be in accordance with the best interest of established family. Once the underage party comes of age the action for nullity will no longer be available. Article 11 FGC provides that no-one who is fully legally incapacitated can marry. When incapacitation has been overcome the marriage cannot be nullified. Article 12 FGC makes marriage voidable if either party suffered from mental illness or was mentally retarded. However, if the state of this person does not endanger the marriage or the health of future issue the court may permit this person to marry. The action for nullity will no longer be available once the illness has ceased. Article 13 provides that someone who is already married cannot marry. The subsequent marriage is not void if the former marriage has been terminated or adjudged a nullity, unless the marriage is terminated through the death of the person who remained in a previous marriage. Another prerequisite to marriage is that the intended spouses must not be closely related. No direct line relatives or siblings can marry. The same applies to persons connected by bond of affinity in direct line (immediate family in-laws). Affinity created by a former marriage continue to be considered impediment to marry. However if there are important reasons, the guardian court may authorise a marriage between in-laws (Article 14 FGC). Finally according to Article 16 FGC it is not possible for adoptive parent and adoptive child to marry unless the adoption has been terminated.

The ground for divorce is complete and irretrievable breakdown of marriage (Article 56 FGC). The breakdown is complete when all fundamental bonds (emotional, physical and economical) between the spouses cease to exist. The term 'irretrievable' means that the breakdown of the relationship is going to be permanent.

However, despite complete and irretrievable breakdown of marriage, a divorce is not permitted if the divorce would be detrimental to the welfare of the common minor children of the spouses or if there are other reasons indicating that to grant a divorce would be against the principles of community life (Article 56 § 2 FGC).

The court may also refuse to grant a divorce if the spouse seeking a divorce is exclusively guilty of the breakdown of the marriage and the innocent spouse does not want to consent to a divorce, unless the refusal to consent to the divorce, at the given circumstances, is against the principles of community life (Article 56 § 3 FGC).

The grounds for obtaining judicial separation are found in FGC Article 60^1 and are almost the same as the grounds for divorce. The separation can be granted in case of the breakdown of marriage. The breakdown must be complete, however, it doesn't have to be irretrievable. The separation cannot be granted when it would be detrimental to the welfare of the common minor children of the spouses or if there are other reasons indicating that to grant a divorce would be against the principles of community life. If the spouses have no common minor children, the separation may be obtained solely on the basis of joint request of the parties without deciding on the guilt for the breakdown of the marriage. In such case, the consequences of separation decree are as if neither of the spouses is guilty.

8. FINANCES/CAPITAL, PROPERTY

8.1 What powers does the court have to allocate financial resources and property on the breakdown of marriage?

At divorce, the court, at the demand of one of the spouses, will divide their community property, as long as this division will not cause undue delay to the divorce proceedings (Article 58 § 3 FGC). If divorce is granted without the division of property, the spouses may employ a separate court's property division procedure; unless they reach their own agreement to divide it (it should be executed in the form of notarial deed if there is real property among the assets).

The court has a substantial range of possibilities with respect to structuring a division of community property. The court may award certain assets to one spouse and certain other assets to the other spouse. Each spouse should receive assets of the same value. To equalise the division of assets the value of individual shares may be compensated by additional cash payments. The payment can be spread out in installments for a maximum period of 10 years. The court also can divide particular assets in kind (eg, money, shares) giving part of it to one spouse and the other part to the other spouse or order that it be sold and the money divided (see Article 46 FGC and Articles 212 and 1035 PCC). When dividing community estate the court must take into the account that pursuant to Article 45 FGC each spouse should repay any expenses and expenditures made from community property to his separate property, except for necessary expenses and expenditures on the assets bringing in an income. A spouse may demand the reimbursement of expenses and expenditures made from separate property on community property. However, it is not possible to claim the reimbursement of expenses and expenditures used to meet the needs of the family unless they increased the value of the property when the community property regime ends.

8.2 Explain and illustrate with reference to recent cases the court's thinking on division of assets

When dividing community property the court is not allowed to divide community debts and liabilities. Therefore one of the most contentious issues concerning the division of community property is a division of the mortgaged real property, notably when a credit from a bank left to be paid by the parties is equal to the value of the property.

The courts have been divided as to how to proceed in such a situation. Some courts have preferred to divide mere value of the real property and not take the bank credit under consideration. Under this approach such bank credit was treated as the debt of the estate and not an asset of the parties and couldn't be taken into the account while dividing the estate (see decision of Supreme Court of December 5, 1978, III CRN 194/78). In more recent decisions the courts have started to observe that although it is not permissible to divide debts along with community property, one may take the value of the debt into account in the process of evaluation of certain asset. Consequently, while calculating the value of such real property, changing market value should be considered (see judgments of Supreme Court of April 2, 2009, IV CSK 566/2008; of January 21, 2010, I CSK 205/2009; of April 20, 2011, I CSK 661/2010).

9. FINANCES/MAINTENANCE

9.1 Explain the operation of maintenance for spouses on an ongoing basis after the breakdown of marriage

The Code Article that provides the reciprocal obligation of spouses to support each other is FGC Article 27. It provides that both spouses are obliged, each according to their strength, earning capacity and resources, to contribute towards meeting the needs of the family founded by their marriage.

After divorce this obligation ceases (see decision of Supreme Court of July 13, 2011, III CZP 39/2011) and the divorced spouse, who has not been found exclusively guilty of the breakdown of marriage and who finds him-/herself in poverty, may demand that the other spouse provides a means of maintenance appropriate for the justified needs of the entitled spouse and the earning capacity and resources of the obligor spouse (Article 60 § 1 FGC). Poverty should be understood as the state in which one cannot meet one's own basic needs. It may result from different reasons (eg, lack of qualifications to get a job as that person took care of the children and household for many years; inability to work because of the need to take care of the children, health problems). Poverty may be the result of the breakdown of marriage or may occur sometime after the divorce. For instance if the obligee spouse loses their job or is forced to significantly reduce work hours as a result of the serious health problems and as a consequence has lower earnings.

The divorced spouse found exclusively guilty of the breakdown of the marriage is not entitled to the spousal support. He/she is obliged, when the divorce results in significant reduction of the standard of living of the innocent spouse, to pay spousal support according to the justified needs of the innocent spouse, even though the innocent spouse is not in poverty. In order to decide whether the standard of living of the innocent spouse has deteriorated, the court has to compare the financial situation after the divorce with the situation which would have been in case if no divorce had been decreed.

The obligation to pay spousal maintenance expires only on the death of the entitled spouse or in case of his/her new marriage. However when the obligor ex-spouse has not been found guilty of the breakdown of marriage, his obligation to pay maintenance expires after five years from the date of the divorce verdict, unless extended by the court at the request of the entitled spouse, due to exceptional circumstances (Article 60 § 3 FGC).

9.2 Is it common for maintenance to be awarded?

Maintenance for an ex-spouse after the divorce is not commonly awarded by the courts in Poland.

9.3 Explain and illustrate with reference to recent cases the court's thinking on maintenance

The court is granted a great deal of discretion with regard to spousal maintenance, including the right not to award it in exceptional circumstances even if all of the requirements described in Article 60 § 2 FGC are fulfilled (judgment of Supreme Court of February 15, 2000, II CKN 391/2000). The court shall consider all the factors indicated in Article 60 FGC and give them due weight.

When considering the obligation of the exclusively guilty spouse to pay support to the innocent spouse (Article 60 § 2 FGC) the court has to compare the factual financial situation of the innocent spouse after divorce to the position that would have existed if the parties were not to divorce and would continue living together (judgment of Posnan Appellate Court of September 9, 2009, I ACa 565/09, Legalis).

The poverty of the spouse as the requirement to award spousal support is of relative character. It means that the spouse has to use all his/her earning capacity to obtain the means necessary to satisfy his/her justified needs before spousal support can be awarded. Therefore a wife who after divorce starts to work and earns 600 PLN is not in poverty, notably when the child support obligation is fulfilled completely by the father of their common child (see judgment of Posnan Appellate Court of February 10, 2004, I ACa 1422/2003, LexPolonica nr 376331). Katowice Appellate Court, in the judgment of March 11, 2010, I ACa 11/10, LEX nr 1120343 underlined that the obligor spouse's duty to support depends also on his justified needs.

10. CHILD MAINTENANCE

10.1 On what basis is child maintenance calculated within the jurisdiction?

The obligation for parental support of minor children is found in several provisions of FGC. FGC Article 133 describes the general obligation of both parents to support their child until the child can provide for him-/herself unless the income from a child's property is sufficient to cover his/her maintenance and upbringing.

The establishment of the amount of child support is left to the discretion of the Family Court. The court will examine the factors that have a bearing on child's standard of living, both before and after the separation of his/her parents, set forth in FGC Article 135 § 1, related to the justified needs of the children and income, earning capacity and resources of both parties. The court applies those factors and determines the amount of support to be paid. Judges applying this standard often come to varying conclusions about an appropriate child-support award.

The amount of child support is based on the actual, justified needs of the child for health, education and maintenance. An important factor in determining the extent of that child's needs is the age of the child. The court may, however, take into account the standard of living that the child would have had if the family had continued to live together. The performance of the child support obligation may rest fully or partially on personal efforts for his/her maintenance and upbringing; in this case child support for the non-custodial parent means covering maintenance and upbringing costs for the child (Article 135 § 3 FGC).

A parent's capacity to pay child support is usually determined by his/her actual income at the time the award is made and all other available sources. If the court concludes that the parent's actual income does not reflect his/her true earning capacity, the court may impute additional income to that parent. This imputation of income may also occur when the court determines that a parent has voluntarily (because of circumstances within the parent's control) reduced his/her actual income. If voluntary and unjustified reduction of income or resources took place in the three years before the court was asked to enter a support order, the reduction is not taken into account when computing child support (Articles 135 § 1 and 136 FGC).

11. RECIPROCAL ENFORCEMENT OF FINANCIAL ORDERS

11.1 Summarise the position in your jurisdiction

Foreign financial orders can be enforced according to international bilateral and multilateral agreements concluded between Poland and other countries. Within the EU the provisions of Council Regulation (EC) No 44/2001 on Jurisdiction and the Recognition and Enforcement of Judgments in Civil and Commercial Matters (Articles 38-52) will apply.

If there is no international convention the rules of PCCP Articles 1150-1152 will be applicable. According to these provisions the enforcement of a foreign decision is possible if it is declared enforceable by the Polish court. That declaration is possible only if the judgment is enforceable in the country of its origin and only if there are no bars to its recognition enumerated in PCCP Article 1146.

12. FINANCIAL RELIEF AFTER FOREIGN DIVORCE PROCEEDINGS

12.1 What powers are available to make orders following a foreign divorce?

If the financial matters were not decided in the foreign divorce decree, either party may apply to the Polish court to make orders regulating these matters, if it has jurisdiction. If the financial matters were decided in a foreign decree, some of them (eg, alimony for the children or spouse maintenance) may be later changed if there is a change of circumstances (FGC Article 138).

D. CHILDREN

13. CUSTODY/PARENTAL RESPONSIBILITY

13.1 Briefly explain the legal position in relation to custody/parental responsibility following the breakdown of a relationship or marriage

FGC Article 58 § 1 provides that at divorce the court shall determine custody over the minor common child/ren of the spouses. The court takes into account the agreement of the spouses on exercising parental authority and visitations if it is in accordance with the best interest of the child. Siblings should not be separated upon divorce, unless it would be in the children's best interest.

FGC Article 58 § 1a provides that the court may designate one parent as the custodial parent, limiting the parental authority of the second parent to specific rights and duties in relation to the child (eg, participation in decision-making concerning the child's education, health and religious upbringing). In determining custody in divorce proceedings, the court must assess what is in the best interest of the child and in doing so should consider a broad range of relevant factors. The gender of the parent still seems to be one of the most important factors. The courts favour mothers of young children as a general matter. The preference for the mother as custodian especially of younger children is traditionally explained by the alleged existence of the greater emotional commitments of women to children (see decision of Supreme Court of December 15, 1998 r., I CKN 1122/98, LexPolonica nr 334439). However, the gender of the parent is not considered for the purposes of matching children with a parent of the same sex (decision of Supreme Court of November 30, 1954, 2 CR 1229/54, LexPolonica nr 376778).

The court may leave the parental authority with both parents only if they present the agreement referred to in Article 58 § 1 FGC, and it is reasonable to believe that they will cooperate in matters concerning the child. There are no specific requirements concerning the content of the agreement referred to in Article 58 § 1 FGC. The courts usually demand that the document signed by both parents contains the basic arrangements concerning the child's place of residence, arrangements as to the contacts of the non-custodial parent with the child, issues that would require joint decisions by the parents, and the mode of communication between them. Sometimes, however, the courts are satisfied with very general provisions of the agreement which in case of later disagreement between the parties may create additional conflicts as to their interpretation.

13.2 Briefly explain the legal position in relation to access/contact/visitation following the breakdown of a relationship or marriage

Pursuant to Article 113 FGC regardless of parental authority, the parents and child have the right and duty to maintain in contact with each other. If the parents living separately are not able to reach an agreement as to the way of maintaining contacts with the child, the court will decide on visitation rights, taking into account the reasonable wishes of the child (Article 113[1] FGC). Article 113 § 2 FCG provides that contacts with the child may include for example, visiting the child, taking the child outside his place of residence, direct and distant communication and maintaining correspondence.

The parent not granted custody in divorce proceedings is entitled to visitation rights (Article 58 FGC), unless it would not be in the child's best interest. If it is in the best interest of the child the court may limit visitation rights. The court may limit contacts by prohibiting the parent from taking the child outside his/her place of residence or allowing the parent to meet the child only in the presence of other parent or another person. The court may also limit access to the child via specific kinds of distance communication or prohibit distance communication at all. The Family and Guardianship Code Article 113[3] states that in extreme situations when the visitation seriously endangers the child (eg, in case of severe physical or sexual abuse) the court may impose a denial of visitation.

FGC Article 113[5], establishes the discretion of the court to change contact awards. The inquiry will focus and depend only upon what is in the best interests of the minor child. Formally, substantial change in circumstances is not required for reconsideration of the order. However examining the best interest of the child will require the court to examine what circumstances have changed so significantly as to influence the interest of the child and prevail on his/her need for stability of contacts.

FGC is silent on the specifics of a visitation plan and therefore the courts have wide discretion in its formulation. In practice the non-custodial parent is usually allowed to spend alternating weekends and one evening visit during the week with the child; holidays and school vacations are equally divided between parents.

14. INTERNATIONAL ABDUCTION

14.1 Summarise the position in your jurisdiction

The 1980 Hague Convention On The Civil Aspects Of International Child Abduction was adopted in Poland in 1992. As with each country that has joined the Convention, Poland established a central authority to receive and proceed requests for assistance in the areas of child return and visitation. In Poland, the Ministry of Justice has been designated as the central authority. The application for assistance is filed with the central authority requesting the return of the child based on his/her wrongful removal or retention. Once it is accepted, it is then sent to the Family Court which has jurisdiction based on the domicile or place of residence of a child.

In seeking the return of an abducted child, the petitioner must show that his/her home country is the child's habitual place of residence and that he/she was lawfully exercising custody rights at the time of removal and that the removal or retention was wrongful. In this situation the return of the child to the home country is mandatory, unless the respondent can establish that specific exceptions apply.

The court may refuse to order the return of the child if:

- more than one year has elapsed since the removal or retention;
- the petitioner was not exercising custody rights or consented to the removal or retention;
- the child objects to the return;
- there is a grave risk of physical or psychological harm or otherwise placing the child in intolerable situation upon his/her return; or
- the return of the child will be contrary to the fundamental principles of the requested state relating to the protection of human rights and fundamental freedoms (Articles 12, 13, 20 of Convention).

The proceedings in many cases last longer than the six weeks required by the Convention (Article 11). If the party is unhappy with the decision of the court, under appropriate circumstances he/she will have the right to appeal decision. The appellate court's decision is final.

The application filed on the basis of the Hague Convention, Article 21 to make arrangements for organising and securing the effective exercise of rights of access is dealt with differently. It is treated as a demand to establish contact with the child and sent to the Family Court as a motion to enforce visitation rights based on Article 113 FGC. The procedure is not treated as privileged but rather as a standard procedure.

Apart from 1980 Hague Convention provisions, Council Regulation (EC) No 2201/2003 of 27 November 2003 concerning jurisdiction and the recognition and enforcement of judgments in matrimonial matters and the matters of parental responsibility, regulating child's abduction issues (see Articles 11 and 60) is also directly applicable in Poland.

15. LEAVE TO REMOVE/APPLICATIONS TO TAKE A CHILD OUT OF THE JURISDICTION

15.1 Summarise the position in your jurisdiction

FGC Article 97 § 2 FGC provides that if both parents have parental authority, then each of them is entitled to exercise it. On important matters concerning the child parents should decide together. If they can't reach agreement, the Family Court will decide. The decision about relocation of a minor child to another jurisdiction is one of the important matters concerning the child within the meaning of Article 97 § 2 FGC. Therefore in case of a disagreement between the parents as to the relocation of the minor child, either of them can apply to the Family Court to resolve the dispute.

15.2 Under what circumstances may a parent apply to remove their child from the jurisdiction against the wishes of the other parent?

FGC does not require the relocating parent to give the other parent any notice prior to the anticipated move. The FGC does not regulate the requirements for the relocation to be considered as justified nor offers any specific standard to resolve the dispute. The courts have wide discretion in deciding this issue and they seem to apply the best interest standard that allows them to take into the account a very broad range of relevant facts. As there are no published courts' decisions on this issue, one may only speculate that these factors include reasons for the move, the quality of life in the new place and feasibility of providing an appropriate visitation schedule for the left-behind parent.

E. SURROGACY AND ADOPTION

16. VALIDITY OF SURROGACY AGREEMENTS

16.1 Briefly summarise the position in your jurisdiction

FGC Article 61^9 provides that a mother of a child is the woman who gave birth to the child. Therefore surrogacy agreements, according to prevailing opinion of jurisprudence, are void as contrary to the law and public policy (Article 58 PCC) and are unenforceable. It also applies to agreements where a surrogate mother gives her consent for the future adoption of the child by genetic parents because according to Article 119^2 FGC, consent to the adoption of the child cannot take place earlier than six weeks after birth.

17. ADOPTION

17.1 Briefly summarise the position in relation to adoption in your jurisdiction. Is adoption available to individuals, cohabiting couples (both heterosexual and same-sex)?

FGC Article 114 provides that one can adopt a minor child only if it is in child's best interest. The criteria of minority must be satisfied at the moment of submitting an application for adoption. The adoptive parent must have full legal capacity and have personal qualifications justifying the belief that he/she will properly carry out the obligations of the parent (Article 114[1] FGC). FGC Article 114[1] § 2 FGC also requires an appropriate age difference between the adopter and adoptee. The adopter is obliged to finish training organised by the specialised adoption centre and obtain the formal opinion of such a centre.

Article 115 § 1 FGC provides that only spouses may jointly adopt a child. Joint adoption is not available to cohabiting couples, either heterosexual and same-sex (see decision of Supreme Court of March 30, 1962, III CR 124/62, Lex 105801). Adoption is available for individuals.

As a general rule an adoption by only one of the spouses is possible only after the consent of the other spouse (Article 116 FGC). An adoption which results in a change of domicile of a child from Poland to a foreign country is allowed only if it is the only way to provide the adoptee with the appropriate substitute family environment (Article 114[2] § 1 FGC). This rule will not apply if there is a relationship of consanguinity or affinity between the adopter and the adoptee or if the adopter has already adopted a brother or sister of the adoptee (Article 114[2] § 2 FGC).

Article 119 FGC requires the consent of the child's parents for the adoption, unless they have been deprived of parental authority or are unknown, or there are significant obstacles in making contact with them. Consent may be given without knowledge of who may adopt the child or without indicating a specified person.

The adoption may create bonds equal to that which exist between parents and children (complete adoption – Article 121 FGC) or may create bonds only between the adopter and adoptee (incomplete adoption – Article 124 FGC).

The adoption can be dissolved by the court for important reasons in proceedings initiated either by the adopter or the adoptee or a prosecutor. However the dissolution of an adoption will not be permitted if, as a result, it will affect the interest of the child (Article 125 FGC).

F. COHABITATION

18. COHABITATION

18.1 What legislation (if any) governs division of property for unmarried couples on the breakdown of the relationship?

There is no specific legislation governing division of property for unmarried couples on the breakdown of their relationship. There are no universal rules indicating how and on the basis of what specific provisions of PCC or FGC the property of cohabitants should be divided. It is clear, however, that cohabitants should not be treated similarly to spouses at dissolution of the relationship in terms of property division and the provisions governing division of marital property should not apply accordingly (see judgments of Supreme Court of May 16, 2000, IV CKN 32/2000 LexPolonica nr 347719; of October 5, 2011, IV CSK 11/2011, Lex Polonica nr 3991028).

Depending on the factual circumstances of the case the courts adopt different approaches to dividing property for unmarried couples. Some courts have tried to employ provisions concerning a civil partnership agreement (Civil Code, Articles 860 ff), but the majority of courts adopt a division of co-ownership (Article 212 PCC ff) or unjust enrichment (Articles 405-414 PCC) approach. The same rules apply to same-sex couples.

G. FAMILY DISPUTE RESOLUTION

19. MEDIATION, COLLABORATIVE LAW AND ARBITRATION

19.1 Briefly summarise the non-court-based processes available in your jurisdiction and the current status of agreements reached under the auspices of mediation, collaborative law and arbitration

The general rule of PCCP is that in matrimonial matters and matters between parents and child it is not permitted to sign a settlement. There are, however, some exceptions. The Supreme Court has explained that the parties may settle in cases concerning contact with the child (decision of Supreme Court of October 21, 2005, III CZP 75/05, LexPolonica 389806), and spouse and child support (decision of Supreme Court of July 16, 1971 r., III CRN 188/71, LexPolonica 322485). These settlements may be reached by the parties during a court's proceedings and are subsequently controlled by the court as to their conformity with law and rules of community life and whether or not they are a circumvention of the law.

19.2 What is the statutory basis (if any), for mediation, collaborative law and arbitration in your jurisdiction? In particular, are the parties required to attempt a family dispute resolution in advance of proceedings?

PCCP Article 436 § 1 PCCP provides that during divorce or judicial separation proceedings, a court may refer the parties to mediation. It is possible only once during divorce proceedings and only after the consent of both parties. If the parties have not chosen a mediator, the court will refer them to a permanent mediator who has knowledge of psychology, pedagogy, sociology or law and also has practical skills in the field of mediation in family matters (Article 436 § 3 PCCP).

In divorce or judicial separation proceedings a court may at every stage of a trial refer the parties to mediation for the purpose of amicable resolution of disputes concerning meeting the needs of family, alimony (maintenance), exercise of parental authority, contact with children, or financial issues which are subject to a court's decision in a future verdict (Article 445^2 PCCP).

In cases concerning the exercise of parental authority a subject of mediation may be the mode of exercising parental authority (570^2 PCCP).

The parties are not required to attempt a family dispute resolution in advance of the institution of proceedings.

H. OTHER

20. CIVIL PARTNERSHIP/SAME-SEX MARRIAGE

20.1 What is the status of civil partnership/same-sex marriage within the jurisdiction?

20.2 What legislation governs civil partnership/same-sex marriage?

In Polish law there is no regulation concerning civil partnership or same-sex marriages. However, in certain circumstances one of the partners can benefit from some law regulations on the basis of 'remaining in cohabitation' status. According to Article 691 § 1 PCC upon the death of the lessee of residential premises (real estate, apartment), the spouse who was not a co-lessee, children of the lessee and the spouse of the lessee, other persons to whom the lessee was obliged to maintain or pay alimony to, and the person the lessee actually cohabited with (both opposite and same-sex), become the new lessees (see decision of Supreme Court of November 28, 2012, III CZP 65/2012, LexPolonica nr 4134116)

21. CONTROVERSIAL AREAS/RAPIDLY DEVELOPING AREAS OF LAW

21.1 Is there a particular area of the law within the jurisdiction that is currently undergoing major change?

There is no particular area of family law that would be currently undergoing major change. There are, however, discussions and legislation initiatives to introduce provisions regulating civil partnerships to Polish law.

21.2 Which areas of law are most out of step and which areas would you most like to see reformed/changed?

We believe that the child support provisions require major changes. The courts are given too much discretion in deciding on the amount of child support. The criteria for making child-support awards should be specific, more predictable and consistent. Polish family law requires child support guidelines that would be based on specific descriptive and numeric criteria and result in a computation of the support obligation.

The legislators should also rethink the concept of delegation of parental authority at divorce or in case of a breakdown of the parents' informal relationship. Currently, in many cases, the opposition of one of the parents (usually the mother) results in an absence of agreement between the parents. Consequently it forces the court to give custody to the mother and limit the parental authority of the father as non-custodial parent. The courts should be allowed to leave full parental authority to both parents even in the absence of a written parental agreement.

Another area of family law that strives for amendments is enforcement of visitation rights of the non-custodial parent. Current remedies for custodial interference are not effective.

Republic of Ireland

Mason Hayes & Curran Jennifer O'Brien

A JURISDICTION AND CONFLICT OF LAW

1. SOURCES OF LAW

1.1 What is the primary source of law in relation to the breakdown of marriage and the welfare of children within the jurisdiction?

The Constitution of Ireland, specifically Articles 41 and 42, recognises the family as the most important social unit in the State and accord a special position to the 'family' based on marriage. While the Constitution dates from 1937, accession to the European Union and other international treaties facilitated the development of modern Irish family law, which is now primarily sourced within a statutory framework. The Judicial Separation and Family Law Reform Act 1989 first introduced the concept of judicial separation and extensive ancillary relief orders. That Act was subsequently amended and enhanced by the Family Law Act 1995 which remains in operation. Divorce was introduced by a narrow majority following a referendum on 24 November 1995 which resulted in new provisions at Article 41 and the enactment of the Family Law (Divorce) Act, 1996.

The Constitution continues to afford special protection to the 'family' based on marriage, a proposition which seems outdated given the recent introduction of civil partnership and a protective statutory regime for certain 'qualified' cohabitants, see the Civil Partnership and Certain Rights and Obligations of Cohabitants Act, 2010.

1.2 Which are the main statutes governing matrimonial law in the jurisdiction?

The following are the main statutes (in alphabetical order):

- Adoption Act 2010
- Child Abduction and Enforcement of Custody Orders Act 1991
- Child Care Act 1991
- Child Care (Amendment) Act 2011
- Children Act 1997
- Civil Partnership and Certain Rights and Obligations of Cohabitants Act 2010
- Civil Registration (Amendment) Act 2012
- Domestic Violence Acts 1996-2002
- Domicile and Recognition of Foreign Divorces Act 1986
- Family Home Protection Act 1976
- Family Law Act 1981
- Family Law Act 1995
- Family Law (Divorce) Act 1996

- Family Law (Maintenance of Spouses and Children) Act 1976
- Guardianship of Infants Act 1964
- Maintenance Act, 1994
- Judicial Separation and Family Law Reform Act 1989
- Status of Children Act 1987

2. JURISDICTION

2.1 What are the main jurisdictional requirements for the institution of proceedings in relation to divorce, property and children?

Domicile and/or ordinary residence in Ireland for a period of 12 months prior to the application forms the basis for jurisdiction in respect of the Judicial Separation and Family Law Reform Act 1989 (the 1989 Act), the Family Law Act 1995 (the 1995 Act), the Family Law (Divorce) Act 1996 (the 1996 Act) and (insofar as it relates to civil partnership), the Civil Partnership and Certain Rights and Obligations of Cohabitants Act, 2010 (the 2010 Act) (together the Family Law Acts).

The Irish courts also have jurisdiction where the provisions of the revised Brussels II Regulation (Council regulation) (EC) No. 2201/2003 of 27 November 2003 (the Regulation) concerning jurisdiction and the recognition and enforcement of judgments in matrimonial matters and in matters of parental responsibility apply.

The Regulation is now generally cited in Irish family law proceedings and has introduced a number of changes to the basis for jurisdiction in respect of divorce, separation, nullity and also in proceedings regarding children. Unfortunately, its provisions can result in a 'race for the line' as each party attempts to acquire a preferred jurisdiction.

The Circuit Court and High Court each have full jurisdiction to deal with proceedings for divorce, separation, nullity and dissolution of civil partnership. Both courts also have jurisdiction to deal with preliminary applications, interim applications and applications for ancillary (including financial) relief. 'Ample resource' cases and/or more complex matters are generally instituted in the High Court whereas the Circuit Family Court deals with a higher volume of family law matters. The District Court, being the lowest court, deals with maintenance, guardianship, custody, access and domestic violence applications.

3. DOMICILE AND HABITUAL RESIDENCE

3.1 Explain the concepts of domicile and habitual residence as they apply to the jurisdiction

Domicile and habitual residence are not specifically defined in either common law or statute.

Domicile is generally understood as the country that a person treats as his permanent home and to which he has the closest legal attachment. The person cannot be without a domicile and cannot have two domiciles at once. At birth an individual acquires a domicile of origin which he retains until he acquires a domicile of choice in its place. A domicile of choice is acquired by making a home in a country with the intention that it should be a permanent base. It may be acquired at any time after a person becomes 16 and can be replaced at will by a new domicile of choice.

Habitual residence is interpreted in accordance with European case law which has been endorsed by the Irish courts and applied in individual cases. The term has been interpreted as meaning the place or country in which a person has his home with an intention to reside there, coupled with a physical presence for a reasonable length of time. The court has held that habitual residence is not a 'term of art', but a matter of fact, to be decided on the evidence in each particular case. See McGuinness J.'s decision in *CM & OM v Delegacion de Malaga & Others* [1999] 2 IR 363. For further judicial discussion on this subject see *PAS v AFS* [2005] IILRM 306, *SR v MMR[2006] IESC 7, AS v CS* [2009] IEHC 345 and *BU v BE* [2010] IEHC 77.

4. CONFLICT OF LAW/APPLICABLE LAW TO BE APPLIED

4.1 What happens when one party applies to stay proceedings in favour of a foreign jurisdiction? What factors will the local court take into account when determining forum issues?

Where proceedings are issued in more than one member state, the Regulation provides that the court properly and first seised with proceedings retains that jurisdiction and any second or subsequent court must decline jurisdiction in favour of the first court. The aim of the Regulation is to avoid competing actions and the creation of 'limping' divorces, incapable of recognition in other jurisdictions.

The doctrine of *forum non conveniens* has limited application in Ireland. The Irish courts have followed the reasoning applied in *Owusu v Jackson and Others* [2005] EUECJC 28102 with regard to mandatory application of the Brussels Convention. At 46, the ECJ held: *'The Brussels Convention precludes a court of a Contracting State from declining the jurisdiction conferred on it by Article 2 of that Convention on the grounds that a court of a non-Contracting State would be a more appropriate forum for the trial of the action even if the jurisdiction of no other Contracting State is in issue or the proceedings have no connecting factors to any other Contracting State.'*

The Irish courts apply *'lex fori'* ie, Irish domestic law, in determining family law applications. Irish judges may have regard to foreign law in the context of divorce and ancillary relief applications, however, foreign law is not applied even between two foreign nationals. In this regard, Ireland has opted out of 'Rome III' which aims to establish a consistent set of rules throughout the EU party member states. The Maintenance Regulation (Regulation (EC) No 4/2009 (given effect in Ireland through SI. No. 274/2011) (the EU Maintenance Regulation) became effective in Ireland in June 2011 and Ireland has also opted into the Hague Protocol of 23 November 2007 on the law applicable to maintenance obligations in member states and in this sense an element of applicable law has now been introduced in Ireland.

B. PRE- AND POST-NUPTIAL AGREEMENTS

5. VALIDITY OF PRE- AND POST-NUPTIAL AGREEMENTS

5.1 To what extent are pre- and post-nups binding within the jurisdiction? Could you provide a brief discussion of the most significant recent case law on this issue

There remains considerable discussion and uncertainty with regard to the status of pre- and post-nuptial agreements in Ireland. While no legislation or case law exists, there is a sense that the jurisprudence is shifting towards a greater emphasis on self-determination provided certain procedural safeguards are observed. The Constitution continues to accord a special place to the 'family' based on marriage and in that sense may continue to provide a basis for many of the traditional social and moral objections. More recently a number of factors have arguably diminished the strength of these objections. In particular, the introduction of divorce in 1997 and the enactment of the Civil Partnership and Certain Rights and Obligations of Cohabitants Act 2010 which makes provision such that cohabitants can now regulate financial matters by written agreement.

An expert study group was established by the Irish Government in 2007 for the purpose of reviewing the role and status of pre-nuptial agreements. This comprehensive report recommended the introduction of legislation such that the courts would be required to have regard to pre-nuptial agreements without the terms of such an agreement becoming automatically determinative of the outcome. The report makes recommendations on the formalities necessary for making pre-nuptial agreements including proper disclosure, provision of independent legal advice and execution of the agreement at least 28 days prior to a marriage ceremony. While the recommendations set out in the report have not yet been implemented, pre-nuptial agreements are becoming more prevalent, particularly for wealthier clients.

C. DIVORCE, NULLITY AND JUDICIAL SEPARATION

6. RECOGNITION OF FOREIGN MARRIAGES/DIVORCES

6.1 Summarise the position in your jurisdiction

Where the formal legal requirements of the state where the marriage was celebrated are observed and where both parties have capacity to marry according to the law of their domicile at the time of marriage, a foreign marriage will be recognised as valid in the Republic of Ireland. Where such a marriage does not fall within the general understanding of marriage in Ireland, it may not be recognised on public policy grounds. For instance, in the context of a polygamist marriage.

Special rules apply in the context of recognition of foreign divorce, according to the date when the foreign divorce proceedings were issued. A foreign divorce obtained prior to 2 October 1986 would be subject to common law rules and the Irish courts will now recognise such a decree in circumstances where either or both spouses were domiciled in the foreign state. In some cases, the High Court has recognised such a divorce on the basis of the residence of either spouse, although the precise parameters of such recognition remain unclear.

A foreign divorce obtained on or after 2 October 1986, would be subject to the provisions of the Domicile and Recognition of Foreign Divorces Act 1986 (the 1986 Act). In such cases, the Irish courts will recognise a foreign divorce where either spouse was domiciled in the foreign state at the date of commencement of the proceedings. Special rules apply with regard to cases concerning England and Wales, Scotland, Northern Ireland, the Isle of Man or the Channel Islands, such that the divorce is recognised if either party was domiciled at the relevant time in any of those jurisdictions.

On or after 1 March 2001 (or 1 March 2005 in respect of newer member states), foreign divorces granted in the EU member states (excluding Denmark) receive automatic recognition based on a number of grounds including residence.

Where there is a dispute, it is possible to make an application under the 1995 Act for the purpose of seeking a formal declaration as to marital status.

7. DIVORCE

7.1 Explain the grounds for divorce within the jurisdiction (please also deal with nullity and judicial separation if appropriate)

Divorce was introduced in Ireland as of 27 February 1997, following a referendum which was won by a narrow majority which resulted in a new constitutional provision and the introduction of the Family Law (Divorce) Act 1996 (the 1996 Act). A decree of divorce can only be granted where:

- the spouses have lived apart from one another for a period of, or periods amounting to, at least four years during the previous five years;
- there is no reasonable prospect of a reconciliation between the spouses;
- such provision as the court considers proper having regard to the circumstances exists or will be made for the spouses, any children of either or both of them and any other person prescribed by law.

As such, there is no requirement to illustrate 'fault' for the purpose of grounding an application for divorce in Ireland. Formal evidence must be given to the court in respect of the period spent living apart, although the courts have allowed for periods of time spent living apart 'while under the same roof'.

In most cases, it is necessary to bring judicial separation proceedings in the first instance, the grounds for which are set out in section 2 of the 1989 Act and include adultery, unreasonable behaviour, living apart for a period of three years (or one year where the Respondent consents) and desertion for a period of one year. Where agreement is reached on the terms of judicial separation, same is usually granted on a no-fault basis, ie, no normal marital relationship for a period of one year prior to issue of proceedings. Behaviour is not generally taken into account unless same is 'gross and obvious' and where it would be unjust to disregard it.

Applications for a decree of nullity are less frequent since the introduction of divorce and can be made where a marriage is 'void' or 'voidable'. In Irish law, a marriage may be void due to lack of capacity, non-observance of formalities or absence of consent. Grounds rendering a marriage voidable include impotence and incapacity to enter into and sustain a normal marriage relationship. It is not possible to seek ancillary relief on foot of a decree of nullity, the effect of which is to declare that no marriage ever existed between the parties.

8. FINANCES/CAPITAL, PROPERTY

8.1 What powers does the court have to allocate financial resources and property on the breakdown of marriage?

Initially contained in the 1989 Act and then substantially replaced by the 1995 Act, the court has wide-ranging powers to make financial relief orders in the context of judicial separation.

The 1996 Act replicates many of these provisions in the context of divorce. Whether dealing with judicial separation or divorce, the court has extensive powers to make orders including for the sale or transfer of the any property or assets owned by either or both of the spouses.

Preliminary and interim relief

Once judicial separation/divorce proceedings are instituted, it is possible to apply for preliminary and/or ancillary relief including maintenance pending suit and *inter alia* freezing orders.

Financial provision

The family law courts can make a number of orders including:

- maintenance (periodical payment) orders;
- lump sum orders;
- property adjustment orders for a transfer of any property or assets between the spouses;
- orders conferring on one spouse an exclusive right to reside in the family home;
- orders for the sale of property;
- financial compensation orders, regarding life cover as security for maintenance payments or otherwise;
- pension adjustment orders;
- orders extinguishing Succession Act rights and dealing with relief orders following death.

There is no provision for a 'clean break' in Irish law whether in the context of judicial separation or divorce. Recent case law such as *G v G* [2011] IESC 40, a decision of the Supreme Court delivered on 19 October 2011, is helpful as the Supreme Court remitted the case to the High Court for alteration and stressed that privately reached 'full and final' separation agreements should be given significant weight in divorce orders. This case is also authority for the separate treatment of inherited assets.

In essence, the court's obligation whether in the context of judicial separation or divorce is to ensure that 'proper provision' is made for the spouses and any dependent children. Section 16 of the 1995 Act and Section 20 of the 1996 Act set out the factors to which the court must have regard when considering whether or not to grant financial relief orders. These include the financial position of each party, the standard of living enjoyed by the parties, conduct where it would be unjust to disregard it, contributions made by each spouse, etc. While there are no specific rules governing assessment of 'proper provision', the seminal case *T v T* [2002] 3 IR 335 referred to a 'benchmark of fairness' for the dependent spouse as being between one-third and one half of the net assets.

It should be noted recent cases have departed from this yardstick depending on the precise circumstances, although it remains a helpful guideline.

While the 'yardstick of fairness' and the factors contained in the legislation offer helpful guidance, they are not determinative of the outcome in any given case. Judicial discretion is exercised widely in these matters and will often be heavily influenced by the precise facts and circumstances of the case. Discovery and exchange of financial reports/information is imperative in financially complex cases. For instance, it may be necessary to bring interim applications for discovery orders. More recently, the Irish High Court and the Circuit Family Court have each introduced processes of case management/progression which are designed to ensure that discovery and other pre-trial matters are dealt with prior to listing of the matter for hearing. This process also assists in the management of settlement discussions as each party has greater clarity as to the 'net asset' position.

The approach of the Irish courts in ancillary relief applications has been neatly summarised in the High Court decision of *MB v VB* (Birmingham J, 19 October 2007 (unreported)). In considering the concept of 'proper provision' the court wrote that *'the Supreme Court [in T v T] eschewed any adherence to any particular mathematical formula, making it clear that there was no automatic principle of assets being distributed on the basis of equality and that equally, on the other side of the coin, the claiming spouse was not confined to the share of the assets that would be required to meet their reasonable needs'*. The court further commented that *'there is no right percentage to be applied… I have not approached this case on the basis of deciding on any particular percentage, but rather I have considered percentages only at the final stage and then done so as a form of safety check, so as to confirm to my satisfaction that the approach I was taking was not an unreal one'*.

Recent financial difficulties and the collapse of the Irish property market have resulted in a number of applications for variation of previous maintenance/capital orders, many of which have been successful. See *AK v JK* IEHC [2008] 341 with regard to differentiation between 'fine tuning applications' and 'strategic applications' where variation is sought in a post-separation context. See also *D v D* [2011] IESC 18 where the Supreme Court allowed the husband to adduce new evidence to show a material change in circumstances (namely the reduction in the value of agricultural land). The matter was remitted to the High Court for a determination of how the assets should be divided.

9. FINANCES/MAINTENANCE

9.1 Explain the operation of maintenance for spouses on an ongoing basis after the breakdown of marriage

On application for judicial separation or divorce, the courts may grant a maintenance order for the support of a financially dependent spouse either as a periodical payment, a secured periodical payment or a lump sum payment. The amount of the payment should be specified including the times at which same are to be made.

Consent orders will often provide for increases in accordance with the Consumer Price Index. Such maintenance orders are subject to variation, discharge or suspension in circumstances where they are successfully reviewed at a later date. The court also has power to make retrospective payments in respect of maintenance, although this seldom occurs. While typically open-ended, maintenance orders can be limited in duration.

In addition, in the context of separation or a divorce, the court can make orders for maintenance pending suit or interim maintenance. Alternatively, the court can make a stand-alone maintenance order under the 1976 Act, even where there are no proceedings for separation/divorce in existence.

The obligation to maintain a dependent spouse continues after divorce, even where no maintenance order was made at that time. The obligation of spousal maintenance only terminates upon the death or remarriage of the receiving spouse although a court is unlikely to impose a maintenance payment where a dependent spouse is cohabiting with a new partner, in circumstances similar to that of husband and wife.

The Circuit Family Court and High Court have unlimited jurisdiction with regard to the level of maintenance orders for spouses and children. There are limitations as to the level of maintenance orders which can be made in the District Court.

9.2 Is it common for maintenance to be awarded?

Maintenance is frequently awarded in ancillary relief applications upon judicial separation and divorce where one of the spouses is financially dependent on the other. In recent times, there is a greater emphasis on the ability of the dependent spouse to re-train and return to remunerative employment. Where there are 'ample resources' and valuable assets available for distribution, maintenance is unlikely to be ordered.

9.3 Explain and illustrate with reference to recent cases the courts' thinking on maintenance

Maintenance orders generally form part of a comprehensive range of ancillary relief orders, whether made by agreement or order of the court. See *CD v PD* (High Court, O'Higgins J, 15 March 2006) and *MB v VB* (High Court, Birmingham J, 19 October 2007 (unreported)).

There is no formula for calculation of appropriate maintenance payments and the test is what constitutes 'proper' maintenance support for a spouse and/or any dependent children. The court would have regard to the financial position of each party and the needs of the dependent spouse/ child in reaching a fair assessment of appropriate maintenance. Reference is made to the High Court decision in *JC v MC (No 2)* (Abbott J, 14 November 2007 (unreported)) where an applicant wife sought additional financial relief subsequent to the grant of a 'full and final' decree of divorce, on the basis of a significant improvement in the husband's financial circumstances. The court held that it had jurisdiction to increase the periodical payments order but not the lump sum order. Abbott J stated: *'I am satisfied having carefully considered the evidence that this figure will be sufficient to enable the ex-wife to cater for her own needs and also to keep house for her adult children. It also gives her scope to build up security (by not having to dip into capital) for her future, to cater for any normal contingencies of life and particularly the necessity to provide security in the event of the earlier death of the ex-husband. To avoid needless applications for a review of this figure, the figure should be reviewed annually in accordance with the Consumer Price Index'.*

See also *H v D* [2011] IEHC 233 in which Irvine J held that a reduction in income did not automatically entitle the applicant to a proportionate reduction in his maintenance payments unless he could demonstrate that the maintenance so reduced would be sufficient to meet the ongoing needs of the respondent and their two children.

10. CHILD MAINTENANCE

10.1 On what basis is child maintenance calculated within the jurisdiction?

An application for child maintenance can be made independently or ancillary to judicial separation/divorce proceedings in respect of a 'dependent child'. A child remains dependent under Irish law until they have attained the age of 18 years or 23 years, provided they continue in full-time education. This obligation arises regardless of the marital status of the parents and/or whether a father enjoys rights of guardianship.

The level of maintenance will be determined following consideration of the income and assets of each parent, the needs of the child and in the marital context, the standard of living enjoyed by the parties prior to separation, together with the other factors set out in Section 16 of the 1995 Act and Section 20 of the 1996 Act.

11. RECIPROCAL ENFORCEMENT OF FINANCIAL ORDERS

11.1 Summarise the position in your jurisdiction

The EU Maintenance Regulation (Regulation (EC) No 4/2009) (the EU Maintenance Regulation) with effect from June 2011 together with the Hague Protocol now regulate maintenance obligations and recognition of cross border orders.

These orders were previously recognised and enforced pursuant to the Brussels I Regulation which also facilitated enforcement of lump sum orders and pension orders, where the purpose was to make provision for maintenance. These provisions have now effectively been replaced by the provisions of the EU Maintenance Regulation. The provisions of the revised Brussels II Regulation are confined to recognition and enforcement of decrees of divorce, separation and nullity throughout these states and as such do not assist with recognition and enforcement of ancillary or financial relief orders. Having said that, choice of jurisdiction remains pivotal in many cases concerning international families and undoubtedly has an impact on financial issues.

The Maintenance Act 1994 in effect ratified the 1990 Rome Convention, and the 1956 New York Convention between member states of the United Nations on the recovery abroad of maintenance. Each of these Conventions, together with the EU Maintenance Regulation, provides for the establishment of a Central Authority in each state. As such, a person with a maintenance order can apply through the Central Authority in his or her state for enforcement through the Central Authority in the other jurisdiction. Enforcement proceedings are conducted in accordance with the provisions of the Convention or EU Maintenance Regulation, whichever is applicable. In Ireland, the existing maintenance enforcement procedure is utilised by the Irish Central Authority. The EU Maintenance Regulation simplifies the procedure as between member states. For enforcement of non-EU orders, an application is first made to the Master of the High Court for a determination as to its enforcement under Section 5 of the Jurisdiction of Courts and Enforcement of Judgments Acts 1988 and 1993 (The Brussels and Lugano Conventions).

Enforcement proceedings are thereafter generally processed through the District Court.

12. FINANCIAL RELIEF AFTER FOREIGN DIVORCE PROCEEDINGS

12.1 What powers are available to make orders following a foreign divorce?

Part III of the 1995 Act provides for applications for financial 'relief orders' on foot of the foreign decrees of divorce or separation. These orders are more limited in scope than the ancillary orders available to an applicant for domestic divorce or separation. Special leave must first be sought from the court prior to bringing such an application. In determining an application for relief, the court must consider several factors including the connection the spouse may have with the state, existing financial arrangements and the possibility of seeking relief in the original state. There are very few reported decisions on Part III to date. Reference is made to *MR v PR* (High Court, Quirke J, 5 July 2005), where the court held that the applicant wife was entitled to financial relief as it was satisfied that no remedy was available to her following grant of a Spanish decree of divorce where full disclosure had not been made by the husband. This decision is confirmed in the later decision of *PMY v PC* (High Court, Sheehan J, 23 November 2007) where relief was refused on the basis that the wife was not precluded from seeking financial relief, including maintenance, in Hong Kong, where the original divorce had been granted.

D. CHILDREN

13. CUSTODY/PARENTAL RESPONSIBILITIES

13.1 Briefly explain the legal position in relation to custody/parental responsibility following the breakdown of a relationship or marriage

In all cases involving children in Ireland, their best interests and welfare are considered to be the guiding and paramount consideration in all matters affecting them (Guardianship of Infants Act, 1964, section 3). Where parties are married, joint custody is assumed and as such orders directing joint custody are generally made by the court on the basis that primary care and control is with one of the parents with days and times for access for the other parent set out in detail, or by using the formula 'as agreed between the parties from time to time'.

In non-marital cases, the mother is the sole legal guardian and custodian of the child(ren). The father can apply to court for guardianship and/or custody and access orders. Alternatively, the mother can appoint the father guardian by statutory declaration.

Where there is a dispute between the parties as to the most appropriate custody/access arrangements, in the context of proceedings before the High or Circuit Family Court, the court may direct a section 47 assessment by a child specialist. Generally, the court will be guided by the specialist, in reaching a determination on these issues. It should be noted that there is no panel of child specialists and access to these services is generally limited to litigants who are in a financial position to discharge associated costs.

13.2 Briefly explain the legal position in relation to access/contact/ visitation following the breakdown of a relationship or marriage

Whether between married parents or unmarried parents, it is usual to put in place interim access arrangements immediately following the breakdown of a relationship, whether by agreement or by court order.

Depending on the circumstances of the case, it may be necessary to seek supervision of access, for example, where there is a serious risk to the welfare of the dependent children, on account of the behaviour of one of their parents. Where there is a dispute with regard to access arrangements, the court may direct an assessment to be carried out by an appropriate child specialist pursuant to section 47, as outlined above. Such provision is not generally available in the context of non-marital children. Access to legal aid is limited and can result in difficulties in enforcement of access/contact arrangements.

14. INTERNATIONAL ABDUCTION

14.1 Summarise the position in your jurisdiction

With effect from 1 October 1991, the Child Abduction and Enforcement of Custody Orders Act 1991 incorporated both the Hague and Luxembourg Conventions on International Child Abduction into Irish law. The revised Brussels II Regulation also applies to the Republic of Ireland with regard to international child abduction. While the Convention continues to apply, the Regulation provides that its provisions take precedence in cases of abductions between member states. As with the Hague Convention, the Regulation aims to prevent parental child abduction between member states and, where such abduction takes place, establishes a system to ensure the prompt return of the child to their member state of habitual residence.

Child abduction cases in Ireland are heard in the High Court and legal aid is available to applicants in these cases. The Irish courts adopt a consistent approach and endeavour to return the child speedily to the country of habitual residence. Refusal to return is considered where a grave risk defence is mounted. The courts do not generally hear direct evidence from children in these proceedings, although child specialists and/or guardian *ad litems* may give evidence in certain circumstances. Again, there is no panel of child specialists available to the court in these cases.

Unmarried fathers who do not have any automatic rights of custody and guardianship are somewhat vulnerable in the Irish context. Recent case law held that the removal of a child in the absence of the consent of an unmarried father (who had not been appointed guardian) is not a wrongful removal as a breach of 'rights of custody' had not occurred. Another case found that where the unmarried father had applied to the courts for guardianship and/or access, the court itself has 'rights of custody'. See *CM v Delegacion de Malaga* [1999] 21R 363; *In re J (A Minor)* (Abduction) [1990] 2AC 562; *In re H* (Abduction: Custody Rights) [1991] 2AC 476; *R v R* [2006] IESC 7 and *AS v MS* (child abduction) [2008] IR 341; *A.BU v J.BE* [2010] IEHC 77; *AU v TNU* [2011] IESC 39 which refers to Baroness Hale's decision in *Re D (A Child)* (Abduction: Rights of Custody) [2007] IAC 619, 'there is now a growing understanding of the importance of listening to the children involved in children's cases'. Also see *MN and RN* [2008] IEHC 382 where Finlay Geoghegan J. states: *'A mandatory positive obligation is placed on a court by Article 11(2) to provide a child with an opportunity to be heard, subject only to the exception where this appears inappropriate having regard to his or her age or degree of maturity'.* (Follows *Re F* [2007] EWCA Civ 468). Also see *JMcB and LE* [2010] IEHC 123.

15. LEAVE TO REMOVE/APPLICATIONS TO TAKE A CHILD OUT OF THE JURISDICTION

15.1 Summarise the position in your jurisdiction

Where a parent applies to a court seeking liberty to relocate or remove a child/children to another jurisdiction, the court will determine the matter based on the best interests principle. The court will also consider the best interests of the child in a pragmatic sense having regard to a number of factors set out in the case law. The courts will generally require information on the arrangements which have been made in the proposed new location, with regard to accommodation, education and the availability of support networks.

Where the court grants leave to relocate, it will endeavour to ensure ongoing contact with the other parent. It is often envisaged that orders will be obtained in similar terms in the new jurisdiction depending on mechanisms available for enforcement.

15.2 Under what circumstances may a parent apply to remove their child from the jurisdiction against the wishes of the other parent?

There are an increasing number of cases in Ireland on this subject. At a minimum, very compelling reasons for relocation are required. Flood J sets out factors to which the court should have regard in a 'leave to remove' application. See *EM v AM* (High Court, 16 June 1992 (unreported). These include the following criteria:

'(1) *Which of the two hypothetical outcomes will provide the greater stability of lifestyle for the child.*
(2) *The contribution to such stability that will be provided by the environment in which the child will reside, with particular regard to the influence of his extended family.*
(3) *The professional advice tendered.*
(4) *The capacity for, and frequency of, access by the non-custodial parent.*
(5) *The past record of each parent, in their relationship with the child insofar as it impinged on the welfare of the child.*
(6) *The respect, in terms of the future of the parties, to orders and directions of this Court'.*

See also *GF v DC* (Circuit Court, McMahon J, 10 May 2007 (unreported)), *KB v LO'R* (High Court, Murphy J, 15 May 2009 (unreported)), *PC v PW* [2008] IEHC 469 and *UV v VU* [2011] IEHC 519 in which McMenamin J considers the criteria set out in *EM v AM* in addition to factors such as financial implications, the children's views, schooling, healthcare and an overall appraisal.

E. SURROGACY AND ADOPTION

16. VALIDITY OF SURROGACY AGREEMENTS

16.1 Briefly summarise the position in your jurisdiction

There is no legislation governing surrogacy in Ireland. Surrogacy agreements are unlikely to be valid in the Republic of Ireland. As a result, Irish couples desperately wanting to have children through surrogacy are driven overseas for fertility treatment. The Minster for Justice, on 21 February 2012, published a guidance document (see *www.justice.ie*) for Irish couples on surrogacy arrangements made abroad. The purpose of the guidance document is to provide information to prospective commissioning parents on the steps necessary to ensure that a child born abroad through a surrogacy arrangement may enter and reside in the state. It is intended to develop legislative proposals in the coming years for the purpose of comprehensively dealing with this complex area.

In a recent case before the High Court, the genetic parents on behalf of their two small children born to a surrogate mother sought to have their names listed as the children's parents on their birth certificates. Declarations were sought under the Status of Children Act, that their genetic mother is their legal mother and should be named as such on the birth certificate. The surrogate mother consented to the application. The Registrar General defended the action, stating that the policy in Ireland is that the name of the woman who gave birth to a child, and not the genetic mother, is the name placed on the child's birth certificate. In a decision handed down by the High Court on 5 March 2013, the genetic parents were successful in their application to have the biological (based on DNA testing) mother recognised as legal mother.

Unfortunately, this decision is likely to be appealed to the Supreme Court. It is submitted that the continued lack of a legislative framework for surrogacy arrangements creates unnecessary risk, uncertainty and costs for those involved.

17. ADOPTION

17.1 Briefly explain the legal position in relation to adoption in your jurisdiction. Is adoption available to individuals, cohabiting couples (both heterosexual and same-sex)?

Adoption is on a statutory basis pursuant to the provisions of the Adoption Act 2010. For eligibility, a child (between six weeks and 18 years) must be an orphan, 'illegitimate' (until Constitutional amendment is enacted) or abandoned. The father's consent is required in respect of a non-marital child. Reduced availability has increased demand for the adoption of overseas children.

The child must come within the jurisdiction of the courts and it must be demonstrated that the order, if granted, would be compatible with the principle of the 'welfare of the child as the first and paramount consideration'. Pursuant to section 3(1) of the Adoption Act 2010, the law now states that a 'parent', in relation to a child, 'means the mother or father or both of the child, whether or not they are married to each other'. Section 3(2) of the 2010 Act makes it clear that references to 'adopters'in that Act shall 'include references to an adopter'. As such adoption by a single applicant is now permitted and is for the first time provided for on a statutory basis. Adoption is not available to same-sex and/or cohabiting couples other than on a sole applicant basis. The prospective adopters are assessed by the Health Service Executive as to their eligibility and suitability. Statutory conditions relating to residence, marriage, religion and minimum age must be satisfied if adopters are to satisfy the eligibility criteria.

Neither Irish domicile or nationality is required. Other conditions relating to factors such as maximum age, quality of and lifestyle must also be met by the adopters.

F. COHABITATION

18. COHABITATION

18.1 What legislation (if any) governs division of property for unmarried couples on the breakdown of the relationship?

The Civil Partnership and Certain Rights and Obligations of Cohabitants Act 2010 (the 2010 Act) entered into force in Ireland on 1 January 2011. In addition to introducing civil partnership for same-sex couples, this legislation introduced a new statutory regime for cohabiting couples, whether same-sex or opposite sex, provided they are not married or civilly partnered to each other. The Act establishes a 'presumptive', 'redress' or 'safety net' scheme for certain cohabiting couples. The aim is to protect the economically dependent or vulnerable party at the end of a long-term cohabiting relationship, whether on relationship breakdown or death. 'Qualified' cohabitants can apply to court for certain financial relief, including property adjustment orders, compensatory maintenance orders, pension adjustment orders and other orders for provision from the estate of a deceased cohabitant. 'Qualified cohabitants' are defined as cohabitants residing together as an unmarried couple in an intimate relationship for a period of five years, or two years where there is a child or children of the relationship. The orders available to qualified cohabitants are not as extensive as those available to spouses and/or civil partners. The claiming partner must illustrate financial dependency and the court must have regard to the factors contained in the legislation which include the rights of other parties (such as any spouses or civil partners in existence), the duration of the relationship and the contributions made by each cohabitant, whether financial or otherwise. Section 201 of the Act provides for regulation of financial matters by written agreement between cohabitants thereby facilitating 'opt out' from the statutory regime. The Act provides that such an agreement will be valid and enforceable where it is in writing, signed by both cohabitants with the benefit of independent legal advice and where it accords with contract law.

G. FAMILY DISPUTE RESOLUTION

19. MEDIATION, COLLABORATIVE LAW & ARBITRATION

19.1 Briefly summarise the non-court-based process available in your jurisdiction and the current status of agreements reached under the auspices of mediation, collaborative law and arbitration

Prior to embarking on proceedings, there is a statutory obligation on solicitors to provide their clients with information and advice on the alternatives available to include counselling and mediation.

A number of family lawyers have trained as mediators and collaborative lawyers, and as such these services are now available to clients. A 'proposed agreement' reached through either the mediation process or the collaborative process is not legally binding and as such lawyers are usually instructed for the purposes of drafting consent terms or a deed of separation.

Arbitration is not generally used in family law disputes though this is an area that may develop in the coming years.

19.2 What is the statutory basis (if any), for mediation, collaborative law and arbitration in your jurisdiction? In particular, are the parties required to attempt a family dispute resolution in advance of the institution of proceedings?

At the current time, there is no statutory basis for either mediation or collaborative law. The draft General Scheme of The Mediation Bill 2012 is intended to introduce a definition of 'mediation' which accords with that contained in the EU Mediation Directive 2008/52/EC, that is, 'mediation' means a structured process, however named or referred to, whereby two or more parties to a dispute attempt by themselves, on a voluntary basis, to reach an agreement on the settlement of their dispute with the assistance of a mediator.

There is no concept of requiring the parties to attempt a family dispute resolution in advance of instituting proceedings, although in practice, most good family law solicitors would tend to seek resolution by agreement, in the first instance. This might take place in the form of mediation, collaborative practice or traditional negotiations at a neutral venue.

Solicitors are obliged to certify prior to issue of judicial separation or divorce proceedings, that they have advised and given their clients information on the alternatives available including counselling, mediation and negotiation of a deed of separation.

H. OTHER

20. CIVIL PARTNERSHIP/SAME-SEX MARRIAGE

20.1 What is the status of civil partnership/same-sex marriage within the jurisdiction?

Ireland does not recognise same-sex marriage, however, the Civil Partnership and Certain Rights and Obligations of Cohabitants Act 2010 (the 2010 Act) introduced civil partnership for same-sex couples and provides for extensive rights and obligations once a civil partnership has been registered.

20.2 What legislation governs civil partnership/same-sex marriage?

The 2010 Act governs civil partnership and also sets out the grounds on which civil partnership may be dissolved. As with marriage, civil partnership only ends on the death of one of the civil partners or on dissolution by the court. The Act makes provision for the formalities and procedures surrounding registration of civil partnership and legal effect is given to a range of rights and entitlements that flow from civil partnership. These include provision for maintenance, protection of the shared home, inheritance entitlements and pension provision. The Act also makes provision for the legal right share of the civil partner which are broadly similar to the provisions applicable to spouses. In addition, certain classes of foreign relationship are also recognised under the provisions of the Act on foot of further ministerial order.

No clear guidance is given on the manner in which children issues should be determined and the 2010 Act is silent on these matters.

21. CONTROVERSIAL AREAS/RAPIDLY DEVELOPING AREAS OF LAW

21.1 Is there a particular area of the law within the jurisdiction that is currently undergoing major change?

A recent constitutional referendum concerning children's rights, Thirty-First Amendment of the Constitution (Children) Bill 2012 was held on 10 November 2012.

While the proposal was approved by voters, the signing of the amendment into law has been delayed by a legal challenge brought in the High Court. The amendment seeks to reinforce the paramountcy principle, regardless of the marital status of a child's parents, thereby facilitating adoption of marital children in appropriate circumstances.

As outlined above, the recent introduction of the 2010 Act has effected very significant changes in the legal and social landscape in Ireland, for both civil partners and cohabiting couples. The Irish Law Reform Commission is also currently reviewing the area of rights and entitlements of unmarried fathers and with regard to families generally.

21.2 Which areas of law are most out of step? Which areas would you most like to see reformed/changed?

In the Report on Legal Aspects of Family Relationships (LRC CP55-2009), a more comprehensive and inclusive definition of the 'family' was urged, to take account of the changing reality of modern Irish society and family life. This includes reform concerning the rights and responsibilities of civil partners, step-parents, grandparents, co-habitants, and other members of the contemporary family in Ireland, taking into account the best interests and welfare of children. The Report also includes a draft Children and Parental Responsibility Bill, which would replace the Guardianship of Infants Act, 1964.

New terms 'parental responsibility'; 'day-to-day care' and 'contact' should replace the terms guardianship, custody and access currently used in the Guardianship of Infacts Act, 1964. This would remove the 'possessive' element present in the current terms and is more consistent with the terms used in many other states and in international instruments to which Ireland is a party.

Recent cases before the courts have also opened up the definitions of 'marriage' and 'family' for discussion. See *JMcD and PL and BM* [2009] IESC 81 in which a sperm donor unsuccessfully sought to be appointed as guardian (although as he was known to the parties he was granted access) of his child in circumstances where the child was being raised by a same-sex couple. The rights of the homosexual *de facto* family were considered in the context of the European Convention on Human Rights Act, 2003.

Lawyers and clients alike have recently called for the introduction of legislation with regard to pre-nuptial agreements. Many calls have also been made to legislate in the area of assisted reproductive technologies as there is currently no legislation in place to regulate the myriad legal, social and ethical issues which arise in this context. (See *Mary Roche & Ors v Thomas Roche, Sims Clinic Ltd & A.G.* [2009] IESC 10).

Furthermore, given the complex rules that apply in the recognition of foreign divorces, a simplification and clarification of these rules would be greatly welcomed.

At a consultative seminar organised by the Department of Justice on 6 July 2013, Minister for Justice, Alan Shatter, outlined his vision for a new structure for family courts. A dedicated and integrated family court structure is proposed which would consist of a lower family court of limited jurisdiction and a higher court of unlimited jurisdiction. Both courts would be staffed by specialist judges. A separate court of appeal would be established.

Finally, there are signs that a body of law is starting to develop surrounding the interaction of family law and social networking websites on the internet. Postings on these websites are becoming a feature of an increasing number of cases raising questions with regard to defamation, discovery, privacy and child protection. See *P v Q* [2012] IEHC 593 in which White J accepted the principle of Constitutional Law with regard to inadmissibility of evidence illegally obtained but states that this and rights of privacy have to be balanced against the welfare and interests of a child.

Extensive discovery orders were affirmed in respect of the wife's email and mobile phone accounts.

The discovery so ordered could not be used for the purpose of the financial proceedings but only in respect of matters pertaining to the welfare of the child.

Russia

Divorce in Russia Dr Catherine Kalaschnikova

A. JURISDICTION AND CONFLICT OF LAW
1. SOURCES OF LAW
1.1 What is the primary source of law in relation to the breakdown of marriage and the welfare of children within the jurisdiction?
1.2 What are the main statutes governing matrimonial law in the jurisdiction?

Russia is a civil law jurisdiction. Statutory law is the only source of law in this country. At the top of the hierarchy of laws is the Federal Constitution, followed in the order of precedence by federal legislation and legislation at the regional level, adopted in compliance with and subject to federal law. Family law is predominantly regulated by federal statutes, the most significant of them being:

- the Civil Code of Russia (1996)
- the Family Code of Russia (1996)
- the Federal Law on Acts of Civil Status (1997)
- the Federal Law on Guarantees of the Rights of the Child (1998)

Among the most recent acts of primary importance are: the Federal Law on the Fundamentals of Protection of Public Health in the Russian Federation (2011), the Federal Law on Custody and Guardianship (2008).

Common law and doctrine are not sources of law in Russia. Nevertheless, the Plenum of the Supreme Court of Russia[1] has adopted a number of important resolutions covering family law issues which provide important guidelines for subordinate courts and legal practitioners.

International treaties and conventions signed and ratified by Russia play a fundamental role in its legal system. Upon ratification they become an inherent part of it and prevail over national law in the event of a conflict of laws.[2]

2. JURISDICTION
2.1 What are the main jurisdictional requirements for the institution of proceedings in relation to divorce, property and children?
When parties are Russian nationals

Jurisdictional issues in family proceedings are governed by the Civil Procedure Code and the Family Code of Russia. Russian courts have jurisdiction in divorce, financial settlement, children and virtually all other family matters, where both parties to the proceedings are Russian citizens,

[1] The Supreme Court of Russia is the highest judicial body on civil (including family), criminal, administrative and other matters, within the jurisdiction
[2] Section 15 (4) of the Constitution of Russia, Section 6 of the Family Code

irrespective of their domicile, habitual residency or the location of their assets.

When either or both parties are not Russian nationals

Divorce

A marriage dissolution in Russia proceeds under the provisions of Russian law.[3]

Where one of the spouses is a foreign national or a stateless person, the Russian court will have jurisdiction in their matrimonial matter if:

- either husband or wife is resident in Russia[4];
- either husband or wife is a Russian national[5];
- the defendant has property in Russia[6].

Financial settlement

The Russian court has jurisdiction in financial settlement proceedings, where at least one of the spouses is a foreign national, and:

- the defendant is resident in Russia[7];
- or has property on its territory[8];
- it is a spousal support matter and the plaintiff is a Russian resident[9].

Financial rights and the obligations of spouses are governed by the law of the country where they have a common place of residence. If they don't have one, the law of the state where they last had a common place of residence applies. The rights and obligations of spouses who do not have a common country of residence are governed by Russian law in Russian divorce proceedings.[10]

Pre-nuptial and post-nuptial agreements

When two parties, who do not have citizenship or a place of residence in common, enter into a pre- or post-nuptial agreement, they may choose which country's law will apply to their agreement[11]. Further, they can choose the appropriate forum that will resolve all arguments between themselves should they arise out of the agreement in future. If no forum is chosen, a Russian court will hear the case if the claim arises out of a pre- or post-nuptial agreement, which is to be performed or part-performed on its territory.[12]

Children

Russian courts have jurisdiction in children matters involving foreign nationals where:

- the defendant parent has a place of residence in Russia[13];

[3] Section 160 (1) of the Family Code
[4] Section 402(2), (3) (8) of the Civil Procedure Code
[5] Section 402(3) (8) of the Civil Procedure Code
[6] Section 402 (3)(2) of the Civil Procedure Code
[7] Section 402 (2) of the Civil Procedure Code
[8] Section 402 (3)(2) of the Civil Procedure Code
[9] Section 402 (3)(3) of the Civil Procedure Code
[10] Section161 (1) of the Family Code
[11] Ibid
[12] Section 402 (6) of the Civil Procedure Code
[13] Section 402 (2) of the Civil Procedure Code

- the defendant parent has property in Russia[14];
- in child support and paternity matters the plaintiff is a Russian resident[15].

Parental rights and responsibilities are governed by the law of the state where the parents lived together. If they don't have a common place of residence, their rights and duties are determined by the law of the state of which the child is a national. In child support and other children's matters the court may apply the law of the state where the child is habitually resident, at the plaintiff's request.[16]

3. DOMICILE AND HABITUAL RESIDENCE

3.1 Explain the concepts of domicile and habitual residence as they apply to the jurisdiction in relation to divorce, the finances and children

While there is no concept of domicile or habitual residence in Russian law, the 'permanent residence' (often called 'place of residence') operates as the test to determine jurisdictional matters. The permanent residence means the place where a person primarily or permanently resides.[17] Rather than attachment to land in general, it is defined as 'a house, an apartment or any other dwelling where a person permanently or temporarily resides as an owner, tenant or on other legal basis'.[18]

It is mandatory for all Russian citizens residing in its territory to obtain a 'residency registration'. Even if they relocate and permanently reside overseas, as long as they maintain their 'registration', in the legal sense they are considered to be Russian residents.

As for foreign nationals, they cannot get a 'residency registration' on a permanent basis. Therefore, the court will determine the issue of whether they are permanent Russian residents for the purposes of matrimonial proceedings, by analogy with the tax legislation. The residency test to be applied in such cases is the continuity of the *de facto* presence of a person in Russian territory – 183 days or more in a year[19].

4. CONFLICT OF LAW/APPLICABLE LAW TO BE APPLIED

4.1 What happens when one party applies to stay proceedings in favour of a foreign jurisdiction? What factors will the local court take into account when determining forum issues?

There are no concepts of a 'more appropriate forum' or 'inappropriate forum' in Russian law. As long as the case falls within Russian jurisdiction, the court will hear the case.

Importantly, where there are similar proceedings pending in a court of a different jurisdiction between the same parties, with the same subject matter and grounds, or where a decision has already been granted in such a case, the Russian court will:

[14] Section 402 (3)(2) of the Civil Procedure Code
[15] Section 402 (3)(3) of the Civil Procedure Code
[16] Section 163 of the Family Code
[17] Section 20 (1) of the Civil Code of Russia
[18] Section 2 of the Freedom of Movement Act (1993)
[19] Section 207 of the Tax Code of Russia

- decline to accept the claim[20];
- dismiss the claim[21]; or
- discontinue the proceedings[22].

However, these rules only apply to those cases in which the decisions are capable of being recognised and enforced in Russia.[23] The decision will be recognised in two situations:

- the proceedings are pending in or have been granted by a court of a reciprocating jurisdiction; that is by a jurisdiction that has a treaty on mutual assistance in civil and family matters in force with Russia; it then is capable of enforcement; or
- the nature of the decision is such that it does not require any enforcement (section 409 of the); such as paternity, divorce, marriage and some others.

If analogous proceedings are pending in a court of a jurisdiction whose decision has no prospect of being recognised in Russia, or the decision has already been granted and has no force and effect in Russia, there is no impediment to a Russian court to finding competent to hear the case and granting a decision in it.

B. PRE- AND POST-NUPTIAL AGREEMENTS

5. VALIDITY OF PRE- AND POST-NUPTIAL AGREEMENTS

5.1 To what extent are pre- and post-nups binding within the jurisdiction? Could you provide a brief discussion of the most significant recent case law on this issue?

Pre-nuptial and post-nuptial agreements are two fairly similar legal instruments from the standpoint of Russian law. Both are governed by Chapter 8 of the Family Code, and both carry the name marital contract[24]. The only difference between the two is when they come into force. While a post-nuptial agreement is effective immediately upon its execution and notarial certification, a pre-nuptial agreement signed and certified only comes into force once the parties enter into a valid marriage.

A marital contract is an agreement that determines the financial rights and obligations of spouses (future spouses).[25] It may not regulate any matters apart from those of strictly financial character. Such issues as parenting, child support and spousal duties of a personal nature are beyond its scope. There are further limitations on the content of the contract. It may not restrict the legal capacity of a spouse, or contain any waivers of the right to challenge the contract in court or restrict the right of a disabled spouse to receive maintenance from the other.

The procedural formalities are minimal. The agreement does not need to be witnessed. Independent legal advice for the parties is not a prerequisite either. However, in order to be binding, the contract must be signed by both parties simultaneously in front of a notary.

[20] Section 134 (1)(2) of the Civil Procedure Code
[21] Section 135 (1)(5) of the Civil Procedure Code
[22] Section 220 of the Civil Procedure Code
[23] Section 409 of the Civil Procedure Code
[24] Hereinafter both types of agreement will be called 'marital contract'
[25] Section 40 of the Family Code

In the 17 years of its existence in Russian legal practice, the marital contract has proved to be a fairly robust legal instrument. Courts are quite reluctant to render them void. Grounds for declaring a marital contract void, outlined in the Civil Code, are common to all types of contracts. These include non-compliance with the formal requirements of the contracts, fraud, mistake, misrepresentation, lack of capacity, duress. An additional ground for a challenge is spelt out by Section 44 of the Family Code: a marital contract is voidable if it puts one party in an extremely unfavourable position.

An extremely unfavourable position is an evaluative term which essentially means that one of the spouses is put in a position where their financial rights are significantly compromised and impaired by the terms of the contract; it anticipates an unjust and unfair contract. By way of illustration, a contract under the terms of which all of the spousal assets acquired during marriage or their vast majority go to one spouse; or a contract leaving a spouse without the means to support himself or herself, is likely to be found extremely unfavourable to a spouse.

The stability of a marital contract is additionally secured by the relatively short limitation periods prescribed for challenging it. The limitation period for claims with respect to voidable marital contracts is only one year,[26] and three years in relation to contracts that are void.[27]

C. DIVORCE, NULLITY AND JUDICIAL SEPARATION

6. RECOGNITION OF FOREIGN MARRIAGES/DIVORCES

6.1 Summarise the position in your jurisdiction

Foreign marriages are recognised in Russia provided they are entered into in compliance with the requirements of the law of the respective foreign jurisdiction and do not offend the principle conditions for marriage solemnization, outlined in Section 14 of the Family Code[28]. What are those principles? A marriage cannot be entered into if:

- either party is already married;
- the parties are closely related (ie, relatives in the line directly ascending or descending such as parents and children, grandfather, grandmother and grandchildren; marriages between brothers and sisters, as well as half-brothers and half-sisters, adopted children and their parents); or
- either party is mentally disabled at the time of entering into a marriage.

Further bars to marriage are set out in various other sections of the Family Code. Thus, a valid marriage is a union of a man or a woman, both of whom should be of a marriageable age of at least 18 years (or 16 years in exceptional cases). A marriage solemnised in church does not have validity, either.

However, a same-sex marriage, or a church marriage, or a marriage of spouses under 18 may be perfectly legal in other jurisdictions. Strictly speaking, these further restrictions are not the principles set out by Section 14 of the Family Code. Does this mean that these marriages will be afforded

[26] Section 181 (2) of the Civil Procedure Code
[27] Ibid
[28] Section 158 of the Family Code

legal recognition in Russia? There is no certainty in this, as there is no answer in law, leaving this matter to the discretion of judges in particular cases.

Divorce orders granted by foreign courts are deemed to be valid if neither party objects to them[29]. There is no requirement to register a foreign divorce order with the authorities or any need to go through any court proceedings in order to give the foreign decree force and effect.

7. DIVORCE

7.1 Explain the grounds for divorce within the jurisdiction (please also deal with nullity and judicial separation if appropriate)

Divorce

There are two mechanisms by which a marriage may be terminated in Russia: judicial and administrative.

Where there are no minor children to the marriage and both parties consent to the divorce, the administrative procedure applies.[30] The administrative procedure is also prescribed where one of the spouses is declared missing or legally incompetent by the court or is sentenced to more than three years of imprisonment.[31] Consenting parties must file their joint divorce petition with the Civil Acts Registration Office. The marriage is terminated one month after the submission, if neither has withdrawn their consent since. Russian consulate and diplomatic offices are competent to register divorces of the Russian citizens abroad.[32]

Those couples who have minor children or where one of the spouses contests the divorce[33], have to apply to court for a divorce order. If one of the spouses, despite having no objections to the divorce, is unwilling or unable to attend the Civil Acts Registration Office to lodge a joint divorce petition, the court is the appropriate venue for marriage termination, as well.

The sole ground for divorce is the irretrievable breakdown of a marriage.[34] No separation period is required to establish the breakdown. In essence, the wish to end the marriage as expressed in a divorce petition by one of the spouses is sufficient.

Where one of the spouses contests the divorce, a court may adjourn the final hearing for no longer than three months. If the parties fail to reconcile, and at least one of them insists on the divorce, the court has no discretion to dismiss thc claim.

Nullity

The court may find a marriage void on the following grounds:

- if it was entered into involuntarily;
- if either party was not of marriageable age;
- if either party was married at the date of the marriage;
- where spouses are closely related (ie, relatives in the line directly

[29] Section 409 of the Civil Procedure Code
[30] Section 19 the Family Code
[31] Ibid
[32] Section 160 (2) of the Family Code
[33] Section 21 of the Family Code
[34] Section 22 of the Family Code

ascending or descending such as parents and children, grandfather, grandmother and grandchildren; marriages between brothers and sisters, as well as half-brothers and half-sisters, adopted children and their parents);
- where either party was mentally disabled at the time of entering into a marriage;
- if one of the spouses concealed the fact that they were infected with a venereal disease or HIV;[35]
- if the marriage was fictitious (registered without an intent to make a family).[36]

However, in some cases, where the ground no longer exists at the date of the hearing, court may dismiss a claim for nullity.

A void marriage entails no legal consequences.[37] A pre- or post-nuptial agreement between the parties to a void marriage is also a nullity. Therefore, a financial agreement between spouses or spouses-to-be may not anticipate and provide for the event of the marriage being annulled.

8. FINANCES/CAPITAL, PROPERTY

8.1 What powers does the court have to allocate financial resources and property on the breakdown of marriage?

8.2 Explain and illustrate with reference to recent cases the court's thinking on division of assets

Division of assets

Russia, being an inquisitorial law jurisdiction, widely empowers courts to gather evidence themselves as well as to assist parties to financial settlement proceedings in the discovery process.

What financial resources form the spousal asset pool? Their income, such as employee's remuneration, pension, social security benefits, as well as movable and immovable property purchased with the couple's joint funds, are considered to be owned jointly by both spouses.[38] These can only comprise assets held under the spouses' names[39], whether this is real property, shares in companies, bank accounts or anything else. Assets owned by third parties are excluded. Thus, property in trust or owned by legal entities of which one or both spouses are shareholders will not be included regardless of how much control either or both parties exercise over the respective companies or trusts and whether they are their beneficiaries.

What doesn't fall into the spousal assets pool category? Property acquired by one of the spouses prior to the marriage, or received during the course of the marriage as a gift, inheritance or through other gratuitous deals[40].

Another area of concern in property settlement cases are spousal assets located abroad. Russian courts are generally reluctant to take them into consideration in property settlement proceedings, despite there being no explicit prohibitions in this respect in legislation. This is partly due to the

[35] Section 15(3) of the Family Code
[36] Section 28 of the Family Code
[37] Section 30 of the Family Code
[38] Section 34 of the Family Code
[39] Section 34 of the Family Code
[40] Section 36 of the Family Code

fact that the inclusion of such assets in property settlement cases inevitably complicates proceedings, and does not promote the objective of a quick and inexpensive resolution of the case. Conversely, it often connotes significant delays in case hearings.

Another reason for this is that gathering this information is an exceptionally difficult task from a practical standpoint. A subpoena issued by Russian authorities to a foreign bank, a company or any other organisation, will more often than not remain unanswered, partly due to the fact that Russia has reciprocal international agreements on legal assistance in civil and family cases with very few countries. Those are mainly the former Soviet republics and former satellite states of the USSR. Therefore, the accessibility of information about foreign property is substantially limited, which makes discharging the burden of proof of the existence of foreign assets even more onerous.

A financial settlement can generally be reached during the marriage as well as within three years after its termination.

The husband's and wife's shares in joint property are presumed to be equal. A court can increase or decrease spousal shares in exceptional circumstances, for instance, when one of the spouses did not receive any income during the marriage for no valid reason or when they wasted joint property, thus acting against the interests of the family.[41]

9. FINANCES/MAINTENANCE

9.1 Explain the operation of maintenance for spouses on an ongoing basis after the breakdown of marriage

9.2 Is it common for maintenance to be awarded?

9.3 Explain and illustrate with reference to recent cases the court's thinking on maintenance

Spousal maintenance awards appear to be rare in the Russian legal reality. Despite the fact that the Family Code prescribes the duty of spouses to support each other financially, the grounds upon which a judge may impose this duty on a husband or a wife are very limited. When does such an entitlement exist? Is a spouse or a former spouse entitled to maintenance?

(a) When a spouse is disabled or has reached pension age and has insufficient means to meet the costs of living (the disability must occur during the marriage or within one year of its termination; pension age must be reached within five years)[42]; or

(b) When the wife is pregnant or has care of a child of the marriage under the age of three;

(c) When a spouse has care of a disabled child of the marriage and that spouse has insufficient means to meet the cost of living.

However, even then a spouse whose income is equal to or more than the living wage,[43] is likely to have their case dismissed, as they no longer formally fall into the category of those having insufficient means to meet the cost of living. Despite there being a big gap between the two. The law is not concerned with ensuring that former spouses maintain the same

[41] Section 39 of the Family Code
[42] Sections 89-90 of the Family Code
[43] Established by the Federal Government of Russia

standard of living, but is merely concerned with ensuring basic needs are met. Hence, as a rule, the level of spousal maintenance does not represent large amounts of financial support.

A court may dismiss a maintenance claim or limit the duration of spousal support when the marriage was short lived or the party claiming financial support on the grounds of being disabled as a result of alcohol or drug abuse or their own criminal activity. Another ground for dismissal of a spousal maintenance claim is the spouse's misconduct during marriage.

10. CHILD MAINTENANCE

10.1 On what basis is child maintenance calculated within the jurisdiction?

The parents of a minor child may enter into an agreement governing the issues of child support (the Child Support Agreement) or resolve it through court, if they are unable to achieve a compromise.

In the absence of an agreement the minimum amount of child support is set out by law at the rate of one quarter of a parent's income for one child, one third of the parent's income for two and one half of the parent's income for three or more children[44]. These rates may be increased or decreased by a court depending on the financial and family circumstances of the parties and other relevant conditions, although this is unusual.

Reaching agreement provides a slightly higher degree of flexibility to the parties: it allows the amount of the agreement to be fixed as a monetary equivalent rather than a share of income. Further, the parties may agree to a lump sum payment of the whole amount due, or to the transfer of real or other property in lieu of child support under the terms of such an instrument. However, a child support agreement may not set the amount of child support at a lesser rate than the minimum amount prescribed by Section 81 of the Family Code[45].

11. RECIPROCAL ENFORCEMENT OF FINANCIAL ORDERS

11.1 Summarise the position in your jurisdiction

The enforcement of foreign financial court orders may prove to be problematic in Russia.

A judicial decision granted by a court of a foreign jurisdiction, where it is not voluntarily observed by the parties, and, therefore, requires enforcement, will be recognised by Russian authorities if, and only if, it was granted by a court of a reciprocating jurisdiction; that is by a jurisdiction that has a treaty on mutual assistance in civil and family matters in force between Russia and the relevant state.[46] There are only a few countries Russia has relevant agreements with. Thus, for example, a US or a UK financial court order, as well as the judicial decisions of a large number of other countries, will have no force and effect on Russian territory.

What avenues does a husband or a wife have if the other spouse does not voluntarily comply with foreign court orders in Russia? The only means

[44] Section 81 of the Family Code
[45] See above
[46] Section 409 of the Civil Procedure Code

available to them will be instituting financial settlement proceedings in a competent Russian court. The decision of a court of another jurisdiction will not impede the Russian proceedings or indeed affect them at all. The case will be heard anew.

It is important to note that Russia has exclusive jurisdiction in relation to the real property located on its territory. Therefore, no foreign court orders in respect of Russian real assets will be recognised or given effect to.

12. FINANCIAL RELIEF AFTER FOREIGN DIVORCE PROCEEDINGS

12.1 What powers are available to make orders following a foreign divorce?

If the parties were divorced in another jurisdiction, this fact in itself does not preclude Russian courts from dealing with outstanding financial issues between the ex-spouses. In fact, nothing prevents either of them from applying to a Russian court for financial relief, as long as the Russian court has jurisdiction to hear the case. No special leave is required to commence financial proceedings.

D. CHILDREN

13. CUSTODY/PARENTAL RESPONSIBILITY

There is a presumption of equal parental responsibility. It essentially means that parents have equal rights and equal responsibilities with respect to their children under the age of 18.[47] They have a right and a duty to bring up their children. They are responsible for their children's health, physical, psychological and ethical development.[48]

Parents have the primary right to bring up their children.[49] This means that the courts automatically consider the parents' rights to be superior to anyone else's, unless the parents are proven unfit or abandon the child.

Parents are their children's legal representatives in all organisations and courts by the operation of law. Moreover, it is their duty to defend their children's rights[50].

The presumption of equal parental responsibility is so strong that it is seldom the subject of a challenge and court determination, unless one of the parents files a claim to restrict the parental rights of the other on the grounds that contact with that parent would expose the child to a risk of violence or abuse.

13.1 Briefly explain the legal position in relation to custody/parental responsibility following the breakdown of a relationship or marriage

13.2 Briefly explain the legal position in relation to access/contact/visitation following the breakdown of a relationship or marriage

Parents residing separately from each other may sign a written agreement settling the child custody and contact matters between them[51]).

[47] Section 61 of the Family Code
[48] Section 63 Family Code
[49] Section 63 Family Code
[50] Section 64 Family Code
[51] Section 66 Family Code

If the parents cannot come to an amicable solution and there is a dispute as to who the child should live with, it is within the competence of a court to make the final decision on the application of either parent. A parent living separately from their child has a right to communicate with him or her and participate in his or her upbringing and in decision making about the child's education.[52]

The parent with whom the child primarily resides has a corresponding duty to refrain from hindering such communication, unless such contact causes physical or psychological harm to the child or impedes the child's moral development.[53]

The parent residing separately from his or her child has a right to receive information about the child from educational, medical, social institutions and all other organisations. The provision of information about the child can only be denied if there is a threat to the child's health or life.

In resolving parental disputes and determining what the best interests of the child are in a particular set of circumstances the court takes into consideration the factors spelt out in Section 65 of the Family Code, namely:

- the attachment of a child to each parent and to any siblings;
- the child's age;
- moral and other qualities of the parents;
- their relationship with the child;
- their capacity to provide for the needs of the child, considering their occupation, financial and family circumstances.

Parents' rights are not affected by factors such as their nationality or country of origin or permanent/ habitual residency. However, if the parents reside in different countries, this will inevitably affect the pattern of their contact with the child due to the cost and time involved in international travel for the parent.

Importantly, there is no principle that the presumption of equal responsibility further provides that children have a right to spend meaningful time with both parents. Therefore, a court would normally appoint a primary carer, who the child will reside with, while allocating certain time for the other parent to have contact with the child.

Typically, primary care will be granted to the mother, unless there is evidence that she is unfit to fulfil that role. The father would be allowed to have the child for one or two days during the weekend every fortnight and spend a few weeks with the child during school holidays.

Where cases concern a parent residing abroad, the court would grant him or her a right to visit the child once or twice a year, depending on the parent's capacity to travel to Russia to see the child. It is not uncommon that overseas trips for a child with a parent residing abroad will be restricted by the court on the other parent's application. This is due to the fact that there is a general judicial view that the child may be abducted by a parent residing abroad, while the other parent will have no means or capacity to travel overseas and/or be adequately represented in foreign parenting proceedings.

[52] Section 66 (1) Family Code
[53] Section 66 (2) Family Code

14. INTERNATIONAL ABDUCTION

14.1 Summarise the position in your jurisdiction

Russia is a relatively new party to the Hague Convention on International Child Abduction, and the mechanisms for making the provisions of that Convention work to assist parents left behind are still in the making.

It is a criminal offence punishable by imprisonment of up to 10 years to abduct a minor.[54] However, in practice, parents or close relatives of a child are never charged with the offence if they acted out of falsely interpreted best interests of the child, even where the abduction was in breach of a child custody court order, or the removal resulted in the second parent losing all contact with the child.

15. LEAVE TO REMOVE/APPLICATIONS TO TAKE A CHILD OUT OF THE JURISDICTION

15.1 Summarise the position in your jurisdiction

Under the provisions of Russian law, a second parent's consent to remove a child from Russia is not required. The most typical case, where a court has to deal with a relocation claim, is when a primary carer intends to permanently leave the country and can't get the second parent's permission for their child to relocate for visa purposes.

A court order to leave the country is also required where a child has been placed on a border control watch list on the application of a parent.[55]

Courts are given wide discretion to decide whether to restrict or allow such leave in a given set of circumstances. There is no legal criteria that would form a basis for such decision apart from the general propositions on the child's rights contained in national statutory law, such as the Right of Citizens of the Russian Federation to Freedom of Movement Act (1993) or international treaties signed by Russia (the International Convention on the Rights of a Child, and others). The courts face a problematic task when they have to try to accommodate the interests of the moving parent and main custodian on the one hand, and the interests of the parent remaining in Russia to maintain quality contact with their child, on the other. The moving parent has to prove a good cause for the relocation (whether it is a job offer or marriage or other circumstances), that good care will be taken of the child, that they will be able to continue their education, be provided with suitable accommodation and will be able to maintain communication with the second parent. If the court is satisfied that it is in the best interests of the child to move, it will grant permission for the child to leave the country.

E. SURROGACY & ADOPTION

16. VALIDITY OF SURROGACY AGREEMENTS

16.1 Briefly summarise the position in your jurisdiction

The Federal Act On Fundamentals of Protection of Public Health in the Russian Federation[56] came into force on 1 January 2012. Together with the Family Code and subordinate acts it provided the legal basis for commercial

[54] Section 126 of the Criminal Code of Russia

[55] Section 21 of the Federal Law on the *Procedure* for *Exiting* and *Entering* the *Russian Federation* (1996)

[56] Hereinafter 'the Health Act'

surrogacy in Russia for the first time. The Act defines surrogacy as carrying and giving birth to a child under the terms of a contract between the surrogate mother and potential parents, the donors of the egg and sperm for the embryo; or between a surrogate mother and a single woman, who is unable to carry and give birth to a child for health reasons.[57]

A surrogate mother must be a woman between 25 and 35 years who:

- has given birth to at least one child of her own;
- has received a satisfactory medical report;
- given written informed consent for the medical reproductive treatment.

A married woman can only become a surrogate mother with the written consent of her husband. She must not use her egg in the surrogacy arrangement.[58]

A married couple who consent to implant an embryo in another woman can be registered as the parents of the child only with the surrogate mother's consent.[59] Neither the commissioning parents nor the surrogate mother may challenge the paternity or maternity of the child on the grounds of his birth being a result of a surrogacy arrangement.[60]

Thus, this form of assisted reproductive treatment is now permitted by federal legislation, including commercial surrogacy.

17. ADOPTION

17.1 Briefly summarise the position in relation to adoption in your jurisdiction. Is adoption available to individuals, cohabiting couples (both heterosexual and same-sex)?

The adoption process is governed by Sections 124-165 of the Family Code, Chapter 29 of the Civil Procedure Code and the Federal Act On the State Database of Parentless Children (2001) as well as other regulatory legal acts.

A prospective parent can apply for information on children available for adoption to a regional or federal operator of the Parentless Children Databank. The parents visit the child and inform the operator of the results of their visit and their decision. The applicants have a right to obtain information about the child and his relatives; and to have an independent medical assessment of the child.

Adoption applications are generally heard by local courts. However, adoption by foreign nationals and Russian citizens permanently residing abroad are within the jurisdiction of the Supreme Court of the respective federal territory of Russia.[61]

Candidates for adoption must provide the court with the following documents in support of their application:

- a copy of their birth certificate (if the child is adopted by an unmarried person);
- a copy of the marriage certificate (if adoption is undertaken by married person(s));

[57] Section 55 (9) of the Health Act
[58] Section 55(10) of the Health Act
[59] Section 51 of the Family Code , Section 16 Federal Law on Acts of Civil Status
[60] Section 52 (3) of the Family Code
[61] Section 269 of the Civil Code

- the spouse's consent to adoption, or a document confirming their separation for at least 12 months (if the child is adopted by only one of the spouses);
- a medical certificate;
- documents confirming sufficient income of the prospective parent;
- documents confirming the applicant's appropriate accommodation;
- a certificate that the applicant is registered as a prospective parent.62

Who can adopt? The applicant must be at least 16 years older than the child to be adopted. Adoption may be refused if the applicant's parental rights were revoked in the past, if they have a criminal conviction for an intentional crime and on other grounds set out by Section 127 of the Family Code.

Adoption may be denied for medical reasons, such as:

- tuberculosis;
- substance abuse;
- infectious diseases (until it is recovered from);
- certain types of mental disorders;
- some other health disorders of the prospective parents.

Child adoption applications are considered in a closed hearing, which the candidates for adoption must attend. Children aged between 10 and 14 may be present. Participation of children over the age of 14 is mandatory.[63] The court grants an order for adoption if it finds the candidates to be fit and financially secure to provide for the needs of the child.

The adoptive parent may give a new name to the child, as well as to change the date and place of the adopted child's birth.[64] The child's consent for that is required if the child is 10 years or older.

When a child, who is a Russian citizen, is adopted by foreign citizens, he or she retains their Russian citizenship.

Adoption by unmarried or same-sex couples is not provided for by Russian law.[65]

F. COHABITATION

18. COHABITATION

18.1 What legislation (if any) governs division of property for unmarried couples on the breakdown of the relationship?

Pursuant to Section 1 (2) of the Family Code, a marriage comes into existence only when it is registered by the Civil Acts Registration Office. No other forms of cohabitation or families entail any legal consequences, irrespective of their length, the existence of children or any other circumstances.

Consequently, the separate legal regime applies to property of a non-married couple. In essence, the assets remain the sole individual property of the partner in whose name they are held, and the second partner does not acquire any property or equitable rights towards those assets, and has

[62] Section 271 of the Civil Procedure Code
[63] Section 273 of the Civil Code
[64] Section 134, 134 of the Family Code
[65] Section 127 of the Family Code

no claim to them. From the standpoint of Russian law, the relationship simply does not exist. Since there is no unity of property, the issue of the financial agreement between parties to such a relationship becomes irrelevant.

G. FAMILY DISPUTE RESOLUTION

19. MEDIATION, COLLABORATIVE LAW AND ARBITRATION

19.1 Briefly summarise the non-court-based processes available in your jurisdiction and the current status of agreements reached under the auspices of mediation, collaborative law and arbitration

19.2 What is the statutory basis (if any), for mediation, collaborative law and arbitration in your jurisdiction? In particular, are the parties required to attempt a family dispute resolution in advance of proceedings?

The first use of mediation in Russian legal history dates back to the 19th century, when it was mainly employed for industrial and trade disputes. However, during the Soviet era and later on it was pretty much forgotten.

This is why the recently adopted Federal Act On the Alternative Procedure of Dispute Resolution with the Participation of a Mediator (Mediation Procedure) [66] is greatly significant; and anticipates the introduction of mediation mechanisms in Family Law as well as other areas of law, traditionally associated with using this practice. The Act came into force on 1 January 2011.

For the first time in Russian legal history it defined the procedure of mediation, who can be a mediator and what the requirements of a mediation agreement are.[67]

Mediators are independent individuals engaged by the parties as intermediaries in dispute resolution with the objective of assisting them to reach a decision on the merits of the dispute.

The agreement to use the mediation procedure must be executed in writing. So must the agreement reached by the parties as a result of mediation in relation to their dispute, ie, the mediated agreement.

The principles of the mediation procedure are:

- mutual will of the parties;
- its voluntariness;
- confidentiality;
- cooperation;
- equal rights of the parties;
- impartiality and independence of the mediator.[68]

There is no requirement to attempt family dispute resolution in advance of the institution of judicial proceedings. However, the general rule states that if the parties have entered into an agreement to use the mediation procedure, then for the duration of the period allocated by the parties for the mediation procedure, neither of them may initiate court proceedings in respect of the dispute.[69]

[66] Hereinafter 'the Mediation Act'
[67] Section 2 of the Mediation Act
[68] Section 3 of the Mediation Act
[69] Section 4 of the Mediation Act

The parties may apply for the mediation procedure at any stage of court proceedings. The adjournment of the judicial proceedings in such an event is further regulated by the procedural legislation.

Information concerning mediation is privileged, and may not be sought from a mediator or the organisation that provided the mediation services, subject to exceptions set out in federal laws, and in cases where the parties have waived confidentiality.[70]

The mediated agreement can be further documented as a consent order by the relevant court, if the parties consider it appropriate.[71] The mediated agreement (other than where its terms are spelled out by court orders) has the force and effect of a contract, the breach of which may be remedied by the means provided by civil legislation.

H. OTHER

20. CIVIL PARTNERSHIP/SAME-SEX MARRIAGE

20.1 What is the status of civil partnership/same-sex marriage within the jurisdiction?

20.2 What legislation governs civil partnership/same-sex marriage?

Russian law does not provide for same-sex marriage or civil partnership. Marriage is traditionally understood and interpreted by courts as the union between a woman and a man. Therefore, *de facto* relationships, including same-sex couples relationships are not legally recognised. There is no such legal concept as cohabitation itself in Russian law.

21. CONTROVERSIAL AREAS/RAPIDLY DEVELOPING AREAS OF LAW

21.1 Is there a particular area of the law within the jurisdiction that is currently undergoing major change?

21.2 Which areas of law are most out of step and which areas would you most like to see reformed/changed?

Despite the inclusion of international treaties and conventions ratified by Russia into its national system of law, and their recognition as a source of law of superior power, the approach of the Russian legislator to the regulation of family legal issues remains archaic in some respects and significantly out of step with today's reality.

The non-recognition of *de facto* relationships is one of the examples. Cohabitation has become a mainstream family arrangement. Indeed, the practical difference between a married and a *de facto* couple is often hard to see these days. It is important for the law to reflect the change rather than impede it without any obvious reason. It is important to bring national law in line with international standards allowing *de facto* couples to arrange their financial, parental and other matters on an equal basis with married couples.

With the rapid expansion of global migration and international relationships, the issue of adjusting Russian law so as to provide adequate protection for the children of such relationships, as well as spousal rights, including those in the financial spectrum, has become essential.

[70] Section (4) of the Mediation Act
[71] Section 12 of the Mediation Act

An important step has been made by Russia in this direction by joining the Hague Convention on the Civil Aspects of International Child Abduction (1980). However, the development of a working mechanism allowing the Convention to be effectively implemented in Russia has yet to be seen.

It is important for Russia to continue building diplomatic relationships in the international arena with a focus on furtherance of international legal co-operation with other states and assistance in civil and family cases.

Family law is a traditionally inert sphere of Russian Law. This is why it is particularly inspiring that, in the course of the last three years, there has been remarkable progress in applying the international experience in the matrimonial area of law so as to bring national law in line with international standards. Let us hope it is the start of a new positive tendency.

Scotland

Turcan Connell Alasdair Loudon

A. JURISDICTION AND CONFLICT OF LAW

1. SOURCES OF LAW

1.1 What is the primary source of law in relation to the breakdown of marriage and the welfare of children within the jurisdiction?

Child and family law in Scotland are rooted in common law but legislation is so far reaching that there are effectively two sources of law: legislation passed by the Scottish Executive, the UK government and the EU; and case law as applied by the courts.

1.2 What are the main statutes governing matrimonial law in the jurisdiction?

There are a number of UK, Scottish and EU statutes currently governing matrimonial law in Scotland, which are as follows:

- Domicile and Matrimonial Proceedings Act 1973 (the 1973 Act);
- Divorce (Scotland) Act 1976 (the 1976 Act);
- Matrimonial Homes (Family Protection)(Scotland) Act 1981 (the 1981 Act);
- Family Law (Scotland) Act 1985 (the 1985 Act);
- Family Law Act 1986 (the 1986 Act);
- Children (Scotland) Act 1995 (the 1995 Act);
- Council Regulation (EC) No 2201/2003 (Brussels II bis);
- Family Law (Scotland) Act 2006 (the 2006 Act).

2. JURISDICTION

2.1 What are the main jurisdictional requirements for the institution of proceedings in relation to divorce, property and children?

In divorce actions, Scotland has jurisdiction when it is the place where one of the following applies at the date of commencement of proceedings:

- the spouses are habitually resident;
- the spouses were last habitually resident if one still resides there;
- the defender is habitually resident;
- the pursuer is habitually resident as long as he/she has resided there for at least one year before the application was made;
- the pursuer is habitually resident as long as he/she has resided there for at least six months and is domiciled there; or
- both spouses are domiciled.

In the UK, 'habitual residence' relates to the relevant territorial unit, for example, Scotland (Article 66 Brussels II bis). Scotland is not itself a member state of the European Union. It is a territorial unit. Where Scotland has jurisdiction, proceedings can be brought in either the Court of Session (the Supreme Civil Court in Scotland) or in the local Sheriff Court (provided that the jurisdictional requirements for the Sheriff Court can be met). If no court of a member state has jurisdiction under the above provisions, where either party is domiciled in Scotland when the action is commenced or was habitually resident in Scotland throughout the period of one year, ending with that date, the Court of Session has residual jurisdiction (Article 14, Brussels II bis and section 7, 1973 Act).

A divorce action can only be heard in the Sheriff Court where jurisdiction can be established for the Court of Session and either one of the parties has been resident in the Sheriffdom for 40 days, ending with the date when the divorce action is begun, or has been resident for a period of not less than 40 days, ending not more than 40 days before the action was begun, where that party has no known residence in Scotland (section 8(3), 1973 Act).

In relation to property, a court hearing a divorce action can make orders in relation to the matrimonial property wherever it is situated and there is, therefore, no separate jurisdictional requirement. Outside divorce proceedings, jurisdiction is based on where the property is situated.

In relation to children, jurisdiction regarding parental responsibilities and rights is conferred by Brussels II bis. Note that it does not apply to the establishment of or contesting of the parent/child relationship or naming a child and the 1986 Act governs these situations.

If the child is habitually resident in Scotland at the time the court is seised, the Scottish courts will have jurisdiction (Article 8). There are specific provisions under Brussels II bis which deal with the situation where a child is wrongfully removed from a member state.

Where a Scottish court is exercising jurisdiction in divorce proceedings, the parties can agree that that court will have jurisdiction in respect of the child providing at least one of them has parental responsibilities and the court believes that the exercise of jurisdiction is in the best interests of the child (Article 12). Where no habitual residence can be established and jurisdiction cannot be founded under Article 12, the courts of the member state in which the child is present shall have jurisdiction (Article 13(1)).

If no member state has jurisdiction under Brussels II bis, national law will determine whether Scotland has jurisdiction (Article 14). Domestically, Scotland has jurisdiction if the child is habitually resident there (section 9, 1986 Act). The Court of Session and the Sheriff Court have jurisdiction to make orders relating to parental responsibilities and rights, including within the context of divorce proceedings.

3. DOMICILE AND HABITUAL RESIDENCE

3.1 Explain the concepts of domicile and habitual residence as they apply to the jurisdiction in relation to divorce, the finances and children

Domicile has been stated to be determined from 'a man fixing voluntarily his sole or chief residence in a particular place, with an intention of continuing to reside there for an unlimited time' (*Udny v Udny* (1869) 7 M. (HL 89 at 99).

Habitual residence is not defined by statute either domestically or in a European context but is a question of fact. Domestically, it has been held to be residence 'which is being enjoyed voluntarily for the time being and with the settled intention that it should continue for some time' (*Dickson v Dickson* 1990 SCLR 692, IH at p703). The particular circumstances of each case must be examined and it is to be understood according 'to the ordinary and natural meaning' of the two words (*Re J (a minor) (abduction)* 1990 2 AC 562 at 578).

In relation to the 40-day rule in sheriff court actions, residence has been held to be where a person resides, ie, his ordinary or principal place of residence. Although it does not require the person to be physically based there at all times, the 'nature and quality' of physical presence is a factor to be taken into account (*Williamson v Williamson* 2009 FamLR 44 and 153).

In the context of habitual residence, residence is where the person resides or lives, a person's abode or dwelling (Clive 1997 JR 137 at 139). Thus, physical presence is required but it need not be uninterrupted, which seems to be in line with the test for sheriff court actions. The residence will be habitual if there is an intention to reside there for an appreciable period (*Cameron v Cameron* 1996 SLT 306 at 313).

In cases where Brussels II bis applies, the ECJ has defined habitual residence as being 'the place where the person has established, on a fixed basis, his permanent or habitual centre of his interest, with all the relevant facts being taken into account for the purpose of determining such residence'. It has further held that, in relation to children, physical presence is required but is not the only factor and that the child must be, in some way, integrated in a social and family environment in that country (proceedings brought by A (Case C-523/07), 2nd April 2009).

4. CONFLICT OF LAW/APPLICABLE LAW TO BE APPLIED

4.1 What happens when one party applies to stay proceedings in favour of a foreign jurisdiction? What factors will the local court take into account when determining forum issues?

In Brussels II bis cases, a court of a member state must decline the case where it has no ground of jurisdiction and another member state does (Article 17). Where proceedings have been brought before two member states which both have jurisdiction, the court second seised must stay its proceedings until the jurisdiction of the court first seised is established and, if that jurisdiction is established, the second seised court must decline jurisdiction (Article 19 Brussels II bis).

Within the United Kingdom, in cases of divorce, separation, declarator of marriage or nullity (consistorial actions), the 1973 Act provides for mandatory and discretionary sists (schedule 3, paragraphs 8 and 9). Where, prior to the proof in a divorce action, proceedings for divorce or nullity are continuing in a 'related jurisdiction' (England, Wales, Northern Ireland, Guernsey, Jersey or the Isle of Man), then Scottish court in certain circumstances must stay proceedings in favour of that related jurisdiction. However, for this provision to apply, (a) the parties must have resided together after the date of the marriage, (b) the place where they resided together when the action in the Scottish court was begun or, if they were not residing together at the time, where they last resided together before the date on which that action was begun, is in that jurisdiction, and (c) either party was habitually resident in the related jurisdiction for one year ending with the date on which they last resided together before the date on which the action in the related jurisdiction was begun.

In addition, a discretionary sist may be granted where, prior to the proof in a consistorial action, any other proceedings in respect of the marriage or affecting its validity are continuing in a jurisdiction outside Scotland, and the balance of fairness requires that those proceedings should be completed before further steps are taken in Scotland. The court must have regard to all relevant factors, including the convenience of witnesses and any delay or expense which may result from the proceedings being sisted, or not being sisted (paragraph 9(2)).

In domestic cases of parental responsibility and rights, where proceedings are continuing in another court, then the Scottish court proceedings may be sisted on the basis that it is more appropriate for the proceedings to continue in that other court (section 14, 1986 Act), but it is not mandatory.

B. PRE- AND POST-NUPTIAL AGREEMENTS

5. VALIDITY OF PRE- AND POST-NUPTIAL AGREEMENTS

5.1 To what extent are pre- and post-nups binding within the jurisdiction? Could you provide a brief discussion of the most significant recent case law on this issue?

Although there is an ancient tradition of marriage contracts in Scotland, until quite recently it was very unusual for a couple, either before or after marriage, to execute an agreement regulating the issue of financial provision to be made upon divorce. Recent practice has changed the landscape and both pre-nuptial and post-nuptial agreements are becoming increasingly common.

Both pre-nups and post-nups are, in essence, contracts entered into by a married couple either before or after marriage. The Scottish courts have always been reluctant to interfere with an agreement entered into freely between two adults of sound mind and, although the enforceability of such an agreement has never been fully tested in Scotland, it is generally accepted to be the case that, providing certain conditions are complied with, a pre-nup or a post-nup will be enforced by the Scottish courts.

The most common type of pre-nuptial agreement in Scotland is that which seeks to 'ring-fence' certain assets to exclude them from the definition of 'matrimonial property' which would otherwise be available for division upon separation or divorce. In terms of the Family Law (Scotland) Act 1985, any assets held by a party at the time of marriage, or acquired by that party during the marriage by way of gift from a third party or inheritance, are in any event excluded from the matrimonial property. Pre-nuptial agreements in Scotland generally seek to extend the ring-fencing to include assets derived from assets brought into the marriage as non-matrimonial property.

It is generally accepted that the conditions which need to be met to render a pre-nup or a post-nup enforceable are as follows:

- the agreement must have been presented to the other party for consideration at a time when the circumstances are such that in themselves they do not create a coercive factor, eg, immediately before a wedding;
- both parties must have a proper opportunity to take legal advice; and
- the terms of the agreement must be fair and reasonable at the time they were entered into.

In terms of section 16 (1) (b) of the 1985 Act, where the parties to a marriage have entered into an agreement as to financial provision to be made on divorce, the court may make an order setting aside or varying the agreement or any term of it where the agreement was not fair and reasonable at the time it was entered into. Only in exceptional circumstances has that provision been implemented in relation to agreements made post-separation and the provision has not been fully tested in relation to pre-nups.

In the case of *Kibble v Kibble* 2010 SLT (Sh Crt) 5, it was decided that section 16 does indeed apply to pre-nups, just as it does to agreements made post separation.

C. DIVORCE, NULLITY AND JUDICIAL SEPARATION

6. RECOGNITION OF FOREIGN MARRIAGES/DIVORCES

6.1 Summarise the position in your jurisdiction

Foreign marriages

Under section 38 of the 2006 Act, a marriage is formally valid and thus recognised in Scotland as long as the formalities required by the law of the country in which the marriage took place were complied with. Further, the parties must have had capacity to contract the marriage under the law of his or her respective domiciles. However, where one or both parties was/were placed under any form of duress, then the Scottish courts will not recognise the marriage, even where the above conditions have been satisfied. Further, the foreign marriage will not be recognised where the law of the domicile is contrary to Scots public policy.

For persons domiciled in Scotland, 'capacity' not only refers to a person's mental state, but also includes issues such as age and forbidden degrees of marriage.

Foreign divorces

In relation to those granted within the British Islands, the 1986 Act provides that all divorces granted by a court of civil jurisdiction within the British Islands shall be recognised throughout the UK (section 44(2)), subject to certain grounds for refusal (discussed below). Therefore non-judicial divorces are no longer recognised in Scotland, except those granted before 1 January 1974 (section 54), as long as it was recognised as valid under the law as it stood before that date.

In relation to those granted outside the British Islands, a distinction is made between divorces granted by means of proceedings, judicial or otherwise, and those granted otherwise than by means of proceedings.

An example of a divorce granted by means of proceedings which are not judicial is the Jewish Gett. However, such proceedings still require a certain degree of formality and at least the involvement of some agency of the state, or recognised by it, having a function that is more than simply probative (*Chaudhary v Chaudhary* [1984] 3 All ER 1017 at 1030-1031).

An overseas divorce granted by means of proceedings must be recognised by the Scottish courts if it is effective under the law of the country in which it was obtained. However, either party to the marriage must have been, at the date of commencement of proceedings, either (a) habitually resident in the country in which the divorce was obtained; (b) domiciled in that country; or (c) a national of that country (section 46).

Similarly, an overseas divorce obtained otherwise than by means of proceedings must be recognised by the Scottish courts if the divorce is effective under the law of the country in which it was obtained. However, the remaining conditions are that, on the date on which the divorce was obtained, (a) either (i) both parties were domiciled in that country or (ii) either party was domiciled in that country and the other party was domiciled in a country under whose law the divorce is recognised as valid; and (b) neither party was habitually resident in the UK for one year immediately preceding the date on which the divorce was obtained (section 46).

As stipulated above, there are specific grounds which the court *may* use for refusing to recognise a foreign divorce, which are set out in section 51 of the 1986 Act.

7. DIVORCE

7.1 Explain the grounds for divorce within the jurisdiction (please also deal with nullity and judicial separation if appropriate)

The grounds of divorce are set out in section 1 of the 1976 Act, as amended by the 2006 Act. In an action for divorce, the court may grant decree of divorce if, but only if, it is established that the marriage has broken down irretrievably by reason of one of the following facts being established:

- since the date of the marriage, the defender has committed adultery;
- since the date of the marriage, the defender has at any time behaved (whether or not as a result of mental abnormality and whether such behaviour has been active or passive) in such a way that the pursuer cannot reasonably be expected to cohabit with the defender;
- there has been no cohabitation between the parties at any time during a continuous period of one year after the date of the marriage and the defender consents to the granting of divorce;
- there has been no cohabitation between the parties at any time during a continuous period of two years after the date of the marriage.

The grounds of nullity of marriage are:

(a) that either party at the time of the marriage is already married;

(b) non-age;

(c) that both parties are of the same sex;
(d) that the parties are within the prohibited degrees of relationship specified in the Marriage (Scotland) Act 1977;
(e) non-compliance with the essential requirements of marriage;
(f) defective consent; and
(g) incurable impotency.

Judicial separation (a court order that ends the spouses' obligation to live together) is rare.

8. FINANCES/CAPITAL, PROPERTY

8.1 What powers does the court have to allocate financial resources and property on the breakdown of marriage?

Under the 1985 Act, section 8, either party to the marriage may apply to the court in an action of divorce for one or more specified orders. The main orders which can be sought are:
(a) the payment of a capital sum;
(b) the transfer of property;
(c) the making of a pension sharing order;
(d) an award of periodical allowance.

In terms of section 9 the court is directed to make such an order as is justified by specified principles and is reasonable having regard to the resources of the parties.

The principles to be applied are that:
(a) the net value of the matrimonial property should be shared fairly between the parties to the marriage;
(b) fair account should be taken of any economic advantage derived by either person from contributions by the other, and of economic disadvantage suffered by either person in the interest of the other person or of the family;
(c) any economic burden of caring after divorce for a child under the age of 16 years should be shared fairly between the parties;
(d) a person who has been dependent to a substantial degree on the financial support of the other person should be awarded such financial provision as is reasonable to enable him to adjust, over a period of not more than three years from the date of the decree of divorce, to the loss of that support on divorce;
(e) a person who at the time of the divorce seems likely to suffer serious financial hardship as a result of the divorce should be awarded such financial provision as is reasonable to relieve him of hardship over a reasonable period.

The overriding principle is that which requires the matrimonial property to be shared fairly between the parties. The 'matrimonial property', which is a concept peculiar to Scotland, is defined as all the property held by either party, or by the parties in their joint names, at the date of separation (not the date of divorce) and which has been acquired by them during the course of the marriage. Further, a property acquired before the marriage by the parties as a family home is also part of the matrimonial property. It will be seen, therefore, that capital assets held by either of the parties before the marriage do not form part of the property to be divided.

An exception to the definition of matrimonial property is that assets acquired during the marriage by way of gift from a third party or by way of inheritance are excluded.

There are various factors to which the court shall have regard when considering each of the section 9 principles. These factors are set out in section 11. The conduct of either party is in essence excluded as a factor to be taken into account.

The net value of the matrimonial property (ie, after matrimonial debts have been taken into account) shall be taken to be shared fairly between the parties when it is shared equally or in such other proportions as are justified by special circumstances. 'Special circumstances' are deemed to include the source of the funds or assets used to acquire any of the matrimonial property where those funds or assets were not derived from the income or efforts of the parties during the marriage.

The role of the court is to distribute the assets of the parties which fall within the definition of matrimonial property in such a way that, taking account of the resources available to the parties and special circumstances, a fair division is achieved.

It should be noted that once decree of divorce is granted, no further claim for financial provision of any type, other than child maintenance, can be applied for and the granting of decree of divorce extinguishes any entitlement to financial provision, other than that which has been already awarded by the court or is the subject of a binding agreement.

8.2 Explain and illustrate with reference to recent cases the court's thinking on division of assets

The overriding principle is that there should be a fair sharing of the matrimonial property. A fair sharing shall be an equal sharing unless there are circumstances which justify an unequal sharing. The most common 'special circumstance' used to argue that a departure from the equal sharing principle is justified is a 'source of funds' argument, ie, that the source of the funds used to acquire any of the matrimonial property was not derived from the income or efforts of the parties during the marriage. Cases where such arguments have been deployed successfully include those where the source of the funds was inherited wealth (see *Willson v Willson* 2009 Fam. L.R. 18) and where the source of the funds was a gift to one of the spouses (see *Armstrong v Armstrong* 2008 Fam. L.R. 125).

Claims under s.9(1)(b) of the 1985 Act (fair account to be taken of any economic advantage/disadvantage suffered) can arise where one spouse has given up or has not pursued a career, usually with promotion prospects, so that he or she can raise the children of the marriage. Such spouses may be left without a pension and with limited future earning capacity, while their partners may have derived an economic advantage because, *inter alia*, they have not had to pay for childcare during the marriage. The court has been sympathetic to such claims (see *Burnside v Burnside* 2007 Fam. L.R. 144) but other recent cases (see *B v B* 2012 Fam L.R. 65) show that the court must be satisfied that the claimant would have been in employment had they not been married. Spouses who have contributed, even minimally, to the family income and have seen their partner take an advantage from that contribution have also brought successful s.9(1)(b) arguments (see *Marshall v Marshall* 2007 Fam. L. R. 48 and *Hodge v Hodge* 2008 Fam. L. R. 51).

9. FINANCES/MAINTENANCE

9.1 Explain the operation of maintenance for spouses on an ongoing basis after the breakdown of marriage

In Scotland, different criteria are to be applied to a claim for spousal maintenance before and after divorce. In terms of section 1 of the 1985 Act, spouses owe an obligation of maintenance (known as aliment) to each other. The obligation to aliment only subsists for as long as the parties are married to each other. The amount of aliment to be awarded by a court against one party in favour of the other party shall be determined by the court taking into account the following factors:

- the needs and resources of the parties;
- the earning capacities of the parties; and
- generally all the circumstances of the case.

In the period where the parties remain married to each other and before a final financial arrangement is made, either by agreement or by the court, it is usual for one spouse to aliment the other, essentially to allow both parties as far as possible to maintain the same standard of living which they enjoyed up to the point of separation.

9.2 Is it common for maintenance to be awarded?

After divorce, spousal maintenance, known as periodical allowance, will only be awarded if it is justified on an application of the principles set out in section 9 of the 1985 Act (see number 8 hereof). In essence, a periodical allowance will only be awarded if the financial circumstances of one spouse following divorce are such that he or she requires continuing financial support from the other spouse to allow him or her to adjust to the financial arrangements arrived at as part of the divorce. It is the duty of the court to seek to achieve a clean break and the court must be satisfied before making an award of periodical allowance that the spouse's entitlement cannot be satisfied by an enhanced capital payment.

Controversially, in terms of section 9 (1) (d) of the 1985 Act, periodical allowance cannot be awarded for a period of longer than three years, except in exceptional circumstances. In other words, in almost all cases, the entitlement to spousal maintenance ends a maximum of three years after the granting of divorce.

9.3 Explain and illustrate with reference to recent cases the court's thinking on maintenance

The emphasis on achieving a financial clean break has meant that the court has been reluctant to grant periodical allowance. For example, in *B v B* 2012

Fam. L.R. 65, while it was acknowledged that the pursuer would require time to adjust to a financially independent lifestyle, Lord Tyre made an order for payment by the pursuer to the defender of six installments of capital instead of an order for periodical allowance. The first, in the sum of £4,000, was to be paid within two weeks of divorce. The remaining five installments, in the sum of £2,000 each, were to be paid at six monthly intervals commencing six months after divorce. This would allow the defender greater flexibility with regard to financial planning during the three years following divorce.

In a case in which periodical allowance was granted, *W v W* 2012 Fam. L.R. 99, the property owned by the parties was roughly equal in value, and the wife was not to receive a substantial capital sum. An award of periodical allowance was granted in her favour at a rate of £1,000 for 18 months in terms of s.9(1)(d) of the 1985 act, to allow her to adjust to the loss of her husband's financial support. This would enable the pursuer to pay off her car loan, make provision for major household bills and make further progress with her degree qualification.

10. CHILD MAINTENANCE

10.1 On what basis is child maintenance calculated within the jurisdiction?

In cases where the parents of a child live apart and the child lives with one of them, the calculation and collection of child maintenance being paid to the 'parent with care' (the parent with whom the child lives) by the 'non-resident parent' (NRP) is governed by the Child Support Act 1991. The Child Maintenance and Enforcement Commission (CMEC), of which the Child Support Agency (CSA) is a part, has exclusive jurisdiction in respect of child maintenance in Scotland.

With the exception of cases where there are four or more children, the rules state that an application can be made by either the parent with care, the non-resident parent or, in certain circumstances, the child. There are four rates applied to child maintenance, which are based on the non-resident parent's net weekly income (NWI), up to a maximum of £2,000.

(a) Basic rate

The basic rate is applied where the NWI is £200 or more. The following percentages of the non-resident parent's NWI requires to be paid to the parent with care:

- 15 per cent where there is one child;
- 20 per cent where there are two children;
- 25 per cent where there are three or more children.

(b) Reduced rate

The reduced rate is applied where the NWI is more than £100 but less than £200; the non-resident parent pays £5, plus the following percentages of their NWI over £100:

- 25 per cent for one child;
- 35 per cent for two children;

- 45 per cent for three or more children.

(c) Flat rate

The flat rate is applied where the NWI is between £5 and £100. A flat rate of £5 is due no matter how many children require maintenance from the non-resident parent. This is also the rate that is paid if the non-resident parent or their partner whom they live with receives income-related benefits or pension credit, or the non-resident parent is in receipt of certain benefits.

(d) Nil rate

The nil rate is applied where the NWI is less than £5, in which case no payment will be due from the non-resident parent for child maintenance.

The basic and reduced rates can be affected if (i) the child or children stay overnight with the non-resident parent on average one night or more per week; or (ii) where there are children living with the non-resident parent for whom they or their partner receive child benefit (relevant other children).

CMEC may also take special expenses into account, such as where the child has a disability. There are also various grounds for applying to CMEC for a variation of the maintenance calculation. The most useful of these arise where the NRP has assets in excess of £65,000 or where the NRP's income is inconsistent with declared income.

In early 2013, changes came into effect for cases where there are four or more children of a relationship. Firstly, the maintenance calculation will be based on the non-resident parent's gross income. Secondly, on the first £800 per week earned, the NRP will pay 12 per cent for one child, 16 per cent for two children and 19 per cent for three or more children. Lastly, on the proportion of gross weekly income exceeding £800 per week, the NRP will pay 9 per cent for one child, 11 per cent for two children and 16 per cent for three or more children.

Every parent in Scotland owes an obligation of aliment to his or her children up until each child reaches the age of 18, or 25 where a child is undergoing appropriate training or education (section 1, 1985 Act). The level of aliment will be determined by the parties' needs and resources, their earning capacities and all the circumstances of the case. This obligation covers all matters not dealt with under the exclusive jurisdiction of CMEC, such as private school fees, additional maintenance where the NRP's NWI exceeds the maximum taken into account by CMEC or in respect of older children still in education.

11. RECIPROCAL ENFORCEMENT OF FINANCIAL ORDERS

11.1 Summarise the position in your jurisdiction

Within the UK

The relevant legislation for enforcement of financial orders in one territorial unit of the UK where the order is made in a different territorial unit of the UK is the Maintenance Orders Act 1950. Under section 16, Scotland *may* enforce a financial order made in another part of the UK if it is registered in Scotland in accordance with the Act. The orders to which this section relates include capital payments as well as maintenance.

Where a 'superior court' granted the order, it should be registered in the Court of Session (section 17). Any other order should be registered in the sheriff court within the jurisdiction of which the defender appears to be residing.

Where such an order has been registered, it may be enforced in Scotland as if it were a Scottish judgment (section 18) and, therefore, diligence can be effected under the Debtors (Scotland) Act 1987, for example, by serving an arrestment against the debtor's earnings.

Brussels and Lugano Conventions and Regulation 44

The above instruments all provide that a 'judgment' from one of the contracting or member states shall be enforced in Scotland when, on the application of any interested party, it has been declared enforceable there (Article 38 Regulation 44; Article 31 Brussels Convention 1968; Article 38 Lugano Convention 2007). Paragraph 2 of each respective Article provides for enforcement in the separate territorial units within the UK.

The application must be submitted to the Court of Session or, in respect of a maintenance judgment, the Sheriff Court, on transmission by the Secretary of State (Article 39(1) and Annex II Regulation 44 and Lugano; Article 32 Brussels Convention). The particular sheriffdom will be that in which (i) the party against whom enforcement is sought is domiciled or (ii) the enforcement is to be carried out. It is, therefore, not necessary that the debtor is domiciled in Scotland. It is sufficient if he or she has assets held in Scotland. The debtor may appeal against the declaration of enforceability.

There are various other Conventions which apply to Scotland in relation to enforcement of financial provisions, for example, the Hague Convention 1973 and the New York Convention 1956.

12. FINANCIAL RELIEF AFTER FOREIGN DIVORCE PROCEEDINGS

12.1 What powers are available to make orders following a foreign divorce?

The relevant legislation in Scotland is Part IV of the Matrimonial and Family Proceedings Act 1984. Where the parties have divorced abroad, an application can be made to either the Court of Session or the sheriff court for an order for financial provision, whether or not a financial order was made in terms of those divorce proceedings. However, in order to establish jurisdiction in a Scottish court, the following must apply (section 28(2)):

- the applicant was domiciled or habitually resident in Scotland on the date of the application; and
- the other party to the marriage:
  - (i) was domiciled or habitually resident in Scotland on either the date when the application was made or when the parties last lived together as husband and wife; or
  - (ii) on the date of the application, was an owner or tenant of, or had a beneficial interest in, property in Scotland which had at some time been the matrimonial home.

For the application to be made in the Sheriff Court, one of the following must apply, either (a) one of the parties was, on the date of the application, habitually resident in the sheriffdom or, (b) where point (ii) above applies, the property is wholly or partially within the sheriffdom.

The court must apply Scots law and must place the parties in the financial position in which they would have been had the divorce been obtained in Scotland on the date on which the foreign divorce took effect, so far as is reasonable and practicable (section 29). The parties' resources and any financial provision or transfer of property order made by a foreign court in or in connection with the divorce proceedings must be taken into account. The court may award interim periodical allowance where it appears that an order for financial provision is likely to be made and the court considers that such an interim award is necessary to avoid hardship to the applicant.

Taking the judgment from the case of *Agbaje v Agbaje* [2010] UKSC 13, which is persuasive in Scotland but not binding, in order to establish a 'substantial connection' with Scotland, it is not necessary to have lived in Scotland for the length of the marriage. It could, in fact, be established even where the parties spent the majority of their married life in a different country, so long as there are other factors which point to a substantial connection with Scotland. Further, in determining the level of financial provision, the court will not necessarily 'top-up' the award in order for it to be in line with what the Scottish court would have ordered. However, the court also need not merely make an award to 'the minimum extent necessary to remedy the injustice'.

D. CHILDREN

13. CUSTODY/PARENTAL RESPONSIBILITY

13.1 Briefly explain the legal position in relation to custody/parental responsibility following the breakdown of a relationship or marriage

The relevant legal term in Scotland is 'residence'. Mothers and married fathers have automatic parental responsibilities and rights (see s.3 of the 1995 Act). Unmarried fathers can acquire parental responsibilities and rights by entering into an agreement with the mother or by application to the court. In respect of children born on or after 4 May 2006, fathers who register the birth jointly with the mother will also acquire parental responsibilities and rights. Parental rights include the right to have the child living with the parent and to control, direct or guide the child's upbringing and parental responsibilities include safeguarding and promoting the child's health, development and welfare.

Each parent with parental responsibilities and rights has the same right to have their child living with them. Following the breakdown of a relationship, parents may agree that one parent will have residence of the child and the other will have contact. Mediation is the preferred forum in which to discuss such matters should the parties require assistance in making arrangements for their children following separation. Otherwise, the court can grant a residence order under s.11 of the 1995 Act. A series of child welfare hearings will consider the issues in any particular case.

In considering whether or not to make an order and what order to make, the court must regard the welfare of the child concerned as its paramount consideration and shall not make any such order unless it considers that it would be better for the child that the order be made than that none be made at all. Taking account of the child's age and maturity, the court is obliged to give him an opportunity to express a view. A child aged 12 or more is presumed competent to express a view.

13.2 Briefly explain the legal position in relation to access/contact/visitation following the breakdown of a relationship or marriage

The relevant legal term in Scotland is 'contact'. Many parents are able to agree contact, failing which the non-resident parent can apply to the court for a contact order. The same principles must be considered by the court in determining the granting of a contact order as are considered in determining the granting of a residence order, such as the welfare of the child being paramount and the principle of non-intervention. Shared care arrangements are becoming increasingly common, whereby parents agree a regime in which the child spends broadly equal amounts of time with each parent.

14. INTERNATIONAL ABDUCTION

14.1 Summarise the position in your jurisdiction

UK cases

Orders in relation to parental responsibilities and rights for children under the age of 16 made in any other part of the UK must be recognised by the Scottish courts as having the same effect as if it had been made by the Court of Session in Scotland (section 25, 1986 Act). However, the order cannot be enforced unless and until it has been registered in the Court of Session by a person having those rights and responsibilities by virtue of the order (section 25 and 27). Once an order has been registered, the Court of Session has the same powers of enforcement as if it had made the order and proceedings for enforcement can be taken accordingly (section 29).

International cases

The Hague Convention on the Civil Aspects of International Child Abduction 1980 governs cases of child abduction between contracting states and its object in such cases is 'to secure the prompt return of children wrongfully removed to or retained in any contracting state'. The main concern is not the welfare of the child but the return of the child to the country of its habitual residence so that the courts of that country can decide on a dispute over the child. The implementing legislation is the Child Abduction and Custody Act 1985.

Where it is thought that a child has been wrongfully removed to or retained in Scotland, an application for his or her return can be made to either the central authority within the contracting state of the child's habitual residence or directly to the central authority in Scotland, which is the Scottish Executive Justice Department (Civil and International Division) (SEJD) on behalf of the Secretary of State. Under Article 7, the central authorities, in securing the prompt return of the child, must take appropriate measures, for example, to discover the whereabouts of the child and initiate or facilitate proceedings with a view to the return of the child (the appropriate court in Scotland in which to bring these proceedings being the Court of Session). However, voluntary return of the child is also envisaged.

A retention or removal is wrongful where it is in breach of 'custody' rights under the law of the contracting state in which the child was habitually resident immediately before the removal or retention (Article 3). Therefore, it is necessary that an explanation of the law, in relation to custody rights of the contracting state in which the child was habitually resident, is produced to the Court of Session. In *BJZ Petitioner*, Lady Smith, 2009 CSOH 136 (September 16 2009), the court refused to return the child because the institution presenting the petition did not provide sufficient evidence of their custody rights over the child under Dutch law. A further qualification for the removal or retention to be wrongful is that the custody rights must have been actually exercised, or would have been exercised by the person with such 'custody' rights but for the removal or retention, at the time of the removal (Article 3).

Where proceedings have been brought, the default position is that the child must be returned where it has been less than one year since the wrongful removal or retention, then it must be done 'forthwith'. However, where the period of one year has expired, the Scottish court must order the return unless the child is settled in Scotland (Article 12).

Further, where there is a grave risk that the return would expose the child to physical or psychological harm, or otherwise place the child in an intolerable situation, then the child need not be returned (Article 13). Similarly, the court does not have to order the return where the child objects and he/she is of sufficient age and maturity, such that it is appropriate to take his/her views into consideration. In the case of *Urness v Minto* (1994) SLT 988, which took both of these issues into account, the court took the child's views into account and allowed the child to stay in Scotland. However, the court also ordered that the younger brother, whose views could not be taken into account, also stay in Scotland on the basis that ordering his return to the United States without both his brother and mother would place the child in an intolerable situation.

Where a child has been taken from a member state (except Denmark) to Scotland, further provisions must be applied to such cases. The European Convention on Custody of Children applies where a child is brought from a Contracting State of the European Convention that is not a party to the Hague Convention or Brussels II bis. Its main purpose is the recognition and enforcement of decisions relating to custody, however, for such an order to be recognised and enforced in Scotland, it must be registered in the Court of Session. The Court can refuse to recognise the order under specific grounds (section 15 and 16 Child Abduction and Custody Act 1985). The Court of Session can enforce the order as if it had made the order and had jurisdiction to do so (section 18).

Non-Brussels/Hague cases

Where a child has been brought to Scotland from a country other than those within the UK or Isle of Man and which is not a signatory to the Brussels Regulation or the Hague Convention, the Scottish courts must recognise an order in relation to parental responsibilities or rights granted by that country, as long as it is the country in which the child was habitually resident (section 26, 1986 Act). There is also a Pakistan protocol of 17 January 2003, between members of the judiciary in the UK and Pakistan, to the effect that judges should not exercise jurisdiction over a child who is habitually resident in the other country unless it is necessary in order for the court to make a ruling on the return of the child to its habitual residence. It is specifically stated that the welfare of the child is best determined by the courts of the country of the child's habitual residence.

15. LEAVE TO REMOVE/APPLICATIONS TO TAKE A CHILD OUT OF THE JURISDICTION

15.1 Summarise the position in your jurisdiction

Section 2 of the 1995 Act provides that a child habitually resident in Scotland cannot be removed from, or retained outside, the UK without the consent of a person who has, and is exercising, a right of residence or contact over the child. However, where both parents have such rights, one cannot provide such consent alone to the removal or retention of the child thus defeating the other parent's rights; the consent of the other parent is required in order to lawfully remove the child from, or retain it outside, the UK.

15.2 Under what circumstances may a parent apply to remove their child from the jurisdiction against the wishes of the other parent?

Section 11 allows a parent to bring proceedings in respect of his or her child in relation to parental rights. Therefore, a parent could seek a specific issue order or a residence order from the court allowing him or her to remove the child from the UK. The court can grant such orders even where the other parent refuses to provide their consent. In making its decision the court must, as with all orders relating to children, have the welfare of the child as its paramount consideration. Further, the court must not make an order unless it considers that it would be better for the child that it be made than that none should be made at all. The court must also have regard to the child's views where that child is of sufficient age and maturity for these views to be taken into account and where that child wishes to express a view (section 11(7)).

It should also be noted that, under section 6 of the Child Abduction Act 1984, a person commits an offence if he or she takes or sends the child out of the UK without the appropriate consent, but only if there is (i) an order of a court in the UK awarding custody to any person, (ii) an order of a court in England and Wales or Northern Ireland making the child a ward of court, or (iii) if there is an order of a court in the UK prohibiting the removal of the child from the UK or any part of it. The appropriate consent can be provided by leave of the court.

E. SURROGACY & ADOPTION

16. VALIDITY OF SURROGACY AGREEMENTS

16.1 Briefly summarise the position in your jurisdiction

Under s.27 of the Human Fertilisation and Embryology Act 1990, a woman who has carried a child as a result of the placing in her of (a) an embryo; or (b) sperm and eggs, is to be treated as the mother of the child, regardless of her biological relationship to the child. Therefore, any surrogacy agreement which has been entered into will have no effect on her having full parental responsibilities and rights, including the right to have the child living with her. Surrogacy agreements are not enforceable in court, and a surrogate can only receive 'reasonable expenses'.

17. ADOPTION

17.1 Briefly summarise the position in relation to adoption in your jurisdiction. Is adoption available to individuals, cohabiting couples (both heterosexual and same-sex)?

The law on adoption is governed by the Adoption and Children (Scotland) Act 2007. Individuals, married couples, civil partners and persons who are living together as if husband and wife or civil partners in an enduring family relationship, aged 21 or over, can apply for an adoption order by submitting an adoption petition to the court. Where the child has been placed with the adopters by an adoption agency, or the adopters are related to the child, the child must have been living with the adopters for at least 13 weeks prior to lodging the adoption petition. The birth parents must consent to the adoption, or the court must be satisfied that their consent should be dispensed with on one of the grounds set out in the 2007 Act, for example that the welfare of the child requires consent to be dispensed with. Where a child is older than 12, the child's consent is also required. Parental responsibilities and rights are transferred to the adoptive parents if the petition is granted.

F. COHABITATION

18. COHABITATION

18.1 What legislation (if any) governs division of property for unmarried couples on the breakdown of the relationship?

Sections 25 to 29 of the 2006 Act, govern the breakdown of relationships of unmarried couples. The provisions cover heterosexual couples who are (or were) living together as if they were husband and wife and persons of the same sex who are (or were) living together as if they were civil partners. However, there are other factors which the court must take into account in deciding whether the couple are, or were, cohabiting. These are (i) how long they have been living together (or lived together); (ii) the nature of their relationship during that period; and (iii) the nature and extent of any financial arrangements subsisting, or which subsisted, during that period. Therefore, it is not entirely clear who will fall within the definition and this will be very much a matter for the courts.

When a cohabiting couple separate, the court can order, upon the application of one of the parties, that (i) a capital sum be paid from the defender to the applicant; or (ii) that an amount is to be paid by the defender to the applicant in respect of the economic burden of caring for their child or children (section 28). In deciding whether to make such an award, the court must take into account any economic advantage to the defender by reason of the applicant's contributions and any disadvantage suffered by the applicant in the interests of the defender or any child of the family. The economic advantages and disadvantages of both parties must then be balanced against each other. Further, and crucially, the application must be made to the court within one year of separation. The leading case brought under this piece of legislation, *Gow v Grant* [2012] UKSC 29, was appealed to the Supreme Court on 24 May 2012. However, the law is still very much evolving in this field.

G. FAMILY DISPUTE RESOLUTION

19. MEDIATION, COLLABORATIVE LAW AND ARBITRATION

19.1 Briefly summarise the non-court-based processes available in your jurisdiction and the current status of agreements reached under the auspices of mediation, collaborative law and arbitration

Non-court-based processes available in Scotland include negotiation, mediation, collaborative law and arbitration. Any agreement signed by the parties and registered in the Books of Council and Session, whether reached by way of mediation, collaborative law or other means, has the same status as a court order in relation to financial issues. In the case of arbitration, the parties agree to be bound by the decision of the arbiter, but the decision on a point of law can be sent to the Court of Session.

19.2 What is the statutory basis (if any), for mediation, collaborative law and arbitration in your jurisdiction? In particular, are the parties required to attempt a family dispute resolution in advance of proceedings?

There is no statutory basis for mediation or collaborative law in Scotland. Arbitration is governed by the Arbitration (Scotland) Act 2010. If all that is stipulated in an agreement is that the parties will go to arbitration, then all of the Scottish Arbitration Rules set out in the 2010 Act will apply. There are, however, mandatory rules that will trump whatever is in the agreement, and default rules that will not. It is not possible for an arbiter to grant divorce.

There is no requirement for the parties to attempt a family dispute resolution in advance of proceedings.

H. OTHER

20. CIVIL PARTNERSHIP/SAME-SEX MARRIAGE

20.1 What is the status of civil partnership/same-sex marriage within the jurisdiction?

Scotland recognises civil partnerships and has done since 5 December 2005. The Scottish Government published the draft Marriage and Civil Partnership

(Scotland) Bill in December 2012 which would legalise same-sex marriage, and is currently consulting on the Bill.

20.2 What legislation governs civil partnership/same-sex marriage?

Part 3 of the Civil Partnership Act 2004 governs civil partnerships in Scotland. Anyone over the age of 16 and who is single can enter into a civil partnership provided the parties are not related in a forbidden degree and they are both of the same sex. Several rights stem from entering into a civil partnership, including those relating to occupying a 'family home', intestacy, recognition for immigration purposes and life assurance policies. A civil partnership can be formally ended by way of dissolution, which can be brought in the Court of Session or Sheriff Court. The grounds for dissolution are irretrievable breakdown of the partnership or where an interim gender recognition certificate has been issued after the date of the civil partnership. Irretrievable breakdown is established where either the couple have been separated for one year and both parties consent; the couple have been separated for two years; or there has been unreasonable behaviour on the part of the defender.

21. CONTROVERSIAL AREAS/RAPIDLY DEVELOPING AREAS OF LAW

21.1 Is there a particular area of the law within the jurisdiction that is currently undergoing major change?

There are no areas of family law within Scotland currently undergoing major change, with the exception of the Marriage and Civil Partnership (Scotland) Bill, as noted above.

21.2 Which areas of law are most out of step and which areas would you most like to see reformed/changed?

Family law in Scotland is going through a particularly settled period. The implementation of the 2006 Act ironed out some anomalies created by the 1985 Act in relation to changes in the value of matrimonial property between the date of separation and the date of divorce. It also sought to codify the circumstances in which a cessation of cohabitation could give rise to a financial claim. A raft of recent cases have developed the law in this area, but there remains considerable uncertainty as to the extent to which particular circumstances ought properly to be taken into account.

One area where change ought to be considered is the fact that spouses do not have an entitlement to share in the increase in value of non-matrimonial property during the course of the marriage. For example, if one party owns a house or a farm or shares in a private company before the marriage, and the marriage subsists for decades, there can be a very substantial increase in the value of those assets, but because they are non-matrimonial property, the non-owning spouse does not have an entitlement to share in the increase of that value. This can clearly cause anomalous results.

Singapore

Drew & Napier LLC Randolph Khoo & Shu Mei Hoon

A. JURISDICTION AND CONFLICT OF LAW

1. SOURCES OF LAW

1.1 What are the primary sources of law in relation to the breakdown of marriage and the welfare of children within the jurisdiction?

The Singapore legal system traces its historical roots to the English common law that was received during its colonial past. The two primary sources of law in question are legislative enactments and the common law as applied in Singapore, with a hierarchy of binding precedent from decided cases.

1.2 Which are the main statutes governing matrimonial law in the jurisdiction?

The Women's Charter (Cap 353) is the main statute dealing with the breakdown of non-Muslim marriages in Singapore. Islamic divorce law is codified under the Administration of Muslim Law Act (Cap 3). The main legislation governing the welfare of children in Singapore is the Guardianship of Infants Act (Cap 122).

2. JURISDICTION

2.1 What are the main jurisdictional requirements for the institution of proceedings in relation to divorce, property and children?

Section 93(1) of the Women's Charter empowers Singapore courts to entertain proceedings for divorce, judicial separation or nullity of marriage only if either of the parties to the marriage is:

(1) domiciled in Singapore at the start of proceedings; or
(2) habitually resident in Singapore for at least three years before the start of proceedings.

In proceedings for nullity of marriage on the ground that a marriage is void or voidable, the court may, notwithstanding that the two requirements above are not fulfilled, grant relief sought where both parties to the marriage reside in Singapore at the time proceedings commence.

Proceedings in relation to division of matrimonial property are ancillary to granting of a judgment for divorce, judicial separation or nullity. However, spouses may enter into property litigation with each other under ordinary principles of common property law.

The statutory restrictions above are no bar to proceedings relating to children of married or unmarried couples. Parties residing in Singapore may file such proceedings under the Guardianship of Infants Act, subject to the court declining to exercise jurisdiction on the principles of *forum non conveniens.*

Section 94(1) of the charter provides that no writ for divorce shall be filed unless at the date of the filing of the writ, three years have passed since the date of the marriage. There are exceptions: a writ for divorce may still be filed before three years have passed on the grounds of (a) exceptional hardship suffered by the plaintiff or (b) exceptional depravity on the part of the defendant.

3. DOMICILE AND HABITUAL RESIDENCE

3.1 Explain the concepts of domicile and habitual residence as they apply to the jurisdiction in relation to divorce, the finances and children

Tan Yock Lin, *Conflict Issues in Family & Succession* Law (Butterworths Asia, 1993) writes, '[d]omicile simply means home'. In *TQ v TR* [2007] 3 SLR(R) 719, the Singapore High Court described 'domicile' in these terms:

'The domicile of a person is determined by the intention of the person's choice, not of the place where he chooses to live, but the place where he chooses to die. In modern times, it is sufficient to include the place where the person intends to return permanently at the end of his or her sojourn elsewhere in the world.'

Section 3(5) of the Women's Charter states that a Singapore citizen is presumed to be domiciled in Singapore until the contrary is proven.

Section 47(1) of the charter provides that a wife's domicile is to be determined 'by reference to the same factors as in the case of any other individual capable of having an independent domicile'.

Beyond the guidance afforded above, an individual's domicile in a given case is a question of fact. An individual may also have domicile acquired by choice.

In *Didier Von Daniken v Sanaa Von Daniken Born El Kolaly* [2005] SGDC 80, the Family Court held that to acquire domicile of choice in Singapore, two elements must be satisfied 'beyond a mere balance of probabilities': proof of the facts of (a) residence in Singapore; and (b) an intention of permanent or indefinite residence in the country.

In *Ho Ah Chye v Hsinchieh Hsu Irene* [1994] 1 SLR(R) 485, the High Court referred to the definition of 'habitual residence' in the English case of *Cruse v Chittum* [1974] 2 All ER 940 as follows:

'"Habitual residence" denoted a regular physical presence enduring for some time. Ordinary residence was different from habitual residence because the latter was something more than the former and was similar to the residence required as part of domicile, but there was no need of animus, so necessary in domicile ...'

A later High Court decision of *Lee Mei-Chih v Chang Kuo Yuan* [2012] 4 SLR 1115 held that 'habitual residence' was the same as 'ordinary residence', holding that these concepts referred to a voluntarily adopted residence for settled purposes. On the facts of the case, the plaintiff was often travelling and away from Singapore for 12 out of the previous 36 months. The court held that she failed to prove the jurisdictional requirement of 'habitual residence' of three years.

4. CONFLICT OF LAW/APPLICABLE LAW TO BE APPLIED

4.1 What happens when one party applies to stay proceedings in favour of a foreign jurisdiction? What factors will the local court take into account when determining forum issues?

Decisions from Singapore's apex court like *Oriental Insurance Co Ltd v Bhavani Stores Pte Ltd* [1997] 3 SLR(R) 363 and *Rickshaw Investments Ltd v Nicolai Baron von Uexkull* [2007] 1 SLR(R) 377 affirm that the principles applied in Singapore to the question of a stay of proceedings in favour of a foreign jurisdiction on the ground of *forum non conveniens* are those generally set out in the English decision of *Spiliada Maritime Corporation v Cansulex Ltd* [1987] AC 460.

In *VH v VI* [2008] 1 SLR(R) 742, the Singapore High Court reiterated the applicability of those principles in the matrimonial context as follows:

(a) The basic principle is that a stay will only be granted on the ground of *forum non conveniens* where the court is satisfied that there is some other available forum, having competent jurisdiction, which is the appropriate forum for trial.

(b) The burden of proof is generally on the defendant to persuade the court to grant a stay. If the court is satisfied that there is another available forum which is *prima facie* the appropriate forum for trial of the action, the burden will shift to the plaintiff to show that there are special circumstances by reason of which justice requires that the trial should nevertheless take place in Singapore.

(c) The defendant not only has to show that the forum of the action is not the natural or appropriate forum for the trial. He has to establish that there is another available forum which is clearly or distinctly more appropriate than the forum of the action.

(d) The 'natural forum' is that with which the action had the most real and substantial connection. These include not only factors affecting convenience or expense (such as availability of witnesses), but also other factors such as the law governing the relevant transaction.

(e) If the court concludes that there is no other available forum which is clearly more appropriate for the trial of the action, it will ordinarily refuse a stay.

(f) If, however, the court concludes that there is some other available forum, which *prima facie* is clearly more appropriate for the trial of the action, it will ordinarily grant a stay unless there are circumstances by reason of which justice requires that a stay should nevertheless be granted.

The High Court in *VH v VI* had to decide whether to stay Singapore proceedings in favour of a Swedish divorce. It held that the crucial question was not whether Sweden was an appropriate forum, but whether Sweden was a *more* appropriate forum than Singapore. The parties and children were all resident in Singapore. The husband was working in Singapore. The children were attending school in Singapore. The parties owned several properties in Singapore. In addition, both parties had initially been content to proceed with the divorce in Singapore. The husband was held to be unable to show that Sweden was a more appropriate forum than Singapore.

For this reason, the judge found it unnecessary to consider the second *Spiliada* principle in (b) above.

An important factor in family cases is the place where children of the marriage are settled (*Low Wing Hong Alvin v Kelso Sharon Leigh* [1999] 3 SLR(R) 993). In *Mala Shukla v Jayant Amritanand Shukla* [2002] 1 SLR(R) 920, the High Court stayed proceedings in Singapore in favour of Indian proceedings, holding that:

'As regards custody of and access to the children, they are children of Indian citizens and are residing in India. India is the most appropriate forum to make orders in respect of them. Even for maintenance, while a court may wish to consider the previous standard of living of the family in Singapore, it may also want to consider the cost of living at the place where the mother and children are at present residing.'

In *ABR v ABS* [2009] SGHC 196, the fact of one spouse living and working in Singapore and of both parties having Singapore permanent residence was insufficient to tilt the balance in favour of litigation in Singapore, when the child concerned was living and studying in India.

In *BDA v BDB* [2013] 1 SLR 607, a wife claimed maintenance from her husband in Singapore in late 2011. Both parents were Indian citizens. Both parties had also been Singapore permanent residents since 2009. In January 2008, the couple moved to Singapore from Hong Kong. In October 2010, the wife and the parties' son left for India. The wife expressed the intention to return to live in Singapore. The husband remained resident in and employed in Singapore. The husband filed for divorce in India a couple of months after the wife's application for maintenance.

The court held that nationality *per se* was of limited significance in the modern age, and that residency and/or domicile were better indicators of the strength of a party's connection to a particular forum. The court considered the divorce started by the husband in India to be distinct from the wife's claim for maintenance in Singapore. It also held that the Singapore court would not be at a complete disadvantage, compared with an Indian court, in determining the proper quantum of maintenance as it needed to take into account the standard of living enjoyed by the wife when the parties were living together in Singapore. The court concluded that the husband had not discharged the burden of showing that India was clearly or distinctly a more appropriate forum and refused to stay the Singapore maintenance claim.

B. PRE- AND POST- NUPTIAL AGREEMENTS

5. VALIDITY OF PRE- AND POST-NUPTIAL AGREEMENTS

5.1 To what extent are pre- and post-nups binding within the jurisdiction? Could you provide a brief discussion of the most significant recent case law on this issue?

Singapore law does not treat pre-nuptial and post-nuptial agreements as being automatically binding in the jurisdiction. Spouses may challenge such agreements as all such agreements are subject to the scrutiny of the court. The Singapore courts reserve the right to determine whether and to what extent pre-nuptial and post-nuptial agreements are enforceable. The most significant recent decision concerning pre-nuptial and post-nuptial agreements is the Court of Appeal decision in *TQ v TR* [2009] 2 SLR(R) 961.

The Singapore courts have long held that pre-nuptial agreements that enable a spouse to negate a marriage and its legal obligations are against public policy and unenforceable. However, agreements that regulate marital relations (eg dictating how the couple should live and conduct themselves as spouses in line with Chinese customary practices) would not be invalid: *Kwong Sin Hwa v Lau Lee Yen* [1993] 1 SLR(R) 90.

Sections 116, 119 and 129 of the Women's Charter empower the Singapore court to review and vary agreements relating to maintenance and custody. Amendments to the charter in 1997 included a new section 112(2)(e) which provides that when exercising powers to divide marital assets, the court shall have regard to 'any agreement between the parties with respect to the ownership and division of matrimonial assets made in contemplation of divorce'.

The Court of Appeal in *TQ v TR* [2009] 2 SLR(R) 961 decided that, *'...where one or more of the provisions of the [Women's Charter] expressly covers a certain category of pre-nuptial agreement, then that provision or those provisions will be the governing law. Where, however, the Act is silent, then the legal status of the pre-nuptial agreement concerned will be governed by the common law. In this regard, it will be assumed that any pre-nuptial agreement which contravenes any express provision of the Act and/or the general or specific legislative policy embodied within the Act itself will not pass muster under the common law.'*

Where a pre-nuptial agreement relates to maintenance of a wife and children, *TQ v TR* decided that the courts cannot be barred from reviewing it. Any covenant to preclude judicial scrutiny of such agreements would not be valid. The courts would be especially vigilant and would be slow to enforce agreements that are apparently not in the best interests of the children. There is a presumption that pre-nuptial and post-nuptial agreements relating to the welfare of the children are unenforceable unless the party relying on the agreement proves that it is in the best interests of the children concerned.

A pre-nuptial or post-nuptial agreement cannot be enforced, in and of itself. However, such an agreement is one of the factors considered by the court in exercising its power for the division of matrimonial assets. A valid pre-nuptial agreement would, to the extent that it was considered relevant, be reflected in an order of court itself. 'Such an agreement cannot oust the jurisdiction of the court': *AOO v AON* [2011] 4 SLR 1169.

TQ v TR concerned a pre-nuptial agreement governed by Dutch law. The pre-nuptial agreement provided that '[t]here shall be no community of matrimonial assets whatsoever between the spouses'. The Court of Appeal held that if a pre-nuptial agreement is 'entered into by foreign nationals and that agreement is governed by and valid according to foreign law, significant (even critical) weight to the terms of the agreement would be accorded'. Where the agreement concerned is valid according to its proper law and not repugnant to any overriding public policy of Singapore, it could be taken into account by the court in deciding the issues covered by the agreement. The court went on to hold that the pre-nuptial agreement was valid under Dutch law and not repugnant to Singapore public policy. The pre-nuptial agreement was accorded 'the highest significance'. This led to there being no order made on the division of assets in favour of the wife.

Post-nuptial agreements have generally also been enforced by the court. In the case of *Tan Siew Eng v Ng Meng Hin* [2003] 3 SLR(R) 474, the parties entered into an agreement providing for a divorce and all ancillary matters. One of its clauses called for the wife to commence divorce proceedings. The wife did not do so. It was accepted by the husband that she had repudiated the agreement. Nevertheless, the courts chose to enforce the terms of the agreement in so far as they related to the division of matrimonial assets.

C. DIVORCE, NULLITY AND JUDICIAL SEPARATION

6. RECOGNITION OF FOREIGN MARRIAGE/DIVORCES

6.1 Summarise the position in your jurisdiction

Section 105 read with section 108 of the Women's Charter, provides that a foreign marriage may be treated as invalid for lack of capacity or other grounds of invalidity under the law of the place where the marriage was celebrated. Formal validity of a foreign marriage is governed by the law of the place of celebration of the marriage: *Arpinya Rongchotiawattana v Wee Oh Keng* [1997] 3 SLR(R) 378.

Essential validity of a foreign marriage under Singapore law is governed by the ante-nuptial domiciliary laws of parties, under the 'dual domicile' rule. This means that each party must have capacity to marry according to the laws of the country from which they each are from: *Re Maria Huberdina Hertogh; Inche Mansor Adabi v Adrianus Petrus Hertogh* [1951] MLJ 164 and *Moh Ah Kiu v Central Provident Fund Board* [1992] 2 SLR(R) 440.

Singapore courts generally recognise a foreign divorce as a matter of international comity and where recognition of the divorce accords with public policy and the court's sense of 'good morals'. The validity of a foreign divorce is not tested solely by reference to domicile of the parties: *Ho Ah Chye v Hsinchieh Hsu Irene* [1994] 1 SLR(R) 485. Where a foreign divorce has been pronounced under circumstances that do not offend against natural justice, the foreign divorce ought to be recognised: *Ng Sui Wah Novina v Chandra Michael Seitawan* [1992] 2 SLR(R) 111.

In *Weschler Mouantri Andree Marie Louise v Mouantri Karl-Michael and Another* [2009] SGHC 83, the High Court held that the courts could not grant a divorce to a petitioner whose marriage had already been dissolved by the Swedish Court, whose jurisdiction it recognised.

7. DIVORCE

7.1 Explain the grounds for divorce within the jurisdiction (please also deal with nullity and judicial separation if appropriate)

There is only one ground for divorce in Singapore, being the irretrievable breakdown of marriage. Sections 95(3)(a)-(e) of the Women's Charter list five facts which prove an irretrievable breakdown of the marriage:

(a) that the defendant has committed adultery and the plaintiff finds it intolerable to live with the defendant;
(b) that the defendant has behaved in such a way that the plaintiff cannot reasonably be expected to live with the defendant;
(c) that the defendant has deserted the plaintiff for a continuous period of at least two years immediately preceding the filing of the writ;
(d) that the parties to the marriage have lived apart for a continuous period of at least three years immediately preceding the filing of the writ and the defendant consents to a judgment being granted; or
(e) that the parties to the marriage have lived apart for a continuous period of at least four years immediately preceding the filing of the writ.

Section 101(1) of the charter allows for an application for a judgment of judicial separation to be made on proof of one of the five facts set out above. Section 101(2) provides that spouses who are separated no longer need to cohabit with each other. Section 103 makes clear that a judicially separated spouse cannot claim in the intestacy of the other spouse.

Section 104 of the charter provides that a spouse may file for a judgment of nullity in respect of his or her marriage. A marriage may be adjudged void or voidable. Under section 105, marriages are rendered void where either party is below the age of 18; where the parties are within prohibited degrees of relationship as set out in the charter and have not obtained a special statutory marriage licence to wed; where either party has committed bigamy; where the parties are not respectively male and female; or if the marriage is not formally solemnised under Singapore law.

Section 106 further provides that a marriage may be held voidable on the grounds of:
(a) non-consummation owing to the incapacity of either party to consummate it or wilful refusal of the defendant to consummate it;
(b) either party not validly consenting to marriage, 'whether in consequence of duress, mistake, unsoundness of mind or otherwise';
(c) either party, though capable of giving a valid consent, suffering (whether continuously or intermittently) from a mental disorder so as to be unfit for marriage;
(d) the defendant suffering from venereal disease in a communicable form; or
(e) the defendant being pregnant by some person other than the plaintiff.

A claim that a marriage is voidable can be defeated if it can be shown that the claimant, knowing that it was open to him to have the marriage avoided, so conducted himself to lead the other spouse 'reasonably to believe that he would not seek to do so': section 107(1) of the charter. Claims for nullity on grounds (b)-(e) above, have also be made within three years from the date of marriage.

8. FINANCES/CAPITAL, PROPERTY

8.1 What powers does the court have to allocate financial resources and property on the breakdown of the marriage?

Section 112(1) of the Women's Charter empowers the court when granting a judgment of divorce, judicial separation or nullity of marriage, to order the division or sale of matrimonial assets, 'in such proportions as the court thinks just and reasonable'.

The court's power is discretionary. Where a wife disavowed liability for a property which was initially loss-making in affidavits and a formal agreement, she was precluded from claiming a share in the property after it turned out that the property had become a lucrative investment: *Ong Boon Huat Samuel v Chan Mei Lan Kristine* [2007] 2 SLR(R) 729.

Unless a judgment for divorce, judicial separation or nullity has been pronounced, the court generally has no jurisdiction to hear matters concerning the division of assets: *Ng Sui Wah Novina v Chandra Michael Setiawan* [1992] 2 SLR(R) 111. Narrow statutory exceptions exist for financial relief consequent upon foreign matrimonial proceedings.

Section 112(10) of the charter defines divisible 'matrimonial assets' as being generally any asset of any nature acquired during marriage by one or both parties. Any asset acquired by a party before marriage is not treated as a matrimonial asset unless the asset 'is ordinarily used or enjoyed by both parties or one or more of their children for shelter or transportation or for household, education, recreational, social or aesthetic purposes' or, if the asset 'has been substantially improved during the marriage by the other party or both parties'. Any asset acquired at any time by gift or inheritance is not divisible, unless 'substantially improved during the marriage by the other party or by both parties to the marriage'.

A party staking a claim to assets of the other spouse acquired prior to marriage or by gift or inheritance, has to prove direct significant contributions to their substantial improvement: *Chen Siew Hwee v Low Kee Guan* [2006] 4 SLR(R) 605.

In *Wan Lai Cheng v Quek Seow Kee* [2012] 4 SLR 405, it was clarified that:

(a) Gifts from third-parties are not included in the pool of matrimonial assets, unless the 'substantial improvement' exception is satisfied.

(b) 'Pure'inter-spousal gifts (ie, gifts that are not acquired by the donee spouse by way of a third-party gift or an inheritance) are included in the pool of matrimonial assets without the need to satisfy any further conditions.

(c) Inter-spousal 're-gifts' (ie, an unconditional gift made by a donor spouse of what was originally a third-party gift or an inheritance) are not included in the pool of matrimonial assets. The 'substantial improvement' exception is not applicable to inter-spousal 're-gifts'.

Tan Hwee Lee v Tan Cheng Guan [2012] 4 SLR 785 clarified further that where *de minimis* inter-spousal gifts were concerned, the court had the discretion to exclude such gifts from the pool of divisible assets. If a gift was made under an agreement in contemplation of divorce, the court could exclude it from division if it is 'clearly inequitable' to divide it.

8.2 Explain and illustrate with reference to recent cases the court's thinking on division of assets

There is no legal presumption that the 'just and equitable' division of assets under Section 112 of the Women's Charter means an equal split of the matrimonial assets: *Yow Mee Lan v Chen Kai Buan* [2000] 2 SLR(R) 659, *Lim Choon Lai v Chew Kim Heng* [2001] 2 SLR(R) 260; *Lock Yeng Fun v Chua Hock Chye* [2007] 3 SLR(R) 520.

The power to divide assets under the charter is exercised in a 'broad brush' fashion. There is no 'account of every minute sum each party has paid or incurred in the acquisition of the matrimonial assets' or meticulous investigation of obligations rendered to the family: *NK v NL* [2007] 3 SLR(R) 743.

The statutory criteria considered under section 112 include the extent of contributions by either party in money, property or work to acquisition, improvement or maintenance of marital assets, debts or obligations undertaken for benefit of the family, needs of children, extent of contributions to care of the family and relatives, income, earning capacity and financial needs of the parties in the foreseeable future, duration of the marriage, age of the parties etc.

Generally for short, childless marriages, a wife tends to get a share of assets equal to her direct contribution to their acquisition and where possible, lump sum maintenance: *Ong Boon Huat Samuel v Chan Mei Lan Kristine* [2007] 2 SLR(R) 729. *Koh Kim Lan Angela v Choong Kian Haw* [1993] 3 SLR(R) 491.

In *Chan Yuen Boey v Sia Hee Soon* [2012] 3 SLR 402, the High Court observed that in the division of assets in long marriages:

'... the proportion awarded to homemaker wives who have made modest financial contributions for marriages lasting 17 to 35 years with children ranged between 35% to 50% of the total matrimonial assets... Where the wife also worked and supported the family financially, the courts have not hesitated to award her up to 60% of the total assets... The exceptions, where the apportionment in favour of the wife was less than 35%, typically concerned cases where the total pool of matrimonial assets had been very substantial, in excess of $100 million'

Failure to provide full and frank disclosure of assets and means can lead the court to drawing adverse inferences against the culpable party. In *Chan Siew Fong v Chan Fook Kee* [2002] 1 SLR(R) 93, a wife in a 30-year marriage received 100 per cent of the sole disclosed marital asset, in circumstances where the court disbelieved that the husband had made full and frank disclosure of assets abroad. In *Yeo Chong Lin v Tay Ang Choo Nancy* [2011] 2 SLR 1157, the Court of Appeal held that a court faced with an absence of full and frank disclosure had at least two alternatives. It could either order a higher proportion of assets to be given to the 'innocent' spouse, or give a value to what assets it considered to be 'undisclosed'. The court in *Yeo Chong Lin* (ibid) approved the lower court's remedy of adding a further 10 per cent to the marital assets as representing the husband's undisclosed assets.

9. FINANCES/MAINTENANCE

9.1 Explain the operation of maintenance for spouses on an ongoing basis after the breakdown of the marriage

Only wives can claim maintenance. Maintenance can be claimed on an interim basis pending the hearing of matrimonial proceedings and at the final hearing of ancillary matters.

Section 114(1) of the Women's Charter requires the court to have regard to all the circumstances of the case in awarding maintenance. This includes income, earning capacity, property, the parties' age, financial resources, needs and obligations, the standard of living of the family before the breakdown of the marriage, duration of marriage, any disability and financial and non-financial contributions.

Section 114(2) of the charter calls for parties to be, as far as is practicable, put in the financial position they would have been had the marriage not broken down and where each party properly discharged his or her financial responsibilities to the other. There is no broad principle that a husband who has not maintained a wife during the marriage is automatically absolved of the need not do so after a divorce: *Foo Ah Yan v Chiam Heng Chow* [2012] 2 SLR 506.

9.2 Is it common for maintenance to be awarded?

Maintenance is often claimed and awarded pending the conclusion of matrimonial proceedings and as part of the ancillary matters.

9.3 Explain and illustrate with reference to recent cases the court's thinking on maintenance

Interim maintenance pending a final divorce is usually conservative. It is intended to provide a 'tide over' sum for the applicant until the final hearing. It does not usually preserve the *status quo* during the marriage. Evidence of what the standard of living was, is considered by the court on a rough and ready basis. A final award for maintenance would usually exceed an interim award of maintenance: *Lee Bee Kim Jennifer v Lim Yew Khang Cecil* [2005] SGHC 209.

In *Tan Sue-Ann Melissa v Lim Siang Bok Dennis* [2004] 3 SLR(R) 376, it was held that the rationale behind imposing a duty on a former husband to maintain his former wife is to even out any financial inequalities between the spouses, taking into account any economic prejudice suffered by the wife during marriage.

Where an order for the division of the matrimonial assets has been made and where this does not amount to much in money's worth, the court may make an order of maintenance that is substantial. (*BG v BF* [2007] 3 SLR(R) 233.) The converse is also true: *Lock Yeng Fun v Chua Hock Chye* [2007] 3 SLR(R) 520.

Maintenance awards are determined flexibly with 'a common sense dose of realities' and without reference to any single formula: *Foo Ah Yan v Chiam Heng Chow* [2012] 2 SLR 506.

10. CHILD MAINTENANCE

10.1 On what basis is child maintenance calculated within the jurisdiction?

Section 127 of the Women's Charter allows the court to order a parent to pay maintenance for the benefit of 'a child of the marriage' under 21 years old during matrimonial proceedings. Like spousal maintenance, child maintenance can be sought on an interim basis and at the final hearing of ancillary matters.

Section 92 of the charter defines 'a child of the marriage' to mean 'any child of the husband and wife, and includes any adopted child and any other child (whether or not a child of the husband or of the wife) who was a member of the family of the husband and wife at the time when they ceased to live together or at the time immediately preceding the institution of the proceedings, whichever first occurred'.

A child above 21 years of age is still entitled to be maintained if under mental or physical disability, compulsory military service or undergoing educational or vocational training, under section 69(5) of the charter.

Section 69(4) of the charter provides that the court when ordering maintenance for a child shall have regard to all of the circumstances of the case, including the financial needs of the child, income, earning capacity (if any), property and financial resources, any disability of the child, the age of the parents, duration of their marriage, the standard of living enjoyed by the child before the parent ceased providing reasonable maintenance for the child.

11. RECIPROCAL ENFORCEMENT OF FINANCIAL ORDERS

11.1 Summarise the position in your jurisdiction

There is no reciprocal enforcement legislation providing for enforcement of foreign financial orders. *Prima facie*, a party intending to enforce such foreign orders may have to start a civil action based on the foreign judgment: *Hong Pian Tee v Les Placements Germain Gauthier Inc* [2002] 1 SLR(R) 515, *Murakami Tokako v Wiryadi Louise Maria* [2007] 4 SLR(R) 565.

Two concurrently operative statutes, the Maintenance Orders (Facilities for Enforcement) Act (Cap 168) (MOFEA) and Maintenance Orders (Reciprocal Enforcement) Act (Cap 169) (MOREA), allow a person to enforce maintenance orders against a party who lives in a reciprocating country, and *vice versa*. Whether an application should be made to MOFEA or MOREA is dependent on the act which the reciprocating country is a party to.

12. FINANCIAL RELIEF AFTER FOREIGN DIVORCE PROCEEDINGS

12.1 What powers are available to make orders following a foreign divorce?

Amendments to the Women's Charter in 2011 empower the court to allow parties divorced in a foreign country to apply for orders for ancillary relief in Singapore if one of the parties was domiciled in Singapore or habitually resident in Singapore for a year prior to the application or foreign divorce. The court must be satisfied that there are 'substantial grounds' for granting such relief. It will consider a range of statutory criteria in deciding whether Singapore is an appropriate forum. These include consideration of the connection of the parties to Singapore and the foreign country, the financial relief already available abroad, the presence of assets here, whether an applicant for such relief had good reasons for omitting to seek relief abroad, the enforceability of a foreign ancillary matters order and the time since the date of the foreign divorce, annulment or judicial separation.

D. CHILDREN

13. CUSTODY/PARENTAL RESPONSIBILITY

13.1 Briefly explain the legal position in relation to custody/parental responsibility following the breakdown of a relationship or marriage

Section 68 of the Women's Charter places a duty on both parents to maintain or contribute to the maintenance of their children. In making a maintenance order, the Court will have regard to the parent's means and station in life.

13.2 Briefly explain the legal position in relation to access/contact/ visitation following the breakdown of a relationship or marriage

Section 125 of the Women's Charter empowers the court to place a child in the custody of either parent.

A parent with custody over the child has control and responsibility over the upbringing, education, health, and religion of the child. A parent with care and control of the child has the right to make daily decisions about a child's upbringing. This right naturally belongs to the parent with whom the child lives: *AQL v AQM* [2012] 1 SLR 840. The court usually grants access to the parent who does not have care and control of the child. Access gives the parent regular hours of contact with the child. Access may be unsupervised. Access is usually supervised if there is emotional, physical or sexual abuse.

In *CX v CY* [2005] 3 SLR(R) 690, the highest court endorsed the concept of joint parental responsibility, even where parents harbour acrimony towards each other. Singapore courts now generally place children in the joint custody of both parents. Exceptional circumstances where this does not happen may be those of physical, sexual or emotional abuse of the child by one parent, or where the relationship of the parties is such that co-operation is impossible even after the avenues of mediation and counseling have been explored, and where lack of co-operation is harmful for the child.

Orders for joint care and control are comparatively rare in Singapore. In deciding which parent should be given care and control of the children, the following trends may be observed from local case law — (i) all things being equal, the mother is preferred if the child is young: *Soon Peck Wah v Woon Che Chye* [1997] 3 SLR(R) 430; (ii) a preference towards preserving the *status quo* and continuity of living conditions: *Wong Phila Mae v Shaw Harold* [1991] 1 SLR(R) 680; and (iii) siblings should not be separated: *Kim Chun Ahe v Ng Siew Kee* [2002] SGDC 276.

14. INTERNATIONAL ABDUCTION

14.1 Summarise the position in your jurisdiction

Section 13 of the Guardianship of Infants Act (Cap 122) empowers the court to direct a parent having custody of a child to produce the child to the judge to make any temporary custody or protection order as may be necessary. Section 14 provides that where a child is removed from custody of his lawful guardian, the sheriff of the court may 'seize' the child and deliver him to his lawful guardian.

Singapore acceded to the Hague Convention on Civil Aspects of International Child Abduction 1980 on 28 December 2010 and enacted the International Child Abduction Act 2010 which came into force in Singapore on 1 March 2011. Singapore therefore subscribes to the Hague Convention regime of ensuring the prompt return of children who have been wrongfully removed from their state of habitual residence, unless the child has been shown to have settled into his or her new environment. The Ministry of Social and Family Development is the designated Central Authority to implement Singapore's obligations under the Convention.

As at 14 June 2013, the countries and territories that have mutual reciprocal enforcement protections for children under the Convention with Singapore are Argentina, Australia, Bahamas, Belgium, the Czech Republic, Estonia, France, Germany, Greece, Hong Kong SAR, Ireland (with effect from 1 July 2013), Israel, Italy, Latvia, Lithuania, Macau, Malta, New Zealand, Norway, Serbia, Seychelles (with effect from 1 July 2013), Slovakia, Spain, Sweden, Switzerland, Ukraine, the United States of America and Uruguay.

When making decisions in relation to the international abduction of children, the Family Court applies the provisions of the International Child Abduction Act 2010 together with the relevant Articles of the Convention. This was done in *BDU v BDT* [2013] SGHC 106 where Justice Judith Prakash ordered the return of a child to his home in Germany.

The decisive factors that a Singapore court will consider in any 'abduction' case are therefore a child's habitual residence and stability when making orders as to whether a child ought to be returned to Singapore or another country. The court will also consider the child's welfare and whether the parent requesting the child's return originally consented to or acquiesced in the removal.

15. LEAVE TO REMOVE/APPLICATIONS TO TAKE A CHILD OUT OF JURISDICTION

15.1 Summarise the position in your jurisdiction

The Singapore court will be concerned mainly with whether the decision to remove the child from the jurisdiction is reasonable in all the circumstances of the case. This involves a balancing exercise, taking into account the effects on children when the wishes of the parent with primary care desiring to take them abroad are interfered with, whether the primary carer may harbour resentment against the children, should his or her wishes to leave be prevented from being fulfilled and whether the application is made in good faith and for good reasons.

15.2 Under what circumstances may a parent apply to remove their child from the jurisdiction against the wishes of the other parent?

No person is allowed to take a child who is subject to an order of custody out of Singapore 'except with the written consent of both parents or the leave of court': section 126(3) Women's Charter.

In *Tan Kah Imm v D'Aranjo Joanne Abigail* [1998] SGHC 247, a mother successfully applied for children aged 18, 15 and 10 to leave for studies in the US. She was found to bear no ill-will or grudge against her ex-husband. The court accepted she truly believed that it was in the best interests and welfare of the children that they should be allowed to pursue their choice of study in the US.

In *Re C (an infant)* [2003] 1 SLR(R) 502, grandparents of a child whose father was serving a jail term, were allowed to leave with the child for Australia. The Court of Appeal held:

'It is the reasonableness of the party having custody to want to take the child out of the jurisdiction which will be determinative, and always keeping in mind that the paramount consideration is the welfare of the child. If the motive of the party seeking to take the child out of jurisdiction was to end contact between the child and the other parent, then that would be a strong factor to refuse the application'.

In *AZB v AYZ* [2012] 3 SLR 627, it was also held that:-

'... the welfare of the child is often so inextricably intertwined with the general well-being and happiness of the primary caregiver that the court is loath to interfere with important life decisions of the primary caregiver, so long as they are reasonably made and are not against the interests of the child'.

The court in *AZB v AYZ* decided that a wife's decision to relocate to the US, where she was originally from, was genuine and reasonable. The court took into account the wife's alienation, isolation and vulnerability in Singapore, as well as benefits which relocating to the US would have on the wife's emotional and financial well-being as the child's main carer. The court concluded that the wife's decision to relocate was in the best interest of the child and also that the husband had not been a good influence on the child.

E. SURROGACY AND ADOPTION

16. VALIDITY OF SURROGACY AGREEMENTS

16.1 Briefly summarise the position in your jurisdiction

Currently, it is illegal for a woman to become a surrogate mother in Singapore and childless couples are prohibited from seeking surrogacy in Singapore. It is also unlawful for local doctors to perform surrogacy procedures.

17. ADOPTION

17.1 Briefly explain the legal position in relation to adoption in your jurisdiction. Is adoption available to individuals, cohabiting couples (both heterosexual and same-sex)?

Adoption is governed by the Adoption of Children Act (Cap 4). Under the act, an applicant must be at least 25 years of age and must be at least 21 years older than the child. The court may waive these requirements if it thinks fit where: (i) either the applicant and the child are close blood relatives within the prohibited degrees of consanguinity; or (ii) as an exceptional measure, it is right to allow the adoption. A sole male applicant is generally not allowed to adopt a girl unless there are special circumstances that justify adoption as an exceptional measure. The act also requires that both the applicant and child are resident in Singapore.

A joint application to adopt a child must be by a married couple. Hence, cohabiting couples may not jointly adopt a child.

In addition to the above requirements, the court will only make an adoption order if: (i) the adoption serves the welfare of the child; (ii) the consent of every parent or guardian of the child, or person who has actual custody of the child, or who is liable to contribute to support the child, is obtained; and (iii) there is no payment in connection with the adoption.

F. COHABITATION

18. COHABITATION

18.1 What legislation (if any) governs division of property for unmarried couples on the breakdown of the relationship?

There is no legislation in Singapore that specifically governs the division of property for unmarried couples on breakdown of their relationship: *Chia Kum Fatt Rolfston v Lim Lay Choo* [1993] 2 SLR(R) 793. Property and assets of cohabitees are dealt with under ordinary principles of general property law.

G. FAMILY DISPUTE RESOLUTION

19. MEDIATION, COLLABORATIVE LAW AND ARBITRATION

19.1 Briefly summarise the non-court based processes available in your jurisdiction and the current status of agreements reached under the auspices of mediation, collaborative law and arbitration

Currently, mediation is available in Singapore as a means of family dispute resolution. Mediation may be conducted by a judge-mediator at the Family Resolution Chambers for disputes relating to divorce, custody, care and control of children, maintenance and division of matrimonial assets. Agreements made between parties become enforceable when they have been made into orders of court: *AOO v AON* [2011] 4 SLR 1169, *AYM v AYL* [2013] 1 SLR 924. Collaborative law and family law arbitration are not part of the legal landscape yet, although they are being considered for possible implementation.

19.2 What is the statutory basis (if any), for mediation, collaborative law and arbitration in your jurisdiction? In particular, are the parties required to attempt a family dispute resolution in advance of the institution of proceedings?

Sections 50(1) and 50(2) of the charter empower the court to refer disputing parties to mediation or counselling. Since 2011, the court may, under Section 50(3A) of the charter, order mandatory mediation or counselling where there are children to the marriage who are under the age of 21 years. This has become the norm for cases filed from 1 July 2013 beginning with couples having at least one child of 14 years of age or less. Such mediation or counselling takes place at the Child Focused Resolution Centre. The aim is to get divorcing parents to focus on the welfare of their children during proceedings.

H. OTHER

20. CIVIL PARTNERSHIP/SAME-SEX MARRIAGE

20.1 What is the status of civil partnership/same-sex marriage within the jurisdiction?

20.2 What legislation governs civil partnership/same-sex marriage.

Singapore does not have any law recognising civil partnerships. Same-sex marriages are treated as void. However, a marriage between a person who has undergone a sex reassignment procedure and a member of the opposite sex is valid.

21. CONTROVERSIAL AREAS/RAPIDLY DEVELOPING AREAS OF LAW

21.1 Is there a particular area of the law within the jurisdiction that is currently undergoing major change?

In 2013, the Chief Justice of Singapore announced various reforms to the family justice system aimed at reducing the acrimony inherent in family disputes and providing holistic solutions to parties in family disputes. These include the possible establishment of a separate Family Justice Court and the setting up of an international family law division within the Subordinate Courts, which will be equipped with specialised expertise for the timely resolution of cases with a cross-border or international dimension.

Another significant future development would be the promotion of the use of collaborative law and possibly the use of arbitration in the family justice system.

21.2 Which areas of law are most out-of-step? Which areas would you most like to see reformed/changed?

First, there is room for greater certainty in the structuring of fair and effective guidelines for care and control and access orders which would help reduce the scope for litigation and attendant anxiety of parents.

Second, greater clarity in how pre-nuptial and post-nuptial agreements would be weighed during ancillary matters hearings would be useful. This would guide practitioners in structuring such agreements and foster a clearer understanding as to the utility and impact of such agreements.

Third, the courts have stressed that non-financial contributions ought not to be undervalued in the division of matrimonial assets. However an examination of the case law reveals a trend of 'home maker husbands' who have made significant non-financial contributions towards home making and caring for the children, and less significant financial contributions as compared with their breadwinner wives being awarded a smaller share of the matrimonial assets as compared with home maker wives who have made similar contributions.

Men in Singapore are precluded from claiming maintenance. As gender inequality recedes, it may be time for these aspects of the law to be reformed.

Lastly, the courts are encountering serious cases involving parental alienation or emotional abuse and efficient remedies need to be in place to address such concerns.

South Africa

Catto Neethling Wiid Inc. Amanda Catto

A. JURISDICTION AND CONFLICT OF LAW

1. SOURCES OF LAW

1.1 What is the primary source of law in relation to the breakdown of marriage and the welfare of children within the jurisdiction?

1.2 Which are the main statutes governing matrimonial law in the jurisdiction?

The sources of South African law relating to marriage, the dissolution of marriage and the welfare of children are common law, customary law, precedent, statute, the writings of jurists and of primary reference, the Constitution.

Regard is always had to the Constitution of the Republic of South Africa as the supreme law when interpreting sources of law. The High Court and the Constitutional Court have held that the Bill of Rights must be interpreted in such a way as to afford protection to the core elements of the institution of marriage and family life.

The common law is Roman Dutch-based with asignificant English law influence. It has been developed through the decisions of the courts and influenced significantly by a number of cultures that make up the South African way of life.

The primary statutes that have application to family law are the following:

- the Marriage Act, 1961 (25 of 1961), which deals with the solemnisation of marriages;
- the Matrimonial Property Act, 1984 (88 of 1984), which regulates the distinct matrimonial property systems;
- the Divorce Act, 1979 (70 of 1979), which determines the grounds for divorce, based on the irretrievable breakdown of a marriage and the determination of the person and proprietary consequences of the divorce for the spouses;
- the Maintenance Act, 1998 (99 of 1998), which regulates the determination and enforcement of maintenance claims;
- the Domicile Act, 1992 (3 of 1992), which amends the common law relating to domicile and regulates the acquisition and determination of domicile;
- the Children's Act, 2005 (38 of 2005), which consolidates the law relating to children and determines the exercise of parental responsibilities and rights.

2. JURISDICTION

2.1 What are the main jurisdictional requirements for the institution of proceedings in relation to divorce, property and children?

A court has jurisdiction in a divorce action if one or both of the parties are either:

(i) domiciled in the area of jurisdiction of the court on the date on which the divorce action is instituted; or

(ii) are ordinarily resident in the jurisdiction of the court on the date of institution of the proceedings and has or have been ordinarily resident in the Republic of South Africa for a period of not less than one year immediately prior to that date.

The South African courts have not definitively defined the term 'residence'. There is no fixed minimum period of physical presence to constitute residence. The term 'ordinarily resident' denotes a residence that is not casual or occasional.

A court that has jurisdiction in respect of a divorce action, has jurisdiction in respect of all relevant claims between the parties, including claims relating to the payment of maintenance, the exercise of parental responsibilities and rights relating to children and property claims. These issues are generally determined simultaneously with the granting of the divorce.

The court which made the original order of divorce, or another court where the parties are both domiciled (or where the applicant is domiciled if the respondent consents) may rescind, vary or suspend the order in respect of the children or the payment of maintenance.

The High Court is the upper guardian of all minor children that fall within the jurisdiction of South Africa and thus has jurisdiction over all matters pertaining to minor children in South Africa.

3. DOMICILE AND HABITUAL RESIDENCE

3.1 Explain the concepts of domicile and habitual residence as they apply to the jurisdiction

In terms of South African law, no person can be without a domicile or have more than one domicile at any time. The Domicile Act 3 of 1992 adapted the common law. The Act must be read in conjunction with the common law.

Any person over the age of 18 years is competent to acquire a domicile of choice. A domicile of choice is acquired by a person when they are lawfully present at a particular place and have the intention to settle there for an indefinite period.

The private legal status of a person in South African law is determined by the law of the country in which he is domiciled.

A minor or a person lacking in mental capacity is not capable of acquiring a domicile of choice. Section 2(1) of the Act states that domicile is determined by operation of law at the place with which they are factually most closely connected.

A domicile of choice is acquired by a person having the requisite legal capacity who establishes their lawful presence in the chosen area with the intention of settling for an indefinite period. A person must be habitually and physically present at the place of intended domicile. No minimum period of physical presence is required, but more than a visit is necessary. The person's presence in the relevant jurisdiction must be lawful to acquire a domicile of choice.

The term 'habitual residence' is known to South African law within the context of applications in terms of the Hague Convention on Civil Aspects of International Child Abduction which was ratified in 1996 and incorporated into South African law in October 1997.

The term 'habitual residence' has been considered in local courts with reference to international precedent. The term has no technical definition, but is decided on the facts of each case, by applying an ordinary meaning to the words. The courts have held that the word 'habitual' implies a stable, territorial link, achieved through length of stay or through evidence of a particularly close tie between person and place, which is not temporary. (*Central Autority of the Republic of South Africa v L G* 2011 (2) SA)

4. CONFLICT OF LAW/APPLICABLE LAW TO BE APPLIED

4.1 What happens when one party applies to stay proceedings in favour of a foreign jurisdiction? What factors will the local court take into account when determining forum issues?

It often occurs that matrimonial proceedings are instituted simultaneously in competing jurisdictions. In determining whether proceedings should be stayed, the court will take into account a number of factors.

The court will consider whether it has jurisdiction to hear the action. The doctrine of effectiveness is fundamental to the consideration of a court's jurisdiction in a matter. The court must have the power to make its order effective. Whether the court has jurisdiction in a divorce is determined in terms of the jurisdictional requirements stipulated in the Divorce Act as detailed above.

Once it is determined that the court has jurisdiction, the court will have regard to whether the issue is already pending adjudication in another court, the doctrine of *lis alibi pendens*. It is within the court's discretion to consider whether an action brought before it should be stayed pending the decision of another previously brought action between the same parties, for the same cause and in respect of the same subject-matter, or whether it is more just and equitable or convenient that it should be allowed to proceed.

In considering a plea of *lis alibi pendens* the court will consider which court will more conveniently consider the issue. The plea is not an absolute bar to the matter proceeding; the court has a discretion whether or not to uphold it and may refuse the stay application.

In *Kerbel v Kerbel* 1987(1)SA 562 W, it was held that once the plea of *lis alibi pendens* has been taken, the court should be inclined to uphold it, unless there is good reason to determine why the court where the action first commenced should not be allowed to carry on with the proceedings.

A court may also decline to exercise jurisdiction if it is more convenient or more fitting for another forum to do so, the doctrine of *forum non conveniens*.

B. PRE- AND POST-NUPTIAL AGREEMENTS

5. VALIDITY OF PRE- AND POST-NUPTIAL AGREEMENTS

5.1 To what extent are pre- and post-nups binding within the jurisdiction? Could you provide a brief discussion of the most significant recent case law on this issue?

South African law recognises a validly concluded ante-nuptial or post-nuptial contract, save to the extent that the contract violates public policy considerations.

Where there is no ante-nuptial contract, the patrimonial consequences of the marriage are determined by the husband's domiciliary law at the time of the marriage. The principle of immutability applies so that there is certainty regarding the law that applies to the patrimonial consequences of the marriage.

Once the legal system governing the proprietary regime of the marriage is determined, that legal system cannot be changed. If, however the husband's domiciliary law at the time that a post-nuptial contract is executed recognises such a contract, then South African law will recognise the contract.

A South African court must authorise the execution of a post-nuptial contract for it to be valid in South Africa, whether against spouses or third parties.

In terms of section 7(9) of the Divorce Act, when a South African court grants a decree of divorce in respect of a marriage, the patrimonial consequences of which are, according to the South African private international law, governed by the law of a foreign state, the court shall have the same power that a competent court of the foreign state concerned would have had at that time to order that assets be transferred from one spouse to the other spouse. This will include applying a validly concluded foreign ante- or post-nuptial contract.

Although subject to some debate, the essential validity of an ante-nuptial contract is determined by the law of the husband's domicile in respect of movable assets and by the law of the place where the property is situated, *lex situs*, in respect of immovable property.

Where parties insert a choice of law clause in an ante-nuptial contract, the validity of such a clause is determined in accordance with the law of the matrimonial domicile.

The *lex loci contractus*, or the law of the place where the contract was concluded, determines the formal validity of an ante- or post-nuptial contract.

Where an ante-nuptial contract is executed outside of South Africa by a husband who is domiciled in South Africa, the contract must be registered in South Africa to be effective against third parties. Registration is not required where the husband is not a South African domiciliary to be recognised by South African law.

South African law does not require an ante-nuptial contract be concluded in writing, formally executed or registered for it to be valid between the parties, but such a contract will not be valid as against third parties.

C. DIVORCE, NULLITY AND JUDICIAL SEPARATION

6. RECOGNITION OF FOREIGN MARRIAGES/DIVORCES

6.1 Summarise the position in your jurisdiction

The validity of a foreign marriage is tested according to the *lex loci celebrationis*, the law of the place where the marriage was celebrated.

The *fraus legis* doctrine, or doctrine of evasion, determines that where a man or woman, one or both of whom were domiciled in the court's jurisdiction, have their marriage deliberately solemnised elsewhere to escape a formal requirement of the *lex domicilii*, they act *in fraudem legis*, and the validity of their marriage is then tested in accordance with local law as *lex domicilii*.

Where the application of the *lex loci celebrationis* is repugnant to the moral principles of the court, it will refuse legal recognition of the marriage. An example of this would be where the marriage is tainted by incest.

Section 13 of the Divorce Act determines that the validity of a divorce order, order for annulment or judicial separation granted in a court of a foreign country or territory shall be recognised by a South African court if, on the date on which the order was granted, either party to the marriage was: domiciled in the country or territory concerned (either in terms of South African law or in terms of the law of that country or territory); was ordinarily resident in that country or territory; or was a national of that country or territory.

It is implicit that the divorce granted must be effective under the law of the country in which it was granted.

7. DIVORCE

7.1 Explain the grounds for divorce within the jurisdiction (please also deal with nullity and judicial separation if appropriate)

The two grounds for divorce are determined in terms of section 3 of the Divorce Act. They are: irretrievable breakdown of the marriage/civil union; and mental illness or continuous unconsciousness.

In terms of section 4 of the Divorce Act, a court may grant a decree of divorce on the ground of irretrievable breakdown of the marriage if it is satisfied that the marriage has reached such a state of disintegration that there is no reasonable prospect of reconciliation or the restoration of a normal marriage relationship between them.

The court will not grant a decree of divorce where appropriate safeguards are not in place to secure the interests of dependent(s) and/or minor children.

The court determining whether the marriage has broken down irretrievably, may consider, as proof of the irretrievable breakdown of the marriage, evidence that: the parties have not lived together as husband and wife for a continuous period of one year prior to the proceedings; that the defendant committed adultery and the plaintiff finds it irreconcilable with a continued marital relationship; or that the defendant has been declared an habitual criminal and is undergoing imprisonment as a consequence of such a sentence.

In addition to the above factors, the court may consider any other circumstances that indicate the marriage has irretrievably broken down. The test is not burdensome.

Section 5A of the Divorce Act provides that the court may refuse to grant a decree of divorce unless it is satisfied that the spouse in whose power it is to have a religious impediment to divorce removed has done all that is necessary to dissolve the religious marriage and to remove the religious barriers to remarriage.

In the absence of compliance with various legal requirements for a valid marriage, the marriage can be determined to be void or voidable.

In circumstances of a void marriage, there is no marriage and no consequences of marriage result. The parties usually seek a declaratory order. A void marriage cannot be validated, save in certain specific circumstances, usually where the offending issue is a formal requirement.

A voidable marriage is distinct from a void marriage. Here, a valid marriage is concluded unless it is invalidated and annulled by a court. Until it is set aside, all the consequences of a valid marriage apply. The annulment usually applies retrospectively to the date of the marriage. Examples of voidable marriages include:

- a marriage by a minor without the consent of his or her guardian;
- a marriage concluded under duress or by fraud or error;
- a marriage by someone impotent at the time of the marriage.

A putative marriage may result as a consequence of a void or voidable marriage. A putative marriage is not a marriage and arises where either both or one party is, in good faith, ignorant that their marriage is invalid. The law attaches some consequences to a union declared to be a putative marriage by a court. Certain proprietary claims may assist the innocent party. Children born of the union are regarded to be legitimate.

There is no longer any concept of judicial separation in South Africa.

8. FINANCES/CAPITAL, PROPERTY

8.1 What powers does the court have to allocate financial resources and property on the breakdown of marriage?

8.2 Explain and illustrate with reference to recent cases the court's thinking on division of assets

A court granting a decree of divorce will determine the proprietary and financial claims of the parties.

In terms of section 7(1) of the Divorce Act, a court granting a decree of divorce may make an order with regard to the division of assets or the payment of maintenance by one party to the other, in accordance with a written settlement agreement entered into between the parties. The parties may, at anytime prior to or following the institution of divorce proceedings, settle their disputes in terms of such an agreement and request that the court incorporate the terms of the agreement into the final decree of divorce.

In terms of section 7(2) of the Divorce Act, where the parties do not conclude an agreement with regard to the payment of maintenance, the court may make an order regarding the maintenance payable by one spouse to the other following the divorce.

The court may also make orders regarding the division of assets (including pension interests) in accordance with the regime that dictates the patrimonial consequences of the marriage. The division of assets will take into account the matrimonial property regime under which the parties were married. Distinct consequences arise if the spouses are married in community of property, or in terms of an ante-nuptial contract excluding accrual sharing before 1 November 1984 or in terms of an ante-nuptial contract concluded thereafter which either includes or excludes accrual sharing. In certain circumstances, the court can also consider ordering one spouse to forfeit the patrimonial consequences of the marriage.

All marriages entered into without a valid ante-nuptial contract are presumed to be in community of property and of profit and loss. The presumption can be rebutted. On divorce, the joint estate, which includes the sum total of the assets and liabilities of the parties, is divided equally between them. The assets that do not fall within the joint estate, being the separate assets as determined in terms of the Matrimonial Property Act (and including inherited assets and donations specifically excluded and certain damages awards) are retained by the relevant spouse. The division of the assets of the joint estate is based upon the principle that the parties are owners of undivided equal shares of the joint estate.

Marriages entered into after 1 November 1984 in terms of an ante-nuptial contract, which excludes community of property and of profit and loss, will automatically be subject to the accrual system, unless accrual sharing is specifically excluded. In a marriage governed by the accrual system, the parties retain separate estates during the marriage and are not responsible for each other's debts. On dissolution of the marriage, the parties share in the accrual of (or growth in) the estate of the other party. The accrual is the difference between the net asset value of each spouse's estate at the commencement of the marriage and the value on dissolution thereof.

In calculating the accrual, the value of assets specifically excluded from accrual sharing at the commencement of the marriage in terms of the ante-nuptial contract, are similarly excluded upon dissolution of the marriage. Certain assets acquired by gift, inheritance or donation are also excluded from the accrual calculation and retained by the relevant spouse. On dissolution of the marriage, regard is had to the change in value of money from the date of commencement until the date of dissolution of the marriage and the commencement values of the parties estates are adjusted accordingly.

The court can order that one party to a marriage in community of property, or to which the accrual system applies, should forfeit the patrimonial benefits of the marriage in favour of the other party, either wholly or in part. The court will do so if it considers that, having regard to the duration of the marriage, the circumstances which gave rise to the breakdown and any substantial misconduct on the part of one of the parties, the other party would be unduly benefited if the forfeiture order was not granted. This discretion is exercised cautiously. In respect of marriages in community of property, this would mean that all assets are not necessarily divided equally. In respect of marriages subject to the accrual system, this could mean that the right to share in the accrual to the other party's estate is forfeited.

Where spouses enter into an ante-nuptial contract after 1 November 1984, where accrual sharing is explicitly excluded, the court does not have a discretion to direct a redistribution of assets between the parties. If the contract provides for any property claims, these will be given effect to. If the parties have jointly owned assets, their rights will be determined in accordance with their respective rights to the assets.

Where spouses entered into an ante-nuptial contract prior to 1 November 1984, in terms of which accrual sharing is excluded, sections 7(3) to 7(6) of the Divorce Act provide for the court granting a decree of divorce to direct that the assets of one spouse be transferred to the other spouse on such basis as the court considers to be just and equitable, having regard to the direct and indirect contributions made by the one spouse to the growth or maintenance of the estate of the other spouse during the marriage.

In directing a redistribution of assets, the court will take into account: the means and obligations of the parties; any donations made between the parties; an order for the transfer of assets in terms of a foreign proprietary regime and any other factor which the court deems relevant. The court is required to exercise its discretion in making a value judgment in respect of the value of the contribution made. There are several considerations that are taken into account in exercising this very wide discretion. Each case is determined on its own merits. Although South Africa has adopted a no fault system of divorce, in exercising its discretion, the court can take into account the misconduct of one or both of the parties, but only where it would be unjust to disregard the misconduct.

More recently, greater consideration has been taken of the assets of discretionary trusts created during the marriage in redistributing assets and in dividing joint and accrued estates. Frequently the trustees of the trusts are joined to divorce actions and relief is sought in respect of the assets of the trusts.

Where the proprietary consequences of a marriage are determined in accordance with the law of a foreign state, the court granting the decree of divorce has the power to make orders in respect of the transfer of assets between spouses on the same basis as a competent court would have to do so on divorce in that jurisdiction.

9. FINANCES/MAINTENANCE

9.1 Explain the operation of maintenance for spouses on an ongoing basis after the breakdown of marriage

The duty of support between spouses in a marriage arises as a consequence of the contract of marriage and is an invariable consequence of the marriage, that cannot be regulated by an ante-nuptial contract. The reciprocal duty of support between spouses comes to an end when the marriage terminates, whether by death or divorce.

Section 7(2) of the Divorce Act provides that a court granting a divorce order may make an order in respect of the payment of maintenance by one party to another following their divorce on the basis that a court finds just. Only the court granting a decree of divorce may extend the maintenance obligation beyond the date of divorce. Another court cannot make an order for the payment of maintenance to a divorced spouse. The court has the discretion to direct that the maintenance obligation should be extended until the death or remarriage of a party or for any other period, the latter provision being styled 'rehabilitative maintenance'. Neither spouse has a right to maintenance upon divorce. The claim arises as a consequence of section 7(2) of the Divorce Act.

When the court considers the making of an order in respect of the payment of maintenance post divorce, it has regard to certain factors which are detailed in section 7(2) of the Divorce Act, namely:

- the existing or prospective means of each of the parties;
- their respective earning capacities;
- financial needs and obligations;
- their age;
- the duration of the marriage;
- their standard of living prior to divorce;
- their conduct insofar as it may be relevant to the breakdown of the marriage;
- an order for the division of assets;
- any other factor which, in the court's opinion, should be taken into account.

None of these factors should be regarded as dominant.

Certain of the factors introduce moral considerations. As divorce is not fault based, the predominant considerations in determining maintenance are financial need and ability of the parties. The court's discretion in respect of the award of maintenance is unfettered.

A maintenance order made in terms of the Divorce Act may be rescinded or varied at any time either by the court which made the order, ordinarily the High Court, or a divorce court or by a maintenance court.

A maintenance order can be revisited and varied or set aside in the event that there is sufficient reason for the variation or setting aside of the order.

9.2 Is it common for maintenance to be awarded?

9.3 Explain and illustrate with reference to recent cases the court's thinking on maintenance

The court regards it as preferable to achieve a clean break on divorce so that the parties are become economically independent. To the extent that the court has a discretion regarding the transfer of assets, it will apply such discretion to terminate the financial dependence of the one party on the other.

This is most likely achieved in circumstances where the court has a discretion in respect of a redistribution order in terms of section 7(3) of the Divorce Act. The court cannot otherwise direct the payment of a lump sum to effect a clean break as maintenance is required to be a periodic payment of sums of money. In certain circumstances, for example, in regard to the provision of household necessities, the court has awarded a lump sum payment to enable an ex-spouse to purchase household necessaries and establish a home as opposed to making monthly payments in this regard. Furthermore, it has been ordered that accommodation requirements of an ex-spouse be met by an appropriate order for maintenance to provide directly for the accommodation of that spouse.

It is relatively common that an order for maintenance of a spouse post divorce is granted, particularly where the marriage has been a long one and the earning abilities and financial resources of the parties are significantly distinct.

10. CHILD MAINTENANCE

10.1 On what basis is child maintenance calculated within the jurisdiction?

The obligation to maintain a child arises by operation of law and not as a consequence of a contractual obligation.

Both parents are required to support a child in accordance with their means. The obligation to maintain a child cannot be contracted out of on divorce, for example by the payment of a lump sum, as to do so is contrary to public policy. The duty of support between a parent and a child is mutual and exists between descendants and ascendants without limitation.

In terms of the Children's Act, one of the four recognised parental responsibilities and rights that a parent has in respect of a child is to contribute to the maintenance of the child.

The Divorce Act provides for the payment of maintenance of dependant and minor children of divorcing couples and a court granting a decree of divorce shall not grant a decree of divorce unless it is satisfied that the provisions made with regard to the welfare of any minor or dependant child are satisfactory.

In calculating the maintenance that is payable in respect of a child, a determination is made in respect of the reasonable needs of the child according to their standard of living, the situation of the child and of the respective parent's ability to meet the needs of the child. It may be required of parents to use both income and capital to meet the reasonable maintenance requirements of a child. Each case is determined on its own merits and there is no specific table or formula in determining the quantum of maintenance payable.

On divorce, maintenance awards are included to provide a monetary payment for general living expenses and for the payment of medical and related costs and educational and related costs. Due regard is had to the time spent with each party and to the costs that are incurred when the child is with them, in addition to medical and educational costs.

11. RECIPROCAL ENFORCEMENT OF FINANCIAL ORDERS

11.1 Summarise the position in your jurisdiction

In terms of the Reciprocal Enforcement of Maintenance Orders Act, 80 of

1963, a maintenance order of a proclaimed country can be enforced in South Africa. A South African maintenance order may be transmitted to a similarly designated foreign country for enforcement against the debtor residing there.

The maintenance order of a proclaimed foreign country must be registered in a South African court before it can be enforced in South Africa. If a person residing in South Africa is entitled to be maintained by a person living in a proclaimed foreign country, an enquiry under the Maintenance Act must be held. A provisional order is granted, which only becomes final when confirmed by the appropriate authority in the foreign country and the order is then enforced in terms of the laws of that country.

In terms of the Enforcement of Foreign Civil Judgments Act, 32 of 1988, civil judgments given in designated countries may be enforced in South Africa in the Magistrate's Court of the district where the person against whom the judgment in question was given resides, carries on business, or is employed or owns movable or immovable property.

Only a final judgment or order for the payment of money by any court in civil proceedings in a designated country, which is enforceable by execution in the country in which it was given or made, may be enforced. The relevant judgment must then be registered in the manner prescribed in the Act. When such a judgment has been registered, the judgment has the same effect as a civil judgment of the relevant South African court and can be enforced in accordance with South African law.

12. FINANCIAL RELIEF AFTER FOREIGN DIVORCE PROCEEDINGS

12.1 What powers are available to make orders following a foreign divorce?

To the extent that a foreign court has made an order in respect of the patrimonial consequences of a marriage, and such order is final and valid in terms of the law of the foreign country, such order will not be revisited by a South African court.

As the High Court is the upper guardian of minor children within its jurisdiction, it has inherent jurisdiction to consider any order in respect of a child within its jurisdiction so as to ensure the protection and of the best interests of that child. In the circumstances, foreign orders in respect of the exercise of parental responsibilities and rights relevant to a child in South Africa can be varied by the South African High Court.

Once a foreign maintenance order has been granted and registered in South Africa, such order can be varied by the relevant Maintenance Court having jurisdiction in the matter should sufficient reason exist for the variation of the foreign order. If no order in respect of post-divorce maintenance of a spouse has been made by a foreign court, such an order cannot be made by a South African court as the maintenance obligation cannot be revived.

D. CHILDREN

13. CUSTODY/PARENTAL RESPONSIBILITY

13.1 Briefly explain the legal position in relation to custody/parental responsibility following the breakdown of a relationship or marriage

The Children's Act determines the regulation of parental responsibilities and rights, including following the breakdown of a relationship or marriage.

Parents of children born in wedlock or of children born out of wedlock, where the parents lived together at the birth or where the father showed his commitment to the child by consenting to being identified as the father (by contributing to the child's upbringing and expenses, or attempting in good faith to do so) enjoy shared parental responsibilities and rights in respect of their child.

Parental responsibilities and rights include the responsibility and right to: act as guardian of the child; care for the child; have contact with the child; contribute to the maintenance of the child.

All of these responsibilities and rights are exercised and regulated against the standard of the best interests of the child. Parental responsibilities and rights can be suspended, terminated or extended by a court.

Parties who share parental responsibilities and rights in respect of a child can reach agreement regarding how they wish to regulate their shared responsibilities and rights in terms of a parenting plan. It is common to incorporate provision for mediation into parenting plans. Although arbitration is precluded in matrimonial matters, parties to a parenting plan frequently agree to defer decision making in respect of disputed issues to a third party mediator, called a facilitator, in terms of a parenting plan. This delegation of decision making is always subject to a court determining the issue and does not divest the co-holders of parental responsibilities of his or her responsibilities or rights.

In terms of the Act there is significant emphasis placed on children having a voice in decisions affecting them and it is an imperative in the Act that due consideration be given to their views.

The term 'custody' has essentially been replaced by the term 'care'. The term care is an all encompassing term relating to the protection of and the regulation of the wellbeing and development of a child.

13.2 Briefly explain the legal position in relation to access/contact/visitation following the breakdown of a relationship or marriage

The term 'access' has been replaced by the term 'contact'.

Contact is defined in the Children's Act as 'maintaining a personal relationship with a child' and where a child resides with someone else, includes visiting and being visited by the child and communication, including by post, telephone and other electronic media.

Contact can be regulated by agreement between the parties, frequently in terms of a parenting plan referred to above, or it can be regulated by the court. The views of the child are considered, taking into account their age and stage of development, and are tested against what is in the best interests of the child.

14. INTERNATIONAL ABDUCTION

14.1 Summarise the position in your jurisdiction

South Africa is a party state to the Hague Convention on Civil Aspects of International Child Abduction. South Africa ratified the Convention in 1996 and the Hague Convention on the Civil Aspects of International Child Abduction Act 72 of 1996 came into operation on 1 October 1997. South Africa abides by the principles espoused in the Convention, which the courts enforce with reference to international precedent. Emphasis is placed on securing the prompt return of children wrongfully removed to or retained in a contracting state.

In practice applications are generally heard on an urgent or semi-urgent basis by way of motion proceedings. The overriding principle espoused in the Constitution and the Children's Act with regard to applying the Convention, is that the best interests of the child are a priority.

In terms of Section 18(2)(c) of the Children's Act, 38 of 2005, a person who has parental responsibilities and rights in respect of a child has the right to act as guardian of the child. Section 18(3)(c)(iii) of the Children's Act requires a guardian to consent to the child's departure or removal from South Africa. Where more than one person has guardianship of a child they must all consent to the departure or removal of a child from South Africa.

The parental responsibilities and rights in terms of the Children's Act include the duty to care for the child, to maintain contact with the child and to contribute to the maintenance of the child. To the extent that these rights and responsibilities are held and exercised by any person in respect of a child, they would have rights of custody for the purposes of the Hague Convention.

Where a child is removed to or from a country that is not a party state to the Convention, the South African High Court as the upper guardian of minor children would and has applied the principle of the best interests of the minor child and has in effect given application to the principles espoused in the Convention in determining whether a child should be returned to or retained in(as the case may be) their habitual residence.

15. LEAVE TO REMOVE/APPLICATIONS TO TAKE A CHILD OUT OF THE JURISDICTION

15.1 Summarise the position in your jurisdiction

It frequently occurs that one spouse is desirous of relocating from South Africa to a distinct jurisdiction with the parties' minor children. As is detailed above, section 18(3)(c)(iii) of the Children's Act requires that a guardian must consent to the child's departure or removal from South Africa. Where more than one person has guardianship of the child both must consent to the departure or removal of the child.

15.2 Under what circumstances may a parent apply to remove their child from the jurisdiction against the wishes of the other parent?

In circumstances where a co-holder of parental responsibilities and rights and/ or the co-guardian of a minor child does not consent to the removal of the child, then the removal of the child from South Africa would be unlawful.

The party desirous of removing the child, in the absence of consent, is required to seek the authority of the High Court for the removal and the authority of the court will only be awarded if the removal is considered to be in the best interests of the child. South African law has developed in this regard with reference to contemporary international precedent in regard to the relocation of children.

Frequently, when orders are granted allowing the relocation of children, provision is made for the registration of orders regulating the continued exercise by both parents of their parental responsibilities and rights including orders in respect of contact.

E. SURROGACY AND ADOPTION

16. VALIDITY OF SURROGACY AGREEMENTS

16.1 Briefly summarise the position in your jurisdiction.

The Children's Act defines a 'surrogate motherhood agreement' as:

'an agreement between a surrogate mother and a commissioning parent in which it is agreed that the surrogate mother will be artificially fertilized for the purpose of bearing a child for the commissioning parent and in which the surrogate mother undertakes to hand over such child to the commissioning parent upon its birth, or within reasonable time thereafter, with the intention that the child concerned becomes the legitimate child of the commissioning parent.'

A surrogacy agreement is not valid unless: it is in writing and signed by all the parties thereto; it is entered into in South Africa; at least one commissioning parent (of if single that parent) is domiciled in South Africa; the surrogate mother and her husband/partner are domiciled in South Africa at the time; and the agreement is confirmed by the High Court.

The written consent of a spouse/partner of both the commissioning parent and of the surrogate mother is required and they must be parties to the agreement. The court may dispense with the consent of the partner of the surrogate mother if she is not the genetic parent.

The agreement is furthermore not valid unless the gamete of both commissioning parents, or if not possible for valid reasons, one of the commissioning parents' gamete is used for the conception of the child. If there is a lone commissioning parent, clearly a gamete from them will need to be used.

The commissioning parents must be unable to give birth to a child. The surrogate mother must have a living child of her own. She must assist for altruistic not commercial reasons. The agreement must stipulate the care and welfare arrangements for the child.

The effect of a valid surrogate motherhood agreement is that the child born is the child of the commissioning parents from birth.

17. ADOPTION

17.1 Briefly explain the legal position in relation to adoption in your jurisdiction. Is adoption available to individuals, cohabiting couples (both heterosexual and same-sex)?

In terms of Chapter 15 of the Children's Act, a child is adopted if they have been placed in the permanent care of a person in terms of a court order that, unless otherwise provided, has the effect of terminating the parental responsibilities that any person had in respect of the child prior to the order. The order confers full parental responsibilities and rights on the adoptive parent.

In terms of section 231 of the Children's Act, a child may only be adopted jointly by a husband and wife; by partners in a permanent domestic life-partnership or persons sharing a common household forming a permanent family unit: by a widow, widower, divorcee or unmarried person; by a person whose spouse or permanent life partner is the parent of the child; by the biological father of a child born out of wedlock; or by the foster parent of the child.

The Act does not distinguish between same-sex and heterosexual couples. The adoption must be in the best interests of the child.

South Africa is a party state to the Hague Adoption Convention.

F. COHABITATION

18. COHABITATION

18.1 What legislation (if any) governs division of property for unmarried couples on the breakdown of the relationship?

There is no law in South Africa regulating the rights of parties to a cohabitative relationship and cohabitation is not recognised as a legal relationship.

Cohabitation is regarded to be a stable, common, monogamous relationship where a couple who do not wish to, or are not allowed to get married, live together as spouses. In order to establish a cohabitative relationship, it is required that there be a sexual relationship between the couple, a factual cohabitative relationship and a measure of durability and stability of the relationship.

Although cohabitation is not a formally recognised legal relationship, in certain circumstances the word 'spouse' has been interpreted to include a partner in a cohabitation relationship in relation to the awarding of benefits. This has included in respect of damages claims, domestic violence disputes, provision for pension benefits and medical aid and the like.

A cohabitee whose partner dies without a valid will has no right to inherit under the Intestate Succession Act. A partner can similarly not rely on the provisions of the Maintenance of Surviving Spouses Act to secure maintenance on the death of a partner.

There is no obligation between cohabitees to maintain one another and thus no enforceable right to claim maintenance, unless an agreement to pay maintenance can be proved.

In certain circumstances partners have been assisted by the courts who have found that a universal partnership, whether express or implied, exists between the couple and have awarded a share of assets acquired during the course of the partnership so that there is a sharing of assets acquired during the cohabitation relationship.

In order to establish a universal partnership, the following requirements ought to be satisfied: that the aim of the partnership is to make a profit; both parties must contribute to the enterprise; the partnership must operate for the benefit of both parties; and the contract between the parties is legitimate. These parameters have been recently quite broadly interpreted.

It is becoming more prevalent that partners in a cohabitative relationship enter into a contract which regulates their relationship, including the personal and proprietary consequences thereof.

G. FAMILY DISPUTE RESOLUTION

19. MEDIATION, COLLABORATIVE LAW AND ARBITRATION

19.1 Briefly summarise the non-court-based processes available in your jurisdiction and the current status of agreements reached under the auspices of mediation, collaborative law and arbitration

Alternatives to litigation are a frequently considered by parties to disputes. Mediation is favoured in matrimonial disputes where, as detailed below, arbitration is prohibited. A few statues refer to the referral of family disputes to mediation prior to resorting to litigation, for example the Children's Act and the Mediation in Certain Divorce Matters Act, 24 of 1987.

In respect of disputes relating to children, sections 33 and 34 of the Children's Act make provision for parties who share parental responsibilities and rights in respect of a child to enter into a parenting plan to regulate by agreement their shared exercise of parental responsibilities and rights. Provision is made for the agreements to be made an order of court. Parenting plans generally provide for compulsory mediation by a mediator appointed in terms of the plan, who is mandated with powers, including to decide a dispute and to issue a directive where agreement is not achieved. Such an agreement binds the parties until the matter is referred to a court. This form of alternative dispute resolution has enjoyed much support from practitioners and the courts.

The courts promote mediation, particularly in family law disputes. In the decision of *MB v NB* 2010 (3) SA 220 (GSJ) (the *Brownlee* decision) the court chastised the parties' attorneys for not advising their clients to consider mediation and issued a punitive costs order against the attorneys.

Collaborative law is in its infancy in South Africa. Among family law practitioners a collaborative approach to dispute resolution is gaining in popularity as they begin to understand the merits of collaborative law.

19.2 What is the statutory basis (if any), for mediation, collaborative law and arbitration in your jurisdiction? In particular, are the parties required to attempt a family dispute resolution in advance of the institution of proceedings?

South Africa does not have a statutory basis, other than in very limited respects, for mediation, collaborative law or arbitration in matrimonial matters. In fact, section 2 of the Arbitration Act 42 of 1965 (as amended) states that arbitration shall not be permissible in respect of any matrimonial cause, any matter incidental to any such cause or any matter relating to status.

A system of compulsory mediation in respect of all litigated matters has been proposed for several years and pilot project has been mooted. Some concerns have been raised regarding the practicality of compulsory mediation in all matters and a practical efficient way forward remains the subject of lobbying and debate.

H. OTHER

20. CIVIL PARTNERSHIP/SAME-SEX MARRIAGE

20.1 What is the status of civil partnership/same-sex marriage within the jurisdiction?

The concept of a civil union was introduced into South African law in terms of the Civil Union Act 17 of 2006 and is defined as a voluntary union of two persons, who are both 18 years of age or older, which is solomnised and registered by way of either a marriage or a civil partnership, in accordance with the procedures prescribed in the Act to the exclusion, while it lasts, of all others.

The Act defines a civil union partner as a spouse in a marriage or a partner in a civil partnership. Spouses in a civil union can elect to call their union a marriage or a civil partnership. Both a marriage and a civil partnership can be entered into by partners of either the opposite or the same sex.

A civil union allows only a monogamous relationship. The law regarding the prohibition of marriages within limited degrees of affinity and consanguinity applies to civil unions.

The dissolution of a civil union, other than by death, is dealt with in accordance with the Divorce Act. The proprietary consequences of a civil union are determined on the same basis as a marriage in terms of the Matrimonial Property Act. That is where no ante-nuptial contract is signed, a union will be automatically in community of property and, where an ante-nuptial contract is signed which does not expressly exclude the accrual system, the accrual system will apply.

A civil union has the legal consequences of a marriage, including the common law, and reference in any law to a husband, wife or spouse includes a partner in civil union. Similarly, the duty of support applies between spouses to a civil union and will be extinguished on dissolution of the civil union by divorce, unless otherwise determined by the court hearing the divorce in terms of section 7(2) of the Divorce Act.

20.2 What legislation governs civil partnership/same sex marriage?

The legislation which governs civil partnerships and same-sex marriages is the Civil Union Act 17 of 2006.

21. CONTROVERSIAL AREAS/RAPIDLY DEVELOPING AREAS OF LAW

21.1 Is there a particular area of the law within the jurisdiction that is currently undergoing major change?

The most anticipated development in respect of family law will be in the recognition and regulation of domestic partnerships and of religious marriages.

There is a dire need for the formal recognition and regulation of both these areas of law that impact on the rights of several family units in South Africa, particularly when measured against constitutional imperatives. The law as it currently exists is uncertain and requires the intervention of the courts and the legislature to address the consequent difficulties for the families concerned.

21.2 Which areas of law are most out-of-step? Which areas would you most like to see reformed/changed?

The area of South African family law which is most out of step with recent developments and constitutional imperatives is the recognition of religious marriages. Marriages entered into in terms of the tenets of a religion, for example, Muslim marriages, Hindu marriages and the like, are not recognised as being valid marriages.

Section 15(1) of the Constitution provides that everyone has the right to freedom of conscience, religion, thought, belief and opinion and the fact that religious marriages are not regulated is problematic within this context.

Significant recognition has been given to the rights of spouses within religious marriages in terms of precedent. The rights of spouses in religious marriages have been extended through legislation, however, religious marriages are still not afforded equal recognition to civil marriages and civil unions. The South African Law Commission proposed a draft bill for an Islamic Marriages Act in 2002 and it is anticipated that the recognition of Islamic and other religious marriages is imminent.

Spain

Alberto Perez Cedillo Spanish Lawyers & Solicitors
Alberto Perez Cedillo & Paula Piquer Ruz

A. JURISDICTION AND CONFLICT OF LAW

1. SOURCES OF LAW

1.1 What is the primary source of law in relation to the breakdown of marriage and the welfare of children within the jurisdiction?

The sources of law in the Spanish legal system are legislation, custom and general principles of law, in that order.

The Spanish system is one of civil law. It is not created by jurisprudence, but rather by legislation and custom, which is applied by judges. However, the Jurisprudence of the Spanish Supreme Court is of great importance in relation to the interpretation and application of the laws, customs and general principles of justice, although it never rises to the level of judicial regulation.

Custom applies in the absence of applicable law, as long as it is not contrary to moral or public order. The general principles of law apply in the absence of legislation and custom, without prejudice to their informative nature in respect of the legal order.

The primary source of law in relation to the breakdown of marriage and the welfare of children within the Spanish jurisdiction is the Spanish Civil Code of 1889, as amended. In addition, some of the autonomous communities, into which Spain is divided, have devised their own set of family laws which are applicable within the boundaries of their territories.

1.2 Which are the main statutes governing matrimonial law in the jurisdiction?

In Spain the main statutes governing Spanish matrimonial family law by default, if there is no specific legislation from any autonomous community, are found in the Spanish Civil Code of 1889 as amended (hereinafter SCC) and in particular Book I, Title IV. Articles 42 to 107.

The Spanish Constitution reserves for state jurisdiction exclusively certain fields of competence relating to such questions as international relations, all cases dealing with rules on the application and enforcement of rules of law, legal and civil relations concerning matrimony, public registers and instruments, bases of contractual obligations and rules to solve conflicts between laws.

In relation to other matters, including the financial consequences of marriage, autonomous communities have their own civil law systems covering certain matters, with rules (known as interregional law) determining when the relevant civil law must be applied as opposed to the national Civil Code.

For this reason, it is vital to ascertain whether the specific autonomous community in question has its own provisions which apply to the matter. For Spanish nationals, the applicable family law shall be determined by the *vecindad civil,* ie, regional citizenship of the persons concerned (relationship between a person and a particular place, which determines the local law applicable, if any).

2. JURISDICTION

2.1 What are the main jurisdictional requirements for the institution of proceedings in relation to divorce, property and children?

In order to determine the applicable jurisdiction, the Spanish court shall first indentify if there are any international treaties in place between the potential jurisdictions.

(a) International jurisdictional requirements with non-EU member states

As a general rule, Spanish courts have jurisdiction when both parties have submitted themselves expressly or implicitly to the tribunals of Spain as well as if the defendant has his/her residence in Spain.

Specifically, this applies in issues of personal and patrimonial relationships between spouses, matrimonial nullity, separation and divorce when both spouses are habitually resident in Spain at the time of issuing proceedings, or when the defendant is a Spanish national and has his/her habitual residence in Spain, or when both spouses are Spanish nationals regardless of their place of habitual residence as long as the proceedings are by mutual agreement.

This also applies in matters of *paterno filial* relationships when the child has his/her place of habitual residence in Spain at the time of issuing proceedings, or the defendant is a Spanish national or resides habitually in Spain.

(b) International jurisdictional requirements between EU members

Depending on the main subject of the proceedings, different jurisdictional requirements will apply as follows:

(b)(i) Divorce

In accordance with Article 3 of Council Regulation No 2201/2003 of 27 November 2003 concerning jurisdiction and the recognition and enforcement of judgments in matrimonial matters and the matters of parental responsibility, repealing Regulation (EC) No 1347/2000II Revised Regulation (hereinafter Brussels II revised) Spanish courts will have jurisdiction when:

- the spouses are habitually resident in Spain; or
- the spouses were last habitually resident in Spain, insofar as one of them still resides there; or
- the respondent is habitually resident in Spain; or

- in the event of a joint application, either of the spouses is habitually resident in Spain; or
- the applicant is habitually resident in Spain if he or she resided there for at least a year immediately before the application was made; or
- the applicant is habitually resident in Spain if he or she resided there for at least six months immediately before the application was made and is a Spanish national; or
- if both spouses are Spanish nationals.

(b)(ii) Maintenance for spouses and children

In accordance with Council Regulation (EC) No 4/2009 of 18 December 2008 on jurisdiction, applicable law, recognition and enforcement of decisions and cooperation in matters relating to maintenance obligations (hereinafter Maintenance Regulation), Spanish courts shall have jurisdiction when:

- the defendant is habitually resident in Spain; or
- the creditor is habitually resident in Spain; or
- when Spanish courts, according to their own law, have jurisdiction to entertain proceedings concerning the status of a person if the matter relating to maintenance is ancillary to those proceedings, unless the jurisdiction of the Spanish courts is based solely on the nationality of one of the parties; or
- when Spanish courts, according to their own law, have jurisdiction to entertain proceedings concerning parental responsibility if the matter relating to maintenance is ancillary to those proceedings unless that jurisdiction is based solely on the nationality of one of the parties.

(b)(iii) Property

As there is no international treaty or European legislation, internal Spanish law applies. Article 22 of the Spanish Organic Act of the Judicial Power 6/1985 of 1 July (hereinafter SOJP) establishes, as a general rule, that Spanish courts will have jurisdiction where both parties have submitted themselves expressly or implicitly to the tribunals of Spain, as well as when the defendant has his/her residence in Spain.

Specifically when dealing with the distribution of capital assets between spouses, when both spouses are habitually resident in Spain at the time of issuing proceedings or the defendant is a Spanish national and has his/her habitual residence in Spain or when both spouses are Spanish nationals, regardless of their place of habitual residence, as long as the proceedings are by mutual agreement, the Spanish courts will have jurisdiction.

(b)(iv) Parental responsibility

Brussels II revised applies. In accordance with Article 8 of the said Regulation, Spanish courts will have jurisdiction to deal with matters regarding parental responsibility when the child is habitually resident in Spain at the time the Spanish court is seised.

3. DOMICILE AND HABITUAL RESIDENCE

3.1 Explain the concepts of domicile and habitual residence as they apply to the jurisdiction in relation to divorce, the finances and children

The concept of domicile, as understood under English law, does not exist in Spanish Law. The word 'domicile', when used in certain articles of Spanish legislation, has therefore a different meaning. Indeed, in most instances where reference is made to a person as domiciled in Spain, it is understood under Spanish law that the person is habitually resident in Spain.

Under Spanish law, the concept of habitual residence and the factors to be taken into account when determing it, vary depending on the context in which it is to be used.

In the majority of cases involving a dispute about habitual residence in connection with Article 40 of SCC the focus will be on two questions:

(a) Has the individual moved to a country for a 'settled purpose?'

(b) Has the individual been in that country for an 'appreciable period?'

This has been made clear by the reiterate jurisprudence of the Spanish Supreme court '*...For a place to be the domicile of a person it is not sufficient to reside there at a particular moment, it is necessary for that residence to be permanent; that is, it is necessary besides the objective requirement of residence in a place, the subjective aspect that this residence is to have permanent or habitual character as has been established for a long time by the Spanish Supreme Court in judgments such as judgments dated 28th November 1940, [RJ1940/1019) 26 May 1944 (RJ 1944/799), 18 September 1947, 25 September 1954 (RJ1954/1049), 21 January 1968, 21 April 1972 (RJ1972/1859) 30 December 1992(RJ 1992/10569) and 13 July 1996 (RJ 1996/5583)-, in accordance with which it is not sufficient to have a place as domicile remaining there more or less continuously but to have the will to effectively and permanently reside in that place*'.

When dealing with an appreciable period of time, the Spanish Supreme court has declared '*...that it is implicit as a fundamental factor of the concept of habitual residence, not the longer or shorter length of time in which a person remains uninterruptedly in a specific place, but the willingness of that person to remain effectively and permanently in that place.(STS 28-XI-40,26-V-44,27-IX-45,18-IX-47,25-IX-54,21-IV-72')*.

As to the evidence of habitual residence, the Spanish Supreme Court has established that the parties may '*.... avail themselves of whatever evidence may be available and is acceptable by Law being the last decision left to the discretion of the judge. In terms of relevant facts that may be indicative of habitual residence, the following evidence is usually mentioned: registration with the local Town Hall, to operate a business in that particular place, to maintain a property there, to be registered wit the electoral census etc*'.

Important factors to consider are the following:

- where does the family usually/always live, work and/or enjoy leisure time?;
- if you move out of Spain, is this move only temporary?;
- do you intend to move your centre of affairs to another country?;
- where have you retained your properties and furniture, even if rented out?;

- where are your cars registered?;
- where is your mailing address?;
- where are you registered with doctors, etc.?;
- where are your financial arrangements based, eg, banks accounts, financial advice, tax status, NI contributions, etc.?;
- Registration with the local Town Hall.

The Spanish concept of habitual residence is the same in relation to divorce, finances and children.

The concept of habitual residence faces considerable uncertainty within the EU. In issues regarding parental responsibility, attentions should be drawn to the autonomous concept being developed by the ECJ case law.

4. CONFLICT OF LAW/APPLICABLE LAW TO BE APPLIED

4.1 What happens when one party applies to stay proceedings in favour of a foreign jurisdiction? What factors will the local court take into account when determining forum issues?

Articles 63 and 64 of the Spanish Civil Procedural Act 1/2000 of 7 January (hereinafter 'SCPA') set up the '*declinatory*' action as the adequate procedure to stay any legal proceedings:

'By means of the 'declinatory action', the defendant and those who may be legally entitled to be a party to the proceedings may claim the lack of jurisdiction of the court on the grounds that the hearing of the case corresponds to foreign courts.

The declinatory action shall be filed within the first ten days following the date of service.'

For proceedings taking place between EU members, the court first seised will consider the grounds alleged by the applicant to gain jurisdiction, that is, habitual residence and nationality of the parties in accordance with Brussels II Revised Regulation. If the grounds alleged are in compliance with Brussels II revised, the court first seised will gain jurisdiction and for that purpose the time and date in which the application was lodged at Court's Dean Office will be the determining factor.

Between non-EU members, Article 22 of the SOJP applies and determines the factors that the court will take into account when deciding forum issues:

(a) if the parties have expressly or tacitly submitted themselves to Spanish courts;
(b) if the defendant has his/her habitual residence in Spain;
(c) if both spouses have habitual residence in Spain at the time of lodging the petition;
(d) if the petitioner is a Spanish national and has his/her habitual residence in Spain;
(e) if both parties are Spanish nationals, regardless of the place of habitual residence if they are filing proceedings by mutual consent.

If none of these factors appear, the Spanish courts will declare themselves non-competent.

B. PRE- AND POST-NUPTIAL AGREEMENTS

5. VALIDITY OF PRE- AND POST-NUPTIAL AGREEMENTS

5.1 To what extent are pre- and post-nups binding within the jurisdiction? Could you provide a brief discussion of the most significant recent case law on this issue?

Pre- and post-nuptial agreements are binding within the Spanish jurisdiction, with the following restrictions:

Spouses' maintenance and household work compensation

Courts generally consider these provisions valid, provided that they do not imply that any of the spouses renounce their right to receive maintenance and that they are not seriously damaging to one of the spouses. Courts are not bound by such agreements and can either enforce them or merely consider them as one of the relevant circumstances of the case.

Children's maintenance and parental responsibility

Such arrangements are not enforceable and do not have any significant effect on orders that might be made by a court following the breakdown of a marriage, as the interest of the child is paramount as a yardstick when making those orders.

Occupation of the matrimonial home

Courts shall enforce these provisions provided that, if there are children, an appropriate place of residence is provided for them and that the provision is not seriously damaging to one of the spouses.

For a pre- and post-nuptial agreement to be valid and enforceable in Spain, it must be signed simultaneously by both parties before a notary public.

The pre- or post-nup will not be valid against third parties acting in good faith until it is registered at the Spanish Civil Registry.

According to Article 1325 SCC, the spouses can stipulate, amend or replace their matrimonial finance regime at any moment by executing a pre- or post-nuptial agreement. This can also contain additional provisions on the consequences of the separation or divorce, as the same refers to *'other dispositions by virtue of marriage'*.

The spouses may regulate any financial or personal matters not included within the scope of the matrimonial finance regime, provided that such provisions are not unlawful, contrary to the customs or contrary to the general principle of equality between the parties to the marriage, otherwise it will be null and void. The general rules of contract apply.

In accordance with the SCC it can be signed any time before, after or on the day of marriage. However Article 1334 SCC clearly establishes that: *'All provisions of marriage articles for the event of a future marriage shall become without force and effect in the event that such marriage should not take place within one year'*.

Most of the autonomous communities follow the same formal requirements, but sometimes there are differences as to the statutory periods within which marriage should take place after completion of the pre-nuptial agreement. For example, in the autonomous community of Cataluña, marriage should take place within the 30 days following the signing of the agreement.

C. DIVORCE, NULLITY AND JUDICIAL SEPARATION

6. RECOGNITION OF FOREIGN MARRIAGES/DIVORCES

6.1 Summarise the position in your jurisdiction

Recognition of foreign marriages

A foreign marriage will be valid if it has taken place in a civil or religious way with the intention that it be legally binding, in accordance (i) with the law of the place of where the marriage has taken place; or (ii) in accordance with the personal law of any of the spouses.

In Spanish International Private Law there is no one single law applicable to all the requirements of marriage. On the contrary, there are rules of conflict that separately determine the law applicable to the matrimonial capacity, the law applicable to matrimonial consent and the law applicable to the form of celebration of the marriage, as follows:

(i) Law applicable to the form of celebration of the marriage

Marriages are normally celebrated in a formal way and the 'form' of the marriage should be understood to mean the way and circumstances that demonstrate the consent to marry.

In order to determine the law applicable to the form of marriage celebration, we have to differentiate different groups:

- Marriage celebrated in Spain between a Spanish national and a foreigner: in accordance with Article 49 of the SCC, the applicable law is exclusively Spanish law as this is the law of the place where the marriage was celebrated.
- Marriages celebrated in Spain between foreigners: 'it will be necessary for at least one of the parties to be habitually resident in Spain. Article 50 of the SCC, establishes that the marriage may be performed in Spain in accordance with the form provided for Spanish nationals or in compliance with the form set forth in the personal law applicable.
- Marriages celebrated abroad between a Spanish national and a foreigner or between Spanish nationals. Article 49.1 and 2 of SCC contain alternative connecting points, so the applicable law will either be:
  (a) the law of the place where the marriage was celebrated; or
  (b) Spanish law.
- Marriage celebrated abroad between foreigners: There is no specific international conflict law rule applicable to such a situation. By analogy, it is possible to apply Article 50 of the SCC and therefore the marriage will only be valid if it has been celebrated in a way which legally valid in accordance with the law of the place where the marriage was celebrated or by the personal law of either of the spouses-to-be.

(ii) Law applicable to the matrimonial capacity

There are no international rules for conflict of law that determines the law applicable to the matrimonial capacity. However, case law indicates that matrimonial capacity is a particular aspect of the general capacity and therefore Article 9.1 of SCC is applicable, hence the law regulating the matrimonial capacity is the national law of each of the spouses at the time the marriage was celebrated.

Matrimonial capacity comprises questions such as the minimum marriage age, persons with whom it is possible to marry, and the physical and psychical qualities for marriage, etc.

Any issues that are contrary to Spanish public policy may prevent the marriage being recognised as valid in Spain.

Recognition of foreign divorce

EU members

Judgment given in another member state, and against which no further appeal lies, may be recognised in the Jurisdiction of Spain in accordance with Article 21 of Brussels II bis. A judgment given in a member state shall be recognised in the other member states without any special procedure being required.

Non-EU members

A special internal procedure called *exequatur* is required. This procedure is regulated in articles 951 and follows the Spanish Civil Procedural Act of 1881. The judgment may be recognised by a Spanish court if the following circumstances apply:

- it has been issued as a result of exercising a personal action;
- it has not been issued by default;
- the judgment is not contrary to Spanish public policy;
- the judgment meets the requirements necessary for it to be enforceable in the country of origin.

It is also necessary to take into account bilateral conventions with third countries such as Switzerland.

7. DIVORCE

7.1 Explain the grounds for divorce within the jurisdiction (please also deal with nullity and judicial separation if appropriate)

After the reform of 15/2005 of 8 July, divorce in Spain does not need any grounds. It does not require concurrence of any cause. A minimum term of three months to be counted from the celebration of the marriage before issuing for divorce (save in some exceptional cases) is required.

8. FINANCES/CAPITAL, PROPERTY

8.1 What powers does the court have to allocate financial resources and property on the breakdown of marriage?

It is a peculiarity of the Spanish system that spouses are only entitled to apply for maintenance and compensation orders during the divorce proceedings. The allocation of property upon the breakdown of a marriage will be dealt with by different and separate proceedings.

Allocation of financial resources within the divorce proceedings

The Spanish courts may make two orders within the divorce proceedings:

- Spouses' maintenance shall be granted where the divorce results in an imbalance between one of the spouses in relation to the position of the other which involves a worsening of the situation that he or she had during the marriage and which aims to address the financial imbalance in which the claimant spouse may be immediately after the divorce.
- Household work compensation: upon termination of the separation of assets regime, compensation can be computed on the basis of the contribution to the household by one of the spouses, to be set up by the Judge in the absence of an agreement. This right or remedy is compatible with any other economic rights to which the favoured spouse may be entitled, as it aims to redress an imbalance which took place during the marriage, whereas spouses' maintenance is applied to the situation in which the claimant spouse finds him/herself immediately after the divorce.

Use of the matrimonial home may also be allocated within the divorce proceedings.

The allocation of property in separate and independent proceedings

The Spanish courts are bound by the applicable matrimonial economic regime with regards to distribution of the parties' property and under no circumstances can they depart from or override the applicable matrimonial economic regime. Therefore, while the divorce proceedings are ongoing, the parties, or more often separately, may apply to the courts for the liquidation of their matrimonial finance regime of community of assets. The distribution of marital assets is carried out in accordance with the rules governing this matrimonial economic regime. In the case of a separation of the assets regime, there is no special procedure for its liquidation, as there is no community of assets and therefore separate civil proceedings will have to be filed for the dissolution of co-ownership. for example.

The matrimonial economic regime of separation of assets is the regime applicable by default in the autonomous communities of Catalonia, Balearic Islands and Valencia.

In the remaining autonomous communities, including Madrid, the default economic regime is that of a community of assets, with the exception of Vizcaya, Navarra and Aragon, which have their own local specific regimes applicable by default.

In the matrimonial economic regime of separation of assets, the property held by each spouse at the start and any which he/she may subsequently acquire pursuant to any title shall belong to such spouse. Likewise, each spouse shall have the administration, enjoyment and free disposal of such property.

The community of joint assets makes any gains or profits obtained indistinctly by either spouse common to the spouses, and shall be allocated by halves upon dissolution thereof. The community of joint assets shall begin upon entering the marriage or upon agreement in a pre- or post-nuptial.

In the matrimonial economic regime of community of assets, the following property is exclusive to each of the spouses:

- property and rights which belonged to each spouse at the start of the marriage;
- those which are acquired subsequently, pursuant to gratuitous title;
- those acquired at the cost of, or as a replacement for, exclusive property;
- those acquired pursuant to a right of pre-emption pertaining to a single spouse;
- patrimonial property rights inherent to the person and which are not transferable *inter vivos*;
- compensation and damages to one of the spouses or to their exclusive property;
- clothes and objects for personal use which are not of significant value;
- the instruments necessary for the conduct of their profession or work, unless they form integral part of or are appurtenances of an establishment or undertaking held in common.

Property mentioned in sections 4 and 8 shall not lose its nature as exclusive property if its acquisition was made with common funds; however, in this case, the community shall be the creditor of the spouse who owns it for the value paid for it.

The following property is held in common:

- property obtained pursuant to the work or industry of either spouse;
- fruits, income or interest generated by exclusive and common property;
- property is acquired for valuable consideration charged to the assets held in common, irrespective of whether the acquisition is made to the community or for only one of the spouses;
- that which is acquired pursuant to a right of pre-emption held in common, even if it should be acquired with funds held on an exclusive basis, in which case the community shall owe the spouse for the value paid;
- undertakings and establishments founded during the life of the community by either spouse at the expense of common property. If, at the time of setting up the undertaking or establishment, both exclusive and common capital is used, it shall correspond pro indiviso to the community of joint assets, and to the spouses in proportion to the value of their respective contributions.

8.2 Explain and illustrate with reference to recent cases the court's thinking on division of assets

Not applicable. As explained above, Spanish courts are bound by the matrimonial economic regime.

9. FINANCES/MAINTENANCE

9.1 Explain the operation of maintenance for spouses on an ongoing basis after the breakdown of marriage

As already explained, Spanish courts have jurisdiction when granting the judicial decree of divorce to make two orders for financial provisions between spouses:

(a) Spouse's maintenance (*pensión compensatoria*)

Regardless of the matrimonial economic regime applicable, spouses may be entitled to receive maintenance as explained in point 8.1 above.

When deciding upon an application for maintenance, the court shall have regard to the following matters:

- any agreements that the spouses may have reached;
- their age and health;
- the professional qualifications and the probability of their obtaining employment;
- past and future dedication to the family;
- collaboration with his or her own labour, in the commercial, industrial or professional activities of the other spouse;
- the duration of their marriage and of cohabitation before marriage;
- the eventual loss of a right to a pension by reason of dissolution of the marriage;
- the wealth and property means and needs of the spouses;
- any other circumstance that the court may consider relevant to the case.

The wealth and economic means of both spouses are assessed in order to establish whether an imbalance has occurred and whether the spouse who would have to pay maintenance can actually afford it.

The main aim of spouses' maintenance is not to provide the support that the ex-spouse needs to cover his or her needs, but to rederess the financial imbalance in which the claimant spouse finds themselves immediately after the divorce.

This maintenance aims to bridge specifically the worsening in situation of one of the spouses caused by the divorce when it produces an economic imbalance in relation to the position of the other spouse. Therefore, offsetting this imbalance is not a subsidiary aim but the main aim of spouses' maintenance.

Depending on the specific circumstances of the case, the court may issue an order for open-ended or fixed-term periodical payments or for a lump sum, although it is common practice that maintenance is usually paid in periodic payments. It is usual to decide on a certain period, after which the debtor will be released.

Where an order for periodic payments has been made, its amount may be modified at any moment by the court, upon the party's application, should a substantial alteration in the financial situation of any of the parties to the marriage occur.

Exceptionally and subject to the condition that the spouses agree, Article 99 SCC provides that '*the substitution of an annuity, the usufruct of certain property, or the delivery of capital in assets other than in money, instead of the award judicially fixed pursuant Article 97 SCC may be agreed upon at any time.*'

The right to receive maintenance shall be extinguished as a result of the removal of the cause which motivated it or in the event of remarriage or cohabitation of the party receiving maintenance.

Article 101 SCC further establishes that: '*...The right to receive maintenance shall not be extinguished by the mere fact of the debtor's death. Notwithstanding* *the foregoing, the latter's heirs may request to the Judge to reduce or suppress it if the estate cannot satisfy the requirements of the debtor or if it should affect their right to a forced share.'*

(b) Household work compensation (*compensación por trabajo para la casa*)
In a separation of assets regime, since there is no allocation of assets, what must be taken into account are other rights that the law confers on the spouses and especially those contemplated at Article 1438 of SCC. This Article provides that, in the separation of assets regime, as the one agreed upon by the parties, housework shall generate a right to compensation upon termination of the matrimonial economic regime.

The aim is therefore to compensate the spouse who has undergone an impoverishment which is correlative to the enrichment of the other spouse for having worked for the household either by looking after the home or caring for the family or for the other spouse without receiving any payment or receiving a payment which is insufficient.

In the absence of an agreement, it is left to the courts' discretion to decide upon the amount to be awarded and the ways in which this compensation will be paid and secured.

This right or remedy is compatible with any other economic rights to which the favoured spouse may be entitled, as it aims to compensate a situation of imbalance which took place during the marriage, whereas spouses' maintenance is applied to a situation in which the claimant spouse finds him/herself immediately after the divorce.

The amounts awarded for the household work of the spouse will be taken into account for the calculation of the amount awarded as maintenance.

9.2 Is it common for maintenance to be awarded?

Awarding spouses' maintenance is becoming less and less common and when granted, unless there are specific circumstances, rarely exceeds two years, reflecting the fact that couples nowadays tend to marry at a later stage and when both have a professional career.

9.3 Explain and illustrate with reference to recent cases the court's thinking on maintenance

Spouses' maintenance

Judgment of the Supreme Court of 10 February 2005: 'As *it has been established by the doctrine the essential premise is the inequality that results of the confrontation between the economic conditions of each one of the spouses before and after the break up*. *There is no need to prove the existence of need- the spouse most at a disadvantage because of the rupture could be entitled to the compensation even if he had sufficient means to sustain him/herself-, but it is necessary that there has been a worsening in his/her situation in relation to that one that she/he used to enjoy during the marriage and in respect of the situation the other spouse enjoys. But it is not about attempting to equiparate economically their wealth*'.

Judgment of the Court of Appeal of Asturias, Section 7 347/2011 of 13

July '*What is intended is to place the spouse who has suffered disadvantage in a position that may enable him/her to sort out his/her own economic problems if by reason of the marriage he/she has relinquished his/her professional or working life making possible that the person who is to benefit from the pension may be in a position to confront in an autonomous way the economic position that may correspond to him/her in accordance with his/her aptitudes and capacities...*'

The Court of Appeal of Asturias, Section 7 in Judgment 347/2011 of 13 July '*The factors to be taken into account to value the possibility of granting a compensatory pension are many and of impossible individual enumeration. Among the most relevant without trying to be exhaustive can be quoted: age ,effective duration of the matrimonial live, dedication to the house and the children, how many of them require future attention, health issues, work that the creditor is carrying out or may be able to carry out due to his/her professional qualifications, employment market conditions in accordance with the occupation of the creditor, possibilities of gaining access to a remunerated work –real and effective perspectives of gaining employment -;possibilities of recycling or returning to the previous job (that was given up because of the marriage); qualifications and previous professional experience; opportunities that society offers...*'.

Household work compensation

Since household work compensation (*compensacion por trabajo para la casa*) was first recognised in 1981, the concept has evolved substantially.

The Judgment of the Court of Appeal of Madrid 508/2007 17 April 2007 establishes '*...For the art. 1438 of SCC to be applicable it is necessary an economic regime of separation of assets and the contribution in kind of the spouse of the creditor to the financial burdens of the marriage, this is an exclusive and direct dedication to household work...*'

Judgment of the Court of Appeal of Madrid dated 1 February 2006 '*...The compensation to which art 1438 refers is not granted in consideration to the future dedication to the family or the economic imbalance produced as a consequence of the divorce to one of the spouses in relation to their previous situation, but exclusively in the objective analysis of the past dedication to the family during the existence of the economic regime of separation of assets...*'.

Judgment of the Supreme Court 534/2011 establishes '*... the right to obtain compensation for having contributed one of the spouses to the burdens of the marriage with household work in the economic regime of separation of assets, requires that having agreed this regime the contributions to the burdens of the marriage have taken place only with the work carried out for the household. It is therefore excluded that in order to obtain compensation is necessary that an increase in the wealth of the other spouse had occurred...*'

Lately, this judicial trend which required an exclusive dedication to the household has been relaxed, allowing for the spouse claiming compensation to combine dedication to the household work with other external works that permit some extra income for the economy of the family. In this sense Judgment of the Supreme Court of 12 of July 2011 (7362/2011) establishes '... what *excludes the right to the compensation is not any other activity outside the home but the collaboration by both spouses in equal terms to the household work. This is the inexistence of a larger contribution and participation of the creditor to the household work...'*

10. CHILD MAINTENANCE

10.1 On what basis is child maintenance calculated within the jurisdiction?

Article 146 of the SCC establishes that the amount of the support shall be proportional to the estate or resources of the person who provides it and the needs of the person receiving it.

Therefore when calculating the amount for maintenance, the judge will take into account the income and liabilities of the creditor and the needs of the child. The amount ordered as maintenance covers what it is known as ordinary expenses. Extraordinary expenses shall be paid by both parties by half unless otherwise established.

Child maintenance may be proportionally reduced or increased in accordance to the increase or reduction in the needs of the child and the wealth of the person obliged to satisfy it.

There are no tables or percentages which apply for the calculation of child maintenance, as in other jurisdictions. However, nowadays, certain judges have adopted tariffs for calculating maintenance which apply in their own courts.

11. RECIPROCAL ENFORCEMENT OF FINANCIAL ORDERS

11.1 Summarise the position in your jurisdiction

Financial orders relating to maintenance for spouse or children who are EU members will be enforced in accordance with the Maintenance Regulation. For non-EU members it will be necessary to look into the Hague Convention of 2 October 1973 or identify any other international bilateral treaty, such as the one subscribed with Uruguay on 4 November 1987.

Any other financial order which does not relate to maintenance will fall out of the scope of European legislation and will have to follow the special procedure contained in the internal Spanish legislation known as exequatur as explained in point 6.1 above.

In Spain, the following means of execution are available:

- attachment of earnings
- withholding of tax rebates;
- seizure of bank accounts;
- withholding of social security benefits;
- seizure of goods and public sale thereof;
- imprisonment in certain cases.

12. FINANCIAL RELIEF AFTER FOREIGN DIVORCE PROCEEDINGS

12.1 What powers are available to make orders following a foreign divorce?

As already explained, Spanish procedural law differentiates between divorce proceedings where maintenance is decided and proceedings for the dissolution of matrimonial economic regimes.

Spanish courts will have the power to vary a maintenance order on the grounds that the circumstances of the spouse or the child have changed from the date the order was given by the foreign court.

Separate proceedings to deal with the dissolution of the Spanish matrimonial economic regime, if they have been left unresolved by the foreign divorce proceedings, may be dealt with by the Spanish courts

D. CHILDREN

13. CUSTODY/PARENTAL RESPONSIBILITY

13.1 Briefly explain the legal position in relation to custody/parental responsibility following the breakdown of a relationship or marriage

In accordance with Article 92 of the SCC, the breakdown of a relationship or marriage shall not release parents from their obligations towards their children.

Both parents shall have parental authority over their children and therefore share the ability to decide and resolve all matters that affect a minor, even though only one of them may have been awarded custody. However, the parents may agree or the judge may decide that parental authority is to be exercised in whole or part by one of the parents.

Article 92.5 establishes that 'Shared care and custody of the children shall be decreed where the parents should request it in the settlement agreement proposal or where both of them should agree on this during the proceedings...'

Moreover Article 92.8 states: 'Exceptionally, even in the absence of the circumstances provided in section five of this article, the Judge, at the request of one of the parties, with the favourable report of the Public Prosecutor, may decree the shared care and custody based on the argument that only thus is the minor's higher interest suitably protected.'

However, the current trend in Spain in accordance with the latest jurisprudence is to grant shared custody, if it is considered to be in the best interest of the children, and it is now often granted even in cases where there is no agreement between the parents.

13.2 Briefly explain the legal position in relation to access/contact/visitation following the breakdown of a relationship or marriage

In accordance with Article 94 of SCC, the parent who does not live with the children shall be entitled to visit them, communicate with them and have them in his company. If no agreement is reached between the parties the judge shall determine the time, manner and place in which visitation rights may be exercised.

The interest of the child is paramount; therefore, this is the main issue to take into account when granting visiting rights. Also, the circumstances of each parent should be taken into account when establishing contact.

It is necessary to take into account that certain autonomous communities have established their own regulations with regards to shared custody.

Currently, more and more courts are tending to grant a generous contact time to the parent with whom the children do not live.

Even if there is an agreement between the parties, it will be necessary to set up the basic arrangements for contact, that is, days, times and place, for the judge and the public prosecutor to consider the suitability of the arrangements, taking into account the child's interests.

14. INTERNATIONAL ABDUCTION

14.1 Briefly summarise the position in your jurisdiction

Since 1987, the Hague Convention of 25 October 1980 on the Civil Aspects of International Child Abduction hads applied in Spain.

The receiving agency is the Ministry of Justice. The accusation is carried out by the Public Prosecutor.

15. LEAVE TO REMOVE/APPLICATIONS TO TAKE A CHILD OUT OF THE JURISDICTION

15.1 Summarise the position in your jurisdiction

The place where the child is to live is an issue that falls within the scope of parental responsibility and therefore a parent needs the consent of the other to remove the child from the jurisdiction.

In case of disagreement the parties may apply to the court for permission. It depends on the local court, but generally this may be requested during the divorce proceedings or afterwards in proceedings related to parental responsibility.

When deciding, the court will take into account the specific circumstances of the case, such as the place where one of the parents intends to relocate, the schedule of visits from the other parent, the interest of the child, the possibility of having access etc.

After hearing both parents, and the child if old enough, then without further recourse the judge attributes the power of deciding to the father or mother, and if the disagreements are repeated or some other cause arises that seriously impedes the exercise of parental authority, the judge may assign totally or partially to one of the parents the ability to decide, including sharing their functions between them.

15.2 Under what circumstances may a parent apply to remove their child from the jurisdiction against the wishes of the other parent?

Different circumstances will apply to different situations. To be reunited with siblings or close family, to receive specific medical treatment, to enjoy a scholarship or any other reason based on the health of the child are circumstances upon which leave to remove may be granted. The interests of the child will always be paramount. Relocation due to the specific circumstances of one of the parents, generally speaking, are more difficult to obtain as there is a general trend not to alter the child's environment if this is suitable to him/her. However, the impossibility of earning a living and/or support for bringing up the child from close family may also justify relocation. The distance between the current and the new location is always relevant and removing the child to a new country located far away such as Australia, New Zealand or South America will be extremely difficult.

The voice of the child will be heard if it is understood that they have the sufficient grade of maturity. There was a well-set-up trend followed by the courts of allowing mothers to relocate with the children on the grounds of freedom of movement granted under the EU but there are growing calls to reverse this pattern. The situation is always uncertain and it is difficult to generalise.

E. SURROGACY AND ADOPTION

16. VALIDITY OF SURROGACY AGREEMENTS

16.1 Briefly summarise the position in your jurisdiction

Law 14/2006 of 26 May (which deals human assisted reproduction techniques) sets up in its Article 10.1 that a contract under which a woman who agrees to be a surrogate (with or without receiving consideration) renounces her maternal relationship in favour of the person entering the contract or a third party will be null and void.

In this instance in the second paragraph of the said Article it is established that for those cases filiation of children born by surrogacy shall be determined by parturition.

It will remain possible for the biological father to claim paternity in accordance with the general rules of Spanish legislation.

In those cases in which it is required that the birth of a child born abroad using a surrogate mother must be registered at the Spanish Civil Registry, the registration of a it will be necessary to produce a resolution which clearly establishes filiation or alternatively to obtain the recognition of the order in Spain by means of an *exequatur* as explained in point 6.1 above.

17. ADOPTION

17.1 Briefly explain the legal position in relation to adoption in your jurisdiction. Is adoption available to individuals, cohabiting couples (both heterosexual and same-sex)?

Adoption requires that the prospective adoptive parent is older than 25. In an adoption by both spouses, it will be sufficient for one of them to have reached such an age. In any event, the prospective adoptive parents must be at least 14 years older than the adoptee.

Only non-emancipated minors may be adopted. As an exception, it will be possible to adopt a person of legal age or an emancipated minor when, immediately prior to the emancipation, there should have existed an uninterrupted situation of foster care or of cohabitation, initiated before the prospective adoptee became 14.

A person cannot adopt a descendant, a relative in the second degree in the collateral line by consanguinity or affinity. A ward cannot be adopted by his/her guardian until final approval of the accounts of the guardianship. Nobody may be adopted by more than one person, unless the adoption is performed jointly or successively by both spouses. Marriage performed subsequently to the adoption shall allow the spouse to adopt the children of his/her consort.

Spanish legislation allows adoption by homosexuals both as spouses or individually and some autonomous communities such as Cataluña have passed legislation allowing homosexual and heterosexual cohabiting couples to adopt.

F. COHABITATION

18. COHABITATION

18.1 What legislation (if any) governs division of property for unmarried couples on the breakdown of the relationship?

Neither the Spanish constitution nor the Spanish Civil Code refers to cohabitation.

Once again, the autonomous communities such as Andalucia, Aragon, Asturias, Baleares, Canarias, Cantabria, Castilla La Mancha, Castilla León, Cataluña, Extremadura, Galicia, Madrid, Navarra, País Vasco and Valencia have however produced legislation in this respect.

Some of this legislation include rights and obligations of the parties towards themselves and their children, even inheritance rights, maintenance and/or compensation rights. However, no measures as to the distribution of assets for unmarried couples are contemplated.

G. FAMILY DISPUTE RESOLUTION

19. MEDIATION, COLLABORATIVE LAW AND ARBITRATION

19.1 Briefly summarise the non-court-based processes available in your jurisdiction and the current status of agreements reached under the auspices of mediation, collaborative law and arbitration

With respect to separation and divorce procedures, the courts promote the resolution of such conflicts by means of mutual agreement between the parties, given that proceedings initiated contentiously between the parties can be settled on a non-contentious basis at any time.

Mediation is contemplated for the resolution of conflicts within proceedings. When an agreement is reached within mediation it has to be filed at court for the judge's approval and issued as a judgment, as otherwise it will not be binding or enforceable.

Collaborative law is not yet contemplated in Spain.

19.2 What is the statutory basis (if any), for mediation, collaborative law and arbitration in your jurisdiction? In particular, are the parties required to attempt a family dispute resolution in advance of the institution of proceedings?

Law 15/2005 of 8 July sets up mediation as a voluntary alternative for resolution in family disputes by using an impartial and neutral mediator. It is possible for the parties to stay separation or divorce proceedings in order to try to reach an agreement.

Other than the above reference, there are no general provisions regulating family mediation at a national level. However, most autonomic communities such as Andalucia, Aragon, Asturias, Canarias, Cantabria, Castilla la Mancha, Castilla y Leon, Cataluña, Comunidad Valenciana, Galicia, Islas Baleares, Madrid, Navarra, Pais Vasco, have set up specific rules on family mediation.

H. OTHER

20. CIVIL PARTNERSHIP/SAME-SEX MARRIAGE

20.1 What is the status of civil partnership/same-sex marriage within the jurisdiction?

Same-sex marriage is contemplated and regulated in Spain. Same-sex spouses have exactly the same rights and obligations as heterosexual spouses. There is no legal equivalent under Spanish law to the figure of civil partnership as understood under English law.

20.2 What legislation governs civil partnership/same-sex marriage?

Article 44 of the Spanish Civil Code establishes that men and women have the right to marry in accordance with the provisions contained in the code. This same Article specifically establishes that the marriage will have the same requirements and effects whether both spouses are the same sex or opposite sexes.

21. CONTROVERSIAL AREAS/RAPIDLY DEVELOPING AREAS OF LAW

21.1 Is there a particular area of the law within the jurisdiction that is currently undergoing major change?

Once again, we will draw attention to the local legislation produced by the autonomous communities which may substantially differ from each other and from the law applicable at a national level.

21.2 Which areas of law are most out-of-step? Which areas would you most like to see reformed/changed?

Not applicable.

Sweden

Advokaterna Sverker och Mia Reich Sjögren AB
Mia Reich Sjögren **Advokaterna Nyblom & Sarvik AB**
Johan Sarvik **Lindskog Malmström Advokatbyrå KB**
Fredric Renström

A. JURISDICTION AND CONFLICT OF LAW

1. SOURCES OF LAW

1.1 What is the primary source of law in relation to the breakdown of marriage and the welfare of children within the jurisdiction?

1.2 Which are the main statutes governing matrimonial law in the jurisdiction?

The primary source of law in relation to the breakdown of marriage, as well as to all Swedish matrimonial law, is the Marriage Code of 1987. Regarding cohabitation, the primary source of law is the Cohabitation Act of 2003.

In the area of welfare of children, the Code Relating to Parents, Guardians and Children of 1949 is the primary source of law.

2. JURISDICTION

2.1 What are the main jurisdictional requirements for the institution of proceedings in relation to divorce, property and children?

Within Sweden, the competent court is the court located where the respondent has his or her habitual residence (Code of Judicial Procedure chapter 10 section 1). In international cases, among others, Brussels II *bis* applies. There is also a 1904 Swedish law enabling, for instance, Swedish citizens to initiate divorce proceedings, among others, in Sweden, as applicants, under certain conditions.

3. DOMICILE AND HABITUAL RESIDENCE

3.1 Explain the concepts of domicile and habitual residence as they apply to the jurisdiction in relation to divorce, the finances and children

The determination of a person's habitual residence depends on whether the matter concerns domestic family law or international family law.

If the matter regards domestic family law, the habitual residence is determined from a person's residential registration within Sweden. If the person is registered in a municipality in Sweden, the city/village where they were registered as at 1 November in the previous year is considered their domicile. If a person does not have a national registration the proper forum for initiating proceedings against this person would be where they currently reside or were last known to reside.

The definition of habitual residence in Swedish international private law originates from the law (1904) regarding certain international legal relations concerning marriage and guardianship. In the current version of the relevant paragraph, section 2 of section 7 of this law states: *'An individual who is resident in a certain state is, for the application of this law, considered to have habitual residence there if the residency, with regard to the duration of the stay and other circumstances, is to be considered permanent'.*

The same definition is used in the law (1990) about international matters regarding division of property between spouses and cohabitants. This definition is considered to be authoritative within Swedish international private law. The 'other circumstances' mentioned above have been described in Swedish case law and in preparatory work on the laws in question. The courts apply these circumstances in the procedure to determine habitual residence.

In order to determine if habitual residency in Sweden is at hand, a Swedish court should examine the objective and the subjective circumstances in the case and for the parties. Objective circumstances include the time spent in Sweden, as well as social and other personal and/or professional relations to Sweden, as compared with other countries. Consideration should also be given to the intent to stay in (or leave) the country, as well as to other subjective circumstances. Subjective circumstances should generally be given less significance in the procedure/examination.

Swedish law does not recognise habitual residence and domicile as separate concepts.

4. CONFLICT OF LAW/APPLICABLE LAW TO BE APPLIED

4.1 What happens when one party applies to stay proceedings in favour of a foreign jurisdiction? What factors will the local court take into account when determining forum issues?

If one party applies to stay proceedings in favour of a foreign jurisdiction, Brussels II *bis* is primarily applicable. Unless this is the case, and Swedish courts are found to be competent in accordance with Swedish law, and if one of the parties objects that divorce proceedings are already pending in another state, the Swedish courts are still, under some circumstances (see below), competent to accept a divorce application from one of the parties. However, the proceedings in Sweden can be stayed if a decision resulting from the proceedings in the other state can be expected to be valid in Sweden.

However, there is some case law determining that, if the proceedings in the other state could not be expected to be finished within reasonable time, this could also be reason for Swedish courts being seen as competent to deal with matters that are already pending in another country.

B. PRE- AND POST-NUPTIAL AGREEMENTS

5. VALIDITY OF PRE- AND POST-NUPTIAL AGREEMENTS

5.1 To what extent are pre- and post-nuptial agreements binding within the jurisdiction? Could you provide a brief discussion of the most significant recent case law on the issue?

Pre-nuptial as well as post-nuptial agreements are legally binding in Sweden if they meet the requirements stipulated by law. The agreement has to be in writing and signed by both spouses. If the parties have habitual residence in Sweden, the agreement also has to be submitted to the court for registration in order to be valid.

Foreign pre and post-nuptial agreements are valid in Sweden if they meet the requirements stipulated in the law that was applicable on the parties' financial circumstances when the document was drawn up.

In a case from the Supreme Court, NJA 1993 s.583, the Court found that under very special circumstances an agreement can be adjusted by the court. The case regards adjustments of a pre-nuptial agreement. The court states that the possibility to adjust a pre-nuptial agreement shall be applied in a restrictive fashion. A pre-nuptial agreement is an expression of the spouses' joint will and adjustments should only be used if the pre-nuptial agreement, to a great extent, treats one of the spouses unfairly, at least if the unfair result is due to circumstances that already existed when the agreement was met. Furthermore, adjustments should only be applied if a large amount of property, through the pre-nuptial agreement, has been excluded from the division of marital assets and this leads to a grossly uneven distribution of the spouses assembled possessions.

Validity of a pre- or post-nuptial agreement does, to date, not require that the parties have obtained independent legal advice prior to entering into the agreement. Nor does it require that full disclosure has been made prior to the signing of the agreement.

C. DIVORCE, NULLITY AND JUDICIAL SEPARATION

6. RECOGNITION OF FOREIGN MARRIAGES/DIVORCES

6.1 Summarise the position within your jurisdiction

If Brussels II *bis* is not applicable, the recognition of foreign divorces may also depend on whether or not Sweden has an international agreement with the country in question. Switzerland, all Nordic countries and all countries that have ratified the Hague Convention on the recognition of divorces and legal separations have such an agreement with Sweden. The general rule according to a law from 1973 is that all verdicts issued in these states are valid in Sweden if the requirements in paragraph 2 are met. Paragraph 2 states that one of several listed connections between the spouses and the country in question have to be at hand. For example, this is the case if one of the spouses has their habitual residence in the country or if both spouses are citizens of the state.

Divorces that are not covered by the situations above are determined in accordance with paragraphs 7 to 9 in the third chapter in the law (1904) regarding certain international legal relations concerning marriage and guardianship. Divorces shall be recognised in Sweden if, with regards to the spouses citizenship, habitual residence or other affiliation, there was a valid reason for the divorce to be dealt with in the other country.

7. DIVORCE

7.1 Explain the grounds for divorce within the jurisdiction (please also deal with nullity and judicial separation if appropriate)

In Sweden the same rules apply to heterosexual marriages as to same-sex marriages. As a fundamental rule, a spouse's will to end the marriage shall be respected. Everybody has the right to divorce if they wish to and the grounds for divorce should not have to be explained.

Divorce can be filed for through a joint written application, or by one of the spouses filing a written application for summons against the other spouse. If one of the spouses is living with a child under the age of 16 (not necessarily their own child or even a child of which they are guardian), a six-month consideration period is required before the court can issue its final ruling. The six-month consideration period is also required if one spouse opposes the divorce. However, if the spouses have been living apart for more than two years, each one of them can ask for an immediate divorce without a consideration period.

8. FINANCES/CAPITAL, PROPERTY

8.1 What powers does the court have to allocate financial resources and property on the breakdown of marriage?

8.2 Explain and illustrate with reference to recent cases the court's thinking on division of assets

In Sweden the same rules apply to heterosexual marriages as to same-sex marriages. As a general principle, each spouse owns his/her respective property and is responsible for his or her own debts. The spouses may also dispose of their own property even within the marriage, unless otherwise specified by law. There are exceptions to this in relation to the matrimonial home and real estate that is not the spouse's private (separate) property, which has become private (separate) through a marriage contract.

Unless specified, all property is each spouse's marital property.

Private (or separate) property may be created either through:

- a pre-nuptial or a post-nuptial agreement;
- a deed of gift from the donor, where it is specified that the gift should be the separate property of the beneficiary;
- a last will, in which it is specified that the inherited property should be the separate property of the beneficiary.

On divorce, all property that is marital property is, in principle, to be divided equally between the spouses. This is also the case if one of the spouses has died. The division then takes place between the widow/widower and the deceased's estate.

Private (or separate) property is kept by the owner (with some exceptions for the joint matrimonial home) after divorce.

Joint ownership of property can be open or concealed. Concealed joint ownership occurs if three criteria are met:

- the property is bought by one of the spouses for joint purposes;
- the spouse who is not the buyer contributes financially to the purchase in some way (eg, that the non-registered owner becomes responsible for a loan taken at the purchase of the property);
- the buying spouse realises that the purpose of the contribution is joint ownership.

A division of property basically means that each spouse should receive property or funds equalling half of the combined net value of the marital property. If a spouse's debts exceed his or her assets, he or she cannot subtract a negative number from the summary. This means that even if one spouse would be heavily indebted, the other spouse can always keep half of his or her net value.

The general rule is to ignore who earned the most or brought most into the relationship, but if the result is unreasonably unfair due to, for example, a short relationship, this may be considered and lead to a different division of the property.

If the parties themselves cannot agree on the division of property, an independent property division executor is appointed by the court to carry it out, upon demand from one of the spouses. If the executor cannot make the parties come to an agreement, a decision will be made. The decision of the executor can be appealed to the District Court.

According to Swedish international private law, couples may choose which law to be applicable in relation to division of assets in case of a divorce or death. The choice can be stated in a marriage contract or in a written agreement. The agreement is valid and binding if it refers to the law of a country where either of them were habitually resident or a citizen at the time when the agreement was made. Furthermore, the agreement has to be in compliance with the law that was applicable on the spouse's financial relations when the agreement was made.

Regardless of whether the spouses have chosen a foreign law to be applied, some of the Swedish rules regarding the marital home, and regarding the possibility to adjust the division of assets when the result is unfair, cannot be set aside.

If the parties choose not to, or ignore deciding on applicable laws in advance, the law (1990) about international matters regarding division of property between spouses and cohabitants states that if a couple (married or co-habiting) has had their residence in a country for more than two years, that country's law would be applicable to the financial relations between the parties. A person should be considered to have residence in a country if the stay in that country can be 'regarded as permanent when considering the duration and other circumstances'. Furthermore, if the couple has just married, the law of the country in which they had (or took) residence in, in close connection with the marriage, will be applicable on their financial relations.

The law from 1990 does not relate to maintenance between the spouses (see below).

9. FINANCES/MAINTENANCE

9.1 Explain the operation of maintenance for spouses on an ongoing basis after the breakdown of marriage.

9.2 Is it common for maintenance to be awarded?

9.3 Explain and illustrate with reference to recent cases the court's thinking on maintenance

Following a divorce each of the spouses are, according to the general rule, responsible for their own support and one spouse should not, in principle, be required to maintain the other spouse. The end of the marriage, in principle, cuts off all financial liabilities between the spouses (apart from dividing the assets).

Stipulated maintenances can be adjusted according to the Marriage Code. If maintenance is granted, the obligation always comes to an end when either the obligated or the entitled spouse dies. This is an important principal rule in Sweden. When determining whether to grant maintenance or not, children always have priority over adults.

As indicated above, maintenance orders are given restrictively. However, maintenance can be granted if two exceptions apply. The first exception regards the situation where one of the spouses needs a contribution during a transitional period of time. For example, this can be the case if the spouse needs time to find employment, begin an education or undertake relevant training.

Maintenance for longer than a transitional period of time is given very restrictively. This is granted if one of the spouses has difficulties providing for him- or herself and the marriage has been of long duration. It can also be granted if other particular reasons apply. If this is the case, in rare situations, maintenance can be granted for an unlimited period of time. According to case law, there has to be a causal connection between the marriage and the spouse's financial difficulties in order to grant maintenance for an unlimited period of time. This is not only the case if maintenance is asked for on the grounds of particular reason, but also if the marriage has been of long duration. When deciding whether to grant maintenance or not, the court looks into the needs of the spouse and if this need has arisen because of the marriage.

There are also some circumstances which reduce the maintenance obligation. These are, for example, the right to state pension, accommodation allowance and study grant (without need obligation of repayment).

The Swedish Court has, prior to Hague Protocol of 2007, applied foreign law if the dependent spouse that seeks the maintenance order is resident outside of Sweden. Now, of course, the Hague Protocol is in effect.

10. CHILD MAINTENANCE

10.1 On what basis is child maintenance calculated within the jurisdiction?

According to the Code Relating to Parents, Guardians and Children, parents are obliged to fulfill their maintenance obligations until the child is 18 years old or until the child finishes upper secondary school, which normally is up to one and a half years after the 18th birthday. The obligation can never last longer than the child's 21st birthday.

When determining maintenance payments to children, the courts look to each parent's capacity to pay. The parent who is going to make maintenance payments to the child is entitled to withhold a sum to cover living expenses. One also looks into the child's need.

As a general rule, children have the right to the same financial standard as their parents, but, in general, the maintenance orders can be said to be very low in comparison with many other countries, even if the obligated parent is of great means.

In some cases, a step-parent might be forced to pay maintenance to his or her spouse's child. For this to be applicable, the step-parent has to be either married to the biological parent or have a joint child with them.

If the parent who is obliged to pay maintenance is unable, for some reason, to fulfil the obligation, the parent who is living with the child can be granted payments from the state instead. The obligated parent then has to pay money back to the state.

Again, the Swedish Court has, prior to the Hague Protocol of 2007, applied foreign law if the dependent child/children that seeks the maintenance order is resident outside of Sweden. Now, of course, the Hague Protocol is in effect.

11. RECIPROCAL ENFORCEMENT OF FINANCIAL ORDERS

11.1 Summarise the position within your jurisdiction

As a general rule, foreign orders will not be acknowledged nor enforced in Sweden without special regulation in law.

Before the introduction of the 2007 Convention on the international recovery of child support and other forms of family maintenance, this has been an area of complexity in Sweden. However, the Convention is now in force and applied in Sweden, which hopefully will simplify matters.

In relation to orders as to division of assets, such orders may, under some circumstances, be acknowledged and enforceable in Sweden.

If a foreign divorce has also dealt with financial relations and the order has become final, this order should be acknowledged in Sweden if:

- the law of the state where the order was made applies to the spouse's financial relations;
- the order was made in the state in which the respondent was habitually resident

However, the foreign order will not be acknowledged in Sweden if:

- the order was made against a party who has not responded to the application and was not aware of the application in time to be able to respond, or against a party who otherwise was not given reasonable opportunity to represent themself in the foreign proceedings;
- the order is in conflict with a Swedish order;
- the order is in conflict with a foreign order, valid in Sweden and resulting from proceedings commenced before the other foreign proceedings;

- proceedings pending in Sweden can lead to a conflicting order;
- proceedings pending abroad can lead to a conflicting order, if those proceedings commenced before the other foreign proceedings and can be expected to result in an order valid in Sweden.

A foreign order that is enforceable in the country which delivered the order, and is acknowledged in Sweden, may be enforceable if the order has been declared enforceable here. Again, the Court of Appeal in Stockholm hears the application.

12. FINANCIAL RELIEF AFTER FOREIGN DIVORCE PROCEEDINGS

12.1 What powers are available to make orders following a foreign divorce?

When a foreign divorce has been obtained, the parties can make applications to the courts in Sweden for financial relief regarding division of property, provided the requirements set up for such applications are met. Those requirements (apart from when divorce takes place in Sweden) are that:

- the respondent has habitual residence in Sweden;
- the applicant has habitual residence in Sweden and Swedish law applies to the spouse's financial relations;
- the matter regards property in Sweden;
- the respondent has accepted the competence of the Swedish courts or has responded and failed to object to it.

An application for financial relief should generally be dismissed or stayed if proceedings pending abroad can lead to a conflicting order and if those proceedings can be expected to result in an order that will be valid in Sweden.

D. CHILDREN

13. CUSTODY/PARENTAL RESPONSIBILITY

13.1 Briefly explain the legal position in relation to custody/parental responsibility following the breakdown of a relationship or marriage

If the parents had joint custody of the child before the breakdown of the relationship or marriage, the main rule is that the custody remains joint. If the parents agree that one of them should have sole custody they can draw up a written agreement stating that the custody of the child shall be due to one of them. In order to be valid the agreement has to be approved by the social services.

The social services shall approve the agreement unless it is obvious that it is not in the child's best interest. If the parents cannot agree in the question of custody the parent who wishes to have sole custody has to bring an action before a court against the other parent. It is then up to the court to decide whether the custody shall continue to be joint or if one of the parents shall have sole custody.

When deciding if the custody shall be joint or not the court shall particularly pay attention to the parents' capability to cooperate over the child. The court cannot decide that custody shall be joint if both parents oppose this.

If custody of the child continues to be joint the parents may draw up an agreement regarding the child's living arrangements. The agreement must be in writing and has to be approved by the social services in order to be enforceable. If the parents cannot agree regarding the living arrangements, it is up to the court to decide this after one of the parents has brought actions against the other before a court.

13.2 Briefly explain the legal position in relation to access/contact/visitation following the breakdown of a relationship or marriage

The child has a right to visits with the parent that he/she is not living with. The visits can take place by the parent and the child seeing each other or through another form of contact, eg, by phone or Skype. The parents are both responsible for the child's contact with the parent that he/she is not living with.

The parents may draw up an agreement regarding visits. In order to be enforceable the agreement has to be in writing and approved by the social services. If the parents cannot agree regarding visits, it is up to the court to decide this after one of the parents has brought actions against the other before a court.

14. INTERNATIONAL ABDUCTION

14.1 Summarise the position within your jurisdiction

Sweden has ratified the Hague Convention on the Civil Aspects on Child Abduction. The Swedish Foreign Ministry is central authority for the convention. All cases regarding return orders are dealt with by the Stockholm District Court. Applications to the court are made by the left behind parent. The central authority mainly assists the applicant in finding competent representation in Sweden. Legal aid can be granted to applicants subject to usual Swedish requirements.

If a child is taken out of Sweden to a country that has ratified The Hague Convention, the central authority will assist in the process of trying to bring the child back. This also applies when a child is taken to a non-convention state, although the same instruments are then not available.

Furthermore, the rules of Brussels II *bis* and the European Convention of 1980 apply to child abductions.

15. LEAVE TO REMOVE/APPLICATIONS TO TAKE A CHILD OUT OF THE JURISDICTION

15.1 Summarise the position in your jurisdiction

Upon divorce in Sweden, custody over a child remains a joint custody, unless the court decides otherwise. Decisions regarding custody, in a divorce case or after filing for custody, are made only if specifically requested by one or both parties.

The court can decide that both parents should have joint custody after divorce.

The court can also, in combination with this, decide that the child should reside with one of the parents. The court can also decide that one of the parents shall have sole custody.

15.2 Under what circumstances may a parent apply to remove their child from the jurisdiction against the wishes of the other parent?

The current situation in Sweden regarding leave to remove a child from the country is uncertain. In a recent decision from a District Court, the court ruled that it is not possible to grant leave to relocate abroad unless the parent requesting leave is also granted sole custody. The court found that it has no power, under current legislation, to make such an order, since the non-residential parent under joint custody always has the right to oppose international relocation. The Supreme Court finally gave leave for the applicant, but the matter was solved differently, meaning that it is still uncertain how the Swedish courts will deal with cases regarding international relocation combined with joint custody.

If the court would grant a request to relocate internationally under joint custody, the residential parent would still face many practical problems. The other custodian could still refuse to sign necessary papers, such as an application for a passport, etc. All important decisions regarding the child still involve both parents if they are both custodians. The conclusion is that the only way a parent can be guaranteed to be able to do what she or he wants in terms of relocation, choice of school, healthcare etc, is to obtain sole custody. This means that a relocation case, in reality, easily turns into a custody case.

As in most countries, the court will try to determine what the effects will be for the child if one alternative or the other is selected. After considering all the relevant circumstances, the court will decide in accordance of the best interests of the child, in their opinion.

The court, will among other things, consider:

- to which of the parents, if any, the child has the closest relation;
- what effect the relocation will have on the relationship with the other parent;
- what effect the relocation will have on the child's relationship with their other relatives;
- if the child is well adjusted in school, social life, etc;
- what the living conditions, material standard, schooling and education, etc, will be in the new country compared with the old country;
- the opinion of the child depending on age and maturity.

In short, basically the same things that are considered when a parent wants to relocate within the country are considered when an international relocation is involved, but it is more difficult to be allowed to relocate internationally. As mentioned above, the parent wanting to relocate is often forced to also request full custody. It is possible, in the near future, that the higher courts will clarify the possibilities to obtain leave to relocate while maintaining joint custody, but there is also a risk that orders like that first requires an adjustment of the current legislation.

For those who wish to relocate to Sweden, it is important to know that Swedish courts do not make mirror orders of orders from other countries, and foreign court orders are not valid or enforced in Sweden without special regulation in law.

E. SURROGACY AND ADOPTION

16. VALIDITY OF SURROGACY AGREEMENTS

16.1 Briefly summarise the position in your jurisdiction

Surrogacy is not allowed according to Swedish law and hence agreements regarding this are not valid.

17. ADOPTION

17.1 Briefly summarise the position in relation to adoption in your jurisdiction. Is adoption available to individuals, cohabiting couples (both heterosexual and same-sex)?

Swedish laws regarding adoption differ slightly whether the adoption is national or international.

If the adoption is national the court has to approve the adoption. Anyone who has reached the age of 25 may file an application of adoption with a court. A person who has reached the age of 18 but not 25 may adopt if the adoption concerns a spouse's child or if there are certain grounds for this. If the person who wishes to adopt is married, he or she may only file for adoption together with their spouse. Only married couples may adopt together which means that cohabitants cannot adopt together. One of them may file alone, but it is most likely that the court will find this unsuitable.

Married couples include both heterosexual and same-sex couples. Adoption is also available to individuals.

If the adoption is international it is the social services that decide whether an adoption shall be allowed or not. The social services conduct an extensive investigation before the decision is made. The adoption must also be approved by the country that the adoptive child is adopted from. The same rules regarding who is allowed to adopt are applicable on international adoptions. This means that adoption is open to married couples or individuals. However, certain countries may not allow individuals or same-sex couples to adopt.

F. COHABITATION

18. COHABITATION

18.1 What legislation (if any) governs division of property for unmarried couples on the breakdown of the relationship?

Cohabitation is regulated in the Cohabitation Act of 2003, which in many ways resembles the Marriage Code. However, it does differ in some areas when it comes to the breakdown of a relationship. The legislation provides a minimum protection for the weaker partner when a cohabiting relationship ends.

The Act states that, on dissolution of the cohabitation, an equal division of the value of the home and household goods which have been acquired for common use shall take place. The Act only regulates the division of the joint home and the household goods. The rights for a cohabitee to take over a joint home are regulated and there are some limitations on a party's right to dispose of the joint home. It is important to know that this act provides a limited protection compared with what is provided for married couples and registered partners.

The act is applicable to couples who are living together on a permanent basis. They have to be sharing household and they have to be in a relationship.

If the home was obtained before the cohabitation started, there is a possibility for the party who is not the owner to be awarded to stay in the home after separation and also, under some limited circumstances (only applying to rented homes and tenant owners homes), to take over a home.

The Cohabitation Act is not imperative; it can be set aside by an agreement. The agreement does not have to be of a specific form and is valid without any further measures as registration.

Cohabitants do not have a legal right to inherit one another; hence the right to inherit must be declared in a will.

G. FAMILY DISPUTE RESOLUTION

19. MEDIATION, COLLABORATIVE LAW AND ARBITRATION

19.1 Briefly summarise the non-court-based processes available in your jurisdiction and the current status of agreements reached under the auspices of mediation, collaborative law and arbitration

If the parents cannot agree on questions regarding custody, the child's living arrangement and/or visitations the court may appoint a mediator. The task for the mediator is to help the parents come to an agreement that is in the child's best interest. The mediator shall report back to the court within the time that is set by the court. The time set by the court may not exceed four weeks. If an agreement is met it can either be established through a written agreement that is approved by the social services or through a court decision.

19.2 What is the statutory basis (if any), for mediation, collaborative law and arbitration in your jurisdiction? In particular, are the parties required to attempt a family dispute resolution in advance of proceedings?

Mediation is regulated in the Parental Code Chapter 6 Paragraph 18a. Mediation is a method that the courts can use in order to help the parents reach an agreement. Hence it is not necessary for the parties to attempt mediation before the commencement of proceedings.

H. OTHER

20. CIVIL PARTNERSHIP/SAME-SEX MARRIAGES

20.1 What is the status of civil partnership/same-sex marriage within the jurisdiction?

20.2 What legislation governs civil partnership/same-sex marriage?

As of 1 May 2009, Swedish law no longer makes a difference between same-sex marriages and marriages between men and women. All matters regarding same-sex spouses are dealt with in the same way as between spouses of opposite sex. Partnerships registered before 1 May 2009 will continue as such until they are dissolved or transformed into marriages. A registered partnership is transformed into a marriage by way of a simple registration procedure or if the partners wed in accordance with the 4th chapter of the Marriage code.

Formally married couples of the same sex now have the same rights as spouses of the opposite sex when it comes to adoption.

21. CONTROVERSIAL AREAS/RAPIDLY DEVELOPING AREAS OF LAW

21.1 Is there a particular area of the law within the jurisdiction that is currently undergoing major change? Which areas of law are most out-of-step?

21.2 Which areas would you most like to see reformed/changed?

See section 15 above.

Switzerland

Langner Stieger Trachsel & Partner Dr. iur. Daniel Trachsel

A. JURISDICTION AND CONFLICT OF LAW

1. SOURCES OF LAW

1.1 What is the primary source of law in relation to the breakdown of marriage and the welfare of children within the jurisdiction? Which are the main statutes governing matrimonial law in the jurisdiction?

Swiss substantive law

Swiss family law is essentially governed by two statutes:

- the Swiss Civil Code (CC; *Schweizerisches Zivilgesetzbuch* or ZGB) of 10 December 1907 (SR 210), which came into force on 1 January 1912 (with numerous amendments over subsequent years); and
- the Federal Law on Registered Partnerships for Same-Sex Couples (*Bundesgesetz über die eingetragene Partnerschaft gleichgeschlechtlicher Paare* or PartG) of 18 June 2004 (PartG; SR 211.231), which came into force on 1 January 2007).

Other important legal sources are decisions handed down by the cantonal courts and, in particular, by the Federal Supreme Court of Switzerland, as well as comprehensive literature.

Swiss private international law

The jurisdiction of the Swiss courts or authorities, applicable law and the recognition and enforcement of foreign decisions, are governed by the Federal Act on International Private Law of 18 December 1987 (PIL act/SR 291). However, according to Article 1. 2 PIL, the terms and conditions of international agreements take precedence over the Swiss legislation.

Switzerland is a signatory to many international treaties. The most important conventions and treaties applicable in Switzerland include:

- The Hague Convention of 2 October 1973 on the law applicable to maintenance obligations (SR 0.211.213.01);
- The Hague Convention of 19 October 1996 on the jurisdiction, applicable law, recognition, enforcement and co-operation in respect of parental responsibility and measures for the protection of children (SR 0.211.231.01/MSA II);
- The Hague Convention of 29 May 1993 on protection of children and co-operation in respect of intercountry adoption (SR 0.211.221.311);
- The Hague Convention of 25 October 1980 on the civil aspects of international child abduction (SR 0.211.230.02);
- The (Lugano) Convention of 30 October 2007 on jurisdiction and

enforcement of judgments in civil and commercial matters (Brussels I; SR 0.275.12, in force in Switzerland since 1 January 2011);

- The Hague Convention of 1 June 1970 on the recognition of marital divorces and legal separations (SR 0.211.212.3); and
- The European Convention of 20 May 1980 on recognition and enforcement of decisions concerning child custody and on restoration of custody of children (SR 0.211.230.01)

For further information see also *www.hcch.e-vision.nl.*

2. JURISDICTION

2.1 What are the main jurisdictional requirements for the institution of proceedings in relation to divorce, property and children?

The Swiss courts at the defendant's or the plaintiff's place of residence, if the latter has been a resident of Switzerland for one year or is a Swiss citizen, have jurisdiction to entertain an action for divorce or separation (Article 59 PIL). In addition, when the spouses are not domiciled in Switzerland and at least one of them is a Swiss national, the courts at the place of origin (*Heimatort*) have jurisdiction to entertain an action for divorce or separation, provided the action cannot be brought at the domicile of either spouse or cannot reason-ably be required to be brought there (Article 60 PIL).

Under the same circumstances, the court may supplement and/or amend an absolute decree which the court itself handed down or was handed down by a court abroad (Article 64 PIL).

Switzerland applies the principle of 'the unity of the divorce ruling' (Article 63. 2 PIL). According to this principle, the court having jurisdiction over a petition for divorce or separation rules not only on the dissolution of the marriage or separation itself but, in addition, on all incidental legal consequences ('secondary effects') including:

- all matters pertaining to children (however, in general, only if the children have their habitual residence in Switzerland);
- support payments for children and marital and post-marital maintenance for spouses;
- the division of assets in pension funds; and
- the distribution of property.

Which law may be applicable for the structuring of incidental legal consequences is determined under prevailing international agreement laws and, subsequently, under Swiss private international law (see below).

3. DOMICILE AND HABITUAL RESIDENCE

3.1 Explain the concepts of domicile and habitual residence as they apply to the jurisdiction

According to Article 20 PIL, an individual:

- has his or her domicile (*Wohnsitz*) in the state where he or she resides with the intent of establishing permanent residence;
- has his or her habitual residence (*Aufenthalt*) in the state where he or she lives during a certain period of time, even if this period initially appears to be of limited duration.

The definition of 'domicile' (*Wohnsitz*), according to PIL, has, on the one hand, an objective element (ie, the necessity of a physical presence of a person at one place), as well as a subjective element (ie, the intention to remain at this place permanently) on the other (BGE 119 II 167 ff.). Where a person has his or her domicile is to be determined in accordance and with a view of all relevant circumstances of the individual case. The domicile is located where the centre of the vital interests of a person is adjudged to be. This must also be apparent to outside parties. The actual centre of a person's vital interests is where their familial and social interests are predominantly located. Further important points of reference are the vocational and financial interests of a person. The place where a person is registered and pays their taxes has an indicative effect. However, the question of where the actual centre of the relevant vital interests is remains decisive. A minimum length of stay is not necessary. However, the person's conduct must clearly indicate that he or she considers remaining at this place. If this is the case, it is then possible to conclude that a person is already domiciled at a place already from the first day of settling in. The impression must be clearly made that a person has left the previous centre of vital interests in order to establish a new one.

No individual may have more than one domicile at the same time. This can lead to difficulties in cases where a family has several homes and stays in each one for a certain period of time. In such cases, the decision of where the domicile is located depends solely on where it appears that a party is most rooted and where the centre of the most essential vital living interests is found.

If a domicile is given up and a new one has not yet been established, the habitual residence (*Aufenthalt*) takes its place as the point of reference (BGE of 30 April 2003, 4 C.298/2002).

Domicile is always determined using these criteria – irrespective of whether this relates to jurisdiction for divorce proceedings, marital law settlements, maintenance or matters concerning children. Insofar as the 'domicile' is a relevant factor in an international treaty, the definition given in the treaty applies, not that given under Swiss international private law.

4. CONFLICT OF LAW/APPLICABLE LAW TO BE APPLIED

4.1 What happens when one party applies to stay proceedings in favour of a foreign jurisdiction? What factors will the local court take into account when determining forum issues?

It is important to note that Swiss private international law clearly differentiates between:

- jurisdiction (*Zuständigkeit*);
- applicable law (*anwendbares Recht*);
- recognition and enforcement of foreign decisions (*Anerkennung und Vollstreckung ausländischer Entscheidungen*).

It is entirely possible that Swiss jurisdiction exists but that a Swiss court, in turn, applies foreign law.

The principle of *forum non conveniens* (literally, a 'forum which is not convenient' or 'inappropriate forum') is not known in Swiss private international law. The factors which the local court takes into account when determining forum issues are set out in Article 9 PIL:

'When an action having the same subject matter is already pending between the same parties in a foreign country, the Swiss court shall stay the case if it is to be expected that the foreign court will, within a reasonable time, render a decision capable of being recognised in Switzerland.

'In order to determine when an action has been initiated in Switzerland, the conclusive date is that of the first act that is necessary to initiate the proceeding. A notice to appear for conciliation is sufficient.

'The Swiss court shall terminate its proceedings as soon as it is presented with a foreign decision capable of being recognised in Switzerland'.

Therefore, the following preconditions must be present in order to stay the Swiss action:

- the action must have the same subject matter (for example, if one spouse has filed suit for separation abroad, the other spouse may still file for divorce in Switzerland, because the two legal matters are not identical);
- the action must be between the same parties, which is regularly the case in legal family procedures; and
- the action must have become pending abroad at a time earlier than that in Switzerland. (At what time the suit has become pending abroad is determined under the laws of the foreign court. Clarifying this is often not easy. It is possible that the applicable foreign law uses, as the determining factor, the point in time when a conciliation petition was introduced, the assignment of the suit to a court, or when the suit papers were delivered to the counterparty).

Swiss law has established a very early point in time: the filing of a request for conciliation, an action, an application to the court or a joint petition for divorce establishes *lis pendens* (Art. 62 Swiss Code of Civil Procedure [CCP]).

If the Convention on Jurisdiction and the Enforcement of Judgements in Civil and Commercial Matters of 30 October 2007 (SR0.275.12; Lugano Convention/Brussels I) applies, the term of the institution of legal proceedings is not determined in accordance with Article 9 PIL, but rather by taking Article 27 Lugano Convention into consideration.

The Swiss court will only stay or terminate its proceedings when it is to be expected that the foreign court will hand down a decision within an appropriate period that can be recognised in Switzerland. If it is clear from the outset that the foreign decision cannot be recognised in Switzerland (because, for example, the conditions for recognition under the Hague Convention on the Recognition of Divorces and Legal Separations of 1 June 1970 are not fulfilled), the Swiss court will then continue its proceedings even though the suit was first filed abroad.

If the states involved are members of the Hague Convention on the recognition of Divorces and Legal Separations of 1 June 1970, the provisions of said Convention must, of course, be taken in to account. The Convention has precedence over Swiss national law (Article 1.2 PIL).

B. PRE- AND POST-NUPTIAL AGREEMENTS

5. VALIDITY OF PRE- AND POST-NUPTIAL AGREEMENTS

5.1 To what extent are pre- and post-nups binding within the jurisdiction? Could you provide a brief discussion of the most significant recent case law on this issue

Pre-nuptial agreements are an important instrument in the area of legal family risk management in Switzerland. For the validity of a pre-nuptial agreement, it is not necessary (but advisable) that:

- the agreement was entered into a certain time before the marriage was celebrated;
- each party received clarification about the content and consequences of the agreement from an independent legally-trained person of their own choice; and
- the parties have provided complete information and full disclosure about their financial circumstances.

A pre-nuptial agreement can be entered into before or after the marriage was celebrated (Article 182. 1 CC). The form of a marital property agreement is valid if it fulfils the requirements of the law applicable to the substance or of the law of the place where the agreement was entered into. If a pre-nuptial agreement is entered into in Switzerland, it must be in the form of a public deed (Article 184 CC).

The areas a pre-nuptial agreement can cover are fairly limited. The following cannot be determined in advance:

- The preconditions for a divorce, nullification or separation of a marriage are ultimately governed by law. Any agreements in variance to it are not binding.
- Agreements on arrangements for children, in particular about parental responsibility, visiting rights or maintenance, made in advance, are not binding.
- Any amounts saved in pension funds during a marriage are divided in the event of a divorce. Waiving such a division is only possible under very restrictive conditions. Agreements in a marital contract that are at variance to this are invalid.

The primary area of application for pre-nuptial agreements is the legal arrangement for a property settlement. The partners to a marriage are able to modify the ordinary matrimonial property regime of sharing of acquired property in a wide variety of ways. Or they can make themselves subject to a separation of property regime or a community of property regime. Such agreements are valid without restrictions and cannot be reviewed by the court that has jurisdiction to entertain actions for a divorce, a separation, or for measures relating to marital property. The distribution of the marital goods is carried out in accordance with the pre-nuptial agreement. The court cannot alter this at the request of one of the partners. Therefore, if the marriage partners subject themselves to a separation of property regime, a division of the assets saved during the marriage will not take place, even if this is found to be unfair. Also, if the marriage ends through the death of one partner, marital agreements are an important instrument in estate planning. Firstly, marital assets will be divided according to existing pre-nuptial or post-nuptial agreements. The result constitutes the estate of the deceased spouse. Secondly, the estate will then be divided according to inheritance law and, in particular, according to the rules set out in last wills or inheritance agreements. In the same way, inheritance agreements between spouses are binding. Property and inheritance arrangements are often combined in one agreement.

In contrast to this, the binding effect of agreements about marital and post-marital support is very restricted. They are not binding to the extent that such agreements are at variance with standard legal principles. If, for example, one spouse agrees, before getting married, to waive post-marital support, he or she can, notwithstanding the previous renouncement, successfully demand support payments in divorce proceedings when the marriage had lasted a long time or if that spouse must care for the children or because they are no longer or only marginally able to work for reasons of health or advanced age.

Pre-nuptial agreements entered into abroad are recognised in Switzerland if they were drawn up and executed in a valid form and the arrangements are not in violation of Swiss '*ordre public*.' For example, a separation of property agreed to in Sweden is valid in Switzerland. However, a clause in a German marital agreement, wherein the spouses waive a pension rights adjustment in accordance with section 1587 lit. o) BGB as part of a legal divorce settlement, is not binding if assets in a Swiss pension fund are being taken into account.

C. DIVORCE, NULLITY AND JUDICIAL SEPARATION

6. RECOGNITION OF FOREIGN MARRIAGES/DIVORCES

6.1 Summarise the position in your jurisdiction

A marriage that was validly celebrated in a foreign country shall be recognised in Switzerland (Article 45 PIL). Swiss law is oriented to the principle of '*favor recognitionis*', under which, according to prevailing doctrine, a marriage is recognised in Switzerland when it is valid in the country where the marriage took place or in the country where at least one of the parties to the marriage is domiciled or habitually resides or is a national. Therefore, marriages which were entered into before a religious, military or consular person can be recognised if they are able to be considered valid in this way under prevailing foreign law. However, exceptions always remain for Swiss *ordre public*. Bigamous or polygamous marriages or marriages between directly related persons or between siblings cannot be recognised. The Hague Convention of 14 March 1978 on Celebration and the Recognition of the Validity of Marriages has not been ratified in Switzerland, which does not cause any problems since Article 45 PIL is more liberal, in terms of recognition, than the Convention.

The Hague Convention of 1 July 1970 on the Recognition of Divorces and Legal Separations is primarily applied for the recognition of divorce and separation decrees handed down abroad. Articles 17 and 18 of the Convention, however, expressly have reservations for a more favourable autonomous (national) recognition law. Therefore, in Switzerland, said Hague Convention is of no great importance, because the Swiss national law is more favourable for recognition. Article 65 PIL stipulates as follows:

"Foreign decrees of divorce or separation shall be recognised in Switzerland if they have been rendered in the state of domicile or habitual residence, or in the national state, of either spouse, or if they are recognised in one of these states.

However, a decree that was rendered in a state of which neither spouse or only the plaintiff spouse is a national shall be recognised in Switzerland only:

- *if, at the time of filing the action, at least one of the spouses was domiciled or had his or her habitual residence in that state and the defendant spouse was not domiciled in Switzerland;*
- *if the defendant spouse submitted to the jurisdiction of the foreign court without reservation; or*
- *if the defendant spouse expressly consented to recognition of the decree in Switzerland."*

Naturally, this is also subject to the *ordre public*, which can be violated through so-called private divorces or through repudiations under Islamic law.

7. DIVORCE

7.1 Explain the grounds for divorce within the jurisdiction (please also deal with nullity and judicial separation if appropriate)

Switzerland has had no-fault divorce since 1 January 2000. A marriage may only be terminated by a court, which has to settle all consequential matters related to the divorce under the 'principle of unity in divorce decrees'. (Article 283 CCP: In its decision on the divorce, the court also determines the consequences of the divorce. Only the division of matrimonial property can be referred to separate proceedings for good cause). The law recognises three reasons for a divorce.

Divorce upon joint petition (Articles 111 and 112 CC)

In a divorce upon joint petition, the spouses submit a joint petition to the court in which a joint will of the spouses to divorce provides sufficient grounds for divorce. The breakup of the marriage must not be substantiated and is also not verified by the court. The court only needs to be convinced that both parties after careful consideration want to dissolve their marriage.

In a divorce by joint petition with complete agreement, the parties to the marriage are in agreement about the divorce petition and all of the consequences of the divorce (Article 111. 1 CC). In the divorce agreement, arrangements for the children, post-marriage support and distribution of occupational pension funds, as well as the division of marital property, must all be settled. The court examines whether the divorce petition, the agreement about the consequences of the divorce and the joint petitions relating to the children are made based on the free will and after careful consideration of the parties to the marriage. To do this, the court questions each spouse individually and both together (Article 111. 1 CC). The children are heard with regard to the arrangements that have been made for them. If the court comes to the conclusion that the divorce and the agreement are based on free will, it issues a divorce decree and approves the agreement.

In a divorce by joint petition with only partial agreement, under Article 112 CC, the spouses are in agreement about the will to divorce when submitting the petition, but not about all consequences of the divorce. The parties to the marriage must expressly declare their will that the court should settle any consequences in dispute and that they will hold to their joint divorce petition irrespective of how the court rules. Each party can submit his or her petition on the disputed divorce consequences. The court then issues an overall judgment on the dissolution of the marriage and the consequences of the divorce.

Divorce by petition of one spouse after having lived apart (Article 114 CC)

If the conditions for a divorce by joint petition are not present, one party to the marriage may petition for divorce if the couple have lived apart for at least two years at the time the petition is submitted. After the end of this period, an absolute right to divorce exists. A factual separation is sufficient. Thus no judicial separation is required, it is sufficient to establish that the couple is no longer living under the same roof (discontinuation of the joint household). On the grounds that he or she would like to begin the two-year separation period, each party to the marriage may demand the dissolution of the common household.

Divorce by petition of one spouse because the continuation of the marriage cannot reasonably be expected (Article 115 CC)

One partner to the marriage may file for divorce before the end of the two-year separation period if the continuation of the marriage can no longer be considered reasonable for serious reasons for which he or she is not at fault. 'Serious reasons' can include, for example, spousal abuse by the other, disreputable or dishonourable moral conduct or an infamous criminal activity. In principle, the court must establish strict criteria when judging the severity of the action since the formalised divorce requirements mentioned above would otherwise lose their importance. This reason for divorce has taken on little practical importance: Court procedures under Article 115 CC generally last longer than two years. For this reason it makes more sense to wait for the end of the two-year separation period (cf. above lit. b).

Annulment not subject to time limit (Article 105 et seq. CC)

This is established if, at the time the marriage took place, one of the parties to the marriage was already married, not of sound mind and since then has not regained the capacity to judge for themselves, the marriage was forbidden through blood relationship or stepchild relationship between the parties under Article 95 CC, or when one of the parties to the marriage does not establish a joint living situation but rather wants to circumvent the laws regarding the admission and residence of foreigners. A petition may be filed by anyone who has an interest at the domicile of the married couple (Article 106 CC). The petition for annulment is open-ended and not subject to statute of limitations (Article 106. 3 CC).

Annulment subject to time limit (Article 107 et seq. CC)
This is established if, at the time the marriage took place, one of the spouses, for a temporary reason, did not have the capacity to make a rational judgement at the wedding ceremony, if one of the spouses, by error, consented to the marriage (either because the spouse did not want to get married or did not want to marry the respective person), if one of the spouses consented to the marriage because the spouse was intentionally deceived as to essential personal qualities of the other person, or if one of the spouses consented to the marriage under threat of imminent and severe danger to the spouse's life, health or honour or that of a person close to them. The petition for the dissolution of the marriage under Article 107 CC may only be submitted within six months since the time the reason for the annulment became known, although the absolute statute of limitations of five years since the time of marriage should be noted (Article 108. 1 CC).

The annulment ruling is not retroactive to the point in time of the marriage. Until the ruling, the marriage has all of the consequences of a valid marriage with the exception of inheritance claims.

Legal separation (Article 117 et seq. CC)
If a reason for a divorce is present, the parties to the marriage may individually or jointly petition the court for a separation order for a specified or unspecified period instead of filing for divorce. Separation is intended for couples who do not want to divorce for religious reasons, because of their age or because of estate consequences, or because dissolution of the marriage would have a negative impact on the widow's or widower's pension under the rules of the existing occupational pension plan. By law, a division of property takes place (Article 118. 1 CC). The practical importance of separation in accordance with Article 117 CC is minimal.

The dissolution of the joint household (Article 175 et seq. CC)
One spouse is entitled to discontinue the joint household for as long as 'their personage, economic security or the well-being of the family is seriously endangered by living together' (Article 175 CC). Adjudication allows for a separation, in particular, when one spouse would like to begin the two-year separation period according to Article 114 CC (see above). The presiding marriage mediation court (*Eheschutzgericht*) settles all necessary modalities for living separately. The practical importance of this so-called 'minor divorce' is substantial.

8. FINANCES/CAPITAL, PROPERTY

8.1 What powers does the court have to allocate financial resources and property on the breakdown of marriage? Explain and illustrate with reference to recent cases the court's thinking on division of assets

Applicable law
According to Article 52 1 PIL, a choice of law is possible in the area of

marital property regime. The spouses may choose the law of the state in which they are both domiciled or will be domiciled after the marriage celebration, or the law of a state of which either of them is national (Article 52. 2 PIL. The choice of law must be done in writing (Article 53. 1 PIL). The chosen law remains applicable as long the spouses have not amended or revoked such choice (Article 53.3 PIL).

In the absence of a choice of law, the division of property under the marital property regime is carried out according to the law of the country where both spouses are domiciled or were last domiciled at the same time (Article 54.1 PIL). If the spouses were never domiciled at the same time in the same state, their common national law applies. In the absence of a common nationality, the property regime of separation of property according to Swiss law applies (Article 54. 3 PIL).

If the spouses' domicile is transferred from one state to another, the law of the new domicile applies and has retroactive effect as of the day of the marriage (Article 55.1 PIL). However, the couple may exclude the retroaction or agree to the continued application of the previous law.

Division of matrimonial property according to Swiss law

A consequence of the dissolution of the marriage is that the marital assets must be divided between the parties to the marriage. The division of property takes place according to the marital property regime the couple is subject to.

Ordinary regime of sharing of acquired property

This marital property regime always applies when the spouses have not selected another marital property regime. In a divorce, the dissolution of the marital property regime is set back to the day on which the petition was filed (Article 204. 2 CC).

The first step is that each spouse shall take back property of his that is in the possession of the other (Article 205.1 CC). If there is no agreement on the allocation of jointly owned assets, the court shall assign the matter in question to that party that can prove an overriding interest in it (Article 205. 2 CC).

A distinction is made between the own property of one spouse (*Eigengut*) and the acquired property (*Errungenschaft*). Own property includes the assets which were present before the beginning of the marriage or were received through gifts or inheritance during the marriage. Acquired property includes assets which resulted through work or as income from own property during the marriage. Every asset is assigned either to acquired or own property. Own property is not subject to the division of property.

Furthermore, the spouses must settle what they owe each other and the debts which they have with outside parties (liabilities). A debt is charged to the property to which it is objectively connected or, in case or doubt, to the property acquired during marriage (Article 209. 2 CC). During the division of property, a compensation claim exists when acquisition debts were paid from the own property of one spouse or own property debts from acquisitions of one spouse (Article 209. 1 CC).

Increases or decreases of value must be calculated and assigned. If a spouse has contributed without compensation to the acquisition, improvement or preservations of assets of the other, and if an added value exists at the time of division, then the spouse shall have a claim which is proportional to the amount of their contribution For example, spouse X inherited from their parents a house with a value of CHF 1,000,000.00 Spouse Z invested CHF 200,000.00, which was their own property. At the time of division, the real estate has a value of CHF 2,000,000.00 Accordingly, spouse Z has a share in added value of CHF 200,000.00 Together with the invested amount spouse Z then receives CHF 400,000.00.

After the liabilities have been deducted from the assets and the own property segregated, it can be established whether a net gain ('surplus', *Vorschlag*) or net loss ('deficit', *Rückschlag*) exists. Each spouse is entitled to half of the surplus of the other (Article 215. 1CC). However, a deficit shall not be taken into account; such a loss has to be carried by the spouse who caused it.

The claim resulting from the property division is a monetary claim. The existing ownership relationships cannot be amended by the court. If, for example, a real estate or shares in a limited company are registered in the name of only one spouse, the court cannot transfer the house or shares into the ownership of the other spouse against the will of the current owner. The settlement is done through a payment.

The following example shows how the calculation is normally done:

Position	Husband	Wife	Position
1. Assets			**1. Assets**
Real estate	500,000.00	0	
Life insurance	100,000.00	0	
Shares	400,000.00	100,000.00	Shares
Cash	100,000.00	50,000.00	Cash
Car	50,000.00	30,000.00	Car
Art	-	20,000.00	Art
subtotal	**1,150,000.00**	**200,000.00**	**subtotal**
2. Liabilities			**2. Liabilities**
Mortgage	350,000.00	0	
subtotal	**350,000.00**	**0**	**subtotal**
3. Own property			**3. Own property**
At the time of marriage	100,000.00	0	

Inheritance	100,000.00	100,000.00	Inheritance
subtotal	**200,000.00**	**100,000.00**	**subtotal**
4. Surplus (Position 1 minus Positions 2 and 3)	**600,000.00**	**100,000.00**	**4. Surplus**
5. Husband's debt	**-250,000.00**	**+250,000.00**	**5. Wife's debt**
6. Result of division	**350,000.00**	**350,000.00**	**6. Result of division**

Community of property regime

In a divorce, irrespective of the pre-nuptial agreement, each spouse shall retake from the property held in common what, under a sharing in acquired property regime, would be his or her own property. The remaining property held in common is divided in half (or according to the rules set out in the marriage agreement).

Separate property

If the couple has agreed to the marital property regime of separation of property, a division of property is, of course, not necessary. Each spouse retains their assets and no settlement is undertaken for the assets accumulated during the marriage.

9. FINANCES/MAINTENANCE

9.1 Explain the operation of maintenance for spouses on an ongoing basis after the breakdown of marriage.
9.2 Is it common for maintenance to be awarded?
9.3 Explain and illustrate with reference to recent cases the court's thinking on maintenance

Maintenance

Applicable law

Maintenance obligations between spouses are governed by the Hague Convention of 2 October 1973 on the law applicable to Maintenance Obligations (SR 0.211.213.01). The provisions of the Convention are applied *erga omnes* in Switzerland.

Swiss substantive law

If a spouse cannot be reasonably expected to adequately provide for himself or herself, the other spouse owes an adequate contribution to him or her. The following criteria are important when establishing the post-marital support payments:

- the task sharing during the marriage;
- the duration of the marriage;
- the standard of living during the marriage;
- the age and the state of health of the spouses;
- the income and the assets of the spouses;
- the extent and duration of future caring for the children by the spouses;
- the professional education and the prospective income; and
- the expected entitlements of private or public pension plans.

Any possible fault of the entitled party for the dissolution of the marriage is not considered. Case law and doctrine have developed various support types, such as childcare support, support in order to improve old age provision and mutual solidarity support. The calculation is done using an individual case-related basis. Support tables or fixed guidelines are unknown in Swiss practice.

In practice, the determination of post-marital support is done in five steps.

Firstly, it must be clarified how long the marriage has lasted, whether it was a 'short' or a 'long' marriage. A marriage was short when it lasted less than five to 10 years and did not produce any children. For a short marriage, only a short transitional pension is awarded, if any at all. This is intended to compensate for any disadvantages linked to the marriage (for example, the wife had to take a less well-paid job at the new place of residence after the marriage; this financial deficit is compensated through a one-year transition pension). In contrast, there is a claim related to the continuation of the customary standard of living experienced during a long marriage. To the extent that this cannot be financed through one's own income, the lacking amount can be demanded in the form of support payments from the higher-earning spouse.

Secondly, what was the standard of living experienced during the marriage? The marital standard of living constitutes the upper limit for post-marital maintenance. This is a very important measurement factor and it must be demonstrated by the party claiming support.

Thirdly, what income can the spouse who is entitled to support earn for himself or herself? The relevant criteria are the duration of the marriage, the assignment of roles within the marriage, education, possible adverse health effects, marketplace circumstances, origins in another culture and, in particular, the necessity to continue to care for the children. According to Swiss practice, the spouse who raises one or more children until they have reached the age of 10 is not required to engage in gainful occupation. After that, working part-time (50 per cent) is required, and after the youngest child reached the age of 16, the caretaking parent is expected to work full-time. This is a general rule, modifications with a view to the individual circumstances are, of course, possible. The interests of assets which a spouse receives under the division of matrimonial property are taken into account. Future expected inheritances can play a role. If one spouse clearly has a shortfall in comparison to the last marital living standard after taking reasonable earning capacity into account, this spouse is fundamentally entitled to support.

Fourthly, does the spouse required to pay support have sufficient earning capacity? If the other spouse cannot make up this gap because of a lack of earning capacity, then the post-marital support payments are dropped or reduced. In other words, the party required to pay support in any case has the right to cover their own familial minimum existence needs. This also applies when support payments for children are in question.

Finally, how long does the support requirement last? Pension payments are generally time limited, usually at the point in time when the youngest child turns 16 (or 18) or until the age of ordinary retirement is reached. Life-long support payments are only granted in exceptional cases.

Post-marital support is regularly paid in the form of periodic, usually monthly, instalments. If circumstances justify it, the court may also grant a lump sum payment (Article 126. 2 CC). Lump sum payments and periodic payments have different tax consequences, and this has to be taken into account when calculating them.

The support payment is regularly adjusted to inflation. Under very restrictive circumstances, the amount of support may be increased after the divorce (Article 129. 3 CC). A support amount may be cancelled or reduced when it is obviously inequitable. According to Article 125. 3 CC, this would be the case if the spouse entitled to support grossly violated their obligation to contribute to the support of the family, wilfully manipulated their neediness, or committed a serious crime against the supporting party or a person closely related to them. However, Article 129. 3 CC has a very limited practical importance. Support obligations expire upon remarriage. Cohabitation may lead to a reduction or a termination of support payments.

If there is a change in circumstances, if the spouse required to pay support earns less or the spouse entitled to support has a higher income than expected, an adjustment can then be petitioned for if the change in circumstances is considerable in amount, lasting and was not foreseeable.

Old-age provision

Applicable law

As a general rule, only Swiss law is applied.

Swiss substantive law

Sufficient provisions for old age belong to marital support. In Switzerland, the so-called 'Three Pillar Principle' is anchored in the constitution (Article 111).

The 'first pillar' is the Federal Old Age and Survivors Insurance (*Alters- und Hinterlassenenversicherung* [AHV, OASI]). This insurance is compulsory throughout Switzerland and covers the minimum basic needs in old age (currently the maximum monthly AHV pension is CHF 2,340.00. The AHV contributions, which the spouses have saved throughout the years of a marriage and which are credited to their individual accounts, are divided and split equally between the two spouses when they divorce (Article 29^quinquies^, 3 lit. c AHVG; so-called splitting). This is done in accordance with the law and agreements at variance to this are not possible.

The 'second pillar' is the occupational pension. In Switzerland both employer and employee have to contribute to a pension scheme wherein a capital is accumulated. These capitals can accrue to a significant amount. Since only an employed spouse has such a work-related pension, the spouse whose work it has been to raise the children should have a share of this saved capital. According to Article 122. 1 CC, each spouse has a right to half of the retirement benefits saved by the other spouse during the course of the marriage. It should be noted that the spouse receiving the entitlement does not get a cash payment but rather vested benefits. The court will instruct the pension fund of the obligated spouse to transfer the corresponding amount either to the pension fund of the other spouse or to a vested benefits account (a blocked account, which can be accessed five years before reaching the normal age of retirement, at the earliest).

If one spouse has become disabled before the divorce or reached the age of retirement and, therefore, already draws a pension from a pension fund, there are then no longer any retirement benefits 'upon leaving' available to be split. The settlement form is then the payment of an appropriate compensation (Article 124. 1 CC). The amount of the payment is established by the court taking all specific circumstances into account. A capital payment as well as a pension payment may be granted as compensation. The same principles are applied when assets in foreign pension funds are involved.

Under very restrictive circumstances, a spouse may renounce their claim in whole or in part if an equivalent provision for old age and disability is ensured in a different manner. However, the judge may refuse the splitting in whole or in part if it obviously would be inequitable due to the liquidation of the marital property regime or the financial situation after the divorce (Article 123 CC).

The 'third pillar' is voluntary, individual retirement savings. The asset growth occurring during the marriage is settled according to the terms of the marital property regime.

10. CHILD MAINTENANCE

10.1 On what basis is child maintenance calculated within the jurisdiction?

Both parents are jointly responsible for supporting a child irrespective of whether they are married, separated or divorced. In cases of joint or sole parental responsibility, the parent not having custody must make monetary payments to support the child (Article 276 CC).

When assessing the amount of support payments, the needs of the child must be taken into account as well as the parents' financial situation and ability to pay (Article 285 CC). According to a widely used rule of thumb, the parent required to pay support generally contributes 17 per cent of their net income for one child, 27 per cent for two children and 37 per cent for three children. The calculation of these figures is done using average circumstances, although a monthly amount of CHF 2,500.00 per child is rarely exceeded in practice. Extraordinary expenses, in particular for private schooling, are paid in addition if the ability to pay allows. The support payment per child is separate to any possible support payments for a spouse. Child allowances are to be paid to the person having parental custody, in addition to support payments.

The support payments are established for children who are still minors at the time of the divorce. However, under Article 133.1 CC, it is possible that support payments continue beyond the age of majority if the child has not completed their education. Children who have reached the age of majority (which is 18 in Switzerland) and are still in education have their own independent right to support and their own claim against both parents.

11. RECIPROCAL ENFORCEMENT OF FINANCIAL ORDERS

11.1 Summarise the position in your jurisdiction

Recognition and enforcement of a foreign absolute decree follow the guidelines described in section 6. If the conditions mentioned there are fulfilled, the foreign order on the division of marital property is recognised and can be enforced in Switzerland (Article 58.2 PIL). A 'mirror order' is not necessary. As far as the enforcement of support claims is in question, the Lugano Convention (Brussels I) in particular must be heeded.

It frequently happens in practice that the parties to the marriage stand before a foreign judge in divorce proceedings and some assets (for instance, property or bank accounts) are located in Switzerland. Even if the foreign court hands down a restraining order against one of the parties to the marriage, this ultimately cannot hinder that person from having access to these assets. A foreign court may not order a bank domiciled in Switzerland or a Swiss court land registry office to block an asset. In such cases, a freezing injunction should be obtained at the place in Switzerland where the asset in question is located. Such an injunction can be obtained very quickly *ex parte* provided the preconditions below can be established:

- According to the applicable law, the requesting spouse has a legal claim to a share of the marital property. (This is not the case, for example, for spouses who live under the regime of separation of property; in such a case, the argument must be made that future support payments are endangered).
- There is a serious danger that one spouse disposes of the assets in Switzerland to the detriment of the other spouse. It must be showed that the enforcement of the division of the property within a marital property regime is endangered. (This is not the case, for example, when there are other assets somewhere else with which the claim of the other spouse can be settled).
- It cannot be expected that the foreign court can issue a decision enforceable in Switzerland within a reasonable period. (This precondition will be regularly fulfilled, since it is necessary to act very quickly in such cases by taking *ex parte* measures in order to achieve the necessary surprise effect).

12. FINANCIAL RELIEF AFTER FOREIGN DIVORCE PROCEEDINGS

12.1 What powers are available to make orders following a foreign divorce?

Supplementing a foreign divorce decree

If a foreign divorce decree does not address all legal consequences of the divorce, ie, when there is a loophole, a supplementing decision may be obtained in Switzerland under some circumstances in accordance with Article 64 PIL. In practice, the necessity for a supplementing decision in Switzerland can primarily arise when the marriage is dissolved abroad and one or both parties to the marriage have assets in a Swiss pension fund (cf. section 9 above). Foreign divorce decrees involving the division of assets in Swiss pension funds are only recognised and enforced under very restricted circumstances, for which reason it is very often necessary to petition for a supplementing decision in the court holding jurisdiction at the domicile of the pension fund in Switzerland.

Amending a divorce decree

An absolute divorce decree can be amended in Switzerland with regard to arrangements made for children and with regard to support for spouses and children. Swiss courts have jurisdiction to entertain an action to amend if they have rendered the decree or if they have jurisdiction according to the principles described in section 2 above (and – as far as parental responsibility and/or visitation is in question – when the children have habitual residence in Switzerland).

Amending is possible when the circumstances on which the divorce decree is based have changed considerably, permanently and in an unforeseeable way. Under Article 8 of the Hague Convention of 2 October 1973 on the Law Applicable to Maintenance Obligations, which is used *erga omnes* in Switzerland, the amendment of a post marital support decision is made in using the law which governed the divorce itself.

D. CHILDREN

13. CUSTODY/PARENTAL RESPONSIBILITY

13.1 Briefly explain the legal position in relation to custody/parental responsibility following the breakdown of a relationship or marriage

When a Swiss court has jurisdiction in a divorce where the spouses have children, the judge will have to decide on all necessary arrangements for the children (Article 133 CC: parental responsibility, daily care and custody and personal contact). The 'no order policy' is not known in Switzerland.

In Switzerland, a clear distinction is drawn between parental responsibility and authority (*Sorgerecht*) and daily care and custody (*Obhut*). Parental responsibility means the comprehensive right to make all important decisions as far as education, religious upbringing; medical interventions of some consequence of the child are concerned. The parent who has care and custody decides on all issues concerning the daily care. More importantly, the caretaking parent also has, according to a recent decision of the Swiss Federal Court (BGE 5D_171/2009 of 1 June 2010), the right to determine where the child has its habitual residence (so called *Aufenthaltsbestimmungsrecht*).

Generally, a court in Switzerland assigns parental responsibility (or parental authority) to one parent alone (Article 133. 1 CC). The most important consideration when assigning parental responsibility is the wellbeing of the child. The circumstances to be taken into consideration include:

- the parents' ability to raise the child and cooperate with each other;
- the ability to personally look after the child, where considerable emphasis is placed on the previous assignment of roles during the period the parents lived together;
- the relationship between the child and the parents;
- the ability to respect and enable the relationship of the child to the parent not having custody; and
- the child's wishes regarding assignment.

If possible, siblings should be kept together. Today, the mother is not given assignment preference anymore, even in the case of infants. The parent who has sole parental responsibility has also sole care and custody.

Only upon joint request by the parents shall the judge leave the parental authority with both parents (joint parental responsibility and authority; Article 133. 3 CC). Joint parental responsibility may not be assigned against the will of one of the parents. This legal situation, which in practice greatly favours the mother, is increasingly criticised. Reform efforts, which would make joint parental responsibility standard practice, are currently pending. Today, joint parental authority is assigned in around one-third of all divorces. The tendency is increasing, however. If the parents petition for a joint parental responsibility they also have to agree which parent is the primary caretaker and consequently has care and custody. This is of great relevance since this parent ultimately decides where the child has its habitual residence (which includes, in general, the right to determine if a child can be removed from one country to another). It is possible to agree on a joint care and custody with the consequence that the parents have to come to an agreement if the relocation of the child is in question.

The children are interviewed by the court when parental responsibility, daily care and custody and visiting rights are under consideration (Article 144 CC). They can ask for their own counsellor, who may submit petitions in the child's interests.

14. INTERNATIONAL ABDUCTION

14.1 Summarise the position in your jurisdiction

(This section has been composed by Margherita Bortolani-Slongo, lawyer and partner of Langner Stieger Trachsel Partner, Zurich)

The Hague Convention on the civil aspects of international child abduction, dated 25 October 1980 (HAC), took effect in Switzerland on 1 January 1984. The same applies to the EC, the Convention on the Recognition and Enforcement of Decisions Concerning Custody of Children and on Restoration of Custody of Children, dated 20 May 1980. Moreover, the Convention on the jurisdiction, the applicable law, recognition, enforcement and co-operation in respect of parental responsibility and measures for the protection of children, dated 19 October 1996 (HKsÜ), has been in effect since 1 July 2009.

As part of the national legislation, Switzerland enforced the Federal Act on International Child Abduction and the Hague Convention on the protection of children and adults of 21 December 2007 (BG-KKE), which has been in force since 1 July 2009. By applying the aforementioned conventions, the law aims to give more priority to children's interests through a more child-friendly process and judgement of repatriation claims and also in terms of the enforcement of repatriation decisions.

In view of procedural aspects, the most important innovations are detailed below.

- The national central authority, in co-operation with the cantons, ensures a network of specialists and institutions, which is available to offer advice, mediation and child representation services, and is able to act with the speed and urgency required by the Convention (Article 3 BG-KKE). If the central authority receives a request for repatriation, it no longer passes this on immediately to the court, as was done previously, but shall instead initiate a mediation process, with the help of this network (Article 4 BG-KKE).
- The only authority eligible to judge repatriation requests is now the Cantonal High Court in which the child is being held at the time the request is lodged (Article 7.1 BG-KKE). If the parties and the court receiving the request agree, the court can transfer the proceedings to the High Court of a different canton (eg, if said court has more experience, Article 7.2 BG-KKE).
- The court makes its decision in rapid proceedings (Article 8. 2 BG-KKE).
- The court personally hears the parties and child (the latter perhaps with the aid of an expert) and officially orders child representation (Article 9 BG-KKE).

With regard to the more child-friendly judgement of the repatriation request, Article 5 BG-KKE specifies the reason for refusal stated in Article 13.1 b HAC, ie, the 'unacceptable situation' into which the child can be brought as a result of the repatriation. Based on the exemplary list in Article 5a to c, the reason for refusal in Article 13. 1 b) HAC exists in particular if:

- lodging with the petitioning parent clearly does not benefit the child's wellbeing;
- taking into account all the circumstances, the abducting parent is not able or can clearly not be expected to look after the child in the country where it resided immediately prior to the abduction;
- lodging with third parties clearly does not benefit the child's wellbeing (Article 5a to c. BG-KKE).

The child's wellbeing must be taken into account when enforcing repatriation decisions (Article 12. 2 BG-KKE). Repatriation decisions can now be changed if the circumstances change drastically after said decisions have been pronounced (Article 13 BG-KKE).

15. LEAVE TO REMOVE/APPLICATION TO TAKE A CHILD OUT OF THE JURISDICTION

15.1 Summarise the position in your jurisdiction

Even if the parents have joint parental responsibility (*gemeinsames Sorgerecht*), from a Swiss point of view, the decisive question is whether the child is subject to joint care and custody (*gemeinsame Obhut*), or whether one parent has sole care and custody (*alleinige Obhut*), which is very often the case in a Swiss divorce.

The parent with sole care and custody must, indeed, inform the other parent and obtain their opinion for the intended change of the child's domicile within the country or abroad. However, when the parents are not of a like mind, the parent with sole care and custody decides alone, although the child's welfare must be heeded (and, in addition, a manifest abuse of rights [ie, an intended alienation of the other parent] is, of course, not allowed). If the parent decides to leave Switzerland with the child, a court will only intervene (and possibly grant parental responsibility and care and custody to the parent remaining in Switzerland) if the situation at the new domicile does not appear to be reconcilable with the welfare of the child, for example, because the educational possibilities appear to be considerably worse. The children will be questioned about a change of domicile and their wishes have a significant influence when they are of an age that they can weigh the consequences of the decision to some extent, which is generally considered to be after the age of 12. In case of emigration, visiting rights will be amended in accordance with the new circumstances.

If joint care and custody exists and the parents are not in agreement about the move, then two procedures are observed in practice: There are courts that decide the issue themselves, in other words, whether the relocation is in the child's interests or not. All pertinent criteria are taken into consideration, such as the child's age and their wishes, schooling possibilities, on-going existing contact with the remaining parent, etc. Other courts weigh the discontinuation of joint care and custody in light of the apparent existence of a conflict between the parents and their not having the ability to cooperate and communicate anymore (which, of course, is required for joint care and custody). As a consequence, care and custody (and very often parental responsibility!) is settled anew and granted to one parent solely. This parent can then decide alone about the change of domicile.

Given these legal circumstances a parent who wants to prevent a child being removed from the jurisdiction without their consent must insist that the following principles become part of the divorce settlement:

- joint parental responsibility;
- joint care and custody;
- a provision which clearly states that a change of the children's habitual residence is mandatory needs the consent of both parents.

A pending statutory amendment aims to ensure that parents with joint custody may decide only jointly about a relocation of the domicile of their children. If it is not possible to reach an agreement, the court or the guardianship authority must decide which solution is in the best interest of the children.

E. SURROGACY AND ADOPTION

16. VALIDITY OF SURROGACY AGREEMENTS

Surrogacy is prohibited in Switzerland.

17. ADOPTION

Adoption is regulated by Article 264 – 269c CC. Switzerland recognises the joint adoption of a child by a married couple (who must have been married for at least five years; in addition, both spouses must be at least 35 years old and 16 years older than the child), as well as individual adoption by an unmarried person. Such persons may adopt if they are at least 35 years old and 16 years older than the child.

An adoption is possible only if the adopting party or parties do not have children of their own. Same-sex couples may not jointly adopt a child, nor may they adopt a child of their respective partner.

F. COHABITATION

18. COHABITATION

18.1 What legislation (if any) governs division of property for unmarried couples on the breakdown of the relationship?

There is no legislation which explicitly governs cohabitation. No mutual support claims exist, even after a long period of living together. There are some rulings where the court passed judgment on certain financial aspects of such a living arrangement under the laws governing a simple partnership (Article 530 ff. OR (Swiss Code of Obligations)). Because of this lack of legal basis, couples are encouraged to establish the modalities of their living together contractually, according to the requirements of each individual case.

G. FAMILY DISPUTE RESOLUTION

19. MEDIATION, COLLABORATIVE LAW AND ARBITRATION

19.1 Briefly summarise the non-court-based processes available in your jurisdiction and the current status of agreements reached under the auspices of mediation, collaborative law and arbitration

The overwhelming majority of all divorce cases in Switzerland are settled amicably. This may mean that a comprehensive legal agreement is reached in advance of the divorce proceedings, or may mean that an agreement is reached in respect of all unsettled aspects during the course of the divorce proceedings with the help of the court. In contested divorce proceedings, a settlement hearing (*Einigungsverhandlung*) is conducted first (Article 291 CCP). At subsequent stages of the legal proceedings the court will repeatedly attempt to establish an agreement between the parties.

Mediation is widespread in Switzerland. By contrast, collaborative legal proceedings are relatively rare. Arbitration proceedings, which anyway may only address the question of marital property settlements in international cases, are in practice unknown in Switzerland.

19.2 What is the statutory basis (if any), for mediation, collaborative law and arbitration in your jurisdiction? In particular, are the parties required to attempt a family dispute resolution in advance of proceedings?

The Swiss Code of Civil Procedure (*Zivilprozessordnung* [CCP]) came into force on 1 January 2011. The new law governs the whole of Switzerland. Article 213

– 218 CCP stipulates the preconditions under which a court may recommend that parties subject themselves to mediation. However, the parties are not under any obligation to subject themselves to mediation before or during the divorce proceedings.

H. OTHER

20. CIVIL PARTNERSHIP/SAME-SEX MARRIAGE

20.1 What is the status of civil partnership/same sex-marriage within the jurisdiction?

20.2 What legislation governs civil partnership/gay marriage?

With effect from 1 January 2007 it has been possible for persons of age to register their same-sex partnerships and legally secure their relationships (Swiss federal act on Registered Partnerships for Same-Sex Couples). By doing so, they have a legal status equal to married couples in questions of inheritance, social security, occupational pension plans, insurance, taxes and immigration. The same-sex registered partner of a Swiss citizen, therefore, has access to permanent residence status. Medical reproduction procedures are forbidden. Same-sex couples may not adopt children.

By law the rules of the regime of separation of property apply. However, the partners may enter into an agreement with the consequence that the provisions of the ordinary regime of sharing of acquired property (see above section 8) will apply.

Both partners may petition the court together for dissolution of the civil partnership. Each partner may also ask that the partnership be dissolved if the couple has lived separately for at least one year.

21. CONTROVERSIAL AREAS/RAPIDLY DEVELOPING AREAS OF LAW

21.1 Is there a particular area of the law within the jurisdiction that is currently undergoing major change?

21.2 Which areas of law are most out of step? Which areas would you most like to see reformed/changed?

Currently reform efforts are underway in the right of parental responsibility (the issue is to make joint parental responsibility the standard case) and the splitting of assets in occupational pension plans. The issue here is, among others, to ensure a split of the capital also after one or both spouses have reached ordinary retirement age.

Ukraine

AGA Partners
Aminat Suleymanova, Ivan Kasynyuk & Irina Moroz

A. JURISDICTION AND CONFLICT OF LAW

1. SOURCES OF LAW

1.1 What is the primary source of law in relation to the breakdown of marriage and the welfare of children within the jurisdiction?

The provisions on the breakdown of marriage and welfare of children are mostly detailed in the chapters II-IV of the Family Code of Ukraine 2002. Child protection law in the Ukraine is based on the Constitution of Ukraine and on the Convention on the Rights of the Child. Some provisions on welfare in the Convention on the Rights of the Child have been codified in the Family Code of Ukraine and in the law on the protection of children.

Ukraine ratified the Convention on the Rights of the Child in 1991. International conventions (treaties) that have been ratified by the Supreme Council of Ukraine are a substantial part of the Ukrainian legislation.

1.2 Which are the main statutes governing matrimonial law in the jurisdiction?

Ukraine is a civil law jurisdiction. The overarching code of Ukrainian civil law is the Civil Code of Ukraine 2003, which is supplemented by the Family Code of Ukraine 2002. The Ukrainian courts rely upon the codes, and there is no formally recognised doctrine of precedent.

The Family Code of Ukraine 2002, determines matters relating to marriage, personal non-property and property rights, the duties of the married couple, the content of personal non-property and property rights, and the duties of parents and children, foster parents and adopted children and relatives.

2. JURISDICTION

2.1 What are the main jurisdictional requirements for the institution of proceedings in relation to divorce, property and children?

The Civil Procedural Code of Ukraine 2005 aims for the just and timely consideration and settlement of family cases in the courts of Ukraine for the protection of rights and the freedom and interests of the persons involved.

A separate chapter in the Civil Procedural Code defines the procedure for cases involving the participation of foreigners. Foreigners in family disputes have procedural rights and duties equal to those of natural persons of Ukraine.

The choice of jurisdiction, according to Ukrainian legislation, has some peculiarities where one of the spouses is not a Ukrainian national. In this instance, the Ukrainian court has jurisdiction to consider disputes with a foreign element (if one of the party is a foreigner, stateless person or Ukrainian national living abroad) only in specific cases, namely:

- if the spouses invoked the jurisdiction of the Ukrainian courts by agreement;
- if the defendant spouse has residence, immovable or movable property in the territory of Ukraine;
- if the plaintiff has his residence in Ukraine in cases that concern payment of maintenance or establishment of fatherhood;
- if the ground for the claim took place in the territory of Ukraine (eg, a pre-nuptial agreement was concluded in the territory of Ukraine; or the spouses got married in the territory of Ukraine);
- in other cases foreseen by international agreements and the laws of Ukraine.

Ukrainian courts have exclusive jurisdiction over disputes that concern real estate located in the territory of Ukraine and over cases involving relationships between children and parents where both parties have residence in Ukraine.

In a case where both spouses are nationals of Ukraine, they may apply to a Ukrainian court irrespective of their place of residence.

3. DOMICILE AND HABITUAL RESIDENCE

3.1 Explain the concepts of domicile and habitual residence as they apply to the jurisdiction in relation to divorce, the finances and children

Ukrainian law follows the concept of domicile (residence), rather than habitual residence.

The term 'residence' is understood according to the Article 3 of Law of Ukraine on Freedom of Movement and Free Choice of Place of Residence in Ukraine adopted on 11 December 2003. The place of residence is the administrative unit, where an individual resides more than six months per year.

Ukrainian law has a requirement for registration of place of residence. As the general rule, claims in family/civil matters shall be brought to the court locally situated at the place of registration of residence. However, registration of the place of residence or temporary address of the person or the absence of such shall not be a condition or grounds for exercising the rights and freedoms provided for by the Constitution, laws or international agreements of Ukraine. Therefore, even if the person has no registration of place of residence, but resides in an administrative unit over six months per year it is considered that they reside at that administrative unit and it is possible to bring a claim at the place of their residence.

A claim to the Ukrainian court may be initiated, if:

Divorce

- the defendant spouse has their residence in the territory of Ukraine.

Finances

- the defendant spouse has their residence in the territory of Ukraine;
- the plaintiff spouse has their residence in Ukraine in cases involving payment of maintenance.

Children

- the defendant spouse has their residence in the territory of Ukraine;
- the plaintiff has their residence in Ukraine in the cases involving payment of maintenance or establishment of fatherhood;
- both parties have residence in Ukraine.

The procedural capacity and capability for foreigners in Ukraine are equal to Ukrainian citizens and determined according to Ukrainian legislation.

4. CONFLICT OF LAW/APPLICABLE LAW TO BE APPLIED

4.1 What happens when one party applies to stay proceedings in favour of a foreign jurisdiction? What factors will the local court take into account when determining forum issues?

In deciding the issue of whether to stay the proceedings or close the proceedings for the reason that the Ukrainian court is not appropriate forum to determine the dispute, the Ukrainian court is governed by the requirements of Civil Procedural Code of Ukraine 2004 and Law of Ukraine on International Private Law 2005.

If an application to stay the proceedings was made before the court opened the proceedings the court shall refuse to open the proceedings on the basis of Article 75(2) of Law of Ukraine on International Private Law, stipulating that, the Ukrainian court shall refuse to open proceedings if a court or other jurisdictional authority of a foreign state considers the dispute between the same parties on the same subject and on the same grounds.

If an application to stay the proceedings was made after the court opened the proceedings, article 207 (1) (4) of Civil Procedural Code of Ukraine shall be applied. According to this article the court is obliged to leave the claim without consideration if a dispute between the same parties on the same subject and the same grounds is considered in another court.

For instance if a divorce application was filled first in a foreign jurisdiction and thereafter a application for the dissolution of the marriage was initiated in Ukraine between the same parties and on the same basis the Ukrainian court shall refuse to open the proceedings or leave the application without consideration.

Four elements must exist for the court to refuse to open the proceedings or leave the application without consideration in favour of a foreign court:

1. the dispute is between the same parties;
2. the dispute concerns the same subject;
3. the dispute is on the same grounds; and
4. the dispute is already under consideration in a foreign court.

B. PRE AND POST-NUPTIAL AGREEMENTS

5. VALIDITY OF PRE- AND POST-NUPTIAL AGREEMENTS

5.1 To what extent are pre- and post-nups binding within the jurisdiction? Could you provide a brief discussion of the most significant recent case law on this issue?

Pre-nuptial agreements are valid and enforceable under Ukrainian legislation. A Ukrainian pre-nuptial agreement is described as a marriage agreement and dealt with in chapter 10 of the Family Code of Ukraine. The nub of any agreement will be a clause to misapply or vary Article 60 of the Family Code, which creates the common joint property regime for spouses.

Therefore, there are three primary purposes of a marriage agreement:

- to regulate the division of common joint property arising from the marriage;
- to regulate or exclude the division of common joint property arising from any pre-marital cohabitation;
- to anchor governing jurisdiction and law.

The Family Code of Ukraine states that a marriage agreement may be concluded between the persons who applied for the registration of marriage, as well as between married couples. If it has been concluded before the registration of the marriage, it shall come into effect from the date of the state registration or the marriage. It shall not regulate the personal relations of a married couple, or personal relations between the married couple and children. A marriage agreement deals only with privity (property relationships) and specifies the rights and duties of the spouses. A marriage agreement may be cancelled on the demand of one of the parties only on the basis of a judicial decision or by the mutual consent of both spouses.

The formalities for executing the agreement are minimal. Both parties must attend before a Ukrainian notary public official and sign the agreement in front of them. If required by the circumstances, an agreement in Ukrainian and an official translation into the other language of any party must be signed in front of notary public official. No lawyers, translators or witnesses are required to be present or to sign the agreement. There is no obligation for legal advice or full and frank disclosure of assets or liabilities. There is also no obligation to show that either side has taken legal advice and no obligation at this point to show that no undue pressure has been put on either party. There is no assessment at this point of whether the agreement is arguably fair.

It is possible under the Family Code to include expenses for children in the main text of an agreement. This arrangement would make these expenses enforceable in most other jurisdictions which allow provision for children's maintenance within the body of such agreements.

The Ukrainian courts do not recognise the doctrine of precedent and rely only upon Ukrainian legislation (codes, laws). The judge deciding a case may take into account interpretations of law stated by the Supreme Court of Ukraine.

A Ukrainian pre-nuptial agreement can be challenged by the court on the basis that it places one spouse in an 'extremely unfavourable material position', under Article 93 Family Code of Ukraine. However, the question for the court is whether the spouse has, as a result of an agreement, been placed in a position significantly less favourable than the position they would have been in under the Family Code.

C. DIVORCE, NULLITY AND JUDICIAL SEPARATION

6. RECOGNITION OF FOREIGN MARRIAGES/DIVORCES

6.1 Summarise the position in your jurisdiction

Article 58 of the Law of Ukraine on International Private Law 2005 provides that a marriage between citizens of Ukraine, marriage between a citizen of Ukraine and a foreigner, marriage between a citizen of Ukraine and a stateless person, registered outside of Ukraine under the law of foreign country is valid in Ukraine, subject to the condition that the citizen of Ukraine complied with the requirements of the Family Code of Ukraine and concluded the marriage without the grounds of invalidity of marriage under Ukrainian law.

Marriage between foreigners, marriage between a foreigner and a stateless person and marriage between persons without citizenship, concluded under the law of a foreign country are valid in Ukraine.

Foreign divorce is recognised in Ukraine on the basis of international multilateral or bilateral agreements ratified by the Supreme Council of Ukraine or under the principle of reciprocity.

The order of recognition of foreign divorce in Ukraine is provided in Articles 399-401 of Civil Procedural Code of Ukraine.

7. DIVORCE

7.1 Explain the grounds for divorce within the jurisdiction (please also deal with nullity and judicial separation if appropriate)

The Family Code of Ukraine envisages that if the spouses do not have children, they may get a divorce in bodies of civil state acts registration. If spouses have children they may get divorced only through court proceedings.

The formal grounds for divorce are breakdown of the marriage, breakdown of common housekeeping, failure of other spouse to perform marital rights and obligations, physical or moral harm toward other spouse or the children. In a case where one of the spouses does not give his or her consent to the dissolution of the marriage, the court will give a reconciliation period. After this period of time has elapsed, the court will grant a divorce if it is found that the further joint life of the spouses and continuance of their marriage is contradictory to the interests of either party and the interests of their children. The marriage is considered to be dissolved from the moment of registration of the divorce with the bodies civil state acts registration if the marriage was dissolved by the body of registration of civil status acts. If the marriage was dissolved by the court order the marriage is considered to be dissolved from the moment the court order entered into force.

Nullity of marriage

Upon the application of an interested person, the body of registration of civil status acts nullifies the marriage if:

- the marriage was registered with a person who at the same time remained in another registered marriage;

- the marriage was registered between people who are relatives in a 'straight line' relationship, as well as between siblings, brother and sister;
- the marriage was registered with a person who is recognised as 'incapable'.

The marriage shall be nullified by the Ukrainian court order if:

- the marriage was registered without the free will of the wife or husband (where a party to the marriage did not fully realise his/her actions and was unable to control it);
- the registered marriage was fictitious;

The marriage may be nullified by the Ukrainian court order if:

- the marriage was concluded with a person under the age of consent and legally not allowed to marry;
- the marriage was registered between an adopter and the adoptee in violation of the requirements of art. 26 (5) of the Family Code of Ukraine;
- the marriage was to a person with hidden serious illness or a disease which is dangerous for the other spouse and (or) their descendants;
- the marriage was registered between cousins; between aunt and uncle and nephew and niece;

Those who have the right to apply to the court for the nullity of the marriage are spouses, other people whose rights are affected by the registration of the marriage, parents, guardians, custodians, guardians of 'incapable' parties, the prosecutor and the custody and care body.

The marriage is considered to be nullified from the date of its state registration.

Judicial separation

Article 119 of the Family Code of Ukraine provides that upon the application of one or both spouses, the court may order a separate arrangement for the residence of the parties in cases where there is inability or unwillingness of a wife and (or) husband to live together. Before a court grants a judicial separation, there are many factors to be taken into account. These will include the current and future financial situations of both of the spouses, accommodation and property, and dependent children and their future needs and welfare.

Establishing a regime of judicial separation does not terminate the rights and responsibilities of the spouses as established by the Family Code of Ukraine or the rights and duties as are prescribed by a marriage agreement. However, the judicial separation of spouses has some peculiarities:

(i) property acquired by one of the spouses during the period of judicial separation is considered to be separate personal property;
(ii) a child born more than 10 months after the date of the judicial separation will not be considered to be the child of the husband.

Judicial separation ceases in the event of reconciliation of family relationships or by acourt order upon application of one of the spouses.

8. FINANCES/CAPITAL, PROPERTY

8.1 What powers does the court have to allocate financial resources and property on the breakdown of marriage?

The Family Code of Ukraine determines the procedure for the division of property acquired before, as well as during, the marriage between the spouses upon divorce.

A 'common joint property' regime is the default position for the property of spouses within Ukraine, established by Article 60 of the Family Code.

'Separate personal property', by contrast, are assets acquired prior to the marriage, or by gift or for personal money (Article 57). If separate personal property produces income during the marriage, that income will also be separate personal property.

However, if an increase in the value of one spouse's separate personal property has been due to the efforts or contribution of the other spouse, that separate personal property may be held as common joint property by the court and the other spouse will be entitled to a share of it.

Property acquired by a man and a woman who live together as a family, but who are not married (under a cohabitation regime), will be considered joint property, unless a written agreement (marriage agreement) between them provides otherwise.

The spouses may wish to vary this default regime in their agreement, re-designating present and future separate personal property and common joint property.

The court has a wide range of powers to share a spouse's common joint property. The court has the power:

(i) to share common joint property between the wife and husband;
(ii) to award indivisible items to one spouse unless otherwise agreed between the parties;
(iii) to award assets relating to professional occupations (eg, musical instruments; office, medical, photography equipment etc.) to the spouse who used them in their professional activities. The cost of these things is taken into account when awarding other property to the other spouse;
(iv) to award the other spouse a lump-sum as compensation instead of their share in the joint common property, including a house, apartment and land. However, the court may exercise this power only with the consent of that spouse, except in cases foreseen by the Civil Code of Ukraine. The awarding of monetary compensation is possible only if the second spouse makes an advance deposit of the respective sum of money into the court account;
(v) to recognise that some or all items of separate personal property are common joint property or recognise that some or all items of common joint property are separate personal property if the appropriate circumstances are proven.

8.2 Explain and illustrate with reference to recent cases the court's thinking on division of assets

The court practice in division of assets is generalised in the Decree of the

Plenum of Supreme Council of Ukraine dated 21 of December 2011 No.11.

The division of a spouse's assets is carried out in accordance with Articles 69-72 of Family Code of Ukraine and Article 372 of the Civil Code of Ukraine. The value of property subject to division is determined by agreement between the spouses, or is based on its actual value at the time of the hearing.

If the marriage agreement has modified the statutory regime of joint property, then a court must proceed and divide the property according to the terms of any such agreement.

In resolving disputes between spouses it is necessary for the court to decide on the amount of property which has been jointly acquired and find out the source and time of its acquisition. Joint assets of spouses that are subject to division may include any kind of property, except those excluded from civil turnover, regardless of whose the property was purchased in.

Property owned by a spouse can be designated as joint property by signing the parties signing a marriage agreement or recognised as such by the court on the grounds that during the marriage the value of this property has significantly increased due to the efforts of financial investnment of the other spouse, or both.

Under the general rule of Article 70 of the Family Code of Ukraine, during the division of the spouses' joint property, the wife's and husband's shares in the assets are equal unless otherwise provided for by agreement between them or under a marriage agreement.

In resolving any dispute over the division of property the court may deviate from equality of shares in circumstances that are of essential importance, particularly if one party did not care about the material support of the family, hid, destroyed or damaged joint property or spent property to the detriment of his family.

A spouse's share in the joint assets may be increased if children or disabled adult children are living with him/her.

9. FINANCES/MAINTENANCE

9.1 Explain the operation of maintenance for spouses on an ongoing basis after the breakdown of marriage

Under Article 76 of the Family Code of Ukraine, divorce does not release spouses from maintenance obligations that originated during marriage. A former spouse is obliged to support the other in certain circumstances described in Article 75 of the Family Code of Ukraine if that spouse became disabled during the marriage or within a year from the date of the marriage breakdown; if the spouse is pregnant; raising a child under the age of three or caring for a disabled child; is set to reach pension age within five years; or in other certain cases listed in the Family Code.

9.2 Is it common for maintenance to be awarded?

Article 77 of the Family Code of Ukraine provides that spouses are free to decide the manner of maintenance.

If the parties have not reached an agreement, maintenance may be imposed by the court order with a certain percentage of the total net income and/or a fixed sum of money. Alimonies are to be paid on a monthly basis. The court has the discretion to increase or decrease these sums to reflect other relevant circumstances. In certain circumstances, where the spouse responsible for the alimony leaves the territory of Ukraine, they may be obliged to pay alimonies in advance.

9.3 Explain and illustrate with reference to recent cases the court's thinking on maintenance

The Supreme Court of Ukraine has interpreted the provisions of the Family and Civil code of Ukraine on the maintenance of spouses and decided that divorce does not release a former spouse from their obligations in relation to maintenance and a cohabitant spouse has the right to maintenance where they are unable to work during cohabitation.

10. CHILD MAINTENANCE

10.1 On what basis is child maintenance calculated within the jurisdiction?

According to the Family Code of Ukraine, after the breakdown of the marriage, a parent is required to pay child support (alimonies). Maintenance can also be paid under a support agreement. The Family Code of Ukraine states that child support is to be imposed by the court allowing a certain part of the total net income for one child or it could be fixed in money.

Pursuant to Article 182 of the Family Code of Ukraine, the court has the discretion to increase or decrease the level of alimony to reflect other relevant circumstances, such as the health and welfare of a child; the health and welfare of the spouse responsible for paying the alimony; the availability of other family members, presence of legally incapable wife (or husband) and/or children from a new marriage, and other circumstances which may be relevant for the court.

The Family Code of Ukraine provides that alimonies should not be decreased lower than 30 per cent of the minimum level of wage for one child. The minimum level of wage will be revised every year according to the law of Ukraine on State Budget upon the establishment of a minimum living wage.

11. RECIPROCAL ENFORCEMENT OF FINANCIAL ORDERS

11.1 Summarise the position in your jurisdiction

A common and acknowledged method of enforcing foreign court orders is according to international bilateral and multilateral treaties which exist between Ukraine and other countries.

The enforcement proceedings available in each case depend on the terms of the treaty or other arrangements that are in place between Ukraine and the other country concerned.

The Civil Procedure Code of Ukraine 2005 defines the order of enforcement of foreign financial orders in Articles 390-398.

In Ukraine, the judgment of an international court shall be enforced during a period of three years from the moment the judgment comes into force. An exception to this rule is periodical payments, which may be enforced and collected during the whole period of sanction.

The principle of reciprocal enforcement of foreign court orders may be applied only if there are no international bilateral and multilateral treaties between Ukraine and the foreign country. The principle of reciprocal enforcement of foreign court orders including financial orders is rather new in Ukraine and Article 390 of the Civil Procedural Code of Ukraine stipulates if the recognition and enforcement of foreign court order depends on the principle of reciprocity, it is believed that it exists, unless proven otherwise. The principle of reciprocity has only been applied in few court cases.

There is no special procedure for the enforcement of court orders, including financial orders, on the principle of reciprocity as there is no list of countries whose court orders will be enforced in Ukraine in accordance with the principle of reciprocity. The general interpretation of the principle of reciprocity under Ukrainian law means that if Ukrainian court orders are enforced in a particular foreign country, the court orders of that foreign country shall be enforced in Ukraine.

12. FINANCIAL RELIEF AFTER FOREIGN DIVORCE PROCEEDINGS

12.1 What powers are available to make orders following a foreign divorce?

Under Ukrainian law there is no special procedure allowing the receipt of financial relief after a foreign divorce. After a foreign divorce, either spouse may apply to the Ukrainian court to settle financial matters (eg, property division, child alimony, maintenance obligations between spouses) if the Ukrainian courts have jurisdiction to consider such matters on the general basis provided by the Civil Procedural Code of Ukraine and the Law of Ukraine on International Private Law.

D. CHILDREN

13. CUSTODY/PARENTAL RESPONSIBILITY

13.1 Briefly explain the legal position in relation to custody/parental responsibility following the breakdown of a relationship or marriage

The breakdown of a marriage does not influence the scope of parental rights and obligations toward the child provided by the Family Code of Ukraine. Even after the breakdown of a marriage, the parents have equal rights to participate in the child's upbringing. The parents retain the full scope of personal non-property and property rights and obligations towards the child. After the breakdown of the marriage each of the parents is obliged to contribute towards the child's maintenance until they attain the age of majority (18 years in Ukraine) and in some circumstances maintain the child after the age of 23 years old. Under Ukrainian legislation the parents are also obliged to share additional expenses for the child, which may include medical treatment and other costs for the improvement of the child's health and development of the child's skills etc.

The parent who does not live with the child has a right to personal communication with the child. The parent with whom the child lives has no right to prevent the parent who lives separately from participating in the upbringing of the child and communicating with the child unless such communication negatively affects the normal development of the child.

The parents have the right to enter into an agreement dealing with the implementation of parental rights and responsibilities of the parent who lives separately. The agreement shall be in writing and notarised.

13.2 Briefly explain the legal position in relation to access/contact/ visitation following the breakdown of a relationship or marriage

The place of residence of child after breakdown of marriage

The place of residence of a child under the age of 10 is determined by the parents' mutual consent. The place of residence of a child who has reached 10 years is agreed by the mutual parents' consent and the child. If the parents live separately, the place of residence of a child who has reached 14 years of age is determined by the child.

If the parents cannot reach an agreement about the child's place of residence the dispute may be solved by custodian bodies or by the court. The following circumstances are taken into account when considering such a dispute: the parents' attitude towards their parental obligations, the personal feelings of the child towards each of the parents, the child's age, state of health, the financial conditions of each of the parents (ownership of personal apartments), steady income, the living conditions of each parent, the current marital status of each parent and the presence of other children etc. Custodian bodies or the court are unlikely to allow the child to live with a parent who has no independent income, is abusing alcohol or drugs or who, by his/her immoral behaviour, may harm the development of child.

Visitation order

If the parent with whom the child lives prevents the parent who lives separately from involvement with the child and the child's upbringing and, in particular, avoids the enforcement of the decision of custodian bodies, the other parent may apply to the court for a visiting order.

In such a case the court determines the level of participation of the other parent in the child's upbringing: periodic and systematic access, the ability to spend vacations together, visiting a child at his/her place of residence, places and times for communication etc.

In a case of non-enforcement of a visiting order by the person with whom child lives, the court, upon the application of the other parent, may order the child to live with the parent who lives separately.

14. INTERNATIONAL ABDUCTION

14.1 Summarise the position in your jurisdiction

In 2006, the Supreme Council of Ukraine passed the Act of Ukraine on Accession of Ukraine to the Convention on the Civil Aspects of International Child Abduction. The Convention is applied between Ukraine and countries that have accepted Ukrainian accession to this convention.

The Convention is enforced and executed in Ukraine according to the Order of Execution in Ukraine of the Convention on the Civil Aspects of International Child Abduction, adopted by the Decree of the Cabinet of Ministers of Ukraine on 10 June 2006 No 952.

The application forms on child return and access to children and a list of necessary documents are provided at the Decree of the Cabinet of Ministers of Ukraine No 952.

The Competent authority in Ukraine to deal with the Convention is the Ministry of Justice of Ukraine. Upon receipt of an application for the return of a child, the Ministry of Justice will firstly take measures to obtain the agreement of the other parent to return the child voluntarily. If the other parent refuses to return the child voluntarily, the Ministry of Justice of Ukraine, on behalf of the parent, can initiate court proceedings concerning the child's return.

The parents are also free to initiate proceedings regarding the return of the child directly in a Ukrainian court without involving the Ministry of Justice of Ukraine under Article 29 of the Convention.

All the actions and services of the Ministry of Justice of Ukraine, including court representation, are free of charge. However, it is always advisable to have a private lawyer to assist with the case and represent the parent's interests in the court.

15. LEAVE TO REMOVE/APPLICATIONS TO TAKE A CHILD OUT OF THE JURISDICTION

15.1 Summarise the position in your jurisdiction

The general rules for removing a child outside the border of Ukraine are provided in the Law of Ukraine On the Procedure for Leaving and Entering Ukraine by Ukrainian Citizens adopted on 21 January 1994.

Under Ukrainian law, citizens who have not reached the age of 16 can only travel outside of Ukraine with the consent of both parents (adoptive parents) or guardians and accompanied by them, or by persons authorised by them.

Otherwise, travelling outside of Ukraine where a Ukrainian citizen has not attained the age of 16, is not accompanied by one parent or accompanied by persons who are authorised by a parent is only possible with the notarised consent of the other parent or both parents, indicating the state of destination and the corresponding length of stay in this state.

A departure from Ukraine without notarised consent from the other parent is possible when:

- the other parent is a foreigner or a stateless person, and this is confirmed on the child's birth certificate;
- the passport for travelling abroad or the child's travel document shows evidence of permanent residence outside Ukraine or evidence of consular registration in Ukrainian embassies abroad. (Ukrainian nationals who live abroad can rely on consular registration and the registration mark of the Ukrainian embassy of 'permanent residence abroad' or 'consular

registration' in the child's passport or travel document).

The child may travel abroad without the notarised consent of the other parent in a case where they are able to show at the points of crossing of state borders, an original document or notarised copy of one of the following:

- the death certificate of the other parent;
- a court order demonstrating the termination of the parental rights of the other parent;
- a court order recognising that the other parent has 'disappeared';
- a court order recognising the other parent as incapable;
- a court order granting permission to travel outside Ukraine for a citizen who has not reached the age of 16 and is without the consent and support of the other parent;
- a certificate of birth issued by the bodies of civil status acts registration, specifying that the record about the father was made on the basis of first paragraph of Article 135 of the Family Code of Ukraine.

15.2 Under what circumstances may a parent apply to remove their child from the jurisdiction against the wishes of the other parent?

If the other parent refuses to give notarised consent for removing a child abroad, the only way to gain permission to take the child abroad is through an application to a Ukrainian court.

While applying to a Ukrainian court, the parent shall prove that the travel is in the best interests of the child (eg, travel to relatives, for rest, tourism, education, improvement of health). It is necessary to indicate the aim of travel, and the duration of travel, as proof of a present invitation for travelling, hotel booking, tickets booking etc. The court gives permission for travel specifically to some period of time and this permission relates to specific travel.

If the applicant wishes to obtain permission to remove a child abroad without the consent of the other parent for numerous trips, it is recommended that the applicant ask the court to allow the making of a travel document to remove a child from Ukraine without the consent of the other parent and to allow for a parent temporary trips abroad with a child without the consent and accompaniment of the other parent.

Upon consideration of an application, the court issues an order and may grant permission to take the child abroad without the consent of the other parent. To deny such a claim, the respondent must provide reasonable evidence to demonstrate that a trip abroad does not meet the child's interests, the child's stay with one parent harms the child, and/or that the other parent does not participate in proper upbringing of the child and child support.

However, in practice. these circumstances are rarely proven and as a general rule, permission is granted to take the child abroad.

E. SURROGACY AND ADOPTION

16. VALIDITY OF SURROGACY AGREEMENTS

16.1 Briefly summarise the position in your jurisdiction

Assisted reproductive technologies and surrogacy in particular, are legally recognised in Ukraine by law and are regulated by the Family Code of Ukraine 2002, the decree of the Ministry of Health Care of Ukraine No. 771 adopted on 23 December 2008 On the Approval of the Instruction about the Order of Assisted Reproductive Technologies Application. As a rule, in practice, in order to settle the arrangements for the surrogacy, the parties conclude a surrogacy agreement which presents their consent to the surrogacy arrangement. Ukrainian law is silent as to the necessity of signing such a surrogacy agreement, its form, content and the party's rights and responsibilities under such agreement. Therefore the parties may upon their own discretion decide whether to sign the surrogacy agreement and the terms on which they would like to do so.

The content of this agreement shall not contradict the provisions of the Family Code of Ukraine, or other acts of civil legislation.

It is necessary to point out some requirements for the successful conclusion of surrogacy agreements which are necessary to secure its validity under Ukrainian law:

- The surrogacy agreement should be concluded prior to the conception of the embryo and its transference to the surrogate mother. A surrogacy agreement concluded after the child's conception may be considered as an agreement on the transfer of a child and may be invalidated;
- A person cannot be the subject of a civil agreement, therefore the wording of the subject of the surrogacy agreement cannot provide for the transfer of a child or the transfer/relinquishment of parental rights;
- Assisted reproductive technologies may be used only by spouses who have registered their marriage, consequently the surrogacy agreement shall be concluded only by the spouses who have registered their marriage (art. 123 of the Family Code of Ukraine 2002);
- The surrogate mother shall be an adult capable woman who has her own healthy child, who has entered into the agreement freely and has no medical contraindications. The surrogate mother shall be objectively informed concerning the procedure of surrogacy treatment.

Special attention shall be paid to the wording of the surrogacy agreement in relation to payments. The payments cannot be made for the transfer of a child or the transfer or deprivation of the parental rights of the surrogate mother, as this will conflict with Ukrainian legislation. At the same time, Ukrainian law does not prohibit the provision of special remuneration to the surrogate mother for the rendering of services of pregnancy and childbirth and/or compensation of all reasonable expenses connected with the rendering of such services, in particular costs for loss of salary, medical treatment, medicines, clothes, housing etc. A surrogacy agreement is usually made in simple written form.

17. ADOPTION

17.1 Briefly explain the legal position in relation to adoption in your jurisdiction. Is adoption available to individuals, cohabiting couples (both heterosexual and same-sex)?

Adoption procedure is regulated in Ukraine by Articles 207-242 of Family

Code of Ukraine and Decree of the Cabinet of Ministers of Ukraine dated 8 October 2008 No. 905 On Approval of the Procedure of the Adoption and Supervision the Rights of Adopted Children.

An adoption can be made only by court order. The adopter of the child must be a capable person over the age of 21 years, unless the adopter is a relative of the child.

The adopter may be a person who is at least 15 years older than the child. In the case of an adoption of an adult person, the age difference cannot be less than 18 years.

Adopters may be spouses. However, adopters may not be a person of the same sex. Legislation also establishes the possibility of one spouse adopting a child if the other spouse does not want to become an adoptive parent. In this case, the second spouse gives notarised consent to the adoption of the child. With such a legal construction the other spouse only agrees to the adoption, and does not acquire the legal status of the adoptive parentor the rights and obligations of the adopter.

Individuals who are not married, but who cohabitat may adopt a child if the court allows them to do so. A child may be adopted by a single man or woman if the child has only a mother or a father who will lose their legal connection with the child due to adoption. The number of children who may be adopted by an adoptive parent is not limited.

The procedure of adoption is rather complicated and strictly regulated by law.

F. COHABITATION

18. COHABITATION

18.1 What legislation (if any) governs division of property for unmarried couples on the breakdown of the relationship?

Ukrainian law recognises cohabitation and allocates property rights to cohabitating couples. Article 74 of the Family Code of Ukraine provides that if a woman and man live as a family but are not married to each other or to any other person, property acquired during their cohabitation belongs to them as joint property, unless otherwise provided for by written agreement between them. The provisions of Chapter 8 of the Family Code apply to the property that is the subject of joint ownership by the cohabitating couple.

These provisions means that property acquired during cohabitation belongs to the couple as common joint property. Although, in each case, the fact of cohabitation must be proven if the matter regarding division of property is put before the court. The fact of cohabitation may be established if it is proven that parties lived together, have common housekeeping, and were registered at the same place, rent an apartment together etc. According to Ukrainian law, a cohabitating couple may conclude an agreement to exclude the joint property regime and to agree a different property regime and to regulate the order of disposition of the property.

This makes it all the more important that cohabitating spouses follow the suggested alternative of Article 74, and designate separate personal property and common joint property in any agreement.

G. FAMILY DISPUTE RESOLUTION

19. MEDIATION, COLLABORATIVE LAW AND ARBITRATION

19.1 Briefly summarise the non-court-based processes available in your jurisdiction and the current status of agreements reached under the auspices of mediation, collaborative law and arbitration

Arbitration

The non-court-based processes for the settlement of disputes which are generally available in Ukraine are mediation and arbitration.

The availability of arbitration in family disputes is very limited in Ukraine.

Under Ukrainian law the parties are not allowed to refer matters to an arbitral tribunal for settlement if the dispute concerns immovable property; disputes where one party is non-resident or disputes that arise from family relations (with the exception of disputes that arise from a marriage agreement).

So, the parties may only refer to arbitration disputes that arise from a marriage agreement where both parties are residents of Ukraine and the disputes do not concern immovable property.

Mediation

There is no legal basis for mediation in Ukraine. However, there are a number of mediation centres that may assist parties in resolving their dispute. Mediation is a sphere that is rapidly developing in Ukraine and a numbers of laws are discussed nowadays in Ukraine that attempt to provide legal regulation for mediation.

There is no legal regulation of agreements reached under the auspices of mediation, collaborative law or arbitration in Ukraine.

In order to be enforceable and binding upon the parties, any agreement reached between the parties in the course of mediation or arbitration must meet the special and general requirements of the Family Code of Ukraine (2004) and/or the Civil Code of Ukraine (2004) which apply to agreements of this specific type..

19.2 What is the statutory basis (if any), for mediation, collaborative law and arbitration in your jurisdiction? In particular, are the parties required to attempt a family dispute resolution in advance of the institution of proceedings?

Currently there is no legal basis for mediation and collaborative law in Ukraine. The legal basis for arbitration in Ukraine is the Law of Ukraine on Arbitral Courts adopted on 11 May, 2004. However, as described above, the availability of arbitration in family disputes is very limited.

There is no requirement that the parties must attempt dispute resolution before issuing court proceedings.

The parties are free to try prejudicial dispute resolution. Prejudicial dispute resolution does not affect their right to apply directly to the court at any time and any stage.

H. OTHER

20. CIVIL PARTNERSHIP/SAME-SEX MARRIAGE

20.1 What is the status of civil partnership/same-sex marriage within the jurisdiction?

20.2 What legislation governs civil partnership/same sex marriage?

According to Article 21 of the Family Code of Ukraine, the family is defined as a 'union between a man and a woman who live together, who are connected by common everyday life and who have mutual rights and duties'. There is no legal allowance for same-sex marriage/civil partnership in Ukrainian legislation.

21. CONTROVERSIAL AREAS/RAPIDLY DEVELOPING AREAS OF LAW

21.1 Is there a particular area of the law within the jurisdiction that is currently undergoing major change?

Recent changes of importance in the area of Family Law in Ukraine concerns the application of assisted reproductive technologies.

The Supreme Council of Ukraine has recently adopted changes to the Family Code of Ukraine, allowing an application for surrogacy treatment to be made only by a married couple (a man and a woman).

The Supreme Council of Ukraine is currently actively discussing new amendments regarding the application of ART, in particular, an upper age limit of 51 years on the age of a woman who can apply for ART. Furthermore, there is a restriction on the availability of surrogacy treatment for foreigners, in particular, it is proposed that surrogacy treatment should only be available to the citizens of Ukraine and foreigners – citizens of the countries in which this method of assisted reproductive technology is not prohibited by law, and in cases where foreigners live in a state other than the state of their citizenship – by the law of the state of their residence. A proposed obligatory precondition for making an application for surrogacy is a genetic connection of the child to at least one of the future parents and an absence of direct genetic connection of the child with the surrogate mother.

It is probable that these discussed amendments (albeit with some corrections) will be adopted in law.

Recent changes also mean that the minimum age of marriage is now 18 years for both men and women.

21.2 Which areas of law are most out-of-step? Which areas would you most like to see reformed/changed?

Ukrainian family law is one of most innovative and advanced within Europe. Nevertheless, there are some areas which need to be reformed.

The execution of court orders for children or alimony payable by the other spouse still needs to be reformed and innovated. In practice the enforcement of court alimony orders is at a very low level.

The other area of family law which needs to be reformed is surrogacy. The legal framework in Ukraine is rather developed compared with most European countries, however, some issues still need to be addressed. The majority of difficulties arise after the child's birth and espceially when the foreign parents encounter problems in getting the child abroad to their home. Surrogacy is allowed only in 15 countries; all other counties forbid surrogacy, and some even make the practice a crime or only allow surrogacy under certain conditions. For these reasons, the parents often encounter problems in getting their surrogate born child abroad and in having their paternity recognised in the country of their residence.

The most common gaps in Ukrainian surrogacy legislation, which need reform, include:

(i) To provide obligatory legal advice to parents regarding the legal status of their surrogate-born child in Ukraine as well as in the country of the parents' residence, the possibility to recognise their paternity in the country of their residence;

(ii) To provide legal regulation for surrogacy agreements: to define in law the subject of such agreements and addressthe issue of payments under the surrogacy agreement and, the order of execution of the agreement.

Ukraine needs to adopt a law preventing domestic violence and creating a social network to counteract domestic violence. A draft of such a law is now being debated at the Supreme Council of Ukraine.

United Arab Emirates

Expatriate Law Alexandra Tribe

A. JURISDICTION AND CONFLICT OF LAW

1. SOURCES OF LAW

1.1 What is the primary source of law in relation to the breakdown of marriage and the welfare of children within the jurisdiction?

Dubai is one Emirate within the United Arab Emirates (UAE). Seven Emirates make up the UAE, being Dubai, Sharjah, Abu Dhabi, Fujeirah, Ras Al Khaimah, Um al Quwaim and Ajman. Each Emirate is governed individually.

The laws of the UAE are codified. In addition, judgments from the Court of Cassation in Abu Dhabi (the final court for the whole of the UAE) constitute precedents binding in Dubai. These cases assist with the interpretation of the statutory provisions. There are not a great number of family law precedents as these cases tend not to reach the Court of Cassation.

The laws that are relevant to family matters are the Federal Law 11 of 1992 concerning Civil Procedure matters (the Civil Procedure Law), the Federal Law 5 of 1985 issuing the Law of Civil Transactions (the Law of Civil Transactions) and the Federal Law 28 of 2005 concerning Personal Status matters (the Personal Status Law). The Personal Status Law was developed from traditional Shari'a laws and principles, but importantly has taken into account the changing times and modern society.

There are a number of different schools for the interpretation of Shari'a principles. If precedents cannot assist with the interpretation of statutory provisions, such schools would be referred to.

It is possible for non-Muslim expatriates to ask for the laws of their home countries to be applied by the courts of the UAE. The Law of Civil Transactions determines the applicable law for different types of cases, and in this regard the following articles are relevant to family law matters (in summary):

Article 13: *'The law of the state in which the husband is a national at the time the marriage is contracted shall apply to divorce and the division of property following divorce.'*

Article 16: *'Substantive matters relating to guardianship, trusteeship and maintenance are governed by the law of the person requiring to be protected.'*

Article 18: *'Possession, ownership and rights over property shall be governed by the law of the country in which the property is located.'*

However, in practice, foreign laws are very rarely applied for the following reasons:

(a) The application of foreign laws is a time-consuming and difficult procedure. It is necessary to have all the possibly relevant laws of that country translated into Arabic and put before the court. The application of precedents and case law makes this an overwhelmingly onerous task.
(b) Foreign laws will not be applied if they are contrary to public order, morals or Islamic Shari'a (Article 27 Civil Procedure Law).
(c) Foreign laws will not be applied if their effect cannot be determined (Article 28 Civil Procedure Law). Therefore if a Dubai judge cannot clearly interpret the foreign laws, local Dubai laws will instead be applied.
(d) Where the foreign law to be applied is the law of one party's nationality, UAE law will instead be applied if that party has dual nationality or his nationality is unknown (Article 24 Civil Procedure Law).
(e) Under the statutory provisions, each party may seek their own laws to be applied. However, in practice, the UAE courts will only apply foreign laws if both parties agree to such law being applied, or if the husband asks for foreign laws to apply and the wife does not object to this.

For the remainder of this chapter, it will be assumed that UAE laws are being applied, not foreign laws.

1.2 Which are the main statutes governing matrimonial law in the jurisdiction?

Federal Law 28 of 2005 concerning personal status matters (the Personal Status Law).

2. JURISDICTION

2.1 What are the main jurisdictional requirements for the institution of proceedings in relation to divorce, property and children?

There are a number of exceptions, but in general, the Courts of First Instance (the lowest tier of court) have jurisdiction over a family case filed against a citizen or foreigner domiciled or resident in the UAE (following Article 5 of the Personal Status Law and Article 20 of the Civil Procedure Law). In addition a citizen or foreigner may commence a divorce in the UAE even if their spouse resides abroad, as long as the spouse is effectively served with the proceedings.

3. DOMICILE AND HABITUAL RESIDENCE

3.1 Explain the concepts of domicile and habitual residence as they apply to the jurisdiction in relation to divorce, the finances and children

In practice, a party would be seen to be domiciled or resident in the UAE for jurisdiction purposes, if they hold a residence visa (or visa entitling them to reside in the UAE). Wider jurisdictional bases are sometimes accepted without opposition.

The English concept of domicile does not apply under UAE law. Under UAE law, domicile is defined under Article 81 of the Law of Civil

Transactions as a place where an individual resides or works, and at which 'habitual conditions' arise, regardless of periods of temporary absence or long intervals of residence. In other words, domicile is where a party sees their long term home to be. Residence can be more temporary than domicile.

The concept of 'habitual residence' is not a connecting factor for jurisdiction purposes, nor a term relevant for any purpose in the UAE.

4. CONFLICT OF LAW/APPLICABLE LAW TO BE APPLIED

4.1 What happens when one party applies to stay proceedings in favour of a foreign jurisdiction? What factors will the local court take into account when determining forum issues?

The UAE courts will apply a 'first in time' rule, but only in respect of judgments rather than ongoing litigation. Therefore one party is able to apply to stay proceedings issued within the UAE courts if they can prove that a final judgment has been issued by a foreign court having jurisdiction. Stays based on *forum conveniens* are not available in family law cases.

B: PRE- AND POST-NUPTIAL AGREEMENTS

5. VALIDITY OF PRE- AND POST-NUPTIAL AGREEMENTS

5.1 To what extent are pre- and post-nups binding within the jurisdiction? Could you provide a brief discussion of the most significant recent case law on this issue?

Muslim couples (Emirati and expatriate) will have entered into a marriage contract (*nikah*) if they are to be married in a Muslim jurisdiction or elsewhere through an Islamic marriage ceremony. Within the marriage contract is a section which allows for dowry (*meher*) to be specified. The dowry is the payment of a sum or sums of money or other valuables to the wife, which may be paid on marriage (immediate dowry or *mokadam*) but which may also consist in part of the deferred dowry payable to the wife in the event of divorce or the husband's death (*moakher*). The dowry is an important part of the marriage contract and is a prerequisite to its legal validity. Because of this dowry element, the marriage contract has been likened by some to a pre-nuptial agreement, but it is in truth quite distinct. There are restrictions as to what can be enforced within the marriage contract; those that are contrary to public order or Islamic Shari'a will not be enforced.

The specified dowry can be substantial and this term within the marriage contract is fully enforceable. However, some wives may use the dowry term to give them a bargaining position, and agree to receive a lesser dowry on alternative terms to their advantage, for instance as a quid pro quo for the wife to have the right herself to pronounce *talaq*. The marriage contract is negotiated and agreed by the husband and the wife's father or other male guardian, often with the benefit of legal advice (although this is not required).

If a Muslim couple wished to rely on a pre-nuptial agreement validly drafted in another jurisdiction, it is likely that the UAE courts would not choose to enforce the terms especially in relation to children. This is because under Shari'a law a couple could not enter into an agreement concerning children who have not yet been born.

There are no specific laws relating to pre-nuptial agreements in the UAE. The UAE courts would view such agreements, if at all, as a civil contract between two parties, but not specifically as a contract relating to marriage or divorce.

Any nuptial agreement would be void or voidable if any term in the agreement conflicts with 'Islamic Shari'a, public order or morals in the UAE' (Article 27 Civil Procedure Law). Public order is defined at Article 3 Civil Procedure Law as 'matters relating to personal status such as marriage'. This means that any terms in the contract which are against UAE morals (for example reference to unmarried cohabiting couples, or adultery, both of which are criminal offences in the UAE) would be void. In addition, any terms conflicting with Shari'a laws would be void. For example under Shari'a law (and the Personal Status Law derived from it) it is not possible for a woman to remarry until after the *eddah* (waiting period) following a divorce. A pre-nuptial agreement that specifically stated that a husband agreed to his wife's immediate remarriage in the event of a divorce would be void as this term conflicts with Shari'a laws. Similarly if a Muslim couple attempted to enter in to a pre-nuptial agreement attempting to restrict the husband's right to take a second wife, this term would be void as it is his right to do this under Shari'a law.

C. DIVORCE, NULLITY AND JUDICIAL SEPARATION

6. RECOGNITION OF FOREIGN MARRIAGES/DIVORCES

6.1 Summarise the position in your jurisdiction

In order for a marriage contracted outside the UAE to be recognised, the marriage certificate should be legalised by the Ministry of Foreign Affairs in the country in which the marriage took place, and then attested by the UAE embassy in that country. Further attestations should take place at the Ministry of Foreign Affairs in the UAE.

In certain circumstances even a validly attested marriage certificate would not be sufficient to allow a marriage to be recognised in the UAE. This is because in Islam, certain marriages are not capable of recognition. These are as follows:

- A marriage between a Muslim man and a woman who is not Muslim, Christian or Jewish.
- A marriage between a Muslim woman and a non-Muslim man.
- A civil marriage between Muslims where there has not been a valid religious marriage ceremony.

7. DIVORCE

7.1 Explain the grounds for divorce within the jurisdiction (please also deal with nullity and judicial separation if appropriate).

For Muslims in the UAE, divorce is the 'cancelling' of the valid contract of marriage between the parties. The divorce can be commenced by the husband, or by the wife if her husband gave her the right to do so (*isma*) in the marriage contract. If the wife is not given the right to divorce the husband within her marriage contract, she may still do so for reasons of 'harm'. The definition of harm in this context is wide ranging and includes the seven categories for divorce set out below (taken from the Personal Status Law).

There are two routes to obtain a divorce. The first is by pronouncing the *Talaq* (which means 'I divorce you' in Arabic). The husband or wife (if she has *isma*) must say or write 'I divorce you' or '*Talaq*' in the presence of a witness. For Muslims, religiously this is a valid method of divorce without further steps being taken. However, for the divorce to be legally recognised, it should be registered with the court: Article 106 Personal Status Law states 'divorce is considered valid when... the judge authenticates it'. Such registration allows documentary evidence of the divorce to be produced so that it can be relied upon in future. If there is a dispute as to whether the *Talaq* was pronounced, the witness would be able to give evidence at court. There are financial implications for a spouse who commences a divorce by pronouncing the *Talaq* without the consent of their spouse.

The second means of obtaining a divorce is by application to court ('separation by way of a judgment'). The applicant will issue a divorce case and the parties will be referred to the Family Guidance Committee, which forms part of the court. Article 98 of the Personal Status Law states that the court should try and reconcile the parties before separating them. This is the purpose of the Family Guidance Committee. The family guidance counsellors are not legally trained, but have experience in meditation and counselling. They meet with both parties and if there cannot be reconciliation, the matter is listed for hearing before a judge. The judge will determine whether there is valid reason for the divorce. These include:

(i) Separation due to 'defects'

(a) Defects such as madness, leprosy, impotence and venereal disease. A party can only rely on such a 'defect' as a ground for divorce if he or she was not aware of the defect at the time of marriage. It is possible for the court to adjourn the case for a period of up to a year to determine whether the defect is capable of being 'removed' (Article 113 Personal Status Law).

(b) Deceit. If there has been serious deceit between the parties during the formation of the marriage, if one party would not have entered into the marriage contract had they been aware of the deceit, they are entitled to rely on this as a basis for divorce (Article 114 Personal Status Law)

(c) Adultery.

(ii) Separation for non-payment of the immediate dowry (*mokadam*)

(iii) Separation due to harm or disputes

One spouse has the right to ask for divorce if he or she is being harmed by the other, and such harm makes it impossible for the parties to live together (Article 117 Personal Status Law). In this situation, the court may instruct two arbitrators to investigate the reasons for the discord between the parties and report back to the court. A finding of fault on one party may have financial implications.

(iv) Separation due to lack of financial support during the marriage
A wife is entitled to ask for a divorce if the court determines that the husband has funds to support her but has failed to do so.

(v) Separation due to absence of one party
A wife may be entitled to divorce if her husband has disappeared. However, the divorce judgment would not be pronounced until a year has passed from the date of her application for divorce, without the husband returning during this time.

(vi) Separation due to jail sentence
A wife is entitled to divorce if her husband is sentenced to more than three years in prison and at the time of the divorce he has been in prison for more than one year.

(vii) Separation due to desertion (*hajr*)
If the husband leaves the family home and does not return within four months of his wife's request that he should resume cohabitation, she is entitled to a divorce.

The waiting period or *'eddah'* is an important concept within Muslim divorces. This is a three-month period (or specifically three menstrual cycles) that commences after the *talaq* has been pronounced or divorce pronounced by the court. During the waiting period, the wife must stay single. The purpose of the waiting period is to firstly ensure that the wife is not pregnant, but also as a period of reflection for the parties to determine whether there is a chance for reconciliation. The husband must pay expenses to the wife during the waiting period, regardless of whether the wife divorced the husband or the husband the wife. If the wife is pregnant at the date of the *talaq*, the waiting period does not conclude until after she has given birth.

There are two types of divorce, revocable and irrevocable. The revocable divorce will not bring an end to the marriage until the conclusion of the waiting period. This means that the parties can reconcile and maintain a valid marriage at any time before the conclusion of the waiting period. After the conclusion of the waiting period, if they wish to reconcile, they must do so by entering in to a new marriage contract.

The irrevocable divorce ends the marriage as soon as it is pronounced. There are two types of irrevocable divorce, the irrevocable divorce with 'small intent', where the divorced woman can reconcile with her husband only with a new marriage contract and dowry, or the irrevocable divorce with 'big intent' where the divorced woman can only return to her husband after marrying another husband, having sexual intercourse with him, divorcing him and waiting until the conclusion of that waiting period.

8. FINANCES/CAPITAL, PROPERTY

8.1 What powers does the court have to allocate financial resources and property on the breakdown of marriage?

The courts will not automatically consider the financial position of a separating couple unless an application is made to the court. Unless the parties are Muslim and a marriage contract is in place which they seek to enforce, a financial application can only be made by the receiving party, not the giving party. This means that a husband (expatriate or Emirati) who divorces his wife in the UAE cannot force a settlement on her in this jurisdiction.

Capital

There are no family laws in the UAE that deal with the allocation of property on the breakdown of marriage. On divorce, each party retains the assets and property held in their respective names. The division of any jointly-owned property is dealt with under general civil laws. One party may apply to the court for an order for sale of a jointly-owned property, or for the other party to buy out their share. The starting point is the assumption that parties hold jointly-owned property in equal shares. If one party is able to show the court that they made a greater financial contribution towards the property in terms of purchase price or mortgage payments, they may retain a larger share of capital. The courts may instruct an accounting expert to examine the parties' respective financial contributions. It is important to note that the UAE courts only have jurisdiction over property owned within the UAE, not abroad. Other jointly-owned bank accounts or other assets will be dealt with in the same way. It is important to note that the UAE courts only have jurisdiction over property owned (or bank accounts sited) within the UAE, and not any which are abroad.

8.2 Explain and illustrate with reference to recent cases the court's thinking on division of assets

As set out above, raising such issues or seeking such relief is not dealt with by the family courts. Instead division of jointly-owned assets would be dealt with by the civil courts.

9. FINANCES/MAINTENANCE

9.1 Explain the operation of maintenance for spouses on an ongoing basis after the breakdown of marriage

Under UAE laws, a wife may make financial claims for herself and her children irrespective of her own wealth and income. It is never possible for a husband to make income claims from a wife, even if he holds custody of the children. The wife's claims for herself are compensation-type claims, as follows:

- The first of these is called *'nafket motaa'*. This claim is for a year's worth of expenses to cover the wife's 'moral damage' that she may suffer as a result of her husband divorcing her against her will. The claim could equate to as much as 40 per cent of a husband's income for one year (payable by one lump sum) but is usually 25 per cent.
- The second is for the wife to claim compensation from her husband, for not having supported her during the last year of her marriage (if appropriate). Again this could equate to a further 25 per cent (but up to

40 per cent) of the husband's income for one year.
- Thirdly is the *'nafket eddah'*. This is the financial claim that a wife could make from her husband for him to support her financially during the waiting period. As set out above, this is usually three months, but can be longer if for example the wife is pregnant.

9.2 Is it common for maintenance to be awarded?

Apart from the compensation type claims above, and a nominal 'carer's allowance' as part of child maintenance, a wife may not make financial claims for herself on divorce.

10. CHILD MAINTENANCE

10.1 On what basis is child maintenance calculated within the jurisdiction?

The court will consider the standard of living that the children experienced during the marriage to determine the appropriate level of child maintenance. Child maintenance will cover all expenses required by the wife to care for the child. These could be for example rent for housing, schooling, food, medical expenses, housemaid, gardener, clothes for children, flights, extracurricular activities. The wife claiming child maintenance would be required to provide documentary evidence of the expenses that her husband met for the children during the marriage for example shopping receipts, tenancy agreement, receipts for flights and travel, receipts for petrol and car expenses, school fees receipts etc. In addition, the wife can claim a monthly figure as a 'carer's allowance'. This figure depends on the level of the husband's income.

11. RECIPROCAL ENFORCEMENT OF FINANCIAL ORDERS

11.1 Summarise the position in your jurisdiction

The UAE is not a territory where the principles of Reciprocal Enforcement of Maintenance Orders are applied. However, foreign financial orders may be enforceable in the same way as foreign contracts, although there can be difficulties as set out below. Enforcement of a foreign order initially requires the commencement of an 'attestation case' (this broadly equates to an application for a mirror order). Under Article 235 of the Civil Code, foreign orders may be enforced in the UAE by applying the laws of the foreign country within the local courts. The provisions are as follows[1]:

'1. *Judgments and orders passed in a foreign country may be ordered for execution and implementation within UAE under the same conditions provided for in the law of foreign state for the execution of judgments and orders passed in the state.*

2. *Petition for execution order shall be filed before the Court of First Instance under which jurisdiction execution is sought under lawsuit filing standard procedures. Execution may not be ordered unless the following was verified:*
   a. *State courts have no jurisdiction over the dispute on which the judgment*

[1] Taken from the English translation of the Civil Procedure Law on Emirati Law (*www.emiratilaw.com*)

or the order was passed and that the issuing foreign courts have such jurisdiction in accordance with the International Judicial Jurisdiction Rules decided in its applicable law.

b. Judgment or order was passed by the competent court according to the law of the country in which it was passed.

c. Litigants in the lawsuit on which the foreign judgment was passed were summoned and duly represented.

d. Judgment or order had obtained the absolute degree in accordance with the law of the issuing court.

e. It does not conflict with or contradict a judgment or order previously passed by another court in the State and does not include any violation of moral code or public order'.

The effect of this Article is that foreign financial orders can be enforced in the UAE courts if:

- the UAE courts did not have jurisdiction to deal with the original litigation;
- the English order was made by a competent court applying the laws of England and Wales;
- both parties were given notice of the hearing and attended or were represented;
- that the court had jurisdiction to make the orders that it did; and
- the order does not conflict with orders previously made by the Dubai courts, and the orders do not breach public order or morals.

Once the attestation case has concluded, the resulting mirror order could be enforced or 'executed' through an execution case. The UAE courts have very wide powers of enforcement for example:

- **Attachment of earnings**
  The judge may make an order that the employer disclose details of the husband's salary and bonuses, then make an order that the maintenance owed is paid at source from the salary. A maximum of one-third of the respondent's periodic salary can be deducted in this way.
- **Enquiry of banks, or traffic and land departments**
  The judge can order an enquiry to determine whether, for example, a respondent has funds in their bank account to pay a lump sum, or a car or property that could be sold to meet an outstanding debt.
- **Freezing bank accounts**
  An order may be made to freeze a bank account if the judge believes that the respondent is likely to dissipate assets to avoid meeting their obligations under the original order.
- **Seizing goods**
  To ensure the repayment of a debt, a judge may order the seizure of a property, or other goods. The executive judge may transfer the matter to the executive judge of another court, in whose jurisdiction the property lies (for example in another Emirate).
- **Imprisonment**
  This is likely if respondent shows a wilful refusal to pay despite being able to afford to, or if the judge fears that they will flee the country.

Imprisonment can be for periods not totalling more than three years. Imprisonment does not negate the need for the respondent to meet the terms of the original order.

- **Travel ban**
  The judge can make an order preventing the respondent from leaving the country.

Once a mirror order has been obtained, it remains in force for such future enforcement as may be required. For instance the mirror order could be retained by a wife and used to enforce each and every future breach of a maintenance order.

If it is apparent in relation to a financial agreement reached or reflected in an order made outside the UAE, that it may be necessary for the agreement/order to be enforced within the UAE, it is advisable to take precautionary measures.The parties could cooperate to obtain a mirror order in the UAE at that stage through an attestation case. Alternatively, a quicker and cheaper option is for an agreement to be drafted in similar terms and put by both parties before the Family Guidance Committee (also known as the Reconciliation Committee) of the UAE, resulting in a judicially-approved document capable of enforcement.

12. FINANCIAL RELIEF AFTER FOREIGN DIVORCE PROCEEDINGS

12.1 What powers are available to make orders following a foreign divorce?

There are no specific statutory provisions dealing with financial provision after a foreign divorce. It would be for one party to rely on an order made by a foreign court (for example through an attestation then execution case) and the other party to put forward why it should not be enforced, for example by claiming that the UAE had jurisdiction at the time and should therefore determine the outcome.

D. CHILDREN

13. CUSTODY/PARENTAL RESPONSIBILITY

13.1 Briefly explain the legal position in relation to custody/parental responsibility following the breakdown of a relationship or marriage

Parents do not share equal parental responsibility for the child. Following a divorce, the mother will become the 'custodian' of young children, and the father the 'guardian'. The custodian is responsible for the nurture and care of the child, and for meeting the child's day-to-day needs and have the child live within their home.

As set out at Article 143 and 144 of the Personal Status Law, a custodian must:

- be rational;
- be mature enough and have attained the age of puberty;
- be honest;
- be able to bring up and take care of a child;
- be free from infectious disease;
- not have been sentenced for a crime of 'honour' ;

- if the custodian is the mother, she must:
  - not re-marry unless the court decides it is in the best interests of the child; and
  - share the same religion as the child; or
- if the custodian is the father, he must:
  - have a suitable woman living within his home to care for the child (such as a female relative);
  - share the same religion as the child.

As set out at Article 146 Personal Status Law, the mother will have custody of young children. Unless the court orders otherwise, custody will move from the mother to the father once the children reach the age of approximately 10-and-a-half for a boy and 12-and-a-half for a girl. The exact ages as set down in the Personal Status Law (Article 156) are 11 and 13 respectively, but these ages are set using the lunar calendar (which is approximately 11 days shorter each year than the Gregorian calendar generally employed elsewhere). The court is able to move custody to father, maternal grandmother, paternal grandmother, maternal sisters, paternal sisters, maternal niece etc (in that order or precedence) if it is determined that the mother does not meet the criteria for a custodian as set out above. However when determining such matters, the court will consider the welfare of the child as the primary concern and make a decision based on the child's best interests in each particular case. It is common these days for the court to be flexible in respect of the custody criteria to ensure that the child's best interests are met.

Guardianship involves supervising, protecting, educating and preparing a child for life, and (when required) giving the necessary consent for the child to marry. The guardian makes the decisions regarding a child's schooling, or medical treatment for example. Guardianship involves guiding the child in the right direction in terms of morals, right and wrong, education and religion. The guardian must be rational, mature, honest and able to fulfil the requirements of guardianship. He must also be able to arrange his affairs as well as those of the child.

The father is ordinarily the guardian of his child. However the guardian will be removed if he commits rape, disgracing conduct or prostitution or led the child in those ways, or if the guardian is sentenced to punishment for a felony crime or misdemeanour that affects the 'soul' of the child. Guardianship can be permanently or temporarily removed if the guardian is sentenced to imprisonment, or if he subjects the child to excessive danger in terms of health, security, honour, behaviour or education. When investigating such cases, it is possible for the court to commit guardianship of a child to a specialised social organisation as a temporary measure.

13.2 Briefly explain the legal position in relation to access/contact/visitation following the breakdown of a relationship or marriage

Contact with a child post divorce is called 'visitation'. The guardian is entitled to visit the child regularly. The custodian may not move the child permanently to another country if it would prevent the guardian from exercising contact with the child. A guardian (usually the father) may make an application to court for an order to allow him to exercise his right to visit the child. Usually such contact would take place for an afternoon each weekend, and for additional time during school holidays. Staying contact would only be permitted where the child is over the age of two.

14. INTERNATIONAL ABDUCTION

14.1 Briefly summarise the position in your jurisdiction

The UAE is not a signatory to the Hague Convention. Within UAE laws, there are no statutory provisions specifically dealing with child abduction.

15. LEAVE TO REMOVE/APPLICATIONS TO TAKE A CHILD OUT OF THE JURISDICTION

15.1 Summarise the position in your jurisdiction

After divorce, if the custodian of the child is other than the child's mother, he or she must obtain the written agreement from the guardian before taking the child out of the UAE. If such permission is withheld by the guardian, the custodian may obtain permission for the child's travel from a Judge (Article 149 Personal Status Law).

During the marriage, a mother must not take the child out of the UAE without written permission from the guardian, who during his lifetime will, in most circumstances, be the father. After divorce (and the conclusion of the waiting period), the mother may take the child out of the country without the father's consent unless it harms the child in some way (Article 150 Personal Status Law).

The guardian of a child has the right to hold the child's passport for safekeeping, but must hand the passport over to the custodian when it is required for the child's travel. The judge may order the passport to be kept with the custodian if she experiences difficulty dealing with the guardian when the passport is requested (Article 157 Personal Status Law).

15.2 Under what circumstances may a parent apply to remove their child from the jurisdiction against the wishes of the other parent?

The custodian of the child may not permanently settle the child in another country if it would cause 'harm' to the other parent or if the distance between the two countries prevented the non-resident parent from visiting the child and returning home within one day (Article 151 Personal Status Law).

If the guardian can prove that his residence in the UAE has expired due to valid reasons such as the end of his employment or due to any other reason, which the court finds to be well founded and not arbitrary, the court may allow the guardian to take the children to live abroad. The mother has the choice whether or not to follow or join them.

E. SURROGACY AND ADOPTION

16. VALIDITY OF SURROGACY AGREEMENTS

16.1 Briefly summarise the position in your jurisdiction

Surrogacy agreements are not allowed within the UAE. They can only be made and implemented abroad.

17. ADOPTION

17.1 Briefly summarise the position in relation to adoption in your jurisdiction. Is adoption available to individuals, cohabiting couples (both heterosexual and same-sex)?

The laws of the UAE prohibit adoption within the UAE by non-Emirati couples. This means that only Emirati citizens holding UAE passports may adopt abandoned children from the UAE. Expatriate couples residing in the UAE must look abroad for children to adopt. The adoption process for expatriates can still be conducted from the United Arab Emirates, regardless of the nationality of the parents.

Abandoned children that have been born in the UAE can obtain UAE citizenship and a UAE passport. The law states that a child will be deemed abandoned in the UAE unless proved otherwise.

Under Shari'a law, parents are encouraged to care for a child who is not their biological child, and to nurture that child like their own. However, it is prohibited for those parents to give the child their own surname. The Personal Status Law adapts this position by allowing the adoptive parents to nominate the child's first name, whereas the court would order the child's surname.

Adoption by same-sex couples, or unmarried couples is not permitted by law.

F. COHABITATION

18. COHABITATION

18.1 What legislation (if any) governs division of property for unmarried couples on the breakdown of the relationship?

This area of law is not relevant in the UAE as cohabitation outside marriage is a criminal offence. Any attempt to commence a court case concerning assets accrued during cohabitation of an unmarried couple would be unwise, as it would highlight the fact that a criminal offence had been committed.

G. FAMILY DISPUTE RESOLUTION

19. MEDIATION, COLLABORATIVE LAW AND ARBITRATION

19.1 Briefly summarise the non-court-based processes available in your jurisdiction and the current status of agreements reached under the auspices of mediation, collaborative law and arbitration

In relation to family law, the only use of mediation is through the court-based Family Guidance Committee (also known as the Reconciliation Committee) as set out above. When commencing most family cases, the matter must be referred to the Family Guidance Committee. The committee is made up of a number of counsellors with mediation/counselling training. They are not legally trained. Their job is to discuss the dispute with the parties and assist them to either reconcile or amicably resolve the issue(s) in dispute. Both parties would be given notice by telephone or post that they are required to attend a meeting. The counsellor can ask for a number of meetings to give the parties time to seek legal advice, or reconsider any proposed settlement. Any agreement reached within the Family Guidance Committee meetings would be drafted into documentary form, and signed by both parties before a judge. The resulting judgment is binding on the parties and can be enforced as required through the courts. For divorce for example, any agreement concerning children or finances reached through the Family Guidance committee meetings could be submitted within divorce proceedings, ensuring that the case concludes swiftly and amicably.

In the event that one party refuses to attend the Family Guidance Committee, or the counsellor determines that an agreement cannot be reached, a 'no objection letter' is issued to enable the parties to progress court proceedings.

19.2 What is the statutory basis (if any), for mediation, collaborative law and arbitration in your jurisdiction? In particular, are the parties required to attempt a family dispute resolution in advance of the institution of proceedings?

The Personal Status Law sets out that parties must meet before the Family Guidance Committee at the court for mediation before their case can proceed within the court. An agreement reached at the Family Guidance Committee can be drafted and signed by the parties before a judge, forming a binding agreement between the parties that is capable of enforcement.

Collaborative law is not practised (save by a limited number of specialist family lawyers serving the expatriate community).

Arbitration in family matters has not yet found a place in the UAE family law system.

H.OTHER

20. CIVIL PARTNERSHIP/SAME-SEX MARRIAGE

20.1 What is the status of civil partnership/same-sex marriage within the jurisdiction?

20.2 What legislation governs civil partnership/same-sex marriage?

Same-sex relationships are strictly against the law in the UAE and may give rise to criminal prosecution and sanctions.

Accordingly, any attempt to resolve issues in the UAE which arise from a same-sex marriage (or civil partnership) that took place outside the UAE should not be contemplated.

21. CONTROVERSIAL AREAS/RAPIDLY DEVELOPING AREAS OF LAW

21.1 Is there a particular area of the law within the jurisdiction that is currently undergoing major change?

Very sadly in 2012, a case came before the courts in the UAE in which a father had killed his child following years of child abuse. The case shocked the Emirati and expatriate communities alike. Child protection laws were in the process of being drafted at this time. The UAE Government was praised for the speed with which it ensured those draft laws were finalised and approved. This child protection law has been informally named 'Wadeema's law' after the child.

His Highness Sheikh Mohammed bin Rashid al Makhtoum, the Vice President, Prime Minister and Ruler of Dubai said: 'Every child has the right to a secure life, permanent care and emotional and psychological stability. We will be uncompromising with whoever infringes upon the rights of children, for the protection of our children is a protection of our future'.

One of the results of this new law is that doctors, teachers and others who deal with children are under a statutory obligation to report suspected cases of child abuse.

21.2 Which areas of law are most out-of-step? Which areas would you most like to see reformed/changed?

It is to be hoped that in years to come the accessibility of UAE laws to the international community will improve further. Until recently, UAE precedents were only available in Arabic. Various online portals now provide English translated family cases that have set a precedent. This has been useful to show international lawyers how the statutory provisions are interpreted in practice.

The author would like to thank Hassan Elhais and Diana Hamade and Sir Peter Singer for their assistance in editing this chapter.

USA – California

Harris Ginsberg LLP Suzanne Harris, Larry A. Ginsberg, Andrea Fugate Balian, Fahi Takesh Hallin, David L. Marcus, Evan C. Itzkowitz, Johnna K. Boylan, Dena J. Kravitz, Jessica M. Spiker, Michelle H. Chen & Jennifer R. Morra

A. JURISDICTION AND CONFLICT OF LAW

1. SOURCES OF LAW

1.1 What is the primary source of law in relation to the breakdown of marriage and the welfare of children within the jurisdiction?

The primary source of law in California related to the dissolution of a marriage and issues relating to children in a dissolution action is the California Family Code (hereinafter referred to as FC)) and published case law from the California appellate courts and the California Supreme Court.

1.2 Which are the main statutes governing matrimonial law in the jurisdiction?

The main statutes governing matrimonial law in California are codified in the California Family Code.

2. JURISDICTION

2.1 What are the main jurisdictional requirements for the institution of proceedings in relation to divorce, property and children?

California must have jurisdiction over the subject matter raised by the pleadings (the marriage *res*) and the parties (personal jurisdiction). The Superior Court has jurisdiction in all proceedings under the FC and all matters that are necessary incidents of the parties' family rights and obligations, such as marital and/or domestic partnership status, child custody/visitation, child and spousal support, parentage, and settlement of the parties' property rights (FC sections 200 and 2010).

To the extent that a party is only seeking to terminate his or her marital status, personal jurisdiction over both spouses is not required if at least one spouse is domiciled in California for at least six months and notice of the proceeding is provided to the other party (FC section 2320; *Mungia v Superior Court* (1964) 225 California App. 2d 280).

With regard to child custody cases, however, the court's ability to exercise jurisdiction is further limited by the Federal Parental Kidnapping Prevention Act (FPKPA) and the Uniform Child Custody Jurisdiction and Enforcement Act. (UCCJEA) (28 USC section 1738A and FC section 3400 *et seq.*). These Acts ensure that only one state has exclusive jurisdiction to make an initial custody determination and to modify any such orders. With certain exceptions,

California has jurisdiction to make an initial custody determination if it is the home state of the child on the date of the commencement of the action, that is, that the child has lived in California with a parent for at least six consecutive months prior to the commencement of a child custody proceeding (FC sections 3402(g) and 3421).

With regard to property, a California court lacks jurisdiction to make orders that directly affect the title or interest in real property located outside California. However, if it has jurisdiction over both parties, the court can make a determination as to the parties' respective interests in such property and order the parties to execute conveyances accordingly (FC section 2660).

3. DOMICILE AND HABITUAL RESIDENCE

3.1 Explain the concepts of domicile and habitual residence as they apply to the jurisdiction, in relation to divorce, the finances and children

Domicile requires the physical presence in the jurisdiction and the intent to remain in the jurisdiction indefinitely (*Smith v Smith* (1955) 45 C 2d. 235, 239). A person may have a residence (a place where they live) within the jurisdiction but not be domiciled in that jurisdiction. A person can have only one domicile, but they can have several residences. If there is a dispute about whether a person resides in the jurisdiction or is domiciled in the jurisdiction, the parties must present evidence regarding the person's intent to remain in the jurisdiction, such as the location of bank accounts, voting registration, a driver's licence and tax return filings (*Marriage of Dick* (1993) 15 CA 4th 144, 152).

4. CONFLICT OF LAW/APPLICABLE LAW TO BE APPLIED

4.1 What happens when one party applies to stay proceedings in favour of a foreign jurisdiction? What factors will the local court take into account when determining forum issues?

The rule in California is that if two courts of different states or countries have concurrent jurisdiction over the same parties and subject matter, the California court has the discretion to determine whether to keep the case or relinquish jurisdiction to the foreign state. This issue is determined on a case-by-case basis. Pertinent considerations include comity, the prevention of multiple and vexatious litigation, judicial economy, the interests of the forum and the convenience of the parties (*Leadford v Leadford* (1992) 6 CA 4th 571, 574-575).

Subject to limited exceptions set forth in the FC, before hearing a child custody proceeding, if California determines that a child custody proceeding has previously been commenced in another UCCJEA jurisdiction, California is required to stay its proceeding and communicate with the other court. California will defer to the other jurisdiction's determination as to which court is the more appropriate forum, and if that state determines it is the more appropriate forum, California will dismiss the custody proceeding. (FC 3426.)

A California court must 'treat a foreign country as if it were a state of the United States.' (FC 3405(a).) A child custody determination made in a foreign country under factual circumstances in conformity with the UCCJEA must be enforced (FC 3405(b)), unless the child custody law of the foreign country violates fundamental principles of human rights. (FC 3405(c).)

Once a California court has made a 'child custody determination', that court obtains 'exclusive, continuing jurisdiction' and no other court may have jurisdiction to modify the custody order. (FC 3402 (c).)

In child support cases, only one state can have child support jurisdiction at any given point in time. In the case of jurisdictional conflict over a petition to establish a child support order, the state with controlling jurisdiction is determined under the Full Faith and Credit for Child Support Orders Act (FFCCSOA, 28 USC section 1738B) and the Uniform Interstate Family Support Act (UIFSA, FC section 4900 *et seq*).

Under UIFSA, the definition of 'state' includes a foreign jurisdiction that has enacted a law or established procedures for issuance and enforcement of support orders which are substantially similar to the procedures under UIFSA (FC section 4901(s)(2)).

In spousal support cases, UIFSA also applies. Once a California court issues a spousal support order, it has continuing, exclusive spousal support jurisdiction throughout the existence of the support obligation (FC section 4909(f) (UIFSA)). Under UIFSA, if another appropriate state renders a spousal support order and maintains continuing jurisdiction over the order, California may only enforce (but not modify) this order.

B. PRE- AND POST-NUPTIAL AGREEMENTS

5. VALIDITY OF PRE- AND POST-NUPTIAL AGREEMENTS

5.1 To what extent are pre- and post-nups binding within the jurisdiction? Could you provide a brief discussion of the most significant recent case law on this issue?

The requirements for a valid premarital agreement entered into after 1 January 1986 are set forth in FC sections 1600 to 1617. A premarital agreement must be in writing and signed by both parties. No consideration is required.

A premarital agreement may cover any subject except for child support, child custody or any issue which violates public policy, nor ones promoting divorce, raising children in a particular religion or penalising a party for fault (ie, causing the end of the marriage).

A premarital agreement is presumed valid and the spouse challenging the agreement bears the burden of proving it is unenforceable. An agreement is unenforceable if, at the time of execution, a party did not execute the agreement voluntarily, or if the agreement was unconscionable, and if before the agreement was executed all of the following applied:

- the party was not provided a disclosure of the other party's assets and debts; or
- the party did not waive that disclosure; and
- the party did not know, or reasonably could not have had knowledge of, the other party's assets and debts.

If an agreement covers spousal support, the party against whom enforcement was sought must have been represented by an attorney. A spousal support provision is unenforceable if it is 'unconscionable' at the time of enforcement.

There are no FC sections specifying a framework for enforceability for post-nuptial agreements. Post-nuptial agreements are subject to the parties' fiduciary obligations to each other pursuant to FC 721(b). If one spouse gains an unfair advantage, the agreement is presumed to have been obtained by undue influence.

C DIVORCE, NULLITY AND JUDICIAL SEPARATION

6. RECOGNITION OF FOREIGN MARRIAGES/DIVORCES

6.1 Summarise the position in your jurisdiction

Pursuant to FC 308, a marriage contracted outside the state of California, 'that would be valid by the laws of the jurisdiction in which the marriage was contracted' is valid in California. California's recognition of marriages that occur in other jurisdictions includes recognition of a marriage between two persons of the same sex entered into outside of California that would be valid pursuant to the laws of the jurisdiction where the marriage occurred.

California's recognition and enforcement of foreign country judgments is predicated on principles of comity or voluntary cooperation (*In re Stephanie M.* (1994) 7 C 4th 295, 313-314). California courts will recognise and enforce foreign country judgments provided that the judgment was valid in the country where rendered (*Burt v Burt* (1960) 187 CA 2d 36, 9 CR 440) and at least one of the parties was domiciled in the foreign country at the time of the dissolution proceeding (*Harlan v Harlan* (1945) 70 CA 2d 657).

7. DIVORCE

7.1 Explain the grounds for divorce within the jurisdiction (please also deal with nullity and judicial separation if appropriate)

California is a no-fault state. As set forth in FC 2310, there are two grounds for commencing a dissolution action. A party must contend that there are 'irreconcilable differences, which have caused the irremediable breakdown of the marriage', or 'incurable insanity', as delineated in FC sections 2311 and 2312.

A legal separation action can be maintained on the same grounds as dissolution, ie, irreconcilable differences or incurable insanity (FC 2310). An action for legal separation permits the parties to settle their responsibilities towards each other and/or their minor children without terminating the marital status.

If a party has not met the six-month residency requirements for filing a dissolution in California but wants to commence an action and obtain orders, they may commence a legal separation action because it does not have the six-month residency requirement. Other reasons to file for legal separation and not obtain a termination of the parties' marital status include religious reasons, retirement benefit issues and/or healthcare concerns.

A marriage is void when the marriage is incestuous (FC 2200), or bigamous or polygamous (under FC 2201). In these instances the marriage is declared to never have existed.

A marriage is voidable if, at the time the marriage was entered into, any of the following existed:

- the petitioner was under the age of 18;
- there was a prior existing marriage, but the prior spouse had been absent for at least five years and was not known by the petitioner to be alive, or was generally reputed or believed by the petitioner to be dead;
- either party was not of sound mind;
- consent of either party was obtained by fraud;
- consent of either party was obtained by force;
- either party was physically incapable of entering into the marriage state and the incapacity continues and appears to be incurable.

8. FINANCES/CAPITAL, PROPERTY

8.1 What powers does the court have to allocate financial resources and property on the breakdown of marriage?

In California, upon filing and serving the petition and summons, both parties are restrained from transferring, conveying or disposing of any property, whether community or separate, during the pendency of the action. These automatic temporary restraining orders (ATROs) are specifically listed on the summons filed with the petition. Exceptions to the ATROs exist if either party must access community assets to pay for the basic necessities of life, attorney fees or if such assets are used as part of the ordinary course of business.

8.2 Explain and illustrate with reference to recent cases the court's thinking on division of assets

Pursuant to the FC 2550, the court must divide the community estate of the parties equally. Property held in joint title and/or property acquired during the marriage is presumed by the court to be community property (FC 2580 and 2581). While the court must divide the community estate equally between the parties, the court has the discretion to award a community asset entirely to one party (FC 2601) to effectuate an overall equal division of the community estate. The court also has the power to effectuate an unequal division or award additional assets to a party if there has been a determination of misappropriation of assets or exclusion of community assets by the other party. (FC 2602).

To overcome the presumption of community property set forth in FC sections 2580 and 2581, a party asserting a separate property claim (ie, that the property was acquired by inheritance, gift, bequest or prior to the date of marriage or after the date of separation), has the burden to trace the asset to a separate property source.

9. FINANCES/MAINTENANCE

9.1 Explain the operation of maintenance for spouses on an ongoing basis after the breakdown of marriage.

9.2 Explain and illustrate with reference to recent cases the court's thinking on maintenance

Each party has a duty to support the other party (FC 4300). Spousal support after the breakdown of the marriage is apportioned into two parts: *pendente lite* support and permanent support orders.

During the proceeding, the court has the authority to order a party to pay spousal support in an amount necessary to support the other spouse (FC 3600). In determining an amount for *pendente lite* support, the court need only consider the moving party's need and the other party's ability to pay, subject to the restrictions of FC sections 4320(i), 4320(m) and 4325, which prevent a spouse who has been the victim of domestic violence from having to support his or her abuser. The benchmark typically used by the court in determining the appropriate amount of this temporary support award is the standard of living the parties enjoyed during the marriage. This goes to the purpose of *pendente lite* support, which is to allow the parties to maintain the status quo of the marital standard of living.

In making a determination of permanent support, the court is bound by statutory guidelines of FC 4320. While the need and ability to pay are a part of these guidelines, they are merely two in a long list of factors the court must consider. Other factors included in FC 4320 include the skills and abilities of each party to support themselves, the duration of the marriage, the assets and debts of each party, the age and health of the parties, history of violence or domestic abuse, the balance of the hardships to each party and any other factors the court determines are just and equitable.

Pursuant to FC 4330, the court may order a party to pay spousal support for a duration of time that the court deems reasonable based on the factors set forth in FC 4320. The court also has the discretion to advise the supported spouse that he or she must make efforts to become self supporting. (FC 4330 (b) and *In re Marriage of Gavron* (2003) CA 3rd 705).

A presumption in California exists that a marriage of 10 years or more is a marriage of long duration (FC 4336). For a marriage of long duration, the court retains jurisdiction to make or modify spousal support orders in the future, unless the parties expressly agree in writing to terminate the court's jurisdiction regarding spousal support or expressly state in such written agreement that support is not modifiable. (See *Marriage of Hibbard* (2013) 212 CA 4th 1007)

9.3 Is it common for maintenance to be awarded?

Spousal support is ordered in most cases in which there is a discrepancy of income between the parties. While the amount and duration of support varies widely from case to case, unless the parties affirmatively waive support, do not seek support, or make close to identical salaries, there is typically an award of support.

10. CHILD MAINTENANCE

10.1 On what basis is child maintenance calculated within the jurisdiction?

In California, both parents have the duty to support their minor child to the best of his or her ability until the child is 18 years old (or 19 years old if they are still in high school), married or emancipated (FC sections 3900 and 3901). To ensure that parents equally share in this responsibility, California adopted a statewide formulaic guideline to determine the amount of child support payable by one parent to the other (FC sections 4050-4076). The California courts may not depart from the statutory guideline child support calculation except for specific and limited circumstances delineated by the legislature (FC sections 4050 and 4052).

The components of California's statutory guideline child support calculation include the amount of both parents' gross income and the approximate percentage of time that the higher earner has or will have primary physical responsibility for the children compared with the other parent. Computer software programs calculate the complex algebraic formula set forth in the California child support guidelines.

The most notable exception to the child support formula occurs when the 'parent being ordered to pay child support has an extraordinarily high income and the amount determined under the formula would exceed the reasonable needs of the children'. (FC 4057(b)(3).) What constitutes an 'extraordinarily high income' or the 'reasonable needs of the children' is determined on a case-by-case basis.

The court can order additional child support to cover portions of specific expenses such as child care costs, uninsured health care costs, travel expenses for visitation and costs related to the education or other special needs of the child. (FC 4062.)

11. RECIPROCAL ENFORCEMENT OF FINANCIAL ORDERS

11.1 Summarise the position in your jurisdiction

California will typically enforce financial orders from other states within the United States. Support orders (child support, spousal support and family support) are enforced via California's version of the Uniform Interstate Family Support Act (UIFSA, FC 4900 *et seq*). A support order from another country is enforceable if that country's laws and procedures for issuing support orders are substantially similar to California's laws and procedures. Both the federal government and the California government maintain a list of countries that qualify for reciprocal enforcement of support orders.

A simplified procedure exists for the enforcement of child and spousal support or spousal support orders from other states by attachment of wages. Federal law requires all states to use the same form for an attachment, which must be honoured in every state. Pursuant to California statutory law, an employer in California must comply with an order for attachment of wages issued in another state for the payment of support in the same manner as the employer would comply with a California order. (FC 5230.1)

Non-support financial orders from another country must be enforced by the filing of a civil action. California's statutory procedure for enforcement of foreign-country money judgments (California Code of Civil Procedure section 1713 *et seq*) excludes from its provisions monetary orders made 'in connection with domestic relations'. California will enforce a foreign order under principles of comity, which prescribes that a court of the United States recognise the judgment of a court of a foreign nation when the foreign court had proper jurisdiction and enforcement does not prejudice the rights of United States citizens or violate domestic public policy. (*In re Stephanie M.* (1994) 7 C 4th 295). Courts have also stated that they will enforce an order which comes from 'a system of jurisprudence likely to secure an impartial administration of justice between the citizens of its own country and those of other countries'. An action to enforce a foreign order should show that the debtor had notice of the foreign proceedings and a full opportunity to participate in the proceedings.

12. FINANCIAL RELIEF AFTER FOREIGN DIVORCE PROCEEDINGS

12.1 What powers are available to make orders following a foreign divorce?

For California to have jurisdiction to modify a child support order made in a foreign jurisdiction, both parties and the child must no longer be residing in the foreign jurisdiction that issued the order or both parties must have filed written consents with the initiating jurisdiction allowing California to modify the order and assume continuing and exclusive jurisdiction. The supporting parent must also be subject to the personal jurisdiction of the California court in which the relief is sought for California to modify the order. Any aspect of the child support order that may not be modified under the law of the issuing foreign jurisdiction also may not be modified by a California court. (FC 4960(c))

FC 4910(c) provides that a California court which does not have continuing, exclusive jurisdiction over a spousal support order may not modify a spousal support order of a foreign jurisdiction. The foreign jurisdiction that issued the spousal support order has exclusive jurisdiction to modify the order, but California will enforce the spousal support order issued in the foreign jurisdiction.

D. CHILDREN

13. CUSTODY/PARENTAL RESPONSIBILITY

13.1 Briefly explain the legal position in relation to custody/parental responsibility following the breakdown of a relationship or marriage

Following the breakdown of a relationship or marriage, the court is called upon to fashion custody orders that are in the child's best interests, taking into consideration the health, safety and welfare of the child, and any history of abuse by a parent. (FC 3011.) It is the public policy of the state to assure that the health, safety and welfare of the children is the court's primary concern. (FC 3020(a).)

In awarding custody, as between the parents, there is 'neither a preference nor a presumption for or against joint legal custody, joint physical custody, or sole custody[.]' (FC 3040(a), (c).) Nor shall a parent be disqualified from receiving custody based on his or her immigration status. (FC 3040(b).) Rather, courts are conferred with the 'widest discretion to choose a parenting plan that is in the best interest of the child.' (FC 3040(c).)

There are a variety of factors a court must consider in determining the child's best interests. Among others, courts consider the presence of child abuse (FC sections 3011, 3020, 3030, 3031, 3044, and 6323), drug or alcohol abuse by either parent (FC 3041.5), the child's ability to maintain frequent and continuing contact with the non-custodial parent (FC sections 3020 and 3040); and risk of abduction by one parent (FC 3048). Factors a court is not permitted to consider in issuing custody orders include a parent's gender (FC 3040(a)(1)); one parent's superior financial conditions (*In re Marriage of Fingert* (1990) 221 CA 3d 1575); racial prejudice (see, *Palmore v Sidoti* (1984) 466 U.S. 429); and, absent a showing of harm, a parent's religious background (*In re Marriage of Mentry* (1983) 142 CA 3d 260).

In California, courts shall consider and give due weight to a child's preference if the child 'is of sufficient age and capacity to reason so as to form an intelligent preference as to custody or visitation'. (FC 3042(a).) If a child is 14 years of age or older, and wishes to address the court regarding custody or visitation, the court shall permit the child to testify unless the court finds that such testimony is not in the child's best interests. (FC 3042(c).)

13.2 Briefly explain the legal position in relation to access/contact/visitation following the breakdown of a relationship or marriage

It is also the policy of the state to 'assure that children have frequent and continuing contact with both parents...and to encourage parents to share the rights and responsibilities of child rearing in order to effect this policy[.]' (FC 3020(b).) It is well established that custody should be given to the parent who promotes frequent and continuing contact. (See *Marriage of Lewin* (1986) 186 CA 3d 1482.) While a custodial parent has the presumptive right to change the residence of the child (FC 7501), the change in residence by the custodial parent for the purpose of frustrating visitation should be considered in the court's decision to change custody. (See, *In re Marriage of Ciganovich* (1976) 61 CA 3d 289.)

Notably, although 'frequent and continuing contact' is a legislative mandate, it can not be used to overcome the presumption that awarding custody to a parent who has perpetuated domestic violence is detrimental to the child. (FC 3044 (b)(1).)

14. INTERNATIONAL ABDUCTION

14.1 Summarise the position in your jurisdiction

International abduction cases have civil and criminal remedies. The Government uses criminal processes to hold the abductor responsible for criminal parental kidnapping. A parent uses civil remedies to seek an abducted child's return.

A parent may be criminally charged under state or federal law, such as the Federal International Parental Kidnapping Crime Act (FIPKCA). The FIPKCA makes it a felony (punishable by fine and/or up to three years imprisonment) for anyone to remove or attempt to remove, or to retain a child under the age of 16 outside the US 'with intent to obstruct the lawful exercise' of parental custody or visitation rights 'arising by operation of law, court order or legally binding agreement of the parties'.

California Penal Code, sections 277 to 280 address the issue of child abduction. Section 278.5(a) states in pertinent part that: 'Every person who takes, entices away, keeps, withholds or conceals a child and maliciously deprives a lawful custodian of a right to custody, or a person of a right to visitation, shall be punished'. If charged under state law, the prosecutor may apply for a federal Unlawful Flight to Avoid Prosecution warrant if the abductor has fled the country to avoid prosecution.

Criminal charges do not address child recovery. A parent must simultaneously pursue civil means to locate and recover a child. FC sections 3130 to 3135 provide the guidelines for locating a missing child.

When children are wrongfully removed to or retained in countries that are Hague Convention treaty partners, a parent may use the Hague Convention's administrative and legal remedies to seek the child's return or access rights.

15. LEAVE TO REMOVE/APPLICATIONS TO TAKE A CHILD OUT OF THE JURISDICTION

15.1 Summarise the position in your jurisdiction

Once a family law action has been commenced in a California court, a party will become subject to the Automatic Temporary Restraining Orders (ATROs) listed on the Summons for Petition of Dissolution, Legal Separation, Nullity, to Establish Parentage. The ATROs will apply to the petitioner on the date the petition is filed and will apply to the respondent on the date that the respondent is served with the petition and summons. One of the ATROs prohibits a party from travelling outside of the State of California with the minor children without the written permission of the other party or a court order. In the event that the party will not permit the other party to temporarily travel or vacation with the minor children outside of the State of California, the party seeking to travel will need to bring an application before the court to obtain the court's permission to travel.

15.2 Under what circumstances may a parent apply to remove their child from the jurisdiction against the wishes of the other parent?

A sole primary custodial parent has a presumptive right to relocate with the minor child(ren). It is often the case that a parent will not consent to the other parent relocating with the minor children outside of California. When this occurs, the parent seeking to relocate will need to bring a request before the court on a regular motion to seek the court's permission to be able to move outside of California with the minor children. The non-custodial parent opposing the relocation may seek and obtain a custody modification based on a proper showing pursuant to the changed circumstance rule (*In re Marriage of Brown & Yana* (2006) 37 C 4th 947).

Pursuant to the case *In re Marriage of LaMusga* (2004) 32 C 4th 1072, some factors to be considered when deciding whether to modify a custody order in light of the custodial parent's proposal to change the residence of the child are:

- the reason for the proposed move;
- the children's interest in stability and continuity in the custodial arrangement;
- the distance of the move;
- the age of the children;
- the children's relationship with both parents;
- the relationship between the parents including, but not limited to, their ability to communicate and cooperate effectively and their willingness to put the interests of the children above their individual interests;
- the wishes of the children if they are mature enough for such an inquiry to be appropriate;
- the reasons for the proposed move; and
- the extent to which the parents currently are sharing custody.

Applying the aforementioned factors to the particular circumstances of any given case will often involve the court's appointment of a child custody evaluator to perform a child custody evaluation and provide written recommendations to the court as to whether or not the move is in the children's best interest. Child custody evaluations often take months to complete and a party can oppose the evaluator's recommendations and request an evidentiary hearing regarding the issues of child custody and the move-away request. A party who wishes to relocate to another jurisdiction with their minor children needs to consider bringing an application several months prior to their intended move.

E. SURROGACY AND ADOPTION

16. VALIDITY OF SURROGACY AGREEMENTS

16.1 Briefly summarise the position in your jurisdiction

California's new surrogacy statute became effective 1 January 2013. Part of the Uniform Parentage Act found at FC 7960 *et seq.*, it requires a surrogate mother and the intended parent or intended parents, as defined, to be represented by separate independent counsel of their choosing prior to executing an assisted reproduction (ART) agreement for gestational carriers, as defined. The statute also requires the ART agreement to be signed by the parties, be notarised or witnessed, and prohibits any embryo transplant procedure or injectable medication until the agreement has been fully executed pursuant to the requirements of the statute. An action to establish the parent-child relationship may be filed before the child's birth, under the new statute. An ART agreement made in compliance with the statute is not open to inspection except by the parties to the proceeding, their attorneys and the State Department of Social Services.

17. ADOPTION

17.1 Briefly explain the legal position in relation to adoption in your jurisdiction. Is adoption available to individuals, cohabiting couples (both heterosexual and same sex)?

In California, there are two basic types of adoption: independent and agency. An independent adoption is usually arranged by an attorney, with the birth and adoptive parents knowing each other or at least meeting. The birth mother must select the adopting parents in this type of adoption. In an agency adoption, the children are placed via licensed public agencies with the adopting families. They usually do not know or meet each other. The agency first requires a home study of the adoptive parent prior to placement. Then, the relinquishment of the birth mother (and the father, if available) is taken. For six months, the agency supervises the placement and then advises the court if placement should be approved. There is a brief court hearing attended by adoptive parents and the child, for approval. A child who is 12 or over must consent to their adoption.

California permits singles and single LGBT individuals to petition to adopt. In 2003, the California Supreme Court affirmed that a same-sex co-parent can petition to adopt his or her partner's child or child of the relationship (*Sharon S. v Superior Court*). Registered domestic partners can use the state's stepparent adoption laws to adopt each other's children or children of the relationship pursuant to FC 9000(b) and, of course, same-sex couples who are legally married are entitled to equal marriage rights under state law, as are same-sex couples legally married in other jurisdictions who move to California.

F. COHABITATION

18. COHABITATION

18.1 What legislation (if any) governs division of property for unmarried couples on the breakdown of the relationship?

A party to a cohabitation arrangement does not automatically have the same rights to property division and spousal support as a party to a proceeding ending a marriage. Any rights to property and support must be established by the filing of a civil lawsuit alleging breach of contract and other claims.

The basis for these claims emerges from case law and general civil law and not from the FC or any statutes specific to cohabitation. The leading case applying these general contract and civil law principles to cohabitation arrangements is *Marvin v Marvin* (1976) 18 C.3d 660, known as '*Marvin*' actions.

The cases refer to causes of action which include breach of an express contract (for example, to pool earnings or to provide support), a contract implied by the parties' conduct, action to enforce a partnership or a joint venture, or to recover the reasonable value of services rendered, among others. A contract which includes the providing of sexual services which is inseverable from the other contract provisions is unenforceable.

With regard to contracts implied by the parties' behaviour, living together is insufficient, by itself, to establish an implied contract. Other relevant factors a court will consider include the reasons the parties did not marry, how title to bank accounts are held (joint instead of separate accounts), whether the parties incurred joint or separate debts, the parties' pooling of finances to purchase property, how title to property (joint ownership) is held, joint interest in a business venture, an understanding between the parties to share profits and losses, and joint or shared rights of control over a business.

G. FAMILY DISPUTE RESOLUTION

19. MEDIATION, COLLABORATIVE LAW AND ARBITRATION

19.1 Briefly summarise the non-court-based processes available in your jurisdiction and the current status of agreements reached under the auspices of mediation, collaborative law and arbitration

Mediation is governed by the California statutes and the case law interpreting those statutes. The concept of mediation is that of confidentiality. All statements and offers made in mediation are precluded from being introduced into evidence at a hearing unless both parties have waived the mediation confidentiality privilege. This creates a setting wherein both parties may attempt to make concessions and offers to resolve an issue, which otherwise they may not for fear that the court will be made aware of the offer. The mediation statutes are contained in California Evidence Code sections 703.5 and 1115 to 1128. Mediation is required by the California court with a court-provided mediation service prior to the court hearing any requests regarding child custody pursuant to FC 3183. Depending on the county in which the matter is heard, the mediator may be required to submit a recommendation to the court as to the custody or visitation issues.

19.2. What is the statutory basis (if any), for mediation, collaborative law and arbitration in your jurisdiction? In particular, are the parties required to attempt a family dispute resolution in advance of proceedings?

The Collaborative Law process is governed by the Collaborative Family Law Act set forth in FC 2013, in which 'the parties and any professionals (their lawyers, accountant, family counselors, etc) engaged by the parties to assist them to use their best efforts and to make a good faith attempt to resolve disputes related to their dissolution, legal separation or nullity matter' on an agreed basis without resorting to adversary judicial intervention. (FC 2013 (b).) Attorneys representing clients in a collaborative process are not considered attorneys of record, but are considered advisory attorneys. While a case is in a 'collaborative process' pursuant to written agreement of the parties, no contested matters may be filed. If an action is filed, the collaborative process is automatically terminated.

Arbitration may be ordered by the court as judicial arbitration in civil matters but not in family law matters. Parties in a family law proceeding may enter into a private arbitration agreement to expedite the resolution process. Private arbitration is governed by Code of Civil Procedure section 1280 *et seq.* and is a binding agreement between the parties to submit to arbitration.

H. OTHER

20. CIVIL PARTNERSHIP/SAME-SEX MARRIAGE

20.1 What is the status of civil partnership/same-sex marriage within the jurisdiction?

Effective from 1 January 2005, California enacted domestic partnership legislation, which provides to same-sex partners who register with the office of the Secretary of State significant benefits similar to legal marriage. The same domestic partnership rights are also afforded to different sex couples when one of the partners is over age 62. These include rights *vis-a-vis* the birth of children during the registered domestic partnership, rights of support, accumulation of most property and related issues.

Issues also exist as to whether the new rights and duties emanating from the law, which became effective 1 January 2005, are retroactive to certain earlier dates. The retroactivity of such provisions remains unsettled.

Those persons registered with the State of California prior to 1 January 2005 were sent letters from the Secretary of State letting those partners know that they had the opportunity to opt out of the new law, but that if the partners did not opt out, the expanded rights and duties imposed on registered domestic partners as of 1 January 2005 would automatically apply to them. This process has resulted in unintended consequences in that many persons did not become aware of their rights and/or responsibilities upon the enactment of the new law, therefore, they did not opt out and are now included under the new, expanded law automatically.

On 26 June, 2013, the US Supreme Court issued a ruling in the case of *United States v Windsor,* which held as unconstitutional a key provision of the federal law known as the Defense of Marriage Act (DOMA). The Court held that Section 3 of DOMA, which provided that the US Government need not recognise nor provide benefits to same-sex married couples, was unconstitutional. The *Windsor* decision considered only the constitutionality of the subject provision of DOMA, and did not specifically address federal recognition of domestic partnerships and civil unions. The *Windsor* decision also did not consider the constitutionality of one state refusing to recognise a same-sex marriage contracted in another state for purposes of state law. The *Windsor* decision will allow married same-sex couples to have the same federal tax and property rights as married couples of the opposite sex.

On 26 June, 2013, in connection with a case arising from a challenge to the ballot initiative passed in 2008 known as Proposition 8, which outlawed same-sex marriages in the State of California, the US Supreme Court issued a ruling which permitted same-sex marriages to resume in California. Therefore, the current state of the law in California allows same-sex couples to marry in California.

20.2 What legislation governs civil partnership/same-sex marriage?

The FC applies to domestic partnership. The legislation that addresses registration, termination and the legal effect of registration is found in the FC sections 297 through to 299.6. FC 300 defines marriage as *'a personal relation arising out of a civil contract between a man and a woman, to which the consent of the parties capable of making that contract is necessary'.*

FC 308 states that California shall recognise marriages between two people of the same sex where the marriage is contracted outside of California and is valid in the jurisdiction in which the marriage was contracted. FC 2320 allows for two people of the same sex to be divorced in California if the marriage was entered into in California (during the brief time period such marriages were allowed) and neither party resides in a jurisdiction that will dissolve the marriage.

21. CONTROVERSIAL AREA/RAPIDLY DEVELOPING AREAS OF LAW

21.1 Is there a particular area of the law within the jurisdiction that is currently undergoing major change?

An area of California community property law which is unsettled and undergoing change is that of the fiduciary duty owed between spouses during marriage. FC 721(b) provides that spouses are subject to the general rules governing fiduciary relationships of persons in confidential relationships and are subject to the same duties of non-marital business partners as provided in certain California Corporations Code sections. The enumerated duties referenced deal with rendering, upon request, information about transactions concerning marital property, providing access to books and records and providing an accounting or holding profits derived from marital property for the benefit of the other spouse.

A breach of a fiduciary duty by one spouse gives the other an array of remedies ranging up to an award of 100 per cent of any asset not disclosed to the other spouse. FC 721 and related statutes were enacted in 1992, but few California family law cases construing the statutes have been published to date.

21.2 Which areas of law are most out of step? Which areas would you most like to see reformed/changed?

Same-sex marriage is an area of the law that is undergoing major change but is still out of step with the needs of clients. The court's *Windsor* ruling did not hold that same-sex couples have an affirmative constitutional right to marry. States in which same-sex marriage is not legal may still refuse to provide state benefits to legally married couples of another state.

USA – Connecticut

Nusbaum & Parrino PC
Edward Nusbaum & Thomas P. Parrino

PREFACE

Any practitioner or student of international matrimonial law recognises that summaries of the law in any jurisdiction are a gloss on the law, presenting a shiny, but deceptive simplicity. Our statutory law bristles with cross-references among the statutes, while reference to our case law, as in many jurisdictions, is necessary to determine interpretation and application of the statutes, particularly where our statutes use terms of art or different words to refer to the same concept. Thus we offer cautionary advice that this comparative law study is insufficient to guide the practitioner whose client seeks relief under Connecticut family law.

In Connecticut family law statutes, 'foreign' refers to another state in the United States. For clarity in the context of this volume comparing family laws internationally, we have substituted 'another US state' or 'other US states' where our statutes refer to 'foreign' and reserve foreign in this summary to refer to a sovereign country other than the United States. And, we have substituted 'divorce' where Connecticut uses 'dissolution' or 'dissolution of marriage'.

A. JURISDICTION AND CONFLICT OF LAW

1. SOURCES OF LAW

1.1 What is the primary source of law in relation to the breakdown of marriage and the welfare of children within the jurisdiction?

Connecticut family law is statutory. Family law matters are heard by the Family Division of our Superior Court, (after this, Family Court), by our Probate Courts, and by the Family Support Magistrate Division of the Superior Court.

1.2 Which are the main statutes governing matrimonial law in the jurisdiction?

Connecticut General Statutes [CGS] Title 46b, Family Law, organises our family law statutes under the following topics:

- Court Proceedings in Family Relations Matters
- Family Matters
- Marriage
- Civil Union [repealed]
- [Divorce], Legal Separation and Annulment
  - I. General Provisions
  - II. Enforcement of [Other US States] Matrimonial Judgments

III. Support of Child and Spouse, Transfer of Property

- Uniform Child Custody Jurisdiction and Enforcement Act
  I. General Provisions
  II. Jurisdiction
  III. Enforcement
  IV. [Other US States] Child Custody
- Juvenile Matters
  I. General Provisions
  II. Interstate Compact for Juveniles
- Paternity Matters
- Support
  I. Uniform Reciprocal Enforcement of Support
  II. Uniform Interstate Family Support Act
  III. Obligation of Relatives
  IV. Family Support Magistrate's Act

CGS Title 46b Sections 231-236 provide for the duties and powers of the Family Support Magistrate Division. Family support magistrates are charged with enforcing child and spousal support per orders issued by the Family Court, and, under the Uniform Reciprocal Support Act, child and spousal support orders issued by both other US states and by foreign countries.

CGS Title 45a, Probate Courts and Procedure, sets our Probate Courts' authority regarding adoption and termination of parental rights.

Appeals of matters originating in the Probate Courts or Family Support Magistrates' Courts are first heard in the Family Court.

2. JURISDICTION

2.1 What are the main jurisdictional requirements for the institution of proceedings in relation to divorce, property and children?

The Family Court has exclusive subject matter jurisdiction of all complaints for divorce, annulment, or legal separation, and the associated issues of maintenance, property division, and custody of children.

A person need only be a resident of Connecticut to file a complaint for divorce and obtain temporary orders for spousal and/or child maintenance, but, domicile must be established for the court to issue a judgment of divorce, including custody, distribution of property, and permanent maintenance. Domicile may be established by residency in Connecticut for 12 months prior to filing the complaint, or 12 months prior to the date the Family Court issues the divorce decree.

Jurisdiction may be contested at any time during the pendency of a family law matter. A party who enters an appearance (notification to the court of self-representation or representation by an attorney) in response to process notifying them of a family law proceeding waives any defects in process, but does not waive either domicile or subject matter jurisdiction. There is no need to file a special appearance to contest domicile or subject matter jurisdiction.

Under both Connecticut's version of the Uniform Child Custody Jurisdiction and Enforcement Act, (UCCJEA), and Connecticut's version of the Uniform Interstate Family Support Act (UIFSA), both of which provide jurisdiction to enforce foreign country's orders concerning the care, custody, education, visitation and/or support of a minor child, jurisdiction is based on the child's residency in Connecticut for more than six months.

Under both the UCCJEA and UIFSA, Connecticut's jurisdiction is subject to a factual hearing to determine whether another US state or foreign country has entered orders concerning the child, whether the other US state's or foreign country's orders comport with certain due process and Connecticut public policy, and/or whether the child's presence is the result of 'unjustifiable conduct' on the part of the person bringing the child to Connecticut from another US state or foreign country.

And, in any case, the Family Court may assert temporary emergency jurisdiction whenever a child has been abandoned or is under threat of abuse, harm, or mistreatment.

3. DOMICILE AND HABITUAL RESIDENCE

3.1 Explain the concepts of domicile and habitual residence as they apply to the jurisdiction in relation to divorce, the finances and children

Domicile consists of actual residence in Connecticut joined with the intention of permanently remaining. A person's domicile persists until the person acquires a new domicile, thus proof of acquisition of the new domicile requires evidence of abandonment of the old.

Residence is not coupled with intent. For instance, as mentioned above in 2.1, a person who is resident in the State of Connecticut finds jurisdiction in the Family Court for filing a divorce action and obtaining temporary alimony and support, but must establish domicile to obtain a final judgment.

Residency is a fact determination based on a wide variety of factors, none of which have markedly more weight than any other. A sample of factors considered:

- the real property the individual owns or rents in the state;
- the frequency and amount of time present in the state;
- the state authority to which the individual pays resident income taxes;
- the address the individual states on tax returns, bank statements and on other forms or correspondence critical to the individual's public and private financial obligations;
- the address the individual states in the individual's correspondence to and from federal and state public agencies or authorities;
- the address on the individual's automobile registration;
- the state from which the individual receives public benefits;
- the address where the individual spends the most time when not working;
- whether the individual is listed in a Connecticut phone directory;
- whether the individual has been called for jury duty; and
- where the individual registered to vote in state and local elections.

The Family Court need not have personal jurisdiction over the non-resident and/or non-appearing spouse to enter final judgment of divorce, so long as requirements of process have been met. To enter final orders of alimony, custody and distribution of assets, however, the Family Court must have personal jurisdiction over both parties.

4. CONFLICT OF LAW/APPLICABLE LAW TO BE APPLIED

4.1 What happens when one party applies to stay proceedings in favour of a foreign jurisdiction?

Family Courts may grant a motion for stay because of family law proceedings in another US state, but must enter a stay where a matrimonial judgment in the other US state is under appeal. There are no statutory provisions governing response to a motion for stay based on matrimonial proceedings pending in a foreign country, nor is there guiding principle in case law.

4.2 What factors will the local court take into account when determining forum issues?

Any list of factors would be incomplete because the Family Court is not limited in considering factors the court may deem relevant. The following list of 'inconvenient forum' factors found in Connecticut's adoption of the Uniform Child Custody Enforcement and Jurisdiction Act is a useful, but not definitive, reference. (In this context, 'state' means both other US states and foreign countries.)

- whether family violence has occurred and is likely to continue in the future and which state could best protect the parties and the child;
- the length of time the child has resided outside this state;
- the distance between the court in this state and the court in the state that would assume jurisdiction;
- the relative financial circumstances of the parties;
- any agreement of the parties as to which state should assume jurisdiction;
- the nature and location of the evidence required to resolve the pending litigation, including testimony of the child;
- the ability of the court of each state to decide the issue expeditiously and the procedures necessary to present the evidence; and
- the familiarity of the court of each state with the facts and issues in the pending litigation.

B. PRE- AND POST-NUPTIAL AGREEMENTS

5. VALIDITY OF PRE- AND POST-NUPTIAL AGREEMENTS

5.1 To what extent are pre- and post-nups binding within the jurisdiction?

Pre-nuptial and post-nuptial agreements are valid and binding in Connecticut if the trial court finds the agreement enforceable at the time of divorce.

Enforcement of pre-nuptial agreements depends on the date of execution. Our Supreme Court's decision in *McHugh v McHugh*, 181 Conn. 482 (1980), governs enforcement of pre-nuptial agreements executed before 1 October, 1995, while Connecticut's Premarital Agreement Act, CGS Title 46b Sections

36g, *et seq.*, governs the enforcement of agreements executed on or after 1 October, 1995.

Until recently, post-nuptial agreements have been enforced, if at all, on a case-by-case basis. Our Supreme Court has now formally provided for the validity and enforceability of post-nuptial agreements, but requires standards for enforcement more rigorous than those for pre-nuptial agreements. *Bedrick v Bedrick*, 300 Conn. 691(2011).

Enforcement of both is dependent on Connecticut's 'second look' doctrine, which allows the court, as a matter of law, to determine whether the pre- or post-nuptial agreement concerned is unconscionable at the time of enforcement in addition to determining whether the agreement met the formation, disclosure and fairness tests at the time the parties signed the agreement.

5.2 Could you provide a brief discussion of the most significant recent case law on this issue?

Our Supreme Court recently ruled that determining unconscionability at the time of enforcement depends on four factors:

- the parties' intent and circumstances when they signed the agreement;
- the circumstances of the parties at the time of the divorce;
- whether those circumstances are so far beyond the contemplation of the parties at the time of execution; and
- if the circumstances are beyond the parties' initial contemplation, whether enforcement would cause an injustice.

In the same breath, the Supreme Court reminded that 'courts of law must allow parties to make their own contracts... whether provident or improvident, an agreement moved on calculated considerations is entitled to the sanction of law'. *Crews v Crews*, 295 Conn. 153 (2010)

The leading case in Connecticut on the Premarital Agreement Act resulted from the Supreme Court's review of our trial of *Friezo v Friezo*, where the opposing party contested enforceability. The Supreme Court reversed the trial court's finding that the agreement was unenforceable, substantiating our points in our final argument at trial. Two critical points were that '...a 'reasonable opportunity to consult with independent counsel' means simply that the party against who enforcement is sought must have had sufficient time before the marriage to consult with an attorney other than the attorney representing the party's future spouse' and that '...it is the party's responsibility to delay the signing of an agreement that is not understood'. *Friezo v Friezo*, 281 Conn. 166, 204 (2006). This significantly limited the scope of grounds for challenging pre-nuptial agreements under the Act where the contesting party asserts micro-compliance based on the party's subjective perceptions of the quality of advice and/or disclosure.

C. DIVORCE, NULLITY AND JUDICIAL SEPARATION

6. RECOGNITION OF FOREIGN MARRIAGES/DIVORCES

6.1 Summarise the position in your jurisdiction

To determine the validity of a marriage in a foreign country, Connecticut will look for compliance with the civil law of the foreign country or political subdivision.

Where a 'citizen of Connecticut' is a party to a marriage in a foreign country, or under the auspices of certain officers or licensed clergymen in US consular jurisdictions, the marriage is valid.

Connecticut recognises divorce decrees from foreign countries, and, usually, the mandates and dispositions in those decrees. The recognition of a foreign divorce decree, whether determining status, child custody, alimony, and/or child support requires registration of the decree with our courts. The registration may be made simultaneously with a motion requesting relief.

7. DIVORCE

7.1 Explain the grounds for divorce within the jurisdiction (please also deal with nullity and judicial separation if appropriate)

CGS Section 46b-40, states the grounds for divorce, annulment, and legal separation.

(a) A marriage is dissolved only by
  (1) the death of one of the parties; or
  (2) a decree of annulment or dissolution of the marriage by a court of competent jurisdiction.

(b) An annulment shall be granted if the marriage is void or voidable under the laws of this state or of the state in which the marriage was performed.

(c) A decree of dissolution of a marriage or a decree of legal separation shall be granted upon a finding that one of the following causes has occurred:
  (1) the marriage has broken down irretrievably; ['no fault']
  (2) the parties have lived apart by reason of incompatibility for a continuous period of at least the 18 months immediately prior to the service of the complaint and that there is no reasonable prospect that they will be reconciled;
  (3) adultery;
  (4) fraudulent contract;
  (5) wilful desertion for one year with total neglect of duty;
  (6) seven years' absence, during all of which period the absent party has not been heard from;
  (7) habitual intemperance;
  (8) intolerable cruelty;
  (9) sentence to imprisonment for life or the commission of any infamous crime involving a violation of conjugal duty and punishable by imprisonment for a period in excess of one year;
  (10) legal confinement in a hospital or hospitals or other similar institution or institutions, because of mental illness, for at least an accumulated period totaling five years within the period of six years next preceding the date of the complaint.

Virtually all complaints for divorce in Connecticut allege the no fault grounds in the form 'the marriage has broken down irretrievably, with no hope of reconciliation'. Allegation of irretrievable breakdown by one spouse is sufficient, notwithstanding the opinion or objection of the other.

Connecticut's statute listing 'Kindred Who May Not Marry' provides the only statutory grounds for annulment. Common law claims for annulment based on fraud are largely unsuccessful because Connecticut embraces the concept that the fraud must involve the 'essentialia [sic] of the marriage' and because fraud must be proved by clear and convincing evidence.

8. FINANCES/CAPITAL, PROPERTY

8.1 What powers does the court have to allocate financial resources and property on the breakdown of marriage?

Connecticut is an equitable distribution state. Upon personal jurisdiction over both parties to a divorce, annulment or legal separation, the Family Court has full authority to make a fair and equitable distribution of all real and personal property in which the divorcing spouses have an interest, individually or jointly, without regard to title or location, sometimes referred to as an 'all property' equitable division scheme.

Family Courts zealously guard the assets in the marital estate during the pendency of the divorce by application of the courts' 'Automatic Orders', imposed at the beginning of the divorce process. The orders preserve the financial status quo until the court issues final judgment. A violator is subject to contempt of court. The Family Court's statutory authority to order the division of assets, however, exists only on the date of dissolution. Accordingly, the value of the assets subject to division is their value on the date of divorce.

Per CGS Title 46b Section 81(c), the Family Court must consider the following statutory factors when determining division of assets.

- length of the marriage;
- causes for the dissolution of marriage [fault];
- age;
- health;
- station [standard of living];
- vocational skills;
- occupation;
- employability;
- estate;
- liabilities;
- needs of each of the parties;
- opportunity of each for future acquisition of capital assets and income;
- contribution of each of the parties in the acquisition, preservation or appreciation in value of their respective estates.

We note that where the last factor specifies 'contribution of each of the parties…' the Family Court considers both financial and non-financial contributions, specifically including a spouse's responsibilities for raising children and maintaining a home, while the other spouse earns the family's income.

The Court needs only to state in its memorandum of decision that the Court considered each factor, and our Appellate and Supreme Courts give considerable deference to the Family Court's judgment in determining the division of assets repeatedly reaffirming that: 'Our standard of review in domestic relations cases is a very narrow one. We will not reverse a trial court's rulings with regard to... financial orders unless the court incorrectly applied the law or could not reasonably have concluded as it did'.

8.2 Explain and illustrate with reference to recent cases the court's thinking on division of assets

The Family Court's thinking on division, or not, of certain assets has been fairly fixed in certain areas. For instance:

- Premarital assets and inherited funds are part of the marital estate, and may be divided by the Family Court in the Court's discretion.
- A professional's licence to practise law, medicine, dentistry, or the like, has no monetary value, therefore the Court cannot compensate, by division of other assets, a spouse's financial and/or non-financial support of the other spouse's education in pursuit of the licence. *Simmons v Simmons*, 244 Conn. 158 (1998).
- A beneficiary's interest in a will of a living person is not divisible in a divorce because the beneficiary has only a 'mere expectancy'. *Rubin v Rubin*, 204 Conn. 224 (1987).

Our Supreme Court later added unvested awards of compensation for future services to the 'mere expectancy' category. *Bornemann v Bornemann*, 245 Conn. 508 (1998)

We gained the first successful application of the Court's ruling when we successfully argued the principle should apply to a husband's unvested stock options awarded during the marriage for our client's future services. The Family Court agreed, as did the Appellate Court on appeal. *Hopfer v Hopfer* 59 Conn. App. 452, 458 (2000). Language stating that restricted stock and/or stock options were awarded 'for future services only', began to appear in corporate documents.

But the law did not remain settled. The Supreme Court subsequently upheld a Family Court's award to the wife of a proportional share of the husband's unvested municipal fireman's pension, despite the fact the husband had yet to perform six of the 25 years of employment that would vest the pension benefits. The definition of property advanced by the Supreme Court appeared to undermine precedent. *Bender v Bender*, 258 Conn. 733 (2001).

The Appellate Court subsequently upheld a Family Court's determination that future contributions to a pension made after the divorce can be considered property subject to equitable distribution. *Ranfone v Ranfone*, 103, Conn. App. 243 (2007). In the same year, the Appellate Court held that an 'unvested investment certificate' 80 per cent earned during the marriage, but to which the husband had no enforceable right, was subject to division. *Czarzasty v Czarzasty*, 101 Conn. App. 583 (2007). Our Supreme Court declined review, letting stand the Appellate Court's observation in *Czarzasty* that:

'...Our Supreme Court's precedents seem] to have recast the analysis used to

determine whether an interest or benefit is property... to a more probabilistic assessment untethered to the existence of a presently existing enforceable right. ... (Family Courts] must make an assessment on a case-by-case basis of the likelihood of the person's receiving the asset claimed by his or her spouse. If the likelihood is not too speculative, then it is property subject to valuation and distribution.'

9. FINANCES/MAINTENANCE

As maintenance takes the form of alimony, child support, or unallocated alimony and child support, the following addresses common elements among the three.

Spousal and child maintenance is based on a party's 'continuing duty to support', a phrase embedded in the Connecticut law of maintenance.

US federal income tax and Connecticut state income tax regulations have a significant role in the award of maintenance. Alimony awarded to a spouse reduces the payor's taxable income and increases the payee's taxable income. Child support does not reduce the payor's taxable income and does not increase the payee's income. If a child support payor has a combined effective annual federal and state tax rate of 30 per cent, then the payor must earn $1,300 to pay each $1,000 of child support, while the payee need not report the $1,000 received on the payee's income tax returns.

Where the case permits an exception to the Child Support Guidelines (see 10.1, below), the court may order 'unallocated alimony and child support', which, like alimony, reduces the taxable income of the payor and increases the taxable income of the payee. In most cases, the tax effects of an order of unallocated alimony and child support mean the payor, usually having a higher effective tax rate, can pay more to the payee, usually having a lower effective tax rate, than if alimony and child support were awarded separately, increasing the net after-tax income for both.

Notwithstanding the tax regulations, our courts have discretion to direct that the award of alimony, or unallocated alimony and child support, shall be taxable to the payor and non-taxable to the payee.

A party may move for modification of temporary or permanent maintenance based upon a 'substantial change in circumstances'. Any modification may be retroactive to the date the proponent served the motion for modification. The proponent must first show that the instant circumstances demonstrate a 'substantial change' in circumstances compared with the circumstances pertaining at the time of the previous maintenance order. Only changes in financial status occurring since the time of the prior maintenance order may be considered.

9.1 Explain the operation of maintenance for spouses on an ongoing basis after the breakdown of marriage

Our Appellate Court recently and concisely stated the purpose of spousal maintenance:

'[T]he purpose of alimony [is] the obligation of support that spouses assume toward each other by virtue of the marriage. ...This court has stated that... [a]limony is always represented by money and is damages to compensate for loss of marital support and maintenance. ...In other words, alimony represents the court's finding, measured in dollars, of the financial needs of the receiving spouse at the time of the [divorce].' (Internal citations and quotation marks omitted.) *Wiegand v Wiegand*, 129 Conn. App. 526, 535-36 (2011).

Per CGS 46b-83, the court must consider the following statutory factors in determining the term and amount of alimony: (see 10.1, below, for the factors considered in awarding child support)

- the length of the marriage;
- the causes for the ... [divorce] ... ([fault]);
- the age;
- health;
- station;
- occupation;
- amount and sources of income;
- vocational skills;
- employability;
- estate;
- the needs of each of the parties;
- the award, if any, which the court may make pursuant to Section 46b-81; and
- in the case of a parent to whom the custody of minor children has been awarded, the desirability of such parent's securing employment.

The factors apply in determinations of both temporary and permanent alimony, except 'cause of the breakdown of the marriage' is omitted in temporary alimony hearings. We note in this context that Connecticut's trial courts are split on the authority of the court to order a party to pay temporary alimony from assets.

No formula or presumptions direct the court's determination of the amount and term of alimony. Neither the statute nor our appellate courts specify the weight to be given to any factor.

The statutory factors mandated for awarding alimony differ from the statutory factors mandated for dividing assets, only in that the factor 'contribution of each of the parties in the acquisition, preservation or appreciation in value of their respective estates', applies to division of assets only.

9.2 Is it common for maintenance to be awarded?

The award of temporary and permanent alimony, child support, or unallocated alimony and child support, is common to all Connecticut divorces.

9.3 Explain and illustrate with reference to recent cases the court's thinking on maintenance

Our courts may order alimony based on a party's 'earning capacity', which may be determined by the court from the facts of the case.

'While there is no fixed standard for determination of an individual's earning

capacity, it is well settled that earning capacity is not any amount which a person can theoretically earn, nor is it confined to actual income, but rather it is an amount which a person can realistically be expected to earn considering such things as his vocational skills, employability, age and health.' (Citations omitted; internal quotation marks omitted). *Bleuer v Bleuer*, 59 Conn. App. 167, 170 (2000).

Ordering sale of an asset to pay alimony post judgment is not permissible, but the court may order an alimony award that has the effect of causing the payor to convert or deplete assets. *Simms v Simms*, 283 Conn. 494 (2007).

Recent case law appears to imply that a court may order alimony in excess of a party's needs. *Dan v Dan*, 137 Conn. App. 728 (2012), but our Supreme Court has now taken the matter on appeal. If the implications of the Appellate Court's decision pass muster with the Supreme Court, the Family court's discretion in alimony matters would expand considerably.

In a case involving a remarkably wealthy family, this firm argued the wife's claim for temporary maintenance for herself and her children, aggressively emphasising the statutory factors 'station' and 'needs of each of the parties'. The resulting decision by the court awarded the wife non-taxable unallocated alimony and child support in the amount of $273,000 per month, ($3,276,000 per year, non-taxable), the highest reported award of temporary support in US history.

10. CHILD MAINTENANCE

10.1 On what basis is child maintenance calculated within the jurisdiction?

Child maintenance, except in certain limited circumstances, terminates when the child concerned reaches the age of 18 or graduates from secondary education (high school, 12th grade), whichever is later, but in no event later than the child's 19th birthday. Unallocated alimony and child support often terminates more than six months after a child turns 18 because of certain presumptions in our federal tax code that must be avoided.

Our statutes require that the court consider the following factors in awarding child maintenance:

- the age;
- health;
- station;
- occupation;
- earning capacity;
- amount and sources of income;
- estate;
- vocational skills and employability of each of the parents; and
- the age, health, station, occupation, educational status and expectation, amount and sources of income, vocational skills, employability, estate and needs of the child.

Up to a combined parental net income of $4,000 per week, Connecticut courts determine child support by application of Connecticut's Child Support Guidelines, which specify what income shall be considered in calculating the average net weekly income of each parent and the amount of child support that must be ordered based on the net average weekly income and number of minor children. Use of the Guidelines is mandatory.

A simplified example:

In a family with two children, the father earns $75,000 per year, and the mother works part time to earn $28,000 per year. After calculations per Connecticut's Child Support Guidelines Worksheet:
The combined weekly NET income of the parties = $1,550
The basic child support obligation from the Guidelines table = $373
The mother's share of the basic child support obligation is 32 per cent, $119
The father's share of the basic child support obligation is 68 per cent, $254
Assuming the children reside primarily with the mother, and assuming there are no allowable deviations from the Guidelines, the father will pay child support to the mother in the amount of $254 per week, $1,101 per month.

If the parties' total net weekly income exceeds $4,000 per week, the presumptive child support is the maximum amount provided for in the child support guidelines, (one child, $473/wk.; two children, $636/wk.; ...six children, $916/wk.). The court must have evidence of needs of the children that exceed the presumptive amount to award a higher amount.

The Child Support Guidelines provide specified exceptions that allow the court to deviate from the mandated guideline amounts, but the Court must review and approve such deviations. Among the reasons for deviation are: other financial resources available to a parent, extraordinary expenses for care and maintenance of a child, extraordinary parental expenses and coordination of total family support.

11. RECIPROCAL ENFORCEMENT OF FINANCIAL ORDERS

11.1 Summarise the position in your jurisdiction

Connecticut's strong public policy is that obligors should pay their child and spousal support obligations.

Connecticut's implementation of the Uniform Interstate Family Support Act (UIFSA) provides for enforcement of orders made by another 'state', and includes foreign countries in the definition of 'state'.

12. FINANCIAL RELIEF AFTER FOREIGN DIVORCE PROCEEDINGS

12.1 What powers are available to make orders following a foreign divorce?

Per statute, a 'support order' is '...a judgment, decree, order or directive whether temporary, final or subject to modification, issued by a tribunal for the benefit of a child, a spouse or a former spouse, which provides for monetary support, health care, arrearages or reimbursement, and may include related costs and fees, interest, income withholding, attorney's fees and other relief'.

A 'tribunal' is '...a court, administrative agency or quasi-judicial entity authorised to establish, enforce or modify support orders or to determine paternity'.

Accordingly, assuming proper registration and the Family Court's recognition of the foreign order per the terms of the UIFSA, the Family Court may exercise all statutory and inherent powers to enforce the child and spousal support orders, including wage withholding and penalties for civil contempt.

D. CHILDREN

13. CUSTODY/PARENTAL RESPONSIBILITY

13.1 Briefly explain the legal position in relation to custody/parental responsibility following the breakdown of a relationship or marriage

From our point of view, the phrase 'custody/parental responsibility' appearing in 13.1 embraces all the concepts represented by the phrase 'access, contact, visitation' in 13.2, thus we see no distinction between 13.1 and 13.2.

13.2 Briefly explain the legal position in relation to access, contact, visitation following the breakdown of a relationship or marriage

Our statutes require that, where children are involved in the divorce, the parents must attend Connecticut's Parenting Education Program, and must, by the 90th day after the process has been returned to the court, establish a temporary parenting plan that attends to the needs and best interests of the children. If the parents cannot agree on a parenting plan by the 90th day, the Family Court orders the parents to undergo mediation and counseling with the Court's Family Services Division. If the mediation is unsuccessful, the court, based in part on the report provided by the Family Services Division, must order a temporary parenting plan. The temporary parenting plan ordered by the Court must conform to numerous, detailed factors listed in CGS Title 46b Section 56, which are both too complex and too lengthy to summarise here.

14. INTERNATIONAL ABDUCTION

14.1 Summarise the position in your jurisdiction

CGS Title 46b Section 115jj provides for enforcement of foreign child custody orders under the Hague Convention:

'A court of this state shall enforce a foreign child custody determination or an order of a federal court or [another US State] court for return of a child under The Hague Convention on the Civil Aspects of International Child Abduction made under factual circumstances in substantial conformity with the jurisdictional standards of this chapter, including reasonable notice and opportunity to be heard to all affected persons, as a child custody determination of another state under sections 46b-115u to 46b-115gg, inclusive, unless such determination was rendered under child custody law which violates fundamental principles of human rights or unless such determination is repugnant to the public policy of this state.'

15. LEAVE TO REMOVE/APPLICATIONS TO TAKE A CHILD OUT OF THE JURISDICTION

15.1 Summarise the position in your jurisdiction

The courts' Automatic Orders direct that neither parent may permanently move the child(ren) from Connecticut during the pendency of the divorce.

The parents may include provisions for traveling with the child(ren) outside Connecticut in their temporary parenting plan, and the court may order same if the parents are unable to agree on a parenting plan. Restrictions on travel depend on the facts of the case.

15.2 Under what circumstances may a parent apply to remove their child from the jurisdiction against the wishes of the other parent?

Where consent is not given by voluntary agreement between the parties, the issue is brought before the court by motion. If the parties are subsequently unable to agree through mediation by the Family Services Division, the Court adjudicates the issue.

In high conflict custody cases, where the parents are unable to agree at all on custody and parenting of the children, the parties, Guardian Ad Litem, attorney for the minor child, and attorneys for the parties attempt to negotiate agreement for such trips, resorting to the court if agreement cannot be achieved. Voluntary agreements in such circumstances tend to be stipulations between the parties that are presented to, reviewed, approved, and ordered by the court. Failure to obey the resulting court order subjects the violator to contempt of court.

E. SURROGACY AND ADOPTION

16. VALIDITY OF SURROGACY AGREEMENTS

16.1 Briefly summarise the position in your jurisdiction

Connecticut recognises surrogacy agreements, referring to them primarily as 'gestational agreements'.

Our Supreme Court's ruling in *Roftopol v Ramey*, 299 Conn. 691 (2011), established that, even when the intended parents have no biological relationship to the child, if two partners, [sex of the partners is irrelevant], have a valid surrogacy agreement in Connecticut, they are legally entitled to have both names put on the birth certificate, which establishes both as the legal parents prior to the child's birth.

In the course of the opinion, the Court summarised Connecticut law:

'Our statutes and case law establish that a gestational carrier who bears no biological relationship to the child she has carried does not have parental rights with respect to that child. Raftopol, supra, at 690.... [CGS Section] 7-48a allows an intended parent who is a party to a valid gestational agreement to become a parent without first adopting the children, without respect to that intended parent's genetic relationship to the children.' Raftopol, supra, at 698.

Accordingly, adoption procedures do not apply to a child born pursuant to a gestational agreement.

17. ADOPTION

17.1 Briefly summarise the position in relation to adoption in your jurisdiction. Is adoption available to individuals, cohabiting couples (both heterosexual and same-sex)?

Connecticut law provides for three types of adoptions:

(1) statutory parent adoptions;
(2) stepparent adoptions; and
(3) blood relative adoptions.

Statutory parent

The birth parents agree on an adoption plan. Following the birth of the child the Probate Court will, after certain procedures and reports, terminate the parental rights of the birth parents, and appoint a private or state child-placing agency as statutory parent of the child. The agency will then monitor the placement and adjustment of the child in the adoptive home for a specified period of time before the adoption becomes final.

Stepparent adoptions

Where the child is not related to the adopting parents, the adoption must be from an appropriate private or state child-placing agency.

Blood relative adoptions

Connecticut law supports the mutual identification of birth parents and perspective adoptive parents, but a licenced agency must be involved in the process and a placement may only occur with a family whose home has been approved by a licenced agency.

F. COHABITATION

18. COHABITATION

18.1 What legislation (if any) governs division of property for unmarried couples on the breakdown of the relationship?

There is no legislation governing the division of property between unmarried couples.

G. FAMILY DISPUTE RESOLUTION

19. MEDIATION, COLLABORATIVE LAW AND ARBITRATION

19.1 Briefly summarise the non-court-based processes available in your jurisdiction and the current status of agreements reached under the auspices of mediation, collaborative law and arbitration

Many family law attorneys in Connecticut provide 'collaborative law' services, where, in the most common design, the parties to the divorce have individual 'consulting counsel' but attempt to work out disputes with the aid of the collaborative attorney and/or other social or financial counselors allied with the collaborative process. Our firm advises against such collaborative law services because financial disclosure is voluntary and the advice of the 'consulting attorney' is confined by the client's knowledge, limited negotiating skills and emotional involvement.

Retired judges and family attorneys offer professional mediation services to resolve either particular disputes or to resolve the entire case. The process is confidential, non-binding, and frequently successful. Reference to these mediators as 'private judges' is appropriate.

19.2 What is the statutory basis (if any), for mediation, collaborative law and arbitration in your jurisdiction? In particular, are the parties required to attempt a family dispute resolution in advance of the institution of proceedings?

There is no requirement for family dispute resolution prior to instituting proceedings. When proceedings have been instituted, if the dispute is not solely a matter of law, the court requires that the parties attempt resolution of the matter by mediation in the Family Services Division. If the mediation by Family Services is unsuccessful, the court proceeds to adjudicate the dispute.

H. OTHER

20. CIVIL PARTNERSHIP/SAME-SEX MARRIAGE

20.1 What is the status of civil partnership/same-sex marriage within the jurisdiction?

Connecticut has repealed statutes providing for civil unions. From 23 April, 2009, anyone who engaged in a civil union in Connecticut prior to that date may apply for and be given a marriage licence, upon issuance of which the civil union shall be merged into the marriage. All Connecticut civil unions prior to 1 October, 2010 are deemed merged into marriage, except where a divorce or annulment was pending, as of that date. Persons having engaged in a civil union outside Connecticut may elect to be married in Connecticut.

On 26 June, 2013, the United States Supreme Court ruled that same-sex couples married in states that recognise same-sex marriages cannot be denied federal benefits. *US v Windsor*, 570 US ____ (2013). While the full scope and application of the ruling awaits further analysis, legislative reaction and test cases, same-sex couples married in Connecticut now have access to federal benefits previously unavailable to them.

20.2 What legislation governs civil partnership/same-sex marriage?

- CGS Sections 46b-38pp – 38 ss.
- Sec. 46b-38pp. Applicability of estate tax, gift tax and income tax to parties to a civil union.
- Sec. 46b-38qq. Merger of civil union into marriage by action of the parties.
- Sec. 46b-38rr. Merger of civil union into marriage by default. Exception.
- Sec. 46b-38ss. Savings clause.

21. CONTROVERSIAL AREAS/RAPIDLY DEVELOPING AREAS OF LAW

21.1 Is there a particular area of the law within the jurisdiction that is currently undergoing major change?

The United States Supreme Court's ruling in *US v Windsor*, cited in 20.1 above, that barred denial of federal benefits to same-sex couples married in states that recognise same-sex marriages, will cause both test cases in certain areas of application of federal benefits, as well as major revisions of current federal benefit and entitlement laws where definitions embedded in the laws and regulations may need to be changed because they are gender specific. We expect a period of instability as both state and federal courts begin to interpret and apply the Supreme Court's ruling.

21.2 Which areas of law are most out-of-step? Which areas would you most like to see reformed/changed?

As discussed above, Connecticut's law of distribution of contingent assets remains unpredictable, subject to further fragmentation as courts sort through conflicting precedents. There is no indication that the legislature might intervene and no indication that the Supreme Court sees necessity to revisit previous, possibly conflicting decisions. The degree of uncertainty tends to increase litigation on property issues.

The law of pre-nuptial agreements has become so complex, particularly with regard to the 'second look' allowed to the court at the time a party seeks enforcement, that, despite careful attention to the detailed formality, procedures and disclosures attendant to the formation of the agreement, a party is almost compelled to contest enforceability, often at the other party's expense. The current state of the law does not support certainty, which is the heart of pre-nuptial agreements.

This firm represented a wife against a husband who failed to provide an accurate financial affidavit and to respond to repeated discovery requests and orders. Despite this, the trial court, in 2003, compelled trial of the matter in spite of our objections based on the husband's incomplete financial disclosure. The Supreme Court, in 2007, reversed, setting forth authority for punishing discovery misconduct in divorce cases. *Ramin v Ramin*, 281 Conn. 324 (2007). Upon retrial , in 2012, the husband having fled to a foreign country, and this firm having again engaged in what the Family Court described as 'Herculean' efforts to track and value of the husband's assets, the court allocated all the husband's assets in the United States as security for the alimony and assets to the wife. Discovery should neither take years nor resemble the labours of Hercules. Full disclosure should be meaningful, based on the duty to disclose rather than leaving the other party adrift to discover the nature and physical location of assets.

USA – Maryland & Washington D.C.

Offit Kurman Cheryl Lynn Hepfer

A. JURISDICTION AND CONFLICT OF LAW

1. SOURCES OF LAW

1.1 What is the primary source of law in relation to the breakdown of marriage and the welfare of children within the jurisdiction?

Maryland

The primary source of law in relation to the breakdown of marriage and the welfare of children within Maryland is case law and statutory law.

Washington D.C.

Statutory law and case law are the primary sources of law concerning divorce and children in Washington, D.C.

1.2 What is the primary source of law in relation to the breakdown of marriage and the welfare of children within the jurisdiction?

Maryland

The main statutes governing matrimonial law in Maryland are the Maryland Family Law Code Annotated and Maryland Rules, Title 9, Family Law Actions.

Washington D.C.

Specifically, Titles 11 and 16 of the D.C. Code address the issues of divorce and children.

2. JURISDICTION

2.1 What are the main jurisdictional requirements for the institution of proceedings in relation to divorce, property and children?

Maryland

One spouse must be a resident of Maryland to file for divorce. If the grounds for divorce occurred outside of Maryland, a spouse may not file for divorce unless one of the spouses has resided in Maryland for at least one year before the application is file. Md. Code Ann., Fam. Law § 7-101. If the grounds for divorce occurred within Maryland, only one spouse must be a resident in Maryland at the time of filing for divorce. Md. Code Ann., Fam. Law § 7-103.

Under Md. Code Ann., Fam. Law § 8-202, when the court grants a divorce, it may resolve any dispute between spouses with respect to the ownership of personal property. Thus, because Maryland has jurisdiction over divorce under Md. Code Ann., Fam. Law § 1-201, it has jurisdiction over property.

The main jurisdictional requirement in relation to custody determinations is found under the Uniform Child Custody Jurisdiction Enforcement Act (UCCJEA). The UCCJEA determines the child's 'home state' as the state in which the child lived with a parent or person acting as a parent for at least six consecutive months. Md. Code Ann., Fam. Law § 9.5-101(h).

Washington D.C.

In Washington, D.C., no action for divorce or legal separation shall be maintainable unless one of the spouses has been a *bona fide* resident for at least six months. D.C. Code § 16-902.

In the absence of a valid agreement disposing the property rights of the spouses, D.C. Code § 16-910 provides that the court rules on property rights upon the entry of a final decree of a divorce.

D.C. Code § 16-4601.01(8) provides that the child's 'home state' is the state in which the child lived with a parent or person acting as a parent for at least six (6) consecutive months in Washington, D.C.

3. DOMICILE AND HABITUAL RESIDENCE

3. Explain the concepts of domicile and habitual residence as they apply to the jurisdiction in relation to divorce, the finances and children

Maryland

In Maryland, a spouse may have a domicile that is different from the domicile of the other spouse. Md. Code Ann., Fam. Law § 4-201(a). In *Fletcher v Fletcher*, the issues of personal and subject matter jurisdiction were before the court. *Fletcher,* 95 Md. App. at 114. 'The two more important factors being where a person actually lives and where he votes.' *Id.*

If a child is domiciled in Maryland for six months prior to the commencement of a custody filing, Maryland has jurisdiction as it is considered the 'home state' under Md. Code Ann., Fam. Law § 9.5-101(h). However, if a child has been removed from the state, but Maryland was the child's residence for six months immediately prior to the commencement of a custody action, Maryland will still have 'home state' jurisdiction. *Id.*

Washington D.C.

In Washington, D.C., one spouse must be domiciled in the district for six months in order to file for divorce. D.C. Code § 16-902

If a child is domiciled in Washington, D.C. for six months prior to the commencement of a custody filing, Washington, D.C. has jurisdiction as it is considered the 'home state' under D.C. Code § 16-4601.01. However, if a child has been removed from the state, but Washington, D.C. was the child's residence for six months immediately prior to the commencement of a custody action, Washington, D.C. will still have 'home state' jurisdiction. *Id.*

4. CONFLICT OF LAW/APPLICABLE LAW TO BE APPLIED

4.1 What happens when one party applies to stay proceedings in favour of a foreign jurisdiction? What factors will the local court take into account when determining forum issues?

Maryland

Unless there is a temporary emergency situation, Maryland may not exercise its jurisdiction if there is a proceeding concerning custody of a child pending in another state. Md. Code Ann., Fam. Law § 9.5-206. If a custody action is filed in Maryland, and the court determines that a custody action has commenced in another state, the Maryland court shall stay its proceeding and communicate with the court of the other state. *Id.* If the court of the foreign state does not believe that Maryland is a more appropriate forum, Maryland shall dismiss the proceeding. *Id.*

Washington D.C.

In Washington, D.C. unless there is a temporary emergency situation, a court may not exercise its jurisdiction if, at the time of the commencement of the proceeding, there is another action concerning custody pending in another jurisdiction, unless the proceeding has been terminated or is stayed by the court of the other state. D.C. Code § 16-4602.06. If a custody action is filed in Washington, D.C., and the court determines that a custody action has commenced in another state, the District court shall stay its proceeding and communicate with the court of the other state. *Id.* If the court of the foreign state does not believe that Washington, D.C. is a more appropriate forum, Washington, D.C. shall dismiss the proceeding. *Id.*

B. PRE- AND POST-NUPTIAL AGREEMENTS

5. VALIDITY OF PRE- AND POST-NUPTIAL AGREEMENTS

5.1 To what extent are pre- and post-nups binding within the jurisdiction? Could you provide a brief discussion of the most significant recent case law on this issue?

Maryland

Maryland's highest court has decided that the State has an interest in assuring that a spouse is supported adequately, that the obligations of marriage are carried out, and that planning for such an event is not against public policy. *Frey v Frey,* 298 Md. 552, 471 A.2d 705 (1984).

In the absence of a terminal date (sometimes called a 'Sunset provision') the pre-marital agreement lives on until its conditions are performed or enforced upon the divorce (or separation depending on the terms of the agreement) of the parties or the earlier death of one of them. *Cannon v Cannon,* 384 Md. 537, 865 A.2d 563 (2005). Such agreements can also provide for support and property transfers during the marriage or provide for the method of titling of property during the marriage, where separation or divorce is not even contemplated.

A pre-nuptial agreement is viewed in an atmosphere that a confidential relationship is presumed as a matter of law between the parties entering into a pre-nuptial agreement. To the contrary, a confidential relationship is not presumed between spouses entering into a post-nuptial agreement. Thus, the party supporting the agreement must prove the contract is fair and reasonable. When attacking an agreement for unconscionability, the determination is made at the time the parties entered into the agreement, not at the time a party seeks to enforce it. *Martin v Farber,* 68 Md. App. 137, 510 A.2d 608, 611 (1986).

Post-Marital Agreements are also favoured by the courts and sanctioned by statute. Family Law Art., Sec. 8-101(a), Anno. Code of Md., as amended.

Washington D.C.

The District of Columbia has adopted the Uniform Premarital Agreement Act (UPAA). The D.C. Version of the UPAA provides that such an agreement is not enforceable if the party against whom enforcement is sought proves that that party did not execute the agreement voluntarily or that the agreement was unconscionable when it was executed and, before execution of the agreement, that party was not provided a fair and reasonable disclosure of the property or financial obligations of the other party; did not voluntarily and expressly waive in writing, any right to disclosure of the property or financial obligations of the other party beyond the disclosure provided; and did not have, or reasonably could not have had, adequate knowledge of the property or financial obligations of the other party. Section 46-506, D. C. Ann. (2005 & Supp. 2008). Thus, even an unconscionable agreement is enforceable so long as it was executed voluntarily. Even lack of financial disclosure will not invalidate an pre-marital agreement if the parties have waived financial disclosure in writing or had actual or constructive knowledge of the other's financial affairs.

C. DIVORCE, NULLITY AND JUDICIAL SEPARATION

6. RECOGNITION OF FOREIGN MARRIAGES/DIVORCES

6.1 Summarise the position in your jurisdiction

Maryland

Foreign marriages are recognised in Maryland if valid where performed, including those that are prohibited within Maryland. However, if contrary to Maryland's public policy, or expressly prohibited by its legislature, the marriage will not be honoured. *See Port v Cowan,* 426 Md. 435, 444-45, 44 A.3d 970 (2012).

Maryland recognises divorce decrees issued in another state, if that state had personal jurisdiction over the parties. However, the courts may refuse to recognize foreign decrees issued following an *ex parte* proceeding, if the appearing party was not domiciled in the issuing state. See *Madaio v Madaio,* 256 Md. 80, 83, 259 A.2d 524 (1969). Divorce decrees issued by foreign countries are not entitled to full faith and credit. They will, however, be recognised under the principle of comity, unless the decree:

- was obtained by a procedure that denied due process;
- was obtained by fraud;
- offends public policy; or
- was obtained where jurisdiction was lacking.

See *Wolff v Wolff*, 40 Md. App. 168, 177-78, 389 A.2d 413 (1978).

Washington D.C.

Valid foreign marriages are recognised in the District. See *Rosenbaum v Rosenbaum*, 210 A.2d 5, 7 (D.C. 1965). That general rule is not applicable if: the parties were domiciled in the District when married and their marriage would be prohibited by District law; or the marriage would violate the District's public policy. See *Hitchens v Hitchens*, 47 F.Supp. 73 (D.D.C. 1942).

The District will recognise foreign divorce decrees if both parties participated in the proceedings and the issue relating to residence was 'fully and fairly tried.' *Wilburn v Wilburn*, 210 A.2d 832, 834 (D.C. 1965).

7. DIVORCE

7.1 Explain the grounds for divorce within the jurisdiction (please also deal with nullity and judicial separation if appropriate)

Maryland

A limited or absolute divorce can be obtained in Maryland. See Md. Code Ann., Fam. Law §§ 7-102 and 7-103. A limited divorce gives one the right to live separate and apart from their spouse, but does not end the marriage, whereas absolute divorce completely severs the marital bond and entitles either party to remarry. See *Ricketts v Ricketts*, 393 Md. 479, 486, 903 A.2d 857 (2006).

The grounds for limited divorce are:

(1) cruelty of treatment;
(2) excessively vicious conduct;
(3) desertion; and
(4) voluntary separation.

The grounds for absolute divorce are:

(1) adultery;
(2) desertion lasting 12 months;
(3) conviction of a felony or misdemeanour;
(4) twelve-month separation;
(5) insanity;
(6) cruelty of treatment; and
(7) excessively vicious conduct.

Marriages can be annulled in Maryland 'when it is procured by abduction, terror, fraud or duress, or when the fraud complained of relates to essential matters affecting the health or well being of the parties themselves'. *Picarella v Picarella*, 20 Md. App. 499, 506, 316 A.2d 826 (1974).

Washington D.C.

D.C. Code Section 16-904(a) provides two divorce grounds:

(1) six-month separation; or
(2) one-year separation.

Legal separations can also be obtained pursuant to D.C. Code Section 16-904(b), where there is:

(1) mutual and voluntary separation; or

(2) one-year separation.

D.C. Code Section 16-904(d) states when a marriage can be annulled, specifically:

(1) where either party has a living spouse from another marriage not lawfully dissolved;
(2) the insanity of a party at the time of marriage, unless voluntary cohabitation continues after discovery of insanity;
(3) where marriage is procured by fraud or coercion;
(4) the incapacitation of a party at the time of marriage without the knowledge of the other party; and
(5) where a party had not reached the age of legal consent at the time of marriage, unless voluntary cohabitation continues after the age of legal consent is obtained.

8. FINANCES/CAPITAL, PROPERTY

8.1 What powers does the court have to allocate financial resources and property on the breakdown of marriage?

Maryland

Under Section 8-201 *et seq.* of the Family Law Article, courts may resolve property ownership disputes at the time of divorce. Generally, the court may not transfer ownership from one party to the other. However, it may transfer ownership interest in:

- a pension, retirement, profit sharing or deferred compensation plan;
- 'family use' personal property; and
- jointly-owned real property used by the parties as their principal residence during their marriage.

Courts can also make monetary awards, as an adjustment of the rights and equities of the parties.

Washington D.C.

Under Section 16-910 of the D.C. Code, courts may make determinations of property rights in a divorce. The court must: assign each party his or her property acquired before the marriage, as well that acquired by gift, bequest, devise or descent; and value and distribute all other property and debt accumulated during the marriage regardless of title. Distribution must be 'equitable, just, and reasonable' after all relevant factors are considered.

8.2 Explain and illustrate with reference to recent cases the court's thinking on division of assets

Maryland

When division of marital property by title is inequitable, the court 'may adjust the equities by granting a monetary award'. The intent of a marital award 'is to compensate a spouse who holds title to less than an equitable portion of that property.' *Brown v Brown*, 195 Md. App. 72, 109, 5 A.3d 1144 (2010); see also *Dave v Steinmuller*, 157 Md. App. 653, 663, 853 A.2d 826 (2004).

Washington D.C.

The court has 'considerable discretion and broad authority in distributing marital property as part of a judgment of divorce' and if the court considers the statutory factors 'in a manner that is equitable, just and reasonable,' its conclusions will not be disturbed. *Bansda v Wheeler*, 995 A.2d 189, 197 (D.C. 2010); see also *Abulqasm v Mahmoud*, 49 A.3d 828, 840 (2012); *Sudderth v Sudderth*, 984 A.2d 1262, 1267-68 (2009).

9. FINANCES/MAINTENANCE

9.1 Explain the operation of maintenance for spouses on an ongoing basis after the breakdown of marriage

Maryland

Alimony is available to either party in a proceeding for alimony, divorce, or annulment. Md. Code Ann., Fam. Law § 11-101. Three types of alimony are available: *pendente lite* alimony, alimony for a specific period and indefinite alimony. To obtain an award, the party seeking alimony must either obtain a divorce, or be able to prove facts that show he or she is entitled to a divorce. See *Cruz v Silva*, 189 Md. App. 196, 225, 984 A.2d 295 (2009).

The purpose of *pendente lite* alimony 'is to maintain the status quo of the parties pending the final resolution of the divorce proceedings,' and is based upon the financial need of the requesting party. *Guarino v Guarino*, 112 Md. App. 1, 10-11, 684 A.2d 23 (1996).

For alimony awards following a merits hearing, the court must decide the amount and duration. Md. Code Ann., Fam. Law § 11-106(a). The court must consider the factors set forth in Section 11-106(b) in making a 'fair and equitable' award.

Indefinite alimony can be awarded only if the court finds that:

(1) 'due to age, illness, infirmity, or disability, the party seeking alimony cannot reasonably be expected to make substantial progress toward becoming self-supporting;' or

(2) 'even after the party seeking alimony will have made as much progress toward becoming self-supporting as can reasonably be expected, the respective standards of living of the parties will be unconscionably disparate.'

Md. Code Ann., Fam. Law § 11-106(c)(1)-(2).

Washington D.C.

The District recognises *pendente lite* alimony, term-limited alimony, and indefinite alimony. D.C. Code §§ 16-911 and 16-913.

If such relief is sought, the Court may order that *pendente lite* alimony be paid by either party to the other, to provide interim maintenance during the pendency of the proceedings. *See* D.C. Code § 16-911; *Bowie v Nicholson*, 705 A.2d 290, 292 (D.C. 1998).

At the time of divorce, the court may award alimony if just and proper. D.C. Code § 16-913(a). Either indefinite alimony or alimony for a set term can be awarded. *Id.*, § 16-913(b). The court must consider all relevant factors 'necessary for a fair and equitable award.'

9.2 Is it common for maintenance to be awarded?

Maryland

Alimony awards are not automatic, and the court 'has broad discretion in making an award of alimony.' *Ware v Ware*, 131 Md. App. 207, 228, 748 A.2d 1031 (2000).

Washington D.C.

Alimony awards are not required and are decided on a case-by-case basis. *Sudderth v Sudderth*, 984 A.2d 1262, 1266 (D.C. 2009). Rather, those matters 'entrusted to sound judgment of the trial court'. *Cefaratti v Cefaratti*, 315 A.2d 142, 144 n. 8 (D.C. 1974).

9.3 Explain and illustrate with reference to recent cases the court's thinking on maintenance

Maryland

Maryland 'generally favours fixed-term or so-called rehabilitative alimony, rather than indefinite alimony'. *Whittington v Whittington*, 172 Md. App. 317, 336, 914 A.2d 212 (2007). That preference arises from the 'conviction that the purpose of alimony is not to provide a lifetime pension, but where practicable to ease the transition for the parties from the joint married state to their new status as single people living apart and independently.' *Whittington*, 172 Md. App. at 336; see also *Jensen v Jensen*, 103 Md. App. 678, 693, 654 A.2d 914, 921 (1995) (focus of alimony is seen as a 'bridge' to self-sufficiency rather than as a form of a lifetime pension). Indefinite alimony should be awarded only in exceptional circumstances. *Dave v Steinmuller*, 157 Md. App. 653, 673, 853 A.2d 826 (2004).

Washington D.C.

The objective of alimony is 'to provide reasonable and necessary support.' *Lake v Lake*, 756 A.2d 917, 921 (D.C. 2000). Alimony is 'not intended as a penalty to be imposed upon the [payor spouse] nor as compensation to solace the [payee recipient spouse]…' rather, the policy is to prevent the recipient spouse from becoming a public charge. *Alibrando v Alibrando*, 375 A.2d 9, 13 (D.C. 1977); see also *Primus v Primus*, 768 A.2d 543, 545 (D.C. 2001).

10. CHILD MAINTENANCE

10.1 On what basis is child maintenance calculated within the jurisdiction?

Maryland

In Maryland, child support is determined by using statutory child support guidelines, as set forth in Md. Code Ann., Fam. Law §§ 12-101 *et seq*. The guidelines are based upon the Income Shares Model, which is premised on the idea that a child 'should receive the same proportion of parental income, and thereby enjoy the standard of living, he or she would have experienced had the child's parents remained together'. *Voishan v Palma*, 327 Md. 318, 322, 609 A.2d 319 (1992).

With limited exceptions, the use of the child support guidelines is required. Md. Code Ann., Fam. Law § 12-202(a)(1).

The statutory schedule of basic child support obligations is based upon the number of children and the combined adjusted actual income of the two parents. See *id.*, § 12-204(e). Where the parents' combined adjusted actual income exceeds the highest level set forth in the schedule, 'the court may use its discretion in setting the amount of child support'. *Id.*, § 12-204(d).

Child support is always modifiable 'upon a showing of a material change of circumstances'. *Id.*, § 12-104(a).

Washington D.C.

Child support in the District is calculated pursuant to the guideline codified at D.C. Code § 16-916.01. Child support awards shall be made in accordance with the guideline. *Id.*, § 16-916.01(a). The guideline's application is presumptive, and 'shall be applied unless its application would be unjust or inappropriate in the circumstances of the particular case.' *Id.*, § 16-916.01(p).

The parties' basic child support obligations are calculated pursuant to the statutory procedures and take into account, among other things, the combined adjusted gross incomes of the parties and the number of children. See *id.*, §§ 16-916.01 (e), (f)(1) and (q). Where the parties' combined adjusted gross income exceeds the maximum level in the guideline, the court 'may exercise its discretion to order more child support [than would have been ordered under the guideline], after determining the reasonable needs of the child based on actual family experience'. *Id.*, § 16-916.01(h).

Child support may be modified 'upon a showing that there has been a substantial and material change in the needs of the child or the ability of the responsible relative to pay'. D.C. Code § 46-204(a).

11. RECIPROCAL ENFORCEMENT OF FINANCIAL ORDERS

11.1 Summarise the position in your jurisdiction

Maryland

Maryland has adopted the Uniform Interstate Family Support Act ('UIFSA'), codified at Md. Code Ann., Fam. Law §§ 10-301 *et. seq*. UIFSA applies to both child support and spousal support orders. Under UIFSA, a support order issued in another state may be registered in Maryland for enforcement.

Washington D.C.

The District has enacted the Uniform Interstate Family Support Act (UIFSA), codified at D.C. Code § 46-301.01 *et. seq*. Under UIFSA, foreign support orders can be registered in the District for enforcement.

12. FINANCIAL RELIEF AFTER FOREIGN DIVORCE PROCEEDINGS

12.1 What powers are available to make orders following a foreign divorce?

Maryland

If an annulment or divorce decree was issued in another jurisdiction,

Maryland courts may make an award of alimony if: the other court lacked jurisdiction to make an award; and the party seeking alimony was domiciled in Maryland for at least one year prior to the annulment or divorce. Md. Code Ann., Fam. Law § 11-105. Similarly, a court can exercise its powers pertaining to property and marital awards if: one of the parties was domicile in Maryland when the foreign proceeding was commenced; and the other court lacked jurisdiction over the party domiciled in Maryland or the property at issued. *Id.*, § 8-212.

Washington D.C.

Where a former spouse has obtained a foreign *ex parte* divorce, the court may order reasonable spousal support, on application of the other spouse and with personal service of process upon the former spouse in the District. See D.C. Code § 16-916.

D. CHILDREN

13. CUSTODY/PARENTAL RESPONSIBILITY

13.1 Briefly explain the legal position in relation to custody/parental responsibility following the breakdown of the marriage

Maryland

In Maryland, the law related to child custody is primarily found in case law rather than statute. Child custody may apply to both legal and physical custody. Legal custody includes the right to make decisions with respect to the child's education, religion, medical care and other significant issues. Physical custody refers to the actual home and daily care of the child. An award of custody may be sole, joint, or shared.

The court must consider the best interest of the child, *Taylor v Taylor*, 306 Md. 209, 508 A.2d 964 (1986). Parents must be able to communicate jointly in order to reach a shared decision for the benefit of the minor child for there to be an award of joint legal custody. *Taylor, supra.*

Washington D.C.

In the District of Columbia child custody law is codified. A parent may be awarded: sole legal custody; sole physical custody; joint legal custody; joint physical custody; or any other custody arrangement that the court deems to be in the child's best interest. See D.C. Code §16-914. Again, the best interest of the child is of paramount concern.

In the District of Columbia, there is a rebuttable presumption that joint custody is in the best interest of the child unless there is a finding by preponderance of the evidence of domestic violence, child abuse, neglect or parental kidnapping.

13.2 Briefly explain the legal position in relation to access/contact/visitation following the breakdown of a relationship or marriage.

Maryland

Maryland recognises the importance of a non-custodial parent to have visitation and access to the minor child. *Radford v Matczuk*, 223 Md. 483, 164

A.2d 904 (1960). A non-custodial parent should only be denied access to a child in extraordinary circumstances. *Id.*

Washington D.C.
In the District of Columbia, the best interest of the child governs the establishment of visitation and access. D.C. Code §16-914. It is considered preferable for there to be frequent and continuing contact between the child and both parents. *Wilkins v Ferguson*, 928 A.2d 655 (D.C. App., 2007). .

14. INTERNATIONAL ABDUCTION

14.1 Summarise the position in your jurisdiction

The United States is a party to the Hague Convention which, along with the International Child Abduction Remedies Act (ICARA)(102 Stat. 437, 42 U.S.C. §11601, *et. seq.*, applies to matters involving international child abduction. Maryland and the District of Columbia ascribe to the federal law with respect to international child abduction.

The ICARA grants federal and state courts concurrent jurisdiction over matters related to international child abduction. The courts have the authority to order the prompt return of the child to the country of habitual residence and also to order the payment of attorneys' fees, costs, and transportation expenses associated with returning the children. 42 U.S. C.S. §11601 and §11607.

Until recently, once a child was returned to the country of habitual residence, the matter was considered moot, which created some problems because the Hague Convention mandated a prompt return. In February, 2013, the United States Supreme Court found that a return order issued pursuant to the ICARA may not be moot for purposes of appeal if disputes remained between the parents, including as to where the child would be raised. *Chafin v. Chafin*, 2013 U.S. Lexis 1122 (Feb. 19, 2013).

15. LEAVE TO REMOVE/APPLICATIONS TO TAKE A CHILD OUT OF THE JURISDICTION

15.1 Summarise the position in your jurisdiction

Maryland
When the custodial parents cannot make a joint decision or when a custodial parent seeks to remove the child from the jurisdiction against the wishes of the non-custodial parent. A parent may file a complaint in the circuit court of the county in which the child resides in order prevent the relocation.

Washington D.C.
Every parent has a constitutional right to travel. *Shapiro v.Thompson,* 394 U.S. 618 (1969). Both parents have a fundamental right to the care, control, and custody of their child. *Troxel v Granville*, 530 U.S. 57 (2000). The District of Columbia enforces these rights.

When custodial parents cannot make a joint decision or when a custodial parent seeks to remove the child from the jurisdiction against the wishes of the non-custodial parent, one parent may seek a change in custody to prevent the relocation.

15.2 Under what circumstances may a parent apply to remove their child from the jurisdiction against the wishes of the other parent?

Maryland

As of 1991, the Courts in Maryland have employed the 'best interest of the child' standard in child relocation proceedings. *Domingues v Johnson*, 323 Md. 486, 593 A.2d 113 (1991); *Goldmeier v Lepselter*, 89 Md.App. 301, 598 A.2d 482 (1991).

Typically, when the custodial parent seeks to relocate with the minor child, and the non-custodial parent opposes and seeks a change in custody, Maryland courts have considered the extent to which the non-custodial parent has been involved in the child's life and exercised significant visitation prior to the relocation. Moreover, they consider whether relocation would disrupt substantial and meaningful contact with the non-custodial parent. *Id.*; *Braun v. Headley*, 131 Md. App. 588, 750 A.2d 624 (2000).

The guiding principle in Maryland when determining a change of custody as a result of a child's relocation is 'whether the interest of the child is best served by the certainty and stability of a primary caretaker, or by ensuring significant day-to-day contact with both parents.' *Domingues*, 323 Md. at 501.

Washington D.C.

One D.C. case outlines the factors the court must consider where the parties to a relocation case share joint legal and physical custody. D.C. Code § 16-914(a)(1)(A) (2009 Supp.); *Boras v Osterberg,*127 Daily Wash. Law Rptr. 1069, 1075 (D.C. Super. Ct. July 29, 1998). In *Boras,* the court determined that it is necessary to apply a balancing test in which the court must consider four relocation-specific factors in addition to the statutory 'best interest of thechild' factors:

- the success of the current custody agreement;
- the motivations of the parents in proposing or opposing relocation;
- the advantages of the move; and
- the possibility of an alternative visitation schedule.*Id.*

E. SURROGACY AND ADOPTION

16. VALIDITY OF SURROGACY AGREEMENTS

16.1 Briefly summarise the position in your jurisdiction

Maryland

Surrogacy contracts are illegal in Maryland. *In Re Roberto d.B.*, 399 Md. 267, 293, 923 A.2d 115, 130-131 (Md. 2007).

Two Maryland statutes have been interpreted to outlaw surrogacy contracts.

Md. Ann. Code, Family Law § 5-327(a)(1) provides:

'Except as otherwise provided, an agency, institution, or individual who renders any service in connection with the placement of an individual for adoption, or in

connection with an agreement for the custody of an individual in contemplation of adoption, may not charge or receive from or on behalf of either the natural parent or the individual to be adopted, or from or on behalf of the individual who is adopting the individual, any compensation for the placement or agreement.'

Although the predecessor for this statute was enacted in 1947, long before the advent of the technology that allowed for surrogacy, the statute has since been amended, to confirm that it applies to surrogacy contracts. In 1992, the Maryland legislature 'added the prohibition on payments in connection with an agreement for the custody of an individual in contemplation of adoption'. 85 Op. Att'y 348, 352 (Dec. 19, 2000). Amendments such as this 'were designed to ensure that the statute applied to certain surrogacy agreements that might otherwise fall outside its purview…' 85 Op. Att'y at 352.

In 1989, due to two well-publicised cases involving allegations of baby-selling that were feared not to be covered by § 5-327, the Legislature enacted Maryland Ann. Code, Article 27, § 35E, which provides: *'A person may not sell, barter, or trade, or offer to sell, barter, or trade a child for money or property, either real or personal, or anything else of value.'*

In one of the more recent cases in Maryland involving surrogacy, the Court of Appeals of Maryland held that a genetically unrelated surrogate was not required to have her name listed as the mother on the birth certificate of children born to her as a result of in vitro fertilization. *See In Re Roberto d.B.*, 399 Md. 267, 923 A.2d 115 (Md. 2007).

Washington D.C.

Surrogacy is expressly prohibited by District of Columbia law. D. C. Code Ann. § 16-402(a) provides: 'Surrogate parenting contracts are prohibited and rendered unenforceable in the District.'

D.C. Code Ann. § 16-401(4) defines a surrogate parenting contract as *'any agreement, oral or written, in which:*

(A) A woman agrees either to be artificially inseminated with the sperm of a man who is not her husband, or to be impregnated with an embryo that is the product of an ovum fertilization with the sperm of a man who is not her husband; and

(B) A woman agrees to, or intends to, relinquish all parental rights and responsibilities and to consent to the adoption of a child born as a result of insemination or in vitro fertilization as provided in this chapter.'

17. ADOPTION

17.1 Briefly explain the legal position in relation to adoption in your jurisdiction. Is adoption available to individuals, cohabiting couples (both heterosexual and same-sex)?

Maryland

Maryland law provides that 'any adult' may petition a court to adopt. Md. Ann. Code, Family Law § 5-331(b)(1); 5-3A-29. Maryland law specifically prohibits discrimination based on marital status with regard to petitions for adoption, stating that a court cannot deny a petition for adoption 'solely because the petitioner is single or unmarried.' Md. Ann. Code, Family Law § 5-337; 5-A-34; 5-3B-19. Whether a person is heterosexual or homosexual does not determine whether the person may adopt. Maryland Ann. Code, Family Law § 5-3B-19, which governs independent adoptions, also provides that the court may not deny the petition solely because the petitioner has a disability.

Washington D.C.

D.C. Code § 16-302 provides that: 'Any person may petition the court for a decree of adoption.'

In general, if a petitioner is married, the petitioner's spouse must also join in the petition. D.C. Code § 16-302. Unmarried couples and same-sex couples in a committed personal relationship may be granted adoptions under this statute. *In re M.M.D.,* 662 A.2d 837 (D.C. 1995).

In the District of Columbia, the petition for adoption must include the race and religion of the prospective adoptee, or his natural parent or parents, and the race and religion of the petitioner. D.C. Code § 16-305 (4), (5). The court is not required to consider these factors, however, in determining whether to grant the petition for adoption. See *In re: Petition of D.I.S.,* 494 A.2d 1316 (D.C. 1985).

F. COHABITATION

18. Cohabitation

18.1 What legislation (if any) governs division of property for unmarried couples on the breakdown of the relationship?

The legislation governing division of property for unmarried couples on the breakdown of the relationship would be the legislation concerning Domestic Partnerships. See section 21 below.

G. FAMILY DISPUTE RESOLUTION

19. MEDIATION, COLLABORATIVE LAW AND ARBITRATION

19.1 Briefly summarise the non-court-based processes available in your jurisdiction and the current status of agreements reached under the auspices of mediation, collaborative law and arbitration

The courts of Maryland and the District of Columbia encourage litigants to reach settlement agreements in family law matters. Mediation is used predominantly. Mediation is a non-binding process which allows parties to present their issues and arguments in a non-court setting, receive feedback from the mediator, and reach a voluntary agreement. Mediators do not issue a decision; they facilitate a settlement. An arbitrator will hear evidence, and render a decision in the case, which typically is binding upon the parties, although the parties may agree to non-binding arbitration. With collaborative law, each party retains a collaboratively trained attorney. A participation agreement is entered into which defines that the parties and their lawyers will work collaboratively toward a settlement and avoid pursuing litigation to resolve the case. The hallmarks of the collaborative process are open and honest disclosure, cooperation in the process, and a desire to work toward a final resolution

In order for a settlement agreement to be upheld, it must be the product of voluntary negotiations with full disclosure of all relevant facts. Agreements that are the product of mediation, collaborative law, conciliation, or arbitration are routinely incorporated into a divorce decree and are often adopted by the court as the final resolution in a family law matter. If the court finds that provisions of the agreement that pertain to the children are not in the best interest of the children, the court may not accept the parties' agreement on that point, leaving the parties to negotiate a new settlement or litigate the issue. See Md. Code Ann., Family Law § 8-103(a); *Cooper v Cooper*, 472 A.2d 878 (DC 1984).

19.2 What is the statutory basis (if any), for mediation, collaborative law and arbitration in your jurisdiction? In particular, are the parties required to attempt a family dispute resolution in advance of the institution of proceedings?

Maryland

In Maryland, Rule 9-205(b)(3) provides *'If the court concludes that mediation is appropriate and likely to be beneficial to the parties or the child and that a qualified mediator is available, it shall enter an order requiring the parties to mediate the custody or visitation dispute. The order may stay some or all further proceedings in the action pending the mediation on terms and conditions set forth in the order.'* Similarly, Rule 17-201, *et seq.*, provides the authority for a court to order the mediation of financial matters between the parties, such as division of marital property or spousal support.

Washington D.C.

Under § 11–1102 of the District of Columbia Family Court Act of 2001, *'To the greatest extent practicable and safe, cases and proceedings in the Family Court of the Superior Court shall be resolved through alternative dispute resolution procedures, in accordance with such rules as the Superior Court may promulgate.'* Similar to Maryland courts, courts of the District of Columbia often refer cases at their initial stage to mediation, or if the parties elect, arbitration or conciliation

H. OTHER

20. CIVIL PARTNERSHIP/SAME-SEX MARRIAGE

20.1 What is the status of civil partnership/same sex marriage within the jurisdiction?

Maryland

Maryland recognises domestic partnerships for limited health, tax and insurance rights. Maryland recently began recognising and permitting same-sex marriages.

Washington D.C.

The District of Columbia recognises and permits both domestic partnerships and same-sex marriages.

20.2 What legislation governs civil partnerships/same sex marriage?

Maryland

a. Domestic partnerships

Domestic partnerships are defined and recognised in the Health-General Article and in the Tax-Property Article of the Maryland Code Annotated.

Under Maryland Health – General Code Annotated § 6-101, a 'domestic partnership' is defined as *'a relationship between two individuals who:*

(1) are at least 18 years old;

(2) are not related to each other by blood or marriage within four degrees of consanguinity under civil law rule;

(3) are not married or in civil union or domestic partnership with another individual; and

(4) agree to be in a relationship of mutual interdependence in which each individual contributes to the maintenance and support of the other individual and the relationship, even if both individuals are not required to contribute equally to the relationship.'

The definition of domestic partnership under Section 12-101(e-2) of the Tax-Property Article of the Maryland Code is almost exactly the same definition as that of the Health-General definition, except that in addition to the above requirements, it adds the requirement that the two individuals:

'(5) share a common residence where both domestic partners life, even if:

(i) only one of the domestic partners has the right to legal possession of the common residence; or

(ii) one of the domestic partners has an additional residence.'

There is no registry of domestic partnerships in Maryland. Instead, in certain instances, evidence of a domestic partnership may be required, in which case such evidence is defined as:

'(1) an affidavit of such domestic partnership; and

(2) two documents reflecting: joint ownership of property, joint liability for a lease, mortgage or loan, joint responsibility for child care, the designation by one domestic partner of the other in a durable power of attorney or as a beneficiary of life insurance or retirement benefits, or a 'relationship or cohabitation contract'.'

See Md. Health-General Code Ann. § 6-101(b), and Md. Tax-Property Code Ann. § 12-101(e-3).

In general, the establishment of a domestic partnership permits domestic partners to visit each other in a healthcare facility or in case of a medical emergency, make medical decisions in the event an individual is incapable of making them. Md. Health-General Code Ann. §§ 5-605(a)(2), 6-201(a), 6-202 and 6-203. It also permits the transfer of residential property between domestic partners without incurring transfer or recordation tax, and permits domestic partners to inherit property from each other and be exempt from state inheritance tax. Md. Tax-Property Code Ann. §§ 12-101(e-4), 12-108(c)(1)(ix), 13-207(a)(2), and 13-403; Md. Tax-General Code Ann. § 7-203(l). The exemptions from transfer and recordation tax also apply to former domestic partners who have evidence of the dissolution of their domestic partnership, either by a death certificate, or an affidavit signed by both members of the domestic partnership stating that it has been dissolved. Md. Tax-Property Code Ann. §§ 12-101(e-4), 12-108(c)(1)(ix), 13-207(a)(2), and 13-403. There is no requirement of a court order to dissolve a domestic partnership.

b. Same-sex marriage

Effective 1 January, 2013, Maryland began permitting and performing same-sex marriages. In November 2012, Maryland became the first of three states in the United States to recognise same-sex marriage by popular vote/referendum. Earlier that year, in May 2012, before same-sex marriage was authorised within the state, the Maryland Court of Appeals held that same-sex marriages validly performed in other states would be recognised in Maryland for purposes of obtaining a divorce. *Port v Cowan*, 426 Md. 435; 44 A.3d 970 (2012).

Maryland Family Law Code § 2-201, entitled 'Valid marriages' now reads, in part, that 'Only a marriage between two individuals who are not otherwise prohibited from marrying is valid in this State.' Md. Fam. L. Code Ann. § 2-201(b). As a result, a same-sex married couple may now terminate their marriage in the same manner, and on the same grounds, as an opposite-sex married couple.

Washington D.C.

a. Domestic partnerships

Under D.C. Code § 32-701 *et seq.*, the District of Columbia permits and recognises domestic partnerships. This statute defines domestic partnerships, and provides domestic partners with healthcare benefits and rights, including the right of D.C. government employees to include a domestic partner and his or her dependents on the employee's health insurance, and the right to visit one's domestic partner in a hospital. Based on the definition in this statute, other areas of D.C. law treat domestic partners the same as married couples, such as with regard to divorce or the termination of the domestic partnership.

A domestic partnership designation is permitted between two individuals in a 'familial relationship' that is 'characterised by mutual caring and the sharing of a mutual residence.' D.C. Code § 32-701(1). A domestic partner must be:

(a) at least 18 years of age and competent to contract;
(b) the sole domestic partner of the other person; and
(c) not married.

D.C. Code § 32-701(3).

This statute, therefore, permits domestic partnerships between blood relations (adult child and elderly parent, for example), provided that both partners meet the requirements of: a mutual caring relationship, sharing a residence, being over 18, not being the domestic partner of anyone else, and not being married to anyone else.

In order to be recognised as a domestic partnership, a couple must register by executing a declaration of domestic partnership, signed under oath and filed with the Mayor. Each partner must affirm under the penalty of perjury that he or she:

- is at least 18 years old and competent to contract;
- is the sole domestic partner of the other person; and
- is not married.

D.C. Code § 32-702(a).

There are a number of ways a domestic partnership may terminate. First, both partners may file with the Mayor a 'termination statement' declaring that the domestic partnership is terminated. Second, one partner may file a termination statement, provided that he or she also includes a declaration that the termination statement has been served on the other partner. Third, one partner may terminate on the ground of the other partner's 'abandon[ing] the domestic partnership' by filing a termination statement in which he or she declares:

(a) that the domestic partnership is terminated;
(b) that the other partner permanently departed the mutual residence at least six months before filing, or has not been in contact with the filing partner for at least six months; and
(c) if the location of the other partner is known, a copy of the termination statement has been served on the other domestic partner.

Fourth, a domestic partnership terminates by law if the domestic partners marry each other. Fifth, the domestic partnership terminates upon the death of either partner. D.C. Code § 32-702(d).

When terminating a domestic partnership, the partners have the same rights to, and responsibilities for, equitable distribution of property, child support and alimony, as divorcing spouses do. D.C. Code 16-901 *et seq.*

b. Same-sex marriage

Since 2010, the District of Columbia has recognised same-sex marriage. D.C. Code § 46-401, entitled 'Equal access to marriage,' provides, in part, that *'[m]arriage is the legally recognized union of 2 persons. Any person may enter into a marriage in the District of Columbia with another person, regardless of gender, unless the marriage is expressly prohibited by § 46-401.01 or § 46-403.'* D.C. Code § 46-401(a)[1].

A same-sex married couple may terminate their marriage in the same manner, and on the same grounds, as an opposite-sex married couple. In order to maintain an action for divorce, the District of Columbia requires that one member of the couple has been a resident of the District of Columbia for at least six months next preceding the filing of the action. D.C. Code § 16-902(a). If, however, a same-sex couple marries in the District of Columbia and then moves to a state that does <u>not</u> recognise their marriage, and will not allow them to obtain a divorce, the couple can obtain a divorce in the District of Columbia. D.C. permits an action for divorce by a same-sex couple, even if neither party resides in the District of Columbia, if:

[1] D.C. Code § 46-401.01 prohibits marriages between certain close relations, and marriages where one of the persons is married and the marriage has not been terminated by death or divorce. Such marriages are automatically void. D.C. Code § 46-403 prohibits marriages where one of the parties is mentally incapacitated, where the marriage has been procured by force or fraud, or where one or both of the parties is under the age of 16. Such marriages or void when so declared by a court order.

(A) the marriage was performed in the District of Columbia; and
(B) Neither party to the marriage resides in a jurisdiction that will maintain an action for divorce.

D.C. Code § 16-902(b). This section grants subject matter jurisdiction only, not personal jurisdiction, suggesting that it is intended for same-sex couples where both spouses consent to, and participate in, the divorce. It is unclear and doubtful, whether such subject matter jurisdiction for out-of-state, same-sex couples would permit the court to determine contested disputes over divorce grounds, property or support. To date, there have been no reported cases on this issue.

21. CONTROVERSIAL AREAS/RAPIDLY DEVELOPING AREAS OF LAW

21.1 Is there a particular area of the law within the jurisdiction that is currently undergoing major change?

Yes, with the recent United States Supreme Court decision striking down portions of the Defense of Marriage Act, legally married same-sex couples should be entitled to more federal rights than previously, and to more state rights where the state law was governed by the Federal definition of marriage. State and federal agencies are still processing the decision and preparing the necessary regulations concerning issues such as: the right to file joint US income tax returns; division of federally-regulated retirement plans upon divorce; and the rights of former spouses of federal employees to various benefits. States that previously depended on the federal definition of marriage may need to re-define their definitions of marriage for benefits such as a same-sex spouse's right to the unlimited exemption from estate tax.

21.2 Which areas of law are most out of step and which areas would you most like to see reformed/changed?

The partial solution of the recent US Supreme Court decisions leave a morass of regulations and conflicting states' laws to contend with in determining the rights of legally married same-sex couples. A national recognition of marriage equality, or a national requirement that states give full faith and credit to the marital status of any legally married couple would provide same-sex married couples the same benefits and obligations as opposite-sex married couples.

The author would like to thank Sandra A. Brooks, Ronald L. Ogens, Christopher M. Wachter, Catherine H. McQueen and Alex M. Allman for their help in compiling this chapter

USA – Minnesota

Walling, Berg & Debele, P.A. Nancy Zalusky Berg,
Lilo D Kaiser, Tara L Smith Ruesga & Laura Sahr Schmit

A. JURISDICTION AND CONFLICT OF LAW

1. SOURCES OF LAW

1.1 What is the primary source of law in relation to the breakdown of marriage and the welfare of children within the jurisdiction?

In the United States and, specifically, in Minnesota, the primary sources of law are the state statutes and opinions issued by the appellate courts. The terms 'dissolution', 'marital dissolution', and 'divorce' are used throughout chapter 518 and have the same meaning.

Provisions within chapter 518 concern the welfare of children in dissolutions of marriage. Chapter 257 governs legitimacy and custody of children born outside of the marriage. Chapter 257C governs third party custody of children and chapter 260C governs children in need of protection and services.

Minnesota has an intermediate appellate court, the Court of Appeals, which considers all appeals properly brought. The Supreme Court will accept and review matters of state-wide significance. Published opinions issued by the Court of Appeals and the Supreme Court are the second primary source of law. The Court of Appeals also issues unpublished opinions, which are not considered binding precedent.

1.2 Which are the main statutes governing matrimonial law in the jurisdiction?

The main statutes governing matrimonial law in Minnesota are contained in the following chapters of the Minnesota Statutes:

517 Marriage
518 Marriage Dissolution
518A Child Support
518B Domestic Abuse
518C Uniform Interstate Family Support Act
518D Uniform Child Custody Jurisdiction and Enforcement Act
519 Married Persons; Rights, Privileges

2. JURISDICTION

2.1 What are the main jurisdictional requirements for the institution of proceedings in relation to divorce, property and children?

Jurisdiction over the dissolution of marriage is established by personal service. One of the spouses must have been a resident or domiciled in

Minnesota for at least 180 days immediately preceding the commencement of the action. Residence is defined by the statute as 'the place where a party has established a permanent home from which the party has no present intention of moving' (Minnesota Statutes section 518.003, subd. 9). Domicile is not defined by statute, but has been defined in case law as 'the union of residence and intention…' (*Davidner v Davidner*, 304 Minn. 491, 494, 232 N.W.2d 5,7 (Minn. 1975).

Residency is a fundamental requirement for jurisdiction; a divorce granted in violation of this provision is void for lack of jurisdiction. The Uniform Child Custody Jurisdiction and Enforcement Act (UCCJEA), codified as Minnesota Statute chapter 518D, governs Minnesota's jurisdiction to determine child custody. The UCCJEA is applicable in marriage dissolution matters as well as proceedings involving children of unmarried parents.

3. DOMICILE AND HABITUAL RESIDENCE

3.1 Explain the concepts of domicile and habitual residence as they apply to the jurisdiction in relation to divorce, the finances and children

Domicile is not defined by statute and, in the context of family law matters, has the same meaning as residency. The terms 'domicile' and 'residency' are used interchangeably. (See discussion of domicile and residency *supra.*)

Minnesota law defines 'residence' as as 'the place where a party has established a permanent home from which the party has no present intention of moving'. (Minnesota Statute section 518.009, subd.9.) The Minnesota Supreme Court has defined 'domicile' as 'the union of residence and intention'. *Davidner v Davidner*, 304 Minn. 491, 493, 232 N.W.2d 5, 7 (1975).

Minnesota law does not have a definition for habitual residence. Under Minnesota Statute chapter 518D (UCCJEA), a court has jurisdiction over custody and parenting time if Minnesota is the child's home state or the state in which the child lived with a parent or a person acting as a parent for at least six consecutive months immediately before the commencement of a child custody proceeding. If a child is less than six months' old, the term means the state in which the child has lived from birth. A period of temporary absence of any of the persons subject to the statute is part of the period (Minnesota Statute section 518D.102(h)).

For the purposes of child support and child-related finances, Minnesota courts have jurisdiction to establish child support in all initial determinations where both parents reside in Minnesota. In cases where the custodial parent resides in Minnesota but the non-custodial parent does not, Minnesota courts may exercise personal jurisdiction over the nonresident individuals in certain circumstances pursuant to Minnesota Statute section 518C.201.

4. CONFLICT OF LAW/APPLICABLE LAW TO BE APPLIED

4.1 What happens when one party applies to stay proceedings in favour of a foreign jurisdiction? What factors will the local court take into account when determining forum issues?

The analysis will depend on whether the proceeding involves children.

Proceeding without children

When children are not involved, the court will first apply the residency test pursuant to Minnesota Statute section 518.07, as described above. If the petitioning party meets the residency requirement, then the court will analyse whether Minnesota and the foreign court have concurrent jurisdiction. Generally, when courts have concurrent jurisdiction, the first court to acquire jurisdiction has priority in deciding the case (*Minnesota Mut. Life Ins. v Anderson*, 410 N.W. 2d 80 (Minn.App. 1987), citing, *Orthmann v Apple River Campground, Inc.*, 765 F.2d 119, 121 (8th Cir.1985)).

Minnesota's 'first to file' rule is described as follows: '*Where two actions between the same parties, on the same subject, and to test the same rights, are brought in different courts having concurrent jurisdiction, the court which first acquires jurisdiction,* its power being adequate to the administration of complete justice, *retains its jurisdiction and may dispose of the whole controversy, and no court of coordinate power is at liberty to interfere with its action. This rule rests upon comity and the necessity of avoiding conflict in the execution of judgments by independent courts, * * *. Minnesota Mut. Life Ins. v Anderson*, 410 N.W. 2d 80 (Minn.App. 1987), citing, State ex rel. *Minnesota National Bank of Duluth v. District Court*, 195 Minn. 169, 173, 262 N.W. 155, 157 (1935).'

In determining whether to dismiss an action when a concurrent action has been commenced in a different forum court, a court may consider the following factors: 'Judicial economy, informal comity between courts, cost and convenience to the litigants, and the possibility of vexatious conflict and overlap of multiple determinations of the same dispute.' *Id.*

Proceeding with children

In proceedings involving children, the court must apply the Uniform Child Custody Jurisdiction and Enforcement Act (UCCJEA), which is codified as Minnesota Statute chapter 518D, see section 3 above. There are three steps in determining jurisdiction under the UCCJEA:

- determine whether the court has jurisdiction to make an initial child custody determination pursuant to Minnesota Statute section 518D.201;
- if it determines that it does have jurisdiction, then determine whether another custody proceeding is pending in a court of another state which has jurisdiction similar to the provisions of section 518D.201 of the UCCJEA;
- if a concurrent proceeding is pending pursuant to a similar law as the UCCJEA, then analyse inconvenient forum pursuant to section 518D.207 (*Abu-Dalbouh v Abu-Dalbouh*, 547 N.W. 2d 700 (Minn.App. 1996), citing *Schmidt v Schmidt*, 436 N.W.2d 99, 104 (Minn. 1989)).

Once a court has proper subject-matter jurisdiction under section 518D.201, it is presumed to have exclusive, continuing jurisdiction over child-custody determinations. The UCCJEA expressly provides that a foreign country shall be treated as if it is a state of the United States for the purpose of applying Minnesota Statute sections 518D.101 to 518D.210. A Minnesota court must recognise and enforce a child custody determination made in a foreign country under factual circumstances in substantial conformity with the jurisdictional standards of Minnesota Statute section 518D.

Secondly, even if the court determines that Minnesota is the home state of a child, the court must inquire whether a proceeding involving custody of the child is simultaneously pending before a foreign court. When a simultaneous proceeding is pending, the court must follow the provisions set forth in Minnesota Statute section 518D.206 of the UCCJEA. Under section 518D.206, a Minnesota court may not exercise jurisdiction unless the proceeding in a foreign court has been terminated or is stayed because the Minnesota court is a more convenient forum.

Thirdly, if the court determines that concurrent jurisdiction exists with a foreign court, then it must analyse whether Minnesota is an inconvenient forum according to the following factors set forth in Minnesota Statute section 518D.207. The factors include the following:

- whether domestic violence has occurred and is likely to continue;
- the length of time the child has resided outside Minnesota;
- the distance between the Minnesota court and the foreign jurisdiction;
- the relative financial circumstances of the parties;
- any party agreement on jurisdiction;
- the nature and location of required evidence, including child testimony;
- the ability of each court to decide the issue expeditiously and procedures necessary to present evidence;
- the familiarity of each court with the facts and issues.

B. PRE- AND POST-NUPTIAL AGREEMENTS

5. VALIDITY OF PRE- AND POST-NUPTIAL AGREEMENTS

5.1 To what extent are pre- and post-nups binding within the jurisdiction? Could you provide a brief discussion of the most significant recent case law on this issue?

In Minnesota, pre- and post-nups are known as ante-nuptial and post-nuptial contracts, respectively. Because ante-nuptial and post-nuptial agreements are considered contracts, the basic contractual concepts of offer, acceptance and consideration must be met. In addition, the Minnesota legislature set forth further standards for testing the validity of ante-nuptial and post-nuptial contracts in the Minnesota Statute section 519.11. The statute is applicable to all ante-nuptial contracts executed on or after 1 August 1979 and all postnuptial contracts executed on or after 1 August 1994.

Ante-nuptial contracts

Under Minnesota Statute section 519.11, ante-nuptial contracts must meet procedural and substantive fairness standards to be enforceable contracts. Some refer to the test required as the *McKee-Johnson* test. In the 1989 *McKee-Johnson v Johnson* case, the Minnesota Supreme Court determined that an ante-nuptial contract must pass three tests:

(1) procedural fairness at execution;
(2) substantive fairness at execution; and
(3) substantive fairness at enforcement.

Firstly, to be procedurally fair, the statute requires the ante-nuptial contract be made between a man and woman of legal age, as well as be in writing and signed by both parties in the presence of two witnesses at least one day prior to the marriage ceremony, and notarised. In addition, each party must make a full and fair disclosure of his or her earnings and property. Each party must also have had an opportunity to consult with an attorney of his or her choice. However, there is no requirement that the party actually consult with an attorney. A finding of procedural unfairness at execution will invalidate the agreement.

Secondly, to be substantively fair at execution, the court will evaluate whether the ante-nuptial contract was unconscionable when executed. For example, an agreement under which a spouse with little or no assets agrees to waive a claim to any marital property or maintenance upon divorce in exchange for no alternative rights to property or maintenance, may be found by the court to be substantively unfair at the time of execution. A finding of substantive unfairness at execution provides a basis to invalidate part or all of the agreement.

Thirdly, to be substantively fair at enforcement, the court will evaluate whether the ante-nuptial contract is unconscionable or oppressive at the time of enforcement. This stresses the importance of drafting an agreement that not only provides for the reasonable expectations of each party but also addresses any anticipated intervening events, such as the birth of a child and changes in employment or health. A finding of substantive unfairness at enforcement provides a basis to invalidate part or all of the agreement.

It is important to distinguish the burdens of proof in Minnesota. A party contesting an ante-nuptial contract has the burden of showing the agreement was procedurally unfair at execution or substantively unfair relative to the division of non-marital property. However, the proponent of an ante-nuptial contract has the burden of showing the agreement was substantively fair relative to the division of marital property. Ultimately, Minnesota courts will carefully consider whether there was any overreaching by one party over the other that resulted in an unfair ante-nuptial contract.

Post-nuptial contracts

Under Minnesota Statute section 519.11, legally married spouses may enter into post-nuptial contracts. The Statute requires procedural and substantive fairness at the time of execution and enforcement. In fact, post-nuptial contracts should not only comply with the requirements of ante-nuptial contracts, but must also meet additional requirements in order to be enforceable contracts. Notably, each spouse must at the time of execution actually be represented by separate counsel. In addition, neither spouse may commence an action for legal separation or dissolution within two years of the date of its execution. Violation of either of these additional terms will deem the post-nuptial contract unenforceable. Furthermore, parties to post-nuptial contracts are forbidden from using the contract to determine child support, custody or parenting time.

Finally, only a valid post-nuptial contract may amend or revoke an ante-nuptial contract. Only a later and valid post-nuptial contract may amend or revoke an earlier post-nuptial contract.

C. DIVORCE, NULLITY AND JUDICIAL SEPARATION

6. RECOGNITION OF FOREIGN MARRIAGES/DIVORCES

6.1 Summarise the position in your jurisdiction

Marriages

Minnesota, like most, if not all, states in the US, will recognise foreign marriages valid under the law where contracted, unless the marriage is contrary to strong public policy. Some foreign marriages thought to violate public policy that are specifically prohibited under Minnesota law include same-sex marriages, as well as those entered into before the dissolution of an earlier marriage, certain religious marriages and those between certain family members (eg, ancestor and descendant, brother and sister, uncle and niece, aunt and nephew and first cousins (Minnesota Statute. section 517.03)). However, a marriage between an uncle and niece, aunt and nephew or first cousins may be recognised if permitted by established customs of aboriginal cultures.

Divorces

The validity of a foreign divorce is generally governed by the rule of comity but only if the foreign tribunal had jurisdiction and there was an opportunity for a full and fair trial. However, Minnesota may still refuse to enforce a judgment if it is contrary to its public policy.

7. DIVORCE

7.1 Explain the grounds for divorce within the jurisdiction (please also deal with nullity and judicial separation if appropriate)

Under Minnesota Statute section 518.06, the grounds for divorce in Minnesota are an irretrievable breakdown of the marriage relationship. The court has jurisdiction to dissolve a marriage when one or both parties allege a desire to end the marriage because efforts towards reconciliation would not be fruitful. Should a dispute arise over whether an irretrievable breakdown exists, the court must find that either the parties have separated and lived apart for at least 180 days or that there is serious marital discord lending itself to irreconcilable differences. Fault, such as adultery, physical or mental cruelty, desertion or failure to provide support, are not relevant in Minnesota.

In Minnesota, marriages that are prohibited are null and void as a matter of law. The following marriages are prohibited pursuant to Minnesota Statute section 517.03, and thus, a nullity:

- marriage entered into before the dissolution of an earlier marriage of one of the parties becomes final;
- marriage between an ancestor and descendant, brother and sister, uncle and niece, aunt and nephew or first cousins, whether by half or whole blood, except marriages permitted by the established customs of aboriginal cultures;

Under certain circumstances, a Minnesota court can declare a marriage null and void. The circumstances are defined in Minnesota Statute section 518.02, which provides that a marriage shall be declared a nullity if:

- a party lacked capacity to consent to the marriage at the time the marriage was solemnised, either due to mental incapacity or infirmity, and the other party was unaware of the incapacity at that time;
- a party lacked the physical capacity to consummate the marriage through sexual intercourse and the other party was unaware of the incapacity at the time the marriage was solemnised;
- a party was under the legal age for marriage, which is 18 years of age in Minnesota (or 16 years of age with consent of a parent).

In Minnesota, a judicial separation is entitled 'legal separation' and is the determination of the rights and responsibilities of a husband and wife arising out of the marital relationship. A decree of legal separation does not terminate the marital status of the parties and it is granted when one or both parties petition for a decree of legal separation and neither party contests the petition (Minnesota Statute section 518.06). A decree of legal separation will address all of the issues that a decree of dissolution would address, including custody, parenting time, child and spousal support and division of property, without dissolving the parties' marriage.

8. FINANCES/CAPITAL, PROPERTY

8.1 What powers does the court have to allocate financial resources and property on the breakdown of marriage?

Minnesota law presumes all property acquired during marriage is marital property. (Minnesota Statute section 518.58). A party to a marriage dissolution proceeding may claim property is non-marital because it was acquired before the marriage or by a specific gift or inheritance during the marriage. (Minnesota Statute section 518.003). If one claims property as non-marital, he or she must prove the non-marital character of the asset. Title and form of ownership are not controlling. Proof of a non-marital claim requires determination of value at the time of marriage or acquisition and tracing the continued existence of the asset until the time of division. The court, alternatively, has the option to award up to one half of the non-marital property to prevent an unfair hardship.

Property identified and classified as either marital or non-marital in character is next valued. Non-marital issues will again need to be addressed because passive and active appreciation of the asset may have marital or non-marital features. The date of valuation is the day of the initially scheduled pre-hearing settlement conference, unless the parties agree otherwise or the court finds another valuation date is fair and equitable. Minnesota is an equitable division property state. This means that property acquired by individuals during marriage will be divided equitably and fairly by the court based on relevant factors set forth in Minnesota Statute section 518.58, which include the length of the marriage, any prior marriage of a party, the age, health, station, occupation, amount and sources of income, vocational skills, employability, estate liabilities, needs, opportunity for future acquisition of capital assets and income of each party. Note that marital misconduct is not a factor. The court may also consider the contribution of each party in the acquisition, preservation, depreciation or appreciation in the amount or value of the marital property, as well as the contribution of a spouse as a homemaker. It is presumed that each spouse made a substantial contribution to the acquisition of property and income while they were living together as husband and wife. While a 50/50 division is not required top meet the equitable standard, it is the norm. A court's decision to divide property inequitably must be based on facts justifying such a division.

8.2 Explain and illustrate with reference to recent cases the court's thinking on division of assets

In general, the market value of an asset is used to value property for division in a marital dissolution (*Prahl v Prahl*, 627 N.W.2d 698 (Minn.App. 2001)). The following aspects of property division frequently present controversies on which the higher courts have recently ruled.

Non-marital property

Non-marital property is often combined with marital property in common interest without anticipation of future division. Upon dissolution of marriage, when the property must be divided, it is often difficult to determine proper allocation of marital and non-marital property.

Pensions

Valuing and dividing a pension is generally left to the trial court's discretion. (Minnesota Statute section 518.58.) In determining whether retirement benefits should be divided at the time of dissolution or upon future receipt by an employee spouse, the trial court should consider the advantages and disadvantages of each option in light of the particular facts of the case. Dividing future retirement benefits acquired during the marriage when the parties are divorcing is preferred where there are sufficient assets available at that time to divide present value of retirement benefits (*Taylor v Taylor*, 329 N.W.2d 795 (Minn. 1983)). If the present value of a pension is speculative, the court has ruled that the proper method is application of a fixed percentage payable when received (*Taylor* at 799).

Business

Valuation of a business in a marriage dissolution proceeding is always problematic because the business is rarely actually for sale; a willing buyer always being the best measure. The courts typically eschew continued joint ownership of any asset after a marriage has been dissolved. The outcome in a particular case will largely depend on the nature of the business, the ownership interest and the transactional models available to accomplish the division.

9. FINANCES/MAINTENANCE

9.1 Explain the operation of maintenance for spouses on an ongoing basis after the breakdown of marriage

Minnesota refers to spousal support, formerly alimony, as spousal maintenance. It is awarded based upon the recipient's need and the obligor's ability to pay. Minnesota Statute section 518.552 further defines a recipient in need as one who lacks sufficient property or who is unable to provide adequate self-support. Spousal maintenance may either be temporary and rehabilitative or permanent, depending on the circumstances of the parties during the marriage. However, the law makes it clear that there is to be no preference toward an award of temporary over permanent maintenance. While marital misconduct is irrelevant in determining the amount and duration of spousal maintenance, the court will look at several other relevant factors in accordance with Minnesota's statutory guidelines. These factors include the financial resources and obligations of the recipient; the time necessary for the recipient to acquire sufficient education or training and the probability (given the party's age and skills) of self-support; the marital standard of living; the marriage duration (including a homemaker's absence from employment, outmoded skills and diminished earning capacity); loss of earnings and opportunities forgone by recipient; the recipient's age and physical and emotional conditions; the obligor's ability to pay and the contribution of each party in the amount or value of marital property, as well as the recipient's contribution as a homemaker to further the obligor's employment or business. Income producing assets acquired as a result of the dissolution of the marriage will offset the need of the dependent spouse.

Spousal maintenance payments are tax deductible for the obligor, thus reducing his or her taxable income. However, these payments are income to the recipient. Cost of Living Adjustments (COLA) may also be applied every two years. Either party may seek to modify a spousal maintenance award under Minnesota Statute section 518A.39 if there is a substantial change in circumstances making the existing obligation unreasonable or unfair. A change warranting modification may include a substantial increase or decrease in a recipient or obligor's gross income; a substantial increase or decrease in the need of a recipient; receipt of public assistance; or a change in either party's cost of living as measured by the Federal Bureau of Labor statistics. To avoid the risk of modification, the parties may negotiate a '*Karon* waiver' for the purpose of preventing any further court review of a spousal maintenance award. Governed by case law and statute, the judgment and decree must set forth the stipulation to waive modification as well as state specific findings in accordance with the provisions set forth in Minnesota Statute section 518.552. The stipulation must be fair, equitable, supported by consideration and set forth that full disclosure of each party's financial circumstances has occurred. A *Karon* waiver can only be obtained by stipulation between the parties. Spousal maintenance awards terminate upon the death of either party or remarriage of the recipient.

9.2 Is it common for maintenance to be awarded?

Spousal maintenance for a dependent spouse in a long-term marriage is favoured (Minnesota Statute section 518.552, sub-division 3). Equity and the ability to meet one's needs and those of the children will govern.

9.3 Explain and illustrate with reference to recent cases the court's thinking on maintenance

In 2004, the Minnesota Court of Appeals held in *Peterka v Peterka*, 675 N.W.2d 353, 358 (Minn.App. 2004), that 'the purpose of a maintenance award is to allow the recipient and the obligor to have a standard of living that approximates the marital standard of living, as closely as is equitable under the circumstances'. Subjective determinations, such as standard of living and reasonable capacity for self-support, permit a wide degree of variability in spousal maintenance awards.

10. CHILD MAINTENANCE

10.1 On what basis is child maintenance calculated within the jurisdiction?

In Minnesota, child maintenance is referred to as child support and is governed by Minnesota Statute section 518A and interpreted by case law. Since 2007, child support has been set according to an 'income shares' model obligating each parent to contribute to the child's support.

Child support is based upon both parties' gross income with income imputed to an unemployed or underemployed parent. Child support consists of three distinct components: basic support; work or school-related child care costs; and medical support. Basic support means the child's housing, food, clothing, transportation, education costs and other expenses relating to the child's care.

To calculate support, it must be determined which party is the obligee and which is the obligor. The parent with 'primary physical custody of the child' is presumed (not conclusively) to be the obligee (Minnesota Statute section 518A.26, subd 14).

Each party's income for child support purposes must be determined. This includes any actual income pursuant to Minnesota Statute section 518A.29 and any potential income imputed pursuant to Minnesota Statute section 518A.32. All parents are presumed to be capable of working full-time (40 hours per week). A parent's income for child support purposes is reduced according to Minnesota Statute section 518A.33 if the parent has a non-joint child in their care. Each parent's income for child support purposes is referred to as their Parental Income for Child Support (PICS).

The procedure laid out in Minnesota Statute section 518A.34 must be followed. The parents' PICS added together determine their combined PICS. The combined PICS are divided by each parent's individual PICS to determine their percentage of contribution.

The combined basic support according to guidelines set forth in Minnesota Statute section 518A.35 must be determined. The obligor's basic child support amount is their percentage (as determined in the previous step) of this combined basic support amount. The obligor's basic support obligation is subject to reduction if the parenting expense adjustment applies. Minnesota Statute. section 518A.36. This means that an obligor is entitled to a 12 per cent reduction in basic support if they have the child between 10 per cent and 45 per cent of the time (determined by number of overnights with the child).

If a parent has between 45.1 per cent and 50 per cent of the time with the child, then parenting time is presumed to be equal. If this is the case, a different calculation is used, offsetting the two parents' respective obligations (Minnesota Statute section 518A.36.) This means that the higher income-earning parent will have an obligation to pay support to the lower income-earning parent.

In determining child care contributions, unless otherwise agreed to by the parties and approved by the court, the court must order that work-related or education-related child care costs of joint children be divided between the obligor and obligee, based on each parent's PICS percentage (see above).

Medical support means providing health care coverage or contributing to the cost of health care coverage, public coverage, unreimbursed medical expense and uninsured medical expenses of the joint child. The court must order that the cost of health care coverage and all unreimbursed and uninsured medical expenses under the health plan be divided between the obligor and obligee based on the parents' PICS percentage. (Minnesota Statute section 518A.41).

The Department of Human Services has developed a child support calculator whereby the above information is inputted and child support is calculated. See Minnesota Child Support calculator, *www.childsupportcalculator.dhs.state.mn.us*.

The statutory guidelines child support amount is presumed to be appropriate. If the court deviates from the guidelines amount, it must make written findings as to the reason for the deviation (Minnesota Statute sections 518A.37 and 518A.43.)

Modifications of existing child support orders are governed by Minnesota Statute section 518A.39. The party requesting the modification must show both a change in circumstances and that the changed circumstances make the existing order 'unreasonable and unfair'.

11. RECIPROCAL ENFORCEMENT OF FINANCIAL ORDERS

11.1 Summarise the position in your jurisdiction

Orders including financial provisions regarding child and/or spousal support are enforced pursuant to Minnesota Statute section 518C and the Uniform Interstate Family Support Act (UIFSA). UIFSA has been enacted in every state in the United States. According to the UIFSA, a support order or an order for income withholding issued by a tribunal of another state must be registered in Minnesota for enforcement (Minnesota Statute section 518C.601).

'State', as defined by UIFSA, includes a foreign jurisdiction that has enacted a law or established procedures for issuance and enforcement of support orders that are substantially similar to the procedures included in

UIFSA or procedures included in the Uniform Reciprocal Enforcement of Support Act (URESA) or the Revised Uniform Reciprocal Enforcement of Support Act (URESA-revised). Minnesota has not enacted URESA or URESA-revised and only Georgia, Iowa, Missouri and Michigan follow URESA or URESA-revised.

To register an order for child or spousal support in Minnesota, the following documents or information must be sent to the court:

- a letter of transmittal to the tribunal requesting registration and enforcement;
- two copies, including one certified copy, of all orders to be registered, including any modification of an order;
- a sworn statement by the party seeking registration or a certified statement by the custodian of the records showing the amount of any arrearage;
- the name of the obligor and, if known, the obligor's address and social security number, the name and address of the obligor's employer and any other source of income of the obligor, a description and the location of any property of the obligor in the state not exempt from execution;
- the name and address of the obligee and, if applicable, the agency or person to whom support payments are to be remitted.

Once the information is received by the court, it must file the order as a foreign judgment (Minnesota Statute section 518C.602). Thereafter, the judgment is enforceable in the same manner and subject to the same procedures as an order issued by a Minnesota court.

12. FINANCIAL RELIEF AFTER FOREIGN DIVORCE PROCEEDINGS

12.1 What powers are available to make orders following a foreign divorce?

After a foreign judgment is registered, a Minnesota court will recognise and enforce the judgment. However, it may not modify the order if the court that issued the judgment had jurisdiction (Minnesota Statute section 518C.603). In other words, a Minnesota court has limited authority to issue orders subsequent to a foreign order's registration. (See Minnesota Statute section 518C.611.)

D. CHILDREN

13. CUSTODY/PARENTAL RESPONSIBILITY

13.1 Briefly explain the legal position in relation to custody/parental responsibility following the breakdown of a relationship or marriage

Custody is defined in MSA section 518.003, subd 3 wherein there are essentially two elements, legal (authority over major decisions such as education or religion) which is presumed to be joint under MSA section 518.17, subd 2 with certain exceptions and physical custody which will be awarded based on a best interests standard outlined in MSA section 518.17, subd 1.

Custody has become a less meaningful term since 2006 when several new laws removed the financial and removal advantages. Most disputes are over parenting time which will be addressed in a parenting plan, (MSA section 518.705) and through the use of early neutral evaluators working with the parties to address parenting concerns.

In all instances if there is a history of domestic violence there will be some limitations or qualifications on custody and parenting time.

Third parties may pursue custody of a child who has resided with them without a parent present for certain periods of time. (MSA Chapter 257C.)

13.2 Briefly explain the legal position in relation to access/contact/visitation following the breakdown of a relationship or marriage

Parenting time is established under MSA section 518.175 as is in the best interests of the child. Parenting time cannot be restricted unless there is a specific finding by the court, after a hearing, parenting time between the child and the parent is likely to endanger the child's physical or emotional heath or impair the child's emotional development. If that finding is made the court may restrict, condition such as supervision or deny entirely.

Grandparents have the right to secure visitation with grandchildren pursuant to MSA 257C.08.

14. INTERNATIONAL ABDUCTION

14.1 Summarise the position in your jurisdiction

The United States, and hence Minnesota, is bound by the Hague Convention on the Civil Aspects of International Child Abduction (Hague Convention). When a family is involved in an international child custody dispute, the Hague Convention will apply if both countries are parties to the treaty.

In the event the child's home country is not a signatory of the Hague Convention but a foreign child custody determination has been issued, Minnesota Statute chapter 518D (UCCJEA) provides several different processes for the foreign child custody determination to be recognised and the abducted child ordered to be returned.

15. LEAVE TO REMOVE/APPLICATIONS TO TAKE A CHILD OUT OF THE JURISDICTION

15.1 Summarise the position in your jusridiction

The parent with whom the child resides may move out of a state with a child upon agreement of the parties or order of the court. The parent wishing to move has the burden of showing that the proposed move is in the best interests of the child prior to the move.

15.2 Under what circumstances may a parent apply to remove their child from the jurisdiction against the wishes of the other parent?

Relocation with a child when a parent desires to move outside the state of Minnesota is governed by Minnesota Statute section 518.175, subd 3. The statute was enacted in 2006 and it overruled the previously court-created rule on relocation found in *Auge v Auge*, 334 N.W.2d 393 (Minn. 1983) which held it was presumed that the custodial parent of a child is entitled to permission to remove the child from the state (Id. at 399).

Now a parent must show the court why a proposed move out of state is in a child's best interests unless there has been domestic violence before the move actually occurs, and that the purpose of the move is not to interfere with the other party's parenting time with the child. The statute sets forth eight best-interest factors that are unique to the consideration of a move out of state. If there has been domestic abuse, the burden shifts to the parent opposing the move.

To date, there is little appellate guidance in interpreting this new statute (Minnesota Statute section 518.175, subd 3). The State's Court of Appeals interpreted the relocation statute in its 2010 decision *Hagen v Schirmers*, 783 N.W.2d 212 (Minn.App. 2010), recognising that while one parent relocating to another state will diminish the child's relationship to the non-relocating parent, one negative factor does not require rejection of a relocation.

E. SURROGACY AND ADOPTION

16. VALIDITY OF SURROGACY AGREEMENTS

16.1 Briefly summarise the position in your jurisdiction

The United States has no national policies governing surrogacy. Each individual state determines its own laws regarding surrogacy.

Several states prohibit surrogacy, declaring all such agreements void and unenforceable as a matter of public policy. A few make it a crime to compensate the surrogate. Other states allow surrogacy but restrict it to married couples or to cases where at least one parent has a genetic link to the child. The majority of states have no laws regarding surrogacy, so families are in legal limbo. See Surrogacy Laws by State from the Human Rights Campaign: *www.allaboutsurrogacy.com*

17. ADOPTION

17.1 Briefly summarise the position in relation to adoption in your jurisdiction. Is adoption available to individuals, cohabiting couples (both heterosexual and same-sex)?

Adoption is available to individuals and cohabitating couples, whether heterosexual or same sex. Adoption is governed by Minnesota Statutes §§ 259.20, *et seq*. and the Minnesota Rules of Adoption Procedure. Case law has established that adoption statutes are to be liberally construed to accomplish their purpose, *Petition of Jordet*, 248 Minn. 433, 439 80 N.W.2d 642, 646 (1957). The best interests of the child are paramount in any adoption proceeding.

There are many different types of adoption including: agency placement, direct placement, step-parent, relative, co-parent, adult, foreign and foster parent. A person who has resided in the state for more than one year may petition the court to adopt a child or an adult. A single person may adopt a child provided all the requirements for adoption are met. There is a preference for placement of a child with relatives. In an agency or a direct placement adoption, an adoption petition must be filed within 12 months after the child is placed in the prospective adoptive home.

An adoption proceeding is commenced in Minnesota by filing a petition for adoption, a motion for a direct placement pre-adoptive custody order, or by filing a motion for waiver of agency placement in the juvenile courts. Minnesota Rules of Adoption Procedure, Rule 26.01 require that certain documents accompany the petition at filing: the adoption study; the biological parents' social and medical history forms, unless the petitioner is the child's step-parent; any requests to waive a post-placement assessment and report; background check; and proof of service of the petition on any other parties, if service is required under the rules or statute.

When a child is adopted under the laws of a foreign country, the adoption is valid and binding under the laws of Minnesota if the validity of the foreign adoption is verified by the granting of an IR-3 visa for the child by the United States Citizenship and Immigration Services (USCIS), Minnesota Statute § 259.60. If the adoption is recognised by USCIS, then it is recommended that the adoptive family obtain an amended birth record so that the child has a birth certificate from the United States by petitioning the district court in the county where the adoptive parent resides for a decree 'confirming' and recognising the adoption, which then authorises the Commissioner of Health to issue a new birth record for the child. A court must issue this decree upon receipt of the following documents: signed, sworn, notarised petition requesting that the adoption be recognised; a copy of the child's original birth record, if available; a copy of the final adoption certificate or equivalent issued in the foreign jurisdiction; a copy of the child's passport, including the US visa indicating IR-3 immigration status; and, a certificated English translation of any of these documents that are not written in English. When a court issues a decree under this section, the court has to forward a copy to the Commissioner of Health and Human Services.

In the event the foreign-born child has no actual birth record because of war in its place of birth, the courts generally accept an affidavit of the petitioner or petitioners stating what information they have about the child's birth or a statement from an orphanage where the child had been located. An adoption of a child in the United States under an IR-4 visa needs to be completed as an agency placement adoption. When a child is in the United States illegally and there is a desire by the child's parents to have the child adopted, immigration issues should be addressed by a qualified immigration attorney familiar with adoption so as to avoid deportation of the child or a risk that the child may never be able to become a United States citizen.

F. COHABITATION

18. COHABITATION

18.1 What legislation (if any) governs division of property for unmarried couples on the breakdown of the relationship?

There is very little legislation directly governing division of property for unmarried couples on the breakdown of the relationship. Minnesota does not recognise common law marriage. However, Minnesota will recognise a common law marriage that was created in another jurisdiction prior to the couple's moving to Minnesota (*Laikola v Engineered Concrete*, 277 N.W.2d 653, 655-56 (Minn.1979) (quoting *In re Estate of Kinkead*, 239 Minn. 27, 30, 57 N.W.2d 628, 631 (1953)).

Minnesota has what is commonly referred to as an 'anti-palimony' statute found in Minnesota Statute section 513.075. This statute was enacted shortly after the landmark case of *Marvin v Marvin* in California 18 Cal.3d 660 (1976). The Minnesota Supreme Court followed California's lead in *Marvin* shortly thereafter (see *Carlson v Olson*, 256 N.W.2d 249 (Minn. 1977)), holding that the district court has the equitable power to divide real and personal property in a partition action between persons who had lived together for 21 years as if married. Not long after *Carlson*, however, the Minnesota legislature attempted to foreclose this type of legal proceeding by enacting a statute that provides if sexual relations between the parties are contemplated of a man and a woman who are living together or are about to commence living together, then a cohabitation contract between them is not valid unless the contract is in writing and enforcement is sought after termination of the relationship. (Minnesota Statute section 513.075.) If the parties have not executed a written cohabitation contract, then the courts are divested of jurisdiction to hear claims for entitlement to property based upon cohabitation (Minnesota Statute section 513.076). The terms of the statute are vague and, by its explicit terms, it only applies to a man and a woman residing together. Thus, arguably, this statute does not bar the courts from reaching a conclusion similar to the *Marvin* case if it involves a same-sex couple.

Equitable remedies and limitations

In re *Estate of Palmen*, 588 N.W.2d 493 (Minn.1999), statutory jurisdictional bar to recovery by one cohabitant from the other on an oral contract applies only when the sole consideration for the contract is contemplation of sexual relations out of wedlock and, thus, a claim by a cohabitant to recover, preserve or protect their own property, which they acquired independent of any service contract related to cohabitation, is enforceable.

In *Obert v Dahl*, 574 N.W.2d 747 (Minn.App. 1998), unless sexual relationship constitutes sole consideration for property agreement, cohabitants may maintain actions against each other under anti-palimony statute, providing that contracts regarding the property and financial relations of the parties living together out of wedlock are enforceable only if in writing and signed by both parties, regarding their own earnings or property, based on equitable theories such as constructive trust or unjust enrichment.

In *re Estate of Eriksen*, 337 N.W.2d 671 (Minn.1983), statutes governing financial and property agreements and contracts between an unwed, cohabitating man and woman were not applicable to the woman's claim to preserve or protect her own property which she acquired for cash consideration and wholly independent of any service contract related to her cohabitation, and the creation of a constructive trust consisting of one-half interest in the home was required to prevent unjust enrichment of the estate.

G. FAMILY DISPUTE RESOLUTION

19. MEDIATION, COLLABORATIVE LAW AND ARBITRATION.

19.1 Briefly summarise the non-court-based processes available to your jurisdiction and the current status of agreements reached under the auspices of mediation, collaborative law and arbitration

The majority of Minnesota's judicial districts operate under an Early Case Management (ECM) model in which, after the filing of an initial pleading for divorce, the court schedules an Initial Case Management Conference (ICMC). At the ICMC, the judicial officer discusses and explains the various Alternative Dispute Resolution (ADR) options available to the parties, including Early Neutral Evaluation (ENE) and mediation. The decision to participate in any ADR process is voluntary and one made at the ICMC by the parties. Two other ADR options available to parties outside of the ECM process are collaborative and cooperative law.

Early Neutral Evaluation (ENE) is a voluntary, confidential process established in Minnesota that is intended to move families through the court system as efficiently and fairly as possible. There are two types of ENE:

(i) Social Early Neutral Evaluation (SENE) involves a two-person, male/female team of evaluators whom, after meeting with the parties and their attorneys to hear each party's position, provide feedback, recommendations and viable settlement options regarding custody and parenting time based on their opinions; and

(ii) Financial Early Neutral Evaluation (FENE) involves one evaluator whom likewise, after meeting with the parties and their attorneys to hear their respective positions, provides feedback, recommendations and viable settlement options regarding financial issues such as property division, maintenance and support.

At conclusion, generally within 45 to 60 days, evaluators only report to the court whether the parties reached an agreement, not the terms of any agreement, unless approved by the parties. Agreements reached through SENE or FENE are binding only to the extent that the terms are memorialised in writing and signed by the parties.

Mediation is a voluntary, confidential process in which parties may or may not participate with the assistance of their attorneys with the goal of reaching full settlement without litigation. Any agreements reached through mediation must be memorialised in writing and signed by the parties in order to be binding.

Collaborative law allows parties and their trained collaborative lawyers to enter into a formal agreement to attempt settlement without seeking court action other than for approval of a final settlement agreement; if settlement is not reached, the collaborative lawyers must withdraw and new counsel must be retained prior to the parties participating in any further proceedings. A complete settlement agreement reached by the parties through the collaborative law process is generally submitted to the court for administrative review and approved for filing without a final hearing when all parties are represented by lawyers.

Cooperative law allows participants and their lawyers to enter into a formal and flexible agreement outlining the process in which the participants seek to utilise in working towards reaching a final resolution. If the participants reach an impasse, however, the cooperative process allows participants to seek court intervention as necessary without retaining new lawyers. Participants in the cooperative law process may also engage in litigation for a limited issue and return to a variety of negotiation models, including mediation, neutral evaluation or moderated settlement conference. The complete settlement agreement reached by the parties through the cooperative law process is generally submitted to the court for administrative review and approved for filing without a final hearing if all parties are represented by lawyers. If all parties are not represented by lawyers, the court will hold a final hearing.

19.2 What is the statutory basis (if any), for mediation, collaborative law and arbitration in your jurisdiction? In particular, are the parties required to attempt a family dispute resolution in advance of the institution of proceedings?

In Minnesota, all family law matters in district court, including those requesting post-decree relief, are subject to Alternative Dispute Resolution (ADR) processes, pursuant to the General Rules of Practice for the District Courts, Rules 114 and 310, except when there is domestic abuse, contempt, or a public agency is either a party or providing services such as in maintenance, support and parentage actions. Further, unless ADR is not required, the moving party must file a Certificate of Settlement Efforts no later than 24 hours before the scheduled hearing, certifying that there was an attempt to resolve the issue(s) raised by the motion.

Rule 114 specifically delineates the various ADR processes in categories such as:

(i) adjudicative types, including arbitration, Consensual Special Magistrate, summary jury trial;
(ii) evaluative types, including Early Neutral Evaluation (ENE) and non-binding advisory opinion;
(iii) an investigative and report process type, including neutral fact finding;
(iv) a facilitative type, including mediation;
(v) hybrid types, including mini-trial and mediation-arbitration; and
(vi) other as created by agreement of the parties.

This final 'other' category provides the basis for collaborative law, also codified at Rule 111.05, and cooperative law.

H. OTHER

20. CIVIL PARTNERSHIP/SAME-SEX MARRIAGE

20.1 What is the status of civil partnership/same-sex marriage within the jurisdiction?

Historically, marriage between persons of the same sex in Minnesota was prohibited. However, the passage of recent legislation will make Minnesota's marriage law gender neutral and same-sex marriage legal in August 2013.

20.2 What legislation governs civil partnership/same-sex marriage?

Effective 1 August, 2013, Minnesota Statute sections 517.01, 517.03, 517.08 , 517.09, 517.201, 517.23, 518.07 will be amended to allow civil marriage between persons of the same sex, as well as to define residency for purposes of the dissolution of a civil marriage.

21. CONTROVERSIAL AREAS/RAPIDLY DEVELOPING AREAS OF LAW

21.1 Is there a particular area of the law within the jurisdiction that is currently undergoing major change?

The segregation of marital property to be divided in the dissolution of the marriage from property acquired outside the marriage remains conflicted and wanting a logical and consistent rationale. The issues include separation of asset from a stream of income available for support. For example, are the retained earnings from a non-marital asset available for the support of the family? Are the undistributed earnings available for division as a marital asset acquired during the marriage due to marital efforts? And the like. Why are minimal efforts expended to manage a non-marital retirement account which result in appreciation capable of giving this asset a marital character?

Child custody is no longer a substantive issue. Since the enactment of the child support guidelines, which take into consideration the income of both parents and allocate the child support by the percentage of time the child is with each parent, as well as the enactment of a law taking away the blanket authority physical custodial parents had to relocate out of state or county, the historic tensions around child custody have abated. The remaining task is allocation of parenting time, which far more parents are able to resolve without high conflict.

21.2 Which areas of law are the most out-of-step? Which areas would you most like to see reformed/changed?

Minnesota enacted laws to permit same sex marriage only in May of 2013. Suddenly what was once impossible will now become common place.

USA – New York

Teitler & Teitler, LLP
John M Teitler, Nicholas W Lobenthal & Paul D Getzels

A JURISDICTION AND CONFLICT OF LAW

1. SOURCES OF LAW

1.1 What is the primary source of law in relation to the breakdown of marriage and the welfare of children within the jurisdiction?

1.2 Which are the main statutes governing matrimonial law in the jurisdiction?

Family law is governed primarily by the Domestic Relations Law (DRL), Family Court Act (FCA), Social Services Law (SSL), Civil Practice Law and Rules (CPLR), the Official Compilation of Codes, Rules & Regulations of the State of New York (NYCRR), and case law interpreting the foregoing.

2. JURISDICTION

2.1 What are the main jurisdictional requirements for the institution of proceedings in relation to divorce, property and children?

Exclusive subject matter jurisdiction over divorce is vested in the Supreme Court of the State of New York, which, despite its name, is a trial-level court of general jurisdiction (*Graves v Graves*, 177 Misc. 2d 358, 360, 675 N.Y.S.2d 843, 846 (Supreme Court (Sup. Ct.) Richmond County 1998); *Fine v Fine*, 65 Misc. 2d 87, 88, 93, 316 N.Y.S.2d 725, 727, 731 (Fam. Ct. N.Y. County 1970); see also *Lacks v Lacks*, 41 N.Y.2d 71, 76-77, 359 N.E.2d 384, 388, 390 N.Y.S.2d 875, 879 (1976)). The Supreme Court also has exclusive jurisdiction to distribute the parties' property (see *Kolar v Kolar*, 113 Misc. 2d 995, 996, 509 N.Y.S.2d 245, 246 (Fam. Ct. Onondaga County 1986) (the Family Court has no jurisdiction to enforce equitable distribution award); *Davidow v Davidow*, 97 Misc. 2d 220, 226-27, 410 N.Y.S.2d 989, 994 (Fam. Ct. Richmond County 1978) (the Family Court had no power to make property award unless it related directly to support)).

Within a divorce action, the Supreme Court also determines spousal maintenance (formerly alimony), and child support and custody (see *Graves v Graves*, 177 Misc. 2d 358, 360, 675 N.Y.S.2d 843, 846 (Sup. Ct. Richmond County 1998)). The Family Court has certain concurrent power to determine spousal maintenance, child support and child custody (*H.M. v E.T.*, 14 N.Y.3d 521, 526, 930 N.E.2d 206, 208, 904 N.Y.S.2d 285, 287 (2010); see N.Y. Const. Article 6, section 13 (enumerating Family Court's powers); FCA section 115 (same)). Appeals from the Supreme Court and the Family Court are taken to the Appellate Division of the Supreme Court of the State of New York, an intermediate appellate court that is divided into four geographic departments (New York Constitution (N.Y. Const.) Article 6, section 4(a); CPLR 5701; FCA section 1111; Judiciary Law (Jud. Law) section 70).

Appeals from the Appellate Division are taken to the Court of Appeals of the State of New York, the state's highest court (see N.Y. Const. art. VI; CPLR 5601, 5602).

Service of process may be effected anywhere in the United States or, subject to any applicable treaties, anywhere in the world (CPLR 313 (McKinney 2010); *Volkswagenwerk Aktiengesellschaft v Schlunk*, 486 U.S. 694, 699 (1988); *Morgenthau v Avion Resources Ltd.*, 11 N.Y.3d 383, 390, 848 N.E.2d 929, 934, 869 N.Y.S.2d 886, 891 (2008); *Sardanis v Sumitomo Corp.*, 279 A.D.2d 225, 228-29, 718 N.Y.S.2d 66, 68 (1st Dep't 2001); see *Wood v Wood*, 231 A.D.2d 713, 647 N.Y.S.2d 830 (2d Dep't 1996)).

The plaintiff's domicile within New York is a sufficient basis for the court to dissolve the marriage, but an independent basis for personal jurisdiction over the defendant must exist for the court to grant economic relief (see CPLR 302(b); *Julien v Julien*, 78 A.D.3d 584, 912 N.Y.S.2d 42 (1st Dep't 2010); *Babu v Babu*, 229 A.D.2d 758, 758-59, 645 N.Y.S.2d 899, 900 (3d Dep't 1996)). The court may determine child custody if New York's codification of the Uniform Child Custody Jurisdiction and Enforcement Act, DRL sections 75 to 76–i, is satisfied.

In a divorce action, residence is a substantive element of the cause of action to be pleaded and proved (*Lacks*, 41 N.Y.2d at 72-73, 359 N.E.2d at 385, 390, N.Y.S.2d at 876).

3. DOMICILE AND HABITUAL RESIDENCE

3.1 Explain the concepts of domicile and habitual residence as they apply to the jurisdiction in relation to divorce, the finances and children

A 'domicile' is a person's fixed and permanent home, to which they always intend to return (*Senhart v Senhart*, 18 A.D.3d 642, 643, 795 N.Y.S.2d 642, 643 (2d Dep't 2005)). A 'residence' is a place to which a person has a significant connection because they have lived there for some length of time during the course of a year (*Deazle v Miles*, 77 A.D.3d 660, 662, 908 N.Y.S.2d 716, 718 (2d Dep't 2010); *Wittich v Wittich*, 210 A.D.2d 138, 139, 620 N.Y.S.2d 351, 352 (1st Dep't 1994)). A person can have only one domicile, but they can have more than one residence (*Laufer v Hauge*, 140 A.D.2d 671, 672, 528 N.Y.S.2d 878, 879 (2d Dep't 1988)).

In New York, an action to annul a marriage, or to declare the nullity of a void marriage, or for divorce or separation may be maintained only when:

- the parties were married in this state and either party is a resident thereof when the action is commenced and has been a resident for a continuous period of one year immediately preceding the commencement of the action; or
- the parties have resided in this state as husband and wife and either party is a resident thereof when the action is commenced and has been a resident for a continuous period of one year immediately preceding the commencement of the action; or

- the cause occurred in the state and either party has been a resident thereof for a continuous period of at least one year immediately preceding the commencement of the action; or
- the cause occurred in the state and both parties are residents thereof at the time of the commencement of the action; or
- either party has been a resident of the state for a continuous period of at least two years immediately preceding the commencement of the action.

(DRL section 230).

4. CONFLICT OF LAW/APPLICABLE LAW TO BE APPLIED

4.1 What happens when one party applies to stay proceedings in favour of a foreign jurisdiction? What factors will the local court take into account when determining forum issues?

A New York court may dismiss a cause of action if, *inter alia*, 'there is another action pending between the same parties for the same cause of action in a court of any state or the United States; instead of dismissing, the court 'may make such order as justice requires' (CPLR 3211(a)(4)). A different rule applies if the other action is pending outside the United States (*Steiner v Steiner*, N.Y. L.J., March 5, 1997, at 25, col. 5 (N.Y. Sup. Ct. N.Y. County) (n.o.r.); *Mary F.B. v David B.*, 112 Misc. 2d 475, 477, 447 N.Y.S.2d 375, 377 (Fam. Ct. N.Y. County 1982)), in which case the court will consider *forum non conveniens*, codified at CPLR 327, whose factors include:

- the burden on the New York courts;
- the potential hardship to the defendant;
- the unavailability of an alternative forum in which plaintiff may bring suit;
- whether both parties to the action are non-residents; and
- whether the transaction out of which the cause of action arose occurred primarily in a foreign jurisdiction.

(*Islamic Republic of Iran v Pahlavi*, 62 N.Y.2d 474, 479, 467 N.E.2d 245, 248, 478 N.Y.S.2d 597, 600 (1984); accord *Salzstein v Salzstein*, 70 A.D.3d 806, 807, 894 N.Y.S.2d 510, 512 (2d Dep't 2010) (potential hardship to witnesses is another factor); *Nasser v Nasser*, 52 A.D.3d 306, 306-07, 859 N.Y.S.2d 445, 445-46 (1st Dep't 2008) (whether foreign law would apply is another factor.))

Litigants in actions pending outside New York or the United States may seek discovery within New York (CPLR 328, 3102(e)).

New York courts will usually apply the law of the state that has the greatest nexus with the dispute (*see Boronow v Boronow*, 111 A.D.2d 735, 737, 490 N.Y.S.2d 230, 232 (2d Dep't 1985), affirmed without consideration of point, 71 N.Y.2d 284, 519 N.E.2d 1375, 525 N.Y.S.2d 179 (1988)).

Contractual choice of law provisions can also be recognised. When a contract governs a transaction of at least US$250,000 in the aggregate, the parties may select New York law, regardless of whether the contract bears a 'reasonable relation' to New York, with exceptions not directly relevant to marital agreements (N.Y. Gen. Oblig. Law section 5-1401). New York will honour a choice of law provision in a marital agreement where the selected law has the most significant contacts with the dispute (see *Anonymous v Anonymous*, N.Y. L.J., August 22, 1997, at 22, col. 6 (N.Y. Sup. Ct. N.Y. County) (n.o.r.), affirmed in part, reversed in part without consideration of point, 253 A.D.2d 696, 677 N.Y.S.2d 573 (1st Dep't 1998); *Strebler v Wolf*, 152 Misc. 859, 273 N.Y.S. 653 (Sup. Ct. N.Y. County 1934); *Lupien v Lupien*, 68 A.D.3d 1807, 1808, 891 N.Y.S.2d 785, 785-86 (4th Dep't 2009).

B. PRE- AND POST-NUPTIAL AGREEMENTS

5. VALIDITY OF PRE- AND POST-NUPTIAL AGREEMENTS

5.1 To what extent are pre- and post-nups binding within the jurisdiction? Could you provide a brief discussion of the most significant recent case law on this issue.

Pre-nuptial or post-nuptial agreements are required to be 'in writing, subscribed by the parties and acknowledged or proven in the manner required to entitle a deed to be recorded' (DRL section 236B(3)). This is a 'bright line' test of enforceability. (*Matisoff v Dobi*, 90 N.Y.2d 127, 681 N.E.2d 376, 659 N.Y.S.2d 209 (1997)).

Pre- and post-nuptial agreements are accorded the same presumption of legality as other contracts (*Bloomfield v Bloomfield*, 97 N.Y.2d 188, 193, 764 N.E.2d 950, 952, 738 N.Y.S.2d 650, 652 (2001)), it being 'the policy of the courts of this state to encourage parties to settle their differences privately'. including relating to marital financial issues (*Bronfman v Bronfman*, 220 A.D.2d 314, 315, 645 N.Y.S.2d 20, 21 (1st Dep't 1996)). As such, courts will strictly enforce and not merely look to them as one consideration or factor. However, such agreements can be challenged on the grounds of fraud and duress and, respecting maintenance, if not 'fair and reasonable' at the time the agreement was made, or if 'unconscionable' when the final judgment of divorce is entered (DRL section 236B(3); see, eg, *Cioffi-Petrakis v Petrakis*, 103 A.D.3d 766, 960 N.Y.S.2d 152 (2d Dep't 2013); *Petracca v Petracca*, 101 A.D.3d 695, 956 N.Y.S.2d 77 (2d Dep't 2012); *Kabir v Kabir*, 85 A.D.3d 1127, 926 N.Y.S.2d 158 (2d Dep't 2011); *Infante v Infante*, 76 A.D.3d 1048, 908 N.Y.S.2d 263 (2d Dep't 2010); *Santini v Robinson*, 68 A.D.3d 745, 891 N.Y.S.2d 100 (2d Dep't 2009); *Logiudice v Logiudice*, 67 A.D.3d 544, 889 N.Y.S.2d 164 (1st Dep't 2009); *Chapin v Chapin*, 12 A.D.3d 550, 786 N.Y.S.2d 65 (2d Dep't 2004); *Wisniewski v Cairo*, 305 A.D.2d 788, 759 N.Y.S.2d 798 (3d Dep't 2003); *Gibson v Gibson*, 284 A.D.2d 908, 726 N.Y.S.2d 195 (4th Dep't 2001)). The spouse seeking to set an agreement aside has the burden of establishing such defence (*Matter of Greiff*, 92 N.Y.2d 341, 344, 703 N.E.2d 752, 754, 680 N.Y.S.2d 894, 896 (1998)).

Foreign marital agreements may be recognised (see, eg, *Van Kipnis v Van Kipnis*, 11 N.Y.3d 573, 900 N.E.2d 977, 872 N.Y.S.2d 426 (2008) (recognising French agreement executed pre-enactment of N.Y. DRL section 236B(3)); *Stawski v Stawski*, 43 A.D.3d 776, 843 N.Y.S.2d 544 (1st Dep't 2007)) (recognising German agreement executed pre-enactment of N.Y. DRL section 236B(3)); *Crowther v Crowther*, 27 Misc. 3d 1211(A), 910 N.Y.S.2d 404, 2010 N.Y. Slip Op. 50677(U), 2010 WL 1531415 (Sup. Ct. Kings County Apr. 6, 2010) (n.o.r.) (applying Dutch law to determine validity)).

C. DIVORCE, NULLITY AND JUDICIAL SEPARATION

6. RECOGNITION OF FOREIGN MARRIAGES/DIVORCES

6.1 Summarise the position in your jurisdiction

Generally, if a marriage is valid in the place where it was solemnised (either in a sister state or in another country), it will be recognised in New York (*In re May's Estate*, 305 N.Y. 486, 114 N.E.2d 4 (1953); *Masocco v Schaaf*, 234 A.D. 181, 186, 254 N.Y.S. 439, 445-46 (3d Dep't 1931)). In appropriate circumstances, however, a court may also look to the law of the jurisdiction that, respecting a particular issue, has the most significant relationship to the spouses and the marriage, even if not where the marriage was solemnised (*Matter of Farraj*, 72 A.D.3d 1082, 900 N.Y.S.2d 340 (2d Dep't 2010) (marriage solemnised in New Jersey would have been void there but was deemed valid under New York law where parties were married in New Jersey solely for religious reasons, parties' intended and actual domicile was New York and parties to marriage held themselves out in New York as married)).

New York will generally also recognise a foreign-country divorce judgment under principles of comity if the judgment was not the product of fraud, coercion or oppression, or does not offend New York public policy (*Gotlib v Ratsutsky*, 83 N.Y.2d 696, 699-700, 635 N.E.2d 289, 290-91, 613 N.Y.S.2d 120, 121-22 (1994)).

7. DIVORCE

7.1 Explain the grounds for divorce within the jurisdiction (please also deal with nullity and judicial separation if appropriate)

New York's new 'no-fault' law (DRL sec. 170(7)), which applies to actions commenced on or after 12 October, 2010 (Ch. 384, 2010 N.Y. Laws), added to the traditional grounds for divorce a no-fault provision requiring merely that '[t]he relationship between husband and wife has broken down irretrievably for a period of at least six months, provided that one party has so stated under oath.' The law prohibits the grant of a divorce on this ground unless all ancillary issues are resolved.

One of New York's intermediate appellate courts, without discussion, has affirmed a trial court's determination that a trial is not available on grounds on a no-fault cause of action. *Palermo v Palermo*, 100 A.D.3d 1453, 953 N.Y.S.2d 533 (4th Dep't 2012), aff'g 35 Misc. 3d 1211(A), 950 N.Y.S.2d 724, 2011 N.Y. Slip Op. 52506(U), 2011 WL 7711557 (Sup. Ct. Monroe County Oct. 20, 2011) (n.o.r.), leave to appeal denied, 103 A.D. 3d 1193, 959 N.Y.S.2d 85 (4th Dep't 2013). Previously, New York trial courts had reached conflicting conclusions on whether a defence may be asserted or a trial held on grounds on a no-fault cause of action. See *Townes v Coker*, 35 Misc. 3d 543, 546-51, 943 N.Y.S.2d 823, 825-29 (Sup. Ct. Nassau County 2012) (granting plaintiff wife's motion for summary judgment for no-fault divorce; no-fault statute did not permit defence to plaintiff's sworn statement that marriage had irretrievably broken down; defendant's motion undermined by his having previously commenced an action for divorce against wife based on constructive abandonment); *Palermo v Palermo*, 35 Misc. 3d 1211(A), 2011 N.Y. Slip Op. 52506(U), 2011 WL 7711557 (Sup. Ct. Monroe County Oct. 20,

2011) (n.o.r.) (defendant husband not entitled to trial on no-fault ground and motion to dismiss denied; plaintiff wife's allegation of irretrievable breakdown sufficient to support divorce; requiring trial would violate legislature's intent to curtail time and expense of fault trials; also denying motion to dismiss for *res judicata* based on wife's prior unsuccessful action for divorce on cruelty ground), aff'd, 100 A.D.3d 1453, 953 N.Y.S.2d 533 (4th Dep't 2012), leave to appeal denied, 103 A.D.3d 1193, 959 N.Y.S.2d 85 (4th Dep't 2013); *Schiffer v Schiffer*, 33 Misc. 3d 795, 930 N.Y.S.2d 827 (Sup. Ct. Dutchess County 2011) (denying plaintiff husband's motion for summary judgment granting no-fault divorce; statute did not remove 'defendant's basic right to contest grounds'; affidavits on motion raised question of fact whether marriage had irretrievably broken down); *A.C. v D.R.*, 32 Misc. 3d 293, 304-08, 927 N.Y.S.2d 496, 505-07 (Sup. Ct. Nassau County 2011) (legislature did not intend defence to no-fault cause of action; however, plaintiff wife's motion for summary judgment denied because statute did not permit grant of no-fault divorce until resolution of financial issues), aff'd without consideration of point sub nom. *Charasz v Rozenblum*, 95 A.D.3d 1057, 945 N.Y.S.2d 117 (2d Dep't 2012); *Strack v Strack*, 31 Misc. 3d 258, 916 N.Y.S.2d 759 (Sup. Ct. Essex County 2011) (complaint's allegations held sufficient to state cause of action; legislature did not intend to abolish right to trial on no-fault ground; treating defendant's motion as one for summary judgment, finding questions of fact requiring trial).

For other noteworthy decisions construing the new no-fault ground, see *Rinzler v Rinzler*, 97 A.D.3d 215, 947 N.Y.S.2d 844 (3d Dep't 2012) (complaint in action seeking divorce based on irretrievable breakdown held not to allege same cause of action as complaint in pending action commenced before effective date based on cruelty and abandonment; reversing grant of motion to dismiss complaint in second action); *Dayanoff v Dayanoff*, 96 A.D.3d 895, 946 N.Y.S.2d 624 (2d Dep't 2012) (dismissal of prior action for failure to make out *prima facie* case for abandonment held not *res judicata* or collateral estoppel bar against subsequent action based on no-fault where no-fault ground had not been enacted at time of prior divorce action and no-fault had not been litigated in prior action); *Tuper v Tuper*, 98 A.D.3d 55, 946 N.Y.S.2d 719 (4th Dep't 2012) (affirming denial of motion to dismiss complaint; complaint adequately pleaded; even if allegations were deficient, any deficiency was cured by admissions in defendant's affidavit in support of amended motion to dismiss; action also held not time-barred by statute of limitations); *C.M.S. v W.T.S.*, 37 Misc. 3d 1228(A), 2012 N.Y. Slip Op. 52221(U), 2012 WL 6062535, at *1 & n.2 (Sup. Ct. Monroe County Dec. 5, 2012) (n.o.r.) (granting divorce based on irretrievable breakdown claim in amended complaint in action commenced before effective date of irretrievable breakdown statute); *G.C. v G.C.*, 35 Misc. 3d 1211(A), 2012 N.Y. Slip Op. 50653(U), 2012 WL 1292729 (Sup. Ct. Monroe County Apr. 16, 2012) (n.o.r.) (permitting amendment of complaint in action commenced before no-fault statute's effective date to add cause of action based on no-fault ground); *Vahey v Vahey*, 35 Misc. 3d 691, 693-95, 940 N.Y.S.2d 824, 827-28 (Sup. Ct. Nassau County 2012) (denying motion to dismiss no-fault cause of action; no-fault complaint not required to allege specific facts demonstrating misconduct and irretrievable breakdown); *Heinz v Heinz*, 31 Misc. 3d 601, 920 N.Y.S.2d 870 (Sup. Ct. Nassau County 2011) (husband's complaint in action seeking divorce based on irretrievable breakdown held not barred by wife's prior pending commenced before effective date based on cruelty and abandonment; 'pendency of an action by one spouse does not, by itself, bar an action by the other spouse on a different ground or grounds'); *A.C. v D.R.*, 31 Misc. 3d 517, 921 N.Y.S.2d 791 (Sup. Ct. Nassau County) (directing joint trial of husband's prior action based on constructive abandonment and wife's second action based on irretrievable breakdown, recognising husband's wish to preserve commencement date of his action for equitable distribution purposes and wife's wish to take advantage of 2010 temporary maintenance statute), vacated in part, 32 Misc. 3d 293, 927 N.Y.S.2d 496 (Sup. Ct. Nassau County 2011), aff'd without consideration of point sub nom. *Charasz v Rozenblum*, 95 A.D.3d 1057, 945 N.Y.S.2d 117 (2d Dep't 2012).

The other grounds for divorce are:

- The cruel and inhuman treatment of the plaintiff by the defendant such that the conduct of the defendant so endangers the physical or mental well being of the plaintiff as renders it unsafe or improper for the plaintiff to cohabit with the defendant.
- The abandonment of the plaintiff by the defendant for a period of one or more years.
- The confinement of the defendant in prison for a period of three or more consecutive years after the marriage of plaintiff and defendant.
- The commission of an act of adultery.
- The husband and wife have lived apart pursuant to a decree or judgment of separation for a period of one or more years after the granting of such decree or judgment, and satisfactory proof has been submitted by the plaintiff that they have substantially performed all the terms and conditions of such decree or judgment.
- The husband and wife have lived separate and apart pursuant to a written agreement of separation, subscribed by the parties thereto and acknowledged or proved in the form required to entitle a deed to be recorded, for a period of one or more years after the execution of such agreement and satisfactory proof has been submitted by the plaintiff that they have substantially performed all the terms and conditions of such agreement.

(DRL section 170).

The grounds for separation in New York are set forth in DRL section 200.

A marriage is void or may be declared null if it is between an ancestor and a descendant, a brother and sister, a half-brother and half-sister, an uncle and niece, or an aunt and nephew (DRL section 5).

A marriage may be declared null on the ground that the former husband or wife of one of the parties is still alive and that prior marriage is still in force (DRL section 140(a) (McKinney 2010)).

A marriage may be annulled on the grounds that one of the parties was below the age of consent, one of the parties was mentally ill or retarded, one of the parties was physically incapable of entering into the marriage state, the consent of one of the parties was obtained by force, duress or fraud or one of the parties has been incurably mentally ill for five years or more (DRL section 140(b)-(f)).

8. FINANCES/CAPITAL, PROPERTY

8.1 What powers does the court have to allocate financial resources and property on the breakdown of marriage?

8.2 Explain and illustrate with reference to recent cases the court's thinking on division of assets

Parties must provide full disclosure of finances (DRL section 236B(4)(a)). Pre-trial disclosure includes statutory form statements of net worth listing detailed monthly living expenses, assets, liabilities and transfers of assets made for lack of consideration, among other information (DRL section 236B(4)(a); 22 NYCRR section 202.16(b); 22 NYCRR part 202 app. A). The form is available at *www.nycourts.gov/forms/matrimonial/networth.pdf*. Disclosure also includes broad document demands and responses, interrogatories (ie, written questions and answers), and depositions (oral questioning under oath) all from the parties (see CPLR 3101(a)) (authorising disclosure from 'a party or the officer, director, member, agent or employee of a party'); CPLR 3102(a) (listing permissible disclosure devices); CPLR 3106-3107 (oral depositions); CPLR 3120, 3122 (document disclosure); CPLR 3130-3133 (interrogatories); *MacKinnon v MacKinnon*, 245 A.D.2d 690, 691, 665 N.Y.S.2d 123, 124 (3d Dep't 1997) ('full financial disclosure spanning the entire marriage'); *De La Roche v De La Roche*, 213 A.D.2d 208, 208, 624 N.Y.S.2d 1, 1 (1st Dep't 1995) ('broad financial disclosure'); *Colella v Colella*, 99 A.D.2d 794, 794, 472 N.Y.S.2d 124, 125 (2d Dep't 1984) (disclosure in matrimonial action 'includes any appropriate disclosure device authorised in CPLR article 31'); *Wilbur v Wilbur*, 89 A.D.2d 686, 686, 454 N.Y.S.2d 36, 37 (3d Dep't 1982) (same)) and via some of these devices from non-parties (see CPLR 3101(a) (disclosure from persons in addition to parties); CPLR 3106-3107 (oral depositions available from 'any person'); CPLR 3120, 3122 (document disclosure available from 'any other party' or 'any other person'); *Reich v Reich*, 36 A.D.3d 506, 830 N.Y.S.2d 29 (1st Dep't 2007) (document disclosure from and deposition of non-party closely held corporation of which husband was 2.5 per cent shareholder); *De La Roche v De La Roche*, 213 A.D.2d 208, 208-09, 624 N.Y.S.2d 1, 1 (1st Dep't 1995) ('such discovery is not restricted to the parties but is obtainable from appropriate third parties'); see also *Kooper v Kooper*, 74 A.D.3d 6, 7-18, 901 N.Y.S.2d 312, 316-23 (2d Dep't 2010) (discussing disclosure available from non-parties; affirming quashing of subpoena because defendant should have awaited response to disclosure requests served on plaintiff before serving subpoena on non-parties)).

Marital property is equitably distributed (DRL section 236B(5)(c)). Marital property includes 'all property acquired by either or both spouses during the marriage and before the execution of a separation agreement or the commencement of a matrimonial action, regardless of the form in which title is held' but excludes 'separate property' (DRL section 236B(1)(c)). Distribution is based on 13 factors, including economic and non-economic contributions to a spouse's career potential and wasteful dissipation of marital assets (DRL section 236B(5)(d)).

'Separate property' is narrowly defined as:

- property acquired before marriage or property acquired by bequest, devise or descent, or gift from a party other than the spouse; or
- compensation for personal injuries; or
- property acquired in exchange for, or the increase in value of, separate property, except to the extent that such appreciation is due in part to the contributions or efforts of the other spouse; or
- property described as separate property by written agreement of the parties pursuant to subdivision three of this part.

(DRL sections 236B(1)(d) and 236B(5)(b)).

Separate property may transmute into marital property in a variety of ways (see eg, *Johnson v Johnson*, 99 A.D.3d 765, 766, 952 N.Y.S.2d 243, 244 (2d Dep't 2012) (rental income traced to certificate of deposit naming defendant husband as beneficiary and describing proceeds as 'joint money from the rental of the apartment' held transmuted into marital property); *Popowich v Korman*, 73 A.D.3d 515, 516, 520, 900 N.Y.S.2d 297, 300, 302 (1st Dep't 2010) (commingling in brokerage account); *Wiener v Wiener*, 57 A.D.3d 241, 241-42, 868 N.Y.S.2d 197, 199 (1st Dep't 2008) (deposit of proceeds of sale of separate-property apartment in joint account); *Schwalb v Schwalb*, 50 A.D.3d 1206, 1209, 854 N.Y.S.2d 802, 805 (3d Dep't 2008) (deposit of proceeds of sale of separate property stock in joint account); *London v. London*, 21 A.D.3d 602, 604, 799 N.Y.S.2d 646, 649 (3d Dep't 2005) (deposit of separate-property inheritance into joint account); *Lynch v King*, 284 A.D.2d 309, 309-10, 725 N.Y.S.2d 391, 392 (2d Dep't 2001) (conveyance of separate-property land)). In addition, the increase in value (or a portion of such increase in value) of separate property may be marital property if due to the active efforts of the non-titled spouse (*Johnson v Chapin*, 12 N.Y.3d 461, 466-67, 909 N.E.2d 66, 69-70, 881 N.Y.S.2d 373, 376-77 (2009) (real property); *Hartog v Hartog*, 85 N.Y.2d 36, 45-49, 647 N.E.2d 749, 753-56, 623 N.Y.S.2d 537, 541-44 (1995) (family business); *Price v Price*, 69 N.Y.2d 8, 503 N.E.2d 684, 511 N.Y.S.2d 219 (1986) (family business); *Biagiotti v Biagiotti*, 97 A.D.3d 941, 943, 948 N.Y.S.2d 445, 448 (3d Dep't 2012) (marital residence owned by defendant husband before marriage); *Scher v Scher*, 91 A.D.3d 842, 844, 938 N.Y.S.2d 317, 320-21 (2d Dep't 2012) (home health attendant business); *Keane v Keane*, 25 A.D.3d 729, 731, 809 N.Y.S.2d 133, 135-36 (2d Dep't) (vacation property), modified on other grounds without consideration of point, 8 N.Y.3d 115, 861 N.E.2d 98, 828 N.Y.S.2d 283 (2006)). These citations are only a small fraction of the extensive body of case law on this issue, which is extremely fact-specific.

Professional licences, degrees and other like career-enhancing assets can be marital property (see, eg, *Grunfeld v Grunfeld*, 96 N.Y.2d 696, 731 N.E.2d 142, 709 N.Y.S.2d 486 (2000) (law licence and practice); *O'Brien v O'Brien*, 66 N.Y.2d 576, 489 N.E.2d 712, 498 N.Y.S.2d 743 (1985) (medical license);

Greisman v Greisman, 98 A.D.3d 1079, 1081, 951 N.Y.S.2d 219, 222 (2d Dep't 2012) (certification as public accountant and accounting firm); *Esposito-Shea v Shea*, 94 A.D.3d 1215, 1215-18, 941 N.Y.S.2d 793, 795-97 (3d Dep't 2012) (law degree and doctorate); *McAuliffe v McAuliffe*, 70 A.D.3d 1129, 1136-37, 895 N.Y.S.2d 228, 235-36 (3d Dep't 2010) (degree); *Haspel v Haspel*, 78 A.D.3d 887, 889-91, 911 N.Y.S.2d 408, 410-11 (2d Dep't 2010) (securities dealer's and real estate broker's licences); *Schwartz v Schwartz*, 67 A.D.3d 989, 991, 890 N.Y.S.2d 71, 73 (2d Dep't 2009) (securities licences); *Kriftcher v Kriftcher*, 59 A.D.3d 392, 393, 874 N.Y.S.2d 153, 155 (2d Dep't 2009) (law degree); *Evans v Evans*, 55 A.D.3d 1079, 1080-81, 866 N.Y.S.2d 788, 790 (3d Dep't 2008) (engineering degree); *Higgins v Higgins*, 50 A.D.3d 852, 853, 857 N.Y.S.2d 171, 173 (2d Dep't 2008) (academic degrees and professional licences); *Midy v Midy*, 45 A.D.3d 543, 544, 846 N.Y.S.2d 220, 221-22 (2d Dep't 2007) (master's degree); *Finkelson v Finkelson*, N.Y. L.J., July 10, 1996, at 30, col. 4 (N.Y. Sup. Ct. N.Y. County) (n.o.r.), modified, 239 A.D.2d 174, 657 N.Y.S.2d 629 (1st Dep't 1997)).

'The valuation date or dates [for each asset] may be any time from the date of commencement of the action to the date of trial' (DRL section 236B(4)(b)). An 'active' asset – that is, affected by a party's direct efforts – is often valued as of the date the action is commenced (*Grunfeld v Grunfeld*, 96 N.Y.2d 696, 707-08, 731 N.E.2d 142, 148, 709 N.Y.S.2d 486, 492 (2000) (law practice); *Rich-Wolfe v Wolfe*, 83 A.D.3d 1359, 1359-60, 922 N.Y.S.2d 593, 594-95 (3d Dep't 2011) (construction and demolition businesses); *Wechsler v Wechsler*, 58 A.D.3d 62, 87, 866 N.Y.S.2d 120, 138 (1st Dep't 2008)). A passive asset – affected primarily by market forces – is often valued as of the date of trial (*Donovan v Szlepcsik*, 52 A.D.3d 563, 564, 860 N.Y.S.2d 585, 586 (2d Dep't 2008) (marital residence); *Pulver v Pulver*, 40 A.D.3d 1315, 1319-20, 837 N.Y.S.3d 369, 374-75 (3d Dep't 2007) (individual retirement account)). These are general rules that depend upon the facts and circumstances of each individual case.

The division and distribution of the parties' property rests largely in the trial court's discretion (eg, *Lurie v Lurie*, 94 A.D.3d 1376, 1378, 943 N.Y.S.2d 261, 263 (3d Dep't 2012); *McAuliffe v McAuliffe*, 70 A.D.3d 1129, 1137, 895 N.Y.S.2d 228, 236 (3d Dep't 2010); *Schwartz v Schwartz*, 67 A.D.3d 989, 990-91, 890 N.Y.S.2d 71, 73 (2d Dep't 2009); *Fields v Fields*, 65 A.D.3d 297, 303, 882 N.Y.S.2d 67, 72 (1st Dep't 2009), affirmed, 15 N.Y.3d 158, 931 N.E.2d 1039, 905 N.Y.S.2d 783 (2010); *Quinn v Quinn*, 61 A.D.3d 1067, 1069, 876 N.Y.S.2d 720, 722 (3d Dep't 2009)).

In determining value, courts may 'tax impact' (ie, discount for embedded taxes due upon liquidation) based upon a variety of factors (see, eg, *Wyser-Pratte v Wyser-Pratte*, 68 A.D.3d 624, 625, 892 N.Y.S.2d 334, 336-37 (1st Dep't 2009) (deferred incentive fees); *Wechsler v Wechsler*, 58 A.D.3d 62, 81, 866 N.Y.S.2d 120, 133-34 (1st Dep't 2008) (proceeds from sale of securities); *Harmon v Harmon*, 173 A.D.2d 98, 105, 578 N.Y.S.2d 897, 901 (1st Dep't 1992) (no tax impacting absent occurrence of taxable event despite embedded capital gains); *Estate of Jelke v Comm'r*, 507 F.3d 1317 (11th Cir. 2007) (trend in tax court of discounting for embedded capital gain even if no imminent taxable event)).

9. FINANCES/MAINTENANCE

9.1 Explain the operation of maintenance for spouses on an ongoing basis after the breakdown of marriage

9.2 Is it common for maintenance to be awarded?

9.3 Explain and illustrate with reference to recent cases the court's thinking on maintenance

For actions commenced before 12 October, 2010: The court may order maintenance or temporary maintenance 'in such amount as justice requires, having regard for the standard of living of the parties established during the marriage, whether the party in whose favo[u]r maintenance is granted lacks sufficient property and income to provide for their reasonable needs and whether the other party has sufficient property or income to provide for the reasonable needs of the other and the circumstances of the case and of the respective parties' (DRL section 236 note (former DRL section 236B(6)(a))). The court must consider 11 factors in determining maintenance, including the ability of the party seeking maintenance to become self-supporting, economic and non-economic contributions to a spouse's career potential and wasteful dissipation of marital assets.

For actions commenced on or after 12 October, 2010: Temporary maintenance maintenance is governed by DRL section 236B(5-a); see also *www.nycourts.gov/divorce/TMG-Worksheet.PDF* (worksheet promulgated by State of New York Unified Court System for calculating temporary maintenance). The statute has been criticised by commentators. (See, eg, N.Y. State Law Revision Comm'n, Final Report on Maintenance Awards in Divorce Proceedings 11 (May 15, 2013); Lee Rosenberg, Multiple Flaws Abound in New Interim Spousal Support Statute, N.Y. L.J., Feb. 25, 2011, at 4, col. 1.)

The court may order post-divorce maintenance 'in such amount as justice requires, having regard for the standard of living of the parties established during the marriage, whether the party in whose favo[u]r maintenance is granted lacks sufficient property and income to provide for their reasonable needs and whether the other party has sufficient property or income to provide for the reasonable needs of the other and the circumstances of the case and of the respective parties (DRL section 236B(6)(a)). The court must consider 20 factors in determining maintenance, including the ability of the party seeking maintenance to become self-supporting, economic and non-economic contributions to a spouse's career potential and wasteful dissipation of marital assets. The amount and duration of maintenance is discretionary based on the factors. There is a wide disparity in maintenance awards as to both amount and duration.

The New York State Law Revision Commission has recently issued a report proposing changes to New York's statutes for both temporary and post-divorce maintenance. (N.Y. State Law Revision Comm'n, Final Report on Maintenance Awards in Divorce Proceedings (15 May, 2013).)

10. CHILD MAINTENANCE

10.1 On what basis is child maintenance calculated within the jurisdiction?

The court must determine child support when the parties have dependent children 'without requiring a showing of immediate or emergency need' (DRL section 236B(7)(a)).

The amount of child support is governed by the Child Support Standards Act, which is codified at DRL section 240(1-b) and FCA section 413(1) (*Bast v Rossoff*, 91 N.Y.2d 723, 697 N.E.2d 1009, 675 N.Y.S.2d 19 (1998); *Cassano v Cassano*, 85 N.Y.2d 649, 651 N.E.2d 878, 628 N.Y.S.2d 10 (1995)).

First, the court calculates the 'basic child support obligation' by determining the 'combined parental income,' multiplying that figure by a 'child support percentage' based on the number of children and, based on the first US$136,000 of combined parental income, pro-rates the amount between the parents based on their respective incomes. The court then performs the same calculation for income over US$136,000 and determines whether to apply the percentages to that additional income after considering 10 factors, incluidng the parents' respective financial resources, the standard of living the child would have enjoyed if the marriage had stayed intact and either parent's educational needs. In high-income cases in recent years, courts have capped combined parental income at between US$300,000 and US$500,000 for basic child support. (See, eg, *Huffman v Huffman*, 84 A.D.3d 875, 876, 923 N.Y.S.2d 583, 585 (2d Dep't 2011); *Bean v Bean*, 53 A.D.3d 718, 725, 860 N.Y.S.2d 683, 690 (3d Dep't 2008); *DeVries v DeVries*, 35 A.D.3d 794, 795-96, 828 N.Y.S.2d 142, 144-45 (2d Dep't 2006); *Fleischmann v Fleischmann*, 24 Misc. 3d 1225(A), 897 N.Y.S.2d 669, 2009 N.Y. Slip Op. 51614(U), 2009 WL 2217384, at *1, *18-*19 (Sup. Ct. Westchester County July 22, 2009) (n.o.r.); *K.J. v M.J.*, 14 Misc. 3d 1235(A), 836 N.Y.S.2d 500, 2007 N.Y. Slip Op. 50310(U), 2007 WL 602225, at *13-*14 (Sup. Ct. Westchester County Feb. 9, 2007) (n.o.r.).)

Second, the court must determine and pro-rate child care expenses ('where the custodial parent is working, or receiving elementary or secondary education, or higher education or vocational training which the court determines will lead to employment, and incurs child care expenses as a result thereof') and health insurance expenses and may award and pro-rate child care expenses (where 'the custodial parent is seeking work and incurs child care expenses as a result thereof') and educational expenses.

11. RECIPROCAL ENFORCEMENT OF FINANCIAL ORDERS

11.1 Summarise the position in your jurisdiction

As noted above, New York will generally recognise a divorce judgment rendered in a foreign country under principles of comity if the judgment was not the product of fraud, coercion or oppression, or does not offend New York public policy.

Under New York's codification of the Uniform Foreign Country Money-Judgments Recognition Act, certain foreign-country judgments that are 'final, conclusive and enforceable where rendered' are also conclusive and enforceable in New York unless 'the judgment was rendered under a system which does not provide impartial tribunals or procedures compatible with the requirements of due process of law', or is repugnant to the state's public policy (CPLR 5304(a), (b); *Bridgeway Corp. v Citibank*, 45 F. Supp. 2d 276 (S.D.N.Y. 1999), affirmed, 201 F.3d 134 (2d Cir. 2000); *Bachchan v India Abroad Publ'ns Inc.*, 154 Misc. 2d 228, 585 N.Y.S.2d 661 (Sup. Ct. N.Y. County 1992)). The definition of 'foreign country judgment' under the Act expressly excludes 'a judgment for support in matrimonial or family matters' (CPLR 5301(b)). It is uncertain whether a lump sum in a divorce is for 'support' in whole or part (compare *Burelle v Gilbert*, 9 Misc. 3d 127(A), 806 N.Y.S.2d 443, 2005 N.Y. Slip Op. 51471(U), 2005 WL 2276677, at ***1 (App. Term 9th & 10th Dists. September 16, 2005) (n.o.r.) (equitable distribution 'is not an award of support, even though entered in a matrimonial proceeding') with *Downs v Yuen*, 298 A.D.2d 177, 177, 748 N.Y.S.2d 131, 131-32 (1st Dep't 2002) (questioning whether some part of a US $10 million award was for support)). However, such a judgment would still be enforceable in New York under principles of comity (see CPLR 5307 (Uniform Foreign Country Money-Judgments Recognition Act does not prevent the recognition of a foreign country judgment in situations not covered by the Act)). *S.B. v W.A.*, 38 Misc. 3d 780, 805-07, 959 N.Y.S.2d 802, 823-24 (Sup. Ct. Westchester County 2012)).

12. FINANCIAL RELIEF AFTER FOREIGN DIVORCE PROCEEDINGS

12.1 What powers are available to make orders following a foreign divorce?

New York courts can entertain proceedings to distribute property subsequent to a foreign judgment of divorce (DRL section 236B(2), (5)(a) (referring to 'proceedings to obtain maintenance or a distribution of marital property following a foreign judgment of divorce')). Generally, they will not do so subsequent to a foreign judgment that actually distributed marital property (*Braunstein v Braunstein*, 114 A.D.2d 46, 497 N.Y.S.2d 58 (2d Dep't 1985); *Nikrooz v Nikrooz*, 167 A.D.2d 334, 561 N.Y.S.2d 301 (2d Dep't 1990)) or that could or should have (*Caiazza v Merola*, 90 A.D.3d 491, 491, 935 N.Y.S.2d 8, 8-9 (1st Dep't 2011); *DeGanay v DeGanay*, 269 A.D.2d 157, 701 N.Y.S.2d 434 (1st Dep't 2000); *Bourbon v Bourbon*, 300 A.D.2d 269, 751 N.Y.S.2d 302 (2d Dep't 2002)).

A New York court may modify a maintenance or child support award made in a foreign divorce judgment if changed circumstances are shown (see *Rauss v Johnson*, 243 A.D.2d 849, 850, 674 N.Y.S.2d 135, 136 (3d Dep't 1997); see also DRL section 236B(9)(b) ('upon a showing of the recipient's inability to be self-supporting or a substantial change in circumstance')).

D. CHILDREN

13. CUSTODY/PARENTAL RESPONSIBILITY

13.1 Briefly explain the legal position in relation to custody/parental responsibility following the breakdown of a relationship or marriage

13.2 Briefly explain the legal position in relation to access/contact/visitation following the breakdown of a relationship or marriage

The court may determine custody if the requirements of New York's codification of the Uniform Child Custody Jurisdiction and Enforcement Act, DRL sections 75 to 76-i, are met. Substantively, custody and visitation are governed by DRL sec. 240 and case law. The Supreme Court may refer custody and visitation issues to the Family Court. (FCA sec. 467(a).) In addition, where no matrimonial action is pending, custody may be determined by writ of *habeas corpus* under DRL sec. 70. The Supreme Court may refer a *habeas corpus* proceeding respecting a child to the Family Court. (FCA sec. 651(a).) Further, a custody or visitation proceeding may be commenced directly in the Family Court. (FCA sec. 651(b).)

A person who has attained the age of 18 years can no longer be subject to a custody order. (DRL sec. 2; *Herschorn v Herschorn*, 92 A.D.3d 500, 501, 938 N.Y.S.2d 528, 529 (1st Dep't 2012); *Larock v Larock*, 36 A.D.3d 1177, 1177-78, 829 N.Y.S.2d 253, 254 (3d Dep't 2007); *Darisa D. v Bienvenida D.*, 26 A.D.3d 222, 223, 809 N.Y.S.2d 49, 50 (1st Dep't 2006); *Lazaro v Lazaro,* 227 A.D.2d 402, 402, 642 N.Y.S.2d 67, 68 (2d Dep't 1996); *Toppel v Toppel*, 67 A.D.2d 628, 628, 412 N.Y.S.2d 17, 18 (1st Dep't 1979).)

Custody and visitation is determined in the best interests of the child. (DRL sec. 240(1)(a); *Wilson v McGlinchey*, 2 N.Y.3d 375, 381, 811 N.E.2d 526, 529, 779 N.Y.S.2d 159, 162 (2004); *Eschbach v Eschbach*, 56 N.Y.2d 167, 171, 436 N.E.2d 1260, 1262, 451 N.Y.S.2d 658, 660 (1982); *Friederwitzer v Friederwitzer*, 55 N.Y.2d 89, 93-95, 432 N.E.2d 765, 767-68, 447 N.Y.S.2d 893, 895-96 (1982).) Relevant factors include the child's wishes, the relative fitness of the parents, the quality of the respective home environments, each parent's financial status, each parent's ability to provide for the child's emotional and intellectual development, which parent has been the primary caregiver, which parent is more likely to foster a relationship between the child and the other parent, each parent's history of domestic violence, and the existence of any agreement (See, eg, *Wilson*, 2 N.Y.3d at 381, 811 N.E.2d at 529, 779 N.Y.S.2d at 162; *Eschbach*, 56 N.Y.2d at 172, 436 N.E.2d at 1263, 451 N.Y.S.2d at 661; *Friederwitzer*, 55 N.Y.2d at 94, 432 N.E.2d at 767-68, 447 N.Y.S.2d at 895-96; *Gordon v Richards*, 103 A.D.3d 929, 930-31, 956 N.Y.S.2d 562, 563-64 (3d Dep't 2013); *Xiomara M. v Robert M., Jr.*, 102 A.D.3d 581, 582, 958 N.Y.S.2d 391, 392 (1st Dep't 2013); *Maraj v Gordon*, 102 A.D.3d 698, 957 N.Y.S.2d 717 (2d Dep't 2013); *Williams v Williams*, 100 A.D.3d 1347, 953 N.Y.S.2d 421 (4th Dep't 2012).)

As between a parent and a third person, parental custody may not be displaced absent grievous cause or necessity, such as surrender, abandonment, persistent neglect, or unfitness. (Eg, *Debra H. v Janice R.*, 14 N.Y.3d 576, 591, 930 N.E.2d 184, 189-90, 904 N.Y.S.2d 263, 268-69 (2010); *Matter of Adoption of L.*, 61 N.Y.2d 420, 426-27, 462 N.E.2d 1165, 1168-69, 474 N.Y.S.2d 447, 450 (1984); *Dickson v Lascaris*, 53 N.Y.2d 204, 208-09, 423 N.E.2d 361, 363-64, 440 N.Y.S.2d 884, 886 (1981); *Bennett v Jeffreys*, 40 N.Y.2d 543, 546-47, 356 N.E.2d 277, 281-82, 387 N.Y.S.2d 821, 824-25 (1976); *Rodriguez v Delacruz-Swan*, 100 A.D.3d 1286, 954 N.Y.S.2d 692 (3d Dep't 2012); *Revis v. Marzan*, 100 A.D.3d 1004, 954 N.Y.S.2d 217 (2d Dep't 2012); *Hezekiah L. v Pamela A.L.*, 92 A.D.3d 506, 506, 938 N.Y.S.2d 87, 88 (1st Dep't 2012); *Rosso v Gerouw-Rosso*, 79 A.D.3d 1726, 914 N.Y.S.2d 829 (4th Dep't 2010).)

The Domestic Relations Law expressly authorises a court to grant visitation to a grandparent in appropriate circumstances. (DRL secs. 72, 240(1)(a).)

14. INTERNATIONAL ABDUCTION

14.1 Summarise the position in your jurisdiction

New York has adopted the Uniform Child Custody Jurisdiction and Enforcement Act (UCCJEA), whose purpose is 'to provide an effective mechanism to obtain and enforce orders of custody and visitation across state lines and to do so in a manner that ensures that the safety of the children is paramount and that victims of domestic violence and child abuse are protected' (DRL section 75(2)). A foreign country is considered a state of the United States for certain purposes under the UCCJEA (DRL section 75-d(1)). A court 'may enforce an order for the return of the child made under the Hague Convention on the Civil Aspects of International Child Abduction as if it were a child custody determination' (DRL section 77-a). The UCCJEA was enacted to bring state law into conformity with federal law, including the Parental Kidnapping Prevention Act, 28 U.S.C. section 1738A (PKPA) (*Bowman v Bowman*, 82 A.D.3d 144, 151 n.3, 917 N.Y.S.2d 379, 385 n.3 (3d Dep't 2011); *Stocker v Sheehan*, 13 A.D.3d 1, 4, 786 N.Y.S.2d 126, 128 (1st Dep't 2004)), one of whose purposes is to 'deter interstate abductions and other unilateral removals of children undertaken to obtain custody and visitation awards' (Pub. L. No. 96-111, sec. 7(c)(6), 94 Statutes at Large 3566, 3568 (1980)).

15. LEAVE TO REMOVE/APPLICATION TO TAKE A CHILD OUT OF THE JURISDICTION

15.1 Summarise the position in your jurisdiction

15.2 Under what circumstances may a parent apply to remove their child from the jurisdiction against the wishes of the other parent?

The 'predominant emphasis' is 'on what outcome is most likely to serve the best interests of the child' (*Tropea v Tropea*, 87 N.Y.2d 727, 739, 665 N.E.2d 145, 150, 642 N.Y.S.2d 575, 580 (1996)). The relevant factors include each parent's reasons for seeking or opposing the move; the quality of the relationship between the child and the custodial and noncustodial parents; the impact of the move on the quantity and quality of the child's future contact with the noncustodial parent; the degree to which the custodial parent's and the child's lives may be enhanced economically, emotionally and educationally by the move; and the feasibility of preserving the relationship between the non-custodial parent and the child through suitable visitation arrangements (*Tropea*, 87 N.Y.2d at 740-41, 665 N.E.2d at 151, 642 N.Y.S.2d at 582). Recent illustrative cases include *Rose v Buck*, 103 A.D.3d 957, 962 N.Y.S.2d 356 (3d Dep't 2013); *Karen H. v Maurice G.*, 101 A.D.3d 1005, 956 N.Y.S.2d 154 (2d Dep't 2012); *Mineo v Mineo*, 96 A.D.3d 1617, 946 N.Y.S.2d 391 (4th Dep't 2012); *Koegler v Woodard*, 96 A.D.3d 454, 946 N.Y.S.2d 139 (1st Dep't), appeal dismissed, 19 N.Y.3d 1013, 976 N.E.2d 235, 951 N.Y.S.2d 708 (2012); *Alaire K.G. v Anthony P.G.*,

86 A.D.3d 216, 925 N.Y.S.2d 417 (1st Dep't 2011); *Rubio v Rubio,* 71 A.D.3d 862, 897 N.Y.S.2d 170 (2d Dep't 2010); *Schwartz v Schwartz,* 70 A.D.3d 923, 895 N.Y.S.2d 206 (2d Dep't 2010); *Solomon v Long,* 68 A.D.3d 1467, 891 N.Y.S.2d 528 (3d Dep't 2009); *Dickerson v Robenstein,* 68 A.D.3d 1179, 889 N.Y.S.2d 319 (3d Dep't 2009); *Mathie v Mathie,* 65 A.D.3d 527, 884 N.Y.S.2d 433 (2d Dep't 2009); *Martino v Ramos,* 64 A.D.3d 657, 884 N.Y.S.2d 427 (2d Dep't 2009); and *Winston v Gates,* 64 A.D.3d 815, 881 N.Y.S.2d 684 (3d Dep't 2009).

E. SURROGACY AND ADOPTION

16. VALIDITY OF SURROGACY AGREEMENTS

16.1 Briefly summarise the position in your jurisdiction

Surrogate parenting contracts are contrary to public policy, and are void and unenforceable. (DRL sec. 122.)

17. ADOPTION

17.1 Briefly explain the legal position in relation of adoption in your jurisdiction. Is adoption available to individuals, cohabiting couples (both heterosexual and same-sex)?

Adoption is governed by DRL secs. 109-117. The Family Court and Surrogate's Court have jurisdiction over adoptions. (N.Y. Const. art. 6, secs. 12(d), 13(b); DRL secs. 109(2), 109(3).) Adoption is available to individuals and cohabiting couples, both heterosexual and same-sex. (DRL sec. 110; see Governor's Approval Memorandum, ch. 509, 2010 N.Y. Laws (Sept. 17, 2010), reprinted in 2010 N.Y. Laws 1515, 1515 (McKinney) ('adult intimate partners' 'includes same-sex couples, regardless of whether they are married'); Memorandum in Support, ch. 509, 2010 N.Y. Laws, reprinted in 2010 N.Y. Laws 2075, 2076 (McKinney) ('by replacing references to 'husband and wife' with the gender-neutral term 'married couple', this measure will help ensure that all married couples, regardless of their sexual orientation, will have equal rights to adopt a child together'); *Matter of Adoption of a Child Whose First Name Is Chan,* 37 Misc. 3d 358, 364, 950 N.Y.S.2d 245, 250 (Sur. Ct. N.Y. County 2012).)

F. COHABITATION

18. COHABITATION

18.1 What legislation (if any) governs division of property for unmarried couples on the breakdown of the relationship?

No legislation governs the division of property for unmarried couples on the breakdown of the relationship.

G. FAMILY DISPUTE RESOLUTION

19. MEDIATION, COLLABORATIVE LAW AND ARBITRATION

19.1 Briefly summarise the non-court-based processes available in your jurisdiction and the current status of agreements reached under the auspices of mediation, collaborative law and arbitration.

19.2 What is the statutory basis (if any) for mediation, collaborative

law and arbitration in your jurisdiction? In particular, are the parties required to attempt a family dispute resolution in advance of the institution of proceedings?

Divorce mediation and collaborative law processes are available; in addition to private mediators and lawyers trained in collaborative law, a court-based mediation program is available if matrimonial proceedings are already under way (see *www.nycourts.gov/ip/adr/divorcemediation.shtml*) and a court-sponsored Collaborative Family Law Center opened 1 September, 2009. Arbitration is available if the parties agree to it and is governed by CPLR art. 75. Generally, 'an agreement to refer a matter concerning marriage to arbitration suffers no inherent invalidity'. (*Avitzur v Avitzur*, 58 N.Y.2d 108, 114, 446 N.E.2d 136, 138, 459 N.Y.S.2d 572, 574 (1983).) Child support may be arbitrated, but is subject to vacatur if it fails to comply with the Child Support Standards Act and is not in the best interest of the child. (*Frieden v Frieden*, 22 A.D.3d 634, 635, 802 N.Y.S.2d 727, 728 (2d Dep't 2005); see *Shapiro v Sanders*, 50 A.D.3d 429, 429, 855 N.Y.S.2d 477, 478 (1st Dep't 2008).) However, custody of and visitation with minor children cannot be arbitrated. (*Schechter v Schechter*, 63 A.D.3d 817, 819, 881 N.Y.S.2d 151, 152 (2d Dep't 2009); *Hirsch v Hirsch*, 4 A.D.3d 451, 452, 774 N.Y.S.2d 48, 49 (2d Dep't 2004); *Glauber v Glauber*, 192 A.D.2d 94, 600 N.Y.S.2d 740 (2d Dep't 1993); *Harris v Iannaccone*, 107 A.D.2d 429, 431, 487 N.Y.S.2d 562, 564 (1st Dep't) (dictum), aff'd, 66 N.Y.2d 728, 487 N.E.2d 908, 496 N.Y.S.2d 998 (1985).)

New York does not require the parties to attempt out-of-court dispute resolution before instituting a matrimonial action in a court.

H. OTHER

20. CIVIL PARTNERSHIP/SAME-SEX MARRIAGE

20.1 What is the status of civil partnership/same-sex marriage within the jurisdiction?

20.2 What legislation governs civil partnership/same-sex marriage?

New York recognises same-sex marriages effective 24 July, 2011 (Marriage Equality Act, Chs. 95-96, 2011 N.Y. Laws, codified at DRL secs. 10-a, 10-b, 11, 13).

New York has not recognised civil unions contracted within the state (*Debra H. v Janice R.*, 14 N.Y.3d 576, 612, 930 N.E.2d 184, 205, 904 N.Y.S.2d 263, 284 (2010) (Smith, J., concurring); *Langan v State Farm Fire & Cas. Co.*, 48 A.D.3d 76, 849 N.Y.S.2d 105 (3d Dep't 2007); *Langan v St. Vincent's Hosp.*, 25 A.D.3d 90, 802 N.Y.S.2d 476 (2d Dep't 2005)), but has recognised civil unions validly contracted in other states (see *Debra H.*, 14 N.Y.3d at 601, 930 N.E.2d at 197, 904 N.Y.S.2d at 276 (recognising Vermont civil union for purposes of determining custody and visitation); *Dickerson v Thompson*, 88 A.D.3d 121, 928 N.Y.S.2d 97 (3d Dep't 2011) (New York courts have jurisdiction to entertain an action to dissolve a civil union validly contracted in another state; dissolution granted)). For a recitation of examples of the extent to which New York and various localities therein extend protection and benefits to parties to same-sex unions, see *Dickerson v Thompson*, 73

A.D.3d 52, 54-56, 897 N.Y.S.2d 298, 300-01 (3d Dep't 2010).

21. CONTROVERSIAL AREAS/RAPIDLY DEVELOPING AREAS OF LAW

21.1 Is there a particular area of the law within the jurisdiction that is currently undergoing major change?

21.2 Which areas of law are most out-of-step? Which areas would you most like to see reformed/changed?

Grounds

New York became the last United States jurisdiction to allow no-fault divorce, effective 12 October, 2010 (Ch. 384, 2010 N.Y. Laws, codified at DRL sec. 170(7)).

Same-sex marriage

New York recognises same-sex marriages effective 24 July, 2011. See the above discussion for recent developments in this area.

On 26 June, 2013, the Supreme Court of the United States, in *United States v Windsor*, ___ U.S. ____, ____, 2013 WL 3196928, at *15-*18 (26 June, 2013), held that section 3 of the Defense of Marriage Act (DOMA), 1 U.S.C. sec. 7, violated the due process and equal protection clauses of the fifth amendment to the US Constitution. Section 3 of DOMA, for the purposes of federal law, defines 'marriage' as 'only a legal union between one man and one woman as husband and wife' and 'spouse' as 'only... a person of the opposite sex who is a husband or a wife.' The statute was held unconstitutional because it denies same-sex married couples certain 'benefits and responsibilities' under federal law that are available to opposite-sex married couples, in such areas as estate tax (at issue in the *Windsor* case), Social Security, housing, other taxes, criminal sanctions, copyright, health benefits, and veterans' benefits.

The effect of the decision is not to compel the individual states to recognise same-sex marriage, but rather to prevent the federal government from treating same-sex married couples differently from opposite-sex married couples. As a result, it would appear settled that same-sex couples in states recognising same-sex marriages can provide for tax-deductible alimony or 'maintenance' and so deduct federal as well as state taxes. However, because the US Supreme Court left open the constitutionality of states refusing to recognise same-sex marriages performed in other states, it is conceivable that same-sex couples married elsewhere but residing in states not recognising such marriage will not be deemed married for federal purposes. (See Estates, Gifts and Trusts Portfolios: Estate Planning/Business Planning Portfolio 849-2nd: Marital Agreements, sec. XI(H)(5) & n.1719.1 (BNA).)

Trusts

New York law on trusts in the equitable distribution context is not well developed. The few cases tend to examine whether the trust's purpose is legitimate; if a trust was an attempt to defeat equitable distribution, the court will instead most likely disregard or set aside the trust and distribute its assets. If the trust was created for a legitimate purpose, the court will then consider whether further intervention is necessary to promote a fair result in the matrimonial action.

For examples of divorce actions involving trusts, see *Spector v Spector*, 18 A.D.3d 380, 797 N.Y.S.2d 437 (1st Dep't 2005) (ordering defendant husband, over whom court had jurisdiction, to cooperate in any action wife might take to dissolve trust); *Riechers v Riechers*, 267 A.D.2d 445, 701 N.Y.S.2d 113 (2d Dep't 1999) (granting distributive award of one-half of value of trust); *Ciaffone v Ciaffone*, 228 A.D.2d 949, 953, 645 N.Y.S.2d 549, 554 (3d Dep't 1996) (granting distributive award of portion of value of marital property conveyed to trust; affirming dismissal of causes of action to set trust aside where established for legitimate purpose); *Goldberg v Goldberg*, 172 A.D.2d 316, 316-17, 568 N.Y.S.2d 394, 395 (1st Dep't 1991) (granting distributive award where husband had secreted marital assets in trusts that served as his 'personal pocket book'); *Contino v Contino*, 140 A.D.2d 662, 529 N.Y.S.2d 14 (2d Dep't 1988) (court must consider secreted assets in determining equitable distribution); *Villi v O'Caining-Villi*, 2005 N.Y. Slip Op. 52049(U), 2005 WL 3442966 (Sup. Ct. Westchester County December 16, 2005) (n.o.r.) (no distributive award where trust not created to defeat equitable distribution); *Surasi v Surasi*, 2001 N.Y. Slip Op. 40408(U), 2001 WL 1607927 (Sup. Ct. Richmond County Nov. 20, 2001) (n.o.r.) (setting aside trust created during action's pendency with intent to deny plaintiff's equitable distribution claim); *Papson v Papson*, No. 10065-1997, 1998 WL 1177948, at *2-*3 (N.Y. Sup. Ct. N.Y. County July 31, 1998) (n.o.r.) (terminating trust where it was 'a bald attempt by defendant to place marital property out of the plaintiff wife's reach' in violation of public policy).

Trend in equitable distribution

In determining what percentage of marital property a spouse is entitled to, the courts in recent years have applied greater scrutiny to the issue of contribution toward the acquisition and increase in value of that property, particularly respecting licences, degrees, and the like, and certain business assets (see, eg, *Johnson v Chapin*, 12 N.Y.3d 461, 466-67, 909 N.E.2d 66, 69-70, 881 N.Y.S.2d 373, 376-77 (real property); *Elias v Elias*, 101 A.D.3d 938, 939, 957 N.Y.S.2d 231, 232-33 (2d Dep't 2012) (business entities); *Nicodemus v Nicodemus*, 98 A.D.3d 605, 606, 949 N.Y.S.2d 741, 743 (2d Dep't 2012) (auto restoration business); *Quarty v Quarty*, 96 A.D.3d 1274, 1277-79, 948 N.Y.S.2d 130, 133-34 (3d Dep't 2012) (nursing degree and certification); *D'Ambra v D'Ambra*, 94 A.D.3d 1532, 1535, 943 N.Y.S.2d 698, 701 (4th Dep't 2012) (business); *Esposito-Shea v Shea*, 94 A.D.3d 1215, 1217-18, 941 N.Y.S.2d 793, 797-98 (3d Dep't 2012) (law degree and Ph.D. degree); *Safi v Safi*, 94 A.D.3d 737, 737-38, 941 N.Y.S.2d 661, 663 (2d Dep't 2012) (business); *Gallagher v Gallagher*, 93 A.D.3d 1311, 1314, 941 N.Y.S.2d 392, 395-96 (4th Dep't) (master's degree), leave to appeal denied, 96 A.D.3d 1514, 945 N.Y.S.2d 587 (4th Dep't), motion for leave to appeal dismissed in part, leave to appeal denied, 19 N.Y.3d 1022,

976 N.E.2d 246, 951 N.Y.S.2d 717 (2012); *Sadaghiani v Ghayoori*, 83 A.D.3d 1309, 1310-11, 923 N.Y.S.2d 236, 238-39 (3d Dep't 2011) (marital portion of enhanced earnings capacity flowing from medical licence); *Bayer v Bayer*, 80 A.D.3d 492, 492, 914 N.Y.S.2d 169, 170 (1st Dep't 2011) (medical licence and career); *Davis v O'Brien*, 79 A.D.3d 695, 697, 912 N.Y.S.2d 644, 646 (2d Dep't 2010) (law partnership); *Popowich v Korman*, 73 A.D.3d 515, 520, 900 N.Y.S.2d 297, 302 (1st Dep't 2010) (brokerage account); *McAuliffe v McAuliffe*, 70 A.D.3d 1129, 1136-37, 895 N.Y.S.2d 228, 235-36 (3d Dep't 2010) (enhanced earning capacity from degree); *Albanese v Albanese*, 69 A.D.3d 1005, 1006, 892 N.Y.S.2d 631, 633 (3d Dep't 2010) (law practice); *Wyser-Pratte v Wyser-Pratte*, 68 A.D.3d 624, 624-25, 892 N.Y.S.2d 334, 336 (1st Dep't 2009) (business assets); *Schwartz v Schwartz*, 67 A.D.3d 989, 991, 890 N.Y.S.2d 71, 73 (2d Dep't 2009) (enhanced earning capacity from securities licences); *Zaretsky v Zaretsky*, 66 A.D.3d 885, 888, 888 N.Y.S.2d 84, 87 (2d Dep't 2009) (real property); *Peritore v Peritore*, 66 A.D.3d 750, 752-53, 888 N.Y.S.2d 72, 74 (2d Dep't 2009) (dental practice); *Mairs v Mairs*, 61 A.D.3d 1204, 1206-07, 878 N.Y.S.2d 222, 224-25 (2d Dep't 2009) (medical license and practice); *Guha v Guha*, 61 A.D.3d 634, 877 N.Y.S.2d 151 (2d Dep't 2009) (marital residence and medical licence); *Quinn v Quinn*, 61 A.D.3d 1067, 1069, 876 N.Y.S.2d 720, 722 (3d Dep't 2009) (medical business); *Kriftcher v Kriftcher*, 59 A.D.3d 392, 393, 874 N.Y.S.2d 153, 155 (2d Dep't 2009) (law degree); *Evans v Evans*, 55 A.D.3d 1079, 1080-81, 866 N.Y.S.2d 788, 790 (3d Dep't 2008) (engineering degree); *Schwartz v Schwartz*, 54 A.D.3d 400, 402, 864 N.Y.S.2d 35, 38 (2d Dep't 2008) (law practice); *Kaplan v Kaplan*, 51 A.D.3d 635, 637, 857 N.Y.S.2d 677, 679 (2d Dep't 2008) (dental practice and licence); *Higgins v Higgins*, 50 A.D.3d 852, 853, 857 N.Y.S.2d 171, 173 (2d Dep't 2008) (academic degrees and professional licences); *Ciampa v Ciampa*, 47 A.D.3d 745, 747, 850 N.Y.S.2d 190, 192 (2d Dep't 2008) (business interests); *Schorr v Schorr*, 46 A.D.3d 351, 351, 848 N.Y.S.2d 614, 615 (1st Dep't 2007) (business interests); *Midy v Midy*, 45 A.D.3d 543, 544, 846 N.Y.S.2d 220, 221-22 (2d Dep't 2007) (master's degree); *Griggs v Griggs*, 44 A.D.3d 710, 713, 844 N.Y.S.2d 351, 355 (2d Dep't 2007) (medical practice)).

Spousal maintenance

There is a wide disparity in outcomes in cases regarding maintenance regarding both the amount and duration of spousal maintenance. Legislation imposing detailed guidelines for temporary maintenance during the pendency of a divorce action and directing further study was enacted in 2010.

Counsel and expert fees

In 2010 (Ch. 329, 2010 N.Y. Laws), DRL section 237 was amended to: (1) allow an award of expert fees as well as counsel fees; and (2) include a presumption of an award of counsel fees to the less-monied spouse in a matrimonial action. DRL section 238 was amended for proceedings to enforce or modify an order or judgment rendered in a matrimonial action (Ch. 329, 2010 N.Y. Laws). The new regime applies to actions and proceedings commenced on or after October 12, 2010 (Ch. 415, 2010 N.Y. Laws).

USA – Texas

Fullenweider Wilhite PC Donn C. Fullenweider

A. JURISDICTION AND CONFLICT OF LAW

1. SOURCES OF LAW

1.1 What is the primary source of law in relation to the breakdown of marriage and the welfare of children within the jurisdiction?

Texas law concerning the marriage, dissolution of marriage and parent-child relationship issues has been codified in the comprehensive Texas Family Code. This Code incorporated prior rudimentary Texas statutes and a large body of Texas case law based on written options of the Texas Supreme Court and numerous Courts of Civil Appeals. These courts issue written opinions interpreting and clarifying the Family Code and these decisions are binding on the trial courts.

1.2 Which are the main statutes governing matrimonial law in the jurisdiction?

The Texas Family Code (Tex. Fam. Code) is divided into five titles:

- The Marriage Relationship, Tex. Fam. Code sections 1.001 to 9.302;
- Child in Relation to the Family, Tex. Fam. Code sections 31.001 to 45.106;
- Juvenile Justice Code, Tex. Fam. Code sections 51.01 to 61.107;
- Protective Orders and Family Violence, Tex. Fam. Code sections 71.001 to 92.001;
- The Parent-Child Relationship and the Suit Affecting the Parent Child Relationship, Tex. Fam. Code sections 101.001 to 266.010.

2. JURISDICTION

2.1 What are the main jurisdictional requirements for the institution of proceedings in relation to divorce, property and children?

Residency requirements

A suit for divorce cannot be maintained unless, at the time the suit is filed, one spouse has been a domiciliary of Texas for the preceding six-month period and a resident of the county in which the suit is filed for the preceding 90-day period (Tex. Fam. Code section 6.301). If one spouse has been a domiciliary of Texas for at least six months, a spouse who resides in another state or nation may sue for divorce in the Texas county in which the domiciliary spouse resides at the time the petition is filed (Tex. Fam. Code sections 6.302).

Acquiring personal jurisdiction over a non-resident respondent

Texas courts acquire personal jurisdiction over a non-resident respondent if

the respondent is:
(i) amenable to process under the Texas long-arm statute;
(ii) would have constitutional guarantees of due process met;
(iii) is properly served with process while in Texas;
(iv) waives service of process; or
(v) makes a general appearance.

The Texas court will have personal jurisdiction over a non-resident under the Texas long-arm statute if:
(i) the petitioner is a resident or domiciliary of Texas when the divorce is filed;
(ii) the petitioner and respondent's last marital residence is Texas;
(iii) the suit is filed within two years after the date the marital residence ended; and
(iv) the court's exercise of jurisdiction over the non-resident would comport with the standards of fair play and substantial justice (Tex. Fam. Code section 6.305(a)(1), (2)).

General divorce jurisdiction

To grant a divorce, the court must have *in rem* jurisdiction (ie, jurisdiction over a thing). See *Williams v North Carolina*, 317 US 287, 297 (1942). A party's domicile in a state creates a relationship with the state that is sufficient to invoke a court's *in rem* jurisdiction over the party's marital status and empower it to change the marital status of a spouse domiciled within its borders, even if the other spouse is not present in the state (*Id.* at 298-99; *Dosamantes v Dosamantes*, 500 S.W.2d 233, 236 (Tex.App. Texarkana 1973, writ dismissed)). For a Texas court to acquire *in rem* jurisdiction over a suit for divorce, two requirements must be met:
(i) one of the spouses must qualify as a Texas domiciliary; and
(ii) service of process on a non-resident spouse must be proper (see *Heth v Heth*, 661 SW, 2d 3-3, 304-05 (Tex.App. Fort Worth 1983, writ dismissed)).

If either of the requirements is not met, the court does not have the power to grant the divorce and any judgment rendered is void.

The Texas court's power to render a divorce or annulment does not, by itself, give the court jurisdiction to divide the spouses' property (see *Dawson-Austin v Austin*, 968 SW, 2d 309, 324 (Tex. 1998).

Jurisdiction to divide and confirm marital property

Two factors are relevant in determining whether a Texas court has the power to divide and confirm the spouses' marital property (which in Texas is called community property), the location of the property and whether the court has personal jurisdiction over both spouses.

Property outside Texas

A Texas court can affect property located outside of the state by:
(i) determining the value of the out of state property and consider that value in dividing the property within the state;

(ii) characterising and confirming out of state property as one spouse's separate property;
(iii) compelling the sale of out of state property and distributing the proceeds between the parties; or
(iv) awarding the out of state property to one spouse and ordering the other spouse to execute instruments convening an interest in that property.

An order that compels a party to execute instruments conveying an interest in out of state property is viewed as imposing a personal obligation on a party, but not directly affecting title (see *McElreath v McElreath*, 345 SW, 2d 733 (Tex.1961)).

Dividing property when the court lacks personal jurisdiction over the respondent

In relation to property within Texas, if a Texas court does not have personal jurisdiction over the respondent, the court may be still be able to divide and confirm marital (community) property located in Texas through its exercise of *in rem* jurisdiction. If the court finds that the non-resident spouse purposefully availed themself to the benefits of owning property within Texas, the court will have the power to divide and confirm that property. See *Dawson-Austin*, 968 SW, 2d at 327. However, the court will not have the power to divide property within Texas if one spouse acquired the property within Texas without the consent of the other spouse, or acted unilaterally in bringing the property to Texas (*Id.*; *Schaffer v Heitner*, 433 US, 186, 207-09 (1977)).

In relation to property outside Texas, if a Texas court lacks personal jurisdiction over the respondent, and does not have *in rem* jurisdiction over the property (because it is located outside Texas), the court cannot divide or confirm that out of state property.

Child custody suits

For Texas to have authority to act in a child custody suit (a Suits Affecting Parent-Child Relationship – SAPCR), the court must have *in rem* jurisdiction (ie, jurisdiction over a thing), established when one of the bases for jurisdiction in the Uniform Child Custody Jurisdiction & Enforcement Act (UCCJEA) is met. Under the UCCJEA, the following will confer *in rem* jurisdiction in order of priority:
(i) home-state jurisdiction;
(ii) significant-connection jurisdiction; and
(iii) default jurisdiction

(Tex. Fam. Code section 152.201).

'Home state', for the purposes of establishing home-state jurisdiction, means the state or country in which the child lived with a parent or person acting as a parent for at least six consecutive months immediately before the custody proceeding commenced. If the child is less than six months' old, home state means the state or country in which the child lived with a parent or person acting as a parent since birth (Tex. Fam. Code section 152.102(7)).

Default jurisdiction

A Texas court will acquire jurisdiction over a child-custody determination if all other states or nations with jurisdiction to make an initial child-custody determination have declined to exercise that jurisdiction, or if no other state has jurisdiction to make an initial child-custody determination.

For other types of SAPCRs, such as child-support suits, Texas courts must have jurisdiction over the persons. Most courts in Texas will decline to exercise jurisdiction over only some of the issues in a SAPCR if another court has jurisdiction to resolve all pending issues.

Child support and parentage suits

For a Texas court to decide issues regarding child support or parentage, a court must have personal jurisdiction over the parties (Tex. Fam. Code section160.604(a). A court acquires jurisdiction over a non-resident respondent if

(i) a Texas statute authorises exercising jurisdiction; and
(ii) exercising jurisdiction follows due process.

In re S.A.V, 837 SW, 2d 80, 85 (Tex.1992). The Family Code sets forth these grounds for exercising personal jurisdiction over a non-resident:

- the respondent is served with citation within Texas, personally or through a representative;
- the individual consents to exercising personal jurisdiction by entering a general appearance, seeking affirmative relief, or otherwise waiving a contest to personal jurisdiction;
- the individual, by his or her own acts or directives, caused the child to live in Texas;
- the individual lived with the child in Texas;
- the individual lived in Texas and provided prenatal expenses or child support;
- the person engaged in sexual intercourse in Texas, if the child may have been conceived from that act;
- the person registered with the paternity registry maintained by the Texas Bureau of Vital Statistics; or
- if the Texas or US Constitution provides any basis for personal jurisdiction over the person. Tex. Fam. Code section 102.011(b)(1)-(8).

The Texas and federal constitutional test of due process is that a court can exercise personal jurisdiction over a person who has minimum contacts with the state if doing so would comport with fair play and substantial justice (*In re S.A.V*, 837 SW 2d at 85-86).

Child custody modification suits

In the absence of temporary emergency jurisdiction, a Texas court cannot modify a child custody determination made by a court of another state or nation, unless a Texas court has jurisdiction to make an initial custody determination and

- the other state or nation determines it no longer has exclusive, continuing jurisdiction or that Texas would be a more convenient forum; or

- a court determines that the child, the child's parents and any person acting as a parent, do not presently reside in the other state or nation. Tex. Fam. Code section 152.203(1), (2).

Temporary emergency jurisdiction
Temporary emergency jurisdiction is reserved for extraordinary circumstances. A court has temporary emergency jurisdiction if the child is present in Texas and the child has been abandoned, or it is otherwise necessary in an emergency to protect the child because someone in the family is subjected to or threatened with mistreatment or abuse (Tex. Fam. Code section 152.204(a)).

3. DOMICILE AND HABITUAL RESIDENCE

3.1 Explain the concepts of domicile and habitual residence as they apply to the jurisdiction in relation to divorce, the finances and children

Qualifications for domicile – State of Texas
To establish a Texas domicile, the person must live in Texas with the express intention of making it their fixed and permanent home (see *Skubal v Skubal*, 584 S.W.2d 45, 46 (Tex.App., San Antonio, 1979, writ dismissed)).

Qualifications for residence – county in Texas
To meet the Texas county residency requirement, the person must be physically living in the county (see *Wilson v Wilson*, 494 S.W.2d 609, 611 (Tex.App., Houston [14th Dist.] 1973, writ dismissed)). Temporary absences from the county are permissible (see *Therwhanger v Therwhanger*, 175 S.W.2d 704, 707 (Tex.App., Eastland 1943, no writ)).

4. CONFLICT OF LAW/APPLICABLE LAW TO BE APPLIED

4.1 What happens when one party applies to stay proceedings in favour of a foreign jurisdiction? What factors will the local court take into account when determining forum issues?

The mere pendency of an action in a foreign jurisdiction will not be grounds for staying a suit in Texas. As a matter of comity, however, it is customary for the court in which the later action is instituted to stay proceedings until the prior action is determined. The custom has grown into a general rule that strongly urges the court in which the subsequent action is instituted to stay or abate its proceedings (see *Space Master Intern., Inc. v. Porta-Kamp Mfg. Co., Inc.*, 794 S.W.2d 944, 946 (Tex.App.-Houston [1st Dist.] 1990, not pet.)). However, an exception to this general rule arises when the party filing in the foreign jurisdiction unreasonably delays in serving process on the other party. In this case, the court does not abuse its discretion in refusing to stay the later filed case (see *Reed v Reed,* 158 Tex. 298, 311 S.W.2d 628, 631 (Tex.1958)).

B. PRE- AND POST-NUPTIAL AGREEMENTS

5. VALIDITY OF PRE- AND POST-NUPTIAL AGREEMENTS

5.1 To what extend are pre- and post-nups binding within the jurisdiction? Could you provide a brief discussion of the most significant recent case law on this issue?

Texas has adopted the Uniform Premarital Agreement Act, which has also been adopted by 27 other states, including the District of Columbia to date. (See Tex. Fam. Code, section 4.001 *ad sequa*).

Texas also permits post-marital property agreements, customarily described as partition or exchange agreements.

Pre- and post-marital agreements are not enforceable if the party against whom enforcement is requested proves:

(i) that the party did not sign the agreement voluntarily; or

(ii) that it was unconscionable when it was signed, and before signing the agreement, the party was not provided a fair and reasonable disclosure of the property and financial obligations of the other party and did not voluntarily and expressly waive in writing any right to such disclosure of property or financial obligation of the other party, did not voluntarily and expressly waive in writing any right to such disclosure of property or financial obligations of the other party beyond the discolsure provided, and did not or reasonably could not have had adequate knowledge of the property or financial obligations of the other party.

While unconscionability has not been defined in pre- or post-marital agreements, courts will consider similar factors as in a general breach of contract claim. The remedies and defences by statute are the exclusive remedies for defences. See Tex. Fam. Code sections 4.006, 4.105. However, the court may consider common law contractual defences such as fraud, duress and undue influence in making its involuntariness evaluation. *Sheshunoff v. Sheshunoff*, 172 S.W.3d 686 (Tex. App. Austin 2005, pet. denied).

The difficulty in setting such agreements aside might be demonstrated by the case of *Osorno v Osorno*, 76 SW3d, 509, 510 (Tex.App.-Houston [14th Dist.] 2002, no pet.). In August, the wife-to-be discovered she was pregnant. According to her, the husband-to-be wanted her to have an abortion, which she refused. In September, the husband-to-be agreed to marry her if she signed a pre-marital agreement. Both husband-to-be and wife-to-be signed an agreement in contemplation of marriage on 9 October 1992, and were married the following day. Aside from his moral duties, the husband-to-be had no legal duty to marry the wife-to-be, and his threat to do something he had the legal right to do was insufficient to invalidate the pre-marital agreement. The wife-to-be was faced with difficult choices, but the court ruled that the agreement was voluntary.

C. DIVORCE, NULLITY AND JUDICIAL SEPARATION

6. RECOGNITION OF FOREIGN MARRIAGES/DIVORCES

6.1 Summarise the position in your jurisdiction

Foreign judgments are generally recognised in United States courts under principles of international comity where (i) there was an opportunity in the foreign country for a full and fair trial before a court of competent jurisdiction under a system of jurisprudence likely to secure the impartial administration of justice between the citizens of that country and citizens of other countries, and (ii) there is nothing to show prejudice in the court or in the system of laws under which it is sitting, or fraud in producing the judgments (see *Cochran Consulting, Inc. v Uwatec USA, Inc.*, 102 F.3d 1224 (Fed. Cir. 1996)). A foreign country's judgment need not be accepted if the country does not reciprocate in accepting judgments of US courts or, if there are other, significant countervailing public policy reasons.

The Full Faith and Credit Clause of the United States Constitution does not require that binding effect and validity be given to a foreign country's divorce judgment (see *Reading & Bates Const. Co. v Baker Energy Res. Corp.*, 976 S.W.2d 702, 712 (Tex.App., Houston [1st Dist.] 1998, pet. denied)). A Texas court is not required to recognise the validity of a divorce judgment of a foreign country, especially where such judgment is invalid (see *Dunn v Tiernan*, 284 S.W.2d 754, 756 (Tex. Civ App.- El Paso 1955, writ ref'd n.r.e.).

7. DIVORCE

7.1 Explain the grounds for divorce within the jurisdiction (please also deal with nullity and judicial separation if appropriate)

There are several grounds for divorce in Texas, including mental cruelty, living apart for more than three years, confinement in a mental health facility, adultery, felony conviction and abandonment for one year. The most commonly used is the no-fault ground of 'insupportability'. There is no defence to this ground of divorce. Tex. Fam. Code section 6.001 provides 'the court may grant a divorce without regard to fault if the marriage has become insupportable because of discord or conflict of personalities that destroys the legitimate ends of the marital relationship and prevents any reasonable expectation of reconciliation'. This no-fault divorce dispenses with any burden to establish the source of the conflict in the marriage.

Texas does not have a provision for judicial separation or permanent separation. Texas has statutes for a marriage annulment, but such are seldom used.

8. FINANCES/CAPITAL, PROPERTY

8.1 What powers does the court have to allocate financial resources and property on the breakdown of marriage?

At the time of divorce, the trial court may divide the community property to be 'just and right'. A just and right division can be a 50-50 split or a disproportionate split, depending on the circumstances. An unequal property division may be justified on these non-exclusive factors:

(i) the need for future support;
(ii) children of the marriage;
(iii) education and employability;
(iv) the size of a separate estate;
(v) health;
(vi) age;

(vii) liquidity;
(viii) income production;
(ix) wrongdoing of a party in bringing about the dissolution of the marriage;
(x) actual or constructive fraud in transactions involving community property;
(xi) tax consequences of the division;
(xii) length of the marriage; and
(xiii) nature of the property to be divided (see *Twyman v Twyman,* 855 SW2d 619, 625 (Tex. 1993).

8.2 Explain and illustrate, with reference to recent cases, the court's thinking on division of assets

The division is based upon the net equity (marital assets minus liabilities awarded) each spouse receives from the division of the marital estate. *In re Marriage of Jeffries,* 144 S.W.3d 636, 641-42 (Tex App. Texarkana 2004, no pet.). As mentioned above in section 8.1, the court can consider nonexclusive factors in making its just and right division, and the facts of each marriage affect those factors that the court considers in the division. See *Medrano v. Medrano,* No. 04-08-00856-CV (Tex. App. San Antonio 2009, no pet.).

9. FINANCES/MAINTENANCE

9.1 Explain the operation of maintenance for spouses on an ongoing basis after the breakdown of marriage

Texas traditionally had no provision for post-divorce maintenance or alimony. In 1995, however, the Texas legislature adopted a maintenance statute. Maintenance is intended to provide a divorced spouse limited support after the divorce and has since been expanded to protect disabled spouses, spouses caring for disabled children, and/or spouses affected by family violence. Temporary spousal support is also available to help protect the financial welfare of a dependent spouse during the divorce.

The duration of spousal maintenance after divorce, if awarded, is determined by the duration of the marriage: the maximum duration for a marriage of between 10 and 20 years is no more than five years; between 20 and 30 years is no more than seven years; and a marriage of 30 years or more only entitles the claimant spouse to a spousal maintenance award for up to 10 years. However, if the spouse is disabled or there is a disabled child of the marriage, then spousal maintenance is indefinite if the spouse satisfies the eligibility requirements.

9.2 Is it common for maintenance to be awarded?

No, it is not common. To be eligible to make a maintenance claim, the claimant must prove that:
(i) he/she is a spouse;
(ii) he/she lacks adequate property (including property distributed to the spouse upon divorce) to provide for his/her minimum reasonable needs;

and

(iii) he/she meets one of the following requirements:
   (a) Establish that the marriage between the claimant and spouse has been 10 years or longer and the claimant lacks the ability to earn sufficient income to provide for his/her minimum reasonable needs after having diligently tried to earn sufficient income to provide for his/her minimum reasonable needs or developing the skills necessary during the separation period and time the divorce suit is pending. Tex. Fam. Code §8.053(a).
   (b) The other spouse was convicted of or received deferred adjudication for a criminal offence that was an act of family violence against the claimant spouse or their child that occurred within two years of or during the divorce suit. Tex. Fam. Code §8.051(1).
   (c) The claimant cannot earn sufficient income for his/her minimum reasonable needs due to an incapacitating physical or mental disability. Tex. Fam. Code §8.051(2)(A).
   (d) The claimant cannot earn income to meet his/her minimum reasonable needs because that person is the custodian of a child of the marriage who is disabled. Tex. Fam. Code §8.051(2)(C).

9.3 Explain and illustrate with reference to recent cases the court's thinking on maintenance

It is not common for post-divorce maintenance to be awarded in Texas. The maintenance awarded during the pendency of the case depends on the status quo and the responsibility of the spouses to support each other and follows lifestyle, needs and ability to pay.

10. CHILD MAINTENANCE

10.1 On what basis is child maintenance calculated within the jurisdiction?

Child maintenance or support is calculated on a guideline based on the monthly net financial resources of the obligor. For one child the obligor will pay 20 per cent of the net resources, and each additional child is a 5 per cent increase (eg, two children – 25 per cent). (Tex. Fam. Code section 154.125). There is a cap on the guidelines for net resources at $7,500 per month. However, additional factors may bring the amount due over that established by the guidelines, if evidence rebuts the presumption that applying the guidelines are in the best interest of the child and proven needs of the child justifies the variance. If these additional factors are not proven, the cap for one child would be set at $1500, even if the obligor earns $1 million or more per year.

11. RECIPROCAL ENFORCEMENT OF FINANCIAL ORDERS

11.1 Summarise the position in your jurisdiction

Enforcement of foreign orders dividing marital property

A Texas court may render an order enforcing the division of property set forth in a foreign decree of divorce (Tex. Fam. Code section 9.007(a)). The power of the court is limited to rendering an order to assist in implementing or to clarify the prior order, and may not alter or change the substantive division of property (*Id*).

Enforcement of foreign child support or spousal support order

A child support or spousal support order rendered in a foreign country may be enforced by a Texas court under the rules and procedures contained in the Uniform Interstate Family Support Act (UIFSA). When Texas has jurisdiction over the party owing child support, then the steps in UIFSA, stated below, should be followed.

Direct enforcement

There are two methods to have a spousal support or child support order enforced in Texas without assistance from a court. First, a notice may be sent directly to the obligor's employer in Texas (Tex. Fam. Code section 159.501) which triggers income withholding by that employer without the necessity of a hearing, unless the employee objects. The act provides for direct administrative enforcement by the support enforcement agency (Tex. Fam. Code section159).

Registration and enforcement

Enforcement of a support order of another nation involving a tribunal of the forum nation begins with the registration of the existing support order in a Texas court (Tex. Fam. Code sections 159.605-159.608). The role of the Texas court is limited to enforcing the order, except in limited circumstances.

12. FINANCIAL RELIEF AFTER FOREIGN DIVORCE PROCEEDINGS

12.1 What powers are available to make orders following a foreign divorce?

Foreign judgments are recognised in United States courts under principles of international comity where (i) there was an opportunity in the foreign country for a full and fair trial before a court of competent jurisdiction under a system of jurisprudence likely to secure the impartial administration of justice between the citizens of that country and citizens of other countries; and (ii) there is nothing to show prejudice in the court, or in the system of laws under which it is sitting, or fraud in producing the judgments (see *Cochran Consulting, Inc. v Uwatec USA, Inc.*, 102 F.3d 1224 (Fed. Cir. 1996)).

Modification of division of marital property

A Texas court may not amend, modify, alter or change the division of property made or approved in the decree of divorce or annulment, although a court may enforce the decree of divorce or annulment (Tex. Fam. Code section 9.007(a)). An order enforcing the division is limited to an order to assist in implementing or to clarify the prior order and may not alter or change the substantive division of property (*Id).*

Modification of spousal support order

A Texas court may grant financial relief following the rendition of a foreign order as permitted by the Uniform Interstate Family Support Act (UIFSA). Under UIFSA, a Texas court may not modify a spousal support order issued by a tribunal of another country having continuing, exclusive jurisdiction over that order under the foreign country's law (Tex. Fam. Code section 159.211).

Modification of child support order

A Texas court may modify a child support order issued by a foreign country and registered in Texas when neither the party nor the child reside in the issuing country and, after notice and hearing, the Texas court finds that:

(i) the following requirements are met:
- the child, the obligee and the obligor do not reside in the issuing state;
- a petitioner, who is a non-resident of Texas, seeks modification; and
- the respondent is subject to the personal jurisdiction of the Texas court;

Or

(ii) Texas is the state of residence of the child, or a party is subject to the personal jurisdiction of the tribunal of this state, and all of the parties have filed consents in a record in this issuing foreign tribunal for a tribunal of Texas to modify the support order and assume continuing, exclusive jurisdiction (see Tex. Fam. Code section 159.611);

(iii) notwithstanding the provisions of Tex. Fam. Code section 159.611), if a foreign country refuses to modify or cannot modify its order under its law, a Texas court may assume jurisdiction to modify the child support order and bind all individuals subject to the personal jurisdiction of the tribunal (Tex. Fam. Code section 159.615).

D. CHILDREN

13. CUSTODY/PARENTAL RESPONSIBILITY

13.1 Briefly explain the legal position in relation to custody/parental responsibility following the breakdown of a relationship or marriage

Texas requires that children have frequent and continuing contact with parents who have shown the ability to act in the best interest of the children and encourages parents to share in the rights and duties of raising their child after parents have separated or divorced. Tex. Fam. Code section 153.001. The best interest of the child is always the paramount concern for the court and evidence is usually necessary to show which parent(s) care for the child in order for either parent to obtain any rights or duties regarding the child.

13.2 Briefly explain the legal position in relation to access/contact/visitation following the breakdown of a relationship or marriage

Typically, one parent is designated the primary parent with the right to designate the child's primary residence. The other parent then, assuming the child is three years of age or older, is awarded access to the child on the first, third and fifth weekends; every Thursday night during the school year, and 30 days during the summer. Holidays are rotated each year between the parents. If the child is younger than three, there is no determinative legal position and the courts decide access/contact/visitation on a case-by-case factual basis depending on what is in the best interest of the child.

14. INTERNATIONAL ABDUCTION

14.1 Summarise the position in your jurisdiction

In an effort to effectuate the return of children who are wrongfully removed or retained across international boundaries and to ensure that the rights of the parent in one country are respected by other countries, the United States has adopted the Hague Convention. The Convention does not grant authority to address the underlying merits of a child custody claim, but empowers courts to determine the existing rights of the parties.

In countries that have adopted the Convention, the petitioner may (i) try to obtain a voluntary return, which can be negotiated by the central authority or an attorney, or (ii) file a formal Notice of Petition Under the Hague Convention and Petition for Return of Children to Petitioner. Any court of competent jurisdiction can hear a Hague Convention case and the International Child Abduction Remedies Act (ICARA) gives both United States federal and state courts jurisdiction over Hague cases (ICARA, 42 U.S.C.11603(a) & (b)).

If a child is abducted from the United States to a country that is not party to the Hague Convention, the parent can petition a court in that country to enforce a custody order made by a US court.

15. LEAVE TO REMOVE/APPLICATIONS TO TAKE A CHILD OUT OF THE JURISDICTION

15.1 Summarise the position in your jurisdiction

It is customary in a Texas court's order affecting the parent-child relationship to include a 'residency restriction' that identifies a specific location within which a parent must establish the residence of the children.

When one parent wishes to relocate outside of the geographic restriction with the child, Texas courts consider a non-exhaustive list of factors when evaluating whether the decision to relocate is in the child's best interest, including:

- the relationship with and presence of extended family;
- the presence of a stable and supportive environment for the child;
- the relocating parent's improved financial or job situation and ability to provide a better standard of living;
- the reasons for and against the move;
- comparison of education, health and leisure opportunities;
- the child's age, community ties, preferences and health and educational needs;
- each parent's plans for the child;
- cooperation between the parents;
- each parent's parenting skills.

15.2 Under what circumstances may a parent apply to remove their child from the jurisdiction against the wishes of the other parent?

When one parent wishes to relocate outside of Texas with the child when a valid court order exists restricting the child's residence to a location within Texas, the parent must modify the prior court order and prove the occurrence of a material and substantial change in the circumstances of the child or a parent since the rendition of the prior order. Sometimes, the need for the move may be a sufficient material and substantial change when a conservator wishes to relocate outside of Texas with a child.

E. SURROGACY & ADOPTION

16. VALIDITY OF SURROGACY AGREEMENTS

16.1 Briefly summarise the position in your jurisdiction

Traditional surrogacy arrangements (whereby the surrogate mother uses her own eggs and is artificially inseminated with the sperm of the intended father) are not legally recognised in Texas. Instead, Texas recognises 'gestational agreements' if the agreement complies with several statutory prerequisites. (Tex. Fam. Code sections 160.751-160.763.) The intended parents must be married to each other, and the intended mother must show either that she is unable (i) to carry a pregnancy to term and give birth to a child; or (ii) to carry the pregnancy to term and give birth without placing her mental or physical health at unreasonable risk or the unborn child's health. (Tex. Fam. Code section 160.756(b)(2).) As for the gestational mother, she must have had at least one previous pregnancy and delivery, and it must be shown that carrying another pregnancy to term would not pose an unreasonable risk to her physical or mental health or the unborn child's health. (Tex. Fam. Code section 160.756(b)(6).)

The gestational agreement needs to be in writing, entered into before conception, between the intended parents, gestational mother (and father if she is married), and the donor of the egg or sperm. (Tex. Fam. Code §160.754(a), (b), (e).) There are also several statutory provisions required to be in the gestational agreement. (See Tex. Fam. Code section 160.754.) Notably, the parties are at risk with the lack of legal protection for non-authorised agreements, both written and oral.

17. ADOPTION

17.1 Briefly explain the legal position in relation to adoption in your jurisdiction. Is adoption available to individuals, cohabiting couples (both heterosexual and same-sex)?

Adoption is available to individuals and cohabiting couples, both heterosexual and homosexual. If the petitioner is married, both spouses must join the petition for adoption, and the adoption can occur at any age of the child. (Tex. Fam. Code section 162.002.) If the petitioner is unmarried but in a relationship, so long as the child is two years' old, the non-parent seeking adoption will need to have exercised actual care, custody, and control over the child for at least six months to one year depending on the circumstances. (Tex. Fam. Code section 162.001.) If the individual is unmarried, then there is no minimum age of child to adopt. (Tex. Fam. Code section 162.001.) If the child is not related to the adopting parent, then a report must be performed on the available health, social, educational, and genetic history of the child to be adopted. (Tex. Fam. Code section 162.005.)

F. COHABITATION

18. COHABITATION

15.1 What legislation (if any) governs division of property for unmarried couples on the breakdown of the relationship?

No community property or other marital rights arise from a meretricious relationship. Unless the parties have entered into, for example, joint banking accounts, then neither party has a claim to the other's property. A court cannot award spousal maintenance to a party to a non-marital relationship (Tex. Fam. Code section 8.051). Texas recognises common law marriage, referred to as an 'informal marriage' (Tex. Fam. Code section 2.401). An informal marriage may be established by proving the man and woman agreed to be married and, after the agreement, lived together in Texas as husband and wife and, in Texas, represented to others that they were married.

G. FAMILY DISPUTE RESOLUTION

19. MEDIATION, COLLABORATIVE LAW AND ARBITRATION

19.1 Briefly summarise the non-court-based processes available in your jurisdiction and the current status of agreements reached under the auspices of mediation, collaborative law and arbitration

The Texas Family Code authorises parties to resolve their dispute through mediation, collaborative law, an informal settlement conference, or arbitration. (See Tex. Fam. Code sections 6.601 (arbitration), 6.602 (mediation), 6.604 (informal settlement conference), 15.001-15.116 (collaborative law).) Some Texas courts even require parties to participate in an alternative dispute resolution process before their case can go to trial.

In a divorce, if the parties agree to binding arbitration, then the court must enter an order reflecting the arbitrator's award. (Tex. Fam. Code section 6.601(b).) If the parties enter into an informal settlement agreement, then the court may review the agreement to decide whether it is just and right. (Tex. Fam. Code section 6.604(d), (e).) With a mediated settlement agreement, a court's review is limited to whether the agreement is illegal or was obtained by fraud, duress, coercion, or other dishonest means.

19.2 What is the statutory basis (if any), for mediation, collaborative law and arbitration in your jurisdiction? In particular, are the parties required to attempt a family dispute resolution in advance of the institution of proceedings?

The Texas Family Code authorises parties to resolve their dispute through mediation, collaborative law, an informal settlement conference, or arbitration. (See Tex. Fam. Code section 6.601 (arbitration), 6.602 (mediation), 6.604 (informal settlement conference), 15.001-15.116

(collaborative law).) Many local trial courts require parties to attempt mediation before their case can be called for trial.

H. OTHER

20. CIVIL PARTNERSHIP/SAME-SEX MARRIAGE

20.1 What is the status of civil partnership/same-sex marriage within the jurisdiction?

A marriage licence will not be issued to marry another person of the same sex. (Tex. Fam. Code section 2.001(b).) If a same-sex couple obtains a marriage licence in Texas, the marriage is void and has no legal effect. Id. section 6.204(b), (c); see *Mireles v Mireles*, No. 01-08-00499-CV, 2009 WL 884815 (Tex. App. Houston [1st Dist.] Apr. 2, 2009, pet. denied) (mem. op.). If the same-sex couple is married or enters into a civil union outside of the state, Texas will not recognise that union. (Tex. Fam. Code section 6.204(b)); see Texas Constitution Article 1, section 32 (stating marriage in this state is a union of only one man and one woman).

Also, one Texas court has held that a male-to-female transsexual – a person born male but surgically changed to resemble a female – is legally a male because of their genetic makeup and cannot marry another male. *Littleton v Prague*, 9 S.W.3d 223, 231 (Tex. App. San Antonio 1999, pet. denied).

20.2 What legislation governs civil partnership/same-sex marriage?

The Defense of Marriage Act, 28 U.S.C.section 1738C; The Texas Constitution, Article 1, section 32; The Texas Family Code sections 2.001, 2.401, 6.204.

21. CONTROVERSIAL AREAS/RAPIDLY DEVELOPING AREAS OF LAW

21.1 Is there a particular area of the law within the jurisdiction that is currently undergoing major change?

Spousal maintenance

Texas was without spousal maintenance or alimony when a very limited spousal maintenance act was adopted in 1995.

To be eligible for spousal maintenance, the requesting spouse must prove she lacks sufficient property to provide for her minimum reasonable needs and:

(i) has been married for 10 years;
(ii) the spouse from whom maintenance is sought was convicted of family violence as defined by the Texas Family Code;
(iii) the spouse is suffering from an incapacitating physical or mental disability; or
(iv) is the custodian of a child of the marriage who requires substantial care and personal supervision because of a physical or mental disability that prevents the spouse from earning sufficient income to provide for the spouse's minimum reasonable needs.

Tex. Fam. Code § 8.051.

The duration for which a spouse is eligible depends on the duration of the marriage and the basis of the award. It is no longer automatically limited to three years. A spouse may be eligible for spousal maintenance for up to 10 years if the duration of the marriage was 30 years or longer. If the spouse is disabled or caring for a disabled child, the duration has no cap. (See Tex. Fam. Code section 8.054.)

Finally, the monthly spousal maintenance was increased from $2,500 to $5,000 per month, or 20 per cent of the paying spouse's gross income, whichever is less. It still remains capped at what is necessary to provide for the spouse's minimum reasonable needs. (Tex. Fam. Code section 8.051).

21.2 Which areas of law are most out-of-step? Which areas would you most like to see reformed/changed?

Characterisation of marital property

In Texas, all property identified and characterised as a spouse's separate property must be confirmed to that spouse and may not be divided by the court between the parties during the division of marital property (Tex. Fam. Code section 7.002(b)(c)). In characterising property as either community or separate, Texas follows the 'inception of title' rule, which provides that a property's character is based on the time and manner in which a person first acquires an ownership interest in the property (see *Jensen v Jensen*, 665 S.W.2d 107, 109 (Tex. 1984)). Thus, if a person first acquires an ownership interest in the property before marriage, the property is considered separate property, regardless of the manner in which it was acquired (Tex. Fam. Code. section 3.001). However, if a person first acquires an ownership interest in property during the marriage, the property is considered community property unless evidence of the manner in which it was acquired would make the property separate, for example, the property was acquired by gift, inheritance, or property agreement or premarital funds (Tex. Fam. Code. section 3.002). In certain factual circumstances, this body of Texas law can present a very inequitable situation at the time of divorce.

Division of marital property

In Texas, all community property must be divided between the spouses in a 'just and right' manner, considering the rights of each spouse and any children of the marriage (Tex. Fam. Code section 7.001). A 'just and right' division may be an equal division of community property or a disproportionate division awarding one spouse a greater portion of the marital estate. In rendering a 'just and right' division of marital property, Texas courts may consider several non-exclusive equitable factors, which is a vague criterion. A Texas family law attorney's ability to predict the manner in which a court will divide the spouses' marital estate is, therefore, limited.

Texas child support guidelines

In Texas, the amount of child support payable by an obligor is determined by applying child support guidelines to the obligor's monthly net resources (monthly income less federal and state income tax, social security tax, union dues and the cost of the child's health insurance). A parent with two children born of the marriage will be ordered to pay 25 per cent of his or her monthly net resources as guidelines child support. If the obligor's monthly net resources exceed $7,500 month, the court only looks to the first $7,500 in the obligor's net resources in calculating guidelines child support (Tex. Fam. Code section 154.125).

For a court to order child support in excess of the guidelines, the court must find that the child's proven needs exceed the guidelines support amount (Tex. Fam. Code section 154.126). If the child's needs exceed the guidelines support amount, the responsibility for meeting the child's needs is allocated between the parties based upon their circumstances (Tex. Fam. Code section 154.126(b)). The 'needs' of the child include more than life's bare necessities, but they do not turn on the parent's ability to pay or the family lifestyle. The court cannot order the obligor to pay more than the presumptive amount of guidelines support or 100 per cent of the child's proven needs, whichever is greater (Tex. Fam. Code section 154.126(b)). In high income cases, this limit is often inequitable.

USA – Virginia

The Maddox Law Firm, PC
Katharine W. Maddox & Julie C. Gerock

A. JURISDICTION AND CONFLICT OF LAW

1. SOURCES OF LAW

1.1 What is the primary source of law in relation to the breakdown of marriage and the welfare of children within the jurisdiction?

The primary source of law in family law proceedings within the Commonwealth of Virginia is Title 20 of the Virginia Code. Title 20 covers practically all issues arising out of the dissolution of a marriage. With respect to cases where the parties are unmarried or they do not have grounds for divorce, then Title 16.1 of the Virginia Code includes a variety of laws regarding children or involving children, including protective orders, abuse and neglect proceedings, juvenile delinquency issues, custody and visitation, child support, and spousal support.

1.2 Which are the main statutes governing matrimonial law in the jurisdiction?

The main statutes governing matrimonial law can be found in Chapter 6 and Chapter 6.1 within Title 20 of the Virginia Code.

2. JURISDICTION

2.1 What are the main jurisdictional requirements for the institution of proceedings in relation to divorce, property and children?

Divorce

In Virginia, at least one of the parties must be and have been an actual *bona fide* resident and domiciliary of Virginia for at least six months preceding the divorce action. These requirements are jurisdictional. Without satisfaction of both requirements, a divorce cannot be granted.

Domicile and residence are not synonymous. 'Residence' is where a person maintains a permanent abode or residence. See *Hiles v Hiles*, 1 64 Va. 131 (1935). 'Domicile' is typically defined as physical presence combined with the intention to live there permanently or indefinitely. While a person may have multiple residences at any one time, a person can only have one domicile. Residency is more objective, domicile is more subjective.

Va. Code section 20-97 addresses jurisdiction issues concerning military and foreign service officers. If a member of the armed forces has been stationed or resided in Virginia for six months or more prior to the divorce action, he is presumed to be domiciled in and to have been a *bona fide* resident of Virginia. If an armed forces member or a foreign service officer is stationed outside of

Virginia but was domiciled in Virginia for six months before such station, he is deemed to have been domiciled in and to have been a *bona fide* resident during the six months before the divorce action.

Property

The domicile and residency requirements confer subject matter jurisdiction. However, without personal jurisdiction over a defendant, the Court cannot enter orders creating, modifying or extinguishing spousal support or marital property rights. A divorce may be granted to a plaintiff without personal jurisdiction over the defendant (*ex parte* divorce), but in the absence of personal jurisdiction, consent or having a significant connection to Virginia, no support or property rights affecting the defendant can be determined.

Personal jurisdiction may be obtained over a defendant as follows:

- Persons found in Virginia: by delivering a copy of the summons and complaint directly to the party in person (Va. Code section 8.01-296);
- By substituted service wherein the summons and complaint are delivered to a person 16 years or older at the party's residence if he/she is not found there; or posting at the front door or main entrance of the party's residence (Va. Code section 8.01–296);
- For residents and non-residents of Virginia: By defendant's acceptance of service or waiver of service in a notarized writing, or by the defendant's filing of an answer in the action (Va. Code section 20–99.1:1).

Personal jurisdiction will not be conferred on a non-resident defendant even if there is valid service of process as stated above, unless the defendant also has a significant connection to Virginia. Pursuant to Va. Code section 8.01–328.1, one may obtain long-arm jurisdiction over a party if the person has a significant connection to the Commonwealth of Virginia, for example by transacting business in Virginia, causing tortious injury in Virginia, entering into contracts in Virginia, having an interest in real property in Virginia, contracting for insurance in Virginia, executing an agreement to pay support in Virginia, having maintained a matrimonial domicile in Virginia at the time of separation, etc. In divorce actions, however, the most compelling basis for exercising long-arm jurisdiction would be the parties having maintained a matrimonial domicile in Virginia at the time of separation.

Child support

The Uniform Interstate Family Support Act (UIFSA) in Chapter 5.3 of Title 20 of the Code of Virginia, sections 20-88.32-88.82, provides the jurisdictional bases for the establishment and enforcement of child support orders over a non-resident parent. In general, personal jurisdiction may be exercised over a non-resident parent if there is personal service in Virginia; he consents to jurisdiction; he resided with the child in Virginia; he resided in Virginia and paid support for the child; the child resides in Virginia due to the acts of the non-resident parent; personal jurisdiction is authorised by law; or there is any other basis consistent with the constitutions of Virginia and the United States.

The bases above are generally not available for the purpose of modifying a support order of another state. A 'state' may be a foreign country if such country is declared a foreign reciprocating country, has established reciprocity with Virginia, or has laws substantially similar to Virginia concerning the establishment and enforcement of child support orders.

Custody

For a discussion as to jurisdictional issues in custody cases, see section on Domicile and Habitual Residence below.

3. DOMICILE AND HABITUAL RESIDENCE

3.1 Explain the concepts of domicile and habitual residence as they apply to the jurisdiction

Virginia may only decree a divorce if at least one of the parties is domiciled within the state for at least six months prior to the filing of divorce action. In a Virginia divorce, the concept of domicile depends not just on that party's presence within the state but their intention that Virginia will be their home 'permanently or certainly for an indefinite period.' See *Howe v Howe*, 179 Va. 111, 119 (1942). In addition to the domiciliary requirement, at least one of the parties must be a resident of Virginia for a period of six months prior to filing for divorce. Establishing a residence in Virginia requires a permanent abode as opposed to a transitory abode. See *Hiles v Hiles*, 164 Va. 131 (1935).

The six month requirement also applies to habitual residence, which within the United States is referred to as the 'home state'. However, home state does not necessarily equate with the concept of habitual residence as used in the 1980 Hague Convention on the Civil Aspects of International Child Abduction.

Virginia has enacted the Uniform Child Custody and Enforcement Act (UCCJEA) to address multi-jurisdictional custody battles. Virginia may assert jurisdiction over a custody dispute under the UCCJEA where Virginia is the 'home state of the child at the date of the commencement of custody proceeding, or was the home state of the child within six months before the commencement of the proceeding and the child is absent [from Virginia] but a parent or person acting as a parent continues to live in [Virginia].' See Code section 20-146.12(A). However, a temporary absence from the state does not interrupt the home state status. See Code section 20-146.1.

4. CONFLICT OF LAW/APPLICABLE LAW TO BE APPLIED

4.1 What happens when one party applies to stay proceedings in favour of a foreign jurisdiction? What factors will the local court take into account when determining forum issues?

When one party applies to stay proceedings in Virginia in favour of a foreign jurisdiction, the Virginia court will first look to whether Virginia properly has jurisdiction over the pending action. If the court determines it does have jurisdiction, it will determine whether it is appropriate to defer to a foreign court. However, if Virginia has jurisdiction, it is rare for Virginia to defer to a foreign court. In these instances, there may be a race to judgment between Virginia and the foreign court. Where the issue involves child custody proceedings, the UCCJEA governs. Factors the Virginia court will consider in a child custody proceedings include:

(a) Whether the court has initial child custody jurisdiction. See Code section 20-146.12.
(b) Whether another state has temporary emergency jurisdiction. Under the UCCJEA, a state may assert temporary emergency jurisdiction where the child is present in the state and the child has been abandoned or it is necessary to protect the child because the child or another family member has been abused or reasonably fears abuse. See Code section 20-146.15.
(c) Whether there are simultaneous proceedings in two jurisdictions. If so, Virginia will usually stay its proceedings if the matter was previously commenced in a foreign court which exercised jurisdiction in substantial conformity with the UCCJEA. In these situations under Virginia law, the Virginia court is required to speak with the foreign court to determine whether Virginia would be the more appropriate forum. See Code section 20–146.17.
(d) Whether Virginia is an inconvenient forum. Under the inconvenient forum analysis, Virginia may decline to assert jurisdiction if the court 'determines that [Virginia] is an inconvenient forum under the circumstances and that a court of another state is a more appropriate forum'. See Code section 20-146.18.
(e) Finally, Virginia may decline jurisdiction even if it could properly assert jurisdiction on the basis of a party's 'unjustifiable conduct'. See Code section 20-146.19.

B. PRE- AND POST-NUPTIAL AGREEMENTS

5. VALIDITY OF PRE- AND POST NUPTIAL AGREEMENTS

5.1 To what extent are pre- and post-nups binding within the jurisdiction? Could you provide a brief discussion of the most significant recent case law on this issue?

Pre- and post-nuptial agreements are usually binding in Virginia. Virginia has adopted the Uniform Premarital Agreement Act (the Act) designed to ensure that such agreements are declared as valid and enforceable contracts. This Act also applies to post-nuptial agreements. See Code sections 20-147 – 20-155. These agreements may relate to the disposition of property after separation, divorce, death, or any other event and will be treated as binding contracts. See *Dowling v Rowan*, 270 Va. 510, 516 (2005), citing Code section 20-150. So long as the agreement is in writing and signed by both parties, the agreement is enforceable regardless of consideration (monetary or otherwise) and is effective upon marriage. See Code section 20-149. Married persons may also enter into such agreements which are binding immediately upon execution. See Code section 20-155.

Under the Act, an agreement is not enforceable if: '1. That person did not execute the agreement voluntarily; or 2. The agreement was unconscionable when it was executed and, before execution of the agreement, that person (i) was not provided with a fair and reasonable disclosure of the property or financial obligations of the other party; and (ii) did not voluntarily and expressly waive, in writing, any right to disclosure of the property or financial obligations of the other party beyond the disclosure provided.' See Code section 20-155.1(A).

An important case concerning premarital agreements is *Flanary v Jackson*, 263 Va. 20 (2002). In *Flanary*, the court held that settlement terms relating to the marriage must be in writing and signed by both parties in order to be enforceable. It is noteworthy, however, that even where pre and post-nuptial agreements are in writing and signed by both parties, the agreement will not be binding if the parties later reconcile unless the agreement specifically stated that it would survive reconciliation. Code section 20-155. Therefore, if the parties enter into a settlement agreement (as opposed to a court order being entered) and they later reconcile, unless the agreement states that it would remain binding despite a reconciliation, the agreement would not be binding post-reconciliation even if the parties thereafter separated a second time.

There are several instances where a such agreements will not be enforceable as set forth in Va. Code section 20-151:

(1) the agreement was not executed voluntarily;

(2) the agreement was unconscionable when executed and fair and reasonable disclosure was not provided and the parties did not waive in writing additional disclosure beyond what was provided; or

(3) if a marriage is later declared to be void, the 'agreement shall be enforceable only to the extent necessary to avoid an inequitable result.'

In addition, several cases outline the circumstances where such agreement will not be enforced:

- *Chaplain v Chaplain*, 54 Va. App. 762, 776 (2009): A pre- or post-nuptial agreement will not be enforced if the court determines the agreement was unconscionable at the time it was entered into and the party challenging enforcement establishes the factors set forth under Virginia Code section 20-155.1(A). In order to prove an agreement is unconscionable, the party challenging the agreement must show '(1) a gross disparity existed in the division of assets and (2) overreaching or oppressive influences' as at the date of execution of the agreement.
- *Derby v Derby*, 8 Va. App. 19 (1989): A pre- or post-nuptial agreement may be unenforceable where duress is proven by clear and convincing evidence.
- *Gaffney v Gaffney*, 45 Va. App. 655, 667 (2005): Post-nuptial agreements will not be enforceable unless they are in writing and signed by both parties, subject to two narrow exceptions under Code section 20-155: (1) The attorneys for the parties endorse a court order containing relevant terms; or (2) the terms are recorded and transcribed by a court reporter and the parties themselves affirm the terms on the record.

C. DIVORCE, NULLITY AND JUDICIAL SEPARATION
6. RECOGNITION OF FOREIGN MARRIAGES/DIVORCES
6.1 Summarise the position in your jurisdiction
Recognition of foreign marriages
The general rule in Virginia is that a marriage valid where celebrated is valid everywhere, unless it is against Virginia's strong public policy. See *Heflinger v Heflinger*, 136 Va. 289 (1923); *Kleinfeld v Veruki*, 7 Va. App. 183 (1988).

Pursuant to Va. Code section 20-38.1, bigamous, polygamous and incestuous marriages are prohibited. Va. Code section 20-45.2 also prohibits marriages between persons of the same sex and Code section 20-45.3 prohibits civil unions between persons of the same sex. Virginia will not recognise same-sex marriages or civil unions obtained outside Virginia and as such, they are considered void and any contractual rights created thereby are void and unenforceable. Marriages between one or more individuals under the age of 18, unless certain exceptions apply, are also considered invalid.

Recognition of foreign divorces
The United States is not a signatory to the Hague Convention on the Recognition of Divorce and Legal Separations, 978 United Nations Treaty Series 399 (1975). The question of whether divorces obtained outside Virginia and outside the United States will be enforced is a matter of comity. *' 'Comity', in the legal sense, is neither a matter of absolute obligation, on the one hand, nor one of mere courtesy and good will, upon the other. But it is the recognition which one nation allows within its territory to the legislative, executive or judicial acts of another nation, having due regard both to international duty and convenience, and to the rights of its own citizens or of other persons who are under the protection of its laws.'* See *Oehl v Oehl*, 221 Va. 618, 622 (1980) quoting *Hilton v Guyot*, 159 U.S. 113, 163-64 (1895).

If the foreign jurisdiction has requirements similar to those of Virginia, such as domicile and residence, then it is likely that Virginia would recognise a divorce entered by that foreign jurisdiction.

7. DIVORCE
7.1 Explain the grounds for divorce within the jurisdiction (please also deal with nullity and judicial separation if appropriate)
Va. Code section 20-91 provides the grounds on which an absolute divorce may be granted by a Virginia court. It provides three 'fault grounds' for divorce and one 'no-fault' ground based on the parties' separation.

No-fault divorce
Most divorces are granted on the no-fault ground of the parties living separate and apart without any cohabitation and without interruption for more than one year. See *Hooker v Hooker*, 215 Va. 415 (1975); Va. Code section 20-91(A)(9)(a). A divorce may be granted after only six months if a separation agreement has been executed and there are no minor children. Va. Code section 20-91(A)(9)(a).

Fault divorce

The three fault grounds for divorce are:
(1) Adultery, sodomy, or buggery committed outside the marriage ('adultery')
(2) Conviction of a felony
(3) Cruelty or desertion

To be granted a divorce in Virginia, it is not enough for one or both of the parties to testify to the separation or to the fault, nor can they stipulate to it. To prevent collusion, a third party must corroborate the grounds for divorce.

Divorce from bed and board (judicial separation)

A divorce from bed and board is different than an absolute divorce in that the marriage is not permanently terminated. When an absolute divorce is granted, the marriage is terminated and each party is free to remarry. If a divorce from bed and board is granted, the parties are declared indefinitely separated, but, they are unable to remarry unless and until an absolute divorce is later granted.

The grounds for a divorce from bed and board are:
(1) Cruelty or reasonable apprehension of bodily hurt;
(2) Wilful desertion or abandonment; or
(3) Constructive desertion.

See Va. Code section 20-95. The grounds for a bed and board divorce are similar to cruelty and desertion grounds as in an absolute divorce, except that there is no one-year waiting period. At the end of the year, the divorce from bed and board action can be merged into an action for absolute divorce.

Defences to divorce actions

Defences available to divorce actions include:
(1) Connivance: Consent (conspiracy together).
(2) Collusion: Fabrication or fraud.
(3) Condonation and cohabitation: Conditional forgiveness.
(4) Recrimination: Both guilty.
(5) Justification.
(6) Insanity: Insanity may be a bar to a fault-based divorce only.
(7) Lack of jurisdiction or due process notice.
(8) Lack of corroboration.
(9) Fraud and duress.
(10) *Laches* and *estoppel*.
(11) *Res judicata*.

See Peter Nash Swisher, Lawrence D. Diehl, & James Ray Cottrell, *Family Law: Theory Practice And Forms* 210-218 (Virginia Practice Series, Vol. 10, 2011).

Nullity

Pursuant to Va. Code section 20-89.1, a marriage may be annulled and considered void, for any of the reasons set forth in Code section 20-13 (lack of license and solemnisation), section 20-38.1 (bigamy, polygamy, incest), section 45.1 (lack of capacity, underage) or fraud or duress. A marriage may also be annulled in cases of natural or incurable impotency existing at the time of the marriage; or prior to the marriage without knowledge of the other, a party was convicted of a felony; or at the time of the marriage without knowledge by the husband, the wife was pregnant with another man's child; or where the husband without knowledge of the wife, had fathered a child born to a woman other than his wife within 10 months of the marriage; or where prior to the marriage, without knowledge of the other, either party had been a prostitute. In these latter situations, an annulment will not be granted if the parties had been married for two years prior to the annulment action.

8. FINANCES/CAPITAL, PROPERTY

8.1 What powers does the court have to allocate financial resources and property on the breakdown of marriage?

Va. Code section 20-107.3 ('ED statute') governs the equitable distribution of property as part of a divorce. In Virginia, property is divided 'equitably' and there is no requirement for equal division of property. The first step is to classify the property as marital, separate or hybrid. The second step is to value the property. The final step is to divide the property taking into account the 11 factors of the ED statute.

Classification

For each item of property, the court must determine whether it is marital, separate, or part marital and part separate ('hybrid property').

(i) Marital property

Includes all property titled in the joint names of both parties, and all other property acquired by each party during the marriage that is not separate property (this can include property titled in only the name of one spouse). All property acquired during the marriage and before the final separation of the parties is presumed to be marital property. Marital property is presumed to be jointly owned unless there is a deed or other clear indicia that it is not jointly owned.

Upon divorce, all marital property is subject to equitable distribution. A court can divide or transfer jointly owned marital property, order a monetary award to either party, and apportion marital debts. There is no statutory presumption that marital property will be equally divided, but in practice, that is often the most likely result.

(ii) Separate property

Separate property is not subject to equitable distribution. It includes all property acquired before the marriage, all property acquired by inheritance or gift from a source other than from the other party during the marriage, and all property acquired in exchange for or from the proceeds of sale of separate property, provided that property acquired during the marriage is maintained as separate property (ie, not 'commingled' with marital property). If there is commingling of separate property with marital property, it may be classified as hybrid property.

(iii) Hybrid property

Hybrid property is part marital and part separate. The ED statute provides situations that would cause property to fall within this classification. For example subsection A.3(e) of the ED statute provides:

'(W)hen marital property and separate property are commingled by contributing one category of property to the other, resulting in the loss of identity of the contributed property, the classification of the contributed property shall be transmuted to the category of property receiving the contribution. However, to the extent the contributed property is retraceable by a preponderance of the evidence and was not a gift, the contributed property shall retain its original classification.'

Valuation

Once the property has been classified, it must then be valued. The value of property must be based on more than mere guesswork. See Peter Nash Swisher, Lawrence D. Diehl, and James Ray Cottrell, *Family Law: Theory Practice And Forms* 742-767 (Virginia Practice Series, Vol. 10, 2011). The generally accepted standard is fair market value which is 'the value at which property would change hands between a willing buyer and a willing seller, neither one being under any compulsion to either buy or sell and both having a reasonable knowledge of the relevant facts.' See Id. at 736.

In Virginia, however, the court may also consider the intrinsic worth to the parties. See *Howell v Howell*, 31 Va. App. 332, 338, 523 S.E.2d 414, 517 (2000). As stated in *Bosserman v Bosserman*, 9 Va. App. 1, 6, 384 S.E.2d 104, 107 (1989), 'Intrinsic value is a very subjective concept that looks to the worth of the property to the parties. The methods of valuation must take into consideration the parties themselves and the different situations in which they exist. The item may have no established market value, and neither party may contemplate selling the item; indeed, sale may be restricted or forbidden. Commonly, one party will continue to enjoy the benefits of the property while the other must relinquish all future benefits. Still, its intrinsic value must be translated into a monetary amount. The parties must rely on accepted methods of valuation, but the particular method of valuing and the precise applicable of that method to the singular facts of the case must vary with the myriad situations that exist among married couples."

Given the complex nature of valuing assets, expert opinions are often necessary to value real property, businesses, artwork, and other assets where the value is not easily ascertainable. If credible and based on sufficient knowledge, the testimony of the owner as to value may be admissible. See Swisher, Diehl and Cottrell, at 751.

Division

Once the assets have been classified and valued, the court must determine how the assets will be distributed. There are 10 factors and one catch-all factor including:

(1) monetary and non-monetary contributions (contributions) to the well-being of the family;

(2) contributions of each in the acquisition and care and maintenance of marital property;
(3) duration of the marriage;
(4) ages, physical and mental condition of the parties;
(5) circumstances and factors which contributed to the dissolution of the marriage;
(6) how and when items of marital property were acquired;
(7) debts and liabilities of each spouse;
(8) liquid or non-liquid character of all marital property;
(9) tax consequences;
(10) use or expenditure of marital property for a nonmarital purpose or dissipation of funds, in anticipation of divorce or separation or after separation of the parties; and
(11) such other factors necessary or appropriate to arrive at a fair and equitable monetary award.

See Code section 107.3.E. It is notable that in Virginia, 'need' is not a factor in the distribution of marital property.

8.2 Explain and illustrate with reference to recent cases the court's thinking on division of assets

Judges in Virginia have wide discretion in dividing marital property and it is difficult to ascertain a particular trend. A few cases, however, depict how certain unique issues were resolved.

- *McIlwain v McIlwain*, 52 Va. App. 644 (2008): The husband who lived in the home from the parties' separation in 2001 to the date of their divorce in 2007 was charged with a payment to the wife equal to one-half the fair rental value of the home. He had changed the locks, exercised full control over the home, there was no mortgage, and the wife bore a disproportionate financial burden during the separation as she had to pay for a place to live of her own. The court applied the catch-all factor 'other factors as the court deems necessary or appropriate to consider in order to arrive at a fair and equitable monetary award'.
- *Fadness v Fadness*, 52 Va. App. 833 (2008): The husband received 52-55 per cent of the marital assets. The husband argued that the court 'failed to give sufficient weight to his argument that his wife was the sole cause of the dissolution of the marriage.' Id. at 842. The husband alleged that the wife was guilty of cruelty and sought a divorce on that ground. The husband believed that due to wife's acts of cruelty, he should have received more than 55 per cent of the assets. The court did not agree.
- *Gilliam v McGrady*, 53 Va. App. 476 (2009): The trial court incorrectly classified a tax debt as marital when it determined that the family benefited from the debt because the family had more disposable income to pay bills and maintain the parties' lifestyle as a result of the husband's failure to pay taxes (ie, the debt). 'By considering only who benefited from the failure to pay the debt, the trial court erred in not considering the purpose of the original debt, ie, the 'trust fund tax'. Without consideration of the purposes of the debt, the logical extension of the

trial court's ruling would be to always find marital debt resulting from gambling, criminal fines, and restitution if any of the proceeds from the illegal activity in any way benefited the marriage.' See Id. at 480 (emphasis added).

- *Duva v Duva*, 55 Va. App. 286 (2009): The trial court incorrectly classified a house purchased by the husband before marriage as marital property finding that it was transmuted from separate property to marital property due to mortgage payments made during the marriage. The Court of Appeals held that the classification of the property is not determined by a process or when value is created. Classification is based on the date of acquisition. See Id. at 298.
- *Schuman v Schuman*, 282 Va. 443, 717 S.E.2d 410 (2011): The trial court held and the Supreme Court of Virginia affirmed that for the purposes of equitable distribution, the wife's restricted stock awards constituted deferred compensation for work performed during the marriage and were marital property, even though they did not vest until after the parties had separated.
- *Patel v Patel*, S.E.2d , 2013 WL 1403344 (2013) : The Court of Appeals affirmed the trial court's refusal to assign a negative value to certain of the husband's assets, despite the fact that neither of the parties disputed that the assets had a negative value.

9. FINANCES/MAINTENANCE

9.1 Explain the operation of maintenance for spouses on an ongoing basis after the breakdown of marriage

Va. Code section 20-107.1 provides courts with authority to award spousal support. There is no formula or guideline. In determining the nature, amount and duration of support, 13 factors must be considered, which include among other things: obligations, needs and financial resources; standard of living during marriage; duration of marriage; age, physical and mental condition of the parties; employment opportunities; contributions to the well-being of the family; property interests of the parties; division of marital property; earning capacity; education, training to improve earning capacity; decisions during marriage regarding employment and career; contributions to attainment of education, training, career or profession of the other; and such other factors, including tax consequences.

Support may be ordered for a defined duration, an undefined duration, or in lump sum, or in any combination thereof. See Va. Code section 20-107.1

Unless otherwise provided by stipulation or contract, spousal support will terminate by statute upon the death of either party or the recipients' remarriage. See Va. Code section 20-109.D. Support may also terminate if the spouse receiving support cohabits with another person in a relationship analogous to marriage for one year or more. See Va. Code section 20-109.A.

In addition, support may be modified if support was ordered by the court, or if it was made modifiable by written agreement of the parties. Support of an undefined duration is subject to termination or modification as to amount or duration, as the circumstances may make proper. See Va. Code section 20-109.A. If support is of a defined duration, upon consideration of the factors set forth in subsection E of section 20-107.1, the court may increase, decrease or terminate the amount or duration of the award upon making certain findings as set forth in Va. Code section 20-109.B

Marital fault is relevant to the entitlement to receive support. However, the only fault ground which is an absolute bar to receiving spousal support is adultery (subject to a narrow exception of a 'manifest injustice'). See Code section 20-107.1(B).

9.2 Is it common for maintenance to be awarded?

It is common for spousal support to be awarded to a spouse, if he or she is entitled to the same after consideration of the spousal support factors. Much of the litigation concerning support awards centres around income earning capacity, particularly in cases where one spouse has stopped working to raise the parties' children or where one spouse has been guilty of adultery, which in most cases is an absolute bar to any spousal support award.

9.3 Explain and illustrate with reference to recent cases the court's thinking on maintenance

A number of cases in Virginia focus on the role of fault and the application of the 'manifest injustice' exception, which is applied to cases in which spousal support may be denied due to adultery of the spouse seeking support. If the court determines from clear and convincing evidence that a denial of support and maintenance would constitute a 'manifest injustice', based upon the respective degrees of fault during the marriage and the relative economic circumstances of the parties, support may be awarded despite the statutory bar.

- *Congdon v Congdon*, 40 Va. App. 255, 264-265 (2003): The wife was awarded support despite her adultery. The husband was abusive, frequented strip clubs, talked crudely about sexual matters and directed profanity at the children. The parties were married 22 years, the husband earned $250,000 per year and had $6 million interest in stocks, etc. The wife made only $10 per hour.
- *Wright v Wright*, 38 Va. App. 394 (2002): The wife admitted post-separation adultery. The parties had a history of violent fights and drinking and the wife had mental and physical health problems. There was credible evidence that the respective degrees of fault weighed against the husband and support was awarded.
- *Dailey v Dailey*, 59 Va. App. 734, 722 S.E.2d 321 (2012): The issue in this case was whether the husband's retirement following divorce was reasonably foreseeable such that it did not constitute a material change in circumstances sufficient to modify the husband's spousal support obligation. Prior to the husband's retirement, the wife received $1,000 per month in spousal support. Following husband's retirement, the wife received a total of $3,900 per month taking into account the support and her share of the husband's retirement. The court held that the husband's retirement was a material change in circumstances and remanded the case

back to the trial court to determine whether the change in circumstances warranted a change in the amount of spousal support, stating that 'the object of spousal support is to 'provide a sum for such period of time as needed to maintain the spouse in the manner to which the spouse was accustomed during the marriage, balanced against the other spouse's ability to pay'.' Id. at 59 Va.App. 743, 722 S.E.2d 325 (2012) quoting *Blank v Blank*, 10 Va.App. 1, 4, 389 S.E.2d 723, 724 (1990)

- *Wright v Wright*, 61 Va. App. 432, 737 S.E.2d 519 (2013): In this 22-year marriage, the trial court awarded the wife, and the Court of Appeals affirmed, spousal support of $10,000 per month for a defined duration of only four years. She had requested an indefinite award of $30,000 per month. The wife held a degree in Economics and a Master's degree in Business Administration, but had not been employed since the birth of the parties' first child. The husband's vocational expert opined that the wife could foreseeably earn $85,000 annually. The husband was a partner at a law firm, and while his income is not recited in the opinion except to say that he was compensated at the third-highest compensation level out of 16 levels for equity partners, the marital value of his law practice was determined to be $1,492,000.

10. CHILD MAINTENANCE

10.1 On what basis is child maintenance calculated within the jurisdiction?

Child support is presumptively calculated based on codified Virginia Child Support Guidelines. See Va. Code section 20-108.2. The guidelines are based on the parties' respective gross incomes, the time-sharing arrangements, the costs of work-related childcare, and health insurance costs for the children. To rebut the presumption, the court is required to make written findings, taking into account the factors set forth in section 20-108.1. Some of the factors include support provided to other family members, custody arrangements, visitation costs, imputation of income, debts related to the child, life insurance costs, educational costs, special needs of a child, a child's independent financial resources, the standard of living during the marriage, and other such factors.

The court has the authority to order a party to maintain an existing life insurance policy for the benefit of the children, and to require the parents to share the reasonable and necessary unreimbursed medical and dental expenses of a child. Child support is generally paid until a child reaches the age of 18, however, if a child is still in high school on his or her 18th birthday, then child support continues to be paid until the child graduates from high school or turns 19 years of age, whichever first occurs.

11. RECIPROCAL ENFORCEMENT OF FINANCIAL ORDERS

11.1 Summarise the position in your jurisdiction

Virginia gives full faith and credit to foreign orders so long as the foreign court had proper jurisdiction over the matter. Virginia may also recognise such orders on the basis of comity even where not required to under the Full

Faith and Credit Clause of the US Constitution. See *Price v Price*, 17 Va. App. 105 (1993). Comity allows Virginia to treat a foreign order as if it were a Virginia order for purposes of enforcement. However, this is premised upon the foreign order not violating Virginia's public policy. See *McKeel v McKeel*, 185 Va. 108 (1946).

The Uniform Interstate Family Support Act (UIFSA) has been enacted in all 50 US states and mandates the terms of enforcement of support orders arising in other states and countries. See Va. Code section 20-88.32 *et seq.*

UIFSA allows for the enforcement of support obligations in proceedings involving multiple states. Under UIFSA, Virginia will enforce foreign support orders and determine the amount (if any) of support arrearages together with directing the appropriate method of payment. See *Gagne v Chamberlain*, 31 Va. App. 533, 537 (2000).

In order for Virginia to enforce a foreign financial order, the foreign order must first be registered within Virginia. Procedures to register support orders or income withholding orders of another state are set forth in Code section 20-88.67. Once properly registered, the foreign order 'is enforceable in the same manner and is subject to the same procedures as an order issued by a tribunal of this Commonwealth.' See Code section 20-88.68 (B). However, unless specifically excepted elsewhere in section 20-88.32 et seq., such foreign registered orders may only be enforced but not modified if the foreign state/country had jurisdiction over the matter. See Code section 20-88.68(C). Procedures to register a child support order of another state for modification are set forth in Va. Code section 20-88.74.

12. FINANCIAL RELIEF AFTER FOREIGN DIVORCE PROCEEDINGS

12.1 What powers are available to make orders following a foreign divorce?

Following entry of a foreign divorce order, pursuant to Va. Code section 20-107.3(J), a court in Virginia may enter an equitable distribution order 'if (i) one of the parties was domiciled in this Commonwealth when the foreign proceedings were commenced, (ii) the foreign court did not have personal jurisdiction over the party domiciled in the Commonwealth, (iii) the proceeding is initiated within two years of receipt of notice of the foreign decree by the party domiciled in the Commonwealth, and (iv) the court obtains personal jurisdiction over the parties pursuant to subdivision A 9 of section 8.01-328.1, or in any other manner permitted by law.' This is known as the 'divisible divorce' doctrine.

D. CHILDREN

13. CUSTODY/PARENTAL RESPONSIBILITY

13.1 Briefly explain the legal position in relation to custody/parental responsibility following the breakdown of a relationship or marriage

In Virginia, legal custody refers to a parent's ability to make decisions on behalf of his/her child. A court may order joint or sole custody. See Va. Code section 20-124.1.

Both legal and physical custody are governed by a variety of factors, which are codified at Va. Code section 20-124.3. These factors are often referred to as the 'best interest' factors, and must be considered by the court in making custody determinations.

In determining custody, whether legal or physical, there is no presumption of law in favour of either parent. See Va. Code section 20-124.2(B.) as amended ('as between the parents, there shall be no presumption or inference of law in favor of either').

Finally, the Virginia General Assembly recently passed a new law, effective 1 July, 2013: 'A parent has a fundamental right to make decisions concerning the upbringing, education, and care of the parent's child.' See Va. Code section 1-240.1. No one yet knows the effect or impact this law will have in custody cases, however, there are concerns that it may be used to argue that the court and others do not have the right to interfere in a parent's decision-making authority or to alter a parent's 'fundamental right' to make decisions regarding the child, such as education, medical care, corporal punishment, and the like.

13.2 Briefly explain the legal position in relation to access/contact/visitation following the breakdown of a relationship or marriage

In Virginia, the concept of access to the child is called physical custody and is defined as 'physical care and supervision of a child'. See Va. Code section 20-146.1.

The court can order joint physical custody to both parents or sole physical custody to only one parent. Joint physical custody means 'both parents share physical and custodial care of the child'. See Va. Code section 20-124.1. Sole physical custody means that one parent has primary or sole custodial care of the child. Physical custody also encompasses rights of visitation or access. As such, while one parent may be granted sole physical custody, the other parent will most often be granted rights of visitation or access.

The factors the court considers when making a determination of legal and/or physical custody are set forth in Va. Code § 20-124.3, such as the ages of the child and parents, the physical and mental condition of the child and parents, the relationships between the parent and child; sibling and other familial relationships; the role each parent has played; the ability of each parent to maintain a close and continuing relationship with the child; the ability of parents to resolve disputes; the reasonable preference of the child; history of family abuse; and other such factors.

Virginia law provides some additional protections, including an expedited trial and the issuance of temporary, deployment-specific orders, for the custodial rights of parents who are in the military and are facing deployment. See Military Parent's Equal Protection Act, Va. Code sections 20-124.7 to 20-124.10.

14. INTERNATIONAL ABDUCTION

14.1 Summarise the position in your jurisdiction

The United States is a signatory to the Hague Convention on the Civil Aspects of International Child Abduction (the Hague Convention). This is mandated by federal law, and all states are required to comply with the mandates of the International Child Abduction Remedies Act (ICARA), 42 U.S.C. section 11601 *et seq*, which codifies federal law as it relates to the Hague Convention.

Issues of international abduction or wrongful retention must be presented to the Central Authority, (US Department of State, Office of Children Issues). The National Center for Missing and Exploited Children (NCMEC) also provides assistance and support.

A party seeking the return of a child based may bring a claim in either federal or state court. See 42 U.S.C. section 11603(a),(b). However, federal courts will only address the merits of the abduction or a wrongful retention claim; underlying child custody matters such as rights of access must be raised in state courts. Under the Hague Convention, priority of custody decisions is afforded to the country of the child's habitual residence, and a competing state custody decision is not by itself a valid basis to refuse to return the child to the country of habitual residence. See *Miller v Miller,* 240 F.3d 392 (4th Cir. 2001).

ICARA requires a party seeking the return of a child to show 'by a preponderance of the evidence' that 'the child has been wrongfully removed or retained within the meaning of the [Hague] Convention.' See 42 U.S.C. section 11603(e)(1). A court will find removal to be wrongful where:

(1) the child was a habitual resident of the petitioner's country upon removal;
(2) the removal violated the custody rights of the petitioner under the laws of his country; and
(3) at the time of removal the petitioner had been exercising his custody rights. See *Bader v Kramer,* 484 F.3d 666, 668 (4th Circuit 2007).

Habitual residence is not defined in the Hague Convention nor is it defined by ICARA. However, the Fourth Circuit (which includes Virginia federal courts) uses a two-part analysis to determine habitual residence: (1) '[W]hether the parents shared a settled intention to abandon the former country of residence' (regardless of whether the intention was present upon departure or formed after departure); and (2) 'whether there was an actual change in geography coupled with the passage of an appreciable period of time, one sufficient for acclimatisation by the children to the new environment.' See *Maxwell v Maxwell,* 588 F.3d 245 (4th Cir. 2009) (internal citations omitted). Therefore, if the court finds both the intent to change habitual residence to Virginia and that the child has acclimatised to Virginia, the court will not order the return of the child back to the country of prior residency.

When a petitioner has proven wrongful removal, Virginia will order the return of a child unless there is 'grave risk' of 'physical or psychological harm', violations of fundamental human rights or freedoms, one year or more delay by the petitioner in seeking the return of the child, consent or acquiescence, or custodial rights not being exercised when the child was removed. See *Bader,* 484 F.3d at 668-669. See also ICARA, section 11603(e)(2)(A), (B).

Virginia courts will also turn to the Uniform Child Custody Jurisdiction and Enforcement Act (UCCJEA). See Code section 20-146 *et seq*. Under the UCCJEA, Virginia may assert jurisdiction over custody matters if Virginia has been the child's home state or was the home state within six months of the proceedings. 'Home state' is similar to the Hague's reference to 'habitual residence' and is likewise undefined, but a period of residency for six months will usually be sufficient. Where the child was in Virginia in excess of six months due to wrongful retention, Virginia will most likely not recognise Virginia as the child's home state under the UCCJEA. See *Moscona v Shenhar*, 50 Va. App. 238 (2007).

The UCCJEA was enacted to deter child abductions between states or countries where one party may have obtained an unfavourable award in one jurisdiction and is seeking a more favourable award from a court in another jurisdiction. See *Johnson v Johnson*, 26 Va. App. 135 (1997).

15. LEAVE TO REMOVE/APPLICATIONS TO TAKE A CHILD OUT OF THE JURISDICTION

15.1 Summarise the position in your jurisdiction

Virginia courts analyse requests to relocate (move or otherwise take the child out of the local jurisdiction) in the same manner as custody and visitation matters. See *Petry v Petry*, 41 Va.App. 782 (2003).

Any order for custody or visitation must require that each of the parties provide 30 days' advance written notice to the court and to the other party of any intent to relocate. See Code section 20-124.5. If the other parent objects to relocation, he/she may file a motion to enjoin the child's relocation pending a full custody and relocation trial.

15.2 Under what circumstances may a parent apply to remove their child from the jurisdiction against the wishes of the other parent?

The issue of relocation is not governed by any Virginia statute. Accordingly, there is no restriction on the ability of either parent to apply to remove the child from the jurisdiction against the wishes of the other parent. Often the custodial parent will inform the other parent of their intent to relocate, and in order to stop the relocation, the non-custodial parent will file a Motion to Enjoin Relocation which many courts will hear on an expedited basis. Usually the court will then set a trial date to determine whether the parent may relocate the child out of the jurisdiction against the other party's wishes.

Assuming the relocation matter is not the initial custody determination, the party seeking to relocate must prove (1) a material change in circumstances has occurred since custody was previously adjudicated; and (2) that relocation is in the child's best interest (as opposed to simply being what the parent wants or in the parent's best interest). See *Wheeler v Wheeler*, 42 Va. App. 282, 288 (2004).

Factors the court will consider include the economic outlook in Virginia versus the new location, the presence of extended family members in each location, and the child's social and educational development in Virginia. The court will also scrutinise the relationship between the non-custodial parent and child to determine whether the relationship can be substantially maintained post-relocation. The overall analysis centres around whether relocation would be in the child's best interest taking all relevant factors into consideration. See *Wheeler*, 42 Va. App. 288; *Scinaldi v Scinaldi*, 2 Va. App. 571 (1986); *Cloutier v Queen*, 35 Va. App. 413 (2001).

E. SURROGACY AND ADOPTION

16. VALIDITY OF SURROGACY AGREEMENTS

16.1 Briefly summarise the position in your jurisdiction

Surrogacy agreements are governed by Va. Code sections 20-156 to 20-165. A surrogacy contract in Virginia is defined as an agreement between the intended parents and a surrogate, in which the surrogate agrees to be impregnated through the use of assisted conception, to carry any resulting fetus, and to relinquish to the intended parents the custody of and parental rights to any resulting child. Va. Code section 20-156.

'Intended parents' are defined as a man and a woman, married to each other, who enter into an agreement with a surrogate under the terms of which they will be the parents of any child born to the surrogate. At this time, there is no separate definition for an unmarried man or an unmarried woman.

Surrogacy contracts in Virginia are permissible. There is a distinction between who will be considered the resulting child's parents depending on whether or not the surrogacy agreement is approved by the court. If a surrogacy contract is approved by the court, then the intended parents shall be deemed to be the parents of any resulting child. Generally speaking, if the agreement is not approved by the court, then the gestational mother may be deemed the child's parent(s). The intended parents would need to adopt the child to obtain parental rights.

An order approving a surrogacy agreement is only valid for 12 months. Agreements must contain provisions to guarantee the payment of reasonable medical and ancillary costs for the surrogate. Agreements for the payment of compensation to the surrogate are void and unenforceable. A surrogate must have had at least one pregnancy and experienced at least one live birth. All parties must undergo physical and psychological evaluations. Other requirements are mandated in order for approval by the court. See Va. Code section 20-160.

17. ADOPTION

17.1 Briefly explain the legal position in relation to adoption in your jurisdiction. Is adoption available to individuals, cohabiting couples (both heterosexual and same-sex)?

The laws related to adoptions in Virginia are complicated and include a number of different types of adoptions. The majority of the law related to adoptions can be found in Chapter 12 of the Va. Code, sections 63.2-1200 to 63.2-1253. These Code provisions deal with the recognition of foreign adoptions, agency adoptions, parental placement adoptions, stepparent adoptions, close relative adoptions and adult adoptions.

There is no provision under Virginia law prohibiting an unmarried individual to adopt a child. However, when an individual seeks to adopt a child, he/she must go through an invasive investigation as to that individual's background to include physical, mental, social and psychological information; and he/she will be subjected to a home study and recommendations will be made as to the suitability of the placement with that individual. While the Code does not specifically differentiate an unmarried individual on the basis of sexual orientation, it is unclear whether a homosexual individual or an individual involved in a same-sex relationship would be prohibited from adopting a child based on lifestyle or morality issues.

There is no case in Virginia which addresses this issue directly. However, in the case of *Doe v Doe*, 222 Va. 736, 284 S.E. 2d 799 (1981), the Supreme Court of Virginia reversed a stepmother's adoption petition that relied solely on the father and stepmother's argument that the mother should not have parental rights because she was a lesbian. While the court did not make a determination as to whether or not the fact that the mother was a lesbian rendered her unfit, the court did say that 'If Jane Doe is an unfit parent, it is solely her lesbian relationship which renders her unfit, and this must be to such an extent as to make the continuance of the parent-child relationship heretofore existing between her and her son detrimental to the child's welfare.' Id. at 746, 284 S.E.2d at 805.

Currently, however, Virginia law does not recognise same-sex marriages and as such, while Virginia's public policy is not in favour of same-sex relationships, the *Doe v Doe* case might give prospective same-sex adoptive individuals some hope of success.

Another case, although not directly on point, may also provide some support for same-sex adoptive parents. In the case of *Davenport v Little-Bowser*, 269 Va. 546, 611 S.E.2d 366 (2005), same-sex adoptive parents and their children filed a complaint against the Registrar of Vital Records for refusing to issue new birth certificates listing both adoptive parents on the children's birth certificates. Their children were adopted pursuant to out-of-state adoption orders. At the trial court level, the court held that birth certificates can only list the name of a mother and of a father. In addition, the court held it could not recognise a status (same-sex relationship) that public policy does not allow. Although the Supreme Court ruled in favour of the adoptive parents, it also made clear that this case was not about same-sex relationships.

F. COHABITATION

18. COHABITATION

18.1 What legislation (if any) governs division of property for unmarried couples on the breakdown of the relationship?

There is no legislation which governs division of property for unmarried couples on the breakdown of the relationship. Virginia does not recognise common law marriage. In Virginia, 'lewd and lascivious cohabitation' (unmarried persons cohabitating together in a romantic relationship) is a crime. See Code section 18.2-345. A relationship based upon a crime bars relief in Virginia courts under Virginia's public policy. However, the authors are not aware of any Virginia case where lewd and lascivious cohabitation has been prosecuted in recent years.

G. FAMILY DISPUTE RESOLUTION

19. MEDIATION, COLLABORATIVE LAW AND ARBITRATION

19.1 Briefly summarise the non court based processes available in your jurisdiction and the current status of agreements reached under the auspices of mediation, collaborative law and arbitration

Virginia permits mediation, collaboration and arbitration.

Mediation is frequently used in Virginia. As defined under Virginia law, mediation '*means a process in which a mediator facilitates communication between the parties and, without deciding the issues or imposing a solution on the parties, enables them to understand and to reach a mutually agreeable resolution to their dispute*'. Va. Code Ann. § 8.01-581.21.

Collaborative law is defined by the International Academy of Collaborative Professionals (IACP) as 'a voluntary dispute resolution process in which parties settle without resort to litigation'.

In Virginia, if collaboration fails neither party may litigate using their collaborative attorneys or other professionals who assisted them with the collaborative process. This approach is different from some other states which do allow the parties to continue with their collaborative attorneys and professionals in the event collaboration fails and the matter proceeds to contested litigation.

Virginia also permits arbitration. Arbitration is very similar to litigation although the parties jointly engage an arbitrator to decide the matter. Similar to litigation, both parties present evidence, call witnesses, the lawyers make opening and closing statements, etc. A significant difference between arbitration and litigation is that in arbitration, many of the rules of evidence which govern litigation do not apply. Another significant difference between arbitration and litigation is that generally, arbitration awards cannot be appealed, challenged, or vacated except under very specific circumstances.

19.2 What is the statutory basis (if any), for mediation, collaborative law and arbitration in your jurisdiction? In particular, are the parties required to attempt a family dispute resolution in advance of the institution of proceedings?

In Virginia, the parties are not required by law to attempt a family dispute resolution in advance of the institution of proceedings.

The statutory authority for mediation is Va. Code §§ 8.01-581.21 – 8.01-581.26. A mediated agreement will be treated by the courts as any other settlement agreement would be. See Va. Code Ann. § 8.01-581.25.

Like arbitration awards, vacating mediation orders and/or agreements is quite difficult. See Va. Code Ann. § 8.01-581.26.

There is no statutory basis for collaborative law in the area of domestic relations.

Virginia has adopted the Uniform Arbitration Act, which governs the arbitration process. See Va. Code § 8.01-577 (Submission of controversy; agreement to arbitrate; condition precedent to action).

It is very difficult to vacate an arbitration award in Virginia. Va. Code § 8.01-581.010 details the various ways an arbitration award may be vacated.

Modification or correction of an arbitration award is governed by Va. Code 8.01-581.11.

Finally, under Va. Code §8.01-581.08, a court may order the arbitrator to modify or correct the arbitration award under §8.01-581.11(1) and (3) or for the purpose for clarifying the award.

H. OTHER

20. CIVIL PARTNERSHIP/SAME-SEX MARRIAGE

20.1 What is the status of civil partnership/same-sex marriage within the jurisdiction?

Virginia does not recognise civil partnership/same-sex marriage, nor does it appear likely that Virginia will recognise such unions in the near future. However, a key issue with respect to enforcement of rights for same-sex couples is whether their rights 'arose' due to their same-sex partnership. For example, Virginia recognised and enforced a Vermont court order providing a non-biological parent rights of custody because her rights were not created by their same-sex union, but rather arose on the basis of the biological parent filing court papers which named the child as the 'biological or adoptive' child of both parties. See *Miller-Jenkins v Miller-Jenkins*, 49 Va. App. 88 (2006); *Miller-Jenkins v Miller-Jenkins*, 276 Va. 19 (2009). This is an important distinction in Virginia because Virginia will not recognise nor enforce any rights which arise or are created on the basis of a same-sex partnership.

20.2 What legislation governs civil partnership/same sex marriage?

The United States has enacted a federal law which allows states to independently decide whether to recognise civil unions/same-sex marriage, the Defense of Marriage Act (DOMA, 28 U.S.C. 1738C). This federal law effectively voids the Full Faith and Credit Clause of the US Constitution with respect to recognition of same-sex relationships legally entered into in other jurisdictions. Individual states are not required to recognise such unions nor are they required to recognise rights or claims arising from such relationships (including contractual rights, inheritance rights and rights to be considered 'family' for purposes of making end of life medical decisions). On 26 June, 2013, the US Supreme Court ruled that a portion of DOMA was an unconstitutional violation of the Equal Protection Clause of the US Constitution. The impact is that the federal government can no longer define marriage as only existing between opposite-sex couples and cannot limit federal benefits to opposite-sex couples. However, the decision does not require individual states to recognise same-sex marriage. As a result, as of 1 August 2013, same-sex marriage is only legal in 13 states and the District of Columbia.

Virginia has enacted specific legislation prohibiting marriage between persons of the same sex, and mandating that any such marriages entered into in other jurisdictions will be treated as void and unenforceable in Virginia. See Code section 20-45.2. In addition, civil unions are prohibited in the same manner as same-sex marriages. See Code section 20-45.3. Virginia will not recognise any contractual rights created by such relationships. While it is difficult to say what effect the Supreme Court's recent ruling will have on same-sex couples in Virginia, the ruling may help pave the way for challenges to the constitutionality of the Virginia laws and the laws of other states which prohibit same-sex unions.

21. CONTROVERSIAL AREAS/RAPIDLY DEVELOPING AREAS OF LAW

21.1 Is there a particular area of the law within the jurisdiction that is currently undergoing major change?

Since the last edition of this chapter, obtaining a divorce has become less cumbersome under certain circumstances, allowing for some divorces to be granted on the papers and pleadings, without requiring an appearance in court.

Another area of controversy is what happens when a now deceased employee fails to change his beneficiary designations for his retirement account or life insurance policy such that his ex-wife is still listed as the beneficiary, and the plan administrator pays the benefits in favour of the ex-wife rather than the current wife, despite the ex-wife's explicit waiver of the benefits in the order of divorce. This is a controversial issue and essentially involves the pre-emption of state law by federal law. The Supreme Court of the United States recently heard the case of *Hillman v Maretta* on 22 April, 2013 and on 3 June, 2013, decided that federal law continues to pre-empt Virginia law, specifically Va. Code section 111.1(D) which states that the former spouse is liable for insurance proceeds to whoever would have received them under applicable law, but for the beneficiary designation. Under the code provision, the current wife was seeking reimbursement of the proceeds paid to the former spouse. The trial court found in favour of current wife and found the former wife liable to the current wife. The Virginia Supreme Court reversed and the US Supreme Court granted certiorari to resolve the conflict between federal and state law. The US Supreme Court held that Va. Code section 111.1(D) is pre-empted by federal law and therefore the former wife is not liable to the current wife for the life insurance proceeds she received.

21.2 Which areas of law are most out-of-step? Which areas would you most like to see reformed/changed?

Virginia's policy set forth in Code sections 20-45.2 and 20-45.3 in refusing to recognise contractual rights created by marriages and civil unions between persons of the same sex in another state or jurisdiction is likely most out-of-step.

Other areas of law that appear out-of-step, in the opinion of the authors, include the lack of a family court, emphasis on the role of fault, failure to allow the court to draw an adverse inference against a party refusing to answer questions regarding adultery, the lack of revision and modification to the child support guidelines at least equivalent to the cost of inflation, and the failure of the child support guidelines to consider the cost of extra-curricular activities that a child may be involved in together with other expenses such as educational tutoring, music lessons, and other such common additional activities.

The authors would like to see all of the issues identified above as out-of-step be reformed or modified. However, the authors consider the issues concerning the contractual rights of same-sex couples to be most in need of immediate reform.

USA – Washington State

Flexx Law, PS Marguerite C. Smith

A. JURISDICTION AND CONFLICT OF LAW

1. SOURCES OF LAW

1.1 What is the primary source of law in relation to the breakdown of marriage and the welfare of children within the jurisdiction? Which are the main statutes governing matrimonial law in the jurisdiction?

The primary source of law relating to the breakdown of marriage and welfare of children is the Revised Code of Washington (RCW) 26. This is the governing statute in Washington State. There is a large body of case law applying and supplementing it.

A practice pointer is that you should always go to the RCW 26 first and then look to the case law to see how the statute is applied, explained or augmented.

2. JURISDICTION

2.1 What are the main jurisdictional requirements for the institution of proceedings in relation to divorce, property and children?

Divorce

A sufficient nexus with the marriage and the state is necessary for the state to have jurisdiction to end the marriage (and to establish full faith and credit to the decree to enable enforcement in other states). Domicile is such a nexus. Washington uses the term 'residence' (*RCW 26.09.030*), but this has been interpreted to mean 'domicile' (see *In re Marriage of Strohmaier*, 34 Wn. App. 14,659 P.2d 534 (1983)). Only one party needs to be a resident (either the petitioner or respondent). 'The indispensible elements of domicile are residence in fact coupled with the intent to make a place or residence one's home...' (see *In re Marriage of Strohmaier*, 34 Wn. App. at 17; and also *Stevens v Stevens*, 4 Wn. App. 79, 480 P.2d 238 (1971)).

Special rules are provided in RCW 26.09.030, 040, to establish domicile for divorce in military families.

Maintenance and child support

All support/maintenance proceedings require *in personam* jurisdiction over the person, the obligor. If the required *in personam* jurisdiction is not present, an order is void in Washington (see *In re Marriage of Powell*, 84 Wn. App.432, 438, 927 P2d. 1154 (1996)). In Powell it was held that the lower court could not order equalisation payments against the obligor as no personal jurisdiction over the husband was established, as was necessary in a personal obligation order.

Property

The court can exercise long arm jurisdiction (see Long arm jurisdiction, below) over causes of action listed in RCW 4.28.185. Under RCW 4.28.185(1)(f) long arm jurisdiction is extended to a person who has lived

'...in a marital relationship within the state notwithstanding subsequent departure from the state, as to all proceedings authorised by chapter 26.09 RCW, so long as the petitioning party has continued to reside in this state or has continued to be a member of the armed forces stationed in this state'.

Where a person has insufficient connections with this state to permit *in personam* jurisdiction, a court, which could dissolve the marriage due to the other party's residency, can not divide property (see *In re Marriage of Tsarbopoulos*, 125 Wn. App.273,104 P.3d 692 (2004)). This was a case in which the husband, who resided in Greece, in a marital dissolution, had no judicially recognisable connections within the state of Washington to which his wife had relocated with the children. Because of this deficiency, the court was precluded from awarding property in the dissolution action.

Washington long-arm jurisdiction

Long-arm jurisdiction is the ability of a state to have personal jurisdiction over a person who is not resident in the state. Washington has two relevant long-arm statutes: RCW26.21A.100 and RCW 4.28.185

RCW 26.21A.100 (Uniform Interstate Family Support Act) authorises courts to exercise personal jurisdiction over non residents in a support proceeding under specified circumstances listed in the section. The list covers a wide spectrum of circumstances including a very broad coverage under subsection (h) which provides for *'any other basis consistent with the Constitutions of this state and the United States for the exercise of personal jurisdiction'* (RCW 26.21A .100 (h)).

RCW 4.28.185 provides that the following persons are submitted to personal jurisdiction:

'(1) Any person, whether or not a citizen or resident of this state, who in person or through an agent does any of the acts in this section enumerated, thereby submits said person, and, if an individual, his personal representative, to the jurisdiction of the courts of this state as to any cause of action arising from the doing of any of said acts:

(e) the act of sexual intercourse within this state with respect to which a child may have been conceived;

(f) living in a marital relationship within this state notwithstanding subsequent departure from this state, as to all proceedings authorised by chapter 26.09 RCW, so long as the petitioning party has continued to reside in this state or has continued to be a member of the armed forces stationed in this state.'

Custody

The Uniform Child Custody Jurisdiction and Enforcement Act 1997 (UCCJEA), codified in Washington by Chapter 26.27 RCW, is the exclusive Washington State source for subject matter jurisdiction in a Washington State Court (RCW 26.27.201, .221). However, see below the discussion of the Hague Convention At the time of writing this chapter, the UCCJEA has been accepted by almost all of the states in the USA and may, by the time of printing, be accepted by all.

The UCCJEA premises jurisdiction on the state's contacts with the child, not *in personam* jurisdiction over the parent. This is in contrast to parentage/ paternity actions under RCW 26.26.515, which requires *in personam* jurisdiction over the person who is to be adjudicated a parent. Note that this can lead to a situation where a parent is sued for support under a parentage action but that court does not have jurisdiction over the child so a visitation action under UCCJEA may have to be started in the child's state.

The court in Washington must treat foreign countries in the same way as it would a sister state in determining whether it must defer jurisdiction to the foreign 'home state' state (RCW 26.27.051).

Generally (with a few exceptions), under the UCCJEA the home state must exercise jurisdiction in custody proceedings. Home state is defined as the state where the child has lived with a parent or person acting as a parent since birth or for six consecutive months immediately before the commencement of the custody proceedings (28 U.S.C. Section 1738A (b)(4); RCW26.27.021(7)).

If neither state fits the home state definition, the court can determine jurisdiction based on the significant connection basis (RCW 26.27.201(1)(b)).

The court shall (with some exceptions listed in the section) decline jurisdiction based on 'unjustifiable conduct' (RCW 26.27.271). An example of this could be a parent wrongfully taking a child from the original home state. *In re Marriage of Ieronimakis* 66, Wn. App. 83, 831 P.2d. 172 (1992), the Appeals Court held that Washington was clearly not the home state. The court reasoned that to allow Washington to assert jurisdiction based on significant contacts brought about by the mother's abduction of the children from Greece would circumvent the intent of the jurisdictional laws. See also the Arizona case of *Welch-Doden v Roberts*, 202 Ariz.201, 42P.3d 1166 (Ariz. App.2002) where the Arizona court refused to accept jurisdiction because of the mother's removal of the child from the prior home state of Oklahoma.

3. DOMICILE AND HABITUAL RESIDENCE

3.1 Explain the concepts of domicile and habitual residence as they apply to the jurisdiction

The importance of domicile and habitual residence in deciding jurisdictional issues are discussed in detail under Jurisdiction, above, and under International Abduction, below.

4. CONFLICT OF LAW/APPLICABLE LAW TO BE APPLIED

4.1 What happens when one party applies to stay proceedings in favour of a foreign jurisdiction? What factors will the local court take into account when determining forum issues?

Forum issues are frequently reasonably self evident after consideration of the basic jurisdiction rules referenced above under Jurisdiction. However, an area of greater complexity, where parties frequently attempt to stay proceedings, is child custody. Under the UCCJEA, if Washington does not have initial jurisdiction under RCW 26.27.201, and if the situations which could justify temporary emergency jurisdiction under RCW 26.27.231 do not apply, the court will decline to accept jurisdiction.

The court may also decline to exercise jurisdiction on the grounds of inconvenient forum (RCW 26.27.261).

The court shall decline jurisdiction if it is obtained by the unjustifiable conduct of the party invoking that jurisdiction (with some exceptions listed in the section) (RCW 26.27.271).

See also the discussion of the 1980 Hague Convention, under International Abduction, below.

B. PRE- AND POST-NUPTIAL AGREEMENTS

5. VALIDITY OF PRE- AND POST-NUPTIAL AGREEMENTS

5.1 To what extent are pre- and post-nups binding within the jurisdiction? Could you provide a brief discussion of the most significant recent case law on this issue?

Pre- and post-nuptial agreements follow much the same rules. Generally, they must be in writing and signed by the party to be charged in order to meet the Statute of Frauds requirements (agreements in consideration of marriage RCW 19.36.010).

One of the most cited cases is *In re Marriage of Matson* 107 Wn. 2d 479,730 P.2d 668 (1986). This was a pre-nuptial case which established a two-prong test for validity: if it is not fair then the court must carefully scrutinise all the circumstances leading up to the signing. The Matson Appeals Court (affirmed by the WA Supreme Court) refused to enforce the contract. The provisions were held to be unfair and there were several procedural problems, such as the shortness of time before the marriage; the wife did not choose the attorney who drafted the contract; and a lack of independent counsel which resulted in the wife not understanding the contract.

In *re Marriage of Bernard,* 165, Wn.2d 895, 204 P.3d 907 (2009), the Washington Supreme Court, in applying the two pronged test of Matson, found that the pre-nuptial was not fair as to the provisions for the wife. The court then considered the second prong of the test and held that there was sufficient evidence to uphold the trial court's holding of procedural unfairness as the wife had been rushed into the agreement just before the wedding and did not have time to properly address it. She signed it the day before the wedding on the understanding that it would be renegotiated. In addition, the side agreement they made on the wedding day to renegotiate was so limited in its scope as not to cure the unfairness.

In *re Marriage of Hadley*, 88 Wn.2d 649,565 P2d 790 (1977) involved property status agreements entered after marriage. (The trial court referred to this particular agreement as neither pre-nuptial, nor post-nuptial, nor made in contemplation of dissolution but rather 'analogous to a community property agreement'.) The Supreme Court ruled that the test that should be applied was (1) whether full disclosure has been made by the respondent of the amount, character and value of the property involved, and (2) whether the agreement was entered into fully and voluntarily on independent advice and with full knowledge by the spouse of her rights. It concluded that both of these tests had been met. It was not wrong to enforce an agreement merely because the wife had not availed herself of the opportunity to have the advice of independent legal counsel.

In re Marriage of Zier, 136 Wn.App.40,147 P.3d 624 (2006) review denied,162 Wn.2d 1008 (2007) the Court of Appeals rejected the wife's challenge to the post-marital community property agreement on the grounds that she had not had independent legal counsel. The Court of Appeals held that the *Matson* standard (supra) was not applicable to an item-specific post-marital community property agreement and that such an agreement was not the same as a pre-nuptial agreement. The Court of Appeals noted that the trial court did not find the wife to be credible in her assertion that she had not understood the agreement. Practice pointer: It is beyond the scope of this material to review the many possible safeguards the practitioner might adopt in facilitating pre-marital or marital agreements and the standard of proof in a disputed action. (Note that there are particular requirements for estate planning purposes ((see for example, RCW 26.16.120)) not referenced here). However, the better practice is always to provide as many safeguards as possible whether or not one thinks one might need it.

C. DIVORCE, NULLITY AND JUDICIAL SEPARATION

6. RECOGNITION OF FOREIGN MARRIAGES/DIVORCES

6.1 Summarise the position in your jurisdiction

Marriages

Pursuant to RCW 26.04.020 (3) 'a marriage between two persons that is recognised as valid in another jurisdiction is valid in this state only if the marriage is not prohibited or made unlawful under subsection(1)(a), 1(c),or (2) of this section'.

Subsection (1)(a) provides: 'When either party thereto has a spouse or registered domestic partner living at the time of such marriage, unless the registered domestic partner is the other party to the marriage;...' . Subsection (2) provides: 'It is unlawful for any person to marry his or her sibling, child, grandchild, aunt, uncle, niece, or nephew'.

It is notable that, where under subsection (1) (b) marriages between first cousins are prohibited in Washington, those marriages are not excluded from recognition if valid in the jurisdiction in which they were solemnised.

Divorces

In *Tostada v Tostada* 137 Wn. App. 136, 151 P.3d 1060 (2007), the

Washington Appeals Court ruled that the trial court erred in declining to recognise the parties' agreed Mexican dissolution decree, in making a custody determination and ordering child support because, as the Appeals Court stated at page 144 Wn. App, 'substantial evidence does not support the trial court's conclusion that a valid marriage and a cognisable dissolution did not occur in Mexico'. Also, the factual circumstances surrounding the Mexican dissolution process substantially conformed to the recodified Uniform Child Custody Jurisdiction and Enforcement Act's (UCCJEA) requirements for acknowledging the validity of a foreign jurisdiction's custody determination (chapter 26.27 RCW).

The Appeals Court held that the wife did not articulate procedural due process violations capable of invalidating the Mexican decree. They petitioned together for a mutual consent divorce; there was no evidence that she did not receive proper notice or opportunity to have counsel; and the wife provided no evidence or legal citation concerning a waiting period for a mutual consent divorce in Mexico. There was also no evidence of coercion or domestic violence resulting in her acquiescence in the decree.

The Appeals Court therefore concluded at page 148 Wn. App. 'Consequently, we vacate the trial court's order denying the validity of the Mexican decree, vacate its custody and child support orders because it lacked jurisdiction to make an initial custody determination, and remand to the trial court for reconsideration and entry of fact.'

7. DIVORCE

7.1 Explain the grounds for divorce within the jurisdiction (please also deal with nullity and judicial separation if appropriate)

Dissolution of marriage or domestic partnerships and legal separation

Washington State is a 'no-fault' state. The requirements for a dissolution of marriage (divorce) and for dissolution of domestic partnerships and legal separation (the term 'judicial separation' is not used) are set out in RCW 26.09.030 as follows: *'When a party who is (1) a resident of this state, or (2) is a member of the armed forces and is stationed in this state, or (3) is married or in a domestic partnership to a party who is a resident of this state or who is a member of the armed forces and is stationed in this state, petitions for a dissolution of marriage or dissolution of domestic partnership and alleges that the marriage or domestic partnership is irretrievably broken, and when ninety days have elapsed since the petition was filed and from the date when service of summons was made upon the respondent, the court shall proceed as follows:...'*

The court under subsection (e) shall not use a party's pregnancy as the sole basis for denying or delaying the entry of the decree of dissolution of marriage or domestic partnership.

The court may, under RCW 26.09.030 (b), enter a decree of legal separation *in lieu* of dissolution if requested, unless the other party objects and petitions for a decree of dissolution or invalidity.

Declaration that the marriage or domestic partnership is invalid

RCW 26.09.040 sets out the grounds on which a court, upon petition, shall declare the alleged marriage or domestic partnership invalid (the term 'nullity' is not used). These include, under (b)(i), age, parental or court approval, existing marriage or domestic partnership, consanguinity, incapacity to consent, force, duress or fraud, failure to ratify by voluntary cohabitation after the age or capacity to consent, or after cessation of force or duress or discovery of the fraud.

Under (c), if the court finds that a marriage or domestic partnership contracted in another jurisdiction was void or voidable under the law of that jurisdiction and was not subsequently validated in that jurisdiction or a subsequent domicile.

8. FINANCES/CAPITAL, PROPERTY

8.1 What powers does the court have to allocate financial resources and property on the breakdown of marriage?

(See discussion under Jurisdiction above).

If real property is located outside the state, courts cannot directly affect title in another state, although there can be an order to convey (see *Brown v Brown*, 46 Wn 2d. 370,372,281 P2d 850 (1955)).

Some federal laws prohibit awards of certain federal benefits. A practitioner should be mindful of the fact that there are special rules applicable to federal benefits and Indian trust land which are outside the scope of this chapter. However, even where the state is precluded from disposing of the asset, the state court may consider the property in the overall 'just and equitable' disposition of property and liabilities in a dissolution of marriage (see *In re Marriage of Konzen*, 103 Wn. 2d 470,693 P.2d 97, cert.denied, 473 U.S.906 (1985); *In re Marriage of Jennings*,138 Wn.2d 612,980 P.2d 1248 (1999)).

8.2 Explain and illustrate with reference to recent cases the court's thinking on division of assets

The division of assets is regulated by statute in Washington under RCW 26.09.080. The case law interprets or supplements the statute.

RCW 26.09.080 requires the court to divide property in a way that is just and equitable after considering all relevant factors including, but not limited to, the nature and extent of the community property; the nature and extent of the separate property; the duration of the marriage or domestic partnership; and the economic circumstances of each spouse or domestic partner at the time the division of property is to become effective, including the desirability of awarding the family home or the right to live therein for reasonable periods to a spouse or domestic partner with whom the children reside the majority of the time.

These four factors are not exclusive and neither of them has more weight as a matter of law than another (see *In re Marriage of Konzen*,103 Wn. 2d 470,478,693 P.2d 97 (1985), cert.denied,473 U.S. 906 (1985)).

The trial court may consider other factors to those four factors listed in RCW 26.09.080. *Urbana v Urbana* 147 Wn.App.1 ,195 P3d 959 (2008). Among those listed by the Urbana Court for possible consideration are the health and ages of the parties, the prospects for future earnings, education, employment history, foreseeable future acquisitions and obligations and squandering of assets.

9. FINANCES/MAINTENANCE

9.1 Explain the operation of maintenance for spouses on an ongoing basis after the breakdown of marriage

RCW 26.09.090 provides that the court shall consider all relevant factors when awarding maintenance including (but not limited to) the following:

- the financial resources of the party seeking maintenance, including separate or community property apportioned to them, and their ability to meet their needs independently, including the extent to which a provision for support of a child living with the party includes a sum for that party;
- the time necessary to acquire sufficient education or training to enable the party seeking maintenance to find employment appropriate to their skills, interests, style of life and other attendant circumstances;
- the standard of living established during the marriage;
- the duration of the marriage;
- the age, physical and emotional condition and financial obligations of the spouse seeking maintenance; and
- the ability of the spouse from whom maintenance is sought to meet their needs and obligations while meeting those of the spouse seeking maintenance.

9.2 Is it common for maintenance to be awarded?

It is common for maintenance to be awarded. The duration and extent depends on what is fair, considering all of the circumstances.

9.3 Explain and illustrate with reference to recent cases the court's thinking on maintenance

Recent cases tend to rely heavily on the older cases applying RCW 26.09.090. The following frequently cited cases give a flavour of the court's thinking.

Maintenance should be available as a flexible tool. Simply because one is capable of self-support does not automatically preclude maintenance. For example, *In re the Marriage of Washburn,* 101 Wn.2d. 168,178-79,677P.2d.152 (1984), the court stated that 'the ability of the spouse seeking maintenance to meet his or her needs independently is only one factor to be considered... The duration of the marriage and the standard of living established during the marriage must also be considered, making it clear that maintenance is not just a means of providing bare necessities, but rather a flexible tool by which the parties' standard of living may be equalised for an appropriate period of time.'

In re Marriage of Bulicek, 59 Wn. App.630, 800 P.2d.394 (1990) the Court of Appeals affirmed the trial court's award of maintenance to the wife citing the wife's ill health and limited work skills and experience. The court at 59 Wn.App 630, 634, recognised that it is a valid goal to disentangle the spouses and set each on a road to self-sufficiency, but that goal must not be followed blindly.

Maintenance can be awarded in lieu of property 'if the assets of the parties are insufficient to permit compensation to be effected entirely through a property division, a supplemental award of maintenance is appropriate' (see *In re Marriage of Barnett,* 63 Wn.App.385,388,818 P2d 1382 (1991)).

Post decree modification of maintenance

The court in Washington has the power to modify decrees ordering child support or spousal maintenance under RCW 26.09.170. 'The provisions of any decree respecting maintenance or support may be modified only as to instalments accruing subsequent to the motion for modification and only upon a showing of a substantial change of circumstances...' (see Maintenance and Child Maintenance). Naturally, this assumes jurisdiction over the cause of action (see Jurisdiction).

The substantial change in circumstances must not be in the contemplation of the parties at the time the decree was entered (see *Lambert v Lambert,* 66 Wn.2d 503,508-10,403 P.2d 664 (1965), and see also *In re Marriage of Chapman,* 34 Wn. App. 216,660 P.2d 326 (1983)).

The parties can expressly agree not to permit post-decree modification but the court cannot order this without that agreement.

It is clear from RCW 26.09.070 (7) and .170 (1) that the legislation did not intend to empower the trial courts to limit or preclude the modification of a spousal maintenance award in the absence of an express and written agreement to that effect, freely and voluntarily entered into by the parties (see *In re Marriage of Short,* 71 Wn. App. 426,443,859 P.2d 636 (1993), aff'd in part, rev'd in part, 125 Wn. 2d 865,890 P.2d 12 (1995)).

In re Marriage of Hulscher, 143 Wn. App 708,180 P.3d 199 (2008), a non-modifiable maintenance agreement in the decree, with no separate written separation contract, was found to be valid and enforceable. In this case the Court of Appeals held there was sufficient evidence that the agreement was written in the decree as it had been negotiated and performed according to its terms before the decree.

10. CHILD MAINTENANCE

10.1 On what basis is child maintenance calculated within the jurisdiction?

Child support (the word 'maintenance' is generally used for spousal support) is governed in Washington by RCW 26.19.

RCW 26.19.001 provides that *'the legislature intends, in establishing a child support schedule, to ensure that child support orders are adequate to meet a child's basic needs and to provide additional child support commensurate with the parents' income, resources and standard of living. The legislature also intends that the child support obligation should be equitably apportioned between the parents'.*

Standards and instruction for setting child support are found throughout RCW 26.19. Child support worksheets and instructions are issued by the administrative office of the courts which shall 'attempt, to the greatest extent possible, to make the worksheets and instructions understandable by persons who are not represented by legal counsel' (RCW 26.19.050 (1)).

Modification of child support

RCW 26.09.170 lists diverse grounds for modification without a showing of substantial change in circumstances.

If a case does not fit within the exceptions above, a substantial change in circumstances must be shown under RCW 26.09.170 (1).

However, there are non-statutory circumstances where child support can be modified in the following situations without a substantial change of circumstances:

- when a default order is entered, a *de novo* hearing can be brought as to the amount of support (*Lahart v Lahart,*13 Wn. App. 452,535 P.2d 145,review denied, 85 Wn.2d 1015 (1975));
- when the court failed to review an agreed order to see it was reasonable (*Pippins v Jankelson,* 110 Wn.2d 475,754 P.2d 105 (1998)).

11. RECIPROCAL ENFORCEMENT OF FINANCIAL ORDERS

11.1 Summarise the position in your jurisdiction

The Uniform Interstate Family Support Act, (UIFSA), codified in Washington under RCW 26.21A regulates interstate enforcement of orders of support.

'State' is defined broadly in RCW 26.21A.010 (21) as follows:

'(21) 'State' means a state of the United States, the District of Columbia, Puerto Rico, the United States Virgin Islands, or any territory or insular possession subject to the jurisdiction of the United States. The term includes:

(a) An Indian Tribe; and

(b) A foreign country or political subdivision that:

(i) Has been declared to be a foreign reciprocating country or political subdivision under federal law;

(ii) Has established a reciprocal arrangement for child support within this state as provided in RCW 26.21A.235; or

(iii) Has enacted a law or established procedures for issuance and enforcement of support orders which are substantially similar to the procedures under this chapter'

Enforcement can be private or through the Washington State Department of Social and Health Services, Division of Child Support (DCS).

The UIFSA permits Washington DCS to enforce across state lines in other states by, for example, serving wage withholding on employers in other states. If the enforcement structure in the foreign state does not facilitate Washington direct enforcement, the WA DCS can request the foreign state to enforce the Washington support order. Enforcement of foreign state support orders within Washington can be done by the DCS with or without formal registration of the order, depending on whether the obligor objects to administrative enforcement of the order (RCW 26.21A.425 in Washington's version of UIFSA 2001); Washington Administrative Code (WAC) 388-14A-3304(5)). An obligor has a limited time to object to the registration (RCW 26.21A.525(1));WAC 388-14A-7100(2)). Objections to registration are restricted to certain defences (see

RCW 26.21A.530). A confirmed order may be enforced as if it was originally entered in Washington (see *Marriage of Owen*, 126 Wn. App.487, 108 P.3d 824, review denied, 155 Wn.2d 1022 (2005)).

Private enforcement of orders of another state can be made under UFISA without going through the DCS (RCW 26.21A.240). For example, procedures are set out for direct wage withholding against the obligor's employer (see RCW 26.21A.400 and .425). A foreign state's support order may be registered for enforcement in Washington. Procedures, notice and defences are set out in RCW 26.21A.500-.535.

Section 459A of the Social Security Act (42 U.S.C. 659A) authorises the Secretary of State, with the concurrence of the Secretary of Health and Human Services, to enter into agreements with foreign countries for family support enforcement. This has led to a confusing mix of agreements, depending on the country. This could change if the 23 November 2007 Convention on the International Recovery of Child Support and Other Forms of Family Maintenance gains momentum. At present, only the USA and Burkina Faso have signed it but they have not taken further steps (a signature is evidence of intention but there is no obligation to take further action).

Foreign judgments may also be filed and enforced in Washington pursuant to RCW 6.36. Under RCW 6.36.010 'foreign judgment' is defined as 'any judgment, decree or order of the United States or of any state or territory which is entitled to full faith and credit in this state'. A filed authenticated copy of a foreign judgment is treated by the court clerk in the same way as a judgment of this state. The authentification must be in accordance with an act of Congress or statute of this state. Such orders have the same effect, defences, set-offs etc and enforcement procedures as this state's orders. (see RCW 6.30.025).

12. FINANCIAL RELIEF AFTER FOREIGN DIVORCE PROCEEDINGS

12.1 What powers are available to make orders following a foreign divorce?

Due to the divisible nature of divorce and family law proceedings in Washington (see Jurisdiction for differing bases for establishing jurisdiction depending upon the subject to be adjudicated upon), it is possible to have a divorce in a foreign state or country and to have, for example, child support and/or custody determined in Washington. However a court in Washington may not make new orders when a procedurally valid foreign order has dealt with the case (see *Tostada v Tostada* 137 Wn. App. 136, 151 P.3d 1060 (2007)), supra.

The court in Washington has the power to modify decrees ordering child support or spousal maintenance under RCW 26.09.170. *'The provisions of any decree respecting maintenance or support may be modified only as to instalments accruing subsequent to the motion for modification and only upon a showing of a substantial change of circumstances...'* (see Maintenance for spousal maintenance and Child Maintenance for child support and discussions therein of exceptions to the general rules). Naturally, this can only occur if the court has jurisdiction to decide the matter (see Jurisdiction).

D. CHILDREN

13. CUSTODY/PARENTAL RESPONSIBILITY

13.1 Briefly explain the legal position in relation to custody/parental responsibility following the breakdown of a relationship or marriage

Establishment of a parent child relationship is regulated by RCW 26.26.101.

RCW 26.26.106 provides that a child born to parents who are not married to each other or in a domestic partnership with each other has the same rights under the law as a child born to parents who are married to each other or who are in a domestic partnership with each other.

There are presumptions of paternity in certain marital and domestic partner situations pursuant to 26.26.116 such as when a child is born during a marriage or domestic partnership.

Upon a judgment determining parentage (under RCW 26.26, the Parentage Statute) the court shall make financial and other orders including support and residential provisions although, in a parentage action, shall only order a parenting plan if requested by a party. RCW 26.26.130. Note that RCW 26.26.130(7) incorporates the residential provisions of RCW 26.09 to parentage actions.

Among the primary sections on child support are RCW 26.18, 26.19 and RCW 26.23.050.

13.2 Briefly explain the legal position in relation to access/contact/ visitation following the breakdown of a relationship or marriage

See section 13.1 above. In addition the following:

RCW 26.09 contains the requirements for a parenting plan. The policy directives are stated as follows:

'*...In any proceeding between parents under this chapter, the best interests of the child shall be the standard by which the court determines and allocates the parties' parental responsibilities. The state recognizes the fundamental importance of the parent-child relationship to the welfare of the child, and that the relationship between the child and each parent should be fostered unless inconsistent with the child's best interests...*'. RCW 26.09.002

RCW 26.09.184 lists the objectives and contents of the permanent parenting plan. These include, *inter alia*, such matters as the care of the child, responsibilities for the child, protecting the best interests of the child and decision making.

Under 26.09.194, a parent may obtain a temporary parenting plan before the permanent plan.

14. INTERNATIONAL ABDUCTION

14.1 Summarise the position in your jurisdiction

Some of the most important legislation is the Uniform Child Custody Jurisdiction and Enforcement Act 1997 (UCCJEA), codified in Washington by RCW 26.27; the 1980 Hague Convention on the Civil Aspects of International Child Abduction (the Hague Convention), implemented in the

USA on 1 July 1988; and the federal 1993 International Parental Kidnapping Crime Act.

Pursuant to RCW 26.27.051 Washington courts must recognise and enforce a foreign nation's custody decree if it was rendered in the foreign country in substantial conformity with the jurisdictional standards set out in RCW 26.27. However, Washington courts need not enforce it if the child custody law of the foreign nation violates fundamental principles of human rights.

Under RCW 26.27.201 the Washington court will decide if it has initial jurisdiction to determine custody under the UCCJEA (see under Jurisdiction and Custody). The court can assume temporary emergency jurisdiction in situations where it may not have initial child custody jurisdiction (RCW 26.27.231).

The 1980 Hague Convention on the Civil Aspects of International Child Abduction (the Hague Convention)

The 1980 Hague Convention on the Civil Aspects of International Child Abduction (the Hague Convention) was implemented in the USA on 1 July 1988 by the International Child Abduction Remedies Act, (ICARA), 42 U.S.C. sections 11601-11610. Under this convention, member countries agree to return a child under 16 years of age to the country of 'habitual residence'. There is no provision for a child custody hearing on its merits. The Convention mandates that each ratifying country establish a central authority to process requests for locating and returning the child. The State Department is the central authority in the USA (see section 11606 of ICARA). The State Department provides useful information about child abduction on its website at *www.travel.state.gov*.

Under section 11603 of ICARA an application for return of the child can be processed through federal or state courts. It is the responsibility of the applicant for return of the child to initiate timely proceedings.

A court is required to defer any consideration of custody upon receipt of notice that an application for return of the child has been made under the Hague Convention until the appropriate state or federal court has decided that the child is not to be returned. (see Article 16 of the Hague Convention).

The Washington State statute RCW 26.27.411 authorises a Washington State court (as opposed to federal) to enforce an order for the return of the child under the Hague Convention as if it were a child custody determination.

Under RCW 26.27.541 a Washington State prosecutor or the attorney general may take any lawful action under the Hague Convention.

The International Parental Kidnapping Crime Act 1993

Codified as 18 U.S.C. section 1204, this provides for up to three years of imprisonment and fines for removing or attempting to remove a child from the USA or retaining a child outside the USA with 'intent to obstruct the lawful exercise of parental rights'. The act broadly defines 'parental rights' as including joint or sole custody or visitation rights which may arise by operation of law, court order or legally binding agreement of the parties.

15. LEAVE TO REMOVE/APPLICATIONS TO TAKE A CHILD OUT OF THE JURISDICTION

15.1 Summarise the position in your jurisdiction

RCW 26.09.430-.480 (Relocation Statute) mandates notice of a residential move by the parent with whom the child resides the majority of the time to any person entitled to court ordered time. If a move is outside the child's school district, this can be objected to within 30 days of notice. The court will conduct a hearing to allow or prohibit the relocation of the child. There are special provisions for exigent circumstances and domestic violence.

15.2 Under what circumstances may a parent apply to remove their child from the jurisdiction against the wishes of the other parent?

Pursuant to a hearing under RCW 26.09.430 relocation, the courts are directed to consider factors listed in RCW 26.09.520 in determining whether or not to allow the parent to remove the child's residence outside the school district. These enquiries, while considering the impact on the child, also consider such factors as the reasons of each person for seeking or opposing the relocation and the good faith of each of the parties in requesting or opposing the relocation and the financial impact and logistics of the relocation or its prevention.

E. SURROGACY AND ADOPTION

16. VALIDITY OF SURROGACY AGREEMENTS

16.1 Briefly summarise the position in your jurisdiction

RCW 26.26.260 provides: *'If a child is born to a surrogate mother pursuant to a surrogate parentage contract, and there is a dispute between the parties concerning custody of the child, the party having physical custody of the child may retain physical custody of the child until the superior court orders otherwise. The superior court shall award legal custody of the child based upon the factors listed in RCW 26.09.187(3) and 26.09.191'*. The referenced sections are criteria for establishing residential provisions in a permanent parenting plan and restrictions where appropriate.

RCW 26.26.230: *'No person, organization, or agency shall enter into, induce, arrange, procure, or otherwise assist in the formation of a surrogate parentage contract, written or unwritten, for compensation.'*

RCW 26.26.220: *'A person shall not enter into, induce, arrange, procure, or otherwise assist in the formation of a surrogate parentage contract under which an unemancipated minor female or a female diagnosed as having an intellectual disability, a mental illness, or developmental disability is the surrogate mother'*.

17. ADOPTION

17.1 Briefly explain the legal position in relation to adoption in your jurisdiction. Is adoption available to individuals, cohabiting couples (both heterosexual and same-sex)?

RCW 26.33.010: *'The legislature finds that the purpose of adoption is to provide stable homes for children. Adoptions should be handled efficiently, but the rights of all parties must be protected. The guiding principle must be determining what is in the best interest of the child. It is the intent of the legislature that this chapter be used only as a means for placing children in adoptive homes and not as a means for parents to avoid responsibility for their children unless the department, an agency, or a prospective adoptive parent is willing to assume the responsibility for the child'.*

RCW 26.33.140(1) Any person may be adopted, regardless of his or her age or residence.

Any person who is legally competent and who is 18 years of age or older may be an adoptive parent.

F. COHABITATION

18. COHABITATION

18.1 What legislation (if any) governs division of property for unmarried couples on the breakdown of the relationship?

Those unmarried persons who do not have a Washington registered domestic partnership are still governed by case law which does not give nearly as many rights at the end of the union. In *Connell v Francisco,*127 Wn.2d 339,898 P.2d 831 (1995) the Washington Supreme Court stated at 127 Wn.2d at 349-50:

'While portions of RCW 26.09.080 may apply by analogy to meretricious relationships, not all provisions of the statute should be applied. The parties to such a relationship have chosen not to get married and, therefore, the property owned by each party prior to the relationship should not be before the court for distribution at the end of the relationship. … We conclude a trial court may not distribute property acquired by each party prior to the relationship at the termination of a meretricious relationship. Until the Legislature, as a matter of public policy, concludes meretricious relationships are the legal equivalent of marriages, we limit the distribution of property following a meretricious relationship to property that would have been characterised as community property had the parties been married'.

For the court to conclude that a mere cohabitation amounts to a 'meretricious relationship' justifying a distribution of property, the Washington Supreme Court has stated that it must be established that 'the parties jointly pooled their time, effort, or financial resources enough to require an equitable distribution of property…' (see *In re Marriage of Pennington and Chesterfield v Nash,* 142 Wn.2d 592, 14 P. 3d 764 (2000) at 142 Wn.2d 607).

G. FAMILY DISPUTE RESOLUTION

19. MEDIATION, COLLABORATIVE LAW AND ARBITRATION

19.1 Briefly summarise the non-court-based processes available in your jurisdiction and the current status of agreements reached under the auspices of mediation, collaborative law and arbitration

Parties can obtain mediators, collaborative attorneys and arbitrators.

CR2A (Civil Rule 2A): *'No agreement or consent between parties or attorneys in respect to the proceedings in a cause, the purport of which is disputed, will be regarded by the court unless the same shall have been made and assented to in open court on the record, or entered in the minutes, or unless the evidence thereof shall be in writing and subscribed by the attorneys denying the same.'*

Practice pointer: The courts tend to uphold out of court agreements as contracts, if basic procedural fairness has been observed. However, when it comes to children's interests they will scrutinse those provisions. See for example, RCW 26.09.070(3) which provides that the parenting and child support provisions of a separation contract is not binding on the court.

19.2 What is the statutory basis (if any), for mediation, collaborative law and arbitration in your jurisdiction? In particular, are the parties required to attempt a family dispute resolution in advance of the institution of proceedings?

The mediation process is statutorily governed by RCW 7.07; RCW 26.09.015 and .016 One should also consult the state and local rules to see if and when mediation is required. Local rules can differ and, of course, can change over time. Alternative dispute resolution is a hot topic and is subject to frequent discussion and review.

Arbitration can be used in family law cases and is a recognised alternative dispute model for parenting plans. RCW 26.09.015(3)(a)(ii): *'If a postdecree mediation-arbitration proceeding is required pursuant to a parenting plan and the same person acts as both mediator and arbitrator, mediation communications in the mediation phase of such a proceeding may be admitted during the arbitration phase, and shall be admissible in the judicial review of such a proceeding under RCW 26.09.184(4)(e) to the extent necessary for such review to be effective.'*

Practice pointer: Some practitioners like to use arbitration in family law others do not. The reality is, at least for children's issues the court will likely overturn any arbitrated decision (or agreement) which it believes does not meet statutory requirements or is not in the child's best interests.

The Uniform Collaborative Law Act was enacted by Washington State in April 2013 and shall become effective as of 28 July, 2013.

H. OTHER

20. CIVIL PARTNERSHIP/SAME-SEX MARRIAGE

20.1 What is the status of civil partnership/same-sex marriage within the jurisdiction?

Washington State now permits same-sex marriages. As of November 2012 the voters voted to approve the enacted 2012 law enabling same-sex couples to marry as of 6 December, 2012.

RCW 26.04.010 provides:

'(1) Marriage is a civil contract between two persons…

(2) Where necessary to implement the rights and responsibilities of spouses under the law, gender specific terms such as husband and wife used in any statute, rule, or other law must be construed to be gender neutral and applicable to spouses of the same sex.'

Prior to enactment of same-sex marriage, the state provided for Registered Domestic Partnerships under RCW 26.60.

Under the new provisions to RCW 60 registered domestic partners may marry under 26.04.010; for those registered domestic partners where at least one of them is under 62 years of age, their registered domestic partnership automatically becomes a marriage on 30 July, 2014, unless proceedings are pending for dissolution, legal separation or annulment on that date. For those registered domestic partners who become married, the date to determine their rights and responsibilities goes back to the date of the registration of the domestic partnership. However the section states that nothing in the section prohibits a different date on the marriage licence. See RCW 26.60.100

Note for those couples, where at least one partner is 62, they may still form registered domestic partnerships. RCW 26.60.010. (As the section states, this is preserved to accommodate people of retirement age who may not find it practical to marry due to social security and pension laws. This applies to people of the same and different sexes where one person is 62 or older).

20.2 What legislation governs civil partnership/same-sex marriage?
See above.

21. CONTROVERSIAL AREAS/RAPIDLY DEVELOPING AREAS OF LAW

21.1 Is there a particular area of the law within the jurisdiction that is currently undergoing major change?

The treatment of same-sex marriages has recently (as of 26 June 2013) undergone a dramatic change with the US Supreme Court decisions in *Windsor v Schlain*, No. 12-307 (U.S 2013). Another case which was excitedly anticipated in the US, *Hollingsworth v Perry*, No.12-144 (U.S. 2013) was not decided on its merits due to lack of standing but may, nonetheless, still be noteworthy as an indication of trends in this area of law.

The law prior to the afore referenced 26 June, 2013 decisions was as follows:

Whereas Washington and an increasing number of states in the US adopted same-sex marriage, same-sex married couples still faced unequal treatment on a federal level because of the Federal Defense of Marriage Act (DOMA). DOMA, under Section 3, defined 'marriage' and 'spouse' as between a man and a woman. Section 2 permitted states to refuse to recognise same-sex marriages of other states. The effect of the two decisions on 26 June 2013:

The *Windsor* case, cited *supra*, struck down the definition of 'marriage' and 'spouse' as between a man and a woman in Section 3. However, it left Section 2 standing which permits states to refuse to recognise the marriages performed in other states.

The *Windsor* case concerned a suit by Edith Windsor who married her same-sex spouse in Ontario, Canada. The couple resided in New York, US where their marriage was deemed valid. Windsor's spouse died leaving her entire estate to Windsor. The federal government under DOMA did not recognise her marriage and did not permit her the federal marital exemption. Estate taxes were charged. Windsor sued for a refund arguing that DOMA violated the guarantee of equal protection which is applied to the federal government through the Fifth Amendment. The justices in a 5-4 decision agreed that the restrictive definition under Section 3 was unconstitutional as it violated basic due process and equal protection principles applicable to the federal government.

Hollingsworth v Perry, cited *supra*, was widely anticipated but had a less dramatic result. Nonetheless, it may be an indicator of the strength of the pro same-sex marriage momentum. In this case the US Supreme Court ruled that the petitioner interest groups had no standing to appeal a decision relating to the unconstitutionality of California's Proposition 8. Proposition 8 prohibited same-sex marriages. The officials responsible for enforcing the law did not defend it. As a result of the US Supreme Court's ruling, the federal district court's decision that Proposition 8 is unconstitutional was left intact.

21.2 Which areas of law are most out-of-step? Which areas would you most like to see reformed/changed?

Same-sex relationships are given inconsistent treatment by states. Washington State's registered domestic partnerships may not be recognised in some other states. Washington State's same-sex marriages may also not be recognised in some other states. We have not yet seen all the results of the *Windsor* case as it is too new. No doubt we will know more soon. However, it seems likely that situations will arise where there is a conflict between state and federal treatments of marriage. A same-sex couple married in a state which permits same-sex marriage might move to a state which does not do so. Presently questions have arisen as to whether federal law would recognise the married status of a same-sex couple if the couple move to a non-recognition state. The lack of certainty in this area is causing considerable debate and may necessitate clarifying regulations, legislation and/or litigation.

Contact details

GENERAL EDITOR

James Stewart
Manches LLP
Aldwych House
81 Aldwych
London WC2B 4RP
United Kingdom
T: +44 (0)20 7753 7409
F: +44 (0)20 7430 1133
E: james.stewart@manches.com
W: www.manches.com

ARGENTINA

Diego Horton
Perez Maraviglia & Horton Abogados
Azcuénaga 950 (1638)
Vicente Lopez
Buenos Aires
Argentina
T: +54 11 4797 7015
F: +54 11 4797 7015
E: dhorton@pmhabogados.com
W: www.pmhabogados.com

AUSTRALIA

Max James Meyer
Meyer Partners Family Lawyers
Level 14, 59 Goulburn St
Sydney
NSW 2000
Australia
T: +61 02 8202 9202
F: +61 02 8202 9292
E: mp@meyerpartners.com.au
W: www.meyerpartners.com.au

AUSTRIA

Dr Alfred Kriegler
Rechtsanwalt Dr. Alfred Kriegler
Hoher Markt 1
1010 Vienna
T: +43 (0)1 533 42 65
F: +43 (0)1 533 42 65 – 4
E: kriegler@divorce.at
W: www.divorce.at

BELGIUM

Jehanne Sosson, Silvia Pfeiff &
Sohelia Goossens
Wouters Sosson & Associés
Avenue Louise, 87 bte 17
Brussels 1050
Belgium
T: +32 2 537 94 31
F: +32 2 538 81 55
E: wouters.sosson@skynet.be
W: www.wouters-sosson.com

BERMUDA

Rachael Barritt, Adam Richards &
Georgia Marshall
Marshall Diel & Myers Limited
31 Reid Street
Hamilton
HM 12
Bermuda
T: +1 441 295 7105
F: +1 441 292 6814
E: rachael.barritt@law.bm
adam.richards@law.bm
georgia.marshall@law.bm
W: www.law.bm

CANADA

Esther Lenkinski & Lisa Eisen
Lenkinski Family Law & Mediation
Professional Corporation
94 Scollard Street
Toronto
Ontario M5R 1G2
Canada
T: +1 416 924 1970 ext. 23
F: +1 416 924 2356
E: elenkinski@lenkinskilaw.com

W: www.lenkinskilaw.com

CHILE

Daniela Horvitz Lennon
Horvitz & Horvitz
Huérfanos 770, Oficina 2303
Santiago 8320193
Chile
T: +56 2 638 5439
F: +56 2 638 0485
E: dhorvitz@horvitz.cl
W: www.horvitz.cl

DENMARK

Maryla Rytter Wróblewski
Nyborg & Rørdam
Store Kongensgade 77, 2. sal
DK 1264 København K.
Denmark
T: +45 33 12 45 40
F: +45 33 93 45 40
E: mw@nrlaw.dk
W: www.nrlaw.dk

DOMINICAN REPUBLIC

Dr Juan Manuel Suero &
Elisabetta Pedersini
Aaron Suero & Pedersini
Avenida Francia No 123
Edificio Khoury – Suite 101
Santo Domingo 10205
Dominican Republic
T: +1 (809) 532 7223
+1 (866) 815 0107
F: +1 (809) 532 6376
+1 (888) 297 8227
E: jsuero@dlawyers.com
epedersini@dlawyers.com
W: www.dlawyers.com

ENGLAND & WALES

James Stewart & Louise Spitz
Manches LLP
Aldwych House
81 Aldwych
London WC2B 4RP
United Kingdom
T: +44 (0)20 7404 4433
F: +44 (0)20 7430 1133
E: james.stewart@manches.com;
E: louise.spitz@manches.com
W: www.manches.com

FINLAND

Hilkka Salmenkylä
Asianajotoimisto Juhani Salmenkylä
Ky, Attorneys at law
Pakilantie 40
Helsinki 00630
Finland
T: +358 9724 0166
F: +358 924 8120
E: hilkka.salmenkyla@salmenkyla.fi
W: www.salmenkyla.fi

FRANCE

Véronique Chauveau,
Charlotte Butruille-Cardew &
Alexandre Boiché
Cabinet CBBC
8, Boulevard de Sébastopol
Paris 75004
France
T: +33 1 55 42 55 25
F: +33 1 55 42 55 29
E: v.chauveau@cbbc-avocats.com
c.butruille-cardew@cbbc-avocats.com
a.boiche@cbbc-avocats.com
W: www.cbbc-avocats.com

GERMANY

Dr. Daniela Kreidler-Pleus
Anwaltskanzlei Dr. Kreidler-Pleus &
Kollegen
Bahnhofstraße 29
Ludwigsburg
D-71638
Germany
T: +49 7141 920005
F: +49 7141 902900
E: kanzlei@kreidler-pleus.de
W: www. kreidler-pleus.de

GIBRALTAR
Charles Simpson
Triay & Triay
28 Irish Town
Gibraltar
T: +350 200 72020
F: +350 200 72020
E: charles.simpson@triay.com
W: www.triay.com

GUERNSEY
Advocate Felicity J Haskins
F Haskins & Co
College Chambers
3-4 St James Street
St Peter Port
GY1 2NZ
Guernsey
Channel Islands
T: +44 (0)1481 721316
F: +44 (0)1481 721317
E: haskins@haskins-co.com
W: www.haskins-co.com

HONG KONG
Catherine Por
Stevenson, Wong & Co.
4/F & 5/F
Central Tower
28 Queen's Road
Central, Hong Kong
T: +852 2533 2555
F: +852 2157 5531
E: catherinepor.office@sw-hk.com
W: www.sw-hk.com

INDIA
Dr. Pinky Anand
Senior Advocate
A-126 Niti Bagh
New Delhi 110 049
India
T: +91 11 41640960
F: +91 11 4174 0656
E: pinkyanand@gmail.com

ISRAEL
Edwin Freedman
Law Offices of Edwin Freedman
154 Menachem Begin Road
Tel Aviv 64921
Israel
T: +972 3 6966611
F: +972 3 6092266
E: edwin@edfreedman.com
W: www.edfreedman.com

ITALY
Avv. Andrea Russo &
Avv. Benedetta Rossi
Pirola Pennuto Zei & Associati
122, Viale Castro Pretorio
Rome 00185
Italy
T: +36 06 570 282658
F: +39 06 570 282733
E: benedetta.rossi@studiopirola.com
andrea.russo@studiopirola.com
W: www.pirolapennutozei.it

JAPAN
Mikiko Otani
Tokyo Public Office, Mita Branch
Honshiba Bldg. 2F, 4-3-11 Shiba,
Minato-ku
Tokyo 108-0014
Japan
T: +81 3 6809 6200
F: +81 3 5765 5750
E: motani2@nifty.com
W: www.t-pblo.jp/fiss

JERSEY
Advocate Barbara Corbett
Hanson Renouf
12 Hill Street
St Helier, JE2 4UA
Jersey
Channel Islands
T: +44 (0)1534 767764
F: +44 (0)1534 767725
E: barbara.corbett@hansonrenouf.com
W: www.hansonrenouf.com

MALAYSIA

Foo Yet Ngo & Kiran Dhaliwal
Messrs Y N Foo & Partners
H-2-12, Block H, Plaza Damas
Jalan Sri Hartamas 1
50480 Kuala Lumpur
Malaysia
T: +603 6203 2848
F: +603 6203 2847
E: ynfoo@ynfoolaw.com

MEXICO

Alfonso Sepúlveda García
& Habib Diaz Noriega
Müggenburg, Gorches, Peñalosa
& Sepúlveda SC
Paseo de los Tamarindos 90, Torre I,
8th Floor
Bosques de las Lomas
05120 Distrito Federal,
México
T: +52 55 5246 3400
F: +52 55 5246 3450
E: alfonso.sepulveda@mgps.com.mx
habib.diaz@mgps.com.mx
W: www.mgps.com.mx

MONACO

Christine Pasquier-Ciulla
& Alison Isabella Torti
PCM Avocats
Athos Palace
2 rue de la Lüjerneta
98000 Monaco
Principality of Monaco
T: +377 97 98 42 24
F: +377 97 98 42 25
E: cpasquierciulla@pcm-avocats.com
atorti@pcm-avocats.com
W: www.pcm-avocats.com

THE NETHERLANDS

Carla Smeets & Caroliene Mellema
Smeets Gijbels BV
Postbus 78067,
1071 KP Amsterdam
The Netherlands
T: +31 (0) 20 574 77 22
F: +31 (0) 20 574 77 33
E: carla.smeets@smeetsgijbels.com
caroliene.mellema@smeetsgijbels.com
W: www.smeetsgijbels.com

NEW ZEALAND

Anita Chan
Barrister
Princes Chambers
3rd Floor, 155 Princes Street
Dunedin 9016
New Zealand
T: +64 3 477 8781
F: +64 3 477 8382
E: anita@princeschambers.net
W: www.familylaw.net.nz

POLAND

Dr Joanna Kosinska-Wiercinska & Dr
Hab. Jacek Wiercinski
Wiercinski Kancelaria Adwokacka
T. Boya-Zelenskiego 4a/7, 00-621
Warsaw
Poland
T: +48 607 453 732
+48 601 547 119
F: +48 022 845 50 05
E: jkw@wiercinski.pl
j.wiercinski@wiercinski.pl

REPUBLIC OF IRELAND

Jennifer O'Brien
Mason Hayes & Curran
6th Floor, South Bank House
Barrow Street
Dublin 4
Republic of Ireland
T: +353 1 614 5000
F: +353 1 614 5001
E: jobrien@mhc.ie
W: www.mhc.ie

RUSSIA

Dr Catherine Kalaschnikova
Divorce in Russia
Moscow Bar of Arbitration Lawyers

Pechatnikov Pereulok 22
Moscow 103045
Russia
T: +7 926 710 1100
F: +7 495 6287839
E: info@divorceinrussia.com
W: www.divorceinrussia.com

SCOTLAND

Alasdair Loudon
Turcan Connell
Princes Exchange
1 Earl Grey Street
Edinburgh
EH3 9EE
Scotland
T: +44 (0)131 228 8111
F: +44 (0)131 228 8118
E: alasdair.loudon@turcanconnell.com
W: www.turcanconnell.com

SINGAPORE

Randolph Khoo & Hoon Shu Mei
Drew & Napier LLC
10 Collyer Quay
#10-01 Ocean Financial Centre
049315
Republic of Singapore
T: +65 6531 2418
+65 6531 2223
F: +65 6532 7149
E: randolph.khoo@drewnapier.com
shumei.hoon@drewnapier.com
W: www.drewnapier.com

SOUTH AFRICA

Amanda Catto
Catto Neethling Wiid Inc
6th Floor, Waalburg Building
28 Wale Street
Cape Town 8001
South Africa
T: +27 21 487 9300
F: +27 21 487 9301
E: amanda@cattonw.co.za
W: www.cattonw.co.za

SPAIN

Alberto Perez Cedillo
& Paula Piquer Ruz
Alberto Perez Cedillo Spanish
Lawyers & Solicitors
London office
1 New Square, Lincoln's Inn,
London WC2A 3SA
United Kingdom
T: +44 (0) 20 3077 0000
F: +44 (0) 20 7404 7821
E: cedillo@apcedillo.com
W: www.apcedillo.com

Madrid office
Paseo de la Castellana n.166
Esc 1-1o izq.
28046 Madrid
Spain
T: (+34) 91 230 6393
E: cedillo@apcedillo.com
W: www.apcedillo.com

SWEDEN

Mia Reich Sjögren
Advokaterna Sverker och Mia Reich
Sjögren AB
Ängelholmsvägen 1
Box 1010
SE-269 21 Båstad
Sweden
T: +46 (0)43 176120
F: +46 (0)43 175105
E: mia@reichsjogren.com

Johan Sarvik
Advokaterna Nyblom & Sarvik AB
Stortorget 17,
S-211 22 Malmö,
Sweden
T: +46 (0)40 772 50
F: +46 (0)40 611 09 25
E: johan@nyblom-sarvik.se
W: www.nyblom-sarvik.se

Fredric Renström
Lindskog Malmström Advokatbyrå

Box 27707
Stockholm 115 91
Sweden
T: +468 5992 9000
F: +468 5992 9001
E: fredric.renstrom@lmlaw.se
W: www.lmlaw.se

SWITZERLAND

Dr. Daniel R. Trachsel
Langner Stieger Trachsel & Partner
Heuelstrasse 21
Postfach
8032 Zürich
Switzerland
T: +41 43 222 62 62
F: +41 43 222 62 72
E: D.Trachsel@lstp.ch
W: www.lstp.ch

UKRAINE

Aminat Suleymanova, Irina Moroz
& Ivan Kasynyuk
AGA Partners
11A Nauki prospect
Kiev 03028
Ukraine
T: +38 044 206 06 75/76
F: +38 044 206 06 75/76
E: office@agalawyers.org
W: www.agalawyers.org

UNITED ARAB EMIRATES

Alexandra Tribe
Expatriate Law within Al Rowaad Advocates
P.O. Box 40073
6th Floor, H Tower
1 Sheikh Zayed Road
Dubai
United Arab Emirates
T: +971 4358 9444
F: +971 4358 9494
E: Alexandra@expatriatelaw.com
W: www.expatriatelaw.com

USA – CALIFORNIA

Suzanne Harris, Larry A. Ginsberg, Andrea Fugate Balian, Fahi Takesh Hallin, David L. Marcus, Evan C. Itzkowitz, Johnna K. Boylan, Dena J. Kravitz, Jessica M. Spiker, Michelle H. Chen & Jennifer R. Morra
Harris Ginsberg LLP
6420 Wilshire Blvd. 16th Floor
Los Angeles, CA 90048
T: +1 310 444 6333
F: +1 310 444 6330
E: sharris@harris-ginsberg.com
W: www.harris-ginsberg.com

USA – CONNECTICUT

Edward Nusbaum
& Thomas P. Parrino
Nusbaum & Parrino, P. C.
212 Post Road West
Westport, CT 06880
USA
T: +1 203 226 8181
F: +1 203 226 6691
E: enusbaum@nusbaumparrino.com
W: www.nusbaumparrino.com

USA – MARYLAND & WASHINGTON D.C.

Cheryl Lynn Hepfer
Offit Kurman
4800 Montgomery Lane, 9th Floor
Bethesda MD 20814
USA
T: +1 240 507 1752
F: +1 240 507 1735
E: CHepfer@offitkurman.com
W: www.offitkurman.com

USA – MINNESOTA

Nancy Zalusky Berg, Lilo D. Kaiser, Tara L. Smith Ruesga
& Laura Sahr Schmit
Walling, Berg & Debele, P.A.
121 South 8th Street
Suite 1100
Minneapolis

Minnesota 55402
USA
T: +1 612 340 1150
F: +1 612 340 1154
E. nancy.bcrg@wbdlaw.com
W: www.wbdlaw.com

USA – NEW YORK

John M. Teitler, Nicholas W. Lobenthal & Paul D. Getzels
Teitler & Teitler, LLP
230 Park Avenue
New York, NY 10169
USA
T: +1 212 997 4400
F: +1 212 997 4949
E: jmteitler@teitler.com
nwlobenthal@teitler.com
pdgetzels@teitler.com
W: www.teitler.com

USA – TEXAS

Donn C. Fullenweider
Fullenweider Wilhite
4265 San Felipe, Suite 1400
Houston, TX 77027
USA
T: +1 713 624 4100
F: +1 713 624 4141
E: dcf@fullenweider.com
W: www.fullenweider.com

USA – VIRGINIA

Katharine W. Maddox
& Julie Curran Gerock
The Maddox Law Firm, P.C.
8221 Old Courthouse Road
Suite 101
Vienna
Virginia 22182
USA
T: +1 703 883 8035
F: +1 703 356 6120
E: kmaddox@maddoxlawoffice.com
jgerock@maddoxlawoffice.com
W: www.maddoxlawoffice.com

USA – WASHINGTON STATE

Marguerite C. Smith
Flexx Law, PS
1215 Fourth Ave
Suite 940
Seattle,
WA 98161
USA
T: +1 206 343 6362
E: Maggie@flexxlaw.com
W: www.flexxlaw.com
www.informeddivorce.com